STATISTICS FOR BEHAVIOURAL
AND SOCIAL SCIENCES

STATISTICS FOR BEHAVIOURAL AND SOCIAL SCIENCES

Banamali Mohanty

Professor of Psychology (Retired),
Post-graduate Department of Psychology, Utkal University

Santa Misra

Reader, Department of Psychology,
Sri Sathya Sai College for Women, Bhubaneswar

SAGE | TEXTS
www.sagepublications.com
Los Angeles • London • New Delhi • Singapore • Washington DC

First published in 2016 by

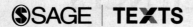

SAGE Publications India Pvt Ltd
B1/I-1 Mohan Cooperative Industrial Area
Mathura Road, New Delhi 110 044, India
www.sagepub.in

SAGE Publications Inc
2455 Teller Road
Thousand Oaks, California 91320, USA

SAGE Publications Ltd
1 Oliver's Yard, 55 City Road
London EC1Y 1SP, United Kingdom

SAGE Publications Asia-Pacific Pte Ltd
3 Church Street
#10-04 Samsung Hub
Singapore 049483

Published by Vivek Mehra for SAGE Publications India Pvt Ltd, typeset in Stone Serif 9.5/11.5pt by Zaza Eunice, Hosur, Tamilnadu, India and printed at Saurabh Printers Pvt Ltd, Greater Noida.

Library of Congress Cataloging-in-Publication Data

Mohanty, Banamali, author.
  Statistics for behavioural and social sciences / Banamali Mohanty, Santa Misra.
    pages cm
  Includes bibliographical references and index.
  1. Psychology—Statistical methods. 2. Social sciences—Statistical methods. I. Misra, Santa, author. II. Title.
  BF39.M64   150.1'5195—dc23   2016   2015031314

ISBN: 978-93-515-0181-7 (PB)

The SAGE Team: Amit Kumar, Indrani Dutta, Vandana Gupta, Anju Saxena and Rajinder Kaur

Dedicated to
Our parents

Brief Contents

Detailed Contents

Preface

We are aware that standard textbooks on the subject of statistics are available and much has been covered in those books, but this time it has been said with a difference in content, approach and style. Our close interaction with both the undergraduate and post-graduate students over a period spanning more than three decades and experience of teaching statistics, research methodology and principles of experimental designs, and guiding research at Utkal University, Bhubaneswar, led us to believe that there was a need for another book on the subject of statistics which could be followed by even those students who did not have sophisticated mathematical background. Since the book is intended for the mathematically unsophisticated, the task of presenting various statistical methods, designs and their analyses comprehensively in simple language was a challenging exercise.

The major objective of this book is to present a clear and usable account of an intricate subject to the students, research workers and the general users of statistics in the behavioural and social sciences. A wide range of content is covered, keeping in mind a variety of potential needs of students and investigators. The presentation of statistical methods aims at much more than a superficial understanding of the principles involved. Many suggestions are offered regarding where and how methods may be appropriately applied as well as their limitations—places where they should not be applied.

Organisation of the Book

This book comprises four parts as follows:

(I) Basic statistics (Chapters 1–12), which are also called as descriptive statistics
(II) Designs of experiments (Chapters 13–15), which are also called as inferential statistics
(III) Distribution-free statistics (Chapters 16 and 17), which are also called as non-parametric statistics
(IV) Test construction (Chapter 18).

Three complementary chapters (Chapters 19–21, mostly from the 'Design of Experiments' part) have been provided for additional reading on the companion website. Please see further for more on this.

This book has been designed as a textbook for both one-semester and full-year courses in statistics. In either case, the instructor has some freedom of choice in the selection of material.

However, for a one-semester course, the selection will include most of Chapters 1–12, and also Sections 16.3 and 16.4 of Chapter 16.

This book presents the basic concepts and practice of statistics to students and researchers of behavioural sciences. Students and researchers in other disciplines, such as biological sciences, life sciences, social sciences, business management, social work, journalism, medicine, engineering, agriculture and elsewhere, may also find the book useful.

The authors have endeavoured hard to put forward, in simple language and style, the application of statistics in designing experiments, drawing samples, presenting the data systematically, analysing experimental results, and making inferences about the hypotheses underlying the investigation. Particular emphasis has been laid on the lucidity and clarity of descriptions and discussions of the topics. Many alternative formulae and methods have been incorporated in this book. Numerous worked out sums have been mentioned in this book to illustrate the application of statistical methods to behavioural measurements. Statistics of correlation and regression (prediction) has been largely elaborated with more illustrative examples.

Various questions and problems are given at the end of each chapter for students to practise. The answers to these problems are also presented chapter-wise at the end of chapters.

The writing of a book of this type demands numerous compromises between a tidy, logical arrangement of materials, sound pedagogy and common usage, which are not always compatible. The desire for completeness has led to the inclusion of occasional sections that are not essential in the introductory text. Instructors can readily identify these sections and omit them if they choose. However, this book may be useful for undergraduate, graduate and post-graduate students of almost all disciplines.

Supplementary Online Resources

The companion website (https://study.sagepub.in/mohanty_SBSS) to the book offers a wealth of resources to the readers. These are:

- Chapters for additional reading:
  - Multiple Comparisons among Treatment Means (Chapter 19)
  - Randomised Block Design (Chapter 20)
  - Analysis of Covariance: Single Factor (Chapter 21)
- Instructor's resources:
  - Summary of the key points
  - Essay questions and answers
  - Multiple choice questions
  - Power Point presentations

Acknowledgements

The authors will deem their labour rewarded if the readers, researchers and students find the book useful.

The authors are deeply indebted to Dr Sadasib Nanda, Mrs Banabasini Mohanty, Biswadeep Mohanty and Soumen Nanda for their unwavering support and cooperation in bringing out this book.

The authors also convey their appreciation to Mr S.N. Behera and Dr Nalinikanta Acharya and his associates for their assistance in the publication of this volume.

The suggestions and opinions provided by the reviewers have been of immense help in preparing the contents and designing the book. The authors acknowledge Dr Avdhesh S. Jha, Entrepreneurship Development Institute of India, Ahmedabad, and Professor V.D. Swaminathan, Department of Psychology, University of Madras.

Banamali Mohanty
Santa Misra

About the Authors

Banamali Mohanty is the Professor Emeritus at the Srusti Academy of Management, Bhubaneswar, Odisha, and also a Guest Teacher at the Trident Academy of Creative Technology, Bhubaneswar, Odisha. He started his professional career as a lecturer in psychology at Kendrapara Autonomous College, Odisha, in 1972, and then joined as a lecturer in psychology at the Post-graduate Department of Psychology, Utkal University, Bhubaneswar, Odisha, in 1973, and retired from the University service as a professor of psychology in 2008. During his 35 years of service at Utkal University, Dr Mohanty served in various positions. Formerly, he was the head of the Department of Psychology, and then he served as a member of various committees of the university such as Subject Research Committee, Board of Studies, Academic Council, Post-Graduate Council and also some professional bodies.

In 1986, Dr Mohanty received his D.Litt. degree in experimental psychology from Utkal University. In 1991, he was awarded the Indo-French Cultural Exchange Fellowship by the University Grants Commission (UGC) of India to work at foundation maison des sciences de l' homme, Paris, France.

He is the author of three books, namely, *Theories of Personality* (in Odia), *Effects of Repeated ECS on Body and Behaviour* and *Perceptual Experiences and Behaviour*. Besides this, he has also contributed some chapters in a few edited books. Dr Mohanty has completed six research projects sponsored by UGC. He has published over 50 research papers in national and international professional journals and more than 50 popular Odia articles in various magazines and periodicals, presented 60 research papers at various national and international conferences and delivered more than 100 popular talks on different psychological topics at professional meetings and on television.

Dr Mohanty has also taught post-graduate psychology courses at Utkal University. His major teaching interests include experimental psychology, experimental designs, comparative and physiological psychology, applied psychology, research methodology and statistics.

Santa Misra is a Reader and Head, Department of Psychology, Sri Sathya Sai College for Women, Bhubaneswar, Odisha. She started her professional career as a lecturer in Psychology in 1982 at Banki College, Odisha, and subsequently served at Godavaris Mahavidyalaya, Banpur, Odisha; Nimapara Autonomous College Odisha; and Nayagarh Autonomous College, Odisha.

Dr (Mrs) Misra received her M.Phil. degree in 1981 and Ph.D. degree in 2000, both in experimental psychology from Utkal University, Bhubaneswar, Odisha. She is a member of professional bodies and associations, such as Odisha Psychology Association, National Academy of Psychology, Indian Psychology Institute, E-journal Antimatters, Biocyburnout Institute of Canada and World Gerontology Board of Japan.

Dr (Mrs) Misra is the author of two books, namely, *Sleep Learning: Theory and Practices* and *Metacognitive Awareness and Academic Performance*, co-author of one book entitled *Psychology of Deviants* and has contributed a chapter in an edited book entitled *Psychology of*

Women Studies. She has completed seven research projects sponsored by the UGC and United Nations Population Fund-India (UNFPA). Dr (Mrs) Misra has successfully guided and supervised two Ph.D. scholars; published 19 research papers in national , 3 in *Social Science Research Network* (SSRN) journal and 26 in international professional journals; presented 58 research papers in national and 15 in international conferences; delivered around 50 popular talks on various psychological topics at professional meetings and on television. She visited Russia (April 2011), Japan (April 2012) and France (July 2014) to present her papers in international conferences. She was a post-doctoral fellow in the Post-graduate Department of Psychology, Utkal University for two years (January 2009–January 2011) to do research for her D.Litt. degree. Dr (Mrs) Misra is teaching graduate Psychology courses at graduate colleges, with her major teaching interest being cognitive psychology, experimental psychology, experimental designs, research methodology and statistics.

CHAPTER 1

Basic Ideas in Statistics

Learning Objectives

After reading this chapter you will be able to:

- Define statistics as a measure of the sample.
- Differentiate between samples and population, and statistics and parameter.
- Describe the nature, aims and applications of statistics as a science.
- Explain the uses and misuses of statistics.
- Elucidate the classification of statistical procedures, and limitations and fallacies of statistics.
- Define sampling as a process of drawing a sample from the population.
- Illustrate the difference between probability (random) and non-probability (non-random) sampling methods.
- Define measurement as a process of mapping or assigning numbers to objects or observations.
- Identify the differences between different scales or levels of measurement.
- Discuss the variables and their classification.

1.1   Introduction

This book is concerned with the elementary statistical treatment of experimental data in behavioural sciences. The data resulting from any experiment are usually the collection of observations or measurements. The inferences or conclusions to be drawn from the data cannot be reliably ascertained to by a simple direct inspection of the data. Classification, analysis, summary description and rules of evidence for the drawing of experimentally valid inference are required. Statistics provide the methodology to do this. Moreover, this book deals with the basic principles of experimental design and analysis, and is addressed to the students and researchers in behavioural sciences. More particularly, it is an attempt to set forth the principles of designing experimental methods of data collection, analysis and interpretation of results. Furthermore, this book deals with not only the parametric statistical tests but also the non-parametric or distribution-free statistical tests for the analysis of the research data, depending upon the experimental designs as well as the research methodology.

The knowledge of statistics is an essential part of training of all students in various disciplines of behavioural sciences, particularly, psychology, education, sociology, biology and so on. There are many reasons for this. First, an understanding of the modern literature of different disciplines of behavioural sciences requires the knowledge of statistical methods and modes of thought. Many current books and journal articles either report experimental findings in a statistical form or present theories or arguments using statistical terms and concepts. These terms and concepts play an increasingly important role in our thought process about behavioural problems quite apart from the treatment of data. Second, training in various disciplines of behavioural sciences at an advanced level requires that the students themselves design and conduct experiments. The design of an experiment is inseparable from the statistical treatment of the results. Experiments must be designed to facilitate the treatment of results in such a way that they permit clear and unbiased interpretation and fulfil the purposes or objectives that motivated the experiment in the first place. If the design of an experiment is faulty, no amount of statistical manipulation can lead to the drawing of valid inferences. Experimental design and statistical procedures are two sides of the same coin. Thus, not only students must conduct advanced-level experiments and interpret results, but also they must plan their experiments in such a way that the interpretation of results can conform to known rules of scientific evidence. Third, training in statistics is training in a scientific method. Statistical inference is scientific inference, which in turn is inductive inference, the making of general statements from the study of a particular case. These terms are, for all practical purposes and at a certain level of generality, synonymous. Statistics attempt to make induction rigorous. Induction is regarded by some scholars as the only way in which new knowledge comes into the world. In a modern society, the role of induction in scientific discovery is of great importance because scientific discovery is possible through induction. For this reason, no serious student and researcher of behavioural sciences, or any other discipline, can afford not to know something of the rudiments of the scientific approach to a problem. Statistical procedures and ideas play an important role in this approach and help researchers to solve the problems.

Statistics, as will be found, is one of those subjects that cumulate. One topic leads to another, and the second is built upon the first. The work has to be kept up to date. If the knowledge of statistics is built on an incomplete foundation, the whole structure will surely topple. The questions and problems found at the end of each chapter will help to test the stability of the student's progress. Understanding statistical analysis has important practical consequences in life.

1.2   Meaning of Statistics

An experiment is the heart of science. The behavioural scientists have the ability to think about the behaviours of the organisms in a novel way. They want to acquire a variety of knowledge about the behavioural problems through scientific experiments. By reasoning or through intuition, the scientist designs an experiment to objectively study or test a particular phenomenon. The data from the experiment are then analysed statistically. For this reason, the scientists or researchers need statistics (singular: statistic).

In the opinion of Baron (2002), statistics are mathematical procedures used to describe data (singular: datum) and draw inferences from them. All scientists require two types of tools in their research, such as equipment for collecting data and some means of interpreting their findings. In psychology, statistics are often used for the latter purpose. To understand the findings of their research and, hence, important aspects of human and animal behaviour, psychologists make use of statistics, or more accurately, the statistical analysis of the data they have collected. Thus, statistics is a science which provides tools for analysis and interpretation to be used on raw data collected for the purpose of decision-making in various fields of scientific inquiry. Broadly speaking, it deals with the collection, classification and tabulation of numerical facts as basis for explanation, description and comparison of phenomena.

In order to know the meaning of statistics, we have to discuss four important terms: population, sample, parameter and statistics. Population means all sets of individuals, animals, objects, elements or reactions that can be described as having a unique pattern of qualities. In brief, a population is the complete set of individuals, objects or scores that the investigator is interested in studying. Population may be either infinite or finite. An infinite population is so vast and widespread that it is not possible or practical to count the number of its members and to know its precise size, for example, the populations of all diabetic humans on the earth, all white rats of a particular strain on the earth, all Acquired Immune Deficiency Syndrome (AIDS) patients in the world and so forth. In contrast, a finite population is so limited in size and location that enables a precise statement of its size by counting of all its members, for example, the populations of all examinees in a school learning examination, all participants in an Olympiad, all university students of the Odisha (old name: Orissa) state and so on.

A sample is defined as a relatively small group of individuals, elements, objects, items, events, cases and the like of a corresponding, relevant population, and it is a true representative of the population from which it is drawn. A representative sample is the one in which the distribution of scores in the sample closely parallels that of the population. In other words, a representative sample is the one that contains the relevant characteristics of the population in the same proportions as they are included in that population. However, non-probability samples and small samples are not the true representatives of their parent population. Briefly, a sample is a subset of the population (Pagano, 1994). In other words, a sample is a collection of some, but not all, of the elements of the population under study, used to describe the population. A good sample will contain at least some of the elements that the population does, which shows that there must be an effective relation between the sample and the population. One way of providing this is to ensure that everyone in the population has a known chance of being included in the sample, and also it seems reasonable to make these chances equal. We also want to be certain that the inclusion of one population member does not affect the chance of others being included in the sample. So the choice is made by some element of chance, such as fishbowl draw (or lottery system), spinning a coin or in large population and samples, by use of computer programs or table of random numbers. For example, we want to know the intelligence quotient (IQ) of the newcomers admitted into the Master of Business Administration (MBA) course in a particular college in the year 2014. The total number of students is 300. Let us take this as a population of size $N=300$. We want a sample of size $n=20$. If we select/draw these 20 samples from a population of 300 by a lottery system or by any other techniques of randomisation as mentioned earlier, then these samples are called random samples, which are the true representatives of the parent population.

A parameter is a measure of the population. It refers to the indices of a central value, dispersion, correlation and so on, of all the individuals of a population. In other words, a parameter is a value or numerical index, such as the mean, median, standard deviation, and the like of the scores for the entire population. Briefly, a parameter is a number calculated on population data that quantifies a characteristic of a population. It is usually difficult to study a population in its entirety. So a parameter cannot be directly measured or precisely known in most cases. But a fairly close idea of the parameter may be made from the corresponding measures of the variables in the samples randomly drawn from the population. Although not precisely known, a parameter is regarded as a fixed reference value as it is not expected to change so long as the population continues to remain unaltered. For example, the total number of students in the 12th class of a particular school is 200. Let us take it as a finite population of size $N=200$. We want to know the average height of the students of this population. For this purpose, we measured the height of each and every individual student and found that the average height is 5′4″ (5 feet and 4 inches). It is also known as the population mean, which is symbolically expressed as Mu (μ). This μ is called a population parameter. The value of this parameter, that is, $\mu=5′4″$, remains unchanged till the size (N) and the same individual students constituting the population have not been changed. In other words, so far as the size (N) and constituents of a particular population are unchanged, the parameter remains constant. It serves as a fixed reference value for the average values of different groups of samples of a particular size (n) drawn from the same population, because the sample statistics fall around the population parameter. For instance, three groups of samples of size, $n=10$ each, were drawn from this parent population of students. The mean height of these three groups (1 through 3) were $\bar{X}_1 = 5′3″$, $\bar{X}_2 = 5′4″$ and $\bar{X}_3 = 5′5″$, respectively. If we analyse these three-sample statistics, one value is less than, one is equal to and one value is greater than the parameter value.

A statistic is a measure of the sample. In other words, a statistic is a number calculated on the sample data that quantifies a characteristic of the sample. It refers to a value or a numerical index, such as the mean, median, standard deviation, and the like of a variable for a particular sample. Unlike a parameter, it can be directly computed from the scores of the variables measured, and then can be used in estimating the corresponding parameter. A statistic may vary from sample to sample drawn from the same population due to the difference in their composition, that is, the differences in the individuals, events or cases included in the different sets of samples. A statistic may be equal to or more or less than the parameter of a particular population. In other words, the values of a statistic for different samples are distributed around the value of the corresponding parameter to form a sampling distribution of that statistic. The deviation of a statistic from the corresponding parameter (e.g., $\bar{X} - \mu$) is called the sampling error. This sampling error may be positive or negative depending on the statistic, whether it exceeds or recedes the parameter, respectively. The sampling error, whether positive or negative, can be decreased with an increase in the sample size. In spite of its variations, the sample statistic is usually a good estimate of the population parameter provided the sample is an impartial, unbiased representative of the population. For example, the sample mean ($\bar{X}$) is a good estimate of the population mean (μ), because the grand mean ($\bar{\bar{X}}$), that is, the mean of all the possible sample means, is equal to the population mean or parameter (i.e., $\bar{X} = \mu$). To make it clearer, let us take a certain finite population containing four individuals (say, A, B, C and D), that is, $N=4$, whose body weights are 50, 50, 52 and 48 kg, respectively. The population mean (μ) is 50 kg. Thus, the parameter value is 50 kg. Now, let us take all possible simple random sample combinations of size $n=2$, without replacement from this population of size $N=4$. There are six such possible sample combinations $\left(\text{i.e., } C_n^N = \dfrac{N!}{n!(N-n)!} = \dfrac{4!}{2!(4-2)!} = \dfrac{4!}{2!2!} = \dfrac{4 \times 3 \times 2 \times 1}{2 \times 1 \times 2 \times 1} = 6\right)$. These six combinations of samples of size $n=2$ are AB, AC, AD, BC, BD and CD, whose mean ($\bar{X}$) body weights are 50, 51, 49, 51, 49 and 50 kg, respectively. The mean of these six sample means, called a grand mean, is $\bar{\bar{X}} = 50$ kg. Thus, the population mean is equal to the sample grand mean (i.e., $\mu = \bar{\bar{X}}$). Therefore, the sample statistic (say, mean $\bar{X}$) is an unbiased estimate of the population parameter (say, mean μ).

Some statistical symbols corresponding to the parametric symbols, where X is the variable, are given in Table 1.1.

Although statistic (plural: statistics) has been diversely defined from Bowley's 'science of counting' or 'science of averages' to Harlow's 'science and art of handling aggregate of facts—observing, their enumeration, recording, classifying and otherwise systematically treating

Table 1.1 Statistcal symbols corresponding to parametric symbols of a variable X

Measure	Statistic	Parameter
Mean	$\overline{X}$	μ
Standard deviation	s, s_x	σ, σ_x
Variance	s^2, s_x^2	σ^2, σ_x^2
Correlation coefficient	r	ρ
Standard error of the mean	$s_{\overline{x}}$	$\sigma_{\overline{x}}$
Standard error of the difference between means	$s_{\overline{x}_1 - \overline{x}_2}$	$\sigma_{\overline{x}_1 - \overline{x}_2}$

them', most statisticians prefer to examine the nature and characteristics of a statistical process as a way of understanding statistics as if it is a young science.

1.3 Nature of Statistics

With regard to the nature of statistics, the following points are noteworthy.

 (i) Statistics is the science of observation, recording and enumeration of facts relating to a social phenomenon.
 (ii) It involves the process of organisation, classification and analysis of numerical facts.
(iii) It provides the basis for explanation, description and comparison of different phenomena.
(iv) It helps the process of interpretation, prediction and decision-making about a scientific inquiry.
 (v) Statistics is not only a science but also an art because it provides the percept to determine the application of the statistical tools, thus facilitating the accomplishment of the ultimate objectives of scientific enquiry.

1.4 Aims and Applications of Statistics as a Science

The word 'statistics' is used in two senses. First, statistics is the science of the methodology for the scientific collection, systematic presentation, mathematical analysis and interpretation of the data, and for making predictions about future outcomes, and drawing inferences about the observed phenomenon in the relevant population from which the samples are drawn. Second, statistics are the useful measures, such as means, medians, standard deviations, and the like, derived from the numerical data of an experiment or test. Thus, statistics is a flexible tool that can be used for many different purposes.

In view of these senses, statistics have the following aims and applications.

1. Statistics help in designing experiments more scientifically and in minimising experimental errors.
2. They are used in drawing a representative sample from the relevant population for a study and also in fixing the size of that sample for the drawing of reliable inferences.

3. Statistics are employed in summarising or describing a large amount of data being collected.

4. Statistics are used for the systematic arrangement, mathematical analysis and interpretation of the observed data for a meaningful description of the studied property or phenomenon. They aim to present the data by such graphical and/or computational methods so as to offer some common forms of expression of the empirical findings for better and effective communication among the researchers.

5. Statistics are used for comparing individuals or groups of individuals in various ways. In other words, statistics are applied in the study, analysis and prediction of individual differences in physical and psychological characteristics.

6. Statistics are employed to accomplish the task of determining whether certain aspects of behaviour are related or not (whether they vary together in a systematic manner). In other words, statistics explore and quantify the magnitude and the direction of a relationship between two or more properties, events or phenomena in a given population.

7. Statistics also find application in predicting future behaviour from current information. Put it into other words, statistics may be applied to predict mathematically the most probable value of a characteristic, property or trait in an individual, from the observed values of other related characteristics, properties or traits in the same individual. Predictions are done by statistical techniques known as correlation and regression.

8. They also explore the cause-and-effect relationships between two or more properties or events.

9. In psychological and educational experiments, tests or surveys, the raw data are collected mostly from samples instead of the entire population. So there is always a probability that the obtained results have occurred by chance in the sample drawn, and would not have occurred if the entire population was studied. Therefore, statistics are used to assess the probability of the results occurring by chance. In other words, statistics estimate the probability of not getting such results, had the entire population been subjected to the same investigation instead of a limited sample. The inference is then drawn accordingly as such a probability is too low or too high. Thus, statistics help to generalise the experimental findings in a sample to the entire population from which the samples are randomly drawn.

10. Statistics are also used to estimate the probability of errors in the inference, thus stipulating the degree of precision of the inference.

11. Statistics are used in estimating the reliability of a test in measuring the specific relevant property or trait of the individuals. This is done by the statistical assessment of the consistency of results on repeating the same test on the same sample.

12. Statistics are applied to estimate the validity of a test, that is, whether a test measures what it intends or purports to measure. This is done by assessing the capacity of that test to measure the specific property in exclusion of other closely related ones.

13. Statistics also estimate variations of a property in the population and explore the possible causative factors for these variations by analysing the variances which are some statistical measures of the variations.

14. Statistics are used universally in diverse aspects of human activities and problems, such as psychological problems, educational problems, scientific research, employment surveys, market research, industrial or organisational development and so on.

15. The performance of one group can be compared with that made by another, and the significance of any differences can be tested by using appropriate statistical tests.

1.5   Classification of Statistical Procedures

Statistical procedures are broadly classified into three major categories: descriptive statistics, sampling or inferential statistics and prediction statistics, which are discussed below.

1.5.1   Descriptive Statistics

Baron (2002) defined descriptive statistics as 'statistics that summarise the major characteristics of an array of scores'. In the opinion of Ferguson (1981), statistical procedures used in describing the properties of a sample, or of population where complete population data are available, are referred to as descriptive statistics. Statistics such as mean, median, standard deviation and correlation coefficients express either some average value of a variable or the dispersion of its individual scores around the average, or the relation between two variables in the sample studied. They, thus, describe the properties of a sample with respect to a variable or variables, and are consequently called descriptive statistics. For instance, if we measure the IQ of the complete population of students in a particular university and compute the mean IQ, then mean (μ) is a descriptive statistic because it describes a characteristic of the complete population. If, on the other hand, we measure the IQ of a sample of 100 students and compute the mean IQ for the sample, then mean ($\bar{X}$) is also a descriptive statistic because it describes a characteristic of that sample which is randomly drawn from the population of university students.

These descriptive statistics may belong to three categories according to the properties of the sample described by them. These three categories are: (i) statistics of location, (ii) statistics of dispersion and (iii) statistics of correlation. The statistics of location include the measures of central tendency—mean, median and mode; frequency distribution, percentiles, quartiles, deciles and normal curve—skewness and kurtosis, and so forth. The statistics of dispersion include the measures of variability, such as standard deviation, mean deviation, quartile deviation, range and variance. The statistics of correlation include correlation coefficients like Pearson's product-moment r, Spearman's rank-order correlation (rho $= \rho$) and Kendall's rank correlation (tau $= \tau$), which describe the degree and direction of the relationship between two or more variables in the individuals of a sample.

1.5.2   Sampling or Inferential Statistics

Statistical procedures used in the drawing of inferences about the properties of populations from sample data are frequently referred to as inferential statistics. If, for example, we wish to make a statement about the mean IQ in the complete population of students in a particular university (say Utkal University) from the knowledge of the mean IQ computed on the sample of 100 students drawn randomly from that population of university students, and to estimate the error involved in this statement, we use procedures from the inferential statistics. The application of these procedures provides information about the accuracy of the sample mean as an estimate of the population mean; that is, it indicates the degree of assurance we may place in the inferences or conclusions we draw from the sample to the population. In short, statistical procedures that permit us to determine whether differences between individuals or groups are the ones that are likely or unlikely to have occurred by chance are known as inferential statistics.

Inferential statistics, otherwise known as sampling statistics, include statistics, such as standard errors, which are not restricted within the limits of a sample. Although computed from the descriptive statistics of a sample, such inferential or sampling statistics go beyond the sample, help in generalising inferences from the sample to the entire population and also fix the probability of errors in such inferences. These inferential statistics find wide applications in testing the experimental hypotheses and the significance of difference between the statistics of different samples. They are also used in estimating the sampling error and the confidence intervals of population parameters.

In simpler terms, it can be said that psychologists use inferential statistics to determine whether differences between individuals or groups are significant or real. Inferential statistics assume that the mean difference in question is zero, and that observed differences are distributed normally around this value. If an observed difference is large enough that it would occur by chance only 5 per cent of the time, it is viewed as significant.

1.5.3   Prediction Statistics

Prediction statistics are better known as forecasting statistics. We can forecast various psychological variables, crops, matters, materials and so on.

Statistical procedures used in predicting future behaviour from current information are referred to as prediction statistics, which include regression coefficients. These are used in predicting the most likely value of a dependent variable (criterion) in an individual on the basis of the known value(s) of one or more independent variables (predictors) in the same individual when those variables have a significant correlation between them. Thus, prediction statistics are computed using descriptive statistics, such as means, standard deviations and correlation coefficients. However, prediction and correlation are closely related topics, and an understanding of one requires an understanding of the other. The correlation coefficients range from –1.00 to +1.00 through zero. The larger the departure from 0.00, the stronger the correlation between the variables in question. The greater the absolute value of the correlation between two variables (e.g., X and Y), the more accurate the prediction of one variable from the other. If the correlation between X and Y is either –1.00 or +1.00, perfect prediction is possible.

In many areas of human endeavour, predictions about the subsequent behaviour of individuals are required. For example, the scholastic performance of a child may be predicted from his/her intelligence test scores, the job performance of an individual from information available at the time of selection, a patient's receptivity to treatment from information obtained prior to treatment, the workshop skill of an engineer from his mechanical aptitude test scores and so on. Such predictions are of great practical benefit to schools, companies, clinics and others wishing to predict future performance from current behaviour.

1.6   Functions (or Use) of Statistics

Statistics are of immediate and practical utility. They help us get our work done more quickly and efficiently. Statistics aid teachers in the assignment of grades and in the construction of tests. They help psychologists interpret the measurements and observations they make. The sociologists find them of similar use in evaluating the data with which they must work. In all behavioural sciences, statistics have become a familiar part of the working day and daily life. In these fields, effectiveness and ease of operation require the knowledge of basic statistical methods. Here, one question arises as to why students would want to study statistics? Such a question calls for the functions of statistics. Now, let us discuss the following functions of statistics.

1.6.1   Collection of Data

The collection of data refers to a purposive gathering of information relevant to the subject matter of study. The task of data collection begins after a research problem is defined and research design/plan is chalked out. There are two sources from which data are collected—the primary source and the secondary source. The primary source provides data by observation and recording during the course of an investigation. This is called primary because the data are obtained from the very source where it is generated. On the other hand, when an individual or organisation processes and publishes data being collected as well as collated by another individual or organisation from the primary sources, it is a secondary source of data. As there are two sources, there are two types of data namely, primary data and secondary data. Primary data are collected from primary sources, whereas secondary data are collected from secondary sources. Put it into other words, the primary data are those which are collected afresh and for the first time, and, thus, happen to be original in character. The secondary data, on the other hand, are those which have already been collected by someone else and which have already been passed through the statistical process. Data which have not passed through the statistical process are also secondary data, if it is passed, presented or used by a third person. The available data are called secondary data because they are being used away from the initial sources and the purpose of original collection. Thus, the data which may be primary in the hands of the one may become secondary in the hands of others. Therefore, the researcher would have to decide which sort of data he/she would be using (thus collecting) for his/her study and accordingly he/she will have to select one or the other method of data collection. The methods of collecting primary and secondary data differ since primary data are to be originally collected, while in the case of secondary data, the nature of data collection work is merely that of compilation.

There are several methods of collecting primary data. Some of the important methods are as follows: (i) observation, (ii) experiment, (iii) interview, (iv) questionnaire and (v) schedules. However, the secondary data can be collected from two sources—published sources (e.g., books, journals, magazines, periodicals, newspapers, reports, records and so on) and unpublished sources (e.g., records maintained by various government and private offices; studies made by research institutions and scholars; diaries, letters, biographies and autobiographies, and so on).

1.6.2   Enumeration

In statistics, two types of enumerations are used. These are census enumeration and sample enumeration. In the census enumeration, information is collected for each and every unit. A unit may be called an individual, a state, a district, a village, a household, a caste, a family, a community, a club, a school, a field, an agricultural plot, a factory, an organisation or any other similar things in any specified geographical area to be covered under study. The aggregate of all units under consideration is called the 'population' or the 'universe'. Sometimes, it may not be possible or even necessary to obtain information for each and every unit of the population. Only the representative characteristics of the sample can warrant an inference on the characteristics of the population. It is called sample enumeration. In most of the psychological studies, sample enumeration is used for the following reasons:

(a) When the universe is inordinately large, there is no alternative but to resort to sampling.
(b) The results are to be obtained more rapidly because data on relatively fewer items can be collected and processed quickly.

(c) With small data, it is possible to have greater precision and depth by a thorough and in-depth study because more detailed information can be sought from a small group of respondents.

(d) It is a more economical method of inquiry. On occasions where the purpose of inquiry does not warrant a complete enumeration, it would be wasteful of efforts to go for it and also a degree of precision higher than what is necessary for the stated purpose.

(e) It is easy to guard against incomplete and inaccurate returns in relatively limited enumeration.

1.6.3   Sampling Design

A sampling design is a definite plan for obtaining a sample from a given population. A sampling design covers all aspects of sampling, such as the system of selection, preparation of a sampling frame from which the selection of units will be made, the size of the sample and so on. In addition, the training of investigators, interviewers and the framing of questionnaires and schedules may also be prescribed in it. There are many sampling designs from which a researcher can choose. Some designs are relatively more precise and easier to apply than others. The researcher must select/prepare a sampling design which should be reliable and appropriate for his research study.

The following are some of the important characteristics of a good sampling design. Therefore, while developing a sampling design, the researcher must pay attention to the following points.

(a) Sampling design must result in a truly representative sample.

(b) Sampling design must be such which results in a small sampling error.

(c) Sampling design must be viable in the context of funds available for the research study.

(d) Sampling design must be such so that systematic bias can be controlled in a better way.

(e) Sampling design should be such that the results of the sample study can be applied, in general, for the universe with a reasonable level of confidence.

1.6.4   Classification of Data

An unorganised mass of data does not allow a proper grasp of the significance of the information contained therein. It is only after classification and tabulation that the data become fit for statistical processing. Although direct methods of calculation may be used when the number of data is very small, it is always advisable to go through the preliminary stages of classification and tabulation before we handle a large mass of data for calculation. In this, advantages lie in precision, accuracy, correctness and time saving.

Classification refers to the process of arranging data into sequences and groups according to their common characteristics, and in separating them into different but related parts. Here, a group, a class or a category has to be determined on the basis of the nature of data and the purpose for which it is going to be used. Classification may be done mentally or actually, but groups have to be formed with elements which have close resemblance. This helps in bringing out the group character of both similarities and diversities within the group as well as among different groups.

(a) *Rules of classification.* The following rules are usually followed in classifying a set of data.

    (i) Each item of information should fit only into one class. In other words, classes must not overlap.

(ii) Classification must be exhaustive. There must be a place for each response in some class.

(iii) The basic principle of classification should be retained throughout; else, the drawing of inferences on the subject matter will become difficult.

(b) *Types of classification.* The following are some of the common modes of classification of data.

  (i) *Alphabetical.* It is the most common form of classification because it helps in locating facts within the table. Reference tables in particular are prepared in an alphabetical form.

  (ii) *Geographical.* It is the classification based on geographical regions. If the existing political boundaries are taken as the basis, the classification may be done by states, districts, or taluks.

  (iii) *Chronological.* Chronological classification is done by time periods such as annual, seasonal, monthly and so on. Such a classification is often combined with one or more of other modes of classification.

  (iv) *Qualitative.* This classification of data is done by the character or the attributes of the subject matter. For example, a classification by the literacy, sex, marital status and so on is said to be a classification by attributes or quality.

  (v) *Numerical.* Numerical or quantitative classification is sought in the cases where magnitude of the attributes can be measured.

1.6.5 Tabulation of Data

The main objective of statistical tables is to summarise a mass of numerical information and to present it in the simplest possible form consistent with the purpose for which it has been designed. The idea is to make a complex mass of data more intelligible and meaningful. This is achieved through systematic arrangement and elegant presentation.

While presenting data in the form of a table, its angularities are removed and it is simplified through proper organisation without sacrificing the quality and usefulness of the data.

(a) *Parts of a statistical table.* Following are the main parts of the table along with suitable comments which will help in preparing an ideal table from a given data.

  (i) *Table number.* A table should always be numbered for easy identification and reference in future. If all the tables are numbered, it will be easy to prepare their list.

  (ii) *Title.* A title should accompany every table. It is customary to place it above in the table. A good title is one which is clearly worded and which offers a brief but unambiguous statement of the nature of the data contained.

  (iii) *Source note.* A source note refers to the source from which information has been taken. Such a note can be useful when the information given is incomplete.

  (iv) *Unit.* The unit of measurement along with the mode of rounding-up should always be given. If the same unit has been used throughout the body of the table, it may be given along with the title.

  (v) *Body.* The body of the table contains the numerical information. The arrangement is made according to the description given for each column and row referred to as caption and stubs, respectively.

    - *Captions.* These refer to headings of vertical columns. A caption has usually a main heading and subheadings.

– *Stubs.* These are the headings of horizontal rows. Much will depend on the choice of arrangements, but normally a relatively important classification with long description is given in the row.

(vi) *Size, shape and style.* A table should be so designed that it is neither very long and narrow nor very short and broad. If need be, it should be adjusted to the space provided for the purpose.

(b) *Types of tables.* Tables can be classified in a number of ways depending on the purpose, stage of inquiry, nature of data used, number of elements covered and so on. Different types of tables are given below:

(i) *General versus specific purpose tables.* The general purpose tables deal with the general descriptive facts about the data. For example, frequency distribution table, mean and standard deviation table, and so forth are general purpose tables. On the other hand, specific purpose tables of the data deal with statistical analyses particularly needed for a specific situation. For example, correlation table, analysis of variance table, and so forth are specific purpose tables.

(ii) *Original versus derived tables.* A table containing actual data is an original table. But a table containing derived results from the original data, results like mean, skewness, coefficient of variation and so on, would constitute a derived table.

(iii) *Process tables.* Process tables are prepared in the early stage of a statistical inquiry to help processing of data for analysis and interpretation. They present the collected data in a classified form to enable quick and proper grasp of its significance.

(iv) *Summary tables.* Summary tables provide summary results of an inquiry at the end of the inquiry. They are condensed tables containing data derived from the inquiry.

(v) *Simple and complex tables.* A simple table deals with only the subclasses of a given phenomenon related to some other variables, whereas a complex table deals with more involved subclasses of one or more variables and is related to various subsections of another variable. It is also called a manifold table with many classes and subclasses of two or more variables.

1.6.6 Measurement

In our day-to-day life, we are often faced with the measurement of physical objects as well as abstract concepts. Thus, measurements are of two types: quantitative and qualitative. The measurements of various features of physical objects, like height, weight, length, breadth and the like, and the amounts of various mental abilities are called quantitative measures, because these can be measured directly with some standard units of measurement. The qualitative measures, on the other hand, refer to the measurement of abstract concepts, like beauty, honesty, aesthetic qualities of a painting, a song and so on. It is not possible to have a direct measurement of abstract concepts. Therefore, measurement means the process of mapping or assigning numbers to objects or observations. The kind or level of measurement which is achieved is a function of the rules under which the numbers were assigned. The operations and relations employed in obtaining the scores define and limit the manipulations and operations which are permissible in handling the scores; the manipulations and operations must be those of the numerical structure to which the measurement is isomorphic.

1.7   Limitations of Statistics

Although statistics are indispensable to almost all sciences—social, behavioural, physical, and natural, and are very widely used in almost all spheres of human activity; yet, they are not without limitations which restrict their scope and utility.

(i) *Statistics do not study qualitative phenomenon.* Statistics are numerical statements in any department of enquiry placed in relation to each other. Since statistic is a science dealing with a set of numerical data, it can be applied to the study of only those phenomena which can be measured quantitatively. However, all human phenomena are not capable of quantitative expression. Abstract concepts or quality characteristics, such as intelligence, health, beauty, honesty, wisdom, welfare, poverty and so on, do not readily lend themselves to quantitative representations, and, thus, cannot be measured quantitatively. For the use of statistical methods in measuring these qualitative characteristics, certain well-defined 'objective scores' have to be devised. The usefulness and application of the techniques of statistical analysis will then depend on how well these scores are devised. For instance, the attribute of intelligence in a group of individuals can be studied on the basis of their IQs, which may be regarded as the quantitative measure of the individual's intelligence.

(ii) *Statistics do not study individuals.* 'By statistics we mean aggregate of facts affected to a marked extent by multiplicity of factors and placed in relation to each other'. Thus, a single or isolated figure cannot be regarded as statistics unless it is a part of the aggregate of facts relating to any particular field of enquiry. Thus, statistical methods do not give any recognition to an object or a person or an event in isolation. In other words, statistical results reveal the average behaviour, the normal or the general trend; they are, therefore, useful for a general appraisal of a phenomenon, and not for substitution to any specific unit or event. This is a serious limitation of statistics. For instance, the price of a single commodity, the profit of a particular concern or the production of a particular business organisation does not constitute statistics since these figures are unrelated and incomparable. However, the aggregate of figures relating to prices and consumption of various commodities, the sales and profits of a business organisation, the income, expenditure, production and so forth, over different periods of time, places and so on, will be statistics. Thus, from a statistical point of view, the figure of the population of a particular country in some given year is useless unless we are also given the figures of the population of the country for different years or of different countries for the same year for comparative studies. Hence, statistics are confined only to those problems where group characteristics are to be studied.

(iii) *Statistical laws are not exact.* Since the statistical laws are probabilities in nature, inferences based on them are only approximate and not exact like the inferences based on physical and natural scientific laws. Statistical laws are true only on average. If the probability of getting a head in a single throw of a coin is 0.5, it does not imply that if we toss a coin 10 times, we shall get five heads and five tails. In 10 throws of a coin, we may get 8 heads, 9 heads or all the 10 heads, or we may not get even a single head. By this, we mean that if the experiment of throwing the coin is carried on indefinitely (i.e., very large number of times), then we should expect on the average 50 per cent heads and 50 per cent tails. In short, statistics are based on approximations and can never be as precise as the figures in physical measurements.

(iv) *Statistics cannot be applied indiscriminately.* The research data are collected with a given purpose or objective. These data are analysed by appropriate statistical techniques. The results of these statistical analyses cannot be applied indiscriminately to any situation. Its validity in a particular situation does not warrant its equal utility in another. Such a use of data (i.e., secondary data) without proper care is likely to lead to fallacious conclusions.

(v) *Statistical relation does not necessarily mean causal relationship.* The statistical relations do not necessarily bring out the cause-and-effect relationship between two phenomena. They only reveal association amongst certain sets of quantities or variables which may not be of cause and effect type. In other words, correlation between two variables does not necessarily indicate the cause-and-effect relationship between these two; it may depict simply the degree of association.

(vi) *Statistics are liable to be misused.* Perhaps the most significant limitation of statistics is that it must be used by experts. Statistics only furnish a tool though imperfect which is dangerous in the hands of those who do not know its use and deficiencies. Statistical methods are the most dangerous tools in the hands of the inexpert. The greatest limitation of statistics is that it deals with figures which are innocent in themselves and do not bear on their face the label of their quality, and can be easily distorted, manipulated, or moulded by politicians, dishonest or unskilled workers, unscrupulous people for personal selfish motives. Statistics neither prove nor disprove anything. It is merely a tool which, if rightly used, may prove extremely useful but if misused by inexperienced, unskilled and dishonest statisticians might lead to very fallacious conclusions, and even prove to be disastrous. It is rightly said, 'statistics are like clay of which you can make a God or Devil as you please'. It is also remarked, 'Science of statistics is the useful servant but only of great value to those who understand its proper use'.

Thus, the use of statistics by the experts who are well experienced and skilled in the analysis and interpretation of statistical data for making predictions about future outcomes and for drawing correct and valid inferences very much increases the importance, utility and popularity of this branch of knowledge.

1.8   Misuses (or Abuses) of Statistics

Instead of serving as a valuable basis for understanding scientific data, interpreting test scores, or making predictions about behaviour, statistics are sometimes employed to confuse, deceive, or mislead their intended victims. To make matters worse, in the wrong hands statistics can be quite effective in this role. According to Baron (2002), the following are the reasons of misuse of statistics: (i) random events do not always seem random; (ii) larger samples provide a better basis for reaching conclusions than smaller ones; (iii) unbiased samples provide a better basis for reaching conclusions than biased ones; (iv) unexpected comparisons are often meaningless; (v) some differences are not really there; and (vi) graphs may distort (or at least bend) reality. In short, although statistics have many beneficial uses, they are often employed to deceive or mislead. Misuse of statistics can involve the use of extremely small or biased samples, unexpected comparisons and misleading graphs and presentations.

The improper use of statistical tools by unscrupulous people with an improper statistical bend of mind has led to the public distrust in statistics. By this we mean that public loses its beliefs, faith and confidence in the science of statistics and starts condemning it. In this context, Gupta (1996, 2005) said that the following are some of the reasons for distrust of statistics. These are enumerated as follows:

(a) Figures are innocent and believable, and the facts based on them are psychologically more convincing. But it is pity that figures do not have the label of quality on their face.

(b) Arguments are put forward to establish certain results which are not true by making use of inaccurate figures or by using incomplete data, thus distorting the truth.

(c) Although accurate, the figures might be moulded and manipulated by irresponsible, inexperienced, dishonest and unscrupulous persons to conceal the truth and present a wrong and distorted picture of the facts to the public for their personal selfish motives, and thus, have discredited the science of statistics.

Hence, if statistics and their tools and techniques are misused, the fault does not lie with the science of statistics; rather, it is the people who misuse it, and who are to be blamed. Utmost care and precautions should be taken for the interpretation of statistical data in all its manifestations. Statistics can effectively be used by expert statisticians.

1.9 Fallacies in Statistics

Although statistics have wide applicability and utility, we often commit some common mistakes in the understanding and interpretation of facts by using statistical methods. These common mistakes are known as fallacies which are unavoidable. The following are the sources of fallacies.

   (i) *Collection of data.* The most important factor to be considered in statistical work is that the original collection of data is proper. If there are inadequacies at the very source of data, even if the best of the statistical methods is used in the analysis and interpretation of results will not serve any useful purpose.

  (ii) *Definition of terms.* The various terms in statistical study should clearly, objectively and unambiguously be defined. The error in collection of data may arise because of faulty definitions which have scope for different interpretations.

 (iii) *Selection of units.* The selection of units or samples should be random, so that they should be the true representative of the universe or population. Serious errors will enter into the collection of data if the units are not the representative of the universe, and thus, the inferences drawn about the universe or population from which the samples are drawn are erroneous or fallacious. In such cases, the data collected should be accompanied with a statement of the deficiencies, so that the users of the results would be warned about the limitations of the study.

 (iv) *Classification.* The fundamental principle of classification is that each group should be homogeneous so that its central value can truly represent the group; the lack of homogeneity often leads to fallacious results.

  (v) *Choice of methods.* An appropriate choice of methods is necessary to obtain reliable inferences from statistical analysis. A wrong method will not throw proper light on the character of data.

 (vi) *Comparisons.* Comparisons are a part of analysis but a good deal of care is required to avoid fallacious conclusions.

1.10 Methods of Sampling

Sampling refers to the process of drawing samples from the population or universe. There are various methods of sampling that may be used singly or along with other methods. The choice will be determined by the researcher based on the purpose of the study for which sampling is sought and on the nature of the population from which the research sample is to be drawn.

Sampling methods are basically of two types, namely, probability sampling and non-probability sampling, which are discussed below.

1.10.1   Probability Sampling

Probability sampling is also known as 'random sampling' or 'chance sampling'. Probability sampling is based on the concept of random selection, which means that each element in the population has an equal and independent chance of selection in the sample. In other words, probability sampling refers to that process in which every item, element or individual of the population/universe has an equal and independent chance of inclusion in the sample. Equal implies that the probability of selection of each element in the population is the same; that is, the choice of an element in the sample is not influenced by other considerations such as personal preference. The concept of independence means that the choice of one element is not dependent upon the choice of another element in the sample; that is, the selection or rejection of one element does not affect the inclusion or exclusion of another. It is, so to say, a lottery method in which individual units are picked up from the whole group not deliberately but by some mechanical process. Here, it is blind chance alone that determines whether one item or the other is selected.

There are seven basic and commonly used types of probability sampling methods: (i) simple random sampling, (ii) systematic random sampling, (iii) stratified random sampling, (iv) cluster sampling, (v) area sampling, (vi) multi-stage random sampling and (vii) sequential sampling. These sampling methods are briefly discussed in the following sections.

1.10.1.1   *Simple Random Sampling*

The controlling factor underlying all major probability sampling plans is 'randomness'. 'Randomness' refers to the fact that all elements or individuals in a given population have an equal and independent chance of being included in a particular sample. In the simple random sampling method, the samples are drawn randomly from the population. A random selection refers to a truly probabilistic selection wherein each unit in the 'universe' has equal chance of being selected. By 'random selection' we do not mean a haphazard or an accidental selection of a certain number of items. Instead, it is a selection of units according to a well chalked out plan which ensures equal chance of selection to each unit in the population. Random sampling ensures the Law of Statistical Regularity which states that if, on an average, the sample chosen is a random one, the sample will have the same composition and characteristics as the universe/population. This is the reason why random sampling is considered as the best technique of selecting a representative sample. In brief, the characteristics of random sampling (or simple random sampling) are as follows:

(a) It gives each element in the population an equal probability of getting into the sample, and all choices are independent of one another.

(b) It gives each possible sample combination an equal probability of being chosen.

To make it clearer, we take a certain finite population consisting of five children (say, A, B, C, D and E), that is, $N=5$. Now let us take all the possible simple random sample combinations of size 2 (i.e., $n=2$) without replacement from this population of size, $N=5$. There are 10 such possible sample combinations of size, $n=2 \left(\text{i.e., } C_n^N = \dfrac{N!}{n!(N-n)!} = \dfrac{5!}{2!3!} = \dfrac{5 \times 4 \times 3 \times 2 \times 1}{2 \times 1 \times 3 \times 2 \times 1} = 10 \right)$.

These 10 combinations of samples of size, $n=2$ are AB, AC, AD, AE, BC, BD, BE, CD, CE and DE. If we choose one of these sample combinations in such a way that each has the probability 1/10 of being chosen, we will then call this a random sample.

The procedure used in simple random sampling is presented below:

Step 1. Determine the size of the present population (N).

Step 2. Identify by a number, an alphabet, or a name, all elements or sampling units in the population.

Step 3. Decide on the sample size (n).

Step 4. Select 'n' cases randomly using the fishbowl draw, the table of random numbers or a computer program.

Merits of simple random sampling

The following are some of the merits or advantages of simple random sampling plan:

(a) All elements in the population have an equal and independent chance of being included in the sample.

(b) The method of simple random sampling is used in conjunction with all other probability sampling plans. Therefore, it serves as a foundation upon which all types of random samples are based.

(c) The researcher does not need to know the true composition of the population beforehand. The simple random sample will theoretically reflect all important segments of the population to one degree or another.

(d) Simple random sampling seems to be the easiest to apply of all probability sampling plans. It is the simplest type of random sampling to understand.

Demerits of simple random sampling

The following are some of the demerits, disadvantages, or limitations of simple random sampling plan:

(a) Simple random sampling plans do not necessarily fully exploit the knowledge the researcher has concerning the population.

(b) Simple random sampling does not guarantee that certain elements existing in small numbers in the population will be included in any given sample.

(c) There is usually a greater sampling error in a simple random sample of size 'n' compared to a stratified random sample of the same size.

Applications of simple random sampling

Simple random sampling is useful for obtaining a probability sample from virtually all sources. It may be used in obtaining random samples from city directories, census tracts, geographical divisions of various territories, schools, prisons, communities, business and industrial organisations, political districts, telephone directories and so on. It may also be used for assignment of elements randomly to different experimental conditions in behavioural sciences. Because all forms of probability sampling must employ simple random sampling at various levels and stages, this sampling plan is indispensable.

1.10.1.2   *Systematic Random Sampling*

Another type of sampling used quite frequently is called as systematic random sampling or simply systematic sampling. In this method, instead of using a table of random numbers or lottery system for selecting all sample cases, we simply go down a list taking every kth individual, starting with a randomly selected case among the first k individuals. Under this method, the kth item is picked up to form the sample frame and k is determined as follows:

$$k = \frac{N}{n},$$

where 'N' is the total size of the population from which the samples are to be drawn, and 'n' is the proposed size of the 'sample' to be drawn. An element of randomness is introduced into this kind of sampling by using the table of random numbers, computer program, fishbowl draw, or lottery system to pick up the unit with which to start. For instance, if we want to select a sample of 90 persons from a population of 1,800, we would take every 20th $\left(k = \frac{N}{n} = \frac{1800}{90} = 20 \right)$ in the list. Any one of the persons would be selected randomly from the first 20 persons as the first sample to start with and thereafter every 20th person would automatically be included in the sample. Suppose the 11th person was selected. The sample would then consist of persons numbered 11, 31, 51, 71, 91, 111, ... Thus, in systematic sampling only the first unit is selected randomly and the remaining units of the sample are selected at fixed intervals. Although a systematic sample is not a random sample in the strict sense of the term, but it is often considered reasonable to treat systematic sample as if it were a random sample.

The procedure used in systematic sampling is presented below:

Step 1. Prepare a list of all the elements in the study population.

Step 2. Decide on the sample size (n).

Step 3. Determine the width of the interval, $k = \dfrac{\text{total population}}{\text{sample size}} = \dfrac{N}{n}$.

Step 4. Using the simple random sampling technique, select an element from the first interval (nth order).

Step 5. Select the same order element from each subsequent interval.

Merits of systematic random sampling

The following are some of the merits or advantages of systematic random sampling plan:

(a) Systematic random sampling can be taken as an improvement over a simple random sample in as much as the systematic sample is spread more evenly over the entire population.

(b) The systematic sampling method is obviously much simpler than the random sampling method whenever a list is extremely long or whenever a large sample is to be drawn.

(c) Moreover, it is an easier and less costly method of sampling, and can be conveniently used even in case of large populations.

Demerits of systematic random sampling

The following are some of the demerits, disadvantages or limitations of systematic random sampling plan:

(a) Systematic sampling is not entirely a random sampling plan; it has the characteristics of both random and non-random sampling designs. Since the selection of the first element from the first interval is random and the selection of other elements from the subsequent intervals is dependent upon the first, it cannot be classified as a random sample.

(b) The individuals may have been ordered so that a trend occurs. If persons in the population have been listed according to office, prestige or seniority, the position of the random start in the systematic random sampling may affect the results.

(c) If there is a hidden periodicity in the population, systematic random sampling will prove to be an insufficient method of sampling. For instance, every 25th item produced by a certain production process is defective. If we are to select a 4 per cent sample of the items of this process in a systematic manner, we would either get all defective items or all good items in our sample depending upon the random starting position.

Applications of systematic random sampling

There are infinite numbers of applications of systematic random sampling. Obtaining elements systematically from a list of labour union members, elementary and secondary school students, college and university students, telephone directories, city directories, membership lists for virtually all types of special interest groups and organisations, employees of companies and businesses, prisoners in penal institutions, neighbourhoods and the like are but a few of the many instances where this sampling form may be applied.

1.10.1.3   *Stratified Random Sampling*

If a population from which samples are to be drawn does not constitute a homogeneous group, a stratified sampling technique is generally applied in order to obtain a representative sample. Under stratified sampling method, first the entire population is divided into several subpopulations that are individually more homogenous than the total population (the different subpopulations are called strata; singular: stratum), and then we select items from each stratum to constitute a sample. Such stratification will lead to greater homogeneity within each stratum, and a marked difference or heterogeneity between several strata. This stratification method is more appropriate when the universe or population is composed of diverse classes of characteristics, and the characteristics of each stratum are relevant to the subject matter under study. Since each stratum is more homogeneous than the total population, we are able to get more precise estimates for each stratum and by estimating more accurately each of the component parts; we get a better estimate of the whole. Briefly, stratified sampling results in more reliable and detailed information.

The following three questions are highly relevant in the context of the stratified sampling technique:

(a) How to form strata?

(b) How should items be selected from each stratum?

(c) How many items can be selected from each stratum or how to allocate the sample size to each stratum?

With regard to the first question, it can be said that the strata can be formed on the basis of common characteristic(s) of the items to be included in each stratum. It means that various strata can be formed in such a way so as to ensure elements being most homogenous within each stratum and most heterogeneous between the different strata. Thus, strata are purposively formed and are usually based on the past experiences and personal judgements of the investigator. One should always remember that careful consideration of the relationship(s) between the characteristic(s) of the population and the characteristic(s) to be estimated are normally used to define the strata.

In respect of the second question, we can say that the usual method for selection of items for the sample from each stratum is the simple random sampling. The systematic random sampling method can be used if it is considered more appropriate in certain situations.

Regarding the third question, we may follow either the proportional stratified sampling method or disproportional stratified sampling method in order to allocate the sample size to each stratum. The sampling fractions $\left(\text{i.e.,}\ \dfrac{n_i}{N_i} = \dfrac{\text{sample size of a particular stratum}}{\text{population size of that particular stratum}} \right)$ for each stratum may be equal, in which case we speak of proportional stratified sampling or the sampling fractions for each stratum may be unequal, in which case we speak of disproportional stratified sampling. Both the proportional stratified sampling and disproportional stratified sampling are otherwise known as proportionate stratified random sampling and disproportionate stratified random sampling, respectively, because the samples from each stratum are drawn randomly by following either the simple random sampling method or systematic random sampling method.

The following is an illustration of the method of proportional allocation under which the sizes of the samples from different strata are kept proportional to the sizes of the strata; that is, if p_i represents the proportion of population included in stratum i and n represents the total sample size, then the number of items/elements to be selected from the stratum i is $n \times p_i$. To illustrate it, let us suppose that we want a sample of size $n=100$ to be drawn from a population of size $N=1,000$, which is divided into four strata of sizes $N_1=400$, $N_2=300$, $N_3=200$ and $N_4=100$, respectively. Adopting proportional allocation, we shall obtain the sample sizes as under for the different strata:

For stratum with $N_1=400$, we have $p_1 = \dfrac{400}{1,000} = 0.40$ and hence n_1 (sample size from first stratum)$= n \times p_1 = 100 \times 0.40 = 40$.

Similarly, for stratum with $N_2=300$, we have $p_2 = \dfrac{300}{1,000} = 0.30$

and hence n_2 (sample size from second stratum)$= n \times p_2 = 100 \times 0.30 = 30$.

For stratum with $N_3=200$, we have $p_3 = \dfrac{200}{1,000} = 0.20$

and hence n_3 (sample size from third stratum)$= n \times p_3 = 100 \times 0.20 = 20$.

For stratum with $N_4=100$, we have $p_4 = \dfrac{100}{1,000} = 0.10$

and hence n_4 (sample size from fourth stratum)$= n \times p_4 = 100 \times 0.10 = 10$.

Thus, using proportional allocation, the sample sizes for different strata are 40, 30, 20 and 10, respectively, which are in proportion to the sizes of the strata, namely, 400: 300: 200: 100. The proportionate stratified random sampling method is considered to be most effective, efficient and an optimal design when the cost of selecting an item is equal for each stratum, there is no difference in within-stratum variances and the purpose of sampling happens to be to estimate of the population value of some characteristic. But in case the purpose is to compare the differences among the strata, then equal sample selection from each stratum would be more efficient even if the strata differ in sizes. In other words, in the latter case, disproportional allocation of sample sizes is more desirable.

To illustrate the disproportionate stratified random sampling method, let us suppose that we want a sample of size $n=120$ to be drawn from a population of size $N=1,200$ which is divided into three strata (k) of sizes $N_1=500$, $N_2=400$ and $N_3=300$. Adopting disproportional allocation, the number of samples (n_j) to be drawn from each stratum or category is:

$$n_j = \frac{n}{k} = \frac{120}{3} = 40,$$

where

n_j=sample size in each stratum
n=total sample size to be drawn from all strata
k=the number of strata or categories.

Thus, the sample size is equal throughout the strata, and 40 items/elements will be randomly drawn from each stratum to be included in the total sample size.

The procedure for selecting a stratified sample is schematically presented below:

Step 1. Identify all elements or sampling units in the sampling population.
Step 2. Decide upon the different strata (k) into which you want to stratify the population.
Step 3. Place each element into the appropriate stratum.
Step 4. Number every element in each stratum separately.
Step 5. Decide the total sample size (n).
Step 6. Decide whether you want to select proportionate or disproportionate stratified sampling and follow the steps below.

Proportionate stratified random sampling	Disproportionate stratified random sampling
Step 7. Determine the proportion of each stratum in the study population (p): $$p = \frac{\text{element numbers in each stratum}}{\text{total population size}}.$$	**Step 7.** Determine the number of elements to be selected from each stratum: $$= \frac{\text{sample size } (n)}{\text{number of strata } (k)}.$$
Step 8. Determine the number of elements to be selected from each stratum = sample size $\times p = n \times p$. **Step 9.** Select the required number of elements from each stratum with a simple random sampling technique or a systematic random sampling technique. As the sample selected is in proportion to the size of each stratum in the population, this method is called proportionate stratified sampling.	**Step 8.** Select the required number of elements from each stratum with a simple random sampling technique or a systematic random sampling technique. As this method does not take the size of the stratum into consideration in the selection of the sample, it is called disproportionate stratified sampling.

Merits of proportionate stratified random sampling

The following are some of the merits or advantages of the proportionate stratified random sampling plan:

(a) Proportionately stratifying the sample enhances the representativeness of it in relation to the population. The representativeness is strengthened by making certain that those elements that exist in few numbers will be included accordingly. This is not necessarily guaranteed under the simple random sampling plan.

(b) The resulting sample is actually a better estimate of the true population characteristics as compared with a simple random sample.

(c) Another important advantage is that the sampling error associated with the sample as a population estimator is reduced over that found to occur with a simple random sample of the same size. In this sense, proportionate stratified random samples are more efficient than simple random samples, where increased efficiency is a function of decreasing the sampling error.

(d) The proportionate stratified random sampling plan estimates the necessity of having to weight the elements according to their original distribution in the population. The weight of any particular value is the frequency of it in the population.

Demerits of proportionate stratified random sampling

Some of the more important limitations, demerits, or disadvantages of the proportionate stratified random sampling plan are the following:

(a) Proportionate stratified random sampling is somewhat more difficult to obtain. It requires that the researcher should know something about the composition of the population and distribution of population characteristics prior to the draw of the elements. This is often an unrealistic assumption.

(b) This method involves more time to obtain elements from each of several strata.

(c) When several strata are to be identified, there is always the likelihood that classification errors might result. Classification error will occur if some elements in the population are categorised into the wrong strata.

(d) Proportionate stratified random sampling plans are usually more costly than simple random sampling plans.

Merits of disproportionate stratified random sampling

The important merits or major advantages of the disproportionate stratified random sampling plan are the following:

(a) It is less time consuming compared with proportionate stratified random sampling. The researcher is not necessarily as concerned about the proportionate representativeness of his or her resulting sample compared with the proportionate stratified random sampling plan. He/she does not have to be as careful in drawing specified number of elements from each of the substrata he/she identifies.

(b) Weighting of particular groups of elements is more likely with this type of sampling plan. The investigator is able to give greater weight to certain elements that are not represented as frequently in the population compared with other elements.

Demerits of disproportionate stratified random sampling

Some of the major limitations, disadvantages, or demerits of this sampling method are the following:

(a) This method does not give each substratum proper representation relative to its distribution throughout the original population. When some substrata are represented more heavily than others, a certain amount of bias enters. The assignment of greater weight to one set of elements in a particular substratum may cause the sample to become more biased, and hence, less representative.

(b) The disproportionate stratified random sampling method requires that the researcher should know something about the composition of the population and the distribution of population characteristics prior to the draw of elements. This is often an unrealistic assumption.

(c) In this method, there is possibility of committing classification error by the researcher, because he/she may misclassify certain elements in the population. However, the simple random sampling plan can overcome the hazards of classification.

Applications of stratified random sampling

When the population is large having heterogeneity, then stratified random sampling is applied.

Proportionate stratified random sampling is applied in the situation where it might be warranted to include school systems where year in school, academic measure, age, or sex would be important. Military studies might successfully employ this sampling plan where military rank, special arrangement and the like would theoretically affect other variables in the research project. It is possible to stratify according to attitudinal characteristics.

The primary use of disproportionate stratified random sampling in research design is when elements exist few in number among certain substrata within the dimension one stratifies. If there is a strong likelihood that one or more substrata will not be included in a simple random sampling of elements, then the researcher should take steps to see that elements from those particular substrata will be included.

1.10.1.4   *Cluster Sampling*

If the total area of interest happens to be a big one, a convenient way in which a sample can be taken is to divide the total area into a number of smaller non-overlapping areas and then to randomly select a number of these small areas (usually called clusters), with the ultimate sample consisting of all (or samples of) units in these small areas or clusters. Thus, in cluster sampling the total population is divided into a number of relatively small subdivisions which are themselves clusters of still smaller units, and then some of these clusters are randomly selected for inclusion in the overall sample. In brief, the cluster sampling pre-supposes the division of a population into a finite number of divisions and other identifiable groups. Cluster sampling consists in forming suitable clusters of units and surveying all the units in some clusters selected according to an appropriate sampling scheme. The clusters of units are formed by grouping neighbouring units or units which can be conveniently surveyed together.

Suppose the investigator wants to study the political attitudes of residents in a given state. It would not be feasible to study all persons, not only from the standpoint of the cost involved and the manpower requirements for field interviewing, but also because a sample of state residents would probably give us comparable information. He divides the state into sections with several horizontal and vertical grid lines. He then numbers each section from 1 to N, N being equal to the total number of sections. Using a random procedure, he draws a specified number of sections to constitute the sample he will study. He sends interviewers to study all persons living in the sections he has randomly drawn.

Cluster sampling, no doubt, reduces cost by concentrating surveys in selected clusters. But certainly it is less precise than random sampling. Cluster sampling is used only because of the economic advantage it possesses; estimates based on cluster samples are usually more reliable per unit cost.

Merits of cluster sampling

The important merits or primary advantages of the cluster sampling method are the following:

(a) Cluster or area sampling is much easier to apply when large populations are studied or when large geographical areas are canvassed.

(b) The cost of cluster sampling is much less compared with other sampling methods. The investigators save time and money by not having to travel great distances to interview specific individuals living at random points in a geographical area. In brief, cluster sampling is used only because of economic advantages it possesses.

(c) Another advantage of cluster sampling is that respondents can be readily substituted for other respondents within the same random section.

(d) Another advantage of this sampling method is flexibility. In a multi-stage cluster sampling design, it is possible to employ different forms of sampling (like simple random, systematic random, or stratified random sampling) in several successive stages.

(e) The fifth advantage of this sampling method is that it is possible to estimate the characteristics of clusters of elements drawn. Again, this derives from the fact that the sample, consisting of several clusters of elements is a probability sample and hence is generalisable to other sections from which it was obtained.

(f) If field research, crews are located at different places throughout the state, cluster or area sampling facilitates their contacting of various elements within a specified area. In this sense, area or cluster sampling is more helpful than the other sampling plans.

Demerits of cluster sampling

The following are the major disadvantages, demerits, or limitations of cluster or area sampling plans:

(a) There is no way to ensure that each sampling unit included in an area or cluster sample will be of equal size. The researcher has little control over the size of each cluster. This variation in the uniformity of cluster sizes could increase the bias of the resulting sample.

(b) There is a greater sampling error associated with the cluster or area sampling plans. Because of this factor, in part, the cluster or area sampling method is less efficient than the other probability sampling methods.

(c) It is also difficult to ensure that individuals included in one cluster are independent of other randomly drawn clusters.

Applications of cluster or area sampling

Cluster or area sampling serves many functions. Public opinion polls are frequently conducted using an area sampling plan. Surveys of farming regions that are sparsely populated and cover extensive geographical sections are more easily conducted employing this sampling plan. When lists of specific individuals are unobtainable or are inaccessible, area sampling is recommended. It is applied to large geographical regions, city blocks or urban territories. Not being able to identify the elements to be interviewed in any other type of random sampling plan makes it mandatory that cluster or area sampling be employed. Large-scale surveys of political and social behaviour would also be amenable to area or cluster sampling.

1.10.1.5   *Area Sampling*

If clusters happen to be some geographical subdivisions, in that case cluster sampling is better known as area sampling. In other words, cluster designs, where the primary sampling unit represents a cluster of units based on geographic area, are distinguished as area sampling. The pros and cons of cluster sampling are also applicable to area sampling.

1.10.1.6   *Multi-stage Random Sampling*

Multi-stage random sampling is a further development of the principle of cluster sampling. Under this method, the random selection is made of primary, intermediate and final units from a given population or a stratum. Thus, the area of investigation is scientifically restricted to a smaller number of ultimate units which are representatives of the whole population.

Suppose we want to investigate the working efficiency of nationalised banks in India and we want to take a sample of few banks for this purpose. The first stage is to select large primary sampling unit such as states in a country. Then we may select certain districts and interview all banks in the chosen districts. This would represent a two-stage sampling design with the ultimate sampling units being clusters of districts.

If instead of taking a census of all banks within the selected districts, we select certain towns and interview all banks in the chosen towns. This would represent a three-stage sampling design. If instead of taking a census of all banks within the selected towns, we randomly sample banks from each selected towns, then it is a case of using a four-stage sampling plan. If we select randomly at all stages, then we will have what is known as 'multi-stage random sampling design'.

Ordinarily, multi-stage sampling is applied in big inquiries extending to a considerable large geographical area, say, the entire country. There are two advantages of this sampling design, such as (a) it is easier to administer than most single-stage designs mainly because of the fact that sampling frame under multi-stage sampling is developed in partial units; and (b) a large number of units can be sampled for a given cost under multi-stage sampling because of sequential clustering, whereas this is not possible in most of the simple designs.

1.10.1.7   *Sequential Sampling*

This sampling design is somewhat complex sample design. The ultimate size of the sample under this technique is not fixed in advance, but is determined according to mathematical decision rules on the basis of information yielded as survey progresses. In other words, here a number of sample lots are drawn one after another from a universe depending on the results of earlier sample. Thus, in brief, we can say that in sequential sampling, one can go on taking samples one after another as long as one desires to do so. This sampling is generally adopted in statistical quality control measures.

1.10.2   Non-probability Sampling

Non-probability sampling refers to that sampling procedure which does not afford any basis for estimating the probability that each item in the population has equal chance of being included in the sample. In this type of sampling, items for the sample are selected deliberately by a researcher; his/her choice concerning the items remains supreme. Moreover, many types of research designs do not require that random samples be drawn. For instance, a researcher wishes to test the reliability of an attitudinal measuring instrument which he/she has developed. It is probably not necessary to go to the trouble of obtaining a random sample for this purpose. In this instance, a haphazard selection of people off the street may be sufficient.

The general objective of a non-probability sampling plan is to gain a rough impression of a collection of elements. Such sampling plans can lay the groundwork for a subsequent, more sophisticated probability sampling form.

The primary difference between a probability sample and a non-probability sample is that the former sampling method uses randomness as a primary statistical control, whereas the latter sampling form does not. Therefore, the findings based on probability samples are usually generalisable to similar populations from which the samples are drawn, and the amount of sampling error can be readily determined. However, it is difficult to determine the amount of sampling error for non-probability samples, and the researcher cannot legitimately generalise his findings to any large population. This is because the population remains largely unidentified with any or all non-probability sampling plan variations.

The major non-probability sampling plans are: (i) purposive sampling, (ii) quota sampling, (iii) accidental sampling, and (iv) judgemental sampling, which are discussed below.

1.10.2.1   *Purposive Sampling*

A purposive sample is one that has been handpicked by the investigator to fully ensure that specific elements are included. In other words, depending on the purpose of the study, the investigator deliberately selects the samples basing on his judgements. For example, a researcher wants to study the relationship between labour turnover and job satisfaction. He feels that labour turnover will be particularly high among workers performing a certain type of job that is generally dissatisfying to them. His attention is focused only on those workers from a special section of the plant/factory. He handpicks a number of employees from that section and studies their job satisfaction and propensity to leave the company for another type of employment. It is important to note that the researcher assumes the representativeness of his sample by virtue of the fact that he handpicks elements presumed to be typical of the population from which they were drawn. In other words, purposive sampling guarantees that certain elements will be included, which are relevant to the research design.

1.10.2.2   *Quota Sampling*

Quota sampling is defined as obtaining a described number of elements by selecting those most accessible to the researcher and those that possess certain characteristics of interest to him. In other words, in this type of sampling, the proportions of the various subgroups in the population are determined, and the sample is drawn (usually not randomly) to have the same percentages in it. For example, if a population has an equal number of males and females in it, so does the sample.

Quota sampling is sometimes referred to as the poor man's proportionate stratified random sample, because such samples are geared to ensure that specific elements will be included and represented in the subsequent collection of them. However, quota sampling in no way should be equated with proportionate stratified random sampling plans because the element of randomness is totally lacking.

The primary advantages of the quota sampling method are as follows: (a) this is considerably less costly than most other sampling methods—probability or non-probability; (b) its satisfactory, quick, crude results satisfy the research objectives of the investigator; and (c) this method can also guarantee the inclusion of certain types of population in the sample.

With regard to the disadvantage, it can be said that the quota sampling method provides too much opportunity for the researchers to select the most accessible elements, even their friends as the sample. The most accessible elements are not necessarily typical of whatever population they were drawn from.

Quota sampling is done primarily because of the convenience and lower cost of collecting information. For a largely exploratory study, quota sampling may be an efficient means of gaining a quick impression of things so that a more sophisticated sampling plan can be used later with the same population. Quota sampling can be used to obtain elements from membership lists and virtually any other source that lists individuals (city directories, telephone directories and so forth). The quota sampling method can be applied to select people possessing certain traits, such as race, socio-economic status (SES), religion, some occupational characteristics and so on.

1.10.2.3   *Accidental Sampling*

Accidental samples are also known as incidental samples. It is the crudest sampling method. Here investigators are guided principally by convenience and economy. They do not care about including people with specific traits and take what they can find and are content with it.

The advantages of this sampling technique are primarily convenience and economy. The disadvantages include limited generalisability and much bias in selecting samples.

This sampling method is based on convenience and economy. It is commonly applied by market researchers and newspaper reporters.

1.10.2.4   *Judgemental Sampling*

Purposive samples are frequently called judgemental samples because investigators exercise their judgement to include elements that are presumed to be typical of a given population about which they seek information. They believe that by carefully handpicking certain elements, they will obtain information comparable to that derived from a sample selected according to some probability sampling method. Suppose that a researcher wants to study the attitude of women towards household goods. Here he/she makes his/her judgement to take only housewives as the sample because he/she thinks that housewives are having more experiences regarding the utility of various household goods. Thus, the worth of this method will depend on the sampling design and the objective of the study.

With regard to the advantages, it can be said that judgemental sampling method does not involve any random selection process; consequently, this method is less costly and the samples are more readily accessible to a researcher. Convenience is an additional incentive to employ judgemental samples.

Regarding the disadvantages of this method, we may say that in judgemental sampling, too much emphasis is placed on the ability of the investigator to assess which elements are typical and which are not. Moreover, judgemental samples are subjective samples because they are based on the subjective judgement and assessment of the investigator, and thus, the findings lack generalisability.

Political scientists, public opinion analysts and economists are interested in using this sampling method to say something about voting behaviour, opinions towards political candidates, and issues and socio-economic conditions by examining a handpicked sample of elements presumed typical of a population. Psychologists might employ this method for selecting individuals possessing certain attitudinal dispositions for psychological experiments. It is possible to use this sampling form in conjunction with the many experimental designs that have been developed for psychological studies.

1.11   Scales or Levels of Measurements

The scales or levels of measurements are divided into four types as follows: (a) nominal scale, (b) ordinal scale, (c) interval scale and (d) ratio scale. These scales are discussed below.

1.11.1   The Nominal or Classificatory Scale

Definition. Measurement at its weakest level exists when numbers or other symbols are used simply to classify an object, person or characteristic. When numbers or other symbols are used to identify the groups to which various objects belong, these numbers or symbols constitute a nominal or classificatory scale.

Example 1.1. The psychiatric system of diagnostic groups constitutes a nominal scale. When a diagnostician identifies a person as 'schizophrenic', 'paranoid', 'manic-depressive' or 'psychoneurotic', he/she uses a symbol to represent the class of persons to which this person belongs, and, thus, he/she uses nominal scaling. Similarly, we can categorise people as having 'positive', 'negative' or 'neutral' attitudes towards a social issue by assigning numbers or symbols, which means that we are using nominal scaling. Numbers on automobile license plates, on cricket players' jerseys or on social-security cards are some examples of the use of numbers in nominal or classificatory scaling.

Formal properties. All scales have certain formal properties. These properties provide fairly exact definitions of the scale's characteristics, more exact definitions than we can give in verbal terms. These properties may be formulated more abstractly than we have done here by a set of axioms that specify the operations of scaling and the relations among the objects that have been scaled.

In a nominal scale, the scaling operation partitions a given class into a set of mutually exclusive subclasses. The only relation involved is that of equivalence; that is, the members of any one subclass must be equivalent in the property being scaled. This relation is symbolised by a familiar sign: =. The equivalence relation is reflexive, symmetrical and transitive.

Admissible operations. The nominal scale is said to be 'unique up to a one-to-one transformation', because in any nominal scale, the classification may be equally well represented by any set of symbols. The symbols designating the various subclasses in the scale may be interchanged, if this is done consistently and completely. For example, when new license plates are issued, the license number which formerly stood for one country can be interchanged with that which had stood for another country. Nominal scaling would be preserved if this changeover were performed consistently and thoroughly while issuing all license plates. Such one-to-one transformations are sometimes called 'the symmetric group of transformations'.

Since the symbols which designate the various groups on a nominal scale may be interchanged without altering the essential information in the scale, the only kinds of admissible descriptive statistics which would remain unchanged by such transformation are the mode and frequency counts. In other words, the mode is the only possible measure of central tendency for a nominal scale, and there is generally no used measure of variability. The hypothesis regarding the distribution of cases among categories can be tested by chi-square (χ^2); it is the most common test of statistical significance which can be utilised for nominal scale data. Similarly, the contingency coefficient (C) is the most common measure of association or correlation between nominal data. These tests (i.e., χ^2, C) are appropriate for nominal data because they focus on frequencies in categories, that is, on enumerative data. Moreover, the chi-square (χ^2) and contingency coefficient (C) are non-parametric statistical tests. In short, for a nominal scale, the examples of appropriate statistics are: mode, frequency, chi-square and contingency coefficient, and the appropriate statistical tests are non-parametric statistical tests.

In spite of its limitations, a nominal scale is very useful in surveys and other ex-post-facto research studies when data are classified by major subgroups of the population.

1.11.2   The Ordinal or Ranking Scale

Definition. It may happen that the objects in one category of a scale are not just different from the objects in other categories of that particular scale, but that they stand in some kind of relation to them. Typical relations among the classes/categories are as follows: higher, more preferred, more difficult, more disturbed, more matured and so on. Such relations may be designated by the carat (>) which, in general, means 'greater than'. In reference to particular scales, the symbol '>' may be used to designate 'is preferred to', 'is higher than', 'is more difficult than', and so on. Its specific meaning depends on the nature of the relationship that defines the scale.

Given a group of equivalence classes/categories (i.e., given a nominal scale), if the relation '>' holds between some but not all pairs of classes/categories, then we have a partially ordered scale. If, on the other hand, the relation '>' holds for all pairs of classes or categories so that a complete rank ordering of classes arises, then we have an ordinal scale. In brief, an ordinal scale refers to that scale in which the relation '>' holds true for all pairs of categories of responses.

Example 1.2. Let us divide people on the basis of their SES into three broad classes: upper, middle and lower, each having two sections as upper and lower. Thus, the resultant six classes are as follows: (1) upper-upper, (2) lower-upper, (3) upper-middle, (4) lower-middle, (5) upper-lower and (6) lower-lower. This SES constitutes an ordinal scale. For instance, in prestige or social acceptability, all members of the upper-middle class are higher than (>) all members of the lower-middle class. The lower-middles, in turn, are higher than the upper-lowers. The equivalence (=) relation holds among members of the same class, and the greater-than (>) relation holds between any pair of classes.

The system of grades in the military services is another example of an ordinal scale, for example, Sergeant > corporal > private. Similarly, many personality inventories and tests of ability or aptitude result in scores that have the strength of ranks, and, thus, are viewed as an ordinal scale.

Formal properties. The ordinal scale has the two properties: the relation of equivalence (=) and the 'greater-than' (>) relation. Axiomatically, the fundamental difference between a nominal scale and an ordinal scale is that the nominal scale incorporates only the relation of equivalence (=), whereas the ordinal scale incorporates not only the relation of equivalence (=) but also the 'greater-than' (>) relation. The latter relation is irreflexive, asymmetrical and transitive.

Admissible operations. Since any order-preserving transformation does not change the information contained in an ordinal scale, the scale is said to be 'unique up to a monotonic transformation', that is, it does not matter what numbers we give to a pair of classes or to the members of the class which is 'greater' or 'more preferred'. Of course, one may use the lower numbers for the 'more preferred' grades. Thus, we usually prefer to excellent performance as 'first class' and to progressively inferior performances as 'second class' and 'third class'. So long as we are consistent, it does not matter whether higher or lower numbers are used to denote 'greater' or 'more preferred'. Thus, any or all the numbers applied to classes in an ordinal scale may be changed in any fashion which does not alter the ordering (ranking) of the objects.

The examples of appropriate statistics for the ordinal scale data are as follows: median, percentile, Mann–Whitney U-test, Kruskal–Wallis one-way analysis of variance by ranks (H), Friedman two-way analysis of variance by ranks (χ_r^2), Spearman rank correlation coefficient (rho=ρ), Kendall rank correlation coefficient (tau=τ), Kendall coefficient of concordance (W) and other 'order statistics' or 'ranking statistics'. The appropriate statistical tests are non-parametric statistical tests in nature.

Median is the only measure of describing the central tendency scores in an ordinal scale, because the median is not affected by changes of any scores that are above or below it as long as the number of scores above and below remains the same. Percentiles and quartiles are meaningful measures of variability or dispersion in an ordinal scale. With ordinal scaling, hypotheses can be tested by using that large group of non-parametric statistical tests (e.g., U-test, H-test, χ_r^2 test and the like), which are sometimes called 'order statistics' or 'ranking statistics'. Correlation coefficients based on rankings (e.g., the Spearman ρ or the Kendall τ) are appropriate.

1.11.3   The Interval Scale

Definition. A scale that has all the characteristics of an ordinal scale, and in addition, that does not have an absolute zero point but whose intervals are equal in size is called an interval scale. An interval scale is characterised by a common and constant unit of measurement which assigns a real number to all pairs of objects in the ordered set. In this sort of measurement, the ratio of any two intervals is independent of the unit of measurement and of the zero point. In an interval scale, the zero point and the unit of measurement are arbitrary.

Example 1.3. We measure temperature on an interval scale. In fact, two different scales, namely, Centigrade and Fahrenheit, are commonly used. The unit of measurement and the zero point in measuring temperature are arbitrary; they are different for the two scales. However, both scales contain the same amount and the same kind of information. This is the case because they are linearly related; that is, a reading on one scale can be transformed to the equivalent reading on the other by the linear transformation:

$$F = \frac{9}{5}C + 32,$$

where

　　F=number of degrees on Fahrenheit scale
　　C=number of degrees on Centigrade scale.

It can be shown that the ratios of temperature differences (distances or intervals) are independent of the unit of measurement and of the zero point. For instance, 'freezing' occurs at 0° and 'boiling' occurs at 100° on the Centigrade scale, whereas on the Fahrenheit scale, 'freezing' occurs at 32° and 'boiling' at 212°. Some other readings on the same temperature on the two scales are:

Centigrade (°)	0	10	30	100
Fahrenheit (°)	32	50	86	212

Here, we can notice that the ratio of the differences between temperature readings on one scale is equal to the ratio between the equivalent differences on the other scale. For example, on the Centigrade scale, the ratio of the differences between 30 and 10, and 10 and 0, is $\frac{30-10}{10-0}=2$. For the comparable readings on the Fahrenheit scale, the ratio is $\frac{86-50}{50-32}=2$. The ratio is the same in both cases, that is, 2. Thus, in an interval scale, the ratio of any two intervals is independent of the unit used and of the zero point, both of which are arbitrary.

Formal properties. The interval scale has all the properties of a nominal scale (i.e., equivalence of categories) and an ordinal scale (i.e., greater-than relations); in addition, it has no 'true' zero point (only an arbitrary zero point), and the intervals on the scale are equidistant. The interval scale does not have the capacity to measure the complete absence of a trait or characteristic. For example, there is no zero height or zero intelligence. Similarly, a zero reading on a thermometer does not indicate the total absence of temperature nor a student securing zero in arithmetic indicates a complete absence of that skill in him/her. Equality of interval means that the same numerical distance is associated with the same empirical distance on some real continuum. For example, we can say that an increase in temperature from 30° to 40° involves the same increase in temperature as an increase from 60° to 70°. But we cannot say that the temperature of 60° is twice as warm as the temperature of 30°, because both numbers are dependent on the fact that the zero point on the scale is set arbitrarily at the temperature of the 'freezing' point of water as shown earlier in the Centigrade and Fahrenheit thermometers. The ratio of the two temperatures, 30° and 60°, means nothing because zero is an arbitrary point.

Therefore, while constructing an interval scale, one must not only be able to specify equivalences, as in a nominal scale, and greater-than relations, as in an ordinal scale, but one must also be able to specify the ratio of any two intervals.

Admissible operations. Any change in the numbers associated with the position of the objects measured in an interval scale must preserve not only the ordering of the objects but also the relative differences between the objects; that is, the interval scale is 'unique up to a linear transformation'. Thus, the information yielded by the scale is not affected if each number is multiplied by a positive constant and then a constant is added to this product, that is, $F(x)=ax+b$. (In the temperature example, $a=\frac{9}{5}$ and $b=32$).

We have already noticed that the zero point in an interval scale is arbitrary. This is inherent in the fact that the scale is subject to transformations which consist of adding a constant to the numbers making up the scale.

The interval scale is a truly quantitative scale. It provides more powerful measurement than ordinary scales because it incorporates the concept of equality of intervals along with the magnitude and direction of difference. Hence, a number of powerful statistical measures can be used with interval scales. All the common parametric statistics (e.g., means, standard deviations, Pearson product-moment correlations, multiple product-moment correlations and the like) are applicable to data in an interval scale. In other words, mean is the appropriate measure of central tendency, and standard deviation is the most widely used measure of dispersion. Pearson product-moment correlation coefficient is the most appropriate technique of finding out the association between variables. Multiple correlations are also used to predict the value of a particular variable based on our knowledge of another variable. Similarly, for testing the hypotheses in an interval scale, the common parametric statistical tests, such as *t*-test and *F*-test are also used.

1.11.4   The Ratio Scale

Definition. A scale that has all the characteristics of an interval scale, and in addition, has a true zero point as its origin, is called a ratio scale. In a ratio scale, the ratio of any two scale points is independent of the unit of measurement.

Example 1.4. We measure mass or weight in a ratio scale. The scales of ounces, pounds and grams have a true zero point. The ratio between any two weights is independent of the unit of measurement. For example, if we determine the weights of two different objects not only in pounds but also in grams, we find that the ratio of the two pound weights is identical to the ratio of the two gram weights.

Formal properties. Ratio scales, most commonly encountered in the physical sciences, have the following four important properties: (i) equivalence, (ii) greater than, (iii) known ratio of any two intervals and (iv) known ratio of any two scale values.

Admissible operations. The numbers associated with the ratio scale values are 'true' numbers with a true zero. However, only the unit of measurement is arbitrary. Thus, the ratio scale is 'unique up to multiplication by a positive constant'; that is, the ratios between any two numbers are preserved when the scale values are all multiplied by a positive constant, and, thus, such a transformation does not alter the information contained in the scale.

Any statistical test, whether parametric or non-parametric, is usable with ratio scales. In addition to the statistics previously mentioned as being appropriate for use with data in interval scales, one may use such statistics (which require the knowledge of the true zero point) as the geometric means, harmonic means and the coefficient of variation with ratio scales.

In summary, four of the most general scales are discussed: the nominal, ordinal, interval and ratio scales. Nominal and ordinal measurements are the most common types of scales used in behavioural sciences. Data measured by either nominal or ordinal scales should be analysed by non-parametric statistical techniques. Data measured in interval or ratio scales may be analysed by parametric statistical tests, if the assumptions of the parametric statistical model are tenable; otherwise, it may be analysed by non-parametric statistical tests. Thus, proceeding from the nominal scale (the least precise scale) to the ratio scale (the most precise scale) relevant information is obtained increasingly. The nominal scale signifies neither the direction nor magnitude; the ordinal scale sets the direction but not magnitude; the interval scale describes both magnitude and direction of the variable without having a true zero point; and the ratio scale brings out the direction and magnitude of the variable along with an absolute zero in the scale. Hence, if the nature of the variables permits, the researcher may use the scale that provides the most precise description.

1.12   Variables and Their Classification

The term 'variable' refers to a property or characteristic whereby the members of a group or set differ one from another. The members of a group may be individuals, and may be found to differ in sex, age, eye colour, intelligence, auditory acuity, reaction time to a stimulus, attitude towards a political issue, anxiety, learning ability, memory capacity, height, weight, body surface area, heart rate, blood pressure, blood sugar level and many other ways. Such properties are variables. In other words, a variable is any property or characteristic of some event, object or person that may have different values at different times depending on the conditions (Pagano, 1994). In contrast, the term 'constant' refers to a property whereby the members of a group do not differ one from another.

A variable may vary in two ways: (a) spatial variation and (b) temporal variation. When a variable varies from individual to individual, place to place, organ to organ, at any given time, it is known as spatial variation. On the other hand, when a variable varies in the same individual at different times, it is called temporal variation.

The particular values of a variable are referred to as variates or variate values. To illustrate, in considering the height of adult males, height is the variable, whereas the height of any particular individual is a variate or a variate value.

Variables are categorised into three broad categories: (i) dependent and independent variables, (ii) continuous and discrete (discontinuous) variables, and (iii) statistical variables—nominal, ordinal, interval and ratio variables, which are discussed in the following sections.

1.12.1   Dependent and Independent Variables

In an experiment or study, the variable whose changes are assessed or measured is called the dependent variable in that experiment. On the contrary, the variable(s) whose effects on the dependent variable are being investigated is called the independent variable(s) in that experiment. Thus, the changes in the dependent variable may be considered to be dependent on the changes of the independent variable(s). The relationship between independent and dependent variables is the relationship between cause and effect, with the independent variable being the cause and the dependent variable being the effect. In short, Pagano (1994) opined that the independent variable in an experiment is the variable that is systematically manipulated by the investigator. The dependent variable in an experiment is the variable that the investigator measures to determine the effect of the independent variable.

In behavioural sciences, the dependent variable is generally called the criterion or criterion variable, whereas the independent variable is called the predictor or predictor variable. For example, if we want to assess the effects of different periods of practice on the learning performance of the subjects in an experiment, then learning performance is the dependent variable or criterion, while the periods of practice constitute the independent variable or the predictor.

An independent variable used in an experiment may be either a treatment variable or a classification variable. A treatment variable is one which involves a modification of the experimental subjects, a modification which is controlled by the experimenter. The treatment variables are under the extensive control of the investigator. Their qualitative forms, values or applied doses are altered by the investigator in deliberate, predetermined and precise (fixed) manner in an experiment to study the effects of such changes on the dependent variable, and are not allowed to change or fluctuate at random. Different dosage of a drug, different methods of learning, different periods of practice, different pitches of a stimulating sound and so on are some of the examples of treatment variables, which are randomly administered to different groups of subjects. In effect, the subjects are treated in some way by the experimenter.

Experimental subjects may, however, be classified on a characteristic which was present prior to, and quite apart from, the experiment, and does not result from the manipulations of the experimenter. Such a variable is called a classification variable, for example, sex, age, disease entity, IQ level, SES, race, breeds, phenotypes, religion, blood groups and so on. Although the values of a classification variable are not, as were, created by the experimenter, as is the case with a treatment variable, the investigator, nonetheless, selects the classification variables that are included in the experiment or are the objects of attention.

In each experiment, there is always a single dependent variable, but there may be one or more independent variables. Where two or more independent variables are used in an experiment, they may belong either to the same type (treatment variables or classification variables) or even to two different types.

Any independent variable, whether of the treatment or classification type, is spoken of as a factor. Experiments that investigate the effect of a particular factor or an independent variable are called single-factor or one-way classification experiments; that investigate simultaneously the effects of two independent variables are called two-factor or two-way classification experiments; that investigate simultaneously the effects of three factors/independent variables are called three-factor or three-way classification experiments; and so on.

The different values or categories of the independent variable are spoken of as levels; thus, we may have two or three or more levels of a factor.

1.12.2   Continuous and Discrete Variables

A continuous variable is one which may take any value within a defined range of values. Between any two values of a variable, an indefinitely large number of values may occur. The possible values or scores of such a variable form a continuous series with no intervening gaps; the variable may, thus, possess any value within this range or domain. Height, weight, length, temperature and chronological age are some examples of continuous variables.

A discrete variable is also called a discontinuous variable that can take specific values only. The size of a family is a discontinuous variable. A family may comprise one, two, three or more children, but values in-between these numbers are not possible. The values obtained in rolling a dice are 1, 2, 3, 4, 5 and 6. Values between these numbers are not possible. Because a discrete variable can have only certain fixed values, its scores form discontinuous data with real gaps between consecutive scores. Some examples of discrete/discontinuous variables are the size of a family, the number of children in a family, the values in rolling a dice, the number of books in a library, the number of words spelled correctly and so on.

1.12.3   Statistical Variables

The statistical variables are otherwise known as measurement variables. Their magnitudes may be measured or counted and expressed in numerical units. A class of variables which is of particular interest to the statisticians includes four types of variables: nominal variable, ordinal variable, interval variable and ratio variable. These variables are discussed in the further.

A nominal variable is a property of the members of a group defined by an operation which permits the making of statements only of equality or difference. Thus, we may state that one person or member is the same as or different from another member with respect to the property in question. For example, individuals may be classified by the colour of their eyes. Colour is a nominal variable. Similarly, some variables, such as sex, race, religion, species, profession, blood group, mother tongue, eye colour, skin colour, hair colour, living–nonliving, pregnant–non-pregnant, success–failure, HIV positive–negative, personality types and so on are called attributes or nominal variables. Such variables can only be assessed, studied or expressed qualitatively, but not quantitatively.

An attribute divided into only two classes is called a dichotomous variable, for example, sex, living–nonliving, pregnant–non-pregnant, success–failure and so on.

An ordinal variable is a property defined by an operation which permits the rank ordering of the members of a group—statements like 'greater than' or 'less than'. Aggressiveness, co-operativeness, attentiveness, social adjustment, trustworthiness, punctuality, honesty, beautifulness and leadership quality are the examples of the ordinal variable. These variables vary distinctly in magnitude or intensity among the members of a population, but their magnitudes cannot be measured quantitatively. The individuals of a sample may be graded into ranks in ascending or descending orders with respect to such a variable. The ranks indicate relative magnitudes only, that is, whether an individual possesses a higher or a lower magnitude of that variable than another individual. These ranks give neither any quantitative measure of the individual values nor the magnitudes of differences between such values. In other words, it can be known or stated from the ranks whether one individual is higher or lower than another with respect to the given variables, but by how much one is higher or lower than the other, cannot be inferred from the ranks. Moreover, there is no indication about whether the difference in magnitude of the variable between any two consecutive ranks equals, exceeds or falls short of the difference in magnitude of the variable between two other consecutive ranks. For example, the difference in punctuality between two individuals ranked 1 and 2, respectively, may very well be equal to, higher than or lower than the difference in punctuality between two individuals ranked 2 and 3.

An interval variable is a property defined by an operation which permits the making of statements of equality of intervals, in addition to the statements of sameness or difference, or greater than or less than. An interval variable does not have a true zero point although a zero point may for convenience be arbitrarily defined. Fahrenheit and Centigrade temperature measurements constitute interval variables. Let us consider three objects, such as, A, B and C; with temperatures 12°, 24° and 36°, respectively. It is appropriate to say that the difference between the temperatures of A and B is equal to the difference in the temperature of B and C. It is also appropriate to say that the difference between the temperature of A and C is twice the difference between the temperature of A and B or B and C. However, it is not appropriate to say that B has twice the temperature of A or that C has three times the temperature of A. Calendar time is also an interval variable with an arbitrarily defined zero point. Intelligence, aptitude, learning, memory and anxiety cannot be absolutely absent and cannot have a zero value anywhere or in any individual or case. These variables are the examples of interval variables.

A ratio variable is a property defined by an operation which permits the making of statements of equality of ratios in addition to all other kinds of statements discussed earlier. This means that one variate value or measurement may be spoken of a double or triple of another and so on. An absolute zero is always implied. Height, weight, length, loudness and pitch are the examples of ratio variables. These variables can totally be absent so as to possess a zero value at some places or in some individuals or cases. These variables are, therefore, measured and expressed in ratio scales, each starting from a true zero point.

Summary

In this chapter, we have discussed the meaning, nature, aims and applications, uses and misuses, limitations, and fallacies of statistics in order to have some basic ideas in statistics. Four important terms—population, sample, parameter and statistics—that enhance the statistical knowledge of the researchers have also been discussed.

Statistical procedures can be classified into three broad categories: descriptive statistics, which organise and summarise data; inferential statistics, which use sample data to draw inferences about population from which the research samples are drawn; and prediction statistics, which predict future outcomes from current information.

Sampling is defined as the process of drawing samples from the population. The difference between two basic types of sampling methods—probability/random, and non-probability/non-random—were discussed. The merits, demerits and applications of different types of probability sampling methods as well as non-probability sampling methods were discussed.

A measurement scale consists of a set of categories that are used to classify individuals. The properties of four types of measurement scales—nominal, ordinal, interval and ratio scales—were discussed in detail.

Variable refers to a property whereby the members of a group differ one from another. The importance of three broad categories of variables—dependent and independent, continuous and discrete, and statistical variables (nominal, ordinal, interval and ratio)—were discussed.

Key Terms

- Descriptive statistics
- Experiment
- Inference
- Inferential statistics
- Non-probability sampling
- Measurement
- Measurement scales: nominal; ordinal; interval; ratio
- Parameter
- Population
- Population: finite, infinite
- Prediction statistics

- Probability sampling
- Sample
- Sampling design
- Sampling statistics
- Statistical variable: nominal; ordinal; interval; ratio
- Statistics
- Variable
- Variable: continuous; discrete
- Variable: dependent; independent
- Variate value

Questions and Problems

1. Explain the terms: population, sample, parameter and statistics.
2. What do you mean by statistics? Enumerate its nature, aims and applications.
3. Write notes on the following:

   (a) Classification of statistical procedures   (b) Functions of statistics
   (c) Limitations of statistics   (d) Fallacies in statistics
   (e) Misuses of statistics

4. What is sampling? Discuss the procedures, advantages and limitations of different methods of random sampling.
5. Differentiate between random sampling and non-random sampling. Discuss about the various methods of non-random sampling.
6. Compare between the procedures of simple random sampling and systematic random sampling.
7. Write notes on the following:

   (a) Classification of data   (b) Tabulation of data

8. What do you mean by measurement? Discuss about the various scales or levels of measurements.
9. What is a variable? Describe different types of variables with examples.

10. Classify the following variables into continuous and discrete series:

    (a) Intelligence test scores   (b) Scores on an achievement test
    (c) Height   (d) Weight
    (e) Age   (f) Number of children in a family
    (g) The values in rolling a die   (h) Number of books in a library
    (i) Number of electric poles in a street   (j) Number of individuals sitting in a bus
    (k) Distance travelled by a train   (l) Size of a family

11. What type of scale—nominal, ordinal, interval or ratio—may be used in measuring each of the following variables?

    (a) Temperature   (b) Length
    (c) Sex   (d) Eye colour
    (e) Height   (f) Weight
    (g) Calendar time   (h) Rating of performance in a task
    (i) Scores on an achievement test   (j) Scores on an intelligence test
    (k) The outcomes of heads and tails in throwing a coin 10 times
    (l) Attitudes of individuals towards a social issue

12. Fill in the blanks:

    (i) Statistics are mathematical procedures used to describe _____ and draw _____ from them.
    (ii) Population may be either _____ or _____.
    (iii) A statistic is a _____ of the sample.
    (iv) 'All AIDS patients in the world' is an example of _____ population.
    (v) A sample is the true _____ of the population from which it is drawn.
    (vi) A random sampling is also referred to as _____ sampling.
    (vii) The sampling error usually _____ with increase in sample size.
    (viii) Purposive sampling is a type of _____ sampling.
    (ix) The system of grades in the military service is an example of a _____ scale.
    (x) The qualitative measures refer to the measurement of _____ concepts.

13. Write whether the following statements are True or False.

    (i) Parameter is a measure of the population.
    (ii) Statistic deals with aggregate of facts.
    (iii) Statistics cannot be misused.
    (iv) Statistics help in minimising experimental errors.
    (v) The conclusions obtained statistically are universally true.
    (vi) A sample study is less expensive than a census study.
    (vii) Cluster sampling is a type of non-probability sampling.
    (viii) Systematic sampling has the characteristics of both random and non-random sampling designs.
    (ix) Statistical laws are not exact.
    (x) The relationship between independent and dependent variables is the relationship between cause and effect.

14. Find out the correct answer from among the four alternatives.

   (i) The difference between a parameter and a statistic is called as:

      (a) Sampling error   (b) Non-sampling error
      (c) Standard error   (d) None of the above

   (ii) Statistics help in designing experiments more:

      (a) Erroneously   (b) Fallaciously
      (c) Scientifically   (d) None of the above

   (iii) Inferential statistics are otherwise known as:

      (a) Descriptive statistics   (b) Sampling statistics
      (c) Prediction statistics   (d) None of the above

   (iv) Stratified random sampling is applied when the population is:

      (a) Large having homogeneity   (b) Large having heterogeneity
      (c) Small having homogeneity   (d) None of the above

   (v) Statistics can best be considered as:

      (a) An art   (b) A science
      (c) Both an art and a science   (d) None of the above

   (vi) When population under investigation is infinite, we should use:

      (a) The sample method   (b) The census method
      (c) Either the census or the sample method
      (d) None of the above

   (vii) Precision of a random sample:

      (a) Increases with decrease in sample size
      (b) Decreases with increase in sample size
      (c) Increases with the increase in the sample size
      (d) None of the above

   (viii) Statistics that summarise the major characteristics of an array of scores are known as:

      (a) Descriptive statistics   (b) Inferential statistics
      (c) Prediction statistics   (d) None of the above

   (ix) A classificatory scale is otherwise known as:

      (a) An ordinal scale   (b) A nominal scale
      (c) An interval scale   (d) None of the above

   (x) In behavioural sciences the dependent variable is called:

      (a) The criterion   (b) The predictor
      (c) Either the predictor or the criterion
      (d) None of the above

CHAPTER 2

Presentation of Data

Learning Objectives

After reading this chapter, you will be able to:

- Show the difference between scores and data.
- Convert raw data to useful information.
- Understand important concepts and principles of the graphic presentation of data.
- Develop the skills of tabulating data into frequency tables.
- Construct and use frequency distributions.
- Prepare graph frequency distributions with histograms, polygons, Ogives, bar diagrams and pie diagrams.
- Describe advantages and limitations of each graphical representation of data.
- Use frequency distributions to make decisions.

2.1 Introduction

Data obtained from the conduct of experiments or surveys are frequently collections of numbers or numerical scores. Mere inspection of a set of numerical scores will ordinarily communicate very little to the understanding of an investigator. Moreover, the numerical data are collected with a definite purpose. But that purpose is not achieved by merely collecting the scores. It is extremely difficult to make any sense out of the individual scores or numbers. Similarly, it is also difficult to know the group characteristics directly from the raw scores. Therefore, for understanding, analysing and interpreting data, for more precise communication and for comparison with other sets of data, raw data are required to be frequently arranged, classified, described and graphically represented. Before going to describe the tabular and graphical forms of the presentation of data, we should discuss about the scores and data.

2.2 Scores and Data

Data are figures, ratings, checklists and other information collected in experiments, surveys and descriptive studies. Measurements that are made on the subjects of an experiment are called data (Pagano, 1994). Usually, data consist of the measurements of the dependent variable or of other subject characteristics, such as age, sex, number of subjects and so on. Data as originally measured are often referred to as raw or original scores. In common parlance, the term *data* is generally synonymously used with statistics. For example, one may say that he or she has seen the data of industrial accidents in India during the last year instead of saying that he or she has seen the statistics of industrial accidents in India. Thus, 'data' is a broad term signifying a number of attributes about a fact or a phenomenon.

A *score*, on the other hand, is a numerical value representing a point or distance along a continuum. A score is usually a part, and sometimes, the most basic about data. The structure of data is most commonly built up on the basis of scores. As scores are the numerical representation of the attributes of a variable, it is dependent on the nature of the variable. There are two types of scores called *continuous scores* and *discrete scores* relating to the nature of the variable being measured.

2.2.1   Continuous Score

A continuous variable is one that theoretically can have an infinite number of values between adjacent units on the scale. A continuous score is thought of as a distance along a continuum, rather than as a discrete point. An inch is the linear magnitude between two divisions on a foot rule, and in the same manner, a score in an intelligence test is a unit distance between two limits. For example, a score of 120 upon an intelligence examination represents the interval 119.5 up to 120.5. The exact midpoint of this score interval is 120 as shown in the diagram below.

Score 120

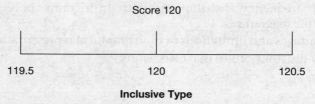

| 119.5 | 120 | 120.5 |

Inclusive Type

This score interval is known as *inclusive type* because both the upper and lower limits are included in the given score.

Other scores may be interpreted in the same way. A score of 22, for instance, includes all values from 21.5 to 22.5, that is, any value from a point 0.5 unit below 22 to a point 0.5 unit above 22. This means that 21.7, 22.0 and 22.4 would all be scored 22. The usual mathematical meaning of a continuous score is an interval that extends along some dimension from 0.5 unit below to 0.5 unit above the face value of the score.

There is another and somewhat different meaning that a test score may have. According to this second view, a score of 120 means that an individual has done at least 120 items correctly, but not 121. Hence, a score of 120 represents any value between 120 and 121. Any fractional value greater than 120, but less than 121, for example, 120.3 or 120.8, since it falls within the interval of 120–121, is scored simply as 120. The middle of the score is 120.5, as shown in the below diagram.

Score 120

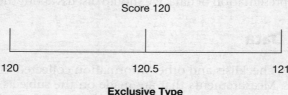

| 120 | 120.5 | 121 |

Exclusive Type

This score interval is called as *exclusive type* because the upper limit is excluded from the given score and is included in the immediate next higher score.

Both of the above ways of defining a score are valid and useful. But which one to be used will depend upon the way in which the test is scored and on the meaning of the units of measurement employed. For example, if each of the 10 boys recorded as having a height of 65 inches, this will ordinarily mean that these heights fall between 64.5 and 65.5 inches (middle value 65 inch) and not between 65 and 66 inches (middle value 65.5 inch). On the other hand, the ages of 20 children, all recorded as being 8 years old, will most probably lie between 8 and 9 years, will be greater than 8 and less than 9 years (middle value 8.5 years). But 8 years old must be taken in many studies to mean 7.5 up to 8.5 years with a middle value of 8 years. One point to remember is that results obtained from treating scores under our second definition will always be 0.5 unit higher than results obtained when scores are taken under the first mathematical definition. The student will often have to decide, sometimes arbitrarily, what meaning a score should have. In general, it is quite safer to take the mathematical meaning of a score unless it is clearly indicated otherwise. This is the method followed throughout this book. For instance, scores of 60 and 120 will remain 59.5–60.5 and 119.5–120.5, respectively, and not that of 60 up to 61 and 120 up to 121.

2.2.2   Discrete Score

Scores for which individual values fall on the scale only with distinct, real gaps are called discrete scores. Such scores usually take only integer values. Those are absolute and no approximate measure of the attribute in question. For example, 365 runs in a cricket match means 365 runs absolutely. It cannot be any fraction less or more of it. We can never say it as 365.5 runs. Similarly, members present in a meeting are a definite integer. We cannot say that there were 56.3 members present in the meeting; rather, we can say that 56 members were present in the meeting. Moreover, we can say that the size of a family is 4 or the number of children in a family is 2. These are discrete scores. But as a matter of fact, most of the psychological and educational measurements do not use discrete scores because of the underlying continuity in the nature of the attributes of a variable. In some cases, there are only purposive uses of the discrete scores to facilitate the collection of data when, in fact, the attribute is in a continuous scale.

2.3   Drawing Up Frequency Distributions

One of the most fundamental and important methods of condensing, summarising and putting order into a disarray of data is the frequency distribution. A frequency distribution is a series where a number of scores with similar or closely related values are put in separate bunches or groups, arranged in order of magnitude in a grouped series. An orderly arrangement in magnitude is called an array or a series. Such a series has two parts: on its left, there are magnitudes of values and, on its right, there is the number of times a value or a group of values (frequency) is repeated. The frequency is juxtaposed to its value or group. In other words, a frequency distribution is a table showing the number (frequency) of individuals, cases, events or scores of a sample in each of the classes into which the variable under investigation has been classified. The main purpose of a frequency table is to simplify the presentation and to facilitate comparison. According to the nature of the variable under study, the frequency distribution is of two principal types, such as the qualitative frequency distribution and the quantitative frequency distribution, which are discussed in the following sections.

Table 2.1 Frequency distribution of religion groups

Religion Groups	Frequency (f)
Hindu	120
Muslim	50
Christian	30
Total (N)	200

2.3.1   Qualitative Frequency Distribution

A *qualitative frequency distribution* is a table showing the number of individuals or cases of a sample in different classes of an attribute or nominal variable, such as honesty, beauty, sex, employment, intelligence, occupation, literacy, blood group, phenotype, hair colour, eye colour, personality, race, religion and so forth. The attributes or nominal variables that are not capable of quantitative measurement are termed as qualitative or descriptive attributes. An attribute or a nominal variable cannot be measured or expressed quantitatively in numerical units, so it is divided into classes depending only on the qualitative distinction between the individuals of a sample with respect to the presence or absence of a particular property or characteristic. Therefore, the classes are given names or numbers as simple labels without any quantitative significance or numerical range, and are separated from each other by intervening gaps. The classes may be assumed to be located at specific points on the scale or domain of that variable; no individual or case falls in the gap between two such points. Such frequency distributions of attributes are, thus, known as *point distributions*. For such a qualitative frequency distribution, the classes of the variable are entered in one column of a simple frequency table, while the number of individuals belonging to each such class is counted from the sample and then entered as frequencies in another column against that particular class (see Table 2.1)

2.3.2   Quantitative Frequency Distribution

If the data are classified on the basis of a particular phenomenon which is capable of quantitative measurement, such as age, height, weight and so on, it is termed as quantitative classification. The *quantitative frequency distribution* consists of a table showing the number of individuals or cases of a sample in different classes into which the entire range of scores (numerical values) of a measurement variable has been grouped. The data, arranged into such a frequency distribution, are called grouped data because the scores have been distributed among the classified groups of scores of the variable. The classification of scores in this way reveals the salient features of the variable in the sample in a meaningful way, for example, the class having the lowest or highest frequency, and the pattern of distribution in various classes. It also helps in the application of statistics for the analysis and interpretation of the data.

The quantitative frequency distribution may broadly be divided into two groups: (a) discrete or discontinuous frequency distribution and (b) continuous frequency distribution.

2.3.2.1   *Discrete or Discontinuous Frequency Distribution*

A much better way of the representation of the data is to express it in the form of a discrete or ungrouped frequency distribution. Because consecutive scores of a discrete variable, such as

Table 2.2   Discrete frequency distribution of families having different number of children

Number of Children	Number of Families
0	1
1	70
2	60
3	9
4	5
5	3
6	2
Total (*N*)	150

family size, number of children in the family or class examination scores of students are separated by real gaps due to the impossibility or impracticability of further fractional subdivision of its measure, the classes of such a variable do not show continuity with each other—the classes are delimited sharply with gaps between them. In framing a discrete or discontinuous frequency distribution, this distinction is retained by recording the class intervals in whole units only and by omitting true class limits in fractional units or decimals. This leaves gaps between the classes; no member of the sample can occur at these gaps. In other words, here the frequency refers to a given discrete value and not to a range of values. In a discrete variable, the exact measurement is possible in whole numbers.

The frequency distribution of a discrete variable is sometimes arranged in the form of a simple frequency table where each single distinct score is entered individually as if to constitute a class by itself; no class is constituted here by the grouping of a range of more than one score in each class. The frequency of a particular score is entered directly against that score. Table 2.2 is an example of a discrete frequency distribution of families having different numbers of children; no family can exist with a fractional number of children like 3.5 or 4.3, and the real gaps exist between the whole numbers of children.

2.3.2.2   *Steps for Discrete Frequency Distribution*

The following steps should be followed for framing a frequency distribution table of a discrete variable:

(i)   Write the name of the variable or 'X' if the name is not given.

(ii)   Below the title/name of the variable or 'X', arrange all the scores in rows carefully putting a comma (,) after each score.

(iii)   Pick up the highest and lowest values from among the scores and write them below the row/(s) of scores. Find out the range of scores by deducting the lowest score from the highest score in the entire series of scores (i.e., Range = Highest score – lowest score) and note it there. Count the number of scores in the entire series and write it below as *N*=?

(iv)   Write the scores in the first column of the frequency table in serial order either in ascending order (i.e., from the lowest to highest scores) or in descending order (i.e., from the highest to lowest scores) according to your convenience.

(v) Then cancel out each score in the series by an oblique stroke (\) and put a vertical stroke (I) in the second column of the frequency table, called the *Tally marks* against the appropriate score (value of the variable) whenever it occurs. After a particular value/score has occurred four times, for the fifth occurrence, put a cross tally mark (\) on the first four tally marks like IIII to give you a block of five tallies. When a particular score occurs for the sixth time, you put another tally mark against it (after leaving some space from the first block of 5) and for the tenth occurrence, you again put a cross tally mark on the sixth to ninth tally marks to get another block of 5 and so on. This process is repeated till all the scores in the series are recorded.

(vi) Count the number of tallies each score/value is repeated, and write the number against the corresponding score/value in the third column, entitled 'Frequency', of the frequency distribution table.

Example 2.1 In a class examination in mathematics, 80 students of class VII obtained the following marks out of a full mark of 10. Prepare a frequency distribution table for the given data.

Marks:

7, 7, 8, 2, 5, 8, 3, 5, 7, 6, 3, 7, 4, 4, 7, 4, 6, 3, 8, 4, 8, 6, 2, 4, 4, 9, 6, 3, 7, 7, 7, 4, 6, 8, 3, 0, 4, 9, 1, 4, 8, 2, 4, 5, 8, 2, 3, 3, 6, 10, 5, 5, 10, 3, 5, 10, 7, 8, 9, 2, 4, 5, 4, 9, 3, 6, 9, 8, 9, 10, 8, 10, 0, 5, 9, 1, 5, 2, 2, 9

Solution

Variable: Mathematics marks; Highest score : 10; Lowest score : 0

Range = Highest score – lowest score = 10 – 0 = 10; N = 80.

See Table 2.3.

2.3.3 Continuous Frequency Distribution

The distribution of frequencies of a continuous variable is known as the continuous frequency distribution. It becomes necessary in the case of some variables which can take any fractional values and in whose case an exact measurement is not possible. There is no real gap between the classes of such a variable so that the consecutive groups or classes are continuous with each other. However, a discrete variable can be presented in the form of a continuous frequency distribution when the discrete distribution is likely to be too long and unwieldy to handle and somewhat odd in presentation.

2.3.4 Facts about Continuous Frequency Distribution

The following are some basic principles for forming a continuous or grouped frequency distribution.

(a) *Number of class intervals.* A class should be clearly defined and should not lead to any ambiguity. Furthermore, they should be exhaustive and mutually exclusive (i.e., non-overlapping) so that any value of the variable corresponds to one and only one of the classes. In other words, there is one-to-one correspondence between the value of the variable and the class.

Table 2.3   Tabulation of a discrete frequency distribution

Mathematics Marks	Tally Marks	Frequency (f)
0	II	2
1	II	2
2	IIII II	7
3	IIII IIII	9
4	IIII IIII II	12
5	IIII IIII	9
6	IIII II	7
7	IIII IIII	9
8	IIII IIII	10
9	IIII III	8
10	IIII	5
		$N=80$

No hard-and-fast rule can be laid down for the number of classes into which a frequency distribution should be divided. If there are too many classes, many of them will contain only a few frequencies, and the distribution may show irregularities, which are not attributable to the characteristics of the variable being measured. If there are too few classes, so many frequencies will be crowded into a class as to cause much information to be lost. Hence, the number of classes to be used depends partly upon the nature of the data and partly upon the number of frequencies in the series. The greater the number of frequencies, the more classes we may have. The following four points are usually considered while deciding about the number of class intervals in a frequency distribution: (i) the total frequency (i.e., total number of observations in the distribution); (ii) the nature of the data (i.e., the size of magnitude of the values of the variable); (iii) the accuracy desired or aimed at and (iv) the ease of computation of the various descriptive measures of the frequency distribution such as mean, variance and so on, for further processing of the data.

However, from a practical point of view, the number of classes should neither be too small nor too large; a balance should be struck between these two factors, namely, the loss of information in the first case (i.e., too few classes) and the irregularity of the frequency distribution in the second case (i.e., too many classes) to arrive at a pleasing compromise, giving the optimum number of classes in view of the statistician. Normally, the number of classes should not be greater than 20 and should not be less than 5, of course keeping in view the points (i)–(iv) mentioned earlier together with the magnitude of the class interval, since the number of class is inversely proportional to the magnitude of the class interval.

A number of thumb rules have been proposed for calculating the proper number of classes. However, an elegant, though approximate, formula is given by Sturges, known as the Sturges rule that reads

$$K=1+3.322\log^{N},$$

where

K = number of class intervals (classes)

N = total frequency or total number of observation in the data.

The value obtained by this formula is rounded to the next higher integer. Since the log of one-digit number is 0, two-digit number is 1, three-digit number is 2, four-digit number is 3 and so on, the use of the Sturges formula restricts the value of K, the number of classes, to be fairly reasonable.

Example 2.2 A test of syllogistic reasoning is administered to 100 students of Grade VIII of a school. Apply the Sturges formula to decide about the number of class intervals:

$$\begin{aligned} \text{Sturges formula: } K &= 1 + 3.322 \log^N \\ &= 1 + 3.322 \log 100 \\ &= 1 + 3.322 \times 2 \\ &= 1 + 6.644 \\ &= 7.644 = 8. \end{aligned}$$

Thus, there would be eight class intervals. This formula very ingeniously restricts the number of classes between 4 and 20, which is a fairly reasonable number from a practical point of view. The rule, however, fails if the number of observations is very large or very small.

(b) *Type of class intervals.* We have discussed that each score in a continuous scale has an upper limit and a lower limit, which are called score limits. Likewise, each class interval is specified by two extreme values called the class limits, the smaller one being termed as the lower limit and the larger one the upper limit of the class. The class limits in a continuous frequency distribution can be presented in any one of the following forms: (i) exclusive or repetition type (A), (ii) inclusive or non-repetition type (B) and (iii) boundary or decimal type (C). These three types are exemplified in the following table.

Example 2.3

(A)			(B)			(C)		
Class Intervals	Midpoints	f	Class Intervals	Midpoints	f	Class Intervals	Midpoints	f
75–80	77	2	75–79	77	2	74.5–79.5	77	2
70–75	72	4	70–74	72	4	69.5–74.5	72	4
65–70	67	5	65–69	67	5	64.5–69.5	67	5
60–65	62	4	60–64	62	4	59.5–64.5	62	4
55–60	57	3	55–59	57	3	54.5–59.5	57	3
50–55	52	2	50–54	52	2	49.5–54.5	52	2
	$N=20$			$N=20$			$N=20$	

All the above three forms of presentation are simply three ways of expressing identically the same facts. In the exclusive type (A), the class interval of 50–55, for instance, is supposed to include all scores beyond 49.5–54.5, and it does not include any score beyond 54.5. The upper limit or upper extreme value 55 is excluded from the respective class and is included in the immediate class. Therefore, these class intervals as depicted under (A) are termed as exclusive classes. In the other inclusive type (B), the class interval of 50–54, for example, also includes all scores between 49.5 and 54.5, which means that as regards functional characteristics both exclusive and inclusive types are the same; however, both the upper and lower limits are included in the respective class intervals of inclusive type as depicted under B (i.e., inclusive classes). The class interval of 49.5–54.5, for instance, in the boundary type (C) also logically includes all the scores between these two limits, and functionally the same as the other two. Furthermore, the class limits, the size of the class interval and the midpoint of the class intervals for all three forms of distributions are the same.

For the rapid tabulation of scores within their proper intervals, method B is to be preferred to 'A' and 'C'. In method A, it is very likely to let a score of 65 slip into the interval of 60–65 simply owing to the presence of 65 at the upper limit of the interval. Method 'C' is clumsy and time-consuming because of the need for writing 0.5 at the lower and upper limits of every class interval. However, this method is helpful when the data contain decimal scores. Method 'B', while easiest for tabulation, offers the difficulty that in later calculations one must constantly remember that the expressed class limits are not the actual class limits; for example, the class interval of 50–54 begins at 49.5 (not at 50) and ends at 54.5 (not at 54). If this is clearly understood, then method 'B' is as accurate as methods 'A' and 'C'. Method 'B' has generally been used throughout this book.

(c) *Size of the class intervals.* Since the size of the class interval is inversely proportional to the number of classes (i.e., class intervals) in a given distribution, from the earlier discussion, it is obvious that as the number of class intervals is decided, the size of the class interval is an automatic consequence where it is proposed to use equal-sized class intervals. However, a choice about the size of the class interval will also largely depend on the sound subjective judgement of the statistician keeping in mind other considerations such as N (total frequency), nature of the data, accuracy of the results and computational case for further processing of the data. Here an approximate value of the magnitude (i.e., width) of the class interval, say, 'i', can be obtained by using the Sturges rule that reads as

$$i = \frac{\text{Range}}{\text{Number of class intervals}} = \frac{\text{Range}}{1 + 3.322 \log^N},$$

where 'Range' is determined by the difference between the largest (L) and smallest (S) scores in the given distribution; that is, Range = Largest score − Smallest score.

Example 2.4 Fifty students of class IX of a school appeared at a school test in mathematics. The student who stood first secured 76 marks and who stood last in the test secured 12 marks out of a full mark of 100. Using the Sturges rule, decide the size of the class interval (i) to tabulate a frequency distribution.

Solution

Largest score = 76;
Smallest score = 12;

$N = 50$.

Range = Largest score − Smallest score
= 76 − 12 = 64.

$$i = \frac{\text{Range}}{\text{Number of class intervals}} = \frac{\text{Range}}{1 + 3.322 \log^N}$$

$$= \frac{64}{1 + 3.322 \log^{50}} = \frac{64}{1 + 3.322} = \frac{64}{4.322} = 14.808 = 15.$$

This shows that the size of the class interval (i) 14.808 may be used as 14 or 15 according to the convenience. On the other hand, given a frequency distribution, the size of the class interval is obtained in two ways: first, from the difference between the true upper limit and lower limit of a particular class interval and second, from the difference between two upper or lower scores or score limits of consecutive intervals, irrespective of the method of distribution used.

Example 2.5 Class interval = 50–54 ; $i = 49.5 \sim 54.5 = 5$,
or

55–60	55–59	54.5–59.5
50–55	50–54	49.5–54.5
$i=5$ 5	5 5	5 5

(d) *Midpoint of the class intervals.* In a continuous frequency distribution, the midpoint of each class interval is used to represent the class. Hence, scores grouped within a given interval in a frequency distribution is supposed to have spread evenly over the entire interval. This assumption is made about a frequency distribution irrespective of the size of the class interval. Therefore, if the spreading of scores around the mid-value is uneven, we run a higher risk of misinterpretation with a greater size of the class interval. But such problems are well taken care of when the numbers of scores in the distribution are large. Even if this condition is not fulfilled, the midpoint assumption is not greatly in error because the lack of balance in one interval will usually be offset by the opposite condition in another interval.

As a rule, the midpoint of a class interval can be obtained as an average of the lower and upper class limits of the said interval. But one should remember that we have discussed three different forms of class intervals, in two of which exact limits are not used. Therefore, providing a method of calculation for each of the forms would make it more convenient.

Example 2.6

(A)	(B)	(C)
Class Interval	**Class Interval**	**Class Interval**
55–60	55–59	54.5–59.5
50–55	50–54	49.5–54.5

Midpoints.

$$\frac{50+55-1}{2} = 52, \quad \frac{50+54}{2} = 52, \quad \frac{49.5+54.5}{2} = 52.$$

As observed in the above example, in the exclusive or repeated type (A), the midpoint of a particular class interval is calculated by subtracting 1 from the sum of the two scores of the interval and then dividing the sum by 2. But in the other two types, inclusive or non-repeated type (B) and boundary or decimal type (C), midpoints are calculated by a simple average of the two scores of the interval.

There is also another simple way to get the midpoints of different class intervals in a distribution where either the uppermost or the lowermost midpoint of the respective class intervals of a distribution is calculated by one of the aforementioned three methods, depending on the type of class intervals. If, for example, the lowermost midpoint of a class interval of a particular distribution is known, the succeeding midpoints can be calculated one by one by adding to it the size of the class interval (i.e., *i*) each time for each class interval. If, on the contrary, the uppermost midpoint of the class interval is known, the midpoints of the following class intervals are obtained one by one by subtracting from it the size of the class interval each time for each class interval. In the above-mentioned example, the lowermost midpoint is 52. As we go on adding 5 (i.e., the size of the class interval) with it, we obtain 57, 62, 67 and 72, which are the midpoints of the succeeding class intervals. On the other hand, if we go on subtracting 5 (i.e., the size of the class interval) from the uppermost midpoint 72, we obtain 67, 62, 57 and 52, which are the midpoints of the following class intervals. However, one should be very careful in using this method because if an error is committed in the first place while calculating the midpoint either of the uppermost or lowermost class interval, then the whole lot of midpoints will be wrong.

2.3.5   Steps for Continuous Frequency Distribution

Generally, there are two methods for the tabulation of scores into continuous frequency distributions. These two methods are known as the *tally method* and the *entry form method*, which are separately discussed in the following, one after another.

2.3.5.1   *Tally Method*

The following are the steps to be followed for framing a continuous frequency distribution of scores under the tally method:

 (i)   Write the name of the variable or 'X' if the name is not given.

 (ii)   Below the title or name of the variable or 'X', arrange all the scores in rows carefully putting a comma (,) after each score.

 (iii)   Pick up the highest and the lowest values from among the scores, and write them below the row(s) of scores. Find out the range of scores and note it below the row(s) of scores.

 (iv)   Count the number of scores in the entire series and write it below the row(s) as $N=?$

 (v)   Decide about the number and size of the class intervals by applying the Sturges rule, if the same are not already given.

 (vi)   Set up the class intervals either beginning from the lowest score in ascending order or from the highest score in descending order by appropriately choosing any one of the three forms of class intervals discussed earlier. It is customary to present class intervals in a column and that too in the first column of the frequency table. Write the heading 'class interval' above it.

 (vii)   Cancel out the first score by an oblique stroke (\) on it and immediately put a vertical stroke (I) against the appropriate class interval below the 'Tally' column. This is how a score is recorded in the frequency distribution. Likewise, cancel out each score to put it as a tally in its appropriate interval. When you get four such tallies against a class interval, for the fifth score to record, put a cross tally (\) on the first four tallies to indicate a block of 5. Continue like this until you record all the scores. The tallies are drawn to facilitate counting.

 (viii)   Write 'Frequency' in the third column and record the number of frequencies against each class interval by correctly counting the tallies. Finally, sum up the frequencies over all the class intervals to indicate the number of cases in the distribution. Check whether or not the number of frequencies tallies with the number of scores (N) written below the row(s) of scores.

Example 2.7 A test of comprehension in English was given to 70 students of Grade VIII. The following marks were obtained by them. Tabulate the data into an appropriate frequency distribution table.

Comprehension Scores:

38, 28, 29, 37, 21, 39, 16, 42, 34, 38, 39, 35, 43, 40, 36, 37, 17, 36, 50, 34, 35, 38, 52, 39, 30, 31, 39, 36, 32, 42, 33, 41, 37, 38, 53, 39, 49, 32, 55, 37, 40, 41, 42, 18, 25, 26, 46, 47, 22, 30, 31, 33, 33, 39, 38, 53, 43, 41, 19, 36, 45, 23, 28, 48, 32, 37, 34, 35, 36, 30

Highest score: 55 $N=70$
Lowest score: 16 $i=5$
Range $=55-16=39$

Class Intervals	Tallies	Frequency
51–55	IIII	4
46–50	IIII	5
41–45	IIII IIII	9
36–40	IIII IIII IIII IIII III	23
31–35	IIII IIII IIII	14
26–30	IIII II	7
21–25	IIII	4
16–20	IIII	4
		$N=70$

The total of the frequency columns is equal to the total of scores, and in statistics, it is known as the number of cases or 'N'. The frequency distribution is the first step for some statistical computation.

2.3.5.2   *Entry Form Method*

The following are the steps to be followed for framing a continuous frequency distribution of scores under the entry form method:

 (i)   Write the name of the variable or 'X' if the name is not given.
 (ii)   Below the title or name of the variable or 'X', arrange all the scores carefully in rows putting a comma (,) after each score.
 (iii) Pick up the highest and the lowest values from among the scores and write them below the row(s) of the scores. Find out the range of scores and note it below the row(s) of scores.
 (iv)   Count the number of scores in the entire series and write it below the row(s) as $N=?$.
 (v)   Decide the number and size of the class intervals by applying the Sturges rule, if the same are not already given.

(vi) Set up the class intervals either beginning from the lowest score or from the highest score by appropriately choosing any one of the three forms of class intervals discussed earlier. It is customary to present the class intervals in a row. Above the row, write the heading 'Class Intervals'.

(vii) Then cancel out the first score by an oblique stroke (\) on it and immediately write the score below the appropriate class interval. Continue like this until you record all the scores in the frequency distribution table. Count the scores in each column to indicate the total frequency against each class interval.

(viii) Sum up the frequencies over all the class intervals and write it in the lower right-hand corner below the column of scores as $N=?$

Example 2.8 Sixty students of Grade IX were given a test of quantitative reasoning, and their scores are given below. Tabulate the data into an appropriate frequency distribution table.

Quantitative reasoning scores:

46, 57, 60, 55, 61, 63, 43, 46, 48, 52, 38, 33, 34, 42, 51, 56, 60, 62, 64, 30, 51, 50, 47, 57, 35, 59, 46, 52, 49, 52, 36, 43, 44, 48, 58, 36, 49, 49, 53, 48, 42, 31, 34, 37, 36, 60, 39, 50, 54, 47, 45, 32, 35, 38, 56, 59, 37, 51, 55, 46

Highest score: 64 $N=60$
Lowest score: 30 $i=5$
Range: $64-30=34$

Class Intervals						
30-34	**35-39**	**40-44**	**45-49**	**50-54**	**55-59**	**60-64**
33	38	43	46	52	57	60
34	35	42	46	51	55	61
30	36	43	48	51	56	63
31	36	44	47	50	57	60
34	37	42	46	52	59	62
32	36	(5)	49	52	58	64
(6)	39		48	53	56	60
	35		49	50	59	(7)
	38		49	54	55	
	37		48	51	(9)	
	(10)		47	(10)		
			45			
			46			
			(13)			
						$N=60$

2.4   The Graphical Representation of the Frequency Distribution

One of the important aims of statistics is to simplify the complex quantitative or numerical data so that it will be meaningful as well as intelligible. Aid in analysing numerical data may often be obtained from a graphic treatment of the frequency distribution. The graphic methods or devices are nothing but pictorial presentations that catch the eye and hold the attention. Such pictorial presentations provide a bird's eye view of the whole mass of data. These are visual aids that involve less thinking and mental manipulations in reflecting on the data than tabular presentation. There is no second opinion that graphic presentations are more impressive and attractive than the tabular presentation of data. It is a psychological fact that the graphs, pictures and diagrams are catchy and have the attention-catching power of visual presentations; they save time, provide scope for an easy comparison and have a lasting effect on the mind of the observer. Moreover, the pictorial or visual presentations translate numerical facts, which are often abstract and difficult to interpret, into a more concrete and understandable form. Sometimes, even complex relations are brought out clearly by these devices, as a result of which analysis, interpretation and explanation of quantitative facts become easier on the part of the researcher. For this and other reasons, the investigator utilises the attention-catching power of visual presentation of the research data.

In general, there are four methods of representing a frequency distribution graphically. These four methods are the *frequency polygon*, the *histogram*, the *cumulative frequency graph* and the *cumulative percentage curve or Ogive*. These graphic devices are treated below one after another. However, first of all, the general principles regarding the graphic presentation of data will be discussed.

2.4.1   General Principles of Graphical Representation of Data

Let us now briefly review the simple algebraic principles which apply to all graphical representation of data. Graphing or plotting is done with reference to two straight lines called coordinate axes. There are two coordinate axes: the one is the vertical or the Y axis and the other is the horizontal or the X axis. These two basic lines are perpendicular to each other; the point where they intersect each other called 0 or the origin. Figure 2.1 represents a system of coordinate axes.

The origin is the zero point (0) or point of reference for both axes. Distances measured along the X axis to the right of 0 are called positive and distances measured along the X axis to the left of 0 are called negative. In a similar vein, distances measured along the Y axis above 0 are called positive and distances measured on the Y axis below 0 are called negative. By intersecting at point 0, the X and Y axes form four divisions or quadrants. Let us designate or label the first, second, third and fourth quadrants as a, b, c and d, respectively. In the upper-right division or the first quadrant (quadrant 'a'), both x and y measures are positive (+ +). In the upper-left division or the second quadrant (quadrant 'b'), x is minus and y is plus (– +). In the lower-left division or the third quadrant (quadrant 'c'), both x and y measures are negative (– –). In the lower-right division or the fourth quadrant (quadrant 'd'), x is positive or plus and y is negative or minus (+ –).

Examples

   (i)   Plot point 'A' whose coordinates are: $x=4$ and $y=3$.
  (ii)   Plot point 'B' whose coordinates are: $x=-2$ and $y=4$.
 (iii)   Plot point 'C' whose coordinates are: $x=-3$ and $y=-5$.
 (iv)   Plot point 'D' whose coordinates are: $x=3$ and $y=-4$.

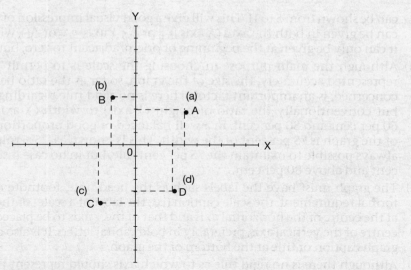

Figure 2.1 System of coordinate axes

Solutions To locate or plot point 'A' whose coordinates are $x=4$ and $y=3$, we go out from 0 to its right four units on the X axis and then up from the origin three units on the Y axis. Where the perpendiculars to these two points intersect, we locate point 'A' (see Figure 2.1).

To locate or plot point 'B' whose coordinates are $x=-2$ and $y=4$, we go from 0 to its left two units along the X axis and then up from 0 four units on the Y axis. Where the perpendiculars to these two points intersect, we locate point 'B' (see Figure 2.1).

Point 'C', whose coordinates are $x=-3$ and $y=-5$, is plotted by going left from 0 three units along the X axis and then down from 0 five units along the Y axis. We locate point 'C' in the place where the perpendiculars to these two points intersect (see Figure 2.1).

In the same manner, point 'D', whose coordinates are $x=3$ and $y=-4$, is plotted by going right from 0 three units along the X axis and then down from 0 four units on the Y axis, as shown in Figure 2.1.

The distance of a point from 0 on the X axis is commonly called the '*Abscissa*' and the distance of a point from 0 on the Y axis is called the 'ordinate'. For instance, the abscissa of point 'A' (see Figure 2.1) is +4 and the ordinate is +3.

In addition to the earlier mentioned general principles regarding both the axes (X and Y), there are some other general rules for the construction of the graph, which are discussed below:

(a) The X axis must run through zero and the Y axis must begin at zero as the origin. This zero is the base, and the curve is to be interpreted in terms of the distance on the baseline. Ordinarily, the curve and the axis lines are drawn heavier than the rest of the graph.

(b) The relationship between the magnitude and distance should be properly maintained in the graph. The equal distance means equal magnitude.

(c) The scale should be chosen carefully. The scale should accommodate the whole data. In this connection, it may be noted that, though both X and Y axes start from zero, it is not always possible to place all the points in either axis by starting the graph from zero value. Say, for example, in a test of the trial-and-error method of learning by mirror drawing apparatus only five trials were taken. The number of errors committed by the subject in these trials ranges from 7 to 11. It is, therefore, not necessary to show errors from 1 to 11 on the Y axis; rather by giving a break in the Y axis with a symbol $\approx$ or $=$, the amount of errors can be shown from 5 to 11. This will give a good visual impression of the graph. Such breaks can be given in both the axes (X axis ⌇⌇, ‖ or ⋀⋁; Y axis ≈, = or ⋀⋁), whenever necessary, but it can only be given at the beginning or origin, adjacent to zero, but not in the middle.

(d) Although the main purpose in choosing the scale is to permit the whole data to be represented accurately, the size of the graph, so far as the ratio between the two axes is concerned, is an important factor. There is no rigid rule regarding the ratio of the axes, but conventionally the ratio of height (Y axis) to width (X axis) may vary between 60 per cent and 80 per cent. In a well-balanced or good proportionate graph, the height of the graph is 75 per cent of the width. This is known as '75% rule'. In practice, it is not always possible to maintain the 75 per cent rule, but in no case it should be below 60 per cent and above 80 per cent.

(e) The graph must have the labels such as the head note, footnote or title. As a matter of formal requirement, the scale caption (i.e., the label of a scale) of the X axis is to be placed at the centre of the horizontal axis and that of the Y axis to be placed on the left side of the centre of the vertical axis, preferably in bold capital letters. It is also customary to place the graph caption or title at the bottom of the graph.

(f) Although there is no rigid rule as to which axis should represent the dependent or independent variable, yet there is a convention that the independent variable is shown in the X axis and the dependent variable in the Y axis.

(g) At times, it is necessary to draw two curves on the same axis. When it becomes necessary to draw two curves on the same base and on the same scale but with different values, the two different curves are to be drawn either in two different colours or in two different ways such as one may be in continuous lines and the other in dotted lines, so that visual differentiation will be easier.

2.4.2   The Frequency Polygon

The frequency distribution of a continuous variable is very often presented graphically as a *frequency polygon*. Polygon means, 'many-angled figure'. The frequency polygon exposes the characteristics of the distribution more easily and clearly, and makes it more convenient to compare the frequency distributions of more than one sample.

The frequency polygon is constructed by plotting a linear graph of frequencies of different class intervals against the midpoints of the respective intervals. It is an area diagram of a continuous frequency distribution; the area enclosed by the polygon represents the total number (*n*) of cases or scores of the sample, and the jagged surface of the polygon visually shows how the frequency changes from class to class in the sample.

For example, Table 2.4 represents the frequency distribution of examination scores of 70 students.

The procedure in plotting a frequency distribution is as follows:

(a) The scores of the variable are scaled along the X axis or the abscissa. In fact, the midpoints (X_C) of the class intervals are marked along the X axis. Besides the X_C scores of the class intervals containing the observed frequencies of data, those of two additional class intervals with zero frequency are also entered on the X axis: one for the class interval just below the lowest class interval (e.g., 45–49) containing observed frequencies and the other for the class interval just above the highest class interval (e.g., 95–99) containing observed frequencies. These two additional class intervals, each having zero frequency, would enable the outline of the frequency polygon to reach or meet the baseline or zero frequency level at both ends and would, thus, close up the area of the frequency polygon. For instance, the midpoints of 42 and 102 have been included in the X axis for two additional

Table 2.4 Scores achieved by 70 students on statistics examination

Class Interval	Frequency
95–99	4
90–94	6
85–89	7
80–84	10
75–79	16
70–74	9
65–69	7
60–64	4
55–59	4
50–54	2
45–49	1
	$N=70$

class intervals with zero frequencies, namely, 40–44 and 100–104, over and above the midpoints of the class intervals containing the score frequencies (see Table 2.5 and Figure 2.2).

(b) The score frequencies are scaled along the Y axis or the ordinate. The scales for scores and frequencies should be so chosen that the ordinate (Y axis) at the peak of the polygon measures 75 per cent or at least 60–80% of its base or abscissa (X axis). The scales for both the X and Y axes should start from zero. However, if the lowest midpoint entered in the X axis is greater than zero, the X axis may be breached or interrupted by a zigzag line (⌇) to bring the lowest midpoint and the polygon closer to the Y axis (see Figure 2.2).

(c) The frequency (f) or the observed frequency (f_o) of each class interval of the frequency distribution is then plotted against the midpoint of the corresponding class interval, including the two additional empty class intervals whose midpoints (X_C) have been entered in the X axis. Evidently, the points for those two empty intervals would lie exactly on the X axis itself since they contain zero frequency.

(d) All the plotted points are then joined together by straight lines to complete the process of drawing or graphing the frequency polygon.

Steps to be followed in constructing a frequency polygon may be summarised as follows:

(i) Draw two straight lines perpendicular to each other: the vertical line near the left side of the paper and the horizontal line bearing the bottom. Label the vertical line (the Y axis) 0Y and the horizontal line (the X axis) 0X. Put 0 where the two lines intersect. This point 0 is the origin.

(ii) Lay off the midpoints (X_C) of the score intervals of the frequency distribution at regular distances along the X axis. Begin with the midpoint of the class interval next below the lowest interval in the distribution and end with the midpoint of the class interval next above the highest interval in the distribution. Label the successive X distances with the midpoints (X_C) of the class intervals. Select an X unit which will allow all of the X_C of the intervals to be represented easily on the graph paper.

Table 2.5 Distribution of observed frequencies (f_o) and smoothed frequencies (f_s) of statistics examination scores given in Table 2.4

Class Intervals	Midpoints (X_c)	f_o	f_s
100–104	102	0	⅓ (0+0+4)=1.33=1.3
95–99	97	4	⅓ (4+0+6)=3.33=3.3
90–94	92	6	⅓ (6+4+7)=5.67=5.7
85–89	87	7	⅓ (7+6+10)=7.67=7.7
80–84	82	10	⅓ (10+7+16)=11.00=11.0
75–79	77	16	⅓ (16+10+9)=11.67=11.7
70–74	72	9	⅓ (9+16+7)=10.67=10.7
65–69	67	7	⅓ (7+9+4)=6.67=6.7
60–64	62	4	⅓ (4+7+4)=5.00=5.0
55–59	57	4	⅓ (4+4+2)=3.33=3.3
50–54	52	2	⅓ (2+4+1)=2.33=2.3
45–49	47	1	⅓ (1+2+0)=1.00=1.0
40–44	42	0	⅓ (0+1+0)=0.33=0.3
		$N=70$	$N=70.0$

(iii) Mark off on the Y axis successive units to represent the frequencies on the midpoints of different intervals. Choose a Y scale which will make the largest frequency (the height) of the polygon approximately 75 per cent of the width of the figure.

(iv) At the midpoint of each class interval on the X axis, go up in the Y direction a distance equal to the number of scores (frequencies) on the corresponding interval. Place points at these locations.

(v) Join these plotted points with straight lines to obtain the surface of the frequency polygon.

2.4.2.1 *Smoothing the Frequency Polygon*

The frequency polygon for small samples is more jagged and more irregular in shape than the frequency polygon for large samples. In other words, the frequency polygon is relatively less jagged and more regular in appearance for large samples. The smaller the sample, the more the irregular jaggedness of the polygon. Therefore, to iron out chance irregularities, and also to give the polygon for a small sample, a less jagged and more regular shape like that expected of a large sample, the frequency polygon may be smoothed as shown in Figure 2.2; the observed frequency (f_o) of each class interval of a small sample may need adjustment or 'smoothing'. Smoothing makes the data more numerous. In smoothing, a series of 'moving' or 'running' averages are taken from which new or adjusted frequencies are determined. The *smoothed frequency polygon* is plotted in the following manner:

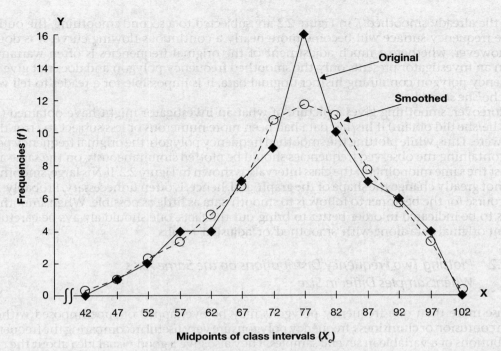

Figure 2.2   Original and smoothed frequency polygons of the distribution of scores given in Table 2.5

(a) The smoothed frequency (f_s) of each class interval may be computed from the observed frequencies (f_o) of a given class and of those two immediately above and below the relevant class interval. In other words, to find an adjusted or smoothed frequency of a particular class interval, we add the f_o on a given interval and the f_o on the two adjacent intervals (the interval just above and the interval just below) and divide the sum by 3, as shown in the following:

$$f_s = \tfrac{1}{3}\,[(f_o \text{ of the relevant class interval})$$
$$+ (f_o \text{ of the next higher class interval})$$
$$+ (f_o \text{ of the next lower class interval})].$$

For example, the smoothed frequency (f_s) for the class interval 75–79 (see Table 2.5) is $(16+10+9)/3 = 11.67 = 11.7$.

(b) The smoothed frequencies are also calculated for the two extreme additional class intervals containing zero observed frequencies. Note that if we omit these last two additional class intervals, N for the smoothed frequency distribution will be less than 70, as the smoothed distribution has frequencies outside the range of the original distribution. Thus, the smoothed frequencies (f_s) for all the class intervals are computed and shown in Table 2.5.

(c) The computed smoothed or adjusted frequencies are then plotted against the midpoints of the respective class intervals.

(d) The plotted points are then joined by straight lines (dotted or broken lines) to give the smoothed frequency polygon (see Figure 2.2). However, unlike the original frequency polygon, the smoothed polygon does not reach or meet the X axis at the two extreme ends.

If the already smoothed f_s in Figure 2.2 are subjected to a second smoothing, the outline of the frequency surface will become more nearly a continuous flowing curve. It is doubtful, however, whether so much adjustment of the original frequencies is often warranted. When an investigator presents only the smoothed frequency polygon and does not give the frequency polygon containing his/her original data, it is impossible for a reader to tell with what he/she started.

Moreover, smoothing gives a picture of what an investigator might have obtained (not what he/she did obtain) if his/her data had been more numerous or less subject to error than they were. Thus, while plotting the smoothed frequency polygon, the original frequency polygon containing the observed frequencies should be plotted simultaneously on the same axes against the same midpoints of the class intervals as shown in Figure 2.2. If N is large, smoothing may not greatly change the shape of the graph, and, hence, is often unnecessary. Probably, the best course for the beginner to follow is to smooth data as little as possible. When smoothing seems to be indicated in order better to bring out the facts, one should always be careful to present original data along with 'smoothed' or 'adjusted' results.

2.4.2.2   *Plotting Two Frequency Distributions on the Same Axes When Samples Differ in Size*

Because more than one frequency polygons may be overlapped or superimposed without much confusion or clumsiness, frequency polygons are very useful in comparing the frequency distributions of a variable in several samples. They also give a good visual idea about the contours of the distribution. But the uneven or jagged surface of the polygon fails to portray precisely the proportionate frequencies in the class intervals because the area of the polygon between the ordinates at the two limits of an interval is hardly proportional to the frequency in the latter.

Table 2.6 gives the distributions of scores on an achievement test made by two groups, A and B, which differ considerably in size. Group A has 60 cases ($N=60$) and Group B has 160

Table 2.6   Achievement test scores of two groups A and B

Scores	Midpoints	Group A (f)	Group B (f)	Group A Percentage Frequencies	Group B Percentage Frequencies
80–89	84.5	0	9	0.0	5.6
70–79	74.5	3	12	5.0	7.5
60–69	64.5	10	32	16.7	20.0
50–59	54.5	16	48	26.7	30.0
40–49	44.5	12	27	20.0	17.0
30–39	34.5	9	20	15.0	12.5
20–29	24.5	6	12	10.0	7.5
10–19	14.5	4	0	6.7	0.0
		60	160	100.1	100.1

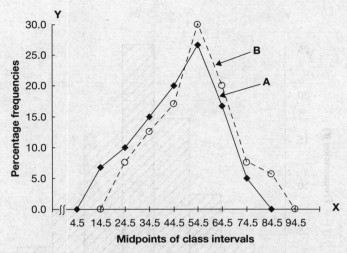

Figure 2.3   Frequency polygons of the two distributions in Table 2.6 scores are laid off on the X axis and percentage frequencies on the Y axis

cases ($N=160$). If the two distributions in Table 2.6 are plotted as polygons on the same coordinate axes, the fact that the frequencies (f's) of Group B are so much larger than those of Group A makes it hard to compare directly the range and quality of achievement in the two groups. A useful device in cases where the N's differ in size is to express both distributions in terms of percentage frequencies as shown in Table 2.6. Now, both N's are 100, and the f's are comparable from interval to interval. Frequency polygons representing the two distributions, in which percentage frequencies instead of original f's have been plotted on the same axes, are shown in Figure 2.3. These polygons provide an immediate comparison of the relative achievement of our two groups. This type of comparison cannot be made by polygons plotted from original frequencies that differ in size.

Percentage frequencies are readily found out by two ways: first, by dividing each f by N, and then multiplying it by 100 (i.e., $f/N \times 100$); and second, by dividing 100 by N, and then multiplying it by each f (i.e., $100/N \times f$). For example, if $N=60$, $f=3$, then percentage frequencies can be calculated as $3/60 \times 100 = 5.0$ or $100/60 \times 3 = 5.0$. What percentage frequencies do, in effect, is to scale each distribution down to the same total N of 100, thus permitting a comparison of f's for each interval.

2.4.3   The Histogram or Column Diagram

Another way of representing a frequency distribution graphically is by means of a histogram or column diagram. In other words, a histogram or a column diagram is a graphical representation of the frequency distribution of a continuous quantitative variable. It is an area diagram of a continuous frequency distribution and consists of a continuous set of bars; consecutive bars are not separated by any intervening space, thus indicating that there is no real gap in the scale of scores of the relevant variable. The total area of the histogram represents the total number (n) of cases in the sample, while the area of each bar is proportional to the frequency of cases in a particular class interval. In the frequency polygon, all of the cases within a given class interval are shown to be located at its midpoint only, whereas in a histogram, the cases in a class interval are shown to be uniformly distributed over the entire length of the interval.

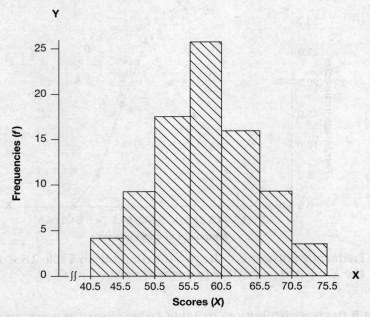

Figure 2.4   Histogram of a frequency distribution of body weights given in Table 2.7

Table 2.7   Frequency distribution of body weights in a sample

Class Intervals		Frequencies (f)
Score Limits	True Limits	
71–75	70.5–75.5	2
66–70	65.5–70.5	8
61–65	60.5–65.5	15
56–60	55.5–60.5	25
51–55	50.5–55.5	17
46–50	45.5–50.5	9
41–45	40.5–45.5	4
		$n=80$

Within each interval of a histogram, the frequency is shown by a rectangle, the base of which is the length of the class interval, and the height of which is the number of cases within the interval. This spares the histogram from a jagged appearance like the frequency polygon and makes it more convenient for a precise visual portrayal of the proportionate frequencies in the class intervals. The outline of the upper surfaces of the bars thus gives an approximate visual idea of the shape of the frequency curve.

However, in comparing the frequency distributions of more than one sample, the histogram is less convenient than the polygons because as many separate histograms have to be used as the number of samples, and they cannot be superimposed on each other without confusion or clumsiness.

The following steps are to be followed in drawing a histogram using the frequency distribution of a sample.

(a) In order to avoid the intervening gaps between consecutive class intervals, true class limits have to be used in plotting the histogram. So, the true class limits of all the class intervals are first computed from their respective score limits. Unlike the frequency polygon, no additional class interval with zero frequency is included below or above the class intervals bearing observed frequencies.

(b) The scores (X) of the variable studied are scaled along the abscissa or X axis on a graph paper—the true class limits of all the class intervals of the frequency distribution are marked on the X axis. If the lower true limits of the lowest class interval are far higher than 0, the X axis may be breached or interrupted by a zigzag line between 0 and that true limit to bring the latter as well as the histogram closer to the Y axis (see Figure 2.4).

(c) The frequencies (f) are scaled along the ordinate or Y axis. The scales for X and f should be so chosen that the ordinate for the highest frequency, that is, the height of the tallest bar measures 60 per cent-80 per cent of the base of the histogram or should follow the 75 per cent rule as discussed earlier.

(d) Two ordinates are raised on the X axis at the true limits of each class interval, and the top end of the rectangle being formed is closed by a horizontal line at the level of the frequency (f) of that class interval indicated by the Y axis scale. A bar is, thus, formed with its base extending over the length of the class interval and its height corresponding to the frequency of cases in that interval. This is repeated for all the class intervals in the data to draw a set of bars.

This type of graph is illustrated in Figure 2.4 basing on the data given in Table 2.7. As long as the class intervals and so, the bases of the bars are of equal lengths, the areas of the bars are proportional to their heights and so, to the frequencies in the respective intervals. When the same number of frequencies/scores is found on two or more adjacent intervals, the rectangles are of the same height. The highest rectangle is of the interval 55.5-60.5, which has 25, the largest frequency, as its height (see Figure 2.4).

The bars, however, differ in the width of their bases if the class intervals are of unequal sizes. In such cases, the areas of the bars fail to give the idea about the proportional frequencies in the class intervals. To remedy this, the frequency (f) of each interval is divided by the class size (i) of that interval to give the frequency density which is the average frequency per unit length of interval, namely, f/i. Each bar is then drawn with its height equalling the frequency density f/i and its base coinciding with the original class size (i) of that interval. The areas of these bars are proportional to the frequencies in the respective class intervals of unequal class sizes (see Figure 2.5).

A histogram with unequal class intervals is illustrated in Figure 2.5 basing on the data given in Table 2.8.

2.4.3.1 Plotting a Histogram and a Frequency Polygon of a Frequency Distribution on the Same Axes

Scores achieved by 50 students on a statistics test are given in Table 2.9, which serves as data for plotting both histogram and frequency polygon (see Figure 2.6).

In plotting a histogram and a frequency polygon for a particular frequency distribution (i.e., data given in Table 2.9) on the same axes, the same rules as followed in drawing individual histograms or frequency polygons are followed.

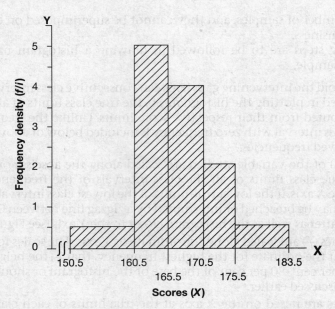

Figure 2.5   Histogram of a distribution of frequency densities with unequal class intervals given in Table 2.8

Table 2.8   Distribution of frequency densities in unequal class intervals

Class Intervals		Size of Interval (i)	Frequencies (f)	f/i
Score Limits	True Limits			
176–183	175.5–183.5	8	4	0.5
171–175	170.5–175.5	5	10	2.0
166–170	165.5–170.5	5	20	4.0
161–165	160.5–165.5	5	25	5.0
151–160	150.5–160.5	10	5	0.5
			$n=64$	

Since each class interval in a histogram is represented by a separate rectangle, it is not necessary to project the sides of the rectangles down to the baseline as has been done in Figure 2.5. The rise and fall of the boundary line shows the increase or decrease in the number of scores/cases from interval to interval and is usually the important fact to be brought out (see Figure 2.6). As in a frequency polygon, the total frequency (n) is represented by the area of the histogram. In contrast to the frequency polygon, however, the area of each rectangle in a histogram is directly proportional to the number of cases within the interval. For this reason, the histogram presents an accurate picture of the relative proportions of the total frequency from interval to interval.

In order to provide a more detailed comparison of the two types of frequency graphs, the distribution in Table 2.9 is plotted upon the same coordinate axes in Figure 2.6 as a frequency polygon and as a histogram.

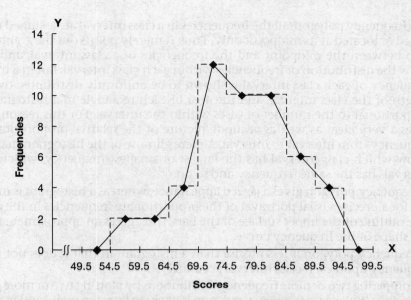

Figure 2.6   Frequency polygon and histogram of 50 statistics test scores as shown in Table 2.9

Table 2.9   Scores achieved by 50 students on a statistics test

Class Intervals (scores)	Midpoints	True Limits	Frequencies
95–99	97	94.5–99.5	0
90–94	92	89.5–94.5	4
85–89	87	84.5–89.5	6
80–84	82	79.5–84.5	10
75–79	77	74.5–79.5	10
70–74	72	69.5–74.5	12
65–69	67	64.5–69.5	4
60–64	62	59.5–64.5	2
55–59	57	54.5–59.5	2
50–54	52	49.5–54.5	0
			$n=50$

2.4.3.2   *Difference Between Frequency Polygon and Histogram*

Although both frequency polygon and histogram are used for the graphical representation of frequency distribution, and are alike in many respects, yet they possess some points of difference. The following are some of these differences.

(i)   A frequency polygon is a line graph of a given frequency distribution, whereas a histogram is essentially a bar graph or a column diagram of the same frequency distribution.

(ii) In a frequency polygon, all the frequencies in a class interval are assumed to be concentrated or located at its midpoint only. Thus, it merely points out the graphical relationship between the midpoint and the frequencies of a class interval, and is unable to show the distribution of frequencies within each class interval. But in a histogram, the frequency of each class interval is shown to be uniformly distributed over the entire length of the class interval, and the area of each rectangle in a histogram is directly proportional to the number of cases within the interval. For this reason, a histogram gives a very clear as well as accurate picture of the relative proportions of the total frequency from interval to interval. A mere glimpse of the histogram makes us able to know which class interval has the largest or smallest frequency, which pair of class intervals has the same frequency and so on.

(iii) A frequency polygon gives a jagged appearance, whereas a histogram is more convenient for a precise visual portrayal of the proportionate frequencies in the class interval. The outline of the upper surface of the bars, thus, gives an approximate visual idea of the shape of the frequency curve.

(iv) A frequency polygon is less precise than a histogram in that it does not represent the frequency upon each class interval accurately.

(v) In comparing two or more frequency distributions by plotting two or more graphs on the same axes, however, a frequency polygon is likely to be more useful and practicable than a histogram as the vertical and horizontal lines in the histograms will often coincide.

(vi) In comparison to a histogram, a frequency polygon gives a much better conception of the contours of the frequency distribution. With a part of the polygon curve, it is easy to know the trend of the distribution, but a histogram is unable to tell us about it.

(vii) Both the frequency polygon and the histogram tell the same story and enable us to show how the scores in the group are distributed in a graphical form—whether they are piled up at the low or high end of the scale or are evenly and regularly distributed over the scale. If the test is too easy, scores accumulate at the high end of the scale, whereas if the test is too tough, scores will crowd the low end of the scale. When the test is well suited to the abilities of the group, scores will be distributed symmetrically around the mean—a few individuals scoring quite high, a few quite low and the majority falling somewhere near the middle of the scale. When this happens, the frequency polygon approximates to the idea of the normal frequency curve. In this situation, the use of a frequency polygon is preferred to that of a histogram.

2.4.4   The Cumulative Frequency Graph

The cumulative frequency graph is another way of representing a frequency distribution by means of a diagram. It is essentially a line graph drawn on a graph paper by plotting actual upper limits of the class intervals on the X axis and the cumulative frequencies of these class intervals on the Y axis. Let us take the data given in the cumulative frequency distribution in Table 2.10 to explain the process of the construction of a cumulative frequency graph (see Figure 2.7).

A cumulative frequency graph is a graphical representation of the distribution of cumulative frequencies in the class interval of the sample. It is drawn in the following manner, using the frequency distribution given in Table 2.10:

(a) The actual or true upper limits (X_u) of all the class intervals in the frequency distribution are computed and entered against the respective intervals (see Table 2.10). The X_u is computed as follows:

$X_u = \frac{1}{2}$ (upper score limit of the given interval + lower score limit of the next higher interval)

Table 2.10   Cumulative frequency distribution of reading scores in a sample

Class Interval	True Upper Limits	Frequency (f)	Cumulative Frequency (cf)
95–99	99.5	4	70
90–94	94.5	6	66
85–89	89.5	7	60
80–84	84.5	10	53
75–79	79.5	16	43
70–74	74.5	9	27
65–69	69.5	7	18
60–64	64.5	4	11
55–59	59.5	4	7
50–54	54.5	2	3
45–49	49.5	1	1
		$n=70$	

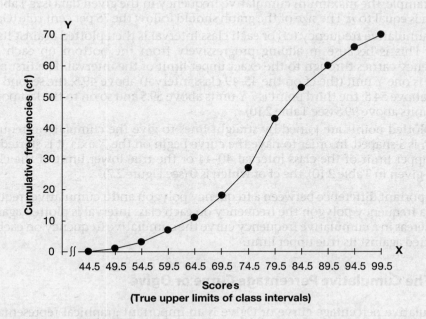

Figure 2.7   Cumulative frequency graph for the data given in Table 2.10

(b) The cumulative frequencies (cf) of all the class intervals are determined and written against the respective class intervals. The cumulative frequency (cf) of a class interval is the sum of the frequencies (f) of all the k number of intervals from the lowest interval to the upper limit of kth interval under consideration. Where cf_1, cf_2, cf_3, ..., cf_k are the cumulative frequencies and f_1, f_2, f_3, ..., f_k are the observed frequencies of the successive class intervals of the frequency distribution in an ascending order of the intervals:

$$cf_1 = f_1; \ cf_2 = f_1 + f_2; \quad cf_3 = f_1 + f_2 + f_3;$$
$$cf_k = f_1 + f_2 + f_3, \ldots, + f_k = n.$$

Another way to determine the cumulative frequencies of the class intervals in ascending order is the following:

$$cf_1 = f_1; \quad cf_2 = cf_1 + f_2; \quad cf_3 = cf_2 + f_3;$$
$$cf_k = cf_{k-1} + f_k = n.$$

To illustrate (see Table 2.10), the first cf is 1; 1+2, from the low end of the distribution, gives 3 as the next entry; 3+4=7; 7+4=11; 11+7=18; 18+9=27 and so on. The last cumulative frequency is equal to 70 or n, the total frequency.

(c) The scores (X) are scaled along the X axis, marking the true upper limits of all the class intervals on it. In addition, the true lower limit of the lowest class interval is also marked on the X axis as the true upper limit of the next lower interval with a cf of 0. From the given Table 2.10, it is evident that the lowest class interval is 45–49, whose true lower limit is 44.5. The cumulative frequencies are scaled along the Y axis of the graph (see Figure 2.7). For example, the maximum cumulative frequency in the given data (see Table 2.10) is 70, which is equal to n. The size of the graph should follow the 75 per cent rule (Garrett, 1966).

(d) The cumulative frequency (cf) of each class interval is then plotted against its true upper limit. This is because in adding progressively from the bottom up each cumulative frequency carries through to the exact upper limit of the interval. The first point on the curve is one Y unit (the cf on the 45–49 class interval) above 49.5; the second point is 3 Y units above 54.5; the third point is 7 Y units above 59.5 and so on to the last point which is 70 Y units above 99.5 (see Table 2.10).

(e) The plotted points are joined by straight lines to give the cumulative frequency graph which is S-shaped. In order to have the curve begin on the X axis, it is started at 44.5 (the true upper limit of the class interval 40–44 or the true lower limit of the class interval 45–49 given in Table 2.10), the cf of which is 0 (see Figure 2.7).

An important difference between a frequency polygon and a cumulative frequency curve is that in a frequency polygon the frequency on each class interval is plotted against its midpoint, whereas in a cumulative frequency curve the cumulative frequency on each class interval is plotted against its true upper limit.

2.4.5   The Cumulative Percentage Curve or Ogive

The cumulative percentage curve or Ogive is an important graphical representation of the cumulative percentage frequency distribution of a continuous variable. It is essentially a line graph drawn on a piece of graph paper by plotting the true upper limits of the class intervals on the X axis and their cumulative percentage frequencies on the Y axis. In this way, the Ogive differs from the cumulative frequency graph in the sense that in an Ogive the cumulative percentage frequencies are plotted on the Y axis instead of cumulative frequencies.

Table 2.11 Cumulative percentage frequency distribution of reading scores in a sample

Class Interval	True Upper Limit	Frequency (f)	Cumulative Frequency (cf)	Cumulative Percentage Frequency (cP)
75–79	79.5	1	125	100.0
70–74	74.5	3	124	99.2
65–69	69.5	6	121	96.8
60–64	64.5	12	115	92.0
55–59	59.5	20	103	82.4
50–54	54.5	36	83	66.4
45–49	49.5	20	47	37.6
40–44	44.5	15	27	21.6
35–39	39.5	6	12	9.6
30–34	34.5	4	6	4.8
25–29	29.5	2	2	1.6
		N=125		

The cumulative percentage frequency (cP) of a class interval is its cumulative frequency (cf) expressed as a percentage of the total frequency (n) of a sample:

$$cP = \frac{cf}{n} \times 100.$$

A cumulative percentage distribution is a tabulated form of the cumulative percentage frequencies according to the class interval of the scores in the grouped data of a sample (see Table 2.11). The cumulative percentage curve or cumulative percentage Ogive is the graphic expression of the cumulative percentage frequency in the class intervals of a sample.

The process of construction of an Ogive may be better understood through the following graphical representation (see Figure 2.8) based on the data given in Table 2.11.

The cumulative percentage (cP) curve or Ogive is drawn in the following way from the classified data of a sample given in Table 2.11:

(a) The actual or true upper limits (X_u) of all the class intervals in the frequency distribution are computed and entered against the respective intervals.

The computation of the true upper limit (X_u) of class intervals is done in the following manner:

$$X_u = \frac{1}{2} \text{(upper score limit of the given interval} + \text{lower score limit of the next higher interval)}$$

(b) The cumulative frequencies (cf) of all the class intervals are computed and tabulated, starting from the lowest class interval or from the low end of the distribution upward as described before by the drawing of the cumulative frequency. For example, the cf for the kth interval will be determined as:

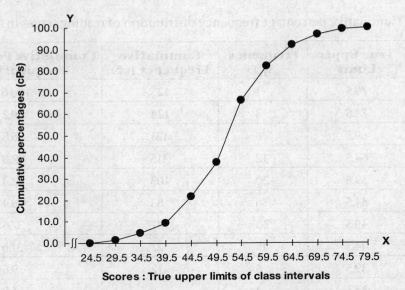

Figure 2.8 Cumulative percentage curve or Ogive plotted from the data of Table 2.11

$$\text{cf}_k = f_1 + f_2 + f_3 + \cdots + f_k \text{ or cf}_k = \text{cf}_{k-1} + f_k,$$ and then it will be entered against the respective class interval.

(c) The cumulative percentage frequency (cP) of each class interval is then computed and tabulated, using the sample size (*n*) and the cf of that interval (see Table 2.11):

$$cP = \frac{\text{cf}}{n} \times 100.$$

Another method of computing cP of each class interval is as follows:

$$cP = \frac{1}{n} \times \text{cf} \times 100.$$

In this method, first we have to determine the reciprocal, $1/n$, called the rate, and multiply each cf in order by this fraction, and then the resultant amount will be multiplied by 100 in order to obtain the percentage. For example, as per the data given in Table 2.11, the rate is $1/n = 1/125 = 0.008$. Hence, multiplying 2 (the cf of the class interval 25–29 in Table 2.11) by 0.008, we obtain 0.016, which is then multiplied by 100 and we obtain 1.6 per cent. Similarly, $6 \times 0.008 = 0.048 \times 100 = 4.8$ per cent; $12 \times 0.008 = 0.096 \times 100 = 9.6$ per cent and so on. The cumulative percentage distribution is, thus, obtained, and the last cumulative percentage frequency is equal to 100, which means that *n* is converted to 100.

(d) The scores (X) of the variable are scaled along the *X* axis on a piece of graph paper, marking the true upper limits of all the class intervals on that line. In addition, the true lower limit of the lowest class interval is also marked on the *X* axis as the true upper limit of the next lower interval with a cP of 0. From the given Table 2.11, it is quite evident that the lowest class interval is 25–29, whose true lower limit is 24.5. The cumulative percentage frequencies (cP) are scaled along the *Y* axis of the curve (see Figure 2.8). The size of the graph should follow the '75% rule'.

(e) The cumulative percentage (cP) frequencies of each class interval are then plotted against its true upper limit (see Figure 2.8). The first point on the Ogive is placed 1.6 Y units (i.e., the cP on the 25–29 class interval) just above 29.5; the second point is 4.8 Y units just above 34.5 and so on. The last point is 100 Y units above 79.5, the exact or true upper limit of the highest class interval (see Table 2.11).

(f) The plotted points are joined by straight lines to complete the cumulative percentage curve or Ogive. In order to have the curve begin on the X axis, it is started at 24.5 (the true upper limit of the class interval 20–24 or the true lower limit of the class interval 25–29 given in Table 2.11), the cP of which is 0 (see Figure 2.8).

One important difference between the cumulative frequency (cf) curve and the cumulative percentage (cP) curve is that in the cf curve the cfs are plotted against the true upper limits of the respective class intervals, whereas in the cP curve or Ogive cPs are plotted against the true upper limits of the respective class intervals.

2.4.5.1 *Smoothing of the Ogive*

One question may be asked as to why do we need smoothing of a frequency polygon or an Ogive. The appropriate answer to this question is that many times the frequency curves obtained from frequency distributions are so irregular and disproportionate that it becomes quite difficult to give some useful interpretation to them. It usually happens in the situation where the total number of frequencies (n) in a sample is small and the frequency distribution is somewhat irregular. These irregularities in frequency distributions and the effects of sampling fluctuations on the frequencies in different class intervals can be minimised by a fairly large sample. An increase in the sample size (n) always results in reducing or eliminating sample irregularities or chance irregularities. However, it is not always possible on the part of the researcher to increase the sample size owing to his/her limitations with regard to time, money and labour. In these situations, the kinds and irregularities in the frequency curves may be removed through the process of smoothing the curve. Thus, to iron out chance irregularities and also to obtain a better notion of how the figure of the curve might look if the data were more numerous, obtained from a fairly large sample, the curve needs to be smoothed.

Therefore, the Ogive is to be smoothed in order to iron out minor kinds and irregularities in the curve. Owing to the smoothing process, the Ogive is more regular and continuous than the original Ogive (see Figure 2.9).

The process of construction and smoothing of an Ogive may be better understood through the following graphical representation (see Figure 2.9) based on the data given in Table 2.12.

The smoothed cP Ogive is drawn in the following way from the classified data of a sample given in Table 2.12.

(a) The class intervals containing the frequencies (f) as well as two additional class intervals, located, respectively, just below and above that range of intervals, and each having zero frequency, are tabulated along with their respective frequencies.

(b) The true upper limits (X_u) of all the class intervals are then computed and entered against the respective intervals. The computation of X_u of class intervals will be done by following the same formula as described earlier by the drawing of cumulative frequency curves or cumulative percentage frequency curves.

(c) The cumulative frequencies (cf) of all the class intervals are then computed and tabulated, starting from the lowest class interval, and the computed cfs are entered against the respective intervals. The procedure for computing the cfs of all class intervals is the same as described earlier while drawing the cumulative frequency graph or the cumulative percentage frequency curve.

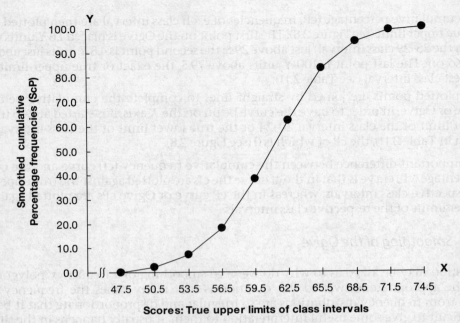

Figure 2.9   Smoothed cumulative percentage frequency (ScP) curve or Ogive of the scores in Table 2.12

Table 2.12   Distribution of cumulative percentages and smoothed cumulative percentages of an arithmetic reasoning test scores in a sample

Class Intervals	X_u	f	cf	cP	Smoothed cP
72–74	74.5	0	80	100.0	100.0
69–71	71.5	3	80	100.0	98.8
66–68	68.5	8	77	96.3	94.2
63–65	65.5	15	69	86.3	83.4
60–62	62.5	28	54	67.5	62.1
57–59	59.5	14	26	32.5	38.3
54–56	56.5	7	12	15.0	17.9
51–53	53.5	5	5	6.3	7.1
48–50	50.5	0	0	0.0	2.1
		N=80			

(d)   The cumulative percentage frequency (cP) of each interval is then computed, tabulated and entered against the respective class intervals. The procedure for computing the cP of all class intervals is the same as described earlier while drawing the cP curve or Ogive.

(e)   The only difference between the process of smoothing an Ogive and smoothing a frequency polygon is that we average cumulative percentage frequencies in the Ogive instead of the actual frequencies. The smoothed cumulative percentage (cP) frequency is computed for each class interval, using the cP of that interval and those of the two intervals just below and above of the given interval. The smoothed cP of a particular class interval can be computed as given below:

Smoothed cP = ⅓ [(cP of the given interval) + (cP of the next lower interval) + (cP of the next higher interval)].

The smoothed cumulative percentage frequencies (ScP) are given in Table 2.12. For example, the smoothed cP to be plotted against 53.5 (the X_u of the 51–53 interval given in Table 2.12) is

$$\frac{6.3 + 0.0 + 15.0}{3} = \frac{21.3}{3} = 7.1.$$

Care must be taken at the extremes of the distribution where the procedure is slightly different. With reference to Table 2.12, for example, the smoothed cumulative percentage frequency at 50.5 is

$$\frac{0.0 + 0.0 + 6.3}{3} = 2.1 \text{ and at } 74.5 \text{ is } \frac{100.0 + 100.0 + 100.0}{3} = 100.0$$

This is because of the fact that the cP of the class interval just below the class interval of 48–50 is 0.0, and the cP of the class interval just above the class interval of 72–74 is 100.0.

Note that the smoothed Ogive extends one class interval beyond the original at both extremes of the distribution.

(f)   The scores (X) of the variable are scaled along the X axis on a piece of graph paper, marking the true upper limits of all the class intervals, including the two additional class intervals, on that line. In addition, the true lower limit of the lowest class interval (in this case, the additional class interval in the low end of the original distribution) is also marked on the X axis as the true upper limit of the next lower interval with a smoothed cP of 0. From the given Table 2.12, it is quite evident that the lowest class interval is 48–50, whose true lower limit is 47.5. The smoothed cumulative percentage frequencies (ScP) are scaled along the Y axis of the Ogive (see Figure 2.9). The size of the graph should follow the '75% rule'.

(g)   The smoothed cumulative percentage frequencies (ScP) of each class interval are then plotted against its true upper limit (see Figure 2.9). The first point on the smoothed Ogive is placed 2.1 Y units just above 50.5, the second point is 7.1 Y units just above 53.5 and so on. The last point is 100 Y units just above 74.5, the true upper limit of the highest class interval, which is the additional class interval at the high end of the distribution (see Table 2.12).

(h)   The plotted points are then joined by straight lines to complete the smoothed cumulative percentage curve or smoothed Ogive. In order to have the curve begin on the X axis, it is started at 47.5 (the true upper limit of the class interval 45–47 or the true lower limit of the class interval 48–50, given in Table 2.12), the ScP of which is 0 (see Figure 2.9).

There are *two important differences* between the cumulative percentage frequency curve and the smoothed cumulative percentage frequency curve. These two differences are: (i) in drawing the cP curve, two additional class intervals, located, respectively, just below and just above the range of original class intervals and each having zero frequency, are not needed, whereas in drawing the smoothed cP curve these two additional class intervals are needed, and scaled on the X axis of the graph; and (ii) in the cP curve the cumulative percentage frequencies of the class intervals are plotted against the true upper limits of the respective intervals, whereas in the smoothed cP curve the smoothed cumulative percentage frequencies of the class intervals are plotted against the true upper limits of the respective intervals.

2.4.5.2   *Uses of the Cumulative Percentage Frequency Curve or Ogive*

The following are some of the uses of the cumulative percentage frequency curve or Ogive:

 (i) The statistics such as median, quartiles, quartile deviations, deciles, percentiles and percentile ranks may be determined quickly and fairly accurately from the Ogive.

 (ii) Percentile norms (a type of norm representing the typical performance of some designated group or groups) may be easily and accurately determined from the Ogive.

(iii) A useful overall comparison of two or more groups is provided when Ogives representing their scores on a given test are plotted upon the same coordinate axes.

2.5   Other Graphic Methods

In addition to the four important graphic methods of representing data that we have already discussed, there are several other graphic methods that deal with data showing the changes attributable to growth, practice, learning and fatigue and so on. These types of data are mostly ungrouped data (data not grouped into a frequency distribution). Widely used devices are the line graph, the bar diagram or bar graph and the pie diagram or circle graph. These are illustrated in the following sections.

2.5.1   The Line Graph

The line graph is a simple mathematical graph that is drawn on the graph paper by plotting the independent variable on the horizontal or X axis and the dependent variable on the vertical or Y axis. With the help of such graphs the effect of one variable upon another variable during an experiment or normative study may be clearly demonstrated. The construction of a line graph can be better understood through the following example.

Example 2.9 A word-learning task consisting of 20 words was administered on a student of class I to demonstrate the effect of practice on learning. He was administered 10 trials, each word carries 1 score, and the following result was obtained:

Trial No.	1	2	3	4	5	6	7	8	9	10
Scores	3	4	6	8	9	10	10	13	12	15

In order to draw the line graph on a piece of graph paper for the data of 10 trials mentioned earlier, first of all, the independent variable (trials) is represented on the horizontal or X axis and the dependent variable (scores, i.e., the number of words learned) is marked off on the vertical or Y axis of the graph. Then the scores of the student are plotted against the respective trials in accordance with the measures marked off on the Y axis. The plotted points are then joined by the straight lines and the lower end of the graph is joined to zero, the meeting point of X and Y axes to complete the line graph (see Figure 2.10).

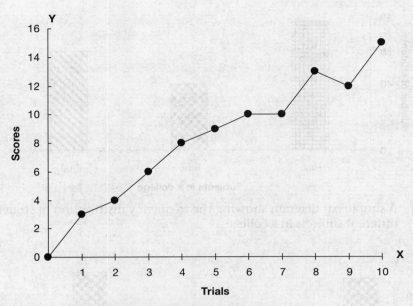

Figure 2.10   Line graph: The effect of practice on learning

2.5.2   The Bar Diagram

In a bar diagram, data are represented by bars or columns. Generally, these diagrams are drawn on graph papers. Therefore, these bar diagrams are also referred to as bar graphs. A bar diagram consists of one or more sets of bars or columns, used frequently for the graphical representation and comparison of the frequency distribution of particularly attributes and discrete variables. Bar diagrams may be conveniently used for comparing the class-wise frequency distribution of a variable in one or more samples.

Bar diagrams are usually available in two forms: vertical and horizontal. While constructing both these forms, the lengths of the bars are kept proportional to the amount of variable or trait (i.e., height, intelligence, number of individuals, educational achievements and so on) possessed. The width of bars is not governed by any set of rules. It is an arbitrary factor. Similarly, the space between two bars is also arbitrary in size.

Bar diagrams are generally of three types: simple bar diagram, multiple bar diagram and proportional bar diagram. These bar diagrams have been discussed as follows:

Simple bar diagram. A simple bar diagram consists of a set of several parallel bars or rectangles, one for each group or class of the variable. The bars may be *vertical* or *horizontal,* have equal widths chosen arbitrarily by the researcher and do not overlap with each other. The bars are separated from each other by small intervening gaps/space indicating that real gaps exist between the classes of the variables. The intervening gaps are, however, arbitrary in size. Frequencies, amounts or percentages are scaled parallel to the lengths of the bars, starting from a zero value to avoid any misleading impression about the relative lengths of the bars. The length or height of each bar is made to correspond to the frequency, amount or percentage in the relevant class. Because the widths of the bars are of equal size, their areas are directly

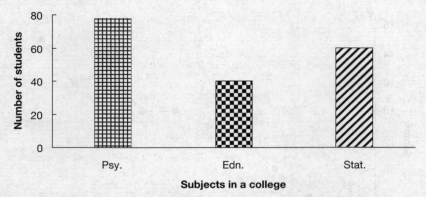

Figure 2.11   A simple bar diagram showing the frequency distribution of students of three different subjects in a college

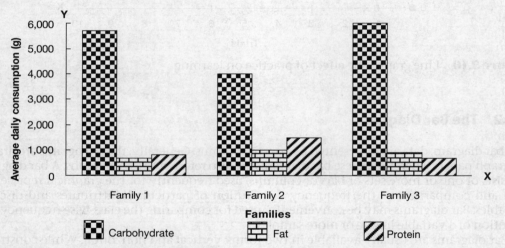

Figure 2.12   A multiple bar diagram showing average daily consumption of three macro-nutrients by three families

proportional to their respective lengths and consequently to the frequencies, amounts or percentages in the respective classes. The distribution in different classes may be studied by comparing the lengths of their respective bars.

Figure 2.11 shows the frequency distribution of students in three different subjects—Psychology, Education and Statistics—in a college. The number of students in Psychology (Psy.) is 78, in Education (Edn.) 40 and in Statistics (Stat.) 60.

Multiple bar diagram. To show the frequency distributions in the groups of more than one sample, a multiple bar diagram is drawn with as many sets of bars as the number of samples. The bars of each set show the frequency distribution of a particular sample in the classes of the variable and are as many as the number of classes. The set of bars of each sample is separated from those of neighbouring samples by gaps (see Figure 2.12).

Example 2.10 The following data describe the average daily consumption of three macro-nutrients by three families:

Sample	Average Daily Consumption of Nutrients in Grams		
	Carbohydrate	**Fat**	**Protein**
Family 1	5,700	700	800
Family 2	4,000	1,000	1,500
Family 3	6,000	900	700

Note: These data are graphically represented in Figure 2.12.

Proportional bar diagrams. This type of diagram consists of a set of *vertical* or *horizontal* bars of identical length for the graphic comparison of the proportional distribution of frequencies, percentage or amounts in different classes or groups of several samples. It presents a more explicit comparative view of the class-wise frequency distribution in different samples than the pie diagram.

In this type of diagram each sample is assigned a bar, the entire area of which represents the total frequency (*n*) of that sample. The widths of all the bars are identical. The frequencies, percentage or amounts are scaled along an axis parallel to the lengths of the bars (see Figure 2.13). Each bar is divided into as many segments as the number of classes or groups. The lengths of the segments are determined by the frequencies, percentages or amounts in the relevant classes or groups. Consequently, their areas are proportional to the frequencies, percentage or amounts in the respective classes or groups. Thus, a comparison of the lengths of different segments of the bars gives an idea about the frequency distribution in the different classes of the samples. For easy comparison, the classes or groups of all the samples should be arranged in the same order and shaded or coloured similarly in all the bars.

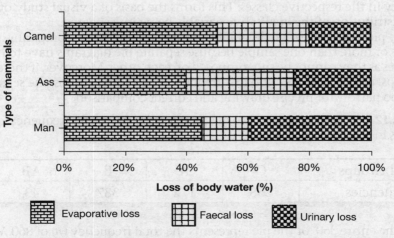

Figure 2.13 A proportional bar diagram showing the proportional loss of body water through three different channels as the percentage of the total daily water loss in three different mammals

Example 2.11 The data presented here show the loss of body water through different channels as the percentage of the total daily water loss in different mammals.

Type of Mammals	Channels of Loss of Body Water (in percentage)		
	Evaporative Loss	Faecal Loss	Urinary Loss
Camel	50	30	20
Ass	40	35	25
Man	45	15	40

Note: These data are represented graphically in Figure 2.13.

2.5.3 Pie Diagram

Pie diagrams are circular graphs used for the graphical representation of the frequency distribution of attributes or qualitative nominal variables. The name pie diagram is given to a circle graph because in determining the circumference of a circle we have to take into consideration a quantity known as 'pie' (written as π).

The diagram consists of a circle (pie) divided into segments having areas proportional to the percentages of the total frequency (n) falling in different classes of the variable. The entire area of the circle represents the total frequency (n) of cases in the sample. The angle 360° at the centre of the circle is divided by a protractor so that the area of the circle is cut into segments, each proportional in area to the relative frequency of a particular class in the sample. The angle $\theta°$ (theta degree) to be cut off from 360° for a segment is given by $\theta = 360° \times f/n$, where f is the frequency of cases in the relevant class and n is the sample size or total frequency. The areas of different segments in the circle, thus, represent graphically the proportions of the net frequency in the respective classes. This forms the basis of a visual study of the class-wise frequency distribution of the qualitative variable being investigated.

However, pie diagrams or circle graphs are inconvenient for comparing the frequency distributions of more than one sample because separate pie diagrams have to be used for different samples as they cannot be superimposed on each other. Moreover, if there are too many classes (groups) or too few cases (too low frequencies) in some groups, the segments for such groups are too narrow for precise drawing and correct comparison.

Example 2.12 We have to draw a pie diagram for the following frequency distribution of blood groups in a sample:

Blood Groups	O	A	B	AB	Total
Frequencies	258	172	387	43	860

Solution The entire 360° of the pie represents the total frequency (n) of 860. Where $\theta°$ is the angle of a segment and f is the frequency of cases in the class represented by that segment:

Since $\theta = 360 \times f/n$; hence,

for   O group, $\theta = 360° \times 258/860 = 108°$,

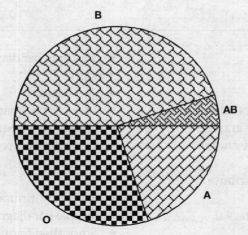

Figure 2.14 A pie diagram of the frequency distribution of blood groups in a sample

$$\text{for} \quad \text{A group,} \ \theta = 360° \times 172/860 = 72°,$$
$$\text{for} \quad \text{B group,} \ \theta = 360° \times 387/860 = 162°,$$
$$\text{for} \quad \text{AB group,} \ \theta = 360° \times 43/860 = 18°.$$

Using a protractor, segments of 108°, 72°, 162° and 18° are then cut off successively from the circle to represent the frequencies of the O, A, B and AB groups, respectively (see Figure 2.14). The segments are shaded or coloured distinctly from each other and labelled.

Summary

In this chapter, we have discussed frequency distributions and how to present them in tables and graphs. In descriptive statistics, we are interested in characterising a set of scores in the most meaningful manner. When faced with a large number of scores, it is easier to understand, interpret and communicate about the scores when they are presented as a frequency distribution. A frequency distribution is a listing of the score values in rank order along with their frequency of occurrence. If there are many scores existing over a wide range, the scores are usually grouped together in equal intervals to allow a more meaningful interpretation. The scores can be presented as an ordinary frequency distribution, a relative frequency distribution, a cumulative frequency distribution or a cumulative percentage distribution. We have discussed each of these and also how to construct them.

When graphing frequency distributions, frequency is plotted on the vertical axis (Y axis) and the score value on the horizontal axis (X axis). Six main types of graphs are used: the frequency polygon, the cumulative frequency curve, the cumulative percentage curve, the histogram, the bar graph and the pie diagram. We have discussed the use of each type and how to construct them. Frequency curves can also show some irregularities and jaggedness. To iron these chance irregularities out, and to give the curve a more regular shape, the frequency polygon and the Ogive may be smoothed. Smoothing makes the data more numerous.

Key Terms

- Bar diagram
- Class interval
- Column diagram
- Continuous frequency distribution
- Cumulative frequency graph
- Cumulative percentage curve
- Data
- Discrete frequency distribution
- Entry form method
- Exact limits of class interval
- Frequency
- Frequency distribution
- Frequency polygon
- Histogram
- Line graph
- Lower limit of class interval
- Midpoint of class interval

- Multiple bar diagram
- Ogive
- Pie diagram
- Proportional bar diagram
- Qualitative frequency distribution
- Quantitative frequency distribution
- Range
- Score
- Score: continuous, discrete
- Simple bar diagram
- Smoothed frequency polygon
- Smoothed Ogive
- Tally method
- Upper limit of class interval
- X axis (abscissa)
- Y axis (ordinate)

Questions and Problems

1. What do you understand by the term 'graphical representation of data'? Enumerate its advantages and general principles.
2. Differentiate between:
   (a) Data and scores
   (b) Qualitative and quantitative frequency distributions
3. What do you mean by 'discrete frequency distribution'? Enumerate the steps for its construction.
4. What is a 'continuous frequency distribution'? Enumerate the basic principles for its formation.
5. What is a 'frequency polygon'? Discuss the steps to be followed for its construction.
6. What do you mean by the term 'cumulative frequency'? Discuss the process of the construction of a cumulative frequency graph.
7. What is a cumulative percentage curve or Ogive? Discuss about the procedures of its construction.
8. What is meant by the term 'smoothing of a curve'? Why it is essential to smooth a frequency polygon or an Ogive? Discuss the process of smoothing a frequency polygon and an Ogive with the help of suitable examples.

9. What is a histogram? Enumerate the steps leading to its construction. Illustrate with the help of a suitable example.

10. Write notes on:

    (a) Difference between a frequency polygon and a histogram

    (b) Uses of an Ogive

11. What are the various modes utilised for the graphical representation of ungrouped data? Discuss them in brief.

12. Point out the various methods utilised for the graphical representation of grouped data (frequency distribution). Discuss them in brief.

13. What do you mean by a line graph? What is its utility? Illustrate its construction with the help of some hypothetical data.

14. What is a bar diagram? Illustrate the construction procedures of various types of bar diagrams with the help of some hypothetical data.

15. What do you mean by a pie diagram? Illustrate its construction with an example.

16. The following are marks obtained by a group of 40 class X students in an English examination.

42	88	37	75	98	93	73	62	96	80
52	76	66	54	73	69	83	62	53	79
69	56	81	75	52	65	49	80	67	59
88	80	44	71	72	87	91	82	89	79

Prepare a frequency distribution and a cumulative frequency distribution for these data using a class interval of 5.

17. Write down the exact limits and the midpoints of the class intervals for the frequency distribution obtained by answering the Problem 16 above.

18. Prepare a frequency distribution for the following test scores ($i=2$).

2	11	6	4	18	1	9	2	2	15
8	16	12	11	17	3	3	5	3	7
11	9	5	16	16	16	4	9	5	7
4	10	4	4	15	15	5	5	11	18
5	10	9	8	7	7	2	6	13	1

Obtain a cumulative percentage frequency distribution for these data.

19. Prepare histograms for the data in Problems 16 and 18 above.

20. Prepare frequency polygons for the data in Problems 16 and 18 above.

21. Prepare cumulative frequency polygons for the data in Problems 16 and 18 above.

22. Represent the following two frequency distributions as two frequency polygons. Plot both frequency polygons on the same axes.

Class Interval	Frequency (Mathematics)	Frequency (English)
90-99	2	4
80-89	5	11
70-79	7	10
60-69	7	6
50-59	6	4
40-49	6	2
30-39	3	2
20-29	3	1
10-19	0	0
0-9	1	0
Total	40	40

23. Draw both a histogram and a frequency polygon on the same axes for the following data:

Class Interval	21-25	26-30	31-35	36-40	41-45	46-50	51-55	56-60	61-65	66-70
Frequency	4	10	16	20	27	18	12	8	6	4

24. Plot frequency polygons, cumulative frequency curves and Ogives separately on different axes for the following distributions:

(a)		(b)	
Class Interval	f	Class Interval	f
75-79	1	37-39	2
70-74	3	34-36	4
65-69	5	31-33	6
60-64	8	28-30	10
55-59	11	25-27	12
50-54	18	22-24	7
45-49	10	19-21	7
40-44	8	16-18	3
35-39	6	13-15	2
30-34	3	10-12	1
25-29	1		
20-24	1		
N=75		N=54	

25. Smooth the curves of the frequency polygon and Ogive constructed from the data given for the two distributions in Problem 24 above.

26. The following scores are obtained by a group of 40 students on an achievement test:

32	78	27	65	88	83	63	52	86	70
42	66	56	44	63	59	73	52	43	69
59	46	71	65	42	55	39	70	57	49
78	70	34	61	62	77	81	72	79	69

Prepare a frequency distribution table and extend it to a cumulative frequency distribution and cumulative percentage frequency distribution tables for the above data by using a class interval of 5.

27. The following scores were obtained by a group of 30 university students in an English examination.

70	68	75	70	85	75	68	85	88	88
61	65	63	63	90	90	75	88	90	72
72	65	70	68	78	78	76	70	64	60

Construct a frequency distribution of the ungrouped scores ($i=1$).

28. Draw a smoothed frequency polygon and a smoothed Ogive from the data given in Problem 23.

29. The following table gives the weekly earnings of various types of workers in a state of India. Construct a bar graph for these data.

Category of Workers	Weekly Earnings (₹)
Professional and technical	2,770
Manager, administrators	3,020
Sales workers	2,250
Clerical workers	1,670
Craft and kindred workers	2,590

30. Draw a pie diagram to represent the following data relating to the monthly expenditure of a particular college.

Type of Expenses	Amount (₹)
Salary of the staff	60,000.00
Electricity, water, telephone	15,000.00
Other stationary	10,000.00
Miscellaneous expenses	15,000.00
Total	1,00,000.00

31. Fill in the blanks:
    (i) The measurements that are made on the subjects of an experiment are called _____.
    (ii) A score is a _____ value representing a point or distance along a continuum.
    (iii) There are two types of scores called _____ and _____.
    (iv) Score intervals may be of _____ and _____ types.
    (v) An attribute that is not capable of quantitative measurement is termed as _____ attribute.
    (vi) A variable that is capable of quantitative measurement is termed as _____ variable.
    (vii) The two types of quantitative frequency distributions are _____ and _____ frequency distributions.
    (viii) Graphing or plotting of the frequencies is done with reference to two straight lines called as _____ axes.
    (ix) In a graph, the distance of a point from 0 on the X axis is commonly called the _____.
    (x) In a frequency polygon, the frequencies of different class intervals are plotted against the _____ of the respective intervals.

32. Write whether the following statements are True or False.
    (i) Polygon means 'many-angled figure'.
    (ii) In a graph, the distance of a point from O on the Y axis is called the ordinate.
    (iii) Histogram is usually a line graph of a given frequency distribution.
    (iv) Data classified qualitatively can be presented on a line graph.
    (v) A cumulative frequency distribution enables us to find out how many observations lie above or below a certain value.
    (vi) Smoothing makes the data more numerous.
    (vii) Ogive refers to the cumulative percentage curve.
    (viii) The area of each rectangle in a histogram is directly proportional to the number of cases within the interval.
    (ix) In a cumulative frequency graph, the cumulative frequency of each class interval is plotted against its midpoint.
    (x) A pie diagram is a circle broken down into component sectors.

33. Find out the correct answers from among the four alternatives.

    (i) Diagrams and graphs are tools of:
       (a) Collection of data
       (b) Analysis of data
       (c) Summarisation
       (d) None of the above

    (ii) Frequency distribution of a nominal variable is called:
       (a) Qualitative frequency distribution
       (b) Quantitative frequency distribution
       (c) Qualitative or quantitative frequency distribution
       (d) None of the above

    (iii) Continuous frequency distribution is a type of:
       (a) Discrete frequency distribution
       (b) Qualitative frequency distribution
       (c) Quantitative frequency distribution   (d) None of the above

    (iv) In a graph, the two basic lines—OY axis and OX axis—are:
       (a) Parallel to each other
       (b) Perpendicular to each other
       (c) Tilted towards each other
       (d) None of the above

    (v) The diagram in which the frequencies of each class interval are shown to be uniformly distributed over the entire length of the class interval is called
       (a) Histogram
       (b) Pie diagram
       (c) Frequency polygon
       (d) None of the above

    (vi) In comparison to histogram, the frequency polygon is less
       (a) Jagged appearance
       (b) Precise
       (c) Irregular
       (d) None of the above

    (vii) Which of the following is quickly and accurately determined from the Ogive?
       (a) Mode
       (b) Mean
       (c) Median
       (d) None of the above

    (viii) In an Ogive, the cumulative percentage frequencies of each class interval are plotted against its:
       (a) True upper limit
       (b) True lower limit
       (c) True midpoint
       (d) None of the above

    (ix) Which one of the following bar diagrams is appropriate for representing the average daily consumption of three macronutrients by three families?
       (a) Simple bar diagrams
       (b) Proportional bar diagrams
       (c) Multiple bar diagrams
       (d) None of the above

    (x) Which one of the following is suitable for representing the frequency distribution of four blood groups in a sample?
       (a) Ogive
       (b) Pie diagram
       (c) Frequency polygon
       (d) None of the above

CHAPTER 3

Measures of Central Tendency

After reading this chapter, you will be able to:

- Apply summary statistics to describe collections of data.
- Use the mean, median (symbol Mdn) and mode to describe how data 'bunch up'.
- Explain the meaning of central tendency.
- Describe the requisites of a good average.
- Compute the mean, median and mode from both ungrouped and grouped data.
- Describe the properties, merits and demerits of the mean, median and mode.
- Enlist situations where the mean, median or mode is used as the most appropriate measure of central tendency.
- Compare the three measures of central tendency for their relative importance in a given context.
- Compute weighted mean.
- Select an appropriate measure of central tendency as per the nature of data and purpose of study.

3.1   Introduction

In Chapter 2, we discussed how to organise and present data in meaningful ways. The frequency distribution and its many derivatives such as tables, diagrams, graphs, charts and so on, for summarising and condensing data, are useful in this regard, but they themselves do not allow quantitative statements that characterise the distribution as a whole to be made nor do they allow quantitative comparisons to be made between two or more distributions. For example, suppose a psychologist has conducted an experiment to determine whether boys and girls differ in mathematical aptitude. He or she has two sets of scores: one from the boys and one from the girls in the experiment. How can he/she compare the distributions? To do so, he/she needs to quantify them. Most often this is done by computing average score for each group and then comparing the averages. The measure computed is a measure of the central tendency of each distribution. Thus, central tendency is the middle point of a distribution. Measures of central tendency are also called measures of location.

For instance, if we take the achievement scores of all the students of a class and arrange them in a frequency distribution, we will find that there are very few students who either score very high or very low. The marks of most of the students lie somewhere between the highest and the lowest scores of the whole class. This tendency of a group about distribution is named as central tendency and the typical score lying between the extremes and shared by most of the students is referred to as a measure of central tendency or central position. In this way, a measure of central tendency, as Tate (1948) defines, 'is a sort of average or typical value of the items in the series and its function is to summarize the series in terms of this average value'.

The value of a measure of central tendency is twofold. First, it is an 'average' that represents all of the scores made by the group, and as such gives a concise description of the performance of the group as a whole. Second, it enables us to compare two or more groups in terms of typical performance.

The most important objective of statistical analysis is to determine a single value for the entire mass of data so that it describes the overall level of the group of observations and can be considered a representative value of the whole set of data. It tells us whether the centre of the distribution of data is located on the scale that we are using. In other words, the measures of central tendency are otherwise known as the measures of central values or central locations because they indicate the location of some central points of the frequency distribution on the scale of the variable.

There are three 'averages' or measures of central tendency in common use. These are: the arithmetic mean (AM), the median and the mode. The 'average' is the popular term for the AM. However, in statistical work, 'average' is the general term for any measure of central tendency. While the AM is the most commonly used measure of a central location, the median and the mode are more suitable measures under a certain set of conditions and for a certain type of data. However, each measure of central tendency should meet the requisites as mentioned in the following section.

3.2 Requisites of a Good Average or Measure of Central Tendency

The following are the desiderata or requirements to be satisfied by an ideal average or measure of central tendency.

(i) *It should be rigidly defined.* That is, the definition should be clear and unambiguous so that it leads to one and only one interpretation by different persons. As a result, the personal prejudice and bias of the investigator do not affect the value of its usefulness. In other words, the definition should not leave anything to the discretion of the investigator or the observer. If it is not rigidly defined, then the bias introduced by the investigator will make its value unstable and render it unrepresentative of the distribution.

(ii) *It should be easy to understand and calculate even for a non-mathematical person.* In other words, it should be readily comprehensible and should be computed with sufficient ease and rapidity, and should not involve heavy arithmetical calculations.

(iii) *It should be based on all the observations.* Thus, in the computation of an ideal average, the entire set of data at our disposal should be used and there should not be any loss of information resulting from not using the available data. Obviously, if the whole data is not used in computing the average, it will be unrepresentative of the distribution.

(iv) *It should be representative of the data.* If it is calculated from a sample, then the sample should be random enough to be accurately representing the population.

(v)   *It should have sampling stability.* It should not be affected by sampling fluctuations. This means that if we take independent random samples of the same size from a given population and compute the average for each of these samples, then, for an ideal average, the values so obtained from different samples should not vary much from one another; we should expect to get approximately the same value from each of these samples.

(vi) *It should not be affected much by extreme values.* By extreme values we mean very small or very large values or scores. Thus, a few very small or very large observations should not unduly affect the value of a good average. If few very small or very large items are present in the data, they will unduly influence the value of the average by shifting it to one side or the other, so that the average should not be really typical of the entire series. Hence, the average chosen should be such that it is not unduly affected by such extreme values or observations.

(vii) *It should be suitable for further mathematical treatment.* In other words, the average should possess some important and interesting mathematical properties so that its use in further statistical theory is enhanced. For example, if we are given the averages and sizes (frequencies) of a number of different groups, then, for an ideal average, we should be in a position to compute the average of the combined group. If an average is not amenable to further algebraic manipulation, then obviously its use will be very much limited for further applications in statistical theory.

3.3   Various Measures of Central Tendency

The following are the three measures of central tendency or measures of location, which are commonly used in practice. These three most often used measures of central tendency are the AM, the median and the mode. In the following sections, we shall discuss them in detail one by one.

It is mathematically appropriate to use X_i as the symbol of the individual score in one or a number of samples and n_i and $\bar{X}_i$ as the individual sample sizes and means of a number of samples, respectively. In this text, however, these values are mostly represented by X, n and $\bar{X}$, respectively, to make them easier to comprehend.

3.3.1   The Arithmetic Mean (AM)

The AM is the simplest but most useful measure of central tendency or central location. It is also commonly known as simply the mean. The mean is the arithmetic average of the observed scores. Even though 'average', in general, means any measure of central location, when we use the word 'average' in our daily routine, we always mean the arithmetic average. The term is widely used by almost everyone in daily communication. We speak of an individual being an average student or of average intelligence. We always talk about average family size or average family income, or grade point average (GPA) for students and so on. Thus, from the statistical point of view, the AM is defined as the sum of the scores divided by the number of scores. In general, if there are n values in a sample, then the sample mean ($\bar{X}$ or $\bar{X}_i$) will be expressed in the following equation form:

$$\bar{X} = \frac{\sum X_i}{n} = \frac{X_1 + X_2 + X_3 + \cdots + X_n}{n}$$

$$\text{or } \bar{X} = \frac{\sum_{i=1}^{n} X_i}{n} = \frac{X_1 + X_2 + X_3 + \cdots + X_n}{n},$$

where

$X_1,\ldots,X_n$=raw scores
$\overline{X}$ (read 'X bar')=mean of sample set of scores
Σ (read 'Sigma')=summation sign
n=number of scores
$i=1,2,3,\ldots,n.$

The above formula states, *add up all the* values of X_i, where the value of i starts at 1 and ends at n with unit increments so that $i=1,2,3,\ldots,n.$

If instead of taking a sample we take the entire population in our calculation of the mean, then the symbol for the mean of the population is μ (the Greek letter mu; read 'mew') and the size of the population is N, so that the equation form becomes

$$\mu = \frac{\sum X_i}{N} = \frac{X_1+X_2+X_3+\cdots+X_N}{N}$$

$$\text{or } \mu = \frac{\sum_{i=1}^{N} X_i}{N} = \frac{X_1+X_2+X_3+\cdots+X_N}{N},$$

where

$$i=1,2,3,\ldots,N.$$

If we have the data in a grouped discrete form with frequencies (f), then the sample mean is given by the following formula:

$$\overline{X} = \frac{\Sigma fX}{\Sigma f} = \frac{\Sigma fX}{n},$$

where

$\overline{X}$=mean of the sample
Σf=summation of all frequencies=n
ΣfX=summation of each value of X multiplied by its corresponding frequency (f).

Note that we use two symbols for the mean: $\overline{X}$ if the scores are sample scores and μ if the scores are population scores. The computations, however, are the same regardless of whether the scores are sample or population scores.

3.3.1.1 *Computation of Mean from Ungrouped Data*

The AM or more simply the mean for the data not arranged into a frequency distribution is computed by dividing the sum of the individual raw scores (X) with the total number (n) of individuals in the sample. The formula for the sample mean of a series of ungrouped measures is

$$\overline{X} = \frac{\sum X_i}{n} = \frac{\sum_{i=1}^{n} X_i}{n}.$$

For example, a sample of five students obtained 60, 65, 55, 70 and 40 scores on an achievement test. The mean of their scores is

$$\bar{X} = \frac{\sum X_i}{n} = \frac{\sum_{i=1}^{n} X_i}{n} = \frac{X_1 + X_2 + X_3 + X_4 + X_5}{5}$$

$$\frac{60 + 65 + 55 + 70 + 40}{5} = \frac{290}{5} = 58.0.$$

Similarly, if a casual labourer earns ₹50, ₹60, ₹40, ₹80 and ₹70 on five successive days, then his or her mean daily wage is

$$\bar{X} = \frac{\sum X_i}{n} = \frac{₹\,50.00 + ₹\,60.00 + ₹\,40.00 + ₹\,80.00 + ₹\,70.00}{5}$$

$$= \frac{₹\,300.00}{5} = ₹\,60.00.$$

3.3.1.2 Computation of Mean from Frequency Tables

Frequency distributions of the discrete variables are often arranged in simple frequency tables in which the frequencies are entered against single distinct scores, each forming a class by itself (see Table 3.1). In such cases, one or more individuals possess identical scores so that the scores are repeated in the data, but the data cannot be classified continuously. The mean is computed here from the frequencies (repetitions) of the individual scores, where $f_1, f_2, \ldots, f_k$ are the frequencies of the individual scores like $X_1, X_2, \ldots, X_k$ and n is the total frequency or sample size. The following is the formula for computing the mean from a frequency table:

$$\bar{X} = \frac{\Sigma f\,X}{n} = \frac{f_1 X_1 + f_2 X_2 + \cdots + f_k X_k}{n}.$$

Let us compute the mean of the data presented in Table 3.1, where the relevant variable, namely the number of children per family, is a discrete variable.

Table 3.1 Frequency table for the number of children for the computation of mean

Number of Children (X)	Number of families (f)	fX
0	7	0
1	35	35
2	67	134
3	43	129
4	32	128
5	10	50
6	3	18
Total	197 (n)	494 (ΣfX)

From the data, arranged in a simple frequency table (see Table 3.1),

$$\bar{X} = \frac{\sum fX}{n} = \frac{494}{197} = 2.51.$$

3.3.1.3   Computation of Mean from Grouped Data

Computation by the direct method or long method

When measures have been grouped into a frequency distribution, the mean is calculated by a slightly different method from that given above. It is known as a direct method. This method is used for directly computing the mean of a continuous measurement variable whose scores have been arranged into regular frequency distributions.

The entire range of the observed scores should be divided into class intervals of either equal or unequal lengths, and the scores should be arranged into a frequency distribution in terms of those intervals. Because the score of each observation in a class interval is assumed to be identical with the midpoint (X_c) of that interval, the sum of the scores of each interval is obtained by multiplying the number of scores or frequencies (f) of that interval by its midpoint (X_c), and may be represented by fX_c. Thus, the sum of the fX_c values of all the intervals gives the net sum of all the scores (i.e., $\sum fX_c$) of the sample. Hence,

$$\bar{X} = \frac{\text{Sum of all scores}}{\text{Sample size}} = \frac{\sum fX_c}{n}$$

Minor discrepancies may arise in the mean computed in this way if the scores are grouped in a different set of class intervals. Moreover, the mean computed from midpoints of class intervals may differ slightly from that computed directly from individual scores of ungrouped data.

Furthermore, the mean cannot be computed in this way if the data have been arranged in an incomplete distribution with some open class intervals, because the midpoint is not available for such an interval.

To illustrate, let us consider Table 3.2, which represents the distribution of achievement test scores in a sample as given below.

The following steps are involved in the computation of the mean from a frequency distribution by the direct method (or long method).

First, calculate the midpoints of all class intervals. Then the midpoint (X_c) of each class interval is computed as follows and entered against that interval in the table:

$$X_c = \tfrac{1}{2}\,(\text{upper score limit} + \text{lower score limit}).$$

For example, for the interval 20–24,

$$X_c = \tfrac{1}{2}\,(24 + 20) = \tfrac{1}{2} \times 44 = 22$$

$$\text{or}\quad \tfrac{1}{2}\,(24.5 + 19.5) = \tfrac{1}{2} \times 44 = 22.$$

Second, multiply each midpoint by the corresponding frequency. In other words, each X_c is multiplied by the frequency (f) of cases in an interval to compute fX_c as the total of the scores in that interval. For example, the sum of the scores of all cases in the interval 30–34 is given by $fX_c = 6 \times 32 = 192$.

Third, sum the products of midpoints by frequencies. For example, from Table 3.2, it is found that: $\sum fX_c = 1612$.

Table 3.2   Frequency distribution for computing the mean achievement test score by the direct method

Class Intervals	Midpoint (X_c)	Frequency (f)	fX_c
45–49	47	1	47
40–44	42	2	84
35–39	37	3	111
30–34	32	6	192
25–29	27	8	216
20–24	22	17	374
15–19	17	26	442
10–14	12	11	132
5–9	7	2	14
0–4	2	0	0
Total		76 (n)	1612 (ΣfX_c)

Fourth, divide this sum of the fX_c by n to obtain the mean. In other words, the mean is finally computed from the sum of the fX_c values of all the class intervals and the total frequency (n) of the cases in the sample, as shown below:

$$\bar{X} = \frac{\Sigma fX_c}{n} = \frac{1612}{76} = 21.21.$$

Computation by the code method or short method

In Table 3.2, the mean was calculated by multiplying the midpoint (X_c) of each class interval by the frequency (number of scores) on the interval, summing these values (the fX_c column) and dividing it by n (the total number of scores). This straightforward or direct method (also called the long method) gives accurate results but often requires the handling of large numbers and entails tedious calculation. Because of this, the code method (also called the assumed mean method) or simply the short method has been devised for computing the mean. This short method is applicable only to continuous frequency distributions having class intervals of equal size. Moreover, the short method does not apply to the calculation of the median or the mode. These measures are always found by the methods previously described.

The most important fact to remember in computing the mean by the code method or short method is that we 'guess' or 'assume' a mean at the outset, and later, apply a correction to this assumed mean (AM) in order to obtain the actual mean (M).

To illustrate, let us consider Table 3.3 that represents the distribution of memory test scores in a sample, as given below.

The following steps are involved in the computation of a mean from a frequency distribution by the code method (or short method):

(i)   The midpoint of each class interval is computed as done previously (see Table 3.2) and entered against that class interval in the table.

Table 3.3 Frequency distribution for computing the mean memory test score by the code method (or short method)

Class Intervals	Midpoint (X_c)	Frequency (f)	x'	fx'
36–38	37	5	+3	15
33–35	34	10	+2	20
30–32	31	15	+1	15
27–29	28 (AM)	23	0	0
24–26	25	13	–1	–13
21–23	22	9	–2	–18
18–20	19	5	–3	–15
Total		80 (n)		+4 ($\Sigma fx'$)

Notes:

$AM = 28.0$

$\bar{X} = M = AM + ci$
$= 28.0 + 0.15 = 28.15$

$c = \dfrac{\Sigma fx'}{n} = \dfrac{4}{80} = 0.05$

$i = 3$
$ci = 0.05 \times 3 = 0.15.$

(ii) There is no set rule for assuming a mean. (The method outlined here gives consistent results no matter where the mean is tentatively placed or assumed.) The best plan is to take the midpoint of an interval somewhere near the centre of the distribution, and if possible, the midpoint of that interval which contains the largest frequency. In other words, the midpoint of an interval, preferably containing the largest frequency, near the centre of the distribution is arbitrarily chosen as the AM, and assigned a code number of 0 to show that this midpoint does not deviate from AM, in the column x' (see Table 3.3). The x' is regularly used to denote the deviation of a score X from the AM, and x is the deviation of a score X from the actual mean (M) of the distribution.

In Table 3.3, the largest frequency (f) is on interval 27–29, which also happens to be in the centre of the distribution. Hence, the AM is taken at 28.0, the midpoint of the class interval.

(iii) The midpoints of class intervals, rising progressively higher than that of the AM, are assigned the code numbers such as +1, +2, +3 and so on, in ascending order. Similarly, those of the intervals, running progressively downwards from the interval of the AM, are given the code numbers such as –1, –2, –3 and so on, in descending order. These code numbers (x') indicate the magnitudes of positive or negative deviations of the respective midpoints from the AM in terms of the interval units or code units which equal the size i of the intervals, that is,

$$x' = \frac{X - AM}{i}.$$

(iv) The code number (x') of each interval is multiplied by the frequency (f) of that interval, and, thus, the product of fx' is found for each class interval. All fx' on intervals above (greater than) the AM are positive, and all fx' on intervals below (smaller than) the AM are negative, since the signs of the fx' depend upon the signs of the x'. For example, the products of f and x' in the intervals 33–35 and 18–20 (see Table 3.3) are given by $fx'=10\times2=20$ and $fx'=5\times(-3)=-15$, respectively.

(v)   The algebraic sum $(\sum fx')$ of all these products (i.e., fx') is found out by deducting the sum of all negative values $(-\sum fx')$ from the sum of all positive values $(+\sum fx')$. In Table 3.3, the sum of all positive values in the fx' column is +50, and the sum of all the negative values in the fx' column is –46. Therefore, the algebraic sum of all these products is $\sum fx'=50-46=+4$.

(vi)   The algebraic sum $(\sum fx')$ of all these products is divided by the sample size (n) to obtain the correction term (c) in code units. From Table 3.3, it is found that $n=80$, $\sum fx'=+4$; therefore, the correction term (c) is

$$c = \frac{\sum fx'}{n} = \frac{+4}{80} = 0.05.$$

(vii)   Then, c is reconverted to the original unit of the scores by multiplying it with the size of the class interval (i). In the given example (see Table 3.3), $i=3$. Therefore, $ci=0.05\times3=0.15$.

(viii)   Next, the algebraic sum of the AM and the correction term in original units (ci) gives the actual mean $(M$ or $\bar{X})$. Therefore,

$$\bar{X} = \text{AM} + ci = \text{AM} + \frac{\sum fx'}{n} \times i$$

where

$\bar{X}$=actual mean of the sample
AM=assumed mean
c=correction term
i=size of the class interval
f=respective frequency of the midvalues of the class intervals
x'=code numbers (the quotient obtained after the division of the difference between the midvalue of the class interval and the AM by the size i of the interval, that is,

$$x' = \frac{X_c - \text{AM}}{i}$$

$\sum fx'$=Algebraic sum of all the products of fx'.
n=sample size or total frequency.

The sample mean of the distribution given in Table 3.3 will be found as

$$\bar{X}=\text{AM}+ci=28.0+(0.05)\,(3)=28.0+0.15=28.15.$$

The process of computing the mean from the grouped data (continuous frequency distribution) by the code method or short method is summarised as follows:

(i)   Tabulate the scores or measures into a continuous frequency distribution having class intervals of equal sizes.

(ii)   Compute the midpoint or midvalue of each class interval and designate it as X or X_c.

(iii) Take the midpoint of an interval as near the centre of the distribution as possible, and preferably, containing the largest frequency, as the AM.

(iv) Find the deviation of the midpoint of each class interval from the AM in units of interval

$$\left(\text{i.e., } x' = \frac{X_c - AM}{i} \right).$$

(v) Multiply or weight each deviation (x') by its corresponding frequency (f).

(vi) Find the algebraic sum ($\Sigma fx'$) of all the products of fx' by deducting the sum of the negative fx' from the sum of the positive fx'; and divide this sum ($\Sigma fx'$) by n (the sample size) to obtain the correction term (c) in units of class interval.

(vii) Multiply c by i (the interval length) to obtain ci (the score correction).

(viii) Add ci algebraically to the AM to obtain the actual mean of the sample. Sometimes ci will be positive and sometimes negative, depending upon where the mean has been assumed. The method works equally well in either case.

Computation of weighted mean

The weighted mean is otherwise known as the overall mean or the combined mean. Occasionally, the situation arises where we know the mean of several samples or groups of scores, and we want to calculate the mean of all the scores combined. Of course, we could start from the beginning again and just sum all the raw scores and divide them by the total number of scores. However, there is a shortcut available if we already know the mean of the groups and the number of scores in each group. The equation for this method derives from the basic definition of the mean.

The sample means ($\bar{X}_1, \bar{X}_2$ and so on) of a number of samples may be used to compute the weighted mean ($\bar{X}$) of the full set, using the sample sizes (n_1, n_2 and so on) as the weights for the respective sample means. Thus, the formula for the weighted mean (or overall or combined mean) reads

$$\bar{X} = \frac{n_1 \bar{X}_1 + n_2 \bar{X}_2 + \cdots + n_k \bar{X}_k}{n_1 + n_2 + \cdots + n_k},$$

where

n_1 = number of scores in the first sample

n_2 = number of scores in the second sample

n_k = number of scores in the kth (last) sample

$\bar{X}_1$ = mean of the first sample

$\bar{X}_2$ = mean of the second sample

$\bar{X}_k$ = mean of the kth (last) sample.

To illustrate how this equation is used, suppose a psychology professor gave a final examination to two classes. The mean of one of the classes was 90, and the number of scores was 20. The mean of the other class was 70, and 40 students took the examination. Calculate the mean of the two classes combined.

The solution is as follows.

$$\text{Given that } \bar{X}_1 = 90 \text{ and } n_1 = 20$$

$$\text{and that } \bar{X}_2 = 70 \text{ and } n_2 = 40$$

$$\bar{X}_{(comb)} = \frac{n_1 \bar{X}_1 + n_2 \bar{X}_2}{n_1 + n_2} = \frac{20(90) + 40(70)}{20 + 40} = \frac{1,800 + 2,800}{60} = \frac{4,600}{60} = 76.67.$$

Note that the overall or combined mean is much closer to the average of the class with 40 scores than the class with 20 scores. In this context, we can see that each of the means is being weighted by its number of scores. We are counting the mean of 70 forty times and the mean of 90 only twenty times. Thus, the overall mean or the combined mean really is a weighted mean, where the weights are the number of scores used in determining each mean.

3.3.1.4 *Properties or Characteristics of the Arithmetic Mean*

The AM, or simply the mean, possesses some very interesting, useful and important properties or characteristics as given below.

(i)   The mean is sensitive to the exact value of all the scores in the distribution. Since to calculate the mean we have to add all the scores, a change in any of the scores will cause a change in the mean. This is not true of the median or the mode.

(ii) The sum of all the scores of a sample is given by the product of their mean and the sample size, as shown below:

$$\sum_{i-1}^{n} X_i = n\bar{X}_i, \quad [i = 1, 2, \dots, n].$$

(iii) Mean may be considered as the score which each individual would have possessed if the total score of the sample $\left(\sum_{i=1}^{n} X_i \right)$ were equally distributed among all the individuals.

(iv) The algebraic sum of the deviations of all the individual scores from the mean amounts to zero. Thus, when $X_i - \bar{X}$ represents the deviation of each individual score from the sample mean, then

$$\sum_{i=1}^{n} (X_i - \bar{X}) = 0, \quad [i = 1, 2, \dots, n]$$

because the sum of the positive deviations of some scores from the mean equals that of the negative deviations of the remaining scores from the same mean.

(v)   The sum of the squared deviations of all the scores about their mean is a minimum. In other words, the sum of squares of deviations from the AM is less than the sum of squares of deviations from any other value. This means that if we take differences between individual values and the mean, and square these differences individually, and then add these squared differences, then the final figure will be less than the sum of the squared deviations around any value other than the mean. Stated algebraically, it means that

$$\sum_{i=1}^{n} (X_i - \bar{X})^2 = \text{Minimum}, [i = 1, 2, \dots, n].$$

(vi) The mean is very sensitive to extreme scores. The mean is the balance point of the distribution. Had we added an extreme score (one far from the mean) to the series, it would have greatly disrupted the balance. The mean would have to shift a considerable distance to re-establish the balance. Thus, the extreme score would make the mean unrepresentative of the data. The mean is more sensitive to extreme scores than the median or the mode.

(vii) If the individual scores of a sample are all multiplied or divided by a constant number, say k, the mean also gets, respectively, multiplied and divided by the same number. Symbolically, it means that

$$\frac{\sum_{i=1}^{n} Xk}{n} = \bar{X}k; \quad \frac{\sum_{i=1}^{n} X}{nk} = \frac{\bar{X}}{k}.$$

(viii) If a constant number, say k, is added to or subtracted from each individual score of a sample, the mean also gets, respectively, increased and decreased by the same number. Symbolically, it is stated as

$$\frac{\sum_{i=1}^{n}(X+k)}{n} = \bar{X}+k; \quad \frac{\sum_{i=1}^{n}(X-k)}{n} = \bar{X}-k.$$

(ix) If the scores (Y) of a variable are the linear functions of the scores (X) of another variable, then the mean $\bar{Y}$ of the former is also a linear function of the mean $\bar{X}$ of the latter. Thus, if a is the vertical intercept and b is the slope of the straight line formed by plotting the Y scores against the X scores of the respective individuals in a sample, then

$$Y = a + bX$$
$$\therefore \bar{Y} = a + b\bar{X}.$$

(x) The weighted mean $(\bar{X})$ or the overall mean $(\bar{X}_{overall})$ or the combined mean $(\bar{X}_{comb})$ of several groups can be determined from the group means and their respective sample sizes. For example, when there are k sets of X scores (namely, $X_1, X_2, \ldots, X_k$) of the same variable in as many groups, the weighted mean $(\bar{X})$ of all the groups combined is computed from the group means, namely, $\bar{X}_1, \bar{X}_2, \ldots, \bar{X}_k$, and their respective sizes, namely, $n_1, n_2, \ldots, n_k$. The group sizes are the weights given to the respective group means. Symbolically, it means that

$$\sum X_1 = n_1 \bar{X}_1, \quad \sum X_2 = n_2 \bar{X}_2, \quad \sum X_k = n_k \bar{X}_k$$
$$\therefore \bar{X} = \frac{\sum X_1 + \sum X_2 + \cdots + \sum X_k}{n_1 + n_2 + \cdots + n_k}$$
$$= \frac{n_1 \bar{X}_1 + n_2 \bar{X}_2 + \cdots + n_k \bar{X}_k}{n_1 + n_2 + \cdots + n_k}$$
$$\text{or } \bar{X} = \frac{\sum[(\text{group size})(\text{group mean})]}{\sum(\text{group size})} = \frac{\sum n_i \bar{X}_i}{\sum n_i}.$$

(xi) Under most circumstances, of the measures used for central tendency, the mean is least subject to sampling variation. If we were repeatedly to take samples from a population on a random basis, the mean would vary from sample to sample. The same is true for the median and the mode. However, the mean varies less than these other measures of central tendency. This is very important in inferential statistics, and is a major reason as to why the mean is used in inferential statistics whenever possible.

3.3.1.5   *Merits and Demerits of the Arithmetic Mean*

The following are some of the merits (advantages) and demerits (disadvantages) of the AM, or simply the mean, as a measure of central tendency or central location.

Merits. In the light of the properties or characteristics laid down above for an ideal measure of central tendency, the AM possesses the following merits:

(i)   It is rigidly defined. Its concept is familiar to most people and intuitively clear.

(ii) It is easy to calculate and understand. Every data set has a mean. It is a measure that can be calculated, and it is unique because every data set has one and only one mean.

(iii) It is based on all the observations. It takes into account all scores in the series for its determination.

(iv) It is suitable for further mathematical treatment. For example, the mean of the combined series, which is known as the weighted mean, or overall mean or combined mean, can be found out by the help of individual group means and group sizes, where the group sizes are the weights given to the respective group means.

(v)   It possesses many useful and important mathematical properties because of which it has very wide applications in statistical theory. The mean is useful for performing statistical procedures such as comparing the means from several data sets.

(vi) Of all the averages or measures of central tendency, the AM is least affected by the fluctuations of sampling. Put it into other words, the AM is a stable average.

Demerits. The following are some of the demerits or disadvantages of the AM as a measure of central location:

(i)   The strongest drawback of the AM is that, although the mean is reliable in that it reflects all the values in the dataset, it is very much affected by extreme values that are not representative of the rest of the data in the series. Two or three very large values of the variable may unduly affect the value of the AM.

(ii) The AM cannot be used in the case of open-ended classes such as less than 10, more than 80 and so on since for such classes we cannot determine the midpoint or mid-value (X_c) of the class intervals. In such cases, the median or the mode may be used.

(iii) The AM cannot be determined by inspection nor it can be located graphically.

(iv) The AM cannot be used if we are dealing with qualitative characteristics, such as beauty, honesty, punctuality and so on, unless it is measured quantitatively. In such cases, the median is the only average to be used.

(v)   The AM cannot be obtained if a single observation in the series is missing or lost or is illegible unless we drop it out and compute the mean of the remaining values.

(vi) In an extremely asymmetrical (skewed) distribution, usually the AM is not a true representative of the distribution, and hence it is not a suitable measure of location.

(vii) The AM may lead to wrong conclusions or to a fictitious average if the details of the data from which it is obtained are not available.

3.3.1.6 *Uses of the Arithmetic Mean*

Of the three commonly used measures of central tendency, the mean is most frequently encountered. However, there are cases when the use of the mean is not justified. Therefore, the following are some of the appropriate conditions where we can use the AM as a measure of the central tendency or central location:

(i) The AM is the most reliable and accurate measure of the central tendency or central location of a distribution in comparison to the median and the mode. The mean has the greatest stability as there are less fluctuation in the means of samples repeatedly drawn randomly from the same population. In other words, the mean, as a measure of central location, is least subject to sampling variation compared to other measures of central tendency. Therefore, in the situation where a reliable, an accurate and a stable measure of central tendency is wanted, we compute the AM for the given data.

(ii) The AM is the centre of gravity in the distribution, a suitable measure of location, and each score contributes to its determination. Therefore, when the scores are distributed symmetrically around a central point, that is, when the distribution is not badly skewed, then we need to compute the AM for the given data as a suitable and appropriate measure of the central tendency.

(iii) The AM can be given an algebraic treatment, and it is suitable for further arithmetical computation or mathematical treatment. Many statistics are based upon the mean. Therefore, mean can be easily employed for the computation of various statistics such as standard deviation (SD), coefficient of correlation (r) and so on. Hence, when the further computations of other statistics such as SD, r and so on are needed, we compute the AM for the given data as a reliable and dependable measure of the central tendency.

(iv) In the computation of the AM, we give equal weightage to every item in the series, because it is affected by the value of each item in that series. Each score of the series contributes to its determination. A mean is the balance point of the distribution. The extreme score in the series would greatly disrupt the balance. Therefore, it is not proper to compute the AM for the series that has extreme scores. But when there are more or less homogeneous scores in the series and a well-balanced point in the distribution is needed, then mean is to be computed for the given data.

3.3.2 The Median (Mdn)

Another commonly used and most frequently encountered measure of the central tendency (or central location) is the median. The median (symbol Mdn) is defined as the scale value below which 50 per cent of the scores fall. In other words, a median is that point in the frequency distribution, above and below which lie equal numbers, or 50 per cent of scores or cases of the sample. In short, a median is a value such that half the observations fall above it and half below it, which means that half the data will have values greater than the median and half will have values less than the median.

If the items of a series are arranged in ascending or descending order of magnitude, the value of the central item in the series is termed as the median. In this sense, we can say that 'the median of a distribution is the point on the score scale below which one-half or 50 per cent of the scores fall'. Thus, a median is the score or value of that middlemost or most central item that divides the series into two equal parts. For example, if we arrange the marks of five students in ascending or descending order, then the marks obtained by the third student from either side will be taken as the median of the scores of the group of students under consideration.

3.3.2.1   *Computation of the Median from Ungrouped Data*

To find the median from an ungrouped data set, first array or arrange the data (or scores or measures) in ascending (from lower to higher) or descending (from higher to lower) order. With regard to the computation of the median from the ungrouped data, two situations may arise: (a) the data set contains an odd number of items and (b) the data set contains an even number of items. These two procedures are discussed in detail in the following:

(i) *When 'n' is an odd number.* If there is an odd (not divisible by 2) number of items or scores in the sample data set, the median (Mdn) coincides with the observed score that occupies the middlemost or central most position of the array. In formal language, the median is

$$\text{Median} = \frac{n+1}{2}\text{th item in a data array,}$$

where

$n=$ number of items in the data array (sample).

Suppose we wish to find the median of the following seven scores in a sample or data set. The scores are 10, 11, 8, 12, 9, 14 and 16. We have to first arrange them into a data array, as given below:

$$8, 9, 10, 11, 12, 14, 16 \ [n=7].$$

According to the equation, the median is

$$\text{Median} = \frac{n+1}{2} = \frac{7+1}{2} = \frac{8}{2} = \text{4th item or score in the array.}$$

Therefore, for the above data set, the median is 11.

(ii) *When 'n' is an even number.* If there is an even (divisible by 2) number of items or scores in the sample data set, the $\frac{n+1}{2}$th score falls midway between two consecutive middle observed scores, and thus the median is given by the average of these two scores. In other words, if there is an even number of items in a data set, the median is the average of the two middle items. The formula for the median of this type of data reads

$$\text{Median} = \frac{\text{the value of } (n/2)\text{th item} + \text{the value of } (n/2+1)\text{th item}}{2}.$$

Suppose we want to find out the median of the following scores obtained by eight students in a psychological test. The scores are 47, 17, 15, 50, 44, 35, 39 and 25.

As a part of solution, first we have to arrange the scores in ascending order:

$$\text{Data array: } 15, 17, 25, 35, 39, 44, 47, 50 \ [n=8]$$

$$n/2\text{th score} = 8/2 = \text{4th score} = 35$$

$$(n/2+1)\text{th score} = 8/2+1 = 4+1 = \text{5th score} = 39.$$

$$\text{Then, Median} = \frac{35+39}{2} = \frac{74}{2} = 37.$$

(iii) Besides the above two situations regarding the computation of the median from the ungrouped data, a third, rather a complex, situation arises if the median or $\frac{n+1}{2}$ th score falls within a set of identical scores in the data. In this problematic situation, the value of the median (Mdn) is found by interpolation. For this, all the observed identical scores of that data set are assumed to occupy one unit interval extending from 0.5 below the score to 0.5 above the given score. Each identical score of the set is assumed to cover that fraction of this unit interval as is given by the reciprocal of the number of scores in that set. The median is computed by adding to the lower limit of this unit interval as many of these fractions of the interval as the number of identical scores of the set covered in counting of 0.5n scores, starting from the lowest score of the data set.

Suppose we want to find out the median for the following body weight (kg) data obtained from a sample of 11 individuals ($n=11$). The scores are 55, 57, 58, 59, 61, 61, 61, 63, 67, 68 and 70. Then, the solution is given as

$$n = 11, \quad \therefore \text{Mdn} = \frac{n+1}{2} \text{th score} = \frac{11+1}{2} = 6\text{th score.}$$

Thus, five scores lie below the median and the remaining five above it. But in counting off five scores from the lowest one in the series, the first of three identical scores, namely, the first 61, gets included in those of five scores. The three identical scores forming the set of 61 may be assumed to occupy one unit interval extending from 60.5 to 61.5, each score occupying 1/3 or 0.33 of this interval. On counting off only one of these three identical scores for arriving at the median, the upper limit of that score is reached at 60.5 + 0.33 = 60.83. This, therefore, is the median.

$$\therefore \text{Mdn} = 60.8 \text{ kg.}$$

3.3.2.2   *Computation of the Median from Grouped Data*

For a continuous frequency distribution, grouped into class intervals, the median is computed by the help of two methods, such as the interpolation method and the equation method, which are discussed in detail in the following. These two methods will be illustrated with reference to the data given in Table 3.4.

(a) *Interpolation method.* A median (Mdn) may be computed for a grouped frequency distribution by the simple interpolation of cumulative frequencies (cf) and use of the true upper and lower limits (X_U and X_L) of the class interval that contains the median.

The following are the steps involved in the process of computing the median for a grouped data by the interpolation method.

First, record the cumulative frequencies as shown in Table 3.4. Second, determine $n/2$, one-half the number of cases, in this example 26 (since $n=52$, $\therefore n/2 = 52/2 = 26$). Third, find the class interval in which the 26th case, the middle case, falls. The 26th case falls within the 21–25 interval, and the exact lower limit and the upper limit of this interval are 20.5 and 25.5, respectively. Clearly, the 26th case falls very close to the above of the lower limit of this interval because we know from an examination of our cumulative frequencies that 34 cases fall below the upper limit of this interval, that is, below 25.5. Fourth, interpolate between the exact limits of the interval to find a value above and below which 26 cases fall. To interpolate, observe that 10 cases fall within the limits 20.5 and 25.5, and we assume that these 10 cases are uniformly distributed in a rectangular fashion between

Table 3.4 Computing the median from grouped data

Class Intervals	Frequency (f)	Cumulative Frequency (cf)
36–40	4	52
31–35	6	48
26–30	8	42
21–25	10	34
16–20	9	24
11–15	7	15
6–10	5	8
1–5	3	3
Total	52 (n)	

these exact limits. Now to arrive at the 26th or middle case, we require 2 of the 10 cases within this interval because 24 cases fall below a value of 20.5; we need two more scores to make up 26. This means that we must find a point between 20.5 and 25.5 such that two cases fall below and eight cases fall above this point. Given that there are 10 scores in the said interval and the interval is 5 units wide, the proportion of the interval we require is 2/10, which is 2/10 × 5 units of score or 1.0. We add this to the lower limit of the interval to obtain the median. Thus,

$$\text{Median} = 20.5 + 1.0 = 21.5.$$

Let us summarize the steps involved:

(i)   Compute the cumulative frequencies.
(ii) Determine $n/2$, one-half the number of cases.
(iii) Find the class interval in which the middle case falls and determine the exact limits of this interval.
(iv) Interpolate to find a value on the scale above and below which one-half the total number of cases fall. This is the median.

(b) *Equation method.* The first three steps involved in the computation of a median by the interpolation method are also involved in the computational procedures of a median by the equation method. However, in addition, a simple formula is employed to calculate the median from a grouped data as given in Table 3.4.

This formula or the equation reads

$$\text{Median} = L + \left(\frac{n/2 - F}{f_{\text{m}}} \right) \times i,$$

where

L = exact lower limit of the class interval upon which the median lies
n = total number of frequencies
$n/2$ = one-half the total number of frequencies

F=sum of the frequencies on all intervals below L

f_m=number of frequencies within the interval upon which the median falls

i=size of the class interval.

In the present example (see Table 3.4), L=20.5, F=24, f_m=10, n=52, and i=5. We then have

$$\text{Median} = L + \left(\frac{n/2 - F}{f_m}\right) \times i$$

$$= 20.5 + \frac{52/2 - 24}{10} \times 5 = 20.5 + \frac{26 - 24}{10} \times 5$$

$$= 20.5 + \frac{2}{10} \times 5 = 20.5 + 1.0 = 21.5.$$

This method assumes that the observations within the interval containing the median are uniformly distributed over the range of that interval, and simple linear interpolation is appropriate.

Data for a discrete variable may be encountered which have been arranged in the form of a frequency distribution. With such data, the median is the midpoint (X_c) of the interval containing the median.

Tables 3.5–3.7 show some special situations in the computation of the median. These are discussed further.

3.3.2.3   Computation of the Median When the Frequency Distribution Contains Gaps

Difficulty arises when it becomes necessary to compute the median from a distribution in which there are gaps or zero frequency upon one or more intervals. In other words, the median may fall in a vacant interval containing no case; the midpoint (X_c) of this interval is then taken as the median (see Table 3.5).

It is clearly evident from Table 3.5 that the class interval 127–136 is a vacant interval with no frequency. The following steps are to be followed for the computation of the median.

(i)   The true lower and upper limits (X_L and X_U) and the cumulative frequency (cf) of each class interval are computed.

(ii)   The size of the class interval (i) is obtained either by subtracting the X_U of any interval from the X_U of the next higher interval or subtracting the X_L of any interval from the X_L of the next higher interval. Thus, for instance,

$$i=116.5-106.5=10$$

or $i=106.5-96.5=10$.

(iii)   One-half of the number of cases is determined by $n/2$, which is 16 in the present example, since n=32.

(iv)   The inspection of data given in Table 3.5 reveals that exactly up to the upper limit (X_U) of the class interval 117–126 has the cf of 16. The next higher interval 127–136, in which the median should fall, is a vacant interval with no case, but also has the cf of 16. So, the midpoint (X_c) of this vacant interval is taken as the median (Mdn). For this interval,

$$X_c = ½(X_L + X_U) = ½(126.5 + 136.5) = 131.5.$$

Therefore, Mdn=131.5.

Table 3.5 Computation of the median when there is one gap in the distribution

Class Intervals	True Limits		Frequency (f)	Cumulative Frequency (cf)
	Lower (X_L)	Upper (X_U)		
147–156	146.5	156.5	5	32
137–146	136.5	146.5	11	27
127–136	126.5	136.5	0	16
117–126	116.5	126.5	8	16
107–116	106.5	116.5	5	8
97–106	96.5	106.5	3	3
Total			32 (n)	

Table 3.6 Computation of the median when there are more than one gaps in the distribution

Class Intervals	True Limits		Frequency (f)	Cumulative Frequency (cf)
	Lower (X_L)	Upper (X_U)		
20–21	19.5	21.5	2	10
18–19	17.5	19.5	1	8
16–17	15.5	17.5	0	7
14–15	13.5	15.5	0	7
12–13	11.5	13.5	2	7
10–11	9.5	11.5	0	5
8–9	7.5	9.5	0	5
6–7	5.5	7.5	2	5
4–5	3.5	5.5	1	3
2–3	1.5	3.5	1	2
0–1	–0.5	1.5	1	1
Total			10 (n)	

With reference to Table 3.6, if we add the frequencies from below, we find that five cases ($n/2$) lie up to the class interval 6–7. By adding the frequencies from above, we also find that five cases lie up to the class interval 12–13. The median should then fall mid-way between the two class intervals 8–9 and 10–11. It should be the common score represented by both these classes. This score is nothing but the upper limit of the class interval 8–9 and the lower limit of the class interval 10–11, and, therefore, it should be 9.5. So, the median for the distribution given in Table 3.6 is 9.5.

The median may fall between two class intervals; in such cases, the true upper limit X_U of the lower of those two intervals is taken as the median (see Table 3.7).

Table 3.7   Computation of the median when it falls in two consecutive class intervals

Class Intervals	True Limits		Frequency (f)	Cumulative Frequency (cf)
	Lower (X_L)	Upper (X_U)		
55–59	54.5	59.5	5	68
50–54	49.5	54.5	3	63
45–49	44.5	49.5	8	60
40–44	39.5	44.5	18	52
35–39	34.5	39.5	15	34
30–34	29.5	34.5	10	19
25–29	24.5	29.5	7	9
20–24	19.5	24.5	2	2
Total			68 (n)	

With reference to Table 3.7, if we add the frequencies from below, we find that 34 cases (i.e., $n/2$) lie up to the class interval 35–39. By adding the frequencies from above, we also find that 34 cases lie up to the class interval 40–44. The median, therefore, falls between the intervals 35–39 and 40–44. So, the upper limit of the lower interval between these two, namely, 35–39, is taken as the median. Thus, median = 39.5, which is also the lower limit of the class interval 40–44. Therefore, in this case, the median is 39.5.

3.3.2.4   Graphical Determination of the Median

After drawing a cumulative percentage (cP) curve or ogive, a line is drawn parallel to its X axis from that point on the Y axis which corresponds to the cP of 50. From where this line meets the ogive, an ordinate is dropped to the X axis. The point of intersection of this ordinate with the X axis gives the median. (This point will be discussed in detail while discussing about the percentiles and percentile ranks in Chapter 5.)

3.3.2.5   Properties or Characteristics of the Median

The following are some of the important properties or characteristics of the median (Mdn):

(i)   Median is that point in the frequency distribution above and below which lie an equal number of cases of the sample. It is one of the partition values or fractiles and is identical to D_5, P_{50} and Q_2 (discussed later).

(ii) The ordinate drawn on the X axis at the median bisects the area of a frequency distribution into two equal halves.

(iii) In a symmetric unimodal distribution, the median coincides with the mean and the mode, and the algebraic sum of deviations of the observed scores from the median amounts to zero.

(iv) In an asymmetric distribution, the median differs from the mean and the mode, with the mean being located further than the median towards the longer tail of the distribution.

(v)   In an asymmetric distribution, the algebraic sum of deviations of the scores from the median differs from zero in value, and its positive or negative sign indicates, respectively, a longer positive or negative tail of the distribution. The degree of asymmetry or skewness of a distribution is estimated from the difference between its median and its mean—extreme observations predominate on that side of the median where the mean is situated, or on that side of the mode where the median is located.

(vi) The median is less sensitive or less deflected than the mean to extreme scores in the data set. For this reason, when the distribution is strongly skewed or asymmetric, it is probably better to represent the central tendency with the median rather than the mean. In other words, the median is more reliable and representative as a central value than the mean in an asymmetric distribution.

(vii) The median can be computed even for the frequency distributions with open class intervals or unequal class sizes, and also for ranked data of psychological and achievement tests.

(viii) The sum of absolute deviations (deviations without sign) about the median is less than the sum of absolute deviations about any other value. If we denote an absolute deviation from the median as $|X-\text{Mdn}|$, then the median is a value such that $\Sigma|X-\text{Mdn}|$ is a minimum.

(ix) Under usual circumstances, the median is more subject to sampling variability than the mean but less subject to sampling variability than the mode. Because the median is usually less stable than the mean from sample to sample, it is not as useful in inferential statistics.

(x)   The median finds its applications in the computations of further statistics such as mean deviation, coefficient of mean deviation and coefficient of skewness, and the median test.

3.3.2.6   *Merits and Demerits of the Median*

The following are some of the merits (or advantages) and demerits (or disadvantages) of the median as a measure of central tendency:

Merits. In the light of the properties or characteristics discussed above, the median has the following merits or advantages:

(i)   The median is rigidly defined. Its concept is familiar as well as clear to most people.

(ii) The median is easy to understand and easy to calculate even for a non-mathematical person.

(iii) The extreme values in the data set do not affect the median as strongly as they do the mean. In other words, since the median is a positional average, it is not affected at all by extreme observations, and as such is very useful in the case of skewed or asymmetric distributions. So, in the case of extreme observations, the median is a better average to use than the AM since the latter gives a distorted picture of the distribution.

(iv) A median can be computed even for grouped data with open-ended classes unless the median falls in an open-ended class.

(v)   A median can sometimes be located by simple inspection and can also be computed graphically.

(vi) A median is the only average to be used while dealing with qualitative characteristics which cannot be measured quantitatively but can still be arranged in the ascending or descending order of magnitude, for example, to find the average beauty, average honesty and the like, among a group of people.

Demerits. The following are some of the demerits or disadvantages of the median as a measure of central tendency:

 (i) Certain statistical procedures that use the median are more complex than those that use the mean.

 (ii) Because the median is the value at the average position, we must array the data before we can perform any computation. This is time consuming for any data set with a large number of elements. Therefore, if we want to use a sample statistic as an estimate of a population parameter (measure), the mean is easier to use than the median.

 (iii) In the case of an even number of observations for an ungrouped data, the median cannot be determined exactly. We merely estimate it as the AM of the two middle items. In fact, any value lying between the two middle observations can serve the purpose of median.

 (iv) The median, being a positional average, is not based on each and every item of the distribution. It depends on all the observations only to the extent whether they are smaller than or greater than it, the exact magnitude of the observations being immaterial. Let us consider a simple example. The median value of 30, 11, 5, 35 and 40, that is, 5, 11, 30, 35, 40 is 30. Now, if we replace the values of 5 and 11 by any two values which are less than 30, and the values of 35 and 40 by any two values greater than 30, the median value, that is 30, is unaffected. This property is sometimes described by saying that the median is sensitive.

 (v) A median is not suitable for further mathematical treatment, that is, given the sizes and the median values of different groups we cannot compute the median of the combined group.

 (vi) A median is relatively less stable than mean, particularly for small samples since it is affected more by fluctuations of sampling as compared with the AM.

3.3.2.7 *Uses of the Median*

The following are some of the important situations where we can use the median as a measure of central location or central tendency.

 (i) The median is the exact midpoint or the 50 per cent point of a data set as half of the cases lie below and above it. Therefore, when the exact midpoint of a distribution is required, then the median is to be computed as a central value.

 (ii) The median is not affected by the extreme scores in the series. Therefore, when a series contains extreme scores, the median is the most representative central measure.

 (iii) In the case of an open-ended distribution (i.e., incomplete distribution like '80 and above' or '20 and below' and so on), it is not possible to compute the mean. In such cases, the median is the most reliable measure that can be computed, because the median is the value above which and below which 50 per cent of the cases lie.

 (iv) The median, but not the mean, can be computed graphically. Therefore, when the data are given in terms of frequency curves, polygons, cumulative frequency curves, cumulative percentage frequency curves or ogives, we can compute the median as a measure of central location.

 (v) The median is especially useful for the qualitative data, the data which cannot precisely be measured quantitatively, for example, qualities such as honesty, beauty, health, culture, punctuality and so on.

 (vi) The median finds its application in the computations of mean deviation, coefficient of mean deviation, coefficient of skewness and the median test.

3.3.3   The Mode (Mo)

The mode is defined as the most frequent score in the distribution. It is the point on the score scale that corresponds to the maximum frequency of the distribution. In any series, it is the value of the item which is most characteristic or common and is usually repeated maximum number of times. Put it into other words, the mode (Mo) is that score of the variable which belongs to the largest number of individuals in a sample. For example, the mode of the scores 4, 5, 6, 5, 7, 5 and 8 is 5, since it occurs more often than any other value in these data.

3.3.3.1   *Computation of the Mode (MO) from Ungrouped Data*

In a simple series of scores or in the ungrouped data of a simple frequency distribution, the mode is the most frequent score. It can be easily computed by merely looking at the data. All that one has to do is to find out the score, which is repeated maximum number of times. Consider the observations 11, 12, 12, 13, 13, 13, 13, 13, 14, 15, 16. Here the value 13 occurs five times, more frequently than any other value; hence, the mode in this case is 13.

In situations where all values of X occur with equal frequency, where that frequency may be equal to or greater than 1, no modal value can be calculated. Thus, for the set of observations 2, 5, 7, 8, 4, 20, 25 and 27, no mode can be obtained. Similarly, the observations 3, 3, 3, 5, 5, 5, 7, 7, 7, 16, 16, 16, 20, 20, 20 do not permit the calculation of a modal value. All values occur with a frequency of 3.

In the case where two adjacent values of X occur with the same frequency, which is larger than the frequency of occurrence of other values of X, the mode may be taken rather arbitrarily as the mean of the two adjacent values of X. Consider the observations 11, 11, 12, 12, 12, 13, 13, 13, 13, 14, 14, 14, 14, 15, 16. Here, both the values 13 and 14 occur with a frequency of 4, which is greater than the frequency of occurrence of the remaining values. The mode may be taken as (13+14)/2 or 13.5.

When two non-adjacent values of X occur such that the frequencies of both are greater than the frequencies in adjacent intervals, then each value of X may be taken as a mode and the set of observations may be spoken of as bimodal. Consider the observations 9, 9, 10, 10, 11, 11, 12, 12, 12, 13, 13, 13, 13, 13, 14, 14, 14, 15, 15, 15, 15, 16, 16, 16, 17, 17, 18, 19, 20. Here, the value 13 occurs five times, and this is greater than the frequency of occurrence of the adjacent values. Also, the value 15 occurs four times, and this is also greater than the frequency of occurrence of the adjacent values. This set of observations may be said to be bimodal.

Usually, distributions are unimodal, that is, they have only one mode. However, it is possible for a distribution to have many modes, called multi-modal. When a distribution has two modes, as is the case with the scores, 1, 2, 3, 3, 3, 3, 4, 5, 6, 7, 7, 7, 7, 8, 9, the distribution is called bimodal.

3.3.3.2   *Computation of the Mode from Grouped Data*

With data grouped in the form of a frequency distribution, the mode is roughly taken as the midpoint of the class interval with the largest frequency. However, when data are available in the form of the frequency distribution, the mode may be computed approximately from the mean and the median of the same distribution, by the following formula:

$$\text{Mode (Mo)} = 3\,\text{Mdn} - 2\bar{X} = 3\,\text{Median} - 2\,\text{Mean},$$

where

Mdn = the median of the given distribution
$\bar{X}$ = the mean of the given distribution.

Let us find out the Mo from the distribution given in Table 3.8.

First of all we have to find out the mean and then median of the distribution given above. On the basis of values of both the mean and median, we can compute the mode of the distribution:

(i)

$$\bar{X} = \frac{\sum fX_c}{n} = \frac{8540}{50} = 170.8.$$

(ii)

$$\text{Mdn} = L + \left(\frac{n/2 - F}{\text{fm}}\right) \times i = 169.5 + \left(\frac{25 - 20}{10}\right) \times 5$$

$$= 169.5 + \frac{5}{10} \times 5 = 169.5 + 2.5 = 172.0.$$

(iii)

$$\text{Mo} = 3\,\text{Mdn} - 2\bar{X}$$

$$= 3 \times 172.0 - 2 \times 170.8 = 516.0 - 341.6 = 174.4.$$

Therefore, the 'empirical' mode is 174.4.

However, the 'crude' mode falls on the class interval having the largest frequency: 170–174 (see Table 3.8). So, the crude mode is the midpoint (X_c) of this class interval, that is, 172.0.

3.3.3.3   *Alternative Method of Computing the Mode from Grouped Data*

Mode can be computed directly from the data grouped into a frequency distribution without calculating the mean and the median for the given distribution. The mode occurs in the interval having the highest frequency of scores. The class interval that contains the mode is called the modal class.

For the purpose of computing the mode from the frequency distribution, we can use the following formula, which reads

$$\text{Mo} = X_L \left(\frac{d_1}{d_1 + d_2}\right) \times i,$$

where

X_L = lower limit of the modal class
d_1 = difference between the frequencies of the modal class and the class directly below it
d_2 = difference between the frequencies of the modal class and the class directly above it
i = size of the class interval.

Before calculating the mode, we must find d_1 and d_2 from the distribution given in Table 3.9:

$$d_1 = f_m - f_{m-1},$$

$$d_2 = f_m - f_{m+1}.$$

where

f_m = frequency of the modal class
f_{m-1} = frequency of the class that directly below (or following) the modal class
f_{m+1} = frequency of the class that directly above (or preceding) the modal class.

Table 3.8 Computing the mode from grouped data

Class Interval	Midpoint (X_c)	Frequency (f)	fX_c	Cumulative frequency (cf)
195–199	197	1	197	50
190–194	192	2	384	49
185–189	187	4	748	47
180–184	182	5	910	43
175–179	177	8	1416	38
170–174	172	10	1720	30
165–169	167	6	1002	20
160–164	162	4	648	14
155–159	157	4	628	10
150–154	152	2	304	6
145–149	147	3	441	4
140–144	142	1	142	1
Total		50	8540	
		(n)	(ΣfX_c)	

From Table 3.9, it is evident that the crude mode lies within the class interval 40–44, which is the modal class. Hence, the $X_L = 39.5$, $f_m = 11$, $f_{m-1} = 8$, $f_{m+1} = 9$ and $i = 5$:

$$d_1 = f_m - f_{m-1} = 11 - 8 = 3,$$

$$d_2 = f_m - f_{m+1} = 11 - 9 = 2.$$

Therefore,

$$\text{Mo} = X_L + \left(\frac{d_1}{d_1 + d_2} \right) \times i = 39.5 + \left(\frac{3}{3+2} \right) \times 5$$

$$= 39.5 + \frac{3}{5} \times 5 = 39.5 + 3.0 = 42.5.$$

So, the 'empirical' mode of the given distribution is 42.5.

3.3.3.4   Properties or Characteristics of the Mode

The following are some of the important properties or characteristics of the mode (Mo):

(i)   A frequency distribution is called unimodal, bimodal or multimodal according to the presence of one, two or more peaks, respectively, and as many mode values.

(ii)   There is no mode if all scores in the data set are identical or have the same frequency.

(iii)   In a perfectly symmetric unimodal distribution, the mean, median and mode are identical and they coincide on the same point at the middle of the distribution.

Table 3.9   Computation of mode from grouped data

Class Intervals	Frequency (f)
65–69	1
60–64	3
55–59	4
50–54	7
45–49	9
40–44	11 (Modal class)
35–39	8
30–34	4
25–29	2
20–24	1
Total	50 (n)

(iv)   In an asymmetric unimodal distribution, the median lies between the mode and the mean, while the mode lies on that side of the median which leads to the shorter tail of the distribution.

(v)   The mode, unlike the median and mean, does not change even if some extreme scores occur in only one tail of the frequency distribution.

(vi)   The amount and algebraic sign of the deviation of the mean from the mode indicate, respectively, the degree and direction of asymmetry of the distribution.

(vii)   Although the mode is the easiest measure of central tendency to determine, it is not used very much in behavioural sciences, because it is not very stable from sample to sample, and often there is more than one mode for a given set of scores.

(viii)   The mode is a statistic of limited practical value. It does not lend itself to algebraic manipulation.

(ix)   For distributions with two or more modes, such modes are obviously not measures of central location.

(x)   The mode can be considered a measure of central location only for distributions that taper off symmetrically towards the extremities.

3.3.3.5   Merits and Demerits of the Mode

The following are some of the merits (advantages) and demerits (disadvantages) of the mode as a measure of central location.

Merits. In the light of the properties or characteristics discussed earlier, the mode has the following merits or advantages:

(i)   The mode is easy to calculate and understand. In some cases, it can be located merely by inspection.

(ii)   The mode, like the median, can be used as a central location for qualitative as well as quantitative data.

(iii) The mode is not at all affected by extreme observations and as such is preferred to the AM while dealing with extreme observations. In other words, like the median, the mode is not unduly affected by extreme values. Even if the high values are very high and the low values very low, we choose the most frequent value of the data set as the modal value. We can use the mode no matter how large, how small or how spread out the values in the data set happen to be.

(iv) The mode can conveniently be obtained from a distribution even containing one or more open-ended classes which do not pose any problems here.

Demerits. Despite the advantages discussed earlier, the following are some of the demerits or disadvantages of the mode as a measure of central tendency:

(i) Despite the above advantages, the mode is not used as often to measure central tendency as are the mean and median. Too often there is no modal value because the data set contains no values that occur more than once. Other times, each value is the mode, because each value occurs the same number of times. Clearly, the mode is a useless measure in these cases.

(ii) Mode is not rigidly defined. It is ill defined if the maximum frequency is repeated or if the maximum frequency occurs either, in very beginning or at the end of the distribution; or if the distribution is irregular.

(iii) Another disadvantage is that when data sets contain two, three or many modes, they are difficult to be interpreted and compared.

(iv) Since the mode is the value of X corresponding to the maximum frequency, it is not based on all the observations of the series. Even in the case of the continuous frequency distribution, the mode depends on the frequencies of the modal class and the classes preceding or succeeding it.

(v) The mode is not suitable for further mathematical treatment. For example, from the modal values and the sizes of two or more series, we cannot find the mode of the combined series.

(vi) As compared to the mean, the mode is affected to a greater extent by the fluctuations of sampling.

3.3.3.6   *Uses of the Mode*

The following are some of the important situations where we can use the mode as a measure of central tendency:

(i) In many cases, the crude mode can be computed by just having a look at the data. It gives the quickest, although approximate, measure of central tendency. Therefore, in situations where a quick and approximate measure of central tendency is all that is wanted, we compute the mode for the given data set.

(ii) A mode is that value of an item which occurs most frequently or is repeated the maximum number of times in a given series. So, when we need to know the most often recurring score or value of the items in a series, we compute the mode.

(iii) Being the point of maximum density, the mode is especially useful in finding the most popular size in studies relating to marketing, trade, business and industry. On account of this characteristic, the mode has unique importance in the large-scale manufacturing of consumer goods. It is the appropriate average to be used to find the ideal size, for example, in business forecasting, in the manufacture of shoes or readymade garments which fit most men or women, in sales, in production and so forth.

(iv) The mode can be used in a situation where we describe the style of dress, the most popular fashion and the modal wage in a certain industry. In other words, when the measure of central tendency should be the most typical value, we compute the mode.

(v) The mode can be computed from the histogram and other frequency curves. So, when the original data are in terms of such graphs, it is appropriate to compute the mode, instead of a mean as a measure of central tendency for the given set of data.

3.4   Comparison of the Mean, Median, and Mode

The three commonly used measures of central tendency—the mean, median and mode—are compared with each other on the following points:

(i) The AM or simply the mean may be regarded as an appropriate measure of central location for interval and ratio variables. All the particular values of the variable are incorporated in its calculation. The median is an ordinal statistic. Its calculation is based on the ordinal properties of the data. If the observations are arranged in order, the median is the middle value. Its calculation does not incorporate all the particular values of the variable, but merely the fact of their occurrence above or below the middle value. Thus, the sets of numbers 7, 11, 25, 27, 30 and 12, 15, 25, 50, 60 have the same median, namely 25, although their means are quite different. The mode, the value or class with the greatest frequency, is a nominal statistic. Its calculation does not depend on particular values of the variable or their order, but merely on their frequency of occurrence.

(ii) A comparison of the mean, median and mode may be made when all three have been calculated for the same frequency distribution. If the frequency distribution is represented graphically, the mean is a point on the horizontal axis which corresponds to the centroid or the centre of gravity of the distribution. If a cutout of the distribution is made from a heavy cardboard and balanced on a knife edge, the point of balance will be the mean. The median is a point on the horizontal axis where the ordinate divides the total area under the curve into two equal parts. Half the area falls to the left and half to the right of the ordinate at the median. The mode is a point on the horizontal axis which corresponds to the highest point of the curve.

(iii) If the frequency distribution is symmetrical, the mean, median and mode coincide, that is, all of them fall on the same point at the middle of the distribution. If the frequency distribution is skewed or asymmetrical, these three measures do not coincide.

Figure 3.1(a) shows the mean, median and mode for a symmetrical frequency distribution. We note that these three measures of central tendency coincide on the same point at the middle of the distribution. In other words, in a symmetrical frequency distribution, the mean, median and mode are equal. Figure 3.1(b) shows the mean, median and mode for a positively skewed frequency distribution. We note that the mean is greater than the median, which, in turn, is greater than the mode. In other words, in a positively skewed distribution (one skewed to the right), the mode is at the highest point of the distribution, the median is to the right of that and the mean is to the right of both the median and mode. If the distribution is negatively skewed, the reverse relation holds. For instance, Figure 3.1(c) shows the mean, median and mode for a negatively skewed frequency distribution. We note that the mean is smaller than the median, which, in turn, is smaller than the mode. Put it into other words, in a negatively skewed distribution (one skewed to the left), the mode is still at the highest point of the distribution, the median is to the left of that and the mean is to the left of both the median and mode.

(iv) A question may be raised regarding the appropriate choice of a measure of central location. In practical situations, this question is rarely in doubt. The AM is usually to be

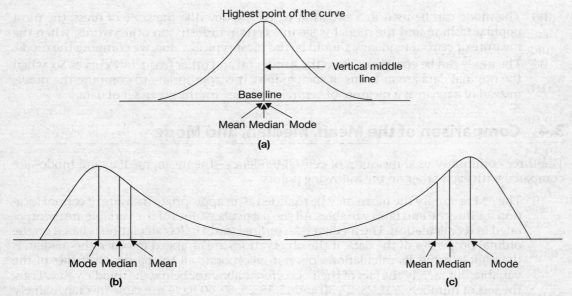

Figure 3.1   Relationship between the mean, median and mode in (a) a symmetrical, (b) positively skewed and (c) negatively skewed frequency distribution

preferred to either the median or the mode. It is rigorously defined, easily calculated and readily amenable to algebraic treatment. It also provides a better estimate of the corresponding population parameter than either the median or the mode. Therefore, although the mean, median and mode are identical in a symmetrical distribution, we rather prefer to apply the mean rather than the median or mode.

The median is, however, to be preferred in some situations. Observations may occur which appear to be atypical of the remaining observations in the set. Such atypical or extreme observations may greatly affect the value of the mean. For example, consider the observations 2, 3, 4, 5, 7, 9, 11, 13, 90. Observation 90 is quite atypical of the remaining and its presence greatly affects the value of the mean. The mean is 16, a value greater than eight of the nine observations or scores in the set. The median is 7. Under circumstances such as this, it may prove advisable in treating the data to use statistical procedures that are based on the ordinal properties of the data in preference to the procedures that incorporate all the particular values of the variable and may be grossly affected by atypical or extreme values. The median, an ordinal statistic, may, under such circumstances, be preferred to the AM. In the aforementioned example, the set of observations is grossly asymmetrical. If the distribution of the variables shows gross asymmetry, the median may be the preferred statistic, because, regardless of the asymmetry of the distribution, it can always be interpreted as the middle value. In other words, when the population is skewed negatively or positively, the median is often the best measure of location because it is always between the mean and the mode. The median is not as highly influenced by the frequency of occurrence of a single value as the mode, nor is it pulled by as extreme values as the mean. Thus, the median may be the best location measure in skewed distributions.

For a strictly nominal variable, the mode, the most frequently occurring class or value, is the only 'most typical' statistic that can be used. It is rarely used with interval, ratio and ordinal variables where means and medians can be calculated.

When we work statistical problems, we must decide whether to use the mean, the median or the mode as the measure of central tendency or central location. However, there are no universal guidelines for applying the mean, median or mode as the measure of central tendency for different populations. Each case must be judged independently, according to the guidelines we have already discussed.

Summary

In this chapter, we have discussed the central tendency of distributions. The most common measures of central tendency are the arithmetic mean, the median and the mode. The arithmetic mean gives the average of the scores and is computed by summing the scores and dividing by N. The median divides the distribution in half and, hence, is the scale value that is at the 50th percentile point of the distribution. The mode is the most frequent score in the distribution. The mean possesses special properties that make it by far the most commonly used measure of central tendency. However, if the distribution is quite skewed, the median should be used instead of the mean, since it is less affected by the extreme scores. In addition to presenting these measures, we showed how to calculate each from both ungrouped and grouped data, and elaborated their most important properties, uses, merits and demerits. We also showed how to obtain the overall mean when the average of several means is desired. Finally, we compared the three measures of central tendency with each other, and also discussed the relationship between the mean, median and mode of a distribution and its symmetry.

Key Terms

- Arithmetic mean
- Average
- Central tendency
- Median
- Mode

- Overall mean
- Raw score
- Skewness: positive; negative
- Symmetrical distribution
- Weighted mean

Questions and Problems

1. What do you mean by the term 'measures of central tendency'? Discuss about the requisites of a good measure of central tendency.
2. Define central tendency. Point out the most common measures of central tendency.
3. What is an arithmetic mean? How can it be computed in the case of ungrouped as well as grouped data? Illustrate with the help of hypothetical data.
4. Discuss about the properties, uses, merits and demerits of the arithmetic mean.
5. Define the median. How can it be computed in the case of ungrouped as well as grouped data? Illustrate with examples.
6. Enumerate the properties, uses, advantages and limitations of the median.
7. What do you understand by the term mode of a data? Point out the methods of its computation in grouped and ungrouped data. Explain through examples.
8. Describe the characteristics, uses, merits and demerits of the mode.
9. Define the mean, median and mode. Make a comparison among them.

10. What are the most commonly used measures of central tendency? Discuss when each one of them should be used and why.

11. In the following situations which measures of central tendency would you like to compute?

   (a) The average achievement of a group.
   (b) The most popular fashion of the day.
   (c) Determining the midpoint of the scores of a group in an entrance examination.

12. If the mean of a set of scores equals $\bar{X}$, what will the mean equal if:

   (a) a constant 'a' is added to each score in the set?
   (b) a constant 'a' is subtracted from each score in the set?
   (c) each score of the set is multiplied by a constant 'a'?
   (d) each score of the set is divided by a constant 'a'?

13. Given the following values of central tendency for each distribution, determine whether the distribution is symmetrical or positively skewed or negatively skewed:

   (a) Mean=14, median=12, mode=10.
   (b) Mean=14, median=16, mode=18.
   (c) Mean=14, median=14, mode=14.

14. A student kept track of the number of hours he studied each day for a two weeks period. The following daily scores were recorded (scores are in hours): 2.5, 3.2, 3.8, 1.3, 1.4, 0, 0, 2.6, 5.2, 4.8, 0, 4.6, 2.8, 3.3. Calculate:

   (a) The mean number of hours studied per day.
   (b) The median number of hours studied per day.
   (c) The modal number of hours studied per day.

15. For the following distributions, state whether you would use the mean or the median to represent the central tendency of the distribution. Explain why.

   (a) 2, 3, 8, 5, 7, 8.   (b) 10, 12, 15, 13, 19, 22.
   (c) 1.2, 0.8, 1.1, 0.6, 25.

16. Calculate the mean, median, and mode for the following scores:

   (a) 5, 2, 8, 2, 3, 2, 4, 0, 6.   (b) 30, 20, 17, 12, 30, 30, 14, 29.
   (c) 1.5, 4.5, 3.2, 1.8, 5.0, 2.2.

17. Find the mean, median and mode for the scores in the following frequency distribution:

X	f
5	1
4	3
3	4
2	6
1	2

18. A sample of $n=8$ scores has a mean of $\bar{X}=12$. A new score of $X=4$ is added to the sample.

    (a) What is ΣX for the original sample?
    (b) What is ΣX for the new sample?
    (c) What is n for the new sample?
    (d) What is the mean for the new sample?

19. A sample of $n=10$ scores has a mean of $\bar{X}=23$. One score is removed from the sample and the mean for the remaining score is $\bar{X}=25$. Find the value of the score that was removed.

20. A sample has a mean of $\bar{X}=20$.

    (a) If each X value is multiplied by 6, then what is the value of the new mean?
    (b) If five points are added to each of the original X values, then what is the value of the new mean?

21. Find the mean, median and mode for the following sets of scores:

    (a) 24, 18, 19, 12, 23, 20, 21, 22.
    (b) 20, 14, 12, 14, 19, 14, 18, 14.
    (c) 24, 18, 19, 20, 22, 25, 23, 12.
    (d) 9, 14, 8, 13, 10, 10, 11, 12, 10.

22. The following is a frequency distribution of examination marks. Compute the mean, median and mode for this distribution.

Class Interval	Frequency
90–94	1
85–89	4
80–84	2
75–79	8
70–74	9
65–69	14
60–64	6
55–59	6
50–54	4
45–49	3
40–44	3
	$N=60$

23. Compute the mean, median and mode for the following distribution.

Class Interval	Frequency
60–64	1
55–59	4
50–54	7
45–49	9
40–44	12
35–39	8
30–34	5
25–29	3
20–24	1
	N=50

24. Calculate the mean, median and mode for the following frequency distributions. Use the short method in computing the mean.

(a)		(b)	
Scores	f	Scores	f
120-122	2	100-109	5
117-119	2	90-99	9
114-116	2	80-89	14
111-113	4	70-79	19
108-110	5	60-69	21
105-107	9	50-59	30
102-104	6	40-49	25
99-101	3	30-39	15
96-98	4	20-29	10
93-95	2	10-19	8
90-92	1	0-9	6
	N=40		N=162

25. Fill in the blanks:

(i) Measures of central tendency are also called measures of _____.

(ii) Central tendency is the _____ point of a distribution.

(iii) In statistical work, _____ is the general term for any measure of central tendency.

(iv) In a sample, if $n=5$ and $\sum X=50$, then $\bar{X}$ is _____.

(v) In a series of scores: 5, 8, 7, 6, 9 and 10, the median is _____.

(vi) Given mean $=25$, median 24, the mode would be _____.

(vii) The arithmetic mean is the centre of _____ in the distribution.

(viii) The median is better suited for _____ interval series.

(ix) The mode of a distribution is the value that has the greatest of _____.

(x) In a symmetric unimodal distribution, the mean, median and mode _____ on the same point at the middle of the distribution.

26. Write whether the following statements are True or False.

(i) The value of the median is affected more by sampling fluctuations than the value of the arithmetic mean.

(ii) The arithmetic mean is always the best measure of central tendency.

(iii) The values of the median and mode can be determined graphically.

(iv) The median is that point in the frequency distribution, above and below which lie the equal number of cases of the sample.

(v) The mean is less sensitive to extreme scores in the series in comparison to the median.

(vi) If a constant number is added to each individual score of a sample, the mean is increased by the value of the constant.

(vii) An average alone is sufficient to understand the basic characteristics of a frequency distribution.

(viii) In a positively skewed distribution, the value of the mode is greater than that of the mean.

(ix) In a negatively skewed distribution, the mean is smaller than the median.

(x) There is no mode if all scores in the data set have the same frequency.

27. Find out the correct answer from among the four alternatives.

(i) Which one of the following gives equal weightage to each score in the series for its computation?

(a) Mean   (b) Median
(c) Mode   (d) None of the above

(ii) Which one of the following is not a proper measure of central tendency for a series of scores that has extreme scores?

(a) Mode   (b) Mean
(c) Median   (d) None of the above

(iii) The algebraic sum of the deviations of all the individual scores in a series amounts to zero, if the deviations are from:

(a) Mode   (b) Median
(c) Arithmetic mean   (d) None of the above

(iv) Which one of the following is the most unstable measure of the central tendency?

(a) Mode (b) Median

(c) Arithmetic mean (d) None of the above

(v) For dealing with qualitative data, the best measure of central tendency is:

(a) Arithmetic mean (b) Median

(c) Mode (d) None of the above

(vi) The positional measure of central tendency is:

(a) Mean (b) Mode

(c) Median (d) None of the above

(vii) Which one of the following is a formula for determining mode?

(a) Mode = 2 Median – 3 Mean (b) Mode = 3 Median – 2 Mean

(c) Mode = 3 Median + 2 Mean (d) None of the above

(viii) Which one of the following measures of central tendency will be used to determine the average size of the shoe sold in the shop?

(a) Arithmetic mean (b) Median

(c) Mode (d) None of the above

(ix) Which one of the following measures of central tendency will be used to find out the average beauty among a group of girl students in a class?

(a) Mode (b) Arithmetic mean

(c) Median (d) None of the above

(x) In the case of an open-ended distribution, the most reliable measure of central tendency is:

(a) Median (b) Arithmetic mean

(c) Mode (d) None of the above

CHAPTER 4

Measures of Variability

After reading this chapter you will be able to:

- Explain the meaning and importance of the measures of variability.
- Describe the characteristics of an ideal measure of variability.
- Use the range, quartile deviation, average deviation (AD) (or mean deviation, MD), standard deviation (SD) and variance to describe how data is 'spread out'.
- Compute the range, quartile deviation, AD/MD, SD and variance from a set of data.
- Describe the properties, uses, merits and demerits of R, Q, AD/MD and SD.
- Enlist situations where the different measures of variability can be specifically used.
- Compute the coefficient of variation.
- Describe the meaning and purpose of moments about the mean.
- Interpret different measures of variability.

4.1   Introduction

In the previous chapter, we have discussed about the measures of central tendency—mean, median and mode. These measures reduce the whole set of data into one single figure, called average, which represents the entire data. But the average alone cannot adequately describe a set of observations, unless all the observations are the same. It is necessary to describe the variability or dispersion of the observations.

Variation in the events of nature is of great concern to the statisticians. The variation of one measurement from another is a persisting characteristic of any sample of measurements. Measurements of intelligence, reaction time, skin resistance and eye colour, for example, exhibit variation in any sample of individuals. Anthropometric measurements such as body height, weight, diameter of the skull and length of the forearm show variation between individuals. Anatomical and physiological measurements vary; also the measurements made by the physicist, chemist, botanist and agronomist. Statistics has been spoken of as the study of variation. The experimental scientist is frequently concerned with the different circum-stances, conditions or sources which contribute to the variation in the measurements he or she obtains. Thus, the study of variation is an important concept in statistics. Moreover, the populations that are the object of statistical study always display variation in one or more respects.

4.2   Meaning and Importance of the Measures of Variability

Averages or measures of central tendency give us an idea of the concentration of the observa-tions about the central part of the distribution; they provide central value or typical represen-tative of a set of scores as a whole. In spite of their great utility in statistical analysis, they have their own limitations. If we are given only the average of a series of observations, we cannot form complete idea about the distribution since there may exist a number of distributions whose averages are the same but which may differ widely from each other in a number of ways. The following example will illustrate this viewpoint.

Let us consider the following three series A, B and C of 10 items each:

Series	Scores	Total	Mean
A	20, 20, 20, 20, 20, 20, 20, 20, 20, 20	200	20
B	17, 18, 18, 19, 20, 20, 21, 22, 22, 23	200	20
C	3, 4, 5, 17, 18, 19, 20, 36, 38, 40	200	20

All these series have the same size ($n=10$) and the same mean, namely, 20. Thus, if we are given that the mean of a series of 10 observations is 20, we cannot determine whether we are talking of the series A, B or C. In fact, any series of 10 items with total 200 will give mean 20. Thus, we may have a large number of series with entirely different structures and compositions but having the same mean.

All the test scores in series A are constant, whereas in series B they range from 17 to 23 and in series C they range from 3 to 40. Therefore, the variation of scores is more in series C than in B and A, although the mean is the same. Thus, if we measure only the mean of these three dis-tributions, we will miss an important difference among the three series. Likewise, for any data, the mean, median and mode tell us only part of what we need to know about the characteris-tics of the data. To increase our understanding of the pattern of data, we must also measure its variability—its dispersion or its spread.

From the above illustration, it is obvious that the measures of central tendency are inad-equate to describe the distribution completely. Thus, the measures of central tendency must be supported and supplemented by some other measures. One such measure is variability or dispersion. The literal meaning of dispersion is 'scatteredness'. We study dispersion to have an idea of the homogeneity (compactness) or heterogeneity (scatter) of the distribution. In the above illustration, we say that series A is stationary, that is, it is constant and shows no variability. Series B is slightly dispersed, and series C is relatively more dispersed. Thus, we say that series B is more homogeneous (or uniform) as compared to series C or the series C is more heterogeneous than series B.

Variability is the tendency of dispersion of individual scores around the mean, median or mode of a frequency distribution. Its measurement gives a quantitative idea of the shape of the distribution and is essential for statistical inference because the significance of any observation must be judged in the context of variability of scores in a sample or population. Statistics of dispersion serve as measures of variability of scores.

The statistical measures of dispersion estimate and numerically express the deviations of individual scores of a sample from a given central value like a mean and median. They are, thus, numerical measures of variability of scores in a sample and their spread or scatter around a central value. Because they describe this property of a sample with respect to a variable, they belong to the class of descriptive statistics.

There are two broad classes of these measures of dispersion or variability, namely, absolute and relative measures.

4.2.1   Absolute Measure of Dispersion

The measures of dispersion which are expressed in terms of the original units of a series are termed as absolute measures. Such measures are not suitable for comparing the variability of two distributions which are expressed in different units of measurement. To become clearer, it can be stated that the absolute measures of dispersion are expressed in the same unit as that of the variable concerned. Consequently, they cannot be used in comparing the variabilities of more than one variable when they are measured and expressed in different units. For example, the variabilities of body heights (cm) and body weights (kg) in a sample cannot be compared on the basis of an absolute measure of dispersion like standard deviation (SD) as their SDs are expressed in cm and kg, respectively.

Moreover, the absolute measures of dispersion are not the proper statistics for comparing the variabilities in two sets of scores, expressed in the same unit but having widely divergent central value like means. For example, the SD is not suitable for comparing the variabilities of femur lengths of giraffes and rats, both in cm units—because the mean and consequently the SD of the variable in giraffes far surpass those of rats—nor are the absolute measures suitable for comparing more than one set of data to find whether the different sets of data differ in precision. The absolute measures of dispersion are, however, very widely used except in the above cases. They include the range, MD, SD, quartile deviation, variance and moments.

4.2.2   Relative Measures of Dispersion

The relative measures of dispersion are obtained as a ratio or percentage and are, thus, pure numbers independent of the units of measurement. For comparing the variability of the two distributions (even if they are measured in the same units), we compute the relative measures of dispersion instead of absolute measures of dispersion.

To be clearer, we can state that the relative measures are computed from the absolute measures of dispersion and the corresponding measures of central values. Each relative measure is derived from a ratio of an absolute measure like the SD and a measure of central value like the mean, and is expressed as a percentage of the latter. Thus, the relative measures do not have other unit. This makes them very suitable for comparing the variabilities of two sets of scores given in different units. Being expressed as the percentage of central values, they are also preferable in comparing two sets of scores given in the same unit but diverging very widely in the central values. Moreover, they can also compare the precision in different sets of data. The relative measures include the coefficient of variation, the coefficient of quartile deviation (CQD) and the coefficient of MD.

4.2.3   Importance of Dispersion or Variability

The dispersion or variability of the distribution is an important characteristic to understand and measure because of the following reasons. First, it gives us additional information that enables us to judge the reliability of our measure of central tendency. If data are widely dispersed, such as those in series C, as illustrated earlier, the central location is less representative of the data as a whole than it would be for data more closely centred around the mean, as in series B. Second, because there are problems peculiar to widely dispersed data, we must be able to identify the data as widely dispersed before we can tackle problems related to it. Third, we may wish to compare dispersions or variabilities of various samples. If a wide spread of values away from the centre is undesirable or presents an unacceptable risk, we need to be able to recognise and avoid choosing the distributions with the greatest dispersion.

4.3   Characteristics of an Ideal Measure of Variability

The desiderata for an ideal measure of variability or dispersion is the same as those for an ideal measure of central tendency, namely:

   (i)   It should be rigidly defined.
  (ii)   It should be easy to calculate and easy to understand.
 (iii)   It should be based on all the observations.
 (iv)   It should be amenable to further mathematical treatment.
  (v)   It should be affected as little as possible by fluctuations of sampling.
 (vi)   It should not be affected much by extreme observations.

   All these properties have already been explained in Chapter 3 on the measures of central tendency.

4.4   Types of Measures of Variability

There are mainly four measures of variability or dispersion commonly used in the behavioural sciences. They are as follows:

1. The range (R)
2. The quartile deviation (Q)
3. The average deviation (AD) or the Mean Deviation (MD)
4. The standard deviation (SD)

   Each of the above measures of variability quantifies the extent of dispersion and gives us the degree of variability by the use of a single number, and also tells us how the individual scores are scattered or spread over throughout the distribution of the given data. These four principal measures of variability are discussed below one after another.

4.4.1   The Range (R)

The range is the simplest of all the measures of variability or dispersion. It is defined as the difference between the highest and lowest scores in the distribution. In other words, a range is calculated by subtracting the lowest score from the highest score in the series. In the equation form:

$$\text{Range} = \text{highest score} - \text{lowest score}.$$

   In the case of the grouped frequency distribution (for discrete values or the continuous frequency distribution), the range is defined as the difference between the upper limit of the highest class interval and the lower limit of the smallest class interval.

The range is easy to calculate but gives us only a relatively crude or rough measure of dispersion or variability of a series, because the range really only measures the spread of the extreme scores and not the spread of any of the scores in between. For example, the range for the measurements 2, 8, 10, 15, 20, 22 and 28 is 28 minus 2 or 26.

4.4.1.1   *Absolute and Relative Measures of the Range*

The range as defined earlier (i.e., highest score–lowest score) is an absolute measure of dispersion and depends upon the units of measurement. Thus, if we want to compare the variability of two or more distributions with the same units of measurement, we may use the definition of range as mentioned earlier that is, the difference between highest and lowest score in a series. However, to compare the variability of the distributions given in different units of measurement, we cannot use the aforementioned definition of range, but we need a relative measure which is independent of the units of measurement. This relative measure is called the coefficient of range, which is defined as follows:

$$\text{Coefficient of range} = \frac{(\text{highest score}) - (\text{lowest score})}{(\text{highest score}) + (\text{lowest score})}.$$

In other words, the coefficient of range is the ratio of the difference between two extreme observations (biggest and smallest) of the distribution to their sum. It is a common practice to use the coefficient of range even for the comparison of variability of distributions given in the same units of measurement.

4.4.1.2   *Merits and Demerits of the Range*

The following are some of the merits (or advantages) and demerits (or disadvantages) of the range as a measure of variability.

Merits. The merits or advantages of the range are discussed below:

(i)   The range is the simplest though crude measure of variability.

(ii)   It is rigidly defined, readily comprehensible and is perhaps the easiest to compute, requiring very little calculations.

(iii)   The range may be effectively used in the application of tests of significance with small samples.

Demerits. The following are some of the disadvantages, demerits, limitations or drawbacks of the range as a measure of variability.

(i)   The range is not based on the entire set of data. It also ignores a good deal of information about the spread and variability of the set of observations, since the value of range is based only on two extreme values from the entire distribution. As such a range cannot be regarded as a reliable measure of variability.

(ii)   The range is very much affected by fluctuations of sampling. Its value varies very widely from sample to sample.

(iii)   The range is an unstable descriptive measure for large samples. The sampling variance of the range for small samples is not much greater than that of the SD but increases rapidly with increase in sample size (n).

(iv)   The range is not independent of sample size, except under special circumstances. For distributions that taper to 0 at the extremities, a better chance exists of obtaining extreme values for large sample than that for small samples. Consequently, ranges calculated on samples composed of different numbers of cases are not directly comparable.

(v) If the smallest and largest values of a distribution are unaltered, and all other values are replaced by a set of observations within these two extreme values, the range of the distribution remains the same or constant. Moreover, if any item is added or deleted on either side of the extreme value, then the value of the range is changed considerably, though its effect is not so pronounced if we use the coefficient of range. Thus, the range does not take into account the composition of the series or the distribution of the observations within the extreme values. Consequently, it is fairly unreliable as a measure of dispersion or variability of the values within the distribution.

(vi) The range cannot be used if we are dealing with the incomplete frequency distribution with open-ended class intervals, because in such cases, the lowest and/or the highest scores of the sample are not available, and thus the range cannot be found.

(vii) The range is not suitable for further mathematical treatment.

(viii) The range indicates only two extreme scores of the sample with no information about the magnitudes and frequencies of intermediate scores.

(ix) The range gives no indication about the form of the distribution of scores—whether symmetrical or skewed (i.e., positively or negatively skewed); unimodal, bimodal or multimodal; mesokurtic, leptokurtic or platykurtic.

(x) The range is very unstable and varies greatly with the sample size—the larger the sample, the greater the chance of including more extreme scores and so the wider the range. In other words, the range is very sensitive to the size of the sample. As the sample size increases, the range tends to increase, though not proportionately.

(xi) Even when all other scores are close to each other, a single extreme score may increase the range disproportionately.

(xii) The range is too indefinite to be used as a practical measure of variability or dispersion.

4.4.1.3   *Uses of the Range*

In spite of the aforementioned limitations, the range, as a measure of variability or dispersion, has its applications in a number of fields, which are discussed as follows:

(i) The range may be used when the data are too scant or too scattered to justify the computation of a more precise measure of variability.

(ii) When the knowledge of extreme scores or of total spread is all that is wanted, the range is used as a measure of variability.

(iii) The range is used in the fields where the data have small variations such as the stock market fluctuations, the variations in money rates and the rate of exchange.

(iv) The range is used in the industry for the statistical quality control of the manufactured products by the construction of the control chart for the range.

(v) The range is by far the most widely used measure of variability in our day-to-day life. For example, the answers to the problems such as 'daily sales in a departmental store', 'monthly wages of workers in a factory' or 'the expected return of fruits from an orchard', are usually provided by the probable limits in the form of a range.

(vi) The range is also used as a very convenient measure by the meteorological department for weather forecasts since the public is primarily interested to know the limits within which the temperature is likely to vary on a particular day.

(vii) When very quickly, within no time, we want to know about the variability of the scores in a series, and when the computation of other measures of variability is not much useful, then we go for the use of the range as a measure of dispersion.

4.4.2   The Quartile Deviation (Q)

The quartile deviation or Q is a measure of variability, which can be calculated by the following formula:

$$Q = \frac{Q_3 - Q_1}{2}.$$

where

$Q_1 =$ the first quartile on the score scale—the point below which lie 25 per cent of the scores; it is also known as the 25th percentile (P_{25}) in a frequency distribution.

$Q_3 =$ the third quartile on the score scale—the point below which lie 75 per cent of the scores; it is also known as the 75th percentile (P_{75}) in a frequency distribution.

The difference between the Q_3 and Q_1 is known as the inter-quartile range. In other words, the inter-quartile range of a frequency distribution extends from the first quartile (Q_1 or P_{25}) to the third quartile (Q_3 or P_{75}). Thus, it contains the middle 50 per cent of the scores of a distribution:

$$\text{Inter – quartile range} = Q_3 - Q_1.$$

Quartile deviation (Q) constitutes half of this middle 50 per cent range of scores, and is, therefore, known as the semi-inter-quartile range. In other words, the quartile deviation is obtained from the inter-quartile range on dividing by 2.

The quartile deviation (Q) defined as $\dfrac{Q_3 - Q_1}{2}$ is an absolute measure of dispersion and is expressed in the same unit as the scores. For comparative studies of variability of two distributions, we need a relative measure which is known as the CQD and is given by the following formula:

$$\text{Coefficient of } Q = \frac{Q_3 - Q_1}{Q_3 + Q_1}.$$

4.4.2.1   *Properties or Characteristics of Quartile Deviation (Q)*

Some of the properties or characteristics of the quartile deviation or semi-inter-quartile range are discussed in the following:

(i) Because the lowest 25 per cent and the highest 25 per cent of the scores lie beyond the inter-quartile range from which Q is computed, the latter is independent of the scores at the two tails of the distribution. Thus, Q is unaffected by the extreme scores at the two ends of the distribution. So, it can be computed even for incomplete distributions with open-class intervals at one or both ends.

(ii) The quartile deviation or Q is not affected by scores other than Q_3 and Q_1. Thus, it gives no idea about the distribution and variability of other scores both within the inter-quartile range and beyond it. This is a serious deficiency or drawback of Q as a measure of dispersion.

(iii) Kurtosis or degree of peakedness of a frequency distribution is proportional to Q. The smaller the Q, the greater the concentration of scores at the middle of the distribution and the more the distribution leptokurtic with a high peak and a narrow body. A large Q shows a long inter-quartile range owing to a wider dispersal of scores of the middle order, making the distribution platykurtic with a low peak and a broad body.

(iv) In unimodal and bilaterally symmetric distributions like the normal distribution, Q_2 or median coincides with the mean and the mode at the centre of the distribution. In such cases, Q_3 and Q_1 are equidistant from Q_2. Thus, Q contains exactly 25 per cent of the total scores on either side of the median and equals 0.6745σ. The range $\bar{X} \pm Q$ includes 50 per cent of the scores in such a distribution. In a normal distribution, Q is called the probable error or PE.

(v) In asymmetric distributions, one tail of the distribution is skewed or more drawn out than the other. In such cases, Q_3 and Q_1 are no longer equidistant from Q_2 or median. So, the midpoint of the inter-quartile range gets displaced towards the skewed tail. On two sides of the median, Q now covers unequal percentages of the total scores. The degree and direction of skewness can, therefore, be assessed from Q and the relative distances between Q_1, Q_2 and Q_3.

4.4.2.2 *Computation of Q from the Frequency Distribution*

The quartile deviation or Q is found from the following formula:

$$Q = \frac{Q_3 - Q_1}{2}.$$

To find Q, it is clear that we must first compute the 75th (Q_3) and 25th (Q_1) percentiles from the frequency distribution. These statistics are found in exactly the same way as was the median, which is, of course, the 50th percentile or Q_2. The only difference is that 1/4 of N is counted off from the low end of the distribution to find Q_1 and that 3/4 of N is counted off to find Q_3. The formulae are as follows:

$$Q_1 = \ell + \left(\frac{N/4 - \text{Cumf}_1}{f_q} \right) \times i,$$

$$Q_3 = \ell + \left(\frac{3N/4 - \text{Cumf}_1}{f_q} \right) \times i,$$

where

ℓ = the exact lower limit of the class interval in which the quartile falls,

i = the length of the class interval,

Cumf_1 = cumulative frequency up to the class interval which contains the quartile,

f_q = the frequency on the class interval containing the quartile.

Table 4.1 shows the computations needed to obtain Q in the frequency distribution of achievement test scores in a group of students.

Since the computation of Q depends upon the values of Q_1 and Q_3, first of all, we must compute these two values and then the value of Q. The following are the steps generally followed in the process of computing Q, Q_1 and Q_3:

(i) The data are entered in a table, and the cumulative frequencies (cf) of each class interval are computed as shown in Table 4.1.

Table 4.1   Computation of the quartile deviation (Q) from data grouped into a frequency distribution

Class Intervals	Frequency (f)	Cumulative Frequency (cf)
131–140	4	80
121–130	14	76
111–120	24	62
101–110	19	38
91–100	12	19
81–90	7	7
Total	80 (N)	

(ii) The size of the class interval (i) is obtained by subtracting the upper limit of a particular class interval (X_U) from that of the next higher one. For example, the X_U of the interval 101-110 is 110.5 and that of the interval 111-120 is 120.5. Thus, $i = 120.5 - 110.5 = 10$.

(iii) For computing Q_1 or P_{25}, we should determine 1/4 of N. In the given data, $N = 80$; 1/4 $N = 1/4 \times 80 = 20$.

On counting off 20 scores from the lowest interval of the distribution, the interval 101-110 (see Table 4.1) is reached, in which P_{25} (Q_1) lies. The true lower limit (X_ℓ) and the frequency (f_q) of that interval, and the cumulative frequency (cf$_1$) up to its lower limit (X_ℓ) are noted from Table 4.1. Therefore,

$$\ell = 100.5; 1/4 \text{ of } N = 20; \quad f_q = 19; cf_1 = 19; i = 10;$$

$$\therefore Q_1 = \ell + \left(\frac{1/4N - cf_1}{f_q}\right) \times i = 100.5 + \left(\frac{20 - 19}{19}\right) \times 10$$

$$= 100.5 + \frac{1}{19} \times 10 = 100.5 + \frac{10}{19} = 100.5 + 0.5 = 101.0.$$

(iv) For computing Q_3 or P_{75},

$$N = 80; 3/4 \text{ of } N = 3/4 \times 80 = 60.$$

On counting off 60 scores from the lowest interval, the interval 111-120 is reached in which P_{75} (Q_3) lies. The true lower limit (X_L) and the frequency (f_q) of that interval, and the cumulative frequency (cf$_1$) up to its lower limit (X_L) are noted from Table 4.1. Therefore,

$$\ell = 110.5; 3/4 \, N = 60; \quad f_q = 24; cf_1 = 38; i = 10;$$

$$\therefore Q_3 = \ell + \left(\frac{3/4N - cf_1}{f_q}\right) \times i = 110.5 + \left(\frac{60 - 38}{24}\right) \times 10$$

$$= 110.5 + \frac{22}{24} \times 10 = 110.5 + \frac{220}{24} = 110.5 + 9.2 = 119.7.$$

(v) The quartile deviation (Q) is then computed as follows:

$$Q = \frac{Q_3 - Q_1}{2} = \frac{119.7 - 101.0}{2} = \frac{18.7}{2} = 9.35$$

4.4.2.3   Merits and Demerits of the Quartile Deviation

Merits. Quartile deviation is quite easy to understand and calculate. It has a number of obvious advantages over range as a measure of dispersion. For example,

  (i) As against the range which is based on two observations (i.e., the highest and lowest values in a series) only, the quartile deviation (*Q*) makes use of 50 per cent of the data and as such is obviously a better measure than the range.

 (ii) Since the quartile deviation ignores 25 per cent of the data from the beginning of the distribution and another 25 per cent of the data from the top end, it is not affected at all by extreme observations.

(iii) The quartile deviation can be computed from the frequency distribution with open-end class. In fact, *Q* is the only measure of dispersion which can be obtained while dealing with a distribution having open-end classes.

Demerits. The following are some of the disadvantages or limitations of the quartile deviation:

  (i) The quartile deviation is not based on all the observations since it ignores 25 per cent of the data at the lower end and 25 per cent of the data at the upper end of the distribution. Hence, it cannot be regarded as a reliable measure of variability.

 (ii) The quartile deviation is affected considerably by fluctuations of sampling.

(iii) The quartile deviation is not suitable for further mathematical treatment.

Thus, quartile deviation is not a reliable measure of variability, particularly for distributions in which the variation is considerable.

4.4.2.4   Uses of the Quartile Deviation

The application or use of the quartile deviation (*Q*) is recommended:

  (i) When the measurement of skewness and kurtosis of a distribution is wanted.

 (ii) When the median is the measure of central tendency.

(iii) When there are scattered or extreme scores which would influence the SD disproportionately.

(iv) When the concentration around the median—the middle 50 per cent of cases—is of primary interest.

 (v) When the distribution is incomplete having some open-end classes.

(vi) When the various percentiles and quartiles have already been computed.

4.4.2.5   Coefficient of Quartile Deviation (CQD)

The CQD is a relative measure of variability or dispersion. It is defined as the quartile deviation (*Q*) expressed as a percentage of the median (Mdn). The CQD can be computed by the following formula:

$$CQD = \frac{Q}{Mdn} \times 100.$$

Because it is independent of specific units, it can be used to compare variabilities of two sets of scores in different units. Its use, however, is very limited.

4.4.3 The Average Deviation or Mean Deviation (AD or MD)

As already pointed out, the two measures of variability or dispersion discussed so far, namely, range and quartile deviation are not based on all the observations, and also they do not exhibit any scatter of the observations from an average and, thus, completely ignore the composition of the series. The AD or MD overcomes both these drawbacks. As the name suggests, this measure of dispersion is obtained on taking the average (arithmetic mean) of the deviations of the given values from a measure of central tendency such as mean, median or mode. In other words, the AD or MD is the mean of the deviations of all the separate scores in the series taken from their mean (occasionally from the median or mode). In averaging deviations to find the AD or MD, the algebraic signs of the deviations are disregarded, and all deviations whether plus or minus are treated as positive, because the algebraic sum of all the deviations from the mean, namely, $\sum(X - \bar{X})$ or $\sum x$ amounts to zero.

The AD or MD is the simplest measure of variability that takes into account the fluctuations or variations of all the items in a series. All MDs are absolute measures of dispersion and are expressed in the same unit as that of the raw scores.

4.4.3.1 *Computation of AD or MD from Ungrouped Data*

The formula for computing the AD from an ungrouped data reads

$$AD = \frac{\sum |x|}{N},$$

where $x = X - \bar{X}$ = deviation of a raw score from the mean $\bar{X}$ of the series and the bars | | enclosing x (i.e., $|x|$) indicate that the algebraic signs are disregarded in arriving at the sum. Thus, x is always a deviation of a score from the mean. The use of the above formula may be explained through the following example.

Let us find the AD of the scores 6, 8, 10, 12 and 14 of a series. Here, $N=5$; $\sum X=6+8+10+12+14=50$; $\bar{X} = \frac{\sum X}{N} = \frac{50}{5} = 10.$

The deviations (x) of the separate scores from this mean are: $6-10=-4$, $8-10=-2$, $10-10=0$, $12-10=2$ and $14-10=4$. The sum of these five deviations disregarding algebraic signs ($\sum|x|$) is $4+2+0+2+4=12$. Therefore, the AD is

$$AD = \frac{\sum |x|}{N} = \frac{12}{5} = 2.4.$$

4.4.3.2 *Computation of AD or MD from Grouped Data*

The AD or MD can be computed from the grouped data by the following formula:

$$AD = \frac{\sum |fx|}{N},$$

where

  N=number of cases

  $\sum fx$=sum of the products of f and x over all the class intervals.

Table 4.2 Computation of the average deviation (AD) from data grouped into a frequency distribution

Class Intervals	Frequency (f)	Midpoints (X)	fX	x (X − X̄)	fx	|fx|
110–114	4	112	448	11.75	47.00	47.00
105–109	4	107	428	6.75	27.00	27.00
100–104	3	102	306	1.75	5.25	5.25
95–99	3	97	291	−3.25	−9.75	9.75
90–94	3	92	276	−8.25	−24.75	24.75
85–89	2	87	174	−13.25	−26.50	26.50
80–84	1	82	82	−18.25	−18.25	18.25
	20 (N)		2005 (ΣfX)			158.50 (Σ|fx|)

The vertical bars \| \| enclosing the fx indicate that the algebraic signs are disregarded in arriving at the sum.

Let us find out the AD from the grouped data given in Table 4.2.

The following steps are involved in the computation of the AD or MD from a frequency distribution.

(i)   The data are entered in a table, and the midpoints (X or X_c) of each class interval are calculated as shown in Table 4.2.

(ii) Each midpoint is multiplied by the frequency (f) of cases in that interval to compute fX or fX_c as the total of the scores in that interval.

(iii) Sum the products of midpoints by frequencies. For example, from Table 4.2, it is found that $\Sigma fX = 2005$.

(iv) Divide this sum of the fX by N to obtain the mean. Therefore,

$$\bar{X} = \frac{\Sigma fX}{N} = \frac{2{,}005}{20} = 100.25.$$

(v)   To find out the deviation score (x) from the mean ($\bar{X}$), the midpoints of each class interval will serve as the raw scores (X) from which the mean ($\bar{X}$) will be subtracted to obtain x (i.e., $x = X - \bar{X}$), and these deviation scores are entered against each class interval keeping the algebraic signs as shown in Table 4.2.

(vi) Each x deviation is now 'weighed' by the frequency which it represents to give the fx. In other words, each x is multiplied by the f of cases in that interval to compute fx as the total deviation scores in that interval, keeping the algebraic signs intact.

(vii) Sum the products of x deviation scores by frequencies (fx) of all class intervals disregarding the algebraic signs ($\Sigma\|fx\|$). For example, from Table 4.2, it is found that, $\Sigma\|fx\| = 158.50$.

(viii) Divide this sum by N to obtain the AD or MD, as shown in the following:

$$AD = \frac{\Sigma\|fx\|}{N} = \frac{158.50}{20} = 7.925 = 7.92.$$

In figuring deviations from the mean, it is helpful to remember that the mean is always subtracted from the midpoint of the interval, that is, X (midpoint) minus $\bar{X}$ (mean) equals x (the deviation). The computation is algebraic: plus and minus signs are recorded. Hence, when the midpoint is numerically greater than the mean, then x will be plus, and when numerically less than the mean, the x will be minus.

In the normal distribution, the AD when measured off on the scale above and below the mean includes the middle 57.5 per cent of the cases. The AD is, therefore, always somewhat larger than the Q which includes the middle 50 per cent of cases.

4.4.3.3 *Properties or Characteristics of the Average Deviation*

The following are some of the important properties or characteristics of the AD or MD:

(i)   Usually, we obtain the AD or MD about any one of the three averages—mean (M), median (Mdn) or Mode (Mo). Thus,

$$\text{AD or MD (about mean)} = \frac{1}{n}\sum f|X - M|$$

$$\text{AD or MD (about median)} = \frac{1}{n}\sum f|X - \text{Mdn}|$$

$$\text{AD or MD (about mode)} = \frac{1}{n}\sum f|X - \text{Mo}|.$$

(ii)   The sum of the absolute deviations (after ignoring the signs) of a given set of scores is minimum when taken about median. Hence, the MD or AD is minimum when it is calculated from the median. In other words, the AD or MD calculated about the median will be less than the AD or MD about the mean or mode.

(iii)   As already pointed out in the first characteristic, usually, we compute the MD about any one of the three averages—mean, median or mode. But since the mode is generally ill defined, in practice, the MD is computed about the mean or median. Furthermore, as a choice between the mean and median, theoretically the median should be preferred since the MD or AD is minimum when calculated about the median. But because of a wide application of mean in statistics as a measure of central tendency, in practice, the AD or MD is generally computed from the mean.

(iv)   There is no mathematical justification in ignoring the signs of the deviations. However, a simple reason may be that, if we do not ignore the signs of the deviations, then

$$\text{AD or MD (about mean)} = \frac{1}{n}\sum(X - M) \quad \text{(for ungrouped data)}$$

$$\text{AD or MD (about mean)} = \frac{1}{n}\sum f(X - M) \quad \text{(for grouped data)},$$

which is always zero because of the property of the arithmetic mean, namely, 'algebraic sum of the deviations of a given set of observations from their mean is always zero'. Furthermore, for a symmetrical distribution $M=\text{Mdn}=\text{Mo}$. Thus, MDs about the median or mode would also be approximately zero for a moderately asymmetrical (skewed) distribution if the signs of the deviations are not ignored. However, since the main objective of a measure of dispersion or variability is to study the scatter of the given observations from a central value, ignoring the signs of the deviations does not matter much.

(v)　For a symmetrical distribution, the range Mean±MD (about mean) or Mdn±MD (about median) (∴ M = Mdn for a symmetrical distribution) covers 57.5 per cent of the observations of the distribution. If the distribution is moderately skewed, the range will cover approximately 57.5 per cent of the observations. Thus, a small value of the MD would imply that the distribution is uniform (less variable) since in this case a small interval around the average will contain more than 50 per cent of the observations of the series.

(vi)　Since in a normal distribution the AD when measured off on the scale above and below the mean includes the middle 57.5 per cent of the cases, it is always somewhat larger than the quartile deviation (Q) which includes the middle 50 per cent of cases.

(vii)　All MDs or ADs are absolute measures of dispersion, and are expressed in the same unit as those of raw scores.

(viii)　The relative measure of the AD or MD is called the coefficient of MD, which is given by

$$\text{Coefficient of MD (about mean)} = \frac{\text{MD}}{\text{Mean}}$$

$$\text{Coefficient of MD (about median)} = \frac{\text{MD}}{\text{Mdn}}.$$

The coefficients of MD defined earlier are pure numbers, independent of the units of measurement, and are useful for comparing the variability of different distributions.

4.4.3.4　*Merits and Demerits of the Average Deviation*

The following are some of the important advantages and disadvantages of the AD or MD.

Merits. The following are some of the merits of the AD or MD:

(i)　The AD or MD is rigidly defined, and is easy to understand and calculate.

(ii)　The AD is based on all the observations and is, thus, definitely a better measure of dispersion than the range and quartile deviation.

(iii)　The averaging of the absolute deviations from an average irons out the irregularities in the distribution and, thus, the MD or AD provides an accurate and true measure of variability.

(iv)　As compared with the SD, the AD is less affected by the extreme observations.

(v)　Since the MD is based on the deviations about an average, it provides a better measure for comparison about the formation of different distributions.

Demerits. The following are some of the disadvantages of the AD or MD:

(i)　The strongest objection against the MD is that, while computing its value we take the absolute value of the deviations about an average and ignore the algebraic signs of the deviations.

(ii)　The step of ignoring the signs of the deviations is mathematically unsound and illogical. It creates artificiality and renders the MD useless for further mathematical treatment. This drawback necessitates the requirement of another measure of variability which, in addition to being based on all the observations, is also amenable to further algebraic manipulations.

(iii) The AD or MD is not a satisfactory measure when taken about the mode or while dealing with a fairly skewed distribution. As already pointed out, theoretically the MD gives the best result when it is calculated about the median. But the median is not a satisfactory measure when the distribution has great variations.

(iv) The MD is infrequently used. It is not readily amenable to algebraic manipulation. This circumstance stems from the use of absolute values. In general, in statistical work, the use of absolute values should be avoided, if at all possible.

(v) The AD cannot be computed for distributions having open-end classes.

(vi) The MD tends to increase with the size of the sample, though not proportionately and not so rapidly as a range.

4.4.3.5 *Uses of the Average Deviation*

In spite of its mathematical drawbacks, the AD has found favour with economists and business statisticians because of its simplicity, accuracy and the fact that the SD gives greater weightage to the deviations of extreme observations. The MD is frequently useful in computing the distribution of personal wealth in a community or a nation since for this extremely rich as well as extremely poor people should be taken into consideration. Regarding the practical utility of the MD as a measure of variability, it may be worthwhile to quote that in the studies relating to forecasting business cycles, the National Bureau of Economic Research has found that the MD is most practical measure of dispersion to use for this purpose.

In addition to the aforementioned uses of the AD, its following use or application is recommended:

(i) When the distribution of the scores is normal or near to normal.

(ii) When it is desired to weigh all deviations from the mean according to their size.

(iii) When the extreme deviations would influence the SD unduly.

4.4.3.6 *Coefficient of Mean Deviation (CMD)*

The CMD is another relative measure of dispersion and is defined as the MD about a given central value (mean or median), expressed as a percentage of the latter. It bears no specific unit. But the fact that algebraic signs of deviations of scores from the central value are ignored in computing the MD makes it difficult to use this coefficient in further statistical work. The CMD about the mean is computed as follows:

$$\text{CMD} = \frac{\text{MD}}{\overline{X}} \times 100.$$

Similarly, the CMD about the median is computed as follows:

$$\text{CMD} = \frac{\text{MD}}{\text{Mdn}} \times 100.$$

These CMDs are useful for comparing the variability of different distributions.

4.4.4   The Standard Deviation (SD)

The SD, usually denoted by the Greek letter σ (small sigma), was first suggested by Karl Pearson as a measure of dispersion or variability in 1893. It is defined as the positive square root of the arithmetic mean of the squares of the deviations of the given observations from their arithmetic mean. In other words, an SD is the positive square root of the mean of squared deviations of all the scores from the mean. In brief, it is the positive square root of variance. The SD is often called 'root mean square deviation'.

The SD is regarded as the most stable and reliable measure of variability, as it always employs mean for its computation. It is an absolute measure of dispersion and is expressed in the same unit as the original scores.

The SD differs from the AD (or MD) in several respects. In computing the AD, we disregard the algebraic signs of deviations and treat all deviations as positive, whereas in computing the SD, we avoid the difficulty of signs by squaring the separate deviations. Moreover, the squared deviations used in computing the SD are always taken from the mean, never from the median or mode, whereas the MDs are computed about one of the three averages—mean, median or mode.

The SD of a sample—large ($n \geq 30$) and small ($n < 30$)—and of a population are denoted by s or σ (small sigma) and σ (big sigma), respectively. For example,

$$s \text{ or } \sigma = \sqrt{\frac{\sum (X - \bar{X})^2}{n}} = \sqrt{\frac{\sum x^2}{n}} \text{ (when sample is large, } n \geq 30\text{),}$$

$$s \text{ or } \sigma = \sqrt{\frac{\sum (X - \bar{X})^2}{n-1}} = \sqrt{\frac{\sum x^2}{n-1}} \text{ (when sample is small, } n < 30\text{),}$$

where

X = individual scores
$\bar{X}$ = sample mean
$X - \bar{X}$ or x = deviation of a score from mean
n = total frequency or sample size.

Using the symbols for parameters for a population of size N,

$$\sigma = \sqrt{\frac{\sum (X - \mu)^2}{N}},$$

where

X = individual scores
μ = population mean
N = population size.

4.4.4.1   *Properties or Characteristics of the Standard Deviation*

The SD is one of the best measures of dispersion—the higher the SD, the wider the dispersion of scores around the mean. Some of its properties or important characteristics are as follows:

(i)   The SD gives us a measure of dispersion relative to the mean. This differs from the range that tells us directly the spread of the two most extreme scores.

(ii)   The SD is sensitive to each score in the distribution. If a score is moved closer to the mean, then the SD will become smaller. Conversely, if a score shifts away from the mean, then the SD will increase. In other words, because the SD takes all the scores of a sample into consideration, it changes with the change of even a single score.

(iii)   Like the mean, the SD is stable with regard to sampling fluctuations. If samples were taken repeatedly from populations of the type usually encountered in the behavioural sciences, the SD of the samples would vary much less from sample to sample than the range. This property is one of the main reasons why the SD is used so much more often than the range for reporting variability. In other words, in different samples from the same population, SDs differ far less than the other absolute measures of dispersion or variability do.

(iv)   Addition or subtraction of a constant number to or from each individual score leaves the SD unaltered, but the multiplication or division of each score by a constant number produces an identical change in the SD.

(v)   If all the scores have an identical value in a sample, the SD amounts to zero.

(vi)   If the scores of a variable Y are the linear functions of the scores of another variable X, the plotting of the Y scores against the X scores of the respective individuals produces a straight line with 'a' as its vertical intercept and 'b' as its slope:

$$Y = a + bX.$$

In such a case, the SDs of the two variables are related to each other as follows:

$$s_y = |b| s_x,$$

where s_y and s_x are the respective SDs and the vertical bars on the two sides of b indicate that the latter is taken as positive, irrespective of its actual algebraic sign.

(vii)   The composite SD of k number of groups can be computed from their individual group sizes (n_i), the group SDs (s_i) and the deviations (x_i) of the group means ($\bar{X}_i$) from the grand mean ($\bar{X}$) of all the groups:

$$s = \sqrt{\frac{\sum n_i s_i^2 + \sum n_i x_i^2}{\sum n_i}}$$

$$\text{or } s = \sqrt{\frac{(n_1 s_1^2 + n_2 s_2^2 + \cdots + n_k s_k^2) + (n_1 x_1^2 + n_2 x_2^2 + \cdots + n_k x_k^2)}{n_1 + n_2 + \cdots + n_k}}.$$

(viii)   Both the mean and the SD can be manipulated algebraically. This allows mathematics to be done with them for use in inferential statistics.

4.4.4.2   *Computation of the SD from Ungrouped Data*

The SD may be computed by any of the following three formulae from the simple series of original and ungrouped scores (X) if the total frequency (n) of the sample is large ($n \geq 30$):

(i) s or $\sigma = \sqrt{\dfrac{\sum(X - \bar{X})^2}{n}} = \sqrt{\dfrac{\sum x^2}{n}}.$

(ii) s or $\sigma = \sqrt{\dfrac{\sum X^2}{n} - \left(\dfrac{\sum X}{n}\right)^2}.$

(iii) s or $\sigma = \sqrt{\dfrac{\sum X^2 - \dfrac{(\sum X)^2}{n}}{n}}$.

But when the sample is small ($n<30$), the SD may be computed by any of the following three formulae:

(i) s or $\sigma = \sqrt{\dfrac{\sum (X - \bar{X})^2}{n-1}} = \sqrt{\dfrac{\sum x^2}{n-1}}$

(ii) s or $\sigma = \sqrt{\dfrac{\sum X^2 - \dfrac{(\sum X)^2}{n}}{n-1}}$

(iii) s or $\sigma = \sqrt{\dfrac{\sum X^2 - n\bar{X}^2}{n-1}}$

Because in a small sample ($n<30$), extreme scores at the two ends of the frequency distribution may escape inclusion due to their less frequent occurrence in the population. Since the SD depends on all the scores, the exclusion of many extreme scores from the sample tends to lower the SD of a small sample much below the population SD (σ). The SD (s or σ) of a small sample, thus, suffers from a downward bias which is not desirable in testing the significance of experimental results. This downward bias of the SD may be compensated by using its degrees of freedom ($n-1$) instead of n in its computation. Such an SD is called an unbiased SD.

Moreover, even though a sample is large ($n\geq 30$), but smaller than the population, the SD of such a sample, when computed with n as the denominator, suffers from some downward bias, though small enough to be neglected often. Hence, it is preferable to compute the unbiased SD for even large samples, using $n-1$ instead of n as the denominator. Thus, the unbiased SD, computed with its degrees of freedom ($n-1$) as the denominator, is the preferred choice for both small and large samples.

The number of values that are free to vary is called the number of degrees of freedom. A quantity of the kind $\Sigma(X - \bar{X})^2$ is said to have associated with it $n-1$ degrees of freedom, because $n-1$ of the n squared deviations of which it is composed can vary. The concept of degrees of freedom is a very useful and general concept in statistics and is elaborated in more detail later in this book.

For example, let us compute the SD of the following memory test scores of 10 high school students:

Scores: 9, 10, 12, 15, 9, 11, 12, 10, 13, 9.

The solution of this problem consists of the following steps:

(i) The data are entered in Table 4.3.
(ii) The mean is first computed:

$$\bar{X} = \frac{\sum X}{n} = \frac{110}{10} = 11.0$$

(iii) The deviation of each score from the mean, namely $(X - \bar{X})$, is worked out and recorded with its algebraic sign.
(iv) Each deviation is squared and the value entered in the table. All these $(X - \bar{X})^2$ values are then totalled or summed up.

Table 4.3   Computation of mean and SD of memory test scores

Students	Test Scores (X)	(X − X̄)	(X − X̄)²
1	9	−2	4
2	10	−1	1
3	12	1	1
4	15	4	16
5	9	−2	4
6	11	0	0
7	12	1	1
8	10	−1	1
9	13	2	4
10	9	−2	4
10 (n)	110 (ΣX)		36 Σ(X − X̄)²

(v)   The unbiased SD (s) is then computed by the first aforementioned formula, which reads

$$s \text{ or } \sigma = \sqrt{\frac{\sum(X - \bar{X})^2}{n-1}} = \sqrt{\frac{36}{10-1}} = \sqrt{\frac{36}{9}} = \sqrt{4} = 2.0.$$

If we want to compute the unbiased SD of the given scores by the help of the second or the third formula just noted, we must refer to Table 4.4.

The solution of the data given in Table 4.4 consists of the following steps:

(i)   The data are entered in Table 4.4.

(ii)   The mean ($\bar{X}$) is first computed:

$$\bar{X} = \frac{\sum X}{n} = \frac{110}{10} = 11.0.$$

(iii)   Each score (X) is squared and the squared scores are totalled to give $\sum X^2$.

(iv)   The unbiased SD (s) is then computed as follows by the help of the second and third formulae:

$$s \text{ or } \sigma = \sqrt{\frac{\sum X^2 - \frac{(\sum X)^2}{n}}{n-1}} = \sqrt{\frac{1246 - \frac{(110)^2}{10}}{10-1}}$$

$$= \sqrt{\frac{1,246 - 1,210}{9}} = \sqrt{\frac{36}{9}} = \sqrt{4} = 2.0$$

Table 4.4   Computation of the mean and SD of memory test scores

Students	Test Scores (X)	X²
1	9	81
2	10	100
3	12	144
4	15	225
5	9	81
6	11	121
7	12	144
8	10	100
9	13	169
10	9	81
$n=10$	110 ($\sum X$)	1,246 ($\sum X^2$)

or

$$s \text{ or } \sigma = \sqrt{\frac{\sum X^2 - n\bar{X}^2}{n-1}} = \sqrt{\frac{1{,}246 - 10(11)^2}{10-1}}$$

$$= \sqrt{\frac{1{,}246 - 10 \times 121}{9}} = \sqrt{\frac{1{,}246 - 1{,}210}{9}} = \sqrt{\frac{36}{9}} = \sqrt{4} = 2.0.$$

4.4.4.3   *Computation of SD from Simple Frequency Table*

Where n number of scores are arranged individually, without any grouping, in a simple frequency table, the unbiased SD may be computed by using the frequency (f) of each score and the mean ($\bar{X}$) of the scores.

The formula reads

$$s \text{ or } \sigma = \sqrt{\frac{\sum f(X-\bar{X})^2}{n-1}} = \sqrt{\frac{\sum fx^2}{n-1}}.$$

Representing the individual scores by X_i and their respective frequencies by f_i, the same formula may also be written as

$$s \text{ or } \sigma = \sqrt{\frac{\sum f_i(X_i-\bar{X})^2}{n-1}} = \sqrt{\frac{\sum f_i x_i^2}{n-1}}.$$

For example, let us arrange the following memory test scores of 10 students in a simple frequency table and compute their mean and unbiased SD:

Scores: 9, 10, 12, 15, 9, 11, 12, 10, 13, 9.

Table 4.5   Simple frequency table of memory test scores for computing SD

Scores (X)	f	fX	$(X-\bar{X})$	$(X-\bar{X})^2$	$f(X-\bar{X})^2$
15	1	15	4	16	16
13	1	13	2	4	4
12	2	24	1	1	2
11	1	11	0	0	0
10	2	20	–1	1	2
9	3	27	–2	4	12
	10 (n)	110 ($\sum fX$)			36 $\sum f(X-\bar{X})^2$

The solution of this problem consists of the following steps:

(i) The individual scores (X) and their respective frequencies (f) are entered in Table 4.5.

(ii) The mean ($\bar{X}$) of the scores is computed from the sum of the products (fX) of the scores and their respective frequencies

$$\bar{X} = \frac{\sum fX}{n} = \frac{110}{10} = 11.0.$$

(iii) The deviation of each score from $\bar{X}$ is computed and squared to obtain the $(X-\bar{X})^2$ for that score.

(iv) Each squared deviation is multiplied by the frequency (f) of that score, and these products for all the scores are totalled to give $\sum f(X-\bar{X})^2$.

(v) The unbiased SD is then computed:

$$s \text{ or } \sigma = \sqrt{\frac{\sum f(X-\bar{X})^2}{n-1}} = \sqrt{\frac{36}{10-1}} = \sqrt{\frac{36}{9}} = \sqrt{4} = 2.0.$$

4.4.4.4   *Computation of SD from Grouped Data*

The computation of the SD from the data grouped into frequency distributions can be made by the help of two methods such as, the direct method and short method (or code method). These two methods are discussed in the following, one after the other.

Computation by the direct method

This method applies to the data arranged into a frequency distribution with either equal or unequal class intervals. Because all scores of a class interval are assumed to be identical with its midpoint (X_c),

$$\sum X = \sum fX_c; \quad \sum(X-\bar{X})^2 = \sum f(X_c-\bar{X})^2,$$

where f and X_c are, respectively, the frequencies and midpoints of the intervals.

Table 4.6   Computation of the SD for the data grouped into frequency distribution by the direct method

Class Intervals	Frequency (f)	Midpoint (X_c)	fX_c	x $(X_c - \bar{X})$	x^2 $(X_c - \bar{X})^2$	fx^2 $f(X_c - \bar{X})^2$
127–129	1	128	128	13	169	169
124–126	2	125	250	10	100	200
121–123	3	122	366	7	49	147
118–120	1	119	119	4	16	16
115–117	6	116	696	1	1	6
112–114	4	113	452	−2	4	16
109–111	3	110	330	−5	25	75
106–108	2	107	214	−8	64	128
103–105	1	104	104	−11	121	121
100–102	1	101	101	−14	196	196
	24 (n)		2,760 (ΣfX_c)			1,074 Σfx^2 or $\Sigma f(X_c - \bar{X})^2$

For example, let us find out the SD of the following distribution of IQ scores of 24 subjects.

Class Intervals	Frequencies
127–129	1
124–126	2
121–123	3
118–120	1
115–117	6
112–114	4
109–111	3
106–108	2
103–105	1
100–102	1

The solution of this problem consists of the following steps:

(i)   The data are entered in Table 4.6.

(ii) The midpoint (X_c) of each class interval is worked out from the upper and lower limits of that interval

$$X_c = \tfrac{1}{2}(\text{upper limit} + \text{lower limit}).$$

(iii) The frequency (f) of each class interval is multiplied by its X_c and these products are totalled for all class intervals to give $\Sigma f X_c$.

(iv) Basing on $\Sigma f X_c$ and n, the mean ($\bar{X}$) is then computed as follows:

$$\bar{X} = \frac{\Sigma f X_c}{n} = \frac{2760}{24} = 115.0.$$

(v) The deviation of each X_c from the mean ($\bar{X}$) is calculated to obtain x or ($X_c - \bar{X}$) and is squared to obtain x^2 or ($X_c - \bar{X}$)^2 of the relevant interval.

(vi) Each squared deviation is multiplied by f of that interval and the products of all the intervals are totalled or summed up to give $\Sigma f x^2$ or $\Sigma f (X_c - \bar{X})^2$.

(vii) The unbiased SD or s is then computed by the following formula:

$$s \text{ or } \sigma = \sqrt{\frac{\Sigma f(X_c - \bar{X})^2}{n-1}} = \sqrt{\frac{\Sigma f x^2}{n-1}} = \sqrt{\frac{1074}{24-1}} = \sqrt{\frac{1074}{23}} = \sqrt{46.696} = 6.83.$$

Therefore, the unbiased SD = 6.83.

Computation by the short method

The short method is also known as the code method. This method is applicable to grouped data arranged into a frequency distribution with equal class intervals only. The short method of calculating the mean was outlined in Chapter 3 under the measures of central tendency. This method consisted essentially in 'guessing' or 'assuming a mean' and later applying a correction to give the actual mean. The short method may also be used for advantage in calculating the SD. It is a decided time and labour saver in dealing with grouped data and is well-nigh indispensable in the calculation of σ's in a correlation table discussed later.

The short method or code method of calculating the SD (σ or s) is illustrated in Table 4.7. The formula for the SD by the short method is:

$$s \text{ or } \sigma = i \sqrt{\frac{\Sigma f x'^2}{n} - c^2},$$

where

i = size of the class interval

$\Sigma f x'^2$ = the sum of the squared deviations in units of class intervals, taken from the assumed mean

c^2 = the squared correction in units of the class interval.

The calculation or computation of the SD by the short method (or code method) may be followed in detail from Table 4.7.

The following steps are to be followed for computing the SD from the grouped data by short or code method:

(i) The size of the class interval (i) is noted. The length of the intervals (i) is obtained by subtracting the lower (or higher) limit of any interval from the respective limit of the next higher interval. For example,

$$i = 105.5 - 102.5 = 3 \text{ or } 102.5 - 99.5 = 3.$$

Table 4.7   Computation of the SD for the data grouped into the frequency distribution by the short method or code method

Class Intervals	Midpoints (X_c)	Frequency (f)	x'	fx'	fx'^2
127–129	128	1	4	4	16
124–126	125	2	3	6	18
121–123	122	3	2	6	12
118–120	119	1	1	1	1
115–117	116	6	0	0	0
112–114	113	4	–1	–4	4
109–111	110	3	–2	–6	12
106–108	107	2	–3	–6	18
103–105	104	1	–4	–4	16
100–102	101	1	–5	–5	25
$i=3$		24 (n)		–8 ($\Sigma fx'$)	122 ($\Sigma fx'^2$)

(ii)   The midpoint (X_c) of each class interval is determined by

$$X_c = \tfrac{1}{2}(\text{upper limit} + \text{lower limit}).$$

(iii)   The midpoint of an interval near the centre of the distribution is chosen arbitrarily as the assumed mean (AM) and assigned a code number (x') of 0. Then the midpoints of intervals progressively higher than that of the AM are given code numbers such as 1, 2, 3 and so on, in ascending order, while the midpoints of intervals progressively lower than the AM are assigned code numbers such as –1, –2, –3 and so on, in descending order. In the present example (see Table 4.7), the X_c of the class interval 115–117 is arbitrarily chosen as the AM and given the code number (x') of 0. Code numbers 1, 2, 3 and 4 are assigned to the successive higher midpoints and –1, –2, –3, –4 and –5 are given to the successive lower ones. The code number (x') of a particular class interval can also be determined by

$$x' = \frac{X_c - \text{AM}}{i},$$

where

x' = code number of a class interval
X_c = midpoint of a class interval
AM = assumed mean
i = length of a class interval.

(iv)   The code number (x') of each interval is multiplied by its frequency (f) to obtain the fx' value of that interval, and then these products (fx') of all the class intervals are totalled, keeping the algebraic sign intact, to obtain $\Sigma fx'$, which may be positive or negative. In the given example (see Table 4.7), $\Sigma fx' = -8$.

(v) Each fx' is multiplied by the corresponding x' again to obtain the fx'^2 of that interval, so that the product of fx'^2 of each interval becomes positive, and then these products of all intervals are totalled to obtain $\sum fx'^2$. In the given example (see Table 4.7), $\sum fx'^2 = 122$.

(vi) The SD is then computed as

$$s \text{ or } \sigma = i\sqrt{\frac{\sum fx'^2}{n} - c^2} = i\sqrt{\frac{\sum fx'^2}{n} - \left(\frac{\sum fx'}{n}\right)^2}$$

$$= 3\sqrt{\frac{122}{24} - \left(\frac{-8}{24}\right)^2} = 3\sqrt{5.08 - (-0.33)^2}$$

$$= 3\sqrt{5.08 - 0.11} = 3\sqrt{4.97} = 3 \times 2.23 = 6.69.$$

Therefore, SD = 6.69.

4.4.4.5 The Effect on the SD of (a) Adding a Constant to Each Original Score or (b) Multiplying Each Original Score by a Constant

In the following, we will discuss the effect on the SD when: (a) a constant is added to each original score and (b) each original score is multiplied by a constant.

(a) If a constant number is added to all the scores in a sample, the SD remains unchanged. Suppose we may decide to add a constant (c), say 5, to all the original marks assigned. The SD of the original marks will be the same as the SD of marks with the five points added. This result follows directly from the fact that if X is an original score, the corresponding score with the constant c added is $X+c$. If the $\bar{X}$ is the mean of the original scores, the mean with the constant added is $\bar{X}+c$. A deviation of an original score from the mean of the original scores is $X - \bar{X}$. Similarly, a deviation from the mean of the scores with the constant added is then $(X+c)-(\bar{X}+c)$, which is readily observed to be equal to $X-\bar{X}$. Since the deviations about the mean are unchanged by the addition of a constant, the SD will remain unchanged.

Table 4.8 provides a simple illustration. The mean of the original scores is 7 and the SD is 4.74. When each score is increased by 5, the mean is $7+5$ or 12, but the SD is still 4.74. Adding a constant (e.g., 3, 5, 7 or 10) to each original score simply moves the whole distribution up the scale 3, 5, 7 or 10 points. The mean is increased by the amount of the constant added, but the SD is not affected at all. If a constant is subtracted from each original score, the distribution is moved down the scale by that constant amount; the mean is decreased by the amount of the constant, and the SD, again, is unchanged. The SD in both instances is 4.74.

(b) If all original scores in a sample are multiplied by a constant, the SD is also multiplied by the absolute value of that constant. If the SD of examination marks is 4, and all original marks are multiplied by the constant 3, then the SD of the resulting marks is $3 \times 4 = 12$. To demonstrate this result, we observe that if $\bar{X}$ is the mean of a sample of scores, the mean of the scores multiplied by c is $c\bar{X}$. A deviation from the mean is then $cX - c\bar{X} = c(X-\bar{X})$. By squaring, summing over n observations, dividing by $n-1$ and taking the square root of it, we obtain

$$\sqrt{\frac{\sum(cX - c\bar{X})^2}{n-1}} = \sqrt{\frac{c^2\sum(X - \bar{X})^2}{n-1}} = \sqrt{c^2 s^2} = cs.$$

Thus, if all original scores are multiplied by a constant c, the SD (or s) is also multiplied by the absolute value of c. If c is a negative number, say, -3, then s is multiplied by the absolute value 3. In the following, Table 4.9 provides a simple illustration.

Table 4.8 Effect on SD of adding a constant to each original score

Original Scores (X)	x	x^2	Scores with a Constant Added ($X+5$)	x	x^2
1	–6	36	6	–6	36
4	–3	9	9	–3	9
7	0	0	12	0	0
10	3	9	15	3	9
13	6	36	18	6	36
$\sum X = 35$ $n = 5$		90 ($\sum x^2$)	60 ($\sum X$)		90 ($\sum x^2$)

$$\bar{X} = \frac{\sum X}{n} = \frac{35}{5} = 7.0$$

$$SD = \sqrt{\frac{\sum X^2}{n-1}} = \sqrt{\frac{90}{5-1}}$$

$$= \sqrt{\frac{90}{4}} = \sqrt{22.5} = 4.74$$

$$\bar{X} = \frac{\sum X}{n} = \frac{60}{5} = 12.0$$

$$SD = \sqrt{\frac{\sum X^2}{n-1}} = \sqrt{\frac{90}{5-1}} = \sqrt{\frac{90}{4}}$$

$$= \sqrt{22.5} = 4.74$$

Table 4.9 Effect on the SD of multiplying each original score by a constant

Original Scores (X)	x	x^2	Scores with a Constant Multiplied ($X \times 5$)	x	x^2
1	–6	36	5	–30	900
4	–3	9	20	–15	225
7	0	0	35	0	0
10	3	9	50	15	225
13	6	36	65	30	900
$\sum X = 35$		90	175		2250
$n = 5$		($\sum x^2$)	($\sum X$)		($\sum x^2$)

$$\bar{X} = \frac{\sum X}{n} = \frac{35}{5} = 7.0$$

$$SD = \sqrt{\frac{\sum X^2}{n-1}} = \sqrt{\frac{90}{5-1}} = \sqrt{\frac{90}{4}}$$

$$= \sqrt{22.5} = 4.74$$

$$\bar{X} = \frac{\sum X}{n} = \frac{175}{5} = 35$$

$$SD = \sqrt{\frac{\sum X^2}{n-1}} = \sqrt{\frac{2,250}{5-1}} = \sqrt{\frac{2,250}{4}}$$

$$= \sqrt{562.5} = 23.72$$

The mean of the original scores is 7.0 and the SD is 4.74. When each original score is multiplied by a constant, say, 5, then the mean becomes 35, that is, $\bar{X}c$ or 7×5, and also the SD becomes 23.72, that is, σc or $4.74 \times 5 = 23.70$. The slight discrepancy between 23.72 and 23.70 results from the rounding of decimals. Thus, the net effect of multiplying each original score in a sample by a constant (c) is to multiply both the mean and σ by the same constant number.

Similarly, the net effect of dividing each original score in a sample by a constant (c) is to divide both the mean and SD by the same constant number. To demonstrate this result, we observe that if $\bar{X}$ is the mean of the original scores in a sample, the mean of the scores divided by c is $\dfrac{\bar{X}}{c}$. A deviation from the mean is then $\dfrac{X}{c} - \dfrac{\bar{X}}{c} = \dfrac{1}{c}(X - \bar{X})$. By squaring, summing over n observations, dividing by $n-1$ and taking the square root of it, we obtain

$$\sqrt{\frac{\sum\left(\dfrac{X}{c} - \dfrac{\bar{X}}{c}\right)^2}{n-1}} = \sqrt{\frac{\dfrac{1}{c^2}\sum(X - \bar{X})^2}{n-1}} = \sqrt{\frac{1}{c^2}s^2} = \sqrt{\frac{s^2}{c^2}} = \frac{s}{c}.$$

Thus, if all original scores are divided by a constant c, the SD (s) is also divided by the absolute value of the same constant number.

By way of illustration, the original scores 1, 4, 7, 10 and 13 have a mean of 7.0 and the SD of 4.74 (see Table 4.9). If the scores are divided by a constant (c), say, 2, we obtain 0.5, 2.0, 3.5, 5.0 and 6.5. The mean is now $7/2 = 3.5$. The deviations from the mean are –3.0, –1.5, 0, 1.5 and 3.0. By squaring these deviations, we obtain 9.0, 2.25, 0, 2.25 and 9.0. The sum of these squares ($\sum x^2$) is 22.50. The SD is

$$s = \sqrt{\frac{\sum x^2}{n-1}} = \sqrt{\frac{22.50}{5-1}} = \sqrt{\frac{22.50}{4}} = \sqrt{5.625} = 2.37.$$

This obtained s of 2.37 is exactly the half of the original s of 4.74.

4.4.4.6   *Computation of the SD from Combined Distributions*

When two sets of scores are combined into a single lot, it is possible to calculate the SD (s or σ) of the total distribution from the σ's of the two component distributions. The formula for this is

$$\sigma_{\text{comb}} = \sqrt{\frac{n_1(\sigma_1^2 + d_1^2) + n_2(\sigma_2^2 + d_2^2)}{n}},$$

where

σ_1 = SD of distribution 1
σ_2 = SD of distribution 2
$d_1 = (\bar{X}_1 - \bar{X}_{\text{comb}})$
$d_2 = (\bar{X}_2 - \bar{X}_{\text{comb}})$
n_1 = number of cases in distribution 1
n_2 = number of cases in distribution 2
$n = n_1 + n_2$.

The formula for the weighted (or combined) mean is

$$\bar{X}_{\text{comb}} = \frac{n_1\bar{X}_1 + n_2\bar{X}_2}{n_1 + n_2},$$

where the new terms are as follows:

$\bar{X}_{comb}$ = mean of the combined distributions

$\bar{X}_1$ = mean of distribution 1

$\bar{X}_2$ = mean of distribution 2.

An example will illustrate the use of the aforementioned formula. Suppose that we are given the means and SDs on an achievement test for two groups of subjects differing in size and are asked to find the SD of the combined group. Data are as follows:

Group	n	$\bar{X}$	SD
A	25	80	15
B	75	70	25

Then, first of all, we have to find the $\bar{X}_{comb}$, the formula for which reads

$$\bar{X}_{comb} = \frac{n_1\bar{X}_1 + n_2\bar{X}_2}{n_1 + n_2} = \frac{(25 \times 80) + (75 \times 70)}{25 + 75} = \frac{2000 + 5250}{100} = \frac{7250}{100} = 72.50.$$

Second, we have to find d_1, d_1^2, d_2 and $d_2^2, \sigma_1^2, \sigma_2^2$ as follows:

$$d_1 = \bar{X}_1 - \bar{X}_{comb} = 80.0 - 72.5 = 7.5; \quad d_1^2 = (7.5)^2 = 56.25$$

$$d_2 = \bar{X}_2 - \bar{X}_{comb} = 70 - 72.5 = -2.5; \quad d_2^2 = (-2.5)^2 = 6.25$$

$$\sigma_1^2 = (15)^2 = 225; \quad \sigma_2^2 = (25)^2 = 625.$$

Third, we have to find σ_{comb} as follows:

$$\sigma_{comb} = \sqrt{\frac{n_1(\sigma_1^2 + d_1^2) + n_2(\sigma_2^2 + d_2^2)}{n}}$$

$$= \sqrt{\frac{25(225 + 56.25) + 75(625 + 6.25)}{100}} = \sqrt{\frac{(25 \times 281.25) + (75 \times 631.25)}{100}}$$

$$= \sqrt{\frac{7031.25 + 47343.75}{100}} = \sqrt{\frac{54375.0}{100}} = \sqrt{543.75} = 23.32.$$

The above formula for finding out the σ_{comb} may easily be extended to include more than two component distributions by adding n_3, σ_3, d_3 and so on.

4.4.4.7   Merits and Demerits of the Standard Deviation

The following are some of the important advantages and disadvantages of the SD as a measure of variability.

Merits

(i)   The SD is by far the most important and widely used measure of variability or dispersion. It is the best measure of variation because of its mathematical characteristics.

(ii)   The SD is rigidly defined and based on all the observations of the distribution.

(iii) The SD is a more stable or accurate estimate of the population parameter than other measures of variation.

(iv) Of all the measures of dispersion, the SD is affected least by the fluctuation of sampling.

(v) The SD is more amenable to mathematical manipulations or to algebraic treatment than other measures of variability.

(vi) The squaring of the deviations $(X - \bar{X})$ removes the drawback of ignoring the signs of deviations in computing the MD or AD. This step renders it suitable for further mathematical treatment.

(vii) It is possible to calculate the combined SD of two or more groups. This is not possible with any other measure of variability.

(viii) For comparing the variability of two or more distributions, the coefficient of variation is considered to be the most appropriate, and this is based on the mean and SD.

(ix) The SD is most prominently used in further statistical work. For example, in computing skewness, kurtosis, correlation and regression, and tests of significance and so forth, the use is made of the SD.

(x) The SD is a keynote in sampling and provides a unit of measurement for the normal distribution.

Demerits

(i) As compared to other measures of variability, the SD is difficult to compute. However, this does not reduce the importance of this measure because of a high degree of accuracy of results it gives.

(ii) The SD gives more weight to extreme items and less to those which are near the mean. It is because of the fact that the squares of the deviations which are big in size would be proportionately greater than the squares of those deviations which are comparatively small. For example, the deviations 2 and 8 are in the ratio of 1:4 but their squares, that is, 4 and 64, would be in the ratio of 1:16.

Taking into consideration the pros and cons and also a wide application of the SD in statistical theory, such as in skewness, kurtosis, correlation and regression analysis, sampling theory and tests of significance, we may regard the SD as the best and the most powerful measure of variability or dispersion.

4.4.4.8   *Uses of the Standard Deviation*

The use of the SD is recommended

(i) When the statistic having the greatest stability is sought.

(ii) When we need a most reliable and accurate measure of variability.

(iii) When extreme deviations should exercise a proportionally greater effect upon the variability.

(iv) When coefficients of correlation, tests of significance and other statistics are to be subsequently computed.

(v) When the measure of central tendency is available in the form of a mean.

(vi) When the distribution is normal or near to normal.

In conclusion, it can be said that all the four measures of variability have their own strengths and weaknesses. Therefore, a comparison among these measures of dispersion is needed.

4.5   Comparing Measures of Variability

By far the most commonly used measure of variability is the SD. Nonetheless, there are situations where the range (R), the AD or the semi-inter-quartile range (Q) may be preferred. The relative advantages and disadvantages of each of these four measures will be discussed with reference to the factors that affect variability such as (i) extreme scores, (ii) sample size, (iii) stability under sampling and (iv) open-ended distributions.

In simple terms, two considerations determine the value of any statistical measurement. These two important considerations are as follows:

(a)   The measure should provide a stable and reliable description of the scores. Specifically, it should not be greatly affected by minor details in the set of data.

(b)   The measure should have a consistent and predictable relationship with other statistical measurements.

Let us now examine each of these considerations separately in reference to the factors affecting variability.

(i)   *Extreme scores.* Of the four measures of variability, the range is mostly affected by extreme scores. A single extreme value will have a large influence on the range. In fact, the range is determined exclusively by the two extreme scores (the lowest and the highest scores) of the distribution. The SD and the variance (which is defined as the square of the SD) are also influenced by extreme scores. Because these two measures (i.e., SD and variance) are based on squared deviations, a single extreme value can even have a disproportionate effect. For example, a score that is 15 points away from the mean will contribute $(15)^2 = 225$ points to the sum of squares (SS). For this reason, both the SD and variance should be interpreted carefully in distributions with one or two extreme values. Because the algebraic sum of the deviations of a given set of observations from their mean is always zero and the MD is computed by taking the absolute values of the deviations, that is, by disregarding the signs of the deviations, it is least affected by the extreme values. Similarly, because the quartile deviation (Q), also known as the semi-inter-quartile range, focuses on the middle of the distribution, it is least affected by the extreme values. For these reasons, the MD and the quartile deviation (Q) often provide the best measures of variability for distributions that are very skewed (or asymmetrical) or that have a few extreme scores.

(ii)   *Sample size.* As the number of scores in a sample increases, the range also tends to increase because each additional score has the potential to replace the current highest or lowest value in the set. Thus, the range is directly related to the sample size. This relationship between the sample size and variability is unacceptable. A researcher should not be able to influence variability by manipulating the sample size. The SD, variance (σ^2), MD and quartile deviation (Q) are relatively unaffected by the sample size, and, therefore, provide better measures of variability.

(iii)   *Stability under sampling.* If we take several different samples from the same population, we should expect the samples to be similar. Specifically, if we compute variability for each of the separate samples, we should expect to obtain similar values. Because all of the samples come from the same source or the same parental population, it is reasonable that there should be some 'family resemblance'. When the SD and variance are used to measure variability, the samples will tend to have similar variability. For this reason, the SD and variance are said to be stable under sampling. They are the stable measures of variability. Similarly, both MD and quartile deviation also provide reasonably stable measures of variability. The range, however, will change unpredictably from sample to sample, and is said to be unstable under sampling.

(iv) *Open-ended distributions.* When a distribution does not have any specific boundary for the highest score or the lowest score, it is called open ended. This can occur only when we have infinite or undetermined scores. The range, SD, variance and MDs cannot be computed from an open-ended distribution. In this situation, the only available measure of variability is the semi-inter-quartile range or simply quartile deviation (Q).

4.6 Variance

The variance (s^2) or mean square (MS) is the arithmetic mean of the squared deviations of individual scores from their mean. In short, variance is the mean of the squared deviation scores. Deviation refers to the distance from the mean, and deviation score, $x = X - \bar{X}$. Variance is one of the absolute measures of dispersion or variability and is identical with the squared SD (SD^2). This is why the SD is also known as the *root-mean-square* about the mean, that is, $SD = \sqrt{variance}$. Being the squared SD, variance is expressed in squared units such as cm^2, kg^2 and the like. It is a very good absolute measure of variability of scores about the mean and finds important applications in the analysis of variance (ANOVA) tests for finding the significance of differences between sample means.

The sample variance for the ungrouped scores is generally computed as follows:

$$s^2 = \frac{\sum(X - \bar{X})^2}{n-1} = \frac{\sum x^2}{n-1},$$

where $(X - \bar{X})$ or x represents the deviations of individual scores from the sample mean. The numerator, namely $\sum(X - \bar{X})^2$ or $\sum x^2$, is the sum of squared deviations, and is called the sum of squares (SS). The parametric or population variance has the symbol of σ^2, which can be found as follows:

$$\sigma^2 = \frac{\sum(X - \mu)^2}{N} = \frac{SS}{N}.$$

For a grouped frequency distribution divided into regular class intervals, variance is computed as the squared SD (s^2) by the following formula:

$$s^2 = \frac{\sum f(X_c - \bar{X})^2}{n-1},$$

where f and X_c are, respectively, the frequencies and midpoints of the intervals.

For grouped data, the same short method or code method is used as in the case of the SD so as to compute variance as the squared SD (s^2). The formula reads

$$s^2 = i\left[\frac{\sum fx'^2}{n} - c^2\right]$$

or

$$s^2 = i\left[\frac{\sum fx'^2}{n} - \left(\frac{\sum fx'}{n}\right)^2\right].$$

For the computational method and the explanation of the symbols, refer to the computation of the SD by the short method or code method.

4.7   Coefficient of Variation

The SD discussed earlier is an absolute measure of dispersion. The corresponding relative mea-sure is known as the coefficient of variation. In other words, the coefficient of variation, denoted by CV, is a relative measure of dispersion. This measure, developed by Karl Pearson, is the most commonly used measure of relative variation. It is used in such problems where we want to compare the variability of two or more than two series. The series (or group) for which the coefficient of variation is greater is said to be more variable or conversely less consistent, less uniform, less stable or less homogeneous. On the other hand, the series for which the coef-ficient of variation is less is said to be less variable, or more consistent, more uniform, more stable or more homogeneous.

Coefficient of variation (CV) is defined as the SD expressed as a percentage of the mean:

$$CV = \frac{s}{\bar{X}} \times 100.$$

As CV is expressed as a percentage, independent of any particular unit, it is more suitable than the SD and variance in comparing the variabilities of two variables measured in different units. Thus, it can be used in comparing the variabilities of body height scores (cm) and body weight scores (kg). It is also preferred to the SD and variance in comparing variabilities of two sets of scores expressed in the same unit but with widely divergent means, for example, femur lengths (cm) of giraffes and mice. Let us analyse the following two examples.

Example 4.1 Suppose we have the following data for a group of 7-year-old boys. Find the relative variability of the following body height (cm) and body weight (kg) scores:

$$\text{Body height: } \bar{X}_1 = 115\,\text{cm}, \, s_1 = 6.5\,\text{cm}$$

$$\text{Body weight: } \bar{X}_2 = 23\,\text{kg}, \, s_2 = 2.7\,\text{kg}.$$

Solution

(i)   For body height: $CV_1 = \dfrac{s_1}{\bar{X}_1} \times 100 = \dfrac{6.5}{115} \times 100 = 5.6.$

(ii) For body weight: $CV_2 = \dfrac{s_2}{\bar{X}_2} \times 100 = \dfrac{2.7}{23} \times 100 = 11.7.$

(iii) $\dfrac{CV_2}{CV_1} = \dfrac{11.7}{5.6} = 2.09.$

From the obtained results, it appears that these 7-year-old boys are about twice as variable in body weight as in body height.

Example 4.2 Suppose we have the following data on body height for a group of boys and a group of adult men. Find the relative variability in the body height of boys and men.

Group	$\bar{X}$	s
Boys	50 cm	6 cm
Men	160 cm	16 cm

Solution

(i)   For the body height of boys: $CV_b = \dfrac{s}{\bar{X}} \times 100 = \dfrac{6}{50} \times 100 = 12.$

(ii) For the body height of men: $CV_m = \dfrac{s}{\bar{X}} \times 100 = \dfrac{16}{160} \times 100 = 10.$

(iii) $\dfrac{CV_b}{CV_m} = \dfrac{12}{10} = 1.2.$

On the basis of our findings, we may conclude that in terms of their SD (s), the men are approximately three times as variable as the boys, but relative to their means, the men and boys are about equally variable. This last result is the more valuable and informative.

Coefficient of variation (CV) is suitable for physiochemical variables expressed in ratio scales (with the 0 point), but not for psychological and educational data in interval scales (with no true 0 point), because no ratio can be computed with values such as the SD and mean in the latter scale, nor is CV suitable where the mean is close to 0 (zero) because in that case CV may approach infinity.

However, objections have been raised to the use of CV when employed to compare groups on mental and educational tests. Most standard psychological and educational tests are interval scales, that is, are scaled in equal units. But mental or psychological tests are never ratio scales—the zero or reference point is unknown—and many are not scaled in equal units. How does the lack of a true zero point affect CV may be seen in the following example. Suppose we have administered a vocabulary test to a group of school children and have obtained a mean of 25.0 and an s of 5.0, and CV is 20. Now, suppose further that we add 10 very easy items to our vocabulary test. It is likely that all of the children will know the new words added. Hence, the mean score will be increased by 10, whereas the s (or σ) remains unchanged. An increase in the mean from 25 to 35 with no corresponding increase in s drops CV from 20 to 14, and, hence, we could have added 20 or 200 items to the test, CV is clearly a very unstable statistic.

The instability of CV should cause us to exercise caution in its use rather than discard it entirely. CV shows what per cent the s is of the mean. If the range of difficulty in the test is altered, or the units changed, not only CV but the mean ($\bar{X}$) will also change. Accordingly, CV is, in a sense, no more arbitrary than $\bar{X}$, and the objections urged against CV could be directed with equal force against $\bar{X}$. CV is useful in comparing the variabilities of a group upon the same test administered under different conditions, such as, when a group works at a task with and without distraction or CV may be used to compare two groups on the same test when the groups do not differ greatly in mean.

It is perhaps most difficult to interpret CV when the comparative variability of a group upon different mental tests is of interest. If a high school class is compared for variability upon tests of paragraph reading and arithmetic reasoning, it should be made plain that CVs refer only to the specific tests. Other tests of reading and arithmetic may—and probably will—give different results owing to differences in the range of difficulty, in size of units and in the reference point. If we restrict CV to the specific tests used, the coefficient of variation will provide information not otherwise obtainable.

4.8 Moments about the Mean

The mean and the SD are closely related to a family of descriptive statistics known as moments. The term 'moment' originates in mechanics. 'Moment' is a familiar mechanical term which refers to the measure of a force with respect to its tendency to provide rotation. The strength of the tendency depends on the amount of force and the distance from the origin of the point at which the force is exerted. If a number of forces, F_1, F_2, F_n at distances X_1, X_2, X_n are applied, the moment of the first force about the origin is $F_1 X_1$, the moment of the second force is $F_2 X_2$ and so on. These moments are additive so that $\sum FX$ is the total moment about the origin. If the total moment is divided by the total force, the quotient is termed 'a moment'. The formula is $\dfrac{\sum FX}{N}$, where $N = \sum F$ is the total force.

Consider a lever supported by a fulcrum. If a force f_1 is applied to the lever at a distance x_1 from the origin, then $f_1 x_1$ is called the moment of the force. Furthermore, if a second force f_2 is applied at a distance x_2, then the total moment is $f_1 x_1 + f_2 x_2$. If we square the distances x, we obtain the second moment; if we cube the distances x, we obtain the third moment and so on. When we come to consider frequency distributions, the origin is the analogue of the fulcrum, and the frequencies in the various class intervals are analogous to forces operating at various distances from the origin.

A moment about the mean is the arithmetic average of the sum of deviations, raised to a specific power, of individual scores from the mean. It is also known as a central moment. Central moments are absolute measures of dispersion. There are different central moments according to the power to which the sum of deviations has been raised.

In general, the rth moment about the mean is given by

$$m_r = \frac{\sum (X - \bar{X})^r}{n}; \quad r = 0, 1, 2, 3, 4, \ldots.$$

In particular, putting $r=0$, we obtain

$$m_0 = \frac{\sum (X - \bar{X})^0}{n} = \frac{1}{n} \sum f(X - \bar{X})^0$$

$$= \frac{1}{n} \sum f \left[\text{Since } (X - \bar{X})^0 = 1 \right] = \frac{1}{n} \times n = 1 \left[\text{Since } \sum f = n \right]$$

The first central moment (m_1) about the mean is computed from the sum of deviations, raised to the power 1, and amounts to 0 for all symmetric or asymmetric distributions:

$$m_1 = \frac{\sum (X - \bar{X})^1}{n} = \frac{1}{n} \sum f(X - \bar{X})^1 = 0,$$

because the algebraic sum of deviations of a given set of observations from their mean is zero. Thus, the first moment about the mean is always zero [Since $\sum (X - \bar{X})^1 = (0)^1 = 0$].

The second central moment (m_2) about the mean is the arithmetic average of the sum of squared deviations from the mean and is identical with the variance (s^2). It is expressed in squared units such as cm^2 or kg^2, and its square root is the SD:

$$m_2 = \frac{\sum (X - \bar{X})^2}{n} = \frac{1}{n} \sum f(X - \bar{X})^2 = s^2.$$

Hence, the second moment about the mean gives the variance of the distribution.

The third and fourth central moments (m_3 and m_4) are expressed in units raised to the powers 3 and 4, respectively, and are computed as follows:

$$m_3 = \frac{\sum (X - \bar{X})^3}{n} = \frac{1}{n} \sum f(X - \bar{X})^3$$

$$m_4 = \frac{\sum (X - \bar{X})^4}{n} = \frac{1}{n} \sum f(X - \bar{X})^4.$$

The third and higher central moments of the odd order (i.e., m_3, m_5 and so on) amount to 0 in symmetric distributions, but possess positive or negative values accordingly as the distribution is positively or negatively skewed. So, m_3 and higher odd central moments serve as the measures of skewness or asymmetry. The central moments of the even order, namely, m_2 and

m_4, are used in measuring the peakedness or kurtosis of a distribution. In other words, the third moment is used to obtain a measure of skewness and the fourth moment is used to obtain a measure of kurtosis.

4.8.1 Purpose of Moments

The concept of moment is of great significance in statistical work. With the help of moments, we can measure the central tendency of a set of observations, their variability, their symmetry and peakedness. Because of the great convenience in obtaining the measures of the various characteristics of a frequency distribution, the calculation of the first four moments about the mean may well be made the first step in the analysis of a frequency distribution.

The following is the summary of how moments help in analysing a frequency distribution:

	Moment	What It Measures
(i)	First moment about origin	Mean
(ii)	Second moment about the mean	Variance
(iii)	Third moment about the mean	Skewness
(iv)	Fourth moment about the mean	Kurtosis

Summary

In this chapter, we have discussed the variability of distributions. The most common measures of variability are the range (R), quartile deviation (Q), average deviation (AD) or mean deviation (MD), standard deviation (SD) and Variance. The range is a crude measure that tells the dispersion between the two most extreme scores. The SD is the most important and most frequently encountered measure of variability. It gives the average dispersion about the mean of the distribution. The quartile deviation is unaffected by the extreme scores at the two ends of the distribution, and it measures the variability of the median of a distribution. The variance is just the square of the SD. In addition to presenting these measures of variability, we have shown how to calculate each measure from ungrouped and/or grouped data, and also elaborated their most important properties, uses, merits and demerits. We compared different measures of variability with each other and also discussed their relationship with the three measures of central tendency. Finally, the concept of moment about the mean was discussed with an emphasis on its purposes.

Key Terms

- Average deviation
- Coefficient of Variation
- Dispersion
- Mean deviation
- Moments about the mean

- Quartile deviation
- Range
- Standard deviation
- Variability
- Variance

Questions and Problems

1. What do you mean by the term, 'variability or dispersion of scores'? Discuss the importance of the measures of variability.
2. What are the different measures of variability? Discuss them in brief.
3. What is the range? How it is determined? Discuss about the merits, demerits and the uses of the range.
4. Discuss the process of computation of quartile deviation and average deviation with the help of hypothetical data.
5. Enumerate the properties, merits and demerits, and uses of the quartile deviation.
6. Describe the characteristics, uses, advantages and limitations of the average deviation.
7. Discuss the process of computation of standard deviation in both ungrouped and grouped data by the help of some hypothetical data.
8. Discuss the properties, uses, advantages and disadvantages of the standard deviation as a measure of variability.
9. Write notes on the following:

   (a) Coefficient of range
   (b) Coefficient of quartile deviation
   (c) Coefficient of mean deviation
   (d) Coefficient of variation
   (e) Variance
   (f) Moments about the mean

10. Give a comparative statement regarding the situations where the use of range, quartile deviation, average deviation and standard deviation is best recommended.
11. Which measure of variability would you prefer in the following situations?

    (a) The measure of central tendency is available in the form of a median
    (b) The distribution is badly skewed
    (c) The coefficient of correlation is, subsequently, to be computed
    (d) The variability is to be calculated easily within no time
    (e) The distribution of scores is normal or near to normal

12. What happens to the standard deviation of a set of scores if:

    (a) a constant 'a' is added to each score?
    (b) a constant 'a' is subtracted from each score?
    (c) each score is multiplied by a constant 'a'?
    (d) each score is divided by a constant 'a'?

13. For the following sample sets of scores, calculate the range, the standard deviation and the variance:

    (a) 6, 2, 8, 5, 4, 4, 7
    (b) 24, 32, 27, 45, 48
    (c) 2.1, 2.5, 6.6, 0.2, 7.8, 9.3

14. Compute the standard deviation for the following sample scores. Why is s so high in part (b) compared to part (a)?

    (a) 6, 8, 7, 3, 6, 4
    (b) 6, 8, 7, 3, 6, 35

15. Without actually calculating the variability, study the following sample distributions:

    Distribution a : 21, 24, 28, 22, 20
    Distribution b : 21, 32, 38, 15, 11
    Distribution c : 22, 22, 22, 22, 22

    (a) Rank order them according to your best guess of their relative variability
    (b) Calculate the standard deviation of each to verify your rank ordering.

16. For the measurements 2, 5, 9, 10, 15, 19, compute

    (a) The range
    (b) The mean deviation
    (c) The standard deviation
    (d) The sample variance

17. The variance calculated on a sample of 100 cases is 15. What is the sum of squares of deviations about the arithmetic mean?

18. A biased variance estimate calculated on a sample of 5 cases is 10. What is the corresponding unbiased variance estimate?

19. The variance for a sample of N measurements is 20. What will be the variance if all measurements are

    (a) multiplied by a constant 5?
    (b) divided by a constant 5?

20. Calculate the second, third and fourth moments for the observations 4, 6, 10, 14, 16. Compute also the measures of skewness and kurtosis.

21. Compute the average deviation and standard deviation from the following ungrouped data: 30, 35, 36, 39, 42, 44, 46, 38, 34, 35.

22. Compute the average deviation from the following distribution:

Class Interval	Frequency
110–114	1
105–109	3
100–104	3
95–99	0
90–94	3
85–89	4
80–84	4
	N=18

23. Calculate the quartile deviation and standard deviation for the following three frequency distributions:

(a)		(b)		(c)	
Scores	f	Scores	f	Scores	f
70–71	2	100–104	1	90–94	1
68–69	2	95–99	2	85–89	4
66–67	3	90–94	1	80–84	2
64–65	4	85–89	6	75–79	8
62–63	6	80–84	7	70–74	9
60–61	7	75–79	3	65–69	14
58–59	5	70–74	2	60–64	6
56–57	1	65–69	1	55–59	6
54–55	2	60–64	2	50–54	4
52–53	3	55–59	4	45–49	3
50–51	1	50–54	0	40–44	3
		45–49	1		
	$N=36$		$N=30$		$N=60$

24. The following are the measurements obtained for two groups of subjects:

    Group I: 2, 3, 5, 10, 20

    Group II: 2, 4, 8, 12, 14

    Calculate the measures of skewness for both the groups.

25. Compute the mean, median, mode, Q and SD for the following distribution of scores:

Scores	Frequency
90–99	2
80–89	12
70–79	22
60–69	20
50–59	14
40–49	4
30–39	1
	$N=75$

26. Fill in the blanks:

    (i)   Measures of variability are otherwise known as measures of _____.
    (ii)   Statistics of dispersion serve as measures of _____ of scores.
    (iii) In a given set of scores: 5, 10, 25, 15 and 45, the range is _____.
    (iv)   _____ is the simplest of all the measures of variability.
    (v)   The difference between Q_3 and Q_1 is known as the _____.
    (vi)   The mean deviation is minimum when it is calculated from _____.
    (vii) The most stable and reliable measure of variability is _____.
    (viii) When mean = 115, SD = 6.5, then CV = _____.
    (ix)   If the coefficient of variation is 20 and the mean is 40, the standard deviation shall be _____.
    (x)   If $Q = 30$, median = 50, then CQD = _____.

27. Write whether the following statements are True or False.

    (i)   Quartile deviation is more suitable in the case of open-ended distributions.
    (ii)   Range is the best measure of dispersion.
    (iii) Variance is equal to the square of standard deviation.
    (iv)   There is no difference between variance and coefficient of variation.
    (v)   Mean deviation is minimum when deviations are taken from median.
    (vi)   Standard deviation can be calculated from any measure of central tendency.
    (vii) Standard deviation is a more stable and accurate estimate of the population parameter than other measures of variation.
    (viii) Absolute measures of dispersion are not suitable for comparing the variability of two distributions which are expressed in different units of measurement.
    (ix)   Mean deviation and quartile deviation often provide the best measures of variability for distributions having some extreme scores.
    (x)   The first moment about the mean is always zero.

28. Find out the correct answer from among the four alternatives.

    (i)   The measure of variability that is least affected by extreme observations is:

          (a) Mean deviation   (b) Standard deviation
          (c) Range   (d) None of the above

    (ii) The measure of dispersion that is best for asymmetrical distribution is:

          (a) Range   (b) Quartile deviation
          (c) Standard deviation   (d) None of the above

    (iii) Which one of the following is directly related to the increase or decrease of sample size?

          (a) Mean deviation   (b) Quartile deviation
          (c) Range   (d) None of the above

(iv) Which one of the following measures of variability can be computed from an open-ended distribution?

(a) Quartile deviation   (b) Standard deviation

(c) Variance   (d) None of the above

(v) When the measure of central tendency is available in the form of mean, which one of the following is the most reliable and accurate measure of variability?

(a) Mean deviation   (b) Standard deviation

(c) Quartile deviation   (d) None of the above

(vi) Variance is defined as:

(a) Square of MD   (b) Square of Q

(c) Square of SD   (d) None of the above

(vii) When the concentration around the median is of primary interest, then the appropriate measure of variability is:

(a) Quartile deviation   (b) Standard deviation

(c) Range   (d) None of the above

(viii) Coefficient of variation is calculated by the formula:

(a) $\dfrac{\bar{X}}{s} \times 100$ (b) $\dfrac{s}{\bar{X}} \times 100$

(c) $\dfrac{s}{\bar{X}} \times 1,000$ (d) None of the above

(ix) In a normal distribution Q is called the:

(a) Probable error (PE)   (b) Standard error (SE)

(c) Experimental error (EE)   (d) None of the above

(x) For a normal distribution, the most reliable and accurate measure of variability is:

(a) Standard deviation   (b) Quartile deviation

(c) Range   (d) None of the above

Percentiles and Percentile Rank

After reading this chapter you will be able to:

- Explain the meanings of percentiles, deciles, quartiles and percentile ranks (PRs).
- Compute percentiles, deciles, quartiles and PRs from the frequency distributions.
- Compute PRs from the ranked data.
- Determine graphically percentiles, deciles, quartiles and PRs from a cumulative percentage curve.
- Describe the utility of percentiles and PRs.
- Use percentile and PRs to describe the position of individual scores within a distribution.

5.1 Introduction

Some measures other than measures of central tendency are often employed when summarising or describing a set of data where it is necessary to divide the data into equal parts. These are positional measures and are called quantiles (or fractiles) and consist of quartiles, deciles and percentiles.

Quartiles divide the data into four equal parts. They are those points in a frequency distribution below which the specific numbers of quarters of the total frequency lie. Thus, Q_1, Q_2, Q_3 and Q_4 are the scores or values below which, respectively, one-fourth, half, three-fourths and all of the total number of scores lie.

Deciles divide the total ordered data into 10 equal parts. They are those points in a frequency distribution below which the specific numbers of tenth parts of the total distribution lie. Thus, D_1, D_2, D_3, . . . , D_9 and D_{10} are, respectively, known as the first, second, third, . . . , ninth and tenth deciles, and are the scores below which the lowest 10 per cent, 20 per cent, 30 per cent, . . . , 90 per cent and 100 per cent of all the scores lie.

Percentiles divide the data into 100 equal parts, and each point is referred to as centile. Percentiles are those points in a frequency distribution below which the specific percentage of the total number of scores of a sample lie. In other words, percentile (P_p) is a point on the score scale below which a given per cent of the cases lie. Thus, the 50th percentile (P_{50}) is the score below which the lowest 50 per cent of the scores lies. Similarly, P_{25} and P_{75} are the scores below which 25 per cent and 75 per cent of the total scores lie, respectively.

There are some relationships between median, quartiles, deciles and percentiles. For example,

$$\text{Mdn} = Q_2 = D_5 = P_{50}; \ Q_1 = P_{25}; \ Q_3 = P_{75}; \ Q_4 = P_{100} = D_{10}; \ D_1 = P_{10}; \ D_2 = P_{20}; \ D_3 = P_{30};$$
$$D_4 = P_{40}; \ D_5 = P_{50}; \ D_6 = P_{60}; \ D_7 = P_{70}; \ D_8 = P_{80}; \ D_9 = P_{90} \ \text{and} \ D_{10} = P_{100}.$$

In this way, the measures such as quartiles, deciles and percentiles all indicate some fixed points like median on the score scale below which a definite proportion of cases lie. Percentiles are generally used in the research area of psychology, education, sociology and so on, where people are given standard tests and it is desirable to compare the relative position of the subject's performance on the test.

5.2   Computation of Percentiles in a Frequency Distribution

Percentiles can be calculated from the frequency distribution by the following formula:

$$P_p = \ell + \left(\frac{pN - F}{f_p} \right) \times i$$

where

P_p = percentage of the distribution wanted, for example, 10 per cent, 30 per cent, 40 per cent, ...
ℓ = exact lower limit of the class interval upon which P_p lies.

Table 5.1   Computation of percentiles in a frequency distribution

Scores	f	Cum.f	Percentiles
195–199	1	50	$P_{100} = 199.5$
190–194	2	49	
185–189	4	47	$P_{90} = 187.0$
180–184	5	43	
175–179	8	38	$P_{75} = 179.2$
170–174	10	30	$P_{50} = 172.0$
165–169	6	20	
160–164	4	14	$P_{25} = 162.6$
155–159	4	10	
150–154	2	6	$P_{10} = 152.0$
145–149	3	4	
140–144	1	1	$P_0 = 139.5$
$i = 5$	$N = 50$		

N=number of scores/cases in the distribution

pN=part of N to be counted off in order to reach P_p

F=sum of all scores upon intervals below ℓ

f_p=number of scores within the interval upon which P_p falls

i=length of the class interval.

Let us refer to Table 5.1 for the computation of percentiles, for example, P_{10}, P_{25}, P_{50}, P_{75}, P_{90} and P_{100}.

Computation of percentile points

P_{10}=10% of $N(50)$=5	$149.5 + \left(\dfrac{5-4}{2}\right) \times 5 = 152.0$
P_{25}=25% of 50=12.5	$159.5 + \left(\dfrac{12.5-10}{4}\right) \times 5 = 162.6$
P_{50}=50% of 50=25	$169.5 + \left(\dfrac{25-20}{10}\right) \times 5 = 172.0$
P_{75}=75% of 50=37.5	$174.5 + \left(\dfrac{37.5-30}{8}\right) \times 5 = 179.2$
P_{90}=90% of 50=45	$184.5 + \left(\dfrac{45-43}{4}\right) \times 5 = 187.0$
P_{100}=100% of 50=50	$194.5 + \left(\dfrac{50-49}{1}\right) \times 5 = 199.5$

In Table 5.1, the percentile points from P_{10} to P_{100} have been computed by the above-mentioned formula for the distribution of scores made by the 50 college students in an achievement test. The details of computation are given in Table 5.1. We may illustrate the method with P_{90}. Here, pN=45 (i.e., 90 per cent of 50=45), and from the Cum.f, we find that 43 scores take us through 180–184 up to 184.5, the exact lower limit of the interval next above where the pN falls. Hence, P_{90} falls upon 185–189, and, substituting pN=45, F=43, f_p=4 (frequency upon 185–189) and i=5 (class interval) in the aforementioned formula for this purpose, we find that P_{90}=187.0 (for the detailed calculation, see Table 5.1). This result means that 90 per cent of the 50 students (or 45 students) scored below 187.0 in the distribution of achievement test scores. The other percentile values are found in exactly the same way as P_{90}. The reader should verify the calculations of P_p in Table 5.1 in order to become thoroughly familiar with the computational methods and procedures.

It should also be noted here that P_0, which marks the exact lower limit of the first interval (namely, 139.5), lies at the top or bottom of the distribution. On the contrary, P_{100} marks the exact upper limit of the last interval (namely, 199.5) lies at the top end of the distribution. These two percentiles represent limiting points. Their principal value is to indicate the boundaries of the percentile scale.

5.3 Computation of Deciles in a Frequency Distribution

Deciles for a given distribution are 10 in number and are described as 1st to 10th decile. A decile is the point on the score scale below which a given decile of the cases lies. The deciles can be calculated from the frequency distribution by the following formulas:

1st decile	$D_1 = \ell + \left(\dfrac{N/10 - F}{f_d} \right) \times i$
2nd decile	$D_2 = \ell + \left(\dfrac{2N/10 - F}{f_d} \right) \times i$
3rd decile	$D_3 = \ell + \left(\dfrac{3N/10 - F}{f_d} \right) \times i$
4th decile	$D_4 = \ell + \left(\dfrac{4N/10 - F}{f_d} \right) \times i$
5th decile	$D_5 = \ell + \left(\dfrac{5N/10 - F}{f_d} \right) \times i$
6th decile	$D_6 = \ell + \left(\dfrac{6N/10 - F}{f_d} \right) \times i$
7th decile	$D_7 = \ell + \left(\dfrac{7N/10 - F}{f_d} \right) \times i$
8th decile	$D_8 = \ell + \left(\dfrac{8N/10 - F}{f_d} \right) \times i$
9th decile	$D_9 = \ell + \left(\dfrac{9N/10 - F}{f_d} \right) \times i$
10th decile	$D_{10} = \ell + \left(\dfrac{10N/10 - F}{f_d} \right) \times i$

Notes:

ℓ = exact lower limit of the class interval upon which the required decile lies

N = number of scores in the distribution

$N/10$ = one-tenth of N to be counted off in order to reach the needed decile

F = sum of all scores upon interval below ℓ

f_d = number of scores within the interval upon which the needed decile falls

i = length of the class interval.

Let us refer to Table 5.2 for the computation of all deciles.

Computation of decile points:

$D_1 = 9.5 + \left(\dfrac{2.4 - 2}{3}\right) \times 10 = 10.83,$	$D_2 = 9.5 + \left(\dfrac{4.8 - 2}{3}\right) \times 10 = 18.83,$
$D_3 = 19.5 + \left(\dfrac{7.2 - 5}{4}\right) \times 10 = 25.00,$	$D_4 = 29.5 + \left(\dfrac{9.6 - 9}{5}\right) \times 10 = 30.70,$
$D_5 = 29.5 + \left(\dfrac{12 - 9}{5}\right) \times 10 = 35.50,$	$D_6 = 39.5 + \left(\dfrac{14.4 - 14}{3}\right) \times 10 = 40.83,$
$D_7 = 39.5 + \left(\dfrac{16.8 - 14}{3}\right) \times 10 = 48.83,$	$D_8 = 59.5 + \left(\dfrac{19.2 - 19}{2}\right) \times 10 = 60.50,$
$D_9 = 69.5 + \left(\dfrac{21.6 - 21}{3}\right) \times 10 = 71.50,$	$D_{10} = 69.5 + \left(\dfrac{24 - 21}{3}\right) \times 10 = 79.50.$

In Table 5.2, the decile points from D_1 to D_{10} have been computed by the corresponding appropriate formulae cited above (for each of the decile points) for the distribution of scores made by the 24 college students in a performance test. The details of computation are given in Table 5.2. We may illustrate the method and procedure of computation with D_1. Here $D_1 = N/10 = 24/10 = 2.4$, and from the cumulative frequency (Cum.f), we find that two scores take us through 0–9 up to 9.5, the exact lower limit of the interval next above where

Table 5.2 Computation of deciles in a frequency distribution

Scores	f	Cum.f	Deciles
70–79	3	24	$D_{10} = 79.50$
60–69	2	21	$D_9 = 71.50$
50–59	2	19	$D_8 = 60.50$
40–49	3	17	$D_7 = 48.83$
30–39	5	14	$D_6 = 40.83$
20–29	4	9	$D_5 = 35.50$
10–19	3	5	$D_4 = 30.70$
0–9	2	2	$D_3 = 25.00$
			$D_2 = 18.83$
			$D_1 = 10.83$
$i = 10$	$N = 24$		

the D_1 falls. Hence, D_1 falls upon 10–19, and substituting D_1 ($N/10$)=2.4, F=2, f_d=3 (frequency upon 10–19) and i=10 (class interval) in the formula given above for this purpose, we find that D_1=10.83 (for the detailed calculation, see Table 5.2). This result means that D_1=10 per cent of the 24 students (i.e., 2.4 students) scored below 10.83 in the distribution of performance test scores. The other decile values are found in exactly the same way as D_1. The reader should verify the calculations of decile points in Table 5.2 in order to become thoroughly familiar with the computational methods and procedures.

5.4   Computation of Quartiles in a Frequency Distribution

Quartiles for a given distribution of scores are 4 in number. They are named 1st, 2nd, 3rd and 4th quartiles (i.e., Q_1, Q_2, Q_3, Q_4, respectively). A quartile is defined as the point on the score scale below which a given quarter of the cases lies. The quartiles can be computed from the frequency distribution by the following formula:

$$\text{1st quartile: } Q_1 = \ell + \left(\frac{N/4-F}{f_q}\right)i, \quad \text{2nd quartile: } Q_2 = \ell + \left(\frac{N/2-F}{f_q}\right)\times i,$$

$$\text{3rd quartile: } Q_3 = \ell + \left(\frac{3N/4-F}{f_q}\right)\times i, \quad \text{4th quartile: } Q_4 = \ell + \left(\frac{N-F}{f_q}\right)\times i,$$

where

Q_1, Q_2, Q_3, Q_4=the type of quartile wanted
ℓ=exact lower limit of the class interval upon which the desired quartile falls
N=number of scores in the distribution
F=sum of all scores upon intervals below ℓ
f_q=number of scores within the interval upon which the desired quartile falls
i=length of the class interval.

Let us refer to Table 5.3 for the computation of all quartiles.

Computation of quartile points:

1st quartile: $Q_1 = 54.5 + \left(\dfrac{15-10}{6}\right)\times 5 = 58.67$
2nd quartile: $Q_2 = 64.5 + \left(\dfrac{30-22}{14}\right)\times 5 = 67.36$
3rd quartile: $Q_3 = 69.5 + \left(\dfrac{45-36}{9}\right)\times 5 = 74.50$
4th quartile: $Q_4 = 89.5 + \left(\dfrac{60-59}{1}\right)\times 5 = 94.50$

In Table 5.3, the quartile points from Q_1 to Q_4 have been computed by the corresponding appropriate formulae cited earlier (for each of the quartile points) for the distribution of scores

Table 5.3   Computation of quartiles in a frequency distribution

Scores	f	Cum.f	Quartiles
90–94	1	60	$Q_4=94.50$
85–89	4	59	
80–84	2	55	
75–79	8	53	
70–74	9	45	$Q_3=74.50$
65–69	14	36	$Q_2=67.36$
60–64	6	22	
55–59	6	16	$Q_1=58.67$
50–54	4	10	
45–49	3	6	
40–44	3	3	
$i=5$	$N=60$		

obtained by 60 students in an examination. The details of computation are given in Table 5.3. We may illustrate the method and procedure of computation with Q_1. Here $Q_1=N/4=15$; and from the Cum.f we find that 10 scores take us through 50–54 up to 54.5, the exact lower limit of the interval next above where the Q_1 falls. Hence, Q_1 falls upon 55–59, and substituting Q_1 ($N/4$)=15, F=10, f_q=6 (frequency upon 55–59) and i=5 (size of class interval) in the above-mentioned formula for the said purpose, we find that Q_1=58.67 (for detailed calculation, see Table 5.3). This result means that Q_1=25 per cent or one-fourth of the 60 students (i.e., 15 students) scored below 58.67 in the distribution of examination scores. The other quartile values are found in exactly the same way as Q_1. The reader should verify the calculations of quartile points in Table 5.3 in order to become thoroughly familiar with the computational methods and procedures.

5.5   Graphical Determination of Percentiles, Deciles and Quartiles from Cumulative Percentage Curve (Ogive)

Percentiles, deciles and quartiles may be obtained graphically from a cumulative percentage (cP) curve or Ogive. A line is drawn paralleled to the X axis from that point on the Y axis which corresponds to the cP for the required fractile—the cP amounts to 10, 20, 25, 50 and 75 for D_1, D_2, P_{25} (Q_1), P_{50} (Q_2, D_5) and P_{75} (Q_3), respectively. From the point of intersection of this line with the Ogive, an ordinate or perpendicular is dropped to the X axis. The point of intersection of this ordinate with the X axis gives the required percentile, decile or quartile.

To illustrate the graphical determination of percentiles, deciles and quartiles, let us refer to Table 5.4 and Figure 5.1.

Table 5.4   Computation of cumulative percentage in a frequency distribution

(1) Score	(2) f	(3) Cum.f	(4) Cum. Per cent.f	Some Calculated Values of Percentiles, Quartiles and Deciles
75–79	1	125	100.0	
70–74	3	124	99.2	
65–69	6	121	96.8	
60–64	12	115	92.0	$P_{90}=D_9=63.46$
55–59	20	103	82.4	$P_{75}=Q_3=57.19$
50–54	36	83	66.4	$P_{50}=Q_2=Mdn=D_5=51.65$
45–49	20	47	37.6	$P_{25}=Q_1=45.56$
40–44	15	27	21.6	$P_{20}=D_2=43.83$
35–39	6	12	9.6	$P_{10}=D_1=39.67$
30–34	4	6	4.8	
25–29	2	2	1.6	
$i=5$	$N=125$			

Note:
$$\text{Rate}=\frac{1}{N}=\frac{1}{125}=0.008.$$

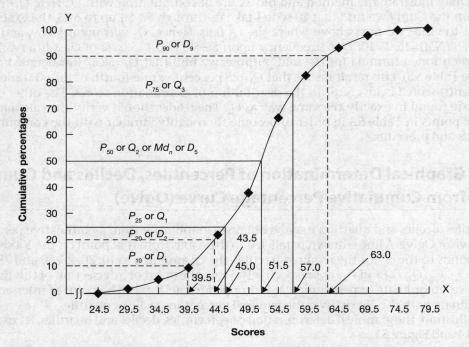

Figure 5.1   Computing percentiles, deciles and quartiles from cumulative percentage curve or Ogive plotted from the data of Table 5.4

The following are some of the calculated values of percentiles, quartiles and deciles based on the data given in Table 5.4.

1.	P_{90} or $D_9 = 59.5 + \left(\dfrac{112.5 - 103}{12}\right) \times 5 = 63.46$
2.	P_{75} or $Q_3 = 54.5 + \left(\dfrac{93.75 - 83}{20}\right) \times 5 = 57.19$
3.	P_{50} or Q_2 or M_{dn} or $D_5 = 49.5 + \left(\dfrac{62.5 - 47}{36}\right) \times 5 = 51.65$
4.	P_{25} or $Q_1 = 44.5 + \left(\dfrac{31.25 - 27}{20}\right) \times 5 = 45.56$
5.	P_{20} or $D_2 = 39.5 + \left(\dfrac{25 - 12}{15}\right) \times 5 = 43.83$
6.	P_{10} or $D_1 = 39.5 + \left(\dfrac{12.5 - 12}{15}\right) \times 5 = 39.67$

The distribution given in Table 5.4 consists of scores obtained by 125 Grade VII children on a reading test. In Columns (1) and (2) class intervals and frequencies are, respectively, noted; and in Column (3), the f's have been cumulated from the low end of the distribution upward. These Cum.f's are expressed as the percentage of $N(125)$ in Column (4). For a clear understanding and the details of the computations of the cumulative percentage frequency and that of the construction of the cumulative percentage curve (or Ogive), the readers should refer to Chapter 2.

The curve in Figure 5.1 represents an Ogive plotted from the data in Column (4) of Table 5.4. Exact interval limits have been laid off on the X axis, and a scale consisting of 10 equal distances, each representing 10 per cent of the distribution, has been marked off on the Y axis. The first point on the Ogive is placed 1.6 Y units just above 29.5, the second point is 4.8 Y units above 34.5 and so on. The last point is 100 Y units above 79.5, the exact upper limit of the highest class interval.

From Figure 5.1, we found that the graphical values of P_{90} (or D_9), P_{75} (or Q_3), P_{50} (or Q_2 or Mdn or D_5), P_{25} (or Q_1), P_{20} (or D_2) and P_{10} (or D_1) are, respectively, 63.0, 57.0, 51.5, 45.0, 43.5 and 39.5, approximately. However, their calculated values are, respectively, 63.46, 57.19, 51.65, 45.56, 43.83 and 39.67. This shows that the graphical values are slightly less than the calculated values. In other words, the percentiles, quartiles and deciles will often be slightly in error when read from an Ogive. This error, however, can be made very small. When the curve is carefully drawn, the diagram fairly large and the scale divisions precisely marked, percentiles (or centiles), quartiles and deciles can be read to a degree of accuracy sufficient for most purposes.

5.6 Percentile Rank

A percentile rank (PR) is a rank or a graded position of a given score on a scale of 100 among all the scores of a sample. It is estimated from the percentage of scores lying below it. In other words, a PR of a given score is the number representing the percentage of the total number of cases lying below the given score.

Table 5.5   Computation of percentile ranks in a frequency distribution

Score	f	Cum.f	Percentile Ranks (PR) for Some Scores (X)
55–59	2	200	PR of $X\,58 = 99.7$
50–54	25	198	PR of $X\,52 = 92.75$
45–49	48	173	PR of $X\,48 = 79.3$
40–44	47	125	
35–39	19	78	PR of $X\,38 = 36.15$
30–34	26	59	
25–29	15	33	
20–24	9	18	PR of $X\,22 = 6.75$
15–19	7	9	
10–14	2	2	
$i = 5$	$N = 200$		

5.6.1   Computation of a Percentile Rank in a Frequency Distribution

We have seen in the last section how percentiles, for example, P_{25}, P_{50} or P_{75} are calculated directly from a frequency distribution. To repeat what has been said earlier, percentiles are points in a continuous distribution below which the given percentages of N lie. We shall now consider the problem of finding an individual's PR or the position on a scale of 100 to which the subject's score entitles him/her.

The distinction between a percentile and a PR will be more clear if a reader can recall that in calculating percentiles he/she starts with a certain per cent of N, say 15 per cent or 60 per cent. He or she then counts into the distribution the given per cent and the point reached is the required percentile, for example, P_{15} or P_{60}. The procedure followed in computing a PR is the reverse of this process. Here, we begin with an individual score and determine the percentage of scores which lie below it. If this percentage is say 60, the score has a PR of 60 on a scale of 100.

With Table 5.5 we shall illustrate the frequency distribution of scores obtained by 200 ten-year-old boys in an arithmetic reasoning test. The PR of a given score belonging to a grouped data or a frequency distribution may be easily computed by employing the following formula:

$$PR = \frac{100}{N}\left[F + \left(\frac{X - \ell}{i} \right) f \right],$$

where

PR = percentile rank for the given score X

F = cumulative frequency just below the interval containing score X

X = score for which PR is wanted

ℓ = exact lower limit of the interval containing X

i=size of the class interval

f=frequency of the interval containing X

N=total number of cases in the given frequency distribution.

Computation of PRs:

$$X = 22 : PR = \frac{100}{200}\left[9 + \left(\frac{22 - 19.5}{5}\right) \times 9\right] = 6.75,$$

$$X = 38 : PR = \frac{100}{200}\left[59 + \left(\frac{38 - 34.5}{5}\right) \times 19\right] = 36.15,$$

$$X = 48 : PR = \frac{100}{200}\left[125 + \left(\frac{48 - 44.5}{5}\right) \times 48\right] = 79.3,$$

$$X = 52 : PR = \frac{100}{200}\left[173 + \left(\frac{52 - 49.5}{5}\right) \times 25\right] = 92.75$$

$$X = 58 : PR = \frac{100}{200}\left[198 + \left(\frac{58 - 54.5}{5}\right) \times 2\right] = 99.7.$$

In Table 5.5, the PRs for scores 22, 38, 48, 52 and 58 taken from the distribution of scores made by the 200 boys in an arithmetic reasoning test are computed by the earlier cited formula. The details of computation are given in Table 5.5. We may illustrate the method with score (X) 52. Here, N=200 and X=52, and from the Cum.f, we find that 173 scores take us through 45–49 up to 49.5, the exact lower limit of the interval next above where X=52 falls. Hence, X=52 falls upon 50–54, and substituting 100/200, F=173, X=52, ℓ =49.5, i=5 (size of class interval) and f=25 in the formula given above for this purpose, we find that the PR of score (X) 52 is 92.75 (for the detailed calculation, see Table 5.5). This result means that 92.75 per cent of 200 boys (i.e., 185 or 186 boys) scored below that boy who has secured the score of 52. The other PRs are found in exactly the same way as X=52. The reader should verify the computations of PRs in Table 5.5 in order to become thoroughly familiar with the computational methods and procedures.

5.6.2 Computing Percentile Ranks from Ranked Data

In the case of ungrouped data, the scores are first arranged into an order, either in a descending order (preferably) or in an ascending order, and then each score is provided a rank or relative position in order of merit. Then either of the following two formulae is employed for the computation of the PR from this ordered data depending upon the nature of ordering— whether *descending order* or *ascending order*.

The following formula is employed to compute the PR when the data are arranged in *descending order*:

$$PR = 100 - \frac{100R - 50}{N}.$$

But where the ranking is in *ascending order*, the PR can be calculated by the following formula:

$$PR = \frac{100R - 50}{N},$$

where

N = total number of individuals in the group

R = rank position of the score of an individual whose PR is to be determined.

Let us illustrate the use of the above two formulae with the help of an example.

Example 5.1 In a statistic test, 15 students of a class have scored as below:

$$10, 50, 30, 45, 60, 55, 80, 75, 70, 35, 15, 20, 40, 25, 65.$$

Find out the PR of the score 70.

Solution

The scores are to be arranged in the descending order, from higher to lower, as shown in the following table.

Ordered Scores	Ranked in Descending Order	Ranked in Ascending Order
80	1	15
75	2	14
70	3	13
65	4	12
60	5	11
55	6	10
50	7	9
45	8	8
40	9	7
35	10	6
30	11	5
25	12	4
20	13	3
15	14	2
10	15	1

Here, $N = 15$, and the rank of the desired score 70 is 3 in descending order and 13 in ascending order. Putting these figures into the formulae, we obtain

$$PR = 100 - \frac{100 \times 3 - 50}{15} = 100 - \frac{300 - 50}{15}$$

$$= 100 - \frac{250}{15} = 100 - 16.67 = 83.33,$$

or

$$PR = \frac{100 \times 13 - 50}{15} = \frac{1300 - 50}{15} = \frac{1250}{15} = 83.33.$$

From the above-mentioned two formulae, it is evident that the PR of a particular score obtained by an individual remains constant, irrespective of the assignment of ranks to the scores either in descending or ascending order. This result of PR=83.33 shows that 83.33 per cent of students of the class scored below the student who secured the score 70.

Example 5.2 In an entrance examination, one candidate ranks 35 (in the descending order of data) out of 150 candidates. Find his PR.

Solution

The PR is given by the formula

$$PR = 100 - \frac{100R - 50}{N}.$$

In this example, $R=35$ and $N=150$.
Hence,

$$PR = 100 - \frac{100 \times 35 - 50}{150} = 100 - \frac{3500 - 50}{150}$$

$$= 100 - \frac{3450}{150} = 100 - 23 = 77.$$

This PR of 77 means that 77 per cent of candidates in the entrance test (i.e., 115 or 116 candidates) scored below the candidate who ranked 35.

If 100 students are ranked for average grade earned throughout the school years, each student will occupy one division on the percentile scale. Hence, the PR of the best student is 99.5 (midpoint of the highest interval 99–100), and the PR of the poorest student is 0.5 (midpoint of the lowest interval 0–1). The PR of the 50th student is $100 - \frac{100 \times 50 - 50}{100}$ or 50.5 (midpoint of the interval 50–51). As a PR is always the midpoint of an interval, it follows that no one can have a PR of 0 or 100. These two points constitute the boundaries or limits of the percentile scale.

The PRs are useful when we want to compare the standing of an individual in one test with his/her standing in another; the N's do not have to be the same in both tests. For example, suppose that Shreyaa ranks 2nd in a class of 30 in English and 10th in a class of 50 in Mathematics. Then, how these two 'standings' can be compared? These two 'standings' of Shreyaa can be compared by the help of her PRs in both the subjects. In English, Shreyaa's PR is $100 - \frac{100 \times 2 - 50}{30}$ or 95; and in Mathematics, her PR is $100 - 100 - \frac{100 \times 2 - 50}{30}$ or 81.

It is evident that relative to the members of her class, Shreyaa is better in English than she is in Mathematics. In many schools, grades in the various subjects are converted into PRs, so that a student's standing or position in classes of different sizes may be compared directly.

5.6.3 Determining Percentile Ranks from Cumulative Percentage Curve (Ogive)

To illustrate the graphical determination of PRs, let us refer to Table 5.6 and Figure 5.2.

Table 5.6 Computation of cumulative percentage in a frequency distribution

(1) Scores	(2) f	(3) Cum. f	(4) Cum. Per cent. f	Some Computed Values of PR
65–69	6	50	100	PR of $X\,67 = 94.0$
60–64	4	44	88	
55–59	4	40	80	PR of $X\,56 = 74.4$
50–54	5	36	72	
45–49	8	31	62	PR of $X\,48 = 57.2$
40–44	6	23	46	
35–39	6	17	34	
30–34	5	11	22	PR of $X\,32 = 17.0$
25–29	4	6	12	
20–24	2	2	4	
15-19	0	0	0	
$i = 5$	$N = 50$			

Note: Rate $= \dfrac{1}{N} = \dfrac{1}{50} = 0.02$.

Computation of PRs:

$$X = 32 : PR = \frac{100}{50}\left[6 + \left(\frac{32 - 29.5}{5}\right) \times 5\right] = 17.0,$$

$$X = 48 : PR = \frac{100}{50}\left[23 + \left(\frac{48 - 44.5}{5}\right) \times 8\right] = 57.2,$$

$$X = 56 : PR = \frac{100}{50}\left[36 + \left(\frac{56 - 54.5}{5}\right) \times 4\right] = 74.4,$$

$$X = 67 : PR = \frac{100}{50}\left[44 + \left(\frac{67 - 64.5}{5}\right) \times 6\right] = 94.0.$$

The distribution given in Table 5.6 consists of scores secured by 50 students in an arithmetic test. In Columns (1) and (2), class intervals and frequencies are, respectively, noted; and in Column (3) the f's have been cumulated from the low end of the distribution upward. These cumulative frequencies (Cum. f's) are expressed as a percentage of $N(50)$ in Column (4).

The curve in Figure 5.2 represents an Ogive plotted from the data in Column (4) of Table 5.6. Exact interval limits have been laid off on the X axis, and a scale consisting of 10 equal distances, each representing 10 per cent of the distribution, has been marked off on the Y axis. The first point on the Ogive is placed 4 Y units just above 24.5, the second point is 12 Y units above 29.5 and so on. The last point is 100 Y units above 69.5, the exact upper limit of the highest class interval.

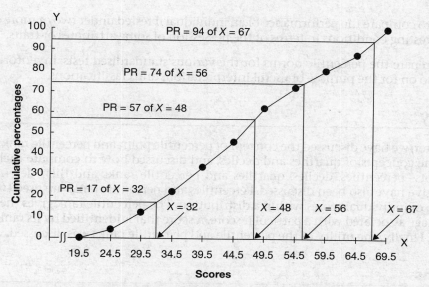

Figure 5.2 Computing percentile ranks from cumulative percentage curve or Ogive plotted from the data of Table 5.6

In order to read the PR of a given score from the Ogive, we reverse the process followed in determining percentiles. Score 67, for example, has a PR of 94, approximately (see Figure 5.2). Here, we start with score 67 on the X axis, go vertically up to the Ogive and then horizontally across to the Y axis to locate the PR at 94 on the cumulative percentage scale. Put it into other words, to be more clear, an ordinate or perpendicular is raised on the X axis of the Ogive at the given score X. A horizontal line is drawn from the point of intersection of the ordinate with the Ogive. The point of intersection of this line with the Y axis gives the PR of the given score. The PRs of scores 32, 48 and 56 are found in the same way to be approximately 17, 57 and 74, respectively. However, the calculated PRs of scores 32, 48, 56 and 67 are, respectively, 17, 57.2, 74.4 and 94.0 (see Table 5.6). This shows a slight difference between the PR values determined from an Ogive and calculated from the cumulative frequency distribution. In other words, PRs will often be slightly in error when read from an Ogive. This error, however, can be made very small. When the curve is carefully drawn, the diagram fairly large and the scale divisions precisely marked, PRs can be read to a degree of accuracy sufficient for most purposes.

5.7 Utility of Percentiles and Percentile Ranks

Percentiles and PRs are used in behavioural and social sciences for the following purposes:

(i) To indicate or determine the relative position of an individual with respect to some attribute (achievement score, presence of some personality trait and so on) in his/her own group.

(ii) For the purpose of comparison, that is,

   (a) to compare two or more individual students belonging to two or more sections, classes or schools

   (b) to compare the performance of two or more classes or schools and

    (c) to compare the performance of an individual if tested under two or more different testing conditions in terms of the possession of some attributes or traits.

(iii) To prepare the percentile norms for the various standardised tests, inventories, scales and so on for the purpose of useful interpretations and classifications.

Summary

In this chapter, we have discussed the concept of percentile point and percentile rank, and also presented the concepts of quartiles and deciles, and discussed how to compute each. All the four concepts—percentiles, deciles, quartiles and percentile ranks and their determination from the Ogive have also been discussed. Percentiles and percentile ranks are used to describe the position of individual scores within a distribution. The percentile rank gives the cumulative percentage associated with a particular score. A score that is identified by its rank is called a percentile. Finally, the utility of the percentile and percentile ranks was discussed.

Key Terms

- Deciles
- Fractiles
- Percentiles
- Percentile ranks
- Quantiles
- Quartiles

Questions and Problems

1. Define the terms percentile, quartile, decile and median. Discuss their mutual relationship.
2. What do you understand by the terms percentile and percentile rank? Discuss the differences between them with an example.
3. Enumerate the utility of percentile and percentile rank in the fields of behavioural sciences.
4. Point out the process of computation of various quartiles, deciles and percentiles with the help of some hypothetical data.
5. Find out the values of (a) 1st and 3rd quartiles (Q_1 and Q_3), (b) 1st decile (D_1) and (c) 90th percentile (P_{90}) from the following distributions of scores:

(a)		(b)	
Scores	**f**	**Scores**	**f**
45-49	2	135-144	1
40-44	3	125-134	2
35-39	2	115-124	8
30-34	17	105-114	22
25-29	30	95-104	33
20-24	25	85-94	22
15-19	15	75-84	9
10-14	3	65-74	2
5-9	2	55-64	1
0-4	1		
	N=100		N=100

6. From the following two distributions of scores, compute the values of (a) P_{30}, P_{70} and P_{90}, and (b) percentile rank of the scores 14, 20 and 26:

I		II	
Scores	**f**	**Scores**	**f**
37-39	2	27-29	1
34-36	10	24-26	3
31-33	15	21-23	6
28-30	19	18-20	10
25-27	16	15-17	9
22-24	8	12-14	11
19-21	9	9-11	10
16-18	7	6-8	3
13-15	3	3-5	3
10-12	1	0-2	1
	N=90		N=57

7. In a particular group of five students, A, B, C, D and E get scores of 42, 60, 31, 50 and 71, respectively, on a certain language test. Find their percentile ranks.

8. Twenty children are put in order of merit for scores on a learning test. What are the PRs of the 1st, 5th, 10th, 15th and 20th children?

9. (a) Sonali ranks 6th in a class of 30 in Mathematics and 6th in a class of 50 in English. Compare her PRs in the two subjects.

   (b) What would Sonali's rank in Mathematics need to be in order for her PR in Mathematics to equal her PR in English?

   (c) Does a PR of 65 earned by a student mean that 65% of the group made scores above him, that 65% of the group made scores below him or that 65% made the same scores?

10. The following distributions represent the achievement of two groups of students—Group A and Group B—upon a memory test.

    (a) Plot Ogives of the two distributions A and B upon the same axes.

    (b) Determine P_{30}, P_{60} and P_{90} graphically from each of the Ogives and compare graphically determined values with calculated values.

    (c) What is the percentile rank of score 55 in Group A's distribution and that in Group B's distribution?

    (d) A percentile rank of 70 in Group A corresponds to what percentile rank in Group B?

Scores	Group A (f)	Group B (f)
79–83	6	8
74–78	7	8
69–73	8	9
64–68	10	16
59–63	12	20
54–58	15	18
49–53	23	19
44–48	16	11
39–43	10	13
34–38	12	8
29–33	6	7
24–28	3	2
	N=128	N=139

11. Fill in the blanks:

    (i) Quartiles, deciles and percentiles taken together are called _____ measures.

    (ii) Quartiles divide the data into _____ equal parts.

(iii)   Deciles divide the total ordered data into _____ equal parts.

(iv)   Percentiles divide the data into _____ equal parts and each point is referred to as _____.

(v)   Median is equal to Q_____, D_____ and P_____.

(vi) Q_1 is equal to P_____ and Q_3 is equal to P_____.

(vii) Q_4 is equal to P_____ and D_____.

(viii) D_1 is equal to P_____.

(ix)   Percentiles and percentile ranks are used to determine the relative _____ of an individual with respect to some attributes in his/her own group.

(x)   A percentile rank is the rank or graded _____ of a given score on a scale of _____ among all the scores of a sample.

12.   Write whether the following statements are True or False.

(i) P_{10} means 10% of N.

(ii) Q_4 is equal to D_8.

(iii) Q_3 is equal to D_3.

(iv) Q_2 is equal to the median.

(v) P_{50} is not equal to D_5.

(vi)   Percentiles and percentile ranks are used to prepare the percentile norms for the various standardised tests, inventories and scales.

(vii)   Percentile is a point on the score scale below which a given per cent of cases lie.

(viii)   A percentile rank of a given score is the number representing the percentage of the total number of cases lying below the given score.

(ix) D_4 is not equal to P_{40}.

(x)   The computational procedures of percentiles and percentile ranks are just opposite to each other.

13.   Find out the correct answer from among the four alternatives.

(i)   A PR of 62 indicates that 62% of the total cases lie

(a)   Below it   (b)   Above it

(c)   Either below or above it   (d)   None of the above

(ii) P_{90} indicates that 90% of the total cases lie

(a)   At par with it   (b)   Below it

(c)   Above it   (d)   None of the above

(iii)   If Mary's PR in English is 66 and in History is 58, then Mary is:

(a)   Better in English than she is in History

(b)   Worse in English than she is in History

(c)   Equal in both English and History

(d)   None of the above

(iv) P_{10} is equal to

    (a) Q_1 (b) D_2

    (c) D_1 (d) None of the above

(v) D_3 is equal to

    (a) P_{30} (b) Q_3

    (c) Q_2 (d) None of the above

(vi) D_5 is equal to

    (a) Q_1 (b) Q_2

    (c) Q_3 (d) None of the above

(vii) Q_3 is equal to

    (a) P_{25} (b) P_{50}

    (c) P_{75} (d) None of the above

(viii)   Deciles divide the total ordered data into

    (a) 4 equal parts   (b) 100 equal parts

    (c) 10 equal parts   (d) None of the above

(ix)   When the data are divided by percentiles, each point is referred to as

    (a) Centiles   (b) Deciles

    (c) Quartiles   (d) None of the above

(x)   The relative merits of a student in two school subjects can be determined by his/her:

    (a) PR   (b) Quartiles

    (c) Deciles   (d) None of the above

CHAPTER 6

Probability, Binomial and Poisson Distributions

After completing this chapter you will be able to:

- Explain the nature of probability.
- Explain the elementary principles of probability.
- Explain different terms in probability.
- Use probabilities to take new information into account: the definition and use of theorems of probability.
- Explain the different ways of arising probabilities.
- Develop rules for calculating different kinds of probabilities.
- Explain permutations and combinations of a particular number of objects.
- Show which probability distribution to use and how to find its values.
- Understand the concept of binomial distribution, its assumptions and properties.
- Understand the concept of Poisson distribution, its assumptions and properties.

6.1   Introduction

In Chapters 2–5, the reader was introduced to certain statistics which are used to describe the properties of frequency distributions or the collections of numbers which frequency distributions comprise. In the present chapter, the nature of probability is considered.

The word 'probability' or 'chance' is very commonly used in our day-to-day conversation. For example, we come across statements such as, 'it will *probably* rain tomorrow'; 'it is *likely* that Mr X may not come today to take his class'; 'it is *possible* that I may not be able to join you at your birthday party'; 'the *chances* of teams A and B winning a certain Cricket match are equal' and so on. All these terms probably, likely, possible and chances convey the same sense, that is, the event is not certain to take place, or, in other words, there is uncertainty about the occurrence of the event in question.

Probability is used to introduce the reader to one particular type of theoretical distribution known as the *binomial distribution*. The binomial distribution is only one of a number of theoretical distributions that are used in practical situations to estimate probabilities. Another discrete probability distribution of rare events belonging to one of the two classes of a dichotomised variable is called the Poisson distribution. The rare events occur at random and are independent of each other in the sample, that is, the probability of occurrence of one rare event is not increased or decreased by the occurrence of any other.

One question arises: Why are experimentalists concerned about probability? In experimental work, a line of theoretical speculation may lead to the formulation of a particular hypothesis. An experiment is conducted and data obtained. How are the data interpreted? Do the data support the acceptance or rejection of the hypothesis? What rules of evidence apply? Questions of these types involve considerations of probability. The answers are in probabilistic terms. The assertions of an investigator are not made with certainty but have some degree of doubt, though small, associated with them.

Let us consider a hypothetical situation. Two methods for the treatment of a disease are under consideration. Two groups of 30 patients each sufferings from the disease are selected. Method A is applied to one group and Method B to the other. Following a period of treatment, 20 patients of the group treated with Method A, and 15 patients of the other group treated with Method B show marked improvement. How may this difference be evaluated? May it be argued from the data that Method A is, in general, superior to Method B? Here, we proceed by adopting a trial hypothesis that no difference exists between the two treatment methods, that is, the one treatment method is not better than the other. We then estimate the probability of obtaining by random sampling under this trail hypothesis a difference equal to or greater than the one observed. If this probability is small, say, the chances are less than 5 in 100, then we may consider this sufficient evidence for the rejection of the trial hypothesis and may be prepared to assert that one method of treatment (i.e., Method A) is better than the other (i.e., Method B). If the probability is not small, say the chances are more than 5 in 100, then we accept the trial hypothesis and conclude that neither treatment method is better than the other.

In general, the interpretation of the data of experiments is in probabilistic terms. The theory of probability is of the greatest importance in scientific work where questions about the correspondences between the deductive consequences of theory and observed data are raised. Probability theory had its origins in games of chance. It has become basic to the thinking of the scientist or investigator.

6.2   The Nature of Probability

Probability may be approached in two ways: (a) from an *a priori* or classical viewpoint and (b) from an *a posteriori* or empirical viewpoint.

A priori means that the probability can be deduced from the reason alone, without experience. From the *a priori* or classical viewpoint, probability is defined as

$$p(A) = \frac{\text{number of events classifiable as A}}{\text{total number of possible events}} \quad (a \text{ priori probability}).$$

The symbol $p(A)$ is read 'the probability of occurrence of event A'. Thus, the equation states that the probability of occurrence of event A is equal to the number of events classifiable as 'A' divided by the number of possible events. To illustrate how this equation is used, let us look at an example involving a die. Each die (the singular of dice is die) has six sides with a different number of spots painted on each side. The spots vary from 1 to 6. Returning to *a priori* probability, suppose that we are going to roll a die once. What is the probability it will come to rest with a '3' (the side with three spots on it) facing upward? Since there are six possible numbers that might occur, and only one of these is 3, the probability of a three in one roll of one die is

$$p(A) = p(3) = \frac{\text{number of events classifiable as 3}}{\text{total number of possible events}} = \frac{1}{6} = 0.1667.$$

Let us try one more problem using the *a priori* approach. What is the probability of getting a number greater than 4 in one roll of one die? This time there are two events classifiable as A (rolling a 5 or 6). Thus,

$$p(A) = p(5 \text{ or } 6) = \frac{\text{number of events classifiable as 5 or 6}}{\text{total number of possible events}} = \frac{2}{6} = 0.3333.$$

Note that the above two problems were solved by the reason alone, without recourse to any data collection. This approach is to be contrasted with the *a posteriori* or empirical approach to probability. *A posteriori* means 'after the fact', and, in the context of probability, it means after some data have been collected. From the *a posteriori* or empirical viewpoint, probability is defined as

$$p(A) = \frac{\text{number of times A has occurred}}{\text{total number of occurrences}} = (\text{a posteriori probability}).$$

To determine the probability of a '3' in one roll of one die using the empirical approach, we would have to take the actual die, roll it many times and count the number of times a '3' has occurred. The more times we roll the die, the better. Let us assume for this problem that we roll the die 1000 times and that a '3' occurs 160 times. The probability of a '3' occurring in one roll of the die is found by

$$p(A) = p(3) = \frac{\text{number of times 3 has occurred}}{\text{total number of occurrences}} = \frac{160}{1000} = 0.16.$$

Note that, with this approach, it is necessary to have the actual die and to collect some data before determining the probability. The interesting thing is that if the die is evenly balanced (spoken of as a fair die), when we roll the die many, many times, the *a posteriori* probability approaches the *a priori* probability. If we roll the die an infinite number of times, the two probabilities will equal to each other. Note also that, if the die is loaded (weighted so that one side comes up more often than the others), the *a posteriori* probability will differ from the *a priori* probability. We can see now that the *a priori* equation assumes that each possible outcome has an equal chance of occurrence. For most of the problems in this chapter and the next, we shall use the *a priori* approach to probability.

6.3 Elementary Principles of Probability

Perhaps the simplest approach to an understanding of the normal probability curve is through a consideration of the elementary principles of probability. In Layman's terminology the word 'probability' connotes that there is uncertainty about the occurrence of the event; for him, all these terms—possibly, likely, probably—convey the same sense, that is, the event is not certain to take place. However, in mathematics and statistics, the term 'probability' is used in a different connotation. As used in statistics, the 'probability' of a given event is defined as the expected frequency of occurrence (or chance of occurrence) of this event among events of the like. This expected frequency of occurrence may be based upon a knowledge of the conditions determining the occurrence of the phenomenon, as in coin-tossing or dice-throwing or upon empirical data, as in mental and social measurements.

The probability of an event may be stated mathematically as a ratio. For example, the probability of an unbiased coin falling head is 1/2 (because a coin has two aspects: head and tail), and the probability of a die showing a two-spot is 1/6 (because a die has six aspects). These ratios are called probability ratios and are defined by that fraction, the numerator of which equals the desired outcome/s and the denominator of which equals the total possible outcomes. Putting more simply, the probability of appearance of any face on a six-faced cube (e.g., four spots) is 1/6 or the $\dfrac{\text{desired outcome/s}}{\text{total number of outcomes}}$. A probability ratio always falls between the limit 0.00 (impossibility of occurrence) and 1.00 (certainty of occurrence). Thus, for example, the probability that the Sun will rise in the west is 0.00, and that a living organism will die one day is 1.00. Between these limits are all possible degrees of likelihood which may be expressed by appropriate ratios.

Let us now apply these simple principles of probability to the specific case of what happens when we toss coins (coin-tossing and dice-throwing furnish easily understood and often used illustrations of the so-called laws of chance). If we toss one coin, obviously it must fall either heads (H) or tails (T) 100 per cent of the time; and furthermore, since there are only two possible outcomes in a given throw, a head (H) or a tail (T) is equally probable. Expressed as a ratio, therefore, the probability of H is 1/2, that of T is 1/2 and

$$(H+T)=1/2+1/2=1.00.$$

If we toss two coins, (a) and (b), at the same time, there are 4 (2^2) possible arrangements which the coins may take. Therefore, the sample space(s) is 4 (2^2):

(1)		(2)		(3)		(4)	
a	b	a	b	a	b	a	b
H	H	H	T	T	H	T	T

Both coins (a) and (b) may fall H; (a) may fall H and (b) T; (a) may fall T and (b) H; or both coins may fall T. Expressed as ratios, the probability of two heads (H H) is 1/4 and the probability of two tails is 1/4. Also, the probability of an HT combination is 1/4 and of a TH combination 1/4. And since it ordinarily makes no difference which coin falls H or which falls T, we may add these two ratios (or double the one) to obtain 1/2, that is (1/4+1/4=1/2) as the probability of an HT or TH combination. The sum of our probability ratios is 1/4+1/2+1/4=1.00.

Suppose we go a step further and increase the number of coins to 3. If we toss these three coins (a), (b) and (c) simultaneously, there are eight possible outcomes and, thus, the sample space(s) is 2^3 or 8:

(1)	(2)	(3)	(4)	(5)	(6)	(7)	(8)
a b c	a b c	a b c	a b c	a b c	a b c	a b c	a b c
H H H	H H T	H T H	T H H	H T T	T H T	T T H	T T T

Expressed as a ratio, the probability of three heads is 1/8 (combination 1), of two heads and one tail is 3/8 (combinations 2, 3 and 4), of one head and two tails is 3/8 (combinations 5, 6 and 7) and of three tails is 1/8 (combination 8). The sum of these probability ratios is $1/8+3/8+3/8+1/8=1.00$.

6.4   Certain Terms in Probability

The following are certain terms that need to be discussed before discussing the procedures for calculating probabilities:

(i) **Experiment and events.** The term experiment refers to describe an act which can be repeated under some given conditions. Random experiments are those experiments whose results depend on a chance such as tossing a coin or throwing a die. The results of a random experiment are called outcomes. If in an experiment all the possible outcomes are known in advance and none of the outcomes can be predicted with certainty, then such an experiment is called a random experiment, and the outcomes are called events or chance events. Events are generally denoted by capital letters such as A, B, C and so on.

An event whose occurrence is inevitable when a certain random experiment is performed is called a certain or sure event. An event which can never occur when a certain random experiment is performed is called an impossible event. For example, in a throw of a balanced dice, the occurrence of any one of the numbers 1, 2, 3, 4, 5 or 6 is a sure event, while the occurrence of 8 is an impossible event. An event which may or may not occur while performing a certain random experiment is known as a random event. The occurrence of 4 is a random event in the above experiment of the throwing of a die.

(ii) **Mutually exclusive events.** Two events are said to be mutually exclusive or incompatible when both cannot occur simultaneously in a single trial; in other words, the occurrence of any one of them precludes the occurrence of the other. For example, if a single coin is tossed, either the head can be up or the tail can be up; both cannot be up at the same time. Thus, the head and tail are the mutually exclusive events. Symbolically, if H and T are mutually exclusive events, then $p(HT)=0$.

It may be pointed out that mutually exclusive events can always be connected by the words 'either ... or'. Events A, B and C are mutually exclusive only if either A or B or C can occur.

(iii) **Independent and dependent events.** Two or more events are said to be independent when the outcome of the one does not affect and is not affected by the other. For example, if a coin is tossed twice, the result of the second throw would in no way be affected by the result of the first throw. Similarly, the results obtained by throwing a die are independent of the results obtained drawing an ace from a pack of cards.

Dependent events are those in which the occurrence or non-occurrence of one event in any one trial affects the probability of other events in other trials. For example, if a card is drawn from a pack of playing cards and is not replaced, this will alter the probability that the second card drawn is, say, an ace. Similarly, the probability of drawing a queen from a pack of 52 cards is 4/52 or 1/13. But if the card drawn (queen) is not replaced in the pack, the probability of drawing again a queen is 3/51 (since the pack now contains only 51 cards, out of which three are queens).

(iv) **Equally likely events.** Events are said to be equally likely when one does not occur more often than the others. For example, if an unbiased coin or dice is thrown, each face may be expected to be observed approximately the same number of times in the long run. Similarly, the cards of a pack of playing cards are so closely alike that we expect each card to appear equally often when a large number of drawings are made with replacement. However, if the coin or the dice is biased, we should not expect each face to appear exactly the same number of times.

(v) **Simple and compound events.** In case of simple events, we consider the probability of the occurrence or not occurrence of a single event. For example, we might be interested in finding out the probability of drawing a red ball from a bag containing 10 white and 6 red balls. On the other hand, in case of compound events, we consider the joint occurrence of two or more events. For example, if a bag contains 10 white and 6 red balls, and if two successive draws of 3 balls are made, we shall be finding the probability of getting 3 white balls in the first draw and 3 red balls in the second draw—we are, thus, dealing with a compound event.

(vi) **Exhaustive events.** Events are said to be exhaustive when their totality includes all the possible outcomes of a random experiment. For example, while throwing a die, the possible outcomes are 1, 2, 3, 4, 5 and 6, and, hence, the exhaustive number of cases is 6. If two dice are thrown once, the exhaustive number (i.e., the sample space) of cases will be 36 ordered pairs (6^2). Similarly, for a throw of 3 dice, the exhaustive number of cases will be 216 (i.e., 6^3) and for n dice they will be 6^n. Similarly, black and red cards are examples of collectively exhaustive events in a draw from a pack of playing cards.

(vii) **Complementary events.** Let there be two events A and B. A is called the complementary event of B (and vice versa) if A and B are mutually exclusive and exhaustive. For example, when a die is thrown, the occurrence of an even number (2, 4 or 6) and an odd number (1, 3 or 5) are complementary events.

Simultaneous occurrence of two events A and B is generally written as AB.

6.5 Theorems of Probability

There are two theorems of probability, namely, the addition theorem and the multiplication theorem, which are discussed in the following sections.

6.5.1 Addition Theorem

The addition theorem states that the probability that any one of a number of mutually exclusive events will occur is the sum of the probabilities of the separate events. In other words, if two events A and B are mutually exclusive, the probability of occurrence of either A or B is the sum of the individual probability of A and B. Symbolically,

$$p(A \text{ or } B) = p(A) + p(B)$$

or

$$p(A \cup B) = p(A) + p(B),$$

where $A \cup B$ is read as 'A union B' and it denotes the union of events A and B.

The theorem can be extended to three or more number of mutually exclusive events. Thus, $p(A \text{ or } B \text{ or } C) = p(A) + p(B) + p(C)$.

Illustration 6.1 One card is drawn from a standard pack of 52. What is the probability that it is either a king or a queen?

Solution There are four kings and four queens in a pack of 52 cards. Therefore, the probability that the card drawn is a king = 4/52, and the probability that the card drawn is a queen = 4/52.

Since the events are mutually exclusive, the probability that the card drawn is either a king or a queen,

$$\therefore p(\text{king or queen}) = p(\text{king}) + p(\text{queen}) = \frac{4}{52} + \frac{4}{52} = \frac{8}{52} = \frac{2}{13}.$$

Illustration 6.2 What is the probability of obtaining either a 1, 2 or 3 in a single throw of a die?

Solution In a single throw of a die, six possible outcomes such as 1, 2, 3, 4, 5 and 6 will occur. Since these outcomes or events are equally likely, the probability of obtaining a 1, 2, 3, 4, 5 or 6 in a single throw is 1/6. Therefore, the probability of obtaining either a 1, a 2 or a 3 in a single throw is

$$p(1 \text{ or } 2 \text{ or } 3) = \frac{1}{6} + \frac{1}{6} + \frac{1}{6} = \frac{3}{6} = \frac{1}{2}.$$

Illustration 6.3 What is the probability of obtaining either two heads or two tails in tossing two coins simultaneously?

Solution In tossing two coins simultaneously, four possible events may occur: HH, TT, HT and TH. The probability of each outcome is 1/4. Thus, the probability of two heads is 1/4 and the probability of two tails is 1/4. Therefore, the probability of obtaining either two heads or two tails is

$$p(\text{two heads or two tails}) = p(\text{two heads}) + p(\text{two tails}) = \frac{1}{4} + \frac{1}{4} = \frac{2}{4} = \frac{1}{2}.$$

Illustration 6.4 In throwing two dice simultaneously what is the probability that the number on the two dice will add up to 3?

Solution In throwing two dice simultaneously 36 (6^2) outcomes will occur, and the probability of each equally likely outcome is 1/36. The probability that the first die is a 1 and the second a 2 is 1/36. The probability that the first die is a 2 and the second a 1 is 1/36. Therefore, the probability of obtaining either 1 and 2, or 2 and 1 is

$$p(1 \text{ and } 2 \text{ or } 2 \text{ and } 1) = p(1 \text{ and } 2) + p(2 \text{ and } 1)$$

$$= \frac{1}{36} + \frac{1}{36} = \frac{2}{36} = \frac{1}{18}.$$

Illustration 6.5 In rolling two dice what is the probability of obtaining either a 7 or an 11?

Solution If we consult the set of possible outcomes in rolling two dice in Section 6.5, we note that a 7 can occur in 6 different ways. Thus, the probability of getting a 7 is 6/36. An 11 can occur in 2 different ways. Thus, the probability of getting an 11 is 2/36. Therefore, the probability of getting either a 7 or an 11 is

$$p(7 \text{ or } 11) = p(7) + p(11) = \frac{6}{36} + \frac{2}{36} = \frac{8}{36} = \frac{2}{9}.$$

Illustration 6.6 Consider a well-shuffled deck of 52 cards. In drawing a single card from the deck, what is the probability of obtaining either the ace, king, queen or jack of spades?

Solution The probability that a single card is the ace of spades is 1/52. The probability that a single card is the king is 1/52, the queen is 1/52 and the jack is 1/52. Therefore, the probability of obtaining either the ace, king, queen or jack of spades in drawing a single card is

$$p(\text{ace, king, queen or jack of spades}) = \frac{1}{52} + \frac{1}{52} + \frac{1}{52} + \frac{1}{52} = \frac{4}{52} = \frac{1}{13}.$$

The illustrative examples above involve the addition of probabilities. Probabilities can be added together when a set of mutually exclusive events can be specified, when the probabilities associated with these events can be stated and when the probability associated with a subset of these events is required.

When events are not mutually exclusive or, in other words, it is possible for both events to occur, the addition theorem must be modified. For example, what is the probability of drawing either a king or a heart from a standard pack of cards? It is obvious that there can be events when king and heart occur together as we can draw a king of hearts (since king and heart are not mutually exclusive events). We must deduce from the probability of drawing either a king or a heart, the chance that we can draw both of them together. Hence, for finding the probability of one or more of two events that are not mutually exclusive, we use the modified form of the addition theorem:

$$p(\text{A or B}) = p(\text{A}) + p(\text{B}) - p(\text{A and B}),$$

where

$p(\text{A or B})$ = probability of occurrence of A or B when A and B are not mutually exclusive
$p(\text{A})$ = probability of occurrence of A
$p(\text{B})$ = probability of occurrence of B
$p(\text{A and B})$ = probability of occurrence of A and B together.

In the example taken, the probability of drawing a king is 4/52 because there are four kings in 52 cards. The probability of drawing a heart is 13/52 because there are 13 hearts in 52 cards. The probability of drawing a king of hearts is 1/52 because there is only one card of king of hearts in 52 cards. Therefore, the probability of drawing a king or heart shall be

$$p(\text{king or heart}) = p(\text{king}) + p(\text{heart}) - p(\text{king and heart}):$$
$$= \frac{4}{52} + \frac{13}{52} - \frac{1}{52} = \frac{4+13-1}{52} = \frac{16}{52} = \frac{4}{13}.$$

6.5.2   Multiplication Theorem

The multiplication theorem states that the probability of the joint occurrence of two or more independent events is the product of their separate probabilities. In other words, if two events A and B are independent, the probability that they both will occur is equal to the product of their individual probability. Symbolically, if A and B are independent, then

$$p(\text{A and B}) = p(\text{A}) \times p(\text{B}).$$

The theorem can be extended to three or more independent events. Thus,

$$p(\text{A, B and C}) = p(\text{A}) \times p(\text{B}) \times p(\text{C}).$$

Illustration 6.7 What is the probability of obtaining four heads in four tosses of a coin?

Solution The probability that any one coin is a head is 1/2. The probability that all four coins are heads is

$$p(4\text{ heads}) = \frac{1}{2} \times \frac{1}{2} \times \frac{1}{2} \times \frac{1}{2} = \frac{1}{16}.$$

Illustration 6.8 What is the probability of obtaining two 6s in rolling two dice?

Solution The probability that the first die is a 6 is 1/6. The probability that the second die is a 6 is 1/6. Thus, the probability that both dice are 6 is

$$p(\text{two 6s}) = \frac{1}{6} \times \frac{1}{6} = \frac{1}{36}.$$

Illustration 6.9 What is the probability of drawing the ace, king and queen of spades in that order, and without replacement, from a well-shuffled deck?

Solution The probability that the first card is the ace of spades is 1/52. Having drawn one card, 51 cards remain, and the probability that the second card is the king of spades is 1/51. Having drawn two cards, 50 cards remain, and the probability that the third card is the queen of spades is 1/50. The probability of the combined events is the product of the separate probabilities. Hence, the probability of drawing the ace, king and queen of spades is

$$p(\text{ace, king and queen of spades}) = \frac{1}{52} \times \frac{1}{51} \times \frac{1}{50} = \frac{1}{132,600}.$$

Illustration 6.10 A bag contains five white and three black balls. Two balls are drawn at random one after the other without replacement. Find the probability that both balls drawn are black.

Solution The bag contains a total of 5+3=8 balls out of which five are white and three are black. The probability of drawing a black ball in the first draw is

$$p(\text{B}) = \frac{3}{5+3} = \frac{3}{8}.$$

The probability of drawing the second black ball given that the first ball drawn is black

$$p(\text{B}) = \frac{2}{5+2} = \frac{2}{7}.$$

The probability that both balls drawn are black is

$$p(2\,\text{B}) = \frac{3}{8} \times \frac{2}{7} = \frac{6}{56} = \frac{3}{28}.$$

The above examples illustrate the multiplication of probabilities. Probabilities may be multiplied together when two or more independent events can be specified, when the probabilities associated with these events can be stated and when the probability associated with the joint occurrence of these events is required.

6.6 Joint and Conditional Probabilities

The multiplication theorem, explained above, is not applicable in the case of dependent events. Two events A and B are said to be dependent when B can occur only when A is known to have occurred (or vice versa). The probability attached to such an event is called the conditional probability and is denoted by $p(A/B)$ or, in other words, probability of A occuring given that B has occurred. If two events A and B are dependent, then the conditional probability of B given A is

$$p(\text{B}/\text{A}) = \frac{p(\text{AB})}{p(\text{A})}.$$

Consider a population of members classified with regard to two characteristics A and B, there being three classes or strata of A and two classes or strata of B, as follows:

	A_1	A_2	A_3	
B_1	0.40	0.15	0.05	0.60
B_2	0.00	0.10	0.30	0.40
	0.40	0.25	0.35	1.00

The probability that a person is B_1 is 0.60, that is, the marginal probability $p(B_1)=0.60$. The probability that he/she is A_1 is 0.40, that is, the marginal probability $p(A_1)=0.40$. The probability that he/she is both A_1 and B_1 is 0.40, that is, $p(A_1B_1)=0.40$. This latter probability is a *joint probability*. It is the probability that a member will fall simultaneously within two classes. All probabilities in the above table are joint probabilities.

Now given the fact that a member is B_1, what is the probability that he or she is A_1, A_2 or A_3? To answer this question, we divide the joint probabilities $p(A_1B_1)=0.40$, $p(A_2B_1)=0.15$ and $p(A_3B_1)=0.05$ by the probability $p(B_1)=0.60$ to obtain $p(A_1/B_1)=0.67$, $p(A_2/B_1)=0.25$ and $p(A_3/B_1)=0.08$. These are *conditional probabilities*. They are the probabilities of A_1, A_2 and A_3 given B_1. Note that the sum of these three probabilities is 1.00. Likewise, if a member is B_2, what is the probability that he or she is A_1, A_2 or A_3? Here, $p(A_1/B_2)=0.00$, $p(A_2/B_2)=0.25$ and $p(A_3/B_2)=0.75$. These conditional probabilities may be written in a tabular form as follows:

	A_1	A_2	A_3
B_1	0.67	0.25	0.08
B_2	0.00	0.25	0.75

Likewise, the conditional probabilities of B given A are as follows:

	A_1	A_2	A_3
B_1	1.00	0.60	0.14
B_2	0.00	0.40	0.86
	1.00	1.00	1.00

6.7   Probability Distributions

In tossing three coins simultaneously, we will get (2^3) eight equally probable (1/8) outcomes, such as

Outcomes:	HHH	HHT	HTH	THH	HTT	THT	TTH	TTT
Number of heads (X):	3	2	2	2	1	1	1	0

Number of Heads (X)	Frequency (f)	Probability (p)
3	1	1/8 = 0.125
2	3	3/8 = 0.375
1	3	3/8 = 0.375
0	1	1/8 = 0.125
Total	8	1.00

The distribution to the right above is a probability distribution.

Similarly, consider a situation where two dice are thrown. The total number of possible outcomes is (6^2) 36, each of equal probability (1/36).

Outcomes = 36						Numbers (values) (X)					
11	21	31	41	51	61	2	3	4	5	6	7
12	22	32	42	52	62	3	4	5	6	7	8
13	23	33	43	53	63	4	5	6	7	8	9
14	24	34	44	54	64	5	6	7	8	9	10
15	25	35	45	55	65	6	7	8	9	10	11
16	26	36	46	56	66	7	8	9	10	11	12

Numbers (X)	Frequency (f)	Probability (p)
12	1	1/36 = 0.0278
11	2	2/36 = 0.0555
10	3	3/36 = 0.0833
9	4	4/36 = 0.1111
8	5	5/36 = 0.1389
7	6	6/36 = 0.1667
6	5	5/36 = 0.1389
5	4	4/36 = 0.1111
4	3	3/36 = 0.0833
3	2	2/36 = 0.0555
2	1	1/36 = 0.0278
Total	36	1.00

The distribution to the right above is a probability distribution.

6.8   Permutations and Combinations

Any arrangement of objects is called *permutation*. Order is the essential idea here. A different order is a different arrangement. Consider two objects labelled A and B. Two arrangements are possible, AB and BA. So here the number of permutation is 2. With three objects labeled A, B and C, six arrangements are possible. These are ABC, ACB, BAC, BCA, CAB and CBA. The number of permutation in this case is 6. In this example, three ways exist for choosing the first object. When the first object is chosen, two ways exist for choosing the second object. When the second object is chosen, one way exists for choosing the third object. The number of permutations in this case is given by $3 \times 2 \times 1 = 6$. In general, if there are n distinguishable objects, the number of permutations of these objects taken n at a time is given by $n!$ or n factorial, which is the product of all integers from n to 1 or $n(n-1)(n-2)...3 \times 2 \times 1$. For $n=4$, $n! = 4 \times 3 \times 2 \times 1 = 24$; for $n=5$, $n! = 5 \times 4 \times 3 \times 2 \times 1 = 120$.

Instead of considering the number of ways of arranging n things n at a time, we may consider the number of ways of arranging n things r at a time, where r is less than n. Thus, the possible arrangements of three objects, A, B and C, taken two at a time are AB, AC, BA, BC, CA and CB. Here, we observe that there are three ways of selecting the first object and two ways of selecting the second object. The number of arrangements is then $3 \times 2 = 6$. Similarly, on considering the number of arrangements of 10 objects taken 3 at a time, we observe that there are 10 ways of selecting the first object, 9 ways of selecting the second and 8 ways of selecting the third. The number of arrangements is then $10 \times 9 \times 8 = 720$. In general, the number of permutations of n things taken r at a time is given by the formula which reads

$$P_r^n = \frac{n!}{(n-r)!}.$$

The number of different ways of selecting objects from a set, ignoring the order in which they are arranged, is the number of *combinations*. For example, given four objects labelled A, B, C and D, the number of permutations, two at a time, is

$$\frac{n!}{(n-r)!} = \frac{4!}{(4-2)!} = \frac{4 \times 3 \times 2 \times 1}{2 \times 1} = 12.$$

The arrangements are AB, BA, AC, CA, AD, DA, BC, CB, BD, DB, CD and DC. Note that each pair occurs in two different orders. If we ignore the order in which each pair of objects is arranged, we have the number of combinations. The number of combinations is then $(4 \times 3)/2 = 6$. In general, the number of different combinations of n objects taken r at a time is given by the following formula:

$$C_r^n = \frac{n!}{r!(n-r)!}.$$

The number of combinations of 10 objects taken 3 at a time is

$$\frac{n!}{r!(n-r)!} = \frac{10!}{3!(10-3)!} = \frac{10!}{3!7!}$$
$$= \frac{10 \times 9 \times 8 \times 7 \times 6 \times 5 \times 4 \times 3 \times 2 \times 1}{3 \times 2 \times 1 \times 7 \times 6 \times 5 \times 4 \times 3 \times 2 \times 1} = 120.$$

The number of combinations of n things taken n at a time is clearly 1, because there is only one way of picking all n objects if we ignore the order of their arrangement.

6.9.   The Binomial Distribution

When a variable is measured on a scale consisting of exactly two categories, the resulting data are called binomial. The term *binomial* can be loosely translated as 'two names', referring to the two categories on the measurement scale. Binomial data can occur when a variable naturally exists with only two categories. For example, people can be classified as male and female, and a coin toss results in either heads or tails. It is also common for a researcher to simplify data by collapsing it into two categories. For example, a psychologist may use personality scores to classify people as either high or low in aggression; similarly, the objects can be categorised as animate or inanimate, and living or nonliving and so on.

As indicated above in tossing three unbiased coins simultaneously, eight possible, equally probable outcomes exist. These are as follows:

Outcomes:	HHH	HHT	HTH	THH	TTH	THT	HTT	TTT
No. of heads:	3	2	2	2	1	1	1	0

The values of X (which stands for the number of heads) are 3, 2, 1 and 0, having frequencies, respectively 1, 3, 3 and 1, and, thus, the probabilities are 1/8, 3/8, 3/8 and 1/8, respectively.

Let us denote the probabilities of head (H) by p and the probabilities of tail (T) by q; here, $p+q=1.0$. The eight possible outcomes with their associated probabilities may be represented as follows:

Outcomes	Probabilities
HHH	p^3
HHT	p^2q
HTH	p^2q
THH	p^2q
TTH	pq^2
THT	pq^2
HTT	pq^2
TTT	q^3

The probabilities of obtaining 3, 2, 1, 0 heads may now be represented as follows:

Number of Heads	Frequency	Probability
3	1	$p^3=1/8$
2	3	$3p^2q=3/8$
1	3	$3pq^2=3/8$
0	1	$q^3=1/8$

Note that since there are three coins, one head may occur in three ways. If there are three coins, two heads can occur in three different ways, which is the number of combinations of three things taken two at a time, that is,

$$\frac{n!}{r!(n-r)!} = \frac{3!}{2!1!} = \frac{3 \times 2 \times 1}{2 \times 1} = 3.$$

If the above probabilities are added together, we obtain $p^3 + 3p^2q + 3pq^2 + q^3 = 1.0$. This is an example of the binominal distribution. The probabilities associated with 3, 2, 1 and 0 heads in the situation described are given by the successive terms of the expansion $(p+q)^3$. In this illustrative example, $p = q = 1/2$, and the required probabilities are as follows:

$$\left(\frac{1}{2} + \frac{1}{2}\right)^3 = \left(\frac{1}{2}\right)^3 + 3\left(\frac{1}{2}\right)^3 + 3\left(\frac{1}{2}\right)^3 + \left(\frac{1}{2}\right)^3 = \frac{1}{8} + \frac{3}{8} + \frac{3}{8} + \frac{1}{8}.$$

The binomial expansion may be applied more usefully to those cases in which there are a large number of independent factors operating. Consider a more complex example involving 10 rather than 3 coins. If we toss 10 coins simultaneously, for instance, we have by analogy with the above $(p+q)^{10}$. This expression may be written as $(H+T)^{10}$. H standing for the probability of a head, T for the probability of a tail (or non-head) and the exponent 10 indicates the number of coins tossed. In tossing 10 coins at the same time what is the probability of obtaining 0, 1, 2, 3, 4, 5, 6, 7, 8, 9 and 10 heads? We are required to determine the probability of obtaining 0 heads and 10 tails, 1 head and 9 tails, 2 heads and 8 tails, 3 heads and 7 tails, 4 heads and 6 tails, 5 heads and 5 tails, 6 heads and 4 tails, 7 heads and 3 tails, 8 heads and 2 tails, 9 heads and 1 tail, and 10 heads and 0 tail. Let us designate the 10 coins by the letters A, B, C, D, E, F, G, H, I and J. Let us assume that all 10 coins are unbiased and that the probability of getting a head or a tail on a single toss of any coin is 1/2.

Let us attend first to the probability of getting 0 head and 10 tails in tossing all coins simultaneously. The probability that coin A is not a head is 1/2, that B is not a head is 1/2, that C is not a head is 1/2 and so on. Therefore, from the multiplication theorem of probability, the probability that all 10 coins are not heads or they are all tails is obtained by multiplying 1/2 ten times, that is, $(1/2)^{10}$ or 1/1024. Thus, in tossing 10 coins simultaneously, there is only one chance in 1024 of obtaining 0 head and 10 tails.

Now consider the problem of obtaining one head and nine tails. The probability that coin A is a head is 1/2. The probability that all the remaining nine coins are tails is $(1/2)^9$. Therefore, the probability that A is a head and all other nine coins are tails is $(1/2)^{10}$. It is readily observed, however, that one head can occur in 10 different ways. Coin A may be a head and all other coins tails, B may be a head and all the others tails and so on. Since one head can occur in 10 different ways, the probability of obtaining one head and nine tails is $10(1/2)^{10} = 10/1024$. Thus, in tossing 10 coins simultaneously, there are 10 chances in 1024 of obtaining one head and nine tails.

Determining the probability of obtaining two heads and eight tails may be similarly approached. The probability that coins A and B are heads is $(1/2)^2$. The probability that all the remaining coins are tails is $(1/2)^8$. The probability that A and B are heads and all the remaining coins are tails is $(1/2)^{10}$. We readily observe, however, that two heads can occur in quite a number of different ways. This number is the number of combinations of 10 things taken 2 at a time, C_2^{10}, which is $10 \times 9/2 = 45$. Therefore, the probability of obtaining two heads and eight tails is $45(1/2)^{10}$ or 45/1024. Similarly, the probability of obtaining three heads and seven tails is $C_3^{10}(1/2)^{10} = 120/1024$, likewise the probability of obtaining four heads and six tails is $C_4^{10}(1/2)^{10} = 210/1024$ and so on. Then the probabilities of obtaining different numbers of heads in tossing 10 coins simultaneously are as follows:

No. of Heads	Probability
10	1/1024
9	10/1024
8	45/1024
7	120/1024
6	210/1024
5	252/1024
4	210/1024
3	120/1024
2	45/1024
1	10/1024
0	1/1024

Similarly, when the binomial $(H+T)^{10}$ is expanded, the terms are

$$(H+T)^{10} = H^{10} + 10H^9T + 45H^8T^2 + 120H^7T^3 + 210H^6T^4 + 252H^5T^5 + 210H^4T^6$$
$$+ 120H^3T^7 + 45H^2T^8 + 10HT^9 + T^{10}.$$

The above results are summarised as follows:

		Probability Ratios
1 H^{10}	=1 chance in 1024 of all coins falling heads	=1/1024
10 H^9T	=10 chances in 1024 of 9 heads and 1 tail	=10/1024
45 H^8T^2	=45 chances in 1024 of 8 heads and 2 tails	=45/1024
120 H^7T^3	=120 chances in 1024 of 7 heads and 3 tails	=120/1024
210 H^6T^4	=210 chances in 1024 of 6 heads and 4 tails	=210/1024
252 H^5T^5	=252 chances in 1024 of 5 heads and 5 tails	=252/1024
210 H^4T^6	=210 chances in 1024 of 4 heads and 6 tails	=210/1024
120 H^3T^7	=120 chances in 1024 of 3 heads and 7 tails	=120/1024
45 H^2T^8	=45 chances in 1024 of 2 heads and 8 tails	=45/1024
10 HT^9	=10 chances in 1024 of 1 head and 9 tails	=10/1024
1 T^{10}	=1 chance in 1024 of all coins falling tails	=1/1024
	Total=1024	1.00

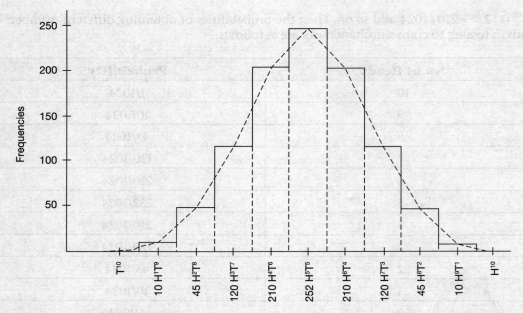

Figure 6.1   Example 12.1 Probability surface obtained from the expansion of $(H+T)^{10}$

These data are represented graphically in Figure 6.1 by a histogram and a frequency polygon plotted on the same axes. The 11 terms of the expansion have been laid off at equal distances along the X axis and the 'chances' of the occurrence of each combination of H's and T's are plotted as frequencies on the Y axis. The result is a symmetrical frequency polygon with the greatest concentration in the centre and the 'scores' falling away by corresponding decrements above and below the central high point. Figure 6.1 represents the results to be expected *theoretically* when 10 coins are tossed 1024 times.

The above probabilities, for obtaining different number of heads while tossing 10 coins simultaneously, are the successive terms in the expansion of the symmetrical binomial $(1/2+1/2)^{10}$. This expansion is

$$\left(\frac{1}{2}+\frac{1}{2}\right)^{10} = \left(\frac{1}{2}\right)^{10} + 10\left(\frac{1}{2}\right)^{10} + \frac{10\times9}{1\times2}\left(\frac{1}{2}\right)^{10} + \frac{10\times9\times8}{1\times2\times3}\left(\frac{1}{2}\right)^{10} + \cdots + \left(\frac{1}{2}\right)^{10}.$$

This is a particular case of the symmetrical binomial $(1/2+1/2)^{n}$, whose terms are

$$\left(\frac{1}{2}+\frac{1}{2}\right)^{n} = \left(\frac{1}{2}\right)^{n} + n\left(\frac{1}{2}\right)^{n} + \frac{n(n-1)}{1\times2}\left(\frac{1}{2}\right)^{n} + \frac{n(n-1)(n-2)}{1\times2\times3}\left(\frac{1}{2}\right)^{n} + \cdots + \left(\frac{1}{2}\right)^{n}.$$

The symmetrical binomial is a particular case of the general form of the binomial $(p+q)^{n}$, where p is the probability that an event will occur and q is the probability that it will not occur, that is, $p+q=1.0$. This binomial may be written as follows:

$$(p+q)^{n} = p^{n} + np^{n-1}q + \frac{n(n-1)}{1\times2}p^{n-2}q^{2} + \frac{n(n-1)(n-2)}{1\times2\times3}p^{n-3}q^{3} + \cdots + q^{n}.$$

The terms of this expansion for $n=2$, $n=3$ and $n=4$ are as follows:

$$(p+q)^2 = p^2 + 2pq + q^2$$

$$(p+q)^3 = p^3 + 3p^2q + 3pq^2 + q^3$$

$$(p+q)^4 = p^4 + 4p^3q + 6p^2q^2 + 4pq^3 + q^4.$$

The binomial $(p+q)^n$ can be readily illustrated by considering a problem involving the rolling of dice. What are the probabilities of obtaining five, four, three, two, one and zero 6s in rolling five dice presumed to be unbiased? The probability of obtaining a 6-spotted face in rolling a single die is 1/6, whereas the probability of not obtaining a 6-spotted face is 5/6. The required probabilities are given by the six terms of the binomial:

$$\left(\frac{1}{6}+\frac{5}{6}\right)^5 = \left(\frac{1}{6}\right)^5 + 5\left(\frac{1}{6}\right)^4\left(\frac{5}{6}\right) + \frac{5\times4}{1\times2}\left(\frac{1}{6}\right)^3\left(\frac{5}{6}\right)^2 + \frac{5\times4}{1\times2}\left(\frac{1}{6}\right)^2\left(\frac{5}{6}\right)^3 + 5\left(\frac{1}{6}\right)\left(\frac{5}{6}\right)^4 + \left(\frac{5}{6}\right)^5.$$

Thus, the probabilities of obtaining five, four, three, two, one and zero 6s in rolling five dice are calculated as follows:

No. of 6s	Probability
5	1/7776
4	25/7776
3	250/7776
2	1250/7776
1	3125/7776
0	3125/7776

From the above data, it is evident that there is one chance in 7776 of obtaining five 6s, 25 chances in 7776 of obtaining four 6s and so on. This distribution is seen to be asymmetrical.

Any term in the binomial expansion may be written as

$$C_r^n \, p^r \, q^{n-r} = \frac{n!}{r!(n-r)!} \, p^r q^{n-r}$$

where C_r^n is the number of combinations of n things taken r at a time. Thus, the probability of obtaining three heads in 10 tosses of a coin is

$$\frac{10!}{3!(10-3)!}\left(\frac{1}{2}\right)^3\left(\frac{1}{2}\right)^{10-3} = \frac{10!}{3!7!}\left(\frac{1}{2}\right)^3\left(\frac{1}{2}\right)^7$$

$$= \frac{10\times9\times8}{3\times2\times1}\left(\frac{1}{2}\right)^{10} = \frac{120}{1024}.$$

The coefficients C_r^n in any expansion are

$$1, n, \frac{n(n-1)}{1\times2}, \frac{n(n-1)(n-2)}{1\times2\times3}, \cdots.$$

These coefficients can be found by the number of combinations of n things taken r at a time.

6.9.1   Properties

The following are some of the important properties or characteristics of the binomial distribution:

   (i)   The binomial distribution is a *discrete probability distribution*. It gives probabilities of whole numbers (e.g., $0,1,2,3,4,5,\ldots,n$) of events or cases of a class. Because there cannot be any fractional occurrence of an event, the whole numbers of events form a discrete or discontinuous series with intervening gaps between them. This makes the distribution discrete.

  (ii)   The binomial distribution is the probability distribution of *dichotomised variables*— the variables that are divided into only two classes according to the presence or absence of some property. Such variables may include male–female, living–nonliving, success–failure, yes–no answers, normal–abnormal and the like.

 (iii)   The events or cases occur at *random* and are *independent of each other*.

 (iv)   Mean (μ), variances (σ^2) and standard deviations (σ) of a binomial frequency distribution are obtained from the sample size (n), and the proportions (p and q) of the cases in the two classes. Thus,

$$\mu = np, \quad \sigma^2 = npq, \quad \sigma = \sqrt{npq}.$$

  (v)   The binomial distribution may be either *unimodal* or *bimodal*.

 (vi)   The *skewness* and *kurtosis* of a binomial distribution depend on the proportions (p and q) of the two classes of the population. The *moment coefficient of skewness* (γ_1) of a binomial distribution is given by

$$\gamma_1 = \frac{q-p}{\sqrt{npq}} = \frac{q-p}{\sigma}.$$

Thus, the distribution is bilaterally symmetrical and has no skewness when $p=q=0.50$. But it has a negative skewness if $p>q$ or $p>0.50$, and its left or low-value tail is more drawn out than the right tail. On the contrary, it has a positive skewness when $p<q$ or $p<0.50$ and its right tail is longer than the left tail.

   The binomial distribution is platykurtic so far as p lies between about 0.2114 and 0.7886, but turns to leptokurtic if p is either below about 0.2114 or above about 0.7886. The *moment coefficient of kurtosis* (γ_2) of a binomial distribution is given by

$$\gamma_r = \frac{1-6pq}{npq}.$$

(vii)   For a symmetrical binomial, where $p=q=1/2$, the mean, variance, skewness and kurtosis are $\mu = n/2, \sigma^2 = n/4, \gamma_1 = 0$ and $\gamma_2 = -2/n$, respectively. Here, we use the symbols μ, σ^2, γ_1 and γ_2 instead of $\bar{X}$, s^2, g_1 and g_2, respectively, because the binomial is a theoretical distribution. The symbols μ, σ^2, γ_1 and γ_2 may be viewed as the population parameters rather than the sample estimates.

6.9.2   Assumptions

For applying the binomial distribution to the observed results, it should be justifiable to make the following assumptions.

(i)   The population is *dichotomised* with an intervening gap between the two classes.

(ii)   The cases or events of each class occur at *random* and are *independent of each other* in the sample so that the occurrence of one event does not influence the probability of occurrence of any other event.

(iii)   The proportion of cases in the two classes of the population has remained *unchanged* during sampling and is known with reasonable accuracy.

(iv)   The mean, standard deviation and variance of the distribution of events of the relevant class are given by the following:

$$\mu = np, \quad \sigma^2 = npq, \quad \sigma = \sqrt{npq}.$$

(v)   The coefficient of dispersion (CD) of the events of one class equals the proportion of cases in the other and falls short of 1

$$CD = \frac{\sigma^2}{\mu} = \frac{npq}{np} = q.$$

6.10   The Poisson Distribution

The Poisson distribution is a theoretical discrete probability distribution that can describe many processes. It is so named after its formulator Simon Denis Poisson, a French Mathematician.

In a population dichotomised with respect to a variable, one of the two classes may sometimes consist of rare events or cases forming a very low proportion of the population. The distribution of relative expected frequencies or probabilities of different numbers of such rare events in a sample from such a population may conform to a theoretical probability distribution called the Poisson distribution. In such cases, the probabilities or relative expected frequencies of 0, 1, 2, 3, ..., n numbers of rare events, among the total number (n) of all the events, are given by the following successive terms of the Poisson distribution:

$$\frac{1}{e^{\mu}}, \frac{\mu}{1!e^{\mu}}, \frac{\mu^2}{2!e^{\mu}}, \frac{\mu^3}{3!e^{\mu}}, \cdots, \frac{\mu^n}{n!e^{\mu}},$$

where μ is the mean of Poisson distribution, n is the sample size and e is the base of the natural logarithm. Using the sample mean $\bar{X}$, these probabilities may be stated in terms of the Poisson distribution in the following series:

$$\frac{1}{e^{\bar{X}}}, \frac{\bar{X}}{1!e^{\bar{X}}}, \frac{\bar{X}^2}{2!e^{\bar{X}}}, \frac{\bar{X}^3}{3!e^{\bar{X}}}, \cdots, \frac{\bar{X}^n}{n!e^{\bar{X}}}.$$

Thus, the probability $P(X)$ of X number of rare events occurring in a sample is given by

$$P(X) = \frac{\bar{X}^X}{X!e^{\bar{X}}} = \frac{\bar{X}^X}{[X(X-1)(X-2)\cdots 2 \times 1](2.7183)^{\bar{X}}},$$

where e approximates to 2.7183.

The absolute expected frequency (*fe*) of the given X number of rare events in the total number (k) of samples, each of size n, may then be obtained by multiplying the relative expected frequency $P(X)$ of a sample by the number (k) of all the samples:

$$fe(X) = kP(X) = \frac{k\bar{X}^X}{X! \, e^{\bar{X}}}.$$

6.10.1   Properties

The following are some of the important properties or characteristics of the Poisson distribution:

(i)   The Poisson distribution may be used as the probability distribution of *rare events* belonging to one of the two classes of a *dichotomised variable*. The class whose events have a distribution in conformity to the Poisson distribution has a very low proportion (p), close to 0, in the population; the other class of far more frequent events has a far higher proportion (q) close to 1 in the population.

(ii) It is a *discrete probability distribution* because it is the probability distribution of the whole numbers (0, 1, 2, 3, ..., n) of elements or events, separated by intervening gaps because of no possibility of occurrence of fractional numbers of events.

(iii) The rare events occur at *random* and are *independent of each other* in the sample—the probability of occurrence of one rare event is not increased or decreased by the occurrence of any other.

(iv) The rare events may occur either *spatially* within a specified space or volume (e.g., Down syndrome patients in a sample of children) or *temporally* within a given time interval (e.g., number of suicide cases in a month).

(v)   The mean (μ) and variance (σ^2) of a Poisson distribution of rare events are identical, finite and very low, less than 5, compared to the total number n of events of both the classes:

$$\mu = np, \quad \sigma^2 = np, \quad \sigma = \sqrt{np}.$$

(vi) The Poisson distribution may be either *unimodal or bimodal*.

(vii) Since μ and σ^2 are identical, the Poisson distribution has a positive skewness, given, thus, by the moment coefficient (γ_1) of skewness,

$$\gamma_1 = \frac{1}{\sqrt{\mu}} = \frac{1}{\sqrt{np}}.$$

For μ as low as 0.1, the distribution is reverse J-shaped with no left tail and a prolonged right tail. As μ rises, a peak appears, but the right or high-value tail is longer than the left one; this positive skewness declines progressively with the rise in μ (see Figure 6.2).

(viii) The Poisson distribution is leptokurtic, its *leptokurtosis* declines with the rise in μ. In terms of the moment coefficient (γ_2) of kurtosis,

$$\gamma_2 = \frac{1}{\mu} = \frac{1}{np}.$$

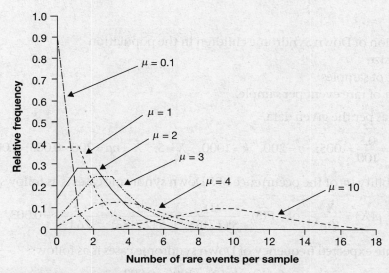

Figure 6.2   Frequency polygons of poisson distribution

Because the shape of the Poisson distribution depends on the mean, probabilities of rare events also depend on the latter.

(ix)   Because μ and σ^2 are identical, the coefficient of dispersion (CD) is 1 or nearly 1 for a Poisson distribution:

$$CD = \frac{\sigma^2}{\mu} = \frac{np}{np} = 1.$$

6.10.2   Assumptions

The following are some important assumptions that the researcher has to make while applying the Poisson distribution to the observed results.

(a)   The variable under investigation is divided into *only two classes* with intervening gaps between the two.

(b)   The proportion (p) of the population, falling in the class whose events are under consideration, is very low—very close to 0—while the proportion q in the other or high-frequency class is correspondingly high.

(c)   The μ and σ^2 of the probability distribution of rare cases are identical, finite, equal to *np* and lower than 5.

(d)   The CD of the distribution is 1 or nearly 1.

(e)   The rare events occur at *random* and are *independent of each other* in the sample.

The understanding about the Poisson distribution will be more clear through the following examples.

Example 6.1 Work out the probability of occurrence of five Down syndrome cases in a sample of 200 children from a population having 0.5% incidence of that genetic disorder. Also, compute the absolute expected frequency of such Down syndrome cases in 1,000 such samples.

Solution

p=proportion of Down Syndrome children in the population
n=sample size
k=number of samples
X=number of rare event per sample.

Therefore, as per the given data,

$$p = \frac{0.5}{100} = .005; \quad n = 200, \quad k = 1000, \quad X = 5, \quad \bar{X} = np = 200 \times 0.005 = 1.00.$$

The probability (p) of the occurrence of 5 Down syndrome cases is as follows:

$$p(X) = \frac{\bar{X}^X}{X!e^{\bar{X}}} \quad \text{or} \quad P(5) = \frac{(1)^5}{5!(2.7183)^1} = \frac{1}{5!(2.7183)} = \frac{1}{326.196} = 0.003.$$

The absolute expected frequency of Down syndrome cases is as follows:

$$fe(X) = kp(X) = 1000 \times 0.003 = 3.$$

Thus, $p(X=5)=0.003$ and $fe(X=5)=3$.

Example 6.2 If 2% of electric bulbs manufactured by a company are known to be defective, what is the probability that a sample of 150 electric bulbs taken from the production process of that company would contain: (a) exactly one defective bulb and (b) more than two defective bulbs.

Solution Let X be the number of bulbs produced by the company. Since the bulbs could be either defective or non-defective, and the probability of bulb being defective remains the same, it follows that X is a binomial variable with parameters $n=150$ and $p=$probability of a bulb being defective$=2/100=0.02$. However, since n is large and p is very small, we can approximate this binomial distribution with the Poisson distribution with parameter $\mu=np=150 \times 0.02=3.0$.

(a) The probability that exactly one bulb would be defective

$$= p(X = 1) = \frac{\bar{X}^X}{X!e^{\bar{X}}} = \frac{(3)^1}{1!(2.7183)^3} = \frac{3}{20.086} = 0.15.$$

(b) The probability that there would be more than two defective bulbs

$$= p(X > 2) = 1 - p(X \leq 2)$$

$$= 1 - \left[p(X = 0) + p(X = 1) + p(X = 2) \right]$$

$$= 1 - \left[\left(\frac{3^0}{0!e^3} \right) + \left(\frac{3^1}{1!e^3} \right) + \left(\frac{3^2}{2!e^3} \right) \right]$$

$$= 1 - \left[\left(\frac{3^0}{0!(2.7183)^3} \right) + \left(\frac{3^1}{1!(2.7183)^3} \right) + \left(\frac{3^2}{2!(2.7183)^3} \right) \right]$$

$$= 1 - \left[\frac{1}{20.086} + \frac{3}{20.086} + \frac{9}{40.172} \right] = 1 - 0.4232 = 0.5768 = 0.58.$$

Summary

In this chapter, we have discussed probability, binomial distribution and Poisson distribution. In presenting probability, we pointed out that probability may be approached from two viewpoints: *a priori* and *a posteriori*. Since probability is fundamentally a proportion or a ratio, it ranges from 0.00 to 1.00. We have also discussed the elementary principles of probability, certain important terms in probability, two theorems of probability(the addition theorem and the multiplication theorem), joint and conditional probabilities, probability distribution, and concepts of permutations and combinations of objects.

Next, we have discussed the binomial distribution, which is a discrete probability distribution of dichotomised variables. We illustrated the binomial distribution through coin-flipping experiments and then showed how the binomial distribution could be generated through the binomial expansion. The binomial expansion is given by $(p+q)^n$, where p is the probability of occurrence of one of the events and q is the probability of occurrence of the other event. In addition, we discussed the properties and assumptions of the binomial distribution.

Finally, we discussed the Poisson distribution that is a theoretical discrete probability distribution of *rare events* belonging to one of the two classes of a dichotomised variable. The Poisson distribution is given by $\dfrac{\mu^n}{n!e^\mu}$, where μ is the mean of the Poisson distribution, n is the sample size and e is the base of the natural logarithm. In addition, we discussed the properties and assumptions of the Poisson distribution.

Key Terms

- *A priori*
- *A posteriori*
- Addition theorem
- Binomial distribution
- Binomial expansion
- Combination
- Complementary events
- Conditional probability
- Dichotomised variable
- Discrete probability distribution
- Equally likely events
- Exhaustive events
- Independent and dependent events
- Joint probability
- Multiplication theorem
- Mutually exclusive events
- Permutation
- Poisson distribution
- Probability
- Probability distribution
- Rare events
- Simple and compound events
- Theorems of probability

Questions and Problems

1. Define probability. Discuss about the elementary principles of probability.
2. Enumerate the different terms in probability.
3. What do you mean by the term 'probability'? Enumerate the theorems of probability with the help of examples.
4. Write notes on:
   (a) Joint and conditional probability
   (b) Probability distribution
   (c) Permutations and combinations
5. What do you understand by the term 'binomial distribution'? Discuss its properties and assumptions.
6. What is meant by the Poisson distribution? Enumerate its properties and assumptions.
7. Which of the following are examples of independent events?
   (a) Obtaining a 3 and a 4 in one roll of two fair dice.
   (b) Obtaining an ace and a king in that order by drawing twice without replacement from a deck of cards.
   (c) Obtaining an ace and a king in that order by drawing twice with replacement from a deck of playing cards.
   (d) A cloudy sky followed by rain.
   (e) A full moon and eating a hamburger.
8. Which of the following are examples of mutually exclusive events?
   (a) Obtaining a 4 and a 7 in one draw from a deck of ordinary playing cards.
   (b) Obtaining a 3 and a 4 in one roll of two fair dice.
   (c) Being male and becoming pregnant.
   (d) Obtaining a one and an even number in one roll of a fair dice.
   (e) Getting married and remaining a bachelor.
9. Which of the following are examples of exhaustive events?
   (a) Flipping a coin and obtaining a head or a tail (edge not allowed).
   (b) Rolling a die and obtaining a 2.
   (c) Taking an examination and either passing or failing.
   (d) Going out on a date and having a good time.
10. If you draw a single card once from a deck of ordinary playing cards, what is the probability that it will be:
    (a) The ace of diamonds?   (b)   A 10?
    (c) A queen or a heart?   (d)   A 3 or a black card?

11. If you roll a pair of fair dice once, what is the probability that you will obtain:

    (a) A 2 on die 1 and a 5 on die 2?
    (b) A 2 and a 5 without regard to order?
    (c) At least one 2 or one 5?
    (d) A sum of 7?

12. If you are randomly sampling one at a time with replacement from a bag that contains eight blue marbles, seven red marbles and five green marbles, what is the probability of obtaining:

    (a) A blue marble in one draw from the bag
    (b) Three blue marbles in three draws from the bag
    (c) A red, a green, and a blue marble in that order in three draws from the bag
    (d) At least two red marbles in three draws from the bag

13. If you are randomly drawing one at a time without replacement from a bag that contains eight blue marbles, seven red marbles and five green marbles, what is the probability of obtaining:

    (a) A blue marble in one draw from the bag?
    (b) Three blue marbles in three draws from the bag?
    (c) A red, a green and a blue marble in that order in three draws from the bag?
    (d) At least two red marbles in three draws from the bag?

14. You want to call a friend on the telephone. You remember the first three digits of her phone number, but you have forgotten the last four digits. What is the probability that you will get the correct number merely by guessing?

15. You are planning to make a 'killing' at the race track. In a particular race, there are seven horses entered. If the horses are all equally matched, what is the probability of your correctly picking the winner and runner-up?

16. A gumball dispenser has 38 orange gumballs, 30 purple ones and 18 yellow ones. The dispenser operates such that one penny delivers 1 gumball.

    (a) Using three pennies, what is the probability of obtaining three gumballs in the order orange, purple and orange?
    (b) Using one penny, what is the probability of obtaining 1 gumball that is either purple or yellow?
    (c) Using three pennies, what is the probability that of the three gumballs obtained, exactly one will be purple and one will be yellow?

17. If two cards are randomly drawn from a deck of ordinary playing cards, one at a time with replacement, what is the probability of obtaining at least one ace?

18. Given a population comprised of 30 bats, 15 gloves and 60 balls, if sampling is random and one at a time without replacement, then

    (a) What is the probability of obtaining a glove, if one object is sampled from the population?

(b)   What is the probability of obtaining a bat and a ball if two objects are sampled from the population?

(c)   What is the probability of obtaining a bat, a glove and a bat in that order if three objects are sampled from the population?

19.   In rolling a die, what is the probability of obtaining either a 5 or a 6?

20.   In rolling two dice on one occasion, what is the probability of obtaining a 7 or an 11?

21.   In rolling two dice, what is the probability that neither a 2 nor a 9 will appear?

22.   In rolling two dice, what is the probability of obtaining a value less than 6?

23.   On four consecutive rolls of a die, a 6 is obtained. What is the probability of obtaining a 6 on the fifth roll?

24.   In dealing four cards without replacement from a well-shuffled deck, what is the probability of obtaining four aces?

25.   An urn contains four black and three white balls. If they are drawn without replacement, what is the probability of the order BWBWBWB?

26.   In tossing five coins, what is the probability of obtaining fewer than three heads?

27.   Assume that the intelligence and honesty are independent. If 10% of a population is intelligent and 60% is honest, what is the probability that an individual selected at random is both intelligent and honest?

28.   A coin is tossed 10 times. What is the probability that the third head will appear on the 10th toss?

29.   In a psychology class of 60 students, there are 15 males and 45 females. Of the 15 men, only 5 are freshmen. Of the 45 women, 20 are freshmen. If you randomly sample an individual from this class,

(a)   What is the probability of obtaining a female?

(b)   What is the probability of obtaining a freshmen?

(c)   What is the probability of obtaining a male freshmen?

(d)   What is the probability of obtaining a female freshmen?

(e)   What is the probability of obtaining a male?

30.   A jar contains 10 black marbles and 20 white marbles.

(a)   If you randomly select a marble from the jar, what is the probability that you will get a white marble?

(b)   If you select a random sample of $n=3$ marbles and the first two marbles are both white, what is the probability that the third marble will be black?

31.   In two throws of a coin, what is the probability of obtaining at least one head?

32.   What is the probability of obtaining exactly one head in three throws of a coin?

33.   Five coins are thrown. What is the probability that exactly two of them will be heads?

34. A box contains 10 red, 20 white and 30 blue marbles. After a thorough shaking, a blindfolded person draws out 1 marble. What is the probability that:
    (a) It is blue?
    (b) It is red or blue?
    (c) It is neither red nor blue?

35. If the probability of answering a certain question correctly is four times the probability of answering it incorrectly, what is the probability of answering it correctly?

36. If two unbiased dice are thrown, what is the probability that the number of spots showing will total 7?

37. (a) In an attitude questionnaire containing 10 statements, each to be marked as True or False, what is the probability of getting a perfect score by sheer guesswork?
    (b) Suppose you know five statements to be True and five False. What is the probability that you will mark the right ones True (select the right five)?

38. A rat has five choices to make of alternate routes in order to reach the food box. If it is true that for each choice the odds are two to one in favour of the correct pathway, what is the probability that the rat will make all of its choices correctly?

39. In seating of eight people at a table with eight chairs, what is the number of possible seating arrangements?

40. In how many ways can two people seat themselves at a table with four chairs?

41. A multiple choice test contains 100 questions. Each question has five alternatives. If a student guesses all questions, what score might he or she expect to obtain?

42. In how many ways can a committee of 3 be chosen from a group of five men?

43. What is the expected distribution of heads in tossing six coins 64 times?

44. What is the expected distribution of 6s in rolling six dice 64 times?

45. What is the probability of obtaining either nine or more heads or three or fewer heads in tossing 12 coins?

46. A man tosses six coins and rolls six dice simultaneously. What is the probability of five or more heads, and five or more 6s?

47. A coin is tossed 10 times. Assuming the coin to be unbiased, what is the probability of getting:
    (a) Four heads?
    (b) At least four heads?
    (c) At most three heads?

48. If 15 dates are selected at random, what is the probability of getting two Sundays?

49. What is the probability of getting two heads on three tosses of a fair coin?

50. Determine the probability of three late arrivals out of six workers, if there is a 0.8 chance of any one worker being late and they arrive independently of one another.

51. Find the mean and the standard deviation of the following binomial distributions:

    (a) $n=16, p=0.40$

    (b) $n=10, p=0.45$

    (c) $n=22, p=0.15$

    (d) $n=350, p=0.90$

    (e) $n=78, p=0.05$

52. The latest nationwide political poll indicates that for Indians who are randomly selected, the probability that they are conservatives is 0.55, the probability that they are liberal is 0.30 and the probability that they are middle of the road is 0.15. Assuming that these probabilities are accurate, answer the following questions pertaining to a randomly chosen group of 10 Indians:

    (a) What is the probability that four are liberal?

    (b) What is the probability that none are conservative?

    (c) What is the probability that two are middle of the road?

    (d) What is the probability that at least eight are liberal?

53. For a binomial distribution with $n=7$ and $p=0.2$, find

    (a) $p(r=5)$ (b) $p(r>2)$

    (c) $p(r<8)$ (d) $p(r\geq4)$

54. Find the mean and standard deviation of the following Poisson distribution:

    (a) $n=15, p=0.20$ (b) $n=8, p=0.42$

    (c) $n=72, p=0.06$ (d) $n=29, p=0.49$

    (e) $n=642, p=0.21$

55. Given $\mu=5$, for a Poisson distribution, find

    (a) $p(X=0)$ (b) $p(X=1)$

    (c) $p(X=2)$ (d) $p(X=3)$

    (e) $p(X=4)$ (f) $p(X=\leq3)$

    (g) $p(X=0 \text{ or } 1 \text{ or } 2)$

56. Fill in the blanks:

    (i) Probability of an event may be stated mathematically as a _____.

    (ii) Probability is defined as _____.

    (iii) The probability of an unbiased coin falling head is _____.

    (iv) The probability of a die showing a two-spot is _____.

    (v) The sample space of two coins tossing simultaneously is _____.

    (vi) If we toss three coins simultaneously, the sample space is _____.

    (vii) If H and T are mutually exclusive events, $p(HT)=$_____.

    (viii) The probability of drawing a queen from a pack of 52 cards is _____.

    (ix) The number of combinations of N things taken N at a time is _____.

    (x) Binomial distribution is the probability distribution of _____ variables.

57. Write whether the following statements are True or False.

   (i)   The number of permutations of four objects labelled A, B, C and D taken two at a time is 12.

   (ii) The number of combinations of 10 objects taken three at a time is 120.

   (iii) The formula for the variance of a binomial frequency distribution is $\sigma^2 = \sqrt{npq}$.

   (iv) In binomial distribution, it is assumed that the population is dichotomised with an intervening gap between the two classes.

   (v)   The binomial distribution is a discrete probability distribution.

   (vi) The Poisson distribution may be either unimodal or bimodal.

   (vii) The sample space of two dice thrown simultaneously is 12.

   (viii) The sample space of four coins tossing simultaneously is 8.

   (ix) The mean and variance of a Poisson distribution of rare events are different.

   (x)   The number of permutations of three objects, named as A, B and C taken 2 at a time is 6.

58. Find the correct answer from among the four alternatives:

   (i)   The probability of drawing an ace from a pack of 52 cards is:

      (a) 1/52   (b) 2/52
      (c) 4/52   (d) None of the above

   (ii) The probability of a die showing a six-spot is:

      (a) 1/6   (b) 6/6
      (c) 3/6   (d) None of the above

   (iii) The number of arrangements of 10 objects taken 3 at a time is:

      (a) 720   (b) 120
      (c) 320   (d) None of the above

   (iv) The number of combinations of 10 objects taken 3 at a time is:

      (a) 30   (b) 120
      (c) 60   (d) None of the above

   (v)   Binomial data can occur when a variable naturally exists with only:

      (a) One category   (b) Two categories
      (c) Tree categories   (d) None of the above

   (vi) The binomial distribution is a:

      (a) Discrete probability distribution
      (b) Continuous probability distribution
      (c) Either discrete or continuous probability distribution
      (d) None of the above

(vii)   Which one of the following formulae is used to compute the variances (σ^2) of a binomial frequency distribution?

(a) $\sigma^2 = np$ (b) $\sigma^2 = \sqrt{npq}$

(c) $\sigma^2 = npq$ (d) None of the above

(viii)   Poisson distribution is so named after its formulator Simon Denis Poisson, who was a:

(a) French Mathematician   (b) French Psychologist

(c) French Physiologist   (d) None of the above

(ix)   If one card is drawn from a standard pack of 52, then which one of the following is the probability that it is either a king or a queen

(a) 4/52   (b) 8/52

(c) 2/52   (d) None of the above

(x)   Which one of the following is the probability of obtaining four heads in four tosses of a coin:

(a) 1/16   (b) 1/2

(c) 1/8   (d) None of the above

CHAPTER 7

Standard Scores and the Normal Probability Curve

After completing this chapter you will be able to:

- Understand the concept of a standard score.
- Explain the characteristics, purposes and application of z-scores.
- Understand the meaning and importance of the normal distribution.
- Explain the equation of the normal probability curve (NPC).
- Describe the properties of the normal curve.
- Transfer a raw score into a z-score.
- Identify areas in a normal curve below or above a particular z-score, and also in between two z-scores.
- Measure skewness and kurtosis as divergence from normality.
- Understand the significance of skewness and kurtosis.
- Understand the process of normalising a distribution of scores.
- Explain the relationships that exist among the constants of the NPC.
- Discuss the common causes of asymmetry.
- Illustrate the various applications of the NPC.

7.1   Introduction

In Chapter 6, the binomial distribution was discussed in detail. The symmetrical binomial $(1/2 + 1/2)^{10}$ was used to illustrate the binomial expansion. Instead of considering $(1/2 + 1/2)^{10}$, we might consider the more general form $(1/2 + 1/2)^n$. As n increases in size, the distribution will approach a continuous frequency curve. This frequency curve, which is bell shaped, is the *normal curve* or *normal distribution*. The frequency distributions of many events in nature are found in practice to be approximated closely by the normal curve, and they are said to be normally distributed. Errors of measurement and errors made in estimating population values from sample values are often assumed to be normally distributed. The frequency distributions of many physical, biological and psychological measurements are observed to approximate the normal form. Because the frequency of occurrence of many events in nature can be shown empirically to conform fairly closely to the normal curve, this curve can be used as a model in dealing with problems involving these events. The present chapter discusses the normal probability curve (NPC) in detail. Before proceeding, however, with a detailed discussion of the normal curve, it may be helpful to the readers to consider briefly the meaning, characteristics, purposes and various applications of standard scores (or z-scores).

7.2   Standard Scores (z-scores)

Hitherto we have considered scores or measurements in the form in which they are originally obtained. Such scores are represented by the symbol X with mean $\bar{X}$ and standard deviation s (or σ). Such scores in their original form are spoken of as raw scores. We have also considered deviations about the arithmetic mean, $x = X - \bar{X}$. These are known as deviation scores, and have a mean of 0 and a standard deviation of s. If now we divide the deviation about the mean by the standard deviation, we obtain what is called a standard score represented by the symbol z. Thus,

$$z = \frac{X - \bar{X}}{s} = \frac{x}{s}.$$

Thus, a standard score is nothing but a z-score. A z-score is a transformed score that designates how many standard deviation units the corresponding raw score is above or below the mean.

Standard scores have a mean of 0 and a standard deviation of 1. As previously shown, if all scores in a sample are multiplied by a constant, the standard deviation is also multiplied by the absolute value of that constant. Deviation scores ($x = X - \bar{X}$) have a standard deviation s. Each score has a constant, $\bar{X}$, added. This leaves s unchanged. If all the deviation scores are divided by s, which is the same thing as multiplying by the constant, $1/s$, the standard deviation of the scores, thus, obtained is $s/s=1$.

Because standard scores have zero mean and unit standard deviation, they are readily amenable to certain forms of algebraic manipulations. Many formulations can be derived more conveniently using standard scores than using raw scores or deviation scores.

To illustrate, the following observations have been expressed in the raw score, deviation score and standard-score form.

Subjects	X	x	z
A	5	−5	−1.12
B	8	−2	−0.45
C	9	−1	−0.22
D	11	1	0.22
E	17	7	1.57
N=5			
Sum	50	00	00
Mean	10	00	00
s	4.47	4.47	1.00

The use of the standard scores means, in effect, that we are using the standard deviation as the unit of measurement. In the above example subject A is 1.12 standard deviations or standard deviation units below the mean, while subject E is 1.57 standard deviation units above the mean.

7.2.1 Characteristics of z-scores

There are three characteristics of z-scores worthwhile to note.

First, the z-scores have the same shape as the set of raw scores. Transforming the raw scores into their corresponding z-scores does not change the shape of the distribution, nor do the scores change their relative positions. All that is changed are the score values. The resulting z-scores will take on the shape of the raw scores.

Second, the mean of the z-scores always equals zero ($\bar{X}_z = 0$). This follows from the observation that the scores located at the mean of the raw scores will also be at the mean of the z-scores. The z-value for raw scores at the mean equals zero. Suppose we have 500 scores of IQ with $\bar{X} = 100$ and $\sigma = 16$. For example, the z transformation for a score that is at the mean of the IQ distribution is given by

$$z = \frac{X - \bar{X}}{\sigma} = \frac{100 - 100}{16} = 0.$$

Thus, the mean of the z-distribution equals zero.

The last characteristic of importance is that the standard deviation of z-score always equals $1 (\sigma = 1)$. This follows because a raw score that is one standard deviation above the mean has a z-score of +1.0:

$$z = \frac{(X - \bar{X})}{\sigma} = \frac{(\bar{X} + 1\sigma) - \bar{X}}{\sigma} = 1.0.$$

7.2.2 Purposes of z-scores

The original, unchanged scores that are the direct result of measurement are often called raw scores. A raw score by itself does not necessarily provide much information about its position within a distribution. To make raw scores more meaningful, or more informative, they are often transformed into new values that contain more information. This transformation is one purpose of z-scores. In particular, we will transform X values into z-scores so that the resulting z-scores tell exactly where the original scores are located.

The second purpose of the z-score is to standardise an entire distribution. A common example of a standardised distribution is the distribution of IQ scores. Although there are several different tests for measuring IQ, all of the tests are standardised so that they have a mean of 100 and a standard deviation of 15. Because all the different tests are standardised, it is possible to understand and compare IQ scores even though they come from different tests. For example, we all understand that an IQ score of 95 is a little below average, no matter which IQ test was used. Similarly, an IQ of 145 is extremely high, no matter which IQ test was used. In general terms, the process of standardising takes different distributions and makes them equivalent. The advantage of this process is that it is possible to compare distributions even though they may have been quite different before standardisation.

In summary, the process of transforming X values into z-scores serves two useful purposes:

(i) Each z-score will tell the exact location of the original X score within the distribution.

(ii) The z-score will form a standardised distribution that can be directly compared to other distributions that also have been transformed into z-scores.

Each of these purposes is discussed as follows:

(i) **z-scores and location in a distribution.** One of the primary purposes of a z-score is to describe the exact location of a score within a distribution. The z-score accomplishes this goal by transforming each X value into a signed number (+ or –) so that (a) the sign tells whether the score is located above (+) or below (–) the mean and (b) the number tells the distance between the score and the mean in terms of the number of standard deviations or standard deviation units. Thus, in a distribution of standardised IQ scores with $\bar{X} = 100$ and $\sigma = 15$, a score of $X = 130$ would be transformed into $z = +2.0$ $\left(z = \dfrac{X - \bar{X}}{\sigma} = \dfrac{130 - 100}{15} = \dfrac{30}{15} = 2.0\right)$. This z-value of +2.0 indicates that the score ($X = 130$) is located above the mean (+) by a distance of 2 standard deviations (30 points).

In toto, a z-score specifies the precise location of each X value (or raw score) within a distribution. The sign of the z-score (+ or –) signifies whether the original score is above the mean (positive) or below the mean (negative). The numerical value of the z-score specifies the distance from the mean by counting the number of standard deviations between X and $\bar{X}$.

(ii) **z-scores and the standardised distribution.** It is possible to transform every X score in a distribution into a corresponding z-score. The result of this process is that the entire distribution of X scores is transformed into a distribution of z-scores. The new distribution of z-scores has characteristics or properties (as discussed earlier) that make the z-score transformation a very useful tool.

The z-score distribution is called the standardised distribution. A standardised distribution is composed of scores that have been transformed to create predetermined values of mean ($\bar{X}$ or μ) and standard deviation (s or σ).

A z-score distribution is an example of a standardised distribution with $\bar{X}$ or $\mu = 0$ and s or $\sigma = 1$. That is, when any distribution (with any mean or standard deviation) is transformed into z-scores, the transformed distribution will always have $\bar{X} = 0$ and $\sigma = 1$. The advantage of standardising is that it makes it possible to compare different scores or different individuals even though they may come from completely different distributions.

The reader should note that the sum of squares of standard scores (Σz^2) is equal to $n - 1$. We observe that $z^2 = (X - \bar{X})^2 / s^2$; hence,

$$\sum z^2 = \frac{\sum (X - \bar{X})^2}{s^2} = \frac{\sum (X - \bar{X})^2}{\sum (X - \bar{X})^2 / n - 1} = \frac{\sum (X - \bar{X})^2 (n-1)}{\sum (X - \bar{X})^2} = n - 1.$$

The reader should note here that if s^2 is defined as $\sum (X - \bar{X})^2 / n$, then the sum of squares of standard scores is n, and not $n - 1$.

7.2.3 Applications of z-scores

The following are some of the important applications or uses of standard scores (or z-scores):

(i) **Transforming X scores into z-scores.** A particular raw score should be converted or transformed into a standard score (or z-score). The formula for transforming raw scores into z-scores is

$$z = \frac{X - \mu}{\sigma} \quad \text{(for poluation)}$$

$$z = \frac{X - \bar{X}}{s} \quad \text{(for sample)}$$

Example 7.1 A distribution of sample scores has a mean of $\bar{X} = 60$ with $s = 12$. Find the z-score for $X = 75$.

Solution

$$z = \frac{X - \bar{X}}{s} = \frac{75 - 60}{12} = \frac{15}{12} = +1.25.$$

Thus, $X = 75$ is 1.25 standard deviation units above the mean.

(ii) **Converting z-scores to X scores.** The raw scores can be determined from the z-scores. The formula for computing X values is directly obtained by solving the z-score formula for X:

$$z = \frac{X - \bar{X}}{s}$$

$zs = X - \bar{X}$ (multipy both sides by s)

$X - \bar{X} = zs$ (transpose the equation)

$X = \bar{X} + zs$ (add $\bar{X}$ to both sides)

Example 7.2 A sample distribution has a mean of $\bar{X} = 60$ and a standard deviation of $s = 12$. What raw score has $z = +0.25$?

Solution

$$X = \bar{X} + zs$$
$$= 60 + (0.25)(12)$$
$$= 60 + 3 = 63.$$

Thus, the corresponding raw score (X) of a $z = +0.25$ is 63.

(iii) **Determining the location of a raw score in a distribution.** The numerical value of the z-score specifies the distance from the mean by counting the number of standard deviations between X and $\bar{X}$. A z-score specifies the precise location of each raw score (X score) within a distribution. The sign of the z-score (+ or –) signifies whether the score is above the mean (positive) or below the mean (negative).

Example 7.3 In a sample distribution of IQ scores, $\bar{X} = 100$ and $s = 10$. What is the location of $X = 120$?

Solution

$$z = \frac{X - \bar{X}}{s} = \frac{120 - 100}{10} = \frac{20}{10} = +2.0.$$

Thus, the z-value indicates that the score ($X = 120$) is located above the mean (+) by a distance of two standard deviations (20 points).

(iv) **Standardising a distribution**. z-scores can be used to standardise an entire distribution of raw scores. Every X score in a distribution can be transformed into a corresponding z-score. The result of this process is that the entire distribution of X scores is transformed into a distribution of z-scores. Because every z-score distribution has the mean of 0 ($\bar{X}=0$ or $\mu=0$) and the standard deviation of 1 ($s=1$ or $\sigma=1$), the z-score distribution is called a standardised distribution. Such a standardised distribution gains a standard meaning, a common reference value and a comparability. Standardised distributions are used to make dissimilar distributions comparable.

(v) **Making comparisons**. Standard scores are frequently used to obtain comparability of observations obtained by different procedures. When two scores come from different distributions, it is impossible to make any direct comparison between them. Suppose, a student of psychology class received a score of $X=60$ in a psychology test and a score of $X=56$ in a statistics test. For which course should he expect the better grades?

Because the scores have come from two different distributions, we cannot make any direct comparison. Moreover, without additional information, it is even impossible to determine whether the student is above or below the mean in either distribution. Before we can begin to make comparisons, we must know the values for the mean and standard deviation for each distribution. Suppose, the psychology test scores had $\bar{X}=50$ and $s=10$, and the statistics test scores had $\bar{X}=48$ and $s=4$. With this new information, we could sketch the two distributions, locate the student's score in each distribution and compare the two locations.

An alternative procedure is to standardise the two distributions. If the psychology test score distribution and the statistics test score distribution are both transformed into z-scores, then the two distributions will both have $\bar{X}=0$ and $s=1$. In the standardised distributions, we can compare the student's z-score for psychology with his z-score for statistics because the z-scores are coming from equivalent, standardised distributions.

However, in practice, it is not necessary to transform every raw score (or X score) in a distribution to make comparisons between two scores belonging to two separate distributions. Here, we need to transform only the two scores in question. In the student's case, we must find the z-score for his psychology and statistics scores.

For psychology, the student's z-score is

$$z = \frac{X-\bar{X}}{s} = \frac{60-50}{10} = \frac{10}{10} = +1.0$$

For statistics, the student's z-score is

$$z = \frac{X-\bar{X}}{s} = \frac{56-48}{4} = \frac{8}{4} = +2.0$$

Note that the student's z-score for statistics is +2.0, which means that his test score is 2 standard deviations above the class mean. On the other hand, his z-score for psychology is +1.0, which means that his test score is 1 standard deviation above the class mean. In terms of relative class standing, the student is doing much better in the statistics class. Note that it is meaningful to make a direct comparison of the two z-scores. A z-score of +2.0 always indicates a higher position or location than a z-score of +1.0 because all z-scores or values are based on the standardised distribution with $\bar{X}$ (or μ)=0 and s (or σ)=1.

7.3   Normal Probability Curve: The Meaning and Importance of the Normal Distribution

In the eighteenth century, gamblers were interested in the chances of beating various gambling games and they asked mathematicians to help them out. DeMoivre (1733) was the first to develop the mathematical equation for the normal curve. Karl Friedrich Gauss and LaPlace (1777–1855) further developed the concept of the curve and probability. They worked on experimental errors in physics and astronomy, and found that the errors of observations made by astronomers are distributed normally. To date, the normal curve is referred to as the curve of error, the bell-shaped curve, the Gaussian curve, or DeMoivre's curve (see Figure 7.1).

A continuous frequency distribution curve, which is bell shaped, bilaterally symmetrical and unimodal, is called the normal distribution curve, or simply the normal curve. Such a curve results in plotting the frequencies (fs) of scores of a continuous measurement variable, observed in a very large sample, against the respective scores (X). The distribution of an identical shape is obtained if the relative frequencies (f/n), obtained by dividing each observed frequency by the total frequency (n), are plotted against the respective standard scores (z-scores) computed from the raw X scores, because z-scores are derived by a linear transformation of X scores $\left(z = \dfrac{X - \bar{X}}{\sigma} = \dfrac{x}{\sigma} \right)$. However, this distribution is called a normal probability distribution or NPC because its y-ordinate gives the relative frequencies or probabilities, instead of the observed frequencies, of the respective z-scores, and hence, of the corresponding X scores (see Figure 7.2).

It is apparent from Figure 7.2 even upon superficial examination that the measures are concentrated closely around the centre and taper off from this central high point or crest to the left and right. There are relatively few measures at the 'low-score' end of the scale, an increasing number up to a maximum at the middle position and a progressive falling-off towards the 'high-score' end of the scale. If we divide the area under the curve (the area between the curve and X-axis) by a line drawn perpendicularly through the central high point to the base line, the two parts, thus, formed will be similar in shape and very nearly equal in area. It is clear, therefore, that the figure exhibits almost perfect bilateral symmetry.

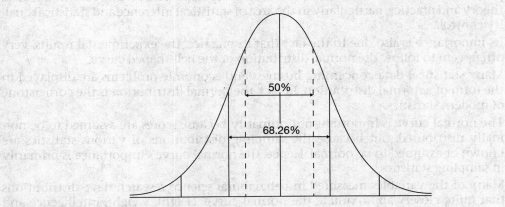

Figure 7.1   Normal distribution curve

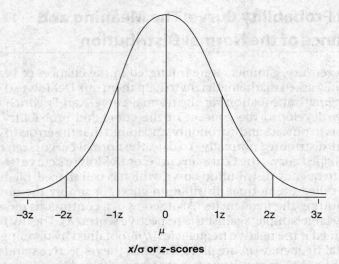

Figure 7.2 Normal probability curve (NPC)

This bell-shaped figure is called the NPC, or simply the normal curve, and is of great value in mental measurement. An understanding of the characteristics of the frequency distribution represented by the normal curve is essential to the students of experimental psychology and mental measurement.

7.3.1 Importance of the Normal Distribution

The normal curve is a very important distribution in the behavioural sciences—in psychology, education, sociology, anthropology and so on. Its importance will be clear from the following points.

(i)   The normal distribution is a continuous distribution that has long occupied a central place in the theory of statistics. It plays a very important and pivotal role in statistical theory and practice, particularly in the area of statistical inference and statistical quality control.

(ii)   Its importance is also due to the fact that in practice, the experimental results, very often seem to follow the normal distribution or the bell-shaped curve.

(iii) Many statistical data concerning business and economic problems are displayed in the form of a normal distribution. In fact, the normal distribution is the cornerstone of modern statistics.

(iv)   The normal curve is important not primarily because scores are assumed to be normally distributed, but because the sampling distributions of various statistics are known or assumed to be normal. Hence, the normal curve's importance is primarily in sampling statistics.

(v)   Many of the variables measured in behavioural science research have distributions that quite closely approximate the normal curve. Height, weight, intelligence and achievement are a few examples.

(vi)   Many of the inference tests used in analysing experiments have sampling distributions that become normally distributed with increasing sample size. The sign test and Mann–Whitney U test are two such tests, which we shall discuss later in the text.

(vii) Many inference tests require sampling distributions that are normally distributed. The z-test, student's t-test, and the F-test are examples of inference tests that depend on this point. Thus, much of the importance of the normal curve occurs in conjunction with inferential statistics.

(viii) Normal distribution occupies a prominent place in statistics because it has some properties that make it applicable to a great many situations in which it is necessary to make inferences by taking samples. Thus, the normal distribution is a useful sampling distribution.

(ix) The normal distribution comes close to fitting the actual observed frequency distributions of many phenomena, including human characteristics (weights, heights, IQs), outputs from physical processes (dimensions and yields) and other measures of interest to managers in both the public and private sectors.

(x) The normal distribution has the remarkable property stated in the central limit theorem (Lindheig and Levy, 1925). According to this theorem as the sample size n increases, the distribution of mean $\bar{X}$ of a random sample taken from practically any population approaches a normal distribution (with mean μ and standard deviation σ). Thus, if samples of large size, n, are drawn from a population that is not normally distributed, nevertheless, the successive sample means will form themselves a distribution that is approximately normal. As the size of the sample is increased, the sample means will tend to be normally distributed. The central limit theorem gives the normal distribution its central place in the theory of sampling, since many important problems can be solved by this single pattern of sampling variability. As a result, the work on statistical inferences is made simpler. This characteristic makes it possible to determine the minimum and maximum limits within which the population values lie. For example, within a range of population means $\pm 3\sigma$ (or $\mu \pm 3z$) 99.73% or almost all the items are covered.

(xi) The normal distribution has numerous mathematical properties which make it popular and comparatively easy to manipulate. For example, the moments of the normal distribution are expressed in a simple form.

(xii) The frequency distributions of many events in nature are found in practice to be approximated closely by the normal curve, and they are said to be normally distributed. Errors of measurement and errors made in estimating population values from sample values are often assumed to be normally distributed. The frequency distributions of many physical, biological and psychological measurements are observed to approximate the normal form. Because the frequency of occurrence (which is called the probability) of many events in nature can be shown empirically to conform fairly closely to the normal curve, this curve can be used as a model in dealing with problems involving these events. To date, the normal probability model is one of the most important probability models in statistical analysis.

7.3.2 Equation of the Normal Probability Curve

In tossing n coins, the frequency distribution of heads or tails is approximated more closely by the normal distribution as n increases in size. The normal curve is the limiting form of the symmetrical binomial. The NPC is a theoretical distribution of population scores. It is a bilaterally symmetrical, unimodal and bell-shaped curve that is described by the following equation. Thus, the equation for the normal curve is

$$y = \frac{N}{\sigma\sqrt{2\pi}} e^{-(x-\mu)^2/2\sigma^2}.$$

where

> y=height of the curve for particular values of X
> N=total frequency of the distribution or the total area under the curve
> π=a constant=3.1416
> σ=standard deviation of the distribution
> e=base of Napierian logarithms=a constant of 2.7183
> X=any score in the distribution
> μ=mean of the distribution.

Note that we have used the notations μ and σ in this above formula to represent the mean and standard deviation, instead of $\bar{X}$ and s, because the formula is a theoretical model. Presumably, μ and σ may be regarded as population parameters. If N, μ and σ are known, then different values of X may be substituted in the equation and the corresponding values of y obtained. If paired values of X and Y are plotted graphically, they will form a normal curve with mean μ, standard deviation σ and area N.

The normal curve is usually written in a standard score form. Standard scores have a mean of 0 and standard deviation of 1. Thus, $\mu=0$ and $\sigma=1$. The area under the curve is taken as unity, that is, $N=1$. With these substitutions, we may write the equation as follows:

$$y = \frac{1}{\sqrt{2\pi}} e^{-z^2/2}.$$

Here, z is a standard score on X and is equal to $(X-\mu)/\sigma$. The score z is a deviation in standard deviation units measured along the base line of the curve from the mean of 0, deviations to the right of the mean being positive and those to the left being negative. The curve has unit area and unit standard deviation. By substituting different values of z in the above formula, different values of y may be calculated. When $z=0$, $y = \frac{1}{\sqrt{2\pi}} = 0.3989$. This follows from the fact that $e^0=1$. Any term raised to the 0 power is equal to 1. Thus, the height of the ordinate (y) at the mean of the normal curve in a standard-score form is given by the number 0.3989. For $z=+1$, $y=0.2420$; for $z=+2$, $y=0.0540$. Similarly, the height of the curve may be calculated for any value of z. In practice, the student is not required to substitute different values of z in the normal-curve formula and solve for y to obtain the height of the required ordinate. These values may be obtained directly from Table A of the appendix. This table shows different values of y corresponding to different values of z and the area of the curve falling between the ordinates at the mean and different values of z.

The general shape of the normal curve can be observed by inspection of Figure 7.3. The curve is symmetrical. It is asymptotic at the extremities; that is, it approaches but never reaches the horizontal axis. It can be said to extend from minus infinity to plus infinity. The area under the curve is finite.

7.3.3   Properties of the Normal Curve

For reference in all cases, the unit normal curve is the standard form. It is computed taking the sample size (n), the standard deviation (σ) and the length of the class intervals (i) of the distribution as 1.0 each. The following are some of the important properties or characteristics of the normal curve:

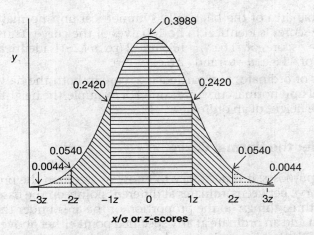

Figure 7.3   Normal curve showing the height of the ordinate at different values of x/σ or z

(i)   The unit NPC is bilaterally symmetrical. The mean, median and mode—the three measures of central tendency coincide; that is, they fall on the same point at the middle of the curve.

(ii)   The maximum ordinate of the curve occurs at the mean, that is, where $z=0$, and in the unit normal curve is equal to 0.3989.

(iii)   The curve is asymptotic. It approaches but does not meet the horizontal axis, and extends from minus infinity $(-\infty)$ to plus infinity $(+\infty)$.

(iv)   The points of inflection of the curve occur at points plus or minus one standard deviation (i.e., $\pm 1\sigma$) unit above and below the mean. Thus, the curve changes from convex to concave in relation to the horizontal axis at these points.

(v)   The area of the unit normal curve is 1 ($N=1$), standard deviation is 1($\sigma=1$), variance is 1 ($\sigma^2=1$) and mean is 0 ($\mu=0$).

(vi)   The mean lies in the middle of the curve and divides the curve into two equal halves. The total area of the NPC is within the $z\pm3\sigma$, below and above the mean.

(vii)   The curve has two tails or ends—right-hand tail or high end and left-hand tail or low end.

(viii)   The $z(x/\sigma)$ or standard score right to the mean is positive and left is negative.

(ix)   Roughly 68% of the area of the curve falls within the limits plus or minus one standard deviation ($\pm 1\sigma$) unit from the mean.

(x)   In the unit normal curve, the limits $z=\pm1.96$ include 95% and the limits $z=\pm2.58$ include 99% of the total area of the curve, 5% and 1% of the area, respectively, falling beyond these limits.

(xi)   The normal distribution gives the probable distribution of scores of a continuous measurement variable according to the laws of probability. It is, thus, a continuous probability distribution.

(xii)   The normal distribution is bilaterally symmetrical and *free from skewness*—its coefficient of skewness amounts to zero.

(xiii)   The normal distribution is taken as a standard for the degree of peakedness or kurtosis. It is *mesokurtic* with its percentile coefficient of kurtosis amounting to 0.263 and its moment coefficient being zero.

(xiv) The fractional area of the bilaterally symmetrical unit normal curve between any two given z-scores is identical in both halves of the curve. Thus, the fractional area between the z-scores of +1 (i.e., $\mu+1\sigma$) and +2 (i.e., $\mu+2\sigma$) is identical with that between the z-scores of – 1 (i.e., $\mu-1\sigma$) and –2 (i.e., $\mu-2\sigma$).

(xv) The heights of ordinates at a particular z-score in both the halves of the bilaterally symmetrical unit normal curve are same. For example, the height of an ordinate at +1z equals to the height of an ordinate at –1z.

7.3.4   Areas under the Normal Curve

For many different purposes, it is necessary to know or ascertain the proportion of the area under the normal curve between ordinates at different points on the base line (or X-axis). We may wish to know three things: (a) the proportion of the area under the curve between an ordinate at the mean and an ordinate at any specified point either above or below the mean; (b) the proportion of the total area above or below an ordinate at any point on the base line; and (c) the proportion of the area falling between ordinates at any two points on the base line.

Table A of the appendix shows the proportion of the area between the mean of the unit normal curve and ordinates extending from $z=0$ to $z=3$. Let us suppose we want to find out the area under the curve between the ordinates at $z=0$ and $z=+1.0$. We note from Table A that this area is 0.3413 of the total. Thus, approximately 34% of the total area falls between the mean and 1 standard deviation unit above the mean. The proportion of the area of the curve between $z=0$ and $z=2$ is 0.4772. Thus, about 47.7% of the area of the curve falls between the mean and 2 standard deviation units above the mean. The proportion of the area between $z=0$ and $z=3$ is 0.49865 or little less than 49.9%.

Since the unit normal curve is bilaterally symmetrical, the proportion of the area falling between $z=0$ and $z=-1$ is also 0.3413; between $z=0$ and $z=-2$ is 0.4772, and between $z=0$ and $z=-3$ is 0.49865. Therefore, the proportion of the area falling between the limits $z=\pm1$ is $0.3413+0.3413=0.6826$, or roughly 68%. The proportion of the area falling between the limits $z=\pm2$ is $0.4772+0.4772=0.9544$ or about 95%. The proportion of the area between the limits $z=\pm3$ is $0.49865+0.49865=0.9973$ or 99.73%. The area outside these latter limits is very small and is only 0.27%. For rough practical purposes, the curve is sometimes taken as extending from $z=\pm3$ (see Figure 7.4).

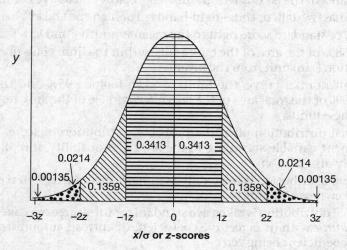

Figure 7.4 Normal curve showing areas between ordinates at different values of x/σ or z

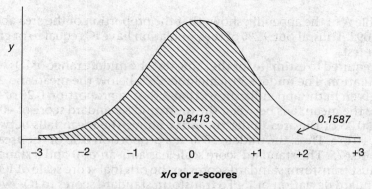

Figure 7.5   Normal curve showing area below and above a point of $z=1$

Let us now consider the determination of the proportion of the total area above or below any point on the base line of the curve. For illustration, let the point be $z=1$. We know that the proportion of area between the mean and $z=1$ is 0.3413. The proportion of the area below the mean or above the mean is 0.5000, because the entire area of the curve is 1, and the mean divides the area of the curve into two equal halves. Therefore, the proportion of the total area below $z=1$ is $0.5000+0.3413=0.8413$. Thus, the proportion of the total area above this point (i.e., above $z=1$) is $1.0000-0.8413=0.1587$ (or $0.5000-0.3413=0.1587$). Similarly, the proportion of the area above or below any point on the base line can be readily determined or ascertained (see Figure 7.5).

Let us consider the problem of finding the area between ordinates at any two points on the base line. Let us assume that we require the area between $z=0.5$ and $z=1.5$. From Table A of the appendix, we note that the proportion of the area between the mean and $z=0.5$ is 0.1915. We also note that the proportion of the area between the mean and $z=1.5$ is 0.4332. Therefore, the area between $z=0.5$ and $z=1.5$ is obtained by subtracting the lower area from the larger area, and thus it is $0.4332-0.1915=0.2417$. The area for any other segment of the curve may be similarly obtained (see Figure 7.6).

On certain occasions we wish to find the values of z which include some specified proportion of the total area. For example, the values of z above and below the mean, which include a proportion 0.95 of the area, may be required. We select a value of z above the mean which includes a proportion 0.475 ($0.95/2=0.475$) of the total area and a value of z below the mean which also includes a proportion 0.475 of the total area. From Table A of the appendix, we observe that the proportion 0.475 of the area falls between $z=0$ and $z=1.96$. Since the curve is symmetrical, the proportion 0.475 of the area falls between $z=0$ and $z=-1.96$. Thus, a proportion 0.95 or 95% of the total area falls within the limits $z=\pm1.96$. Also, a proportion 0.05 or 5% falls outside these limits. Similarly, it may be shown that 99% of the area of the curve falls within and 1% outside, the limits $z=\pm2.58$. Figure 7.7 is a normal curve showing values of z which include a proportion 0.95 of the total area.

7.3.5   Areas under the Normal Curve—Illustrative Example

The distribution of IQ scores obtained by the application of a particular test is approximately normal with a mean of 100 and standard deviation of 15. We are required to estimate what percentage of individuals in the population have IQs of 120 and above. First of all, we will find out the z transformation of the IQ score of 120. The IQ of 120 in standard score form is $z=(120-100)/15=1.33$. Thus, an IQ of 120 is 1.33 standard deviation units above the mean.

Reference to Table A in the appendix shows that the proportion of the area above a standard score of 1.33 is 0.092. Thus, about 9.2% of the population have IQs equal to or greater than 120 in this particular test.

We are also required to estimate for the same test the middle range of IQs which includes 50% of the population. The middle 50% includes 25% below the mean and 25% above the mean. Table A given in the appendix shows that 25% or a proportion 0.25 of the area under the curve below the mean falls between the mean and a standard score of −0.675. Also 25% or a proportion 0.25 of the area under the curve above the mean falls between the mean and a z-score of +0.675. Thus, the middle 50% or a proportion 0.50 of the area falls between the limits of $z = ±0.675$. The standard score scale has a mean of 0 and a standard deviation of 1. Here, we must transform standard scores to the original score scale of IQs with a mean of 100 and a standard deviation of 15. To transform standard scores to IQs, we multiply the standard score by 15 and add 100. That means, $X = z\sigma + \mu$ .The IQ score below the mean is $(−0.675)(15) + 100 = 100 − 10.125 = 89.875 = 90$. The IQ score above the mean is $(+0.675)(15) + 100 = 10.125 + 100 = 110.125 = 110$. Thus, we estimate that about 50% of the populations have IQs within a range of roughly 90–110. Therefore, from a normal curve we can find out the areas corresponding to any raw score and also find out the raw score corresponding to a given area.

7.4   Measuring Divergence from Normality

A normal distribution is described as an exactly perfect bell-shaped curve. However, such a perfect symmetrical curve rarely exists in our actual dealings as we usually cannot measure an entire population. Instead, we work on representative samples of the population. Therefore, in actual practice, the slightly deviated or distorted bell-shaped curve is also accepted as the normal curve on the assumption of normal distribution of the characteristics measured in the entire population.

From the above discussion, it should not be assumed that the distribution of the data in all cases will always lead to normal or approximately normal curves. In the cases where the scores of the individuals in the group seriously deviate from the average, the curves representing these distributions also deviate from the shape of a normal curve. This deviation or divergence from normality tends to vary in two ways: in terms of *skewness* and in terms of *kurtosis*. The *skewness* and *kurtosis* are known as the two types of errors of the normal distribution, which have been discussed in the following.

7.4.1   Skewness

In some frequency distributions, scores are concentrated at one end of the scale and are much fewer towards the other end. Such an asymmetric distribution has its peak or mode towards the former end and a longer and more pointed tail at the other end. Such a distribution is called a *skewed distribution. Skewness* is the degree of asymmetry of the distribution.

7.4.1.1   *Properties of Skewed Distributions*

The following are some of the crucial characteristics or properties of the skewed distributions.

(a)   A skewed distribution cannot be bisected into two symmetrical halves, because one of its tails is longer and more tapering than the other.

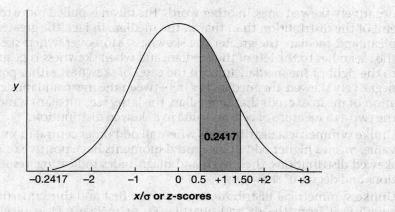

Figure 7.6   Normal curve showing area between ordinates of $z=0.5$ and $z=1.5$

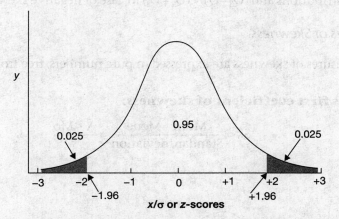

Figure 7.7   Normal curve showing value of z which includes a proportion 0.95 of the total area

(b) Skewness may be positive or negative accordingly as the pointed longer tail rolls down to the high-value (right) end or the low-value (left) end of the scale, respectively. The scores are more concentrated towards the respective opposite ends of the scale.

In other words, a distribution is said to be *skewed* when the three measures of central tendency fall at different points in the distribution, and the balance (or centre of gravity) is shifted to one side or the other—to left or right. A distribution is said to be *positively skewed* or skewed to the right when scores are massed at the low (or left) end of the scale and are spread out gradually towards the high or right end as shown in Figure 7.8. A distribution is said to be *negatively skewed* or skewed to the left when scores are massed at the high end of the scale (the right end) and are spread out more gradually towards the low end (or left) as shown in Figure 7.9.

(c) The mean, median and mode fail to coincide in an asymmetric distribution. Both median and mean are displaced from the mode towards the skewed tail, but the displacement of the mean considerably exceeds that of the median. So, Mean > Median > Mode in positively skewed distributions, while Mode > Median > Mean in negatively skewed ones. In other words, the mean is pulled more towards the skewed end of the distribution than that of the median. In fact, the greater the gap between mean and median, the greater the skewness. Moreover, when skewness is negative, the mean lies to the left of the median; and when skewness is positive, the mean lies to the right of the median. In both the cases of skewness, either positively skewed or negatively skewed, the median lies in between the mean and mode. Because the deviation of mean exceeds that of median, the latter (i.e., median) is more dependable on the two as a measure of central value in a skewed distribution.

(d) Unlike symmetrical distributions where all odd-order central moments possess a zero value, m_3 and higher odd-order central moments have positive or negative values in skewed distributions, their signs and magnitudes indicating, respectively, the directions and degree of skewness.

(e) Unlike symmetrical distributions where the first and third quartiles (Q_1 and Q_3) are equidistant from the second quartile (Q_2 or median), Q_1 is displaced towards the skewed tail in an asymmetric distribution. Therefore, $(Q_3 - Q_2) > (Q_2 - Q_1)$ in positively skewed distributions and $(Q_3 - Q_2) < (Q_2 - Q_1)$ in case of negative skewness.

7.4.1.2   Measures of Skewness

The following measures of skewness are expressed in pure numbers, free from the unit of the variable.

(a) **Pearson's first coefficient of skewness:**

$$Sk = \frac{\text{Mean} - \text{Mode}}{\text{Standard deviation}} = \frac{\bar{X} - Mo}{s}.$$

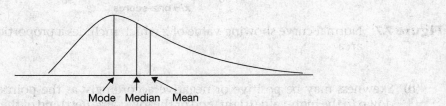

Mode Median Mean

Figure 7.8   Positive skewness (the curve inclines more to the right)

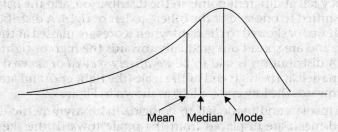

Mean   Median   Mode

Figure 7.9   Negative skewness (the curve inclines more to the left)

(b) Pearson's second coefficient of skewness:

$$Sk = \frac{3(\text{Mean} - \text{Median})}{\text{Standard deviation}} = \frac{3(\bar{X} - \text{Mdn})}{s}.$$

The second coefficient is preferable to the first because of the difficulty in estimating the mode of a distribution precisely.

In symmetric distributions like normal distribution, $\bar{X} = \text{Mdn} = \text{Mo}$; so both the coefficients of Pearson amount to zero in such distributions.

(c) Bowley's quartile coefficients of skewness:

$$Sk = \frac{(Q_3 - Q_2) - (Q_2 - Q_1)}{(Q_3 - Q_1)} = \frac{(Q_3 - Q_2) - (Q_2 - Q_1)}{2Q},$$

where Q is the quartile deviation.

In symmetric distributions like normal distribution, $Q_3 - Q_2 = Q_2 - Q_1$; so the quartile coefficient amounts to zero in such distributions.

(d) Moment coefficient of skewness (γ_1 or g_1):

$\gamma_1 = \dfrac{m_3}{s^3}$, where the third moment m_3 about the mean is divided by the third power of the standard deviation (s). The other formula reads as follows:

$$g_1 = \frac{m_3}{m_2 \sqrt{m_2}},$$

where the third moment m_3 about the mean is divided by the quantity $m_2 \sqrt{m_2}$, the second moment m_2 about the mean. Because the m_3 amounts to 0 for a symmetric distribution, γ_1 or g_1 has a zero value for symmetric distributions like a normal distribution.

(e) Percentile coefficient of skewness:

$$Sk = \frac{(P_{90} + P_{10})}{2} - P_{50}.$$

For all the five coefficients of skewness, a value of 0 indicates a symmetrical distribution without skewness. A positive or negative value indicates, respectively, a positive or negative skewness. The degree of skewness is given by the magnitude of the coefficient.

Example 7.4 Compute the Pearson's second coefficient of skewness for a frequency distribution of alpha scores having a mean of 170.8, standard deviation of 12.63 and median of 172.0.

Solution $\bar{X} = 170.8$, $s = 12.63$, $\text{Mdn} = 172.0$.

$$\therefore Sk = \frac{3(\bar{X} - \text{Mdn})}{s} = \frac{3(170.8 - 172.0)}{12.63}$$

$$= \frac{3(-1.2)}{12.63} = \frac{-3.6}{12.63} = -0.28.$$

This slight negative skewness shows that the distribution is slightly negatively skewed, and the distribution of data approaches the normal form.

Example 7.5 Calculate the percentile coefficient of skewness for a frequency distribution of differential aptitude test scores of 50 students, having $P_{10}=152.0$, $P_{50}=172.0$ and $P_{90}=187.0$.

Solution $P_{10}=152.0$; $P_{50}=172.0$; $P_{90}=187.0$.

$$Sk = \frac{(P_{90}+P_{10})}{2} - P_{50} = \frac{(187.0+152.0)}{2} - 172.0$$

$$= \frac{339.0}{2} - 172.0 = 169.5 - 172.0 = -2.5.$$

This obtained skewness of –2.5 shows that the distribution of data is a negatively skewed curve.

Example 7.6 Compute the quartile coefficient of skewness for the frequency distribution of human body weights, having Q_1, Q_2 and Q_3, respectively, 60.4, 63.3 and 65.8 kg.

Solution $Q_1=60.4\,kg$; $Q_2=63.3\,kg$; $Q_3=65.8\,kg$.

$$\therefore Sk = \frac{(Q_3-Q_2)-(Q_2-Q_1)}{(Q_3-Q_1)} = \frac{(65.8-63.3)-(63.3-60.4)}{(65.8-60.4)}$$

$$= \frac{2.5-2.9}{5.4} = \frac{-0.4}{5.4} = -0.074.$$

$$or\ Q = \frac{Q_3-Q_1}{2} = \frac{65.8-60.4}{2} = \frac{5.4}{2} = 2.7$$

$$Sk = \frac{(Q_3-Q_2)-(Q_2-Q_1)}{2Q} = \frac{(65.8-63.3)-(63.3-60.4)}{2\times 2.7}$$

$$= \frac{2.5-2.9}{5.4} = \frac{-0.4}{5.4} = -0.074.$$

This slight negative skewness shows that the distribution of body weights is slightly negatively skewed and it closely approaches the normal form.

Example 7.7 Find out the moment coefficient of skewness for a distribution of test scores having $m_3=10.80$, $m_2=9.20$ and $s=3.03$.

Solution $m_3=10.80$; $m_2=9.20$; $s=3.03$.

$$Sk = \gamma_1 = \frac{m_3}{s^3} = \frac{10.80}{(3.03)^3} = \frac{10.80}{27.82} = +0.388.$$

$$or\ Sk = g_1 = \frac{m_3}{m_2\sqrt{m_2}} = \frac{10.80}{9.20\sqrt{9.20}} = \frac{10.80}{9.20\times 3.03} = \frac{10.80}{27.88} = +0.387.$$

The difference between γ_1 and g_1 is quite negligible, that is (0.388–0.387), 0.001, which might be due to the rounding up of the decimal points. However, the distribution of scores is a positively skewed curve.

Example 7.8 Compute the moment coefficient of skewness for the following set of scores: 6, 8, 10, 16 and 20.

Solution

Scores (X)	($X - \bar{X}$)	($X - \bar{X}$)²	($X - \bar{X}$)³
6	–6	36	–216
8	–4	16	–64
10	–2	4	–8
16	4	16	64
20	8	64	512
$n=5$ 60 $\Sigma(X)$	0 $\Sigma(X-\bar{X})$	136 $\Sigma(X-\bar{X})^2$	288 $\Sigma(X-\bar{X})^3$

$$\bar{X} = \frac{\sum X}{n} = \frac{60}{5} = 12.0$$

$$SD = \sqrt{\frac{\sum(X-\bar{X})^2}{n}} = \sqrt{\frac{136}{5}} = \sqrt{27.2} = 5.21$$

$$m_2 = \frac{\sum(X-\bar{X})^2}{n} = \frac{136}{5} = 27.2$$

$$m_3 = \frac{\sum(X-\bar{X})^3}{n} = \frac{288}{5} = 57.6.$$

Moment coefficient of skewness (γ_1 or g_1):

$$Sk = \gamma_1 = \frac{m_3}{s^3} = \frac{57.6}{(5.21)^3} = \frac{57.6}{141.42} = 0.407$$

or

$$\therefore Sk = g_1 = \frac{m_3}{m_2\sqrt{m_2}} = \frac{57.6}{27.2\sqrt{27.2}} = \frac{57.2}{27.2 \times 5.21} = \frac{57.6}{141.71} = 0.406.$$

The amounts of skewness obtained by γ_1 and g_1 are almost similar; the difference between these two is very negligible, which may be due to the rounding up of the decimals. However, it is a positively skewed set of numbers.

7.4.2   Kurtosis

The term 'kurtosis' refers to the *flatness* or *peakedness* of a frequency distribution as compared with the normal distribution. Kurtosis is usually of three types: *mesokurtic, leptokurtic* and *platykurtic.* The normal distribution is said to be *mesokurtic* and its peakedness of a medium

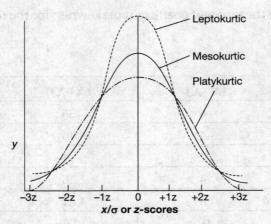

Figure 7.10   Different forms of kurtosis–leptokurtic, mesokurtic and platykurtic curves

order is taken as the standard (see Figure 7.10). A frequency distribution more peaked than the normal is said to be *leptokurtic;* the one flatter than the normal is called *platykurtic.*

A *leptokurtic* distribution has a higher peak, thicker tails and a narrower body than the normal distribution. Thus, a leptokurtic distribution has higher frequencies of scores near its centre and at its two tails than that of a normal distribution with the same mean and variance, but has lower frequencies of scores of intermediate magnitudes.

A *platykurtic* distribution is flatter at its centre, broader in the body and thinner at the tails than that of the normal distribution because compared to the latter, the former carries lower frequencies of scores near its centre and its tails, but higher frequencies of scores of intermediate magnitudes.

7.4.2.1   *Measures of Kurtosis*

(a)   Percentile coefficient of kurtosis (Ku):

$$Ku = \frac{P_{75} - P_{25}}{2(P_{90} - P_{10})} \text{ or } Ku = \frac{Q}{(P_{90} - P_{10})}.$$

For mesokurtic, platykurtic and leptokurtic distributions, kurtosis amount is equal to 0.263, >0.263 and <0.263, respectively. In other words, the amount of kurtosis for a normal curve is 0.263. If the value of kurtosis is greater than 0.263, the distribution is said to be platykurtic, and if the value is less than 0.263, the distribution is called leptokurtic.

(b)   Moment coefficient of kurtosis (γ_2 or g_2):

$$g_2 = \frac{m_4}{m_2^2} - 3; \quad \gamma_2 = \frac{m_4}{s^4} - 3,$$

where s is the standard deviation (SD), and m_2 and m_4 are, respectively, the second and fourth central moments about the mean. For mesokurtic, platykurtic and leptokurtic distributions, γ_2 or g_2 amounts to zero, a negative value and a positive value, respectively. The number 3 comes about because the ratio $m_4 / m_2^2 = 3$ for a normal distribution. This means that $g_2 = 0$ for a normal distribution. For a leptokurtic distribution, g_2 is greater than zero, and for a playkurtic distribution, g_2 is less than zero.

Example 7.9 Compute the percentile coefficient of kurtosis for a frequency distribution of achievement test scores, having a 10th percentile of 152.0, a 25th percentile of 162.62, a 75th percentile of 179.19 and a 90th percentile of 187.0.

Solution $P_{10}=152.0$; $P_{25}=162.62$; $P_{75}=179.19$; $P_{90}=187.0$.

$$\therefore Ku = \frac{P_{75} - P_{25}}{2(P_{90} - P_{10})} = \frac{179.19 - 162.62}{2(187.0 - 152.0)} = \frac{16.57}{2 \times 35} = \frac{1657}{70} = 0.237.$$

or $P_{25}=Q_1=162.62$; $P_{75}=Q_3=179.19$.

$$Q = \frac{Q_3 - Q_1}{2} = \frac{179.19 - 162.62}{2} = \frac{167.57}{2} = 8.285$$

$$Ku = \frac{Q}{P_{90} - P_{10}} = \frac{8.285}{187.0 - 152.0} = \frac{8.285}{35} = 0.237.$$

Since the obtained Ku is less than 0.263, the distribution is slightly leptokurtic.

Example 7.10 Calculate the percentile coefficient of kurtosis for a frequency distribution of differential aptitude test scores, having $P_{10}=80.60$, $P_{25}=88.89$, $P_{75}=108.15$ and $P_{90}=116.03$.

Solution $P_{10}=80.60$, $P_{25}=88.89$, $P_{75}=108.15$ and $P_{90}=116.03$.

$$\therefore Ku = \frac{P_{75} - P_{25}}{2(P_{90} - P_{10})} = \frac{108.15 - 88.89}{2(116.03 - 80.60)} = \frac{19.26}{2 \times 35.43} = \frac{19.26}{70.86} = 0.272.$$

Since the obtained Ku exceeds 0.263, the distribution is slightly platykurtic.

Example 7.11 Calculate the moment coefficient of kurtosis (g_2) for a distribution of test scores whose second and fourth central moments about the mean are 8.0 and 108.80, respectively.

Solution $m_2=8.0$; $m_4=108.80$.

$$\therefore g_2 = \frac{m_4}{m_2^2} - 3 = \frac{108.80}{(8.0)^2} - 3 = \frac{108.80}{64.00} - 3 = 1.7 - 3 = -1.3.$$

Since the obtained g_2 is negative, the distribution is platykurtic.

Example 7.12 Compute the moment coefficient of kurtosis for the following set of scores: 6, 9, 10, 11 and 14.

Solution

Scores (X)	$(X-\bar{X})$	$(X-\bar{X})^2$	$(X-\bar{X})^4$
6	−4	16	216
9	−1	1	1
10	0	0	0
11	1	1	1
14	4	16	216
$n=5$ 50 (ΣX)	0 $\Sigma(X-\bar{X})$	34 $\Sigma(X-\bar{X})^2$	434 $\Sigma(X-\bar{X})^4$

$$\bar{X} = \frac{\sum X}{n} = \frac{50}{5} = 10.0$$

$$SD = \sqrt{\frac{\sum(X - \bar{X})^2}{n}} = \sqrt{\frac{34}{5}} = \sqrt{6.8} = 2.61$$

$$m_2 = \frac{\sum(X - \bar{X})^2}{n} = \frac{34}{5} = 6.8$$

$$m_4 = \frac{\sum(X - \bar{X})^4}{n} = \frac{434}{5} = 86.8.$$

Moment coefficient of kurtosis (γ_2 or g_2):

$$g_2 = \frac{m_4}{m_2^{\,2}} - 3 = \frac{86.8}{(6.8)^2} - 3 = \frac{86.8}{46.24} - 3 = 1.88 - 3 = -1.12.$$

or

$$\gamma_2 = \frac{m_4}{S^4} - 3 = \frac{86.8}{(2.61)^4} - 3 = \frac{86.8}{46.40} - 3 = 1.87 - 3 = -1.13.$$

The amounts of kurtosis obtained by γ_2 and g_2 are almost similar; the difference between these two is very much negligible, which may be due to the rounding up of the decimals. However, it is a platykurtic set of numbers, because the amount of kurtosis is negative.

7.5   Normalising a Distribution of Scores

The process of normalising a distribution of scores is demonstrated below. From the results, the normal curve for the data will be plotted; this normal curve for any set of data will be referred to as the curve of best fit for that set of data. The best-fitting curve for any set of data has the same mean ($\bar{X}$) and standard deviation (s), and is based upon the same number of cases (n) as the original data. Such a best-fitting normal distribution can be computed as follows:

(a)   The observed scores are arranged in a continuous frequency distribution with class intervals of equal length (i).

(b)   The midpoint (X_c) of each class interval as well as $\bar{X}$ and s of the sample is computed.

(c)   Each X_c is transformed into a z-score by the formula that reads as follows:

$$z = \frac{X_c - \bar{X}}{s}.$$

(d)   The unit normal-curve table (Table A in the appendix) is used to find the height of the ordinate (y) of the unit normal curve at each computed z-score.

(e)   The expected frequency of each class interval of the best-fitting normal distribution is computed in the following way (see Table 7.1):

$$fe = \left(\frac{in}{s}\right)y.$$

Table 7.1   Normalising a distribution of scores: Computation of the best-fitting normal distribution

(1)	(2)	(3)	(4)	(5)	(6)	(7)
Class intervals	f_o	X_c	$X_c - \bar{X}$	z	y	fe
90–94	1	92	28.1	2.30	0.0283	1.7
85–89	3	87	23.1	1.89	0.0669	4.1
80–84	8	82	18.1	1.48	0.1334	8.2
75–79	12	77	13.1	1.07	0.2251	13.8
70–74	28	72	8.1	0.66	0.3209	19.7
65–69	36	67	3.1	0.25	0.3867	23.8
60–64	12	62	–1.9	–0.16	0.3939	24.2
55–59	18	57	–6.9	–0.57	0.3391	20.8
50–54	10	52	–11.9	–0.97	0.2492	15.3
45–49	8	47	–16.9	–1.38	0.1539	9.5
40–44	8	42	–21.9	–1.79	0.0804	4.9
35–39	5	37	–26.9	–2.20	0.0355	2.2
30–34	1	32	–31.9	–2.61	0.0132	0.8
	$n=150$					Σfe$=149.0$

(f)   Each fe may be graphically plotted against the X_c of the corresponding class interval for drawing the best-fitting normal curve.

Example 7.13 A psychological test yields a distribution of scores of 150 students as follows with a mean of 63.9 and a standard deviation of 12.2. Compute the expected frequencies of the best-fitting normal distribution.

Class Intervals	30–34	35–39	40–44	45–49	50–54	55–59	60–64	65–69	70–74	75–79	80–84	85–89	90–94
Frequencies	1	5	8	8	10	18	12	36	28	12	8	3	1

Solution

(a)   The data are arranged in the first two columns of Table 7.1. Column 1 lists the intervals and Column 2 shows the observed frequencies (f_o).

$$N=150, \quad \bar{X}=63.9, \quad s=12.2, \quad i=5.$$

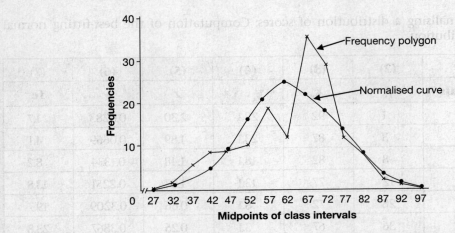

Figure 7.11 Frequency polygon and normalised curve for the data in Table 7.1

(b) The midpoint (X_c) of each class interval is computed and recorded in Column 3 of Table 7.1.

(c) The deviation of each midpoint (X_c) from the mean ($\bar{X}$) is calculated and recorded in Column 4.

(d) Each deviation score ($x = X_c - \bar{X}$) is transformed into the z-score by dividing it by the standard deviation (s). For example, for the interval 90–94,

$$z = \frac{X_c - \bar{X}}{s} = \frac{92 - 63.9}{12.2} = \frac{28.1}{12.2} = 2.30.$$

These z-scores corresponding to each interval are recorded in Column 5 of Table 7.1.

(e) The height (y) of the ordinate at each computed z-score, neglecting the algebraic sign of the latter, is then recorded from the unit normal-curve table (Table A given in the appendix). For example, for the z-score of 2.30, $y = 0.0283$. These heights of ordinates are recorded in Column 6.

(f) The expected frequency (fe) of the best-fitting normal distribution is computed for each z-score by multiplying its y-score with a ratio of in/s, which is a constant for all z-scores in the distribution. For example, for the class interval 90–94,

$$\frac{in}{s} = \frac{5 \times 150}{12.2} = 61.5;\ fe = y \times \frac{in}{s} = 0.0283 \times 61.5 = 1.7.$$

The computed expected frequencies (fe) correspond to the height of the ordinate at the z-scores in the respective class intervals of the best-fitting normal distribution. These computed expected frequencies (fe) are recorded in Column 7 of Table 7.1.

(g) In Figure 7.11, the axes have been set up in the usual manner for constructing a frequency polygon. First the f_o's are plotted and these points connected with a rule as in the usual method for plotting a frequency polygon. Then the values of fe's in Column 7 are plotted and these are connected by means of a smooth curve. In Figure 7.11, we have the curve of best fit for these data superimposed upon the frequency polygon for the original data; the f_o's and fe's are plotted against the midpoints of the respective class intervals.

7.6   Relationships among the Constants of the NPC

Instead of σ, the Q may be used as the unit of measurement in determining areas within given parts of the normal curve. In the NPC, the quartile deviation (Q) is generally called the probable error (PE). The relationship between the PE and σ is given in the following equations:

$$PE = 0.6745\sigma$$

$$\sigma = 1.4826 \ PE$$

from which it is seen that σ is always about 50% larger than the PE.

7.7   Applications of the Normal Probability Curve

The NPC has wide significance and applications in the field of measurement concerning behavioural sciences. Some of its important applications are discussed in the following text with illustrative examples. The solution of the problems given in these examples requires the knowledge of the conversion of raw scores into z-scores and vice versa, and the knowledge of how to use the normal-curve table (Table A given in the appendix) for finding out the fractional parts of the total area of the curve in relation to sigma (σ) distances.

1. To determine the percentage of cases in a normal distribution below, above or within given limits.

Example 7.14 Let us assume that IQs are normally distributed in the population with a mean of 100 and a standard deviation of 15. Find the percentage of people with IQs (a) below 90, (b) above 120 and (c) between 75 and 125.

Solution

(a) $\bar{X} = 100$, $\sigma = 15$. First of all, the raw score 90 should be transformed into a z-score.

$$\text{z-score equivalent to raw score } 90 = \frac{X - \bar{X}}{s} = \frac{90 - 100}{15} = \frac{-10}{15} = -0.67.$$

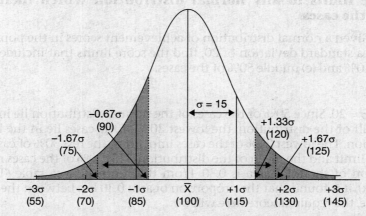

Figure 7.12   Showing the percentage of cases below 90, above 120 and between 75 and 125

The score 90 falls at $-0.67z$ below the mean. From the normal-curve table (Table A in the appendix), it is found that the proportion of area that lies between $\bar{X}$ and $-0.67z$ is 0.2486. Hence, the proportion of area that lies below $-0.67z$ is 0.2514 (i.e., 0.5000 – 0.2486), because the unit normal curve is a bilaterally symmetrical curve, and each half below and above the mean contains an area of 0.5. Therefore, 25.14% of people have IQs below 90, and the chances are about 25 in 100 that any score in the distribution will be less than 90 (see Figure 7.12).

(b) $\bar{X}=100$, $\sigma=15$. First of all, the raw score 120 should be transformed into a z-score.

$$z\text{-score equivalent to raw score } 120 = \frac{X - \bar{X}}{\sigma} = \frac{120 - 100}{15} = \frac{20}{15} = 1.33.$$

Thus, the score 120 falls at $1.33z$ above the mean. From the normal-curve table (Table A), it is found that the proportion of the total area lies between $\bar{X}$ and $1.33z$ is 0.4082. Hence, the proportion of area lies above $+1.33z$ is 0.0918 (i.e., 0.5000 – 0.4082). Therefore, 9.18% of people have IQs above 120, and the chances are about 9 in 100 that any score in the distribution will be larger than 120 (see Figure 7.12).

(c) $\bar{X}=100$, $\sigma=15$. First of all the raw scores 75 and 125 should be transformed into their respective z-scores.

$$z\text{-score equivalent to raw score } 75 = \frac{X - \bar{X}}{\sigma} = \frac{75 - 100}{15} = \frac{-25}{15} = -1.67.$$

$$z\text{-score equivalent to raw score } 125 = \frac{X - \bar{X}}{\sigma} = \frac{125 - 100}{15} = \frac{25}{15} = +1.67.$$

From the normal-curve table (Table A), it is found that the proportion of the total area lies between the $\bar{X}$ and $-1.67z$ is 0.4525. Since the normal curve is bell shaped and bilaterally symmetrical, the proportion of the total area lies between the $\bar{X}$ and $+1.67z$ is also 0.4525. Hence, the proportion of the total area lies between $-1.67z$ and $+1.67z$ is 0.9050 (i.e., 0.4525 + 0.4525). Therefore, 90.5% of people have IQs between 75 and 125, and the chances are about 90 in 100 that any score in the distribution will be found between 75 and 125 (see Figure 7.12).

2. To find the limits in any normal distribution which include a given percentage of the cases.

Example 7.15 Given a normal distribution of achievement scores in the population with a mean of 100 and a standard deviation of 20, find the score limits that include the (a) lowest 20%, (b) highest 10% and (c) middle 50% of the cases.

Solution

(a) $\bar{X} = 100$; $\sigma = 20$. Since 50% of the cases of the normal distribution lie in the right half or left half of the distribution, the lowest 20% of the cases lie in the left half of the distribution. The lowest 20% of the cases imply that the rest 30% of cases lie between its lower limit and the mean of the distribution. This 30% of the cases means that the proportion of the total area is 0.30. From the normal-curve table (Table A in the appendix), it is found that the proportion of area 0.30 lies between the $\bar{X}$ and -0.84σ. Therefore, the required score here will be

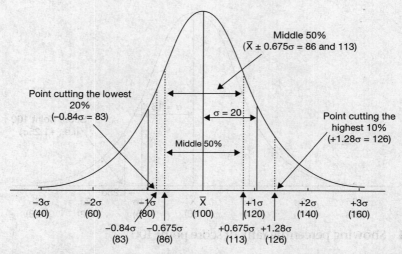

Figure 7.13 Showing the score limits that include lowest 20%, highest 10% and middle 50% of the cases

$$X = \bar{X} + z\sigma = 100 + (-0.84 \times 20) = 100 - 16.8 = 83.2 \text{ or } 83.$$

Here, we will discuss about the limits in terms of scores which include the lowest 20% of the cases. The upper limit of these cases may now be given by the score point 83.2 or 83, and the lower limit will be the lowest score of the distribution. In other words, we may say that the lowest 20% of the distribution lies below the score 83.2 or 83 (see Figure 7.13).

(b) $\bar{X} = 100$; $\sigma = 20$. The highest 10% of the cases lie in the right half of the distribution, and these highest 10% imply that 40% of the cases lie between its lower limit and the mean of the distribution. This 40% of the cases means that the proportion of the total area is 0.40. From the normal-curve table (Table A), we know that 0.3997 proportion of area lies between the mean and 1.28σ. Therefore, the lower score limit of the highest 10% of the cases is

$$X = \bar{X} + z\sigma = 100 + (1.28 \times 20) = 100 + 25.6 = 125.6 \text{ or } 126.$$

Thus, the lower score limit of the highest 10% of the cases of the distribution is 125.6 or 126 and its upper score limit will be the highest score of the distribution. In other words, we may say that the highest 10% of the cases of the distribution lies above the score 125.6 or 126 (see Figure 7.13).

(c) $\bar{X} = 100$; $\sigma = 20$. The middle 50% of the cases in a normal distribution include the 25% just above and the 25% just below the mean. The 25% of the cases means that the proportion of the total area is 0.25. From Table A of the appendix, we find that 0.25 area of the distribution lies between the mean and 0.675σ, and of course, 0.25 area of the distribution also lies between the mean and −0.675σ. The middle 50% of the cases (or proportion of the total area 0.50), therefore, lie between the mean and ±0.675σ. Thus, the score limits that include the middle 50% (or proportion of area 0.50) of the distribution are

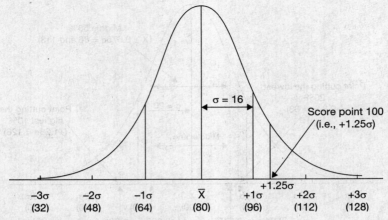

Figure 7.14   Showing percentile rank of score point 100

$$\bar{X} \pm 0.675\sigma$$

or $\bar{X} - 0.675\sigma$ and $\bar{X} + 0.675\sigma$

or $100 - (0.675 \times 20)$ and $100 + (0.675 \times 20)$

or $100 - 13.5$ and $100 + 13.5$

or 86.5 and 113.5 or 86 and 113.

Hence, the middle 50% of the cases in the given distribution lie between the scores 86.5 and 113.5 (i.e., 86.5 is the lower limit and 113.5 is the upper limit). This is depicted in Figure 7.13.

3. To determine the percentile ranks of individuals.

Example 7.16 Given a normal distribution with $\bar{X} = 80$ and $\sigma = 16$, find the percentile rank of an individual scoring 100.

Solution $\bar{X} = 80$; $\sigma = 16$; $X = 100$.

The percentile rank, as we know, is essentially a rank or position of an individual (on a scale of 100) decided on the basis of the individual's score. In other words, here we have to determine the percentage of cases lying below the score point 100. For this, let us first transform the raw score into the standard z-score with the help of the following formula:

$$z = \frac{X - \bar{X}}{\sigma} = \frac{100 - 80}{16} = \frac{20}{16} = +1.25.$$

Now, we have to determine the total percentage of cases lying below $+1.25\sigma$. From the normal-curve table (Table A), we find that the proportion of area that lies between $\bar{X}$ and $+1.25\sigma$ is 0.3944. Thus, the proportion of the total area below $+1.25\sigma$ is equal to the total proportion of area in the left half of the distribution plus the proportion of area between the $\bar{X}$ and 1.25σ. Hence, the total area below $+1.25\sigma = 0.5000 + 0.3944 = 0.8944$, which means 89.44% of individuals whose scores lie below the score point 100. Therefore, we may say that the percentile rank of an individual scoring 100 is 89 (see Figure 7.14).

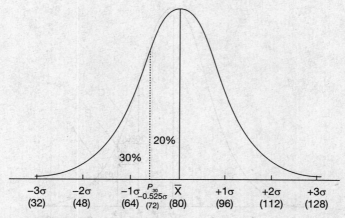

Figure 7.15   Showing score point of percentile P_{30}

4. To determine the percentile points in terms of scores of a given percentage of cases.

Example 7.17 Given a normal distribution with a mean of 80 and standard deviation of 16, determine the percentile P_{30}.

Solution $\bar{X} = 80$; $\sigma = 16$.

In determining P_{30}, we have to find out a score point below which 30% of the cases lie. In the NPC (see Figure 7.15), these 30% of cases fall in the left half. This implies that the rest 20% of cases lie on the left side of the mean. From the table of normal curve (Table A), it is found that 20% of cases or the proportion of area 0.20 lie between the mean and −0.525σ. Therefore, the required score is

$$X = \bar{X} - 0.525\sigma = 80 - 0.525 \times 16 = 80 - 8.4 = 71.6 \text{ or } 72.$$

Therefore, the score point of P_{30} is 72.

5. To compare scores on two different tests.

Example 7.18 A student obtains 90 marks in Mathematics and 50 marks in English. If the mean and standard deviation for the scores in Mathematics are 70 and 20, and for the scores in English are 30 and 10, respectively, in which subject he did better?

Solution From the given data, direct comparison of his relative status in Mathematics and in English cannot be made because the marks achieved by him do not belong to the same scale of measurement. Therefore, his raw scores in both the subjects should be transformed into a common scale—a standard z-score.

In Mathematics: $X = 90$; $\bar{X} = 70$; $\sigma = 20$.

$$z = \frac{X - \bar{X}}{\sigma} = \frac{90 - 70}{20} = \frac{20}{20} = +1.0.$$

In English: $X = 50$; $\bar{X} = 30$; $\sigma = 10$.

$$z = \frac{X - \bar{X}}{\sigma} = \frac{50 - 30}{10} = \frac{20}{10} = +2.0.$$

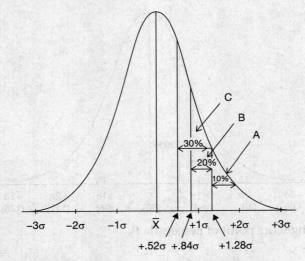

Figure 7.16   Showing the difficulty values of the problems

Thus, the z-score of the student in Mathematics is +1.0 and in English is +2.0. This follows that he did better in English than that in Mathematics.

6. To compare two distributions in terms of 'overlapping'

Example 7.19 Given the distribution of the memory test scores of 300 boys and 250 girls, the boys' mean score is 21.49 with σ of 3.63. The girls' mean score is 23.68 with σ of 5.12. The medians are as follows: boys—21.41 and girls—23.66. Assuming the normality of both the distributions, find out what percentage of boys exceeds the median of the girls' distribution?

Solution Boys: $N=300$; $\bar{X}=21.49$; $\sigma=3.63$;   Mdn = 21.41.

Girls: $N=250$; $\bar{X}=23.68$; $\sigma=5.12$;   Mdn = 23.66.

Both distributions are assumed to be normal. The girls' *median* is 23.66 – 21.49 = 2.17 score units above the boys' *mean*. Dividing 2.17 by 3.63 (the σ of the boys' distribution), we find that the girls' median is 0.60σ above the mean of the boys' distribution. The normal-curve table (Table A) shows that about 23% of a normal distribution lies between the mean and 0.60σ; hence, about 27% of the boys (i.e., 50–23%) exceed the girls' median. In other words, 81 boys $\left(\text{i.e., } \dfrac{27}{100} \times 300\right)$ exceed the girls' median.

7. To determine the relative difficulty of test questions, problems and other test items.

Example 7.20 Three problems A, B and C have been solved by 10%, 20% and 30%, respectively, of a large group. If we assume the capacity measured by the test problems to be distributed normally, what is the relative difficulty of problems A, B and C?

Solution Our first task is to find for Problem A, a cut in the distribution, such that 10% of the entire group (the per cent passing) lies above and 90% (the per cent failing) lies below the given point. The highest 10% in a normally distributed group has 40% of the cases between its lower limit and the mean (see Figure 7.16). From the normal-curve table (Table A), we find that

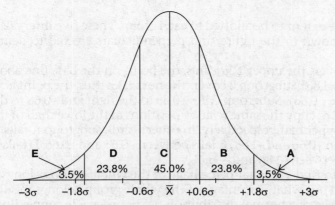

Figure 7.17 Showing percentage or number of students belonging to five subgroups having equal range of ability

39.97% (i.e., 40%) of a normal distribution lies between the mean and $+1.28\sigma$. Hence, Problem A belongs at a point on the base line of the curve, a distance of $+1.28\sigma$ from the mean, and accordingly, $+1.28\sigma$ may be set down as the difficulty value of this problem.

Problem B, passed by 20% of the group, falls at a point in the distribution 30% above the mean. From Table A it is found that 29.95% (i.e., 30%) of the group falls between the mean and $+0.84\sigma$; hence problem B has a difficulty value of $+0.84\sigma$.

Problem C, passed by 30% of the group, falls at a point in the distribution 20% above the mean. From Table A, it is found that 19.85% (i.e., 20%) of the group lies between the mean and $+0.52\sigma$; hence, Problem C has a difficulty value of $+0.52\sigma$. Let us summarise our results as follows:

Problems	Passed By (%)	σ Values	σ Difference
A	10	+1.28	–
B	20	+0.84	0.44
C	30	+0.52	0.32

The σ difference in difficulty between Problems B and C is 0.32, which is roughly 3/4 of the σ difference in difficulty between Problems A and B. Since the percentage difference is the same in the two comparisons, it is evident that when ability is assumed to follow the normal curve, the σ differences, but not the percentage differences, are the better indices of differences in difficulty.

8. To separate a given group into subgroups according to capacity, when the trait is normally distributed.

Example 7.21 Suppose that we have administered an entrance test for admission in the PG Department of Psychology, Utkal University, to a group of 400 undergraduate students. We wish to classify the group into five subgroups A, B, C, D and E, according to ability, the *range* of ability to be equal in each subgroup. On the assumption that the trait measured by our test is normally distributed, how many students should be placed in subgroups A, B, C, D and E?

Solution Let us first represent the positions of the five subgroups diagrammatically on a normal curve as shown in Figure 7.17. If the base line of the curve is considered to extend from -3σ to $+3\sigma$, that is, over a range of 6σ, dividing this range by 5 (the number of subgroups) gives

1.2σ as the base line extent to be allotted to each group. These five intervals may be laid off on the base line as shown in the figure, and perpendiculars erected to demarcate the various subgroups.

Subgroup A covers the upper 1.2σ; thus, the point on the base line above which A falls is +1.8σ (i.e., 3σ–1.2σ=1.8σ). Subgroup B covers the next 1.2σ; thus, the point above which B falls is +0.6σ (i.e., 1.8σ–1.2σ=0.6σ). Subgroup C lies +0.6σ to the right and –0.6σ to the left of the mean. Subgroups D and E occupy the same relative positions in the lower half of the curve that B and A occupy in the upper half, respectively. In other words, subgroup A falls between +1.8σ and +3σ; B falls between +0.6σ and +1.8σ; C falls between –0.6σ and +0.6σ; D falls between –0.6σ and –1.8σ; and E falls between –1.8σ and –3σ.

Now we have to find out what percentage of the whole group belongs to each of the five subgroups. To find out what percentage of the whole group belongs in subgroup A, we must find what percentage of a normal distribution lies between +3σ (upper limit of the subgroup A) and +1.8σ (the lower limit of the subgroup A). From the normal-curve table (Table A), it is found that 49.87% of a normal distribution lies between the mean and +3σ, and 46.41% between the mean and +1.8σ. Hence, 3.46% (49.87–46.41%) or roughly about 3.5% of the total area under the normal curve lies between +1.8σ and +3σ; and accordingly, subgroup A comprises 3.5% of the whole group.

The percentages in the other subgroups are calculated in the same way. Subgroup B covers the cases lying between +.6σ and +1.8σ. From Table A, we find that 46.41% of the normal distribution falls between the mean and +1.8σ (upper limit of subgroup B), and 22.57% falls between the mean and +0.6σ (lower limit of subgroup B). Subtracting, we find that 23.84% (46.41–22.57%) or about 23.8% of the distribution belongs in subgroup B.

Subgroup C extends from –0.6σ to +0.6σ on both sides of the mean. Table A shows that 22.57% of the normal distribution lies between the mean and +0.6σ and the same percentage of cases lies between the mean and –0.6σ. Therefore, Subgroup C includes 22.57%×2=45.14% or about 45% of the distribution.

Finally, subgroup D, which lies between –0.6σ and –1.8σ, contains exactly the same percentage of the distribution as subgroup B; subgroup E, which lies between –1.8σ and –3σ, contains the same percentage of the whole distribution as subgroup A. Therefore, subgroup D contains 23.8% and subgroup E contains 3.5% of the whole distribution.

We may summarise the percentage and number of students in each subgroup as follows.

	Subgroups	A	B	C	D	E
1.	Percentage of the whole group in each subgroup	3.5	23.8	45.0	23.8	3.5
2.	Number of students in each subgroup out of a total of 400	14	95.2	180	95.2	14
3.	Number of students in whole number	14	95	180	95	14

7.8   Common Causes of Asymmetry

Divergence or deviation of a frequency distribution from the normal form is known as asymmetry. Deviations from the normality are called the errors of normal distribution; these errors are of two types—skewness and kurtosis—which have already been discussed earlier in this chapter. Now the question arises as to why frequency distributions deviate from the normal form. The following are some of the common causes of asymmetry:

(i) **Selection.** Selection is a potent cause of skewness and kurtosis. Selection will produce skewness and kurtosis in distributions even when the test has been adequately constructed and carefully administered. Therefore, the samples must be selected randomly from the population; each element of the population should have equal chance of being selected and included in the sample. Moreover, the sample size should be large (i.e., more than 30). In other words, the samples should be large and an unbiased selection.

(ii) **Unsuitable or poorly made tests.** The test administered should be suitable or befitting for the trait being measured. If a test is too easy, scores will pile up at the high-score end of the scale, whereas when the test is too hard, scores will pile up at the low-score end of the scale. Therefore, the test should consist of items having 50% or intermediate difficulty levels. Moreover, the test items should have discriminatory abilities, which can discriminate subjects as having high, medium or low in the trait being measured. The ambiguous or poorly made items should be eliminated.

(iii) **Non-normal distributions.** Skewness or kurtosis or both will appear when there is a real lack of normality in the trait being measured. Non-normality of distribution will arise, for instance, when some of the hypothetical factors determining the strength of a trait are dominant or pre-potent over the others, and hence are present more often than chance will allow. Illustrations may be found in distributions resulting from the throwing of loaded dice. When off-centre or biased dice are cast, the resulting distribution will certainly be skewed and probably peaked, owing to the greater likelihood of combinations of faces yielding certain scores. The same is true of biased coins.

(iv) **Errors in the construction and administration of tests.** Various factors in addition to those mentioned above make for distortions in score distributions. Differences in the size of the units in which test performance has been expressed, for example, will lead to irregularities in some distribution. If the items are very easy at the beginning and very difficult or hard later on, an increment of one point of score at the upper end of the test scale will be much greater than an increment of one point at the low end of the scale. The effect of such unequal or 'rubbery' units jams the distribution and reduces the spread. Scores tend to pile up at some intermediate point and to be stretched out at the low end of the scale.

Errors in timing or in giving instructions, errors in the use of scoring keys, large differences in practice or in motivation, all of these factors, if they cause some subjects to score higher and others to score lower than they normally would, tend to make for skewness in the distribution.

7.9   The Normal Approximation to the Binomial

It has been observed that as n increases in size, the symmetrical binomial is more closely approximated by the normal distribution. This means that the normal distribution may be used to estimate binomial probabilities. If we are given a situation where 10 coins are tossed simultaneously, the exact binomial probability and its normal approximation of occurrence of different number of heads will be as shown in Table 7.2. For the detailed computation of the binomial probability of occurrence of different number of heads, the reader is required to refer to Section 6.7.

Now let us discuss the procedure of determining the normal probabilities of occurrence of different heads while tossing 10 unbiased coins at the same time. Here, $n=10$, mean $(\bar{X})$ of the binomial $= n/2 = 10/2 = 5$, the standard deviation $(\sigma) = \sqrt{\dfrac{n}{4}} = \sqrt{\dfrac{10}{4}} = 1.58$; and variance

Table 7.2 Comparison of binomial probabilities with corresponding normal approximations for $n=10$ and $p=\frac{1}{2}$

Number of Heads	Exact Binomial Probability	Normal-Curve Approximation
10	1/1024=0.001	0.002
9	10/1024=0.010	0.011
8	45/1024=0.044	0.044
7	120/1024=0.117	0.114
6	210/1024=0.205	0.203
5	252/1024=0.246	0.251
4	210/1024=0.205	0.203
3	120/1024=0.117	0.114
2	45/1024=0.044	0.044
1	10/1024=0.010	0.011
0	1/1024=0.001	0.002
Total	1.000	0.999

$(\sigma^2)=n/4=10/4=2.5$. Because the normal distribution is continuous, and not discrete, we consider any value as covering the exact limits 0.5 below to 0.5 above the given value. For example, value 10 ranges from 9.5 to 10.5. These two limits should be transformed into z-scores. The z-score equivalent to a raw score $9.5=\dfrac{X-\bar{X}}{\sigma}=\dfrac{9.5-5.0}{1.58}=2.85$. Similarly, the z-score equivalent to a raw score $10.5=\dfrac{X-\bar{X}}{\sigma}=\dfrac{10.5-5.0}{1.58}=3.48$. Then from the normal-curve table (Table A of the appendix), we should find out the proportion of the area of the normal curve falling between the mean and $+2.85\sigma$ is 0.4978, and the area between the mean and $+3.48\sigma$ is 0.5000. Thus, the area lies between $+2.85\sigma$ and $+3.48\sigma$ is 0.0022 (i.e., $0.5000-0.4978=0.0022$). Hence, the normal approximation of the binomial probability of occurrence of 10 heads is 0.002.

Likewise, the value 9 is covering the exact limits 8.5–9.5. In a standard–score form, the value 8.5 is equivalent to $z=(8.5-5.0)/1.58=2.21$, and 9.5 is equivalent to $(9.5-5.0)/1.58=2.85$. The proportion of the area of the normal curve falls between the mean and $+2.21\sigma$ is 0.4864, and between the mean and $+2.85\sigma$ is 0.4978. Thus, the area lies between $+2.21\sigma$ and $+2.85\sigma$ is 0.0114 (i.e., $0.4978-0.4864$). Hence, the normal approximation of binomial probability of occurrence of 9 heads is 0.011.

The score 8 is covering the exact limits 7.5–8.5. In the standard-score form, the value 7.5 is equivalent to z of 1.58 and value 8.5 is equivalent to z of 2.21. The proportion of the area of the normal curve falls between the mean and $+1.58\sigma$ is 0.4429, and between the mean and $+2.21\sigma$ is 0.4864. Thus, the area lies between $+1.58\sigma$ and 2.21σ is 0.0435 (i.e., $0.4864-0.4429$). Hence, the normal approximation of binomial probability of occurrence of 8 heads is 0.044.

The score 7 is covering the exact limits 6.5–7.5. In the standard-score form, the value 6.5 is equivalent to $+0.95z$ and the value 7.5 is equivalent to $+1.58z$. The proportion of the area of the normal curve falls between the mean and $+0.95\sigma$ is 0.3289, and between the mean and $+1.58\sigma$ is 0.4429. Thus, the area lies between $+0.95\sigma$ and $+1.58\sigma$ is 0.114 (i.e., $0.4429-0.3289$). Hence, the normal approximation of binomial probability of occurrence of 7 heads is 0.114.

In a similar vein, value 6 is covering the exact limits 5.5–6.5. In the standard-score form, the value 5.5 is equivalent to $+0.32z$ and the value 6.5 is equivalent to $+0.95z$. The proportion of the area of the normal curve falls between the mean and $+0.32\sigma$ is 0.1255, and between the mean and $+0.95\sigma$ is 0.3289. Thus, the area lies between $+0.32\sigma$ and $+0.95\sigma$ is 0.2034 (i.e., $0.3289-0.1255$). Hence, the normal approximation of the binomial probability of occurrence of 6 heads is 0.203.

Similarly, value 5 is covering the exact limits 4.5–5.5. In the standard-score form, the value 4.5 is equivalent to $-0.32z$ and the value 5.5 is equivalent to $+0.32z$. The proportion of the area of the normal curve lies between $\pm0.32\sigma$ is 0.251 (i.e., 0.1255×2). Hence, the normal approximation of the binomial probability of occurrence of 5 heads is 0.251.

Since the normal curve is a bilaterally symmetrical and bell shaped, the normal approximations of the binomial probabilities of occurrence of 4, 3, 2, 1, 0 heads are equal to that of the occurrence of 6, 7, 8, 9, 10 heads, respectively. The exact binomial probabilities and the normal-curve approximations to these binomial probabilities are given in Table 7.2.

Let us now compare the normal-curve approximation with the exact binomial probability of obtaining 7 or more heads in tossing 10 coins simultaneously. Thus, using the normal-curve approximation to the binomial, we estimate the probability of obtaining 7 or more heads in tossing 10 unbiased coins as 0.171 (i.e., $0.114+0.044+0.011+0.002$). We may compare this with the exact probabilities obtained directly from the binomial expansion shown in Table 7.2. This binomial probability is 0.172 (i.e., $0.117+0.044+0.010+0.001$). Here, we note that the discrepancy between the estimate obtained from the normal curve and the exact binomial probability is trivial or very negligible.

Table 7.2 compares the binomial and normal probabilities for $n=10$ and $p=1/2$. We note that in this instance the differences between the exact binomial probabilities and the corresponding normal approximations are small.

The accuracy of the approximation depends both on n and p; as n increases in size, the accuracy of the approximation is improved. For any n as p departs from $1/2$, the approximation becomes less accurate.

Summary

In this chapter, we have discussed the standard scores (or z-scores) and the NPC. A z-score is a transformation of a raw score. It designates how many standard deviation units the corresponding raw score is above or below the mean. A z distribution has the characteristics that the z-scores have the same shape as the set of raw scores, the mean of z-scores always equal zero, and the standard deviation of z-scores always equals 1. In addition, we discussed the purposes and applications of z-scores. Next, we discussed the NPC. We pointed out that the normal curve is a bell-shaped curve and gave the equation describing it. Moreover, we discussed the properties of the normal curve, divergence from normality: skewness and kurtosis, common causes of asymmetry, procedures for normalising a distribution of scores, relations that exist among the constants of the NPC, the area contained under the normal curve and its relation to z-scores. Finally, we showed how to use z-scores in conjunction with a normal distribution to find: (a) the percentage or frequency of scores corresponding to any raw score in the distribution and (b) the raw score corresponding to any frequency or percentage of scores in the distribution. In addition, other applications of the NPC and the normal approximation to the binomial were also discussed.

Key Terms

- Asymmetry
- Asymptotic
- Constants
- Deviation score
- Divergence from normality
- Kurtosis
- Normal curve

- Normal probability curve
- Raw score
- Skewness
- Standard score
- Standardised distribution
- z-score
- z-score transformation

Questions and Problems

1. What is a z-score? Discuss the characteristics and purposes of z-scores.
2. Explain the applications of z-scores.
3. Describe exactly what information is provided by a z-score.
4. Define the normal curve. Discuss the importance of the normal distribution.
5. What is the equation of the NPC? Explain the properties of the normal curve.
6. What do you mean by divergence from normality? Discuss the different types of errors in normal distribution.
7. What is skewness? Elucidate the properties of the skewed distribution.
8. What is kurtosis? Analyse the different types of kurtosis.
9. Critically analyse the various applications of the NPC.
10. What do you mean by asymmetry? Examine the various causes of asymmetry.
11. For a population with $\mu=50$ and $\sigma=8$, find the z-score that corresponds to each of the following X values: 58, 34, 70, 46, 62 and 44.
12. For a population with $\mu=80$ and $\sigma=20$, find the scores (X value) that correspond to each of the following z-scores: 2.50, –0.50, –1.50, 0.25, –0.75 and 1.00.
13. A distribution of scores has a standard deviation of $\sigma=10$. Find the z-score corresponding to each of the following values:

    (a) A score that is 20 points above the mean.
    (b) A score that is 10 points below the mean.
    (c) A score that is 15 points above the mean.
    (d) A score that is 30 points below the mean.

14. For a population with $\mu=90$, a raw score of $X=93$ corresponds to $z=+0.50$. What is the standard deviation for this distribution?
15. For a population with $\sigma=8$, a raw score of $X=43$ corresponds to $z=-0.25$. What is the mean for this distribution?
16. Find the height of the ordinate of the normal curve at the following z-values: –2.15, –1.53, +0.07, +0.99 and +2.76.
17. Consider a normally distributed variable with $\bar{X}=50$ and $s=10$. For $N=200$, find the height of the ordinates at the following values of X: 25, 35, 49, 57 and 63.

18. Find the proportion of the areas of the normal curve:

    (a) between the mean and $z=1.49$
    (b) between the mean and $z=-1.26$
    (c) to the right of $z=0.25$
    (d) to the right of $z=-1.50$
    (e) to the left of $z=-1.26$
    (f) to the left of $z=0.95$
    (g) between $z=\pm0.50$
    (h) between $z=-0.75$ and $z=1.50$
    (i) between $z=1.00$ and $z=1.96$

19. Find a value of z such that the proportion of the area:

    (a) to the right of z is 0.25
    (b) to the left of z is 0.90
    (c) between the mean and z is 0.40
    (d) between $\pm z$ is 0.80

20. On the assumption that IQs are normally distributed in the population with a mean of 100 and a standard deviation of 15, find the proportion of people with IQs:

    (a) above 135   (b) above 120
    (c) below 90   (d) between 75 and 125.

21. In a population of scores, $X=58$ corresponds to $z=0.50$ and $X=46$ corresponds to $z=-1.00$. Find the mean and the standard deviation for this population.

22. On a psychology examination with $\mu=72$ and $\sigma=12$, you get a score of $X=78$. The same day, on an English examination with $\mu=56$ and $\sigma=5$, you get a score of $X=66$. For which of the two examinations would you expect to receive the better grade? Explain your answer.

23. A population has $\mu=80$:

    (a) If the standard deviation is $\sigma=2$, would a score of $X=86$ be described as a central score or as an extremely high score?
    (b) If the standard deviation is $\sigma=12$, would a score of $X=86$ be described as a central score or as an extremely high score?

24. On a statistics examination, you have a score of $X=73$. If the mean for this examination is $\mu=81$, would you prefer a standard deviation of $\sigma=8$ or $\sigma=16$?

25. A population consists of the following $N=5$ scores: 8, 6, 2, 4, 5:

    (a) Compute μ and σ for the population.
    (b) Find the z-score for each raw score in the population.
    (c) Transform the original population into a new population of $N=5$ scores with $\mu=100$ and $\sigma=20$.

26. A distribution with $\mu=74$ and $\sigma=8$ is being standardised to produce a new mean of $\mu=100$ and a new standard deviation of $\sigma=20$. Find the standardised value for each of the following scores from the original distribution: 84, 78, 80, 66, 62, 72.

27. In a normal distribution:

    (a) Determine P_{27}, P_{46}, P_{54} and P_{81} in σ units.
    (b) What are the percentile ranks of scores at -1.23σ, -0.50σ, $+0.84\sigma$?

28. Given a normal distribution with a mean of 80 and a standard deviation of 16, determine the percentile points of P_{30}, P_{50}, P_{70} and P_{90}.

29. A statistician studied the records of daily rainfall for a particular geographical locale. She found that the average daily rainfall was normally distributed with a mean $\mu=8.2$ cm and a standard deviation $\sigma=2.4$. What is the percentile rank of the following scores?

    (a) 12.4   (b) 14.3
    (c) 5.8   (d) 4.1
    (e) 8.2

30. Using the same population parameters as in Problem 29, what percentage of scores are above the following scores?

    (a) 10.5   (b) 13.8
    (c) 7.6   (d) 3.5
    (e) 8.2

31. Using the same population parameters as in Problem 29, what percentage of scores are between the following scores?

    (a) 6.8 and 10.2   (b)   5.4 and 8.0
    (c) 8.8 and 10.5

32. A teacher decides to fail 25% of students in a class. Examination marks are roughly normally distributed with a mean of 72 and a standard deviation of 6. What marks does a student make to pass?

33. Scores on a particular statistical test are normally distributed, with a mean of 50 and a standard deviation of 10. The decision is made to use a letter-grade system A, B, C, D and E, with the proportions 0.10, 0.20, 0.40, 0.20 and 0.10 in the five grades, respectively. Find the score intervals for the five letter grades.

34. Four problems, A, B, C and D, have been solved by 50%, 60%, 70% and 80%, respectively, of a large group. Compare the difference in difficulty between A and B with the difference in difficulty between C and D.

35. In a certain college, ten grades, A+, A, A–; B+, B, B–; C+, C, C–; and D, are assigned. If ability in mathematics is distributed normally, how many students in a group of 500 freshmen should receive each grade?

36. The following are data for test scores for two age groups:

	11-year group	14-year group
$\bar{X}$	48	56
S	8	12
N	500	800

Assuming normality, estimate (a) how many of the 11-year olds do better than the average 14-year old, and (b) how many of the 14-year olds do worse than the average 11-year old.

37. Compute the moment coefficient of skewness for the following set of scores:

$$5, 9, 10, 16, 20.$$

38. Compute the moment coefficient of kurtosis for the following set of scores:

$$7, 8, 10, 11, 14.$$

39. Below are the scores of a sample of 130 students on a Minnesota Paper-Form Board Test.

60–62	2
57–59	4
54–56	8
51–53	10
48–50	18
45–47	16
42–44	14
39–41	14
36–38	10
33–35	18
30–32	14
27–29	2
	$N=130$ $\bar{X}=42.8$ $s=8.2$

(a) Assume a normal population distribution and determine what per cent of cases you would expect to find between the mean and the following scores in similar samples: 60, 38, 28.

(b) Find the percentage and number of cases expected to fall between the following pairs of scores: 35 and 40, 50 and 55, 56 and 60.

(c) How many cases would you expect to find above a raw score of 50? Below a score of 35?

40. Apply the normalising process to the data of Problem 39 and plot the best-fitting curve for these data. On the same axes, plot the frequency polygon for the original data.

41. Fill in the blanks:
    (i) A standard score is nothing but a _____ score.
    (ii) Standard scores have a mean of _____ and standard deviation of _____.
    (iii) In the unit normal probability curve, the three measures: mean, median and mode, of the central tendency _____.
    (iv) The normal curve extends from _____ infinity to _____ infinity.
    (v) The area of the unit normal curve is _____ and its standard deviation is _____.
    (vi) The maximum ordinate of the unit normal curve is equal to _____.
    (vii) In the unit normal probability curve, the proportion of areas between the limits $z \pm 3$ is _____.
    (viii) In the unit normal probability curve, the coefficient of skewness amounts to _____ and kurtosis amounts to _____.
    (ix) Skewness is positive when mean is _____ than mode.
    (x) The moment coefficient of the normal curve is _____.

42. Write whether the following statements are True or False.
    (i) In a skewed distribution, quartiles are equidistant from the median.
    (ii) Skewness cannot be calculated in a bimodal distribution.
    (iii) In a symmetrical distribution, mean = median = mode.
    (iv) The normal distribution is said to be mesokurtic.
    (v) g_2 is a measure of kurtosis.
    (vi) In a normal probability curve, PE = 0.6745σ.
    (vii) Deviations from the normality are called the errors of normal distribution.
    (viii) Normal distribution is discrete but not continuous.
    (ix) Normal distribution is bilaterally symmetrical and unimodal.
    (x) Selection is a potent cause of skewness and kurtosis.

43. Find out the correct answer from among the four alternatives.
    (i) When the coefficient of skewness is zero, the distribution is:
       (a) Symmetrical   (b) Asymmetrical
       (c) Non-normal   (d) None of the above
    (ii) In a positively skewed distribution:
       (a) Median > Mean > Mode   (b) Mean > Median > Mode
       (c) Mode > Median > Mean   (d) None of the above
    (iii) In a negatively skewed distribution:
       (a) Mode > Mean > Median   (b) Mean > Mode > Median
       (c) Mode > Median > Mean   (d) None of the above

(iv) If the value of kurtosis is greater than 0.263, the distribution is said to be:

    (a) Normal   (b) Platykurtic

    (c) Leptokurtic   (d) None of the above

(v) When g_2 is greater than 0, the distribution is:

    (a) Leptokurtic   (b) Platykurtic

    (c) Normal   (d) None of the above

(vi) If a frequency distribution is positively skewed, the mean of the distribution is:

    (a) Greater than the mode   (b) Less than the mode

    (c) Equal to the mode   (d) None of the above

(vii) In a symmetrical distribution:

    (a) $Q_3 - Q_2 > Q_2 - Q_1$ (b) $Q_3 - Q_2 < Q_2 - Q_1$

    (c) $Q_3 - Q_2 = Q_2 - Q_1$ (d) None of the above

(viii) In a normal distribution, the quartile coefficient of skewness amounts to:

    (a) Zero   (b) Greater than zero

    (c) Less than zero   (d) None of the above

(ix) The moment coefficient of skewness for a distribution of test scores having $m_3 = 10.80$ and $m_2 = 9.20$ is:

    (a) +0.738   (b) + 0.387

    (c) −0.387   (d) None of the above

(x) The moment coefficient of kurtosis for a distribution of test scores having $m_2 = 8.0$ and $m_4 = 108.8$ is:

    (a) +1.3   (b) +1.7

    (c) −1.3   (d) None of the above

CHAPTER 8

Testing of Hypothesis

After completing this chapter you will be able to:

- Explain the concepts of H_0 and H_1.
- Use samples to decide whether a population possesses a particular characteristic.
- Understand the two types of errors possible when testing hypotheses.
- Decide when to use one-tailed tests and when to use two-tailed tests.
- Determine the region of rejection and the region of acceptance.
- Explain and compute sampling errors.
- Learn how to draw the sampling distribution.
- Compute the standard error (SE) of the mean and proportions.
- Explain and determine the power of a test.
- Understand the logic of hypothesis testing.
- Learn the procedures (four-step process) for hypothesis testing.

8.1 Introduction

Scientific research may be divided into two categories: observational studies and true experiments. In observational studies or such type of research, there are no variables that are actively manipulated by the investigator. Included within this category of research are naturalistic observation, parameter estimation and correlational studies. With naturalistic observation research, a major goal is to obtain an accurate description of the situation being studied. Most of the anthropological and etiological research is of this type. Parameter estimation research is conducted on samples to estimate the level of one or more population characteristics, for example, the population average or percentage. Surveys, public opinion polls and much market research fall into this category. In correlational research, the investigator focuses attention on two or more variables to determine whether they are related.

In true experimental type of research, an attempt is made to determine if changes in one variable produce changes in another variable. With this type of research, an independent variable is manipulated, and its effect on some dependent variable is studied. However, there can be more than one independent variable and more than one dependent variable. In the simplest case, there is only one independent variable and one dependent variable.

In both types of research works described earlier, data are usually collected on a sample of subjects, rather than that on the entire population to which the results are intended to apply. Ideally, of course, the experiment/study would be performed on the whole population, but usually it is far too costly and time consuming, and so a sample is taken. Note that not just any sample will do. The sample should be a *random* sample. Random sampling has been discussed in Chapter 1. For now, it is sufficient to know that random sampling allows the laws of probability to be applied to the data and at the same time helps achieve a sample that is representative of the population. Thus, the results obtained from the sample should also apply to the population. Once the data are collected, they are statistically analysed, and the appropriate conclusions about the concerned population are drawn.

Statistical analysis has been divided into two areas: (a) descriptive statistics and (b) inferential statistics. Both involve analysing data. If an analysis is done for the purpose of describing or characterising the data that have been collected, then we are in the area of descriptive statistics. Thus, descriptive statistics is concerned with techniques that are used to describe or characterise the obtained data. For example, measures of central tendency, measures of variability and graphical representation of data are some of the descriptive statistics.

Inferential statistics, on the other hand, is not concerned with just describing the obtained data. Rather, it embraces techniques that allow one to use the obtained sample data to infer to or draw conclusions about populations. Thus, inferential statistics involve techniques that use the obtained sample data to infer to populations. This is the more complicated part of statistical analysis. It involves probability and various inference tests such as Student's *t*-test and analysis of variance and so on.

To illustrate the difference between descriptive and inferential statistics, suppose that we are interested in determining the average IQ of the entire population of students of various colleges affiliated to a university. Since it will be too costly and time consuming to measure the IQ of every student in the population, we will take a random sample of, say, 100 students, and give each of them an IQ test. Then we will have 100 sample IQ scores, which we will use to determine the average IQ in the population. Although we cannot determine the exact value of the average IQ of the population, we can estimate it, using the sample data in conjunction with an inference test called Student's *t*-test. The results will allow us to make a statement, such as 'We are 95% confident that the interval of 115–120 contains the mean IQ of the population'. Here, we are not describing the obtained scores, but instead we are using the sample scores to infer to a population value. We are, therefore, in the domain of inferential statistics.

We have pointed out earlier that inferential statistics have two main purposes: (a) hypothesis testing and (b) parameter estimation. By far, most of the applications of inferential statistics are in the area of hypothesis testing. Scientific methodology depends on this application of inferential statistics. Without objective verification, science would cease to exist, and objective verification is often impossible without inferential statistics. At the heart of science lies the *scientific experiment* and the experiment provides the basis for an *objective evaluation* of the hypothesis. Usually, the experiment has been designed to test a hypothesis, and the resulting data must be analysed. Occasionally, the results are so clear-cut that statistical inference is not necessary. However, such experiments are rare. Due to the variability that is inherent from subject to subject in the variable being measured, it is often quite difficult to detect the effect of the independent variable without the help of inferential statistics. In this chapter, we shall begin the fascinating journey into the hypothesis testing with the basic terminologies of statistical analysis and the logic of hypothesis testing.

The following are some of the basic terminologies of statistical analysis, which are also the basic concepts concerning testing of hypothesis.

8.2   An Experiment

Experimentation is a classic method of science laboratory where elements manipulated and effects observed can be controlled. Experimentation provides a method of hypothesis testing. After experimenters define a problem, they propose a tentative answer or hypothesis. Then they test the hypothesis and confirm or disconfirm it in the light of the results they have found. It is important to note that the confirmation or rejection of the hypothesis is stated in terms of probability rather than certainty.

An experiment is conducted as per its experimental design. Experimental design is the blue print of the procedures that enable the researcher to test a hypothesis by reaching valid conclusions about the relationship between independent and dependent variables. The selection of a particular design is based upon the purpose of the experiment, the type of variables to be manipulated and the conditions or limiting factors under which it is conducted. The design deals with such practical problems as to how subjects are to be selected from the population and how they are assigned to experimental and control groups, the way variables are to be manipulated and controlled, the way extraneous variables are to be controlled, how observations are to be made and the type of statistical analysis to be employed in interpreting data relationships. Once a particular design is selected, all aspects of the experiment from the initial to the final stages are taken care of.

Suppose we want to conduct an experiment to find out the effect of smoking marijuana on the reaction time of the subjects. In this experiment, marijuana smoking is the independent variable and reaction time is the dependent variable. Suppose that the sample consists of 10 students randomly selected from the population of under-graduate students. The hypothesis we decide to investigate is that marijuana smoking affects reaction time. This will be a basic fact-finding experiment in which we attempt to find out if marijuana smoking has any effect at all, either to speed up the reaction time or to slow it down. Each student is tested under two conditions: a control condition and an experimental condition. Thus, the subjects served as their own controls. Their scores were paired, and the differences between these pairs were analysed. In other words, there are two reaction time scores (in milliseconds) for each student: one from the experimental condition and one from the control condition. If marijuana does really affect the reaction time, we would expect different scores for the two conditions. For example, if marijuana slows the reaction time, the scores should be higher under the experimental condition. If each subject's control score is subtracted from his/her experimental score, we would expect a predominance of positive difference scores.

Thus, the experimental design that we have been using in the marijuana experiment (i.e., the same subjects used in both conditions) is called the repeated measures, replicated measures or correlated group design. The essential features are that there are paired scores in the conditions and the differences between the paired scores are analysed. Student's *t*-test for correlated groups is one of the appropriate statistical inference tests to analyse these types of data.

8.3 Null Hypothesis (H_0)

A hypothesis may be defined as a proposition or a tentative answer to the research problem. For the study in Section 8.2, the hypothesis states that marijuana smoking affects reaction time. Actually, in any experiment, there are two opposing hypotheses that compete for explaining the results. They are the *null hypothesis* (H_0) and *alternative hypothesis* (H_1). Note that both hypotheses are stated in terms of population parameters.

The first and most important of the two hypotheses is the *null hypothesis* and it is identified by the symbol H_0. The null hypothesis is a hypothesis of no difference. It states that in the general population, there is no change, no difference or no relationship. In the context of an experiment, H_0 predicts that the independent variable (treatment) has no effect on the dependent variable for the population. For the experimental study in Section 8.2, the null hypothesis states that marijuana has *no effect* on the reaction time. In symbols, this hypothesis is represented as

$$H_0 : \mu_1 = \mu_2 \text{ or } \mu_1 \sim \mu_2 = 0$$

That is, the means of the two groups are equal or the difference between the means of two groups is zero. In other words, the mean reaction time of the experimental group is equal to that of the control group.

8.4 Alternative Hypothesis (H_1)

The second hypothesis is simply the opposite of the null hypothesis, and it is called the *scientific* or *alternative hypothesis* (H_1). The alternative hypothesis states that there is a change, a difference or a relationship for the general population. In the context of an experiment, H_1 predicts that the independent variable (treatment) will have an effect on the dependent variable. For the present example, the alternative hypothesis claims that marijuana affects the reaction time. In symbols, H_1 is represented as

$$H_1 : \mu_1 = \mu_2 \text{ or } \mu_1 \sim \mu_2 \neq 0.$$

That is, the means of the two groups are not equal or the difference between the means of two groups is not zero. In other words, the mean reaction time of the experimental group is not equal to that of the control group.

The alternative hypothesis (H_1) may be non-directional or directional, which will be examined in detail later in this chapter. If the H_1 is non-directional, it specifies that the independent variable has an effect on the dependent variable. For this non-directional alternative hypothesis, the null hypothesis asserts that the independent variable has no effect on the dependent variable. In the present example, since the alternative hypothesis is non-directional, the null hypothesis specifies that 'marijuana has no effect on reaction time'. We pointed out previously that the H_1 specifies that 'marijuana affects reaction time'. If the alternative hypothesis is directional, then the null hypothesis asserts that the independent variable does not have an effect in the direction specified by the alternative hypothesis. For example, the H_1 asserts that marijuana slows the reaction time, whereas the H_0 asserts that marijuana does not slow the reaction time. Similarly, the H_1:asserts that marijuana accelerates the reaction time, whereas H_0 asserts that marijuana does not accelerate the reaction time. Thus, an alternative hypothesis 'marijuana affects reaction time' is non-directional because it does not specify the direction of the effect. If the hypothesis specifies the direction of the effect, it is a directional hypothesis. 'Marijuana slows reaction time' or 'marijuana accelerates reaction time' is an example of a directional alternative hypothesis.

The null hypothesis is set up to be the logical counterpart of the alternative hypothesis such that if the null hypothesis is false, the alternative hypothesis must be true. Therefore, these two hypotheses (i.e., H_0 and H_1) are mutually exclusive and exhaustive. They both cannot be true. The statistical analysis of the data by the help of inferential statistical tests will determine which one should be rejected and which one should be accepted. So, we always first evaluate the null hypothesis and try to show that it is false. If we can prove it to be false, then the alternative hypothesis must be true. Thus, the alternative hypothesis is not directly tested statistically; rather, its acceptance or rejection is determined by the respective rejection or retention of the null hypothesis in the statistical test. We should also note that both hypotheses refer to a population whose mean is unknown—namely, the population of under-graduate students who are in habit of smoking marijuana.

8.5   Levels of Significance

Levels of significance are called the alpha (α) levels of significance. It is our own decision-making procedure. In advance of the data collection, for the requirement of objectivity, we specify the probability (p) of rejecting the null hypothesis, which is called the significance level of the test. By convention, commonly used alpha levels are $\alpha = 0.05$ (5%) and $\alpha = 0.01$ (1%) as the levels of significance. We reject a null hypothesis whenever the outcome of the experiment has a probability equal to or less than 0.05 or 0.01. The frequent use of 0.05 and 0.01 levels of significance is a matter of convention having little scientific bias.

In contemporary statistical decision theory, this convention of adhering rigidly to an arbitrary 0.05 level has been rejected. In fact, the choice of level of significance should be determined by the nature of the problem for which we seek answer, and the consequences of the findings. For example, in medical research where the efficacy of a particular medicine is being evaluated, 0.05 level may be considered a lenient standard. Perhaps, a stringent level of significance, say, 0.001 is more appropriate in this situation than 0.05 and 0.01 levels of significance.

We always evaluate the results of an experiment by assessing the null hypothesis. The reason we directly assess the null hypothesis instead of the alternative hypothesis is that we can calculate the probability of chance events, but there is no mathematics for the probability of the alternative hypothesis. We evaluate the null hypothesis by assuming that it is true and test the reasonableness of this assumption by calculating the probability of getting the results if *chance alone is operating*. If the obtained probability turns out to be equal to or less than a critical probability level called the *alpha* (α) *level*, we reject the null hypothesis. Rejecting the null hypothesis allows us, then, to accept indirectly the alternative hypothesis since, if the experiment is done properly, it is the only other possible explanation. When we reject H_0, we say that the results are *significant* or *reliable*. If the obtained probability is greater than the *alpha level*, we conclude by failing to reject H_0. Since the experiment does not allow the rejection of H_0, we retain H_0 as a reasonable explanation of the data. When we retain H_0, we say that the results are not significant or reliable. Of course, when the results are not significant, we cannot accept the alternative hypothesis. Thus, the decision rule states:

If the obtained probability $\leq \alpha$, reject H_0

If the obtained probability $> \alpha$, fail to reject H_0, retain H_0.

The *alpha level* is set at the beginning of the experiment. Commonly used alpha levels are $\alpha = 0.05$ and $\alpha = 0.01$.

8.6   Errors of Inference

Hypothesis testing is an inferential process, which means that it uses limited information as the basis for reaching a general conclusion. Specifically, a sample provides only limited or incomplete information about the population, and yet a hypothesis test uses a sample to draw a conclusion about the population. In this situation, there is always the possibility that an incorrect conclusion or decision will be made. Although sample data are usually representative of the population, there is always a chance that the sample is misleading and will cause a researcher to make the wrong decision about the research results.

In making tests of significance, we are likely to be in error in drawing inference concerning the hypothesis to be tested. There are two types of errors that may be made while arriving at a decision about the null hypothesis. These are called Type I and Type II errors.

A Type I error is defined as a conclusion or decision to reject the null hypothesis when, in fact, the null hypothesis is true. In other words, a Type I error occurs when a researcher rejects a null hypothesis that is actually true. In a typical research situation, a Type I error means that the researcher concludes that a treatment does have an effect when, in fact, the treatment has no effect.

A Type II error is defined as a decision to retain or accept the null hypothesis when, in fact, the null hypothesis is false. In other words, a Type II error occurs when a researcher fails to reject a null hypothesis that is really false. In a typical research situation, a Type II error means that the hypothesis test has failed to detect a real treatment effect.

The probability of committing Type I error is associated with the level of significance, that is, the alpha (α) level. The larger the α, the more the likelihood of H_0 getting rejected falsely. In other words, if the level of significance for rejecting H_0 is high, we are more likely to commit Type I error. The Type II error is usually represented by beta (β; read 'bayta'). When H_0 is false and we decide not to reject H_0 on the basis of a test of significance, then we are likely to commit a Type II error:

Probability (p) of Type I error $= \alpha$
Probability (p) of Type II error $= \beta$.

The probability of making Type I error is controlled by the level of significance (or the alpha level), which is at the discretion of the experimenter. For the requirement of objectivity, the specific values of alpha (α) should be specified before conducting the experiment or before beginning data collection.

To help clarify the relationship between the decision process and possible error, we have summarised the possibilities in Table 8.1. The column heading is 'State of Reality'. This means the correct state of affairs regarding the null hypothesis. There are only two possibilities: either H_0 is true (no effect) or it is false (effect exists). The row heading is the decision made when analysing the data. Again, there are only two possibilities. Either we reject H_0 or we retain H_0. If we retain

Table 8.1   Possible conclusions and the state of reality

Decision	State of Reality	
	H_0 is True	**H_0 is False**
Retain H_0	[1]Correct decision	[2]Type II error
Reject H_0	[3]Type I error	[4]Correct decision

Table 8.2   Effect of making alpha more stringent on beta

Alpha Level	Obtained Probability	Decision	State of Reality	
			H₀ is True	H₀ is False
0.05	0.02	Reject H₀	[1]Type I error	[2]Corrct decision
0.01	0.02	Retain H₀	[3]Correct decision	[4]Type II error

that H_0 and H_0 is true, we have made a correct decision (see the first cell in the table). If we reject that H_0 and H_0 is true, we have made a Type I error (see the third cell in the table). If we retain that H_0 and H_0 is false, we have made a Type II error (the second cell). Finally, if we reject that H_0 and H_0 is false, we have made a correct decision (the fourth cell). Note that when we reject H_0, the only possible error is a Type I error. If we retain H_0, the only error we may make is a Type II error.

From the analysis just discussed, we know that there are only two such possibilities: Type I error and Type II error. Knowing these two possibilities, we can design experiments before conducting them so as to minimise the probability of making a Type I error or a Type II error. By minimising the probability of making these errors, we maximise the probability of concluding correctly, regardless of whether the null hypothesis is true or false.

Let us now see how alpha (α) limits the probability of making a Type I error. The alpha level that the scientist sets at the beginning of the experiment is the level to which he or she wishes to limit the probability of making a Type I error. We can see this by considering an example. This example is best understood in conjunction with Table 8.2. Suppose we do an experiment and set $\alpha = 0.05$ (top raw of Table 8.2). We evaluate a chance and obtain a probability of 0.02. We reject H_0. If H_0 is true, we have made a Type I error (the first cell). Suppose, however, that alpha had been set at $\alpha = 0.01$ instead of 0.05 (the bottom row of Table 8.2). In this case, we would retain H_0 and no longer we would be making a Type I error (the third cell). Thus, the more stringent the alpha level, the lower the probability of making a Type I error. In other words, by controlling the alpha level, we can minimise the probability of making a Type I error.

On the other hand, what happens if H_0 is really false (the last column of the table)? With $\alpha = 0.05$ and the obtained probability $= 0.02$, we would reject H_0 and thereby make a correct decision (the second cell). However, if we change the value of α to 0.01, we would retain H_0, and we would make a Type II error (the fourth cell). Thus, making alpha more stringent decreases the probability of making a Type I error, but increases the probability of making a Type II error. Due to this interaction between alpha and beta, the alpha level employed for an experiment depends on the intended use of the experimental results. If the results are to communicate a new fact to the scientific community, the consequences of a Type I error are great, and, therefore, stringent alpha levels are used (α of 0.05 and 0.01). If, however, the experiment is exploratory in nature and the results are to guide the researcher in deciding whether to do a full-fledged experiment, it would be foolish to use such stringent alpha levels. In such cases, alpha levels as high as 0.10 or 0.20 are often used.

8.7   One-tailed and Two-tailed Tests

Depending upon the nature of an alternative hypothesis (H_1) in question, either a two-tailed or a one-tailed statistical test has to be chosen.

A two-tailed test is a non-directional statistical test for finding the significance of the result. The evaluation should always be two-tailed unless the experimenter is willing to retain H_0 if the results are extreme in the direction opposite to that predicted. The term two-tailed comes from the fact that the critical region or area of rejection is located in both tails or ends of the distribution. This format is by far the most widely accepted procedure for hypothesis testing. For example, in our experiment regarding the effect of marijuana smoking on reaction time, we have stated the null hypothesis as

H_0: Marijuana has no effect on reaction time (i.e., $\mu_1 = \mu_2$ or $\mu_1 - \mu_2 = 0$).

H_1: Marijuana affects reaction time (i.e., $\mu_1 \neq \mu_2$ or $\mu_1 - \mu_2 \neq 0$).

The above two statistical hypotheses (H_0 and H_1) are non-directional, and, thus, it is a non-directional hypothesis test or a two-tailed test.

A one-tailed test is a directional test. Usually, a researcher begins an experiment with specific prediction about the direction of the treatment effect. For example, a specific training programme is expected to *increase* student performance, or alcohol consumption is expected to *slow* reaction times. In these situations, it is possible to state the statistical hypotheses in a manner that incorporates the directional prediction into the statement of H_0 and H_1. The result is a directional test, or what commonly is called a one-tailed test. In a directional hypothesis test, or a one-tailed test, the statistical hypotheses (H_0 and H_1) specify either an increase or a decrease in the population mean score. That is, they make a statement about the direction of the effect.

Suppose, for example, a researcher is using a sample of $n=16$ laboratory white rats to examine the effect of a new diet drug. It is known that under regular circumstances these rats eat an average of 10 grams of food each day. The distribution of food consumption is normal with $\sigma=4$. The expected effect of the drug is to reduce food consumption. The purpose of the experiment is to determine whether or not the drug really works.

Because a specific direction is expected for the treatment effect, it is possible for the researcher to perform a directional test. The first step is to state the statistical hypotheses. Remember that the null hypothesis states that there is no treatment effect and that the alternative hypothesis says that there is an effect. For example, the predicted effect is that the drug will reduce food consumption. Thus, the two hypotheses would state:

H_0: Food consumption is not reduced.

H_1: Food consumption is reduced.

To express these directional hypotheses in symbols, it is usually easier to begin with the alternative hypothesis. Again, we know that regular rats eat an average of $\mu=10$ grams of food. Therefore, expressed in symbols, H_1 states

$H_1 : \mu < 10$ (with the drug, food consumption is less than 10 grams per day)

The null hypothesis states that the drug does not reduce food consumption.

$H_0 : \mu \geq 10$ (with the drug, food consumption is at least 10 grams per day).

The critical region or the region of rejection is located entirely in one tail or one end of the distribution. This is why the directional test is called *one-tailed*. In the present example, the treatment is intended to reduce food consumption. Therefore, only sample values that are substantially less than $\mu=10$ would indicate that the treatment worked, thereby leading to rejecting H_0. Here, the region of rejection is located on the left-hand tail of the distribution.

Notice that a directional or one-tailed test requires two changes in the step-by-step hypothesis testing. In the first step of the hypothesis test, the directional prediction is incorporated into the statement of the hypotheses. In the second step of the process, the critical region or area of rejection is located entirely in one tail, either on the left-hand tail or on the right-hand tail, of the distribution. After these two changes, the remainder of a one-tailed test proceeds exactly the same as a regular two-tailed test. Specifically, we calculate the z-score statistic and then make a decision about H_0 depending on whether or not the z-score is in the critical region.

8.8   Critical Region or Region of Rejection

The critical region or the region of rejection of null hypothesis (H_0) is defined with reference to the sampling distribution. The decision rules specify that H_0 should be rejected if an observed statistic has any value in the region of rejection. The probability associated with any value in the region of rejection is equal to or less than alpha (α).

The location of region of rejection is affected by the nature of experimental hypothesis (H_1). If H_1 predicts the direction of the effect, then a one-tailed test is applied. However, if the direction of the effect is not indicated by H_1, then the two-tailed test is applied. It may be noted that one-tailed and two-tailed tests differ only in the location of the region of rejection, but the size of the region is not affected.

The one-tailed region and two-tailed region are presented in Figure 8.1 and Figure 8.2, respectively. It can be seen in Figure 8.1 that the region of rejection is entirely at one end or tail of the sampling distribution, 5% or 1% of the entire area being under the curve. In a two-tailed test (see Figure 8.2), the region of rejection is located at both ends or tails of the sampling distribution, 2.5% or 0.5% of the total area on each side of the distribution.

For a two-tailed test with the alpha (α) chosen to be 0.05, each tail of the H_0 distribution ends with a rejection or critical region ($\alpha/2$) of area 0.025 extending beyond the critical z-score of 1.96 in that tail (see Figure 8.2(a)). If the z-score computed from an observed difference between two sample means lies below -1.96σ or above $+1.96\sigma$, the observed difference

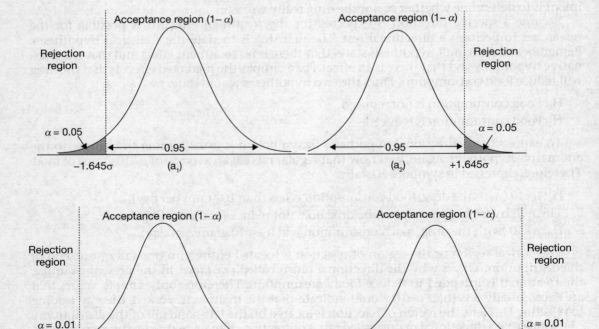

Figure 8.1   Rejection region, acceptance region and critical z values for the (a_1 and a_2) 0.05 level and (b_1 and b_2) 0.01 level of significance in a one-tailed test

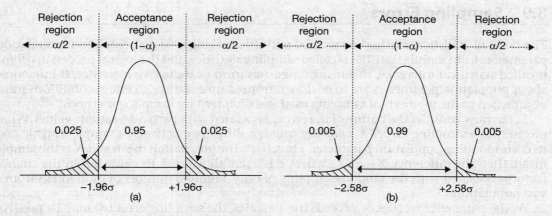

Figure 8.2   Rejection region, acceptance region and critical z values for the (a) 0.05 level and (b) 0.01 level of significance in a two-tailed test

falls within the rejection region and, thus, the H_0 is rejected; and if the computed z-score is less than $\pm 1.96\sigma$, then H_0 falls within the acceptance region, and, thus, the H_0 is accepted. But in a one-tailed test with the alpha (α) chosen to be 0.05, and involving a single tail (either low-tail or high-tail), the critical or rejection region in that tail extends over the entire α level of 0.05, which is the fractional area in that tail beyond the critical z-score of -1.645 (see Figure 8.1(a_1)) or of $+1.645$ (see Figure 8.1(a_2)). If the z-score computed from the observed difference between two sample means amounts to ± 1.645 or more, it lies in the rejection region, and, thus, the H_0 is rejected; and if the computed z-score is less than ± 1.645, it falls in the acceptance region, and, thus, the H_0 is accepted. It is, thus, evident that with an identical alpha (α), an observed difference may be significant in a one-tailed test, though it may fail to be significant in a two-tailed test—a computed z of 1.645 in the aforementioned example is significant for a one-tailed test at the 0.05 level of significance, but is not significant for a two-tailed test at the same 0.05 level.

In a similar footing, let us discuss the significance of an observed difference at the $\alpha = 0.01$ level in both two- and one-tailed tests. For a two-tailed test with the α chosen to be 0.01, each tail of the H_0 distribution ends with a rejection region ($\alpha/2$) of area 0.005 extending beyond the critical z-score of 2.58 in that tail (see Figure 8.2(b)). If the z-score computed from the observed difference between two sample means lies below -2.58 or above $+2.58$, the observed difference falls within the rejection region, and the H_0 is rejected; if the computed z-score is less than ± 2.58, then H_0 is accepted because H_0 falls within the acceptance region. But in a one-tailed test with the α chosen to be 0.01, and involving a single tail, the critical region in that tail extends over the entire α level of 0.01, which is the fractional area in that tail beyond the critical z-score of -2.33 (see Figure 8.1(b_1)) or of $+2.33$ (see Figure 8.1(b_2)). If the obtained z-score computed from the difference between two sample means amounts to ± 2.33 or more, then it falls within the rejection region and then the H_0 is rejected; and if the computed z-score is less than ± 2.33, then H_0 is accepted because this z-score lies within the acceptance region. It is, thus, evident that with an identical α, an observed difference may be significant in a one-tailed test but fails to be significant in a two-tailed test. For example, a computed z of 2.33 is significant for a one-tailed test at the 0.01 level of significance, but is not significant for a two-tailed test at the same 0.01 level of significance.

8.9   Sampling Errors

The body of statistical method concerned with the making of statements about population parameters from sample statistics is called sampling statistics, and the logical process involved is called statistical inference, this being a rigorous form of inductive inference. If inferences about population parameters are to be drawn from sample statistics, certain conditions must be attached to the methods of sampling used (see Chapter 1 for sampling methods).

Let us now consider the nature of the errors associated with particular sample values. What precisely is a sampling error? A *sampling error* is a difference between a sample statistic and its corresponding population parameter. Thus, if μ is the population mean and $\bar{X}$ is the sample mean, then the difference $\bar{X} - \mu = e_i$, where e_i is a sampling error. Its cause lies in the chance factors associated with the random sampling of only a limited number of individuals from a vast population.

As the parameter recedes or exceeds the statistics, the sampling error (e_i) may be positive or negative, respectively. For example, if the finite population of all the participants in an Olympiad has a mean height (μ) of 5'8" and a random sample of the participants has a mean height ($\bar{X}$) of 6'2", the sampling error of $\bar{X}$ is given by

$$e_i = \mu = 6'2'' - 5'8'' = +6 \text{ inches.}$$

Similarly, if the mean IQ on the Stanford–Binet scale amounts to 120 for the entire finite population of IIT-JEE candidates, and to 116 for a small sample of those candidates, the sampling error of the $\bar{X}$ of this sample is given by

$$e_i = \bar{X} - \mu = 116 - 120 = -4.$$

Sampling errors cannot be found directly and precisely in most cases because the parameters, particularly of infinite populations, are not precisely known. However, sampling error may be estimated from the variations of the relevant statistics in samples of equal sizes, drawn from the given population. Note that the variance and standard deviation (SD) of sample means ($\bar{X}$) are the same as the variance and standard deviation of the sampling error (e_i) because μ is a constant.

8.10   Sampling Distribution

A *sampling distribution* is a distribution of statistics obtained by selecting all the possible samples of a specific size from a population. Thus, the distribution of sample means is an example of a sample distribution. In fact, it is often called the sampling distribution of $\bar{X}$.

If many large samples of identical size n are drawn by random sampling from the same population and a particular statistic (say, the mean) is computed from the scores of each sample, the computed values of the statistic are distributed in a frequency distribution called an *experimental sampling distribution* of that statistic. The SD and variance of this distribution serve as measures of variations of the relevant statistic from sample to sample.

Instead of computing the distribution of a statistic from experimentally observed scores of a variable in actually drawn samples, the theory of probability may be used to construct theoretically a frequency distribution of that statistic in the random samples from a population of a known nature. This gives a *theoretical sampling distribution* of that statistics. For example, in a given finite population, the number of members is 8, and we have to draw some samples of four members each. The number of such samples is the number of combinations of eight things taken four at a time; or $C_4^8 = 70$. Each of these 70 samples may be considered equiprobable. The means for the 70 possible samples may be ascertained and a frequency distribution be prepared. This frequency distribution is a *theoretical sampling distribution*. Its SD and variance are the measures of the sample-wise variation of the relevant statistic in that population.

The SD of a sampling distribution of a statistic is, thus, a measure of the dispersion of that statistic around the corresponding population parameter, and is called the standard error (SE) of that statistic. For example, the means of samples drawn from a population form a sampling distribution of means, and the SD of this distribution is called the SE of the means. The SD of a theoretical sampling distribution is the parametric SE of the relevant statistic in the population; on the contrary, the SD of an experimental sampling distribution is an *estimate* of the parametric SE, and is computed from the observed sample data.

Theoretical and experimental sampling distributions can also be framed for the differences with regard to a statistic between samples drawn from two different populations. The SD for such a sampling distribution is a measure of the dispersion of differences between the statistics of each pair of samples around the difference between the two population parameters. It is known as the SE of the difference between the relevant statistics. For example, differences between the means of every pair of samples from two separate populations form a sampling distribution of differences between the means and the SD of this distribution is the SE of the difference between the means.

8.11   Standard Errors

The SE of a statistic is a measure of the deviation of that statistic from the corresponding parameter, and consequently it serves as an index of the sampling error of that statistic. It is the SD of the sampling distribution of the relevant statistic—the SD of the theoretical sampling distribution is the *parametric or true SE*, while the SD of an experimental sampling distribution is an *estimate of the true SE*.

The SE has wide applications. It is computed for a variety of sample statistics such as mean, median, SD, proportion, quartile deviation and correlation coefficients. It may be used in measuring the variability of a statistic between different samples of a population just as the SD serves as a measure of variability of individual scores in a particular sample. The SE may be used in testing the significance or dependability of the relevant statistic. Because the SE is a measure of the sampling error of a statistic, it may be used in computing the limits of a *confidence interval* within which the population parameter has a specified probability of falling. The SE of the statistics of two samples, drawn from the same or different populations, may again be used in computing the *SE of the difference* between such statistics.

The *SE of the difference* between the sample statistics of a particular type is the SD of the sampling distribution of such differences around the difference between the parameters of the populations from which the samples have been drawn. It is a measure of the *variability of such differences*. It finds application in testing the significance of difference between the statistics of two samples exposed to different levels of experimental treatments. It is, thus, useful in testing experimental hypotheses.

8.11.1   Standard Error of the Mean

The means of samples drawn from the same population form a frequency distribution, called the *sampling distribution of means*, around the parametric mean of that population. The mean of this distribution coincides with the population mean (μ), while its SD is the SE of the means. If a theoretical sampling distribution of means has been constructed based on the probability theory instead of actual sampling and experimental determination of the means, the SD of the distribution is the *true or population* SE of the means and is represented by the symbol $\sigma_{\bar{x}}$. The SD of an experimental sampling distribution, computed by determining the sample means experimentally, is an estimate of $\sigma_{\bar{x}}$ and is represented by $s_{\bar{x}}$.

The $s_{\bar{x}}$ is a measure of the deviation of sample means from the population mean. Being an index of the sampling error of means, it is computed to see how far $\bar{X}$ can be used as a dependable estimate of the population mean (μ). It is used in computing a confidence interval in which μ has a specified probability of falling. It is also used in computing the SE *of the difference* between sample means required for testing experimental hypotheses.

Of course, $s_{\bar{x}}$ could be computed experimentally from the data of a large number of samples of equal sizes, drawn repeatedly from the same population. But it can be conveniently estimated even by using a single sample. The value of $s_{\bar{x}}$ is inversely proportional to the square root of the size of the sample used.

The computation of $s_{\bar{x}}$ depends on the nature of the population and the method of sampling. Some examples are given below.

1. Simple random sampling without replacement.

Two types of populations may be subjected to simple random sampling without replacement.

(a)   For a *finite population* of size N exceeding the sample size n,

$$\sigma_{\bar{X}} = \frac{\sigma}{\sqrt{n}} \sqrt{\frac{N-n}{N-1}}.$$

Because the population SD(σ) is usually unknown, the unbiased sample SD (s) computed with ($n-1$) instead of n as the denominator is used in place of σ and the estimated SE ($s_{\bar{x}}$) is, thus, obtained. So, where

$$s = \sqrt{\frac{\sum(X-\bar{X})^2}{n-1}}$$

$$s_{\bar{X}} = \frac{s}{\sqrt{n}} \sqrt{\frac{N-n}{N-1}}.$$

But when the sample SD used has been computed with n instead of ($n-1$) as the denominator,

$$s = \sqrt{\frac{\sum(X-\bar{X})^2}{n}}$$

$$s_{\bar{X}} = \frac{s}{\sqrt{n-1}} \sqrt{\frac{N-n}{N-1}}.$$

(b)   For an *infinite population* ($N=\infty$),

$$\sigma_{\bar{X}} = \frac{\sigma}{\sqrt{n}} \sqrt{\frac{N-n}{N-1}} = \frac{\sigma}{\sqrt{n}} \sqrt{\frac{\infty-n}{\infty-1}}$$

or

$$\sigma_{\bar{X}} = \frac{\sigma}{\sqrt{n}}.$$

On replacing σ by the unbiased SD, computed with $(n-1)$ as the denominator,

$$s_{\bar{X}} = \frac{s}{\sqrt{n}}, \text{ where } s = \sqrt{\frac{\sum(X - \bar{X})^2}{n-1}}.$$

But if the sample SD used has been computed with n instead of $(n-1)$ as the denominator, then

$$s_{\bar{X}} = \frac{s}{\sqrt{n-1}}, \text{ where } s = \sqrt{\frac{\sum(X - \bar{X})^2}{n}}.$$

2. Simple random sampling with replacement.

In case the sampling has been done by this method, irrespective of whether the population is finite or infinite,

$$\sigma_{\bar{X}} = \frac{\sigma}{\sqrt{n}}.$$

Because σ is unknown, the sample SD (s) is used in its place:

$$s_{\bar{X}} = \frac{s}{\sqrt{n}}, \text{ where } s = \sqrt{\frac{\sum(X - \bar{X})^2}{n-1}}$$

or

$$s_{\bar{X}} = \frac{s}{\sqrt{n-1}}, \text{ where } s = \sqrt{\frac{\sum(X - \bar{X})^2}{n}}.$$

3. Stratified random sampling.

Two types of populations may be subjected to stratify random sampling.

(a) For a population in which the means of different strata differ negligibly, $\sigma_{\bar{X}}$ and $s_{\bar{X}}$ are computed by the same formulae as used in the case of simple random sampling.

(b) If there are substantial differences between the means of different strata in the population, then

$$\sigma_{\bar{X}} = \sqrt{\frac{\sigma^2 - \sigma_{st}^2}{n}},$$

where σ^2 and σ_{st}^2 are the population variances of, respectively, the entire population and the strata. The estimated SE ($s_{\bar{x}}$) may be computed similarly using the corresponding sample variances. Where X_1, X_2 and so on are the raw scores of different strata; $\bar{X}_1, \bar{X}_2$ and so on are the respective stratum means; n_1, n_2 and so on are the respective stratum sizes; $\bar{X}$ is the grand mean and s is the unbiased SD of the entire sample, N is the total sample size and s_{st} is the SD of the sample strata:

$$s_{st}^2 = \frac{n_1(\bar{X}_1 - \bar{X})^2 + n_2(\bar{X}_2 - \bar{X})^2 + \cdots + n_k(\bar{X}_k - \bar{X})^2}{N},$$

$$s_{\bar{X}} = \sqrt{\frac{s^2 - s_{st}^2}{N}}.$$

8.11.2   Standard Error of Proportions

Where the population is divided into two classes with respect to a variable and the proportions of cases in those classes are θ and $(1-\theta)$, respectively, the population or the true SE (σ_θ) and the estimated SE (s_p) of the proportion of cases in the first class are obtained as follows:

$$\sigma_\theta = \sqrt{\frac{\theta(1-\theta)}{N}}$$

$$s_p = \sqrt{\frac{p(1-p)}{n}} = \sqrt{\frac{pq}{n}},$$

where p and q are the proportion of cases in the respective classes in a sample of size n.

8.12   Power of the Test

We have already defined alpha (α) as the probability of making a Type I error and beta (β) as the probability of making a Type II error. We have just considered that there is an inverse relation between the likelihood of making the two types of errors, that is, a decrease in α will increase β for a given sample of N elements. If we wish to reduce Type I and Type II errors, we must increase N.

Various statistical tests offer the possibility of different balances between the two types of errors. For achieving this balance, the notion of the power function of a statistical test is relevant.

Conceptually, the power of an experiment is a measure of the sensitivity of the experiment to detect a *real effect* of the independent variable. By *a real effect of the independent variable*, we mean an effect that produces a change in the dependent variable. If the independent variable does not produce a change in the dependent variable, it has no effect, and we say that the independent variable does not have a *real* effect.

In analysing the data from an experiment, we 'detect' a real effect of the independent variable by rejecting the null hypothesis (H_0). Thus, power is defined in terms of rejecting H_0. Mathematically, the power of an experiment is defined as the probability that the results of an experiment will allow the rejection of the null hypothesis if the independent variable has a real effect. In brief, the power of a test is defined as the probability of rejecting the null hypothesis (H_0) when it is, in fact, false, and, thus, must be rejected, that is,

Power = 1 − probability of Type II error = $1 - \beta$.

It may be noted that the power of a test increases with the increase in the size of sample (N).

From the above-noted equation of power, it is also derived that $\beta = 1 -$ power. By maximising power, we minimise beta, which means that we minimise the probability of making a Type II error. Thus, power is a very important topic. Hence, the power of a statistical test is the probability that the test will correctly reject a false null hypothesis.

As the definition implies, the more powerful a statistical test is, the more readily it will detect a treatment effect when one really exists (correctly rejecting H_0). It should be clear that the concepts of power and Type II error are closely related. When a treatment effect exists, the hypothesis test will have one of two results: (a) it can fail to discover the existing treatment effect (a Type II error) and (ii) it can correctly detect the presence of a treatment effect (rejecting a false null hypothesis).

We have already noted that the probability of a Type II error is identified by the symbol beta, β. Thus, the probability of correctly rejecting a false H_0 must be $1 - \beta$. If, for example, a hypothesis test has a probability of 0.20 (20% chance) of failing to detect a treatment effect (Type II error), then it must have a probability of 0.80 (80% chance) of successfully detecting it. Thus, the power of a statistical test refers to the probability of rejecting a false H_0, which is determined by

$$\text{Power} = p \, (\text{rejecting a false } H_0) = 1 - \beta.$$

The power of a statistical test depends on the size of the treatment effect. Therefore, it does not have a single value for every hypothesis test. When a treatment has a large effect, it will be easy to detect this effect, and power will be high. On the other hand, when the treatment effect is very small, it will be difficult to detect, and power will be low. Thus, rather than talking about power as a single value, we must examine the different values of power associated with different magnitudes of treatment effect.

We know that the null hypothesis is rejected whenever sample data are in the critical region. With this in mind, we can restate the definition of power as follows:

Power is the probability of obtaining sample data in the critical region when the null hypothesis is false. Because 'data in the critical region' is equivalent to 'rejecting the null hypothesis', this definition is equivalent to our original definition of power.

Since power is a probability, its value can vary from 0.00 to 1.00. The higher the power, the more sensitive the experiment to detect a real effect of the independent variable. Experiments with as high as 0.80 or higher are very desirable but rarely seen in behavioural sciences. Values of 0.40–0.60 are much more common. It is especially useful to determine the power of an experiment when (a) initially designing the experiment and (b) interpreting the results of experiments that fail to detect any real effects of the independent variable, that is, experiments that retain H_0.

8.13 The Logic of Hypothesis Testing

It is usually impossible or impractical for a researcher to observe every individual in a population. Therefore, researchers usually collect data from a sample and then use the sample data to help answer questions about the population from which the research samples are drawn. Hypothesis testing is a statistical procedure that allows researchers to use sample data to draw inferences about the population of interest.

Hypothesis testing is one of the most commonly used inferential procedures. Although the details of a hypothesis test will change from one situation to another, the general process will remain constant. In this chapter, we will introduce the general procedure for a hypothesis test.

A hypothesis test is a statistical method that uses sample data to evaluate a hypothesis about a population parameter. In very simple terms, the logic underlying the hypothesis-testing procedure is as follows:

(a) First, we state a hypothesis about a population. Usually, the hypothesis concerns the value of a population parameter. For example, we might hypothesise that the mean IQ for registered voters in the Odisha state is $\mu = 110$.

(b) Next, we obtain a random sample from the population. For example, we might select a random sample of $n = 200$ registered voters.

(c) Finally, we compare the sample data with the hypothesis. If the data are consistent with the hypothesis, we will conclude that the hypothesis is reasonable. But if there is a big discrepancy between the data and the hypothesis, we will decide that the hypothesis is wrong.

8.14   Procedure for Hypothesis Testing

To test a hypothesis means to tell (on the basis of the data the researcher has collected) whether or not the hypothesis seems to be valid. In hypothesis testing, the main question is: Whether the null hypothesis should be accepted or not? Procedure for hypothesis testing refers to all those steps that we undertake for making a choice between the two actions, that is, the rejection or acceptance of a null hypothesis.

A hypothesis test is a formalised procedure that follows a standard series of operations. To emphasise the formal structure of a hypothesis test, we will present hypothesis tests as a *four-step process*. For the purpose of demonstration, the following scenario will be used to provide a concrete background for the hypothesis-testing process.

Example 8.1 Alcohol appears to be involved in a variety of birth defects, including low birth weight and retarded growth. A researcher would like to investigate the effect of prenatal alcohol on birth weight. A random sample of $n=16$ pregnant rats is obtained. The mother rats are given daily doses of alcohol. At birth, one pup is selected from each litter to produce a sample of $n=16$ newborn rats. The average weight for the sample is $\bar{X}=15$ grams. The researcher would like to compare the sample with the general population of rats. It is known that regular newborn rats (not exposed to alcohol) have an average weight of $\mu=18$ grams. The distribution of weights is normal with $\sigma=4$. Figure 8.3 shows the overall research situation. Notice that the researcher's question concerns the unknown population that is exposed to alcohol and the data consist of a sample from this unknown population.

The following steps outline the hypothesis test that evaluates the effect of alcohol exposure on birth weight.

Step 1. State the hypotheses and select the alpha level.

Both hypotheses concern the population that is exposed to alcohol where the population mean is unknown (the population on the right-hand side of Figure 8.3). The null hypothesis states that exposure to alcohol has no effect on birth weight. Thus, the population of rats with alcohol exposure should have the same mean birth weight as the regular, unexposed rats. In symbols,

$$H_0: \mu_{\text{alcohol exposure}} = 18 \text{ (even with alcohol exposure, the rats still average 18 grams at birth).}$$

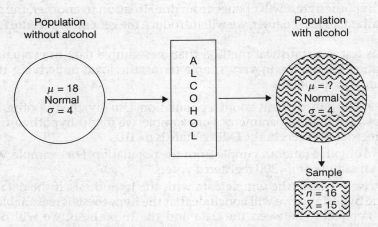

Figure 8.3   The structure of a research study to determine whether prenatal alcohol affects birth weight

The alternative hypothesis states that alcohol exposure does affect birth weight, so the exposed population should be different from the regular rats. In symbols,

H_1: $\mu_{\text{alcohol exposure}} \neq 18$ (alcohol exposure will change birth weight).

Notice that both hypotheses concern the unknown population. For this test, we will use an alpha level of $\alpha = 0.05$, that is, we are taking 5% risk of committing a Type I error.

The formulation of hypotheses is an important step which must be accomplished with due care in accordance with the object and nature of the problem under consideration. It also indicates whether we should use a one-tailed test or a two-tailed test. If H_1 is of the type greater than (i.e., when the hypothesized value of H_1 is greater than that of H_0: $H_1 > H_0$) or of the type lesser than (i.e., when the hypothesized value of H_1 is less than that of H_0: $H_1 < H_0$), we use a one-tailed test, but when H_1 is of the type 'whether greater or smaller' (i.e., when the hypothesized value of H_1 is not equal to that of H_0: $H_1 \neq H_0$), then we use a two-tailed test. Thus, in the present example, we use a two-tailed test.

The hypotheses are tested on a pre-determined level of significance, and as such the same should be specified. Generally, in practice, either 0.05 or 0.01 level is adopted for the purpose. However, in the present study, we take $\alpha = 0.05$. The factors that affect the level of significance are: (a) the magnitude of the difference between sample means, (b) the size of the samples, (c) the variability of measurements within samples and (d) whether the hypothesis is directional or non-directional. A directional hypothesis is one which predicts the direction of the difference between, say, means. In brief, the level of significance must be adequate in the context of the purpose and nature of enquiry.

Step: 2. Set the decision criteria by locating the critical region.

By definition, the critical region consists of outcomes that are very unlikely if the null hypothesis is true. To locate the critical region, we will go through a *three-stage process*. First, we begin with the population of birth weight scores for rats that have been exposed to alcohol. According to the H_0, the mean for this population is $\mu = 18$ grams. In addition, it is known that the population of birth weight scores is normal with $\sigma = 4$. Second, we use the hypothesised population to determine the complete set of sample outcomes that could be obtained if the null hypothesis is true. Because the researcher plans to use a sample of $n = 16$ rats, we construct the distribution of sample means for $n = 16$. This distribution of sample means is often called the *null distribution* because it specifies exactly what kinds of research outcomes should be obtained according to the null hypothesis. For this example, the null distribution is centred at $\mu = 18$ (from H_0) and has an SE of $\sigma_{\bar{x}} = \sigma / \sqrt{n} = 4 / \sqrt{16} = 4 / 4 = 1$. Finally, we use the null distribution to identify the critical region, which consists of those outcomes that are very unlikely if the null hypothesis is true. In our example, with $\alpha = 0.05$ (a two-tailed test), the critical region consists of the extreme 5% of the total distribution—each tail contains 2.5% of the distribution. As we saw earlier, for any normal distribution, z-scores of $z = \pm 1.96$ separate the middle 95% from the extreme 5% (a proportion of 0.0250 in each tail). Thus, if the null hypothesis is true, the most unlikely outcomes correspond to z-score values beyond ± 1.96. This is the critical region or region of rejection for our test.

Step 3: Collect the data and compute the test statistics.

At this point, we would select our random sample of $n = 16$ pups whose mothers had received alcohol during pregnancy. The birth weight would be recorded for each pup and the sample mean computed. As noted, we obtained a sample mean of $\bar{X} = 15$ grams. The sample mean is then converted to a z-score, which is our test statistic

$$z = \frac{\bar{X} - \mu}{\sigma_{\bar{x}}} = \frac{15 - 18}{1} = \frac{-3}{1} = -3.00.$$

Step 4: Make a decision.

The z-score computed in Step 3 has a value of –3.00, which is beyond the boundary of –1.96. Therefore, the sample mean is located in the critical region. This is a very unlikely outcome if the null hypothesis is true, so our decision is to reject the null hypothesis. In addition to this statistical decision concerning the null hypothesis, it is customary to state a conclusion about the results of the research study. For this example, we conclude that prenatal exposure to alcohol does have a significant effect on birth weight.

Summary

In this chapter, we have discussed the topic of testing of hypothesis citing an experiment involving a repeated measures design. The essential features of the repeated measures design are that there are paired scores between conditions and difference scores are analysed. Student's t-test for correlated groups is one of the appropriate statistical inference tests to analyse this type of data.

In any hypothesis-testing experiment, there are always two hypotheses that compete to explain the results. They are called the alternative hypothesis and the null hypothesis. The alternative hypothesis specifies that the independent variable is responsible for the differences in the score values between the conditions. The alternative hypothesis may be directional or non-directional. It is legitimate to use a directional hypothesis when there is a good theoretical basis and good supporting evidence in the literature. If the experiment is a basic fact-finding experiment, ordinarily a non-directional hypothesis should be used. A directional alternative hypothesis is evaluated with a one-tailed probability value, and a non-directional alternative hypothesis with a two-tailed probability value.

The null hypothesis is the logical counterpart to the alternative hypothesis such that if the null hypothesis is false, the alternative hypothesis must be true. If the alternative hypothesis is non-directional, the null hypothesis specifies that the independent variable has no effect on the dependent variable. If the alternative hypothesis is directional, the null hypothesis states that the independent variable has no effect in the direction specified.

In evaluating the data from an experiment, we never directly evaluate the alternative hypothesis. We always first evaluate the null hypothesis. The null hypothesis is evaluated by assuming chance alone is responsible for the differences in scores between conditions. In doing this evaluation, we calculate the probability of getting the obtained result or a result even more extreme if chance alone is responsible. If this obtained probability is equal to or lower than the alpha level, we consider the null hypothesis explanation unreasonable, and, therefore, we reject the null hypothesis. We conclude by accepting the alternative hypothesis, since it is the only other explanation. If the obtained probability is greater than the alpha level, we retain the null hypothesis. It is still considered a reasonable explanation of the data. Of course, if the null hypothesis is not rejected, the alternative hypothesis cannot be accepted. The conclusion applies legitimately only to the population from which the sample was randomly drawn or selected.

The alpha level is usually set at 0.05 or 0.01 to minimise the probability of making a Type I error. A Type I error occurs when the null hypothesis is rejected and it is actually true. The alpha level limits the probability of making a Type I error. It is also possible to make a Type II error. This error occurs when we retain the null hypothesis and it is false. Beta is defined as the probability of making a Type II error. When alpha is made more stringent, beta increases.

In addition, we have discussed in detail the sampling errors, sampling distribution, SE of the mean and proportions, power of the test and also the logic of hypothesis testing. Finally, we have discussed a four-step process for hypothesis testing through an illustrative problem using a z-test.

Key Terms

- Alpha level (α)
- Alternative hypothesis (H1)
- Beta (β)
- Correct decision
- Correlated group design
- Critical region
- Critical value
- Decision criteria
- Decision making
- Directional hypothesis
- Errors of inference
- Hypothesis
- Levels of significance
- Logic of hypothesis testing
- Non-directional hypothesis

- Null hypothesis (H_0)
- One-tailed test
- Power of the test
- Region of acceptance
- Region of rejection
- Repeated measures design
- Replicated measures design
- Sampling distribution
- Sampling errors
- Standard error
- State of reality
- Type I error
- Type II error
- Two-tailed test

Questions and Problems

1. Differentiate between the following:
   (a) Observational and true experimental type of research.
   (b) Descriptive and inferential statistics.

2. Discuss the basic concepts concerning the testing of hypothesis by the help of a hypothetical experiment.

3. What do you mean by a hypothesis? Explain the concepts null hypothesis and alternative hypothesis.

4. Explain the following concepts:
   (a) Levels of significance   (b) Errors of inference
   (c) One-tailed and two-tailed tests

5. Write notes on the following:
   (a) Sampling distribution   (b) Sampling errors

6. What is meant by the standard error of a statistic? Explain the standard error of the mean and proportions.

7. Explain the following with reference to testing of hypothesis:
   (a) Type I and Type II errors   (b) Power of the test

8. What is meant by hypothesis testing? Explain the logic of hypothesis testing.

9. What do you mean by hypothesis testing? Analyse the procedures for hypothesis testing.

10. With the help of examples, explain the nature of null hypothesis and alternative hypothesis in directional and non-directional tests.

11. In the z-score formula as it is used in a hypothesis test:

    (a) Explain what is measured by $\bar{X} - \mu$ in the numerator.
    (b) Explain what is measured by the standard error in the denominator.

12. The term error is used in two different ways in the context of a hypothesis test. First, there is the concept of standard error, and second, there is the concept of a Type I error.

    (a) What factor can a researcher control that will reduce the risk of a Type I error?
    (b) What factor can a researcher control that will reduce the standard error?

13. Why do we test H_0 to establish an effect instead of H_1?

14. A normal population has a mean of $\mu=100$. A sample of $n=36$ is selected from the population, and a treatment is administered to the sample. After treatment, the sample mean is computed to be $\bar{X}=106$.

    (a) Assuming that the population standard deviation is $\sigma=12$, use the data to test whether or not the treatment has a significant effect. Test with $\alpha=0.05$.
    (b) Repeat the hypothesis test, but this time assume that the population standard deviation is $\sigma=30$.
    (c) Compare the results from part (a) and part (b). How does the population standard deviation influence the outcome of a hypothesis test?

15. A mood questionnaire has been standardised so that the scores form a normal distribution with $\mu=50$ and $\sigma=15$. A psychologist would like to use this test to examine how the environment affects mood. A sample of $n=25$ individuals is obtained, and the individuals are given the mood test in a darkly painted, dimly lit room with plain metal desks and no windows. The average score of the sample is $\bar{X} = 43$.

    (a) Do the sample data provide sufficient evidence to conclude that the environment has a significant effect on mood? Test at the 0.05 level of significance.
    (b) Repeat the hypothesis test using the 0.01 level of significance.
    (c) Compare the results from part (a) and part (b). How does the level of significance influence the outcome of a hypothesis test?

16. A psychologist examined the effect of chronic alcohol abuse on memory. In this experiment, a standardised memory test was used. Scores on this test for the general population form a normal distribution with $\mu=50$ and $\sigma=6$. A sample of $n=22$ alcohol abusers has a mean score of $\bar{X} = 47$. Is there evidence for memory impairment among alcoholics? Use $\alpha=0.01$ for a one-tailed test.

17. A school principal is interested in a new method for teaching VIIIth grade social studies, which he believes will increase the amount of material learned. To test this method, the principal conducts the following experiment. The VIII grade students in the school district are grouped in pairs based on matching their IQs and past

grades. Twenty matched pairs are randomly selected for the experiment. One member of each pair is randomly assigned to a group that receives the new method, and the other member of each pair to a group that receives the standard instruction. At the end of the course, all students take a common final examination. The following are the results:

Pair No.	New Method	Standard Instruction
1	95	83
2	75	68
3	73	80
4	85	82
5	78	84
6	86	78
7	93	85
8	88	82
9	75	84
10	84	68
11	72	81
12	84	91
13	75	72
14	87	81
15	94	83
16	82	87
17	70	65
18	84	76
19	72	63
20	83	82

(a) What is the alternative hypothesis? Use a directional hypothesis.
(b) What is the null hypothesis?
(c) Using $\alpha = 0.05_{1\,tail}$, what is your conclusion?
(d) What error may you be making by your conclusion in part (c)?
(e) To what population does your conclusion apply?

18. A new competitor in the scotch whiskey industry conducts an experiment to compare their scotch whiskey (called McPherson's Joy) to the other three leading brands. Two hundred scotch drinkers are randomly sampled from the scotch drinkers

living in the New York city. Each individual is asked to taste the four scotch whiskeys and pick the one they like the best. Of course, the whiskeys are unmarked, and the order in which they are tasted is balanced. The number of subjects that preferred each brand is shown in the following table:

McPherson's Joy	Brand X	Brand Y	Brand Z	Total
58	52	48	42	200

(a) What is the alternative hypothesis? Use a non-directional hypothesis.
(b) What is the null hypothesis?
(c) Using $\alpha = 0.05$, what do you conclude?

19. An experimental psychologist interested in animal learning conducts an experiment to determine the effect of ACTH (adrenocorticotropic hormone) on avoidance learning. Twenty 100-day-old male rats are randomly selected from the University Vivarium for the experiment. Of the 20 randomly chosen rats, 10 rats receive injections of ACTH, 30 minutes before being placed in the avoidance situation. The other 10 receive placebo injections. The number of trials for each animal to learn the task is given below:

ACTH	Placebo
58	74
73	92
80	87
78	84
75	72
74	82
79	76
72	90
66	95
77	85

(a) What is the non-directional alternative hypothesis?
(b) What is the null hypothesis?
(c) Using $\alpha = 0.01_{2\text{-tail}}$, what do you conclude?
(d) What error may you have made by concluding as you did in part (c)?
(e) To what population do these results apply?

20. A researcher in human sexuality is interested in determining whether there is a relationship between sexual gender and time-of-day preference for having intercourse. A survey is conducted, and the results are shown in the following table; entries are the number of individuals who preferred morning or evening times.

Sexual Gender	Intercourse Time		Total
	Morning	Evening	
Male	36	24	60
Female	28	32	60
Total	64	56	120

    (a) What is the null hypothesis?

    (b) Using $\alpha = 0.05$, what do you conclude?

21. A psychologist is interested in whether the internal states of individuals affect their perceptions. Specifically, the psychologist wants to determine if hunger influences perception. To test this hypothesis, she randomly divided 24 subjects into three groups of 8 subjects per group. The subjects are asked to describe 'pictures' that they are shown on the screen. Actually, there are no pictures, just ambiguous shapes or forms. Hunger is manipulated through food deprivation. One group is shown the pictures 1 hr after eating, another group 4 hr after eating and the last group 12 hr after eating. The number of food-related objects reported by each subject is recorded. The following data are collected:

Food Deprivation		
1 hr	4 hr	12 hr
2	6	8
5	7	10
7	6	15
2	10	19
1	15	9
8	12	14
7	7	15
6	6	12

    (a) What is the overall null hypothesis?

    (b) What is your conclusion? Use $\alpha = 0.05$.

    (c) Using the Newman–Keuls test with $\alpha = 0.05_{2\text{-tail}}$ do all possible post hoc comparisons between pairs of means. What is your conclusion?

22. An engineer working for a leading electronics firm claims to have invented a process for making longer lasting TV picture tubes. Tests run on 24 picture tubes made with the new process show a mean life of 1725 hr and an SD of 85 hr. Tests run over the last three years on a very large number of TV picture tubes made with the old process show a mean life of 1538 hr. Is the engineer correct in her claim? Use $\alpha = 0.01_{1\text{-tail}}$ in making your decision.

23. In a study to determine the effect of alcohol on aggressiveness, 17 adult volunteers were randomly assigned to two groups, an experimental group and a control group. The subjects in the experimental group drank vodka disguised in orange juice, and the subjects in the control group drank only orange juice. After the drinks were finished, a test of aggressiveness was administered. The scores below were obtained; higher scores indicate greater aggressiveness.

Orange Juice	Vodka Plus Orange Juice
11	14
9	13
14	19
15	16
7	15
10	17
8	11
10	18
8	

    (a) What is the alternative hypothesis? Use a non-directional hypothesis.

    (b) What is the null hypothesis?

    (c) Using $\alpha = 0.05_{2\text{-tail}}$, what is your conclusion?

24. The dean of admissions at a large university has weighted high school grades heavily when deciding which students to admit to the university, yet he has never seen any data relating the two variables. So he decides to conduct a study to find out the relationship between high school grades and college grades. He randomly samples

15 seniors from his university and obtains their high school and college grades. The following data are obtained:

Subjects	High School Grades	College Grades
1	2.2	1.5
2	2.6	1.7
3	2.5	2.0
4	2.2	2.4
5	3.0	1.7
6	3.0	2.3
7	3.1	3.0
8	2.6	2.7
9	2.8	3.2
10	3.2	3.6
11	3.4	2.5
12	3.5	2.8
13	4.0	3.2
14	3.6	3.9
15	3.8	4.0

(a) Compute r_{obt} for these data.

(b) Is the correlation significant? Use $\alpha = 0.05_{2\text{-tail}}$.

(c) What proportion of the variability in college grades is accounted for by the high school grades?

(d) Is the dean justified in weighting high school grades heavily when determining which students to admit to the university?

25. An experiment is conducted to evaluate the effect of smoking on heart rate. Ten subjects who smoke cigarettes are randomly selected for the experiment. Each subject serves in two conditions. In condition 1, the subject rests for an hour, after which heart rate is measured. In condition 2, the subject rests for an hour and then smokes two cigarettes. In condition 2, heart rate is measured after the subject has finished smoking the cigarettes. The data are given below:

Subject	Heart Beats Per Minute	
	No Smoking	Smoking
1	72	76
2	80	84
3	68	75
4	74	73
5	80	86
6	85	88
7	86	84
8	78	80
9	68	72
10	67	70

(a) What is the non-directional alternative hypothesis?
(b) What is the null hypothesis?
(c) Using $\alpha = 0.05_{2\text{-tail}}$, what do you conclude?

26. You are interested in testing the hypothesis that adult men and women differ in logical reasoning ability. To do so, you randomly selected 16 adults from the city in which you live and administer a logical reasoning test to them. A higher score indicates better logical reasoning ability. The following scores are obtained:

Men	Women
70	80
60	50
82	81
65	75
83	95
92	85
85	93
	75
	90

In answering the following questions, assume that the data violate the assumptions underlying the use of the appropriate parametric test and that you must analyse the data with a non-parametric test.

(a) What is the null hypothesis?
(b) Using $\alpha = 0.05_{2\text{-tail}}$, what is your conclusion?

27. A student believes that physical science professors are more authoritarian than social science professors. She conducts an experiment in which six physics, six psychology and six sociology professors are randomly selected and given a questionnaire measuring authoritarianism. The results are shown below. The higher the score, the more authoritarian is the individual. Assume the data seriously violate normality assumptions. What do you conclude, using $\alpha = 0.05$?

Professors		
Physics	**Psychology**	**Sociology**
75	73	71
82	80	80
80	85	90
97	92	78
94	70	94
76	69	68

28. A sleep researcher is interested in determining whether taking naps can improve performance and, if so, whether it matters if the naps are taken in the afternoon or evening. Thirty undergraduates are randomly sampled and assigned to one of six conditions, napping in the afternoon or evening, resting in the afternoon or evening, or a normal activity control condition again in the afternoon or evening. There are five subjects in each condition. Each subject performs the activity appropriate for his or her assigned condition, after which a performance test is given. The higher the score, the better the performance. The following results were obtained. What is your conclusion? Use $\alpha = 0.05$ and assume that the data are from normally distributed populations.

Time of Day	Activity		
	Napping	**Resting**	**Normal**
Afternoon	8	7	3
	7	6	5
	6	5	6
	9	8	4
	5	4	5
Evening	6	5	4
	7	4	3
	6	4	3
	5	3	2
	4	5	4

29. (a) Define the power of a hypothesis test.
    (b) List the factors that affect the power of an experiment and explain how they can be used to increase power.
    (c) What happens to power as the treatment distribution gets farther from the null distribution?

30. (a) Explain why power for a hypothesis test can never be less than the alpha level for the test. What happens to power as the treatment distribution gets very close to the null distribution?
    (b) Suppose that a researcher normally uses an alpha level of 0.01 for hypothesis tests, but this time used an alpha level of 0.05. What does this change in the alpha level do to the amount of power? What does it do to the risk of a Type I error?
    (c) A researcher wants a statistical test to be powerful, yet he would also like to avoid a Type I error. Which one of the following approaches would achieve these goals? Explain your answer.

    (i) Increase the alpha level (for example, from 0.05 to 0.10).
    (ii) Use a small alpha level, but increase the sample size.
    (iii) Use a one-tailed test.

31. Fill in the blanks:

    (i) In a simple true experiment type of research one _____ variable is manipulated and its effects on some _____ variable is studied.
    (ii) Statistical analysis has been divided into two areas, _____ statistics and _____ statistics.
    (iii) The two main purposes of inferential statistics are _____ and _____.
    (iv) Both null hypothesis and alternative hypothesis are stated in terms of population _____.
    (v) Null hypothesis is a hypothesis of _____ difference.
    (vi) Alternative hypothesis is simply the _____ of the null hypothesis.
    (vii) Type I error occurs when a researcher rejects a null hypothesis that is actually _____.
    (viii) Type II error is made when we accept a null hypothesis which is _____.
    (ix) In _____ tailed tests rejection region is located in one tail.
    (x) The standard deviation of a sampling distribution is called _____.
    (xi) The distribution formed of all possible values of a statistics is called the _____.
    (xii) The mean of the sampling distribution of means is equal to the _____.

32. Write whether the following statements are True or False.

    (i) Probability of Type I error is called α (alpha).
    (ii) Probability of Type II error is called β (beta).
    (iii) H_0 represents null hypothesis and H_1 alternative hypothesis.

(iv) When the null hypothesis is true and our test accepts it, this is called Type I error.

(v) The reciprocal of standard error is a measure of reliability of precision of the sample.

(vi) A two-tailed test is a directional statistical test.

(vii) When the area of rejection is located in both tails of the distribution, it is called the one-tailed test.

(viii) The term standard error of the mean is used to refer to the standard deviation of the distribution of sample means.

(ix) The sample mean $\bar{X}$ is the best estimator of the population mean μ.

(x) Sampling error is a difference between a sample statistic and its corresponding population parameter.

33. Find out the correct answer from among the four alternatives.

(i) The standard error of proportions in a sample of size n is determined by:

(a) $\sqrt{\dfrac{pq}{n}}$ (b) $\sqrt{npq}$

(c) $\sqrt{\dfrac{np}{q}}$ (d)   None of the above

(ii) In a two-tailed test, 95% confidence interval (or fudicial limits) for the population mean is constructed as:

(a) $\bar{X} \pm 3\sigma_{\bar{x}}$ (b) $\bar{X} \pm 1.96\sigma_{\bar{x}}$
(c) $\bar{X} \pm 1.64\sigma_{\bar{x}}$ (d)   None of the above

(iii) In a two-tailed test, 99% fudicial limits of the population mean are:

(a) $\bar{X} \pm 2.33\text{SE}$ (b) $\bar{X} + 1.96\text{SE}$
(c) $\bar{X} \pm 2.58\text{SE}$ (d)   None of the above

(iv) The amount of sampling error for a sample mean $\bar{X} = 6.5$ and population mean $\mu = 5.8$ is:

(a) +0.7   (b)   +1.7
(c) −1.2   (d)   None of the above

(v) If the sample size $n = 64$ and $s = 4$, the standard error of the sample mean is:

(a) 0.5   (b)   0.0625
(c) 16   (d)   None of the above

(vi) Sampling distribution refers to the distribution of

(a) Individual scores   (b)   Sample means
(c) Sample SD   (d)   None of the above

(vii) Power of a statistical test is equal to:

(a) $1 - \alpha$ (b) $1 - \sigma$
(c) $1 - \beta$ (d)   None of the above

(viii) Large sample theory is applicable when:

   (a) $n \geq 30$ (b) $n < 30$
   (c) n is at least 100   (d) None of the above

(ix) Probability of Type II error is

   (a) Alpha (α)   (b) Beta (β)
   (c) Gama (γ)   (d) None of the above

(x) The difference between a sample statistic and its corresponding population parameter is known as:

   (a) Sampling error   (b) Standard error
   (c) Experimental error   (d) None of the above

Correlation

After completing this chapter you will be able to:

- Understand the concepts, usage and limitation of correlation.
- Use a scatter diagram to visualise the relationship between two variables.
- Describe the assumptions, properties and uses of product–moment correlation.
- Compute the Pearson correlation r from both ungrouped and grouped data.
- Interpret various types of coefficients of correlations.
- Understand how different factors affect the correlation coefficient.
- Understand, compare and compute biserial, point biserial, tetrachoric and partial correlation coefficients.

9.1 Introduction

Correlation and regression are very much related. They both involve the relationship between two variables. Regression, however, is primarily concerned with using the relationship for prediction, whereas correlation is primarily concerned with finding out whether a relationship exists and with determining its magnitude and direction.

The data in which we secure measures of one variable for each individual are called a *univariate* distribution. If we have pairs of measures on two variables of each individual, the joint presentation of the two sets of scores is called a *bivariate* distribution. *Bivariate statistics* analyse the data of two variables in a sample, measure the relationship between two variables or predict the most likely value of one variable in an individual from the given value of another variable in the same individual. *Multivariate statistics* analyse the data of more than two variables: measure their relationships or predict the most likely value of one variable from the given values of two or more other variables.

Correlation coefficients are descriptive statistics for measuring the relationship between variables. *Regression* is the prediction statistics for giving the most likely value of a variable depending on the value(s) of one or more other variables. Correlation and regression, involving only two variables, are bivariate statistics. Partial and multiple correlations and multiple regressions involve more than two variables, and are called multivariate statistics. We will read about regression in detail in the next chapter.

9.2   Correlation

Correlation is a statistical technique that is basically used to measure and describe a relationship between two variables. In short, correlation explores the *magnitude* and *direction* of association between two or more variables, that is, how far the variations of a variable are related to those of one or more other variables in the same individual. It, thus, gives the magnitude and the algebraic sign of concomitant variations of variables related to each other.

Coefficient of correlation (or simply, correlation coefficient) is a *numerical index that expresses quantitatively the magnitude and direction of the relationship*. It is a kind of ratio which expresses the extent to which changes in one variable are accompanied by changes in the other variable.

9.2.1   The Characteristics of a Relationship

A correlation measures three characteristics of the relationship between X and Y variables. These three characteristics are as follows.

9.2.1.1   *The Direction of the Relationship*

Correlation can be classified into two basic categories, such as positive and negative.

In a *positive correlation,* the two variables tend to move in the same direction. If the X variable increases, the Y variable also increases; if the X variable decreases, the Y variable also decreases.

In a *negative correlation,* the two variables tend to go in opposite directions. As the X variable increases, the Y variable decreases. That is, it is an inverse relationship.

The direction of a relationship is identified by the sign of the correlation. A positive value (+) indicates a positive relationship; a negative value (–) indicates a negative relationship. The following example provides a description of positive and negative relationships. Suppose that you have noted that when the temperature is high, the seller tends to sell a lot of cold drinks. When the temperature is low, the seller sells relatively less number of cold drinks (see Figure 9.1[a]). This is an example of a positive correlation. At the same time, you have noted a relationship between temperature and coffee sales. In cold days, the seller sells much more coffee than in hot days (see Figure 9.1 [b]). This is an example of a negative relationship.

9.2.1.2   *The Form of the Relationship*

Correlation may be either linear or nonlinear, depending on whether the relation between the variables can be described by a straight or a curved line. In linear correlation, the magnitude of change of one variable bears a constant ratio to that of some other variable. In other words, linear correlation is a ratio of change between the two variables either in the same direction or in the opposite direction, and the graphical representation of the one variable with respect to other variable is a straight line.

Consider another situation in which with an increase of one variable, the second variable increases proportionately up to some point; after that with an increase in the first variable, the second variable starts decreasing. The graphical representation of the two variables will be a curved line. Such a relationship between the two variables is termed as the curvilinear correlation.

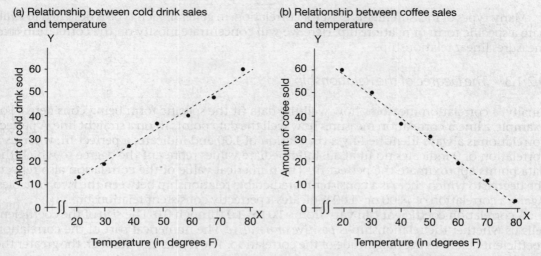

Figure 9.1   Examples of positive and negative relationships: (a) cold drink sales are positively correlated with temperature and (b) coffee sales are negatively correlated with temperature

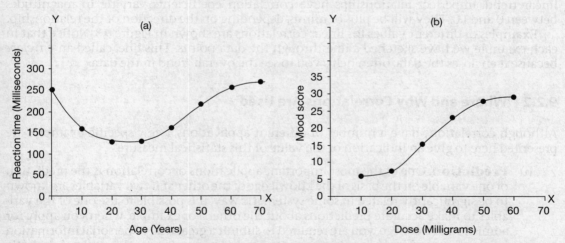

Figure 9.2   Examples of relationship which are not linear: (a) relationship between time and age and (b) relationship between mood and drug dose

In the preceding coffee and cold drink examples, the relationships tend to have a linear form; that is, the points in the scatter plot tend to form a straight line. Notice that (see Figure 9.1(a) and [b]) we have drawn a line through the middle of the data points in each figure to show the relationship. However, you should note that other form of relationship does exist. Figure 9.2(a) shows the relationship between reaction time (RT) and age. In this plot, there is a curved relationship. RT improves with age until the late teens, when it reaches a peak; after that, RT starts to get worse. Figure 9.2(b) shows the typical dose–response relationship. Again, this is not a straight line relationship. In this graph, the elevation in mood increases rather rapidly with dose increases. However, beyond a certain dose, the amount of improvement in mood levels off.

Many types of measurements exist for correlation. In general, each type is designed to evaluate a specific form of relationship. Here we will concentrate mostly on the correlation that measures linear relationships.

9.2.1.3 *The Degree of the Relationship*

Finally, a correlation measures how well the data fit the specific form being considered. For example, a linear correlation measures how well the data points fit on a straight line. A perfect correlation is always identified by a correlation of 1.00 and indicates a perfect fit, whereas a correlation of 0 indicates no fit at all. Intermediate values represent the degree to which the data points approximate the perfect fit. The numerical value of the correlation also reflects the degree to which there is a consistent, predictable relationship between the two variables. Again, a correlation of +1.00 or –1.00 indicates a perfectly consistent relationship.

A correlation coefficient can vary from +1.0 to –1.0 through 0.0. The *sign* of the coefficient tells us whether the relationship is *positive or negative*. The numerical part of the correlation coefficient describes the magnitude of the correlation. The higher the number, the greater the correlation. Since 1.00 is the higher number possible, it represents a perfect correlation. A correlation coefficient of +1.00 means that the correlation is perfect and the relationship is positive. A coefficient of –1.00 means that the correlation is perfect and the relationship is negative. When the relationship is non-existent, the correlation coefficient equals 0, which shows no linear trend. Imperfect relationships have correlation coefficients varying in magnitudes between 0 and 1.0. They will be plus or minus, depending on the direction of the relationship.

Examples of different values for linear correlations are shown in Figure 9.3. Notice that in each example we have sketched a line through the data points. This line, called an *envelope* because it encloses the data, often helps you to see the overall trend in the data.

9.2.2 Where and Why Correlations Are Used

Although correlations have a number of different applications, a few specific examples are presented here to give an indication of the value of this statistical measure.

(i) **Prediction.** One of the most important applications of correlation is the prediction of one variable on the basis of the knowledge of the other(s). If two variables are known to be significantly related in some systematic way, it is possible to use one of the variables to make accurate predictions about the other. For example, when you apply for admission to a college, you are required to submit a great deal of personal information in the form of your curriculum vita, including your scores on the Scholastic Achievement Test (SAT). College officials want this information so that they can predict your chances of success in college. It has been demonstrated over several years that the SAT scores and college grade point averages are correlated. Students who do well on the SAT tend to do well in college; students who have difficulty with the SAT tend to have difficulty in college. Based on this relationship, the college admissions office can make a prediction about the potential success of each applicant. However, this prediction may not be perfectly accurate, because perfectly accurate prediction depends upon the perfect correlation between the variables.

(ii) **Validity.** Correlation is used to determine the validity of a test. Suppose that a psychologist develops a new test for measuring intelligence. How could you show that this test is truly measuring what it claims, that is, how could you demonstrate the validity of the test? One common technique for demonstrating the validity is to use a correlation. If the test actually is measuring intelligence, then the scores on the test

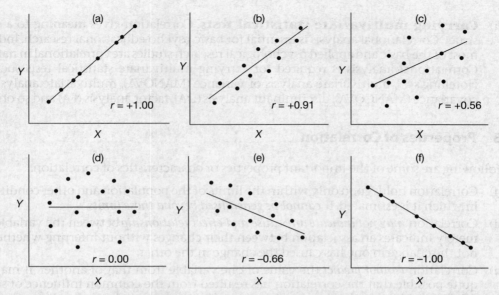

Figure 9.3   Examples of different values for linear correlations: (a) a perfect positive correlation, +1.00. (b) a strong positive relationship, +0.91. (c) a relatively weak positive relationship, +0.56. (d) a zero relationship, 0.00. (e) a relatively weak negative relationship, −0.66. (f) a perfect negative correlation, −1.00

should be related to other measures of intelligence, for examples, standardised IQ tests, performance on learning tasks, problem-solving ability and so on. The psychologist could measure the correlation between the new test and each of these other measures of intelligence in order to demonstrate that the new test is valid.

(iii)   **Reliability**. In addition to evaluating the validity of a measurement procedure, correlations are used to determine the reliability of a test. A measurement procedure is considered reliable to the extent that it produces stable, consistent measurements. That is, a reliable measurement procedure will produce the same (or nearly the same) scores when the same individuals are measured under the same conditions. For example, if your IQ scores were measured as 115 last week, you would expect to obtain nearly the same score if your IQ were measured again this week. One way to evaluate reliability is to use correlations to determine the relationship between two sets of measurements. When reliability is high, the correlation between two measurements should be strong and positive.

(iv)   **Theory verification.** Many psychological theories make specific predictions about the relationship between two variables. For example, a theory may predict a relationship between brain size and learning ability; a developmental theory may predict a relationship between parents' IQs and the child's IQ; a social psychologist may have a theory predicting a relationship between personality type and behaviour in a social situation. In each case, the prediction of the theory could be tested by determining the correlation between the two variables.

(v)   **Grouping variables.** Correlation helps us to group the variables or measures together for parsimonious interpretation of data. The variables having positive relationships among themselves will be grouped together, whereas variables having negative correlations will be grouped separately.

(vi) **Carrying multivariate statistical tests.** Correlation gives meaning to a construct. Correlational analysis is essential for basic psycho-educational research. Indeed, most of the basic and applied psychological research studies are correlational in nature. Correlational analysis is required for carrying multivariate statistical tests such as Hotelling's T², multivariate analysis of variance (MANOVA), multivariate analysis of covariance (MANCOVA), discriminant analysis (DA), factor analysis (FA) and so on.

9.2.3 Properties of Correlation

The following are some of the important properties or characteristics of correlation.

(i) Correlation holds good only within the limits of the population and other conditions in which it is estimated. It *cannot be generalised beyond those limits.*

(ii) Correlation *may not indicate any cause-and-effect relationship* between the variables. It merely indicates an association between their changes without inferring whether or not the change in one has caused the change in the other.

(iii) Correlation *cannot predict* the value of one variable from that of another. It may be quite possible that the correlation has resulted from the common influence of some other variable(s) on the correlated variable. However, regression or prediction can be worked out only if a significant correlation exists between the variables.

(iv) Correlation holds good even if any or all of the variables involved is/are free to *vary at random,* not being fixed or deliberately controlled by the investigator. For example, in the correlation between body height and weight of humans, both variables vary at random beyond the control of the investigator.

(v) Correlation suffers from *sampling errors.* So, correlation coefficients of samples drawn from a population form a sampling distribution around the parametric correlation coefficient as the mean. Both theoretical and experimental *sampling distributions* of correlation coefficients can be worked out. The standard deviation (SD) of such a sampling distribution is the standard error (SE) of the correlation coefficient. The SE of a computed correlation coefficient is used in evaluating its significance.

9.3 Product–Moment Correlation (*r*)

The product-moment coefficient of correlation was formulated by the British Mathematician Karl Pearson (1857-1936). Therefore, it is known as the Pearson correlation or the Pearson product-moment correlation. By far the most common correlation is the Pearson correlation, which is identified by the letter '*r*'. The Pearson correlation (*r*) measures the degree and direction (algebraic sign) of the linear relationship between two variables. It is, thus, a *coefficient of simple linear correlation.* Actually, when the relationship between two variables can be represented graphically by a straight line, it is known as the linear correlation. Such a correlation clearly reveals how the change in one variable is accompanied by a change in the other or to what extent the increase or decrease in one variable is accompanied by an increase or decrease in the other.

9.3.1 Assumptions of Pearson's *r*

The Pearsonian correlation coefficient (*r*) is based on the following assumptions.

(a) Both the variables, *X* and *Y*, are *continuous measurement variables* of either *interval* or *ratio* types, with *r* being inapplicable to nominal and ordinal variables. In other words, the units of measurement are equidistant throughout the range of scores involved in the correlation, and the measurements should be in terms of either in interval or ratio scales of measurement.

(b) The variables X and Y under study have *unimodal and fairly symmetrical distributions* in the population without marked skewness, although they need not be normally distributed. In other words, Pearson's 'r' does not assume the normality of distribution of the two variables involved. No matter what the shape of the distribution of either variable, we are always justified in computing 'r' to determine the strength of the (linear) relationship between the two variables.

(c) The paired scores of the variables in each individual are *independent* of such paired scores of all other individuals in the sample. In other words, the scores have been obtained in independent pairs, with each pair being unconnected with other pairs.

(d) The relationship between the two variables is linear; there exists a *linear relationship* between the two sets of scores of the variables X and Y. Thus, the variables X and Y under the study are *linearly related*. In other words, the scatter diagram of their scores will give a straight line curve.

(e) In computing r, we assume the linearity of regression between two variables involved in the study. In a scatter diagram, regression is linear if, except for chance fluctuations, the means of the successive columns lie on a straight line, and if the means of the successive rows lie on another straight line. If the line connecting the means of the columns and the line connecting the means of the rows do not deviate systematically from a straight line, we have linear regression. Such a line may have a slope which is positive, negative or even zero. If each time the X score increases by 1 unit, the Y score increases or decreases by a constant amount, then regression is linear.

(f) Pearson's r does not assume that whether an increase in the score on one variable is related or not to an increase or decrease in the score on the other variable. Pearson's r measures the strength or amount of the relationship if it exists. That is, we do not assume anything about either the direction or the magnitude of the relationship. Instead, we use r to determine the sign and size of the existing correlation, which may either be positive, zero or negative of any amount, but within the limits of -1.0 to $+1.0$.

9.3.2   Properties or Characteristics of Pearson's *r*

One of the formulae for r that looks simple is $r = \dfrac{\Sigma z_x z_y}{N-1}$, in which r is the Pearson product-moment coefficient of correlation, z_x is a standard score for the X variable, z_y is the corresponding standard score for the Y variable and N is the number of cases. This formula shows us some important characteristics of Pearson's r. Let us see these characteristics or properties in the following.

(i) **Pearson's *r* is a product moment *r*.** In physics or mechanics, a moment is the measure of the tendency to produce motion about a point or axis. Thus, the first moment about zero as an origin is the mean, since $\dfrac{\Sigma X}{N} = \bar{X}$. Also, the first moment about the mean is always zero, since $\dfrac{\Sigma x}{N} = 0$. If we raise scores to the second power, we obtain second moments, and, thus, $\dfrac{\Sigma x^2}{N}$ is the second moment about the mean. This is very similar to the formula for s^2, and if N is large, the two are practically identical. Hence, $\dfrac{\Sigma x^2}{N}$ is the second moment, and it is essentially equal to $\dfrac{\Sigma x^2}{N-1}$ or s^2, which is the square of the SD. If a moment involves the product of two variables, it is called a product–moment.

If other words, the sum of the deviations from the mean, raised to some power, and divided by N is called a 'moment'. When corresponding deviations in x and y are multiplied together, summed and divided by N (to give $\dfrac{\Sigma xy}{N}$) the term 'product-moment' is used. Thus, the fact that the product-moment, $\dfrac{\Sigma z_x z_y}{N-1}$, leads to r has led statisticians to refer to r as the Pearson product-moment coefficient of correlation, developed by Pearson.

(ii) **Pearson's r is a ratio.** This correlation is computed by

$$r = \frac{\text{degree to which } X \text{ and } Y \text{ vary together}}{\text{degree to which } X \text{ and } Y \text{ vary separately}}$$
$$= \frac{\text{covariability of } X \text{ and } Y}{\text{variability of } X \text{ and } Y \text{ separately}}$$

The r is that ratio which expresses the extent to which changes in one variable are accompanied by changes in the second variable. When there is a perfect linear relationship, every change in the X variable is accompanied by a corresponding change in the Y variable. For example, every time the value of X increases, there is either a perfectly predictable increase in Y (see Figure 9.3[a]) or a perfectly predictable decrease in Y (see Figure 9.3[f]). In both the cases, the result is a perfect linear relationship, with X and Y always varying together. In these cases, the covariability (X and Y together) is identical to the variability of X and Y separately, and the formula produces a correlation of +1.00 (Figure 9.3[a]) and a correlation of –1.00 (Figure 9.3[f]), respectively. At the other extreme, when there is no linear relationship, a change in the X variable does not correspond to any predictable change in Y. In this case, there is no covariability, and the resulting correlation is zero.

(iii) r_{xy} **equals to** r_{yx}. For any one person, we obtain the same product of scores regardless of whether we multiply z_x by z_y or z_y by z_x. Mathematicians call this the commutative law, and grade school pupils learn that $(7)(3)=(3)(7)$ when they learn the multiplication tables. If each product remains unchanged by such a reversal, it follows that if we should reverse all of the products, their total would remain the same and, hence, r_{yx} would equal to r_{xy}.

(iv) r **can be either positive or negative.** Standard scores are deviations from the mean, expressed in units of the SDs. Since their sum must be zero, ordinarily about half of them will be positive and half negative. This will be true for both z_x and z_y. If we arbitrarily pair most of the positive z_x values with positive z_y values, and if we also pair most of the negative z_x values with negative z_y values, nearly all of the products will be positive, $\Sigma z_x z_y$ will be positive, and, hence, r will be positive. On the other hand, if we pair positive z_x with negative z_y scores, and negative z_x with positive z_y scores, most of the products will be negative, $\Sigma z_x z_y$ will be negative and, hence, r will be negative.

(v) r **is confined within the limits of –1.00 and +1.00.** In other words, the correction coefficient can vary from a value of –1.00 (which means prefect negative correlation) through zero (which means no correlation) to +1.00 (which means perfect positive correlation)

If each person had exactly the same z_x score as his/her z_y score, the r will take its maximum value, and it becomes

$$r = \frac{\Sigma z_x z_y}{N-1} = \frac{\Sigma z_x^2}{N-1}.$$

The last expression we recognise as the square of the SD of z_x scores. But since we know that the SD of standard scores in a unit normal probability curve is 1.00, the squared SD of standard scores is also 1.00 and, under our assumption, r would be equal to +1.00. At the other extreme, if each person's z_y scores were the negative of his/her z_x scores, r will become

$$r = \frac{\Sigma z_x(-z_y)}{N-1} = \frac{\Sigma(-z_y^2)}{N-1} = -\frac{\Sigma z_y^2}{N-1}.$$

This is the negative of the preceding value, and, hence, r would become –1.00.

(vi) **r may be regarded as an arithmetic mean.** If we call the $z_x z_y$ products by some other name such as $X_5 = z_x z_y$, it becomes clear that r is the sum of X_5 divided by $N-1$, that is, r is approximately the mean of X_5 and, hence, that of the $z_x z_y$ products also. In fact, if the SDs are computed with N instead of $N-1$ in the denominator, then r is exactly the mean of such standard score products, that is, $r = \frac{\Sigma z_x z_y}{N}$, instead of $r = \frac{\Sigma z_x z_y}{N-1}$.

(vii) **The magnitude and the algebraic sign of r** indicate, respectively, the degree and the direction of the linear relationship between the variables. The value of r ranges between –1.00 and +1.00, and does not bear the unit of any of the variables. A value of 0 indicates the absence of any correlation; this means that changes in the scores of one variable are not associated at all with those of the scores of the other in an individual. The closer the value of r to –1.00 or +1.00, the stronger or higher the relation between the variables.

(viii) **Even if a constant number** is added to or subtracted from the scores of the two variables and/or they are divided or multiplied by a constant number, Pearson's r remains the same.

(ix) **A positive r** indicates that an individual, having a high score in one variable, is likely to possess a high score in the other variable, while an individual with a low score in one is expected to have a low score in the other too. A perfect positive correlation is indicated if r amounts to +1.00. In such a case, each individual has the same z_x and z_y scores for his/her X and Y scores, respectively, that is, $z_x = z_y$.

A negative r indicates, on the contrary, that a high score of one variable is likely to be associated with a low score of the other, and vice versa. A perfect negative correlation is indicated if r amounts to –1.00. For each individual in such a case, $z_x = -z_y$.

(x) **r of +0.60** implies the same magnitude of the relationship as r of –0.60. The sign tells us about the direction of the relationship, and the magnitude about the strength of the relationship.

(xi) **Due to random variations of the variables** in samples, r suffers from sampling errors and varies from sample to sample drawn from the same population. So sample r scores form a sampling distribution around the parametric correlation coefficient (ρ). Both theoretical and experimental sampling distributions of r may be framed. The sampling distribution is nearly symmetrical if ρ amounts to zero, but is progressively skewed positively or negatively as ρ approaches –1.00 and +1.00, respectively. The SD of this sampling distribution is the SE of the computed r (s_r) and is used in finding the significance of r.

(xii)

$$r_{xy} = \sqrt{b_{yx} b_{xy}},$$

where

b_{yx} = regression coefficient of Y on X

b_{xy} = regression coefficient of X on Y

r_{xy} = square root of the slopes of the regression lines.

(xiii) **The degrees of freedom (df)** for r is $N-2$, which is used for testing the significance of the obtained r. Testing the significance of r is testing the significance of regression. The regression line involves the slope and intercept; hence, 2 df is lost. So when $N=2$, r is either $+1.00$ or -1.00 as there is no freedom for sampling variation in the numerical value of r.

(xiv) **Pearson's r** (or any other correlation coefficient) does not directly give the percentage relationship or dependence of one variable on another unless its value is $+1.00$, -1.00 or 0.00. In many cases, it is the squared value of the correlation coefficient (r^2), which gives the percentage dependence of the variables and is called the *coefficient of determination*. Thus, if r amounts to $+0.60$, only a 0.36 proportion or 36% of the total variance of one variable may be associated with the variance of the other; the remaining proportion, 0.64 here, is the *coefficient of non-determination* indicating such proportion of the variance of one variable which is not associated with that of the other.

9.3.3   Factors Affecting Correlation Coefficient (r)

If variation in X is responsible for variation in Y, this must be reflected by evidence of some degree of association between X and Y, when the effect of intervening variables is appropriately controlled. The fact that X and Y vary together is a necessary, but not a sufficient condition for one to make a statement about causal relationship between the two variables. In short, evidence that two variables vary together is not necessarily evidence of causation. If one is to speak of causation, it must be on grounds over and above those merely demonstrating association between the two variables.

Four possibilities might exist when the variables X and Y are correlated. First, it may be that the condition of Y is determined, in part, at least, by the condition of X. Second, the situation may be reversed, and Y is causing X to vary. Third, there may be a third factor that is influencing both X and Y; thus, producing the observed association between the two. Fourth, the 'third factor' may not be a unitary characteristic but in fact a complex of interrelated variables.

The following are some of the important factors that affect the correlation coefficient.

(i) **Linearity of regression.** Figure 9.4(a) shows moderately low correlation and Figure 9.4(b) shows a high correlation between the X and Y variables. In both Figures 9.4(a) and (b), the straight lines of best fit have been included.

In the diagram depicting the lower correlation (Figure 9.4[a]), notice that the points scatter rather widely about the line. In the other figure (Figure 9.4[b]), the points tend to hug the line quite closely. In general, the more closely the scores hug the straight line of best fit, the higher

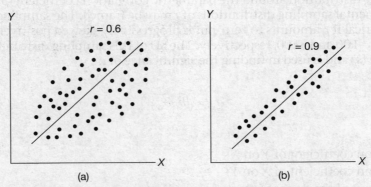

(a)   (b)

Figure 9.4   (a) Moderately low correlation and (b) high correlation between X and Y variables

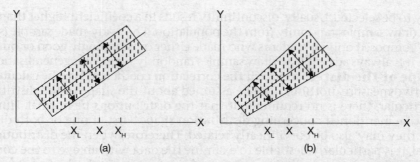

Figure 9.5   Scatter diagram: (a) scatter of values are the same and (b) scatter of values are varied

the value of *r*. When *r* is 0, the scores scatter as widely about the line as possible, and when *r* is 1, the scores hug the line as closely as possible. One meaning of the 'hugging principle' is that the prediction of *Y* from the knowledge of *X* can be made with greater accuracy when the correlation is high rather than when it is low. In a given set of data, a straight line may or may not reasonably describe the relationship between the two variables. When a straight line is appropriate, *X* and *Y* are said to be linearly related. More formally, the data are said to exhibit the property of the linearity of regression.

When the correlation is other than zero and the relationship is nonlinear, Pearson's *r* will underestimate the degree of association.

(ii) **Homoscedasticity.** We found that if the scores scatter widely about the straight line of best fit, the value of *r* would be low, whereas if the scores hugged the line closely, the value of *r* would be high. In Figure 9.5(a), no matter what the value of *X* is chosen, the corresponding value of *Y* scatters to about the same extent. In the second diagram (Figure 9.5(b)), this is not so. Although *Y* does not vary much about the line when the value of *X* is low, it varies more when *X* has an intermediate value, and it varies greatly when *X* has a high value. Since *r* is a function of the degree to which the points hug the regression line, the value obtained for it has a meaning of general significance in the first diagram (Figure 9.5[a]); it describes the close association of *X* and *Y* irrespective of the specific value of *X* (or *Y*).

In Figure 9.5(b), according to the 'hugging criterion', there is a close association of *X* and *Y* for low values of *X*, a lesser degree of association when *X* has an intermediate value and very little association when the values of *X* are high. It follows that if Pearson's *r* is computed on the data in the second situation (Figure 9.5[b]), it will reflect the 'average' degree to which the scores hug the line and will characterise properly only the degree of relationship appropriate to the intermediate values of *X* and *Y*. The strength of association as measured by *r* will not, in these circumstances, have the general meaning that it has for the data of the first diagram (Figure 9.5[a]). In the specific illustration (Figure 9.5[b]), *r* will underestimate the extent of the relationship for low values of *X* and will overestimate the relationship for high values.

When the amount of scatter is the same throughout, the bivariate distribution is said to exhibit the property of homoscedasticity or equal variability. This property implies that if the data were sectioned into columns, the variability of *Y* would be the same from column to column, or if they were sectioned into rows, the variability of *X* would be the same from row to row. We can see that homoscedasticity characterises the data shown in Figure 9.5(a), but not those in Figure 9.5(b). Thus, the lack of homoscedasticity can affect the problem of prediction.

(iii) **Correlation coefficient in discontinuous distribution.** One of the important assumptions of *r* is that the distribution of scores in the population should be continuous. A sample constituted in a discontinuous manner will yield a correlation coefficient different from what would be obtained in drawing a sample so that all elements of the population had an equal opportunity to be selected. Usually, discontinuity results in a coefficient higher than otherwise. One should draw samples randomly from the population. The ready-made sample is a very special sample, composed only of students who made either outstandingly good or outstandingly bad records. It is always advisable to draw samples randomly for greater generalisation.

(iv) **Shape of the distribution**. If the correlation coefficient is to be calculated purely as a descriptive measure, nothing need be assumed about the shape of the distribution of X or Y. In particular, there is no requirement that the distributions be normal. However, two points must be mentioned concerning distribution shape. First, if one or both distributions are skewed, they may also be curvilinearly related. Therefore, when the distributions are not symmetrical, it is particularly desirable to examine the data with an eye to the correctness of the linear hypothesis. Second, obtaining the coefficient is often only the first step in analysis. When additional steps are undertaken, the assumption frequently must be made that X and Y are normally distributed. For example, this assumption is needed in making inferences about the population value of the coefficient and in establishing limits of error in prediction.

(v) **Random variation**. Sometimes we are interested only in describing how things are in the particular group of observations under study; in this case, the correlation coefficient obtained with that group is exactly what we want to know. But in some other circumstances, we want to make an inference about the state of affairs in the population from the knowledge of the state of affairs in the sample. Like all statistics, the value of r varies from sample to sample, depending on the chance factors associated with the selection of the particular sample. Correlation varies according to the sample size. In general, large sample yields values of r that are similar from sample to sample, and, thus, the value obtained from a large sample will probably be close to the population value. For very small samples, r is quite unstable from sample to sample, and its value cannot be depended upon to lie close to the population value. In order to yield reasonable stable r sample size (n) should be large enough.

(vi) **Circumstances under which r is obtained**. In addition to the influence of random sampling variation, other factors such as specific measure, age and grade of samples, economic condition of the families from which the subjects are drawn, types of languages the samples have (i.e., bilingual or unilingual), learning atmosphere (anxiety and normal learning condition) can also affect the amount of correlation. Thus, the degree of association between two variables depends on: (a) the specific measure taken for each of the two variables, (b) the kinds of subjects used for the investigation and (c) the particular circumstances under which the variables are operative. If any of these factors changes over time, the extent of the association may also change. Consequently, it is of utmost importance that a correlation coefficient be interpreted in the light of particular conditions by which it was obtained.

(vii) **Other factors**. In addition to the factors discussed earlier, there are the other two important factors that influence the magnitude of the correlation coefficient. These two factors are: (a) the range of talent and (b) the heterogeneity of samples. The value of the correlation coefficient depends on the degree of variation characterising the two variables as well as on the relationship present. Other things being equal, the greater the restriction of range in X and/or Y, the lower the correlation coefficient. The heterogeneity of the samples will reduce the amount of the correlation coefficient. In other words, correlation will be greater among the pooled data than among the separate samples.

9.3.4   Uses of Pearson's r

The product–moment correlation is one of the most widely used analytical procedures in the field of behavioural sciences, particularly in educational and psychological measurement and evaluation. The following are some of the important uses of r.

(i) Peason's *r* is used to state the extent of the relationship existing between two variables in quantitative terms. In other words, we need Pearson's *r* because we wish to quantify our statements. This makes comparisons possible. For example, the speed of the response test correlates +0.55 with proficiency.

(ii) Besides providing a direct measure of the degree of association existing between two variables, Pearson's *r* occurs in equations which are used in predicting one score (such as success on the job) from another (such as an aptitude test score). In other words, the regression equation is possible because of *r*. The prediction of one variable—the dependent (or criterion) variable on the basis of the independent (or predictor) variable—is possible because of Pearson's *r*.

(iii) There are a great many uses of correlation coefficients in mental measurement and psychological theory. They provide evidence concerning the interrelationships among test scores and other variables. They are often crucial in determining whether certain data are consistent with a hypothesis or whether they refute it.

(iv) Pearson's *r* is often used in determining the reliability and validity of a test. It also determines the degree of objectivity of a test, and helps in decision-making.

(v) Pearson's *r* is useful in determining the relative roles of various correlates to a certain ability.

(vi) When several variables are correlated with each other, many correlations among them can often be explained in terms of a smaller number of underlying factors. These are found by a technical process known as factor analysis. Two variables are correlated because of some common factor. For example, the aptitude-achievement tests have paper-and-pencil tests in common. Correlation coefficients are the basic data that form the foundation upon which all such studies are based. Furthermore, Pearson's *r* is virtually indispensable in evaluating the relative merits of various aptitude and achievement tests, both in vocational guidance and in vocational selection. In short, factor analysis is possible because of the product–moment correlation coefficient.

9.3.5   Applicability of Pearson's *r*

Pearson's *r* is the standard index of the amount of correlation between two variables, and we employ it whenever it is possible and convenient to do so.

The Pearson product-moment correlation is applied to the data: (a) where two variables, *X* and *Y*, are measured on continuous metric (numerical) scales; (b) when the measurements are made in terms of interval and ratio scales; (c) when the data are in terms of scores, not in frequencies and (d) when the regression is linear or the relationship is in the form of a straight line.

9.3.6   Computation of *r* from Ungrouped Data

Of the various correlation coefficients in current use, the one most frequently encountered is called the Pearson product-moment correlation co-efficient (*r*). In the pages that follow, we shall present various methods for computing this coefficient. Usually, there are four general procedures for computing Pearson's *r* from the ungrouped data: (a) Pearson's *r* from original scores or raw scores, (b) Pearson's *r* from the deviation scores from the means, (c) Pearson's *r* from the deviation scores from the assumed mean (AM) and (d) Pearson's *r* from standard scores. These four procedures are discussed in the following one after another.

Table 9.1 Computation of *r* from original scores or raw scores

	(1)	(2)	(3)	(4)	(5)
	X	Y	X²	Y²	XY
	5	1	25	1	5
	10	6	100	36	60
	5	2	25	4	10
	11	8	121	64	88
	12	5	144	25	60
	4	1	16	1	4
	3	4	9	16	12
	2	6	4	36	12
	7	5	49	25	35
	1	2	1	4	2
N=10	ΣX=60	ΣY=40	ΣX²=494	ΣY²=212	ΣXY=288

9.3.6.1 *Pearson's r from Original or Raw Scores*

This procedure deals entirely with original scores or raw scores. It is preferred only when the raw scores are small in both magnitude and number, and when the mean values are in fractions. The formula for finding the Pearson *r* from the raw scores is as follows:

$$r = \frac{N\Sigma XY - (\Sigma X)(\Sigma Y)}{\sqrt{[N\Sigma X^2 - (\Sigma X)^2][N\Sigma Y^2 - (\Sigma Y)^2]}},$$

where

r=product–moment correlation coefficient between the X and Y variables
N=total number of paired scores/observations
ΣX=sum of raw scores in the X variable
ΣY=sum of raw scores in the Y variable
ΣXY=sum of the products of each X score multiplied with its corresponding Y score.
ΣX^2=sum of the squares of raw scores in the X variable
ΣY^2=sum of the squares of raw scores in the Y variable
$(\Sigma X)^2$=square of the sum of the raw scores in the X variable
$(\Sigma Y)^2$=square of the sum of the raw scores in the Y variable.

The use of the above formula may be understood through the following example given in Table 9.1

The necessary steps are illustrated in Table 9.1. They are enumerated here.

Step 1. Enter the X and Y scores in the first and second columns, respectively, as shown in Table 9.1. Then add the X and Y scores separately to give ΣX and ΣY. Note the number of cases (N).

Step 2. Square each X or Y score and then sum the squared scores of each variable to give ΣX^2 and ΣY^2, respectively, as noted in Columns 3 and 4 of Table 9.1.

Step 3. Multiply the X score of each individual with his/her Y score to give the XY value of that individual and then total all the XY values to give ΣXY as noted in Column 5 of Table 9.1.

Step 4. Apply the following formula to compute Pearson's r:

$$r_{xy} = \frac{N\Sigma XY - (\Sigma X)(\Sigma Y)}{\sqrt{[N\Sigma X^2 - (\Sigma X)^2][N\Sigma Y^2 - (\Sigma Y)^2]}}$$

$$= \frac{10 \times 288 - 60 \times 40}{\sqrt{[10 \times 494 - (60)^2][10 \times 212 - (40)^2]}}$$

$$= \frac{2880 - 2400}{\sqrt{(4940 - 3600)(2120 - 1600)}} = \frac{480}{\sqrt{(1340 \times 520)}}$$

$$= \frac{480}{\sqrt{696800}} = \frac{480}{834.74} = +0.57.$$

$$\therefore r = +0.57$$

9.3.6.2   *Pearson's r from the Deviation Scores from the Actual Means*

This procedure deals with the deviation scores taken from the actual means of both the variables X and Y. It is preferred only when the mean values of both the variables are not in fractions and when the number of cases is small. The formula for computing the Pearson r from the deviation scores taken from the actual means of the two variables is as follows:

$$r = \frac{\Sigma xy}{\sqrt{\Sigma x^2 \Sigma y^2}} \text{ or } r = \frac{\Sigma xy}{N\sigma_x \sigma_y},$$

where

r=correlation coefficient between the X and Y variables

x=deviation score of any X score from its mean

y=deviation score of any Y score from its mean

Σxy=sum of all the products of deviation scores of x and y (each x deviation multiplied by its corresponding y deviation)

Σx^2=sum of the squared deviation scores of x series

Σy^2=sum of the squared deviation scores of y series

σ_x=SD of the X scores

σ_y=SD of the Y scores

N=the number of paired scores/observations.

The use of the above formula may be understood through the example given in Table 9.2. The necessary steps are illustrated in Table 9.2. They are enumerated here.

Step 1. Enter the X and Y scores in the first and second columns, respectively, as shown in Table 9.2. Then total the X and Y scores separately to give ΣX and ΣY. Note the N. Find the means of X scores ($\bar{X}$) and Y scores ($\bar{Y}$), and note these means in Table 9.2 which are 7.0 and 8.0, respectively.

Table 9.2 Computation of r from deviation scores taken from the means

	(1)	(2)	(3)	(4)	(5)	(6)	(7)
	X	Y	x $(X-\bar{X})$	y $(Y-\bar{Y})$	x^2	y^2	xy
	13	11	6	3	36	9	18
	12	14	5	6	25	36	30
	10	11	3	3	9	9	9
	8	7	1	−1	1	1	−1
	7	9	0	1	0	1	0
	5	11	−2	3	4	9	−6
	5	3	−2	−5	4	25	10
	5	7	−2	−1	4	1	2
	3	6	−4	−2	16	4	8
	2	1	−5	−7	25	49	35
$N=10$	$\Sigma X=70$	$\Sigma Y=80$	$\Sigma x=0$	$\Sigma y=0$	$\Sigma x^2=124$	$\Sigma y^2=144$	$\Sigma xy=105$

$$\bar{X}=\frac{\Sigma X}{N}=\frac{70}{10}=7.0, \qquad \sigma_x=\sqrt{\frac{\Sigma x^2}{N}}=\sqrt{\frac{124}{10}}=\sqrt{12.4}=3.521,$$

$$\bar{Y}=\frac{\Sigma Y}{N}=\frac{80}{10}=8.0. \qquad \sigma_y=\sqrt{\frac{\Sigma y^2}{N}}=\sqrt{\frac{144}{10}}=\sqrt{14.4}=3.795.$$

Step 2. Find the deviation of each X score from its mean ($\bar{X}=0.7$) and enter it in Column 3 of Table 9.2 as $x(X-\bar{X})$. Similarly, find the deviation of each Y score from its mean ($\bar{Y}=8.0$) and enter it in Column 4 of Table 9.2 as $y(Y-\bar{Y})$. Check them by finding algebraic sums, which should be zero (i.e., $\Sigma x=0$; $\Sigma y=0$).

Step 3. Square all of the x's and all of the y's and enter these squares in Columns 5 and 6 of Table 9.2 as x^2 and y^2, respectively. Total these columns to obtain Σx^2 and Σy^2.

Step 4. Multiply each x with its corresponding y in the same row and enter these products (with due regards to sign) in Column 7 of Table 9.2 as xy. Total the xy column, taking account of sign, to obtain Σxy.

Step 5. Find the SDs of both X and Y scores from $\Sigma x^2 (\sigma_x)$ and $\Sigma y^2 (\sigma_y)$, respectively.

Step 6. Apply the following formula to compute r:

$$r_{xy}=\frac{\Sigma xy}{\sqrt{\Sigma x^2 \Sigma y^2}}=\frac{105}{\sqrt{124\times144}}=\frac{105}{\sqrt{17856}}=\frac{105}{133.63}=+0.79$$

$$\text{or } r_{xy}=\frac{\Sigma xy}{N\sigma_x\sigma_y}=\frac{105}{10\times3.521\times3.795}=\frac{105}{133.62}=+0.79$$

$$\therefore r_{xy}=+0.79.$$

9.3.6.3 *Pearson's r from the Deviation Scores from the Assumed Means*

This procedure deals with the deviation scores taken from the AMs of both the variables X and Y. It is preferred only when the actual means of both the variables are in fractions or decimals, and when the magnitudes of X and Y scores are high. The formula for computing the Pearson r from the deviation scores taken from the AMs of both the variables is as follows:

$$r = \frac{\dfrac{\Sigma x'y'}{N} - C_x C_y}{\sigma'_x \sigma'_y},$$

where

r = correlation coefficient between the X and Y variables

x' = deviation score of any X score from its AM.

y' = deviation score of any Y score from its AM.

$\Sigma x'y'$ = sum of all the products of deviation scores of x' and y' (each x' deviation multiplied by its corresponding y' deviation)

N = total number of paired scores/observations

C_x = correction factor for X scores

C_y = correction factor for Y scores

σ'_x = SD of X scores

σ'_y = SD of Y scores.

The use of the above formula may be understood through the examples given in Table 9.3. The necessary steps are illustrated in Table 9.3. They are enumerated here.

Step 1. Enter the X and Y scores in the first and second columns, respectively, as shown in Table 9.3. Then total the X and Y scores separately to obtain ΣX and ΣY, respectively. Note the N. Find the means of X scores ($\bar{X}$) and that of Y scores ($\bar{Y}$), and note these means in Table 9.3, which are 62.5 and 30.4, respectively.

Step 2. Choose the AM's of both the X and Y scores. For the given data, take AM_X as 60.0 and AM_Y as 30.0.

Step 3. Find the deviation of each X score from its AM ($AM_X = 60.0$) and enter it in Column 3 of Table 9.3 as $x'(\bar{X} - AM_X)$. Similarly, find the deviation of each Y score from its AM ($AM_Y = 30.0$) and enter it in Column 4 of Table 9.3 as $y'(\bar{Y} - AM_Y)$. Total these columns, taking account of signs, to obtain $\Sigma x'$ and $\Sigma y'$, respectively.

Step 4. Square all of the x' and all of the y', and enter these squares in Columns 5 and 6 of Table 9.3 as x'^2 and y'^2, respectively. Total these columns to obtain $\Sigma x'^2$ and $\Sigma y'^2$.

Step 5. Multiply each x' with its corresponding y' in the same row, and enter these products (with due regards to sign) in Column 7 of Table 9.3 as $x'y'$. Total the $x'y'$ column, taking account of signs, to obtain $\Sigma x'y'$.

Step 6. Apply the following formula to compute r:

$$r_{xy} = \frac{\dfrac{\Sigma x'y'}{N} - C_x C_y}{\sigma'_x \sigma'_y} = \frac{\dfrac{334}{12} - (2.5)(.4)}{7.04 \times 4.86} = \frac{27.83 - 1.00}{34.2144} = \frac{26.83}{34.2144} = +0.78$$

$$\therefore r = +0.78.$$

Table 9.3. Computation of r from deviation scores taken from the assumed means

	(1)	(2)	(3)	(4)	(5)	(6)	(7)
	X	Y	x' $(X-AM_x)$	y' $(Y-AM_y)$	x'^2	y'^2	$x'y'$
	50	22	−10	−8	100	64	80
	54	25	−6	−5	36	25	30
	56	34	−4	4	16	16	−16
	59	28	−1	−2	1	4	2
	60	26	0	−4	0	16	0
	62	30	2	0	4	0	0
	61	32	1	2	1	4	2
	65	30	5	0	25	0	0
	67	28	7	−2	49	4	−14
	71	34	11	4	121	16	44
	71	36	11	6	121	36	66
	74	40	14	10	196	100	140
$N=12$	$\Sigma X=750$	$\Sigma Y=365$	$\Sigma x'=30$	$\Sigma y'=5$	$\Sigma x'^2=670$	$\Sigma y'^2=285$	$\Sigma x'y'=334$

$$\bar{X} = \frac{\Sigma X}{N} = \frac{750}{12} = 62.5,$$

$AM_X = 60.0,$

$C_x = \bar{X} - AM^X = 62.5 - 60.0 = 2.5,$

$C_x^2 = (2.5)^2 = 6.25,$

$$\sigma'_x = \sqrt{\frac{\Sigma x'^2}{N} - C_x^2}$$

$$= \sqrt{\frac{670}{12} - 6.25}$$

$$= \sqrt{55.83 - 6.25}$$

$$= \sqrt{49.58} = 7.04.$$

$$\bar{Y} = \frac{\Sigma Y}{N} = \frac{365}{12} = 30.4,$$

$AM_Y = 30.0,$

$C_y = \bar{Y} - AM^Y = 30.4 - 30.0 = 0.4,$

$C_y^2 = (0.4)_2 = 0.16,$

$$\sigma'_y = \sqrt{\frac{\Sigma y'^2}{N} - C_y^2},$$

$$= \sqrt{\frac{285}{12} - 0.16},$$

$$= \sqrt{23.75 - 0.16},$$

$$= \sqrt{23.59} = 4.86.$$

9.3.6.4 *Pearson's r from Standard Scores*

This procedure deals with the standard scores or z-scores of both the variables, X and Y, for computing the Pearson r. It is preferred only when the actual means of both the variables are not in fractions or decimals, the number of paired observations is small and the magnitudes of the X and Y scores are high. The formula for computing the Pearson r, which describes r as the mean z-score product, from the standard scores of both the variables is as follows:

$$r = \frac{\Sigma z_x z_y}{N},$$

Table 9.4   Computation of *r* from standard scores

	(1)	(2)	(3)	(4)	(5)	(6)	(7)	(8)	(9)	(10)
	X	**Y**	**x** $(X-\bar{X})$	**y** $(Y-\bar{Y})$	**x²**	**y²**	**xy**	**z_x** (x/σ_x)	**z_y** (y/σ_y)	**Z_xZ_y**
	72	170	3	0	9	0	0	1.34	0.0	0.00
	69	165	0	−5	0	25	0	0.00	−0.37	0.00
	66	150	−3	−20	9	400	60	−1.34	−1.46	1.96
	70	180	1	10	1	100	10	0.45	0.73	0.33
	68	185	−1	15	1	225	−15	−0.45	1.10	−0.49
N = 5	345 (ΣX)	850 (ΣY)	0 (Σx)	0 (Σy)	20 (Σx^2)	750 (Σy^2)	55 (Σxy)	0.0 (Σz_x)	0.0 (Σz_y)	1.80 (Σz_xz_y)

$$\bar{X}=\frac{\Sigma X}{N}=\frac{345}{5}=69.0,$$
$$\bar{Y}=\frac{\Sigma Y}{N}=\frac{850}{5}=170.0,$$
$$\sigma_x=\sqrt{\frac{\Sigma x^2}{N-1}}=\sqrt{\frac{20}{5-1}}=\sqrt{\frac{20}{4}}=\sqrt{5}=2.24.$$
$$\sigma_y=\sqrt{\frac{\Sigma y^2}{N-1}}=\sqrt{\frac{750}{5-1}}=\sqrt{\frac{750}{4}}=\sqrt{187.5}=13.69.$$

where

 r = correlation coefficient between the *X* and *Y* variables
 N = total number of paired observations
 z_x = standard score of *X* scores
 z_y = standard score of *Y* scores
 Σz_xz_y = sum of all the products of standard scores of *x* and *y*.

The use of the above formula may be understood through the examples given in Table 9.4. The *steps* necessary are illustrated in Table 9.4. They are enumerated here.

Step 1. Enter the *X* and *Y* scores in the first and second columns, respectively, as shown in Table 9.4. Then total the *X* and *Y* scores separately to obtain ΣX and ΣY, respectively. Note the *N*. Find the means of *X* scores ($\bar{X}$) and *Y* scores ($\bar{Y}$), and note these means in Table 9.4, which are 69.0 and 170.0, respectively.

Step 2. Find the deviation of each *X* score from its mean ($\bar{X}=69.0$) and enter it in Column 3 of Table 9.4 as $x(X-\bar{X})$. Similarly, find the deviation of each *Y* score from its mean ($\bar{Y}=170.0$) and enter it in Column 4 of Table 9.4 as $y(Y-\bar{Y})$. Check them by finding algebraic sums, which should be zero (i.e., $\Sigma x=0$; $\Sigma y=0$).

Step 3. Square all of the *x*'s and all of the *y*'s and enter these squares in Columns 5 and 6 of Table 9.4 as x_2 and y_2, respectively. Total these columns to obtain Σx^2 and Σy^2.

Step 4. Multiply each *x* with its corresponding *y* in the same row and enter these products (with due regards to sign) in Column 7 of Table 9.4 as *xy*. Total the *xy* column, taking account of sign, to obtain Σxy.

Step 5. Find the SDs of *X* scores (σ_x) and *Y* scores (σ_y) from Σx^2 and Σy^2, respectively, as shown in Table 9.4, which are $\sigma_x=2.24$ and $\sigma_y=13.69$.

Step 6. Find the standard scores (z_x) of X scores by dividing its each deviation score (x) by its SD (σ_x), and enter these standard scores (with due regards to sign) in Column 8 of Table 9.4 as z_x. Similarly, find the standard scores (z_y) of Y scores by dividing its each deviation score (y) by its SD (σ_y) and enter these standard scores (with due regards to sign) in Column 9 of Table 9.4 as z_y. Check them by finding algebraic sums, which should be zero (i.e., $\Sigma z_x = 0$; $\Sigma z_y = 0$).

Step 7. Multiply each z_x with its corresponding z_y in the same row and enter these products (with due regards to sign) in Column 10 of Table 9.4 as $z_x z_y$. Total the $z_x z_y$ Column, taking account of sign, to obtain $\Sigma z_x z_y$.

Step 8. Apply the following formula to compute r:

$$r_{xy} = \frac{\Sigma z_x z_y}{N} = \frac{1.80}{5} = +0.36$$

$$\therefore r = +0.36.$$

9.3.7 Computation of *r* from Grouped Data

Product–moment *r* may be computed through a scatter diagram or a correlation table. If this diagram or table is not given, then the need of its construction arises. When the number of pairs of measurement (N) of two variables, X and Y, are large or even moderate in size, the customary procedure is to group data in both X and Y and to form a scatter diagram or scattergram or correlation table. It is also called a two-way frequency distribution or *bivariate frequency distribution,* since it represents the joint distribution of two variables. The choice of size of the class interval and limits of intervals follows much the same rules as were given previously under the frequency distribution. Let us illustrate the construction of a scatter diagram or correlation table with the help of some hypothetical data.

9.3.7.1 *Construction of a Scatter Diagram*

Example 9.1 Twenty students have obtained the following scores on test in psychology (X) and statistics (Y). Express these scores through a scatter diagram.

Student No.	Scores in Psychology (X)	Scores in Statistics (Y)	Student No.	Scores in Psychology (X)	Scores in Statistics (Y)
1	25	32	11	10	31
2	41	34	12	25	42
3	53	48	13	44	57
4	12	35	14	32	48
5	26	52	15	42	63
6	28	45	16	45	53
7	51	57	17	31	48
8	54	62	18	23	43
9	50	67	19	28	71
10	48	73	20	22	52

Table 9.5   Scatter diagram for data given in Example 9.1

		X Scores in Psychology					
Y Scores in Statistics	**Class Intervals**	**10–19**	**20–29**	**30–39**	**40–49**	**50–59**	f_y
	70–79		/①		/①		2
	60–69				/①	//②	3
	50–59		//②		//②	/①	5
	40–49		///③	//②		/①	6
	30–39	//②	/①		/①		4
	f_x	2	7	2	5	4	20(N)

Procedure

In setting up a double grouping of data, a table is prepared with columns and rows. Here we classify each pair of variates simultaneously in the two classes, one representing score in psychology (X) and the other in statistics (Y) as shown in Table 9.5. The scores of 20 students in both psychology (X) and statistics (Y) are shown in Table 9.5.

In the construction of a scatter diagram or a bivariate frequency distribution from the given data, we usually proceed as under.

(i)   The construction of a scattergram is relatively simple. Along the left-hand margin, the class intervals of the Y score distribution are laid off from bottom to top (in ascending order), and along the top of the diagram, the class intervals of the X score distribution are laid off from left to right (in ascending order). In the present example, we begin with the class intervals of the X score distribution from 10 to 19 and end with 50–59, and for the Y score distribution from 30 to 39 and end with 70–79. We also add one column and one row to Table 9.5 for the purpose of presenting the summation of the frequencies in the respective rows and columns.

(ii)   Each pair of scores (both in X and Y) of an individual is represented through one tally mark in the respective cell. For example, in the given data, the first student (or student no.1) has secured 25 in psychology (X) and 32 in statistics (Y). His/her score of 25 in X places him/her in the second column and 32 in Y places him/her in the last row. So, for this pair of scores (i.e., 25 and 32), a tally will be marked in the cell which is the resultant of the second column and fifth row. In a similar way, in the case of student no. 2, for scores 41 and 34, we shall put a tally in the fourth column of the fifth row. Likewise, 20 tallies will be put in the respective cells of columns and rows. The columns represent the X scores and rows represent the Y scores.

(iii)   After the completion of task of tallying, these tally marks are translated into cell frequencies. These frequencies are written in each of the cells inside the respective circles.

(iv)   The cell frequencies in each of the rows will be summed up and these sums will be written in the last column under the heading f_y. Similarly, the cell frequencies in each of the columns may also be summed up, and these sums are recorded in the bottom row under the heading f_x.

(v)   The frequencies recorded in the last column under the heading f_y are then summed up. This sum represents the total frequencies (N) for the distribution Y. Similarly, by summing up the frequencies recorded in the bottom row under the head f_x, we may get the total of all the frequencies (N) under the distribution X. Thus, in the present case, the total of f_y column is 20 and the total of f_x row is also 20. It is, in fact, a bivariate distribution because it presents the joint distribution of two variables. The scattergram is then a *correlation table*.

Calculation of *r* from Scattergram or Correlation Table

The following outline of the *steps* to be followed in calculating *r* will be best understood if the student will constantly refer to Table 9.6 as he/she reads through each step.

Step 1. Construct a scattergram for the two variables to be correlated and from it draw up a correlation table as described in Table 9.5.

Step 2. Count the frequencies of each class interval of the distribution X and write it in the f_x row. Similarly, count the frequencies of each class interval of the distribution Y and write it in the f_y column.

Step 3. The distribution of statistic scores (Y) for the 20 students falls in the f_y column at the right of the diagram. Assume a mean for the Y distribution, using the rules given in Chapter 3 and draw double lines to mark off the row (class interval) in which the AM of the Y distribution falls. In the given correlation table (see Table 9.6), let us assume the mean at the class interval of 40–49, and put double lines on this row as shown in the table. The AM for the Y distribution has been taken at 44.5 (midpoint of the interval 40–49) and the y's have been taken from this point. The prime (') of the x's and y's indicates that these deviations are taken from the AMs of the X and Y distributions, respectively. The deviations above the line of the AM will be positive (+ve) and the deviations below it will be negative (–ve). The deviation against the line of the AM, that is, against the class interval where we assumed the mean is marked 0 (zero), and above it the y's are noted as +1, +2, +3, and below it y' is noted to be –1. Now, the y' column is filled up. Then multiply f_y and y' of each row to obtain the f_y' column. Similarly, multiply f_y' and y' of each row to obtain the $f_y'^2$ column.

Step 4. Adopt the same procedure as in Step 3 and compute x', f_x' and $f_x'^2$. For the distribution X, let us assume the mean in the class interval of 20–29 and put double lines to mark off the column (class interval) as shown in the table. The AM for the X distribution has been taken at 24.5 (midpoint of the class interval 20–29), and the x's have been taken from this point. The deviations to the left of this column will be negative (–ve) and right be positive (+ve). Thus, x' for the column where the mean is assumed is marked 0 (zero) and the x' to its left is marked –1 and x's to its right are marked +1, +2 and +3. Now, the x' row is filled up. Multiply the values of f_x and x' of each column to obtain the f_x' row. Similarly, multiply f_x' and x' of each column to obtain the $f_x'^2$ row.

Step 5. In this step, we will determine $\Sigma x'$ and $\Sigma y'$. As this step is an important one, we are to mark carefully $\Sigma x'$ for different class intervals of the Y distribution and $\Sigma y'$ for different class intervals of the X distribution.

(i) $\Sigma x'$ *for different class intervals of the Y distribution.*

- In the *first* row, 1 f is in the cell, 20–29, whose x' is 0 (look at the bottom). The x' entry of this cell is $1 \times 0 = 0$. Again 1 f is in the cell, 40–49, whose x' is 2. The x' entry of this cell is $1 \times 2 = 2$. Therefore, the $\Sigma x'$ for the first row $= (1 \times 0) + (1 \times 2) = 0 + 2 = 2$.

- In the *second* row, 1 f is in the cell, 40–49, whose x' is 2. The x' entry of this is $1 \times 2 = 2$. Again 2 f's are in the cell, 50–59, whose x's are 3, each. The x' entry of this cell is $2 \times 3 = 6$. So the $\Sigma x'$ for the second row $= (1 \times 2) + (2 \times 3) = 2 + 6 = 8$.

Table 9.6 Computation of coefficient of correlation (r)

X Scores in Psychology (columns) — **Y Scores in Statistics** (rows)

Class Intervals	10-19	20-29	30-39	40-49	50-59	f_y	y'	fy'	fy'^2	$\Sigma x'$	$\Sigma x'y'$
70-79		1		1		2	3	6	18	2	6
60-69				1	2	3	2	6	12	8	16
50-59		2		2	1	5	1	5	5	7	7
40-49		3	2		1	6	0	0	0	5	0
30-39	2	1		1		4	−1	−4	4	0	0
f_x	2	7	2	5	4	20(N)		$\Sigma fy'=13$	$\Sigma fy'^2=39$	$\Sigma x'=22$	$\Sigma x'y'=29$
x'	−1	0	1	2	3		Check				
fx'	−2	0	2	10	12	$\Sigma fx'=22$					
fx'^2	2	0	2	20	36	$\Sigma fx'^2=60$	Check				
$\Sigma y'$	−2	4	0	6	5	$\Sigma y'=13$					
$\Sigma x'y'$	2	0	0	12	15	$\Sigma x'y'=29$					

- In the *third* row, 2 f's are in the cell, 20–29, whose x's are 0, each; 2 f's are in the cell, 40–49, whose x's are 2, each; and 1 f is in the cell, 50–59, whose x' is 3. So, the $\Sigma x'$ for the third row $=(2\times0)+(2\times2)+(1\times3)=0+4+3=7$.
- In the *fourth* row, 3 f's are in the cell, 20–29, whose x's are 0, each; 2 f's are in the cell, 30–39, whose x's are 1, each; and 1 f is in the cell, 50–59, whose x' is 3. So the $\Sigma x'$ for the fourth row $=(3\times0)+(2\times1)+(1\times3)=0+2+3=5$.
- In the *fifth* row, 2 f's are in the cell, 10–19, whose x's are –1 each; 1 f is in the cell, 20–29, whose x' is 0; and 1 f is in the cell, 40–49, whose x' is 2. So the $\Sigma x'$ for the fifth row $=(2\times-1)+(1\times0)+(1\times2)=-2+0+2=0$.

(ii) $\Sigma y'$ *for different class intervals of the X distribution.*

- In the *first* column, 2 f's are in the cell, 30–39, whose y's are –1, each. So the $\Sigma y'$ for the first column $=2\times-1=-2$.
- In the *second* column, 1 f is in the cell, 70–79, whose y' is 3; 2 f's are in the cell, 50–59, whose y's are 1, each; 3 f's are in the cell, 40–49, whose y's are 0, each; and 1 f is in the cell, 30–39, whose y's is –1. So the $\Sigma y'$ for the second column $=(1\times3)+(2\times1)+(3\times0)+(1\times-1)=3+2+0-1=4$.
- In the *third* column, 2 f's are in the cell 40–49, whose y's are 0, each. So the $\Sigma y'$ for the third column $=2\times0=0$.
- In the *fourth* column, 1 f is in the cell, 70–79, whose y' is 3; 1 f is in the cell, 60–69, whose y' is 2; 2 f's are in the cell, 50–59, whose y's are 1, each; and 1 f is in the cell, 30–39, whose y' is –1. So the $\Sigma y'$ for the fourth column $=(1\times3)+(1\times2)+(2\times1)+(1\times-1)=3+2+2-1=6$.
- In the *fifth* column, 2 f's are in the cell, 60–69, whose y's are 2, each; 1 f is in the cell, 50–59, whose y' is 1; and 1 f is in the cell, 40–49, whose y' is 0. So the $\Sigma y'$ for the fifth column $=(2\times2)+(1\times1)+(1\times0)=4+1+0=5$.

Step 6. Now, we can calculate $\Sigma x'y'$ for each row of the distribution Y by multiplying the $\Sigma x'$ entries of each row by y' entries of each row. Then, we calculate $\Sigma x'y'$ for each column of distribution X by multiplying $\Sigma y'$ entries of each column by the x' entries of each column.

Step 7. Now, we take the algebraic sum of the values of rows fx', fx'^2, $\Sigma y'$ and $\Sigma x'y'$ for the X distribution. Similarly, we take the algebraic sum of the values of columns fy', fy'^2, $\Sigma x'$ and $\Sigma x'y'$ for the Y distribution.

Step 8. $\Sigma x'y'$ of the X distribution $=\Sigma x'y'$ of the Y distribution

$$\Sigma fx'=\Sigma x'; \Sigma fy'=\Sigma y'.$$

Step 9.

$$\Sigma fx'=\Sigma x'=22; \quad \Sigma fx'^2=60$$
$$\Sigma fy'=\Sigma y'=13; \quad \Sigma fy'^2=39$$
$$\Sigma x'y'=29; \quad N=20.$$

Step 10. In order to compute the coefficient of correlation from a scattergram or correlation table (grouped data), any one of the following formulae can be applied:

$$(1) \quad r=\frac{\dfrac{\Sigma x'y'}{N}-C_xC_y}{\sigma'_x\sigma'_y}.$$

$$(2) \quad r=\frac{N\Sigma x'y'-\Sigma x'\Sigma y'}{\sqrt{[N\Sigma x'^2-(\Sigma x')^2][N\Sigma y'^2-(\Sigma y')^2]}}.$$

Step 11. In order to compute r by the first formula, we must find out C_x, C_y, σ'_x and σ'_y from the given data in Table 9.6:

$$C_x = \frac{\Sigma fx'}{N} = \frac{\Sigma\Sigma x'}{N} = \frac{22}{20} = 1.1; \quad C_x^2 = (1.1)^2 = 1.21$$

$$C_y = \frac{\Sigma fy'}{N} = \frac{\Sigma\Sigma y'}{N} = \frac{13}{20} = 0.65; \quad C_y^2 = (0.65)^2 = 0.4225$$

$$\sigma'_x = \sqrt{\frac{\Sigma fx'^2}{N} - C_x^2} = \sqrt{\frac{60}{20} - 1.21} = \sqrt{3.0 - 1.21} = \sqrt{1.79} = 1.3379$$

$$\sigma'_y = \sqrt{\frac{\Sigma fy'^2}{N} - C_y^2} = \sqrt{\frac{39}{20} - 0.4225} = \sqrt{1.95 - .4225} = \sqrt{1.5275} = 1.2359$$

$$r = \frac{\dfrac{\Sigma x'y'}{N} - C_x C_y}{\sigma'_x \sigma'_y} = \frac{\dfrac{29}{20} - (1.1)(0.65)}{(1.3379)(1.2359)} = \frac{1.45 - 0.715}{1.6535}$$

$$= \frac{0.735}{1.6535} = 0.4445 = 0.44$$

$$\therefore r = +0.44.$$

Let us now apply the second formula given above to calculate r:

$$r = \frac{N\Sigma x'y' - \Sigma x'\Sigma y'}{\sqrt{[N\Sigma x'^2 - (\Sigma x')^2][N\Sigma y'^2 - (\Sigma y')^2]}}$$

$$= \frac{20 \times 29 - (22)(13)}{\sqrt{[20 \times 60 - (22)^2][20 \times 39 - (13)^2]}}$$

$$= \frac{580 - 286}{\sqrt{(1200 - 484)(780 - 169)}} = \frac{294}{\sqrt{716 \times 611}} = \frac{294}{\sqrt{437476}}$$

$$= \frac{294}{661.4197} = 0.4445 = 0.44$$

$$\therefore r = +0.44.$$

9.3.8 Interpretation of the Coefficient of Correlation (r)

Mere computation of correlation does not have any significance unless and until it is interpreted. Therefore, after computing a correlation coefficient between two variables, the next step is to consider what it tells us. In fact, it is computed to tell us about the following important things.

First of all, it tells us whether there is any relationship or association between two variables, and if any such relationship or correlation exists, then indicates the nature and type of relationship. Finally, it indicates the degree of closeness or significance of this relationship. In view of these above purposes, the following facts should be kept in mind for interpreting the coefficient of correlation.

(i) **The sign of the correlation coefficient should be taken into consideration.** A positive sign tells about the existence of positive correlation between two variables, while the negative sign indicates the negative correlation.

(ii) **A correlation coefficient is not a proportion.** It does not give directly anything like a percentage of relationship. We cannot say that an r of 0.60 indicates a degree of relationship twice as great as an *r* of 0.30, nor can we say that an increase in correlation from 0.40 to 0.50 is equivalent to an increase from 0.60 to 0.70. Similarly, the difference between coefficients of 0.40 and 0.60 is not equal to the difference between coefficients of 0.70 and 0.90. Therefore, it should be clearly understood that the coefficient of correlation is an index number, not a measurement on an interval (equal-unit) scale. However, r^2 is not only on an interval scale but a ratio scale. It should be noted that a correlation of –0.60 indicates the same close relationship as a correlation of +0.60. The relation differs only in direction.

(iii) **For the simple verbal description of the correlation coefficient**, help may be taken from the following summary:

Size of Correlation	Interpretation
±1.0	Perfect positive/negative correlation.
From ±0.91 to ±0.99	Very high positive/negative correlation; quite dependable relationship.
From ±0.71 to ±0.90	High positive/negative correlation; marked relationship.
From ±0.51 to ±0.70	Moderate positive/negative correlation; substantial but small relationship.
From ±0.31 to ±0.50	Low positive/negative correlation; definite but small relationship.
From ±0.11 to ±0.30	Very low positive/negative correlation.
From ±0.0 to ±0.10	Markedly low, slight, almost negligible positive/negative correlation.
0 (zero value)	Zero relation, absolutely no relationship.

(iv) **The above verbal interpretation of the correlation coefficient** is altogether a tentative one. However, the task of interpretation should not be considered so simple. The question regarding the significance of the size of the coefficient of correlation cannot be fully answered without referring to the particular purposes and situations under which the coefficient of correlation has been computed. Consequently, we have to interpret the coefficient of correlation in the way we aim to use it for different purposes as noted below.

(a) **In the form of a reliability coefficient for testing the reliability of a test.** For example, the reliability coefficient can be obtained by correlating scores from two alternate, parallel forms of the same test. Similarly, if an intelligence test is administered today and again after a month to the same subjects, the correlation between these two sets of scores will serve as the reliability coefficient of the intelligence test. There has been some consensus that to be a very accurate measure of individual differences in some characteristics, the reliability coefficient should be above 0.90. The truth is, however, that many standard tests with reliability coefficients as low as 0.70 prove to be very useful. And tests with reliabilities lower than that can be useful in research.

(b) **In the form of a validity coefficient for studying the predictive validity of a test.** For example, the correlation between scores on an aptitude test and measures of academic or vocational success gives a validity coefficient which is an index of the predictive value of a test. In the case of using a correlation coefficient for predicting the validity of a test, we will not require the value of the correlation coefficient as much high. Common experience shows that the validity coefficient of a single test may be expected in the range of 0.00–0.60, with most indices within the lower part of this range. It is common experience that a college–aptitude test correlates somewhere near 0.50 with grades in courses.

(c) **In the form of a purely descriptive device for describing the nature of relationship between two variables**. When one is investigating a purely theoretical problem, even very small correlations, if statistically significant, are often very indicative of a psychological law. In research, tests having low-reliability coefficients can also be useful.

(v) **Finally,** the question arises as to how long a correlation coefficient may be and still be of value. The answer to this question requires the knowledge of the technique for testing the significance of correlation. All these techniques will be discussed further.

The practical conclusion to be drawn from this is that a correlation is always relative to the situation under which it is obtained, and the size does not represent any absolute natural fact. Therefore, the coefficient of correlation should be interpreted in the light of those situations or circumstances, very rarely, certainly, in any absolute sense.

9.3.9 Testing the Significance of Pearson's r

We can test the significance of an obtained coefficient of correlation by the help of any one of the following techniques.

9.3.9.1 *Testing r Against the Null Hypothesis (H₀)*

The significance of an obtained r may be tested against the null hypothesis (H_0) which states that the population r is, in fact, zero. If the computed r is large enough to invalidate or cast serious doubt upon this null hypothesis, we accept r as indicating the presence of at least some degree of correlation. It can be done with the help of a table given in the appendix (Table B). From this table, we can read directly, given the degrees of freedom ($N-2$), the values of r that would be significant at 0.05 and 0.01 levels of significance (usually two significance levels 0.05 and 0.01 are taken). Then we will take appropriate decision about the significance of the given or obtained r by comparing it with the tabulated values of r. The obtained r will be significant if it will be equal to or greater than the table values of r.

This method may be employed in the case of large as well as small samples with any obtained value of r. The procedure can be understood easily through the following illustration.

Example 9.2 Given $r = 0.78$, $N = 12$. Test the significance of the given r.

Solution Let us, first of all, set up a null hypothesis saying that the population r is, in fact, zero, and see whether it is accepted or rejected in view of the given data:

$$H_0 : r = 0; \quad H_1 : r \neq 0.$$

Here, $N = 12$. Therefore, the number of degrees of freedom will be $N-2 = 12-2 = 10$. We read the values of r at the 0.05 and 0.01 levels of significance from Table B (given in the appendix) for $df = 10$. These tabulated values are 0.576 and 0.708, respectively. This means that only five times in 100 trials would an r as large as ± 0.576 arises from the fluctuations of sampling alone if the population r were actually 0.00; and only once in 100 trials would an r as large as ± 0.708 appear if the population r were 0.00. It is clear that the given r of 0.78, since it is larger than 0.708, it is highly significant at the 0.01 level of significance. Therefore, $p < 0.01$. This indicates that the H_0 is rejected and the H_1 is accepted in 99% of cases, and we may take the computed value of r as quite trustworthy, genuine and significant.

The 0.05 and 0.01 levels in Table B (given in the appendix) are the only ones needed ordinarily in evaluating the significance of an obtained r. Several illustrations of the use of Table B in determining significance are given in the following table.

Size of Sample (N)	Degree of Freedom (N−2)	Calculated r	Interpretation
10	8	0.70	Significant at 0.05, not at 0.01 level
12	10	0.55	Not significant
27	25	0.50	Significant at 0.05, barely at 0.01 level
100	98	−0.30	Very significant

It is clear from these above examples that even a small r may be significant if computed from a very large sample, and that an r as high as 0.70 may not be significant if N is quite small.

9.3.9.2   Testing r in Terms of t Distribution

This method of testing the significance of r developed by R. A. Fisher by making use of the t distribution and testing the significance of an obtained r against the null t hypothesis shows that the population r is, in fact, zero. Fisher in his work demonstrated that when the population r is zero, a parameter t can be estimated by the formula which reads as follows:

$$t = \frac{r}{s_r} = r\sqrt{\frac{N-2}{1-r^2}}; \quad s_r = SE_r = \sqrt{\frac{1-r^2}{N-2}}.$$

The values of t for different samples are distributed as in a t distribution. In other words, we begin by assuming the null hypothesis that the value of the correlation coefficient is equal to 0 ($H_0 : r = 0$). A test of significance may then be applied using the distribution of t. The t value required is given by the above formula.

The number of degrees of freedom associated with this value of t is $N-2$. The loss of two degrees of freedom results because testing the significance of r from 0 is equivalent to testing the significance of the slope of a regression line from 0. The correlation coefficient is nothing but the slope of a regression line in a standard score form. The number of degrees of freedom (df) associated with the variability about a straight line fitted to a set of points is 2 less than the number of observations.

The procedure can be better understood through the following illustration.

Example 9.3 Given $r = 0.50$; $N = 20$. Test the significance of the given r.

Solution Let us set up null hypothesis stating that the population r is, in fact, zero, and see whether it is accepted or rejected in view of the given data:

$$H_0 : r = 0; \quad H_1 : r \neq 0; \quad N = 20.$$

We can obtain the value of t as follows:

$$SE_r = s_r = \sqrt{\frac{1-r^2}{N-2}}$$

$$t = \frac{r}{s_r} = r\sqrt{\frac{N-2}{1-r^2}} = 0.50\sqrt{\frac{20-2}{1-(0.50)^2}} = 0.50\sqrt{\frac{18}{1-0.25}}$$

$$= 0.50\sqrt{\frac{18}{0.75}} = 0.50\sqrt{24} = 0.50 \times 4.90 = 2.45.$$

Here $N=20$. Therefore, the df $= N-2 = 20-2 = 18$. We read the values of t at the 0.05 and 0.01 levels of significance from Table C (given in the appendix) for df $=18$. These tabulated values are 2.10 and 2.88, respectively. It is clear that the computed $t=2.45$ is greater than the table value of t given for the 0.05 level of significance but smaller than the table value of t given for the 0.01 level of significance. Therefore, the computed 't' of 2.45 is significant at the 0.05, but not at the 0.01, level of significance because in order to be significant, the obtained value of t must be equal to or greater than the table values given for different levels of significance. Therefore, $p<0.05$. This indicates that the H_0 is rejected and H_1 is accepted in 95% of cases, and we may take the computed value of 't', and, thus, the given value of r, as trustworthy, real and significant.

9.3.9.3 Testing r in Terms of Standard Error (SE) of r

When the sample size is large and r is relatively small, we can test the significance of the given r by obtaining the SE of r. The classical formula for the SE of r is

$$s_r = \sigma_r = \frac{1-r^2}{\sqrt{N}}.$$

The procedure will be better understood through the following illustration.

Example 9.4 Given $r=0.50$; $N=100$. Test the significance of the given r.

Solution Here $r=0.50$ and $N=100$.
Therefore,

$$\sigma_r = \frac{1-r^2}{\sqrt{N}} = \frac{1-(0.50)^2}{\sqrt{100}} = \frac{1-0.25}{10} = \frac{0.75}{10} = 0.075.$$

To test the dependability of r in terms of its SE, we assume the sampling distribution of r to be normal. By assuming the sampling distribution of r to be normal, we have the following confidence intervals at the 0.95 (or 95%) and 0.99 (or 99%) levels for delimiting our population r.

The 0.95 confidence interval for the true r is

$$r \pm 1.96\sigma_r$$
$$= 0.50 \pm 1.96(0.075) = 0.50 \pm 0.147$$
$$= 0.353 \underline{\hspace{3cm}} 0.647.$$

0.99 confidence interval for true r is

$$r \pm 2.58\sigma_r$$
$$= 0.50 \pm 2.58(0.075) = 0.50 \pm 0.1935$$
$$= 0.3065 \underline{\hspace{3cm}} 0.6935.$$

We may feel quite certain and, therefore, conclude that the estimated r is at least as large as 0.3065 and is no larger than 0.6935.

Since our obtained r of 0.50 comes within this range of interval, it is significant at the 0.01 level of significance. Therefore, $p < 0.01$. This indicates that the H_0 is rejected and H_1 is accepted in 99% of cases.

9.3.9.4   Testing r in terms of Fisher's z function

A mathematically more defensible method of testing the significance of an r, especially when the sample size is large (N is 30 or greater) and the r is very high or very low, is to convert r into R. A. Fisher's z function (which is known as transformation z or z'), and find out the SE of z. The function z has two advantages over r: (a) its sampling distribution is approximately normal and (b) its SE depends only upon the size of the sample N, and is independent of the size of r.

The conversion of r into Fisher's z function may be done with the help of Table D (given in the appendix). Then we can find out the SE of z by the following formula:

$$\sigma_z = \frac{1}{\sqrt{N-3}}.$$

Subsequently, the 0.95 confidence interval and 0.99 confidence interval can be found out by using formulae $z \pm 1.96\,\sigma_z$ and $z \pm 2.58\,\sigma_z$, respectively. These z values are again converted into r function with the help of the conversion Table D.

The whole process can be better understood through the following illustration.

Example 9.5 Given $r = 0.85$; $N = 52$. Test the significance of the given r.

Solution Here $r = 0.85$ and $N = 52$. First, from Table D we read that an r of 0.85 corresponds to a z of 1.26. The SE of z is

$$\sigma_z = \frac{1}{\sqrt{N-3}} = \frac{1}{\sqrt{52-3}} = \frac{1}{\sqrt{49}} = \frac{1}{7} = 0.14.$$

The 0.95 confidence interval for the true z is

$$z \pm 1.96\sigma_z$$
$$= 1.26 \pm 1.96 \times 0.14 = 1.26 \pm 0.27 = 0.99 \text{ to } 1.53.$$

These values of z are again converted into r values with the help of Table D. Converting these z's back into r's, we obtain a confidence interval of r from 0.76 to 0.91. Thus, the confidence interval of the 0.95 level for the true r varies from 0.76 to 0.91. The fiduciary probability that this interval contains the true r is 0.95.

The 0.99 confidence interval for the true z is

$$z \pm 2.58\sigma_z$$
$$= 1.26 \pm 2.58 \times 0.14 = 1.26 \pm 0.36 = 0.90 \text{ to } 1.62.$$

Converting these z's back into r's, we obtain a confidence interval of r from 0.715 to 0.925. Thus, the confidence interval of the 0.99 level for the true r varies from 0.715 to 0.925. The fiduciary probability that this interval contains the true r is 0.99.

Since the given r of 0.85 is coming within the 0.99 confidence interval, it is significant at the 0.01 level of significance. Therefore, $p < 0.01$. This indicates that the H_0 is rejected and H_1 is accepted in 99% of cases. If the obtained r, on the other hand, would have not come within this range, that is, if it is below the lower limit of this range of interval, it is insignificant.

9.3.10 Factors Influencing the Size of *r*

The following are some of the factors which influence the size of the coefficient of correlation.

(i) The size of *r* is influenced by the range of the two variables, *X* and *Y*. Restricting the range of either of the variables will have the effect of lowering the correlation; the wider the range, the greater the size of *r*. In other words, range restriction reduces the size of *r* because there would be much less systematic changes in *Y* with changes in *X*.

(ii) The size of *r* is very much dependent upon the variability of the measured values in the correlated samples. Everything being equal, the greater the variability, the higher the correlation.

(iii) The size of *r* is altered, when an investigator selects an extreme group of subjects in order to compare these groups with respect to certain behaviour. The *r* obtained from the combined data of the extreme groups would be larger than the *r* obtained from a random sample of the same group.

(iv) The addition or deletion of the extreme cases to or from the group can lead to change in the size of *r*. The addition of the extreme cases to the group may increase the size of *r*, while the deletion of the extreme cases from the group will lower the value of *r*.

9.3.11 Correlation and Causation

A correlation coefficient gives us a quantitative determination of the degree of relationship between two variables *X* and *Y*. But *r* alone gives us no information as to the character of the association, and we cannot assume a causal sequence unless we have evidence beyond the correlation coefficient itself. Causation implies an invariable sequence—A always leads to B—whereas correlation is simply a measure of mutual association between two variables.

When two variables, *X* and *Y*, are correlated, it is tempting to conclude that one of them is the cause of the other. However, concluding so without further experimentation would be a serious error, because whenever two variables are correlated, there are four possible explanations of the correlation. It may be that (a) the correlation between *X* and *Y* is spurious, (b) *X* is the cause of *Y*, (iii) *Y* is the cause of *X* or (iv) a third variable is the cause of the correlation between *X* and *Y*.

The first possibility asserts that it was just due to accidents of sampling unusual people or unusual behaviour that the samples showed a correlation—that, if the experiments were repeated or more samples were taken, the correlation would disappear. If the correlation is really spurious, it is obviously wrong to conclude that there is a causal relation between *X* and *Y*.

It is also erroneous to assume causality between *X* and *Y* if the fourth alternative is correct. Quite often when *X* and *Y* are correlated, they are not causally related to each other, but rather a third variable is responsible for the correlation. For example, the correlation between intelligence and educational achievement over a wide age range is often drastically reduced when the effect of the age variable is removed. This clearly shows that the correlation between intelligence and educational achievement is influenced by the age variable, and, thus, intelligence and educational achievement are not causally related.

Recently, a newspaper article reported a positive correlation between obesity and female crime. Does this mean that if a woman gains 10 kg of body weight, she will become a criminal? Or does it mean that if she is a criminal, she is doomed to being obese? Neither of these explanations seems satisfactory. Frankly speaking, we are not sure how to interpret this correlation. One possibility is that it is a spurious correlation. If not, it could be due to a third factor, namely, socio-economic status. Both obesity and crime are related to a lower socio-economic status.

The point we are trying here to make is that a correlation between two variables is not sufficient to establish causality between them. There are other possible explanations. To establish one variable is the cause of another, we must conduct an experiment in which we systemati-cally vary only the suspected causal variable and measure its effect on the other variable.

9.4   Biserial Coefficient of Correlation (r_b)

The biserial correlation (r_b) is a specialised form of the product-moment correlation (r). It is used as a measure of simple linear correlation between a continuous measurement variable and an apparently dichotomous variable which is reasonably expected to yield a continuous series of normally distributed metric data.

The biserial correlation is especially designed for the situation in which both the variables correlated are really continuously measurable but one of the two is, for some reason, artificially reduced to two categories. This reduction to two categories may be a consequence of the only way in which the data can be obtained. As for example, when one variable is whether or not a student passes or fails to pass a certain criterion of success. The variable which is artificially reduced to two categories of values is called dichotomous. Such apparently dichotomous variables include vari-ables such as pass–fail, successful–unsuccessful, diabetic–non-diabetic, neurotic–non-neurotic, trained–untrained and so on. Thus, r_b should be computed for correlating performance test scores with trained–untrained status, and differential aptitude test scores with pass–fail status.

When one of two traits is scored on a continuous scale and the other on a scale having only two values, the resulting correlation is called a biserial correlation. If the criterion is a scaled trait and the item is dichotomous, a biserial correlation is called for. The item scores are dichotomous if only two answers are possible (such as 'true' or 'false', 'yes' or 'no', 'pass' or 'fail') or if several pos-sible answers are classified into those which are 'acceptable' and those which are 'not acceptable'.

Suppose we want to categorise the students who pass and who fail in a test. For this, we can well assume a criterion or continuum along which individuals differ with respect to ability required to pass this criterion. Those having a degree of ability above a certain crucial point do pass it, and those having a degree of ability below that crucial point fail to pass. In such a case, the biserial correlation method is more profitable and fruitful.

Biserial correlation is often used for *item–total correlation* between a dichotomised test item and the total score of a psychological test, assuming that the dichotomy of the test item rep-resents an apparent dichotomy of a near-normally distributed variable. Likewise, r_b is computed between a dichotomised test item and continuous scores of an external criterion for an attribute (item–criterion correlation) so as to assess the capacity of the test item to measure the attribute.

While correlating two continuous variables, the scores of one variable may sometimes be found to have a truncated distribution in the sample with no score beyond certain scale values, or to have a skewed distribution in the sample, although their population distribution may reasonably be assumed to be normal. In such cases, the distribution of scores of that vari-able may be dichotomised into two classes at a point as near to the median as possible, and r_b is then computed between it and the other continuous variable.

9.4.1   Assumptions of r_b

For applying biserial r, it should be justifiable to assume the following:

1. Both the variables, X and Y, are continuous (even, the dichotomous variable is actually continuous). More specifically, one of the variables is a continuous measurement varia-ble yielding a continuous metric series of scores, while the other is an apparently or arti-ficially dichotomous variable which either may yield a continuous series of metric data on further exploration or has been dichotomised from such continuous scores.

2. The continuous measurement variable involved has a normal or near-normal distribution in the population without much skewness or asymmetry.
3. The distribution of values on the dichotomous variable, when continuously measured, shall be normal. In other words, the continuous metric data, underlying the dichotomised variable, have a unimodal and normal or near-normal distribution in the population.
4. The joint distribution of X and Y is normal bivariate.
5. Since there is normality in the distribution of scores, there is homoscedasticity. For each X, the variance of Y is the same as for every other X. This means that the column and row variances should be approximately equal.
6. There is a linear relationship between the two variables.
7. The dichotomous variable has been dichotomised at a point not far from the median of the continuous distribution of its scores. In other words, the proportion of cases in each class of the dichotomised variable should not be far different from 0.50—the more extreme this dichotomy or the smaller the sample size (n), the higher the SE of r_b and consequently the lower the reliability of the r_b.
8. In each class of the dichotomised variable, every score of the continuous variable occurs at random and is independent of other scores.

9.4.2 Computation of r_b

The principle upon which the formula for the computation of biserial r is based is that with zero correlation there would be no difference between means, and the larger the difference between means, the larger the correlation. For example, if $\bar{X}_p \sim \bar{X}_q$ is large, then the obtained r_b will be more.

The general formula for biserial r is

$$r_b = \frac{\bar{X}_p - \bar{X}_q}{s_t} \times \frac{pq}{y},$$

where

r_b = biserial coefficient of correlation
$\bar{X}_p$ = mean of X values for the higher group in the dichotomous variable
$\bar{X}_q$ = mean of X values for the lower group in the dichotomous variable
p = proportion of the cases in the higher group of the dichotomised variable
q = proportion of the cases in the lower group of the dichotomised variable
y = the height of the ordinate of the unit normal curve at the point of division of the normal curve area into p and q
s_t = SD of the total scores of the sample in the continuously measured variable X.

In many situations, a more convenient formula for the computation of r_b is used. This alternative formula for biserial r reads as follows:

$$r_b = \frac{\bar{X}_p - \bar{X}_t}{s_t} \times \frac{p}{y},$$

where the only new symbol is $\bar{X}_t$, which is the mean of the total sample. The greater advantage of this formula over the other one is that it gives us one less distribution to deal with. It is convenient to use the same zero point for both the component distribution and for the total distribution.

In addition to the just mentioned two formulae, another alternative formula is also available using n_p or the number of cases in the class with the proportion p. This formula reads as follows:

$$r_b = \frac{n_p(\bar{X}_p - \bar{X}_t)}{n s_t y}.$$

The ordinate y is found from the normal curve table (Table A given in the appendix). It is the ordinate of the unit normal curve corresponding to that fractional area from its mean $(\mu = 0)$ which equals the absolute difference, neglecting the algebraic sign, between p and 0.50, the latter being half the area of the unit normal curve.

The procedures involved in the computation of r_b will be better understood through the following examples.

Example 9.6 The following is the distribution of scores of 200 students passed and failed on a psychological test. Calculate the biserial correlation between the two variables and interpret your results.

	\multicolumn{10}{c}{Scores}									
	40–49	50–59	60–69	70–79	80–89	90–99	100–109	110–119	120–129	130–139
Pass	0	1	3	10	27	30	26	21	7	5
Fail	2	6	4	11	21	16	7	3	0	0

Solution The total test scores constitute a continuous measurement variable while the pass/fail on the test constitute an artificial dichotomous variable. So r_b is computed between the two variables (see Table 9.7).

The following *steps* are to be followed for computing biserial correlation between two variables (see Table 9.7).

Step 1. Proportions (p and q) of students passing and failing on the psychological test are worked out

$$p = \frac{n_p}{N} = \frac{130}{200} = 0.65, \quad q = \frac{n_q}{N} = \frac{70}{200} = 0.35.$$

Step 2. Means of test scores of students passing $\bar{X}_p$ and failing $\bar{X}_q$ on the test, and also the grand mean of the total test scores $\bar{X}_t$ are computed (see Table 9.7) following the AM method as described in Chapter 3:

$$\Sigma f_p x' = 49, \quad C_p = \frac{\Sigma f_p x'}{n_p} = \frac{49}{130} = 0.377;$$

$$i = 10, \quad \therefore C_p i = 0.377 \times 10 = 3.77;$$

$$\bar{X}_p = AM + C_p i = 94.5 + 3.77 = 98.27.$$

$$\Sigma f_q x' = -76, \quad C_q = \frac{\Sigma f_q x'}{n_q} = \frac{-76}{70} = -1.086;$$

$$i = 10, \quad \therefore C_q i = -1.086 \times 10 = -10.86;$$

$$\bar{X}_q = AM + C_q i = 94.5 + (-10.86) = 94.5 - 10.86 = 83.64.$$

Table 9.7   Computation of biserial correlation (r_b)

	Scores										n	n/N
	40–49	50–59	60–69	70–79	80–89	90–99	100–109	110–119	120–129	130–139		
Pass	0	1	3	10	27	30	26	21	7	5	$130 = n_p$	$0.65 = p$
Fail	2	6	4	11	21	16	7	3	0	0	$70 = n_q$	$0.35 = q$
Total	2	7	7	21	48	46	33	24	7	5	$200(N)$	1.00

Scores	Midpoint	f_p	f_q	f_t	x'	$f_p x'$	$f_q x'$	$f_t x'$	$f_t x'^2$
130–139	134.5	5	0	5	4	20	0	20	80
120–129	124.5	7	0	7	3	21	0	21	63
110–119	114.5	21	3	24	2	42	6	48	96
100–109	104.5	26	7	33	1	26	7	33	33
90–99	94.5	30	16	46	0	0	0	0	0
80–89	84.5	27	21	48	–1	–27	–21	–48	48
70–79	74.5	10	11	21	–2	–20	–22	–42	84
60–69	64.5	3	4	7	–3	–9	–12	–21	63
50–59	54.5	1	6	7	–4	–4	–24	–28	112
40–49	44.5	0	2	2	–5	0	–10	–10	50
Sum		130	70	200		49	–76	–27	629

$$\Sigma f_t x' = -27, \quad C_t = \frac{\Sigma f_t x'}{n_t} = \frac{-27}{200} = -0.135;$$

$$i = 10, \quad C_t i = -0.135 \times 10 = -1.35;$$

$$\bar{X}_t = AM + C_t i = 94.5 + (-1.35) = 94.5 - 1.35 = 93.15.$$

Step 3. The SD of the total test scores (s_t) is computed by taking the deviation scores from the AM, as described in Chapter 4:

$$s_t = i\sqrt{\frac{\Sigma f_t x'^2}{N} - C_t^2} = 10\sqrt{\frac{629}{200} - (-0.135)^2}$$

$$= 10\sqrt{3.145 - 0.018225} = 10\sqrt{3.126775} = 10 \times 1.768 = 17.68.$$

Step 4. Since $p = 0.65$, the absolute difference between p and 0.50 amounts to $|0.65 - 0.50| = 0.15$. Thus, y is the ordinate at the point limiting the area ($p - 0.50$) or 0.15 from the mean (μ) in the unit normal curve. By extrapolation from Table A (given in the appendix) y amounts to 0.3704 for this area of 0.15.

Step 5. r_b is computed by either of the following formulae:

(i)

$$r_b = \frac{\bar{X}_p - \bar{X}_q}{s_t} \times \frac{pq}{y} = \frac{98.27 - 83.64}{17.68} \times \frac{(0.65 \times 0.35)}{0.3704}$$

$$= \frac{14.63}{17.68} \times \frac{0.2275}{0.3704} = 0.8275 \times 0.6142 = 0.508.$$

or

(ii)

$$r_b = \frac{\bar{X}_p - \bar{X}_t}{s_t} \times \frac{p}{y} = \frac{98.27 - 93.15}{17.68} \times \frac{0.65}{0.3704}$$

$$= \frac{5.12}{17.68} \times \frac{0.65}{0.3704} = 0.2896 \times 1.7549 = 0.508$$

or

(iii)

$$r_b = \frac{n_p(\bar{X}_p - \bar{X}_t)}{ns_t y} = \frac{130(98.27 - 93.15)}{200 \times 17.68 \times 0.3704} = \frac{130 \times 5.12}{3536 \times 0.3704}$$

$$= \frac{665.6}{1309.7344} = 0.508.$$

9.4.3   Test of Significance of r_b

The obtained r_b can be tested for its significance by any one of the following three ways:

9.4.3.1   *In Terms of the Standard Error of r_b*

The SE of r_b is estimated by the following formula:

$$s_{r_b} = \frac{\dfrac{\sqrt{pq}}{y} - r_b^2}{\sqrt{N}}.$$

In Example 9.6, $p = 0.65$, $q = 0.35$, $N = 200$, $y = 0.3704$ and $r_b = 0.508$. Therefore,

$$s_{r_b} = \frac{\dfrac{\sqrt{0.65 \times 0.35}}{0.3704} - (0.508)^2}{\sqrt{200}} = \frac{\dfrac{\sqrt{0.2275}}{0.3704} - 0.2581}{14.1421}$$

$$= \frac{\dfrac{0.4770}{0.3704} - 0.2581}{14.1421} = \frac{1.2878 - 0.2581}{14.1421} = \frac{1.0297}{14.1421} = 0.07.$$

To test the dependability of r_b in terms of its SE, we assume that the sampling distribution of r_b to be normal. By assuming the sampling distribution of r_b to be normal, we have the following confidence intervals at the 0.95 and 0.99 levels for delimiting our population r_b

The 0.95 confidence interval for the true r_b is

$$r_b \pm 1.96 s_{r_b}$$
$$= 0.508 \pm 1.96 \times 0.07$$
$$= 0.508 \pm 0.1372$$
$$= 0.3708 _____ 0.6452.$$

The 0.99 confidence interval for the true r_b is

$$r_b \pm 2.58 s_{r_b}$$
$$= 0.508 \pm 2.58 \times 0.07$$
$$= 0.508 \pm 0.1806$$
$$= 0.3274 _____ 0.6886.$$

We may feel quite certain and, therefore, conclude that the estimated r_b is at least as large as 0.3274 and is no larger than 0.6886.

Since our obtained r_b of 0.508 comes within this range of interval, it is significant at the 0.01 level of significance. Therefore, $p < 0.01$. This indicates that H_0 is rejected and H_1 is accepted in 99% of cases.

9.4.3.2   In Terms of Conversion to z-score

To test the H_0 that there is no correlation between the variables, the computed r_b is converted to z-score, where s_{r_b} is the SE of r_b, which can be computed by the following formula:

$$s_{r_b} = \frac{1}{y} \sqrt{\frac{pq}{N}}.$$

In Example 9.6, $p = 0.65$, $q = 0.35$, $y = 0.3704$, $N = 200$ and $r_b = 0.508$.

Therefore,

$$s_{r_b} = \frac{1}{0.3704} \sqrt{\frac{0.65 \times 0.35}{200}} = \frac{1}{0.3704} \sqrt{\frac{0.2275}{200}}$$

$$= \frac{1}{0.3704} \sqrt{0.0011375} = 2.6998 \times 0.0337 = 0.09.$$

$$z = \frac{r_b}{s_{r_b}} = \frac{0.508}{0.09} = 5.64.$$

Two-tailed probability (p) of the H_0 is given by

$p = 2[0.5000 - (\text{fractional area of unit normal curve from its } \mu \text{ to the } z\text{-score of } 5.64)]$
$= 2 (0.5000 - 0.49997) (\text{Table A in the appendix given up to } z = 4.0)$
$= 2 \times 0.00003 = 0.00006.$

As p is too low, there is a significant correlation between two variables ($p < 0.01$). So the H_0 is rejected and H_1 is accepted in 99% of cases.

9.4.3.3   *In Terms of Transformed z**

To test the significance of the biserial coefficient of correlation, a transformed z^* (read z star) will be made.

In Example 9.6, the $r_b = 0.508 = 0.51$ and $N = 200$

R. F. Tate said that $r = 0.8944r_b$ or $r_b = 1.118r$ and $z^* = 0.8944z$ or $z = 1.118z^*$.

Therefore, $r = 0.8944r_b = 0.8944 \times 0.51 = 0.436144 = 0.44$.

If $r = 0.44$ and $z = 0.47$ (Table D given in the appendix), then $z^* = 0.8944z = 0.8944 \times 0.47 = 0.420368 = 0.42$.

The SE of $z^* = \sigma_z^* = \dfrac{1}{\sqrt{N}} = \dfrac{1}{\sqrt{200}} = \dfrac{1}{14.1421} = 0.07$.

The 0.95 confidence interval of z^* is

$$z^* \pm 1.96\,\sigma_{z^*}$$
$$= 0.42 \pm 1.96 \times 0.07 = 0.42 \pm 0.1372 = 0.42 \pm 0.14$$
$$= 0.28 \underline{\qquad} 0.56.$$

These z^* values are converted into z values. Therefore, the 0.95 confidence interval in terms of z values is

$$1.118 \times 0.28 \underline{\qquad} 1.118 \times 0.56$$
$$= 0.313 \underline{\qquad} 0.626$$
$$= 0.31 \underline{\qquad} 0.63$$

These z values, are transformed into r values:

If $z = 0.31$, $r = 0.30$.
If $z = 0.63$, $r = 0.56$.

So, the 0.95 confidence interval in terms of r values is

$$0.30 \underline{\qquad} 0.56.$$

The above r values are converted into r_b values:

If $r = 0.30$, $r_b = 1.118 \times 0.30 = 0.3354 = 0.33$.
If $r = 0.56$, $r_b = 1.118 \times 0.56 = 0.6261 = 0.63$.

So, the 0.95 confidence interval in terms of r_b values is:

$$0.33 \underline{\qquad} 0.63.$$

Likewise, the 0.99 confidence interval for z^* may be computed as follows:

$$z^* \pm 2.58\sigma_{z^*}$$
$$= 0.42 \pm 2.58 \times 0.07 = 0.42 \pm 0.18$$
$$= 0.24 \underline{\qquad} 0.60.$$

These z^* values are converted into z values as:

$$1.118 \times 0.24 = 0.27 \text{ and}$$
$$1.118 \times 0.60 = 0.67.$$

The above z values are transformed into r values:

$$\text{If } z=0.27, r=0.265.$$
$$\text{If } z=0.67, r=0.585$$

The above r values are converted into r_b values:

$$\text{If } r=0.265, r_b=1.118 \times 0.265 = 0.296 = 0.30.$$
$$\text{If } r=0.585, r_b=1.118 \times 0.585 = 0.654 = 0.65.$$

So, the 0.99 confidence interval in terms of r_b values is 0.30 _____ 0.65.

Since our obtained $r_b=0.508$ or 0.51 lies within this interval, it is significant at the 0.01 level of significance. $\therefore p<0.01$. This indicates that the H_0 is rejected and H_1 is accepted in 99% of cases.

9.4.4   Evaluation of the r_b

Since the biserial coefficient of correlation is a product-moment r and is designed to be a good estimate of the Pearson r, the same requirements as for the latter must be satisfied. This means that the assumptions described earlier must be fulfilled.

The use of the quantities p, q and y in the formulae directly implies the normal distribution of the dichotomised variable. Departures from normality will often lead to a very erroneous estimates of correlation.

An interesting and disconcerting aspect of biserial r is that its values may cross the limits of −1.00 and +1.00, particularly if the continuous scores of the dichotomised variable have a bimodal or skewed distribution.

Biserial r is very useful; in fact, it is sometimes essential, and when properly used, it is a very good substitute for the Pearson r. There are instances in which the Y variable has been continuously measured, but there are irregularities that preclude computing a good estimate of the Pearson r. In such cases, the r_b may be brought into service. One example of this would be a truncated distribution; another would be when there are very few categories for the Y variable and it is doubtful whether they are equidistant on a metric scale; another would be in the case of a badly skewed distribution in Y values owing to a defective measuring instrument. Before computing r_b, we would, of course, need to dichotomise each Y distribution and we should take the division point as close to the median as possible.

Biserial r is less reliable than the Pearson r. Therefore, whenever there is a real choice of computing a Pearson r versus a biserial r, one should favour the former, unless the sample is very large and computation time is an important factor.

The SE for a biserial r is quite a bit larger than that for a Pearson r derived from the same sample. The reason behind this is the real difference in the numerators. One reads $1-r^2$ and another reads $\dfrac{\sqrt{pq}}{y}-r_b^2$.

9.5   Point Biserial Coefficient of Correlation(r_{pbi})

The point biserial r is a specialised form of the product-moment r. It is used as a measure of linear correlation between a continuous measurement variable and a dichotomous nominal variable or attribute. The point biserial r is especially designed for the situation in which both of the variables correlated are really continuously measurable, but one of the two variables is a genuine or real dichotomy. Examples of genuine dichotomies are: male–female, living–nonliving, right–wrong, pregnant–non-pregnant, colour blind–normal, alcoholic–non-alcoholic, criminal–non-criminal, neurotic–non-neurotic and so on.

In giving a final form to a psychological test, r_{pbi} may be computed to correlate the dichotomously scored right–wrong answers to a given test item with the continuous series of total scores of the entire test; this item–total correlation is often undertaken for the selection of test items.

The point biserial coefficient of correlation provides a very simple solution to the problem of biserial correlation.

9.5.1 Assumptions of r_{pbi}

For applying a point biserial r, it should be justifiable to assume the followings:

(a) One of the variables is a continuous measurement variable yielding a continuous series of scores, while the other is a genuinely dichotomous nominal variable that cannot yield a continuous or normal distribution even on further exploration.

(b) The continuous measurement variable involved has a normal or near-normal distribution in the population without much asymmetry or skewness.

(c) In each class of the dichotomous variable, every score of the continuous variable occurs at random and is independent of all other scores.

(d) There is a linear relationship between the two variables.

9.5.2 Computation of r_{pbi}

While computing the r_{pbi} we will come across certain terms where p and q are the proportions of cases or individuals in the two classes of the dichotomous variable, $\bar{X}_p$ and $\bar{X}_q$ are the mean scores of the continuous variable for individuals belonging to the respective classes of the dichotomous variable, $\bar{X}_t$ is the grand mean of the total scores, s_t is the SD of all scores of the continuous variable and n is the number of individuals in the sample.

The general formula for the computation of the point–biserial correlation is

$$r_{pbi} = \frac{\bar{X}_p - \bar{X}_q}{s_t} \times \sqrt{pq}.$$

The only difference between this formula and the one for the ordinary biserial r is that the numerator contains $\sqrt{pq}$ rather than pq, and the constant y is missing from the denominator.

For the same set of data, then the ordinary biserial r would be $\dfrac{\sqrt{pq}}{y}$ times as large as r_{pbi}.

As for the ordinary biserial r, there is an alternative formula for computing r_{pbi}, which may be more convenient in many situations. It reads as follows:

$$r_{pbi} = \frac{\bar{X}_p - \bar{X}_t}{s_t} \times \sqrt{\frac{p}{q}}.$$

The computation of p and q may be avoided by using np and nq, which are the numbers of individuals in the respective classes, and as such the following are the formulae:

$$r_{pbi} = \frac{\bar{X}_p - \bar{X}_q}{ns_t} \times \sqrt{n_p n_q} \quad \text{or} \quad r_{pbi} = \frac{\bar{X}_p - \bar{X}_t}{s_t} \times \sqrt{\frac{n_p}{n_q}}.$$

The values of r_{pbi} range from –1.00 to +1.00, but never reach the extremes. They fall with the increasing extremeness of the point of dichotomy of the nominal variable. So the greater the difference between p and q in the sample, the smaller the value of r_{pbi}.

Let us apply the above formulae to some data given in the following examples.

Example 9.7 In a sample of 51 sixteen-year-old high school students, of whom 24 were male and 27 were female, the mean body weights in kilograms were 67.8 and 56.6, respectively. The SD of the total scores was found to be 13.2 kg. Work out an appropriate correlation coefficient between body weight and sex and interpret the result.

Solution Because body weight is a continuous measurement variable and sex (male–female) status constitutes a genuine dichotomous variable, r_{pbi} should be computed:

$$n_p = 24; \quad n_q = 27; \quad n = n_p + n_q = 24 + 27 = 51$$

$$p = \frac{n_p}{n} = \frac{24}{51} = 0.47; \quad q = \frac{n_q}{n} = \frac{27}{51} = 0.53$$

$$\bar{X}_p = 67.8\,\text{kg}; \quad \bar{X}_q = 56.6\,\text{kg}; \quad s_t = 13.2\,\text{kg}$$

$$r_{pbi} = \frac{\bar{X}_p - \bar{X}_q}{s_t} \times \sqrt{pq} = \frac{67.8 - 56.6}{13.2}\sqrt{0.47 \times 0.53}$$

$$= \frac{11.2}{13.2}\sqrt{0.2491} = 0.848 \times 0.499 = 0.42.$$

Alternatively,

$$r_{pbi} = \frac{\bar{X}_p - \bar{X}_q}{ns_t} \times \sqrt{n_p n_q} = \frac{67.8 - 56.6}{51 \times 13.2}\sqrt{24 \times 27}$$

$$= \frac{11.2}{673.2} \times \sqrt{648} = 0.0166 \times 25.456 = 0.42.$$

The correlation between sex and body weight for 16-year-old high school students is estimated to be 0.42.

Example 9.8 The following is the distribution of extraversion scores of 72 subjects, 42 males and 30 females, on a psychological test. Calculate the point biserial correlation between extraversion and sex of the subjects and interpret your results.

	X: Extraversion						
	6–10	11–15	16–20	21–25	26–30	31–35	n
Male	2	5	10	15	10	0	42
Female	0	0	5	10	10	5	30
Total	2	5	15	25	20	5	72

Solution Total extraversion scores constitute a continuous measurement variable, and sex (male–female) status constitutes a genuine dichotomous variable. So r_{pbi} is computed between the two variables (see Table 9.8).

The following *steps* are to be followed for computing point biserial correlation between two variables (see Table 9.8).

Table 9.8 Computation of point biserial correlation (r_{pbi})

	X: Extraversion							
	6-10	11-15	16-20	21-25	26-30	31-35	n	n/N
Male	2	5	10	15	10	0	$42=n_p$	$0.58=p$
Female	0	0	5	10	10	5	$30=n_q$	$0.42=q$
Total	2	5	15	25	20	5	$72(N)$	1.00

Scores	Midpoint	f_p	f_q	f_t	x'	$f_p x'$	$f_q x'$	$f_t x'$	$f_t x'^2$
31-35	33	0	5	5	2	0	10	10	20
26-30	28	10	10	20	1	10	10	20	20
21-25	23	15	10	25	0	0	0	0	0
16-20	18	10	5	15	-1	-10	-5	-15	15
11-15	13	5	0	5	-2	-10	0	-10	20
6-10	8	2	0	2	-3	-6	0	-6	18
Sums:		42	30	72		-16	15	-1	93

Step 1. Proportions of cases (p and q) in the two sexes are worked out:

$$n_p = 42; \quad n_q = 30; \quad N = 72;$$

$$p = \frac{n_p}{N} = \frac{42}{72} = 0.58; \quad q = \frac{n_q}{N} = \frac{30}{72} = 0.42.$$

Step 2. Means of extraversion scores of males ($\bar{X}_p$) and females ($\bar{X}_q$) and also the grand mean of the total extraversion scores ($\bar{X}_t$) are computed (see Table 9.8) following the AM method as described in Chapter 3:

$$\Sigma f_p x' = -16. \quad C_p = \frac{\Sigma f_p x'}{n_p} = \frac{-16}{42} = -0.38$$

$$i = 5. \quad C_p i = -.38 \times 5 = -1.90$$

$$\bar{X}_p = AM + C_p i = 23 + (-1.90) = 23 - 1.90 = 21.10$$

$$\Sigma f_q x' = 15. \quad C_q = \frac{\Sigma f_q x'}{n_q} = \frac{15}{30} = 0.5$$

$$C_q i = 0.5 \times 5 = 2.5.$$

$$\bar{X}_q = AM + C_q i = 23 + 2.5 = 25.5$$

$$\Sigma f_t x' = -1. \quad C_t = \frac{\Sigma f_t x'}{N} = \frac{-1}{72} = -0.014$$

$$C_t i = -0.014 \times 5 = -0.07$$

$$\bar{X}_t = AM + C_t i = 23 + (-.07) = 23 - 0.07 = 22.93.$$

Step 3. The SD (s_t) of the total test scores (i.e., extraversion scores) is computed by taking the deviation scores from the AM, as described in Chapter 4:

$$s_t = i\sqrt{\frac{\Sigma f_t x'^2}{N} - C_t^2} = 5\sqrt{\frac{93}{72} - (-0.014)^2}$$

$$= 5\sqrt{1.292 - 0.0002} = 5\sqrt{1.2918} = 5 \times 1.136 = 5.68.$$

Step 4. r_{pbi} is computed by either of the following formulae:

(i)
$$r_{pbi} = \frac{\bar{X}_p - \bar{X}_q}{s_t} \times \sqrt{pq} = \frac{21.10 - 25.5}{5.68} \times \sqrt{0.58 \times 0.42}$$

$$= \frac{-4.40}{5.68} \times \sqrt{0.2436} = -0.7746 \times 0.4935 = -0.38$$

or

(ii)
$$r_{pbi} = \frac{\bar{X}_p - \bar{X}_t}{s_t} \times \sqrt{\frac{p}{q}} = \frac{21.10 - 22.93}{5.68} \times \sqrt{\frac{0.58}{0.42}}$$

$$= \frac{-1.83}{5.68} \times \sqrt{1.3809} = -0.3222 \times 1.1751 = -0.38$$

or

(iii)
$$r_{pbi} = \frac{\bar{X}_p - \bar{X}_q}{ns_t} \times \sqrt{n_p n_q} = \frac{21.10 - 25.5}{72 \times 5.68} \times \sqrt{42 \times 30}$$

$$= \frac{-4.40}{408.96} \times \sqrt{1260} = -0.0107 \times 35.4965 = -0.38$$

or

(iv)

$$r_{\text{pbi}} = \frac{\bar{X}_p - \bar{X}_t}{s_t} \times \sqrt{\frac{n_p}{n_q}} = \frac{21.10 - 22.93}{5.68} \times \sqrt{\frac{42}{30}}$$

$$= \frac{-1.83}{5.68} \times \sqrt{1.4} = -0.3222 \times 1.1832 = -0.38.$$

9.5.3   Test of Significance of r_{pbi}

The computed r_{pbi} can be tested for its significance by any one of the following two ways.

9.5.3.1   In Terms of Direct Conversion into t Ratio

To find out the significance of the obtained r_{pbi} the t-test is to be made basing directly on the computed r_{pbi} This formula reads as follows:

$$t = r_{\text{pbi}} \sqrt{\frac{N-2}{1-r_{\text{pbi}}^2}}; \quad \text{df} = N - 2.$$

In Example 9.8, $r_{\text{pbi}} = -0.38$, $N = 72$.
Therefore,

$$t = -0.38 \sqrt{\frac{72-2}{1-(-0.38)^2}} = -0.38 \sqrt{\frac{70}{1-0.1444}}$$

$$= -0.38 \sqrt{\frac{70}{0.8556}} = -0.38 \sqrt{81.8139}$$

$$= -0.38 \times 9.045 = -3.44.$$

Here, $N=72$ and df $= N-2 = 72-2 = 70$. We read the values of t at the 0.05 and 0.01 levels of significance from Table C (given in the appendix) for df=70. These tabulated values are 1.994 and 2.648, respectively. The computed t value is compared with the tabulated or critical t values. If the computed t value is equal to or greater than the tabulated t value(s), then it is said to be significant at that level of significance, and, thus, the computed r_{pbi} is considered significant at the same level of significance. In the present example, it is clear that the computed $t=-3.44$ is greater than (disregarding the algebraic sign) both the table values of t. Therefore, the computed t of -3.44 is significant at the 0.01 level of significance, and, hence, the computed r_{pbi} of -0.38 is significant at the 0.01 level of significance. $\therefore p < 0.01$. This indicates that the H_0, which proposes that there is no correlation between the variables in the population, is rejected and the H_1, which states that there is a relationship, is accepted in 99% of cases. Therefore, it is reasonable to conclude that there is a strong or significant relationship between sex and extraversion trait.

9.5.3.2   In Terms of the SE of r$_{pbi}$

The significance of the obtained r_{pbi} is tested by converting the obtained r_{pbi} into the t ratio by the help of the SE of the r_{pbi}. The SE of the r_{pbi} ($s_{r_{\text{pbi}}}$) can be computed by the following formula:

$$s_{r_{\text{pbi}}} = \sqrt{\frac{1-r_{\text{pbi}}^2}{N-2}} \quad \text{and} \quad t = \frac{r_{\text{pbi}}}{s_{r_{\text{pbi}}}}, \quad \text{df} = N - 2.$$

In Example 9.8, $r_{pbi} = -0.38$, $N = 72$.
Therefore,

$$s_{r_{pbi}} = \sqrt{\frac{1 - r_{pbi}^2}{N - 2}} = \sqrt{\frac{1 - (-0.38)^2}{72 - 2}} = \sqrt{\frac{1 - 0.1444}{70}}$$

$$= \sqrt{\frac{0.8556}{70}} = \sqrt{0.0122} = 0.1104$$

$$t = \frac{r_{pbi}}{s_{r_{pbi}}} = \frac{-0.38}{0.1104} = -3.44.$$

Here, $N = 72$, so $df = N - 2 = 72 - 2 = 70$. With $df = 70$, the table value of t at $0.05 = 1.994$ and at $0.01 = 2.648$. Since the computed t value is greater than both the table values, it is significant at the 0.01 level of significance, and, thus, the obtained r_{pbi} of -0.38 is also significant at the 0.01 level of significance. $\therefore p < 0.01$. This shows that the H_0 is rejected and H_1 is accepted in 99% of cases. This significant t ratio indicates that there is a strong and significant correlation between extraversion trait and sex.

Alternatively, for a very large sample, we can test the significance of the computed r_{pbi} by finding its SE and converting it into the t ratio by the help of the following formulae:

$$s_{r_{pbi}} = \frac{1}{\sqrt{N}}; \quad t = r_{pbi}\sqrt{N}$$

or

$$t = \frac{r_{pbi}}{s_{r_{pbi}}}; \quad df = \text{infinite} (\infty).$$

Suppose that in a sample of 200 (i.e., 130 male and 70 female), the obtained r_{pbi} is 0.50. We have to test whether this r_{pbi} is significant or not.

Here, $r_{pbi} = 0.50$, $N = 200$; $df = N - 2 = 200 - 2 = 198$, which is treated as infinite (∞):

$$s_{r_{pbi}} = \frac{1}{\sqrt{N}} = \frac{1}{\sqrt{200}} = \frac{1}{14.14} = 0.0707$$

$$t = \frac{r_{pbi}}{s_{r_{pbi}}} = \frac{0.50}{0.0707} = 7.07$$

or

$$t = r_{pbi}\sqrt{N} = 0.50\sqrt{200} = 0.50 \times 14.14 = 7.07.$$

The critical value or table value of t, with $df = \infty$, at $0.05 = 1.96$ and at $0.01 = 2.58$ (see Table C given in the appendix). Since the computed $t = 7.07$ is much greater than both the table values of t, it is significant at the 0.01 level of significance. Therefore, the computed r_{pbi} of 0.50 is also significant at the 0.01 level of significance. $\therefore p < 0.01$. This indicates that the H_0 is rejected and H_1 is accepted in 99% of cases.

9.5.4 Evaluation of Point Biserial Correlation (r_{pbi})

Since the r_{pbi} is not restricted to normal distributions in the dichotomous variable, it is much more generally applicable than r_b. When there is doubt about computing r_b, the r_{pbi} will serve. For this reason, it should probably be used more than it is. Although it is a product–moment r in value, r_{pbi} is rarely comparable numerically with a Pearson r, or even with an ordinary biserial r, when computed from the same data. This is its greatest weakness as a descriptive statistics. Under special circumstances, to be described in the following, it may be used as a basis for making an estimate of the Pearson r. In regard to a continuous distribution, when r_{pbi} is computed, the same requirements apply as in computing the Pearson r or the biserial r—they include a rather symmetrical, unimodal continuous distribution.

9.5.5   Mathematical Relation of r_{pbi} to r_b

If r_{pbi} were computed from data that actually justified the use of r_b, the coefficient computed would be markedly smaller than r_b obtained from the same data. Even if the one variable is actually continuous but not normally distributed (in which case, we might better utilise r_{pbi}), the latter would give an underestimate of the amount of correlation. As was pointed out before, r_b is $\sqrt{pq}/y$ times as large as r_{pbi} when they are computed from the same data. This ratio of $\sqrt{pq}/y$ varies from about 1.25 when $p=0.50$ to about 3.73 when p (or q) equals 0.99.

If needed, particularly when the normality of distribution exists, we may make the conversion of r_b into r_{pbi} or vice versa in terms of the following formulae:

$$r_b = r_{pbi}\frac{\sqrt{pq}}{y},$$

$$r_{pbi} = r_b\frac{y}{\sqrt{pq}}.$$

When the dichotomous variable is normally distributed without reasonable doubt, it is recommended that r_b be computed and interpreted. If there is little doubt that the distribution is a genuine dichotomy, r_{pbi} should be computed and interpreted. When in doubt, the point biserial r is probably the safer choice.

9.5.6   Comparison between r_b and r_{pbi}

The following general comment is taken from Tate, "It would seem from the evidence presented that point biserial r is in most cases the better coefficient to use." The two coefficients (r_b and r_{pbi}) may now be compared on several points.

(a) **The statistical model.** For r_b, a normal bivariate universe is assumed. If this is the case, then the distribution of Y variable cannot be normal within the separate categories. For r_{pbi}, no assumption is made as to the distribution of the dichotomous variable, but generalisation is made only to a universe of samples of size N having the same fixed number of cases N_0 and N_1 in the dichotomous categories. For r_{pbi}, it is assumed that Y is normally distributed within each X category and that the two Y distributions have the same variances. The validity of this assumption can be ascertained by testing the two distributions for the equality of variances, and testing, possibly only by inspection, the normality of each distribution.

(b) **Range of values of r.** For the point biserial r, the range is from −1.00 to +1.00. For biserial r, the range is unlimited.

(c) **Sampling distribution and tests of significance.** The exact sampling distribution of biserial r is unknown, and significance can be tested only if the transformation to z^* can be made. This is defensible only when p is near 0.5, N is large and r_b is not near +1.00 or −1.00. The exact sampling distribution of the point biserial r is known and tests of significance and confidence intervals can be obtained for any value of p and any size of N, by referring to the t-test table.

(d) **Use with other r's in a regression equation.** For biserial r, such use is very dubious for the point biserial r legitimate.

(e) **Position of dichotomous cut.** For either coefficient, better results are obtained when $N_0 = N_1$ than when they differ in size.

(f) **The circumstances where we use r_b and r_{pbi}.** It is recommended that when the dichotomous variable is normally distributed without much doubt, r_b should be computed and so interpreted. If there is little doubt that the distribution is genuine dichotomy, r_{pbi} should be computed and so interpreted. When there is a point distribution, r_{pbi} can approach 1.00.

(g) **In r_b,** the dichotomous variable is artificially reduced to two categories, whereas in r_{pbi}, the dichotomy is real or genuine one.

(h) **When properly applied, r_b gives coefficients** that are generally good approximations to Pearson's r that could be computed from the same data had both variables been continuously measured. Consequently, all the usual interpretations that are made of r can also be made of r_b.

(i) **Both r_b and r_{pbi} can be converted to each other.** We can convert r_b to r_{pbi}, and also r_{pbi} to r_b by the help of the formulae described earlier in this chapter under Section 9.5.5 (Mathematical Relation of r_{pbi} to r_b).

(j) **Both r_b and r_{pbi} are used in item analysis** (i.e., item-total correlation or item-criterion correlation), but r_b is not as valid procedure and not as defensible as r_{pbi}.

9.6   Tetrachoric Correlation (r_t)

Tetrachoric correlation (r_t) is a measure of correlation between two artificially dichotomous variables. Such artificially dichotomous variables include normal-abnormal, pass-fail, yes-no, athlete-non-athlete, agree-disagree, favourable-unfavourable, neurotic-non-neurotic, diabetic-non-diabetic, successful-unsuccessful, trained-untrained and so on.

A tetrachoric r is computed from data in which both X and Y variables have been reduced artificially to two categories. Under the appropriate conditions, it gives a coefficient that is numerically equivalent to the Pearson r and may be regarded as an approximation to it. The value of r_t ranges from −1.00 to +1.00.

The difference between biserial r and tetrachoric r is that in the former, one of the two variables is artificially reduced to two categories, but in the latter, both the variables are artificially reduced to two categories.

During item analysis for a psychological test, r_t is often computed for item-criterion correlation between a dichotomously scored test item and an external criterion representing the attribute under study, where the test item and the criterion have been artificially dichotomised. Thus, r_t may assess the power of a test item in measuring the attribute represented by the external criterion.

9.6.1   Assumptions of r_t

The following are some of the important assumptions underlying the tetrachoric correlation (r_t).

(a) Both the variables, X and Y, are artificially dichotomised into two categories. Thus, the data are in a fourfold (2×2) contingency table.

(b) The variables either have continuous metric data that have been dichotomised into two classes or may yield a continuous series of scores on measurements. In brief, both the variables should be continuously measurable.

(c) The continuous series of scores of both dichotomised variables form unimodal and normal distributions in the population. In brief, both variables are normally distributed in the population.

(d) There exists a linear relationship between the continuous scores of the variables. In other words, both variables, X and Y, are linearly related.

(e) The point of dichotomy is close to the median of each variable so that both the proportions p and q of its two classes are not far from 0.50.

9.6.2   Computation of r_t

When we want to find out the relationship between two variables, X and Y, which are artificially dichotomised into two categories, then we apply tetrachoric correlation and find out the amount of relationship between them. In other words, for the computation of r_t, the obtained data should be arranged in a (2×2)-fold (or fourfold) contingency table, and then r_t is computed by the following cosine-pi formula, which is an approximation to a tetrachoric r. In the mathematical form, the cosine-pi formula reads as follows:

$$r_{\text{cos-pi}} = \text{Cos}\left(\pi \frac{\sqrt{bc}}{\sqrt{ad} + \sqrt{bc}} \right).$$

Since for computing purposes, π can be taken to be 180°, the practical form of equation is

$$r_{\text{cos-pi}} = \text{Cos}\left(\frac{180°\sqrt{bc}}{\sqrt{ad} + \sqrt{bc}} \right).$$

By dividing both the numerator and denominator by $\sqrt{bc}$, we have a formula that is more simpler and convenient for computing purposes. In a simpler form, it reads

$$r_{\text{cos-pi}} = \text{Cos}\left(\frac{180°}{1 + \sqrt{\dfrac{ad}{bc}}} \right),$$

where a, b, c and d are the cell frequencies of the fourfold contingency table.

It is well to remember that b and c represent the unlike-signed cases, and a and d are the like-signed cases. When numbers are substituted, the above expression within the parentheses reduces to a single number, which is an angle in terms of degrees of arc. The cosine of this angle is the estimate of r_t. Therefore, $r_{\text{cos-pi}} = r_t$. The angle will vary from 0°, when either b or c (or both) is zero, to 180°, when either a or d (or both) is zero. In the first case, when the angle is zero, the r_t is +1.00, and in the second case, when the angle is 180°, r_t is –1.00. When the product bc equals ad, the angle is 90°, the cosine of which is zero, and r_t is estimated to be zero (see Table F given in the appendix).

In this method, if the angle should prove to be between 90° and 180°, the correlation is negative. This can be anticipated by noting that the product bc is greater than ad. Angles over 90° are not listed in Table F. For an angle between 90° and 180°, deduct the angle from 180°, find the cosine of this difference and give it a negative sign. Or in this case, the following slightly modified formula may be used:

$$r_{\text{cos-pi}} = -\text{Cos}\left(180° - \frac{180°\sqrt{bc}}{\sqrt{ad} + \sqrt{bc}} \right) \quad \text{or} \quad r_{\text{cos-pi}} = -\text{Cos}\left(180° - \frac{180°}{1 + \sqrt{\dfrac{ad}{bc}}} \right).$$

To be more clear, we can say that if the product ad is greater than bc ($ad > bc$), the angle is between 0° and 90°, so that r_t lies between 0 and +1.00. The cosine of this angle, lying between 0° and 90°, is noted from Table F, in the appendix, as the positive, and thus r_t is positive. When $ad = bc$, the computed angle is 90° so that $r_t = \text{Cos } 90° = 0$. When $bc = 0$, the angle is 0°, so that $r_t = \text{Cos } 0° = +1.00$. When $ad = 0$, the computed angle leads to 180°, so that $r_t = \text{Cos } 180° = -1.00$. If the product bc is greater than ad ($bc > ad$), the angle is between 90° and 180°, so that r_t lies between 0 and –1.00.

Table G in the appendix provides a quick solution for $r_{\text{cos-pi}}$ or r_t to two decimal places. Only the ratio ad/bc (or its reciprocal bc/ad) need be known; compute whichever gives a value greater than 1.0. In other words, in order to find out $r_{\text{cos-pi}}$ or r_t, we can take the ratio of ad/bc and then consult the table of the cosine-pi coefficient of correlation (i.e., Table G in the appendix) and find out the appropriate $r_{\text{cos-pi}}$ or r_t. The greater value, either ad or bc, should be taken as a numerator and the less value should be taken as a denominator, in order to make the ratio (either ad/bc or bc/ad) more than 1.0. If bc is greater than ad, find the ratio bc/ad and attach a negative sign to $r_{\text{cos-pi}}$ or r_t.

9.6.3   Significance of r_t

The tetrachoric r is less reliable than the Pearson r, being at least 50% more variable. In other words, the SE of r_t is from 50% to 100% larger than the SE of the Pearson r of the same size and based on the same N. If r is computed from 100 cases, to be equally stable, the r_t should be computed from at least 150–200 cases. The r_t is most reliable when N and r is large, and when the division into two categories is close to the medians.

The SE of r_t (s_{r_t}) is much higher than that of r. So, the complete formula for estimating s_{r_t} is too long to be practical and, hence, it will not be given here. However, to test the H_0 of no correlation (i.e., $r_t = 0$), a simplified formula of s_{r_t} may be used. This formula is much simpler and reads

$$s_{r_t} = \frac{\sqrt{p_1 p_2 q_1 q_2}}{y_1 y_2 \sqrt{n}} = \frac{1}{y_1 y_2} \sqrt{\frac{p_1 p_2 q_1 q_2}{n}},$$

where p_1 and q_1 are the proportions of cases in two classes of the first variable, p_2 and q_2 are the proportions in similar cases of the second variable, and y_1 and y_2 are the ordinates of the unit normal curve at the points of dichotomy of the respective variables into their classes. The y_1 and y_2 can be found from the differences between half the unit normal curve area, namely, 0.500, and p_1 and p_2, respectively.

In order to test the significance of r_t, it is then converted to the t ratio by the following formula:

$$t = \frac{r_t}{s_{r_t}}; \quad df = \infty.$$

The computed t is compared with critical values of t, with df = ∞, for finding the significance. Let us apply the above formulae to the data given in the following example.

Example 9.9 The data represent the number of students responding 'Yes' and 'No' to two questions in a personality questionnaire. Out of 140 replies to both questions, 50 responded 'Yes' to both questions, 40 responded 'No' to Question-I and 'Yes' to Question-II, 20 responded 'Yes' to Question-I and 'No' to Question-II, and 30 responded 'No' to both questions. Is there any significant correlation between the responses of the students to Question-I and Question-II?

Solution As both the variables (i.e., Question I and Question II) are artificially dichotomous, r_t is computed between them.

Table 9.9   Fourfold contingency table from which r_t is computed

		Question I		Total (f_r)	Proportion
		Yes	**No**	**Total (f_r)**	**Proportion**
Question II	Yes	50(a)	40(b)	90	0.64(p_2)
	No	20(c)	30(d)	50	0.36(q_2)
	Total (f_c)	70	70	140.(n)	1.00
	Proportion	0.50(p_1)	0.50(q_1)	1.00	

(a)   The data are entered as cell frequencies in a (2×2)-fold contingency table, representing 'Yes' responses to Question I in the left column and 'Yes' responses to Question II in the top row, as shown in Table 9.9.

(b)   Then we assign small alphabets a, b, c and d to the cell frequencies in such a way that we have the numbers who responded similarly (cells a and d) and the numbers who responded differently to both questions (cells b and c) as given in Table 9.9.

(c)   The cell frequencies are used in computing ad and bc. $ad = 50 \times 30 = 1500$; $bc = 40 \times 20 = 800$; $\therefore ad > bc$.

(d)   The cosine-pi formula is used in computing r_t:

$$r_t = r_{\text{cos-pi}} = \text{Cos}\left(\frac{180°}{1 + \sqrt{\dfrac{1500}{800}}}\right) = \text{Cos}\left(\frac{180°}{1 + \sqrt{1.875}}\right) = \text{Cos}\left(\frac{180°}{1 + 1.369}\right)$$

$$= \text{Cos}\left(\frac{180°}{2.369}\right) = \text{Cos }75.98° = +0.242.$$

The cosine of an angle of 75.98° (as found by interpolating in Table F in the appendix) is 0.242.

Alternatively, we can compute the $r_{\text{cos-pi}}$ or r_t by a shortcut way, which needs only the ratio ad/bc. In the given example, $ad/bc = 1{,}500/800 = 1.875$. This ratio lies between the given ratios 1.838 and 1.888 (see Table G in the appendix), which indicates a correlation of 0.24. Therefore, $r_{\text{cos-pi}} = r_t = 0.24$.

(e)   The computed r_t is converted to Student's t for testing the H_0 of no correlation. Where p_1 and q_1 are the proportions of 'Yes' and 'No' responses to Question-I; p_2 and q_2 are the proportions of 'Yes' and 'No' responses to Question-II; and n is the sample size. Thus,

$$p_1 = 70/140 = 0.50; \quad q_1 = 70/140 = 0.50; \quad p_2 = 90/140 = 0.64; \quad q_2 = 50/140 = 0.36.$$

(f)   The unit normal curve ordinates, y_1 and y_2 at the points of dichotomy of the respective variables, are found out from the differences between half the unit normal curve area, namely, 0.50, and p_1 and p_2, respectively. Thus,

$$0.50 - p_1 = 0.50 - 0.50 = 0.0; \quad y_1 = 0.3989 \text{ (Table A in the appendix)}.$$
$$0.50 - p_2 = 0.50 - 0.64 = -0.14; \quad y_2 = 0.3737 \text{ (Table A in the appendix)}.$$

(g) The computation of SE of r_t (s_{r_t}) is done by the following formula:

$$s_{r_t} = \frac{1}{y_1 y_2}\sqrt{\frac{p_1 p_2 q_1 q_2}{n}} = \frac{1}{(0.3989)(0.3737)}\sqrt{\frac{(0.50)(0.64)(0.50)(0.36)}{140}}$$

$$= \frac{1}{0.1491}\sqrt{\frac{0.0576}{140}} = \frac{1}{0.1491}\sqrt{0.0004} = 6.7069 \times 0.02 = 0.1341.$$

(h) The computed r_t of 0.24 is converted to t as follows:

$$t = \frac{r_t}{s_{r_t}} = \frac{0.24}{0.1341} = 1.7897 = 1.79.$$

(i) The computed t value of 1.79 is compared with the critical values of t obtained from Table C in the appendix with df=∞. Thus, $t_{0.05(\infty)}=1.960$; $t_{0.05(\infty)}=2.576$.

Because the computed t of 1.79 is smaller than both the table/critical values of t, there is no significant correlation between the responses of the students to both the questions in terms of 'Yes' and 'No' ($p>0.05$). In other words, the two qualities represented by the two questions (i.e., Question-I and Question-II) are not correlated in the population. Therefore, the H_0 of no correlation is accepted in 95% of cases.

9.7 Partial Correlation

In addition to the correlation methods involving two variables, there are two special correlation methods that involve more than two variables. These are known as the partial correlation ($r_{12.3}$) and the multiple correlation (R).

Partial and multiple correlations represent an important extension of the theory and techniques of simple or two-variable linear correlation to problems which involve three or more variables. The correlation between two variables is sometimes misleading and may be erroneous if there is little or no correlation between the variables other than that brought about by their common dependence upon a third variable (or several variables). Many attributes increase regularly with age from about 6 to 18 years such as height, weight, physical strength, mental test scores, vocabulary, reading skills and general knowledge. Over a wide age range, the correlation between any two of these traits will almost certainly be positive and probably high, owing to the common maturity factor which is highly correlated with both variables. In fact, the correlation between two traits may drop to zero if the variability caused by age differences is eliminated.

The factor of age can be controlled in two ways: (i) experimentally, by selecting children of the same age and (ii) statistically, by holding age variability constant through partial correlation. In order to get children of the same or of nearly the same age, we may have to reduce drastically the sizes of our sample. A partial correlation, therefore, since it utilises all of the data, is often to be preferred to experimental control. In other words, in studying the correlation between two variables, the interfering influence of other variable(s) may be eliminated, cancelled out or partialed out by partial correlation.

Thus, the partial correlation is a method of *multivariate statistics* involving more than two variables in a sample. It is a special form of correlation between two variables when the influence of other variable(s) is ruled out by keeping the latter at a constant level. It is that part of the product–moment r between two variables which remains after the elimination of the effects of other variable(s) on them. The partial correlation may be of different orders according to the number of variables eliminated or cancelled. The correlation between two variables, involving no elimination of any other variable, is a zero-order r. Thus, the product-moment correlation between two variables is a zero-order r.

9.7.1   Assumptions of Partial r

The following are the assumptions of the partial correlation:

(a)   All the variables involved in the correlation are continuous measurement variables.

(b)   The scores of the samples in these variables have unimodal and fairly symmetrical distributions in the population from which the samples are drawn without marked skewness.

(c)   The paired scores of an individual in each pair of variables are independent of such paired scores of all other individuals in the sample.

(d)   There is a linear correlation or association between the scores of individuals in each pair of variables.

9.7.2   First-order Partial Correlation

The first-order partial r is the correlation between two variables (X_1 and X_2), partialling out another variable (X_3) correlated with both of them. Thus, of the three correlated variables, the first-order partial r holds one constant to remove its effect on the correlation between the other two variables. For example, $r_{12.3}$ represents the partial correlation between X_1 and X_2 when X_3 has been held constant or partialed out. The subscripts 12.3 mean that variable 3 is rendered constant, leaving the net correlation with the variables 1 and 2. The subscripts in the partial correlation $r_{12.34}$ mean that the effects of two variables, namely, 3 and 4, are partialed out from the correlation between variables 1 and 2. The numbers to the *right* of the decimal point represent the variables whose influence is ruled out; those to the *left* represent the two correlated variables. Here, any X_1 score consists of two independent and uncorrelated components, one correlated with X_3 and the other is independent of X_3; similarly, each X_2 score has one component correlated with X_3 and the other component is independent of X_3. The zero-order r (r_{12}) between X_1 and X_2 is partly due to their respective components correlated with X_3; the $r_{12.3}$ partials out or eliminates these components associated with X_3 and measures the correlation between the residual components of X_1 and X_2, free from the influence of X_3.

The partial r of any order is computed using the product-moment r and lower orders of partial r. Thus, the first-order partial r is based upon three zero-order r's. The general formula for this first-order partial r is

$$r_{12.3} = \frac{r_{12} - (r_{13}r_{23})}{\sqrt{(1 - r_{13}^2)(1 - r_{23}^2)}},$$

where we would read $r_{12.3}$ as the correlation between variables 1 and 2 with the effects of variable 3 partialled out; r_{12}, r_{13} and r_{23} are zero-order product-moment r values between variables X_1 and X_2, X_1 and X_3, and X_2 and X_3, respectively. If in a sample of students, r_{12} is the correlation between intelligence test scores (X_1) and anxiety test scores (X_2), r_{13} is the correlation between X_1 and age (X_3), and r_{23} is the correlation between X_2 and X_3, $r_{12.3}$ is the partial r between intelligence and anxiety test scores, eliminating or removing the effects of age. The partial r values range from -1.00 to $+1.00$.

Similarly, it is possible to write comparable equations for other first-order partial r values ($r_{13.2}$, and $r_{23.1}$):

$$r_{13.2} = \frac{r_{13} - (r_{12}r_{23})}{\sqrt{(1 - r_{12}^2)(1 - r_{23}^2)}}$$

$$r_{23.1} = \frac{r_{23} - (r_{12}r_{13})}{\sqrt{(1 - r_{12}^2)(1 - r_{13}^2)}}.$$

where we would read $r_{13.2}$ as the correlation between intelligence test scores (X_1) and age (X_3), partialling out the effect of anxiety test scores (X_2). Similarly, $r_{23.1}$ is the correlation between anxiety test scores (X_2) and age (X_3), partialling out the impact of intelligence test scores.

Example 9.10 Suppose that we have the following three variables.

Variable 1 (X_1): Chronological age
Variable 2 (X_2): Weight
Variable 3 (X_3): Arithmetic test scores

For several hundred students, we compute the correlations among three variables and obtained the following:

$$r_{12} = 0.80$$
$$r_{13} = 0.60$$
$$r_{23} = 0.50$$

From this, we see that we have a correlation between weight and arithmetic test scores (r_{23}) which, with a sample of this size, is statistically significant. Suppose that we investigate the relationship between weight (X_2) and arithmetic test scores (X_3) with the effects of chronological age (X_1) partialed out ($r_{23.1}$):

$$r_{23.1} = \frac{r_{23} - (r_{12}r_{13})}{\sqrt{(1 - r_{12}^2)(1 - r_{13}^2)}} = \frac{0.50 - (0.80)(0.60)}{\sqrt{[1 - (0.80)^2][1 - (0.60)^2]}}$$

$$= \frac{0.50 - 0.48}{\sqrt{(1 - 0.64)(1 - 0.36)}} = \frac{0.02}{\sqrt{0.36 \times 0.64}} = \frac{0.02}{\sqrt{0.2304}}$$

$$= \frac{0.02}{0.48} = 0.04.$$

Now, we see that with the effects of chronological age removed, there is no significant relationship between weight and arithmetic test scores. Since the partial r is a Pearson r, it may be treated as such; the tests for significance are similar, except the df, which is $N-3$. For example, to test the significance, the computed partial r is transformed into the t score and the latter is compared with critical t scores having the same df. For the significance of the computed $r_{12.3}$,

$$s_{r_{12.3}} = \sqrt{\frac{1 - r_{12.3}^2}{N - 3}}$$

$$t = \frac{r_{12.3}}{s_{r_{12.3}}} = r_{12.3}\sqrt{\frac{N - 3}{1 - r_{12.3}^2}}$$

$$\mathrm{df} = N - 3.$$

The transformation of other partial r values into t scores may be computed similarly:

$$S_{r_{13.2}} = \sqrt{\frac{1-r_{13.2}^2}{N-3}}; \quad t = \frac{r_{13.2}}{S_{r_{13.2}}} = r_{13.2}\sqrt{\frac{N-3}{1-r_{13.2}^2}}$$

$$S_{r_{23.1}} = \sqrt{\frac{1-r_{23.1}^2}{N-3}}; \quad t = \frac{r_{23.1}}{S_{r_{23.1}}} = r_{23.1}\sqrt{\frac{N-3}{1-r_{23.1}^2}}.$$

In the above example (see Example 9.10), using a variance interpretation, the proportion overlap between X_2 and X_3 is $r_{23}^2 = (0.50)^2 = 0.25$. The proportion overlap with X_1 eliminated is $r_{23.1}^2 = (0.04)^2 = 0.0016$. The proportion overlap which results from the effects of chronological age is $0.25 - 0.0016 = 0.2484$. It would also be appropriate to state that the percentage of the total association present resulting from the effect of chronological age (X_1) is $0.2484/0.25 \times 100 = 99.36\%$. The remaining per cent of the association results from other factors.

9.7.3 Second-order Partial Correlation

Second-order partial r's are those in which the relationship between two variables is computed with the effects of two other variables partialed out. Thus, the second-order partial r involves four inter-correlated variables and measures the correlation between two of them, partialling out the other two. For example, $r_{12.34}$ correlates the variables X_1 and X_2, eliminating the effects of other two variables X_3 and X_4.

The formula to find out $r_{12.34}$ reads

$$r_{12.34} = \frac{r_{12.3} - r_{14.3}r_{24.3}}{\sqrt{(1-r_{14.3}^2)(1-r_{24.3}^2)}} \quad \text{or} \quad r_{12.34} = \frac{r_{12.4} - r_{13.4}r_{23.4}}{\sqrt{(1-r_{13.4}^2)(1-r_{23.4}^2)}}.$$

The significance of the computed $r_{12.34}$ may be tested by transforming it to t scores and then comparing this transformed t score with the critical t scores. The required t is

$$t = \frac{r_{12.34}}{S_{r_{12.34}}}; \quad S_{r_{12.34}} = \frac{1}{\sqrt{N-4}}; \quad df = N-4.$$

This may be referred to a table of t with $N-4$ degrees of freedom. Since the second and still higher orders of partial r are rarely used, their detailed discussion is not given here.

9.7.4 Significance of Partial r

The null hypothesis (H_0) proposes that the partial correlation between the given variables amounts to zero in the population, and that the computed partial r has resulted only due to chances associated with random sampling. To test the probability (p) of this H_0 being correct, the computed partial r is converted to the t ratio and then this t ratio is compared with the critical values of t noted from Table C in the appendix with $df = N-3$ for the first-order partial r, and $df = N-4$ for the second-order partial r. The formulae for computing the SE of the partial r and converting the computed partial r to the t ratios/scores have already been cited earlier.

Let us apply some of the above formulae to the data given in the following example.

Example 9.11 In a sample of 153 students, the Pearson r values between intelligence test scores (X_1), anxiety test scores (X_2) and chronological age (X_3) were found to be as follows:

$$r_{12} = 0.46; \quad r_{13} = 0.35; \quad r_{23} = 0.17.$$

Compute $r_{12.3}$ and interpret it.

Solution

(a)   The $r_{12.3}$ shows that it is a first-order partial r.

(b)   The zero-order correlations between the given variables are $r_{12}=0.46$, $r_{13}=0.35$, $r_{23}=0.17$ and $N=153$.

(c)   The computation of $r_{12.3}$ is done by the following formula:

$$r_{12.3} = \frac{r_{12} - r_{13}r_{23}}{\sqrt{(1-r_{13}^2)(1-r_{23}^2)}} = \frac{0.46 - (0.35)(0.17)}{\sqrt{[1-(0.35)^2][1-(0.17)^2]}}$$

$$= \frac{0.46 - 0.0595}{\sqrt{(1-0.1225)(1-0.0289)}} = \frac{0.4005}{\sqrt{(0.8775)(0.9711)}}$$

$$= \frac{0.4005}{\sqrt{0.8521}} = \frac{0.4005}{0.9231} = 0.4339.$$

(d)   Computation of the SE of $r_{12.3}$ $(s_{r_{12.3}})$ is done by the following formula:

$$s_{r_{12.3}} = \sqrt{\frac{1-r_{12.3}^2}{N-3}} = \sqrt{\frac{1-(0.4339)^2}{153-3}} = \sqrt{\frac{1-0.1883}{150}}$$

$$= \sqrt{\frac{0.8117}{150}} = \sqrt{0.0054} = 0.0736.$$

(e)   The computed $r_{12.3}$ of 0.4339 is converted to the t ratio by the following formula:

$$t = \frac{r_{12.3}}{s_{r_{12.3}}} = \frac{0.4339}{0.0736} = 5.8954.$$

(f)   The computed t value of 5.8954 is compared with the critical values of t noted from Table C in the appendix with df$=N-3=153-3=150=\infty$. Thus, $t_{05(\infty)}=1.960$; $t_{01(\infty)}=2.576$; $t_{0.01(\infty)}=3.291$. The computed t is, thus, higher than the critical t value for the 0.001 level of significance. So the computed partial r is significant ($p<0.001$). Therefore, the H_0 which proposes a zero partial r between the given variables in the population is rejected in 99.9% cases. So, we may conclude that there is a significant correlation between intelligence test scores and anxiety test scores with the effects of chronological age partialed out.

9.8   Part Correlation

With three variables X_1, X_2 and X_3, the partial correlation is the correlation between residuals on X_1 and X_2 with X_3 removed from both variables by linear regression. A situation may be considered where X_3 is removed from one variable only, say X_2, and X_1 is then correlated with the residual of X_2. This type of correlation is called part correlation or *semipartial correlation*.

The part correlation between X_1 and the residuals on X_2 with X_3 removed is computed by the following formula:

$$r_{1(2.3)} = \frac{r_{12} - r_{13}r_{23}}{\sqrt{1 - r_{23}^2}}.$$

If $r_{12} = 0.55$, $r_{13} = 0.60$ and $r_{23} = 0.50$, then the part correlation is

$$r_{1(2.3)} = \frac{0.55 - (0.60)(0.50)}{\sqrt{1 - (0.50)^2}} = \frac{0.55 - 0.30}{\sqrt{1 - 0.25}} = \frac{0.25}{\sqrt{0.75}} = \frac{0.25}{0.866} = 0.289.$$

An application of part correlation arises where measurements have been obtained prior to an experimental treatment and subsequent measurements on the same subjects under the experimental treatment. It may be informative to calculate the correlation between some other variable and the measurements obtained under treatment with the effects of the initial values removed by linear regression. Part correlation is appropriate here.

9.9   Multiple Correlation

All statistical techniques which simultaneously analyse more than two variables on a sample of observation are called multivariate statistics or multivariate techniques. Multiple correlation comes under *multivariate statistics* and involves more than two variables in a sample. The dependent variable is called the *criterion* and the independent variable is called the *predictor*. The multiple correlation is a measure of the relation between one criterion variable and the weighted sum of two or more predictor variables. The *multiple linear correlation coefficient* (R) is a special form of the product–moment r, and measures the magnitude of the linear relationship between a given variable and the weighted sum of two or more other variables. R increases the accuracy of correlation of a variable with other correlated ones. The coefficient of multiple correlation indicates the strength of relationship between one variable and two or more others combined with optimal weights. Multiple correlation is related to the intercorrelations between independent variables as well as to their correlations with the dependent variable.

9.9.1   Assumptions of R

For computing the multiple correlation, it should be reasonable to assume that:

  (a)   all the variables involved are continuous measurement variables;
  (b)   their scores have unimodal and fairly symmetrical distributions in the population without marked skewness;
  (c)   the paired scores of each pair of variables in an individual are independent of such paired scores of all other individuals in the sample;
  (d)   there is a linear correlation or association between the scores of each pair of variables.

9.9.2   Some Principles of R

Although multiple correlation problems may be extended to any number of variables, before we consider the solution with more than 3, it is desirable to examine some of the general principles which apply for any number of variables but which can be seen more clearly when there are only three variables.

There are two main principles of multiple correlation. First, a multiple correlation increases as the size of correlations between dependent (or criterion) and independent (or predictor) variables increases. Second, a multiple correlation increases as the size of intercorrelations of independent variables decreases. A maximum R will be obtained when the correlations with X_1 (criterion variable) are large and when intercorrelations of $X_2, X_3, \ldots, X_n$ (predictor variables) are small. In building a battery of tests to predict a criterion, test makers should try to maximise the validity of each test and to minimise the correlations between tests.

9.9.3 Advantages of R

The multiple correlation coefficient serves the following purposes:

(a) It serves as a measure of the degree of association between one variable taken as the dependent variable (or criterion) and a group of other variables taken as the independent variables (or predictors).

(b) Multiple correlation also serves as a measure of goodness of fit of the calculated plane of regression and consequently as a measure of the general degree of accuracy of estimates made by reference to the plane of regression.

9.9.4 Limitations of R

The following are some of the important limitations of multiple correlation.

(a) Multiple correlation is based on the assumption that the relationship between the variables is linear. This means that the rate of change in one variable in terms of another is assumed to be constant for all values. But in practice, most relationships are not linear; it may be nonlinear or curvilinear. This limits the use of multiple correlation.

(b) Another important limitation is the assumption that the effects of independent variables on the dependent variables are separate, distinct and additive. When the effects of variables are additive, a given change in one has the same effect on the dependent variable regardless of the sizes of the other two independent variables.

(c) Multiple correlation involves a great deal of work relative to the results frequently obtained. When the results are obtained, only a few students well trained in the method are able to interpret them; other students, because of the lack of understanding, may misuse the correlation results. This resulting misuse is due to the complexity of the method.

9.9.5 Multiple Correlation with Three Variables

The multiple linear correlation coefficient (R) is computed between a criterion variable X_1 and a weighted sum of two predictor variables X_2 and X_3 (i.e., $R_{1.23}$). The computation of $R_{1.23}$ can be done using either the zero-order product–moment r values between the variables of each pair or the beta coefficients (i.e., β_2 and β_3). β_2 and β_3 are the proportions of the total variance of X_1 owing to the effects of, respectively, X_2 and X_3.

Suppose r_{12}, r_{13} and r_{23} are the Pearson r values between the variables X_1 and X_2, X_1 and X_3, and X_2 and X_3, respectively. From these given zero-order product–moment r values, we can compute β_2, β_3 and R as follows:

$$\beta_2 = \frac{r_{12} - r_{13}r_{23}}{1 - r_{23}^2}; \quad \beta_3 = \frac{r_{13} - r_{12}r_{23}}{1 - r_{23}^2}$$

$$R_{1.23} = \sqrt{\beta_2 r_{12} + \beta_3 r_{13}}.$$

Alternatively, we can compute R directly from the Pearson r values if beta coefficients are not known. This formula reads

$$R_{1.23} = \sqrt{\frac{r_{12}^2 + r_{13}^2 - 2r_{12}r_{13}r_{23}}{1 - r_{23}^2}}.$$

If the multiple correlation is perfectly linear, R amounts exactly to 1.00. If R amounts to 0.00, the linear correlation does not exist, but the existence of a nonlinear correlation cannot be straightway denied. A decrease in the magnitude of correlation between the predictor variables (r_{23} here) or an increase in the magnitude of correlations between the criterion variable and the individual predictor variables (r_{12} and r_{13} here) may raise the magnitude of R.

Sometimes the correlation between the criterion X_1 and one of the predictors X_2 (i.e., r_{12}) is substantially reduced by the influence of the other predictor X_3 if the latter (X_3) has a high correlation with X_2 (i.e., r_{23}) but a negative or zero correlation with X_1 (i.e., r_{13}). Then the predictor X_3 is called a *suppression variable*—it has a variance common with the other predictor X_2, but this common variance is absent in the criterion X_1. X_2 may still have a positive correlation with the criterion X_1 because of a variance common to both of them, but this correlation r_{12} is partly suppressed by the negative weight of the other variance common to the two predictors and absent in the criterion. The $R_{1.23}$ minimises this negative weight of the suppression variable and consequently attains a higher value than the zero-order correlation r_{12}.

The multiple correlations $R_{2.13}$ and $R_{3.12}$ are computed similarly like $R_{1.23}$ by the following formulae using zero-order product–moment r values:

$$R_{2.13} = \sqrt{\frac{r_{12}^2 + r_{23}^2 - 2r_{12}r_{13}r_{23}}{1 - r_{13}^2}}$$

$$R_{3.12} = \sqrt{\frac{r_{13}^2 + r_{23}^2 - 2r_{12}r_{13}r_{23}}{1 - r_{12}^2}}.$$

9.9.6   Multiple Correlation with More than Three Variables

Multiple correlation with one criterion variable and more than two predictor variables can also be computed using the beta coefficients and the product-moment r values by the following formula, where m is the total number of variables and g is the number of predictors:

$$R_{1.23,\ldots,m} = \sqrt{\beta_2 r_{12} + \beta_3 r_{13} + \cdots + \beta_m r_{1m}}$$

9.9.7   Interpretation of R

Once computed, a multiple correlation (R) is subjected to the same kinds of interpretation, as to size and importance, that were described for a simple r. One kind of interpretation is in terms of R^2, which is called the *coefficient of multiple determination*. This tells us the proportion of variance in X_1 that is dependent upon, associated with or predicted by X_2 and X_3 combined with the regression weights used. In other words, R^2 is a measure of that proportion of variance of the criterion which comes from the combined contribution of the predictors. Thus,

$$R_{1.23}^2 = \beta_2 r_{12} + \beta_3 r_{13},$$

where $\beta_2 r_{12}$ and $\beta_3 r_{13}$ are the proportions of the total variance of the criterion X_1 due to the effects of the predictors X_2 and X_3, respectively. The remaining proportion of variance of the criterion, which is independent of the combined contribution of the predictors, is given by the symbol K^2 and is known as the *coefficient of multiple non-determination*, which equals $1 - R^2$. This is consistent with the fact that $R^2 + K^2 = 1.0$ just as $r^2 + k^2 = 1.0$ in the simple correlation problem. If R^2 is 0.4578, we can say that 45.78% of the variance in the criterion is accounted for by both the predictors taken together. The remaining percentage of the variance, which is 54.22 $(1 - R^2)$ is still to be accounted for. Thus, where $r_{13.2}$ is the partial r between the criterion X_1 and the predictor X_3 eliminating the effect of other predictor X_2,

$$K^2_{1.23} = 1 - R^2_{1.23} = (1 - r^2_{13.2})(1 - r^2_{12}).$$

9.9.8 Significance of R

The null hypothesis (H_0) proposes that the multiple R between one criterion variable and combination of two predictor variables amounts to zero in the population, and the computed R has resulted only due to chances associated with random sampling. To test the H_0 that the computed R is not significantly different from 0, the R is converted to the t ratio which is compared with the critical values of t noted from Table C in the appendix with df $= N - 3$ in case of R with three variables.

Alternatively, the computed R (either with three or more than three variables) is converted to F ratio which is compared with critical F ratio noted from Table E in the appendix for the specified df_1 and df_2 combination.

When R is computed with three variables, the formulae for computing the SE of R (s_R) and converting the computed R either to t or F ratios are given as follows:

$$s_R = \frac{1}{\sqrt{N-3}}; \quad t = \frac{R}{s_R}; \quad df = N - 3$$

$$F = \frac{R^2(N - g - 1)}{g(1 - R^2)}; \quad df_1 = g; \quad df_2 = N - g - 1,$$

where g is the number of predictors. Thus, for $R_{1.23}, R_{2.13}$ and $R_{3.12}$, respectively, $df_1 = g = 2$; $df_2 = N - g - 1 = N - 2 - 1 = N - 3$:

$$F = \frac{R^2_{1.23}(N - 3)}{2(1 - R^2_{1.23})}; \quad F = \frac{R^2_{2.13}(N - 3)}{2(1 - R^2_{2.13})}; \quad F = \frac{R^2_{3.12}(N - 3)}{2(1 - R^2_{3.12})}$$

When R is computed with more than three variables, the formula for converting the R to F ratio reads

$$F = \frac{R^2_{1.23}\cdots m(N - g - 1)}{g(1 - R^2_{1.23}\cdots m)}; \quad df_1 = g; \quad df_2 = N - g - 1.$$

If the computed F is significant, then the computed R is significantly different from 0 at that level of significance which has a critical F value either equal to or lower than the computed F ratio. In other words, when the computed F ratio becomes equal to or greater than the critical F value for a particular level of significance (either 0.05 or 0.01 levels), then it is said to be significant at that level of significance.

Let us apply some of the above formulae to the data given in the following example.

Example 9.12 In a sample of 153 university freshmen, the product–moment r values between the grade (X_1), psychology test scores (X_2) and mathematics test scores (X_3) were found to be as follows: $r_{12} = 0.50$, $r_{13} = 0.60$ and $r_{23} = 0.40$. Compute the multiple correlation coefficient between the grade and the combination of psychology and mathematics test scores, and interpret it.

Solution

(a) We have to find out the multiple correlation (R) with three variables: one criterion (X_1) and two predictors (X_2 and X_3). The variables are: X_1=grade, X_2=psychology test scores and X_3=mathematics test scores.

(b) The zero-order correlations between the variables are: $r_{12}=0.50$, $r_{13}=0.60$, $r_{23}=0.40$ and $N=153$.

(c) The computation of $R_{1.23}$ is done using the Pearson r values by the following formula:

$$R_{1.23} = \sqrt{\frac{r_{12}^2 + r_{13}^2 - 2r_{12}r_{13}r_{23}}{1 - r_{23}^2}} = \sqrt{\frac{(0.50)^2 + (0.60)^2 - 2(0.50)(0.60)(0.40)}{1 - (0.40)^2}}$$

$$= \sqrt{\frac{0.25 + 0.36 - 0.24}{1 - 0.16}} = \sqrt{\frac{0.61 - 0.24}{0.84}} = \sqrt{\frac{0.37}{0.84}}$$

$$= \sqrt{0.4405} = 0.664.$$

Alternatively, we can compute $R_{1.23}$ using the beta coefficients (β_2 and β_3) which are, in turn, computed using the Pearson r values, as given below:

$$\beta_2 = \frac{r_{12} - r_{13}r_{23}}{1 - r_{23}^2} = \frac{0.50 - (0.60)(0.40)}{1 - (0.40)^2} = \frac{0.50 - 0.24}{1 - 0.16} = \frac{0.26}{0.84} = 0.3095$$

$$\beta_3 = \frac{r_{13} - r_{12}r_{23}}{1 - r_{23}^2} = \frac{0.60 - (0.50)(0.40)}{1 - (0.40)^2} = \frac{0.60 - 0.20}{1 - 0.16} = \frac{0.40}{0.84} = 0.4762$$

$$R_{1.23} = \sqrt{\beta_2 r_{12} + \beta_3 r_{13}}$$

$$= \sqrt{(0.3095)(0.50) + (0.4762)(0.60)}$$

$$= \sqrt{0.15475 + 0.28572} = \sqrt{0.44047} = 0.664.$$

(d) Computation of $S_{R_{1.23}}$ and conversion of the computed $R_{1.23}$ to the t or F ratio can be done as follows:

$$S_{R_{1.23}} = \frac{1}{\sqrt{N-3}} = \frac{1}{\sqrt{153-3}} = \frac{1}{\sqrt{150}} = \frac{1}{12.247} = 0.082$$

$$t = \frac{R_{1.23}}{S_{R_{1.23}}} = \frac{0.664}{0.082} = 8.098$$

$$df = N - 3 = 153 - 3 = 150.$$

Alternatively, the computed $R_{1.23}$ is converted to the F ratio by the following formula:

$$F = \frac{R_{1.23}^2(N-g-1)}{g(1-R_{1.23}^2)}, \text{ where } g = \text{number of predictors} = 2$$

$$= \frac{(0.664)^2(153-2-1)}{2[1-(0.664)^2]} = \frac{0.4409(153-3)}{2(1-0.4409)} = \frac{0.4409 \times 150}{2 \times 0.5591}$$

$$= \frac{66.1350}{1.1182} = 59.1442$$

$$df_1 = g = 2; \quad df_2 = N - g - 1 = 153 - 3 = 150.$$

(e) The computed t value of 8.098 is compared with the critical values of t noted from Table C in the appendix with df= $N-3$=153$-$3=150=∞. Thus, $t_{0.05}(\infty)=1.960$, $t_{0.01}(\infty)=2.576$

and $t_{0.001}(\infty)=3.291$. The computed t is, thus, higher than the critical t for the 0.001 level of significance. So the computed $R_{1.23}$ is significant ($p<0.001$). So the H_0, which proposes a zero $R_{1.23}$ between the given variables in the population, is rejected in 99.9% of cases. Therefore, it is reasonable to conclude that there is a significant multiple correlation ($R_{1.23}$) between the grade (the criterion variable) and the combination of psychology test scores and mathematics test scores (the predictor variables).

Alternatively, the computed F ratio of 59.1442 is compared with the critical F ratios noted from Table E in the appendix with $df_1=2$ and $df_2=150$. Thus, $F_{0.05(2,150)} = 3.06$ and $F_{0.01(2,150)} = 4.75$. Since the computed F far exceeds the critical F for the 0.01 level of significance, the computed $R_{1.23}$ is significantly different from 0 ($p<0.01$). So, the H_0 is rejected in 99% of cases.

Summary

In this chapter, we have discussed the topic of correlation. A correlation is a measure of the association or the relationship that exists between two variables. The magnitude and direction of the relationship are given by a correlation coefficient. A correlation coefficient can vary from +1.0 to –1.0. The sign of the coefficient tells us whether the relationship is positive or negative. The numerical part describes the magnitude of the correlation. When the relationship is perfect, the magnitude is 1 (e.g., +1.0 perfect positive, and –1.0 perfect negative). If the relationship is non-existent, the magnitude is 0. Magnitudes between 0 and 1 indicate imperfect relationships.

There are many correlation coefficients that can be computed depending on the scaling of the data and the shape of relationship. In this chapter, we emphasised the product–moment (Pearson r), biserial, point-biserial, tetrachoric and partial correlation coefficients. We put more emphasis on their assumptions, properties and computational equations and formulae; and several practice problems have been worked out.

As the last topic of simple correlation or product–moment correlation, we discussed correlation and causation. We pointed out that if a correlation exists between two variables X and Y in an experiment, then we cannot conclude that they are causally related on the basis of the correlation alone, because there are other possible explanations. The correlation may be spurious or a third variable (say, variable Z) may be responsible for the correlation between the first two variables (say, variables X and Y). To establish causation, one of the variables must be independently manipulated and its effect on the other variable is measured. All other variables should be held constant or vary unsystematically. Even if the two variables are causally related, it is important to keep in mind that r^2 rather than r indicates the magnitude of the effect of one variable on the other.

Finally, we introduced the topic of multiple correlation (R) with more emphasis on its assumptions, principles, advantages, limitations, computations with three variables as well as more than three variables, interpretation and test of significance.

Key Terms

- Beta coefficients
- Biserial coefficient
- Bivariate distribution
- Bivariate frequency distribution
- Coefficient of alienation
- Coefficient of determination
- Correlation
- Correlation and causality
- Correlation coefficient
- Covariance of X and Y
- Criterion
- Equation for straight line

- Intercept
- Linear correlation
- Linear equation
- Method of least squares
- Multiple correlation
- Multivariate statistics
- Nonlinear correlation
- Part correlation
- Partial correlation
- Pearson r
- Perfect positive correlation
- Perfect negative correlation
- Point biserial coefficient

- Predictor
- Prediction
- Scatter diagram
- Semi-partial correlation
- Slope
- Standard error of estimate
- Sum of products
- Suppression variable
- Tetrachoric coefficient
- Univariate distribution
- X-intercept
- Y-intercept
- Zero-order r

Questions and Problems

1. What is correlation? Discuss the characteristics of a relationship.
2. Define correlation. Where and why correlations are used?
3. What do you mean by correlation? Discuss the properties of correlation.
4. Define the product–moment coefficient of correlation and discuss its properties and assumptions.
5. Briefly discuss the factors that affect the correlation coefficient.
6. Write notes on the followings:

    (a) Assumptions of Pearson's r.
    (b) Uses of Pearson's r.
    (c) Applicability of Pearson's r.
    (d) Interpretation of Pearson's r.
    (e) Testing the significance of Pearson's r.
    (f) Factors influencing the size of r.
    (g) Correlation and causation.

7. What do you mean by biserial correlation? Discuss its assumptions.
8. Discuss the applicability and test of significance of r_b.
9. Make an evaluation of the biserial correlation.
10. Define point biserial correlation. Discuss about its applicability.
11. Write notes on the followings:

    (a) Assumptions of r_{pbi}.
    (b) Test of significance of the r_{pbi}.
    (c) Evaluation of r_{pbi}.

12. Explain the mathematical relation of r_{pbi} to r_b.

13. Compare and contrast between biserial correlation and point biserial correlation.
14. What is tetrachoric correlation? Differentiate between biserial *r* and tetrachoric *r*.
15. Write notes on the followings:

    (a) Assumptions of tetrachoric correlation.
    (b) Uses of r_t.
    (c) Testing of significance of r_t.

16. What is partial correlation? Differentiate between first-order and second-order partial correlations.
17. Write notes on the followings:

    (a) Assumptions of partial correlation.
    (b) Uses of partial correlation.
    (c) Testing of significance of partial correlation.
    (d) Part correlation.
    (e) Difference between partial and multiple correlations.

18. What do you mean by multiple correlation? Discuss its assumptions.
19. Write notes on the followings:

    (a) Principles of *R*.
    (b) Interpretation of *R*.
    (c) Testing of significance of *R*.
    (d) Advantages and limitations of *R*.
    (e) Difference between simple and multiple correlations.

20. Answer the following questions:

    (a) Would you expect the correlation between marks on examination in physics and mathematics to be positive, negative or about 0?
    (b) When *N*=2, what are the possible values of the correlation coefficient?
    (c) Under what conditions will the variance of the sum of two variables equal the variance of the difference between two variables?
    (d) Is the correlation between *X* and *Y* changed by adding a constant to *X* or by multiplying *X* by a constant?
    (e) What is the formula for *r* in the standard-score form if the variance is defined as $s^2 = \Sigma(X - \bar{X})^2 / N$?

21. Find out the correct answer:

    (i) Product–moment correlation coefficient:

        (a) Has no limits   (b) Varies between ±1.0
        (c) Can be more than 1.0   (d) None of these

    (ii) Pearson *r* is obtained by the formula:

        (a) $r = \Sigma xy / N\sigma_x\sigma_y$ (b) $r = \Sigma XY / N\sigma_x$
        (c) $r = \Sigma x\Sigma y / \sigma_x\sigma_y$ (d) None of these

(iii) Coefficient of determination is defined as:

(a) $1+r^2$

(b) r^3

(c) r^2

(d) None of these

(iv) The limits of the population correlation are given by:

(a) $r \pm PE$

(b) $r \pm 2\,PE$

(c) $r \pm 3\,PE$

(d) None of these

(v) If the sum of the products of X and Y scores from their respective means, that is, Σxy is zero, then the coefficient of correlation shall be:

(a) +1.0

(b) 0.0

(c) –1.0

(d) None of these

(vi) While drawing a scatter diagram if all the points are falling on a straight line moving upward from the lower left-hand correlation is said to be:

(a) Perfect positive

(b) Perfect negative

(c) Simple positive or negative

(d) None of these

(vii) In a scattergram, if all the points are lying on a straight line rising from the upper left-hand corner to the lower right-hand corner, the correlation shall be:

(a) 0.0

(b) –1.0

(c) +1.0

(d) None of these

(viii) If the plotted points lie on a straight line parallel to the X-axis of a scatter diagram, it shows:

(a) Perfect negative correlation

(b) Perfect positive correlation

(c) Absence of correlation

(d) None of these

(ix) Two variables, X and Y, varying in an inverse direction is an indicative of a:

(a) Positive correlation

(b) Negative correlation

(c) Both positive and negative correlations

(d) None of these

(x) Probable error (PE) is:

(a) 0.6745 SE

(b) 0.6457 SE

(c) 0.6753 SE

(d) None of these

22. Fill in the blanks:

(a) The statistical tool for discovering and measuring the degree of the relationship between two variables is known as _____.

(b) Product–moment correlation is the contribution of_____.

(c) Rank-order correlation was developed by _____.

(d) If $r = 0.3$, then coefficient of determination will be _____.

(e) The coefficient of correlation is under-root of 2 _____.

(f) The relationship between three or more variables is studied with the help of _____ correlation.

(g) One of the most important assumptions of correlation is that the correlation between two variables should be _____.

(h) Even a high degree of correlation between two variables does not necessarily imply the existence of _____ and _____ relationship between the variables.

(i) In a perfect positive correlation, the magnitude of r will be _____.

(j) A significant positive correlation between two variables implies that both variables vary in the _____ direction.

23. Indicate whether the following statements are True or False:

(a) A negative correlation implies that the values of both the variables are decreasing.

(b) There is no limit to the value of r.

(c) Product–moment correlation was developed by Pearson.

(d) Rank-order correlation was developed by Spearman.

(e) A nonsense correlation between two variables is purely due to chance.

(f) Correlation always signifies a cause-and-effect relationship between the variables.

(g) Pearsonian correlation coefficient is the best under all situations.

(h) Correlation coefficient is independent of change of scale and origin.

(i) Correlation is an analysis of the covariation between two or more variables.

(j) Correlation analysis helps us in determining both the direction and degree of relationship between two or more variables.

24. The following are paired sample scores:

$$X: 1 \quad 4 \quad 7 \quad 10 \quad 13$$
$$Y: 1 \quad 2 \quad 3 \quad 4 \quad 5$$

(a) Calculate the value of Pearson r using the raw score equation. Interpret the results.

(b) Multiply the X scores by 5 and compute r again. Has the value changed?

25. Calculate the product-moment correlation coefficient between the following scores of two variables using the deviation scores from their respective means. Interpret the results.

$$X: 65 \quad 66 \quad 67 \quad 67 \quad 68 \quad 69 \quad 70 \quad 72$$
$$Y: 67 \quad 68 \quad 65 \quad 68 \quad 72 \quad 72 \quad 69 \quad 71$$

26. Find out Pearson's coefficient of correlation between the following X and Y series using the deviation scores from their respective AMs. Interpret the results.

(a)
$$X: 58 \quad 41 \quad 39 \quad 32 \quad 41 \quad 44 \quad 41 \quad 43 \quad 39 \quad 55$$
$$Y: 11 \quad 41 \quad 31 \quad 51 \quad 26 \quad 26 \quad 19 \quad 32 \quad 30 \quad 25$$

(b) $\quad X:$ 15 20 25 30 35 40 45 50 55 60
$\qquad\quad Y:$ 35 36 30 30 25 25 20 20 15 15

27. (a) Total sales turnover and net profit of seven medium-sized companies are given below. Calculate the correlation coefficient between total sales turnover and net profits, using standard score forms. Test its significance.

Total sales turnover:	100	200	300	400	500	600	700
Net profits:	30	50	60	80	100	110	130

(b) Find the correlation between the two sets of scores given below, using the ratio method, that is, the standard score forms. Test its significance.

$X:$	15	18	22	17	19	20	16	21
$Y:$	40	42	50	45	43	46	41	41

28. (a) Calculate Karl Pearson's correlation between X and Y variables from the following data. Test its significance.

$$N=13, \quad \Sigma X=117, \quad \Sigma X^2=1313, \quad \Sigma Y=260, \quad \Sigma Y^2=6580 \quad \text{and} \quad \Sigma XY=2822$$

(b) From the data given below, compute Karl Pearson's coefficient of correlation and test its significance.

	X Series	Y Series
Number of items	15	15
Arithmetic mean	25	18
Sum of squares of deviations from their respective means	136	138
Summation of products of deviations from their respective means	122	

(c) In order to find the correlation coefficient between two variables X and Y from 12 pairs of observations, the following calculations were made.

$$\Sigma X=30, \quad \Sigma Y=5, \quad \Sigma X^2=670, \quad \Sigma Y^2=285, \quad \Sigma XY=334$$

On subsequent verification, it was found that the pair ($X=11$, $Y=4$) was opted incorrectly, the correct value being $X=10$ and $Y=14$. Find the correct value of r and test its significance.

29. Find Pearson's product-moment coefficient of correlation from the following scatter diagram (correlation table) and interpret the results:

		Scores on Test *X*							
	Class Intervals	**0-4**	**5-9**	**10-14**	**15-19**	**20-24**	**25-29**	**30-34**	**Total**
Scores on Test *Y*	15-17			1			1	2	4
	12-14		1	1	3	1	2	1	9
	9-11		1	4	5	5	1		16
	6-8	2	3	5	4	5	2		21
	3-5	2	5	1		1	1		10
	0-2	2	1		1				4
	Total	6	11	12	13	12	7	3	64

30. (a) The following data give the distribution of scores on the Thorndike Intelligence Examination made by entering college freshmen who presented 12 or more recommended units and entering freshmen who presented less than 12 recommended units. Compute biserial *r* and its SE.

Thorndike Scores	**12 or More Recommended Units**	**Less than 12 Recommended Units**
90-99	6	0
80-89	19	3
70-79	31	5
60-69	58	17
50-59	40	30
40-49	18	14
30-39	9	7
20-29	5	4
	186	80

(b) The following data represent the distribution of scores achieved on a music appreciation test by 145 high school seniors with and without training in music. Compute biserial r and its SE.

Scores	Training Group	No Training Group
85–89	5	6
80–84	2	16
75–79	6	19
70–74	6	27
65–69	1	19
60–64	0	21
55–59	1	16
	21	124

(c) The table below shows the distributions of scores on an achievement test earned by those students who answered 50% or more and those who answered less than 50% of the items in an arithmetic test correctly. Compute r_b and the 0.99 confidence interval for the true r_b.

Achievement Test Score	Students Answering 50% or More of the Items	Students Answering Less than 50% of the Items
185–194	7	0
175–184	16	0
165–174	10	6
155–164	35	15
145–154	24	40
135–144	15	26
125–134	10	13
115–124	3	5
105–114	0	5
	120	110

31. (a) The following table shows the total scores achieved by 15 students on a test (used as the criterion). The response of each student to item no.13 on the test is shown. A 1 means that the item was passed and a 0 means that it was failed. Calculate the point biserial r and its SE. Test the significance of the obtained r_{pbi}.

Students	Test Criterion (X)	Item No. 13 (Y)
1	25	1
2	23	1
3	18	0
4	24	0
5	23	1
6	20	0
7	19	0
8	22	1
9	21	1
10	23	1
11	21	0
12	20	0
13	21	1
14	21	1
15	22	1

(b) From the table below, compute r_{pbi} and test its significance.

Scores on Miller Analogies Test	VA Trainees	
	Failed in Programme	Obtained Ph.D.
95–99	0	1
90–94	1	1
85–89	0	6
80–84	2	11
75–79	4	6
70–74	6	9
65–69	8	3
60–64	3	2
55–59	2	1
50–54	6	
45–49	2	
40–44	3	
35–39	1	
30–34	1	
	39	40

32. Compute tetrachoric r for the following tables.

(a) Relation of alcoholism and health in 811 fathers and sons. Entries are expressed as proportions.

		SONS		
		Unhealthy	Healthy	Totals
FATHERS	Unalcoholic	0.343	0.405	0.748
	Alcoholic	0.102	0.150	0.252
	Total	0.445	0.555	1.000

(b) Correspondence of Yes and No answers to two items of a neurosis inventory

		Question 1		
		No	**Yes**	**Total**
Question 2	Yes	83	187	270
	No	102	93	195
	Total	185	280	465

33. (a) The correlation between a general intelligence test and school achievement in a group of children from 8 to 14 years old is 0.80. The correlation between the general intelligence test and age in the same group is 0.70; and the correlation between school achievement and age is 0.60. What is the correlation between general intelligence and school achievement in children of the same age? Comment upon your result.

(b) Given the following data for 100 college freshmen:

X_1 = intelligence test
X_2 = cancellation test
X_3 = controlled association test
$r_{12} = 0.20$; $r_{13} = 0.70$; $r_{23} = 0.45$

What is the 'net' correlation between:

(i) Intelligence and cancellation? and
(ii) Intelligence and controlled association?
Interpret your results.

34. The following are the scores on three variables (X_1, X_2 and X_3) for five subjects. Compute the multiple correlation coefficient between X_1 scores and the combination of X_2 and X_3 scores, and interpret it.

Subjects	X_1	X_2	X_3
1	9	5	15
2	7	3	12
3	6	4	13
4	4	2	7
5	4	1	8

35. Calculate (a) $R_{1.23}$ (b) $R_{3.12}$ and (c) $R_{2.13}$ for the following data:

$\bar{X}_1 = 6.8,$	$\bar{X}_2 = 7.0,$	$\bar{X}_3 = 74$
$S_1 = 1.0,$	$S_2 = 0.8,$	$S_3 = 9$
$r_{12} = 0.60,$	$r_{13} = 0.70,$	$r_{23} = 0.65$

36. Fill in the blanks:

   (a) By squaring $R_{1.23}$ we obtain the coefficient of _____.
   (b) The coefficient of multiple correlation lies between _____ and _____.
   (c) The dependent variable is always denoted by _____.
   (d) Partial correlation coefficients such as $r_{12.3}$ and $r_{13.2}$ are referred to as _____.
   (e) Second-order partial correlation coefficients can be obtained from _____ coefficients.

37. Write whether the following statements are 'True' or 'False'.

   (a) It is possible to obtain $r_{23} = 0.7, r_{31} = -0.4, r_{12} = 0.6$.
   (b) $r_{13.2}$ is the coefficient of partial correlation between X_1 and X_3, keeping X_2 constant.
   (c) The coefficient of multiple correlation ranges from 0 to 1.0.
   (d) $r_{12.3}$ and $r_{21.3}$ are not the same thing.
   (e) In the case of four variables, there are 16 possible first-order coefficients.
   (f) The closer the coefficient of multiple correlation is to 1.0, the better the relationship between variables.
   (g) The coefficient of multiple correlation is denoted by a symbol R.

Regression

After completing this chapter you will be able to:

- Understand the concept, usage and limitation of regression.
- Use regression analysis to estimate the relationship between two variables.
- Compute multiple correlation and regression coefficients.
- Interpret multiple regression and multiple correlation coefficients.
- Understand the difference between correlation and regression.

10.1   Introduction

Regression is a form of prediction statistics. It predicts the most likely values of a variable on the basis of the specific values of another correlated variable or a number of other correlated variables. The variable whose values are predicted is the dependent variable or criterion, whereas the variable whose values form the basis of the prediction is called the independent variable or predictor.

Regression can be computed only if the dependent and independent variables possess a significant correlation between them. Regression translates the association between two variables (or between one variable and a combination of two or more other variables) into an expression of one of them as a function of the other(s). Just like correlation, regression holds good only in a particular population from which the samples are selected, and only for that limited range of scores of the variables from which it has been derived; it cannot be extended beyond these limits.

10.2   Simple Regression

Depending on the number of variables involved, the regression is of two types: *simple regression* and *multiple regression*. In simple regression, only two variables are involved; the criterion or dependent variable is a function of a single independent variable or predictor. In other words, the scores of the criterion are predicted from the given scores of the single predictor, for example, the regression of the statistics test scores on intelligence test scores, or the regression of height of a group of samples on their weight. In multiple regression, on the other hand, more than two variables are involved; the criterion is a function of the combination of two or more predictors. Thus, the scores of the criterion are predicted from the scores of more than one predictor, for example, the regression of the examination marks in science on mathematics and IQ test scores, or the regression of surface area of a person on his/her height and weight.

The regression may be linear or nonlinear depending on the form of relationship between the variables. If the relation between the criterion and the predictor is described in terms of a straight line, it is called linear regression and when it is described in terms of a curved line, it is called nonlinear or curvilinear regression. In other words, the scatter plot/scattergram of the scores of the criterion and predictor should show a linear distribution of its plotted points with an upward or downward slope for a linear regression, whereas for a nonlinear regression, the scatter plot/scattergram should show a curvilinear distribution like elliptical or hyperbolic ones. It is a usual practice to designate the predictor/independent variable by the symbol X and the criterion/dependent variable by Y.

Linear regression expresses the dependent variable Y as the linear function of the independent variable X so that the values of Y predicted from the values of X lie around a straight line called the regression line of Y on X. The regression line is so located in relation to the points plotted from the paired scores of the two variables that the sum of squared vertical distances of those points from the line is kept at a minimum (method of least squares). In other words, it is the best-fitting straight line for the plotted points.

Before we proceed for further discussions about the models, properties, assumptions and computation of simple linear regression, certain terms related to simple linear regression need some clarification; these are discussed further.

10.2.1   Scatter Plot or Scatter Diagram or Scattergram

The simplest and the easiest way to determine if a relationship exists between two variables is to plot the variables on the same graph. The Y variable is plotted on the ordinate (vertical or Y axis) and the X variable on the abscissa (horizontal or X axis). The resulting graph is called a scatter plot. With regard to its definition, we can say that a scatter plot is a graph of paired X and Y values.

To begin our discussion, let us use an illustration where there is a positive linear relationship between the X and Y variables. Table 10.1 shows one month's salary for five salesmen and the rupee value of the merchandise they sold that month.

Table 10.1   One month's salary of five salesmen and value of merchandise they sold in rupees

	X Variable	Y Variable
Salesman	Merchandise Sold (₹)	Salary (₹)
1	0	500
2	1,000	800
3	2,000	1,100
4	3,000	1,400
5	4,000	1,700

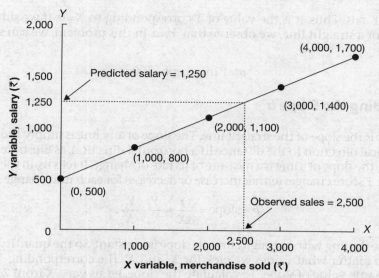

Figure 10.1   Graph of the relationship between salary and merchandise sold

The relationship between X and Y variables can best be seen by plotting a graph using the paired X and Y values for each salesman as the points on the graph. This scatter plot is shown in Figure 10.1. Referring to this figure, we see that all of the points fall on a straight line. When a straight line describes the relationship between two variables, the relationship is called linear. So, with regard to its definition, we can state that a linear relationship between two variables is one in which the relationship can be most accurately represented by a straight line. The graph represented in Figure 10.1 can be used to predict the salary of other salesmen of the same company. For example, if a salesman sells merchandise worth of ₹ 2,500, we would predict his salary to be ₹ 1,250. The graphic solution has been shown in Figure 10.1. By vertically projecting the X value of ₹ 2,500 until it intersects with the straight line, we can read the predicted Y value from the Y-axis. The salesman's salary should be equal to ₹ 1,250.

10.2.2   The Equation for a Straight Line

Although a graphic solution is sometimes used for prediction, it is much more common to predict Y from the equation of the straight line. The general form of the equation of any straight line is given by

$$Y = bX + a,$$

where

   $a = Y$ intercept (value of Y when $X = 0$)
   $b =$ slope of the line.

10.2.3   Finding the Y Intercept a

The quantity a is a constant. It is the distance on the Y axis from the origin to the point where the straight line cuts the Y axis. In short, the Y intercept is the value of Y where the line intersects the Y axis. Thus, it is the value of Y corresponding to $X=0$. If we substitute $X=0$ in the equation for a straight line, we observe that $Y=a$. In this problem, we can see from Figure 10.2 that

$$a = Y \text{ intercept} = 500.$$

10.2.4   Finding the Slope b

The quantity b is the slope of the straight line. The slope of any line is simply the ratio of the distance in a vertical direction to the distance in a horizontal direction, as illustrated in Figure 10.2. In other words, the slope of a line is a measure of its rate of change. It tells us, in the equation form, how much the Y score changes (either increase or decrease) for each unit change in the X score:

$$b = \text{slope} = \frac{\Delta Y}{\Delta X} = \frac{Y_2 - Y_1}{X_2 - X_1}.$$

Since we are dealing with a straight line, its slope is constant. So the quantity b is a constant. This means no matter what values we pick for X_2 and X_1, the corresponding Y_2 and Y_1 scores will yield the same value of slope. To calculate the slope, let us vary X from 2,000 to 3,000. If $X_1 = 2,000$, then $Y_1 = 1,100$. If $X_2 = 3,000$, then $Y_2 = 1,400$. Substituting these values into the slope equation:

$$b = \text{slope} = \frac{\Delta Y}{\Delta X} = \frac{Y_2 - Y_1}{X_2 - X_1} = \frac{1400 - 1100}{3000 - 2000} = \frac{300}{1000} = 0.30.$$

Thus, the slope $= 0.30$. This means that the Y value increases 0.30 of a unit for every 1 unit increase in X. Note that the same slope would occur if we had chosen any other values for X_1 and X_2. For example, if $X_1 = 1,000$ and $X_2 = 2,000$, then $Y_1 = 800$ and $Y_2 = 1,100$. Then the slope is

$$b = \text{slope} = \frac{\Delta Y}{\Delta X} = \frac{Y_2 - Y_1}{X_2 - X_1} = \frac{1100 - 800}{2000 - 1000} = \frac{300}{1000} = 0.30.$$

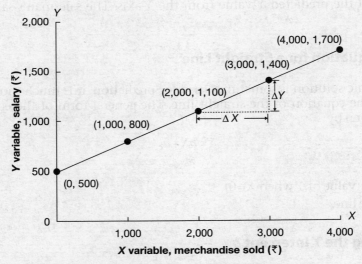

Figure 10.2   Graph of salary and amount of merchandise sold

Figure 10.2 also shows the Y intercept $= a = 500$. Both the slope and Y intercept have been shown in Figure 10.2. If a and b are known, the location of the line is uniquely fixed, and for any given value of X, we can compute a corresponding value of Y.

The full equation for the linear relationship that exists between salary and merchandise sold can now be written as

$$Y = bX + a.$$

Substituting the values for a and b:

$$Y = 0.30X + 500.$$

When used for prediction, the equation becomes

$$Y' = \hat{Y}(Y \, hat/cap) = 0.30X + 500,$$

where $Y' = \hat{Y}$ is the predicted value of the Y variable.

With this equation, we can predict any Y value just by knowing the corresponding X value. For example, if $X = 2,500$ as in our previous problem, then

$$Y' = 0.30X + 500 = 0.30 \times 2,500 + 500 = 750 + 500 = 1,250.$$

Thus, if a salesman sells merchandise worth ₹2,500, his salary would equal ₹1,250. This is, of course, the same value we achieved with a graphical solution as shown in Figure 10.1.

Moreover, the slope of the line tells us whether the relationship is positive or negative. When the relationship is positive, the slope is positive. The previous example had a positive slope, that is, higher values of X were associated with higher values of Y, and lower values of X were associated with lower values of Y. When the slope is positive, the line tends to run upward from left to right, indicating that as X increases, Y increases. Thus, a direct relationship exists between the two variables.

When the relationship is negative, there is an inverse relationship between the variables, making the slope negative. With a negative slope the line runs downward from left to right. Low values of X are associated with the high values of Y, and high values of X are associated with low values of Y. Another way of saying this is that as X increases, Y decreases.

In the relationship we have graphed in Figures 10.1 and 10.2, all of the points have fallen on the straight line. When this is the case, the relationship is a perfect one, and we can exactly predict each Y score just by knowing its corresponding X score. Unfortunately, in the behavioural sciences, perfect relationships are rarely found. However, it is much more common to find imperfect relationships. Thus, a perfect relationship is one in which a positive or negative relationship exists and all of the points fall exactly on the line. An imperfect relationship, on the other hand, is the one in which a relationship exists but all the points do not fall on the line.

There are two regression lines as there are two variables X and Y. When we predict the Y scores basing on the X scores, the prediction line is called the regression line of Y on X. On the other hand, when we predict the X scores based on the Y scores, the prediction line is called the regression line of X on Y. In other words, the regression line goes in the name of the variable whose values are being predicted. Let us discuss those two regression lines.

10.2.5 The Linear Regression of Y on X

Columns 2 and 3 of Table 10.2 contain the abstract reasoning test (ART) scores and mathematics test (MT) scores of a sample of 10 school students. Suppose we are interested in using these hypothetical data to predict the MT scores (Y) from ART scores (X).

Table 10.2   ART and MT scores of 10 school students: Predicting Y from X

(1) Students	(2) ART Scores (X)	(3) MT Scores (Y)	(4) X²	(5) XY	(6) Predicted MT Scores (Y')
1	5	10	25	50	8
2	8	10	64	80	10
3	10	12	100	120	12
4	12	9	144	108	14
5	15	17	225	255	16
6	11	14	121	154	13
7	13	15	169	195	14
8	9	11	81	99	11
9	11	15	121	165	13
10	6	7	36	42	9
Total N=10	100 (∑X)	120 (∑Y)	1,086 (∑X²)	1,268 (∑XY)	

These data are plotted in a graphic form or a scatter plot, which is shown in Figure 10.3. Each pair of scores is represented by a point. Although when plotted graphically the arrangement of points shows considerable irregularity, we observe a tendency for MT scores to increase as ART scores increase. From the scatter plot, it is obvious that the relationship between abstract reasoning (AR) and mathematics (M) is imperfect.

Even though all of the points do not fall on a single line, it is still clear from Figure 10.3 that a relationship exists between X and Y. In this case, the relationship is imperfect and appears to be a positive linear one. When the linear relationship is imperfect, we cannot draw a single straight line through all of the points; the most we can do is to draw a single line which best fits the points. We can, however, construct a straight line that best describes the relationship and then use this line for prediction or estimation. This prediction line is called a *regression line* of Y on X, if we are going to predict Y scores from X scores. Since in an imperfect relationship no single line will hit all of the points, there are many possible regression lines that could be drawn. But the question is: How do we determine which is the best? The answer to this question is the *method of least squares*. In other words, the solution most often used is to construct the straight line that minimises errors of prediction according to a *least-squares* criterion. Then this line is called the *least-squares regression line*.

The least-squares regression line for the data in Table 10.2 is shown in Figure 10.3. In this figure, each value of X has a corresponding Y value and also a Y' value corresponding to a point on the regression line (where Y=actual value and Y'=the predicted Y value). The vertical distance between each point and the line represents the error in prediction. In other words, $Y-Y'$ is equal to the error in prediction for each point. It might seem that the total error in prediction should be the simple algebraic sum of $Y-Y'$ summed over all of the points, i.e.,

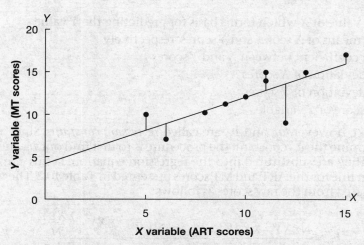

Figure 10.3   Scatter plot of ART and MT scores; least-squares regression line and prediction error

$\sum(Y-Y')$. However, the total error in prediction is not equal to $\sum(Y-Y')$, because some of Y' values will be greater than actual Y values and some will be less. Thus, there will be both positive and negative error scores, and the simple algebraic sums of these would cancel each other. Therefore, instead of just summing $Y-Y'$, we first compute $(Y-Y')^2$ for each score/point. This squaring process removes the negative signs and, thus, eliminates the cancellation problem. Now, if we minimise $\sum(Y-Y')^2$, we shall minimise the total error of prediction. We will construct the line that minimises $\sum(Y-Y')^2$. Thus, the least-squares regression line is the prediction line that minimises $\sum(Y-Y')^2$. Note that, for any linear relationship, there is only one line that will minimise $\sum(Y-Y')^2$. Thus, there is only one least-squares regression line for each linear relationship. The method of least-squares locates the regression line in such a position that the sum of squares of departures of points from the line parallel to the Y axis is minimum, that is, the line is located in a position such that the quantity $\sum(Y-Y')^2$ is a minimum. Thus, the least-squares regression line is used because it gives greater overall accuracy in prediction than any other regression line.

In the present context, the slope of the least-squares regression line for predicting Y from X will be denoted by b_{yx} and the point where the line cuts the Y-axis (i.e., Y intercept) by a_{yx}. The equation for such a regression line is given by

$$Y' = b_{yx}X + a_{yx}$$
$$\text{or} \quad Y' = \bar{Y} + b_{yx}(X - \bar{X})$$
$$\text{or} \quad Y - \bar{Y} = r\frac{\sigma_y}{\sigma_x}(X - \bar{X}),$$

where

Y' = predicted or estimated value of Y

b_{yx} = slope of the regression line for minimising errors in predicting Y

a_{yx} = Y axis intercept for minimising errors in predicting Y

X=any given value of X which forms basis for predicting the Y value

$\bar{X}$ and $\bar{Y}$ =the means of X scores and Y scores, respectively

r=correlation coefficient between X and Y scores

σ_x=standard deviation of X scores

σ_y=standard deviation of Y scores

Y=predicted score of Y variable.

In this context, however, a_{yx} and b_{yx} are called *regression constants*. Since we need the b_{yx} constant to determine the a_{yx} constant, the procedure is to first find out b_{yx} and then a_{yx}. Once both are found, they are substituted into the regression equation. Let us construct the least-squares regression line for the ART and MT scores presented in Table 10.2. The values of b_{yx} and a_{yx} may be calculated from the raw scores as follows:

$$b_{yx} = \frac{N\Sigma XY - \Sigma X\Sigma Y}{N\Sigma X^2 - (\Sigma X)^2} = \frac{\Sigma XY - N\bar{X}\bar{Y}}{\Sigma X^2 - N(\Sigma X)^2} = \frac{\Sigma XY - \dfrac{\Sigma X\Sigma Y}{N}}{\Sigma X^2 - \dfrac{(\Sigma X)^2}{N}},$$

$$a_{yx} = \frac{\Sigma Y - b_{yx}\Sigma X}{N} = \bar{Y} - b_{yx}\bar{X},$$

where

ΣX and ΣY=sums of X and Y, respectively

ΣXY=sum of the products of X and Y

ΣX^2=sum of the squares of X

$\bar{X}$ and $\bar{Y}$ =means of X and Y, respectively.

To illustrate, consider the data of Table 10.2. Columns 2 and 3 of this table provide the ART and MT scores of 10 school students. Column 4 provides the values X^2 and Column 5 provides the products XY. Summing the columns, we obtain

$$\Sigma X=100; \quad \Sigma Y=120; \quad \Sigma X^2=1,086; \quad \Sigma XY=1,268 \text{ and } N=10.$$

Applying the left-hand form of the above equations for b_{yx} and a_{yx}, we have

$$b_{yx} = \frac{N\Sigma XY - \Sigma X\Sigma Y}{N\Sigma X^2 - (\Sigma X)^2} = \frac{10 \times 1268 - 100 \times 120}{10 \times 1086 - (100)^2} = \frac{12680 - 12000}{10860 - 10000} = \frac{680}{860} = 0.7907,$$

$$a_{yx} = \frac{\Sigma Y - b_{yx}\Sigma X}{N} = \frac{120 - 0.7907 \times 100}{10} = \frac{120 - 79.07}{10} = \frac{40.93}{10} = 4.093.$$

The regression line for predicting Y from X is then described by the equation: $Y'=b_{yx}X+a_{yx}=$ $0.7907X+4.093$. By substituting any value of X in this formula, we obtain Y', the estimated or predicted value of Y. Column 6 of Table 10.2 shows the predicted MT scores obtained by applying this regression equation.

10.2.6   The Linear Regression of *X* on *Y*

Thus far, we have been concerned with predicting Y scores from X scores and have drawn the regression line of Y on X (see Figure 10.3). If, however, we wish to predict or estimate X scores from Y scores, a different regression line has to be used. This is called the regression line of X on Y. In an imperfect relationship, these two regression lines will be located in different positions;

but when the relationship is perfect, both regression lines coincide, forming the single line that hits all of the points.

The regression line of X on Y is located in a position such as to minimise the sum of squares of the distances from the point to the line parallel to the X axis. If X is an observed or actual value and X' is a value estimated or predicted from Y value, this line is so located as to make the quantity $\Sigma(X - X')^2$ a minimum.

The *differences* between these two regression lines are that: (a) the regression line of Y on X enables us to predict Y values from X values, whereas the regression line of X on Y helps us to predict or estimate X values from Y values; (b) the regression line of Y on X minimises errors in the Y variable (i.e., minimising Y' errors), whereas the regression line of X on Y minimises errors in the X variable (i.e., minimising X' errors); and (c) in the regression line of Y on X, the errors minimised are represented by vertical lines parallel to the Y axis (see Figure 10.3), but in the regression line of X on Y, the errors minimised are represented by the horizontal lines parallel to the X axis (see Figure 10.4).

To illustrate the computation of the regression line of X on Y, let us use again the same data given in Table 10.2. This time we shall predict ART scores (X) from the MT scores (Y). For convenience, the data are shown in Table 10.3.

The formula for the regression line of X on Y is given by

$$X' = b_{xy}Y + a_{xy}$$

$$\text{or} \quad X' = \bar{X} + b_{xy}(Y - \bar{Y})$$

$$\text{or} \quad X - \bar{X} = r\frac{\sigma_x}{\sigma_y}(Y - \bar{Y}),$$

Table 10.3 ART and MT scores of 10 school students: predicting X from Y

1 Students	2 ART Scores (X)	3 MT Scores (Y)	4 Y^2	5 XY	6 Predicted ART Scores (X')
1	5	10	100	50	8
2	8	10	100	80	8
3	10	12	144	120	10
4	12	9	81	108	8
5	15	17	289	255	14
6	11	14	196	154	12
7	13	15	225	195	12
8	9	11	121	99	9
9	11	15	225	165	12
10	6	7	49	42	6
Total N=10	100 (ΣX)	120 (ΣY)	1,530 (ΣY^2)	1,268 (ΣXY)	

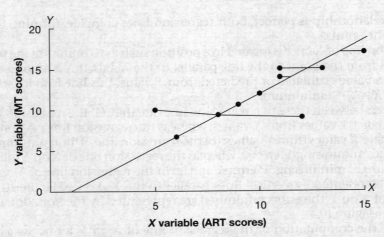

Figure 10.4   Scatter plot of ART and MT scores. Least-squares regression line and prediction error

where

> X'=predicted or estimated value of X
> b_{xy}=slope of the regression line for minimising X' errors
> a_{xy}=X axis intercept for minimising X' errors
> Y=any given value of Y which forms basis for predicting X value
> $\bar{X}$ and $\bar{Y}$ =the means of X scores and Y scores, respectively
> r=correlation coefficient between X and Y scores
> σ_x=standard deviation of X scores
> σ_y=standard deviation of Y scores
> X=predicted score of the X variable.

The values of b_{xy} and a_{xy} may be calculated from the following formulae:

$$b_{xy} = \frac{N\Sigma XY - \Sigma X \Sigma Y}{N\Sigma Y^2 - (\Sigma Y)^2} = \frac{\Sigma Y - N\bar{X}\bar{Y}}{\Sigma Y^2 - N(\Sigma Y)^2} = \frac{\Sigma XY - \dfrac{\Sigma X \Sigma Y}{N}}{\Sigma Y^2 - \dfrac{(\Sigma Y)^2}{N}},$$

$$a_{xy} = \frac{\Sigma X - b_{xy}\Sigma Y}{N} = \bar{X} - b_{xy}\bar{Y}.$$

Table 10.3 shows that ΣX=100; ΣY=120; ΣY^2=1,530; ΣXY=1,268 and N=10. Applying the left-hand side of the above formulae to b_{xy} and a_{xy}, we obtain

$$b_{xy} = \frac{N\Sigma XY - \Sigma X \Sigma Y}{N\Sigma Y^2 - (\Sigma Y)^2} = \frac{10 \times 1268 - 100 \times 120}{10 \times 1530 - (120)^2} = \frac{12680 - 12000}{15300 - 14400} = \frac{680}{900} = 0.7555,$$

$$a_{xy} = \frac{\Sigma X - b_{xy}\Sigma Y}{N} = \frac{100 - 0.7555 \times 120}{10} = \frac{100 - 90.66}{10} = \frac{9.34}{10} = 0.934.$$

The regression line for predicting X from Y is then given by the equation: $X'=b_{xy}Y+a_{xy}=$ $0.7555\,Y+0.934$. By substituting any value of Y in this equation, we obtain X', the estimated or predicted value of X. Column 6 of Table 10.3 shows the predicted ART scores obtained by applying this regression equation. The regression line of X on Y is shown in Figure 10.4.

Although different equations do exist for computing the second regression line (i.e., regression line of X on Y), they are seldom used. Instead, it is a common practice to designate the predicted variable as Y and the given variable as X. Thus, if we wanted to predict ART scores from MT scores, we would designate ART scores as the Y variable and MT scores as the X variable, and then use the regression equation for predicting Y values from X values.

To summarise, for any scatter diagram/plot, two regression lines exist. The first line is used for predicting Y from the knowledge of X. The second line is used for predicting X from the knowledge of Y. The first line is located in order to minimise the sum of squares of deviations from the line parallel to the Y-axis, that is, $\Sigma(Y - Y')^2$. The second line is located in order to minimise the sum of squares of deviations from the line parallel to the X axis, that is, $\Sigma(X - X')^2$. If a perfect correlation exists between the X and Y axes, these two lines coincide. If not, it can be shown that $r = \sqrt{b_{yx} b_{xy}}$.

10.2.7   Regression Lines in a Deviation-score Form

Earlier we have considered the regression line of Y on X and that of X on Y in the raw-score form. Instead of considering raw scores, we may consider regression lines for deviation scores, that is, for scores of the form $x = X - \bar{X}$ and $y = Y - \bar{Y}$. The slopes of the two regression lines expressed in a deviation score form are written very simply as

$$b_{yx} = \frac{\Sigma xy}{\Sigma x^2}; \quad b_{xy} = \frac{\Sigma xy}{\Sigma y^2}.$$

The slopes of the lines in the deviation-score model are, of course, exactly the same as in the raw-score model. The locations of the reference axes have, however, changed. The point of interception of the two regression lines with these reference axes is 0. The two lines pass through the origin: $a_{yx} = a_{xy} = 0$.

10.2.8   The Standard Error of Estimate: Accuracy of Prediction

The regression line, say, of Y on X represents our best estimate of the Y values given their corresponding X values. However, unless the relationship between X and Y is perfect, most of the actual Y values will not fall on the regression line. Thus, when the relationship is imperfect, there will necessarily be prediction errors. It is useful to know the magnitude of the errors, because the accuracy of prediction depends on the amount of prediction errors; if the amount of error is less, then the accuracy of prediction is more and vice versa.

Quantifying prediction errors involves computing the standard error (SE) of estimate. The SE of estimate is much like the standard deviation which gives us a measure of the average deviation about the mean. The SE of estimate gives us a measure of the average deviation of the prediction errors about the regression line. In this context, the regression line can be considered as an estimate of the mean of the Y values for each of the X values. It is like a 'floating' mean of the Y values, which changes with the X values. With the standard deviation, the sum of the deviations, $\Sigma(X - \bar{X})$, equals 0. We have to square the deviations in order to obtain a meaningful average. The situation is the same with the SE of estimate. Since the sum of the prediction errors, $\Sigma(Y - Y')$, equals 0, we must square them also. The average is then obtained by summing the squared values, dividing it by $N-2$, and taking the square root of the quotient (very much like with the standard deviation).

The equation/formula for the SE of estimate for predicting Y from X is

$$s_{y.x} = \sqrt{\frac{\Sigma(Y-Y')^2}{N-2}} = s_y\sqrt{1-r^2}.$$

Note that we have divided by $N-2$ rather than $N-1$, as is done with the simple standard deviation. We divide by $N-2$ because the calculation of the SE of estimate involves fitting the data to a straight line. To do so, we require the estimation of two parameters, slope and intercept, leaving the deviations about the line with $N-2$ degrees of freedom.

The variance of the difference between the actual and predicted values of Y, that is $(Y-Y')$, is denoted by s_{yx}^2. This variance, which is a measure of the accuracy of prediction, can be shown as follows:

$$s_{yx}^2 = \frac{\Sigma(Y-Y')^2}{N-2} = s_y^2(1-r^2).$$

The right-hand side of the above formula shows a relation between the correlation coefficient and the magnitude of errors of prediction.

The SE of estimate varies from 0 to s_y. When $r=1$ and all points fall exactly along a straight regression line, $s_{yx}=0$; when $r=0$, then $s_{yx}=s_y$. The SE of estimate describes the degree of accuracy associated with predicting one variable from another. In a scatter diagram, it predicts how closely the points cluster about the regression line. Moreover, the SE of estimate makes no distinction between a positive and a negative correlation. From a prediction viewpoint, a correlation of –0.80, for example, provides the same accuracy of prediction as a correlation of +0.80. Furthermore, when standard scores (z-scores) are used, the SE of estimate is simply $\sqrt{1-r^2}$. This quantity is sometimes called the *coefficient of alienation*. It is the obverse of the correlation coefficient. The correlation coefficient describes the degree of association between two variables. However, the quantity $\sqrt{1-r^2}$ describes the degree of lack of association or alienation between two variables.

In brief, we can say that the SE of estimate is a quantification of the errors of prediction. The larger its value, the less confidence we have in the prediction, and thus the prediction is less accurate. Conversely, the smaller its value, the more likely the prediction will be accurate.

In the preceding paragraphs, we have discussed errors in predicting Y from X. The arguments involved in predicting X from Y are directly parallel.

10.2.9   Relation of Regression to Correlation

If all points in a scatter plot/diagram fall exactly along a straight line, the two regression lines coincide. Perfect prediction is possible. The correlation coefficient in this case is either –1.0 or +1.0. When the amount of correlation departs from either –1.0 or +1.0, the two regression lines have an angular separation. In general, as the degree of relationship between two variables decreases, the angular separation between two regression lines increases. When no systematic relationship between two variables exists at all, with both the variables being independent, the two regression lines are at right angles to each other.

A simple relation exists between the correlation coefficient (r) and the slopes of the two regression lines (b_{yx} and b_{xy}). As shown earlier, $b_{yx} = \Sigma xy / \Sigma x^2$ and $b_{xy} = \Sigma xy / \Sigma y^2$. It can also be noted, however, that $\Sigma xy = (N-1)\,r\,s_x s_y$, $\Sigma x^2 = (N-1)s_x^2$ and $\Sigma y^2 = (N-1)s_y^2$. By simply substituting these values, we obtain

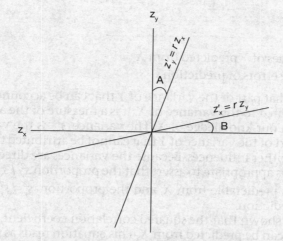

Figure 10.5 Regression lines in the standard-score form. Angle A is equal to angle B

$$b_{yx} = \frac{\Sigma xy}{\Sigma x^2} = \frac{(N-1)rs_x s_y}{(N-1)s_x^2} = r\frac{s_y}{s_x},$$

$$b_{xy} = \frac{\Sigma xy}{\Sigma y^2} = \frac{(N-1)rs_x s_y}{(N-1)s_y^2} = r\frac{s_x}{s_y}.$$

Consider a situation where the scores are in a standard-score form, and, thus, $z_x = (X - \bar{X})/s_x$ and $z_y = (Y - \bar{Y})/s_y$. The standard deviation of standard scores is 1, that is, $s_{z_x} = s_{z_y} = 1$. Thus, in the standard-score model, the slope of each regression line is equal to the correlation coefficient. If pairs of standard scores are plotted graphically, and two regression lines are fitted to the data, the equations of these lines are as follows:

$$z'_y = rz_x \text{ and } z'_x = rz_y,$$

where z'_y and z'_x are the estimated or predicted standard scores. The regression model in the standard-score form is shown in Figure 10.5.

In Figure 10.5, the slope of the line $z'_y = rz_x$ relative to the z_x-axis is the same as the slope of the line $z'_x = rz_y$ relative to the z_y-axis. For perfect correlation, the lines coincide at the 45° angle to the z_x- and z_y-axes. The slope is obviously unity in this case. For a zero correlation, the two regression lines have a 90° angular separation. One regression line will coincide exactly with the z_x-axis and the other with the z_y-axis.

Let us now discuss how the variance of correlation coefficient is related to the variance of Y that can be predicated from X. In discussing the prediction of Y from the knowledge of X, it was noted that a score of Y could be viewed as comprised of two parts. One part is the predicted value of Y'. This is the distance from the X axis to the regression line, corresponding to any particular value of X. All values of Y' lie on the regression line. The other part is the difference between the actual value of Y and the predicted value Y', that is, $Y - Y'$. Hence, $Y = Y' + (Y - Y')$. These two parts are independent of each other, that is, they are uncorrelated. Therefore, the variances of these two parts are directly additive, which may be written as

$$s_y^2 = s_{y'}^2 + s_{y \cdot x}^2,$$

where

s_y^2 = variance of Y

$s_{y'}^2$ = variance of values of Y predicted from X

$s_{y.x}^2$ = variance of the errors of prediction.

The variance $s_{y'}^2$ is that part of the variance of Y that can be accounted for, predicted from, explained by or attributed to the variance of X. It is a measure of the amount of information we have about Y from our knowledge of X. The variance s_{yx}^2 is the variance of the errors of prediction. It is that part of the variance of Y that cannot be attributed to the variance of X, but must be attributed to other influences. Because the variances are directly additive, if $s_y^2 = 200$, $s_{y'}^2 = 150$ and $s_{yx}^2 = 50$, it is appropriate to assert that the proportion $s_{y'}^2 / s_y^2 = 150/200 = 0.75$ or 75% of the variance of Y is predictable from X, and the proportion $s_{yx}^2 / s_y^2 = 50/200 = 0.25$ or 25% comprises errors of prediction.

Similarly, it can be shown that the squared correlation coefficient, r^2, is the proportion of the variance of Y that can be predicted from X. This equation reads as follows:

$$r^2 = s_{y'}^2 / s_y^2.$$

Thus, r^2 is the ratio of two variances, and may, therefore, be viewed as a simple proportion. If $r = 0.60$, then $r^2 = 0.36$. This indicates that 36% of the variance of the Y variable is predicted from the variance of the X variable. In effect, we know 36% of what we would have to know to make a perfect prediction of the Y variable from the X variable. Thus, r^2 can quite meaningfully be interpreted as a proportion, and $r^2 \times 100$ as a per cent. In general, in attempting to conceptualise the degree of relationship represented by a correlation coefficient, it is more meaningful to think in terms of the square of the correlation coefficient instead of the correlation coefficient itself. For example, a correlation of 0.20 represents 4% association and a correlation of 0.50 represents 25% association.

Our discussions regarding the variance interpretation of the correlation coefficient have been illustrated by discussing the prediction of Y from X. All discussions regarding the prediction of Y from X applies also to the prediction of X from Y. In predicting X from Y, $r^2 = s_{x'}^2 / s_x^2$.

10.2.10   Models of Regression

There are three models of regression according to the nature of independent variable(s). These models are discussed in the following:

(a) *Model I regression*. It is the regression of a dependent variable or criterion (Y) on an independent variable or predictor (X), which is a 'fixed' treatment variable, whose values vary under the planned, deliberate control of the investigator, and not at random. Thus, the values of Y suffer from errors due to random variations. But the values of X are free from random errors. A model I regression is used for predicting the values of Y for specific values of X when the latter is varied by the investigator at precise and predetermined manners and rates. It can also estimate how much of the variations of Y may be due to the variations of X, and can thus explore the causation of the changes in the dependent variable Y due to the changes in the independent variable X, that is, their cause-and-effect relationship. This is unlike r which estimates only the association between the variables without assuming any cause-and-effect relationship between them. A simple model I regression is based on one predictor that is a 'fixed' treatment variable. A multiple model I regression is based on two predictors both of which are 'fixed' treatment variables. In an experiment, several predetermined doses of insulin ('fixed' independent variable X) were injected to animals and their blood sugar levels (dependent variable Y) were subsequently estimated. This is a case for simple model I regression of Y on X so that the values of Y may be predicted from the values of X, and the change of X is considered a cause for the change of Y.

(b) *Model II regression.* It is the regression of a criterion (Y) on a predictor (X) which is a classification variable that is beyond the control of the researcher. It predicts the most likely value of Y on the basis of an already existing value of X in the individual; X is measured, but not applied by the investigator. Because the values of the predictor (X) are not 'fixed', controlled deliberately or applied by the investigator, its values suffer from random errors. Thus, both the dependent and independent variables, Y and X, respectively, are free to vary at random and have random errors. Model II regression cannot, therefore, explore the cause-and-effect relationship between the variables; it can merely estimate an interdependence of their changes, sometimes due to a common cause. Model II regression may be worked out between the anxiety test scores (Y) and the intelligence test scores (X); neither of these two are under the control of the investigator. Similarly, the regression of height on body weight, that of mathematical aptitude on ART scores and that of cardiac stroke volume on blood pressure are some of the examples of simple model II regression; each uses a random predictor such as body weight, AR and blood pressure. However, the regression of the body surface area on height and weight is an example of multiple model II regression, because both the predictors—height and weight—are random variables.

(c) *Model III regression.* It is a multiple regression predicting the value(s) of a dependent variable or criterion (Y) from the given values of two or more predictors or independent variables (X_1, X_2 and so on). Some of the independent variables are 'fixed' treatment variables and other(s) are classification variable(s). For example, the regression of mathematical aptitude test scores on periods of practice (fixed treatment variable) and sex (classification variable) of the subjects. Some other examples of model III regression may be the regression of sexual activity of rats on applied doses of a hormone (fixed treatment variable) and age (classification variable) of the animals, the regression of the blood thyroxine level on atmospheric temperature (classification variable) and injected dose of thyrotropin (fixed treatment variable).

10.2.11   Properties of Simple Linear Regression

The following are some of the principal properties of the simple linear regression.

(a) The linear regression of a variable Y on the basis of the scores of another variable X or vice versa can be worked out only when the two variables have a significant linear correlation, r_{yx} or r_{xy}. The scatter diagram, resulting from the plotting of the predicted criterion scores (Y') against the corresponding predictor scores (X) used in their regression, has a linear distribution.

(b) Two separate regression equations may be worked out for each pair of variables X and Y. One of these is the regression equation of Y on X, predicting the Y scores on the basis of X scores; the other is the regression equation of X on Y, predicting the X scores from Y scores. However, the regression of one of the two correlated variables is generally worked out, which is relatively more difficult to measure or is measured less precisely than the other.

(c) The linear regression equation of Y on X is given by (as mentioned earlier)

$$Y' = b_{yx}X + a_{yx}$$
$$\text{or}\quad Y' = \bar{Y} + b_{yx}(X - \bar{X}),$$

where Y' is the predicted Y score from the actual X scores; b_{yx} is the slope of the regression line and a_{yx} is the general level of the regression line (or Y intercept) showing Y as a linear function of X.

(d) The statistic b_{yx} is a prediction statistic and is called the regression coefficient of Y on X. It is the average rate of increase or decrease in the score of the criterion Y for a unit rise or fall in the score of the predictor X. The b_{yx} is given basically by the ratio of the covariance of scores of both variables, X and Y, and the variance of the scores of the predictor (X). This formula reads

$$b_{yx} = \frac{\text{Cov}(X,Y)}{\text{Var}(X)} \quad \text{or} \quad b_{yx} = r_{yx} \frac{s_y}{s_x}.$$

In terms of raw scores X and Y, means $\bar{X}$ and $\bar{Y}$, and standard deviations s_x and s_y, of the respective variables, the sample size n and the correlation coefficient r_{yx} between the variables, the equations for $\text{Cov}(X,Y)$, $\text{Var}(X)$ and r_{yx} read

$$\text{Cov}(X,Y) = \frac{\Sigma(X - \bar{X})(Y - \bar{Y})}{n} = \frac{\Sigma XY}{n} - \frac{\Sigma X \Sigma Y}{n^2}$$

$$\text{Var}(X) = s_x^2 = \frac{\Sigma X^2}{n} - \left(\frac{\Sigma X}{n}\right)^2 = \frac{\Sigma(X - \bar{X})^2}{n}$$

$$r_{yx} = \frac{\text{Cov}(X,Y)}{s_x s_y}.$$

Thus, b_{yx} may be computed by any of the formulae given above.

(e) The statistic a_{yx} is the Y intercept of the regression line of Y on X. It may be computed from b_{yx} as follows:

$$a_{xy} = \bar{Y} - b_{yx}\bar{X}.$$

(f) In a similar vein, the regression equation of X on Y may also be worked out. In this case, X' is the predicted X value from the actual Y value, b_{xy} is the regression coefficient of X on Y (or the slope of the regression line of X on Y), and a_{xy} is the X intercept which gives the general level of the regression line of X on Y, showing X as a linear function of Y. The linear regression equation of X on Y reads

$$X' = b_{xy}Y + a_{xy}$$

or

$$X' = \bar{X} + b_{xy}(Y - \bar{Y}).$$

The following is the equation for b_{xy}:

$$b_{xy} = \frac{\text{Cov}(X,Y)}{\text{Var}(Y)} \quad \text{or} \quad b_{xy} = r_{xy} \frac{s_x}{s_y}.$$

The equations for $\text{Cov}(X,Y)$ and $r_{xy}(r_{yx} = r_{xy})$ have already been cited earlier under point (d). The equation for $\text{Var}(Y)$ is given as follows:

$$\text{Var}(Y) = s_y^2 = \frac{\Sigma Y^2}{n} - \left(\frac{\Sigma Y}{n}\right)^2 = \frac{\Sigma(Y - \bar{Y})^2}{n}.$$

The statistic a_{xy} is computed from b_{xy} as follows:

$$a_{xy} = \bar{X} - b_{xy}\bar{Y}.$$

(g) The above two regression equations (i.e., $Y' = b_{yx}X + a_{yx}$ and $X' = b_{xy}Y + a_{xy}$) as well as the two regression lines (i.e., of Y on X and of X on Y) become identical with each other only when r_{yx} or r_{xy} is perfect, and equals either +1.0 or –1.0. For all other values of the correlation coefficient (r), the regression lines intersect at a single point which corresponds to the means ($\bar{X}$ and $\bar{Y}$) of the two variables. The angle between two regression lines increases with the decrease in the magnitude of r, and reaches 90° when r amounts to 0.0; both b_{yx} and b_{xy} become 0 in this case and no regression is possible.

(h) In the standard-score model, the slope of each regression line is equal to the correlation coefficient. Thus, the equations for these two regression lines are

$$z'_y = rz_x \text{ and } z'_x = rz_y.$$

For perfect correlation, the lines coincide at a 45° angle to the z_x- and z_y-axes. For a zero correlation, the two regression lines have a 90° angular separation.

(i) The geometric mean of the two regression coefficients (or slopes) equals the product–moment r between the two variables. Thus,

$$r_{yx} \text{ or } r_{xy} = \sqrt{b_{yx}b_{xy}}.$$

It follows from the above equation that the two regression coefficients are reciprocals of each other when the product–moment r between the two variables amounts to either +1.0 or –1.0.

(j) The predicted scores of the criterion (say, Y) is merely the most probable score of an individual having a given score of the predictor (say, X). So, in any sample, all the individuals with a given X score are not expected to have their actual Y scores identical to Y' scores. Rather, their actual Y scores, which are experimentally measured, will form a normal or near-normal distribution around the relevant predicted Y' score with the latter (i.e., Y' scores) as the mean.

(k) For all scores of the predictor (say, X), the observed scores of the criterion (say Y) should lie scattered equally around the regression line. In other words, the deviations of the observed Y scores from the respective predicted Y' scores should be uniform all along the regression line.

(l) The difference between the predicted Y' scores and the observed Y scores of the criterion is called the error of prediction. This error increases with the decrease in the magnitude of correlation, and is measured as the SE of estimate (s_{yx}) of Y on X. The equation for s_{yx} reads

$$S_{y.x} = \sqrt{\frac{\Sigma(Y-Y')^2}{n}} = s_y\sqrt{1-r_{yx}^2}.$$

It is well evident from the above equation that when r_{yx} is +1.0 or –1.0, the s_{yx} becomes 0, and all the observed Y scores coincide with the respective Y' scores and fall exactly on the regression line. On the contrary, when r_{yx} is 0.0, s_{yx} equals s_y, and no prediction is possible.

Similarly, the equation for the SE of estimate of X on Y ($s_{x.y}$) is given by

$$S_{x.y} = \sqrt{\frac{\Sigma(X-X')^2}{n}} = s_x\sqrt{1-r_{xy}^2}.$$

10.2.12　Assumptions of Simple Linear Regression

Some important assumptions of simple linear regression are discussed below.

(a) The variables (i.e., dependent variable or criterion, and independent variable or predictor) involved in regression should be either continuous variables or such discrete variables as can be reasonably assumed to have continuous series of values; regression equations cannot be computed for attributes or genuinely discrete variables.

(b) Both the variables, that is, the criterion and the predictor, have unimodal and fairly symmetrical distributions in the population.

(c) The scores of the criterion (say, Y) are a linear function of the scores of the predictor (say, X); the scatter diagram, obtained by plotting the Y scores against the respective X scores, has a linear distribution.

(d) The Y scores of a criterion, measured in a large number of individuals having a given X score of the predictor, are distributed normally, independent of each other, around the predicted Y' scores as the mean, and with equal variances from the latter.

(e) The predictor or the independent variable should be either a 'fixed' treatment variable in model I regression or a classification variable in model II regression.

(f) Deviations of the observed values of the criterion (say, Y) from the corresponding predicted values (i.e., Y' values) are uniform all along the regression line. In other words, the observed values of Y are equally scattered around the line for all values of X (homoscedasticity, meaning equality of variances between row and column values).

10.2.13　Computation of Simple Linear Regression

The regression coefficient, say, b_{yx} for the regression of Y on X is computed by using any one of the following four formulae.

(i) *Using raw scores.*

(a) The X and Y scores of the variables are totalled separately to give ΣX and ΣY, respectively.

(b) Each X score is squared and then all these squared X scores are totalled to give ΣX^2.

(c) Each X score is multiplied by the corresponding Y score of the same subject to obtain XY of that subject, and all such XY scores are totalled to obtain ΣXY.

(d) Then the statistic b_{yx} is computed as follows using the sample size n (Example 10.1):

$$b_{yx} = \frac{n\Sigma XY - \Sigma X \Sigma Y}{n\Sigma X^2 - (\Sigma X)^2}.$$

(ii) *Using the sum of products.*

(a) The means ($\bar{X}$ and $\bar{Y}$) of the variables are computed using ΣX and ΣY and sample size n as follows:

$$\bar{X} = \frac{\Sigma X}{n}, \quad \bar{Y} = \frac{\Sigma Y}{n}.$$

(b) The deviations of X and Y scores from their respective means are computed. The deviations of X scores from $\bar{X}$ and of Y scores from $\bar{Y}$ of each subject are multiplied by each other to give $(X - \bar{X})(Y - \bar{Y})$. Then these are all added up to give the sum of products $\Sigma(X - \bar{X})(Y - \bar{Y})$.

(c) The deviations of X score from $\bar{X}$ are squared for each subject and then these squared deviations are totalled to give the sum of squared deviations of the predictor, namely $\Sigma(X - \bar{X})^2$.

(d) The regression coefficient is then computed as follows (Example 10.2):

$$b_{yx} = \frac{\Sigma(X - \bar{X})(Y - \bar{Y})}{\Sigma(X - \bar{X})^2} = \frac{\Sigma xy}{\Sigma x^2}.$$

(iii) *Using the product–moment r.*
     If the product–moment r (r_{yx}) and the SDs of the variables (s_x and s_y) have already been computed, then b_{yx} may be computed by using them (Example 10.3) as follows:

$$b_{yx} = r_{yx} \frac{s_y}{s_x}.$$

(iv) *Using covariance and variance.*

(a) The ΣX, ΣY, ΣX^2 and ΣXY scores are computed as in steps (a)–(c) of the computation of b_{yx} from raw scores.

(b) Cov(X, Y) and variance of X scores (s_x^2) are then computed using the sample size n:

$$\text{Cov}(X,Y) = \frac{\Sigma XY}{n} - \frac{\Sigma X \Sigma Y}{n^2}$$

$$s_x^2 = \frac{\Sigma X^2}{n} - \left(\frac{\Sigma X}{n}\right)^2.$$

(c) The regression coefficient is then computed using the covariance and the variance as given follows (Example 10.4):

$$b_{yx} = \frac{\text{Cov}(X,Y)}{s_x^2}.$$

After computing b_{yx} by any one of the *four alternative methods* mentioned above, a_{yx} is computed using the means of the two variables as follows:

$$a_{yx} = \bar{Y} - b_{yx}\bar{X}.$$

The computed scores of a_{yx} and b_{yx} are then put in the following equation to give the regression equation of Y on X:

$$Y' = a_{yx} + b_{yx}X.$$

To draw the linear regression line of Y on X, the Y' score for each of the X scores is computed using the regression equation. Each Y' score is then plotted graphically against the corresponding X score.

Example 10.1 The following are the anxiety test scores and final examination scores of 10 college students. Build a regression equation for predicting the final examination score given the anxiety level.

Students	1	2	3	4	5	6	7	8	9	10
Anxiety	28	41	35	39	31	42	50	46	45	37
Final Exam	82	58	63	89	92	64	55	70	51	72

Solution

(a) The data are entered in the first three columns of Table 10.4. The anxiety test scores (X) and final examination scores (Y) are totalled to give ΣX and ΣY, respectively. In the present example, $\Sigma X = 394$ and $\Sigma Y = 696$.

(b) Each Y score is multiplied by the corresponding X score of each student and all these products are totalled to give ΣXY. In the given example, $\Sigma XY = 26,819$.

(c) Each X score is squared and all these squared scores are totalled to give ΣX^2. In the given example, $\Sigma X^2 = 15,946$.

(d) The regression coefficient b_{yx} is then worked out from the raw scores by the appropriate formula as follows:

$$b_{yx} = \frac{n\Sigma XY - \Sigma X \Sigma Y}{n\Sigma X^2 - (\Sigma X)^2} = \frac{10 \times 26819 - 394 \times 696}{10 \times 15946 - (394)^2} = \frac{268190 - 274224}{159460 - 155236}$$

$$= \frac{-6034}{4224} = -1.4285.$$

(e) a_{yx} is then computed using $\bar{X}, \bar{Y}$ and b_{yx}:

$$\bar{X} = \frac{\Sigma X}{n} = \frac{394}{10} = 39.4; \quad \bar{Y} = \frac{\Sigma Y}{n} = \frac{696}{10} = 69.6$$

$$a_{yx} = \bar{Y} - b_{yx}\bar{X} = 69.6 - (-1.4285)(39.4)$$

$$= 69.6 - (-56.2829) = 69.6 + 56.2829 = 125.8829.$$

(f) The values of a_{yx} and b_{yx} are used to build the regression equation for predicting Y values from X values as follows:

$$Y' = a_{yx} + b_{yx}X$$

$$= 125.8829 + (-1.4285)X$$

$$= -1.4285X + 125.8829.$$

Since the regression coefficient (b_{yx}) is negative, the relationship between anxiety test scores (X) and final examination scores (Y) is negative.

Example 10.2 The following are 12 paired measurements. Compute the slope of the regression line for predicting Y from X and also the regression equation for predicting Y given X.

X	50	54	56	59	60	65	64	65	67	71	71	74
Y	22	25	34	28	26	28	30	30	28	33	36	40

Solution

(a) The means of X and Y scores, the deviations of X and Y scores from their respective means, the sum of the products of the deviations of X and Y scores from their respective means and the sum of the squared deviations of X scores from their mean are worked out in Table 10.5.

(b) The regression coefficient or slope of the regression line for predicting Y from X, that is, b_{yx} is computed using the sum of products $\Sigma(X-\bar{X})(Y-\bar{Y})$, and the sum of squared deviations of X scores from $\bar{X}$, that is $\Sigma(X-\bar{X})^2$ as follows:

$$b_{yx} = \frac{\Sigma(X-\bar{X})(Y-\bar{Y})}{\Sigma(X-\bar{X})^2} = \frac{\Sigma xy}{\Sigma x^2} = \frac{311.0}{598.0} = 0.5201.$$

(c) The computed b_{yx} is then used in computing a_{yx} as follows:

$$a_{yx} = \bar{Y} - b_{yx}\bar{X} = 30.0 - (0.5201 \times 63) = 30.0 - 32.7663 = -2.7663.$$

(d) The regression equation for predicting Y given X is then computed with the help of a_{yx} and b_{yx} as follows:

$$Y' = a_{yx} + b_{yx}X = -2.7663 + 0.5201X$$
$$= 0.5201X - 2.7663 = 0.52X - 2.77 \text{ (reduced to two decimals).}$$

Since the regression coefficient or slope of the regression line is positive, the relationship between the X and Y scores is positive.

Table 10.4   For computing regression coefficient from raw scores

(1) Students	(2) Anxiety (X)	(3) Final Exam (Y)	(4) XY	(5) X^2
1	28	82	2,296	784
2	41	58	2,378	1,681
3	35	63	2,205	1,225
4	39	89	3,471	1,521
5	31	92	2,852	961
6	42	64	2,688	1,764
7	50	55	2,750	2,500
8	46	70	3,220	2,116
9	45	51	2,295	2,025
10	37	72	2,664	1,369
Total $n=10$	394 (ΣX)	696 (ΣY)	26,819 (ΣXY)	15,946 (ΣX^2)

Table 10.5   For computing regression coefficient from the sum of products

X	Y	$(X - \bar{X})$ (x)	$(Y - \bar{Y})$ (y)	$(X - \bar{X})^2$ (x^2)	$(X - \bar{X})(Y - \bar{Y})$ (xy)
50	22	−13.0	−8.0	169.0	104.0
54	25	−9.0	−5.0	81.0	45.0
56	34	−7.0	4.0	49.0	−28.0
59	28	−4.0	−2.0	16.0	8.0
60	26	−3.0	−4.0	9.0	12.0
65	28	2.0	−2.0	4.0	−4.0
64	30	1.0	0.0	1.0	0.0
65	30	2.0	0.0	4.0	0.0
67	28	4.0	−2.0	16.0	−8.0
71	33	8.0	3.0	64.0	24.0
71	36	8.0	6.0	64.0	48.0
74	40	11.0	10.0	121.0	110.0
Total N=12	756 (ΣX)	360 (ΣY)		598.0 $\sum(X-\bar{X})^2$ (Σx^2) (Sum of squares)	311.0 $\sum(X-\bar{X})(Y-\bar{Y})$ (Σxy) (Sum of products)

Notes:

$$\bar{X} = \frac{\Sigma X}{N} = \frac{756}{12} = 63.0$$

$$\bar{Y} = \frac{\Sigma Y}{N} = \frac{360}{12} = 30.0$$

Example 10.3 Compute the regression equation of mathematics scores (Y) on the differential aptitude test (DAT) scores (X), using the following data, and work out the SE of estimate.

Sample size $n=12$; $\bar{X}=62.5$; $s_x=7.04$
$\bar{Y}=30.4$; $s_y=4.86$; $r_{yx}=+0.78$.

Solution

(a)   Given, $n=12$; $\bar{X}=62.5$; $s_x=7.04$; $\bar{Y}=30.4$; $s_y=4.86$; and $r_{yx}=+0.78$
(b)   The regression coefficient b_{yx} is then computed using the r_{yx}, s_x and s_y as follows:

$$b_{yx} = r_{yx}\frac{s_y}{s_x} = 0.78\frac{4.86}{7.04} = 0.78 \times 0.69 = 0.5382.$$

Table 10.6 For computing regression coefficient from covariance

	X	**Y**	**XY**	**X²**
	7	1	7	49
	10	2	20	100
	9	4	36	81
	13	3	39	169
	7	3	21	49
	11	4	44	121
	13	5	65	169
Total N=7	70 (ΣX)	22 (ΣY)	232 (ΣXY)	738 (ΣX^2)

(c) The computed b_{yx} is then used to compute a_{yx} as follows:

$$a_{yx} = \bar{Y} - b_{yx}\bar{X} = 30.4 - 0.5382 \times 62.5 = 30.4 - 33.64 = -3.24.$$

(d) The regression equation for predicting Y from X is then computed using a_{yx} and b_{yx} as follows:

$$Y' = a_{yx} + b_{yx}X = -3.24 + 0.5382X = 0.5382X - 3.24.$$

(e) SE of estimate (s_{yx}) is computed using s_y and r_{yx} as follows:

$$s_{y.x} = s_y\sqrt{1 - r_{yx}^2} = 4.86\sqrt{1 - (.78)^2} = 4.86\sqrt{1 - .6084}$$
$$= 4.86\sqrt{0.3916} = 4.86 \times 0.6258 = 3.04.$$

Since the regression coefficient (b_{yx}) is positive the relationship between the X and Y scores is positive.

Example 10.4 Given the set of paired X and Y scores, determine the regression equation for predicting Y given X.

X	7	10	9	13	7	11	13
Y	1	2	4	3	3	4	5

Solution

(a) The data are entered in the first two columns of Table 10.6. The X and Y scores are totalled to give ΣX and ΣY, respectively. In the present example, ΣX=70 and ΣY=22.

(b) Each Y score is multiplied by the corresponding X score, and all these products are totalled to give ΣXY. In the given example, ΣXY=232.

(c) Each X score is squared, and these squared scores are totalled to give ΣX^2. In the given example, ΣX^2=738.

(d) The regression coefficient b_{yx} is computed using the covariance of X and Y scores, and the variance of X score, which are calculated as follows:

$$\text{Cov}(X,Y) = \frac{\Sigma XY}{n} - \frac{\Sigma X \Sigma Y}{n^2} = \frac{232}{7} - \frac{70 \times 22}{(7)^2} = \frac{232}{7} - \frac{1540}{49}$$

$$= 33.143 - 31.429 = 1.714$$

$$\text{Var}(X) = s_x^2 = \frac{\Sigma X^2}{n} - \left(\frac{\Sigma X}{n}\right)^2 = \frac{738}{7} - \left(\frac{70}{7}\right)^2 = \frac{738}{7} - (10)^2$$

$$= 105.429 - 100.0 = 5.429$$

$$b_{yx} = \frac{\text{Cov}(X,Y)}{s_x^2} = \frac{1.714}{5.429} = 0.3157.$$

(e) a_{yx} is then computed by using $\bar{X}, \bar{Y}$ and b_{yx}:

$$\bar{X} = \frac{\Sigma X}{n} = \frac{70}{7} = 10.0; \quad \bar{Y} = \frac{\Sigma Y}{n} = \frac{22}{7} = 3.143$$

$$a_{yx} = \bar{Y} - b_{yx} \ \bar{X} = 3.143 - 0.3157 \times 10 = 3.143 - 3.157 = -0.014.$$

(f) The values of a_{yx} and b_{yx} are used to determine the regression equation for predicting Y given X as follows:

$$Y' = a_{yx} + b_{yx} X = -0.014 + 0.3157 X \ \textbf{or} \ 0.3157 X - 0.014$$

10.3 Multiple Regression

In the previous section, we have considered the simple regression that has involved only two variables—one dependent variable (criterion) and one independent variable (predictor)—predicting the values of the criterion (Y) from the given values of the predictor (X). However, multiple regression is an extension of simple regression to situations that involve two or more predictor variables. Multiple regression is a method of multivariate statistics; it predicts the most likely value of a variable (criterion or dependent variable) from the values of two or more other variables (predictors or independent variables). It can be computed only if the variables possess significant correlations with each other.

Multiple regression translates the relation between the criterion and the combination of two or more predictors into an expression showing the criterion as a function of the predictors. Multiple regression may be linear or nonlinear depending upon whether the criterion is a linear or nonlinear function of the predictors. Multiple regressions belong to models I, II and III as all the predictors are 'fixed' treatment variables or all are classification variables, or some of them are 'fixed' treatment variables and some classification variables.

10.3.1 Multiple Linear Regression with Three Variables

This type of regression predicts the value of the criterion (say, Y) from the given values of two predictors (say, X_1 and X_2). The general multiple regression equation for the straight line, showing Y as the linear function of X_1 and X_2, is as follows:

$$Y' = b_1 X_1 + b_2 X_2 + a,$$

where

Y′=predicted value of Y

b_1=regression coefficient of the first predictor variable

X_1=first predictor variable

b_2=regression coefficient of second predictor variable

X_2=second predictor variable

a= Y-intercept (or prediction constant).

This equation is very similar to the one we used in simple regression except that we have added another predictor variable and its coefficient. As before, the coefficient and constant values are determined according to the least-squares criterion that $\Sigma(Y-Y')^2$ is a minimum. To be clearer, we may say that b_1 and b_2 are otherwise called as *partial regression coefficients*. b_1 is the average rate of change of Y for each unit change of X_1 when the effect of the second predictor X_2 is partialled out; b_1 thus gives the slope of the regression line of Y on X_1 when X_2 is held constant. The other coefficient b_2 is the average rate of change of Y for each unit change of X_2 when the effect of the first predictor X_1 is partialled out; b_2 thus gives the slope of the regression line of Y on X_2 when X_1 is kept constant.

b_1 and b_2 are computed using the SDs (s_y, s_{x_1} and s_{x_2}) of the respective variables and the *beta coefficients* (β_2 and β_3). The values of β_2 and β_3 are multiple regression weights for standard scores. They are also sometimes called *beta coefficients*. With three variables, the values of β_2 and β_3 are given by

$$\beta_2 = \frac{r_{12} - r_{13}r_{23}}{1-r_{23}^2} = \frac{r_{yx_1} - r_{yx_2}r_{x_1x_2}}{1-r_{x_1x_2}^2}; \quad \beta_3 = \frac{r_{13} - r_{12}r_{23}}{1-r_{23}^2} = \frac{r_{yx_2} - r_{yx_1}r_{x_1x_2}}{1-r_{x_1x_2}^2}.$$

The equations for the regression coefficients b_1 and b_2 are as follows:

$$b_1 = \beta_2 \frac{s_y}{s_{x_1}}; \quad b_2 = \beta_3 \frac{s_y}{s_{x_2}}.$$

The Y-intercept or the prediction constant, a, can be computed by the following equation:

$$a = \bar{Y} - b_1\bar{X}_1 - b_2\bar{X}_2.$$

The values of b_1, b_2 and a are then put in the preceding general formula for the multiple regression equation to give the required regression equation for three variables: one criterion (Y) and two predictors (X_1 and X_2).

A composite formula may also be computed directly from *beta weights* as follows:

$$Y' = \beta_2 \frac{s_y}{s_{x_1}} X_1 + \beta_3 \frac{s_y}{s_{x_2}} X_2 + \left(\bar{Y} - \beta_2 \frac{s_y}{s_{x_1}} \bar{X}_1 - \beta_3 \frac{s_y}{s_{x_2}} \bar{X}_2 \right).$$

This is the regression equation in a raw-score form. It may be used to predict a raw score of Y from a raw score on X_1 and X_2 The values $\beta_2 \frac{s_y}{s_{x_1}}$ and $\beta_3 \frac{s_y}{s_{x_2}}$ act as weights. The quantity to the right in the parentheses is constant. The above composite formula for the regression equation may be reduced to the following:

$$Y' = \bar{Y} + \beta_2 \frac{s_y}{s_{x_1}} (X_1 - \bar{X}_1) + \beta_3 \frac{s_y}{s_{x_2}} (X_2 - \bar{X}_2).$$

If the raw scores are converted into standard scores, then the following is a multiple regression equation in a standard-score form. This equation reads

$$z_1' = \beta_2 z_2 + \beta_3 z_3 \quad \text{or} \quad z_y' = \beta_2 z_{x_1} + \beta_3 z_{x_2}.$$

It will yield the best possible linear prediction of a standard score on z_y from the standard scores z_{x_1} and z_{x_2}. The estimated standard score z_y' and the observed standard scores z_{x_1} and z_{x_2} may be written as

$$z_y' = \frac{Y' - \bar{Y}}{s_y}; \quad z_{x_1} = \frac{X_1 - \bar{X}_1}{s_{x_1}}; \quad z_{x_2} = \frac{X_2 - \bar{X}_2}{s_{x_2}}.$$

By substituting these values in the regression equation in a standard-score form, we obtain

$$\frac{Y' - \bar{Y}}{s_y} = \beta_2 \frac{X_1 - \bar{X}_1}{s_{x_1}} + \beta_3 \frac{X_2 - \bar{X}_2}{s_{x_2}}.$$

The SE of estimate $(s_{y \cdot x_1 x_2})$ of Y on X_1 and X_2 is computed using the multiple correlation coefficient $R_{y \cdot x_1 x_2}$, which reads

$$R_{1.23} = \sqrt{\beta_2 r_{12} + \beta_3 r_{13}} \quad \text{or} \quad R_{y \cdot x_1 x_2} = \sqrt{\beta_2 r_{yx_1} + \beta_3 r_{yx_2}}$$

$$s_{1.23} = s_1 \sqrt{1 - R_{1.23}^2} \quad \text{or} \quad s_{y \cdot x_1 x_2} = s_y \sqrt{1 - R_{y \cdot x_1 x_2}^2}.$$

Other three-variable multiple regression equations, for example, the regression of X_1 on Y and X_2 are similarly worked out using specific *beta coefficients*.

10.3.2   Multiple Linear Regression with More than Three Variables

Where m is the total number of independent variables involved (i.e., $m > 3$), the regression of Y on $X_1, X_2, X_3, \ldots, X_m$ is worked out as follows:

$$Y' = a_{y \cdot x_1 x_2 x_3 \cdots x_m} + b_{yx_1 \cdot x_2 x_3 \cdots x_m} X_1 + b_{yx_2 \cdot x_1 x_3 \cdots x_m} X_2 + \cdots + b_{yx_m \cdot x_1 x_2 \cdots (m-1)} X$$

or

$$Y' = \bar{Y} + \beta_2 \frac{s_y}{s_{x_1}} (X_1 - \bar{X}_1) + \beta_3 \frac{s_y}{s_{x_2}} (X_2 - \bar{X}_2) + \cdots + \beta_m \frac{s_y}{s_{x_m}} (X_m - \bar{X}_m).$$

Using the coefficient of multiple determination, the SE of estimate is worked out as follows:

$$s_{y \cdot x_1 x_2 x_3 \cdots x_m} = s_y \sqrt{1 - R_{y \cdot x_1 x_2 x_3 \cdots x_m}^2}.$$

Let us apply all the above formulae regarding the multiple regression equation and solve the problem given in the following example.

Example 10.5 The following are the data on two predictors (X_1 and X_2) and criterion (Y) for five students. Build a multiple regression equation. What is the Y value of a student with $X_1=8$ and $X_2=5$?

Students	1	2	3	4	5
X_1	10	8	7	5	5
X_2	6	4	5	3	2
Y	16	13	14	8	9

Solution

(a) The data are entered in the first four columns of Table 10.7. The X_1, X_2 and Y scores are totalled to give ΣX_1, ΣX_2 and ΣY, respectively. In the present example, it is found that $\Sigma X_1=35$, $\Sigma X_2=20$ and $\Sigma Y=60$.

(b) All individual scores of X_1, X_2 and Y are squared and then these squared scores are totalled to give ΣX_1^2, ΣX_2^2 and ΣY^2, respectively, in Columns 5, 6 and 7 of Table 10.7. From the given example, it is computed that $\Sigma X_1^2=263$, $\Sigma X_2^2=90$ and $\Sigma Y^2=766$.

(c) Each X_1 score is multiplied by the corresponding Y score as well as by the corresponding X_2 score to give the products X_1Y and X_1X_2, respectively. Similarly, each X_2 score is multiplied by the corresponding Y score to give the product X_2Y All these products are then totalled to give ΣX_1Y, ΣX_2Y and ΣX_1X_2, respectively, in Columns 8, 9 and 10 of Table 10.7. In the given example, it is computed that $\Sigma X_1Y=447$, $\Sigma X_2Y=260$ and $\Sigma X_1X_2=152$.

(d) The product–moment correlations (i.e., zero-order r's) between the variables (r_{x_1y}, r_{x_2y} and $r_{x_1x_2}$) X_1, X_2 and Y are computed as follows:

$$r_{x_1y} = \frac{N\Sigma X_1Y - \Sigma X_1\Sigma Y}{\sqrt{[N\Sigma X_1^2-(\Sigma X_1)^2][N\Sigma Y^2-(\Sigma Y)^2]}} = \frac{5\times447-35\times60}{\sqrt{[5\times263-(35)^2][5\times766-(60)^2]}}$$

$$= \frac{2235-2100}{\sqrt{[1315-1225][3830-3600]}} = \frac{135}{\sqrt{90\times230}} = \frac{135}{\sqrt{20700}} = \frac{135}{143.87} = 0.94,$$

Table 10.7   For computing multiple regression coefficient from raw scores

(1)	(2)	(3)	(4)	(5)	(6)	(7)	(8)	(9)	(10)
Students	X_1	X_2	Y	X_1^2	X_2^2	Y^2	X_1Y	X_2Y	X_1X_2
1	10	6	16	100	36	256	160	96	60
2	8	4	13	64	16	169	104	52	32
3	7	5	14	49	25	196	98	70	35
4	5	3	8	25	9	64	40	24	15
5	5	2	9	25	4	81	45	18	10
Total $N=5$	35 (ΣX_1)	20 (ΣX_2)	60 (ΣY)	263 (ΣX_1^2)	90 (ΣX_2^2)	766 (ΣY^2)	447 ΣX_2^2	260 (ΣX_2Y)	152 (ΣX_1X_2)

$$r_{x_2 y} = \frac{N \Sigma X_2 Y - \Sigma X_2 \Sigma Y}{\sqrt{[N \Sigma X_2^2 - (\Sigma X_2)^2][N \Sigma Y^2 - (\Sigma Y)^2]}} = \frac{5 \times 260 - 20 \times 60}{\sqrt{[5 \times 90 - (20)^2][5 \times 766 - (60)^2]}}$$

$$= \frac{1300 - 1200}{\sqrt{[450 - 400][3830 - 3600]}} = \frac{100}{\sqrt{50 \times 230}} = \frac{100}{\sqrt{11500}} = \frac{100}{107.24} = 0.93,$$

$$r_{x_1 x_2} = \frac{N \Sigma X_1 X_2 - \Sigma X_1 \Sigma X_2}{\sqrt{[N \Sigma X_1^2 - (\Sigma X_1)^2][N \Sigma X_2^2 - (\Sigma X_2)^2]}} = \frac{5 \times 152 - 35 \times 20}{\sqrt{[5 \times 263 - (35)^2][5 \times 90 - (20)^2]}}$$

$$= \frac{760 - 700}{\sqrt{[1315 - 1225][450 - 400]}} = \frac{60}{\sqrt{90 \times 50}} = \frac{60}{\sqrt{4500}} = \frac{60}{67.08} = 0.89.$$

(e) The standard deviations (s_{x_1}, s_{x_2} and s_y) of the scores of the three variables are individually computed as follows:

$$\Sigma x_1^2 = \Sigma X_1^2 - \frac{(\Sigma X_1)^2}{N} = 263 - \frac{(35)^2}{5} = 263 - \frac{1225}{5} = 263 - 245 = 18,$$

$$s_{x_1} = \sqrt{\frac{\Sigma x_1^2}{N-1}} = \sqrt{\frac{18}{5-1}} = \sqrt{\frac{18}{4}} = \sqrt{4.5} = 2.12,$$

$$\Sigma x_2^2 = \Sigma X_2^2 - \frac{(\Sigma X_2)^2}{N} = 90 - \frac{(20)^2}{5} = 90 - \frac{400}{5} = 90 - 80 = 10,$$

$$s_{x_2} = \sqrt{\frac{\Sigma x_2^2}{N-1}} = \sqrt{\frac{10}{5-1}} = \sqrt{\frac{10}{4}} = \sqrt{2.5} = 1.58,$$

$$\Sigma y^2 = \Sigma Y^2 - \frac{(\Sigma Y)^2}{N} = 766 - \frac{(60)^2}{5} = 766 - \frac{3600}{5} = 766 - 720 = 46$$

$$s_y = \sqrt{\frac{\Sigma y^2}{N-1}} = \sqrt{\frac{46}{5-1}} = \sqrt{\frac{46}{4}} = \sqrt{11.5} = 3.39.$$

(f) Then the means of the scores of the three variables ($\bar{X}_1, \bar{X}_2$ and $\bar{Y}$) are computed as follows:

$$\bar{X}_1 = \frac{\Sigma X_1}{N} = \frac{35}{5} = 7.0; \quad \bar{X}_2 = \frac{\Sigma X_2}{N} = \frac{20}{5} = 4.0;$$

$$\bar{Y} = \frac{\Sigma Y}{N} = \frac{60}{5} = 12.0.$$

(g) The inter-correlations between two predictors ($\bar{X}_1$ and $\bar{X}_2$) and the criterion (Y), the means and SDs are noted in a tabular form as follows:

	X_2	Y	Means	SD
X_1	0.89	0.94	7.0	2.12
X_2	–	0.93	4.0	1.58
Y		–	12.0	3.39

(h) The beta coefficients/regression weights (β_2 and β_3) are then computed using the zero-order product–moment r's as follows:

$$\beta_2 = \frac{r_{yx_1} - r_{yx_2} r_{x_1 x_2}}{1 - r_{x_1 x_2}^2} = \frac{0.94 - 0.93 \times 0.89}{1 - (0.89)^2} = \frac{0.94 - 0.83}{1 - 0.79} = \frac{0.11}{0.21} = 0.52,$$

$$\beta_3 = \frac{r_{yx_2} - r_{yx_1} r_{x_1 x_2}}{1 - r_{x_1 x_2}^2} = \frac{0.93 - 0.94 \times 0.89}{1 - (0.89)^2} = \frac{0.93 - 0.84}{1 - 0.79} = \frac{0.09}{0.21} = 0.43.$$

(i) The regression coefficients, b_1 and b_2, are then computed using the beta coefficients (β_2 and β_3 and SDs (s_{x_1}, s_{x_2} and s_y) as follows:

$$b_1 = \beta_2 \frac{s_y}{s_{x_1}} = 0.52 \frac{3.39}{2.12} = 0.52 \times 1.60 = 0.83$$

$$b_2 = \beta_3 \frac{s_y}{s_{x_2}} = 0.43 \frac{3.39}{1.58} = 0.43 \times 2.14 = 0.92.$$

(j) The Y intercept or the prediction constant (a) is computed using the regression coefficients (b_1 and b_2) and the means of the scores of the three variables ($\bar{X}_1, \bar{X}_2$ and $\bar{Y}$) as follows:

$$a = \bar{Y} - b_1 \bar{X}_1 - b_2 \bar{X}_2 = 12.0 - 0.83 \times 7.0 - 0.92 \times 4.0$$
$$= 12.0 - 5.81 - 3.68 = 12.0 - 9.49 = 2.51.$$

(k) The multiple regression equation is computed using the values of a, b_1 and b_2 as follows:

$$Y' = b_1 X_1 + b_2 X_2 + a = 0.83 X_1 + 0.92 X_2 + 2.51.$$

(l) Since in Example 10.5 it is mentioned to find out the Y value of a student with $X_1 = 8$ and $X_2 = 5$, we can substitute these values of X_1 and X_2 in the above equation, and, thus, find the Y' score. Thus,

$$Y' = 0.83 \times 8.0 + 0.92 \times 5.0 + 2.51 = 6.64 + 4.60 + 2.51 = 13.75 \text{ or } 14.$$

Therefore, we may conclude that a student's Y value is 13.75 or 14 with $X_1 = 8$ and $X_2 = 5$. Thus, Example 10.5 summarises all the procedures required for computing the multiple linear regression equation with three variables: two predictors and one criterion.

10.3.3   Assumptions of Multiple Linear Regressions

The following are some of the principal assumptions of multiple linear regressions.

(a) The dependent (or criterion) variable is a random variable, whereas the independent (or predictors) variables may not necessarily be random variables.

(b) The relationship between the one dependent variable and two or more independent variables is linear. In other words, the correlation between the criterion and predictors is linear.

(c) The variances of the conditional distributions of the dependent variable, given various combinations of values of the independent variables, are all equal. Moreover, the conditional distributions for the dependent variable follow the normal probability distribution.

10.3.4   Objectives of Multiple Linear Regressions

The following are the three main objectives or purposes of multiple linear regression analysis.

(i)   To derive an equation that provides the predicted or estimated value of the dependent variable (or criterion) from the values of two or more independent variables (or predictors).

(ii) To obtain a measure of the error involved in using this regression equation as a basis for estimation or prediction.

(iii) To obtain a measure of the proportion of variance in the dependent variable accounted for or 'explained by' the independent variables.

The above three purposes can be achieved through the following activities.

The first purpose is accomplished by deriving an appropriate regression equation by the method of least squares. The second purpose is achieved through the calculation of the SE of estimate. The third purpose is accomplished by computing the multiple coefficient of determination.

10.4   Difference Between Correlation and Regression

The following are some of the principal points of difference between a correlation and a regression:

(i)   Correlation coefficients are descriptive statistics for measuring the relationship between variables, whereas regression is the prediction statistics for giving the most likely value of a variable depending on the value(s) of one or more other correlated variables. Correlation and regression involving only two variables are bivariate statistics. Multiple correlations and multiple regressions involve more than two variables and are multivariate statistics.

(ii) Correlation literally means the relationship between two or more variables which vary in sympathy so that the movements in one tend to be accompanied by the corresponding movements in the other(s). Regression, on the other hand, means stepping back or returning to the average value and is a mathematical measure expressing the average relationship between the two variables.

(iii) Correlation need not imply the cause-and-effect relationship between the variables under study, whereas regression clearly establishes this relationship. The variable corresponding to cause is taken as an independent (or predictor) variable and the variable corresponding to effect is taken as a dependent (or criterion) variable. In other words, regression clearly indicates the cause-and-effect relationship between independent and dependent variables.

(iv) A correlation coefficient between two variables X and Y is a measure of the direction and degree of the *linear* relationship between the two variables, which is mutual and symmetric, that is, $r_{xy} = r_{yx}$; and it is immaterial which of X and Y is independent variable and which is dependent variable. Regression analysis, on the other hand, aims at establishing the functional relationship between the two variables X and Y, and then using this relationship to predict or estimate the value of the dependent variable for any given value of the independent variable. Thus, regression definitely makes a difference as to which variable is independent and which is dependent. This means that in the case of regression, the independent and dependent variables have a definite direction. Hence, there are two distinct regression lines, that is, Y on X and X on Y. Therefore, the regression coefficients are not symmetric in X and Y, that is, $b_{yx} \neq b_{xy}$.

(v) A correlation coefficient r_{xy} is a relative measure of the linear relationship between the X and Y variables and is independent of the unit of measurement, whereas the regression coefficients, b_{yx} and b_{xy}, are absolute measures representing the change in the value of the variable $Y(X)$ for a unit change in the value of variable $X(Y)$.

(vi) There may be a *nonsense correlation* between two variables which is purely due to chance and has no practical relevance, for example, the correlation between the increase in income and the size of shoes of a group of individuals. However, there is nothing like *nonsense regression*.

(vii) Correlation analysis is confined only to the study of the linear relationship between the variables and, therefore, has limited applications. Regression analysis, on the other hand, studies both linear and nonlinear relationships between the variables, and, thus, has much wider applications.

In addition to the above points of difference, there is something common in both correlation and regression analyses. First, correlation is simple and multiple. Similarly regression is simple and multiple. The simple correlation and simple regression are called bivariate statistics, whereas both multiple correlation and multiple regression are called multivariate statistics. Second, the coefficient of correlation (r) takes the same sign as the regression coefficients (b_{yx} and b_{xy}). Third, if the value of b is significant at a given level of significance, r is also significant at that level of significance.

10.5 Uses of Regression Analysis

Regression is prediction statistics. It predicts the most likely value of a variable on the basis of a specific value of another related variable or a number of other variables. Regression analysis is a branch of statistical theory that is widely used in almost all the scientific disciplines. For example, in economics, it is the basic technique for measuring or estimating the relationship among economic variables which are very vital for the economic life of individuals. For instance, if we know that two variables, price (X) and demand (Y), are closely related, we can find out the most probable value of Y for a given value of X or vice versa. Similarly, if we know that the amount of tax and the rise in the price of a commodity are significantly related, we can find out the expected price for a certain amount of tax levy. Thus, the study of regression is of great help to the economists and businessmen. However, the uses of regression are not confined to economics and business field only. Its applications are extended to almost all the natural, physical, social and behavioural sciences. The regression analysis attempts to accomplish the following:

(i) Regression analysis provides estimates of the value of a dependent variable (or criterion) from the value of an independent variable (or predictor) or a number of independent variables. The device used to accomplish this estimation procedure is the *regression line*. The regression line describes the average relationship existing between the X and Y variables, that is, it displays the mean value of Y for a given value of X or vice versa. The equation of this regression line is known as the regression equation that provides estimates of the dependent variable when the value of the independent variable is inserted into the equation.

(ii)   Another goal of regression analysis is to obtain a measure of the error involved in using the regression line as a basis for estimation. For this purpose, the SE of estimate is calculated. This is a measure of the scatter or spread of the observed values of the dependent variable Y around the corresponding values estimated from the regression line $(Y - Y')$. If the line fits the data closely, that is, if there is little scatter of the observations around the regression line, good estimates can be made of the Y variable. On the other hand, if there is a great deal of scatter of the observations around the fitted regression line, the line will not produce accurate estimates of the dependent variable (Y).

(iii) With the help of the regression coefficients (b_{yx} and b_{xy}), we can calculate the correlation coefficient (r): $r_{xy} = \sqrt{b_{yx}b_{xy}}$. The square of the correlation coefficient (r^2) is called the *coefficient of determination*, which measures the degree of association that exists between two variables. It assesses the proportion of variance in the dependent variable (Y) that has been accounted for by the regression equation. In general, the greater the value of r^2, the better the fit and the more useful the regression equation as a prediction device.

10.6   Limitations of Regression Analysis

The following are some of the important limitations of regression analysis:

(i)   In making estimate from a regression equation, it is important to remember that the assumption is being made that the relationship has not changed since the regression equation was computed.

(ii)   Another point worth remembering is that the relationship shown by the scatter diagram may not be the same if the equation is extended beyond the values used in computing the equation. For example, there may be a close linear relationship between the yield of a crop, say, wheat, and the amount of fertilizer applied with the yield increasing as the amount of fertilizer is increased. It would not be logical, however, to extend this equation beyond the limits of the experiment for it is quite likely that if the amount of fertilizer were increased indefinitely, the yield would eventually decline as too much fertilizer was applied.

10.7   Miscellaneous Illustrations on Regression

Illustration 10.1 Two random variables have the regression equations:

$$3X + 2Y - 26 = 0,$$
$$6X + Y - 31 = 0.$$

Find the mean values and the coefficient of correlation between X and Y. If the variance of $X = 25$, find the standard deviation of Y from the data given above. [B.A.(H) Econ., Delhi University, 1995; M.Com., Madurai University, 1997; MBA, Kumaun University, 2001].

Solution
Given data:

Equation (i): $3X + 2Y - 26 = 0$ or $3X + 2Y = 26$
Equation (ii): $6X + Y - 31 = 0$ or $6X + Y = 31$.

Mean values of X and Y:

$$3X+2Y=26$$
$$6X+Y=31.$$

Multiplying Equation (i) by 2:

$$6X+4Y=52$$
$$6X+Y=31.$$

Subtracting Equation (ii) from Equation (i):

$$3Y=21$$
$$Y=7 \text{ or } \bar{Y}=7.$$

Putting the value of Y in Equation (i):

$$3X+14=26$$
$$3X=26-14=12$$
$$X=4 \text{ or } \bar{X}=4.$$

Coefficient of correlation. For finding the coefficient of correlation, we determine the values of two regression coefficients from the two regression equations.

Taking Equation (i) as the regression equation of Y on X:

$$2Y=26-3X$$

$$Y=13-\frac{3}{2}X \quad \text{or} \quad b_{yx}=\frac{-3}{2}=-1.5.$$

Taking Equation (ii) as the regression equation of X on Y:

$$6X=31-Y$$

$$X=\frac{31}{6}-\frac{1}{6}Y \quad \text{or} \quad b_{xy}=\frac{-1}{6}.$$

$$\therefore r=\sqrt{b_{yx}\times b_{xy}}=-\sqrt{\frac{3}{2}\times\frac{1}{6}}=-0.5.$$

The variance of $X=\sigma_x^2=25$ (given)
The standard deviation of $X=\sigma_x=\sqrt{25}=5.$
Substituting the values, the standard deviation of $Y(\sigma_y)$ is:

$$b_{yx}=r\frac{\sigma_y}{\sigma_x} \quad \text{or} \quad \frac{-3}{2}=-0.5\frac{\sigma_y}{5}$$

$$\text{or} \quad -1.5=-0.5\frac{\sigma_y}{5} \quad \text{or} \quad 5(-1.5)=-0.5\sigma_y$$

$$\text{or} \quad 0.5\sigma_y=7.5 \quad \text{or} \quad \sigma_y=15.$$

Thus, the obtained values are: $\bar{X}=4$; $\bar{Y}=7$, $r=-0.5$ and $\sigma_y=15$.

Illustration 10.2 For 50 students of a class, the regression equation of marks in statistics (X) on the marks in accountancy (Y) is $3Y-5X+180=0$. The mean marks in accountancy is 44 and the variance of marks in statistics is 9/16th of the variance of marks in accountancy. Find the mean marks in statistics and the coefficient of correlation between marks in the two subjects. [M.Com., Madurai University, 1993; B.Com.(H), Delhi University, 1994]

Solution

Given data:

X stands for marks in statistics
Y stands for marks in accountancy
$\bar{Y} = 44$.

The variance of $X(\sigma_x^2)$ is 9/16th of the variance of $Y(\sigma_y^2)$, which means that if σ_x^2 is 9, then $\sigma_y^2 = 16$.

The regression equation of X on Y is:

$$3Y - 5X + 180 = 0 \text{ or } 3Y + 180 = 5X.$$

Mean marks of X is:

$$5X = 3Y + 180 \quad \text{or} \quad 5X = 3 \times 44 + 180$$
$$\text{or} \quad 5X = 132 + 180 \quad \text{or} \quad 5X = 312$$
$$\text{or} \quad X = \frac{312}{5} = 62.4 \quad \text{or} \quad \bar{X} = 62.4.$$

Hence the mean marks in statistics is 62.4.

For computing the coefficient of correlation, we apply the following formula:

$$b_{xy} = r\frac{\sigma_x}{\sigma_y}.$$

The regression coefficient of X on $Y(b_{xy})$ will be calculated from the given equation as follows:

$$5X = 3Y + 180 \quad \text{or} \quad X = 0.6Y + 36 \quad \text{or} \quad b_{xy} = 0.6.$$

$$\sigma_x^2 = 9 \text{ (given)}, \quad \therefore \sigma_x = \sqrt{9} = 3.$$
$$\sigma_y^2 = 16 \text{ (given)}, \quad \therefore \sigma_y = \sqrt{16} = 4.$$

Substituting the above values, we can find out the coefficient of correlation (r) between the X and Y marks as follows:

$$b_{xy} = r\frac{\sigma_x}{\sigma_y} \quad \text{or} \quad 0.6 = r\frac{3}{4} \quad \text{or} \quad 3r = 2.4 \quad \text{or} \quad r = +0.8.$$

Thus, the obtained mean marks in statistics ($\bar{X}$) is 62.4, and the coefficient of correlation (r) between the marks in two subjects (X and Y) is 0.80, which is a positive relationship.

Illustration 10.3 If two regression lines are $3X + 12Y = 19$ and $3Y + 9X = 46$, then find out: (a) mean value of X and Y, (b) the value of the correlation coefficient and (c) the ratio of variance of X and variance of Y (BBA, Utkal University, 2005).

Solution

Given data:

Equation (i): $3X + 12Y = 19$
Equation (ii): $3Y + 9X = 46$ or $9X + 3Y = 46$.

(a) *Mean value of X and Y:*

$$3X + 12Y = 19$$
$$9X + 3Y = 46.$$

Multiplying Equation (i) by 3:

$$9X + 36Y = 57$$
$$9X + 3Y = 46.$$

Subtracting Equation (ii) from Equation (i):

$$33Y = 11,$$
$$Y = \frac{11}{33} = \frac{1}{3} \quad \text{or} \quad \bar{Y} = \frac{1}{3}.$$

Putting the value of Y in Equation (i):

$$3X + 12 \times \frac{1}{3} = 19.$$
$$\text{or} \quad 3X = 19 - 4 \text{ or } 3X = 15$$
$$\text{or} \quad X = 5 \quad \text{or} \quad \bar{X} = 5.$$

Hence, the mean value of X and Y are 5 and 1/3, respectively.

(b) *The value of correlation coefficient.* For finding the coefficient of correlation, we determine the values of two regression coefficients from the two regression equations.

Taking Equation (i) as regression Equation of Y on X:

$$12Y = 19 - 3X$$
$$Y = \frac{19}{12} - \frac{3X}{12} \quad \text{or} \quad b_{yx} = \frac{-3}{12} = \frac{-1}{4}$$

Taking Equation (ii) as regression Equation of X on Y:

$$9X = 46 - 3Y$$
$$X = \frac{46}{9} - \frac{3}{9}Y \quad \text{or} \quad b_{xy} = \frac{-3}{9} = \frac{-1}{3}$$
$$\therefore r = \sqrt{b_{yx} \times b_{xy}} = -\sqrt{\frac{1}{4} \times \frac{1}{3}} = -\sqrt{\frac{1}{12}} = -\sqrt{0.0833} = -0.29$$

Hence, the value of correlation coefficient, $r = -0.29$

(c) *The ratio of variance of X and variance of Y.*

$$b_{xy} = r\frac{\sigma_x}{\sigma_y} = \frac{r\sigma_x}{\sigma_y} \quad \text{and} \quad b_{yx} = r\frac{\sigma_y}{\sigma_x} = \frac{r\sigma_y}{\sigma_x}$$

$$\therefore \frac{b_{xy}}{b_{yx}} = \frac{r\sigma_x}{\sigma_y} / \frac{r\sigma_y}{\sigma_x} \quad \text{or} \quad \frac{b_{xy}}{b_{yx}} = \frac{r\sigma_x}{\sigma_y} \times \frac{\sigma_x}{r\sigma_y}$$

$$\text{or} \quad \frac{b_{xy}}{b_{yx}} = \frac{\sigma_x^2}{\sigma_y^2} \quad \text{or} \quad \frac{\sigma_x^2}{\sigma_y^2} = \frac{b_{xy}}{b_{yx}} = \frac{-1}{3} / \frac{-1}{4} = \frac{4}{3}$$

Hence, the ratio of variance of X and variance of $Y = \dfrac{4}{3}$.

Illustration 10.4 The equations of two lines of regression obtained in a correlation analysis are the following:

$$2X + 3Y - 8 = 0 \quad \text{and} \quad X + 2Y - 5 = 0$$

Obtain the value of the correlation coefficient and the variance of Y, given that the variance of X is 12 (BBA, Utkal University, 2010).

Solution
Given data:

$$\text{Equation (i):} \quad 2X+3Y-8=0$$
$$\text{Equation (ii):} \quad X+2Y-5=0$$
$$\text{Variance of } X(\sigma_x^2)=12$$

The value of the correlation coefficient. For finding the value of correlation coefficient, we determine the values of two regression coefficients from the two regression equations.

Taking Equation (i) as regression Equation of X on Y:

$$2X=8-3Y$$

$$X = 4-\frac{3}{2}Y \quad \text{or} \quad b_{xy} = -\frac{3}{2}$$

Taking Equation (ii) as regression Equation of Y on X:

$$2Y = 5 - X$$

$$Y = \frac{5}{2}-\frac{1}{2}X \quad \text{or} \quad b_{yx} = -\frac{1}{2}$$

$$\therefore r = \sqrt{b_{xy} \times b_{yx}} = -\sqrt{\frac{3}{2}\times\frac{1}{2}} = -\sqrt{\frac{3}{4}} = -\sqrt{0.75} = -0.866$$

Variance of Y:

$$\text{Variance of } X(\sigma_x^2)=12 \text{ (given)}$$
$$\text{Standard deviation of } X(\sigma_x)=\sqrt{12}$$

Substituting the values, variance of $Y(\sigma_y^2)$ is:

$$b_{yx} = r\frac{\sigma_y}{\sigma_x} \qquad \text{or} \quad -\frac{1}{2} = -0.866\frac{\sigma_y}{\sqrt{12}}$$

$$\text{or} \quad -0.5 = \frac{-0.866}{\sqrt{12}}\sigma_y \quad \text{or} \quad \sigma_y = \frac{0.5\sqrt{12}}{0.866}$$

$$\therefore \quad \sigma_y^2 = \frac{0.25\times 12}{0.75} = 4$$

Thus, the obtained values are:

$$\text{Correlation coefficient } (r)=-0.866$$
$$\text{Variance of } Y(\sigma_y^2)=4$$

Illustration 10.5 Obtain the regression equations from the following data:

$$N=50, \quad \Sigma X=500, \quad \Sigma Y=300, \quad \Sigma X^2=5,450, \quad \Sigma Y^2=2,000, \quad \Sigma XY=3,090$$

(BBA, Utkal University, 2008)

Solution
Given data:

$$N=50, \quad \Sigma X=500, \quad \Sigma Y=300, \quad \Sigma X^2=5,450, \quad \Sigma Y^2=2,000, \quad \Sigma XY=3,090$$

Mean values of X and Y:

$$\bar{X} = \frac{\Sigma X}{N} = \frac{500}{50} = 10$$

$$\bar{Y} = \frac{\Sigma Y}{N} = \frac{300}{50} = 6$$

Regression equation of Y on X:

$$Y' = a_{yx} + b_{yx}X$$

$$b_{yx} = \frac{N\Sigma XY - \Sigma X.\Sigma Y}{N\Sigma X^2 - (\Sigma X)^2} = \frac{50 \times 3090 - 500 \times 300}{50 \times 5450 - (500)^2}$$

$$= \frac{154500 - 150000}{272500 - 250000} = \frac{4500}{22500} = 0.2$$

$$a_{yx} = \bar{Y} - b_{yx}\bar{X} = 6 - 0.2 \times 10 = 6 - 2 = 4$$

$$\therefore Y' = 4 + 0.2X$$

Regression equation of X on Y:

$$X' = a_{xy} + b_{xy}Y$$

$$b_{xy} = \frac{N\Sigma XY - \Sigma X.\Sigma Y}{N\Sigma Y^2 - (\Sigma Y)^2} = \frac{50 \times 3090 - 500 \times 300}{50 \times 2000 - (300)^2}$$

$$= \frac{154500 - 150000}{100000 - 90000} = \frac{4500}{10000} = 0.45$$

$$a_{xy} = \bar{X} - b_{xy}\bar{Y} = 10 - 0.45 \times 6 = 10 - 2.7 = 7.3$$

$$\therefore X' = 7.3 + 0.45Y$$

Illustration 10.6 From the following data, obtain the two regression equations:

X	6	2	10	4	8
Y	9	11	5	8	7

(BBA, Utkal University, 2009)

Solution

	X	Y	X^2	Y^2	XY
	6	9	36	81	54
	2	11	4	121	22
	10	5	100	25	50
	4	8	16	64	32
	8	7	64	49	56
$N=5$	30 (ΣX)	40 (ΣY)	220 (ΣX^2)	340 (ΣY^2)	214 (ΣXY)

Mean values of X and Y:

$$\bar{X} = \frac{\Sigma X}{N} = \frac{30}{5} = 6$$

$$\bar{Y} = \frac{\Sigma Y}{N} = \frac{40}{5} = 8$$

Regression equation of Y on X:

$$Y' = a_{yx} + b_{yx}X$$

$$b_{yx} = \frac{N\Sigma XY - \Sigma X.\Sigma Y}{N\Sigma X^2 - (\Sigma X)^2} = \frac{5 \times 214 - 30 \times 40}{5 \times 220 - (30)^2}$$

$$= \frac{1070 - 1200}{1100 - 900} = \frac{-130}{200} = -0.65$$

$$a_{yx} = \bar{Y} - b_{yx}\bar{X} = 8 - (-0.65 \times 6) = 8 + 3.9 = 11.9$$

$$\therefore Y' = 11.9 + (-0.65X) = 11.9 - 0.65X$$

Regression equation of X on Y:

$$X' = a_{xy} + b_{xy}Y$$

$$b_{xy} = \frac{N\Sigma XY - \Sigma X.\Sigma Y}{N\Sigma Y^2 - (\Sigma Y)^2} = \frac{5 \times 214 - 30 \times 40}{5 \times 340 - (40)^2}$$

$$= \frac{1070 - 1200}{1700 - 1600} = \frac{-130}{100} = -1.3$$

$$a_{xy} = \bar{X} - b_{xy}\bar{Y} = 6 - (-1.3 \times 8) = 6 + 10.4 = 16.4$$

$$\therefore X' = 16.4 + (-1.3Y) = 16.4 - 1.3Y$$

Illustration 10.7 From the following data, obtain the two regression equations and calculate the correlation coefficient.

X	1	2	3	4	5	6	7	8	9
Y	9	8	10	12	11	13	14	16	15

Estimate the value of Y which should correspond on an average to $X=6.2$ (M.Com., Madras University 1996; B.Com., M.G. University, 1997).

Solution

X	$(X-\bar{X})$ x	x^2	Y	$(Y-\bar{Y})$ y	y^2	xy
1	−4	16	9	−3	9	12
2	−3	9	8	−4	16	12
3	−2	4	10	−2	4	4

	4	−1	1	12	0	0	0
	5	0	0	11	−1	1	0
	6	1	1	13	1	1	1
	7	2	4	14	2	4	4
	8	3	9	16	4	16	12
	9	4	16	15	3	9	12
N=9	45 (ΣX)	0 (Σx)	60 (Σx^2)	108 (ΣY)	0 (Σy)	60 (Σy^2)	57 (Σxy)

Mean values of X and Y:

$$\bar{X} = \frac{\Sigma X}{N} = \frac{45}{9} = 5$$

$$\bar{Y} = \frac{\Sigma Y}{N} = \frac{108}{9} = 12$$

Regression coefficients of X and Y:

$$b_{xy} = r\frac{\sigma_x}{\sigma_y} = \frac{\Sigma xy}{\Sigma y^2} = \frac{57}{60} = 0.95$$

$$b_{yx} = r\frac{\sigma_y}{\sigma_x} = \frac{\Sigma xy}{\Sigma x^2} = \frac{57}{60} = 0.95$$

Regression equation of X on Y:

$$X' = a_{xy} + b_{xy}Y$$

b_{xy} was calculated and it was 0.95

$$a_{xy} = \bar{X} - b_{xy}\bar{Y} = 5 - (0.95 \times 12)$$
$$= 5 - 11.4 = -6.4$$
$$\therefore X' = -6.4 + 0.95Y = 0.95Y - 6.4$$

Alternatively, regression equation of X on Y:

$$X - \bar{X} = r\frac{\sigma_x}{\sigma_y}(Y - \bar{Y}) = b_{xy}(Y - \bar{Y})$$

$$\text{or} \quad X - 5 = 0.95(Y - 12)$$
$$\text{or} \quad X - 5 = 0.95Y - 11.4$$
$$\text{or} \quad X = 0.95Y - 6.4$$

Regression equation of Y on X:

$$Y' = a_{yx} + b_{yx}X$$

b_{yx} was calculated and it was 0.95

$$a_{yx} = \bar{Y} - b_{yx}\bar{X} = 12 - (0.95 \times 5)$$
$$= 12 - 4.75 = 7.25$$
$$\therefore Y' = 7.25 + 0.95X = 0.95X + 7.25$$

Alternatively, regression equation of Y on X:

$$Y - \bar{Y} = r\frac{\sigma_y}{\sigma_x}(X - \bar{X}) = b_{yx}(X - \bar{X})$$

or $Y - 12 = 0.95(X - 5)$

or $Y - 12 = 0.95X - 4.75$

or $Y = 0.95X + 7.25$

Correlation coefficient (r): The correlation coefficient (r) is the under-root of the two regression coefficients, that is,

$$r = \sqrt{b_{xy} \times b_{yx}} = \sqrt{0.95 \times 0.95} = 0.95$$

Estimated value of Y when $X=6.2$ is:

$$Y' = 0.95X + 7.25 = (0.95 \times 6.2) + 7.25$$
$$= 5.89 + 7.25 = 13.14$$

Illustration 10.8 Find most likely price in Cuttack corresponding to price ₹75 at Kolkata from the following:

	Kolkata	Cuttack
Average Price	65	67
Standard Deviation	2.5	3.5

Correlation coefficient between the prices of commodities in two cities is 0.85 (BBA, Utkal University, 2008).

Solution
Since Cuttack price depends on Kolkata price, we denote Cuttack price by Y and Kolkata price by X, and fit a regression line of Y on X.

Given data: $\bar{X} = 65, \bar{Y} = 67, \sigma_x = 2.5, \sigma_y = 3.5$ and $r = 0.85$

Regression equation of Y on X:

$$Y' = a_{yx} + b_{yx}X$$

$$b_{yx} = r\frac{\sigma_y}{\sigma_x} = 0.85\frac{3.5}{2.5} = 0.85 \times 1.4 = 1.19$$

$$a_{yx} = \bar{Y} - b_{yx}\bar{X} = 67 - (1.19 \times 65) = 67 - 77.35 = -10.35$$

$$\therefore Y' = -10.35 + 1.19 \times 75 = -10.35 + 89.25 = 78.9$$

Alternatively,

$$Y' = \bar{Y} + b_{yx}(X - \bar{X})$$

$$b_{yx} = r\frac{\sigma_y}{\sigma_x} = 0.85\frac{3.5}{2.5} = 0.85 \times 1.4 = 1.19$$

$$\therefore Y' = 67 + 1.19(75 - 65)$$

$$= 67 + 1.19 \times 10 = 67 + 11.9 = 78.9$$

Alternatively,

$$Y - \bar{Y} = r\frac{\sigma_y}{\sigma_x}(X - \bar{X})$$

or $Y - 67 = 0.85\dfrac{3.5}{2.5}(75 - 65)$

or $Y - 67 = 0.85 \times 1.4(75 - 65)$

or $Y - 67 = 1.19 \times 10$

or $Y = 11.9 + 67 = 78.9$

Thus, the most likely price in Cuttack corresponding to price ₹75 at Kolkata is ₹78.9.

Illustration 10.9 The following results were obtained in the analysis of data on the yield of dry bark in ounces (Y) and age in years (X) of 200 cinchona plants.

	X	**Y**
Average	9.2	16.5
Standard Deviation	2.1	4.2

Coefficient of correlation = 0.8

Construct two lines of regression and estimate the yield of dry bark of a plant of age 8 years (BBA, Utkal University, 2007).

Solution

Given data: $\bar{X} = 9.2, \bar{Y} = 16.5, \sigma_x = 2.1, \sigma_y = 4.2$ and $r = 0.8$

Construction of two lines of regression:

(i)   Regression equation of X on Y:

$$X' = a_{xy} + b_{xy}Y$$

$$b_{xy} = r\frac{\sigma_x}{\sigma_y} = 0.8\frac{2.1}{4.2} = 0.8 \times 0.5 = 0.4$$

$$a_{xy} = \bar{X} - b_{xy}\bar{Y} = 9.2 - (0.4 \times 16.5)$$

$$= 9.2 - 6.6 = 2.6$$

$$\therefore X' = a_{xy} + b_{xy}Y = 2.6 + 0.4Y$$

(ii)   Regression equation of Y on X:

$$Y' = a_{yx} + b_{yx}X$$

$$b_{yx} = r\frac{\sigma_y}{\sigma_x} = 0.8\frac{4.2}{2.1} = 0.8 \times 2 = 1.6$$

$$a_{yx} = \bar{Y} - b_{yx}\bar{X} = 16.5 - (1.6 \times 9.2)$$

$$= 16.5 - 14.72 = 1.78$$

$$\therefore Y' = a_{y_x} + b_{y_x}X = 1.78 + 1.6X$$

(The students may apply other two alternative formulae, as used in Illustration 10.8, to find out these regression equations).

(iii)   Estimation of Y when $X = 8$:

$$\therefore Y' = 1.78 + (1.6 \times 8) = 1.78 + 12.8 = 14.58$$

Thus, the yield of dry bark of a plant of 8 years is 14.58 ounces.

Illustration 10.10 You are given the following information about advertising and sales:

	Advertising Expenditure (₹ in Lakh)	Sales (₹ in Lakh)
Mean	10	9
SD	3	12

Correlation coefficient: 0.8

(i)   Calculate two regression lines
(ii)   Find the likely sales when advertising expenditure is ₹15 lakh
(iii) What should be the advertising expenditure if the company wants to reach a sales target of ₹120 lakh?

(MBA, Kumaun University 1998; BBA, Utkal University, 2004).

Solution

Since sales depend on advertising, we denote sales by Y and advertising expenditure by X.

Given data: $\bar{X} = 10, \bar{Y} = 9, \sigma_x = 3, \sigma_y = 12$ and $r = 0.8$

(i)   Calculation of two regression lines:

(a)   Regression equation of X on Y:

$$X' = a_{xy} + b_{xy}Y$$

$$b_{xy} = r\frac{\sigma_x}{\sigma_y} = 0.8\frac{3}{12} = 0.8 \times 0.25 = 0.2$$

$$a_{xy} = \bar{X} - b_{xy}\bar{Y} = 10 - (0.2 \times 9)$$

$$= 10 - 1.8 = 8.2$$

$$\therefore X' = 8.2 + 0.2Y$$

(b)   Regression equation of Y on X:

$$Y' = a_{yx} + b_{yx}X$$

$$b_{yx} = r\frac{\sigma_y}{\sigma_x} = 0.8\frac{12}{3} = 0.8 \times 4 = 3.2$$

$$a_{yx} = \bar{Y} - b_{yx}\bar{X} = 9 - (3.2 \times 10)$$

$$= 9 - 32 = -23$$

$$\therefore Y' = -23 + 3.2X = 3.2X - 23$$

(ii)   For finding the likely sales when advertising expenditure is ₹15 lakh, we put $X=15$ in Equation (b).

$$Y' = 3.2X - 23 = (3.2 \times 15) - 23$$

$$= 48 - 23 = 25 \text{ lakh}$$

Thus, $Y_{15} = 25$ lakh

(iii)   For determining advertising expenditure for a sales target of ₹120 lakh, we put $Y=120$ in Equation (a).

$$X' = 8.2 + 0.2Y = 8.2 + (0.2 \times 120)$$

$$= 8.2 + 24 = 32.2 \text{ lakh}$$

Thus, $X_{120} = 32.2$ lakh

Summary

In this chapter, we have discussed the topic of regression. Regression is a form of prediction statistics. It predicts the most likely values of a variable (say, variable Y) on the basis of the specific values of another correlated variable (say, variable X). When there is a general linear relationship between two variables, X and Y, it is possible to construct a linear equation that allows us to predict the Y value corresponding to any known value of X, or vice versa. The linear equation generated by regression is called *regression equation*. There are two regression equations, and thus, two regression lines—one, the linear regression line of Y on X and another, the linear regression line of X on Y. By using the method of *least squares*, a best-fitting straight line that minimises the errors of prediction is constructed. This line is called *least-squares regression line*, which minimises the errors between the predicted values and the actual values of a variable (say, either Y or X variable). The accuracy of the prediction is measured by the SE of estimate, which provides a measure of the standard distance (or error) between the predicted value of a variable (say, variable Y) on the line and the actual data point.

Finally, we introduced the topic of multiple regressions, showing how using more than one predictor variable might result in increasing prediction accuracy and the proportion of the variance of Y that is accounted for by the relationship. The computational equations and formulae for simple regression and multiple regression were presented, and several practice problems worked out.

Key Terms

- Beta weights
- Bivariate statistics
- Least-squares regression line
- Linear regression
- Models of regression
- Multiple regression
- Partial regression coefficients

- Regression
- Regression analysis
- Regression coefficient
- Regression line
- Regression weights
- Regression of Y on X
- Regression of X on Y

Questions and Problems

1. Explain the term regression and state the difference between regression and correlation.
2. What do you mean by regression? Explain the relation of regression to correlation.
3. What is a regression line? Why are there generally two regression lines? Under what conditions can there be only one regression line?
4. What are regression coefficients? How are they computed?
5. What do you understand by regression? Differentiate between simple and multiple regressions.
6. Explain the following concepts:

   (a) Slope of a regression line
   (b) Y-intercept
   (c) X-intercept

7. Explain the concept of the standard error of estimate of the linear regression of Y on X. Can you express it in terms of a correlation coefficient? What is the standard error of estimating Y from X if $r=1$?
8. Explain the various models of regression.
9. Define regression. Enumerate the properties of simple linear regression.
10. Write notes on the followings:

    (a) Assumptions of simple linear regression
    (b) Principles of the least-squares regression method

11. What is multiple linear regression? When is it needed?
12. Explain the followings:

    (a) Multiple regression equation
    (b) Assumptions of linear multiple regression
    (c) Objectives of multiple regression

13. Find out the correct answer:

   (i) The coefficient of multiple correlation between X_2 on the one hand and X_1 and X_3 on the other is denoted by:

   (a) $R_{1.23}$

   (b) $R_{2.13}$

   (c) $R_{3.12}$

   (d) None of these

   (ii) In case of three variables, X_1, X_2 and X_3, there are:

   (a) Three partial correlation coefficients

   (b) Two partial correlation coefficients

   (c) Four partial correlation coefficients

   (d) None of these

   (iii) In multiple correlation analysis, there are at least:

   (a) Two variables

   (b) Three variables

   (c) Five variables

   (d) None of these

   (iv) $r_{13.2}$ means the coefficient of partial correlation between:

   (a) X_1 and X_2, keeping the effect of X_3 constant

   (b) X_2 and X_3, keeping the effect of X_1 constant

   (c) X_1 and X_3, keeping the effect of X_2 constant

   (d) None of these

   (v) $r_{12.4}$ is calculated as:

   (a) $\dfrac{r_{12}-(r_{14}r_{24})}{\sqrt{(1-r_{14}^2)(1-r_{24}^2)}}$

   (b) $\dfrac{r_{12}+(r_{14}r_{24})}{\sqrt{(1-r_{14}^2)(1-r_{24}^2)}}$

   (c) $\sqrt{\dfrac{r_{12}-(r_{14}r_{24})}{(1-r_{14}^2)(1-r_{24}^2)}}$

   (d) None of these

   (vi) In case of three variables, the multiple regression equation of X_1 on X_2 and X_3 has the form:

   (a) $X_{1.23}=a_{1.23}+b_{12.3}\,X_2+b_{13.2}\,X_3$

   (b) $X_{1.23}=a_{2.13}+b_{12.3}\,X_2-b_{13.2}\,X_3$

   (c) $X_{1.23}=a_{3.12}-b_{12.3}\,X_2-b_{13.2}\,X_3$

   (d) None of these

   (vii) $b_{12.3}$ is called the partial regression coefficient of:

   (a) X_2 on X_3, keeping X_1 constant

   (b) X_1 on X_2, keeping X_3 constant

   (c) X_1 on X_3, keeping X_2 constant

   (d) None of these

14. The following are paired measurements:

$$X:\ 1\ \ 5\ \ 6\ \ 6\ \ 2$$
$$Y:\ 2\ \ 4\ \ 5\ \ 3\ \ 1$$

Compute:

(a) The correlation between X and Y.

(b) The slope of the regression line for predicting Y from X.

(c) The Y-axis intercept for minimising error in predicting Y.

(d) The regression equation for predicting Y from X.

(e) The slope of the regression line for predicting X from Y.

(f) The X-axis intercept for minimising error in predicting X.

(g) The regression equation for predicting X from Y.

(h) The predicted values of Y corresponding to the given values of X.

(i) The variance of the errors of estimation in predicting Y from X.

(j) The predicted values of X corresponding to the given values of Y.

(k) The variance of the errors of estimation in predicting X from Y.

(l) The slope of the regression line for predicting a deviation score on Y from a deviation score on X.

(m) The Y-axis intercept for minimising error in predicting a deviation score on Y.

(n) The regression equation for predicting a deviation score on Y from the knowledge of a deviation score on X.

(o) The slope of the regression line for predicting a deviation score on X from a deviation score on Y.

(p) The X-axis intercept for minimising error in predicting a deviation score on X.

(q) The regression equation for predicting a deviation score on X from the knowledge of a deviation score on Y.

15. (a) Given the bivariate data:

X: 2 5 3 2 1 1 7 3
Y: 6 1 0 0 1 2 1 5

(i) Fit a regression line of Y on X, and then predict Y, when $X=10$.

(ii) Fit a regression line of X on Y, and then predict X, when $Y=2.5$.

(iii) Calculate Karl Pearson's correlation coefficient.

(b) Obtain the regression equations from the following data:

$N=50$, $\Sigma X=500$, $\Sigma Y=300$, $\Sigma X^2=5,450$, $\Sigma Y^2=2,000$, $\Sigma XY=3,090$

(c) For a bivariate data $\bar{X}=20$, $\bar{Y}=25$, $\sigma_x=5$, $\sigma_y=8$ and $r=0.7$
Find the regression equation of X on Y and estimate the value of X when Y is 30.

16. (a) You are given the following information about advertising and sales:

	Advertising Expenditure (₹ Lakh)		Sales (₹ Lakh)
Mean	10		9
SD	3		12
Correlation Coefficient		0.8	

(i)   Calculate two regression lines.

(ii) Find the likely sales when the advertising expenditure is ₹15 lakh.

(iii) What should be the advertising expenditure if the company wants to reach a sales target of ₹120 lakh?

(b) Given the following information:

	X		**Y**
Arithmetic Mean	6		8
Standard Deviation	5		40/3
Correlation Coefficient		$r=8/15$	

Find:

(i)   Two regression equations.

(ii) The most likely value of Y when $X=100$.

(c) The following results were obtained in the analysis of data on yield of dry bark in ounces (Y) and age in years (X) of 200 cinchona plants:

	X	**Y**
Average	9.2	16.5
Standard Deviation	2.1	4.2
Coefficient of Correlation	=0.8	

Construct two lines of regression and estimate the yield of dry bark of a plant of age 8 years.

(d) Find most likely price in Cuttack corresponding to price ₹75 at Kolkata from the following:

	Kolkata	**Cuttack**
Average Price	65	67
Standard Deviation	2.5	3.5

Correlation coefficient between the prices of commodities in two cities is 0.85

17. (a) Two random variables have the regression equations:

$$3X+2Y-26=0$$
$$6X+Y-31=0$$

Find the mean values of, and the correlation coefficient between X and Y. If the variance of $X=25$, find the standard deviation of Y from the data given.

(b) If the two regression lines are:

$$3X+12Y=19$$
$$3Y+9X=46$$

Then find out:

   (i)   Mean value of X and Y
   (ii) The value of correlation coefficient
   (iii) The ratio of variance of X and variance of Y

(c) The equations of two lines of regression obtained in a correlation analysis are the following:

$$2X+3Y-8=0$$
$$X+2Y-5=0$$

Obtain the value of the correlation coefficient and the variance of Y, given that the variance of X is 12.

(d) In a regression study the two regression lines are obtained as $2X-3Y+6=0$ and $4Y-5X-8=0$. Calculate means of X and Y. If the standard deviation of X is 3, determine the standard deviation of Y.

(e) The two regression equations are $3X-2Y+1=0$ and $3X-8Y+13=0$. Find the arithmetic means of X and Y.

18. (a) Given $b_{xy}=0.85$, $b_{yx}=0.89$ and the standard deviation of $X=6$, find the value of: r and σ_y.

(b) Find the regression coefficients of Y on X and X on Y from the following data.

$$\Sigma X = 50, \bar{X} = 5, \Sigma Y = 60, \bar{Y} = 6, \Sigma XY = 350.$$ Variance of $X=4$ and that of $Y=9$.

(c) The correlation coefficient between two variables X and Y is $r=0.6$.
   If $s_x = 1.5, s_y = 2.0, \bar{X} = 10$ and $\bar{Y} = 20,$ then find the regression lines of:

   (i) Y on X
   (ii) X on Y.

19. (a) Estimate:

   (i) the sale for advertising expenditure of ₹100 lakh and
   (ii) the advertisement expenditure for sales of ₹47 crores from the data given below:

Sales (₹ Crores)	14	16	18	20	24	30	32
Adv. Exp. (₹ Lakh)	52	62	65	70	76	80	78

(b) The following data gives the age of cars of a certain make and annual maintenance costs. Obtain the regression equation for costs related to age.

Age of cars (in years)	2	4	6	8
Maintenance costs (in hundreds of ₹)	10	20	25	30

20. (a) For the following set of data:
   (i) Calculate multiple regression plane of Y on X_1 and X_2.
   (ii) Predict Y for $X_1=36$ and $X_2=16$

Y	8	36	23	27	14	12
X_1	10	37	18	29	14	28
X_2	8	20	14	11	9	4

(b) Find the multiple linear regression equation of X_1 on X_2 and X_3 from the data relating to three variables given below. Also predict the value of X_1 when $X_2=10$ and $X_3=12$.

X_1	4	6	7	9	13	15
X_2	15	12	8	6	4	3
X_3	30	24	20	14	10	4

(c) Given the following, determine the regression of:
   (i) x_1 on x_2 and x_3 (ii) x_2 on x_1 and x_3

(Assume that x_1, x_2 and x_3 represent deviations from their respective means).

$$r_{12}=0.8, \quad r_{13}=0.6, \quad r_{23}=0.5$$
$$\sigma_1=10, \quad \sigma_2=8, \quad \sigma_3=5$$

(d) Compute the multiple linear regression of arithmetic reasoning test scores (X_1) on the combination of mechanical knowledge test scores (X_2) and numerical operation test scores (X_3), using the following data in a sample of 103 students.

$$\bar{X}_1 = 9.7, \quad \bar{X}_2 = 26.2, \quad \bar{X}_3 = 44.0$$
$$s_1=2.20, \quad s_2=6.60, \quad s_3=8.80$$
$$r_{12}=0.46, \quad r_{13}=0.35, \quad r_{23}=0.17$$

21. Fill in the blanks:

    (a) The under-root of two _____ coefficients gives the value of the correlation coefficient.

    (b) If both the regression coefficients are negative, the correlation coefficient would be _____.

    (c) Both the regression coefficients cannot _____ one.

    (d) The variable whose value is going to be predicted is called the _____ variable.

    (e) The variable whose value forms the basis of prediction is called the _____ variable.

    (f) The regression analysis helps us to study the _____ of the relationship between the variables.

    (g) The statistical technique, with the help of which we estimate the _____ value of one variable from the _____ value of another variable, is called _____ analysis.

    (h) Regression coefficient of Y on X is denoted by _____.

    (i) There are _____ types of regression equations.

    (j) b_{xy} denotes the regression coefficient of _____.

    (k) $r\dfrac{S_y}{S_x}$ is equal to _____ regression coefficient.

    (l) $r\dfrac{S_x}{S_y}$ is equal to _____ regression coefficient.

22. Find out the correct answer:

    (a) In a simple regression analysis there are:

        (i) Only two variables   (ii) More than two variables

        (iii) Less than two variables   (iv) None of these

    (b) The two regression lines cut each other at the point of average of:

        (i) Both X and Y (ii) X only

        (iii) Y only   (iv) None of these

    (c) The two regression lines coincide if:

        (i) r is zero   (ii) r is either +1.0 or –1.0

        (iii) r is very low   (iv) None of these

    (d) For a zero correlation the two regression lines have a:

        (i) 90° angular separation   (ii) 60° angular separation

        (iii) 30° angular separation   (iv) None of these

    (e) The regression line of Y on X minimises total of the squares of the:

        (i) Horizontal deviations

        (ii) Vertical deviations

(iii)   Both horizontal and vertical deviations

(iv)   None of these

(f)   When one regression coefficient is negative, the other would be:

(i)   Positive   (ii)   Negative

(iii)   Zero   (iv)   None of these

(g)   The regression line of Y on X passes through the potted points in such a manner that:

(i) $\sum(Y-Y_c)^2=0$ (ii) $\sum(Y-X_c)=0$

(iii) $\sum(Y-Y_c)=0$ (iv)   None of these

(h)   With $b_{xy}=0.5$, $r=0.8$ and variance of $Y=16$, the standard deviation of X equals to

(i)   2.5   (ii)   5.4

(iii)   10.0   (iv)   None of these

(i)   If the degree of relationship between two variables decreases, the angular separation between two regression lines:

(i)   Increases   (ii)   Decreases

(iii)   Both increases or decreases   (iv)   None of these

(j)   Perfect prediction is possible if the correlation coefficient between two variable is:

(i)   Perfect   (ii)   Low

(iii)   High   (iv)   None of these

(k)   Both the regression coefficients will have the:

(i)   Same signs   (ii)   Opposite signs

(iii)   Inverse signs   (iv)   None of these

(l)   If both the regression coefficients are negative, then r will be:

(i)   Positive   (ii)   Negative

(iii)   Positive or negative   (iv)   None of these

23.   Write whether the following statements are True or False.

(a)   Regression analysis reveals average relationship between two variables.

(b)   The term 'regression' was first used by Sir Francis Galton in 1877.

(c)   Regression coefficients are independent of the change of origin but not of scale.

(d)   The regression coefficient of Y on X is denoted by the symbol b_{xy}.

(e)   The regression coefficient of X on Y is denoted by the symbol b_{yx}.

(f)   The two regression lines cut each other at the point of average of X and Y.

(g)   In the regression equation 'a' and 'b' are called numerical constants.

(h) The correlation coefficients, r_{xy} and r_{yx}, are symmetric.
(i) The regression coefficients, b_{yx} and b_{xy}, are not symmetric.
(j) In regression equation of Y on X, Y is the independent variable and X is the dependent variable.
(k) In a regression equation of X on Y, X is the dependent variable and Y is the independent variable.
(l) If the standard error of estimate is zero, then there is no variation about the regression line and the correlation will be perfect.

CHAPTER 11

Significance of the Mean and Other Statistics

After completing this chapter you will be able to:

- Test the significance of a mean in small and large samples.
- Compute the standard error of a mean in small and large samples.
- Determine the confidence intervals of a mean in small and large samples.
- Understand the nature of the t distribution.
- Differentiate between the t distribution and the normal distribution.
- Determine the degrees of freedom (df) associated with a t-test for a single sample.
- Understand the process of determining the significance of a small sample mean.
- Compute the standard error of a median, a standard deviation (SD), a quartile deviation, a percentage/proportion and of a correlation coefficient.
- Understand the significance of a single median, SD, quartile deviation, percentage/proportion and correlation coefficient.

11.1 Introduction

In behavioural sciences, we have to compute the mean and several other parameters for studying the characteristics of certain populations. But many times it is neither feasible nor practicable to study each and every element of the population. For example, if we want to know the average height of Indian women of 20 years of age, then we have to approach all the young women of 20 years of age, measure their heights and calculate the mean/average. This average is the true value of the desired population mean. But to do so is not a simple task. It is quite impracticable. Therefore, a convenient as well as a practical solution to this above problem lies in estimating the population mean from the sample means. Here, we must take a true representative sample of an appropriate size. Suppose we have selected randomly 100 such samples. Then we have to measure their height and calculate the mean which may yield the desired average height of the targeted population. Thus, the primary objective of a *statistical inference* is to enable us to generalise from a sample to some large population of which the sample is a part.

The mean, median, standard deviation (SD) and other measures computed from samples are called *statistics* which are subjected to 'fluctuations of sampling'. Measures which are directly computed from population, on the other hand, are called parameters, which are to be thought of as fixed reference values. Because the statistics are subjected to 'fluctuations of sampling', sometimes they will tend to be larger and sometimes smaller than the parameters. However, the statistics computed from the samples may be used to draw inferences and estimates about the parameters of the parent population from which the samples are drawn. In an ideal situation, we expect any sample statistic to give a true estimate of the population parameter. The degree to which a sample mean (or other statistics) represents its parameter is an *index of the significance* or trustworthiness of the computed sample mean. Therefore, when we have calculated a statistic, we may ask ourselves this question: How good an estimate is this statistic of the parameter based upon the entire parent population from which our samples were drawn? The purpose of this chapter is to provide methods which will enable us to answer this question for the mean, median and for other statistics.

11.2   Significance of the Mean in Large Samples

11.2.1   The Standard Error of the Mean (SE_m or σ_m) in Large Samples

The degree to which a sample mean approximates its parameter depends upon how impartially and randomly we have drawn our samples from the population. Given a random sample, that is to say, a cross-section of the population, the representativeness of a sample mean can be shown to depend mathematically upon two characteristics of the distribution: (a) N, the number of cases and (b) σ, the variability or spread of scores around the mean. For example, let us assume that we have the knowledge of the true mean (i.e., mean of the population). Further, suppose that we have taken 100 representative samples of size 40 each from the population and have computed their respective sample means. If we analyse the distribution of these sample means, we will find that a majority of these sample means are clustered around the population mean (μ), and in the case of a large sample (i.e., $N \geq 30$), the distribution will be found to be normal as shown in Figure 11.1.

The mean of the sample means will be a fairly good or somewhat true estimate of the population mean. Some of these sample means will deviate seriously from the population mean either on the positive or the negative side of the curve while most of them will show negligible divergence.

The measure of dispersion or variability of these sample means from their respective individual scores may also be calculated in the form of SDs (s). Moreover, in an ideal case a sample mean must represent the population mean or true mean, but in application, a sample mean is likely to differ from its parameter or true value. This difference is known as sampling error that may occur in estimating the population mean (or true mean) from a given sample mean, that is, ($\bar{X} - \mu$). The curve representing the distribution of sample means possessing lesser or greater error (i.e., negative or positive error) of estimation for the population mean is called the curve of the error, and SD of this distribution of the sample means is known as the standard error of the mean (SE_m or σ_m). In a large sample, the formula for the standard error of mean is

$$SE_m \text{ or } \sigma_m = \frac{\sigma}{\sqrt{N}},$$

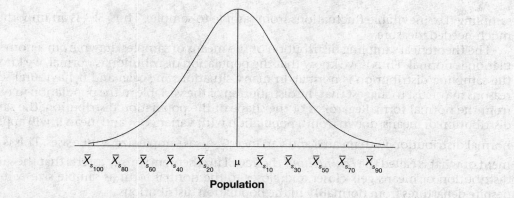

Figure 11.1 Normal distribution of sample means $(\bar{X}_s)$

where

$\sigma=$ the SD of the population

$N=$ the number of cases in the sample.

In the above formula for the SE_m, the σ in the numerator is actually the population SD, but not the sample SD. In practice, σ is usually unknown and is replaced by the sample SD which is designated by s. Therefore, the standard error of the mean is estimated by the formula

$$s_{\bar{X}} = \frac{s}{\sqrt{N}}.$$

This is the formula in common use for estimating the standard error of the mean. But to get a better approximation to the population σ, we should compute SD of a sample by the formula $s = \sqrt{\dfrac{\Sigma x^2}{N-1}}$ instead of by the usual formula $SD = \sqrt{\dfrac{\Sigma x^2}{N}}$.

In the social and behavioural sciences, we may generally omit this correction, as our samples are usually so large that the subtraction of 1 from N makes no appreciable difference in the computed SD. Whenever N is 'large' (it is conventional to call any sample greater than 30 large), it is not worthwhile making the correction. But when N is 'small' (less than 30), it is advisable to use $N-1$, and it is imperative when N is quite small, say less than about 10. The student must remember (a) that theoretically $N-1$ should always be used when the SD is to be an estimate of the population σ and (b) that the distinction between 'large sample statistics' and 'small sample statistics' in terms of a cutting point of $N=30$ is arbitrary, and is in part a matter of convenience.

Examination of the formula $\sigma_m = \dfrac{\sigma}{\sqrt{N}}$ indicates that the standard error of the mean is directly related to the SD of the population and inversely related to the size of the sample. Thus, the greater the variation of the variable in the population, the greater the standard error; also, the larger the size of N, the smaller the standard error. Similarly, the examination of the formula $s_{\bar{X}} = \dfrac{s}{\sqrt{N}}$ indicates that the SE_m varies directly with the amount of the sample SD (or s) and inversely with the sample size N. As it is difficult to influence the amount of the sample SD, our best chance of decreasing the σ_m or $s_{\bar{X}}$ lies in increasing the sample size N. The SE_m measures the degree to which the mean is affected by both errors of measurement and errors of sampling (i.e., inevitable fluctuations from sample to sample). Thus, SE_m is an important and much-needed measure.

The theoretical sampling distribution of the means of samples drawn from a normal population is normal. Thus if we know that the population distribution is normal, we know that the sampling distribution is normal. In many situations in social and behavioural sciences, reasons may exist to suggest that the distribution of the variable in the population may depart from the normal form. Regardless of the shape of the population distribution, the sampling distribution of means, drawn from a population with variance σ^2 and mean μ, will approach a normal distribution with mean μ and variance σ^2/N as sample size N increases. This is a statement of what is called the *central-limit theorem*. This theorem simply asserts that the sampling distribution of means gets closer and closer to the normal form as sample size N increases despite departures from normality in the population distributions.

11.2.2   Confidence Intervals for Means in Large Samples

As we have discussed earlier, a sample mean is employed to estimate the population mean. In the real sense, it is very difficult to say categorically that a sample mean is or is not a dependable and trustworthy estimate of the population mean. We can only give the probability of a given divergence. We know that all the sample means drawn from the same population deviate in one way or other from the population mean and the distribution of these sample means, in the case of large samples ($N>30$), is a normal distribution. The standard error of the mean (SE_m) represents a measure by which the sample means deviate from the overall population mean. Now the question arises as to how much should a sample mean miss the population mean so that it may be taken as a good or trustworthy estimate of the population mean. The answer to this question lies in the setting up of limits of the confidence intervals fixed on the basis of the degree of confidence or trustworthiness required in a particular situation.

In statistics usually we make use of 0.95 (or 0.05) and 0.99 (or 0.01) percentage of probability as the two well-known degrees of confidence for specifying the interval within which we may assert the existence of the population mean. In the case of the normal distribution, we know from the table of normal curve (see Table A in the appendix) that 95% of cases lie within the limits $M \pm 1.96\sigma$ and 99% of cases lie within the limits $M \pm 2.58\sigma$. (For more details, see Chapter 7.) Hence, we can say that the chances are 95 in 100 that the population mean (μ) lies between $\bar{X} \pm 1.96 s_{\bar{x}}$ (or $M \pm 1.96\sigma_m$); thus the upper limit is 1.96 standard error units above the sample mean and the lower limit is 1.96 standard error units below the sample mean. Similarly, there are only 5 chances in 100 that the population means will fall beyond the limits $\bar{X} \pm 1.96 s_{\bar{x}}$.

For greater assurance, we may go for the 0.99 confidence level which states that the chances are 99 in 100 that the population mean falls between $\bar{X} \pm 2.58 s_{\bar{x}}$; thus, the upper limit is 2.58 standard error units above the sample mean and the lower limit is 2.58 standard error units below the sample mean. Likewise, there is only 1 chance in 100 that the population means will fall beyond the limits $\bar{X} \pm 2.58 s_{\bar{x}}$.

The values in terms of scores of the limits $\bar{X} \pm 1.96 s_{\bar{x}}$ and $\bar{X} \pm 2.58 s_{\bar{x}}$ are called confidence limits and the intervals they contain are called confidence intervals for a known or fixed degree or level of confidence, such as the 0.95 or 0.99 confidence levels. The levels of confidence of 0.95 confidence interval and 0.99 confidence interval are also expressed in probabilities like $p=0.95$ and $p=0.99$, respectively. However, in this text, we will be using the terms 5% ($p=0.05$) and 1% ($p=0.01$) levels of confidence in defining the limits, respectively, $\bar{X} \pm 1.96 s_{\bar{x}}$ and $\bar{X} \pm 2.58 s_{\bar{x}}$ beyond which the population mean may be estimated to lie. At the 5% level of confidence, we will say that our population mean may lie within the range of $\bar{X} \pm 1.96 s_{\bar{x}}$, and at the 1% level of confidence, we will say that the population mean may lie within the range $\bar{X} \pm 2.58 s_{\bar{x}}$.

The limits of the confidence interval of a parameter were called by Fisher (1935) the fiduciary limits and the confidence placed in the interval defined by the limits as containing the parameter is called the fiduciary probability. In terms of fiduciary probability, the 0.95 confidence interval would be described as follows. 'The fiduciary probability is 0.95 that population means (M_{pop}) lie within the interval $M \pm 1.96\sigma_m$, and 0.05 that it falls outside of these limits'. Likewise, in terms of the fiduciary probability, the 0.99 confidence interval would be described as follows. 'The fiduciary probability is 0.99 that M_{pop} lies within the interval $M \pm 2.58\sigma_m$, and 0.01 that it falls outside of these limits.'

11.2.3   Computation of Significance of Means in Large Samples

The following example will serve to illustrate the computation and interpretation of SE of the mean ($s_{\bar{x}}$) in large samples.

Example 11.1 The mean on a test of abstract reasoning for 250 students of the first year of Class 12 in Bhubaneswar city was 28.50 with an SD of 4.50. How dependable is this mean? Specifically, how good an estimate is it of the mean which could be expected if all of the first year students of Class 12 in Bhubaneswar city were tested?

Solution

(a)   Given $\bar{X} = 28.50$; SD (s) = 4.50; $N = 250$, the standard error of the mean ($s_{\bar{x}}$) is computed by the following formula that reads:

$$s_{\bar{x}} = \frac{s}{\sqrt{N}} = \frac{4.50}{\sqrt{250}} = \frac{4.50}{15.81} = 0.28 \quad \text{(rounded to two decimals)}.$$

(b)   Then the 0.95 and 0.99 confidence intervals are computed as follows:

(i)   0.95 confidence interval:

$$\bar{X} \pm 1.96s_{\bar{x}} = 28.50 \pm 1.96 \times 0.28$$
$$= 28.50 \pm 0.55 = 27.95 - 29.05$$

Hence, $27.95 \leq \mu \leq 29.05$. This means that we are 95% confident that the population mean lies between 27.95 and 29.05.

This shows that 95 in 100 sample means lie within $\pm 1.96\sigma_m$ of the population mean–miss the population mean by $\pm 1.96 \times 0.28$ or ± 0.55. In other words, the expectation is high (the probability is 0.95) that our sample mean of 28.50 will not miss the population mean (μ) by more than ± 0.55. Conversely, the probability is low ($p = 0.05$) that the sample mean of 28.50 does miss the parameter (the population mean) by more than ± 0.55. Both of these statements express the dependability of the sample mean in terms of the degree to which it estimates accurately the population mean.

(ii)   0.99 confidence interval:

$$\bar{X} \pm 2.58s_{\bar{x}} = 28.50 \pm 2.58 \times 0.28$$
$$= 28.50 \pm 0.72 = 27.78 - 29.22.$$

Hence, $27.78 \leq \mu \leq 29.22$. This means that we are 99% confident that the population mean lies between 27.78 and 29.22.

This shows that 99 in 100 sample means lie within $\pm 2.58\sigma_m$ of the population mean—miss the population mean by $\pm 2.58 \times 0.28$ or ± 0.72. Here, the expectation is high ($p = 0.99$) that our sample mean of 28.50 will not miss the population mean by more than ± 0.72. Conversely, the probability is low ($p = 0.01$) that the sample mean of 28.50 does miss the population mean by more than ± 0.72. Both of these statements express the dependability of the sample mean in terms of degree to which it estimates accurately the population mean.

Example 11.2 The mean and SD of a sample of 144 boys in a test of numerical ability are 50 and 6, respectively.

(i)   Determine the 95% and 99% intervals for the population mean and interpret them.
(ii) Determine the acceptable sampling error at the 0.05 and 0.01 levels of significance.
(iii) It is unlikely that the true mean is larger than what values at 0.95 interval and at 0.99 interval.

Solution Given, $N = 144$, $\bar{X} = 50$, $SD = s = 6.0$, the standard error of mean can be computed as follows:

$$s_{\bar{x}} = \frac{s}{\sqrt{N}} = \frac{6.0}{\sqrt{144}} = \frac{6.0}{12} = 0.50.$$

(i)   95% confidence interval for population mean (μ) ranges between $\bar{X} \pm 1.96 s_{\bar{x}}$. Therefore, the limits of the interval are: $50 \pm 1.96 \times 0.50 = 50 \pm 0.98 = 49.02 - 50.98$.
      Thus, 95% confidence interval for μ ranges from 49.02 to 50.98. From the sample mean ($\bar{X}$) of 50, we estimate the μ to be some fixed value in between 49.02 and 50.98, and in saying so we are 95% confident. In other words, our sample mean of 50 will not miss the population mean by more than 0.98, and this will be true for 95 cases in 100. Alternatively, only in 5 cases in 100 our sample mean of 50 will miss the population mean by more than 0.98.
      Similarly, 99% confidence interval for μ ranges between $\bar{X} \pm 2.58 s_{\bar{x}}$. Therefore, the limits of the interval are as follows: $50 \pm 2.58 \times 0.50 = 50 \pm 1.29 = 48.71 - 51.29$. Thus, the 99% confidence interval for μ ranges from 48.71 to 51.29. From the $\bar{X}$ of 50, we estimate the μ to be some fixed value in between 48.71 and 51.29, and in saying so we are 99% confident. In other words, our $\bar{X}$ of 50 will not miss the μ by more than 1.29, and this will be true for 99 cases in 100. Alternatively, only in 1 case in 100, our $\bar{X}$ of 50 will miss the μ by more than 1.29.

(ii) Critical values at the 0.05 level of significance = 1.96
      Critical values at the 0.01 level of significance = 2.58
      Sampling error = critical value × standard error of mean.
      Thus, the sampling error at the 0.05 level of significance is $1.96 s_{\bar{x}}$ and at the 0.01 level of significance is $2.58 s_{\bar{x}}$.
      An acceptable sampling error at the 0.05 level = $1.96 s_{\bar{x}} = 1.96 \times 0.50 = 0.98$.
      An acceptable sampling error at the 0.01 level = $2.58 s_{\bar{x}} = 2.58 \times 0.50 = 1.29$.

(iii) At the 0.95 confidence interval, our $\bar{X}$ of 50 will not miss the true mean (or population mean) by more than 0.98, that is, the true mean is not larger than 50.98. Similarly, at the 0.99 confidence interval our $\bar{X}$ of 50 will not miss the true mean by more than 1.29, that is, the true mean is not larger than 51.29.

11.3 Significance of the Mean in Small Samples

11.3.1 The Standard Error of the Mean ($s_{\bar{x}}$) in Small Samples

We usually take a sample of 30 cases or more as a large sample, and a sample of less than 30 as a small sample. In case of the small ($N < 30$), the formula for the standard error of the mean ($s_{\bar{x}}$) should read

$$\text{SE}_m \quad \text{or} \quad s_{\bar{X}} = \frac{s}{\sqrt{N}},$$

where

$s =$ SD of the sample mean
$N =$ size of sample.

In this case, the value of s is calculated using the formula as follows:

$$s = \sqrt{\frac{\Sigma x^2}{N-1}}$$

where
$x =$ deviation score from the mean, (i.e., $X - \bar{X}$) instead of the formula

$$\sigma = \sqrt{\frac{\Sigma x^2}{N}}$$

which is used for computing SD in the case of the large sample.

11.3.2 The *t* Distribution

We have seen that the distribution of means of large samples randomly drawn from the population is normal (see Figure 11.1). However, when samples are small, the distribution does not take the shape of a normal curve. Therefore, the significance of the mean of a small sample can be tested in terms of a *t* distribution rather than a normal distribution. The equation for the *t*-test is

$$t = \frac{\bar{X} - \mu}{s_{\bar{X}}}.$$

This ratio contains the variable sample value $\bar{X}$ and $s_{\bar{x}}$ in the numerator and denominator, respectively. This is called a *t* ratio. It departs appreciably from the normal form for small *N*. Its theoretical sampling distribution is called the distribution of *t*. It was originally developed by Gossett in 1908 who wrote under the pen name 'Student'. The *t* distribution is frequently referred to as Student's distribution. Student's *t*-test is a practical, quite powerful test widely used in the behavioural sciences. The *t*-test is very similar to the *z*-test.

The sampling distribution of *t* is a probability distribution of the *t* values that would occur if all possible different samples of a fixed size *N* were drawn randomly from the population. It gives all the possible different '*t*' values for samples of size *N*, and the probability of getting each value if sampling is random from the population. If 100 samples of, say, 5 members each, were randomly drawn from a population, $\bar{X}$ and $s_{\bar{x}}$ calculated for each sample, and 100 values of t obtained, the frequency distribution of these 100 values of t would not be normal. It would be a symmetrical distribution with somewhat thicker tails than the normal distribution.

The following points are some of the important differences between the t distribution and the normal distribution (i.e., z distribution):

(a) The distribution of t is symmetrical about zero with somewhat thicker tails than the normal distribution. In other words, the t distribution is symmetrical but leptokurtic; it becomes more peaked in the middle and has relatively more area in its tails compared to the normal curve.

(b) The theoretical sampling distribution of t for small N is a symmetrical distribution and is thicker at the extremities than the corresponding normal curve. It tapers off to infinity at the two extremities.

(c) When N is small, the t distribution lies under the normal curve, but the tails or ends of the curve are higher than the corresponding parts of the normal curve.

(d) The t distribution does not differ greatly from the normal unless N is quite small; and as N increases in size, the t distribution approaches more and more closely to the normal form.

(e) In contrast to a single normal distribution (or z distribution), the distribution of t is not a single distribution but is a family of distributions. A different t distribution exists for each number of df. As the number of df increases, the t distribution approaches the normal form. Theoretically, when df$=\infty$, the t distribution is identical to the z distribution. It is because of the fact that as the df increase, sample size (N) increases, and the estimate s gets closer to σ. At any df other than ∞, the t distribution has more extreme t values than the z distribution, since there is more variability in t, due to using s to estimate σ. Another way of saying this is that the tails of the t distribution are elevated relative to the z distribution. Thus, for a given alpha level (i.e., the level of significance), the critical value of t is higher than that for z, making the t-test less sensitive than the z-test. That is, for any alpha level, the obtained t value (t_{obt}) must be higher than the obtained z value (z_{obt}) to reject the null hypothesis.

(f) In the normal distribution 95% of the total area under the curve falls within plus and minus 1.96 SD units from the mean (i.e., $\mu \pm 1.96\sigma$) and 5% of the area falls outside these limits. Likewise, 99% of the area under the normal curve falls within plus and minus 2.58 SD units from the mean (i.e., $\mu \pm 2.58\sigma$) and 1% of the area falls outside these limits. In the t distribution, the distances along the baseline of the curve that include 95% and 99% of the total area are different to different numbers of df. It is customary in tabulating areas under the t curve to use df instead of N. Consequently, tables of t by df instead of N are more generally applicable. A more complete tabulation of t with different df is given in Table C of the appendix. Note that as the number of df approaches infinity, t approaches the values 1.96 and 2.58, respectively, at the 5% and 1% levels of confidence, just like the normal curve. The difference between t for about 30 df and t for an indefinitely large number of df is sometimes interpreted for practical purposes as trivial. Therefore, a distinction is often made between large sample and small sample statistics. This distinction resides in the fact that the normal distribution (or z distribution) is frequently found to be an appropriate model for use with sampling problems involving large samples. With small samples, the distribution of t provides for many statistics a more appropriate model.

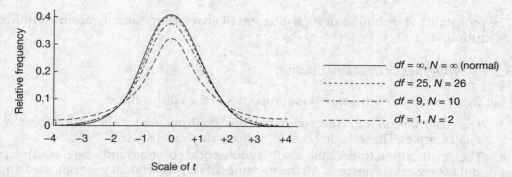

Figure 11.2   Distribution of *t* for various degrees of freedom from 1 to ∞. When df is very large, the distribution of *t* is virtually normal

Figure 11.2 compares the normal distribution with the *t* distribution for various df.

The *t*-distribution curve (Figure 11.2) can be plotted theoretically, using Gossett's equation in computing from each *t* score the height of the ordinate *Y* giving the probability of that *t* score. When Y_0 is a constant for a sample depending on the df and π is the ratio between the circumference and the diameter of a circle, the equation expresses *Y* as a function of *t* in the following manner:

$$Y_0 = \frac{[(df-1)/2]!}{[(df-2)/2]!} \times \frac{1}{\sqrt{\pi\,df}};$$

$$Y = \frac{Y_0}{\left[1+\dfrac{t^2}{df}\right]^{(df+1)/2}}.$$

The difference between two sample means can be transformed into a *t* score by dividing the deviation of that difference from the difference between the corresponding population means, with the SE of the difference between those means. When $\bar{X}_1$ and $\bar{X}_2$ are the means of two samples drawn from two normally distributed populations having μ_1 and μ_2 as the respective parametric means, $s_{\bar{X}_1-\bar{X}_2}$ is the SE of difference between $\bar{X}_1$ and $\bar{X}_2$, $\hat{s}$ is the pooled or common SD of the two sample means, and N_1 and N_2 are the respective sample sizes.

The following are the formulae for computing t, $\hat{s}$ and $s_{\bar{X}_1-\bar{X}_2}$:

$$t = \frac{(\bar{X}_1 - \bar{X}_2)-(\mu_1 - \mu_2)}{s_{\bar{X}_1-\bar{X}_2}}.$$

If the samples have been drawn from the same population, then $\mu_1 = \mu_2$ and the formula for computing *t* becomes

$$t = \frac{\bar{X}_1 - \bar{X}_2}{s_{\bar{X}_1-\bar{X}_2}},$$

$$\hat{s} = \sqrt{\frac{\Sigma(X_1 - \bar{X}_1)^2 + \Sigma(X_2 - \bar{X}_2)^2}{(N_1 -1)+(N_2 -1)}} = \sqrt{\frac{\Sigma x_1^2 + \Sigma x_2^2}{N_1 + N_2 - 2}},$$

$$s_{\bar{X}_1-\bar{X}_2} = \hat{s}\sqrt{\frac{N_1 + N_2}{N_1 N_2}} = \hat{s}\sqrt{\frac{1}{N_1} + \frac{1}{N_2}}.$$

The probability distribution of such difference between two sample means conforms to the *t* distribution.

11.3.2.1   *Properties of the t Distribution*

The following are some of the important properties of the *t* distribution.

   (i)   The *t* distribution is the theoretical model of continuous probability distributions for small samples. The statistic *t* is, thus, a small sample statistic.
   (ii)   The *t* distribution forms a bilaterally symmetrical curve around a single central peak and possesses no skewness. All the measures of central tendency—mean, median and mode—coincide with the centre. Thus, the *t* distribution has a mean of 0. The SD of the distribution amounts to $\sqrt{N/(N-2)}$, where $N-2$ is a positive integer.
   (iii)   The *t* distribution looks like a bell-shaped curve. But its distribution is more variable with zero skewness and kurtosis greater than 3.
   (iv)   The *t* distribution is symmetrical about the line $t=0$. It is unimodal with maximum ordinate at $t=0$.
   (v)   When *N* is small, the *t* distribution lies under the normal curve, but the tails or ends of the curve are higher than the corresponding parts of the normal curve.
   (vi)   The units along the baseline of *t* distribution are actually the sigma (σ) scores, that is,

$$t = \frac{\bar{X} - \mu}{s_{\bar{X}}}.$$

   (vii)   It is evident from Figure 11.2 that there are numerous *t* distributions for different df. With the increase in df (and hence, in the sample size), the *t* distribution progressively approaches the normal distribution in shape; there are negligible differences between the two distributions when *N* equals or exceeds 30, and almost no difference when *N* approaches ∞. Thus, for large samples, the equation for the *t* distribution resembles the one for the unit normal curve:

$$Y = \frac{1}{\sqrt{2\pi}} e^{-t^2/2}.$$

Hence, though a small-sample statistic, *t* is applicable even to large samples because of the close identity of normal and *t* distributions for large samples.
   (viii)   In contrast to the normal distribution, *t* distributions are *leptokurtic*. The leptokurtosis increases with the decrease in the df and hence with the decrement of the sample size. When df approaches infinity (∞), the *t* distribution becomes mesokurtic and coincides with the normal distribution.
   (ix)   Like the normal distribution, *t* distributions are asymptotic with their tails or ends extending to −∞ and +∞.
   (x)   Since probability distributions are showing relative frequencies, the total area under any *t* distribution curve, representing the total frequency *N*, is taken as 1.0.
   (xi)   The fractional area of a *t*-distribution curve between the ordinates at any two *t* scores on the *X*-axis gives the proportion of the total cases which falls between those given *t* scores. However, as *t* distributions vary in shape according to the number of df, such

a distance or range between two t scores along the X-axis that includes a specific fractional area like 0.95 and 0.99 varies with the df.

(xii)   When a t score has been computed for the difference between two sample means, the sum of the fractional areas of the relevant t distribution in its two tails, beyond, respectively, the negative and positive values of the computed t, gives the probability (p) of obtaining by mere chance the observed magnitude of difference between the sample means, irrespective of the algebraic sign of the difference.

(xiii)   A critical t score (t_a) is the highest t score with a given df, up to which the observed results (e.g., an observed difference between two sample means) have a specified probability (p) of occurring by mere chance. The t distributions have wide applications in finding the significance of the observed results and in computing the confidence intervals of population means.

11.3.3   Degrees of Freedom (df)

Although the t distribution varies with the sample size, Gossett found that it varies *uniquely* with the df associated with t, rather than simply with sample size. Though, earlier we made some references of the number of df, this concept requires further elaboration.

The df for any statistic is the number of scores that are free to vary in calculating that statistic. For example, there are N df associated with the mean. For any set of scores, N is given. If there are three scores and we know the first two scores, the last score can take on any value. It has no restrictions on it. There is no way to tell what it must be by knowing the other two scores. The same is true for the first two scores. Thus, all three scores are free to vary when calculating the mean. Thus, there are N df for calculating mean.

In contrast, the df for calculating the SD (s) is $N-1$. Let us consider three raw scores like 6, 8 and 16. The mean is 10.0. These raw scores, when represented as deviations from a mean of 10, become -4, -2 and $+6$. The sum of these deviations is zero. In consequence, if any two deviations are known, the remaining deviation is determined. Therefore, only two of the three deviation scores are free to vary. Whatever values these take, the third is fixed. In calculating s, only $N-1$ deviation scores are free to vary. Thus, there are $N-1$ df associated with the SD.

In calculating t for a single sample, we must first calculate s. Since we lose 1 df in calculating s, there are $N-1$ df associated with t. Thus, for the t-test df $= N-1$.

However, the df is not always $N-1$ in all cases. It varies with the nature of the problem and the restrictions imposed on it. For example, in case of correlation between two variables where we need to compute deviations from two means, the number of restrictions imposed goes up to two, and consequently the df becomes $N-2$. Similarly, the equation of a straight line is $Y' = b X + a$, where b is the slope of the line and a is the Y intercept. Both b and a are estimated from the data. It may be said that 2 df are lost in estimating b and a from the data. Thus, in single linear regression, the df is $N-2$. Likewise, in first-order partial r and in second-order partial r, the number of df are $N-3$ and $N-4$, respectively. Moreover, in case of analysis of variance and contingency tables of chi-square (χ^2), we may have some other different formulae for the computation of the number of df (those will be discussed later on). However, in all cases, we will always have a common feature conveying that the number of observations or values in a given data minus the number of restrictions imposed upon this data constitute the number of df for the data. Thus,

Number of degrees of freedom = Number of observations or
value – Number of restrictions.

11.3.4 Confidence Intervals of Means for Small Samples

The line of reasoning used in determining confidence intervals for small samples is similar to that for large samples. However, with small samples, the t distribution is used instead of the normal distribution in fixing the limits of the interval. For large samples, the 95% and 99% confidence intervals for the mean are given, respectively, by $\bar{X} \pm 1.96 s_{\bar{x}}$ and $\bar{X} \pm 2.58 s_{\bar{x}}$. For small samples, an unbiased estimate of σ^2 is used in estimating the standard error ($s_{\bar{x}}$). Thus, the standard error using the unbiased variance estimate is $s_{\bar{x}} = \dfrac{s}{\sqrt{N}}$. The value of t used in fixing the limits of the 95% and 99% intervals will vary, depending on the number of df. Let us consider an example where $\bar{X} = 25.80$, $s = 8.0$, $N = 16$ and df $= N - 1 = 16 - 1 = 15$. In reference to Table C of the appendix, we observe that for 15 df, 95% of the area of the t distribution falls within a t of ± 2.13 from the mean. The standard error is $s_{\bar{x}} = \dfrac{8}{\sqrt{16}} = \dfrac{8}{4} = 2.0$. Thus, the 95% confidence limits are given by $\bar{X} \pm 2.13 s_{\bar{x}} = 25.80 \pm 2.13 \times 2 = 25.80 \pm 4.26$. These limits are 21.54 and 30.06. We may assert with 95% confidence that the population mean falls within these limits. Hence, $21.54 \leq \mu \leq 30.06$.

Similarly, with 15 df, 99% of the area of the t distribution falls within a t of ± 2.95 from the mean. Thus, the 99% confidence limits are $\bar{X} \pm 2.95 s_{\bar{x}} = 25.80 \pm 2.95 \times 2.0 = 25.80 \pm 5.90 = 19.90$ and 31.70. We may assert with 99% confidence that the population mean lies within these limits. Hence, $19.90 \leq \mu \leq 31.70$.

11.3.5 Process of Determining the Significance of Small Sample Means

The entire procedure may be summarised under the following steps:

(i) **Determining the standard error of the mean.** In the case of the small samples ($N < 30$), the standard error of the mean ($s_{\bar{x}}$) is computed by the formula that reads

$$\text{SE}_\text{m} \quad \text{or} \quad s_{\bar{x}} = \frac{s}{\sqrt{N}}$$

where s is the SD of the sample mean and N is the sample size.

(ii) **Use of the t distribution instead of the normal distribution.** As we have discussed earlier, the distribution of sample means in the case of small samples takes the shape of a t distribution instead of a normal distribution. Therefore, we will try to make use of the t distribution.

(iii) **Determining the degrees of freedom.** As we know, the shape of a t distribution depends upon the number of df. The number of df thus has to be determined by using the formula, df $= N-1$, where N stands for the number of cases in the sample.

(iv) **Using the t-distribution table.** Like the normal distribution table, the t-distribution table is also available. Table C given in the appendix represents such a table. From this table, we can read the value of t for the given df at the specific level of probability (i.e., at 5% or 1%) decided at the beginning of the experiment or data collection.

(v) **Determining the confidence interval.** After finding the critical values of t from Table C given in the appendix at the 5% and 1% levels of confidence with known df, we may proceed to determine the limits of the confidence interval for the population mean, with 95% and 99% confidence, through the procedures as described earlier.

Let us illustrate the above process through an example.

Example 11.3 In a particular test, 16 independent observations were taken with a mean of 50.0 and SD of 10.0. Determine the 0.95 and 0.99 confidence intervals for the population mean.

Solution

(a)   Given the data: $N = 16$, $\bar{X} = 50.0$ and SD or $s = 10.0$, the standard error of the mean ($s_{\bar{x}}$) is computed by the following formula:

$$s_{\bar{X}} = \frac{s}{\sqrt{N}} = \frac{10.0}{\sqrt{16}} = \frac{10.0}{4} = 2.5.$$

(b)   The number of df is

$$df = N - 1 = 16 - 1 = 15.$$

(c)   The critical values of t will be determined from Table C given in the appendix with $df = 15$ for the 0.05 and 0.01 levels of significance. These values are 2.13 and 2.95, respectively.

(d)   Then, the 0.95 and 0.99 confidence intervals are determined as follows:

(i)   The 0.95 confidence interval:

$$\bar{X} \pm 2.13 s_{\bar{x}} = 50.0 \pm 2.13 \times 2.50$$
$$= 50.0 \pm 5.32 = 44.68 \text{ and } 55.32$$

Hence, $44.68 \leq \mu \leq 55.32$, which means μ ranges from 44.68 to 55.32. In other words, with 95% of confidence we can assert that 95% of sample means like 50.0 (the mean of our sample) lie between the population mean μ and $\pm 2.13\ s_{\bar{x}}$ and that 5% fall outside of these limits. If we infer that μ is neither less than 44.68 nor greater than 55.32, then we will be correct in 95% of the times and may be wrong in 5% of the times. So, the probability (p) is 0.95.

(ii)   The 0.99 confidence interval:

$$\bar{X} \pm 2.95\ s_{\bar{x}} = 50.0 \pm 2.95 \times 2.50$$
$$= 50.0 \pm 7.37 = 42.63 \text{ and } 57.37.$$

Hence, $42.63 \leq \mu \leq 57.37$. In other words, with 99% confidence we can say that 99% of sample means lie between μ and $\pm 2.95 s_{\bar{x}}$ and that 1% fall beyond these limits. Thus, if we infer that μ is neither less than 42.63 nor greater than 57.37, then we will be 99% of the times correct and only 1% of the times incorrect. So the probability (p) is 0.99.

Example 11.4 The following scores were obtained by five students in a psychological test. The scores are 11, 13, 9, 12 and 15. Determine the 0.95 and 0.99 confidence interval for the population mean.

Solution

(a)   The given scores are arranged in a tabular form as given below and then the ΣX, N, $\bar{X}$, x and Σx^2 are determined/computed.

Students	Scores (X)	x $(X-\bar{X})$	x^2
1	11	–1	1
2	13	1	1
3	9	–3	9
4	12	0	0
5	15	3	9
$N=5$	60 (ΣX)		20 (Σx^2)

Notes: $\bar{X} = \dfrac{\Sigma X}{N} = \dfrac{60}{5} = 12.0.$

(b)   The SD will be computed using Σx^2 and df $= N-1$ as follows:

$$\text{SD} \quad \text{or} \quad s = \sqrt{\frac{\Sigma x^2}{N-1}} = \sqrt{\frac{20}{5-1}} = \sqrt{\frac{20}{4}} = \sqrt{5.0} = 2.24.$$

(c)   The computed s is used to compute the standard error of the mean ($s_{\bar{x}}$) as follows:

$$s_{\bar{X}} = \frac{s}{\sqrt{N}} = \frac{2.24}{\sqrt{5}} = \frac{2.24}{2.24} = 1.0.$$

(d)   The critical values of t at the 0.05 level of significance (i.e., 95% confidence interval) and at the 0.01 level of significance (i.e., 99% confidence interval) will be determined by the help of df from Table C given in the appendix:

$$\text{df} = N-1 = 5-1 = 4.$$

With df $=4$, the critical t value at the 0.05 level is 2.78 and at the 0.01 level is 4.60.

(e)   Both 95% and 99% confidence intervals of the population mean will be determined using $\bar{X}, s_{\bar{X}}$, and the critical values of t at the respective levels of confidence, as follows.

(i)   The 0.95 confidence interval:

$$\bar{X} \pm 2.78\ s_{\bar{x}} = 12.0 \pm 2.78 \times 1.0 = 12.0 \pm 2.78 = 9.22 \text{ and } 14.78.$$

Thus, the limits of 95% confidence interval are 9.22 and 14.78. This means that $p=0.95$ and that μ lies in the interval 9.22–14.78. Hence, $9.22 \leq \mu \leq 14.78$.

(ii)   The 0.99 confidence interval:

$$\bar{X} \pm 4.60 s_{\bar{x}} = 12.0 \pm 4.60 \times 1.0 = 12.0 \pm 4.60 = 7.40 \text{ and } 16.60.$$

Thus, the limits of 99% confidence interval are 7.40 and 16.60. This means that $p=0.99$ and that μ lies in the interval 7.40–16.60. Hence, $7.40 \leq \mu \leq 16.60$.

Example 11.5 A researcher is investigating a technique purported to decrease the age at which children begin speaking. $\mu=13.0$ months; σ is unknown; the sample of 15 children using the researcher's technique has a mean for the first word utterances of 11.0 months and an SD of 3.34.

   (a) What is the non-directional alternative hypothesis?
   (b) What is the null hypothesis?
   (c) Did the technique work? Use $\alpha=0.05_{2\,\text{tail}}$.

Solution

   (a) *The alternative hypothesis (H_1).* The technique affects the age at which children begin speaking. Therefore, the sample with $\bar{X}=11.0$ is a random sample from a population where $\mu \neq 13.0$.
   (b) *The null hypothesis (H_0).* The sample with $\bar{X}=11.0$ is a random sample from a population with $\mu=13.0$.
   (c) Conclusion using $\alpha=0.05_{2\,\text{tail}}$.

Step 1. We have to apply the appropriate statistics. Since this is a single-sample experiment with unknown σ, t-test is appropriate.

   Given data: $\bar{X}=11.0$; $N=15$; SD or $s=3.34$; $\mu=13.0$; $\sigma=$unknown, first of all, the standard error of the mean ($s_{\bar{X}}$)will be computed using the s as an unbiased estimate of σ as follows:

$$s_{\bar{X}} = \frac{s}{\sqrt{N}} = \frac{3.34}{\sqrt{15}} = \frac{3.34}{3.87} = 0.86,$$

$$t = \frac{\bar{X}-\mu}{s_{\bar{X}}} = \frac{11.0-13.0}{0.86} = \frac{-2.0}{0.86} = -2.32.$$

Step 2. We have to evaluate the obtained t (t_{obt}) value based on its sampling distribution. If the obtained t value is equal to or greater than the critical t (t_{crit}) value, then it falls within the critical region for the rejection of the null hypothesis. The t_{crit} is found in Table C of the appendix under the appropriate alpha level and df. For this example, with $\alpha=0.05_{2\,\text{tail}}$ and df$=N-1=15-1=14$, from Table C, $t_{\text{crit}}=\pm2.14$. $t_{\text{obt}}=-2.32$. Since $t_{\text{obt}} > t_{\text{crit}}$, it falls within the critical region, and, therefore, we reject H_0, and conclude that the technique does decrease the age at which children in the researcher's scale first begin speaking.

11.4 Significance of the Median

As all statistics have sampling distributions and standard errors, the significance of these statistics, such as median (Mdn), quartile deviation (Q), SD (SD or s), percentage/proportions, can be interpreted like that of the mean and we can estimate the parameter.

In terms of s (or σ) and Q, the standard errors of the median (SE_{Mdn} or s_{Mdn}) for large samples can be calculated through the following formulae:

$$s_{\text{Mdn}} = \frac{1.253\sigma}{\sqrt{N}} \quad \text{or} \quad \frac{1.253s}{\sqrt{N}}; \quad s_{\text{Mdn}} = \frac{1.858Q}{\sqrt{N}},$$

where $\sigma=$SD of the population; $s=$SD of the sample; $N=$sample size; $Q=$quartile deviation of the sample.

The fact that the s_{Mdn} is roughly $1\frac{1}{4}$ times the $s_{\bar{x}}$ shows the mean to be in general more dependable (i.e., less subject to sampling fluctuations) than the median.

The limits of confidence intervals at the 95% and 99% levels may be located by taking $\pm 1.96 s_{Mdn}$ and $\pm 2.58\, s_{Mdn}$ about the sample median. The above formulation assumes normality of the parent population and a large sample size (N). In many situations where the median is used, the distribution of the variable is not normal. This, indeed, is one of the reasons for using the median instead of the mean. In consequence, the above formulation is of limited use.

Further examples will illustrate the use and interpretation of the above formulae.

Example 11.6 The performance on an intelligence test of 225 students of Grade X was recorded as follows:

$$\text{Median} = 90.8 \text{ and SD} = 3.5.$$

Determine the confidence limits at the 0.05 and 0.01 levels for the estimation of the population median.

Solution Given the data: $N = 225$; Median $= 90.8$; $s = 3.5$, the standard error of the median (s_{Mdn}) can be calculated by the following formula:

$$s_{Mdn} = \frac{1.253s}{\sqrt{N}} = \frac{1.253 \times 3.5}{\sqrt{225}} = \frac{4.3855}{15} = 0.29.$$

Then the 0.05 and 0.01 confidence intervals are determined as follows:

(i) Confidence limits at the 0.05 (or 5%) level of confidence:

$$\begin{aligned} \text{Mdn} \pm 1.96 s_{Mdn} &= 90.8 \pm 1.96 \times 0.29 \\ &= 90.8 \pm 0.57 = 90.23 \text{ and } 91.37. \end{aligned}$$

Thus, the confidence limits at the 0.05 level of the confidence range from 90.23 to 91.37.

(ii) Confidence limits at the 0.01 (or 1%) level of confidence:

$$\begin{aligned} \text{Mdn} \pm 2.58 s_{Mdn} &= 90.8 \pm 2.58 \times 0.29 \\ &= 90.8 \pm 0.75 = 90.05 \text{ and } 91.55. \end{aligned}$$

Thus, the confidence limits at the 0.01 level of the confidence range from 90.05 to 91.55.

Example 11.7 In a language test 900 ten-year-old children made the following record: Median $= 24.50$ and $Q = 5.61$. How well does this median represent the median of the population from which this sample was drawn?

Solution Given data: $N = 900$; Median $= 24.50$; $Q = 5.61$, the standard error of the median (s_{Mdn}) can be calculated by the formula that reads

$$s_{Mdn} = \frac{1.858Q}{\sqrt{N}} = \frac{1.858 \times 5.61}{\sqrt{900}} = \frac{10.42}{30.0} = 0.35.$$

Since N is large, the sampling distribution may be taken to be normal and the confidence interval can be found from the last line in Table C of the appendix.

The 0.99 confidence interval for the population median (Mdn_{pop}) is $\text{Mdn} \pm 2.58 s_{Mdn} = 24.50 \pm 2.58 \times 0.35 = 24.50 \pm 0.90$ or 23.60 and 25.40. Thus, the limits of the 0.99 confidence interval range from 23.60 to 25.40. We may be 99% confident that the median of the population is not less than 23.60 nor more than 25.40. This narrow range shows a high degree of trustworthiness in the sample median.

11.5   Significance of the Standard Deviation

The standard error of an SD (SE_s or s_s), like standard error of the mean ($s_{\bar{x}}$), is found by computing the probable divergence of the sample SD (s) from its population SD (σ). The formula for SE_s is

$$SE_s \quad \text{or} \quad s_s = \frac{0.71\sigma}{\sqrt{N}} = \frac{0.71s}{\sqrt{N}}; \quad \text{or} \quad s_s = \frac{s}{\sqrt{2N}},$$

where σ=SD of the population and s=SD of the sample.

The sampling distribution of s is skewed for a small sample (N less than about 25). But when samples are large and are drawn randomly from their population, any one of the above two formulae may be applied to compute s_s and interpreted in the same way as $s_{\bar{x}}$. Since sample size is large ($N>30$), the 95% and 99% confidence limits can readily be obtained by taking $s \pm 1.96 s_s$ and $s \pm 2.58 s_s$, respectively. The following example will illustrate the use and interpretation of the above formulae.

Example 11.8 The performance of 225 X grade boys in an abstract reasoning test was recorded as follows:

$$\bar{X} = 27.26; \; s = 11.20.$$

How well does this s represent the σ of the population from which this sample was drawn?

Solution Given data: N=225; $\bar{X}$=27.26; s=11.20, the SE of the SD is computed by the following formulae:

$$s_s = \frac{0.71s}{\sqrt{N}} = \frac{0.71 \times 11.20}{\sqrt{225}} = \frac{7.952}{15} = 0.53.$$

Alternatively,

$$s_s = \frac{s}{\sqrt{2N}} = \frac{11.20}{\sqrt{2 \times 225}} = \frac{11.20}{\sqrt{450}} = \frac{11.20}{21.21} = 0.53.$$

Since N is large, the 0.99 confidence interval for σ can safely be taken at the limits $\pm 2.58 s_s$. Substituting for s_s, we have $s \pm 2.58 s_s = 11.20 \pm 2.58 \times 0.53 = 11.20 \pm 1.37$ or 9.83 and 12.57. Thus, the 0.99 confidence interval limits range from 9.83 to 12.57. If we assume that the σ lies between the limits 9.83 and 12.57, we should be right 99% of the time and wrong 1%.

Another fact is that the SE of an SD is always smaller than the SE of the mean.

11.6   Significance of the Quartile Deviation

In terms of s (or σ) and Q, the standard error of the quartile deviation (SE_Q or s_Q) for large samples can be computed by the following formulae:

$$SE_Q \quad \text{or} \quad s_Q = \frac{0.786\sigma}{\sqrt{N}} = \frac{0.786s}{\sqrt{N}}; \quad \text{or} \quad s_Q = \frac{1.17Q}{\sqrt{N}}.$$

Since the sample size is large, the 95% and 99% confidence limits can readily be obtained by taking $Q\pm1.96s_Q$ and $Q\pm2.58s_Q$, respectively.

The following example will illustrate the use and interpretation of the above two formulae.

Example 11.9 On a language scale, 801 twelve-year-old boys made the following record: $Q=4.90$ and $s=7.30$.

How well does this Q represent the quartile deviation of the population from which this sample was drawn?

Solution Given data: $N=801$; $Q=4.90$; $s=7.30$, the standard error of the Q is calculated through the following formulae, using both s and Q values:

$$s_Q = \frac{0.786s}{\sqrt{N}} = \frac{0.786\times7.30}{\sqrt{801}} = \frac{5.7378}{28.30} = 0.203.$$

Alternatively,

$$s_Q = \frac{1.17Q}{\sqrt{N}} = \frac{1.17\times4.90}{\sqrt{801}} = \frac{5.733}{28.30} = 0.203.$$

Since N is large, the 0.99 confidence interval for population Q is $Q\pm2.58s_Q=4.90\pm2.58\times0.203=4.90\pm0.52$ or 4.38 and 5.42. Thus, the 0.99 confidence interval limits range from 4.38 to 5.42. This narrow range shows that the sample Q is a highly dependable statistic. If we assume that the population Q lies between the limits 4.38 and 5.42, we should be right 99% of the time and wrong 1%.

11.7   Significance of the Percentage/Proportion

There are certain attributes or characteristics which are very difficult or impossible to measure. However, it is often feasible to find the percentage of a given sample which exhibits these behavioural characteristics or possesses a definite attitude. Given the percentage occurrence of behaviour, the question often arises of how much confidence we can place in the figure. How reliable an index is the percentage of the incidence of the behaviour in which we are interested? To answer this question, we must compute the SE of a percentage by the following formula that reads

$$SE_\% \quad or \quad s_\% = \sqrt{\frac{PQ}{N}},$$

where

$P=$ the percentage occurrence of the behaviour

$Q=1-P$

$N=$ number of cases.

The sampling distribution of percentage can be taken as normal when N is large (larger than about 50) and when P is less than 95% and greater than 5%. The $SE_\%$ is interpreted like the $s_{\bar{x}}$. Since N is large, the 0.95 and 0.99 confidence interval limits for the population percentage (P_{pop}) can safely be located by taking $\pm1.96s_\%$ and $\pm2.58s_\%$, respectively, about the sample percentage (P).

The following example will illustrate the use and interpretation of the above formula.

Example 11.10 In a study of cheating among elementary-school children, 200 or 40% of the 500 children from homes of high socioeconomic status were found to have cheated on various tests. Assuming our sample to be representative of children from good homes, how much confidence can be placed in this percentage? How well does it represent the population percentage?

Solution Given data: $N=500$; $P=40\%$, we can find out $Q=1-P$ or $100-40\%=60\%$.

The standard error of percentage can be computed through the following formula:

$$\text{SE}_\% \quad \text{or} \quad s_\% = \sqrt{\frac{PQ}{N}} = \sqrt{\frac{40\% \times 60\%}{500}} = \sqrt{\frac{2400\%}{500}} = \sqrt{4.8\%} = 2.19\%.$$

In the present problem, the 0.99 (or 99%) confidence interval for the population percentage is $40\% \pm 2.58 \times 2.19\% = 40\% \pm 5.6\%$ or from 34.4% to 45.6%. We may be ensure that the percentage of children in general who cheat in tests of the sort used in this study will be at least 34.4% and will not be larger than 45.6%. In other words, we can assume with 99% confidence that the elementary school children of high socioeconomic status would cheat with at least 34.4% and will not be more than 45.6%.

11.8 Significance of the Correlation Coefficient

Various ways of testing the significance of the correlation coefficient (r) are discussed in detail in Chapter 9 under Section 9.3 (product-moment correlation). It needs no further discussion here. However, the classical formula for the SE of r, when N is large, is given as follows:

$$\text{SE}_r \quad \text{or} \quad s_r = \frac{1-r^2}{\sqrt{N}}.$$

The following example will illustrate the use and interpretation of the above formula.

Example 11.11 One hundred twenty children were tested on two variables X and Y. The product-moment correlation between these two variables is 0.60. What are the limits of 99% confidence interval for population r?

Solution Given the data: $N=120$; $r=0.60$,

$$\text{SE}_r \quad \text{or} \quad s_r = \frac{1-r^2}{\sqrt{N}} = \frac{1-(0.60)^2}{\sqrt{120}} = \frac{1-0.36}{10.95} = \frac{0.64}{10.95} = 0.06.$$

To test the dependability of r in terms of its SE, we assume the sampling distribution of r to be normal.

99% confidence interval for the population r is $r \pm 2.58 s_r = 0.60 \pm 2.58 \times 0.06 = 0.60 \pm 0.15$ or 0.45 and 0.75. Thus, the 0.99 confidence interval limits range from 0.45 to 0.75. We can feel quite certain; therefore, r is at least as large as 0.45 and is no larger than 0.75.

Summary

In this chapter, we have discussed the topic of significance of the mean and other statistics, which include the median, SD, quartile deviation, percentage/ proportion and the correlation coefficient. In studying the characteristics of a certain population, many times it is neither feasible nor practicable to study each and every element of the population. Therefore, we usually resort to sampling. A true representative sample of an appropriate size is selected randomly and the desired sample statistics like mean, median, SD and so on are computed. These sample statistics are then used in estimating the corresponding parameters such as the mean, median, SD and the like of the whole population of which the sample is a part. The degree to which a sample statistic represents its population parameter is an *index of the significance* or *trustworthiness* of that sample statistic.

Testing of the significance of trustworthiness of the computed sample mean and that of other statistics as noted above requires the computation of the standard error of those sample statistics. In the case of large samples (i.e., $N > 30$), the distribution of means of a number of samples of a particular size drawn randomly from the same population will be normal, as we have shown it in a normal curve. The SD of this distribution is known as the standard error of the mean. In the case of small samples ($N < 30$), the distribution of sample means takes the shape of the *t* distribution, and not normal as in the case of large samples. The shape of the *t* distribution varies according to the number of df, and when df is very large, the distribution of *t* is virtually normal, as we have already presented.

Finally, the computational equations and formulae for the computation of the standard error of a sample mean, median, SD, quartile deviation, percentage/proportion and correlation coefficient, both in small and large sample cases, were presented; the processes of determining the significance of a sample mean and other statistics, as mentioned above, were discussed, and several practice problems worked out.

Key Terms

- Central limit theorem
- Confidence interval
- Confidence limits
- Critical value of *r*
- Critical value of *t*
- Degrees of freedom
- Fiduciary limits
- Fiduciary probability
- Index of the significance

- Large sample
- Normal distribution
- Small sample
- Standard error
- Statistical inference
- *t* distribution
- *t* statistics
- Test of significance

Questions and Problems

1. What do you mean by *t* distribution? Discuss its important properties.
2. Explain the terms:
   (a) Degrees of freedom
   (b) The *t* distribution
   (c) Statistical inference
3. Explain the concept of standard error for determining the significance of the mean and other statistics.

4. What do you mean by the term 'significance of the sample mean'? Explain in detail with a hypothetical example.

5. Explain the concept of confidence interval and confidence limits as used in determining the significance of the mean and other statistics.

6. How would you proceed to determine the significance of a given sample mean in case of a large sample? Illustrate with the help of a hypothetical example.

7. How does the procedure for determining the significance of the mean of a small sample differ from that of the mean of a large sample? Illustrate with the help of a hypothetical example the process of determining the significance of a small sample mean.

8. Briefly discuss the process of determining the significance of the statistics like median, standard deviation and quartile deviation.

9. Enumerate the procedure for testing the significance of a given percentage or proportion. Explain it with an example.

10. Discuss the different procedures used for determining the significance of a correlation coefficient between two variables in a given sample. Illustrate it with an example.

11. The mean and standard deviation of 400 students in a numerical ability test were found to be 42 and 8, respectively. Can you estimate the population mean (μ) at both 95% and 99% confidence interval?

12. The mean and standard deviation of a sample of 169 boys in an arithmetic addition test were 50 and 6, respectively.

    (a) Determine the 95% confidence interval for the population mean and interpret it.

    (b) Determine the 99% confidence interval for μ.

    (c) Determine the acceptable sampling error of 0.05 and 0.01 levels of significance.

13. For a given group of 500 soldiers the mean AGCT score is 95.00 and SD is 25.

    (a) Determine the 0.99 confidence interval for the true mean.

    (b) It is unlikely that the true mean is larger than what value?

14. From the following data, compute the standard error of mean and establish the confidence interval of the location of the true mean at 0.05 and 0.01 levels

	Sample A	Sample B	Sample C	Sample D
Mean	40	45	50	80
SD	4	6	8	12
N	125	400	900	626

15. For a given group of five students, the mean score is 12 and SD is 2.24. Determine the limits of 95% confidence interval for the population mean.

16. The mean of 16 independent observations of a certain magnitude is 100 and the SD is 24.

   (a) At the 0.05 confidence level, what are the fiduciary limits (0.95 confidence interval) for the true mean?
   (b) Taking the 0.99 confidence interval as our standard, we may be assured that the true mean is at least as large as what value?

17. The following measures of perception span for unrelated words are obtained from 5 children: 5,6,4,7 and 5. Find the 0.99 confidence interval for the true mean of these scores.

18. Suppose it is known that the SD of the scores in a certain population is 20. How many cases would we need in a sample in order that the SE

   (a) of the sample mean be 2?
   (b) of the sample SD be 1?

19. In a language test, 801 eleven-year-old boys made the following record: median 21.40 and $Q=4.90$. How well does this median represent the median of the population from which this sample was drawn?

20. On an attitude scale, the performance of a group of 36 student teachers was recorded as : Mdn = 30.4 and SD = 2.4.
   How well does this median represent the median of the population from which this sample was drawn?

21. Given $M=26.40$; $\sigma=5.20$ and $N=100$, compute the 0.95 confidence interval for the true σ.

22. Given $N=400$, $\sigma=6$.
   How well does this SD represent the SD of the population from which the sample was drawn?

23. Given $N=801$, $Q=4.90$.
   How well does this Q represent the population quartile deviation?

24. In a numerical ability test, 200 12-year-old girls made the following record:

$$\bar{X} = 119.44; \text{SD} = 6.68; Q = 4.49.$$

   How well does this Q represent the quartile deviation of the population from which this sample was drawn?

25. In a study of cheating among elementary school children, 100 or 25% of the 400 children from homes of high socioeconomic status were found to have cheated on various tests. How well does this sample percentage represent the population percentage?

26. Given $r=0.48$, $N=52$. Find the standard error of r and determine the limits of confidence interval at 0.05 and 0.01 levels.

27. $r=0.52$, $N=173$. How well does this sample r represent the population r?

28. Fill in the blanks:

   (i) Various measures computed from samples are called _____.
   (ii) Measures which are directly computed from population are called _____.

(iii)   The degree to which a sample statistic represents its parameter is an _____ of the significance of that sample statistic.

(iv)   The formula used to compute the standard error of the population mean is _____.

(v)   The limits of the confidence interval of a parameter have been called by Fisher as _____.

(vi)   The t distribution is the theoretical model of _____ probability distribution for small samples.

(vii)   In contrast to the normal distribution, t distributions are usually _____.

(viii)   When df approaches infinity (∞), the t distribution becomes _____.

(ix)   For a given data $N=100$, $r=0.60$, the SE_r will be _____.

(x)   The Student's t-test was originally developed by _____.

29.   Write whether the following statements are True or False.

(i)   The t-test is very similar to the z-test.

(ii)   The t distribution is symmetrical but leptokurtic.

(iii)   In the case of the small samples, the standard deviation is calculated by the formula $s = \sqrt{\dfrac{\sum x^2}{N}}$.

(iv)   In a two-tailed test, the z value at $\alpha=.05$ is 2.58.

(v)   The mean of the sample means will be a fairly good estimate of the population mean.

(vi)   The central limit theorem simply asserts that the sampling distribution of means gets closer and closer to the normal form as sample size N increases.

(vii)   In a large sample, the 0.99 confidence interval for the sample mean is determined as $\bar{X} \pm 1.96 s_{\bar{X}}$.

(viii)   For a given data, $N=144$, $\bar{X}=50$, SD$=6.0$; the 95% confidence interval ranges from 49.02 to 50.98.

(ix)   The degrees of freedom for a t-test performed for two independent samples is determined as $N_1 + N_2 - 2$.

(x)   If the sizes of two independent samples are 10 and 12, respectively, then the df for a t-test will be 20.

30.   Find out the correct answer from among the four alternatives.

(i)   Estimation of the parameters of the parent population is made by:

(a)   Sample statistics   (b)   Sampling fluctuations

(c)   Sampling errors   (d)   None of the above

(ii)   The 0.95 confidence interval of the population mean is determined as:

(a) $\bar{X} \pm 2.58 s_{\bar{X}}$ (b) $\bar{X} \pm 1.96 s_{\bar{X}}$

(c) $\bar{X} \pm 1.29 s_{\bar{X}}$ (d)   None of the above

(iii) If $N=144$, $\bar{X}=50$, SD$=6.0$, then the standard error of the mean will be:

(a) 0.25   (b) 0.75

(c) 0.50   (d) None of the above

(iv) If $N_1=20$ and $N_2=22$, then df for a t-test will be:

(a) 40   (b) 41

(c) 38   (d) None of the above

(v) In calculating t for a single sample, the df will be:

(a) $\underline{N-1}$ (b) N_1+N_2-1.

(c) N_1+N_2-2 (d) None of the above

(vi) The 0.95 confidence interval, for the given data having $n=5$, $t_{.05}=2.78$, $s_{\bar{X}}=1.0$, $\bar{X}=120$, ranges from:

(a) 9.22 to 14.78   (b) 18.44 to 29.56

(c) 4.61 to 7.39   (d) None of the above

(vii) The standard error of the median, for the given data having $N=225$, Median 90.8, SD$=3.5$, will be:

(a) 0.584   (b) 0.292

(c) 0.146   (d) None of the above

(viii) For a given data with $N=900$, Median$=24.50$, Q$=5.61$, the standard error of the median is:

(a) 0.694   (b) 0.174

(c) 0.347   (d) None of the above

(ix) The standard error of the standard deviation is computed by:

(a) $s_S = \dfrac{0.71s}{\sqrt{N}}$ (b) $s_S = \sqrt{\dfrac{0.71s}{N}}$

(c) $s_S = \dfrac{0.71s}{N}$ (d) None of the above

(x) The classical formula for the standard error of r, when N is large, reads as:

(a) $SE_r = \sqrt{\dfrac{1-r^2}{N}}$ (b) $SE_r = \dfrac{1-r^2}{\sqrt{N}}$

(c) $SE_r = \dfrac{1-r^2}{N}$ (d) None of the above

CHAPTER 12

Significance of the Difference between Means and Other Statistics

Learning Objectives

After completing this chapter you will be able to:

- Understand the concept of sampling distribution of differences between two sample statistics.
- Understand the concept of z-test.
- Use t-test depending on the nature of the samples.
- Differentiate between z-test and t-test.
- Compute the standard error of the difference between the sample means, medians, standard deviations (SDs) or variances, correlation coefficients and so on.
- Understand the processes of determining the significance of difference between the sample means, medians, SDs or variances, correlation coefficients and so on.
- Determine the degrees of freedom (df) associated with a t-test for testing the significance of the difference between two sample statistics.
- Determine the critical value of t for a specific df associated with it, at the desired level of significance.

12.1 Introduction

In the fields of behavioural sciences, there are many occasions where we are more interested in knowing about the significance of the difference between two sample statistics rather than merely knowing the significance of a computed single sample statistic. For example, suppose a researcher wants to study the effect of Yoga exercises in promoting the intelligence of Grade V students. For this purpose, he or she randomly selects 40 students from the class and divides them into two equal random groups. One group, called the experimental group, is subjected to Yoga exercise practices for three months, while the other group, called the control group, is deprived of these practices. Then the intelligence of these two groups of students is measured by Raven's Coloured Progressive Matrices, and the mean scores of these two groups are computed. The significance of the difference between the mean scores of the experimental and control groups will then help him or her to say whether the Yoga exercise practices are a contributing factor towards the promotion of intelligence. In this situation, the problem is the determination of the significance of the difference between two computed sample means. Here the question is whether the difference, if any, between the two sample means is the result of sampling fluctuations and chance factors (i.e., temporary and accidental factors) which have occurred incidentally or indicates some real, genuine or true difference between the population means.

The significance of the observed results of a study is assessed statistically by working out the probability of such results arising by chance due to random sampling. The observed results are considered significant only if such probability is justifiably too low. For estimating the probability of the observed results arising from chances associated with random sampling, either 'z' or 't' score is computed from the observed data. The computed 'z' or 't' score is then interpreted with reference to the normal or 't' distribution, respectively.

Because the significance of the observed results is inferred statistically in terms of the level of probability of such results arising due to chances of random sampling, there always exists a probability of an error in the inference made.

12.2   Sampling Distribution of Differences

For certain purposes, a knowledge of the *sampling distribution of the difference* between two statistics, such as the difference between two sample means or two proportions, is required. To conceptualise the sampling distribution of the difference between, say, two sample means, let us consider two indefinitely large populations whose means are equal, that is, $\mu_1 = \mu_2$. Let $\bar{X}_1$ be the mean of a sample of N_1 cases drawn at random from the first population and $\bar{X}_2$ be the mean of a sample of N_2 cases drawn from the second population. The difference between their means is $\bar{X}_1 - \bar{X}_2$. Since $\mu_1 = \mu_2$, this difference results from the sampling error. A large number of pairs of samples may be drawn, and a frequency distribution made of the differences. It describes how the differences between means chosen at random from two populations, where $\mu_1 = \mu_2$, will vary with repeated sampling. Sometimes this difference will be positive, sometimes negative and sometimes zero. The distribution of these differences will form a normal distribution around a difference of zero. From this distribution, we may estimate the probability of obtaining a difference of any specified size in drawing samples at random from populations, where $\mu_1 = \mu_2$. By considering an indefinitely large number of pairs of samples, we arrive at the concept of a theoretical sampling distribution of differences between sample means. The standard deviation (SD) of this distribution is called the standard error (SE) of difference ($s_{\bar{X}_1 - \bar{X}_2}$) between means. In this situation, the samples are independent. The means may be viewed as paired at random. No correlation exists between the pairs of means; the individual measurements in the two populations are not paired with one another.

The variance of the sampling distribution of differences describes how the differences vary with repeated sampling. Let us consider the case of independent samples. If $\sigma_{\bar{X}_1}^2 = \sigma_1^2 / N_1$ is the variance of the sampling distribution of means drawn from one population and $\sigma_{\bar{X}_2}^2 = \sigma_2^2 / N_2$ is the corresponding variance from the other population, then the variance of the sampling distribution of differences between means is the sum of the two variances. Thus,

$$\sigma_{\bar{X}_1 - \bar{X}_2}^2 = \sigma_{\bar{X}_1}^2 + \sigma_{\bar{X}_2}^2 = \frac{\sigma_1^2}{N_1} + \frac{\sigma_2^2}{N_2},$$

when $\sigma_1^2 = \sigma_2^2 = \sigma^2$, the variances in the two populations being equal, we may write

$$\sigma^2_{\bar{X}_1 - \bar{X}_2} = \sigma^2 \left(\frac{1}{N_1} + \frac{1}{N_2} \right).$$

Let us now consider a situation where measurements are paired with one another. Such data arise, for example, where measurements are made on the same group of subjects under both control and experimental conditions. The paired measurements may be correlated. In this instance, in approaching the sampling distribution of differences between means, we conceptualise two populations of paired measurements with equal means; thus, $\mu_1 = \mu_2$. Denote the correlation between the paired measurements by the symbol ρ_{12}. Samples of size 'N' are drawn at random, and the differences between the means are obtained. The distribution of differences between means for an indefinitely large number of samples is the sampling distribution of differences for correlated populations.

The variance of the sampling distribution of differences for correlated populations may be shown to be

$$\sigma^2_{\bar{X}_1 - \bar{X}_2} = \sigma^2_{\bar{X}_1} + \sigma^2_{\bar{X}_2} - 2\rho_{12}\sigma_{\bar{X}_1}\sigma_{\bar{X}_2},$$

where ρ_{12} is the correlation in the population. Here, we can note one thing that the formula for the independent samples is a particular case of the more general formula for the correlated samples. It is the particular case which arises when $\rho_{12} = 0$. In the correlated case, $N_1 = N_2 = N$. In practice, the variances are estimated from the data. Thus, the above formula for correlated populations becomes

$$s^2_{\bar{X}_1 - \bar{X}_2} = s^2_{\bar{X}_1} + s^2_{\bar{X}_2} - 2r_{12}s_{\bar{X}_1}s_{\bar{X}_2}.$$

Obviously, when $r_{12} = 0$, the sampling variance of the difference between means is the sum of the separate variances as follows:

$$s^2_{\bar{X}_1 - \bar{X}_2} = s^2_{\bar{X}_1} + s^2_{\bar{X}_2}.$$

12.3   Significance of the Difference between Two Means

Think about a simple experiment. There are only two variables in a simple experiment, which are called independent and dependent variables. As we know that the variable whose changes are studied in the experiment is called the dependent variable in that experiment, whereas the variable whose effect on the dependent variable is being investigated is called the independent variable. Moreover, in a simple experiment, there are two independent groups of samples which are randomly selected from the population. One of these two groups is treated with the independent variable, and, hence, is called the experimental group, whereas the other group does not receive the treatment of the independent variable, and, hence, is called the control group. These two random groups of samples may differ with respect to their mean scores, owing to one of the following reasons.

First, the independent variable may not have produced any effect or change in the dependent variable so that the two samples, though exposed to two different levels of the independent variable, still belong to the same population, and their means are estimates of the same population. But the sample means may still differ because the samples are constituted of two different groups of individuals drawn at random from the population. In other words, such a difference between the sample means may be accounted for by the sampling error of the mean and estimated by the SE of difference between the means.

Secondly, the independent variable may indeed have produced changes in the dependent variable. In such a situation, the two sample means are different from each other, and, thus, these two samples belong to two different populations, and their means are estimates of the respective population means. The difference between such sample means is not due to the chances of random sampling and cannot be accounted for by the sampling error of the means.

Because of the two above alternative possibilities, the significance of the difference between two sample means must be assessed, paying due attention to the SE of that difference. For this, the observed difference between the two sample means is generally transformed into a standard score, either 'z' or 't', using the SE of that difference; the probability of this standard score occurring by mere chance due to random sampling is then found using either the unit normal curve or the 't' distribution with the help of the number of df. If the probability is found to be too high that the observed difference between the sample means may have arisen from the chances associated with random sampling and may be explained by the SE of the difference, the observed difference is not considered to be significant, which means that the independent variable does not have produced a significant change in the dependent variable. On the contrary, if the probability is found to be too low that the observed difference between the sample means may have arisen from the chances of random sampling, the difference is considered to be significant, which means that the independent variable is considered to have produced a significant change in the dependent variable.

12.4   Significance of the Difference between Two Means Using 'z' Scores

With regard to the significance of difference between means, two situations arise: (a) those in which means are uncorrelated or independent and (b) those in which means are correlated. Means are uncorrelated or independent when computed from different samples or from uncorrelated tests administered to the same sample. In such a case, two situations may arise: (a) when means are uncorrelated or independent and samples are large and (b) when means are uncorrelated/independent and samples are small.

The 'z' test is more applicable to the situation where it is desired to test the significance of the difference between means of two large independent or uncorrelated groups of samples. To interpret statistically whether the difference between the means of two large independent groups, each having the sample size (N) equal to or greater than 30 ($N \geq 30$), is significant or not, the unit normal curve areas (Table A given in the appendix) may be used for finding the probability (p) of the null hypothesis (H_0) being correct, because the means of large samples and consequently the differences between such sample means possess sampling distributions identical with the normal distribution. For this reason, the observed difference between two independent sample means is transformed into the corresponding standard score (z) and the probability (p) of obtaining that 'z' score owing to mere chances of random sampling is found, using the unit normal curve areas. Only when the 'p' thus worked out does not exceed the chosen level of significance (alpha level, α), the H_0 is rejected as untenable and the observed difference between two sample means is considered to be significant ($p \leq \alpha$).

For using the 'z' score and the unit normal curve areas in the tests of significance, the variable under investigation as well as the obtained data must fulfil certain criteria. It is, however, not necessary always to test whether the required criteria have actually been fulfilled; it will suffice if it is justifiable to assume that the required criteria have been fulfilled. Such criteria for a statistical test are thus called the *assumptions* for the test.

12.4.1 Assumptions for Using 'z' Test

The following are some of the reasonable assumptions for using 'z' test for testing the significance of difference between two independent sample means:

(a) The dependent variable is a continuous measurement variable.

(b) The scores of the dependent variable have a normal distribution in the population from which the samples are drawn.

(c) Each score occurs in the sample at random and independent of all other scores.

(d) The sample size should be large enough ($N \geq 30$) so that the sample means and consequently the differences between them should have normal sampling distribution in the population.

12.4.2 Two-tailed Test

The *null hypothesis* (H_0) for a two-tailed test states that there is no significant difference between the sample means, that the sample means are estimates of the same population mean, that the observed difference between the sample means has resulted from mere chances of random sampling, and that there would have been no difference between the means if the entire population were used instead of random samples. In other words, if μ_1 and μ_2 are the population means estimated by $\bar{X}_1$ and $\bar{X}_2$, respectively, then

$$H_0: \quad \mu_1 = \mu_2 \quad \text{or} \quad \mu_1 - \mu_2 = 0$$
$$H_1: \quad \mu_1 \neq \mu_2 \quad \text{or} \quad \mu_1 - \mu_2 \neq 0.$$

The following procedure is used to find the probability (p) of this null hypothesis (H_0) being correct:

(a) The observed difference between the sample means ($\bar{X}_1 - \bar{X}_2$) is transformed into 'z' score, assuming that the H_0 is correct and that the population means μ_1 and μ_2, estimated by the sample means, are identical. Where s_1 and s_2 are the SDs of the respective samples, $s_{\bar{X}_1}$ and $s_{\bar{X}_2}$ are the SEs of the respective sample means, $s_{\bar{X}_1 - \bar{X}_2}$ is the SE of the difference between the sample means, N_1 and N_2 are the sizes of the respective samples, and μ_1 and μ_2 are identical,

$$s_{\bar{X}_1} = \frac{s_1}{\sqrt{N_1}}; \quad s_{\bar{X}_2} = \frac{s_2}{\sqrt{N_2}};$$

$$s_{\bar{X}_1 - \bar{X}_2} = \sqrt{(s_{\bar{X}_1})^2 + (s_{\bar{X}_2})^2}; \mu_1 - \mu_2 = 0;$$

$$\therefore z = \frac{(\bar{X}_1 - \bar{X}_2) - (\mu_1 - \mu_2)}{s_{\bar{X}_1 - \bar{X}_2}} = \frac{\bar{X}_1 - \bar{X}_2}{s_{\bar{X}_1 - \bar{X}_2}};$$

$$\text{or} \quad z = \frac{\bar{X}_1 - \bar{X}_2}{\sqrt{(s_{\bar{X}_1})^2 + (s_{\bar{X}_2})^2}} = \frac{\bar{X}_1 - \bar{X}_2}{\sqrt{\dfrac{s_1^2}{N_1} + \dfrac{s_2^2}{N_2}}}.$$

(b) The fractional area beyond the computed 'z' score in each tail of the unit normal curve is then obtained from the difference between 0.50 which is half of the unit normal curve area, and the fractional area of the curve from its centre or μ to the computed 'z' score (Table A given in the appendix). For a two-tailed test, this area gives half of the probability, that is, $p/2$, of obtaining the computed 'z' score by the chances associated with random sampling. So, the probability (p) of obtaining the computed 'z' score as well as the observed difference between the sample means is given by the sum of the fractional areas beyond $\pm z$ in the two tails. Thus,

$$p = 2\,[0.50 - (\text{fractional area of unit normal curve from } \mu \text{ to computed } z)]$$

It should be noted that the fractional areas of the unit normal curve from its μ to different 'z' scores are tabulated in the area column of Table A (given in the appendix).

(c)   The computed 'p' is then compared with the chosen level of significance (α). If 'p' is equal to or less than the chosen α, the probability of chance occurrence of the observed difference, as proposed by the H_0, is considered too low; the H_0 is then rejected and the alternative hypothesis (H_1) is accepted—the observed difference is considered to be significant ($p \leq \alpha$). If, on the contrary, 'p' exceeds the chosen alpha (α), the probability of H_0 being correct is considered too high; so, the H_0 cannot be rejected in that case—the observed difference is then considered not significant ($p > \alpha$). In other words, H_0 is accepted and H_1 is rejected.

12.4.3   One-tailed Test

The *null hypothesis* for a *one-tailed test* proposes that one sample mean is not significantly greater than another, that the observed results showing one sample mean greater than another have arisen by mere chances of random sampling and that no such result would have been obtained if the entire population were studied instead of random samples. In other words, according to H_0 and H_1,

$$\text{either} \quad H_0:\ \mu_1 \ngtr \mu_2;\quad H_1:\ \mu_1 > \mu_2$$
$$\text{or} \quad H_0:\ \mu_1 \nless \mu_2;\quad H_1:\ \mu_1 < \mu_2.$$

The probability (p) of this null hypothesis (H_0) being correct is found in the following way.

(a)   The observed difference ($\bar{X}_1 - \bar{X}_2$) between the sample means is transformed into 'z' score in the same way as in the case of the two-tailed test, assuming the H_0 to be correct:

$$z = \frac{\bar{X}_1 - \bar{X}_2}{S_{\bar{X}_1 - \bar{X}_2}} = \frac{\bar{X}_1 - \bar{X}_2}{\sqrt{\dfrac{s_1^2}{N_1} + \dfrac{s_2^2}{N_2}}}.$$

(b)   The fractional area beyond the computed 'z' score in a single tail (or one tail) of the unit normal curve is then obtained from the difference between 0.50 (which is half the unit normal curve area) and the fractional area of that curve from its centre (or μ) to the computed 'z' score (Table A of the appendix). For a one-tailed test, this area gives the probability (p) of obtaining the computed 'z' score as well as the observed difference between the sample means, where the observed difference bears a given algebraic sign.

$$p = [0.50 - (\text{fractional area of unit normal curve from } \mu \text{ to computed 'z')}].$$

(c)   The computed 'p' is then compared with the chosen level of significance (α). If $p \leq \alpha$, the probability of the H_0 being correct is considered too low; the H_0 is then rejected and the H_1 is accepted—it is inferred that one sample mean is significantly higher (or lower) than another. But if $p > \alpha$, the probability is considered too high for the H_0 being correct; so the H_0 cannot be rejected—it is then inferred that one sample mean is not significantly higher (or lower) than another. This leads to the acceptance of H_0 and the rejection of H_1.

The entire procedure of testing the significance of difference between means using the 'z' test will be more clear through the following examples.

Example 12.1 In a modified form of the Differential Aptitude Test (DAT), the mean score obtained by a sample of 374 girls amounted to 98.7 (SD=14.08), while the mean score of another sample of 255 boys was 95.5 (SD=13.02). Is there any significant difference between the mean scores of the two sexes ($\alpha=0.01$)?

Solution
It is a two-tailed test since the direction is not clear.

Given data: For girls: $X_1 = 98.7$; $s_1 = 14.08$; $N_1 = 374$
For boys: $X_2 = 95.5$; $s_2 = 13.02$; $N_2 = 255$.

To test the significance of an observed difference between two sample means, we can proceed through the following steps:

Step 1. We have to be clear whether we are going to make a two-tailed test or a one-tailed test. Here, as per the given question, we want to test whether there is a significant difference between the mean scores of the two sexes; no clear-cut direction is given. So it is a two-tailed test.

Step 2. We set up a null hypothesis (H_0) which states that there is no significant difference between the two sample means, the observed difference being due only to chances associated with random sampling. In contrast, the alternative hypothesis (H_1) contends that there is a significant difference between the two sample means; the observed difference is a real and genuine difference. So, the H_0 and H_1 are stated as follows:

$$H_0: \quad \bar{X}_1 = \bar{X}_2; \quad H_1: \quad \bar{X}_1 \neq \bar{X}_2$$

or

$$H_0: \quad \bar{X}_1 - \bar{X}_2 = 0; \quad H_1: \quad \bar{X}_1 - \bar{X}_2 \neq 0.$$

Step 3. Then we have to decide the level of significance of the test. In this example, we are to test the difference at the 0.01 level of significance ($\alpha=0.01$).

Step 4. In this example, the sample means are uncorrelated/independent and samples are large. So the SEs of the sample means are first computed using the respective SDs and sample sizes as follows:

$$s_{\bar{X}_1} = \frac{s_1}{\sqrt{N_1}} = \frac{14.08}{\sqrt{374}} = \frac{14.08}{19.34} = 0.728,$$

$$s_{\bar{X}_2} = \frac{s_2}{\sqrt{N_2}} = \frac{13.02}{\sqrt{255}} = \frac{13.02}{15.97} = 0.815.$$

Step 5. The SE of the difference (SE_D) between the sample means is then computed using the SEs of the means by the following formula:

$$s_{\bar{X}_1 - \bar{X}_2} = \sqrt{(s_{\bar{X}_1})^2 + (s_{\bar{X}_2})^2} = \sqrt{(0.728)^2 + (0.815)^2} = \sqrt{0.529984 + 0.664225}$$
$$= \sqrt{1.194209} = 1.093.$$

As an alternative to steps 4 and 5, the SE of the difference between sample means may also be computed directly from the SDs of the sample means. The formula reads as follows:

$$s_{\bar{X}_1 - \bar{X}_2} = \sqrt{\frac{s_1^2}{N_1} + \frac{s_2^2}{N_2}} = \sqrt{\frac{(14.08)^2}{374} + \frac{(13.02)^2}{255}} = \sqrt{\frac{198.2464}{374} + \frac{169.5204}{255}}$$
$$= \sqrt{0.53 + 0.665} = \sqrt{1.195} = 1.093.$$

Step 6. Assuming the H_0 to be correct, the difference between the sample means is converted to 'z' scores through the following formula:

$$z = \frac{\bar{X}_1 - \bar{X}_2}{s_{\bar{X}_1 - \bar{X}_2}} = \frac{98.7 - 95.5}{1.093} = \frac{3.2}{1.093} = 2.93.$$

Step 7. The unit normal curve table (Table A of the appendix) is used to find out the two-tail probability (p) of obtaining the computed 'z' score, and, hence, the observed difference between two sample means by chance due to random sampling.

$p = 2[0.50 - \text{(fractional area of the unit normal curve from its } \mu \text{ to the computed}$
'z' score of 2.93)].
$= 2[0.50 - 0.4983] = 2 \times 0.0017 = 0.0034.$

Step 8. This obtained 'p' of 0.0034 will be compared with the α (alpha) level of 0.01 for testing the significance of mean difference. In this example, because the computed 'p' of 0.0034 is less than the chosen α of 0.01, the probability of the H_0 being correct is considered too low. The H_0 is, therefore, rejected and H_1 is accepted. This shows that the mean DAT scores are considered to be significantly different in the two sexes. So, $p < 0.01$. This indicates that the boys and girls will differ significantly from each other with regard to their mean DAT scores in 99% of cases.

As an alternative to Steps 7 and 8, the computed 'z' value can be compared directly with the critical values of 'z' given in Table A of the appendix for the 0.05 and 0.01 levels of significance. It is evident from Table A that the critical values of 'z', for a two-tailed test, at the 0.05 and 0.01 levels are 1.96 and 2.58, respectively. The obtained 'z' value in order to be significant at the 0.05 level must be equal to or more than 1.96 (i.e., $z_{obt.} \geq 1.96$). Similarly, the obtained 'z' value should be equal to or more than 2.58 (i.e., $z_{obt.} \geq 2.58$) in order to be significant at the 0.01 level of significance. In this example, the obtained value of 'z' is 2.93, which is greater than the critical value of z of 2.58 at the 0.01 level. Therefore, the obtained 'z' value is significant at the 0.01 level of significance. So, $p < 0.01$. This shows that: (a) the H_0 is rejected and H_1 is accepted; (b) the mean DAT scores are significantly different in the two sexes; and (c) the boys and girls will differ significantly from each other with regard to their mean DAT scores in 99% of cases.

Example 12.2 A mathematics teacher divided his class into two random groups. He provided an extra drill in computation skill for an hour daily to the experimental group hoping that such a drill will promote the computation skill of the students of this group. The control group was not provided any such drill. At the end of the session for 30 days, he administered an achievement-test and collected data as follows:

	Experimental Group	**Control Group**
Mean	35.0	30.0
SD	4.0	3.0
N	48	45

Is the gain (difference between means) significant enough to indicate that a drill in mathematics promotes computation skill?

Solution

Given data: Experimental group: $\bar{X}_1 = 35$; $s_1 = 4$; $N_1 = 48$
                 Control group: $\bar{X}_2 = 30$; $s_2 = 3$; $N_2 = 45$.

Step 1. In this example, the teacher is interested to know the significance of difference between two sample means in terms of a particular direction, that is, the gain on account of drill work. There is a clear-cut direction. Therefore, to determine the significance of difference between means, a one-tailed test will be used. So, it is a one-tailed test.

Step 2. We set up an H_0 which states that the gain on account of drill work is not significant; $\bar{X}_1$ is not significantly higher than $\bar{X}_2$. On the contrary, the H_1 states that the gain on account of drill work is significant, that is, $\bar{X}_1$ is significantly higher than $\bar{X}_2$. The H_0 and H_1 are stated as follows:

$$H_0:\ \ \bar{X}_1 \not> \bar{X}_2;\ \ H_1:\ \ \bar{X}_1 > \bar{X}_2.$$

Step 3. Then we have to decide the significance level of the test. In this example, we are to test the difference at the 0.05 and 0.01 levels of significance, since no specific alpha (α) level is given in the above example. Hence, $\alpha = 0.05$ and $\alpha = 0.01$.

Step 4. In the given example, the samples are independent and large. So the SEs of the sample means are first computed using the respective SDs and sample sizes as follows:

$$s_{\bar{X}_1} = \frac{s_1}{\sqrt{N_1}} = \frac{4.0}{\sqrt{48}} = \frac{4.0}{6.93} = 0.58,$$

$$s_{\bar{X}_2} = \frac{s_2}{\sqrt{N_2}} = \frac{3.0}{\sqrt{45}} = \frac{3.0}{6.71} = 0.45.$$

Step 5. The SE of the difference (SE_D) between the sample means is then computed using the SEs of the means by the following formula:

$$s_{\bar{X}_1 - \bar{X}_2} = \sqrt{(s_{\bar{X}_1})^2 + (s_{\bar{X}_2})^2} = \sqrt{(0.58)^2 + (0.45)^2} = \sqrt{0.3364 + 0.2025}$$

$$= \sqrt{0.5389} = 0.73 \text{ (to two decimals)}.$$

As an alternative to Steps 4 and 5, the SE of the difference between sample means may also be computed directly from the SDs of the sample means through the following formula:

$$S_{\bar{X}_1 - \bar{X}_2} = \sqrt{\frac{s_1^2}{N_1} + \frac{s_2^2}{N_2}} = \sqrt{\frac{(4)^2}{48} + \frac{(3)^2}{45}} = \sqrt{\frac{16}{48} + \frac{9}{45}}$$
$$= \sqrt{0.3333 + 0.20} = \sqrt{0.5333} = 0.73 \text{ (to two decimals)}.$$

Step 6. Assuming the H_0 to be correct, the difference between the sample means is converted to 'z' scores through the following formula:

$$z = \frac{(\bar{X}_1 - \bar{X}_2)}{S_{\bar{X}_1 - \bar{X}_2}} = \frac{35.0 - 30.0}{0.73} = \frac{5.0}{0.73} = 6.85.$$

Step 7. The unit normal curve table (Table A of the appendix) is used to find out the one-tail probability (p) of obtaining the computed 'z' score, and, hence, the observed difference between two sample means, by chance due to random sampling:

p=[0.50–(fractional area of unit normal curve from μ to computed z)]
=[0.50–0.49997]=0.00003.

(Note: In Table A of the appendix the fractional area is given up to the 'z' value of 4.0. Since our obtained z=6.85, the probability (p) will be much less than 0.00003).

Step 8. This obtained p of 0.00003 will be compared with the α levels of 0.05 and 0.01 for testing the significance of mean difference. In this example, because the computed 'p' of 0.00003 is much less than the chosen α of 0.05 and 0.01, the probability of the H_0 being correct is considered too low (p<0.05 and p<0.01). The H_0 is, therefore, rejected and H_1 is accepted. This shows that the two sample means are significantly different from each other. In other words, $\bar{X}_1$ is greater than $\bar{X}_2$; the gain on account of drill work is significant in 99% of cases, and, hence, drill work may be taken as a significant factor for the promotion of the computation skill.

As an alternative to Steps 7 and 8, the computed 'z' value can be compared directly with the critical values of 'z' given in Table A of the appendix for the 0.05 and 0.01 levels of significance. It is found from Table A that the critical values of 'z' at the 0.05 and 0.01 levels for a one-tailed test are 1.645 (or 1.65) and 2.325 (or 2.33), respectively. Since the obtained 'z' of 6.85 is much greater than both the critical values, it is significant at both the 0.05 and 0.01 levels of significance. Therefore, we may say that the mean score of the experimental group is significantly higher than that of the control group in 99% of cases. In other words, the gain on account of drill work is significant and drill work may be taken as a significant factor for the promotion of the computation skill of the students. Thus, the H_0 is rejected and H_1 is accepted in 99% of cases (p<0.01).

Example 12.3 In an abstract reasoning test, the mean score of 114 men was 23.7 with the SD of 6.08. Similarly, the mean score of 175 women was 21.0 with the SD of 4.89. (a) Find whether or not there is a significant difference between the means of the two samples (α=0.05). (b) Is the mean of men significantly higher than that of the women (α=0.01)?

Solution

Given data: Men: $\bar{X}_1 = 23.7$; $s_1 = 6.08$; $N_1 = 114$
            Women: $\bar{X}_2 = 21.0$; $s_2 = 4.89$; $N_2 = 175$.

(a) We have to test whether there is a significant difference between the two sample means.

Step 1. Since no direction of difference is given, it is a two-tailed test for the significance of difference between two independent and large sample means.

Step 2. H_0 proposes that the two means, $\bar{X}_1$ and $\bar{X}_2$, do not differ significantly; the observed difference, if any, being due only to chances of random sampling. On the contrary, the H_1 intends to mean that the two means, $\bar{X}_1$ and $\bar{X}_2$, are significantly different, and this difference is a real or genuine difference. So, the H_0 and H_1 are stated as follows:

$$H_0: \ \bar{X}_1 = \bar{X}_2; \ \ H_1: \ \bar{X}_1 \neq \bar{X}_2$$

or

$$H_0: \ \bar{X}_1 = \bar{X}_2 = 0; \ \ H_1: \ \bar{X}_1 - \bar{X}_2 \neq 0.$$

Step 3. With regard to the level of significance of the test, as per the question, we are to test the difference between two sample means at the 0.05 level of significance ($\alpha = 0.05$).

Step 4. The SEs of sample means are first computed using the respective SDs and sample sizes as follows:

$$s_{\bar{X}_1} = \frac{s_1}{\sqrt{N_1}} = \frac{6.08}{\sqrt{114}} = \frac{6.08}{10.68} = 0.57,$$

$$s_{\bar{X}_2} = \frac{s_2}{\sqrt{N_2}} = \frac{4.89}{\sqrt{175}} = \frac{4.89}{13.23} = 0.37.$$

Step 5. The SE_D between the sample means is then computed using the $s_{\bar{X}_1}$ and $s_{\bar{X}_2}$ through the following formula:

$$s_{\bar{X}_1 - \bar{X}_2} = \sqrt{(s_{\bar{X}_1})^2 + (s_{\bar{X}_2})^2} = \sqrt{(0.57)^2 + (0.37)^2} = \sqrt{0.3249 + 0.1369}$$

$$= \sqrt{0.4618} = 0.68 \ \text{(to two decimals)}.$$

As an alternative to Steps 4 and 5, the SE_D (or $s_{\bar{X}_1 - \bar{X}_2}$) between two sample means may also be computed directly from the SDs of the sample means as follows:

$$s_{\bar{X}_1 - \bar{X}_2} = \sqrt{\frac{s_1^2}{N_1} + \frac{s_2^2}{N_2}} = \sqrt{\frac{(6.08)^2}{114} + \frac{(4.89)^2}{175}} = \sqrt{\frac{36.9664}{114} + \frac{23.9121}{175}}$$

$$= \sqrt{0.3243 + 0.1366} = \sqrt{0.4609} = 0.68 \ \text{(to two decimals)}.$$

Step 6. Assuming the H_0 to be correct, the difference $(\bar{X}_1 - \bar{X}_2)$ between the two sample means is first transformed into the 'z' scores as follows:

$$z = \frac{\bar{X}_1 - \bar{X}_2}{s_{\bar{X}_1 - \bar{X}_2}} = \frac{23.7 - 21.0}{0.68} = \frac{2.7}{0.68} = 3.97.$$

Step 7. We can test the significance of the obtained 'z' value in terms of the critical values of 'z' given in Table A of the appendix. It is evident from Table A that the critical value of 'z', for a two-tailed test, at the 0.05 level of significance is 1.96. Since the obtained 'z' value of 3.97 is higher than the critical value of 'z' of 1.96 (i.e., $z_{obt.} > 1.96$), the marked difference between two sample means is significant at the 0.05 level of significance ($p < 0.05$). The H_0 is rejected and H_1 is accepted. This means that the observed difference between the two sample means is statistically significant. In other words, men and women differ significantly from each other with regard to their abstract reasoning in 95% of cases.

(b) Is the mean of men significantly higher than that of the women ($\alpha = 0.01$)?

Step 1. Since a clear-cut direction ($\bar{X}_1 > \bar{X}_2$) is given, it is a one-tailed test for the significance of $\bar{X}_1$ being higher than $\bar{X}_2$.

Step 2. H_0 contends that $\bar{X}_1$ is not significantly higher than $\bar{X}_2$, whereas the H_1 states that $\bar{X}_1$ is significantly higher than $\bar{X}_2$. So, H_0 and H_1 are stated as follows:

$$H_0: \ \bar{X}_1 \not> \bar{X}_2; \ \ H_1: \ \bar{X}_1 > \bar{X}_2.$$

Step 3. With regard to the level of significance of the test, as per the question, we test that $\bar{X}_1$ is not significantly higher than $\bar{X}_2$ at the 0.01 level of significance ($\alpha = 0.01$).

Step 4. Assuming the H_0 to be correct, the difference ($\bar{X}_1 - \bar{X}_2$) between the two sample means is first converted to the 'z' score in the same way as that for the two-tailed test given above. Thus, $z = 3.97$.

Step 5. The significance of the obtained 'z' value can be tested by comparing it with the critical value of 'z' given in Table A of the appendix for the 0.01 level of significance. It is found from Table A that the critical value of 'z' at 0.01, for a one-tailed test, is 2.325 (or 2.33). Since the obtained 'z' of 3.97 is much greater than the critical value of 'z' of 2.33 (i.e., $z_{obt.} > 2.33$), it is significant at the 0.01 level of significance. This leads to the rejection of H_0 and acceptance of H_1. Therefore, we may say that the abstract reasoning mean score of men is significantly higher than that of women in 99% of cases ($p < 0.01$).

12.5 Significance of the Difference between Two Means Using 't' Test

The 't' test is a parametric statistical test which is used for testing the significance of difference between two group means or sample means. These two group means may be uncorrelated/independent or may be correlated/dependent. Two means are uncorrelated when computed from different samples; it is correlated when computed from the same sample or matched samples.

A difference is called significant when the probability is enough high that it cannot be attributed to chance (i.e., temporary or accidental factors), and, hence, represents a true difference between population means. A difference is non-significant or a chance when it appears reasonably certain that it could easily have arisen from sampling fluctuations, and, hence, implies no real or true difference between the population means.

In studies using small samples ($N < 30$) drawn at random from a population in which the variable under investigation has a normal distribution, the scores of a small sample are distributed in the form of a 't' distribution. Therefore, to test the significance of the difference between the means of two small samples, that difference ($\bar{X}_1 - \bar{X}_2$) is converted to Student's 't' score/ratio, which is then interpreted with reference to the appropriate 't' distribution.

12.5.1   Assumptions for '*t*' Test

The following are some of the important assumptions of the '*t*' test:

(a)   The observations must be independent, which implies two things—that the selection of samples from the population should be random and the assignment of scores to the performance of the samples should be impartial and unbiased.

(b)   The dependent variable whose changes are being studied is a continuous measurement variable. In other words, the measurements should be in terms of the interval scale of measurement.

(c)   The sampling distribution of the difference between two sample means, that is $(\bar{X}_1 - \bar{X}_2)$, is normally distributed. This means that the dependent variable or the trait that the researcher is going to measure must be normally distributed in the population from which the samples were drawn.

(d)   Each score of the dependent variable occurs at random and independent of all other scores in the sample.

(e)   The populations from which the samples are selected must have the homogeneity of variances. In other words, the samples are taken from populations having identical/equal variances ($\sigma_1^2 = \sigma_2^2$).

(f)   The '*t*' test for correlated groups requires that the sampling distribution of the mean difference ($\bar{D}$) be normally distributed. This means that '*N*' should be ≥ 30, assuming that the population shape does not differ greatly from normality, or the population scores themselves should be normally distributed.

Thus, it follows from the above assumptions that '*t*' tests cannot be applied or used if the dependent variable in experiment/study is a discrete, ordinal or nominal variable, if it has a non-normal distribution in the population, or if the populations from which the two samples have been drawn differ in their variances.

12.5.2   Degrees of Freedom of '*t*'

The degrees of freedom (df) of the computed '*t*' must always be considered for its interpretation because the '*t*' distributions, unlike the normal distribution, vary with the df. Therefore, the computed '*t*' must be referred to the '*t*' distribution specific for the df of the computed '*t*' for interpretation.

The unit normal curve closely approximates or almost coincides with the '*t*' distribution for high df (i.e., for large sample sizes). So, the '*t*' test can be applied not only to small samples ($N < 30$) but also to large ones, even to those with '*N*' approaching infinite (∞). There are also very close similarities between the critical '*z*' scores and the critical '*t*' scores with df$=\infty$ for identical levels of significance. Thus, it implies that for testing the significance of difference between two large sample means with df$=\infty$, either the '*z*' test or '*t*' test may be applied. But '*t*' tests alone are applicable to small samples because their distributions conform to leptokurtic '*t*' distributions only, instead of the mesokurtic normal distribution.

12.5.3   Two-tailed '*t*' Test

The two-tailed '*t*' test is used to find out whether or not an observed difference between two sample means is significant, irrespective of the algebraic sign of the difference. It investigates the probability (p) of correctness of the null hypothesis (H_0), which states that the two sample means are not significantly different from each other and are estimates of the same population parameter. Thus, the H_0 and H_1 are stated as follows:

$$H_0: \quad \mu_1 = \mu_2 \quad \text{or} \quad \mu_1 - \mu_2 = 0$$
$$H_1: \quad \mu_1 \neq \mu_2 \quad \text{or} \quad \mu_1 - \mu_2 \neq 0.$$

Assuming the H_0 to be correct, the observed difference between two sample means ($\bar{X}_1 - \bar{X}_2$) is transformed into the 't' score using the same basic formula as is used in computing the 'z' score. This formula reads as follows:

$$t = \frac{\bar{X}_1 - \bar{X}_2}{s_{\bar{X}_1 - \bar{X}_2}}.$$

However, the $s_{\bar{X}_1 - \bar{X}_2}$ may be computed here in several alternative ways according to the nature of the sample and the type of experiment.

The probability (p) of the H_0 being correct is obtained from the fractional areas in the two tails of the relevant 't' distribution beyond the computed 't' score. For this purpose, the computed 't' score is compared with the two-tailed critical 't' score having the same df as that of the computed 't', and for the chosen level of significance (α). So long as the computed 't' exceeds or equals the critical 't' score, the 'p' given by the total of the fractional areas in the two tails beyond the computed 't' does not exceed α ($p \leq \alpha$). The H_0 is then considered to have too low a probability of being correct and may be rejected—the means are then considered to differ significantly from each other. But if the computed 't' is lower than the critical 't' score, the total fractional area in the two tails beyond the computed t (and, hence, the p) exceeds the chosen α ($p > \alpha$). The H_0 is then taken to have a high probability of being correct and cannot be rejected—the difference between the two sample means is then considered as not significant.

In simple words, it can be stated that if the obtained 't' value is greater than or equal to the table value of 't' with a particular df and for a specific level of significance for a two-tailed test, then the obtained 't' score is said to be significant at that level of significance ($p \leq \alpha$); so H_0 is rejected and H_1 is accepted, which means that the difference between two sample means is statistically significant. If, on the other hand, the obtained 't' score is less than the table value of 't', then it is not significant ($p > \alpha$); so H_0 is accepted and H_1 is rejected, which means that the difference between two sample means is not statistically significant.

12.5.4 One-tailed 't' Test

The one-tailed 't' test is used to see whether or not one of the two means is significantly higher or lower than the other. It investigates the probability (p) of correctness of the H_0 which states that one mean is not significantly higher (or lower) than the other. The H_0 and H_1 are stated below:

$$H_0: \quad \text{Either} \quad \mu_1 \not> \mu_2 \quad \text{or} \quad \mu_1 \not< \mu_2$$
$$H_1: \quad \text{Either} \quad \mu_1 > \mu_2 \quad \text{or} \quad \mu_1 < \mu_2.$$

Assuming the H_0 to be correct, the observed difference between two sample means ($\bar{X}_1 - \bar{X}_2$) is converted to 't' score in the same way as in the case of a two-tailed test. The probability (p) of the H_0 being correct is obtained from the fractional area in a single tail of the relevant 't' distribution beyond the computed 't' score. For this purpose, the computed 't' score is compared with the one-tailed critical 't' score having the same df as that of the computed 't' and for the chosen alpha (α). If the computed 't' exceeds or equals the critical 't', the fractional area in one tail beyond the computed 't' (and hence, the p) does not exceed α ($p \leq \alpha$). If this is the case, the H_0 is then considered to have too low a probability of being correct and may be rejected, and, thus, one of the means is considered to be significantly higher (or lower) than the other. But if the computed 't' is lower than the critical 't', the fractional area in one tail beyond the computed 't' (and hence the p) exceeds α ($p > \alpha$). Hence, the H_0 is then taken to have a high probability of being correct, and cannot be rejected—one of the sample means is then considered not to be significantly higher (or lower) than the other.

Put it into other words, if the obtained 't' ratio is greater than or equal to the table value of 't' with reference to a particular df and a chosen α for a one-tailed test, then the obtained 't' score is said to be significant at that particular level of significance ($p \leq \alpha$). This indicates that H_0 is rejected and H_1 is accepted, which means that one of the sample means is significantly higher (or lower) than the other. On the contrary, if the obtained 't' score is less than the table value of 't', then it is not significant ($p > \alpha$); so H_0 is accepted and H_1 is rejected, which indicates that one of the sample means is neither significantly higher nor lower than the other mean.

12.5.5   't' Tests for Independent Sample Means

Two or more random samples used in an independent group experiment are drawn from the population independent of each other so that such samples consist of separate groups of individuals, and may or may not be identical/equal in size. One of these random samples serves as the control group that does not receive any treatment with the independent variable, while the other constitutes the experimental group that receives treatment with the independent variable. After a specific period of such differential treatments, the dependent variable being investigated is measured in both the control and experimental groups. The scores of the dependent variable, obtained in this way from such independent groups, constitute *unpaired observations*. The means of the scores of such independent groups are *uncorrelated* to each other. The significance of the difference between two such group means may be estimated by the 't' test in several ways depending upon whether the samples or groups are large or small, equal or unequal in size.

12.5.5.1   *For Small Independent Samples of Unequal Sizes*

For testing the significance of the difference between means of two independent small samples ($N_1 < 30$; $N_2 < 30$) of unequal sizes ($N_1 \neq N_2$), drawn from populations having equal variances, the observed difference between the two sample means ($\bar{X}_1 - \bar{X}_2$) is converted to a 't' score using a pooled standard derivation ($\hat{s}$) or a common variance ($\hat{s}^2$). It is noted here that s_1^2 and s_2^2 are the variances of the respective sample means; $s_{\bar{X}_1}$ and $s_{\bar{X}_2}$ are the SEs of the respective sample means; and $s_{\bar{X}_1 - \bar{X}_2}$ is the SE of the difference between the means. The $\hat{s}$, $s_{\bar{X}_1 - \bar{X}_2}$ and 't' are computed by the following formulae:

$$\hat{s} = \sqrt{\frac{\Sigma(X_1 - \bar{X}_1)^2 + \Sigma(X_2 - \bar{X}_2)^2}{(N_1 - 1) + (N_2 - 1)}} = \sqrt{\frac{\Sigma x_1^2 + \Sigma x_2^2}{N_1 + N_2 - 2}}$$

$$= \sqrt{\frac{s_1^2(N_1 - 1) + s_2^2(N_2 - 1)}{N_1 + N_2 - 2}} \text{ (when values of } s_1 \text{ and } s_2 \text{ are given instead of raw scores)}$$

$$S_{\bar{X}_1-\bar{X}_2} = \sqrt{(s_{\bar{X}_1})^2 + (s_{\bar{X}_2})^2} = \sqrt{\frac{s_1^2}{N_1} + \frac{s_2^2}{N_2}} = \sqrt{\frac{\hat{s}^2}{N_1} + \frac{\hat{s}^2}{N_2}}$$

$$= \hat{s}\sqrt{\frac{N_1 + N_2}{N_1 N_2}} = \hat{s}\sqrt{\frac{1}{N_1} + \frac{1}{N_2}}$$

$$t = \frac{\bar{X}_1 - \bar{X}_2}{s_{\bar{X}_1-\bar{X}_2}}$$

$$df = (N_1 - 1) + (N_2 - 1) = N_1 + N_2 - 2.$$

The entire procedure of testing the significance of difference between means of two independent small samples of unequal sizes using the 't' test will be more clear through the following examples.

Example 12.4 An interest t-test is administered to 6 boys in a vocational training class (VTC) and to 10 boys in a Latin class (LC). Their scores are presented in the first two columns of Table 12.1. Find whether the mean difference between the two groups is significant.

Solution

(a) The H_0 states that there is no significant difference between the two sample means. To find the probability (p) of the H_0 being correct, a two-tailed test is done using the pooled SD ($\hat{s}$) because the samples are of small but unequal sizes. The H_0 and H_1 are stated below:

$$H_0: \ \bar{X}_1 = \bar{X}_2; \quad \text{or} \quad \bar{X}_1 - \bar{X}_2 = 0$$
$$H_1: \ \bar{X}_1 \neq \bar{X}_2; \quad \text{or} \quad \bar{X}_1 - \bar{X}_2 \neq 0.$$

Table 12.1 Computation of means and SDs of interest test scores

1	2	3	4	5	6
Interest Test Scores		$(X_1 - \bar{X}_1)$ (x_1)	$(X_1 - \bar{X}_1)^2$ (x_1^2)	$(X_2 - \bar{X}_2)$ (x_2)	$(X_2 - \bar{X}_2)^2$ (x_2^2)
VTC(X_1)	LC(X_2)				
28	20	−2	4	−4	16
35	16	5	25	−8	64
32	25	2	4	1	1
24	34	−6	36	10	100
26	20	−4	16	−4	16
35	28	5	25	4	16
	31			7	49
	24			0	0
	27			3	9
	15			−9	81
180 (ΣX_1) $N_1=6$	240 (ΣX_2) $N_2=10$		110 $\Sigma(X_1-\bar{X}_1)^2$ or (Σx_1^2)		352 $\Sigma(X_2-\bar{X}_2)^2$ or (Σx_2^2)

(b) Using the data presented in Table 12.1, the sample means $\bar{X}_1$ and $\bar{X}_2$ are first computed:

$$\Sigma X_1 = 180, \quad N_1 = 6, \quad \bar{X}_1 = \frac{\Sigma X_1}{N_1} = \frac{180}{6} = 30.0$$

$$\Sigma X_2 = 240, \quad N_2 = 10, \quad \bar{X}_2 = \frac{\Sigma X_2}{N_2} = \frac{240}{10} = 24.0.$$

(c) The deviations of scores of each sample from the corresponding sample mean are worked out and squared, and the squared deviations of each sample are totalled to give the respective sums of squared deviations. From Table 12.1,

$$\Sigma(X_1 - \bar{X}_1)^2 = \Sigma x_1^2 = 110; \quad \Sigma(X_2 - \bar{X}_2)^2 = \Sigma x_2^2 = 352.$$

(d) The pooled SD ($\hat{s}$) is computed using the sums of squared deviations:

$$\hat{s} = \sqrt{\frac{\Sigma(X_1 - \bar{X}_1)^2 + \Sigma(X_2 - \bar{X}_2)^2}{(N_1 - 1) + (N_2 - 1)}} = \sqrt{\frac{\Sigma x_1^2 + \Sigma x_2^2}{N_1 + N_2 - 2}}$$

$$= \sqrt{\frac{110 + 352}{6 + 10 - 2}} = \sqrt{\frac{462}{14}} = \sqrt{33} = 5.74.$$

(e) The SE of the difference between the means ($s_{\bar{X}_1 - \bar{X}_2}$) is computed using the pooled SD ($\hat{s}$):

$$s_{\bar{X}_1 - \bar{X}_2} = \hat{s}\sqrt{\frac{N_1 + N_2}{N_1 N_2}} = 5.74\sqrt{\frac{6 + 10}{6 \times 10}} = 5.74\sqrt{\frac{16}{60}} = 5.74\sqrt{0.2667}$$

$$= 5.74 \times 0.516 = 2.96.$$

(f) The difference between the two sample means ($\bar{X}_1 - \bar{X}_2$) is converted to the 't' score:

$$t = \frac{\bar{X}_1 - \bar{X}_2}{s_{\bar{X}_1 - \bar{X}_2}} = \frac{30 - 24}{2.96} = \frac{6.0}{2.96} = 2.03$$

$$df = N_1 + N_2 - 2 = 6 + 10 - 2 = 14.$$

(g) Entering Table C (given in the appendix) with df=14, the two-tailed critical value of 't' at the 0.05 level of significance is 2.145 and at the 0.01 level is 2.977. The computed or observed 't' of 2.03 is less than the critical 't' values at both the levels of significance. Hence, the H_0 is accepted and H_1 is rejected. The probability of H_0 being correct is greater than α (i.e., $p > 0.05$). We may conclude that the difference between the two means of interest t-test scores of two small but independent groups of boys is not statistically significant; hence, the given difference in these two sample means being insignificant can only be attributed to some chance factors or random sampling fluctuations.

Example 12.5 Under the assumption that newspaper reading will increase the vocabulary, the experimental group was given 2 hours daily in the library for reading newspapers, while no such facility was provided to the control group. After six months of such differential treatment, both the groups were given a vocabulary test. The scores obtained are given below. Test whether newspaper reading has a significant facilitatory effect on the vocabulary of the subjects.

Experimental group: 120, 122, 111, 112, 120
Control group: 110, 112, 95, 105, 110, 95, 112, 101.

Table 12.2   Computation of means and SD of vocabulary test scores (VTS)

Experimental Group			Control Group		
VTS(X_1)	(x_1) $(X_1 - \bar{X}_1)$	x_1^2	VTS (X_2)	(x_2) $(X_2 - \bar{X}_2)$	x_2^2
120	3	9	110	5	25
122	5	25	112	7	49
111	−6	36	95	−10	100
112	−5	25	105	0	0
120	3	9	110	5	25
			95	−10	100
			112	7	49
			101	−4	16
585 (ΣX_1), $N_1 = 5$		104 (Σx_1^2)	840 (ΣX_2), $N_2 = 8$		364 (Σx_2^2)

Solution

(a)   The given data are entered in Table 12.2 as follows:

(b)   The H_0 contends that the newspaper reading has no significant facilitatory effect on vocabulary of the subjects. A one-tailed test is done to estimate the probability of the H_0 being correct. The H_0 and H_1 are stated below:

$$H_0:\ \bar{X}_1 \not> \bar{X}_2;\quad H_1:\ \bar{X}_1 > \bar{X}_2;$$

(c)   Using the data presented in Table 12.2, the sample means $\bar{X}_1$ and $\bar{X}_2$ are first computed

$$\Sigma X_1 = 585,\quad N_1 = 5,\quad \bar{X}_1 = \frac{\Sigma X_1}{N_1} = \frac{585}{5} = 117.0$$

$$\Sigma X_2 = 840,\quad N_2 = 8,\quad \bar{X}_2 = \frac{\Sigma X_2}{N_2} = \frac{840}{8} = 105.0.$$

(d)   The deviations of scores of each sample/group from the corresponding group mean are worked out and squared, and the squared deviations of each group are totalled to give the respective sums of squared deviations. From Table 12.2,

$$\Sigma(X_1 - \bar{X}_1)^2 = \Sigma x_1^2 = 104;\quad \Sigma(X_2 - \bar{X}_2)^2 = \Sigma x_2^2 = 364.$$

(e)   The pooled SD ($\hat{s}$) is computed using the sums of squared deviations:

$$\hat{s} = \sqrt{\frac{\Sigma x_1^2 + \Sigma x_2^2}{N_1 + N_2 - 2}} = \sqrt{\frac{104 + 364}{5 + 8 - 2}} = \sqrt{\frac{468}{11}} = \sqrt{42.545} = 6.52.$$

(f)   The SE of the difference between the means ($s_{\bar{X}_1-\bar{X}_2}$) is computed using the pooled SD ($\hat{s}$):

$$s_{\bar{X}_1-\bar{X}_2} = \hat{s}\sqrt{\frac{N_1+N_2}{N_1 N_2}} = 6.52\sqrt{\frac{5+8}{5\times 8}} = 6.52\sqrt{\frac{13}{40}} = 6.52\sqrt{0.325}$$

$$= 6.52 \times 0.57 = 3.72.$$

(g)   The difference between the two sample means ($\bar{X}_1 - \bar{X}_2$) is converted to the 't' score as follows:

$$t = \frac{\bar{X}_1 - \bar{X}_2}{s_{\bar{X}_1-\bar{X}_2}} = \frac{117.0 - 105.0}{3.72} = \frac{12.0}{3.72} = 3.23$$

$$\text{df} = N_1 + N_2 - 2 = 5 + 8 - 2 = 11.$$

(h)   Entering Table C (given in the appendix) with df=11, the one-tailed critical value of 't' at the 0.05 level of significance is 1.796 and at the 0.01 level is 2.718. The computed or calculated 't' of 3.23 is higher than the critical 't' values at both the levels of significance. So the probability (p) of the H_0 being correct is less than 0.01 ($p<0.01$). Hence, the H_0 is rejected and H_1 is accepted. We may conclude that $\bar{X}_1$ is significantly higher than $\bar{X}_2$ in 99% of cases; in other words, newspaper reading has a significant facilitatory effect on the vocabulary of the subjects in 99% of cases.

Example 12.6 On an arithmetic reasoning test 11, ten-year-old boys and 6 ten-year-old girls made the following scores:

	Mean	SD	N	df
Boys	40.50	4.5	11	10
Girls	38.00	5.5	6	5

Is the mean difference of 2.50 significant at the 0.05 level of significance?

Solution

(a)   The given data are:

Boys: $\bar{X}_1 = 40.50$; $s_1 = 4.5$; $N_1 = 11$;   df $= N_1 - 1 = 10$
Girls: $\bar{X}_2 = 38.00$; $s_2 = 5.5$; $N_2 = 6$;   df $= N_2 - 1 = 5$.

(b)   The H_0 states that the $\bar{X}_1$ is not significantly higher than $\bar{X}_2$. A one-tailed 't' test is performed to estimate the probability (p) of the H_0 being correct. The H_0 and H_1 are stated below:

$$H_0 : \bar{X}_1 \not> \bar{X}_2; \quad H_1 : \bar{X}_1 > \bar{X}_2.$$

(c)   As the samples are small but unequal, the pooled SD ($\hat{s}$) of the sample means is first computed using their unbiased SDs (s_1 and s_2), as follows:

$$\hat{s} = \sqrt{\frac{s_1^2(N_1-1)+s_2^2(N_2-1)}{N_1+N_2-2}} = \sqrt{\frac{(4.5)^2(11-1)+(5.5)^2(6-1)}{11+6-2}}$$

$$= \sqrt{\frac{20.25 \times 10 + 30.25 \times 5}{15}} = \sqrt{\frac{202.5 + 151.25}{15}} = \sqrt{\frac{353.75}{15}}$$

$$= \sqrt{23.5833} = 4.86.$$

(d) The SE of the difference between the means is then computed using the $\hat{s}$ as follows:

$$s_{\bar{X}_1-\bar{X}_2} = \hat{s}\sqrt{\frac{N_1+N_2}{N_1 N_2}} = 4.86\sqrt{\frac{11+6}{11\times 6}} = 4.86\sqrt{\frac{17}{66}}$$

$$= 4.86\sqrt{0.2576} = 4.86\times 0.51 = 2.48.$$

(e) The difference between the two sample means $(\bar{X}_1 - \bar{X}_2)$ is converted to the 't' score, as follows:

$$t = \frac{\bar{X}_1 - \bar{X}_2}{s_{\bar{X}_1-\bar{X}_2}} = \frac{40.50-38.00}{2.48} = \frac{2.50}{2.48} = 1.01$$

$$df = N_1 + N_2 - 2 = 11 + 6 - 2 = 15.$$

(f) Entering Table C (given in the appendix) with df=15, the one-tailed critical value of 't' at the 0.05 level of significance is 1.753. The computed 't' score is found to be lower than the critical 't' value at the 0.05 level ($t_{0.05}$). So the probability (p) of H_0 being correct is higher than 0.05 ($p>0.05$). Hence, the H_0 cannot be rejected. In other words, H_0 is accepted and H_1 is rejected.

Therefore, we may conclude that mean difference of 2.50 is not significant at the 0.05 level of significance; $\bar{X}_1$ is not significantly higher than $\bar{X}_2$, and, thus, the insignificance of the difference between these two sample means can only be attributed to some chance factors or random sampling fluctuations.

Example 12.7 Two random samples gave the following results:

Sample	Size	Sample Mean	Sum of Squares of Deviations from the Mean
1	10	15	90
2	12	14	108

Test whether the samples have come from the same normal population.

Solution

(a) The given data are:

Sample 1: $\bar{X}_1 = 15.0$; $\Sigma x_1^2 = 90$; $N_1 = 10$

Sample 2: $\bar{X}_2 = 14.0$; $\Sigma x_2^2 = 108$; $N_2 = 12$.

(b) The H_0 states that the samples have come from the same normal population, whereas the H_1 states that the samples have come from different populations. To find the probability (p) of the H_0 being correct, a two-tailed 't' test is done using the pooled SD ($\hat{s}$), because the samples are of small but unequal sizes. The H_0 and H_1 are stated as follows:

$$H_0:\ \bar{X}_1 = \bar{X}_2;\ \text{ or }\ \bar{X}_1 - \bar{X}_2 = 0$$
$$H_1:\ \bar{X}_1 \neq \bar{X}_2;\ \text{ or }\ \bar{X}_1 - \bar{X}_2 \neq 0$$

(c)   As the samples are small but unequal, the $\hat{s}$ of the sample means is first computed using the sums of squares of deviations from the respective means (i.e., Σx_1^2 and Σx_2^2):

$$\hat{s} = \sqrt{\frac{\Sigma x_1^2 + \Sigma x_2^2}{N_1 + N_2 - 2}} = \sqrt{\frac{90 + 108}{10 + 12 - 2}} = \sqrt{\frac{198}{20}} = \sqrt{9.9} = 3.15.$$

(d)   The SE of the difference between the means is then computed using ($\hat{s}$) as follows:

$$s_{\bar{X}_1 - \bar{X}_2} = \hat{s}\sqrt{\frac{N_1 + N_2}{N_1 N_2}} = 3.15\sqrt{\frac{10 + 12}{10 \times 12}} = 3.15\sqrt{\frac{22}{120}} = 3.15\sqrt{0.1833}$$

$$= 3.15 \times 0.428 = 1.35.$$

(e)   The difference between the two sample means ($\bar{X}_1 - \bar{X}_2$) is converted to the 't' score as follows:

$$t = \frac{\bar{X}_1 - \bar{X}_2}{s_{\bar{X}_1 - \bar{X}_2}} = \frac{15.0 - 14.0}{1.35} = \frac{1.00}{1.35} = 0.74$$

$$df = N_1 + N_2 - 2 = 10 + 12 - 2 = 20.$$

(f)   Entering Table C (given in the appendix) with df = 20, the two-tailed critical value of 't' at the 0.05 level of significance is 2.086 and at the 0.01 level of significance is 2.845. The computed 't' score of 0.74 is lower than the critical 't' values at both the levels of significance. So the probability (p) of H_0 being correct is higher than 0.05 ($p > 0.05$). Hence, the H_0 cannot be rejected. In other words, the difference between two sample means is not statistically significant. Therefore, we may conclude that the samples have come from the same normal population.

12.5.5.2   For Both Small and Large Independent Samples of Equal Sizes

If two independent samples have equal sizes ($N_1 = N_2$) and have been drawn from populations having the same variance, the $\hat{s}$, $s_{\bar{X}_1 - \bar{X}_2}$ and 't' may be computed as follows, irrespective of the sample sizes, either small or large, where $N_1 = N_2 = N$:

$$\hat{s} = \sqrt{\frac{\Sigma(X_1 - \bar{X}_1)^2 + \Sigma(X_2 - \bar{X}_2)^2}{2(N-1)}} = \sqrt{\frac{\Sigma x_1^2 + \Sigma x_2^2}{2(N-1)}} = \sqrt{\frac{s_1^2 + s_2^2}{2}}$$

$$s_{\bar{X}_1 - \bar{X}_2} = \sqrt{(s_{\bar{X}_1})^2 + (s_{\bar{X}_2})^2} = \sqrt{\frac{s_1^2 + s_2^2}{N}} = \sqrt{\frac{\hat{s}^2}{N} + \frac{\hat{s}^2}{N}} = \hat{s}\sqrt{\frac{2}{N}}$$

$$t = \frac{\bar{X}_1 - \bar{X}_2}{s_{\bar{X}_1 - \bar{X}_2}}; \quad df = 2(N-1).$$

The entire procedure of testing the significance of difference between the means of two independent small and large samples of equal sizes using the 't' test will be more clear through the following examples.

Example 12.8 In a numerical operations test, the mean and SD of the scores of 16 boys were found to be 40.3 and 8.15, respectively; these values amounted to 37.5 and 6.35, respectively, for 16 girls. Is there a significant difference between the means of boys and girls?

Solution

(a) The given data are:

$$\text{Boys:} \quad \bar{X}_1 = 40.3; \quad s_1 = 8.15; \quad N_1 = 16$$
$$\text{Girls:} \quad \bar{X}_2 = 37.5; \quad s_2 = 6.35; \quad N_2 = 16$$

Size of each sample $= N_1 = N_2 = N = 16$.

(b) The H_0 states that there is no significant difference between two sample means. To find the probability (p) of this H_0 to be correct, a two-tailed 't' test is done using pooled SD ($\hat{s}$), because the samples are of small but equal sizes. The H_0 and H_1 are stated as follows:

$$H_0: \quad \bar{X}_1 = \bar{X}_2; \quad \text{or} \quad \bar{X}_1 - \bar{X}_2 = 0$$
$$H_1: \quad \bar{X}_1 \neq \bar{X}_2; \quad \text{or} \quad \bar{X}_1 - \bar{X}_2 \neq 0.$$

(c) The pooled SD ($\hat{s}$) is computed using the unbiased SDs (s_1 and s_2) of the two independent small samples of equal sizes as follows:

$$\hat{s} = \sqrt{\frac{s_1^2 + s_2^2}{2}} = \sqrt{\frac{(8.15)^2 + (6.35)^2}{2}}$$
$$= \sqrt{\frac{66.4225 + 40.3225}{2}} = \sqrt{\frac{106.745}{2}} = \sqrt{53.3725} = 7.306.$$

(d) Using the formula for independent small samples of equal sizes, the SE of the difference between the means ($s_{\bar{X}_1 - \bar{X}_2}$) is computed using the $\hat{s}$ as follows:

$$s_{\bar{X}_1 - \bar{X}_2} = \hat{s}\sqrt{\frac{2}{N}} = 7.306\sqrt{\frac{2}{16}} = 7.306\sqrt{0.125}$$
$$= 7.306 \times 0.353 = 2.58.$$

(e) The difference between the two sample means ($\bar{X}_1 - \bar{X}_2$) is converted to the 't' score as follows:

$$t = \frac{\bar{X}_1 - \bar{X}_2}{s_{\bar{X}_1 - \bar{X}_2}} = \frac{40.3 - 37.5}{2.58} = \frac{2.8}{2.58} = 1.085$$

$$df = 2(N-1) = 2(16-1) = 2 \times 15 = 30.$$

(f) Entering Table C (given in the appendix) with df = 30, the two-tailed critical values of 't' at the 0.05 level of significance is 2.042 and at the 0.01 level is 2.750. The computed 't' of 1.085 is even lower than the critical 't' value for the 0.05 level of significance. Hence, the probability (p) of the H_0 being correct exceeds 0.05 ($p > 0.05$). Thus, the H_0 cannot be rejected. In other words, H_0 is accepted and H_1 is rejected. Therefore, we may conclude that there is not a significant difference between the means of boys and girls; whatever difference is there between their means, it is attributed to some chance factors or random sampling fluctuations.

Example 12.9 Two groups of students, each having 10 students, got the following scores on an attitude scale:

Group I: 10, 9, 8, 7, 7, 8, 6, 5, 6, 4
Group II: 9, 8, 6, 7, 8, 8, 11, 12, 6, 5.

Test the significance of the difference between these two group means.

Solution

(a) The given data are entered in Table 12.3:

(b) The H_0 states that there is no significant difference between the two group means. To find the probability (p) of the H_0 being correct, a two-tailed 't' test is done using the pooled SD ($\hat{s}$) because the groups are of small but equal sizes. The H_0 and H_1 are stated as follows:

$$H_0: \bar{X}_1 = \bar{X}_2; \quad \text{or} \quad \bar{X}_1 - \bar{X}_2 = 0$$
$$H_1: \bar{X}_1 \neq \bar{X}_2; \quad \text{or} \quad \bar{X}_1 - \bar{X}_2 \neq 0.$$

(c) Using the data presented in Table 12.3, the group means ($\bar{X}_1$ and $\bar{X}_2$) are first computed:

$$\Sigma X_1 = 70, \quad N_1 = 10, \quad \bar{X}_1 = \frac{\Sigma X_1}{N_1} = \frac{70}{10} = 7.0$$

$$\Sigma X_2 = 80, \quad N_2 = 10, \quad \bar{X}_2 = \frac{\Sigma X_2}{N_2} = \frac{80}{10} = 8.0$$

$$N_1 = N_2 = N = 10.$$

(d) The deviations of scores of each group from the corresponding group mean are worked out and squared, and the squared deviations of each group are totalled to give the respective sums of squared deviations. From Table 12.3,

$$\Sigma(X_1 - \bar{X}_1)^2 = \Sigma x_1^2 = 30; \quad \Sigma(X_2 - \bar{X}_2)^2 = \Sigma x_2^2 = 44.$$

Table 12.3 Computation of means and SDs of attitude scores

Group I			Group II		
(X_1)	(x_1) $(X_1 - \bar{X}_1)$	x_1^2	(X_2)	(x_2) $(X_2 - \bar{X}_2)$	x_2^2
10	3	9	9	1	1
9	2	4	8	0	0
8	1	1	6	−2	4
7	0	0	7	−1	1
7	0	0	8	0	0
8	1	1	8	0	0
6	−1	1	11	3	9
5	−2	4	12	4	16
6	−1	1	6	−2	4
4	−3	9	5	−3	9
70 (ΣX_1), $N_1 = 10$		30 (Σx_1^2)	80 (ΣX_2), $N_2 = 10$		44 (Σx_2^2)

(e) The pooled SD ($\hat{s}$) is computed using the sums of squared deviations of the two independent small groups of equal sizes as follows:

$$\hat{s} = \sqrt{\frac{\Sigma x_1^2 + \Sigma x_2^2}{2(N-1)}} = \sqrt{\frac{30+44}{2(10-1)}} = \sqrt{\frac{74}{2 \times 9}} = \sqrt{\frac{74}{18}} = \sqrt{4.1111} = 2.03.$$

(f) The SE of the difference between the means ($s_{\bar{X}_1 - \bar{X}_2}$) is computed using the pooled SD ($\hat{s}$) for two independent small groups of equal sizes as follows:

$$s_{\bar{X}_1 - \bar{X}_2} = \hat{s}\sqrt{\frac{2}{N}} = 2.03\sqrt{\frac{2}{10}} = 2.03\sqrt{0.2}$$
$$= 2.03 \times 0.447 = 0.91.$$

(g) The difference between the two sample means ($\bar{X}_1 - \bar{X}_2$) is converted to the 't' score as follows:

$$t = \frac{\bar{X}_1 - \bar{X}_2}{s_{\bar{X}_1 - \bar{X}_2}} = \frac{7.0 - 8.0}{0.91} = \frac{-1.0}{0.91} = -1.10$$

$$df = 2(N-1) = 2(10-1) = 2 \times 9 = 18.$$

(h) Entering Table C (given in the appendix) with df=18, the two-tailed critical value of 't' at the 0.05 level of significance is 2.101 and at the 0.01 level of significance is 2.878. The computed 't' of 1.10 (disregarding the sign) is lower than even the critical 't' value for the 0.05 level of significance. Hence, the probability (p) of the H_0 being correct is greater than 0.05 ($p > 0.05$). Thus, the H_0 cannot be rejected. In other words, the H_0 is accepted and the H_1 is rejected. Therefore, we may conclude that the difference between the two group means is not statistically significant; the given difference between group means being insignificant can only be attributed to some chance factors or random sampling fluctuations.

Example 12.10 In a body weight measure, the mean and SD of the scores of eight adult males were found to be 57.0 kg and 4.26 kg, respectively; these values amounted to 52.0 kg and 2.72 kg, respectively, for eight adult females. Find whether or not the mean weight of males is significantly higher than that of females.

Solution

(a) The given data are:

Adult males:　$\bar{X}_1 = 57.0$ kg;　$s_1 = 4.26$ kg;　$N_1 = 8$
Adult females:　$\bar{X}_2 = 52.0$ kg;　$s_2 = 2.72$ kg;　$N_2 = 8$

Size of each sample $= N_1 = N_2 = N = 8$.

(b) The H_0 contends that the mean body weight of the adult males is not significantly higher than that of the adult females. To find the probability (p) of this H_0 to be correct, a one-tailed 't' test is done using the pooled SD ($\hat{s}$), because the samples are of small but equal sizes. The H_0 and H_1 are stated as follows:

$$H_0: \quad \bar{X}_1 \not> \bar{X}_2;$$
$$H_1: \quad \bar{X}_1 > \bar{X}_2.$$

(c) The pooled SD ($\hat{s}$) is computed using the unbiased SDs (s_1 and s_2) of the two independent small samples of equal sizes as follows:

$$\hat{s} = \sqrt{\frac{s_1^2 + s_2^2}{2}} = \sqrt{\frac{(4.26)^2 + (2.72)^2}{2}}$$

$$= \sqrt{\frac{18.1476 + 7.3984}{2}} = \sqrt{\frac{25.546}{2}}$$

$$= \sqrt{12.773} = 3.574.$$

(d) The SE of the difference between the means ($s_{\bar{X}_1 - \bar{X}_2}$) of two independent small samples of equal sizes is computed using the $\hat{s}$ as follows:

$$s_{\bar{X} - \bar{X}_2} = \hat{s}\sqrt{\frac{2}{N}} = 3.574\sqrt{\frac{2}{8}} = 3.574\sqrt{0.25}$$

$$= 3.574 \times 0.5 = 1.787 = 1.79.$$

(e) The difference between the two sample means ($\bar{X}_1 - \bar{X}_2$) is converted to the 't' score as follows:

$$t = \frac{\bar{X}_1 - \bar{X}_2}{s_{\bar{X}_1 - \bar{X}_2}} = \frac{57.0 - 52.0}{1.79} = \frac{5.0}{1.79} = 2.793$$

$$df = 2(N-1) = 2(8-1) = 2 \times 7 = 14.$$

(f) Entering Table C (given in the appendix) with df=14, the one-tailed critical value of 't' at the 0.05 level of significance is 1.761 and at the 0.01 level of significance is 2.624. The computed 't' of 2.793 is higher than the critical 't' for the 0.01 level of significance. Hence, the probability (p) of the H_0 being correct is less than 0.01 ($p<0.01$). Thus, the H_0 may be rejected. In other words, the H_0 is rejected and H_1 is accepted. Therefore, it is inferred that the mean body weight of adult males is significantly higher than that of the adult females in 99% of cases.

Example 12.11 A physiological psychologist has the hypothesis that hormone 'A' is important in producing sexual behaviour. To investigate this hypothesis, 20 male rats were randomly selected and then randomly categorised into two equal groups. The animals in Group 1 were injected with hormone 'A' and then were placed in an individual housing cage with a sexually receptive female. The animals in Group 2 were given similar treatment except they were injected with a placebo solution. The number of matings were counted over a 20-minute period. The following results were obtained:

Hormone 'A' (Group 1): 8, 10, 12, 6, 6, 7, 9, 8, 7, 11.
Placebo (Group 2):   5, 6, 3, 4, 7, 8, 6, 5, 4, 8.

Test whether or not hormone 'A' has significantly produced more sexual behaviour than the placebo solution.

Solution

(a) The given data are entered in Table 12.4 as follows:
(b) The H_0 states that hormone 'A' has not significantly produced more sexual behaviour than the placebo solution. To find the probability (p) of this H_0 to be correct, a

one-tailed 't' test is done using the pooled SD ($\hat{s}$) because the groups are of small but equal sizes. The H_0 and H_1 are stated as follows:

$$H_0 : \bar{X}_1 \ngtr \bar{X}_2; \quad H_1 : \bar{X}_1 > \bar{X}_2.$$

(c)   Using the data presented in Table 12.4, the group means, $\bar{X}_1$ and $\bar{X}_2$, are first computed:

$$\Sigma X_1 = 84, \quad N_1 = 10, \quad \bar{X}_1 = \frac{\Sigma X_1}{N_1} = \frac{84}{10} = 8.4$$

$$\Sigma X_2 = 56, \quad N_2 = 10, \quad \bar{X}_2 = \frac{\Sigma X_2}{N_2} = \frac{56}{10} = 5.6$$

Size of each group: $N_1 = N_2 = N = 10$.

(d)   The deviations of scores of each group from the corresponding group mean are worked out and squared, and the squared deviations of each group are totalled to give the respective sums of squared deviations. From Table 12.4,

$$\Sigma(X_1 - \bar{X}_1)^2 = \Sigma x_1^2 = 38.40; \quad \Sigma(X_2 - \bar{X}_2)^2 = \Sigma x_2^2 = 26.40.$$

(e)   The pooled SD ($\hat{s}$) is computed using the sums of squared deviations of the two independent small groups of equal sizes as follows:

$$\hat{s} = \sqrt{\frac{\Sigma x_1^2 + \Sigma x_2^2}{2(N-1)}} = \sqrt{\frac{38.40 + 26.40}{2(10-1)}} = \sqrt{\frac{64.80}{2 \times 9}} = \sqrt{\frac{64.80}{18}} = \sqrt{3.6} = 1.897.$$

Table 12.4   Computation of means and SDs of mating scores

Hormone A (Group I)			Placebo (Group II)		
(X_1)	(x_1) $(X_1 - \bar{X}_1)$	x_1^2 $(X_1 - \bar{X}_1)^2$	(X_2)	(x_2) $(X_2 - \bar{X}_2)$	x_2^2 $(X_2 - \bar{X}_2)^2$
8	−0.4	0.16	5	−0.6	0.36
10	1.6	2.56	6	0.4	0.16
12	3.6	12.96	3	−2.6	6.76
6	−2.4	5.76	4	−1.6	2.56
6	−2.4	5.76	7	1.4	1.96
7	−1.4	1.96	8	2.4	5.76
9	0.6	0.36	6	0.4	0.16
8	−0.4	0.16	5	−0.6	0.36
7	−1.4	1.96	4	−1.6	2.56
11	2.6	6.76	8	2.4	5.76
84 (ΣX_1), $N_1 = 10$		38.40 (Σx_1^2) $\Sigma(X_1 - \bar{X}_1)^2$	56 (ΣX_2), $N_2 = 10$		26.40 (Σx_2^2) $\Sigma(X_2 - \bar{X}_2)^2$

(f)   The SE of the difference between the means ($s_{\bar{X}_1 - \bar{X}_2}$) is computed using the $\hat{s}$ for two independent small groups of equal sizes as follows:

$$s_{\bar{X}_1 - \bar{X}_2} = \hat{s}\sqrt{\frac{2}{N}} = 1.897\sqrt{\frac{2}{10}} = 1.897\sqrt{0.2}$$
$$= 1.897 \times 0.447 = 0.848.$$

(g)   The difference between the two group means ($\bar{X}_1 - \bar{X}_2$) is converted to the 't' score as follows:

$$t = \frac{\bar{X}_1 - \bar{X}_2}{s_{\bar{X}_1 - \bar{X}_2}} = \frac{8.4 - 5.6}{0.848} = \frac{2.8}{0.848} = 3.302$$

$$\mathrm{df} = 2(N-1) = 2(10-1) = 2 \times 9 = 18.$$

(h)   Entering Table C (given in the appendix) with df = 18, the one-tailed critical value of 't' at the 0.05 level of significance is 1.734 and at the 0.01 level of significance is 2.552. The computed 't' of 3.302 is higher than the critical 't' for the 0.01 level of significance. Hence, the probability (p) of the H_0 being correct is less than 0.01 ($p < 0.01$). Thus, the H_0 may be rejected. In other words, the H_0 is rejected and the H_1 is accepted. Therefore, we may conclude that hormone 'A' has produced significantly more sexual behaviour in animals than the placebo solution in 99% of cases.

Example 12.12 The principal of a management college is interested in determining whether there is any difference in the number of credits taken by male and female students during their freshman year per semester. He/she selects a sample of 50 males and 50 females and observes the following information:

$$\text{Males:} \quad \bar{X}_1 = 13.6; \quad s_1 = 1.4$$
$$\text{Females:} \quad \bar{X}_2 = 14.8; \quad s_2 = 1.6.$$

At $\alpha = 0.05$, test the null hypothesis that there is no difference in the number of credits taken by male students as compared to female students.

Solution

(a)   The given data are:

$$\text{Males:} \quad \bar{X}_1 = 13.6; \quad s_1 = 1.4; \quad N_1 = 50$$
$$\text{Females:} \quad \bar{X}_2 = 14.8; \quad s_2 = 1.6; \quad N_2 = 50.$$
$$\text{Size of each sample: } N_1 = N_2 = N = 50.$$

(b)   The H_0 states that there is no significant difference between two sample means. To find the probability (p) of this H_0 to be correct, a two-tailed 't' test is done using the unbaised SDs (s_1 and s_2) of both the samples, because both the samples are large ($N_1 > 30$, $N_2 > 30$) and their sizes are equal ($N_1 = N_2$). The H_0 and H_1 are stated as follows:

$$H_0: \ \bar{X}_1 = \bar{X}_2; \ \text{ or } \ \bar{X}_1 - \bar{X}_2 = 0$$
$$H_1: \ \bar{X}_1 \neq \bar{X}_2; \ \text{ or } \ \bar{X}_1 - \bar{X}_2 \neq 0.$$

(c)   The SE of the difference between the means ($s_{\bar{X}_1 - \bar{X}_2}$) is computed using the s_1 and s_2 of two large independent samples of equal sizes as follows:

$$s_{\bar{X}_1 - \bar{X}_2} = \sqrt{\frac{s_1^2 + s_2^2}{N}} = \sqrt{\frac{(1.4)^2 + (1.6)^2}{50}}$$

$$= \sqrt{\frac{1.96 + 2.56}{50}} = \sqrt{\frac{4.52}{50}} = \sqrt{0.0904} = 0.301.$$

(d) The difference between the two sample means ($\bar{X}_1 - \bar{X}_2$) is converted to the 't' score as follows:

$$t = \frac{\bar{X}_1 - \bar{X}_2}{s_{\bar{X}_1 - \bar{X}_2}} = \frac{13.6 - 14.8}{0.301} = \frac{-1.2}{0.301} = -3.987$$

$$df = 2(N-1) = 2(50-1) = 2 \times 49 = 98.$$

(e) Entering Table C (given in the appendix) with df=98, the two-tailed critical value of 't' at the 0.05 level of significance is 1.9846 (by interpolation). Because the 't' distributions are perfectly bilaterally symmetrical, the negative sign of the computed 't' is ignored and the 't' score of 3.987 is compared with the two-tailed critical value of 't' at the 0.05 level for df=98. As the computed 't' of 3.987 is higher than the two-tailed critical 't' for the 0.05 level of significance, the probability (p) of correctness of the H_0 is less than 0.05 ($p<0.05$). The H_0 may, therefore, be rejected. In other words, H_0 is rejected and H_1 is accepted. Thus, we may conclude that there is a significant difference in the number of credits taken by male students as compared to female students in 95% of cases.

Example 12.13 A mathematics teacher divides his/her class into two random groups. He/she provides an extra drill in computation work for an hour daily to the experimental group hoping that such a drill will promote the computation skill of the students of this group. The control group is not provided any such drill. At the end of the session for one month, he/she administers an achievement-test and collects data as given below:

	Experimental Group	Control Group
Means	35	30
SD	4	3
N	45	45

Is the gain on account of drill work significant enough to indicate that a drill in mathematics promotes computation skill?

Solution

(a) The given data are:

Experimental group: $\bar{X}_1 = 35$; $s_1 = 4$; $N_1 = 45$
Control group: $\bar{X}_2 = 30$; $s_2 = 3$; $N_2 = 45.$

Size of each sample: $N_1 = N_2 = N = 45.$

(b) The H_0 states that the gain on account of drill work is not significant enough to indicate that a drill in mathematics promotes computation skill. In other words, the mean achievement scores ($\bar{X}_1$) of the experimental group is not significantly higher than that of the control group ($\bar{X}_2$). To find the probability (p) of this H_0 to be correct, a one-tailed 't' test is undertaken. The H_0 and H_1 are stated as follows:

$$H_0 : \bar{X}_1 \not> \bar{X}_2; \quad H_1 : \bar{X}_1 > \bar{X}_2.$$

(c) The SE of the difference between the means ($s_{\bar{X}_1-\bar{X}_2}$) is computed using the unbiased SDs (i.e., s_1 and s_2) of two large independent groups of equal sizes as follows:

$$s_{\bar{X}_1-\bar{X}_2} = \sqrt{\frac{s_1^2 + s_2^2}{N}} = \sqrt{\frac{(4)^2 + (3)^2}{45}}$$

$$= \sqrt{\frac{16+9}{45}} = \sqrt{\frac{25}{45}} = \sqrt{0.5555} = 0.745.$$

(d) The difference between the two sample means ($\bar{X}_1 - \bar{X}_2$) is converted to the 't' score as follows:

$$t = \frac{\bar{X}_1 - \bar{X}_2}{s_{\bar{X}_1-\bar{X}_2}} = \frac{35-30}{0.745} = \frac{5}{0.745} = 6.711$$

$$df = 2(N-1) = 2(45-1) = 2 \times 44 = 88.$$

(e) Entering Table C (given in the appendix) with df=88, the one-tailed critical value of 't' at the 0.05 level of significance is 1.6624 and at the 0.01 level of significance is 2.3692 (by interpolation). The computed 't' of 6.711 is higher than the one-tailed critical 't' value for the 0.01 level of significance. Hence, the probability (p) of H_0 being correct is less than 0.01 ($p<0.01$). The H_0 may, therefore, be rejected. In other words, the H_0 is rejected and H_1 is accepted; the mean achievement score of the experimental group ($\bar{X}_1$) is significantly higher than that of the control group ($\bar{X}_2$). So, we may conclude that the gain on account of drill work is significant enough to indicate that a drill in mathematics promotes computation skill.

12.5.5.3   *For Large Independent Samples of Unequal Sizes*

When both the samples are independent and sample sizes are large ($N_1>30$, $N_2>30$) but not equal ($N_1 \neq N_2$), the 't' score is computed for the difference between sample means ($\bar{X}_1 - \bar{X}_2$), using the unbiased SDs of the individual samples and not the pooled SD ($\hat{s}$). If two independent large samples have unequal sizes ($N_1 \neq N_2$) and have been drawn from populations having the same variance, the $s_{\bar{X}_1-\bar{X}_2}$ and 't' may be computed as follows:

$$s_{\bar{X}_1-\bar{X}_2} = \sqrt{(s_{\bar{X}_1})^2 + (s_{\bar{X}_2})^2} = \sqrt{\frac{s_1^2}{N_1} + \frac{s_2^2}{N_2}}$$

$$t = \frac{\bar{X}_1 - \bar{X}_2}{s_{\bar{X}_1-\bar{X}_2}}; \quad df = N_1 + N_2 - 2.$$

The entire procedure of testing the significance of difference between the means of two independent large samples of unequal sizes using the 't' test will be more clear through the following examples.

Example 12.14 Two groups in two schools were given the *Minnesota Paper Formboard* test with the following results:

Group A	Group B
$\bar{X}_1 = 32.0$	$\bar{X}_2 = 36.0$
$s_1 = 6.2$	$s_2 = 7.4$
$N_1 = 145$	$N_2 = 82$

Is there a significant difference between the two means?

Solution

(a) The given data are:

$$\text{Group A:} \quad \bar{X}_1 = 32.0; \quad s_1 = 6.2; \quad N_1 = 145$$
$$\text{Group B:} \quad \bar{X}_2 = 36.0; \quad s_2 = 7.4; \quad N_2 = 82.$$

(b) The H_0 states that there is no significant difference between the two group means. To find the probability (p) of this H_0 to be correct, a two-tailed 't' test is done using the unbiased SDs (s_1 and s_2) of both the samples, because both the samples are large ($N_1 > 30$, $N_2 > 30$) and their sizes are not identical ($N_1 \neq N_2$). The H_0 and H_1 are stated as follows:

$$H_0: \quad \bar{X}_1 = \bar{X}_2; \quad \text{or} \quad \bar{X}_1 - \bar{X}_2 = 0$$
$$H_1: \quad \bar{X}_1 \neq \bar{X}_2; \quad \text{or} \quad \bar{X}_1 - \bar{X}_2 \neq 0.$$

(c) The SE of the difference between the means ($s_{\bar{X}_1 - \bar{X}_2}$) is first computed using the s_1 and s_2 of two large independent samples of unequal sizes as follows:

$$s_{\bar{X}_1 - \bar{X}_2} = \sqrt{\frac{s_1^2}{N_1} + \frac{s_2^2}{N_2}} = \sqrt{\frac{(6.2)^2}{145} + \frac{(7.4)^2}{82}}$$
$$= \sqrt{\frac{38.44}{145} + \frac{54.76}{82}} = \sqrt{0.2651 + 0.6678} = \sqrt{0.9329} = 0.966.$$

(d) The difference between the two sample means ($\bar{X}_1 - X_2$) is converted to the 't' score as follows:

$$t = \frac{\bar{X}_1 - \bar{X}_2}{s_{\bar{X}_1 - \bar{X}_2}} = \frac{32.0 - 36.0}{0.966} = \frac{-4.0}{0.966} = -4.141$$

$$\text{df} = N_1 + N_2 - 2 = 145 + 82 - 2 = 227 - 2 = 225 = \infty.$$

(e) Entering Table C (given in the appendix) with df$=\infty$, the two-tailed critical value of 't' at the 0.05 level of significance is 1.960 and at the 0.01 level of significance is 2.576. Because the 't' distributions are perfectly bilaterally symmetrical, the negative sign of the computed 't' is ignored and the 't' score of 4.141 is compared with the two-tailed critical value of 't' at both the 0.05 and 0.01 levels of significance (df$=\infty$). The computed 't' being found much higher than even the critical 't' score for the 0.01 level of significance, the probability (p) of the H_0 being correct is much lower than 0.01 ($p < 0.01$). Hence, the H_0 is rejected and H_1 is accepted, and it is inferred that there is a significant difference between the two group means in 99% of cases.

Example 12.15 On an arithmetic reasoning test 31 ten-year-old boys and 42 ten-year-old girls made the following scores:

	Means	SD	N
Boys	40.39	8.69	31
Girls	35.81	8.33	42

Is the mean of boys significantly higher than that of girls?

Solution

(a) The given data are:

$$\text{Boys:} \quad \bar{X}_1 = 40.39; \quad s_1 = 8.69; \quad N_1 = 31$$
$$\text{Girls:} \quad \bar{X}_2 = 35.81; \quad s_2 = 8.33; \quad N_2 = 42.$$

(b) The H_0 contends that the mean of boys is not significantly higher than that of girls. To find the probability (p) of this H_0 to be correct, a one-tailed 't' test is done using the SDs (s_1 and s_2) of both the samples, because both the samples are large ($N_1 > 30$, $N_2 > 30$) and their sizes are unequal ($N_1 \neq N_2$). The H_0 and H_1 are stated as follows:

$$H_0: \quad \bar{X}_1 \not> \bar{X}_2$$
$$H_1: \quad \bar{X}_1 > \bar{X}_2.$$

(c) The SE of difference between the means ($s_{\bar{X}_1 - \bar{X}_2}$) is first computed using the s_1 and s_2 of the two large independent samples of unequal sizes as follows:

$$s_{\bar{X}_1 - \bar{X}_2} = \sqrt{\frac{s_1^2}{N_1} + \frac{s_2^2}{N_2}} = \sqrt{\frac{(8.69)^2}{31} + \frac{(8.33)^2}{42}}$$

$$= \sqrt{\frac{75.5161}{31} + \frac{69.3889}{42}} = \sqrt{2.4360 + 1.6521}$$

$$= \sqrt{4.0881} = 2.022.$$

(d) The difference between the two sample means ($\bar{X}_1 - \bar{X}_2$) is converted to the 't' score as follows:

$$t = \frac{\bar{X}_1 - \bar{X}_2}{s_{\bar{X}_1 - \bar{X}_2}} = \frac{40.39 - 35.81}{2.022} = \frac{4.58}{2.022} = 2.265$$

$$df = N_1 + N_2 - 2 = 31 + 42 - 2 = 73 - 2 = 71.$$

(e) Entering Table C (given in the appendix) with df = 71, the one-tailed critical value of 't' at the 0.05 level of significance is 1.6667 and at the 0.01 level of significance is 2.3803 (by interpolation). The computed 't' of 2.265 is higher than the critical 't' score for the 0.05 level but less than the 't' score for the 0.01 level of significance. Hence, the probability (p) of the H_0 being correct is lower than 0.05 ($p < 0.05$). So, the H_0 is rejected and H_1 is accepted. Therefore, it is reasonable to conclude that the mean score of boys is significantly higher than that of the girls in 95% of cases. In other words, if the 10-year-old boys and girls are compared 100 times with regard to their arithmetic reasoning abilities, the boys are better than girls in 95 times.

12.5.5.4   *Interpretation of 't' Computed from Independent Samples*

We have already discussed about the interpretation of 't' scores computed from independent samples in the above 12 examples. However, here we are describing the general procedures for the interpretation of the computed 't'.

The 't' score, computed by any of the above methods, is compared with critical 't' scores having the same df as that of the computed 't' and for different levels of significance, generally, the 0.05 and 0.01 levels of significance. Either two-tailed or one-tailed critical 't' scores are used in this comparison accordingly as a two-tailed or one-tailed 't' test is intended. The algebraic sign of the computed 't' score is ignored during this comparison. If the computed 't' score equals or exceeds the critical 't' score for a chosen level of significance (α), the H_0 is rejected and the H_1 is accepted, and, thus, the observed results are considered to be significant respectively at or below that level of significance ($p \leq \alpha$). On the contrary, if the computed 't' score becomes less than the critical 't' score for a chosen 'α' (alpha), then the H_0 cannot be rejected, and the H_1 is rejected, and, thus, the observed results are not considered to be significant ($p > \alpha$). In behavioural sciences, the observed results are usually not considered significant if 'p' exceeds an 'α' of 0.05.

12.5.6   't' Tests for Correlated Sample Means

The preceding section dealt with the problem of determining whether the difference between two independent sample (whether small or large having equal or unequal sizes) means is significant. A closely related problem is concerned with the significance of the difference between two correlated sample means. The method of testing the significance of the difference between two correlated sample means involves three situations: (a) the single group method, (b) the method of equivalent groups matching by pairs and (c) groups matched for the mean and SD. These methods are discussed in detail in the following sections.

12.5.6.1   *The Single Group Method*

Correlated means are obtained from the same test administered to the same group upon two occasions. This experimental design is called the 'single group' method. In a single group experiment, the same group or sample of individuals, drawn at random from a population, first serves as the control group and subsequently as the experimental group. Prior to any treatment with the independent variable, the dependent variable is initially measured in the individuals of the group which thus serves as the control group. Then the same group is treated with or exposed to the independent variable, followed by the measurement of the dependent variable again, so that the group now serves as an experimental group. The two sets of scores of the dependent variable, obtained from the single group during its use as the control group and the experimental group, respectively, form paired observations because each individual is having one pair of scores. These two sets of scores are also correlated with each other because the same individuals respond to the same items of a particular test at both the times, that is, before and after the treatment. Suppose that we have administered a test to a group of children and two weeks later have repeated the test. We wish to measure the effect of practice or of a special training upon the second set of scores or to estimate the effects of some activity interpolated between the test and retest. For example, the multiplication ability may be initially measured in a group of students (control group); they are then induced with a state of anxiety and the multiplication ability is subsequently measured again in them (experimental group). The two sets of scores of the multiplication ability form paired and correlated observations. The effect of the independent variable (e.g., anxiety) on the dependent one (e.g., multiplication ability) is explored by the statistical estimation of the significance of difference between the means of such paired observations.

In order to determine the significance of the difference between two correlated means obtained from the same group of subjects in both initial and final testing conditions, we must use the following formula to find the SE of difference between two correlated means. The formula reads

$$SE_D = s_{\bar{X}_1 - \bar{X}_2} = \sqrt{(s_{\bar{X}_1})^2 + (s_{\bar{X}_2})^2 - 2r_{12}s_{\bar{X}_1}s_{\bar{X}_2}},$$

where

SE_D or $s_{\bar{X}_1 - \bar{X}_2}$ = SE of the difference between two correlated means
$s_{\bar{X}_1}$ = SE of the initial test mean
$s_{\bar{X}_2}$ = SE of the final test mean
r_{12} = Coefficient of correlation between initial and final test scores.

The difference between two correlated means can be converted to the 't' score by the usual formula that reads

$$t = \frac{\bar{X}_1 - \bar{X}_2}{s_{\bar{X}_1 - \bar{X}_2}}; \quad df = N - 1.$$

In performing the 't' test for the significance of difference between two correlated means obtained from a single group experiment, particularly using a large sample ($N > 30$), the product–moment correlation coefficient (Pearson's r) computed between the paired scores has to be used in computing $s_{\bar{X}_1 - \bar{X}_2}$, as noted above. However, if the single group consists of a small sample ($N < 30$), one can find out the $s_{\bar{X}_1 - \bar{X}_2}$ by the above formula or may prefer a simple procedure called the '*difference method*', which is not appropriate for a single group experiment using a large sample. In other words, to bypass the need for computing the correlation coefficient (r) between the paired scores, a 't' test by the *difference method* is used for finding the significance of the difference between means of paired scores of a small group ($N < 30$) in such a single group experiment.

The nature of *difference method* is simply described. N is the number of paired observations or paired scores. X_1 and X_2 denote any pair of scores. 'D' is the difference between any pair of scores ($X_1 - X_2$). ΣD is the sum of all such differences between paired scores. $\bar{D}$ and S_D are, respectively, the mean and the SD of those differences, and $S_{\bar{D}}$ is the SE of $\bar{D}$.

For a two-tailed 't' test by the difference method, the H_0 contends that the mean difference ($\bar{D}$) between the paired observations does not differ significantly from 0. For a one-tailed 't' test, the H_0 contends that $\bar{D}$ does not have a significant positive (alternatively, negative) value. To estimate the probability (p) of the correctness of the H_0, the mean difference ($\bar{D}$) between the paired observations is converted to a 't' score. The following are the formulae to compute $\bar{D}$, S_D, $S_{\bar{D}}$ and 't':

$$\bar{D} = \frac{\Sigma D}{N}; \quad S_D = \sqrt{\frac{\Sigma(D - \bar{D})^2}{N-1}} = \sqrt{\frac{\Sigma d^2}{N-1}}$$

$$S_{\bar{D}} = \frac{S_D}{\sqrt{N}}; \quad t = \frac{\bar{D}}{S_{\bar{D}}}; \quad df = N - 1$$

The number of df used in evaluating 't' is 1 less than the number of pairs of observations or $N-1$ (1 df is lost since SE_D is computed around the mean of the distribution of differences).

Alternatively, 't' may be computed directly from the differences (D) between the paired scores and the squared values (D^2) of those differences. This formula for calculating 't' is

$$t = \frac{\Sigma D}{\sqrt{\dfrac{N\Sigma D^2 - (\Sigma D)^2}{N-1}}}; \quad df = N-1$$

The computed 't' score is then compared with either the two-tailed or one-tailed critical 't' scores with the same df and for different levels of significance (i.e., for 0.05 and/or 0.01 levels). The difference between the paired scores is considered to be significant if the computed 't' equals or exceeds the critical 't' for the chosen level of significance ($p \leq \alpha$). On the contrary, the difference may not be considered significant if the computed 't' is lower than the critical 't' for the chosen level of significance ($p > \alpha$).

The entire procedure of testing the significance of difference between two correlated means (obtained from a single group experiment using either a large sample or a small sample) using the 't' test will be more clear through the following examples.

Example 12.16 A group of students of Grade V was given a test in addition. Then a state of 'anxiety' was induced in them and the arithmetic test was re-administered. The results are given below:

Pre-test	End-test
$\bar{X}_1 = 70$	$\bar{X}_2 = 67$
$s_1 = 6$	$s_2 = 5.8$
$N_1 = 81$	$N_2 = 81$

r_{12} between pre- and end-test scores is 0.82.
Test whether or not anxiety has a detrimental effect on the arithmetic ability of children.

Solution

(a) The given data are:

Pre-test: $\bar{X}_1 = 70$; $s_1 = 6$; $N_1 = 81$;
$r_{12} = 0.82$
End-test: $\bar{X}_2 = 67$; $s_2 = 5.8$; $N_2 = 81$.

The two means, $\bar{X}_1$ and $\bar{X}_2$, are correlated means because they are obtained from a single group experiment, consisting of a large sample ($N = 81$), and each student was tested twice-before and after the induction of the state of anxiety. These two sets of paired scores are denoted by pretest (X_1) and end test (X_2).

(b) The H_0 contends that anxiety has no detrimental effect on the arithmetic ability of children. To estimate the probability (p) of the correctness of this H_0, a one-tailed 't' test is applicable for the difference between two correlated means obtained from a large single group tested on two occasions.

The H_0 and H_1 are stated as follows:

$$H_0: \ \bar{X}_2 \not< \bar{X}_1$$
$$H_1: \ \bar{X}_2 < \bar{X}_1.$$

(c) The SE of each mean ($s_{\bar{X}_1}$ and $s_{\bar{X}_2}$) is first computed using the s_1 and s_2, respectively, of $\bar{X}_1$ and $\bar{X}_2$, as follows:

$$s_{\bar{X}_1} = \frac{s_1}{\sqrt{N}} = \frac{6}{\sqrt{81}} = \frac{6}{9} = 0.67.$$

$$s_{\bar{X}_2} = \frac{s_2}{\sqrt{N}} = \frac{5.8}{\sqrt{81}} = \frac{5.8}{9} = 0.64.$$

(d) The SE of difference between the two correlated means ($s_{\bar{X}_1-\bar{X}_2}$) is then computed using the r, $s_{\bar{X}_1}$ and $s_{\bar{X}_2}$ of a large single group as follows:

$$\begin{aligned} s_{\bar{X}_1-\bar{X}_2} &= \sqrt{(s_{\bar{X}_1})^2 + (s_{\bar{X}_2})^2 - 2r_{12}s_{\bar{X}_1}s_{\bar{X}_2}} \\ &= \sqrt{(0.67)^2 + (0.64)^2 - 2(0.82)(0.67)(0.64)} \\ &= \sqrt{0.4489 + 0.4096 - 0.7032} \\ &= \sqrt{0.8585 - 0.7032} = \sqrt{0.1553} = 0.3941. \end{aligned}$$

(e) The difference between two correlated means ($\bar{X}_1 - \bar{X}_2$) obtained from a large single group is converted to 't' score as follows:

$$t = \frac{\bar{X}_1 - \bar{X}_2}{s_{\bar{X}_1-\bar{X}_2}} = \frac{70-67}{0.3941} = \frac{3.0}{0.3941} = 7.612$$

$$df = N - 1 = 81 - 1 = 80.$$

(f) Entering Table C (given in the appendix) with df=80, the one-tailed critical value of 't' at the 0.05 level of significance is 1.664 and at the 0.01 level of significance is 2.374. The computed 't' of 7.612 is much higher than the critical 't' score for 0.01 level of significance. Hence, the probability (p) of the H_0 being correct is lower than 0.01 ($p<0.01$). Thus, the H_0 is rejected and H_1 is accepted. Therefore, it is safe to conclude that anxiety has significantly deteriorated the arithmetic ability of children in the end test, which may hold good in 99% of cases.

Example 12.17 The following sets of scores were made by 10 students in a laboratory experiment on perception. Is there a significant difference between the means of two distributions?

Students	1	2	3	4	5	6	7	8	9	10
Test 1	3	6	8	7	8	5	7	3	4	6
Test 2	12	11	12	14	16	10	14	9	11	10

Solution

(a) Since the given data are obtained from a single group experiment having small sample size, one can test the significance of the difference between two correlated means

Table 12.5 't' Test for difference between means of paired scores by the correlation method

Subjects	Test 1 (X_1)	Test 2 (X_2)	X_1^2	X_2^2	X_1X_2
1	3	12	9	144	36
2	6	11	36	121	66
3	8	12	64	144	96
4	7	14	49	196	98
5	8	16	64	256	128
6	5	10	25	100	50
7	7	14	49	196	98
8	3	9	9	81	27
9	4	11	16	121	44
10	6	10	36	100	60
$N=10$	57 (ΣX_1)	119 (ΣX_2)	357 (ΣX_1^2)	1459 (ΣX_2^2)	703 (ΣX_1X_2)

through a 't' test computed by the *correlation method* as in case of the above example (Example 12.16) or by the *difference method*. Let us decide to apply the correlation method to find out the SE of difference between two correlated means ($s_{\bar{X}_1-\bar{X}_2}$), and thus to compute 't'. Let the paired achievement Test 1 and Test 2 scores be denoted by X_1 and X_2, respectively. The above given data are entered in Table 12.5.

(b) The H_0 contends that there is no significant difference between the means of paired scores of two distributions, any observed difference being due to mere chances associated with random sampling fluctuations. To estimate the probability (p) of the correctness of this H_0, a two-tailed 't' test by the correlation method is applied to the paired scores of a small single group. The H_0 and H_1 are stated as follows:

$$H_0 : \bar{X}_1 = \bar{X}_2; \quad \text{or} \quad \bar{X}_1 - \bar{X}_2 = 0; \quad \text{or} \quad \bar{D} = 0$$
$$H_1 : \bar{X}_1 \neq \bar{X}_2; \quad \text{or} \quad \bar{X}_1 - \bar{X}_2 \neq 0; \quad \text{or} \quad \bar{D} \neq 0.$$

(c) Using the data presented in Table 12.5, the coefficient of correlation (r) between the paired scores is first computed by the following formula:

$$
\begin{aligned}
r_{12} &= \frac{N\Sigma X_1 X_2 - \Sigma X_1 \Sigma X_2}{\sqrt{[N\Sigma X_1^2 - (\Sigma X_1)^2][N\Sigma X_2^2 - (\Sigma X_2)^2]}} \\
&= \frac{10 \times 703 - 57 \times 119}{\sqrt{[10 \times 357 - (57)^2][10 \times 1459 - (119)^2]}} \\
&= \frac{7030 - 6783}{\sqrt{[3570 - 3249][14590 - 14161]}} \\
&= \frac{247}{\sqrt{321 \times 429}} = \frac{247}{\sqrt{137709}} = \frac{247}{371.09} = 0.67.
\end{aligned}
$$

(d) Using the data presented in Table 12.5, the means of paired scores are then computed:

$$\text{Size of the group} = N = 10$$

$$\Sigma X_1 = 57, \quad \bar{X}_1 = \frac{\Sigma X_1}{N_1} = \frac{57}{10} = 5.7$$

$$\Sigma X_2 = 119, \quad \bar{X}_2 = \frac{\Sigma X_2}{N_2} = \frac{119}{10} = 11.9.$$

(e) Using the data presented in Table 12.5, the sum of the squared deviations of each set of paired scores (i.e., Σx_1^2 and Σx_2^2), their respective SDs (i.e., s_{X_1} and s_{X_2}) and SE of the means (i.e., $s_{\bar{X}_1}$ and $s_{\bar{X}_2}$) are computed. From Table 12.5,

$$\Sigma X_1 = 57; \quad \Sigma X_1^2 = 357; \quad \Sigma X_2 = 119; \quad \Sigma X_2^2 = 1459; \quad \Sigma X_1 X_2 = 703; \quad N = 10.$$

The sum of squared deviations (Σx_1^2 and Σx_2^2) of both sets of paired scores (X_1 and X_2) are computed using $\Sigma X_1, \Sigma X_1^2, \Sigma X_2, \Sigma X_2^2$ and N, as follows:

$$\Sigma x_1^2 = \Sigma X_1^2 - \frac{(\Sigma X_1)^2}{N} = 357 - \frac{(57)^2}{10} = 357 - \frac{3249}{10}$$
$$= 357 - 324.9 = 32.1$$

$$\Sigma x_2^2 = \Sigma X_2^2 - \frac{(\Sigma X_2)^2}{N} = 1459 - \frac{(119)^2}{10} = 1459 - \frac{14161}{10}$$
$$= 1459 - 1416.1 = 42.9.$$

(f) The SDs of the first and second sets of paired scores (s_{X_1} and s_{X_2}) are computed respectively using Σx_1^2 and Σx_2^2, and df $= N-1$ as follows:

$$s_{X_1} = \sqrt{\frac{\Sigma x_1^2}{N-1}} = \sqrt{\frac{32.1}{10-1}} = \sqrt{\frac{32.1}{9}} = \sqrt{3.57} = 1.89.$$

$$s_{X_2} = \sqrt{\frac{\Sigma x_2^2}{N-1}} = \sqrt{\frac{42.9}{10-1}} = \sqrt{\frac{42.9}{9}} = \sqrt{4.77} = 2.18.$$

(g) The SE of each correlated mean ($s_{\bar{X}_1}$ and $s_{\bar{X}_2}$) is then computed using, respectively, s_{X_1} and s_{X_2} as follows:

$$s_{\bar{X}_1} = \frac{s_{X_1}}{\sqrt{N}} = \frac{1.89}{\sqrt{10}} = \frac{1.89}{3.16} = 0.60.$$

$$s_{\bar{X}_2} = \frac{s_{X_2}}{\sqrt{N}} = \frac{2.18}{\sqrt{10}} = \frac{2.18}{3.16} = 0.69.$$

(h) The SE of difference between two correlated means ($s_{\bar{X}_1-\bar{X}_2}$) is computed using the r_{12}, $s_{\bar{X}_1}$ and $s_{\bar{X}_2}$ of a small single group as follows:

$$s_{\bar{X}_1-\bar{X}_2} = \sqrt{(s_{\bar{X}_1})^2 + (s_{\bar{X}_2})^2 - 2r_{12}s_{\bar{X}_1}s_{\bar{X}_2}}$$
$$= \sqrt{(0.60)^2 + (0.69)^2 - 2(0.67)(0.60)(0.69)}$$
$$= \sqrt{0.3600 + 0.4761 - 0.5548} = \sqrt{0.8361 - 0.5548} = \sqrt{0.2813} = 0.53.$$

(i) The difference between the means of paired scores $(\bar{X}_1 - \bar{X}_2)$ obtained from a small single group is converted to 't' score as follows:

$$t = \frac{\bar{X}_1 - \bar{X}_2}{s_{\bar{X}_1 - \bar{X}_2}} = \frac{5.7 - 11.9}{0.53} = \frac{-6.2}{0.53} = -11.698$$

$$\text{df} = N - 1 = 10 - 1 = 9.$$

(j) Because 't' distributions are perfectly bilaterally symmetrical, the negative sign of the computed 't' is ignored and the 't' score of 11.698 is compared with the two-tailed critical 't' scores, with df=9, for the 0.05 and 0.01 levels of significance. Entering Table C (given in the appendix), with df=9, the two-tailed critical value of 't' at the 0.05 level of significance is 2.262 and at the 0.01 level of significance is 3.250. The computed 't' of 11.698 is much higher than the critical 't' score at 0.01 level of significance. Hence, the probability (p) of the H_0 being correct is lower than 0.01 ($p < 0.01$). Thus, the H_0 is rejected and H_1 is accepted. Therefore, it is reasonable to conclude that there is a significant difference between the means of two distributions in 99% of cases.

Example 12.18 Ten students are given five successive trials upon a digit-symbol test of which only the scores for Trials 1 and 5 are shown. Is the mean gain from the initial to final trial significant?

Students	1	2	3	4	5	6	7	8	9	10
Trial 1	50	42	51	26	35	40	60	41	70	55
Trial 5	62	44	61	35	30	52	68	51	84	63

Solution

(a) Since the given data are obtained from a single group experiment having small sample size, let us decide to apply *the difference method* to compute the SE of difference between means of paired scores and thus to compute the 't' score. Let the paired scores of Trial 1 and Trial 5 be denoted by X_1 and X_2, respectively. The given data are entered in Table 12.6.

(b) The H_0 contends that the mean gain from initial to final trial is not significant. In other words, the mean of final trial ($\bar{X}_2$) is not significantly greater than the mean of the initial trial ($\bar{X}_1$), any observed improvement or gain being due to mere chances associated with random sampling fluctuations. To find the probability (p) of the H_0 being correct, a one-tailed 't' test by difference method is applied to the paired observations of the small single group. The H_0 and H_1 are stated as follows:

$$H_0 : \quad \bar{X}_2 \not> \bar{X}_1; \quad \text{or} \quad \bar{D} = 0$$
$$H_1 : \quad \bar{X}_2 > \bar{X}_1; \quad \text{or} \quad \bar{D} \neq 0.$$

(c) Using the data presented in Table 12.6, the means of paired scores are first computed as follows:

$$\text{Size of the single group: } N = 10$$

$$\Sigma X_1 = 470, \quad \bar{X}_1 = \frac{\Sigma X_1}{N_1} = \frac{470}{10} = 47.0$$

$$\Sigma X_2 = 550, \quad \bar{X}_2 = \frac{\Sigma X_2}{N_2} = \frac{550}{10} = 55.0.$$

Table 12.6 '*t*' test for difference between means of paired scores by the difference method

Subjects	Trial 1 (X_1)	Trial 5 (X_2)	D Difference $(X_2 - X_1)$	$(D - \bar{D})$ (d)	$(D - \bar{D})^2$ (d^2)
1	50	62	12	4	16
2	42	44	2	–6	36
3	51	61	10	2	4
4	26	35	9	1	1
5	35	30	–5	–13	169
6	40	52	12	4	16
7	60	68	8	0	0
8	41	51	10	2	4
9	70	84	14	6	36
10	55	63	8	0	0
N=10	470 (ΣX_1)	550 (ΣX_2)	80 (ΣD)		282 $\Sigma(D-\bar{D})^2$ or (Σd^2)

(d) The difference between the two scores of each pair (*D*) is worked out and totalled to give ΣD, which is used in computing mean difference ($\bar{D}$). *D* is usually found out by deducting a score of a set having a relatively smaller total from its paired score of the other set having a larger total in order to avoid maximum negative values of the difference. In the present example (see Table 12.6) *D* is taken as $X_2 - X_1$, because the total score of X_2 (i.e., ΣX_2) is greater than that of X_1 (i.e., ΣX_1). Moreover, ΣD is found out by adding all positive values of the difference on one hand, all negative values on the other, and deducting the total negative values from the total positive values. In the present example (see Table 12.6), the sum of positive values of *D* is 85 and sum of negative values of D is 5. So the ΣD is (85–5) or 80. From Table 12.6 it is found that $\Sigma D = 80$. Therefore,

$$\bar{D} = \frac{\Sigma D}{N} = \frac{80}{10} = 8.0.$$

(e) The deviation of each *D* from $\bar{D}$ [$(D-\bar{D})$ or *d*] is worked out and squared [$(D-\bar{D})^2$ or d^2], which are recorded in Table 12.6.

(f) The sum of the squared deviations of *D* values from $\bar{D}$ [$\Sigma(D-\bar{D})^2$ or Σd^2] is used in computing the SD of the difference (s_D) which is then used in computing the SE of $\bar{D}$ ($s_{\bar{D}}$). From Table 12.6,

$$\Sigma(D - \bar{D})^2 = \Sigma d^2 = 282$$

$$s_D = \sqrt{\frac{\Sigma(D-\bar{D})^2}{N-1}} = \sqrt{\frac{\Sigma d^2}{N-1}} = \sqrt{\frac{282}{10-1}} = \sqrt{\frac{282}{9}} = \sqrt{31.3333} = 5.5976$$

$$s_{\bar{D}} = \frac{s_D}{\sqrt{N}} = \frac{5.5976}{\sqrt{10}} = \frac{5.5976}{3.1623} = 1.77.$$

(g)   The difference between the means of paired scores $(\bar{X}_1 - \bar{X}_2 = \bar{D})$ obtained from a small single group is converted to the 't' score by using $\bar{D}$ and $s_{\bar{D}}$ as follows:

$$t = \frac{\bar{D}}{s_{\bar{D}}} = \frac{8.0}{1.77} = 4.52, \quad df = N - 1 = 10 - 1 = 9.$$

(h)   Entering Table C (given in the appendix), with df=9, the one-tailed critical value of 't' at the 0.05 level of significance (the 0.05 level is read from the 0.10 column ($p/2=0.05$)) is 1.833 and at the 0.01 level (the 0.01 level is read from the 0.02 column ($p/2=0.01$)) is 2.821. The computed 't' of 4.52 is higher than the critical 't' score at the 0.01 level of significance. Hence, the probability (p) of the H_0 being correct is lower than 0.01 ($p<0.01$). Thus, the H_0 is rejected and H_1 is accepted. Therefore, it is reasonable to conclude that the mean gain from initial to final trial ($\bar{X}_2 > \bar{X}_1$) is significant in 99% of cases.

Example 12.19 A major oil company would like to improve its tarnished image following a large oil spill. Its marketing department develops a short television commercial and tests it on a sample of $N=7$ subjects. People's attitudes about the company are measured with a short questionnaire, both before and after viewing the commercial. The data are as follows:

Persons	A	B	C	D	E	F	G
Before (X_1)	15	11	10	11	14	10	11
After (X_2)	15	13	18	12	16	10	19

Is there a significant change?

Solution

(a)   Since the given data are obtained from a single group experiment having small sample size and the scores are small, let us decide to apply the 'difference method' in which 't' may be computed directly from the difference (D) between the paired scores and the squared values of those differences (D^2). The given data are entered in Table 12.7.

(b)   The H_0 states that there is no significant change in attitudes of persons about the company from before to after viewing the commercial. In other words, the mean difference ($\bar{D}$) is 0; any observed change or difference being due to mere chances associated with random sampling fluctuations. To find the probability (p) of the H_0 being correct, a two-tailed 't' test by difference method is applied to the paired observations of the small single group. The H_0 and H_1 are stated as follows:

$$H_0: \ \bar{X}_1 = \bar{X}_2; \quad \text{or} \quad \bar{D} = 0 \text{ (the mean difference is zero)}$$
$$H_1: \ \bar{X}_1 \neq \bar{X}_2; \quad \text{or} \quad \bar{D} \neq 0 \text{ (there is a mean change in attitudes).}$$

(c)   Using the data presented in Table 12.7, the means of paired scores are first computed as follows:

$$\text{Size of the single group: } N=7$$

$$\Sigma X_1 = 82, \quad \bar{X}_1 = \frac{\Sigma X_1}{N} = \frac{82}{7} = 11.71$$

$$\Sigma X_2 = 103, \quad \bar{X}_2 = \frac{\Sigma X_2}{N} = \frac{103}{7} = 14.71.$$

Table 12.7 't' Test for difference between means of paired scores by the difference method

Persons	Before (X_1)	After (X_2)	D $(X_2 - X_1)$	D^2
A	15	15	0	0
B	11	13	2	4
C	10	18	8	64
D	11	12	1	1
E	14	16	2	4
F	10	10	0	0
G	11	19	8	64
$N=7$	82 (ΣX_1)	103 (ΣX_2)	21 (ΣD)	137 (ΣD^2)

(d) The difference between the two scores of each pair of observation (D) is worked out and recorded in Table 12.7. These differences for all the pairs of scores are totalled to give ΣD, which is used to compute mean difference ($\bar{D}$):

$$\text{From Table 12.7, } \Sigma D = 21, \quad \bar{D} = \frac{\Sigma D}{N} = \frac{21}{7} = 3.0.$$

(e) Each D value is squared and then totalled to give ΣD^2. Table 12.7 shows that $\Sigma D^2 = 137$.

(f) The 't' score is computed, using ΣD, ΣD^2 and the sample size ($N=7$) as follows:

$$t = \frac{\Sigma D}{\sqrt{\dfrac{N\Sigma D^2 - (\Sigma D)^2}{N-1}}} = \frac{21}{\sqrt{\dfrac{7 \times 137 - (21)^2}{7-1}}} = \frac{21}{\sqrt{\dfrac{959 - 441}{6}}}$$

$$= \frac{21}{\sqrt{\dfrac{518}{6}}} = \frac{21}{\sqrt{86.33}} = \frac{21}{9.29} = 2.26$$

$$\text{df} = N - 1 = 7 - 1 = 6.$$

(g) Entering Table C (given in the appendix), with df$=6$, the two-tailed critical value of 't' at the 0.05 level of significance is 2.447 and at the 0.01 level of significance is 3.707. The computed 't' of 2.26 is lower than the critical 't' score even at the 0.05 level of significance. Hence, the probability (p) of the H_0 being correct is greater than 0.05 ($p > 0.05$). Thus, the H_0 is not rejected. In other words, the H_0 is accepted and the H_1 is rejected. Therefore, we may conclude that there is no evidence that the viewing of commercial has significantly changed people's attitudes about the company.

The 'difference method' is only applicable to test the significance of difference between means of paired scores obtained from a single group experiment having small sample size ($N < 30$); it is not applicable for a single group having large sample size ($N > 30$). The 'difference method' is quicker and easier to apply than is the longer method (i.e., correlation method) of calculating SEs for each mean and the SE of the difference, and is to be preferred unless the correlation between paired scores is wanted. Moreover, when the paired scores are of greater magnitude, the 'difference method' outlined in Example 12.18 is preferred whereas the 'difference method' outlined in Example 12.19 is preferred when the paired scores are of smaller magnitude.

In a single group/sample method 't' test is often called as a *repeated-measures* 't' test. A repeated-measures study is one in which a single sample/group of individuals is measured more than once on the same dependent variable. In other words, with a repeated-measures design, two sets of data are obtained from the same sample/group of individuals. For example, a group of patients could be measured before therapy and then measured again after therapy. Or a group of individuals could be tested in a quiet comfortable environment and then tested again in a noisy, stressful environment to examine the effects of stress on performance. In each case, notice that the same variable is being measured twice for the same set of individuals, that is, we literally repeat measurements on the same sample.

The main advantage of a repeated-measure study/design is that it uses exactly the same subjects in all treatment conditions. Thus, there is no risk that the subjects in one treatment are substantially different from the subjects in another. With an independent-measures design, on the other hand, there is always a risk that the results are biased because the individuals in one sample are much different from the individuals in the other sample.

12.5.6.2   *The Method of Equivalent Groups: Matching by Pairs*

In the method of equivalent groups the matching is done initially by pairs so that each individual in the first group has a match in the second group. Two equivalent groups matched by pair is otherwise known as *matched-subjects design*. A matched-subjects design involves two separate samples/groups, but each individual in one sample is matched one-to-one with an individual in the second sample. The matching is done with respect to an initially measured variable that the researcher expects to influence or affect the dependent variable to be studied subsequently. Suppose, for example, a researcher plans to compare learning performance in two different treatment conditions. For this study, the researcher might want to match the subjects in terms of intelligence. If there is a subject with an IQ of 110 in one sample, the researcher would find a matched subject with an IQ of 110 for the second sample. Thus, the two samples are perfectly matched in terms of intelligence. Of course, it is possible to match subjects on more than one variable. For example, a researcher could match pairs of subjects on age, gender, race, socioeconomic status, intelligence, interest, aptitude, previous knowledge of the subjects, etc. The matching is done so that the two individuals are equivalent (or nearly equivalent), and thus, the two resultant groups are equivalent, having equal sample size ($N_1 = N_2$). The two equivalent or matched groups are then exposed to or treated with different levels of the independent variable—one of the groups may, for example, serve as the control group not treated with the experimental factor (independent variable) while the other group serves as the experimental group treated with the independent variable. The dependent variable is subsequently measured in the individuals of both the groups. The two sets of final scores of the dependent variable constitute paired and correlated observations.

In performing 't' test for the significance of difference between means of two such equivalent/matched groups, the product-moment correlation coefficient (Pearson's r) has to be worked out between the two sets of scores and used in computing the SE of the difference between the means ($s_{\bar{X}_1 - \bar{X}_2}$). Thus, for '$N$' pairs of scores of matched groups the following formula is used to compute the SE_D ($s_{\bar{X}_1 - \bar{X}_2}$), as it is in the case of a large single group:

$$SE_D = s_{\bar{X}_1 - \bar{X}_2} = \sqrt{(s_{\bar{X}_1})^2 + (s_{\bar{X}_2})^2 - 2r_{12}s_{\bar{X}_1}s_{\bar{X}_2}}.$$

For the computation of 't' the usual formula is applied as under:

$$t = \frac{\bar{X}_1 - \bar{X}_2}{s_{\bar{X}_1 - \bar{X}_2}}; \quad df = N - 1.$$

The computed 't' is then compared with the one-tailed or two-tailed critical 't' scores, with the same df, for different levels of significance, to find the 'p' of the H_0 being correct. The inference is then drawn according as the 'p' is considered too low or too high, as in the preceding examples of 't' test.

The procedure of testing the significance of difference between means of two equivalent or matched-pair groups using 't' test will become more clear through the following example.

Example 12.20 Two groups of students, 20 in each, of a class were matched in pairs on the basis of IQ. The experimental group was taught by the use of 'film strip' method and the control group by the conventional 'read and discuss' method. The obtained data are given below. Test whether the difference between the mean achievement scores of the two groups is significant.

Experimental Group	Control Group
$N_1 = 20$	$N_2 = 20$
$\bar{X}_1 = 53.20$	$\bar{X}_2 = 49.80$
$s_1 = 7.4$	$s_2 = 6.5$
$r_{12} = 0.60$	

Solution

(a) The given data are:

Experimental group: $N_1 = 20$ $\bar{X}_1 = 53.20$; $s_1 = 7.4$
Control group: $N_2 = 20$ $\bar{X}_2 = 49.80$; $s_2 = 6.5$
$r_{12} = 0.60$

The two means, $\bar{X}_1$ and $\bar{X}_2$, are correlated means because they are obtained from two matched-pair groups, consisting of a small sample ($N_1 = N_2 = N = 20$), one experimental group and other control group.

(b) The H_0 states that there is no significant difference between the mean achievement scores of the two matched-pair groups. To find the probability (p) of this H_0 being correct, a two-tailed 't' test is done using the correlation coefficient between the matched-pair scores of the experimental and control groups. The H_0 and H_1 are stated below:

$$H_0 : \bar{X}_1 = \bar{X}_2; \quad \text{or} \quad \bar{X}_1 - \bar{X}_2 = 0$$
$$H_1 : \bar{X}_1 \neq \bar{X}_2; \quad \text{or} \quad \bar{X}_1 - \bar{X}_2 \neq 0$$

(c) The SE of each mean ($s_{\bar{X}_1}$ and $s_{\bar{X}_2}$) is first computed using the SDs (s_1 and s_2) of $\bar{X}_1$ and $\bar{X}_2$, respectively, as follows:

$$s_{\bar{X}_1} = \frac{s_1}{\sqrt{N_1}} = \frac{7.4}{\sqrt{20}} = \frac{7.4}{4.47} = 1.65$$

$$s_{\bar{X}_2} = \frac{s_2}{\sqrt{N_2}} = \frac{6.5}{\sqrt{20}} = \frac{6.5}{4.47} = 1.45$$

(d) The SE of difference between the means of two matched-pair groups (SE_D or $s_{\bar{X}_1 - \bar{X}_2}$) is then computed using the $s_{\bar{X}_1}, s_{\bar{X}_2}$ and r_{12}, as follows:

$$SE_D = s_{\bar{X}_1 - \bar{X}_2} = \sqrt{(s_{\bar{X}_1})^2 + (s_{\bar{X}_2})^2 - 2r_{12} s_{\bar{X}_1} s_{\bar{X}_2}}$$

$$= \sqrt{(1.65)^2 + (1.45)^2 - 2(0.60)(1.65)(1.45)}$$

$$= \sqrt{2.7225 + 2.1025 - 2.871}$$

$$= \sqrt{4.825 - 2.871} = \sqrt{1.954} = 1.398.$$

(e) The difference between the means of two matched-pair groups having small samples is converted to 't' score or 't' ratio, as follows:

$$t = \frac{\bar{X}_1 - \bar{X}_2}{s_{\bar{X}_1 - \bar{X}_2}} = \frac{53.20 - 49.80}{1.398} = \frac{3.40}{1.398} = 2.432.$$

$$df = N(\text{Number of pairs}) - 1 = 20 - 1 = 19$$

(f) Entering Table C (given in the appendix) with df=19, the two-tailed critical value of 't' at the 0.05 level of significance is 2.093 and at the 0.01 level of significance is 2.861. The computed 't' of 2.432 is higher than the critical 't' value for 0.05 level but lower than the critical 't' score for 0.01 level of significance. Hence, the probability (p) of the H_0 being correct is lower than 0.05 ($p<0.05$). Thus, the H_0 is rejected at the 5% level and H_1 is accepted. It is, therefore, inferred that the difference between the mean achievement scores of two matched-pair groups (i.e., experimental group and control group) is statistically significant in 95% of cases.

12.5.6.3   *Groups Matched for Mean and Standard Deviation*

When it is impracticable or impossible to set up groups in which subjects have been matched person for person, investigators often resort to the matching of groups in terms of mean and SD. The matching variable is usually different from the variable under study but is, in general, related to it and sometimes highly related. Put it into other words, here instead of one-to-one correspondence or matching carried out in pairs on an individual level, the group as a whole is matched with the other group in terms of mean and SD of some variable/variables other than the one under study. No attempt is made to pair off individuals, and the two matched groups are not necessarily of the same size, although a large difference in 'N' is not advisable. In other words, the two matched groups (which are matched for mean and SD) may or may not have equal sample sizes (i.e., $N_1 = N_2$ or $N_1 \neq N_2$), and may have small ($N_1 < 30$; $N_2 < 30$) or large ($N_1 > 30$; $N_2 > 30$) samples.

In comparing final mean scores of two matched groups the procedure is somewhat different from that used with two equivalent or matched-pair groups as illustrated above in Example 12.20. Suppose that 'X' is the variable under study and 'Y' is the variable in terms of which the two groups have been matched or equated as to mean and SD. Then, if r_{xy} is the correlation between 'X' and 'Y' in the population from which the samples have been drawn, the SE of the difference between means in 'X' of two groups matched for mean and SD is found out by the following formula:

$$SE_D = s_{\bar{X}_1 - \bar{X}_2} = \sqrt{[(s_{\bar{X}_1})^2 + (s_{\bar{X}_2})^2] - [1 - (r_{12})^2]}.$$

't' is computed by the usual formula that reads

$$t = \frac{\bar{X}_1 - \bar{X}_2}{s_{\bar{X}_1 - \bar{X}_2}}.$$

With regard to the number of df it is said that whether the two matched groups have equal or unequal sample sizes, and have small or large samples, the df is calculated in the following method:

$$df = [(N_1 - 1) + (N_2 - 1) - 1].$$

We must subtract the one additional df to allow for the fact that our groups are matched in variable 'Y'. The general rule is that 1 df is subtracted for each restriction imposed upon the observations, that is, for each matching variable.

An example will illustrate the procedure for testing the significance of difference between means of two matched groups (matched for mean and SD) using 't' test.

Example 12.21 The achievement of two groups of first-year high-school boys, one from a technical and the other from an academic high school, is compared on a Mechanical Aptitude Test (MAT). The two groups are matched for mean and SD upon a General Intelligence Test (GIT). The following data are obtained on the MAT. Do the two groups differ in mean ability?

	Technical	**Academic**
Sample size (N)	137	125
Mean on MAT($\bar{X}$)	54.38	51.42
SDs on MAT (s)	7.14	6.24
r_{12} between GIT and MAT Scores: 0.30		

Solution

(a) The given data are:

Technical: $N_1 = 137$; $\bar{X}_1 = 54.38$; $s_1 = 7.14$
Academic: $N_2 = 125$; $\bar{X}_2 = 51.42$; $s_2 = 6.24$

$$r_{12} = 0.30$$

The two means, $\bar{X}_1$ and $\bar{X}_2$, are correlated means because they are obtained from two matched groups (which are matched for mean and SD on GIT scores), consisting of large ($N_1 > 30$ and $N_2 > 30$) but unequal sample sizes ($N_1 \neq N_2$).

(b) The H_0 states that the two matched groups do not differ significantly in their mean ability. To find the probability (p) of this H_0 being correct, a two-tailed 't' test is done using the given r. The H_0 and H_1 are stated as follows:

$$H_0: \quad \bar{X}_1 = \bar{X}_2 \quad \text{or} \quad \bar{X}_1 - \bar{X}_2 = 0$$
$$H_1: \quad \bar{X}_1 \neq \bar{X}_2 \quad \text{or} \quad \bar{X}_1 - \bar{X}_2 \neq 0.$$

(c) The SE of each mean $s_{\bar{X}_1}$ and $s_{\bar{X}_2}$ is first computed using the SDs (s_1 and s_2) of $\bar{X}_1$ and $\bar{X}_2$, respectively, as follows:

$$s_{\bar{X}_1} = \frac{s_1}{\sqrt{N_1}} = \frac{7.14}{\sqrt{137}} = \frac{7.14}{11.70} = 0.61$$

$$s_{\bar{X}_2} = \frac{s_2}{\sqrt{N_2}} = \frac{6.24}{\sqrt{125}} = \frac{6.24}{11.18} = 0.56.$$

(d) The SE of difference between the means of two matched-pair groups (SE_D or $s_{\bar{X}_1-\bar{X}_2}$) is then computed using the, $s_{\bar{X}_1}, s_{\bar{X}_2}$ and r_{12}, as follows:

$$\begin{aligned}
SE_D = s_{\bar{X}_1-\bar{X}_2} &= \sqrt{[(s_{\bar{X}_1})^2 + (s_{\bar{X}_2})^2][1-(r_{12})^2]} \\
&= \sqrt{[(0.61)^2 + (0.56)^2][1-(0.30)^2]} \\
&= \sqrt{[0.3721 + 0.3136][1-0.09]} \\
&= \sqrt{[0.6857][0.91]} = \sqrt{0.623987} = 0.79.
\end{aligned}$$

(e) The difference between the means of two matched groups having large but unequal samples is converted to 't' score as follows:

$$t = \frac{\bar{X}_1 - \bar{X}_2}{s_{\bar{X}_1-\bar{X}_2}} = \frac{54.38 - 51.42}{0.79} = \frac{2.96}{0.79} = 3.747$$

$$\begin{aligned}
df &= [(N_1 - 1) + (N_2 - 1) - 1] = [(137-1)+(125-1)-1] \\
&= [136 + 124 - 1] = 260 - 1 = 259
\end{aligned}$$

(f) Entering Table C (given in the appendix) with df=259=∞, the two-tailed critical value of 't' at the 0.05 level of significance is 1.96 and at the 0.01 level of significance is 2.576. The computed 't' of 3.747 is higher than the critical value for the 0.01 level of significance. Hence, the probability (p) of the H_0 being correct is lower than 0.01 ($p<0.01$). Thus, the H_0 is rejected at the 1% level and H_1 is accepted. Therefore, we may conclude that the two matched groups are significantly different in their mean ability in 99% of cases; we are asserting that, in general, boys in the technical high school are higher in mechanical aptitude than the boys of 'equal general intelligence' in the academic high school.

The *repeated-measures design* (single group method), *matched-subjects design* (two equivalent or matched-pair groups) and *matched-groups design* (two groups matched for mean and SD), taken together, are called *related-samples design*. In this research design, the resultant two means are correlated, and the 't' test applied to test the significance of the difference between these two correlated means is known as *related-samples 't' test*.

Let us discuss briefly the uses, advantages and disadvantages, and assumptions of related-samples 't' test.

12.5.6.4   Uses of Related-sample 't' Test

The repeated-measures study differs from the independent-measures study in a fundamental way. In the latter type of study, a separate sample is used for each treatment. In the repeated-measures design, only one sample of subjects is used and measurements are repeated for the same sample in each treatment. There are many situations where it is possible to examine the effect of a treatment by using either type of study. However, there are situations where one type of design is more desirable or appropriate than the other. For example, if a researcher would like to study a particular type of subject that is not commonly found (a rare species, people with an unusual illness, etc.), then a repeated-measure study will be more economical in the sense that fewer subjects are needed. Rather than selecting several samples for the study (one sample per treatment), a single sample can be used for the entire research study.

Another factor in determining the type of design is the specific question being asked by the investigator. Some questions are better studied with repeated-measures design than the independent-measures design, especially those concerning changes in performance across time.

For example, a psychologist may wish to study the effect of practice on how well a person performs a task. To show that practice is improving a person's performance, the investigator would typically measure the person's performance very early in the study (when there is little or no practice) and repeat the measurement later when the person has had a certain amount of practice. Most studies of skill acquisition examine practice effects by using a repeated-measures design. Another situation where a repeated-measures design or study is useful is in developmental psychology. By repeating observations of the same individuals at various points in time, an investigator can watch behaviour unfold and obtain a better understanding of developmental processes.

Moreover, the related-samples studies (i.e., repeated-measures study, two equivalent or matched-pair groups study or a study involving groups matched on mean and SD) have been widely used in a variety of psychological and educational studies. Illustrations are found in experiments designed to evaluate the relative merits of two methods of teaching, the effects of drugs upon efficiency, transfer effects of special training, therapeutic effects of a particular therapy, effects of a particular diet and the like.

Finally, there are situations where a repeated-measures design cannot be used. Specifically, when two different populations are being compared (e.g., men versus women, first-born versus second-born children and the like), we must use separate samples from each population. Typically, these situations require an independent-measures design, but it is occasionally possible to match subjects or match groups with respect to a critical variable and conduct either a matched-subjects study or a matched-group study.

12.5.6.5   *Advantages of Related-samples 't' Test*

Each individual subject enters a research study with his/her own individual characteristics. Factors such as age, gender, race, personality, height, weight, socioeconomic status, intelligence and so on differentiate one subject from another. These individual differences can influence the scores that are obtained for subjects and can create problems for interpreting research results. With an independent-measures design, there is always the potential that the individuals in one sample are substantially different (e.g., smarter, stronger, taller or heavier) than the individuals in the other sample. Although a researcher would like to think that the mean difference found in an independent-measures study is caused by the treatment, it is always possible that the differences are simply due to the preexisting individual differences. However, one of the advantages of a repeated-measures research design is that it eliminates this problem because the same individuals are used in every treatment condition. In other words, there are no individual differences between treatments with a repeated-measures design.

Individual differences can cause another statistical problem. Specifically, large differences from one individual to another tend to increase the sample variance. We know that large variance can obscure any patterns in a set of data and also contributes directly to the magnitude of the SE. In general, as variance increases, it becomes increasingly difficult to demonstrate a significant treatment effect. The repeated-measures design helps to reduce this problem. Specifically, a repeated-measures design removes the individual differences from the data and, therefore, tends to reduce the sample variance. The sample variance is equivalent to noise and confusion in the data. Reducing sample variance makes it easier to see patterns in the data and increases the likelihood of finding significant results.

To demonstrate this fact, consider the sample data in Table 12.8.

Notice that we have taken hypothetical data so that there are large differences between individuals. Subject A consistently has scores in the 70s, Subject B in the 50s, Subject C in the 30s and so on. Normally, large individual differences cause the scores to be spread over a wide range, so that the sample is large. In Table 12.8, the data show that the sum of squared deviation values (Σx_1^2 or Σx_2^2) around 1,900 for the scores in Treatment 1 and Treatment 2. However,

Table 12.8 Hypothetical data showing large individual differences that are eliminated when the difference scores are computed

Subject	Treatment I			Treatment II			D $(X_2 - X_1)$	d $(D - \bar{D})$	d^2
	X_1	x_1	x_1^2	X_2	x_2	x_2^2			
A	70	28	784	76	29	841	6	1	1
B	54	12	144	58	11	121	4	–1	1
C	30	–12	144	36	–11	121	6	1	1
D	14	–28	784	18	–29	841	4	–1	1
$N=4$	168 (ΣX_1) $\bar{X}_1 = 42$		1,856 (Σx_1^2)	188 (ΣX_2) $\bar{X}_2 = 47$		1,924 (Σx_2^2)	20 (ΣD) $\bar{D} = 5$		4 (Σd^2)

with a repeated-measures design, we do not make comparisons between individuals. Instead, this design makes comparisons within individuals; that is, each subject's score in Treatment 1 is compared with the same subject's score in Treatment 2. The comparison is accomplished by computing difference scores (D). Notice in Table 12.8 that when the difference scores are computed, the huge individual differences disappear. The sum of squared deviation values (Σd^2) for the 'D' scores is only 4. The process of subtracting to obtain the difference scores has eliminated the absolute level of performance for each subject (e.g., 70 versus 50) and, thus, has eliminated the individual differences from the sample variance. Reducing the sample variance also reduces the SE and produces a more precise and sensitive test for mean difference.

12.5.6.6 *Disadvantages of Related-samples 't' Test*

The general goal of a repeated-measures 't' test is to demonstrate that two different treatment conditions result in two different means. However, the outcome of a repeated-measures study may be contaminated by other factors that can cause the two means to be different when actually there is no difference between the treatments. Two such factors, especially associated with repeated-measures design are *carryover effects* and *progressive error*.

A carryover effect occurs when a subject's response to the second treatment is altered by lingering aftereffects from the first treatment. Some examples of carryover effect are as follows:

(a) Imagine that a researcher is comparing the effectiveness of two drugs by testing both drugs, one after the other, on the same group of subjects. If the second drug is tested too soon after the first, there may be some of the first drug still in the subject's system, and this residual could exaggerate or maximise the effects of the second drug.

(b) Imagine a researcher comparing performance on two tasks that vary in difficulty. If subjects are given a very difficult task first, their poor performance may cause them to lose motivation, so that performance suffers when they get to the second task.

In each of these examples discussed, the researcher will observe a difference between the two treatment means. However, the difference in performance is not caused by the treatments; instead, it is caused by carryover effects.

Progressive error occurs when a subject's performance or response changes consistently over time. For example, a subject's performance may decline over time as a result of fatigue. Or a subject's performance may improve over time as a result of practice. In either case, a researcher would observe a mean difference in performance between the first treatment and the second treatment, but the change in performance is not due to the treatments; instead, it is caused by progressive error.

In order to distinguish between carryover effects and progressive error, one must remember that carryover effects are related directly to the first treatment. Progressive error, on the other hand, occurs as a function of time, independent of which treatment condition is presented first or second. Both of these factors, however, can influence the outcome of a repeated-measures study, and they can make it difficult for a researcher to interpret the results: Is the mean difference caused by the treatment, or it is caused by other factors?

One way to deal with carryover effects or progressive error is to *counterbalance* the order of presentation of treatments. That is, the subjects are randomly divided into two groups, with one group receiving Treatment 1 followed by Treatment 2, and the other group receiving Treatment 2 followed by Treatment 1. When there is a reason to expect strong carryover effects or large progressive error, the best strategy is not to use a repeated-measures design. Instead, using independent measures with a separate sample for each treatment condition or using a matched-subject design or matched-groups design so that each individual participates in only one treatment condition.

12.5.6.7   *Assumptions of the Related-samples 't' Test*

The related-samples 't' statistic requires two basic assumptions which are discussed as follows:

(a) The observations within each treatment condition must be independent. The assumption of independence refers to the scores within each treatment. Inside each treatment, the scores are obtained from different individuals and should be independent of one another.

(b) The population distribution of difference scores (D values) must be normal. The normality assumption is not a cause for concern unless the sample size is relatively small. In the case of severe departures from normality, the validity of the 't' test may be compromised with small samples. However, with relatively large samples ($N > 30$), this assumption can be ignored.

12.5.7   Robustness of the 't' Test

The 't' test for means of independent samples assumes (a) normality of the distribution of the variables in the population from which the samples are drawn and (b) homogeneity of variance, that is, $\sigma_1^2 = \sigma_2^2$. Experiments have been conducted to determine the effect on the 't' test for independent groups of violating the assumptions of normality of the raw score populations and homogeneity of variance. Fortunately, it turns out that the 't' test is a *robust* test. A test is said to be *robust* if it is relatively insensitive to, or not seriously affected by, violation of its underlying assumptions. 't' test is relatively insensitive to violations of normality and homogeneity of variance, depending on sample size, and the type and magnitude of the violation. If $N_1 = N_2$ and if the size of each sample is equal to or greater than 30, then the 't' test for independent groups may be used without appreciable error despite moderate violation of the normality and/or the homogeneity of variance assumptions. If there are extreme violations of these assumptions, then an alternate test such as Mann–Whitney 'U' test should be used (for details of the 'U' test, see Chapter 17, Section 17.5).

It is worth noting that when the two samples show large differences in their variances, it may indicate that the independent variable is not having an equal effect on all the subjects within a condition. This can be an important finding in its own right, leading to further experimentation into how the independent variable varies in its effects on different types of subjects.

12.5.8 Power of the 't' Test

The general basic formula for computing the 't' score or 't' ratio is: $t = \dfrac{\bar{X}_1 - \bar{X}_2}{s_{\bar{X}_1 - \bar{X}_2}}$. However, the

$s_{\bar{X}_1 - \bar{X}_2}$ may be computed in several alternative ways according to the nature of samples— whether correlated or uncorrelated, small or large, having equal or unequal sample sizes. But in case of paired observations or single group experiment, we rather prefer to compute 't' ratio by *difference method*; the formula for computing 't' score reads $t = \dfrac{\bar{D}}{s_{\bar{D}}}$.

It seems fairly obvious that the larger obtained 't' (t_{obt}) is, the more likely it is that H_0 will be rejected. Hence, anything that increases the likelihood of obtaining high values of t_{obt} will result in a more powerful 't' test. This can occur in several ways. First, the larger the real effect of the independent variable, the more likely it is that $\bar{X}_1 - \bar{X}_2$ or $\bar{D}$ will be large. Since these difference scores are in the numerator of the 't' equation, it follows that *the greater the effect of the independent variable, the higher the power of the 't' test* (other factors held constant).

Second, the denominator of the 't' equation varies as a function of sample size and sample variability, because $s_{\bar{X}_1 - \bar{X}_2}$ is computed using the SD (or variability) of the samples and the number of cases in the sample (size) as follows:

$$s_{\bar{X}_1 - \bar{X}_2} = \sqrt{\frac{\hat{s}^2}{n_1} + \frac{\hat{s}^2}{n_2}}$$ (For independent samples of small and unequal sizes)

$$s_{\bar{X}_1 - \bar{X}_2} = \sqrt{\frac{\hat{s}^2}{n} + \frac{\hat{s}^2}{n}}$$ (For independent samples of small and equal sizes)

$$s_{\bar{X}_1 - \bar{X}_2} = \sqrt{\frac{s_1^2}{n} + \frac{s_2^2}{n}}$$ (For independent samples of large and equal sizes)

$$s_{\bar{X}_1 - \bar{X}_2} = \sqrt{\frac{s_1^2}{n_1} + \frac{s_2^2}{n_2}}$$ (For independent samples of large and unequal sizes)

$$s_{\bar{X}_1 - \bar{X}_2} = \sqrt{(s_{\bar{X}_1})^2 + (s_{\bar{X}_2})^2 - 2r_{12} s_{\bar{X}_1} s_{\bar{X}_2}}$$ (For correlated samples of both small and large sizes)

$$s_{\bar{X}_1 - \bar{X}_2} = s_{\bar{D}} = \frac{s_D}{\sqrt{n}}$$ (For correlated samples of small size: single group method:

by difference method)

As sample size increases, the denominator of the 't' equation, that is, $s_{\bar{X}_1 - \bar{X}_2}$ or $s_{\bar{D}}$ decreases, which, in turn, causes the t_{obt} to increase. *Thus, increasing sample size increases the power of the 't' test.*

The denominator of the 't' equation (i.e., $s_{\bar{X}_1 - \bar{X}_2}$ or $s_{\bar{D}}$) also varies as a function of sample variability, which is measured by the SD of the samples. As the variability increases (or SD increases), the denominator (i.e., $s_{\bar{X}_1 - \bar{X}_2}$ or $s_{\bar{D}}$) also increases, which in turn, causes the t_{obt} to decrease. *Thus, high sample variability decreases the power of the 't' test.* Therefore, it is desirable to decrease the sample variability as much as possible. One way to decrease variability is to carefully control the experimental conditions. For example, in a reaction-time experiment, the experimenter might use a warning signal that directly precedes the stimulus to which the subject must respond. In this way, variability due to attention lapses could be eliminated. Another way is to use the appropriate experimental design. For example, in certain situations, using a correlated-groups design rather than an independent-groups design will decrease variability.

12.6   Significance of the Difference between Two Medians

Just like the means, the medians may be uncorrelated, when obtained from independent samples, or correlated, when obtained from the same group tested on two occasions or from two equivalent matched groups on a final test.

12.6.1   The SE of the Difference between Two Uncorrelated Medians

The significance of the difference between two medians obtained from two independent samples may be tested by the help of 't' test just like that of two independent means. The following formula is used to find out the SE of difference between two uncorrelated medians ($SE_{D_{Mdn}}$ or $s_{Mdn_1 - Mdn_2}$):

$$SE_{D_{Mdn}} = s_{Mdn_1 - Mdn_2} = \sqrt{s^2_{Mdn_1} + s^2_{Mdn_2}}$$

where

s_{mdn_1} is the SE of Mdn_1

s_{mdn_2} is the SE of Mdn_2.

The formula for computing the SE of the median has already been described in Chapter 11.

The entire procedure of testing the significance of difference between medians of two independent samples using 't' test will be more clear through the following example.

Example 12.22 The performance on an intelligence test of 225 boys and 225 girls of Grade X was recorded as follows:

	N	Median	SD
Boys	225	95.8	4.5
Girls	225	90.3	4.0

Test the significance of the difference between these two group medians.

Solution

(a)   The given data are:

$$\text{Boys: } N_1 = 225, \quad Mdn_1 = 95.8, \quad s_1 = 4.5$$
$$\text{Girls: } N_2 = 225, \quad Mdn_2 = 90.3, \quad s_2 = 4.0$$

Size of each sample: $N_1 = N_2 = N = 225$.

(b) The H_0 states that there is no significant difference between the two group medians. To find the probability (p) of the H_0 being correct, a two-tailed 't' test is done. The H_0 and H_1 are stated below:

$$H_0: \quad Mdn_1 = Mdn_2 \quad \text{or} \quad Mdn_1 - Mdn_2 = 0$$
$$H_1: \quad Mdn_1 \neq Mdn_2 \quad \text{or} \quad Mdn_1 - Mdn_2 \neq 0$$

(c) The SE of each median is first computed (as in Chapter 11) using the corresponding SD as follows:

$$s_{Mdn_1} = \frac{1.253 s_1}{\sqrt{N_1}} = \frac{1.253 \times 4.5}{\sqrt{225}} = \frac{5.6385}{15} = 0.376$$

$$s_{Mdn_2} = \frac{1.253 s_2}{\sqrt{N_2}} = \frac{1.253 \times 4.0}{\sqrt{225}} = \frac{5.012}{15} = 0.334$$

(d) The SE of difference between the medians ($s_{Mdn_1 - Mdn_2}$) is computed using the SE of each median (s_{Mdn_1} and s_{Mdn_2}) as follows:

$$s_{Mdn_1 - Mdn_2} = \sqrt{s_{Mdn_1}^2 + s_{Mdn_2}^2} = \sqrt{(0.376)^2 + (0.334)^2}$$
$$= \sqrt{0.141376 + 0.111556} = \sqrt{0.252932} = 0.503$$

(e) The difference between the two sample medians ($Mdn_1 - Mdn_2$) is converted to the critical ratio (CR) of 't', as follows:

$$t = \frac{Mdn_1 - Mdn_2}{s_{Mdn_1 - Mdn_2}} = \frac{95.8 - 90.3}{0.503} = \frac{5.5}{0.503} = 10.934$$
$$df = 2(N-1) = 2(225-1) = 2 \times 224 = 448 = \infty$$

(f) Entering Table C given in the appendix with df $= \infty$, the two-tailed critical value of 't' at the 0.05 level of significance is 1.96 and at the 0.01 level of significance is 2.576. As the computed 't' of 10.934 is much higher than the two-tailed critical 't' for the 0.01 level of significance, the probability (p) of correctness of the H_0 is less than 0.01 ($p < 0.01$).

The H_0 is rejected and H_1 is accepted. Therefore, we may conclude that there is a significant difference between the medians of two independent samples in 99% of cases.

12.6.2 The SE of Difference between Two Correlated Medians

The following formula is used to find out the SE of difference between two correlated medians:

$$SE_{D_{mdn}} = s_{Mdn_1 - Mdn_2} = \sqrt{s_{Mdn_1}^2 + s_{Mdn_2}^2 - 2r_{12} s_{Mdn_1} s_{Mdn_2}}$$

However, when medians are correlated, the value of r_{12} cannot be determined accurately and the reliability of the median cannot be readily computed. Therefore, when samples are not independent, rather they are correlated, it is a better procedure to use means instead of medians. So, further discussion about the significance of the difference between two correlated medians through examples is not needed.

12.7   Significance of the Difference between Two Standard Deviations (SDs) or Variances (s^2)

Like means and medians, the SDs may be uncorrelated or correlated depending upon the nature of samples from which they are obtained. The significance of the difference between two such group SDs may be estimated by the 't' test or 'F' test in several ways depending upon whether the samples are uncorrelated or correlated, whether they are large or small, etc. The various procedures for testing the significance of difference between two SDs or variance (s^2) are discussed further:

12.7.1   Significance of the Difference between Two Uncorrelated Standard Deviations (SDs) or Variances (s^2)

When samples are independent, that is, when different groups are studied or when tests given to the same groups are uncorrelated, the SDs or s^2 obtained from them are called independent or uncorrelated. The SD or s^2 measures the variability among groups. In many studies in behavioural sciences, particularly in psychology and education, the investigator is more interested in knowing whether his/her groups differ significantly in SD or s^2 than in knowing whether they differ in mean achievement. For example, an educational psychologist who is investigating a new method of teaching arithmetic may want to know whether the changed procedures have led to greater variability in scores than that present under the older method.

Thus, occasions arise where a test of the significance of the difference between the SDs or the variances of measurements for two independent samples is required. In the conduct of a simple experiment using control and experimental groups, the effect of the experimental condition may reflect itself not only in a mean difference between the two groups but also in variance/SD difference. For example, in an experiment designed to study the effect of a distracting agent, such as noise, on motor performance, the effect of the distraction may be to greatly increase the variability of performance, in addition possibly to exert some effect upon the mean. The variances obtained in any experiment should always be the object of scrutiny and comparison.

The procedures for testing the significance of difference between two uncorrelated SDs or variances are different depending upon the sizes of the two independent samples—whether they are large or small. These procedures are discussed further:

12.7.1.1   SE of the Difference between Two Uncorrelated SDs or Variances Obtained from Large Independent Samples

When the two SDs or variances are obtained from two uncorrelated or independent large samples, we can find out the SE of difference (SE_{D_s} or $s_{s_1-s_2}$) between these two SDs by the following formula that reads as follows:

$$SE_{D_s} = s_{s_1-s_2} = \sqrt{s_{s_1}^2 + s_{s_2}^2}$$

where

s_{s_1} is the SE of the first SD(s_1)
s_{s_2} is the SE of the second SD(s_2).

Then, the CR of 't' and df are computed as follows:

$$t = \frac{S_1 - S_2}{S_{S_1 - S_2}}$$

$df = (N_1 + N_2 - 2)$ (when N's are large but unequal)
$df = 2\,(N-1)$ (when N's are large but equal)

The entire procedure of testing the significance of difference between two uncorrelated SDs/s^2 obtained from two large independent samples using 't' test will be more clear through the following example.

Example 12.23 In a test of abstract reasoning, a sample of 144 Grade X girls and a sample of 121 Grade X boys scored as shown:

Sex	N	Means	SDs
Girls	144	30.25	11.86
Boys	121	31.95	8.11

Test whether the difference between two SDs is significant?

Solution

(a) The given data are:

Girls: $N_1 = 144$; $\bar{X}_1 = 30.25$; $s_1 = 11.86$
Boys: $N_2 = 121$; $\bar{X}_2 = 31.95$; $s_2 = 8.11$

(b) The H_0 states that there is no significant difference between two group SDs or variances. To find the probability (p) of the H_0 being correct, a two-tailed 't' test is done. The H_0 and H_1 are stated below:

H_0: $s_1 = s_2$ or, $s_1 - s_2 = 0$ (in terms of SDs)
$\quad\quad s_1^2 = s_2^2$ or, $s_1^2 - s_2^2 = 0$ (in terms of variances)
H_1: $s_1 \neq s_2$ or, $s_1 - s_2 \neq 0$ (in terms of SDs)
$\quad\quad s_1^2 \neq s_2^2$ or, $s_1^2 - s_2^2 \neq 0$ (in terms of variances)

(c) The SE of each SD is first computed (as in Chapter 11) using the corresponding SD, as follows:

$$S_{S_1} = \frac{0.71 s_1}{\sqrt{N_1}} = \frac{0.71 \times 11.86}{\sqrt{144}} = \frac{8.4206}{12} = 0.702$$

$$S_{S_2} = \frac{0.71 s_2}{\sqrt{N_2}} = \frac{0.71 \times 8.11}{\sqrt{121}} = \frac{5.7581}{11} = 0.523$$

(d) The SE of difference between two SDs ($s_{S_1 - S_2}$) is computed using the SE of each SD (s_{S_1} and s_{S_2}) as follows:

$$SE_{D_S} = S_{S_1 - S_2} = \sqrt{s_{S_1}^2 + s_{S_2}^2} = \sqrt{(0.702)^2 + (0.523)^2}$$
$$= \sqrt{0.492804 + 0.273529} = \sqrt{0.766333} = 0.875$$

(e) The difference between the two sample SDs $(s_1 - s_2)$ is converted to the CR of 't', as follows:

$$t = \frac{s_1 - s_2}{s_{s_1 - s_2}} = \frac{11.86 - 8.11}{0.875} = \frac{3.75}{0.875} = 4.286$$

$$\mathrm{df} = N_1 + N_2 - 2 = 144 + 121 - 2 = 265 - 2 = 263 = \infty$$

(f) Entering Table C (given in the appendix) with df $= \infty$, the two-tailed critical value of 't' at the 0.05 level of significance is 1.96 and at the 0.01 level of significance is 2.576. As the computed 't' of 4.286 is much higher than the two-tailed critical 't' for the 0.01 level of significance, the probability (p) of correctness of the H_0 is less than 0.01 $(p < 0.01)$. Hence, the obtained difference is significant beyond the 0.01 level. Thus, the H_0 is rejected and H_1 is accepted. Therefore, we may conclude that in the reasoning test, the girls are more variable in general than are the boys in 99% of cases.

12.7.1.2 *Significance of the Difference between Two Uncorrelated SDs or s^2 Obtained from Small Independent Samples*

When the samples are small and independent (uncorrelated), the significance of the difference between two SDs can be determined by the 'F' test, through the use of variances. The formula mentioned earlier in the text for $(s_{s_1 - s_2})$ is not accurate and appropriate when Ns are small, as the SDs from small samples drawn at random from a normally distributed population will tend to exhibit skewed distributions around the population σ.

Let s_1^2 and s_2^2 be two variances based on independent samples. We may consider the difference $s_1^2 - s_2^2$. An alternative and more fruitful procedure is to consider the ratio s_1^2 / s_2^2 or s_2^2 / s_1^2. If the two variances are equal, this ratio will be unity. If they differ and $s_1^2 > s_2^2$, then $s_1^2 / s_2^2 > 1$ and $s_2^2 / s_1^2 < 1$. A departure of the variance ratio from unity indicates a difference between variances, the greater the departure the greater the difference. Quite clearly, a test of the significance of the departure of the ratio of two variances from unity will serve as a test of the significance of the difference between the two variances.

In order to apply such a test of significance of difference, the sampling distribution of the ratio of two variances is required. To conceptualise such a sampling distribution, consider two normal populations A and B with the same variance σ^2. In other words, $\sigma_1^2 = \sigma_2^2 = \sigma^2$. This condition is usually spoken of as *homogeneity of variances*. Draw samples of N_1 cases from population A and N_2 cases from B, calculate unbiased variance estimates s_1^2 and s_2^2, and then compute the ratio s_1^2 / s_2^2. Continue this procedure until a large number of variance ratios is obtained. Always place the variance of the sample drawn from A in the numerator and the variance of the sample drawn from B in the denominator of the ratio. Some of the variance ratios will be greater than unity; others will be less than unity. The frequency distribution of the variance ratios for a large number of pairs of variances is an experimental sampling distribution. The corresponding theoretical sampling distribution of variance ratios is known as the distribution of F. The variance ratio is known as an 'F' ratio, that is, $F = s_1^2 / s_2^2$ or $F = s_2^2 / s_1^2$. In other words, the larger of the two sample variances will be in the numerator and the smaller of the two sample variances will be in the denominator of the 'F' ratio.

In the above illustration, samples of N_1 are drawn from one population (A) and samples of N_2 from another (B). Degrees of freedom $N_1 - 1$ and $N_2 - 1$ are associated with the two variance estimates. A separate sampling distribution of 'F' exists for every combination of df. Table E of the appendix shows values of 'F' required for significance at the 5% and 1% levels for varying combinations of df. This table shows values of F equal to or greater than unity. It does not show values of 'F' less than unity. The number of df associated with the variance estimates in the numerator (i.e., the larger variance or the greater mean square) and denominator (i.e., the smaller variance or the lesser mean square) are shown along the top and to the left, respectively, of Table E. The numbers in lightface type are the values for significance at the 5% (i.e., 0.05) level, and those in boldface type are the values at the 1% (i.e., 0.01) level. These values cut off 5% and 1% of one tail of the distribution of F.

In testing the significance of the difference between two variances, the null hypothesis ($H_0: \sigma_1^2 = \sigma_2^2 = \sigma^2$) is assumed. In calculating the F ratio, it is the general practice that the larger of the two variance estimates is always placed in the numerator and the smaller in the denominator. In consequence the 'F' ratio in this situation is always greater than unity. The 'F' ratio is calculated, referred to Table E of the appendix, and a significance level determined. It should be noted that the 'F' test is a one-tailed test, because we are dealing with the part of the 'F' distribution with values greater than 1. Table E shows values required for significance at the 5% and 1% (i.e., 0.05 or 0.01) levels. In testing the significance of the difference between two variances obtained from two independent small samples, we want a two-tailed test—a test of the probability of Fs below as well as above 1.0. It is not necessary, however, to get a second 'F' ratio by dividing the smaller variance by the larger variance. All we need to do is double the probability of the ratio at the 0.05 and 0.01 points. This gives a two-tailed test at the 0.10 and 0.02 levels. In other words, when we obtain results that are significant, we say that they are significant at the 5% or 1% point. If the table is used for a two-tailed test, an F significant at the 0.05 point must be interpreted at the 0.10 level and an 'F' significant at the 0.01 point at the 0.02 level.

Table E has been prepared for use with the analysis of variance (Chapter 14) which makes extensive use of the 'F' ratio. In the analysis of variance, the decision as to which variance estimate should be put in the numerator and which in the denominator is made on grounds other than their relative size. Consequently, in the analysis of variance, 'F' ratios less than 1 can occur, and Table E provides the appropriate probabilities without any doubling procedure.

To conduct an 'F' test, divide the larger variance by the smaller one, and evaluate the resulting 'F' in terms of the appropriate df referring to Table E of the appendix.

The entire procedure of testing the significance of difference between two uncorrelated variances obtained from two independent small samples using 'F' test will be more clear through the following example:

Example 12.24 Given two independent samples of size 20 with $s_1^2 = 400$ and $s_2^2 = 625$, test the hypothesis that the variances are significantly different from each other.

Solution

(a)   The given data are:

$$\text{Sample I:} \quad N_1 = 20, \quad s_1^2 = 400$$
$$\text{Sample II:} \quad N_2 = 20, \quad s_2^2 = 625$$

(b)   The H_0 states that the two uncorrelated variances are not significantly different from each other. To find the probability of this H_0 being correct, a two-tailed 'F' test is done. The H_0 and H_1 are stated below:

$$H_0: \quad s_1^2 = s_2^2 \quad \text{or} \quad s_1^2 - s_2^2 = 0$$
$$H_1: \quad s_1^2 \neq s_2^2 \quad \text{or} \quad s_1^2 - s_2^2 \neq 0$$

(c)   'F' ratio is calculated by dividing the larger variance estimate (s_2^2) by the small variance estimate (s_1^2), as follows:

$$F = \frac{s_2^2}{s_1^2} = \frac{625}{400} = 1.5625$$

$$\text{df}_1 \text{ for numerator (or larger variance)} = N_2 - 1 = 20 - 1 = 19$$
$$\text{df}_2 \text{ for denominator (or smaller variance)} = N_1 - 1 = 20 - 1 = 19$$

(d)   Entering Table E of the appendix with $\text{df}_1 = 19$ (df for the larger variance) and $\text{df}_2 = 19$ (df for the smaller variance), we get an 'F' of 2.165 at the 0.05 levels of significance and of 3.03 at the 0.01 level of significance. Our obtained 'F' of 1.5625 is far below the smaller of these Fs and, hence, is not significant at the 0.05 level; doubling this we obtain the 0.10 level. There is no evidence that the two groups differ in variability. It is clear, therefore, that the difference between the variances of two independent small samples cannot be considered statistically significant. The evidence is insufficient to warrant rejection of the null hypothesis. In other words, H_0 is accepted and H_1 is rejected.

12.7.2   Significance of the Difference between Two Correlated Standard Deviations or Variances

When the same group of subjects is tested under two experimental conditions, or two equivalent, matched-groups are used in the study, the SDs or the variances obtained from them are called correlated. For example, in an experiment designed to study the effect of an educational programme on attitude change, attitudes may be measured, an educational programme applied and attitudes re-measured. In other words, the attitudes are measured before and after the application of the educational programme in the same sample. It may be hypothesised that some change in variance of attitude-test scores may result. An increase in variance or SD may mean that the effect of the programme is to reinforce the existing attitudes, producing more extreme attitudes among individuals at both ends of the attitude continuum. A decrease in variance may mean that the effect of the programme is to produce an attitudinal regression to greater uniformity.

When we compare the SDs or variances of the same group upon two occasions or of the equivalent, matched groups on a final test, we must take into account possible correlation between the paired observations or between the scores of two equivalent or matched groups being compared.

The procedures for testing the significance of difference between two correlated SDs or variances are different depending upon the sizes of the correlated samples—whether they are large or small. These procedures are discussed further:

12.7.2.1   *SE of Difference between Two Correlated SDs or Variances Obtained from Large Correlated Samples*

When two SDs or s^2 are obtained from correlated samples of large size, we can find out the SE of difference between two SDs (SE_{D_s} or $s_{s_1 - s_2}$) by the following formula that reads as follows:

$$\text{SE}_{D_s} = s_{s_1 - s_2} = \sqrt{s_{s_1}^2 + s_{s_2}^2 - 2r_{12}^2 s_{s_1} s_{s_2}}$$

where

s_{s_1} and s_{s_2} are the SEs of the two SDs
r_{12}^2 is the square of the coefficient of correlation between paired scores of the same group or between final scores of two equivalent or matched groups.

Then, the CR of 't' and df are computed as follows:

$$t = \frac{s_1 - s_2}{s_{s_1 - s_2}}; \quad df = N - 1$$

The entire procedure of testing the significance of difference between two correlated SDs or variances obtained from large correlated samples using 't' test will be more clear through the following example:

Example 12.25 The following data were obtained from an experiment designed to find out the effect of a treatment on a single sample of 50 subjects. Is there a significant increase in the variability in the achievement scores of the subjects after the treatment?

	Pre-treatment	Post-treatment	
Means	74.0	97.0	$r_{12} = 0.75$
SD	10.2	13.6	

Solution

(a) The given data are:

Pre-treatment: $\bar{X}_1 = 74.0$, $s_1 = 10.2$

Post-treatment: $\bar{X}_2 = 97.0$, $s_2 = 13.6$

Size of the sample: $N = 50$; $r_{12} = 0.75$

(b) The H_0 states that there is no significant increase in variability in the achievement scores of the subjects after treatment. To find the probability (p) of this H_0 being correct, a one-tailed 't' test is done. The H_0 and H_1 are stated below:

$$H_0: s_2 \not> s_1; \quad H_1: s_2 > s_1$$

(c) The SE of each SD is first computed (as in Chapter 11) using the corresponding SD, as follows:

$$s_{s_1} = \frac{0.71 s_1}{\sqrt{N}} = \frac{0.71 \times 10.2}{\sqrt{50}} = \frac{7.242}{7.071} = 1.02$$

$$s_{s_2} = \frac{0.71 s_2}{\sqrt{N}} = \frac{0.71 \times 13.6}{\sqrt{50}} = \frac{9.656}{7.071} = 1.37$$

(d) The SE of difference between two correlated SDs is computed using the s_{s_1}, s_{s_2} and r_{12} as follows:

$$\begin{aligned}
SE_{D_s} = s_{s_1 - s_2} &= \sqrt{s_{s_1}^2 + s_{s_1}^2 - 2r_{12}^2 s_{s_1} s_{s_2}} \\
&= \sqrt{(1.02)^2 + (1.37)^2 - 2 \times (0.75)^2 \times 1.02 \times 1.37} \\
&= \sqrt{1.0404 + 1.8769 - 2 \times 0.5625 \times 1.02 \times 1.37} \\
&= \sqrt{2.9173 - 1.5721} = \sqrt{1.3452} = 1.16
\end{aligned}$$

(e) The difference between two correlated SDs $(s_1 - s_2)$ is converted to the CR of 't', as follows:

$$t = \frac{s_1 - s_2}{s_{s_1 - s_2}} = \frac{10.2 - 13.6}{1.16} = \frac{-3.4}{1.16} = -2.931$$

$$\text{df} = N - 1 = 50 - 1 = 49$$

(f) Because 't' distributions are perfectly bilaterally symmetrical, the negative sign of the computed 't' is ignored and the 't' ratio of 2.931 is compared with the one-tailed critical 't' scores. Entering Table C of the appendix with df=49, the one-tailed critical value of 't' at the 0.05 level of significance is 1.677 and at the 0.01 level of significance is 2.405. As the computed 't' of 2.931 is higher than the one-tailed critical 't' for the 0.01 level of significance, the probability (p) of correctness of the H_0 is less than 0.01 ($p<0.01$). Hence, the difference between two correlated SDs is significant beyond the 0.01 level. Thus, H_0 is rejected and H_1 is accepted. Therefore, we may conclude that there is a significant increase in the variability in the achievement scores of the subjects after the treatment.

12.7.2.2   *Significance of the Difference between Two Correlated SDs or Variances Obtained from Small Correlated Samples*

If s_1^2 and s_2^2 are the two unbiased variance estimates and r_{12} is the correlation between the paired observations, the quantity:

$$t = \frac{(s_1^2 - s_2^2)\sqrt{N-2}}{\sqrt{4s_1^2 s_2^2 (1 - r_{12}^2)}}$$

has a 't' distribution with $N-2$ df. Therefore, when samples are correlated and small in size ($N<30$), the difference between two SDs obtained from those samples can be tested for significance in terms of variances by the above formula of the 't' test with df=$N-2$, instead of $N-1$.

The entire procedure of testing the significance of the difference between two correlated SDs in terms of variances obtained from small correlated samples using 't' test with df=$N-2$ will be more clear through the following example.

Example 12.26 An attitude-scale was administered to a sample of 18 subjects before and after the administration of an educational programme. The unbiased variance estimates of attitude-test scores before and after the administration of the educational programme were 153.20 and 102.51, respectively. The correlation between the before-and-after attitude measures was 0.60. Are the two variances significantly different from each other?

Solution

(a) The given data are:

$$\text{Let } s_1^2 = 153.20 \quad \text{and} \quad s_2^2 = 102.51$$

$$\text{Size of the sample: } N=18$$

$$r_{12}=0.60$$

(b) The H_0 states that the two variances are not significantly different from each other. To find the probability (p) of this H_0 being correct, a two-tailed 't' test is done. The H_0 and H_1 are stated as follows:

$$H_0: \quad s_1^2 = s_2^2 \quad \text{or} \quad s_1^2 - s_2^2 = 0$$
$$H_1: \quad s_1^2 \neq s_2^2 \quad \text{or} \quad s_1^2 - s_2^2 \neq 0$$

(c) The computation of the CR of 't' is done directly, as follows:

$$t = \frac{(s_1^2 - s_2^2)\sqrt{N-2}}{\sqrt{4s_1^2 s_2^2(1 - r_{12}^2)}} = \frac{(153.20 - 102.51)\sqrt{18-2}}{\sqrt{4 \times 153.20 \times 102.51[1-(0.60)^2]}}$$

$$= \frac{50.69 \times 4}{\sqrt{62818.128(1-.36)}} = \frac{202.76}{\sqrt{62818.128 \times 0.64}} = \frac{202.76}{\sqrt{40203.60192}}$$

$$= \frac{202.76}{200.51} = 1.011$$

$$df = N - 2 = 18 - 2 = 16$$

(d) Entering Table C of the appendix with df = 16, the two-tailed critical value of 't' at the 0.05 level of significance is 2.120 and at the 0.01 level of significance is 2.921. As the computed 't' of 1.011 is much smaller than the two-tailed critical 't' for the 0.05 level of significance, the probability (p) of correctness of the H_0 is greater than 0.05 ($p > 0.05$). Hence, the difference between two correlated variances obtained from a small sample is not statistically significant. In other words, the evidence is insufficient to warrant rejection of the null hypothesis. Thus, H_0 is accepted and H_1 is rejected. Therefore, we may conclude that the intervening educational programme has not changed the variability of attitudes.

12.8   Significance of the Difference between Two Correlation Coefficients for Independent Samples

Before going to discuss about the procedures of testing the significance of the difference between two correlation coefficients, we should have some knowledge about the sampling distribution. So, let us first discuss about the sampling distribution.

We may draw a large number of samples from a population, compute a correlation coefficient for each sample and prepare a frequency distribution of correlation coefficients. Such a frequency distribution is an experimental sampling distribution of the correlation coefficient. To illustrate, casual observation suggests that a positive correlation exists between height and weight. A number of samples of 20 cases each may be drawn at random from a population of adult males and a correlation coefficient between height and weight computed for each sample. These coefficients will display variation of one from another. By arranging these coefficients in the form of a frequency distribution an experimental sampling distribution of the correlation coefficient is obtained. The mean of this distribution will tend to approach the population value of the correlation coefficient with increase in the number of samples. Its SD will describe the variability of the coefficients from sample to sample.

A further illustration may prove helpful. By throwing a pair of dice, say, a white one and a red one, a number of times, a set of paired observations is obtained. A correlation coefficient may be calculated for the paired observations. Since the two dice are independent, the expected value of this correlation coefficient is zero. However, for any particular sample of 'N' throws, a positive or negative correlation may result. A large number of samples of 'N' throws may be obtained, a correlation coefficient computed for each sample and a frequency distribution of the coefficients prepared. The mean of this experimental sampling distribution will tend to approach zero; the population value of the correlation coefficient and its SD will be descriptive of the variability of the correlation in drawing samples of size 'N' from this particular kind of population. Note that here, as in all sampling problems, a distinction is drawn between a population value and an estimate of that value based on a sample. The symbol 'ρ', the Greek letter 'rho', is used to refer to the population value of the correlation coefficient, and 'r' is the sample value.

The shape of the sampling distribution of the correlation coefficient depends on the population value 'ρ'. As 'ρ' departs from '0', the sampling distribution becomes increasingly skewed. When 'ρ' is high positive, say, $\rho=0.80$, the sampling distribution has extreme negative skewness. Similarly, when 'ρ' is high negative, say, $\rho=-0.80$, the distribution has extreme positive skewness. When $\rho=0$, the sampling distribution is symmetrical and for large values of 'N', say, 30 or above, it is approximately normal.

The SD of the theoretical sampling distribution of ρ, the SE, is given by the formula that reads

$$\sigma_r = \frac{1-\rho^2}{\sqrt{N-1}}$$

When 'ρ' departs appreciably from '0', this above formula is of little use, because the departures of the sampling distribution from normality make interpretation difficult.

Difficulties resulting from the skewness of the sampling distribution of correlation coefficient are resolved by a method developed by R.A. Fisher. According to this method, the values of 'r' are converted to values of z_r, using the following transformation formula:

$$z_r = \frac{1}{2}\log(1+r) - \frac{1}{2}\log(1-r)$$

However, the values of z_r corresponding to particular values of 'r' need not be computed directly from the above formula but may be simply obtained from Table D in the appendix. For example, for $r=0.60$, the corresponding $z_r=0.693$; for $r=0.80$, $z_r=1.099$ and so on. For negative values of 'r' the corresponding z_r values may be given negative signs. In a number of sampling problems involving correlation, rs are converted to z_rs, and a test of significance is applied to the z_rs instead of to the original rs.

There are two important advantages of this transformation of rs to z_rs. One advantage of this transformation resides in the fact that the sampling distribution of z_r is for all practical purposes independent of 'ρ'. The distribution has the same variability for a given 'N' regardless of the size of 'ρ'. Another advantage is that the sampling distribution of z_r is approximately normal. Values of z_r can be interpreted in relation to the normal curve. The SE of z_r is given by:

$$SE_{z_r} = s_{z_r} = \frac{1}{\sqrt{N-3}}$$

The SE is seen to depend entirely on the sample size (N). (The two correlated variables take away 2 df; the transformation into 'z' adds another restriction. Hence, we subtract 3 from N.)

Now let us discuss about the significance of the difference between two correlation coefficients. Consider a situation where two correlation coefficients r_1 and r_2 are obtained from two independent samples. The correlation coefficients may, for example, be correlations between intelligence-test scores and statistics-examination marks for two different freshman classes A and B. We wish to test whether r_1 is significantly different from r_2, that is, whether the two samples can be considered random samples from a common population. The null hypothesis is H_0: $\rho_1=\rho_2$ or $\rho_1-\rho_2=0$.

The significance of the difference between r_1 and r_2 can be readily tested using Fisher's z_r transformation. We have to first convert r_1 and r_2 to z_rs using Table D of the appendix. As stated previously, the sampling distribution of z_r is approximately normal with an SE given by $s_{z_r} = \dfrac{1}{\sqrt{N-3}}$. The following is the formula to find out the SE of the difference between two values of z_r.

$$SE_{z_r} = s_{z_{r_1} - z_{r_2}} = \sqrt{s_{z_{r_1}}^2 + s_{z_{r_2}}^2} = \sqrt{\frac{1}{N_1 - 3} + \frac{1}{N_2 - 3}}$$

where

$s_{z_{r_1}}^2$ and $s_{z_{r_2}}^2$ are the SE of z_{r_1} and z_{r_2}, respectively.

By dividing the difference between the two values of z_r by the SE of the difference ($s_{z_{r_1} - z_{r_2}}$), we obtain the 'z' ratio, as follows:

$$z = \frac{z_{r_1} - z_{r_2}}{s_{z_{r_1} - z_{r_2}}} = \frac{z_{r_1} - z_{r_2}}{\sqrt{\dfrac{1}{(N_1 - 3)} + \dfrac{1}{(N_2 - 3)}}}$$

This is a unit-normal-curve deviate and may be so interpreted. Values of 1.96 and 2.58 are required for significance at the 5% and 1% (or 0.05 and 0.01) levels, respectively.

The entire procedure of testing the significance of the difference between two correlation coefficients for independent samples using 'z' test will be more clear through the following example.

Example 12.27 The correlation coefficients between intelligence-test scores and statistics-examination marks for two different freshman classes A and B are, respectively, 0.52 and 0.82. The sample size of class A is 63 and that of class B is 33. Are the two correlation coefficients significantly different?

Solution

(a) The given data are:

Freshman class A: $N_1 = 63$, $r_1 = 0.52$
Freshman class B: $N_2 = 33$, $r_2 = 0.82$

(b) The H_0 states that the two correlation coefficients are not significantly different from each other. To find the probability (p) of this H_0 being correct, a two-tailed 'z' test is done. The H_0 and H_1 are stated as follows:

H_0: $r_1 = r_2$ or $r_1 - r_2 = 0$
H_1: $r_1 \neq r_2$ or $r_1 - r_2 \neq 0$

(c) First of all we have to transfer the given correlation coefficients to their corresponding z_r values with the help of Table D of the appendix. Thus, the $r_1 = 0.52$ is $z_{r_1} = 0.576$ and $r_2 = 0.82$ is $z_{r_2} = 1.157$. In other words, the corresponding z_{r_1} and z_{r_2} values of $r_1 = 0.52$ and $r_2 = 0.82$ obtained from Table D of the appendix are 0.576 and 1.157, respectively.

(d) The SE of the difference between z_{r_1} and z_{r_2} is computed as follows:

$$s_{z_{r_1} - z_{r_2}} = \sqrt{\frac{1}{N_1 - 3} + \frac{1}{N_2 - 3}} = \sqrt{\frac{1}{63 - 3} + \frac{1}{33 - 3}}$$

$$= \sqrt{\frac{1}{60} + \frac{1}{30}} = \sqrt{0.0167 + 0.0333} = \sqrt{0.05} = 0.224$$

(e) Then, the 'z' ratio is computed by dividing the difference between the two values of z_r by the SE of difference, as follows:

$$z = \frac{z_{r_1} - z_{r_2}}{S_{z_{r_1} - z_{r_2}}} = \frac{0.576 - 1.157}{0.224} = \frac{-0.581}{0.224} = -2.594$$

(f) Because the 'z' ratio is a unit-normal-curve deviate and 'z' distributions are perfectly bilaterally symmetrical, the negative signs of the computed 'z' is ignored and the 'z' ratio of 2.594 is compared with the two-tailed critical 'z' scores given in Table A of the appendix. Table A depicts that the critical values of 'z', for a two-tailed test at the 0.05 level of significance (or 5% level) is 1.96 and at the 0.01 level of significance (or 1% level) is 2.58. Since the obtained 'z' value of 2.594 is higher than the two-tailed critical value of 'z' of 2.58 (i.e., $z_{obt} > 2.58$), the marked difference between two independent correlation coefficients is significant at the 0.01 level of significance. In other words, the probability (p) of correctness of the H_0 is less than 0.01 ($p < 0.01$). Thus, H_0 is rejected and H_1 is accepted. Therefore, we may conclude that the two independent correlation coefficients are significantly different from each other in 99% of cases.

Measurement of the significance of the difference between the rs obtained from the same sample represents certain complications, as rs from the same group are presumably correlated. Formulae for computing the correlation between two correlated rs are not entirely satisfactory and there is no method of determining the correlation between two zs directly. Fortunately, we may feel sure that if the rs are positively correlated in our group, and the CR as determined by the SE of the difference between two 'z' coefficients is significant, that the CR would be even more significant if the correlation between the rs were known.

The 'z' transformation can be usefully employed when rs which differ widely in size are to be averaged or combined.

12.9   Significance of the Difference between Two Proportions or Two Percentages

We have studied in detail some of the ways in which we test the significance of difference between two means, medians, SDs or variances, correlation coefficients, etc. Now we shall consider specifically differences between proportions and percentages. Before we do this, however, we should note that there is a general way of testing the significance of the difference between two statistics. We use a 'z' or 't' test, depending on the size of the sample. Both of these are defined as the difference between two statistics divided by the SE of this difference. Of course, we have to use the correct formula for the SE of the different statistics that we are using.

Like means and other statistics, the proportions or percentages may be uncorrelated or correlated depending upon the nature of samples on which they are based. The significance of the difference between two proportions or percentages may be tested by the help of 'z' test or 't' test depending upon the nature (i.e., uncorrelated or correlated) and size (i.e., large or small) of samples. The different procedures for testing the significance of difference between two proportions or percentages are discussed further.

12.9.1   Significance of the Difference between Two Uncorrelated Proportions or Percentages

When independent samples are used in the study, the obtained data are called uncorrelated (or independent). Often questions arise in the interpretation of experimental results which require a test of significance of the difference between two independent proportions or percentages. The data comprise two samples drawn independently. Of the N_1 members in the first sample, f_1 have the attribute A. Of the N_2 members in the second sample, f_2 have the attribute 'A'. The proportions having the attributes in the two samples are: $\frac{f_1}{N_1} = p_1$ and $\frac{f_2}{N_2} = p_2$.

Similarly, the per cents having the attributes in the two samples are: $\frac{f_1}{N_1} \times 100 = P_1$ and $\frac{f_2}{N_2} \times 100 = P_2$. In other words, per cent (P) is 100 times of proportion (p). That is, $P = p \times 100$, where 'P' stands for percentage and 'p' stands for proportion. Can the two samples be regarded as random samples drawn from the same population? Is p_1 (or P_1) significantly different from p_2 (or P_2)? To illustrate, in a public opinion poll the proportion 0.75 in a sample of urban residents expressed a favourable attitude towards a particular social issue as against a proportion 0.65 in a sample of rural residents. Can the difference between the proportions be interpreted as indicative of an actual urban-rural difference in opinion? To illustrate further, the per cent of boys failed in an examination is 42% and that of girls is 50%. Does this represent a significant change in the per cents of failures or may the difference be attributed to sampling considerations? The answers to these questions depend upon the significance of the difference between two uncorrelated proportions or percentages.

The procedures for testing the significance of the difference between two uncorrelated (or independent) proportions or percentages are different depending upon the sizes of the two independent samples—whether they are large or small. These procedures are as follows:

12.9.1.1   SE of the Difference between Two Uncorrelated Proportions or Percentages Based on Large Independent Samples

The SE of a single proportion is estimated by the formula that reads

$$SE_p = s_p = \sqrt{\frac{pq}{N}}$$

where p is the sample value of a proportion

$$q = 1 - p.$$

When samples are independent but large, the following is the formula to find out the SE of difference between two independent or uncorrelated proportions.

$$SE_{D_p} = s_{D_p} = s_{p_1 - p_2} = \sqrt{s_{p_1}^2 + s_{p_2}^2}$$

where

s_{p_1} is the SE of p_1

s_{p_2} is the SE of p_2.

Before we solve this, we can make the computations easier if we may change the notations as follows:

$$s_{p_1-p_2} = \sqrt{\left(\sqrt{\frac{p_1 q_1}{N_1}}\right)^2 + \left(\sqrt{\frac{p_2 q_2}{N_2}}\right)^2} = \sqrt{\frac{p_1 q_1}{N_1} + \frac{p_2 q_2}{N_2}}.$$

This latter equation should be used in preference to find out the SE of difference between two uncorrelated proportions when samples are large, because we can go into it directly with our 'p' values, and the computation of the two separate SEs of the proportions is not necessary.

Since the samples are independent and large, the difference between two proportions should be converted to 'z' ratio by the help of SEs of difference between proportions ($s_{p_1-p_2}$).

To test the significance of the difference between two uncorrelated proportions, we divide the observed difference between the proportions (p_1-p_2) by the estimate of the SE of difference to obtain 'z' as follows:

$$z = \frac{p_1 - p_2}{s_{p_1-p_2}}$$

The obtained 'z' value may be interpreted as usual as a deviate of the unit normal curve. As usual for a two-tailed test, values of 1.96 and 2.58 are required for significance at the 5% (or 0.05) and 1% (or 0.01) levels, respectively.

With regard to the percentage, we can say that the formula for the SE of a percentage is given as:

$$SE_\% = s_\% = \sqrt{\frac{PQ}{N}}$$

where

P=per cent occurrence of the observed behaviour
$Q=1-P$
N=size of the sample.

The following is the formula to find out the SE of difference between two percentages (P_1 and P_2).

$$SE_{D\%} = s_{D\%} = s_{P_1-P_2} = \sqrt{s_{P_1}^2 + s_{P_2}^2}$$
$$= \sqrt{\left(\sqrt{\frac{P_1 Q_1}{N_1}}\right)^2 + \left(\sqrt{\frac{P_2 Q_2}{N_2}}\right)^2} = \sqrt{\frac{P_1 Q_1}{N_1} + \frac{P_2 Q_2}{N_2}}$$

The difference between two uncorrelated percentages based on large independent samples is converted to 'z' score as follows:

$$z = \frac{P_1 - P_2}{s_{P_1-P_2}}$$

The obtained 'z' value may be interpreted as usual.

From the above discussions about the test of significance of difference between two uncorrelated proportions or percentages based on large samples, the formulae are the same for both except the notations in terms of 'P' and 'Q' (different in size of the letters); for proportions these are in small letters, such as p, q, p_1, q_1, p_2 and q_2, and for percentages these are in capital letters, such as P, Q, P_1, Q_1, P_2 and Q_2.

The entire procedure of testing the significance of the difference between two uncorrelated proportions or percentages based on large independent samples using 'z' test will be more clear through the following examples.

Example 12.28 In a survey it was found that 60 out of 170 females and 32 out of 128 males preferred a certain TV programme over two others. Is there a sex difference in the preference for this programme?

Solution

(a) The given data are:

Females: $N_1 = 170$;   Number preferred $(f_1) = 60$
Males: $N_2 = 128$;   Number preferred $(f_2) = 32$

(b) The H_0 states that there is no significant difference between the two proportions of females and males showing preference for a certain TV programme. To find the probability (p) of this H_0 being correct, a two-tailed 'z' test is done. The H_0 and H_1 are stated below:

$$H_0: \quad p_1 = p_2 \quad \text{or} \quad p_1 - p_2 = 0$$
$$H_1: \quad p_1 \neq p_2 \quad \text{or} \quad p_1 - p_2 \neq 0$$

(c) First we have to compute the proportions of females and males showing preference for a certain TV programme, as follows:

Proportion of females: $\quad p_1 = \dfrac{f_1}{N_1} = \dfrac{60}{170} = 0.35; \quad q_1 = 1 - 0.35 = 0.65$

Proportion of males: $\quad p_2 = \dfrac{f_2}{N_2} = \dfrac{32}{128} = 0.25; \quad q_2 = 1 - 0.25 = 0.75$

(d) Then, we compute the SE of difference between the two proportions as follows:

$$s_{p_1 - p_2} = \sqrt{\frac{p_1 q_1}{N_1} + \frac{p_2 q_2}{N_2}} = \sqrt{\frac{(0.35)(0.65)}{170} + \frac{(0.25)(0.75)}{128}}$$

$$= \sqrt{\frac{0.2275}{170} + \frac{0.1875}{128}} = \sqrt{0.00134 + 0.00146}$$

$$= \sqrt{0.0028} = 0.053$$

(e) Then, the 'z' ratio is computed as dividing the difference between the two proportions ($p_1 - p_2$) by the SE of the difference ($s_{p_1 - p_2}$) as follows:

$$z = \frac{p_1 - p_2}{s_{p_1 - p_2}} = \frac{0.35 - 0.25}{0.053} = \frac{0.10}{0.053} = 1.89$$

(f) Entering Table A of the appendix, the two-tailed critical value of 'z' at the 0.05 level of significance is 1.96 and at the 0.01 level of significance is 2.58. Since the obtained 'z' value of 1.89 is smaller than 1.96, the probability (p) of correctness of the H_0 is greater than 0.05 ($p > 0.05$). Thus, H_0 is accepted and H_1 is rejected. Therefore, we may conclude that there is not a significant sex difference in showing preference for a certain TV programme, and both the samples—females and males—have drawn randomly from the same population.

Example 12.29 In a school of 500 pupils, 52.3% are girls, and in a second school of 300 pupils, 47.7% are girls. Is there a significant difference between the percentage of girls enrolled in the two schools?

Solution

(a) The given data are:

$$
\begin{aligned}
\text{First school:} \quad & N_1=500; \quad \text{Per cent of girls:} \quad P_1=52.3\% \\
& Q_1=100\%-52.3\%=47.7\% \\
\text{Second school:} \quad & N_2=300; \quad \text{Per cent of girls:} \quad P_2=47.7\% \\
& Q_2=100\%-47.7\%=52.3\%
\end{aligned}
$$

(b) The H_0 states that there is no significant difference between the percentage of girls enrolled in the two schools. To find the probability (p) of this H_0 being correct, a two-tailed 'z' test is done. The H_0 and H_1 are stated below:

$$
\begin{aligned}
H_0: \quad & P_1=P_2 \quad \text{or} \quad P_1-P_2=0 \\
H_1: \quad & P_1\neq P_2 \quad \text{or} \quad P_1-P_2\neq 0
\end{aligned}
$$

(c) We first compute the SE of difference between the percentage as follows:

$$
\begin{aligned}
S_{p_1-p_2} &= \sqrt{\frac{P_1Q_1}{N_1}+\frac{P_2Q_2}{N_2}} = \sqrt{\frac{52.3\times 47.7}{500}+\frac{47.7\times 52.3}{300}} \\
&= \sqrt{\frac{2494.71}{500}+\frac{2494.71}{300}} = \sqrt{4.9894+8.3157} = \sqrt{13.3051} = 3.648\%
\end{aligned}
$$

(d) Then, the 'z' ratio is computed by dividing the difference between two percentages (P_1-P_2) by the SE of the difference $(s_{p_1-p_2})$ as follows:

$$
z = \frac{P_1-P_2}{s_{P_1-P_2}} = \frac{52.3-47.7}{3.648} = \frac{4.6}{3.648} = 1.26
$$

(e) Entering Table A of the appendix, the two-tailed critical value of 'z' at the 0.05 level of significance is 1.96 and at the 0.01 level of significance is 2.58. Since the obtained 'z' value of 1.26 is smaller than 1.96, the probability (p) of correctness of the H_0 is greater than 0.05 $(p>0.05)$. Thus, H_0 is accepted and H_1 is rejected. Therefore, we may conclude that there is not a significant difference between the percentage of girls enrolled in the two schools; with respect to the per cent of girls both samples have been randomly drawn from the same population.

12.9.1.2   *SE of Difference between Two Uncorrelated Proportions or Percentages Based on Small Independent Samples*

The above technique works adequately when the Ns are above 100. However, if either of the Ns is less than 100, and either or both of the ps are extreme, that is, less than 0.10 or greater than 0.90, it is better to base the SE of the difference on the proportion or percentage in the two groups combined. In other words, when the two independent samples are of small size, the SE of the difference between two proportions (p) or two percentages (P) is based on a pooled estimate of 'p' or 'P' as the case may be. Since we are testing the null hypothesis that the population proportions (H$_0$: $p_1=p_2$) or population percentages (H$_0$: $P_1=P_2$) are equal, we are justified in doing this.

Let us first discuss about the significance of difference between two proportions based on two independent small samples.

The SE of the difference between two proportions based on two small independent samples is estimated by:

$$S_{p_1-p_2} = \sqrt{pq\left(\frac{1}{N_1}+\frac{1}{N_2}\right)}$$

where

'p' is an estimate of proportion based on the two samples combined.

The value of 'p' is obtained in two ways depending upon the nature of the given data. If the given data are in terms of frequencies, then the value of 'p' is obtained by adding together the frequency of occurrence of the attributes in the two samples and then dividing this by the total number in the two samples. Thus:

$$p = \frac{f_1+f_2}{N_1+N_2}$$

where

f_1 and f_2 are the frequencies of first and second samples

'q' being, of course, $1-p$.

If the given data are in terms of proportions, then the pooled estimate of 'p' is obtained from the following equation by pooling 'p_1' and 'p_2', as follows:

$$p = \frac{p_1N_1 + p_2N_2}{N_1+N_2}$$

where

'p' is an estimated proportion

'p_1' and 'p_2' are the proportions of the first and second samples, respectively

'q' is $1-p$.

Let us now discuss about the significance of difference between two percentages based on two independent small samples.

The SE of the difference between two percentages based on two small independent samples is estimated by:

$$S_{p_1-p_2} = \sqrt{PQ\left(\frac{1}{N_1}+\frac{1}{N_2}\right)}$$

where

'P' is an estimate of percentage based on the two samples combined.

If the given data are in terms of percentages, then the pooled estimate of 'P' is obtained by pooling P_1 and P_2 from the equation as follows:

$$P = \frac{P_1N_1 + P_2N_2}{N_1+N_2}$$

where

'*P*' is an estimated percentage

P_1 and P_2 are the per cents of the first and second samples, respectively

$Q = 1 - P$.

The justification for combining data from the two independent small samples to obtain a single estimate of '*p*' (proportion) or '*P*' (percentage) resides in the fact that in all cases where the difference between either two proportions or two percentages is tested, the null hypothesis (H_0) is assumed. This H_0 states that no difference exists in the population proportions or population percentages. Because the null hypothesis is assumed, we may use an estimate of either '*p*' or '*P*' based on the data combined for the two samples.

In order to test the significance of the difference between two proportions or two percentages based on two small independent samples, the '*t*' test, instead of the '*z*' test, is applied. The CR of '*t*' is obtained by dividing the observed difference between two proportions ($p_1 - p_2$) or between two percentages ($P_1 - P_2$) by the estimate of the SE of the difference as follows:

$$t = \frac{p_1 - p_2}{s_{p_1 - p_2}} \quad \text{(In case of proportions)}$$

$$t = \frac{P_1 - P_2}{s_{P_1 - P_2}} \quad \text{(In case of percentages)}$$

$$\text{df} = N_1 + N_2 - 2 \ (\text{when } N_1 \neq N_2)$$
$$\text{df} = 2(N-1) \ (\text{when } N_1 = N_2 = N)$$

The obtained '*t*' value may be interpreted, taking into account the df, as usual. The above technique (i.e., the '*t*' test) can be used with large samples as well as with small ones. With large samples, the difference in the results will be trivial; with smaller samples, more reliable results are obtained using the '*t*' test, which is based on the observed difference between two proportions (or two percentages) divided by the estimated SE of the difference.

The entire procedure of testing the significance of the difference between two uncorrelated proportions or percentages based on small independent samples using '*t*' test will be more clear through the following examples.

Example 12.30 Thirty-six in a group of 40 and five in a group of 50 respond '*yes*' to a certain attitude test item. Do the responses of the two groups differ significantly?

Solution

(a) The given data are:

Group 1: $N_1 = 40$; Number responded 'Yes' (f_1) = 36
Group 2: $N_2 = 50$; Number responded 'Yes' (f_2) = 5

(b) The H_0 states that the responses of the two groups do not differ significantly. To find the probability (*p*) of this H_0 being correct, a two-tailed '*t*' test is done. The H_0 and H_1 are stated below:

$$H_0: \ p_1 = p_2 \quad \text{or} \quad p_1 - p_2 = 0$$
$$H_1: \ p_1 \neq p_2 \quad \text{or} \quad p_1 - p_2 \neq 0$$

(c) First we have to compute the proportions of subjects responded 'Yes' to a certain attitude test item in both groups, as follows:

Proportion of subjects in group 1: $p_1 = \dfrac{f_1}{N_1} = \dfrac{36}{40} = 0.90$

Proportion of subjects in group 2: $p_2 = \dfrac{f_2}{N_2} = \dfrac{5}{50} = 0.10$

(d) Then, we can find out a pooled estimate of the proportion (p) in one of the two following ways:

$$p = \dfrac{f_1 + f_2}{N_1 + N_2} = \dfrac{36 + 5}{40 + 50} = \dfrac{41}{90} = 0.46$$

Alternatively,

$$P = \dfrac{P_1 N_1 + P_2 N_2}{N_1 + N_2} = \dfrac{0.90 \times 40 + 0.10 \times 50}{40 + 50} = \dfrac{36 + 5}{90} = \dfrac{41}{90} = 0.46$$

If the estimated $p=0.46$, then $q=1-0.46=0.54$

(e) Then, we compute the SE of difference between the two proportions using the estimated 'p' and 'q' values, as follows:

$$s_{p_1 - p_2} = \sqrt{pq\left(\dfrac{1}{N_1} + \dfrac{1}{N_2}\right)} = \sqrt{(0.46)(0.54)\left(\dfrac{1}{40} + \dfrac{1}{50}\right)}$$

$$= \sqrt{0.2484(0.025 + 0.02)} = \sqrt{0.2484 \times 0.045}$$

$$= \sqrt{0.011178} = 0.106$$

(f) The 't' ratio is then computed by dividing the difference between the two proportions ($p_1 - p_2$) by the estimate of the SE of difference ($s_{p_1 - p_2}$) as follows:

$$t = \dfrac{p_1 - p_2}{s_{p_1 - p_2}} = \dfrac{0.90 - 0.10}{0.106} = \dfrac{0.80}{0.106} = 7.55$$

$$df = N_1 + N_2 - 2 = 40 + 50 - 2 = 90 - 2 = 88$$

(g) Entering Table C of the appendix with df=88, the two-tailed critical value of 't' at the 0.05 level of significance is 1.9876 and at the 0.01 level is 2.6334 (by interpolation). As the computed 't' of 7.55 is much higher than the two-tailed critical 't' for the 0.01 level of significance, the probability (p) of correctness of the H_0 is less than 0.01 ($p<0.01$). Hence, the difference between the two uncorrelated proportions is significant beyond the 0.01 level. Thus, H_0 is rejected and H_1 is accepted. Therefore, we may conclude that the responses of the two independent groups differ significantly in 99% of cases.

Example 12.31 In a study of the attitudes of Indians to immigrants and immigration policy, independent samples of Hindi- and non-Hindi-speaking Indians were used. Subjects were asked whether they agree or disagree with present government immigration practices. In the Hindi-speaking sample of 50 subjects, 80% subjects indicated agreement. In the non-Hindi-speaking sample of 50 subjects, 60% subjects indicated agreement. Do the responses in the two groups differ significantly?

Solution

(a) The given data are:

Hindi-speaking group: $N_1 = 50$, $P_1 = 80\%$
Non-Hindi-speaking group: $N_2 = 50$, $P_2 = 60\%$

(b) The H_0 states that the responses of the two groups do not differ significantly. To find the probability (p) of this H_0 being correct, a two-tailed 't' test is done. The H_0 and H_1 are stated below:

$$H_0: \quad P_1 = P_2 \quad \text{or} \quad P_1 - P_2 = 0$$
$$H_1: \quad P_1 \ne P_2 \quad \text{or} \quad P_1 - P_2 \ne 0$$

(c) First we have to compute a pooled estimate of 'P' by pooling P_1 and P_2 as follows:

$$P = \frac{P_1 N_1 + P_2 N_2}{N_1 + N_2} = \frac{80 \times 50 + 60 \times 50}{50 + 50} = \frac{4000 + 3000}{100} = \frac{7000}{100} = 70\%$$
$$Q = 100\% - 70\% = 30\%$$

(d) Then, we compute the SE of difference between the two percentages using the estimated 'P' and 'Q' values as follows:

$$s_{P_1 - P_2} = \sqrt{PQ\left(\frac{1}{N_1} + \frac{1}{N_2}\right)} = \sqrt{70 \times 30\left(\frac{1}{50} + \frac{1}{50}\right)}$$
$$= \sqrt{2100(0.02 + 0.02)} = \sqrt{2100 \times 0.04}$$
$$= \sqrt{84} = 9.165\%$$

(e) The 't' ratio is then computed by dividing the difference between the two percentages ($P_1 - P_2$) by the estimate of the SE of difference ($s_{P_1 - P_2}$) as follows:

$$t = \frac{P_1 - P_2}{s_{P_1 - P_2}} = \frac{80 - 60}{9.165} = \frac{20}{9.165} = 2.18$$
$$\mathrm{df} = 2(N - 1) = 2(50 - 1) = 2 \times 49 = 98$$

(f) Entering Table C of the appendix with df=98, the two-tailed critical value of 't' at the 0.05 level of significance is 1.9846 and at the 0.01 level is 2.6272 (by interpolation). As the computed 't' of 2.18 is higher than the two-tailed critical 't' for the 0.05 level of significance, the probability (p) of correctness of the H_0 is less than 0.05 ($p < 0.05$). Hence, the difference between the two uncorrelated percentages is significant beyond the 0.05 level. Thus, the H_0 is rejected and the H_1 is accepted. Therefore, we may conclude that the responses of the two independent groups differ significantly in 95% of cases.

12.9.2 Significance of the Difference between Two Correlated Proportions or Percentages

Frequently in research work we wish to test the significance of difference between two proportions or percentages based on the same sample of individuals or on matched samples. The data consist of pairs of observations and are usually nominal in type. The paired observations may exhibit a correlation, which must be taken into consideration in testing the difference between proportions or percentages. To illustrate, a test consisting of two different attitude scale items may be administered to a sample of 'N' individuals. Paired observations are available for each individual. One individual may respond 'Yes' to the first and second items. A second individual may respond 'Yes' to the first item and 'No' to the second item. A third individual may respond 'No' to the first item and 'Yes' to the second item. A fourth individual may respond 'No' to both items. The paired observations may be tabulated in a two-by-two table. The data may be represented schematically in the form of a fourfold, or 2×2, table as follows:

		I **Frequencies** Item 2					**II** **Proportions** Item 2					**III** **Percentages** Item 2		
		No	Yes	Total			No	Yes	Total			No	Yes	Total
Item 1	Yes	A	B	A+B	Item 1	Yes	a	b	a+b (p_1)	Item 1	Yes	a	b	a+b (P_1)
	No	C	D	C+D		No	c	d	c+d (q_1)		No	c	d	c+d (Q_1)
	Total	A+C	B+D	N		Total	a+c (q_2)	b+d (p_2)	1.00		Total	a+c (Q_2)	b+d (P_2)	100%

In diagram I, the capital letters represent frequencies. The cell A represents the number of individuals who have responded 'Yes' to item 1 and 'No' to item 2. The cell B represents the individuals who have responded 'Yes' to both items. The cell C represents the individuals who have responded 'No' to both items. The cell D represents the individuals who have responded 'No' to item 1 and 'Yes' to item 2. Thus, cells B and C represent those individuals who have responded in the same direction to the two items. Cells A and D represent the individuals who have answered the two items differently. A+B represents the number of individuals who have responded 'Yes' to item 1, C+D represents individuals who responded 'No' to item 1, A+C represents individuals who responded 'No' to item 2 and B+D represents the number of individuals who responded 'Yes' to item 2.

In diagram II the lower case (or small) letters represent the proportions obtained by dividing the frequencies by $N\left(\dfrac{f}{N}\right)$. The proportions of 'Yes' responses to item 1 and item 2 are, respectively, p_1 and p_2. We wish to test the significance of the difference between p_1 and p_2.

In diagram III the small letters represent the percentages obtained by dividing the frequencies by N and multiplying by 100, that is, $\left(\dfrac{f}{N} \times 100\right)$. The per cents of 'Yes' responses to item 1 and item 2 are, respectively, P_1 and P_2. We wish to test the significance of the difference between P_1 and P_2.

When the data are correlated, the formula for the SE of the difference between two proportions becomes:

$$\text{SE}_{D_p} = s_{p_1 - p_2} = \sqrt{s_{p_1}^2 + s_{p_2}^2 - 2(r_{p_1 p_2})(s_{p_1})(s_{p_2})}$$

where

s_{p_1} is the SE of p_1
s_{p_2} is the SE of p_2
$r_{p_1 p_2}$ is the correlation between p_1 and p_2.

The correlation between the two proportions or per cents is given by the phi coefficient (for details of the phi coefficient, see Chapter 16, Section 16.5), a ratio equivalent to the correlation coefficient in 2×2 tables.

If p_1 and p_2 have been averaged in order to provide an estimate of p, the population parameter, the above formula becomes:

$$s_{p_1-p_2} = \sqrt{2s_p^2\,(1-r_{p_1 p_2})}$$

where

s_p is the SE of the p (averaged or pooled proportion).

Similarly, the formula for the SE of the difference between two correlated percents reads as follows:

$$s_{P_1-P_2} = \sqrt{s_{P_1}^2 + s_{P_2}^2 - 2(r_{P_1 P_2})(s_{P_1})(s_{P_2})}$$

where

s_{P_1} is the SE of P_1

s_{P_2} is the SE of P_2

$r_{P_1 P_2}$ is the correlation between two percentages (P_1 and P_2), which may be computed by the phi coefficient.

Like proportions, if the two percentages, that is, P_1 and P_2, have been averaged in order to provide an estimate of the population parameter, P, the above formula becomes:

$$s_{P_1-P_2} = \sqrt{2s_P^2\,(1-r_{P_1 P_2})}$$

However, McNemar (1962) has developed a technique for testing the significance of the difference between two correlated proportions or percentages that do not necessitate the computation of the correlation coefficient between the two variables. The formula given by McNemar, which does not take into account the correlation between the paired observations, to compute an estimate of the SE of the difference between two correlated proportions or percentages reads as:

$$SE_{D_p} = s_{p_1-p_2} = \sqrt{\frac{a+d}{N}}; \quad SE_{D\%} = s_{p_1-p_2} = \sqrt{\frac{a+d}{N}}$$

(In case of proportions)   (In case of percentages)

When a common population parameter, P, either proportion (p) or percentage (P) has been estimated from p_1 and p_2 (in case of proportions) or from P_1 and P_2 (in case of percentages), the formula, which avoids the calculation of the correlation coefficient, to compute an estimate of the SE of difference between two correlated proportions or percentage is as follows:

$$SE_{D_p} = s_{p_1-p_2} = \sqrt{\frac{b+c}{N}}; \quad SE_{D\%} = s_{p_1-p_2} = \sqrt{\frac{b+c}{N}}$$

(In case of proportions)   (In case of percentages)

In order to test the significance of the difference between two correlated proportions or percentages, we usually apply a 'z' test. A normal deviate 'z' is obtained by dividing the difference between the two correlated proportions or percentages by the SE of the difference. Thus, in case of proportions 'z' is computed by the formula:

$$z = \frac{p_1-p_2}{s_{p_1-p_2}} = \frac{p_1-p_2}{\sqrt{\dfrac{a+d}{N}}} \quad \text{or} \quad \frac{p_1-p_2}{\sqrt{s_{P_1}^2 + s_{P_2}^2 - 2(r_{P_1 P_2})(s_{P_1})(s_{P_2})}}$$

depending upon whether or not we have computed the correlation coefficient between two proportions (i.e., p_1 and p_2).

In case of percentages, 'z' is computed by the formula:

$$z = \frac{P_1 - P_2}{S_{P_1 - P_2}} = \frac{P_1 - P_2}{\sqrt{\dfrac{a+d}{N}}} \quad \text{or} \quad \frac{P_1 - P_2}{\sqrt{s_{P_1}^2 + s_{P_2}^2 - 2(r_{P_1 P_2})(s_{P_1})(s_{P_2})}}$$

depending upon whether or not we have calculated the correlation coefficient between two percentages (i.e., P_1 and P_2).

When the sum of the two cell frequencies, A+D, is reasonably large, this 'z' ratio can be interpreted as a unit-normal-curve deviate, values of 1.96 and 2.58 being required for significance at the 5% and 1% (i.e., 0.05 and 0.01 levels) levels, respectively, for a two-tailed test. In this context, a reasonably large value of A+D may be taken as about 20 or above.

It may be shown that the formula for the value of 'z' given above, for both proportions and percentages, reduces to:

$$z = \frac{D - A}{\sqrt{A+D}} = \sqrt{\frac{(D-A)^2}{A+D}}$$

where

'A' and 'D' are cell frequencies.

For computational purposes, this is the more useful formula.

When a common population parameter, either proportion (p) or percentage (P) is a pooled estimate obtained by pooling the respective proportions (i.e., p_1 and p_2) or respective percentages (i.e., P_1 and P_2), we should apply a 't' test for testing the significance of the difference between two correlated proportions or percentages. The CR of 't' is obtained by dividing the difference between two correlated proportions or percentage by the SE of the difference. Thus, in case of proportions, 't' is computed by the following formula:

$$t = \frac{p_1 - p_2}{S_{p_1 - p_2}} = \frac{p_1 - p_2}{\sqrt{\dfrac{b+c}{N}}} \quad \text{or} \quad \frac{p_1 - p_2}{\sqrt{2s_p^2(1 - r_{p_1 p_2})}}$$

depending upon whether or not we need the correlation coefficient between two proportions (i.e., p_1 and p_2).

In case of pooled percentage (P), 't' is computed by the formula:

$$t = \frac{P_1 - P_2}{S_{P_1 - P_2}} = \frac{P_1 - P_2}{\sqrt{\dfrac{b+c}{N}}} \quad \text{or} \quad \frac{P_1 - P_2}{\sqrt{2s_P^2(1 - r_{P_1 P_2})}}$$

depending upon whether or not the correlation coefficient between two percentages (i.e., P_1 and P_2) is computed.

The entire procedure of testing the significance of the difference between two correlated proportions or percentages, whether pooled or not, using 'z' test or 't' test will be more clear through the following examples.

Example 12.32 The attitudes of 200 adult individuals are measured with an attitude scale item before and after a programme designed to induce attitude change. The following data are obtained. Is the difference between two correlated proportions of individuals agreeing to the item before and after the programme significant?

Frequencies

After

		Disagree	Agree	Total
Before	Agree	10	50	60
	Disagree	110	30	140
	Total	120	80	200

Solution

(a) The data are given in frequencies in a 2×2 table as follows:

Frequencies

After

		Disagree	Agree	
Before	Agree	10 A	50 B	60 (A+B)
	Disagree	110 C	30 D	140 (C+D)
	Total	120 (A+C)	80 (B+D)	200 (N) (A+B+C+D)

Proportions

After

		Disagree	Agree	Total
Before	Agree	0.05 a	0.25 b	0.30 (p_1) (a+b)
	Disagree	0.55 c	0.15 d	0.70 (c+d)
	Total	0.60 (a+c)	0.40 (p_2) (b+d)	1.00 (a+b+c+d)

First of all we have to compute proportions by dividing the frequencies by N (in the given example $N=200$), and prepare a 2×2 proportion table, which is given above right to the frequency table.

(b) The H_0 states that the difference between two correlated proportions is not significant. To find the probability (p) of this H_0 being correct, a two-tailed 'z' test is done. The H_0 and H_1 are stated below:

$$H_0: \quad p_1 = p_2 \quad \text{or} \quad p_1 - p_2 = 0$$
$$H_1: \quad p_1 \neq p_2 \quad \text{or} \quad p_1 - p_2 \neq 0$$

(c) The cell frequencies are assigned A, B, C and D, and the cell proportions are assigned a, b, c and d. The proportion of individuals agreed to the attitude item before the attitude programme was introduced is designated as p_1 and the proportion of individuals agreed after the programme was induced is designated as p_2. Therefore, $p_1 = 0.30$ and $p_2 = 0.40$, as indicated in the proportion table. Thus, $q_1 = 1 - p_1 = 1 - 0.30 = 0.70$ and $q_2 = 1 - p_2 = 1 - 0.40 = 0.60$.

(d) Suppose we want to find out the SE of the difference between two correlated proportions by taking into account the correlation coefficient between the two proportions. In order to do this we have to compute the SE of p_1, SE of p_2 and $r_{p_1 p_2}$.

$$SE_{p_1} = s_{p_1} = \sqrt{\frac{p_1 q_1}{N}} = \sqrt{\frac{0.30 \times 0.70}{200}} = \sqrt{\frac{0.21}{200}} = \sqrt{0.00105} = 0.032$$

$$SE_{p_2} = s_{p_2} = \sqrt{\frac{p_2 q_2}{N}} = \sqrt{\frac{0.40 \times 0.60}{200}} = \sqrt{\frac{0.24}{200}} = \sqrt{0.0012} = 0.035$$

$$r_{p_1 p_2} = \text{Phi}\phi = \frac{AD - BC}{\sqrt{(A+B)(C+D)(A+C)(B+D)}} = \frac{10 \times 30 - 50 \times 110}{\sqrt{60 \times 140 \times 120 \times 80}}$$

$$= \frac{300 - 5500}{\sqrt{80640000}} = \frac{-5200}{8979.978} = -0.58$$

(e) Let us now compute the SE of the difference between two correlated proportions as follows:

$$SE_{D_p} = s_{p_1 - p_2} = \sqrt{s_{p_1}^2 + s_{p_2}^2 - 2(r_{p_1 p_2})(s_{p_1})(s_{p_2})}$$

$$= \sqrt{(0.032)^2 + (0.035)^2 - 2(0.58)(0.032)(0.035)}$$

$$= \sqrt{0.001024 + 0.001225 - 0.0012992}$$

$$= \sqrt{0.002249 - 0.0012992} = \sqrt{0.0009498} = 0.03$$

(f) The 'z' ratio is then computed by dividing the difference between two correlated proportions $(p_1 - p_2)$ by the SE of the difference $(s_{p_1 - p_2})$, as follows:

$$z = \frac{p_1 - p_2}{s_{p_1 - p_2}} = \frac{0.30 - 0.40}{0.03} = \frac{-0.10}{0.03} = -3.33$$

Alternatively, we can compute the SE of the difference between two correlated proportions by the formula given by McNemar, which avoids the computation of SE of each proportion as well as the correlation coefficient between the two proportions. This formula reads as follows:

$$SE_{D_p} = s_{p_1 - p_2} = \sqrt{\frac{a+d}{N}} = \sqrt{\frac{0.05 + 0.15}{200}} = \sqrt{\frac{0.20}{200}} = \sqrt{0.001} = 0.03$$

$$z = \frac{p_1 - p_2}{s_{p_1 - p_2}} = \frac{0.30 - 0.40}{0.03} = \frac{-0.10}{0.03} = -3.33$$

Alternatively, $z = \dfrac{D - A}{\sqrt{A + D}} + \dfrac{30 - 10}{\sqrt{10 + 30}} = \dfrac{20}{\sqrt{40}} = \dfrac{20}{6.32} = 3.16.$

It is worth mentioning here that the value of $(s_{p_1 - p_2})$ obtained from both the formulae applied above is identical, and hence the obtained value of 'z' is the same. Therefore, when the computation of the correlation coefficient between the two proportions is not necessary, it is better and easier to apply McNemar's above formula to find out the SE of the difference between two correlated proportions.

(g) Since 'z' is a unit-normal-curve deviate, the negative sign of 'z' is ignored and it is interpreted as usual. Entering Table A of the appendix, the two-tailed critical value of 'z' at the 0.05 level of significance is 1.96 and at the 0.01 level of significance is 2.58.

Since the obtained 'z' value of 3.33 (or 3.16) is much higher than 2.58, the probability (p) of correctness of the H_0 is less than 0.01 ($p < 0.01$). Thus, H_0 is rejected and H_1 is accepted. Therefore, we may conclude that the difference between two correlated proportions is significant in 99% of cases.

Example 12.33 One hundred children of Grade V were tested on two test items. The following data were obtained regarding their 'pass' and 'fail' on both test items. Is the difference between two correlated percentages of children passing the two items significant?

Frequencies

Item 2

		Fail	Pass	
Item 1	Pass	20	60	80
	Fail	10	10	20
		30	**70**	100

Solution

(a) The data are given in frequencies in a 2×2 table as follows:

Frequencies

Item 2

		Fail	Pass	
Item 1	Pass	20 / A	60 / B	80 (A+B)
	Fail	10 / C	10 / D	20 (C+D)
		30 (A+C)	70 (B+D)	100 (N) (A+B+C+D)

Percentages

Item 2

		Fail	Pass	
Item 1	Pass	20% / a	60% / b	80% (p_1) (a+b)
	Fail	10% / c	10% / d	20% (c+d)
		30% (a+c)	70% (p_2) (b+d)	100% (a+b+c+d)

First, we have to compute the per cents by dividing the frequencies by 'N' and multiplying by 100 $\left(\dfrac{f}{N} \times 100; \text{ in the given example } N = 100 \right)$ and then prepare a 2×2 percentage table as shown above, right to the frequency table.

(b) The H_0 states that the difference between two correlated percentage of children passing the two items is not significant. To find the probability (p) of this H_0 being correct, a two-tailed 'z' test is done. The H_0 and H_1 are stated below:

$$H_0: \quad P_1 = P_2 \quad \text{or} \quad P_1 - P_2 = 0$$
$$H_1: \quad P_1 \neq P_2 \quad \text{or} \quad P_1 - P_2 \neq 0$$

(c) The cell frequencies are assigned A, B, C and D, and the cell percentages are assigned a, b, c and d. The per cent of children passing item 1 is designated as P_1 and passing item 2 as P_2. Therefore, $P_1 = 80\%$ and $P_2 = 70\%$ as indicated in the percentage table. Thus, $Q_1 = 100 - 80\% = 20\%$ and $Q_2 = 100 - 70\% = 30\%$.

(d) Suppose we want to find out the SE of the difference between two correlated percentages by considering the correlation coefficient between the two percentages. In order to do this, we have to compute the SE of P_1, SE of P_2 and $r_{P_1P_2}$.

$$\text{SE}_{P_1} = s_{P_1} = \sqrt{\frac{P_1Q_1}{N}} = \sqrt{\frac{80 \times 20}{100}} = \sqrt{\frac{1600}{100}} = \sqrt{16} = 4.0\%$$

$$\text{SE}_{P_2} = s_{P_2} = \sqrt{\frac{P_2Q_2}{N}} = \sqrt{\frac{70 \times 30}{100}} = \sqrt{\frac{2100}{100}} = \sqrt{21} = 4.58\%$$

$$r_{P_1P_2} = \text{Phi } \phi = \frac{AD - BC}{\sqrt{(A+B)(C+D)(A+C)(B+D)}} = \frac{20 \times 10 - 60 \times 10}{\sqrt{80 \times 20 \times 30 \times 70}}$$

$$= \frac{200 - 600}{\sqrt{3360000}} = \frac{-400}{1833.03} = -0.22$$

(e) Let us now compute the SE of the difference between two correlated percentages as follows:

$$\text{SE}_{D\%} = s_{P_1-P_2} = \sqrt{s_{P_1}^2 + s_{P_2}^2 - 2(r_{P_1P_2})(s_{P_1})(s_{P_2})}$$

$$= \sqrt{(4)^2 + (4.58)^2 - 2(0.22)(4)(4.58)}$$

$$= \sqrt{16.0 + 20.9764 - 8.0608}$$

$$= \sqrt{36.9764 - 8.0608} = \sqrt{28.9156} = 5.38\%$$

(f) The 'z' ratio is then computed by dividing the difference between two correlated percentages $(P_1 - P_2)$ by the SE of the difference $(s_{P_1-P_2})$ as follows:

$$z = \frac{P_1 - P_2}{s_{P_1-P_2}} = \frac{80 - 70}{5.38} = \frac{10}{5.38} = 1.86$$

Alternatively, the SE of the difference between two correlated percentages can be computed by a simpler formula developed by McNemar, if there is no necessity for the correlation coefficient between two percentages. This formula reads

$$\text{SE}_{D\%} = s_{P_1-P_2} = \sqrt{\frac{a+d}{N}} = \sqrt{\frac{0.20 + 0.10}{100}} = \sqrt{\frac{0.30}{100}} = \sqrt{0.003} = 0.0548 = 5.48\%$$

$$z = \frac{P_1 - P_2}{s_{P_1-P_2}} = \frac{80 - 70}{5.48} = \frac{10}{5.48} = 1.82$$

Alternatively, $z = \dfrac{D - A}{\sqrt{A + D}} = \dfrac{10 - 20}{\sqrt{20 + 10}} = \dfrac{-10}{\sqrt{30}} = \dfrac{-10}{5.48} = -1.82$

(g) Entering Table A of the appendix, the two-tailed critical value of 'z' at the 0.05 level of significance is 1.96 and at the 0.01 level of significance is 2.58. Since the obtained 'z' value of 1.86 (or 1.82) is smaller than 1.96, the probability (p) of correctness of the H_0 is greater than 0.05 ($p > 0.05$). Thus, the H_0 is accepted and H_1 is rejected. Therefore, we may conclude that the difference between two correlated percentages of children passing the two items is not significant.

Example 12.34 Given the following responses of 100 individuals to two items on a personality scale, determine whether there is a significant difference in the responses to the two items.

Item 2

		Disagree	Agree
Item 1	Agree	40	20
	Disagree	25	15

Solution

(a) The data are given in frequencies in a 2×2 table as follows:

Frequencies

Item 2

		Disagree	Agree	
Item 1	Agree	40 A	20 B	60 (A+B)
	Disagree	25 C	15 D	40 (C+D)
		65 (A+C)	35 (B+D)	100 (N)

Proportions

Item 2

		Disagree	Agree	
Item 1	Agree	0.40 a	0.20 b	$0.60(p_1)$ (a+b)
	Disagree	0.25 c	0.15 d	0.40 (c+d)
		0.65 (a+c)	$0.35 (p_2)$ (b+d)	1.00

First, we calculate the proportions by dividing the frequencies by N (f/N; in this example $N=100$) and then prepare a 2×2 proportion table as shown above.

(b) The H_0 states that there is no significant difference to the responses to the two items. To find the probability (p) of this H_0 being correct, a two-tailed 't' test is done. The H_0 and H_1 are stated below:

$$H_0: \quad p_1 = p_2 \quad \text{or} \quad p_1 - p_2 = 0$$
$$H_1: \quad p_1 \neq p_2 \quad \text{or} \quad p_1 - p_2 \neq 0$$

(c) The cell frequencies are assigned A, B, C and D, and the cell proportions are assigned a, b, c and d. The proportion of individuals agreed to item 1 is designated as p_1 and agreed to item 2 is p_2. Therefore, $p_1 = 0.60$ and $p_2 = 0.35$. Thus, $q_1 = 1 - p_1 = 1 - 0.60 = 0.40$ and $q_2 = 1 - p_2 = 1 - 0.35 = 0.65$.

(d) Suppose we want to find out the SE of the difference between two correlated proportions by averaging these two proportions and also by taking into consideration the correlation coefficient between the two proportions. For this purpose we have to find out the pooled p, SE of p and $r_{p_1 p_2}$:

$$p = \frac{p_1 + p_2}{2} = \frac{0.60 + 0.35}{2} = \frac{0.95}{2} = 0.475; \quad q = 1 - p = 1 - 0.475 = 0.525$$

$$\text{SE}_p = s_p = \sqrt{\frac{pq}{N}} = \sqrt{\frac{0.475 \times 0.525}{100}} = \sqrt{\frac{0.249375}{100}} = \sqrt{0.00249375} = 0.05$$

$$r_{p_1 p_2} = \text{Phi } \phi = \frac{AD - BC}{\sqrt{(A+B)(C+D)(A+C)(B+D)}} = \frac{40 \times 15 - 20 \times 25}{\sqrt{60 \times 40 \times 65 \times 35}}$$

$$= \frac{600 - 500}{\sqrt{5460000}} = \frac{100}{2336.66} = 0.04$$

(e) The SE of the difference between two correlated proportions is computed by the formula that reads

$$\text{SE}_{D_p} = s_{p_1-p_2} = \sqrt{2s_p^2(1-r_{p_1p_2})}$$
$$= \sqrt{2(0.05)^2(1-0.04)} = \sqrt{2 \times 0.0025 \times 0.96}$$
$$= \sqrt{0.0048} = 0.07$$

(f) The 't' ratio is computed by dividing the difference between two correlated proportions by the SE of the difference ($s_{p_1-p_2}$) as follows:

$$t = \frac{p_1 - p_2}{s_{p_1-p_2}} = \frac{0.60 - 0.35}{0.07} = \frac{0.25}{0.07} = 3.57$$

Alternatively, an estimate of the SE of the difference between two correlated proportions can be computed by the following formula when the correlation coefficient between the proportions is not needed, and 'p' is a pooled estimate by pooling p_1 and p_2. The formula reads as follows:

$$s_{p_1-p_2} = \sqrt{\frac{b+c}{N}} = \sqrt{\frac{0.20+0.25}{100}} = \sqrt{\frac{0.45}{100}} = \sqrt{0.0045} = 0.07$$
$$t = \frac{p_1 - p_2}{s_{p_1-p_2}} = \frac{0.60 - 0.35}{0.07} = \frac{0.25}{0.07} = 3.57$$

which checks the result obtained from the above formula utilising the correlation coefficient.

Just like the 'z' ratio, 't' ratio can also be calculated from the cell frequencies by the formula:

$$t = \frac{D-A}{\sqrt{A+D}} = \frac{15-40}{\sqrt{40+15}} = \frac{-25}{\sqrt{55}} = \frac{-25}{7.42} = -3.37$$

Since the 't' distribution is a perfectly bilaterally symmetrical, the negative signs should be ignored. The 't' values obtained by different methods of computation described earlier in the text are slightly different, which may be attributed to the decimal points involved in the calculation.

$$df = N-1 = 100-1 = 99$$

(g) Entering Table C of the appendix with df=99, the two-tailed critical value of 't' at the 0.05 level of significance is 1.9843 and at the 0.01 level of significance is 2.6266 (by interpolation). As the computed 't' of 3.57 (or 3.37) is much higher than the two-tailed critical value of 't' for the 0.01 level of significance, the probability (p) of correctness of the H_0 is less than 0.01 ($p<0.01$). Hence, the difference between the two correlated proportions is significant beyond the 0.01 level. Thus, the H_0 is rejected and H_1 is accepted. Therefore, we may conclude that there is a significant difference in the responses of the individuals to the two items.

Example 12.35 A large group of politicians ($N=250$) answered as follows the two questions of social relevance. Is the difference between the per cents answering the two questions 'Yes' significant?

Frequencies

Item 1

		No	Yes	
Item 2	Yes	25	100	125
	No	75	50	125
		100	150	250

Solution

(a) The data are given in frequencies in a 2×2 table as follows:

Frequencies

Item 1

		No	Yes	
Item 2	Yes	25 B	100 A	125 (A+B)
	No	75 D	50 C	125 (C+D)
		100 (B+D)	150 (A+C)	250 (N) (A+B+C+D)

Percentages

Item 1

		No	Yes	
Item 2	Yes	10% b	40% a	50%(P_2) (a+b)
	No	30% d	20% c	50% (c+d)
		40% (b+d)	60%(P_1) (a+c)	100% (a+b+c+d)

First, we calculate the percentages by dividing the frequencies by N and then multiplying it by 100 $\left(\dfrac{f}{N} \times 100; \text{ in the present example } N = 250 \right)$, and prepare a 2×2 table of percentages as shown above, right to the frequency table.

(b) The H_0 states that the difference between the per cents answering the two questions 'Yes' is not significant. To find the probability (p) of this H_0 being correct, a two-tailed 't' test is done. The H_0 and H_1 are stated below:

$$H_0: \quad P_1 = P_2 \quad \text{or} \quad P_1 - P_2 = 0$$
$$H_1: \quad P_1 \neq P_2 \quad \text{or} \quad P_1 - P_2 \neq 0$$

(c) The cell frequencies are assigned A, B, C and D, beginning from 'Yes' to both items to 'No' to both items as shown above in the frequency table, and accordingly the cell per cents are assigned a, b, c and d. Moreover, the per cent of politicians answered 'Yes' to item 1 is designated as P_1 and 'Yes' to item 2 is P_2. Therefore, $P_1 = 60\%$ and $P_2 = 50\%$. Thus, $Q_1 = 100\% - P_1 = 100\% - 60\% = 40\%$ and $Q_2 = 100\% - P_2 = 100\% - 50\% = 50\%$.

(d) Suppose we wish to compute SE of the difference between two correlated per cents by averaging these two per cents and also taking the correlation coefficient between these two per cents into consideration. In order to do this, we have to first of all compute the average 'P', SE of 'P' and $r_{P_1 P_2}$.

$$P = \frac{P_1 + P_2}{2} = \frac{60\% + 50\%}{2} = \frac{110\%}{2} = 55\%$$

$$Q = 100\% - P = 100\% - 55\% = 45\%$$

$$SE_\% = s_P = \sqrt{\frac{PQ}{N}} = \sqrt{\frac{55 \times 45}{250}} = \sqrt{\frac{2475}{250}} = \sqrt{9.9} = 3.15\%$$

$$r_{P_1 P_2} = \text{Phi } \phi = \frac{AD - BC}{\sqrt{(A+B)(C+D)(A+C)(B+D)}} = \frac{100 \times 75 - 25 \times 50}{\sqrt{125 \times 125 \times 150 \times 100}}$$

$$= \frac{7500 - 1250}{\sqrt{234375000}} = \frac{6250}{15309.311} = 0.41$$

(e) The SE of the difference between two correlated per cents is computed by the formula as follows:

$$SE_{D\%} = s_{P_1 - P_2} = \sqrt{2s_P^2(1 - r_{P_1 P_2})}$$

$$= \sqrt{2(3.15)^2(1 - 0.41)} = \sqrt{2 \times 9.9225 \times 0.59}$$

$$= \sqrt{11.70855} = 3.42\%$$

(f) The 't' ratio is obtained by dividing the difference between two correlated percents $(P_1 - P_2)$ by the SE of the difference $(s_{P_1 - P_2})$:

$$t = \frac{P_1 - P_2}{s_{P_1 - P_2}} = \frac{60 - 50}{3.42} = \frac{10}{3.42} = 2.92$$

Alternatively, an estimate of the SE of the difference between two correlated per cents can be computed by the following formula, which avoids the computation of the correlation coefficient between two correlated per cents, when 'P' is an average of P_1 and P_2. This formula reads

$$s_{P_1 - P_2} = \sqrt{\frac{b+c}{N}} = \sqrt{\frac{0.10 + 0.20}{250}} = \sqrt{\frac{0.30}{250}} = \sqrt{0.0012} = 0.0346 = 3.46\%$$

$$t = \frac{P_1 - P_2}{s_{P_1 - P_2}} = \frac{60 - 50}{3.46} = \frac{10}{3.46} = 2.89$$

which checks the results obtained from the above two formulae of SE of the difference between two correlated per cents.

$$df = N - 1 = 250 - 1 = 249 = \infty$$

(g) Entering Table C of the appendix with df = 249 (∞), the two-tailed critical value of 't' at the 0.05 level of significance is 1.96 and at the 0.01 level of significance is 2.576 (or 2.58). As the computed 't' of 2.92 (or 2.89) is higher than the two-tailed critical value of 't' for the 0.01 level of significance, the probability (p) of correctness of the H_0 is less than 0.01 ($p < 0.01$). Hence, the difference between the two correlated per cents is significant. Thus, the H_0 is rejected and H_1 is accepted. Therefore, we may conclude that the difference between the per cents of politicians answering the two questions 'Yes' is statistically significant.

Summary

In this chapter, we have discussed the topic of significance of the difference between means and other statistics by using the z-test and t-test. With regard to the significance of difference between two sample means four situations arise: (a) those in which the two means are uncorrelated or independent and samples are large, (b) those in which the two means are uncorrelated or independent and samples are small, (c) those in which the two means are correlated and samples are large and (d) those in which the two means are correlated and samples are small. These four situations are also applicable for testing the significance of difference between two medians, two SDs or variances and two proportions or percentages. However, the first two situations are applicable for testing the significance of difference between two correlation coefficients. The z-test is more applicable to independent or uncorrelated samples of large size, whereas the t-test is applicable to both independent/uncorrelated and correlated samples of large as well as small sizes. It is because in small-sample cases the scores are distributed in the form of a t distribution whereas in large-sample cases there is no difference between the obtained z ratio and t ratio.

A sample having 30 or more cases ($N \geq 30$) is usually treated as a large sample while a sample containing less than 30 cases ($N < 30$) is considered a small sample. Two groups of samples are called independent or uncorrected when they are randomly selected from a totally different or uncorrelated population having equal variances. The means or other statistics obtained from these samples are called independent or uncorrelated measures. On the other hand, the means and other statistics which are obtained from the same test administered to the same group of samples upon two occasions are called correlated measures.

Testing of the significance of the difference between two sample means, two sample medians, two sample standard deviations or variances, two correlation coefficients and two proportions or percentages by using either z-test or t-test requires the computation of the *SE of difference*. The computational equations or formulae for the computation of the *SE of difference* between two sample means or other statistics as noted above, appropriate to the nature of samples, that is, whether samples are large or small, and uncorrelated or correlated, were presented. The procedures for determining the significance of the difference between two sample means and other statistics, as mentioned above, were discussed in detail and several practice problems worked out.

Next, we compared the correlated-groups and independent-groups designs. When the correlation between paired scores is high, the correlated-groups design is more sensitive than the independent-groups design. However, it is easier and more efficient regarding df to conduct an independent-groups experiment. In addition, there are many situations where the correlated-groups design is inappropriate.

Finally, we discussed the robustness and power of the t-test. We pointed out that the t-test is robust with regard to violations of the population normality and homogeneity of variance assumptions. We also pointed that the power of the t-test varies directly with the magnitude of the real effect of the independent variable (i.e., the greater the effect of the independent variable, the higher the power of the t-test), and the N of the sample (i.e., increasing sample size increases the power of the t-test), but varies inversely with the variability of the sample scores (i.e., high sample variability decreases the power of the t-test).

Key Terms

- Alternative hypothesis (H₁)
- Carryover effects
- Control group
- Correlated-groups design
- Correlated means, medians, standard deviations/variances, and proportions/percentages
- Correlated samples
- Correlation of coefficient
- Degrees of freedom of t
- Difference method
- Experimental group
- F distribution
- F ratio
- Groups matched for mean and SD
- Homogeneity of variances
- Independent-groups design
- Independent samples
- Individual difference
- Matched-groups design
- Matched-subjects design
- Method of equivalent groups: Matching by pairs
- Null hypothesis (H₀)
- One-tailed test
- Paired observations

- Pooled variance
- Power of the t-test
- Progressive error
- Related-samples design
- Related-samples t-test
- Repeated measures design
- Robustness of the t-test
- Sample variability
- Samples of equal sizes
- Samples of unequal sizes
- Sampling distribution of differences
- Sampling error
- Sampling error of the means
- Significance of the differences
- Single group method
- Standard error of difference
- t-test
- t-test for correlated groups
- t-test for independent groups
- two-tailed test
- uncorrelated means, medians, standard deviations/variances and proportions/percentages
- unpaired observations
- z-test

Questions and Problems

1. What do you mean by sampling distribution? Discuss about the sampling distribution of differences between two statistics.

2. (a) What is a z-test? Discuss the assumptions for using z-test.

   (b) What is a t-test? Elucidate the assumptions underlying t-test.

3. Write notes on the following:

   (a) t-distribution

   (b) Degrees of freedom (df)

   (c) Concept of standard error of difference

   (d) One-tailed and two-tailed tests

(e)Type I and Type II errors
   (f) Null hypothesis
   (g) Levels of significance

4. Two groups of premedical students belonging to two different colleges were admin-istered a standardised medical aptitude test. The data collected are given below:

	Group A	Group B
Mean	32	36
SD	6.2	7.4
N	145	82

Is there a significant difference between the two means?

5. The students of two classes were taught differently. Class A was taught in an inten-sive coaching facility whereas Class B in a normal class teaching. At the end of the school year, the following data were collected from them. Test whether intensive coaching has facilitated the performance of Class A students.

	Group A	Group B
N	60	80
M	48	45
σ	6.0	7.4

6. The following data were collected from two independent groups of 144 men and 175 women, on an attitude scale. Test the significance of the difference between the two group means at the 0.05 level of significance, and interpret your result.

	Mean	SD
Men	19.7	6.08
Women	21.0	4.89

7. In a psychological study of two large samples, the following data were collected:

Difference between two means = 4.20
Standard error of the difference between means = 2.80

   (a) Is the obtained difference between two means significant at the 0.05 level of significance?
   (b) What difference is necessary for being significant at the 0.01 level of significance?

8. The following are data for two samples of students under two experimental conditions:

Sample A: 2   5   7   9   6   7
Sample B: 4   16   11   9   8

Test the significance of the difference between means.

9. The following data are obtained from two independent samples:

	Sample A	Sample B
$\bar{X}$	124	120
N	50	36
$\Sigma(X - \bar{X})^2$	5.512	5.184

Test whether the mean for Sample A is equal to or greater than that for Sample B.

10. The body weights (kg) of eight adult males and eight adult females are given below. Find whether or not the mean weight of males is significantly higher than that of females.

Males: 50   58   60   55   59   56   54   64
Females: 49   52   51   56   55   53   52   48

11. Given $\bar{X}_1 = 12.8, \bar{X}_2 = 16.9, N_1 = 11, N_2 = 9, \Sigma x_1^2 = 61, \Sigma x_2^2 = 51$ and assuming that these data are uncorrelated, compute t and interpret the results.

12. The following data are obtained from two independent large samples.

	Sample I	Sample II
N	101	101
$\bar{X}$	58.6	56.0
s	8.3	6.2

Test whether the difference between two sample means is statistically significant.

13. A group of students was given a test in addition. Then a state of 'anxiety' was induced and the arithmetic test was readministered. The results are given below:

Pre-test	Post-test
$\bar{X} = 70$	$\bar{X} = 67$
$s = 6.0$	$s = 5.8$
$N = 30$	$N = 30$

r between pre-and post-test scores $= 0.82$
Test whether the post-test mean is significantly lower than the pre-test mean.

14. The following are paired measurements obtained for a sample of eight subjects under two conditions:

Condition A: 8   17   12   19   5   6   20   3
Condition B: 12   31   17   17   8   14   25   4

Test the significance of the difference between means using a non-directional test.

15. For a sample of 26 pairs of measurements, $\Sigma D = 52$ and $\Sigma D^2 = 400$. Compute t and interpret it.

16. Ten subjects are given five successive trials upon a digit—symbol test of which only the scores of Trials 1 and 5 are given. Is the mean gain from initial to final trial significant?

Trial 1:   8   15   12   7   13   9   11   10   14   11
Trial 5:   14   16   10   11   17   13   12   19   10   16

17. In an investigation a researcher wanted to test the effect of a particular drug in reducing anxiety. For this purpose, he used two groups of subjects—experimental and control—matched in pairs. The anxiety scores of the subjects of both the groups are given below. Test the null hypothesis at the 0.05 level of significance.

Experimental group: 115   114   114   110   108   107   105   100   97   95
Control group: 120   117   112   118   102   95   107   106   93   99

18. Two groups of high-school students were matched for mean and SD on a group intelligence test. Then, they were administered a battery of learning tests, and the data collected are given below. Test the significance of the difference between the two group means.

	Group A	Group B
M	48.52	54.61
σ	11.60	15.35
N	58	72

r between intelligence test and learning battery = 0.50

19. The following data are collected from two independent groups on an attitude test.

	Group I	Group II
Median	7	8
SD	1.8	2.2
N	10	10

Test whether the difference between two group medians is statistically significant.

20. In a study of abstract reasoning, a sample of 83 Grade X boys has SD of 11.56 and a sample of 95 Grade X girls has SD of 7.81. Test whether the difference between two SDs is statistically significant.

21. A psychological test was administered to a sample of 31 boys and 26 girls. The sum of squares of deviations (Σx^2) is 1926 for boys and 2875 for girls. Are boys significantly different from girls in the variability of their performance on this test?

22. A group of 38 subjects was administered an attitude scale before and after the administration of an educational programme. The unbiased variance estimates of their attitude-scale scores before and after the administration of an educational programme were 153.20 and 102.51, respectively. The correlation between the before and after attitude measures is 0.60. Are the two variances significantly different from each other?

23. Given two correlated samples of size 20 with $s_1^2 = 400, s_2^2 = 625$ and $r_{12} = .7071$, test the hypothesis that the variances are significantly different from each other.

24. The correlation between psychological test scores and academic achievement for a sample of 147 freshmen is 0.40. The corresponding correlation for a sample of 125 sophomores is 0.59. Do the correlations differ significantly?

25. We find r's of –0.60 and –0.51, N being 85 in both sets of data. Use the formula for uncorrelated r's and test the hypothesis of no significant difference between these two r's.

26. Given two random samples of size 100 each with sample values $p_1 = 0.80$ and $p_2 = 0.60$, test the significance of the difference between p_1 and p_2.

27. In a market survey 24 out of 96 males and 63 out of 180 females indicate a preference for particular brand of cold drinks. Do the data warrant the conclusion that a sex difference exists in brand preference?

28. The following data are obtained from two independent samples:

$$p_1 = 0.90 \quad p_2 = 0.80$$
$$N_1 = 40 \quad N_2 = 30$$

Test the null hypothesis that the population proportions are equal (H_0: $p_1 = p_2$).

29. Consider two test items A and B. In a sample of 100 people, 30 pass item A and fail item B, whereas 20 fail item A and pass item B. Are the proportions passing the two items significantly different from each other?

30. On an attitude scale, 63 and 39 individuals from a sample of 140 indicate agreement to items A and B, respectively, and 29 individuals indicate agreement to both items. Is there a significant difference in the response elicited by the two items?

31. Given the following data for an item in Stanford-Binet: of 100 nine-year-olds, 72% pass; of 100 ten-year-olds, 78% pass. Is the item more difficult for nine-year-olds than for ten-year-olds?

32. Fill in the blanks:

   (i) The standard deviation of the sampling distribution of difference between two means is called the _____ between means.

   (ii) The variance of the sampling distribution of differences between means is the _____ of the two variances.

   (iii) The observed difference between the two sample means is generally transformed into a standard score, either _____ or _____, using the standard error of that difference.

(iv)   The significance of the difference between means of two large independent groups of samples is usually tested by using _____ test.

(v)   The symbol $p \leq \alpha$ indicates the _____ of H_0.

(vi)   For using z-test, the dependent variable should be a _____ measurement variable.

(vii)   One of the assumptions for using z-test is that each score occurs in the sample at _____ and _____ of all other scores.

(viii)   The H_0 states that the two population means are _____.

(ix) t-test is a _____ statistical test.

(x)   For using t-test, the observations must be _____.

33.   Write whether the following statements are True or False.

(i) t-test is used for testing the significance of the difference between two sample means.

(ii)   In a one-tailed test, the z-value at $\alpha = 0.01$ is 2.33.

(iii)   All directional tests are called two-tailed tests.

(iv)   The statement $\mu_1 \neq \mu_2$ is given by the H_0.

(v)   The unit normal curve closely approximates with the t-distribution for high df.

(vi) t-test cannot be applied if the populations from which the two samples have been drawn differ in their variances.

(vii)   The condition $\sigma_1^2 = \sigma_2^2 = \sigma^2$ is usually spoken of as homogeneity of variances.

(viii)   If two variances are unequal, their ratio will be unity.

(ix)   When the population correlation coefficient is zero, the sampling distribution of the correlation coefficient is asymmetrical.

(x)   The standard error of a single uncorrelated proportion is computed by the formula that reads $s_p = \sqrt{\dfrac{pq}{N}}$.

34.   Find out the correct answer from among the four alternatives.

(i) t-test is a test of significance of the difference between:

(a)   Two sample means
(b)   Three sample means
(c)   More than three sample means
(d)   None of the above

(ii)   The null hypothesis for a two-tailed test states that:

(a) $H_0: \mu_1 \neq \mu_2$ (b) $H_0: \mu_1 = \mu_2$
(c) $H_0: \mu_1 > \mu_2$ (d)   None of the above

(iii)   For using z-test for testing the significance of difference between two independent sample means, the sample size should be:

(a)   Large enough   (b)   Small
(c)   Either large or small   (d)   None of the above

(iv)   Which one of the following expresses the statement of the alternative hypothesis?

(a) $\bar{X}_1 = \bar{X}_2$ (b) $\bar{X}_1 - \bar{X}_2 = 0$

(c) $\bar{X}_1 \neq \bar{X}_2$ (d)   None of the above

(v)   The standard error of the difference between two independent sample means is computed by

(a) $s_{\bar{X}_1 - \bar{X}_2} = \sqrt{(s_{\bar{X}_1})^2 + (s_{\bar{X}_2})^2}$ (b) $s_{\bar{X}_1 - \bar{X}_2} = s_{\bar{X}_1}^2 + s_{\bar{X}_2}^2$

(c) $s_{\bar{X}_1 - \bar{X}_2} = \sqrt{s_{\bar{X}_1} + s_{\bar{X}_2}}$ (d)   None of the above

(vi)   The t-test is usually known as the

(a)   Non-student's t-test   (b)   Student's t-test

(c)   People's t-test   (d)   None of the above

(vii) For using t-test, it is assumed that the populations from which the samples are selected must have:

(a)   Homogeneity of variances   (b)   Heterogeneity of variances

(c)   Unequal variances   (d)   None of the above

(viii) If in a given data $\bar{X}_1 = 30, \bar{X}_2 = 24, s_{\bar{X}_1 - \bar{X}_2} = 2.0,$ then the t ratio is

(a)   2.0   (b)   2.5

(c)   3.0   (d)   None of the above

(ix)   For an uncorrelated t-test, the df will be:

(a) $N_1 + N_2 - 2$ (b) $N_1 + N_2 - 1$

(c) $N - 1$ (d)   None of the above

(x)   For the correlated t-test, the df will be determined as:

(a) $N - 2$ (b) $N - 1$

(c) $N + 1$ (d)   None of the above

Experimental Design: An Introduction

After completing this chapter you will be able to:

- Understand the meaning and the importance of the experimental design.
- Describe the various types of variances, and how the experimental design controls them.
- Explain the meaning and types of experimental validity and factors that jeopardise validity.
- Differentiate among the experimental design, quasi-experimental design and the single-case experimental design.
- Conduct experiments involving between-subjects design, within-subjects design, or a mixed design.
- Understand factorial experimental designs.
- Plan and conduct experiments involving either single-factor or multi-factor experimental designs.
- Analyse the data obtained using statistical methods appropriate to the experimental designs.

13.1   Introduction

Some subsequent chapters of this book are concerned with the analysis of variance (ANOVA) and covariance. These procedures are used in the analysis of the data of experiments. A very brief, and elementary, discussion of the experimental design should serve as a useful preliminary to a detailed study of these methods of analysis.

The term experimental design has been used differently by several researchers. However, a look at the available literature on the subject reveals that the term experimental design has been used to convey mainly two different, though *interrelated*, meanings. In the first place, the term is used in general sense to include a wide range of basic activities for carrying out experiments, that is, everything from the statement of the problem to drawing of conclusions. The second definition of the term is comparatively restricted. It contains activities like procedure for the selection of independent variables or factors and their levels for manipulation, identification of extraneous variables that need to be controlled, and procedure for handling experimental units, selection of criterion measure, selection of specific design and analysis of data.

In this book, we shall be dealing with the designs that confirm primarily to the second definition of the term, although other aspects of designing, contained in the first definition of the term, cannot be ignored entirely, because we know that research is an integrated activity, where one step out of a sequence of steps cannot be effectively isolated from the rest. Thus, the knowledge of the basic principles of experimental design covered by both the definitions is a prerequisite for achieving the objectives of research.

13.2   What Is Experimental Design?

The study of the structure and planning of experiments is a field of investigation commonly called the design of experiments. Winer (1971) has compared the design of an experiment to an architect's plan for the structure of a building. The designer of experiments performs a role similar to that of the architect. The prospective owner of a building gives his basic requirements to the architect, who then exercising his ingenuity, prepares a plan or a blue-print outlining the final shape of the structure. Similarly, the designer of the experiment has to do the planning of the experiment so that the experiment on completion fulfils the objectives of research. According to Myers (1980), the design is the general structure of the experiment, and not its specific content. According to Lindquist (1956), 'Research design is the plan, structure and strategy of investigation conceived so as to obtain answer to research question and to control variance'.

Thus, experimental design is the scientific planning of an experiment for exploring the effect of one or more independent variables or factors on a single dependent variable, minimising the experimental errors from uncontrolled random variations, and making the inference more reliable and reasonably unambiguous.

The experimental design has many aspects—some are simple and some are quite complex. All experiments are concerned with the relations between variables. In the simplest types of experiments, only two variables are involved—an independent variable and a dependent variable. For example, an experiment may be conducted to compare three different methods of teaching mathematics, designated A, B and C. Each method may be applied to a different group of experimental subjects. Following a period of differential instructions, performance of each group may be measured using an achievement test. In this simple experiment, the different methods of teaching mathematics constitute the levels or categories of the independent variable (i.e., method of teaching). The investigator decides which methods will be used and the size of the group to which they will be applied, that is, he/she controls the values or categories of the independent variable and the frequency of occurrence of those values or categories. The measures of achievement constitute the dependent variable. The essence of the idea of an experiment lies in the simple fact that the investigator selects the values or categories of the treatment variable and the frequency of their occurrence. It is clearly desirable, therefore, that some of the *principles* underlying such experimentation should be understood.

From the above discussions, it follows that in developing the design of an experiment the investigator must: (1) select the values or categories of the independent variable, or variables, to be compared; (2) select the subjects for the experiment; (3) apply rules or procedures whereby subjects are assigned to the particular values or categories of the independent variable; and (4) specify the observations or measurements to be made on each subject.

13.3 Basic Terminology in Experimental Design

The experimental designs have some important terminologies which have been discussed below. It is essential for the investigators to get acquainted with the terminology for clear understanding of the designs of the experiments and the corresponding analysis of data.

13.3.1 Factor

An independent variable used in an experiment may be either a treatment (or experimental) variable or a classification variable. A treatment or experimental variable is the one which is manipulated in the experimental design by the experimenter. For example, the experimenter manipulates the intensity of illumination to study its effect on visual acuity. Here, illumination is a treatment or an experimental variable. Similarly, different dosage of a drug or different methods of learning are administered to different groups of subjects. In effect, the subjects are treated in some way by the experimenter.

Experimental subjects may, however, be classified on a characteristic which was present prior to, and quite apart from, the experiment and does not result from the manipulations of the experimenter. Such a variable is a classification variable or subject-related variable. The subject-related variables cannot be directly manipulated by the experimenter but can be manipulated through selection. For example, if the experimenter is interested in studying the effect of age on the reaction time of the subjects, then he/she may manipulate the age by selecting subjects of different age levels. When an independent variable is manipulated through selection of subjects, it is generally referred to as a classification variable. Examples of such variables are sex, age, race, disease entity, IQ level, socioeconomic status, home environment, genetic error, atmospheric humidity and so on. Variables of this category allow the researcher to assess the extent of differences between the subjects.

Any independent variable, whether of the treatment or classification type, is spoken of as a factor. Thus, there are two types of factors depending upon the nature of independent variable; one is the treatment factor and the other is the classification factor.

The independent variable or factor that is directly manipulated in the experimental design by the experimenter is also known as the E-type of factor, and one that is manipulated through the selection of subjects is known as the S-type of factor. The S types of factors are generally included in the experiment to classify the subjects for the purpose of control. At times, the experimenter may be interested in evaluating the effect of the S-type of factors. For example, the experimenter may classify subjects into low, medium and high socioeconomic groups to assess the extent of differences in a particular dependent measure among the subjects of the three groups. However, most of the times the classification factor (i.e., S-type of factor) is built into the design, not because of intrinsic interest in the effects but because the results are likely to be difficult to interpret if these factors are not included. These factors are defined by their function in the design and may be either classification or treatment factors.

The factors are denoted by the capital letters A, B, C, D and so on. For example, an experiment is designed to study simultaneously the effects of strain and rearing environment on the maze performance of rats. In this experiment, there are two independent variables or factors; factor *A* refers to the strain and factor *B* refers to the rearing environment.

13.3.2 Levels

Each specific variation in a factor is called the level of that factor. In other words, the different values or categories of the independent variable are spoken of as levels; thus we may have two, three or more levels of a factor. For example, the factor drug dosage may consist of three levels, such as 0, 5 and 10 mg. The experimenter may decide to choose the number of levels of a factor.

The levels of a factor are designated by the corresponding lower case (small) letters of the factor symbol with a subscript. For example, the levels of factor A are designated by the symbols $a_1, a_2, a_3, \ldots, a_p$. Similarly, the levels of Factor B are designated by the symbols $b_1, b_2, b_3, \ldots, b_q$.

13.3.3   Dimensions

The dimensions of a factorial experiment are indicated by both the number of levels of each factor and the number of factors. For example, a three-factor (A, B, C) experiment, in which the first factor (A) has p levels, second (B) has q levels and third (C) has r levels, will be designated as the $p \times q \times r$ factorial experiment. This is the general form and the dimensions in the specific case may assume any value for p, q and r. A factorial experiment, for example, in which there are three factors, first having two levels, second having three levels and third having four levels, is called $2 \times 3 \times 4$ (read as two by three by four) factorial experiment. The dimension of this experiment is $2 \times 3 \times 4$.

13.3.4   Treatment Combinations

In an experiment, the term treatment refers to a particular set of experimental conditions. Though the term treatment and treatment combinations are often used interchangeably, there is some difference between these two. For example, in a single-factor experiment, the levels of the factor constitute the treatments, whereas in a two or more factorial experiment, the product of the levels of all the factors constitutes the treatment combinations. Suppose, in a single-factor experiment the investigator is interested in studying the effect of levels of illumination on visual acuity, and the experimenter decides to have three levels of illumination like 10 ml, 20 ml and 30 ml. Thus, there will be three treatments or treatment conditions. Let us take another example to present a case of treatment combinations. In a two-factorial experiment ($A \times B$), factor A having two levels and factor B having four levels, there will be a total of 2×4 or 8 treatment combinations.

13.3.5   Replication

The term replication refers to an independent repetition of the experiment under as nearly identical conditions as possible. The experimental subjects in the repetitions are independent samples randomly drawn from the population being studied. It may be pointed out that an experiment with 'n' observations per cell is to be distinguished from an experiment having 'n' replications with one observation per cell. Thus, the total number of observations per treatment in the two experiments (i.e., unreplicated and replicated, respectively) is the same, but the manner in which the two experiments are conducted differs. For example, a 2×2 factorial experiment having 4 treatment combinations with 10 observations per treatment is different from an experiment having 10 replications with one observation per treatment. The total number of observations per treatment is the same, that is, 10 in both the experiments. The only purpose of a replicated experiment is to maintain more uniform conditions within each cell (or each treatment combination) of the experiment to eliminate possible extraneous source of variation between cells or treatment combinations. It is quite important that the number of observations per cell for any single replication should be the maximum so as to ensure uniform conditions within all cells of the experiment. However, the partitioning of total variance and degrees of freedom (df) in the replicated and unreplicated experiments will differ.

13.3.6   Main Effects

The difference in performance from one level to another for a particular factor, averaged over other factors, is called main effect of that factor. In a factorial experiment, the mean squares for the levels of factors are called the main effects of the factors. Let us consider an example of a $2 \times 2 \times 3$ (or $A \times B \times C$) factorial experiment in which factor A has two levels, factor B has two levels and factor C has three levels. The A sum of squares corresponds to a comparison between levels a_1 and a_2, the B sum of squares to a comparison between levels b_1 and b_2, and the C sum of squares to a comparison between levels c_1, c_2 and c_3. The difference in performance between levels a_1 and a_2, averaged over levels of factors B and C, is called the main effect of factor A. Similarly, the difference in performance between levels b_1 and b_2, averaged over levels of factors A and C, is called the main effect of factor B. In a similar vein, the difference in performance among levels c_1, c_2 and c_3, averaged over levels of factors A and B, is called the main effect of factor C.

The main effect of a factor can be represented graphically. In the graph, it is the curve joining the points representing the mean performance on the levels of a particular factor averaged over the other factors in the experiment. A significant main effect will have significant slope or, in other words, the curve will not be parallel to the X-axis.

13.3.7   Simple Effects

In a factorial experiment, the effect of a treatment on one factor at a given level of the other factor is called the simple effect. Let us consider an example of a 2×2 factorial experiment in which factors A and B have two levels each. The effect of treatment on two levels of A under each of the two levels of B is called simple effect of A. Similarly, the effect of treatment on two levels of B under each of the two levels of A is called the simple effect of B.

Graphically, the simple effects are represented in the same manner as the two-factor interaction. For example, the simple effect of A, graphically, is the AB interaction profile where the levels of factor A are marked on the X axis, and the two curves represented by the levels b_1 and b_2 are the simple effects at each of the two levels. Similarly, the simple effect of B is the AB interaction profile where the levels of factor B are marked on the X axis, and the two curves represented by a_1 and a_2 are the simple effects at each level.

13.3.8   Interaction Effect

The factorial experiments are important because they allow the investigator to study simultaneously the effects of more than one factor. Apart from the advantage of efficiency of factorial experiments over the single-factor experiment, it at the same time permits the investigator to evaluate the interaction between two or more factors that are studied. Interaction is an important concept in research. It can be evaluated in all experiments having two or more factors.

Let us discuss about a simple interaction effect between two independent variables or factors. Interaction between two factors is said to occur when change in the values of one factor alters the effects on the other. However, it may be noted that the presence of interaction destroys the additivity of the main effects. That is, what is added by one factor at the first level of the other is different from what is added at another level. The absence of interaction, on the other hand, means that the additive property applies to the main effects, that is, they are independent.

Let us explain the concept of interaction with the help of an example. Suppose investigator wants to study the simultaneous effects of two factors: factor A (method of learning) having two levels a_1 (massed method) and a_2 (distributed method), and factor B (intelligence) having two levels b_1 (high intelligence) and b_2 (low intelligence) on the achievement scores of the 8th grade students. It is, thus, a 2×2 factorial experiment having 10 students per cell. The mean scores of the four groups are given below in a 2×2 contingency table.

		A (Method of Learning)	
		a_1 (Massed)	a_2 (Distributed)
B (Intelligence)	b_1 (High)	70.1	90.8
	b_2 (Low)	50.0	60.5

Difference for the high intelligence level $(b_1) = 90.8 - 70.1 = 20.7$,
Difference for the low intelligence level $(b_2) = 60.5 - 50.0 = 10.5$,
Interaction $= 20.7 - 10.5 = 10.2$.

Alternatively,

Difference for the distributed method $(a_2) = 90.8 - 60.5 = 30.3$,
Difference for the massed method $(a_1) = 70.1 - 50.0 = 20.1$,
Interaction $= 30.3 - 20.1 = 10.2$.

In other words, the interaction is measured by the difference between the two differences. It can be observed from the above table that the increase in the mean scores of the high intelligence group under distributed practice is much more than the corresponding increase in the mean scores of the low intelligence group. That is, what is added by the factor of intelligence at the massed practice level is different from that what is added at the distributed practice level. Clearly, the two factors A and B have a combined effect, which is different from the effects when the two factors are applied separately.

Thus, the interaction is indicated by the failure of the differences to be equal. If the differences are equal, it means, there is no interaction. Therefore, we may say that the interaction effect between two factors may be significant, may not be significant or may be zero. If the $A \times B$ interaction effect is significant, it means that the A effect is not the same for the different levels of B, that is, the difference between the means of a_1 and a_2 for the first level of B (i.e., b_1) is significantly different from the difference between the means of a_1 and a_2 for the second level of B (i.e., b_2). It may be noted that in the presence of significant interaction effect, the main effect should be interpreted with caution.

A non-significant $A \times B$ interaction indicates that the difference between the means of a_1 and a_2 for b_1 is not significantly different from the difference between the means of a_1 and a_2 for b_2. In other words, with a non-significant $A \times B$ interaction, we can say that the A effect (the difference between a_1 and a_2) is independent of B, that is, we have approximately the same difference between a_1 and a_2, regardless of the levels of B.

If the $A \times B$ interaction is exactly equal to zero, then the difference between the means of a_1 and a_2 for b_1 would be exactly equal to the difference between the means of a_1 and a_2 for b_2. A zero interaction means that the A effect is quite independent of B.

Another way of examining the nature of an interaction is to represent it graphically. For example, in a two factorial experiment, we take one of the factors, say factor B, for the X-axis and graph the means (or sums) for each level of A. Thus, there would be two lines in the figure, one for a_1 and the other for a_2. If the lines for a_1 and a_2 were exactly parallel, then the $A \times B$ interaction would be zero. If the lines are nearly parallel, within the limits of a random variation, then the $A \times B$ interaction is something other than zero but not significant. In other words, in a non-significant interaction between A and B, the two lines corresponding to a_1 and a_2 are not parallel but within the limits of random variation. The fact that the lines of a_1 and a_2 are not parallel, and are not within the limits of random variation, corresponds to the fact that the $A \times B$ interaction is significant.

13.4   Experimental Design as Variance Control

Variance is the very foundation of experimentation and is an extremely useful concept. Let us, therefore, try to understand its meaning and uses before handling simple ANOVA. Variance is a measure of the dispersion or spread of a set of scores. It describes the extent to which the scores differ from each other. The square root of the variance is called the standard deviation. However, because of its mathematical properties, the variance is more useful than the standard deviation in research. Variance and variation, though, used synonymously are not identical terms. Variance is only one of the several statistical methods of representing variation. Variation is, thus, a more general term which includes variance as one of the methods of representing variation.

Variance control is the central theme of the experimental design. The problem of variance control has three aspects that deserve our full attention. The three aspects of variance are (a) systematic variance, (b) extraneous variance and (c) error variance. The major function of the experimental design is to maximise the effect of systematic variance, control extraneous variance and minimise error variance. These three types of variances are discussed below.

13.4.1   Systematic Variance

Systematic variance is the variability in the dependent measure due to the manipulation of the experimental variable in the experiment by the experimenter. An important task of the experimenter is to maximise this variance. This objective is achieved by making the levels of the experimental variable/s (or factor/s) as unlike or different as possible. Let us suppose, an experimenter is interested in studying the effect of doses of insulin on the blood sugar level. The experimenter decides to study the effect by manipulating three levels of insulin, that is, 0, 5 and 10 mg. As the difference between any two levels of the experimental variable is not substantial, there is little chance of separating its effect from the total variance. Thus, in order to maximise systematic variance, it is desirable to make the experimental conditions (or levels) as different as possible. In this experiment regarding the effect of doses of insulin on the blood sugar level, it would be appropriate, then, to modify the levels of doses of insulin to 0, 10 and 20 mg, so that the difference between any two levels is substantial.

13.4.2   Extraneous Variance

Extraneous variables are those uncontrolled variables (i.e., variables not manipulated by the experimenter) that may have a significant influence upon the results of a study. Many research conclusions are questionable because of the influence of these extraneous variables. In addition to the independent variable/s and dependent variable, which are main concerns in any experiment, extraneous variables are encountered in all experimental situations that can influence the dependent variable. Thus, the extraneous source of variance is contributed by all the variables other than the independent variable/s whose effect is being studied in the experiment. These variables have often been called extraneous variables, irrelevant variables, secondary variables, nuisance variables and so on.

In order to have research conclusions to be reliable and valid, the influence of the extraneous variable/s on the dependent variable under study should be controlled. There are five basic procedures for controlling the extraneous source of variance. These procedures are cited below:

(i)   Randomisation
(ii) Elimination
(iii) Matching
(iv) Additional independent variable
(v)   Statistical control

These above five procedures are discussed in detail below.

13.4.2.1   *Randomisation*

According to Cochran and Cox (1957), 'Randomization is somewhat analogous to insurance in that it is a precaution against disturbances that may or may not occur and that may or may not be serious, if they do occur'. Thus, randomisation is an important method of controlling extraneous variable/s. It is considered to be the most effective way to control the variability due to all possible extraneous sources. If thorough randomisation has been achieved, then the treatment groups in the experiment could be considered statistically equal in all possible ways. Therefore, randomisation is a powerful method of controlling extraneous or irrelevant variables. In other words, randomisation is a procedure for equating groups with respect to the extraneous variables.

Randomisation in the experiment could mean random selection of the experimental units or subjects from the larger population of interest to the experimenter and/or random assignment of the experimental units or subjects to the treatment conditions. Random selection means that each experimental unit/subject has an equal chance of being selected and each choice is independent of any other choice. Random assignment, on the other hand, means that every experimental units/subject has an equal chance of being placed in any one of the treatment conditions or groups. Thus, random selection and random assignment are different procedures. If subjects are not assigned randomly, then confounding may occur. The term 'confounding' is used to describe an operation of variables in an experiment that confuses the interpretation of data. If an independent variable is confounded with an extraneous variable (or a secondary variable), the experimenter cannot separate the effects of the two variables on the dependent measure.

An experimental design that employs randomisation as a method of controlling extraneous variable/s is called randomised group design. For example, in the randomised group design, the extraneous source of variance due to individual differences is controlled by assigning subjects randomly to, say, k treatment conditions in the experiment. According to McCall (1923), 'Just as representativeness can be secured by the method of chance, so equivalence may be secured by chance, provided the number of subjects to be used is sufficiently numerous'. This refers to achieving comparable groups through the principle of chance. It may, however, be noted that randomisation is employed even when subjects are matched. In repeated measures design (within-subjects design), where each subject undergoes all the k treatment conditions, the order in which treatments are administered to the subjects is randomised independently for each subject.

Fisher's most fundamental contribution has been the concept of achieving pre-experimental equation of groups through randomisation. Equating the effects through random assignment of subjects to groups in the experiment is considered to be the overall best tool for controlling various sources of extraneous variation at the same time. Perhaps, the most important discriminating feature of the experimental design, as compared to the quasi-experimental design, is the principle of randomisation.

Randomisation provides the most effective method of eliminating systematic bias and of minimising the effect of extraneous variable/s. The principle is based upon the assumption that through random assignment, differences between groups result only from the operation of probability or chance. These differences are known as *sampling error* or *error variance*.

In an experiment, differences in the dependent variables that may be attributed to the effect of the independent variables are known as *experimental variance*. The significance of an experiment may be tested by comparing experimental variance with error variance. If at the conclusion of the experiment, the differences between the experimental and control groups are too great to attribute to error variance, it may be assumed that these differences are attributable to the experimental variance.

13.4.2.2   *Elimination*

Another procedure for controlling the unwanted extraneous variance is elimination or removal of the variable completely by so choosing the subjects that they become homogeneous, as far as possible, on the variable to be controlled. Suppose, the sex of the subjects, considered as an extraneous variable, is found to influence the dependent measure in an experiment. Therefore, the sex variable (secondary source of variance) has to be controlled. The experimenter may decide to take either all males or all females as the subjects in the experiment, and thus, control through elimination the variability due to sex variable. Let us take another example of controlling extraneous variance by eliminating or removing the variable. Suppose, intelligence of the subjects in the group is found to influence the achievement test scores of the subjects. The experimenter thinks intelligence as an extraneous variable and hence wants to control its potential effect on the dependent variable. This potential effect of intelligence (secondary source of variance) can be controlled by selecting subjects of nearly uniform intelligence. Thus, we can control the extraneous variable by eliminating the variable itself from the experimental design. However, with this procedure we loose the power of generalisation of results. If we select subjects from a restricted range, then we can discuss the outcome of the experiment within this restricted range and not outside it. For example, using only female subjects removes sex as a variable but thereby reduces the generalisation from the study to only females. Elimination procedure for controlling the extraneous source of variance is primarily a non-experimental design control procedure. Elimination as a procedure has the effect as accentuating the between-group-variance through decrease in the within-group-variance (or error variance).

13.4.2.3   *Matching*

Another procedure for controlling the extraneous source of variance is matching. It is also a non-experimental design procedure. In this procedure, the investigator matches the subjects on that extraneous variable which is substantially related to the dependent variable. That is, if the investigator finds that the variable of intelligence is highly correlated with the dependent variable, it is better to control the variance through matching the subjects on the variable of intelligence. Suppose, an investigator is interested in studying the efficacy of the method of instruction on the academic achievement scores of the 8th grade children. The methods to be evaluated are two in number, such as, the lecture method and discussion method. Here, the method of instruction is the independent variable/experimental variable of interest to the investigator. But the investigator finds that the academic achievement scores (the dependent variable) are positively correlated with the intelligence of the subjects, that is, subjects with high intelligence tend to score high on the achievement test, and those who are low in intelligence score low on the achievement test. Thus, the variable of intelligence (not of direct interest to the investigator) needs to be controlled because it is a source of variance that influences the academic achievement scores. In this experiment, the extraneous variable (intelligence) can be controlled by matching the subjects in the two groups on intelligence (concomitant variable). The subjects may be matched subject-by-subject on intelligence, or they may be group-matched.

However, matching as a method of control limits the availability of subjects for the experiment. This method is limited by the difficulty of matching on more than one variable. If the experimenter decides to match subjects on two or three variables, he may not find enough subjects for the experiment. Moreover, matching the subjects on one variable may result in their mismatching on other variables. It is also likely that some subjects will be excluded from the experiment if a matching subject is not available. Furthermore, the method of matching biases the principle of randomisation. However, matching is not considered satisfactory unless the members of the pairs or set are randomly assigned to the treatment groups, a method known as matched randomisation.

13.4.2.4   *Additional Independent Variable*

Sometimes the experimenter may consider elimination inexpedient or unpractical. He/she may not eliminate the extraneous variable from the experiment; rather, may include it into the design as an additional independent variable. Let us cite our previous example in which the experimenter is interested in studying the efficacy of two methods (i.e., lecture method and discussion method) of instruction on the academic achievement scores of 8th grade children. The experimenter does not want to eliminate the variable of intelligence, and hence introduces intelligence as an attribute variable (a characteristic that can be identified and measured). Then he/she creates three groups of subjects on the basis of their intelligence scores. These three groups consist of subjects having above average intelligence, average intelligence and below average intelligence as levels of the additional independent variable (intelligence).

Thus, the outcome of such a control procedure is a factorial design. In the above example, it will be a 3×2 factorial design in which the first independent variable or factor is intelligence having three levels, and the second independent variable or factor is the method of instruction having two levels. The first factor or independent variable is a classification variable or control variable and the second one is the experimental or treatment variable which is directly manipulated by the experimenter in the experimental design. With the help of ANOVA, the experimenter can take out the variance due to intelligence (main effect of intelligence) from the total variance. The experimenter may decide to study the influence of intelligence on academic achievement and also the interaction between intelligence and method of instruction. Thus, the secondary or extraneous source of variance is controlled by introducing the extraneous variable as an additional independent variable in the experiment. In this case, the experimenter gets the advantage of isolating the effect of intelligence on academic achievement and the interaction effect as additional information.

13.4.2.5 *Statistical Control*

Another procedure to control the extraneous source of variance is through the statistical control. In this technique, no attempt is made to restrain the influence of the extraneous or secondary variables, rather one or more concomitant secondary variables (covariates) are measured, and the dependent variable is statistically adjusted to remove the effects of the uncontrolled source of variation. Analysis of covariance (ANCOVA) is one such technique. It is used to remove statistically the possible amount of variation in the dependent variable due to the variation in the concomitant secondary variable. The method has been presented in Chapter 21 (available on the companion website).

The extraneous source of variance can also be controlled with the help of various experimental designs. For example, we can make the extraneous variable constant by 'blocking' the experimental units or subjects as in the randomised complete block design (Chapter 20, available on the companion website). In this design, the subjects pretested on the concomitant secondary variable are grouped in blocks on the basis of their scores on the concomitant variable so that the subjects within each block are relatively homogenous. The purpose is to create between-block differences. Later on, the variance between the blocks is taken out from the total variance. Thus, the variability due to the extraneous variable is statistically held constant.

Let us give an example to illustrate this point. Suppose, an investigator finds that the anxiety level of the subjects (an extraneous variable) influences the dependent variable in the experiment. The experimenter can control this secondary source of variation through elimination, that is, by selecting subjects of low anxiety level only. But this procedure will limit the generality of the experimental results. Therefore, the experimenter may decide to apply statistical technique to control the extraneous variable (i.e., anxiety level). For this purpose, the experimenter can administer an anxiety test to measure the anxiety level (concomitant variable) to all the subjects selected randomly from the population for the experiment. After the administration of the anxiety test, the experimenter may create blocks on the basis of the anxiety scores of the subjects in such a way so that the subjects within each block are as homogeneous as possible and the differences between the blocks are high. In such a design, the variability due to the block differences is taken out from the total variation. Thus, the statistical control technique can be utilised by the experimenter to control the variance contributed by an extraneous variable.

13.4.3 Error Variance

The term error variance (or experimental error) refers to all uncontrolled sources of variation in the experiment. Error variance results from random fluctuations in the experiment. Error variance can be controlled through experimental procedures or some statistical procedures. If the extraneous source of variation is not effectively controlled then it becomes a part of error variance. So, by controlling the extraneous source of variation, one can reduce the amount of error variance.

There are two main sources of error variance. First is the inherent variability in the experimental subjects (or units) to which treatments are applied. Second is the error of measurement which is caused by the lack of uniformity in the physical conduct of experiment and/or by the lack of the standardised experimental technique.

Individuals vary a lot in respect of intelligence, aptitude, interest, anxiety and so on. All these person-related variables tend to inflate the experimental error. The other source of error variance is associated with errors of measurement and could be due to unreliable measuring instrument, fatigue on the part of the experimental subjects, transient emotional states of the subjects, in attention by subjects at some point of time and so on.

Statistical controls can be applied to minimise such error variance. For example, repeated measures design can be used to minimise the experimental error. By this statistical technique, the variability due to individual differences is taken out from the total variability, and thus, the error variance is reduced. ANCOVA is also another technique to reduce the error variance. Moreover, error variance can also be controlled by increasing the reliability of measurements by giving clear and unambiguous instructions regarding the conduction of the experiment and by using reliable measuring instruments or tests and so on.

An important function of the experimental design, as it has been pointed out earlier, is to maximise the systematic variance, control extraneous source of variance and minimise the error variance. The systematic variance or the variance due to experimental variable is tested against the error variance (F-test is discussed in Chapter 14); therefore, the error variance should be minimised to give systematic variance a chance to show the significance.

13.5   Experimental Validity

To make a significant contribution to the development of knowledge, an experiment must be valid. This validity is an important concept in experimental situation. In an experiment, validity is related to the control of extraneous variables which tend to mask the effect of the experimental variable. More the extraneous variation slips into an experiment, greater is the possibility that the independent variable is not wholly responsible for changes in the dependent variable. The extraneous variation may influence the dependent variable to such an extent, where the conclusions drawn from the experimental results become invalid.

The experimental validity is divided into two parts—*internal and external validity*. The internal validity is basic minimum without which the results of any experiment cannot be interpreted. That is, it is concerned with making certain that the independent variable manipulated in the experiment is responsible for the variation in the dependent variable. In other words, an experiment has internal validity to the extent that the factors which have been manipulated (independent variables) actually have a genuine effect on the observed consequences (dependent variables) in the experimental setting. External validity, on the other hand, is concerned with the generalisability of the obtained results of the experiment. That is, to what population, settings, treatment variables and so on, can the results of an experiment be generalised. In other words, external validity is the extent to which the variable relationships can be generalised to other settings, other treatment variables, other measurement variables and other populations.

Experimental validity is an ideal to aspire to, for it is unlikely that it can ever be completely achieved. Internal validity is very difficult to achieve in the non-laboratory setting of the behavioural experiment, where there are so many extraneous variables to attempt to control. When experimental controls are tightened to achieve internal validity, the more artificial, less realistic situation may prevail, reducing the external validity or generalisability of the experiment. Some compromise is inevitable so that a reasonable balance may be established between control and generalisability—between internal and external validity. For detailed discussion on internal and external validity, the reader may refer to Campbell and Stanley (1963).

However, there are several factors that jeopardise the experimental validity. These factors create threats to both internal and external experimental validity. Let us discuss briefly these factors in the following sections.

13.5.1   Threats to Internal Experimental Validity

In any behavioural experiments, a number of extraneous variables are present in the situation or are generated by the experimental design and procedures. These extraneous variables influence the results of the experiment in ways that are difficult to evaluate. In a sense, they introduce rival hypotheses that could account for experimental change not attributable to the experimental variables under consideration. Although these extraneous variables usually cannot be completely eliminated, many of them can be identified. It is important that behavioural researchers anticipate them to occur and take all possible precautions to minimise their influence through experimental design and execution.

A number of factors jeopardise the power of the experimenter to evaluate the effects of independent variables unambiguously. In the opinion of Campbell and Stanley (1966), the following factors threaten the internal validity of an experiment.

13.5.1.1   *Maturation*

The experimental subjects change biologically as well as psychologically in many ways over a period of time, and the changes may be confused with effects of the independent variables under consideration. During the course of a study, the subjects might become more tired, wiser, hungrier, older and so on. Moreover, they may be influenced by the incidental learnings or experiences that they encounter through normal maturation. This threat is best controlled by randomly assigning subjects to experimental and control groups. The difference between these two groups would then be considered to be due to the experimental treatment rather than to maturation.

13.5.1.2   *History*

Certain specific external events which are beyond the control of the researcher may have a facilitating or inhibiting effect on the performance of the subjects. For example, the effect of the emotional tirade of a teacher, the anxiety produced by a pending examination, or a catastrophic event in the community may significantly affect the test performance of a group of students.

In many experiments, these external events will have a similar effect upon both experimental and control subjects, in which case this threat is controlled. However, because they are specific events, they may affect one group but not the other. The effect of these uncontrolled external events is one of the hazards inherent in experiments carried on outside the laboratory. In laboratory experiments, these extraneous variables can be controlled more effectively.

13.5.1.3   *Testing*

The process of pretesting at the beginning of an experiment can produce a change in subjects. Pretesting may produce a practice effect that can make subjects more proficient in subsequent test performance. Testing presents a threat to internal validity that is common to pre-test-post-test experiments. Of course, an equivalent control group would be affected by the test in a similar way as the experimental group. Thus, having experimental and control groups controls for this threat in the same way that it does for the threat of maturation.

13.5.1.4 *Unstable Instrumentation*

Unreliable instruments or techniques used to describe and measure various aspects of behaviour are threats to the validity of an experiment. If tests used as instruments of observation are not accurate or consistent, then a serious element of error is introduced. If human observers are used to describe behaviour changes in subjects, then changes in observers or in their standards due to fatigue, increased insight or skill, or changes in criteria of judgement over a period of time are likely to introduce errors in the experiment.

13.5.1.5 *Statistical Regression*

Statistical regression is otherwise known as *regression to the mean*. It is a phenomenon that sometimes operates when subjects are selected on the basis of extremely high or extremely low pre-test scores and when the measuring device is not totally reliable, which is common. Subjects who score very high in a pre-test may score very low on a subsequent testing or vice versa. Therefore, the purpose of a study may require the researcher to select subjects based on their extreme scores. A study of the effect of differential remedial reading programmes assumes that the subjects must need remedial reading instruction, and therefore, have very low reading scores in the pre-test. To control for *regression to the mean*, the researcher would randomly assign his/her sample of poor readers to the experimental and control groups. Since both groups would be expected to improve equally because of *regression to the mean*, if the experimental group improved significantly more than the control group, the experimenter or researcher could conclude that this was due to the experimental treatment rather than statistical regression.

13.5.1.6 *Selection Bias*

Selection bias is represented by the non-equivalence of the experimental and the control groups, and its most effective deterrent is the random assignment of subjects to treatments. Selection bias is likely when upon invitation, volunteers are used as members of an experimental group; their higher motivation than that of the non-volunteers may introduce a bias that would invalidate reasonable comparison between experimental and control groups.

13.5.1.7 *Interaction of Selection and Maturation*

The interaction of selection and maturation may occur whenever the subjects can select which treatment they will receive. Even though the groups may be equivalent in the pre-test and other cognitive measures, the reasons why some subjects choose one treatment over another may be related to the outcome measure (dependent variables). Therefore, as a precaution against this threat, groups of subjects should be assigned randomly to different treatment conditions.

13.5.1.8 *Experimental Mortality*

Mortality or loss of subjects, particularly likely in long-term experiment, introduces a potentially confounding element. Even though experimental and control groups of subjects are randomly assigned, the survivors might represent groups that are quite different from the unbiased groups that began the experiment. Those who survive a period of experimentation are likely to be healthier, more able, or more highly motivated than those who are absent frequently or who drop out of school, and do not remain for the duration of the experiment. The major concern here is whether the groups experienced different loss rates or reasons for dropouts that might confound the results.

13.5.1.9   *Experimenter Bias*

This is a type of bias introduced when the experimenter or the researcher has some previous knowledge about the subjects involved in an experiment. This knowledge of subject status may cause the experimenter/researcher to convey some clue that affects the subject's reaction or may affect the objectivity of his/her judgement.

    The threat of this factor can be controlled by following blind or double-blind procedures of administration of the treatments. When the researcher has no knowledge about which subject is receiving placebo or which subject is receiving treatment, it is known as blind procedure. On the other hand, when the experimenter and researcher both have no knowledge about the treatment conditions, either placebo or experimental conditions, it is called as double-blind procedure. These two techniques or procedures help to minimise the contamination.

13.5.2   Threats to External Experimental Validity

Laboratory research has the virtue of permitting the experimenter to carefully avoid threats to internal experimental validity. However, the artificial nature of such a setting greatly reduces the generalisability of the findings from such research. According to Campbell and Stanley (1966), the following factors may lead to reduced generalisability of research to other settings, individuals, variables and measurement instruments.

13.5.2.1   *Interference of Prior Treatments*

In some types of experiments, the effect of one treatment may carry over to subsequent treatments. For example, in some educational research/experiment, learning produced by the first treatment is not completely erased and its influence may accrue to the advantage of the second treatment. This is one of the major limitations of the single-group, equated-materials experimental design in which the same subjects serve as members of both control and experimental groups. If an equated-materials design is necessary, a counter balanced design will generally control for threat.

13.5.2.2   *The Artificiality of the Experimental Setting*

In an effort to control the extraneous variables, the researcher imposes certain careful controls which may introduce a sterile or artificial atmosphere that is not at all like the real-life situation about which generalisations are desired. The reactive effect of such an experimental process is a constant threat to external experimental validity.

13.5.2.3   *Interaction Effect of Testing*

The use of a pre-test at the beginning of a study may sensitise individuals by making them more aware of the concealed purposes of the researcher and may serve as a stimulus to change. This is a different potential problem than that of testing discussed earlier as a threat to internal validity.

With testing, the threat was that the pre-test would affect the subjects' performance on the post-test in a direct fashion. That was easily controlled by having a control group. In the case of the interaction effect of testing, we have a more difficult problem. Here, the pre-test may alert the experimental group to some aspect of the interventions that is not present for the control group. That is, the pre-test may interact differently with the experimental intervention than it does with the control or placebo conditions. To avoid this threat requires random assignment and either no pre-test or the Solomon four-group design.

In Solomon's four-group design:

1. Subjects are randomly assigned to four groups.
2. Two groups receive the experimental treatment (X).
3. One experimental group receives a pre-test (O_1).
4. Two groups (control) do not receive treatment (C).
5. One control group receives a pre-test (O_3).
6. All four groups receive post-tests (O_2, O_4, O_5, O_6).

Thus, Solomon's four-group design is as follows:

R	O_1	X	O_2
R	O_3	C	O_4
R		X	O_5
R		C	O_6

ANOVA (F test) is used to compare the four post-test scores, and ANCOVA to compare gains in O_2 and O_4.

Because this design provides for two simultaneous experiments, the advantages of a replication are incorporated. A major difficulty is finding enough subjects to assign randomly to four equivalent groups.

13.5.2.4   Interaction of Selection and Treatment

Researchers are rarely, if ever, able to randomly select samples from the wide population of interest and randomly assign them to different treatment conditions or groups; consequently, generalisation from samples to populations is hazardous. Samples used in most classroom experiments are usually composed of intact groups, not randomly selected individuals. They are based upon an accepted invitation to participate. Some school officials agree to participate; others refuse. One cannot assume that samples taken from cooperating schools are necessarily representative of the target population. Such schools are usually characterised by faculties that have high morale, less insecurity, greater willingness to try new approach and a greater desire to improve their performance.

13.5.2.5   The Extent of Treatment Verification

Due to the potential threat of experimenter bias, most researchers have research assistants or others, who are not directly involved in the formulation of research hypotheses, who deliver the treatment/s. This leads to a potential threat to external experimental validity. Was the treatment administered as intended and described by the researcher? The researcher must have a verification procedure (e.g., direct observation or videotape) to make sure that the treatment was properly administered.

After reading about these threats to both internal and external experimental validity, the beginner is probably ready to conclude that behavioural research is too hazardous to attempt. Particularly, outside of the laboratory, ideal experimental conditions and controls are never likely to prevail. However, an understanding of these threats is important so that the researcher can make every effort to remove or minimise their influence. If one were to wait for a research setting free from all threats, no research would ever be carried on. Knowing the limitations, and doing the best that he/she can under the circumstances, the researcher may conduct experiments, reach valid conclusions, provide answers to important questions and solve significant problems.

13.6   Types of Experimental Designs

The experimental design is the blueprint of the procedures that enable the researcher to test hypothesis by reaching valid conclusions about relationships between independent and dependent variables. Selection of a particular design is based upon the purposes of the experiment, the type of variables to be manipulated and the conditions or limiting factors under which it is conducted. The design deals with practical problems such as how subjects are to be assigned to various treatment conditions (i.e., experimental and control groups), the way independent variables are to be manipulated and controlled, the way extraneous variables are to be controlled, how observations are to be made, how the data are to be collected and the type of statistical analysis to be employed in interpreting the results and drawing inferences.

The adequacy of experimental designs is judged by the degree to which they eliminate or minimise threats to experimental validity. Depending upon the liberty of the experimenter in assigning subjects randomly to the various treatment groups, and in manipulating the independent variable/s in the experiment, the experimental designs are categorised into three classes, such as, *experimental design, quasi-experimental design* and *single-case experimental design*. However, depending upon the number of independent variable/s (or factor/s) studied at a time in an experiment, the experimental designs are categorised into two classes like *single-factor experimental design* and *multi-factor experimental design*. These experimental designs are briefly discussed below.

13.6.1   Experimental Design

The experimental situations in which the experimenter can manipulate the independent variable/s and has liberty to assign subjects randomly to the treatment conditions, and control the extraneous variable/s are designated as true experiments. The designs belonging to this category are called experimental designs. Included in this category are all those designs in which large number of experimental subjects are studied, the subjects are assigned randomly to the treatment groups, the independent variable or factor is manipulated in the experiment by the experimenter, and the experimenter has complete control over the scheduling of independent variable/s.

There are three types of experimental designs, such as, *between-subjects design* (or randomised group design), *within-subjects design* (or repeated measures design) and *mixed design*. In the between-subjects design, each subject is observed only under one of the several treatment conditions. In other words, the number of randomised groups will be equal to the number of k (i.e., treatment conditions), and one group will be randomly assigned to one of the different treatment conditions. In the within-subjects design, each subject is observed under all the treatment conditions involved in the experiment. In other words, all the treatment conditions will be applied randomly on the same group of subjects. Finally, in the mixed design, some factors are between subjects and some within subjects.

13.6.2 Quasi-experimental Design

In behavioural sciences, especially in educational and social research, it is not always possible on the part of the experimenter to exercise full control over the experimental situation. For example, the experimenter may not have the liberty of assigning subjects randomly to the treatment conditions or the experimenter may not be in a position to apply the independent variable whenever or to whomever he/she wishes. Collectively, such experimental situations form part of quasi-experimental designs. In other words, all such experimental situations in which the experimenter does not have full control over the assignment of experimental subjects randomly to the treatment conditions or the independent variable cannot be manipulated are collectively called quasi-experimental designs. For example, in an ex-post-facto study, the independent variable has already occurred and hence the experimenter studies the effect after the occurrence of the variable. Here, the experimenter has nothing to do with the manipulation of the independent variable. Similarly, in another situation only three intact groups are available for the experiment. In this case, the experimenter cannot randomly assign the subjects to the treatment conditions; rather, he/she can only randomly apply treatments to the three intact groups. There are various such situations in which the experimenter does not have full control over the experimental situations. The plan of such experiments constitutes the quasi-experimental design.

Let us give an example to differentiate between experimental and quasi-experimental designs. First, we give an example of an experimental design. Suppose, an investigator is interested to find out the effect of three methods A, B and C of teaching (A = lecture, B = Seminar and C = discussion) mathematics on the mathematics achievement scores of the 8th grade students. The investigator draws a random sample of kn (k = number of treatment conditions; n = number of subjects in each sample) subjects from a large population of 8th grade students. Then the investigator assigns randomly n subjects to each of the k (here k = 3) treatment conditions—A, B and C. Each of the n subjects in each of the k treatment groups is taught mathematics with a method (appropriate for that group) for, say, two months. Thereafter, a common mathematics achievement test is administered to all the subjects of three groups. The outcome of the experiment is evaluated statistically in accordance with the design of the experiment. The present experiment is a randomised group design or single-factor experiment, and thus the outcome can be analysed by Fisher's one-way ANOVA technique (see chapter 14).

Let us now give an example of quasi-experimental design. Suppose, for the aforesaid problem, the investigator cannot draw a random sample of 8th grade students as the schools do not permit the investigator to regroup the classes to provide teaching in mathematics with the methods he/she is interested in. Ideal conditions being unavailable, the investigator finds three schools following the same curriculum in mathematics and each providing/imparting teaching by one of the three above methods. Then the investigator administers a mathematics achievement test to the subjects from the three schools and compares the outcome to evaluate the effect of each method of teaching (ex-post-facto) on mathematics achievement scores.

From the example cited above, it is observed that the investigator/experimenter in the second condition did not have control over the selection of subjects and also over the assignment of subjects to the treatment conditions. Moreover, the investigator could not manipulate the independent variable/ factor (i.e., imparting teaching with the three methods) as the independent variable had already occurred. This experiment constitutes the quasi-experimental design.

We can notice that the objective of the experiment was same in both the designs (i.e., experimental and quasi-experimental design). However, random assignment of subjects to the various treatment conditions was not possible in the quasi-experiment and it was therefore inefficient/handicap in controlling the extraneous variables. These quasi-experimental investigations are as sound as experimental investigations, but are less powerful in drawing causal relationship between independent and dependent variables. The statistical tests applied to the data obtained from quasi-experimental design are the same as those applied to the data collected in experimental design. It is possible to perform even ANCOVA on data of such studies. However, the conclusions cannot be drawn with as much confidence as from the studies employing experimental designs, because some of the assumptions (e.g., randomisation) underlying the statistical tests are violated in the quasi-experimental designs. Besides this, the experimenter does not have full control over the secondary or extraneous variables that might influence the dependent variable/s in the experiment.

Although quasi-experimental investigations have some limitations or lacunas, nevertheless these are advantageous in certain respects. It is possible to seek answers to several kinds of problems about past situations and those situations which cannot be handled by employing experimental designs. The reader may refer to Cook and Campbell (1979) for a comprehensive review of quasi-experimental designs.

13.6.3 Single-case Experimental Design

In another research situation, the objective may be to study intensively a particular individual rather than a group of individuals. In the former case, the researcher may be interested in answering questions about a certain person or about a person's specific behaviour. For example, behaviour of a particular individual may be observed to note changes over a period of time to study the effect of a behaviour modification technique. All such designs in which observations or measurements are made on an individual subject are categorised as single-case or single-subject experimental design, in contrast to the designs in which groups of subjects are observed and the experimenter has full control over the experimental situation (as in experimental design).

Single-subject or single-case experimental designs are an outgrowth of applied clinical research, especially in the area of behaviour modification. In this type of design, repeated measurements are taken across time on one particular individual to note the subtle changes in behaviour. Single-subject or single-case experimental designs are an extension of *before–after design*.

The single-case experimental designs do not lend themselves to clear statistical analysis, and hypothesis testing has not been formalised as in the case of experimental designs. The experimenter relies on the convincingness of the data. In these designs, the experimenter cannot control the order effects. Moreover, these designs do not provide a good basis for generalisation. However, single-case experimental designs provide us such information about human behaviour that is not always obtainable in group designs. It is especially useful in clinical research where individual's behaviour is of paramount importance. For details of the single-case experimental design, the reader may refer to Hersen and Barlow (1976).

13.7 Factorial Experimental Designs

13.7.1 Single-factor Experimental Design

Any experimental design which involves a single treatment or classification variable is called a single-factor experimental design. This factor or variable may have two or more levels. Let us initially consider experiments in which the single factor is a treatment variable with k levels or categories, and not a classification variable. Such experiments are of various types, some of which are discussed here.

First, a group of experimental subjects may be divided into k independent groups, using a random method. A different treatment may then be applied to each group. One group may be a control group, that is, a group to which no treatment is applied. A meaningful interpretation of the findings of the experiment may require a comparison of results obtained under treatment with results obtained in the absence of treatment. In other words, comparisons may be made between treatments and a control, between treatments, or both.

Second, some single-factor experiments involve a single group of subjects. Each subject receives all k treatments. Repeated observations or measurements are made under k conditions, one of which may be a control condition, on the same subjects. In this type of experiment, the measurements made under the k treatment conditions will not be independent. Positive correlations will usually exist between the paired measurements obtained under any two treatment conditions. These correlations will reduce the magnitude of the error in the comparisons of the separate treatment means.

Third, a single-factor experiment may consist of groups that are matched on one or more variables which are known to be correlated with the dependent variable. In an experiment of three methods of teaching mathematics, intelligence quotient (IQ) may be known to be correlated with achievement in mathematics. Three groups of subjects, paired or matched subject by subject by IQ, may be used. The rationale here is that because IQ is correlated with mathematics achievement, a correlation between mathematics achievements scores for paired subjects may result. The error term would be reduced thereby. In some practical experimental situations, the gains made by matching are trivial in relation to the work involved in the process of matching the groups subject by subject. Therefore, an interesting variant of the matched-group experiment is one in which subjects are not matched subject by subject but are group-matched with regard to distribution on one or more control variables. This group matching results in the same error reduction as in the individual matching of subjects (McNemar, 1969).

Thus, the primary objective of this kind of experiment is to compare the relative effectiveness of two or more treatments on a common criterion. The term single factor in this context is used in contrast to the term multi-factor. In multi-factor experiment, the primary objective is to compare the effects of combinations of treatments acting simultaneously on each of the elements. Single-factor designs form a special case of what are called *completely randomised designs*. These form the building blocks for any other designs; they also provide a standard against which efficiency of other types of designs is measured.

Some of the *criteria* for good experimental designs are as follows:

(i) The analyses resulting from the design should provide unambiguous information on the primary objectives of the experiment. In particular, the design should lead to unbiased estimates.

(ii) The model and its underlying assumptions should be appropriate for the experimental material/s.

(iii) The design should provide maximum information with respect to the major objectives of the experiment per minimum amount of experimental effort.

(iv) The design should provide some information with respect to all the objectives of the experiment.

(v) The design must be feasible within the working conditions that exist for the experimenter.

Statistical models are introduced to define and summarise the assumptions that have been made about populations from which the samples are drawn and treatments are applied. Models serve as guides in formalising statistical bases of the data analysis. Models are also useful tools in guiding test procedures. The terms which do or do not appear in a model, however, must reflect corresponding effects that are present in an experiment as it actually is conducted. Furthermore, the distribution assumptions on such terms must also reflect, realistically, corresponding distributions in the actual experiment.

The scope of inferences from an experiment stems not from any formal model but rather from its design and the procedures followed in its conduct. In this sense, the role of the model is secondary rather than primary.

13.7.2   Multi-factor Experimental Design

The experiments discussed just above have involved a single independent variable or factor. This independent variable may be a single treatment, or classification variable having two or more levels. Experiments may, however, be designed to study simultaneously the effects of two or more independent variables or factors. For example, the experiment in which three methods of teaching mathematics are compared may be expended to include a comparison of distributed (or spaced) versus massed learning conditions. Under the distributed/spaced learning conditions, subjects receive short periods of intensive teaching (or instructions) separated by brief time intervals of rest. But under the massed leaning conditions, subjects receive intensive teaching (or instructions) for a prolonged time period without any rest within the teaching session. The effects on mathematics achievement of the six possible treatment combinations of three methods of teaching and two learning conditions may be investigated, each treatment combination being applied to a different group of experimental subjects. Such an experiment is called a factorial experiment or multi-factor experimental design. Experiments in which the treatments are combinations of levels of two or more factors are said simply to be factorial or multi-factorial. If all possible treatment combinations are studied, the experiment is said to be a complete factorial experiment. In some experiments, the factors have two levels only. We may speak of a 2×2 experiment, a $2 \times 2 \times 2$ experiment, or a 2^n experiment, where 'n' is the number of factors.

In our example of 3×2 factorial experiment on teaching mathematics in relation to distributed (or spaced) versus massed learning, three variables are involved. Two of these, method of teaching and learning condition, are independent variables, and one, mathematics achievement test score, is the dependent variable. Thus, three variate values are available for each subject—the teaching method used, the learning condition and mathematics achievement—test score. The teaching method and learning condition are nominal variables.

The purpose of this factorial experiment is to explore the relation between the learning condition and test scores, and the teaching method and test scores. The relations between the six combinations of learning condition and teaching method may also be studied. An important feature of the structure of this experiment is that the two nominal variables, learning condition and teaching method, are independent of each other. By choosing six groups of equal size, the independence of these two variables is assured. If the numbers of cases in the six groups, when written in the form of a 2×3 contingency table, are proportional to the marginal totals, and chi-square (χ^2) for the table is zero (0), then the independence of the two treatment variables will also be assured. In the design of factorial experiments the groups should be either of equal size or proportional. Departures from equality or proportionality should be avoided.

Factorial experiments may have some advantages and disadvantages. One advantage of the factorial experiment is that information is obtained about the interaction between factors. For example, in the experiment on teaching mathematics, one method of teaching may interact with a condition of learning and render that combination either better or worse than any other combination. One disadvantage of the factorial experiment is that the number of combinations may become quite unwieldy, and, from a practical point of view, the experiment may be very difficult to conduct. Moreover, the meaningful interpretation of the interaction effects may prove difficult. In general, in behavioural sciences, particularly, in psychology and education, it is usually advisable to avoid factorial experiments with more than a few factors (that is more than two or three factors).

We should also note that factorial experiments may involve repeated measurement on the same subjects. For example, in a 3×2 factorial design, repeated measurements may be made on the same subjects under each of the six treatment combinations. The result is an $N \times 3 \times 2$ arrangement of numbers.

Summary

In this chapter, we have discussed the topic of experimental design: an introduction. Experimental design is the scientific planning of an experiment for exploring the effect of one or more independent variables on a dependent variable, minimising the experimental errors from uncontrolled random variations, and making the inference more reliable and reasonably unambiguous. It is essential for the investigator to get acquainted with the basic terminology in experimental design for clear understanding of the designs of the experiments and the corresponding analysis of data. The basic terminology includes such terms as factor, levels, dimensions, treatment combinations, replication, main effects, simple effects and interaction effect. We have also discussed the experimental design as variance control because variance control is the central theme of the experimental design. The problem of variance control has three aspects like systematic variance, extraneous variance and error variance. The major function of the experimental design is to maximise the effect of systematic variance, control extraneous variance, and minimise error variance. These three types of variances have been discussed in detail.

Next, we discussed the experimental validity which is divided into two parts—internal and external validity. Several factors that jeopardise both internal and external experimental validity have been presented.

Finally, we discussed the types of experimental designs. The adequacy of experimental design is judged by the degree to which they eliminate or minimise threats to experimental validity. Depending upon the liberty of the experimenter in assigning subjects randomly to the various treatment groups, and manipulating the independent variable/s in the experiment, the experimental designs are categorised into three classes, such as, the *true experimental design*, *quasi-experimental design* and *single case experimental design*. However, depending upon the number of independent variable/s (or factor/s) studied at a time in an experiment, the experimental designs are categorised into two classes like *single-factor experimental design* and *multi-factor experimental design*. Moreover, the true experimental design is of three types: *between-subjects design* (or *randomised group design*), *within-subjects design* (or *repeated measures design*) and *mixed design*. In the *between-subjects design*, each subject is observed only under one of the several treatment conditions. In other words, the number of randomised groups of subjects will be equal to the number of treatment conditions (k), and one group will be randomly assigned to one of the *k* conditions. In the *within-subjects design*, each subject is observed under all the treatment conditions involved in the experiment. In other words, all the *k* conditions will be applied randomly on the same group of subjects. In the mixed design, some factors are between subjects and some within subjects.

Key Terms

- Additional independent variable
- Before–after design
- Between-group variance
- Between-subjects design
- Completely randomised design
- Dimensions
- Elimination
- Error variance
- Experimental design
- Experimental validity
- Experimental variance
- Experimenter bias
- External experimental validity
- Extraneous variance
- Factor
- Factorial experimental designs
- Interaction effect
- Internal experimental validity
- Levels
- Main effects

- Matching
- Mixed design
- Multi-factor experimental design
- Quasi-experimental design
- Randomisation
- Randomised group design
- Repeated measures design
- Replication
- Selection bias
- Simple effects
- Single-case experimental design
- Single-factor experimental design
- Solomon's four-group design
- Statistical control
- Statistical regression
- Systematic variance
- Treatment combination
- Variance control
- Within-group variance
- Within-subjects design

Questions and Problems

1. What do you mean by an experimental design? Discuss the principles underlying in the development of such designs.
2. Define experimental design. Analyse the basic terms necessary for clear understanding of the designs of experiments.
3. What is variance? Elucidate the basic procedures for controlling the extraneous source of variance.

4. Write notes on:

    (a) Systematic variance   (b) Extraneous variance

    (c) Error variance

5. What do you mean by experimental validity? Discuss about the different parts of experimental validity.

6. Briefly discuss the factors that jeopardise the experimental validity.

7. What do you mean by internal experimental validity? Discuss about the threats to internal experimental validity.

8. What is external experimental validity? Discuss the factors that threaten the external validity of an experiment.

9. Critically analyse the different types of experimental designs.

10. What do you mean by a factor? Elucidate various types of single-factor experimental design.

11. What is a multi-factor experimental design? Explain it with suitable examples. Discuss the objectives or purposes of factorial experimental designs.

12. Write notes on the following:

    (a) Criteria for good experimental designs.

    (b) Difference between single-factor and multi-factor experimental designs.

13. Fill in the blanks:

    (i) The designer of experiments performs a role similar to that of the _____.

    (ii) According to Myers, the design is the general _____ of the experiment.

    (iii) All experiments are concerned with the _____ between variables.

    (iv) In the simplest type of experiments two variables, _____ and _____ variables, only are involved.

    (v) The variable whose effects are being studied in an experiment is called_____ variable.

    (vi) The measures of achievement constitute the _____ variable.

    (vii) An independent variable used in an experiment may be either a treatment variable or a _____ variable.

    (viii) Any independent variable, whether of the treatment or classification type, is spoken of as a _____.

    (ix) Each specific variation in a factor is called the _____ of that factor.

    (x) A significant main effect will have significant _____.

14. Write whether the following statements are True or False.

    (i) In a factorial experiment, the effect of a treatment on one factor at a given level of the other factor is called the simple effect.

    (ii) In factorial experiments, the presence of interaction effect destroys the additivity of the main effects.

(iii) Variance control is the central theme of the experimental design.

(iv) The major function of the experimental design is to maximise the error variance.

(v) Experimenter bias is a threat to external experimental validity.

(vi) Interaction effect can be studied in a single-factor experimental design.

(vii) Age is an example of classification variable.

(viii) Sex is a treatment variable.

(ix) In developing the design of an experiment the investigator must specify the observations to be made on each subject.

(x) The joint effect of two factors is known as their interaction effect.

15. Find out the correct answer from among the four alternatives.

(i) The designer of experiments performs a role similar to that of the:

    (a) Architect   (b) Artist

    (c) Poet   (d) None of the above

(ii) Dosage of a drug is an example of

    (a) Classification variable   (b) Treatment variable

    (c) Dependent variable   (d) None of the above

(iii) In an experimental design, any independent variable is called a:

    (a) Dimension   (b) Level

    (c) Factor   (d) None of the above

(iv) In a factorial experiment, $A \times B$ signifies:

    (a) Main effect   (b) Interaction effect

    (c) Simple effect   (d) None of the above

(v) Variability in the dependent measure due to the manipulation of the experimental variable in the experiment by the experimenter is known as:

    (a) Systematic variance   (b) Extraneous variance

    (c) Error variance   (d) None of the above

(vi) Which one of the following is a basic procedure for controlling the extraneous source of variance?

    (a) Generalisation   (b) Replication

    (c) Randomisation   (d) None of the above

(vii) Interference of prior treatments is a factor that jeopardises the

    (a) Internal experimental validity   (b) External experimental validity

    (c) Test validity   (d) None of the above

(viii)   Selection of a particular design of an experiment is based upon the:

    (a)   Purposes of the experiment   (b)   Results of the experiment

    (c)   Statistical analysis of data   (d)   None of the above

(ix)   The between-subjects experimental design is otherwise known as:

    (a)   Within-subjects design   (b)   Repeated measures design

    (c)   Randomised group design   (d)   None of the above

(x)   The experimental situations over which the experimenter does not have full control constitute the:

    (a)   Quasi-experimental designs

    (b)   True experimental designs

    (c)   Either quasi or true experimental designs

    (d)   None of the above

CHAPTER 14

Analysis of Variance (Independent Measures)

After completing this chapter you will be able to:

- Recognise situations requiring the comparison of two means or populations.
- Get acquainted with the concepts and components of analysis of variance (ANOVA).
- Understand the logic of ANOVA.
- Introduce F distribution and learn how to use it in statistical inferences.
- Compare more than two population means using ANOVA.
- Compute and test the significance of the F-ratio in one-way and two-way analysis of variances for independent measures.
- Describe the assumptions underlying the ANOVA.
- Get acquainted with different types of transformation of data.

14.1 Introduction

In Chapters 11 and 12, we learned how to test hypotheses using data from either one or two samples, respectively. We used one-sample test (Chapter 11) to determine whether a mean, median, standard deviation/variance, quartile deviation, percentage/proportion or a correlation coefficient was significantly different from a hypothesised value. In the two-sample tests (Chapter 12), we examined the difference between two means, two medians, two standard deviations/variances, two correlation coefficients, or two proportions/percentages and we tried to learn whether this difference was significant.

Suppose, we have means from three or more than three populations instead of only two. In this case, we cannot apply the methods introduced in Chapter 12 because they are limited to testing for the equality of only two means. The *analysis of variance* (ANOVA) will enable us to test whether *more* than two population means can be considered equal. In this chapter, we will learn a statistical technique known as ANOVA that will enable us to test for the significance of the differences among more than two sample means. Using ANOVA, we will be able to make inferences about whether our samples are drawn from populations having the same mean.

14.2   Nature and Purpose

The ANOVA was developed by Ronald A Fisher, a renowned British Statistician, and was reported by him in 1923. The name F-test was given to it by Snedecor (1946) in Fisher's honour. Since that time it has found wide application in many areas of experimentation. Its early application was in the field of agriculture. This device had made tremendous contribution to designing of experiments and their statistical analysis.

The ANOVA deals with variances rather than with standard deviation or standard error. It is a method for dividing the variation observed in experimental data into different parts, each part assignable to a known source, cause or factor. We may assess the relative magnitude of variation resulting from different sources and ascertain whether a particular part of the variation is greater than expectation under the null hypothesis. The ANOVA is inextricably associated with the design of experiments. Obviously, if we are to relate different parts of the variation to particular causal circumstances, experiments must be designed to permit this to occur in a logically rigorous fashion, because the main function of experimental design is to maximise systematic variance, control extraneous sources of variance and minimise error variance.

The ANOVA technique is useful in testing differences between two or more treatment means. Its special merit lies in testing differences between all of the means at the same time. The ANOVA is a powerful aid to the researcher. It helps him/her in designing experiments efficiently, and enables him/her to take account of the interacting variables. It also aids in testing hypothesis. Thus, ANOVA is a hypothesis-testing procedure that is used to evaluate mean difference between two or more treatments (or populations). As with all inferential procedures, ANOVA uses simple data as the basis for drawing general conclusions about populations. It may appear that F- and t-tests are simply two different ways of doing exactly the same job, testing the mean differences. In some respects, this is true—both tests use sample data to test hypotheses about population means. However, F-test has a tremendous advantage over t-test. Specifically, t-test is limited to situations where there are only two treatments to compare. The major advantage of ANOVA is that it can be used to compare two or more treatments. Thus, ANOVA provides researchers with much greater flexibility in designing experiments and interpreting results. Therefore, ANOVA is much more needed than the t-tests.

Like the t-tests presented in Chapters 11 and 12, ANOVA can be used with either an independent-measures or repeated-measures design. As mentioned earlier, one should recall that an independent-measures design means that there is a separate sample of n subjects for each of the treatments being compared. This design is otherwise known as randomised group design or between-group design. In a repeated-measures design, on the contrary, the same sample of n members is tested in all of the different treatment conditions. This design is otherwise known as within-group design. In addition, ANOVA can be used to evaluate the results of a research study that involves more than one independent variable or factors. For example, an investigator might want to compare the effectiveness of two different teaching methods (independent variable 1) for three different class sizes (independent variable 2). The structure of this research study is a 2×3 factorial design which involves comparing independent sample means from six different treatment combinations; a separate randomised group is used for each treatment condition. The dependent variable for this study would be each subject's score on a standardised achievement test.

As we can see, ANOVA provides researchers with an extremely flexible data-analysis technique. It can be used to evaluate the significance of mean differences in a wide variety of research situations and is one of the most commonly used hypothesis-testing procedures. In a study where the researcher manipulates a variable to create different treatment conditions, the variable is called an *independent variable* or *treatment variable*. On the contrary, when a researcher uses a non-manipulated variable to differentiate groups of subjects, the variable is called *a quasi-independent variable* or *classification variable*. For example, class size and methods of teaching are the independent variables, whereas age and sex are the quasi-independent variables (i.e., they are pre-existing subject variables). In the context of ANOVA, an independent variable or quasi-independent variable is called a *factor*.

14.3   *F*-Test and *t*-Test

The *t*-test is adequate when we want to determine whether or not two treatment means or two sample means differ significantly from each other. It is applied in case of experiments involving only two groups. However, for various reasons, *t*-test is not adequate for comparisons involving more than two means. The most serious objection to the use of *t*-test, when more than two comparisons are to be made, is the large number of computations involved, which would be too cumbersome to carry out. The general formula for determining the number of combinations to be made taking two groups at a time is $\dfrac{N(N-1)}{2}$ or $\dfrac{k(k-1)}{2}$, where N or k refers to the number of treatment groups. For example, if there are 10 groups, we would have to make $\dfrac{10(10-1)}{2} = \dfrac{10 \times 9}{2} = 45$ separate *t*-tests; for 15 groups, we would have to make 105 separate *t*-tests. Thus, as the number of treatment groups increases, the number of comparisons to be made increases rapidly, that is, the computation work increases disproportionately. Furthermore, if a few comparisons (i.e., *t*-ratios) turn out to be significant, it will be difficult to interpret the results. Let us elucidate this point by the help of an example.

Suppose, an investigator is interested in studying the effects of 10 treatments in an experiment, and assigned randomly 10 separate groups of subjects—one group to each of the treatment conditions. Thus, there are 10 group means. Evidently, 45 possible *t*-tests will have to be made for 10 treatment means. That is, first *t*-test $H_0: \mu_1 = \mu_2$; then second *t*-test $H_0 = \mu_1 = \mu_3$, and so on till we perform all the 45 *t*-tests for the difference between every pair of means. Out of the 45 *t*-tests, we expect to find an average of 2 or 3 *t*-ratios/values (0.05×45) to be significant at 5% level by chance alone. Suppose, we find that out of 45 *t*-tests only five are significant at 0.05 level. When *t*-test is being applied, there is no way to know whether these five differences are true differences or within chance expectation. The more *t*-tests we perform, the more likely it is that more differences will be statistically significant purely by chance. Thus, the *t*-test is not an adequate procedure to simultaneously evaluate three or more treatment means. We would like the probability of Type 1 error in the experiment to be 0.05 or less.

The ANOVA or *F*-test, on the other hand, permits us to evaluate three or more means at one time. In making comparisons in experiments involving more than two means, the equality breaks down. Hence the ANOVA or *F*-test should always be preferred. The *F*-test is also an adequate test for determining the significance of two means. For two groups $(df = k - 1 = 2 - 1 = 1)$, $F = t^2$ or $t = \sqrt{F}$. Therefore, in case of two treatment conditions or two randomised groups, either of the two tests (t or F) is used; it is a matter of choice which one of the two tests is used. Both tests yield exactly the same result. This means that the one-way ANOVA and the two-tailed *t*-test can be used interchangeably in comparing the differences between two treatment means. However, it is seen that in the same situation, *F*-test is easier to perform than the *t*-test.

The test statistic for ANOVA is very similar to the t statistic used in earlier chapters. For the t statistic, we computed a ratio with the following structure:

$$t = \frac{\text{Obtained difference between sample means}}{\text{Difference expected by chance (error)}}$$

For ANOVA, the test statistic is called an F-ratio which has the following structure:

$$F = \frac{\text{Variance (differences) between sample means}}{\text{Variance (differences) expected by chance (error)}}$$

Note that the F-ratio is based on variance instead of sample mean difference. The reason for this change is that ANOVA is used in situations where there are more than two sample means and it is impossible to compute a sample mean difference. Hence, variance is used to define and measure the size of the differences among the sample means.

14.4   The Logic of Analysis of Variance

The formulae and computations required in ANOVA are somewhat complicated, but the logic that underlies the whole procedure is fairly straightforward. The present section will give a general picture of ANOVA before we start looking at the details. We will introduce the logic of ANOVA with the help of the hypothetical data in Table 14.1. These data represent the results of an independent-measures experiment comparing learning performance under three methods of teaching—A, B and C.

It is evident from Table 14.1 that there are three separate samples, with $n=5$ in each sample. The dependent variable is the number of problems solved correctly. Table 14.1 shows that the scores are not all the same. The scores are different or are variable. Our goal is to measure the amount of variability (the size of the differences) and to explain its source.

The first step is to determine the total variability for the entire set of data. To compute the total variability, we will combine all the scores from all the separate samples to obtain one general measure of variability for the complete experiment. Once we have measured the total variability, then we can divide it into separate components. The word *analysis* means dividing into smaller parts, and because we are going to analyse variability, the process is called *analysis of variance*. This analysis process divides the total variability into two basic components, such as (a) *between-treatments variance* and (b) *within-treatments variance*. Analysing the total

Table 14.1   Hypothetical data from an experiment examining learning performance under three methods of teaching—A, B and C

Method A (Sample 1)	Method B (Sample 2)	Method C (Sample 3)
2	2	5
1	3	4
0	4	7
3	3	4
4	3	5
$\bar{X}_1 = 2.0$	$\bar{X}_2 = 3.0$	$\bar{X}_3 = 5.0$

variability into these two components is the heart of ANOVA. We will now examine each of the components in more detail.

14.4.1   Between-treatment Variance

If we look at the data given in Table 14.1, we clearly see that much of the variability in the scores is due to general differences between treatment conditions. For example, the scores in the method C tend to be much higher ($\bar{X}_3 = 5.0$) than the scores in method A ($\bar{X}_1 = 2.0$) and in method B ($\bar{X}_2 = 3.0$). We will calculate the variance between treatments to provide a measure of the overall differences between treatment conditions. When you see the term *variance*, you can automatically translate it into the term *differences*. Thus, the between-treatment variance is really measuring the difference between sample means.

In addition to measuring the differences between treatments, the overall goal of ANOVA is to evaluate the differences between treatments. There are always two possible explanations for the between-treatment differences/variance: (i) the differences are caused by the treatment effects and (ii) the differences are simply due to chance.

(i)   **Treatment effect.** The differences or variances are caused by the treatments. For the data in Table 14.1, the scores in sample 1, sample 2 and sample 3 were obtained under different teaching methods A, B and C, respectively. It is possible that the difference between samples is caused by the different teaching methods.

(ii)   **Chance.** The differences/variances are simply due to chance. If there is no treatment effect at all, you would still expect some differences between samples. The samples consist of different individuals with different scores, and it should not be surprising that individual differences exist between samples just by chance. In general, 'chance differences' can be defined as unplanned and unpredictable differences that are not caused or explained by any action on the part of the researcher. The researchers have commonly identified two primary sources for chance differences. These two sources are (a) individual differences and (b) experimental error, which are discussed below.

(a)   **Individual differences.** Individual subjects enter a research study with different characteristics. Although it is reasonable to expect that different subjects will secure different scores, it is impossible to predict exactly what the difference will be.

(b)   **Experimental error.** Whenever we make a measurement, there is potential for some amount of error. For example, if we measure the same individual under the same condition on two occasions, it is possible that we will obtain two different measurements. Because these differences are unexplained and unpredictable, they are considered to be chance.

Thus, when we compute the between-treatment variance, we are measuring differences that could be caused by a treatment effect or could simply be due to chance. The next step in the analysis is to measure how much difference (or variance) is likely to occur just by chance alone. To measure chance differences, we will compute the variance within treatments.

14.4.2   Within-treatments Variance

In addition to the general differences between-treatment conditions, there is variability within each treatment or each sample. The within-treatments variance provides a measure of the variability inside each treatment condition. In each treatment condition, we have a set of

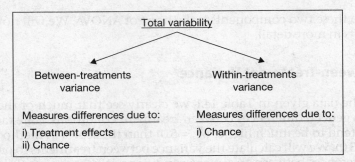

Figure 14.1   Partitioning of total variance into two basic components: Between-treatments variance and within-treatments variance

individuals or subjects who are treated exactly the same, that is, the investigator does not do anything that would cause these individuals to have different scores. In Table 14.1, for example, the data show that five subjects were tested in method A (sample 1). Although these five subjects were all treated exactly the same (i.e., all taught with the help of teaching method A), their scores were different. Now the question is, 'Why are the scores different?' The answer is that the differences within a treatment are simply due to chance.

Thus, the within-treatments variance provides a measure of how much difference is reasonable to expect just by chance.

Figure 14.1 shows the overall analysis of variance and identifies the sources of variability that are measured by each of the two basic components.

14.4.3   The *F*-ratio: The Test Statistic for ANOVA

Once we have analysed the total variability into two basic components (between treatments and within treatments), we simply compare them. The comparison is made by computing a statistic called an *F*-ratio. For the independent-measures ANOVA, the *F*-ratio has the following structure:

$$F = \frac{\text{Between-treaments variance}}{\text{Within-treatments variance}}$$

When we express each component of variability in terms of its sources (see Figure 14.1), the structure of *F*-ratio is:

$$F = \frac{\text{Treatment effect} + \text{Differences due to chance}}{\text{Differences due to chance}}$$

The value obtained for the *F*-ratio will help determine whether or not any treatment effect exists. Let us consider the following two possibilities:

(i)   When the treatment has no effect, then the differences between treatments (numerator) are entirely due to chance. In this case, the numerator and the denominator of the *F*-ratio are both measuring chance differences and should be roughly the same size. With the numerator and denominator roughly equal, the *F*-ratio should have a value around 1.0. In terms of the formula, when treatment effect is zero, we obtain

$$F = \frac{0 + \text{Differences due to chance}}{\text{Differences due to chance}}$$

Thus, an F-ratio near 1.0 indicates that the differences between treatments (numerator) are about the same as the differences that are expected by chance (denominator). When an F-ratio is near 1.0, we will conclude that there is no evidence to suggest that the treatment has any effect.

(ii)   When the treatment does have an effect, causing differences between treatments, then the between-treatment differences (numerator) should be larger than chance (denominator). In this case, the numerator of the F-ratio should be noticeably larger than the denominator, and we should obtain an F-ratio noticeably larger than 1.0. Thus, a large F-ratio indicates that the differences between treatments are greater than chance, that is, the treatment does have a significant effect.

In more general terms, the denominator of the F-ratio measures only uncontrolled and unexplained (often called unsystematic) variability. For this reason, the denominator of the F-ratio is called the *error term*. The numerator of the F-ratio always includes the same unsystematic variability as in the *error term*, but it also includes any systematic variability caused by the treatment effect. The goal of ANOVA is to find out whether or not a treatment effect exists.

In brief, for ANOVA, the denominator of the F-ratio is called the *error term*. The error term provides a measure of the variance due to chance. When the treatment effect is zero (H_0 is true), the error term measures same sources of variance as the numerator of the F-ratio, so the value of the F-ratio is expected to be nearly equal to 1.0.

14.5   One-way Analysis of Variance

One-way analysis of variance (ANOVA) is otherwise known as one-way classification or single-classification ANOVA. One-way ANOVA is applied to analyse the data obtained from single-factor, independent-measures research studies. Those experiments which investigate the effect of only one independent variable (or a factor), having two or more levels to which separate groups of subjects are randomly assigned, on the dependent variable are called the single-factor, independent-measures experiments.

In brief, one-way ANOVA is used to find out the effect of a single independent variable on the dependent variable. The number of applied levels or treatment conditions (k) of the independent variable determines the number of groups in the experiment, because it follows a randomised group design, that is, independent or separate groups of subjects are randomly assigned to different treatment conditions. The number of subjects in each group equals the number of independent observations in each level/treatment condition of the independent variable. Therefore, the sample size (n) of k treatment groups may be equal or unequal. The independent variable (or factor) in the experiment may have only two or more than two levels. In case of two levels, the relationship between F and t is that, $F = t^2$ or $\sqrt{F} = t$.

In one-way analysis of variance, a separate sample is taken for each of the treatment conditions. The goal of ANOVA is to help the researcher decide between the following two interpretations.

1.   There are really no differences between the populations (or treatments). The observed differences between samples are simply due to chance (sampling error).

2.   The differences between the sample means represent real differences between the populations. That is, the populations (or treatments) really do have different means, and the sample data accurately reflect these differences.

You should recognise these two interpretations as corresponding to the two hypotheses (null hypothesis and alternative hypothesis) that are part of the general hypothesis-testing procedure.

The following example will be used to introduce the statistical hypotheses for ANOVA. Suppose that a psychologist examined learning performance of the subjects under three temperature conditions 40°, 60° and 80°. Three separate samples of subjects are selected randomly, one sample for each treatment condition.

The purpose of the study is to determine whether room temperature affects learning performance. In statistical terms, we want to decide between two hypotheses: the null hypothesis (H_0), which says that temperature has no effect, and the alternative hypothesis (H_1), which states that temperature does affect learning performance. In symbols, the null hypothesis states:

$$H_0 : \mu_1 = \mu_2 = \mu_3$$

In words, the null hypothesis states that temperature has no effect on learning performance. That is, the population means for the three temperature conditions are all the same. In general, H_0 states that there is no treatment effect. Once again notice that the hypotheses are always stated in terms of population parameters, even though we use sample data to test them.

For the alternative hypothesis (H_1), we may state that:

H_1: At least one population mean is different from others. In general, H_1 states that the treatment conditions are not all the same, that is, there is a real treatment effect.

Note that we have not given any specific alternative hypothesis. This is because many different alternatives are possible, and it would be tedious to list them all. One alternative, for example, would be that the first two population means are identical, but that the third is different. Another alternative states that the last two means are the same, but that the first is different. Other alternatives might be:

$$H_1: \quad \mu_1 \neq \mu_2 \neq \mu_3 \quad \text{(all three means are different)}$$
$$H_1: \quad \mu_1 = \mu_3, \quad \text{but } \mu_2 \text{ is different}$$

It should be pointed out that a researcher typically entertains only one (or at most a few) of these alternative hypotheses. For the sake of simplicity, we will state a general alternative hypothesis rather than try to list all the possible specific alternatives.

14.5.1   Basic Terminology, Notations, Concepts and Formulae used for ANOVA

Before we introduce the notation, we will first look at some special terminology that is used for ANOVA. As noted earlier, in analysis of variance an independent variable is a *factor*. Therefore, for the experiment shown in Table 14.1, the factor is teaching method. Because this experiment has only one independent variable, it is a single-factor experiment. The next term which we need to know is *levels*. The levels in an experiment consist of the different values or categories used for the independent variable or factor. For example, in the learning experiment (Table 14.1) we are using three categories of the teaching. Therefore, the factor 'teaching method' has three levels. In other words, the individual treatment conditions that make up a factor are called levels of the factor.

Because ANOVA most often is used to examine data from more than two treatment conditions (and more than two samples), we will need a notational system to help keep track of all the individual scores and totals. To help introduce this notational system, we will use the hypothetical data from Table 14.2 along with some of the notations and statistics that will be described. The data given in Table 14.2 represent the results of an independent–measures experiment comparing learning performance under three spacing conditions of distributed practice.

Table 14.2   Hypothetical data from an experiment examining learning performance under three spacing conditions of distributed practice

	Spacing Conditions			
1	**2**	**3**	
(2 Seconds)	**(3 Seconds)**	**(5 Seconds)**	
4	5	8	
3	6	9	
4	5	10	
3	6	8	
5	7	12	
$n:5$	5	5	$N=15; n=5; k=3; kn=N$
$\Sigma X:19$	29	47	$\Sigma\Sigma X=G=95$
$\bar{X}:3.8$	5.8	9.4	$\bar{X}..=6.33$
$\Sigma X^2:75$	171	453	$\Sigma\Sigma X^2=699$

(i)   The letter k is used to identify the number of treatment conditions, that is, the number of levels of the factor. For an independent-measures study, k also specifies the number of independent or separate samples or groups. For the data in Table 14.2, there are three treatment conditions, so $k=3$.

(ii)   The number of scores in each treatment condition is identified by a lowercase letter n. For the data in Table 14.2, $n=5$ for all the treatment conditions. If the samples are of different sizes, we can identify a specific sample by using a subscript. For example, n_1 is the number of scores in treatment condition 1; n_2 is the number of scores in treatment condition 2 and so on.

(iii)   The total number of scores in the entire study is specified by a capital letter N. When all the samples are of the same size (n is constant), then $N=kn$. For the data in Table 14.2, there are $n=5$ scores in each of the $k=3$ treatments. So, $N=kn=3\times5=15$.

(iv)   The total or sum of the scores for each treatment condition is identified by the sigma (Σ) of the capital letter X, that is, ΣX. The total of scores for a specific treatment condition can be identified by adding a numerical subscript to the ΣX. For example, the total of the scores for the third treatment condition in Table 14.2 is $\Sigma X_3=47$.

(v)   The sum of all the scores in the entire research study (the grand total) is identified by G. We can compute G by adding up all N scores or by adding up the treatment totals. So, $G=\Sigma\Sigma X$. For example, the grand total for the data given in Table 14.2 is $G=\Sigma\Sigma X=95$.

(vi)   The mean or average of the scores for each treatment is identified by a bar (horizontal line) over the capital letter X, that is, $\bar{X}$. The mean of the scores for a specific treatment can be identified by adding a numerical subscript to $\bar{X}$. For example, the mean of the scores for the second treatment in Table 14.2 is $\bar{X}_2=5.8$.

(vii)   The mean or average of all the scores in the entire study (the grand mean) is identified by X bar dot dot i.e., $\bar{X}..$). For example, the grand mean for the data given in Table 14.2 is $\bar{X} = 6.33$.

(viii) The total or sum of the squares of the scores for each treatment condition is identified by the sigma (Σ) of the square of the capital letter X, that is, ΣX^2. The total of the squares of the scores for a specific treatment condition can be identified by adding a numerical subscript to the ΣX^2. For example, the total of the squares of the scores for the first treatment condition in Table 14.2 is $\Sigma X_1^2 = 75$.

(ix)   The sum of the squares of all the scores in the entire study (i.e., all N scores) is identified by sum of the sums of the squares of the scores for each treatment condition, that is, $\Sigma\Sigma X^2$. For example, the total of the squares of all N scores given in Table 14.2 is $\Sigma\Sigma X^2 = 699$.

Let us now discuss about the *concepts* that are used in the computation of ANOVA. The following are some of such *concepts*.

(i) Correction term (C).

For computing the sum of squares by the direct method a correction is needed. The correct term (C) is obtained by squaring the grand total (G or $\Sigma\Sigma X$) and then dividing it by the total number of subjects or observations in the experiment ($N = kn$). So, $C = \dfrac{(G)^2}{N} = \dfrac{(\Sigma\Sigma X)^2}{N}$. In the present example, from the data given in Table 14.2,

$$C = \frac{(G)^2}{N} = \frac{(95)^2}{15} = 601.67$$

(ii) Sum of squares (SS)

The sum of the squared deviations around the mean is called sum of squares (Σx^2) or SS in a shortened form. The total sum of squares may be divided into two additive and independent parts, such as, within-groups sum of squares (or within-treatments sum of squares) and between-groups sum of squares (or between-treatments sum of squares). These are discussed below one by one.

(a)   **Total sum of squares**. As the name implies, the total sum of squares (SS_t) is the sum of squares for the entire set of N scores in the experiment. We compute this value by using the computational formula for SS_t which reads

$$SS_t = \Sigma\Sigma X^2 - C$$

Applying this above formula to the set of data in Table 14.2, we obtain

$$SS_t = 699 - 601.67 = 97.33$$

(b)   **Within-groups sum of squares**. The within-groups (or within-treatments) sum of squares (SS_w) is the pooled sum of squares based on the variation of each group about its own mean. The within-groups sum of squares is also called error sum of squares. All the uncontrolled sources of variation are pooled in the within-groups sum of squares. We compute the SS_w by the following formula:

$$SS_w = \Sigma\left[\Sigma X^2 - \frac{(\Sigma X)^2}{n}\right]$$

$$= \left[\Sigma X_1^2 - \frac{(\Sigma X_1)^2}{n_1}\right] + \left[\Sigma X_2^2 - \frac{(\Sigma X_2)^2}{n_2}\right] + \left[\Sigma X_3^2 - \frac{(\Sigma X_3)^2}{n_3}\right]$$

Applying this formula to the set of data in Table 14.2, we obtain

$$SS_w = \left[75 - \frac{(19)^2}{5}\right] + \left[171 - \frac{(29)^2}{5}\right] + \left[453 - \frac{(47)^2}{5}\right]$$

$$= \left[75 - \frac{361}{5}\right] + \left[171 - \frac{841}{5}\right] + \left[453 - \frac{2209}{5}\right]$$

$$= \left[75 - 72.2\right] + \left[171 - 168.2\right] + \left[453 - 441.8\right]$$

$$= 2.8 + 2.8 + 11.2 = 16.8.$$

Alternatively, the SS_w can be obtained by subtraction, taking advantage of the addition theorem characterising this analysis. We know that the total sum of squares has two additive and independent components like between-groups sum of squares (SS_b) and within-groups sum of squares (SS_w). Therefore,

$$SS_t = SS_b + SS_w$$
$$\text{Hence,} \quad SS_w = SS_t - SS_b$$

That is, the SS_w can be obtained by subtracting the SS_b from the SS_t. Applying this formula to the data given in Table 14.2, we obtain

$$SS_w = 97.33 - 80.53 = 16.8$$

However, there can be no verification of the computation of the within-groups sum of squares by the subtraction method. Therefore, beginners would do well to calculate independently the within-groups sum of squares by the previous formula cited above; this formula treats within-groups sum of squares as the pooled sum of squares based on the variation of the individual observations about the mean of the particular group.

If no error or mistake is committed in the computation process, the outcome by the direct method is exactly the same as obtained by the subtraction method.

(c) **Between-groups sum of squares.**
The between-groups sum of squares (SS_b) is a measure of the variation of the group means about the combined or grand mean. If the group means do not differ among themselves at all, the sum of squares between groups will be zero. Thus, greater the variation in the group means, the larger is the sum of squares between groups. The SS_b is called true sum of squares.

The sum of the squares between the various groups can be found by taking the mean of each group, getting its deviation from the grand mean (or combined mean), squaring this deviation, and then multiplying each of these by the number of individuals (n) in each group and lastly adding these values as follows:

$$SS_b = \Sigma(\bar{X} - \bar{X}..)^2(n) = (\bar{X}_1 - \bar{X}..)^2(n_1) + (\bar{X}_2 - \bar{X}..)^2(n_2) + (\bar{X}_3 - \bar{X}..)^2(n_3)$$

Applying this formula to the set of data in Table 14.2, we obtain

$$SS_b = (3.8 - 6.33)^2(5) + (5.8 - 6.33)^2(5) + (9.4 - 6.33)^2(5)$$

$$= (-2.53)^2(5) + (-0.53)^2(5) + (3.07)^2(5)$$

$$= 6.4009 \times 5 + 0.2809 \times 5 + 9.4249 \times 5$$

$$= 32.0045 + 1.4045 + 47.1245 = 80.5335 = 80.53$$

This above method of computing between-groups sum of squares usually is awkward and cumbersome, especially when treatment/group means are not whole numbers, as it is in the case of present example Table 14.2. Therefore, we will use a computational formula for SS_b that uses the treatment totals (ΣX) instead of treatment means ($\bar{X}$). This computational formula to obtain the between-groups sum of squares is called as the *direct method*. In this method, the totals of each of the three groups (as in our example) have been squared and divided by the number of observations/subjects in each group, and then summed $\left[\Sigma \dfrac{(\Sigma X)^2}{n} \right]$. Finally, the correction term (C) has been subtracted from the sum of squares.

Thus, the *direct method* of obtaining SS_b reads as follows:

$$SS_b = \left[\Sigma \frac{(\Sigma X)^2}{n} \right] - C = \left[\frac{(\Sigma X_1)^2}{n_1} + \frac{(\Sigma X_2)^2}{n_2} + \frac{(\Sigma X_3)^2}{n_3} \right] - C$$

Applying this formula to the set of data in Table 14.2, we obtain

$$\left[\frac{(19)^2}{5} + \frac{(29)^2}{5} + \frac{(47)^2}{5} \right] - 601.67 = \left[\frac{361}{5} + \frac{841}{5} + \frac{2209}{5} \right] - 601.67$$

$$= \left[72.2 + 168.2 + 441.8 \right] - 601.67 = 682.2 - 601.67 = 80.53$$

If no error or mistake is committed while computing the SS_b, then the outcome by both the above methods will be the same.

At this point in the analysis, we have computed all three of the SS values and it is appropriate to verify our calculations by checking to see that the two components add up to the total. Using the data from Table 14.2,

$$SS_t = SS_b + SS_w$$
$$97.33 = 80.53 + 16.80$$

Thus, the sum of squares are additive.

The formula for each SS and the relationships among these three values are shown in Figure 14.2.

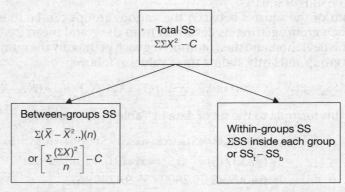

Figure 14.2   Partitioning the sum of squares (SS) for the independent-measures analysis of variance

(iii) **Degree of Freedom**

The analysis of degree of freedom (df) follows the same pattern as the analysis of SS. First, we will find df for the total set of N scores (or kn scores when n is constant in k treatments), and then we will partition this value into two additive and independent components: degrees of freedom between treatments/groups and degrees of freedom within treatment (or groups). In computing degrees of freedom, there are two important considerations to keep in mind.

(i)   Each df value is associated with a specific SS value.

(ii)   Normally, the value of df is obtained by counting the number of items that were used to calculate SS and then subtracting 1 from it. For example, if you compute SS for a set of n scores, then df = $n-1$.

With this in mind, we will examine the degrees of freedom for each part of the analysis.

(a)   **Total degrees of freedom (df$_t$).** The df$_t$ is associated with SS$_t$. To find the df associated with SS$_t$, you must first recall that this SS value measures variability for the entire set of N scores. Therefore, this df value will be df$_t$ = $N-1$. One degree of freedom is lost by taking deviations about the grand mean.

For the data in Table 14.2, the total number of scores is $N=15$, so the total degrees of freedom would be df$_t$ = $N-1 = 15-1 = 14$.

(b)   **Within-groups degrees of freedom (df$_w$).** The df$_w$ is associated with the SS$_w$. To find the df associated with SS$_w$, we must look at how this SS value is computed. Remember, we first find SS inside of each of the treatment (or groups) and then add these values together to get the SS$_w$. Each of the treatment SS value measures variability for the n scores in the treatment/group, so each SS will have df = $n-1$. When all these individual treatment values are added together, we obtain df$_w$ = $\Sigma(n-1)$ = Σdf in each treatment. In each group or treatment, one df is lost by taking deviations from the group mean.

For the data in Table 14.2, each treatment has $n=5$ scores. This means there are $n-1 = 5-1 = 4$ degrees of freedom inside each treatment. Because there are three different treatment conditions having same size (n constant) of subjects or observations, this gives a total of 12 [df = $k (n-1)$] for the within-treatments degrees of freedom. Notice that this formula for df simply adds up the number of scores in each treatment (the n values) and subtract 1 for each treatment. If these two stages are done separately, you obtain, df$_w$ = $N-k$. (Adding up all the n values gives N. If you subtract 1 for each treatment, then altogether you have subtracted k because there are k treatments). For the data in Table 14.2, $N=15$ and $k=3$, so, df$_w$ = $15-3 = 12$.

(c)   **Between-groups degrees of freedom (df$_b$).** The df$_b$ is associated with the SS$_b$. The df associated with SS$_b$ can be found by considering the SS formula. This SS formula measures the variability for the set of treatment totals (ΣX). To find df$_b$, simply count the number of treatment totals (ΣX) and subtract 1. Because the number of treatments is specified by the letter k, the formula for df is df$_b$ = $k-1$. We have k means and one df is lost by expressing the group means as deviations from the grand mean.

For the data in Table 14.2, there are three treatment conditions ($k=3$), so the between-treatments degrees of freedom are computed as follows:

$$df_b = k-1 = 3-1 = 2$$

Note that the two parts we obtained from this analysis of degrees of freedom add up to equal the total degrees of freedom. In other words, the degrees of freedom are additive:

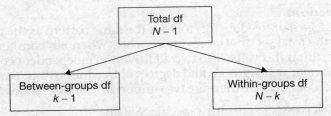

Figure 14.3   Partitioning degrees of freedom (df) for the independent-measures analysis of variance

$$df_t = df_b + df_w \quad \text{or} \quad 14 = 2 + 12$$

The complete analysis of degrees of freedom is shown in Figure 14.3.

(iv) **Mean squares or variance estimates**.

In the terminology of the analysis of variance (ANOVA), the variance is called the mean square or simply MS. In other words, in ANOVA, it is customary to use the term mean square (MS) in place of the term variance. As discussed earlier, variance is defined as the mean of the squared deviations. In the same way that we use SS to stand for the sum of the squared deviations, we now will use MS to stand for the mean of the squared deviations.

The mean squares are otherwise known as variance estimates (VE). The MS is obtained by dividing the SS by the df. Thus, $MS = Variance = \dfrac{SS}{df}$. Since there are three types of SS (i.e., total SS, within-groups SS and between-groups SS) having their own associated degrees of freedom, there would be three types of MS or variance estimates, like total variance estimate or $MS_t(s_t^2)$, within-groups variance estimate or $MS_w(s_w^2)$ and between-groups variance estimate or $MS_b(s_b^2)$. These three types of MS or variance estimates are computed below with reference to the data given in Table 14.2

$$\text{Total VE / MS} \quad (s_t^2) = \frac{SS_t}{df_t} = \frac{97.33}{14} = 6.95$$

$$\text{Within-groups VE / MS} \quad (s_w^2) = \frac{SS_w}{df_w} = \frac{16.80}{12} = 1.40$$

$$\text{Between-groups VE / MS} \quad (s_b^2) = \frac{SS_b}{df_b} = \frac{80.53}{2} = 40.265$$

Thus, we notice that the sum of squares (SS) and degrees of freedom (df) are additive. The variance estimates, which are sometimes spoken of as the mean squares (MS), are not additive.

(v) **The F-ratio**.

We have now the variance estimates (or MS) for the between-groups and within-groups. The between-group variance is called the true variance, whereas the within-group variance is known as the error variance. The F-ratio simply compares these two variances:

$$F = \frac{MS_b}{MS_w} = \frac{s_b^2}{s_w^2}. \text{ For the data given in Table 14.2, the F-ratio is:}$$

$$F = \frac{40.265}{1.40} = 28.76$$

(vi) **The ANOVA summary table.**

It is useful to organise the results of the analysis in one table called an ANOVA summary table. The table shows the source of variation (between groups, within groups, and total variation), SS, df, MS and F, in a serial order. For the previous computations, the ANOVA summary table is constructed as follows:

Source of Variation	SS	df	MS	F
Between Groups	80.53	2	40.265	28.76**
Within Groups	16.80	12	1.40	
Total	97.33	14		

Note:** $p < 0.01$.

(vii) **Test of significance.**

The last step in the analysis is to evaluate the obtained F value. For this example, the obtained value of $F = 28.76$ indicates that the numerator of the F-ratio is substantially bigger than the denominator. In other words, the obtained F value indicates that the differences between treatments or groups are more than 28 times bigger than what would be expected by chance. Stated in terms of the experimental variables, it appears that differential spacing of the distributed practice does have an effect on learning performance. However, to properly evaluate the obtained F value, we must consult the critical values of F given in Table E in the appendix for 2 and 12 degrees of freedom. First, we move along the top row, where degrees of freedom for greater mean square (or for numerator mean square) are given and pause at 2. Then, we proceed downwards in column 2 until we find the row entry corresponding to df 12. The values of F significant at 5% level are given in light-face type (or roman type), and those significant at 1% level are given in bold-face type (or dark-face type). The critical value of F corresponding to 2 and 12 df at $\alpha = 0.01$ is 6.93. Since our obtained value of $F = 28.76$ far exceeds the critical or tabled value of 6.93, we reject the null hypothesis (H_0), and accept the alternative hypothesis (H_1). The overall F indicates that the means of the three groups do not fall on a straight line with zero slope. Hence, the null hypothesis that the three groups are random samples from a common normal population is rejected. On the basis of the results of the experiment, we may conclude that the three differential spacing of the distributed practice produced significant differences in the three groups. As F is an overall index, further tests on means have to be carried to compare the pairs of means. This aspect will be discussed in Chapter 19 (available on the companion website).

14.5.2   Summary of Steps

In summary, to test the significance of the difference between k means using the analysis of variance, the following steps are involved:

1. **Presentation** of the given data in a table having all its notations, like k, n, kn, N, etc.
2. **Computation** of a variety of summary statistics, like, treatment totals (ΣX): $\Sigma X_1, \Sigma X_2$, and ΣX_3; grand total ($\Sigma\Sigma X = G$); treatment means ($\bar{X}$): $\bar{X}_1, \bar{X}_2$ and $\bar{X}_3$; and grand mean ($\bar{X}..$); sum of the squares of treatment scores (ΣX^2): $\Sigma X_1^2, \Sigma X_2^2$, and ΣX_3^2, and sum of the sums of squares ($\Sigma\Sigma X^2$) of treatment scores, etc.

3. **Statement** of the null hypothesis (H_0) and alternative hypothesis (H_1), and selection of an alpha level.

4. **Calculation of the correction term (*C*)** by appropriate formula.

5. **Analysis of sum of squares (SS)**. Computation of the total sum of squares (SS_t) and partitioning the total SS into two additive and independent components—a within-groups (SS_w) and a between-groups (SS_b) sum of squares using the appropriate computation formulae.

6. **Determination of the degrees of freedom (df)**. Determining the total degrees of freedom (df_t) and partitioning the total df into two additive and independent components—within-groups df (df_w) and between-groups df (df_b), using the appropriate computation formulae.

7. **Calculation of mean squares (MS)**. Computing the total mean squares (MS_t), within-groups mean squares (MS_w) and between-groups means squares (MS_b) or variance estimates (s_t^2, s_w^2, s_b^2, respectively) by dividing respectively the total SS, within-groups SS and between-groups SS by their corresponding, associated number of degrees of freedom (i.e., df_t, df_w and df_b, respectively).

8. **Calculation of *F*.** Computing the *F*-ratio by dividing the between-groups mean square (MS_b) or variance estimates (s_b^2) by the within-groups mean squares (MS_w) or variance estimates (s_w^2) as follows:

$$F = \frac{MS_b}{MS_w} \quad \text{or} \quad F = \frac{s_b^2}{s_w^2}$$

9. **Preparation** of the analysis of variance summary table containing source of variation, SS, df, MS and *F*, as given in the example.

10. **Test of significance** of the obtained *F* value with reference to the critical values of *F* (given in Table E in the appendix) with a given df_b and df_w. If the probability of obtaining the observed *F* value is small, say, less than 0.05 or 0.01, under the null hypothesis, then reject that hypothesis (H_0) and accept the alternative hypothesis (H_1) showing the significant treatment effect.

One important point to remember is that the obtained value of *F*, which is less than 1 ($F<1$), indicates nothing but sampling variation. It is only larger values of *F* that suggest treatment effects. Therefore, we refer to the critical values of F table only when the *F*-ratio is greater than 1. If the between-groups MS is smaller than the within-groups MS, then *F* value will be less than 1. In the analysis of variance summary table, we simply ignore the obtained *F* values that are less than 1, and there is no need to refer to the *F* table, as the data offer no evidence against the null hypothesis (H_0).

14.5.3   Illustrative Examples: One-way ANOVA

In the previous section, we have already discussed about various notations and concepts used in ANOVA through an example taking hypothetical data. Now, we will demonstrate the complete computational process (step-wise) of one-way ANOVA through some of the following illustrative examples.

Example 14.1 An investigator is interested in exploring the most effective method of instruction in the classroom. He decides to try three methods: Lecture (1); Seminar (2) and Discussion (3). He randomly selects 5 subjects for each of the three groups from the class of 10th grade students.

After 3 months of instructions, an achievement test is administered to the three groups. The achievement scores are given below. Test whether the three group means are different or not.

Subjects	1	2	3	4	5
Lecture (1)	8	10	11	11	12
Seminar (2)	11	13	13	15	16
Discussion (3)	5	5	8	9	10

Solution

For the solution of the problem the following steps should be followed:

1. **The given data are entered in Table 14.3 having all its notations.**
2. **Computation of a variety of summary statistics for the data in Table 14.3.** Specifically, $n=5$; $k=3$; $kn=N=3\times5=15$; $\Sigma X_1=52$, $\Sigma X_2=68$, $\Sigma X_3=37$; $\Sigma\Sigma X=G=157$; $\bar{X}_1=10.4$, $\bar{X}_2=13.6$, $\bar{X}_3=7.4$, $\bar{X}..=10.47$; $\Sigma X_1^2=550$, $\Sigma X_2^2=940$, $\Sigma X_3^2=295$, $\Sigma\Sigma X^2=1785$.
3. **Statement of the null hypothesis (H_0) and alternative hypothesis (H_1).** The H_0 contends that there is no significant difference among the group/treatment means; any observed difference being due to mere chance or sampling error. The H_1, on the contrary, states that there is a real or genuine difference between the treatment means. The H_0 and H_1 are stated as follows:

$$H_0: \quad \mu_1=\mu_2=\mu_3 \text{ (or } \bar{X}_1=\bar{X}_2=\bar{X}_3)$$
$$H_1: \quad \mu_1\neq\mu_2\neq\mu_3 \text{ (or } \bar{X}_1\neq\bar{X}_2\neq\bar{X}_3)$$

Table 14.3 Achievement test scores of subjects treated by three methods of instructions

Subjects	Method			
	Lecture	Seminar	Discussion	
	(1)	(2)	(3)	
1	8	11	5	
2	10	13	5	
3	11	13	8	
4	11	15	9	
5	12	16	10	
n:	5	5	5	$N=15$; $n=5$; $k=3$; $kn=N$
ΣX:	52	68	37	$\Sigma\Sigma X=G=157$
$\bar{X}$:	10.4	13.6	7.4	$\bar{X}..=10.47$
ΣX^2:	550	940	295	$\Sigma\Sigma X^2=1785$

4. **Calculation of the correction term (C).**

$$C = \frac{(\Sigma\Sigma X)^2}{N} = \frac{(G)^2}{N} = \frac{(157)^2}{15} = \frac{24649}{15} = 1643.27$$

5. **Computation of the sum of squares (SS).**

(a) Total SS $= \Sigma\Sigma X^2 - C = 1785 - 1643.27 = 141.73$

(b) Between-groups SS $= \Sigma\dfrac{(\Sigma X)^2}{n} - C$

$$= \left[\frac{(\Sigma X_1)^2}{n_1} + \frac{(\Sigma X_2)^2}{n_2} + \frac{(\Sigma X_3)^2}{n_3}\right] - C$$

$$= \left[\frac{(52)^2}{5} + \frac{(68)^2}{5} + \frac{(37)^2}{5}\right] - 1643.27$$

$$= \left[\frac{2704}{5} + \frac{4324}{5} + \frac{369}{5}\right] - 1643.27$$

$$= [540.8 + 924.8 + 273.8] - 1643.27$$

$$= 1739.4 - 1643.27 = 96.13.$$

(c) Within-groups SS $=$ Total SS $-$ Between-groups SS
$$= 141.73 - 96.13 = 45.60$$

Alternatively, within-groups SS can also be computed by the following formula, which is rather a tedious method:

$$\text{Within-groups SS} = \Sigma\left[\Sigma X^2 - \frac{(\Sigma X)^2}{n}\right]$$

$$= \Sigma\left[\Sigma X_1^2 - \frac{(\Sigma X_1)^2}{n_1}\right] + \left[\Sigma X_2^2 - \frac{(\Sigma X_2)^2}{n_2}\right] + \left[\Sigma X_3^2 - \frac{(\Sigma X_3)^2}{n_3}\right]$$

$$= \left[550 - \frac{(52)^2}{5}\right] + \left[940 - \frac{(68)^2}{5}\right] + \left[295 - \frac{(37)^2}{5}\right]$$

$$= [550 - 540.8] + [940 - 924.8] + [295 - 273.8]$$

$$= 9.2 + 15.2 + 21.2 = 45.6$$

6. **Determination of the degrees of freedom (df).** Since there are three types of sum of squares, there are three types of degrees of freedom (df).

(a) Total df $= N-1$ or $kn-1$
$$= 15-1 = 14 \text{ or } 3\times5-1 = 14.$$
(b) Between-groups df $= k-1 = 3-1 = 2$
(c) Within-groups df $= N-k$ or $k(n-1)$
$$= 15-3 = 12 \text{ or } 3(5-1) = 3\times4 = 12$$

7. **Computation of mean squares (MS).** Like sum of squares, mean squares are of three types, and each MS is determined by dividing the corresponding SS by its associated df as follows:

(a) Total MS $= \dfrac{\text{Total SS}}{\text{Total df}} = \dfrac{141.73}{14} = 10.12$

Table 14.4   Summary of one-way analysis of variance

Source of Variation	SS	df	MS	F
Between-groups	96.13	2	48.065	12.65**
Within-groups (Error)	45.60	12	3.80	
Total	141.73	14		

*Note:*** $p < 0.01$.

(b)   Between-groups MS $= \dfrac{\text{Between-groups SS}}{\text{Between-groups df}} = \dfrac{96.13}{2} = 48.065$

(c)   Within-groups MS $= \dfrac{\text{Within-groups SS}}{\text{Within-groups df}} = \dfrac{45.60}{12} = 3.80$

8. **Computation of *F*-ratio.** The test statistic of ANOVA is called an *F*-ratio which can be calculated as follows:

$$F = \frac{\text{Between-groups MS}}{\text{Within-groups MS}} = \frac{48.065}{3.80} = 12.65$$

9. **Preparation of ANOVA summary table.** It is useful to organise the results of the analysis in one table called an ANOVA summary table as in the Table 14.4.

10. **Test of significance.** Consulting Table E in the appendix with df=2/12, the critical value of *F* at 0.05 level is 3.88 and at 0.01 level is 6.93. Since the obtained *F*-ratio is 12.65, which is greater than both the tabled values of *F*, it is significant at 0.01 level. $\therefore p < 0.01$. This indicates that the three groups of subjects are different in their mean performances in 99% of cases. The null hypothesis (H_0) is rejected and the alternative hypothesis (H_1) is accepted.

On the basis of the findings of the analysis of data, we may safely conclude that the three methods of instruction produced significant differences in the three groups. In other words, the three group means are significantly different, which shows the effectiveness of the method of instruction. The three groups of subjects are not the random samples from a common normal population.

Example 14.2 The following are the number of nonsense syllables recalled by four groups of subjects (having unequal sample size, *n*) using four different methods of presentation. Test whether different methods of presentation have differential effects on the recall ability of the subjects.

I: 5, 7, 6, 3, 9, 7, 4, 2
II: 9, 11, 8, 7, 7
III: 8, 6, 9, 5, 7, 4, 4
IV: 1, 3, 4, 5, 1, 4

Solution

The steps to be followed are the following:

1. **The given data are presented in Table 14.5 along with its notations.**

2. **Computation of a variety of summary statistics for the given data in Table 14.5.** Specifically, $k=4$, $N=(n_1+n_2+n_3+n_4)=8+5+7+6=26$. Treatment totals $(\Sigma X) : \Sigma X_1 = 43, \Sigma X_2 = 42, \Sigma X_3 = 43, \Sigma X_4 = 18$, and grand total $(\Sigma\Sigma X = G) = 146$; treatment means $(\bar{X}) : \bar{X}_1 = 5.38, \bar{X}_2 = 8.40, \bar{X}_3 = 6.14, \bar{X}_4 = 3.00$ and grand mean $(\bar{X}..) : \Sigma\Sigma X / N = 5.62$; sum of the squares of treatment scores $(\Sigma X^2) : \Sigma X_1^2 = 269, \Sigma X_2^2 = 364; \Sigma X_3^2 = 287, \Sigma X_4^2 = 68$, and sum of the sums of squares of treatment scores $(\Sigma\Sigma X^2) = 988$.

3. **Statement of the null hypothesis (H_0) and alternative hypothesis (H_1) are as follows:**

$$H_0: \quad \mu_1 = \mu_2 = \mu_3 = \mu_4 \ (\text{or } \bar{X}_1 = \bar{X}_2 = \bar{X}_3 = \bar{X}_4)$$
$$H_1: \quad \mu_1 \neq \mu_2 \neq \mu_3 \neq \mu_4 \ (\text{or } \bar{X}_1 \neq \bar{X}_2 \neq \bar{X}_3 \neq \bar{X}_4)$$

4. **Calculation of the correction term (C).**

$$C = \frac{(\Sigma\Sigma X)^2}{N} = \frac{(G)^2}{N} = \frac{(146)^2}{26} = \frac{21316}{26} = 819.85$$

5. **Computation of sum of squares (SS).**

   (a) Total SS $= \Sigma\Sigma X^2 - C = 988 - 819.85 = 168.15$

Table 14.5 Recall scores of four groups of subjects under four different methods of presentation

	Method				
	I	**II**	**III**	**IV**	
	5	9	8	1	
	7	11	6	3	
	6	8	9	4	
	3	7	5	5	
	9	7	7	1	
	7		4	4	
	4		4		
	2				
n:	8	5	7	6	$N=26; k=4$
ΣX:	43	42	43	18	$\Sigma\Sigma X = G = 146$
$\bar{X}$:	5.38	8.40	6.14	3.00	$\bar{X}.. = 5.62$
ΣX^2:	269	364	287	68	$\Sigma\Sigma X^2 = 988$

(b) Between-groups SS

$$= \left[\frac{(\Sigma X_1)^2}{n_1} + \frac{(\Sigma X_2)^2}{n_2} + \frac{(\Sigma X_3)^2}{n_3} + \frac{(\Sigma X_4)^2}{n_4} \right] - C$$

$$= \left[\frac{(43)^2}{8} + \frac{(42)^2}{5} + \frac{(43)^2}{7} + \frac{(18)^2}{6} \right] - 819.65$$

$$= \left[\frac{1849}{8} + \frac{1764}{5} + \frac{1849}{7} + \frac{324}{6} \right] - 819.65$$

$$= \left[231.13 + 352.80 + 264.14 + 54.00 \right] - 819.65$$

$$= 902.07 - 819.65 = 82.22.$$

(c) Within-groups SS = Total SS – Between-groups SS
$$= 168.15 - 82.22 = 85.93$$

Alternative method for within-groups SS:

Within-groups SS $= \left[\Sigma X_1^2 - \frac{(\Sigma X_1)^2}{n_1} \right] + \left[\Sigma X_2^2 - \frac{(\Sigma X_2)^2}{n_2} \right] + \left[\Sigma X_3^2 - \frac{(\Sigma X_3)^2}{n_3} \right] + \left[\Sigma X_4^2 - \frac{(\Sigma X_4)^2}{n_4} \right]$

$$= \left[269 - \frac{(43)^2}{8} \right] + \left[364 - \frac{(42)^2}{5} \right] + \left[287 - \frac{(43)^2}{7} \right] + \left[68 - \frac{(18)^2}{6} \right]$$

$$= [269 - 231.13] + [364 - 352.80] + [287 - 264.14] + [68 - 54]$$

$$= 37.87 + 11.2 + 22.86 + 14.0 = 85.93$$

6. **Determination of degrees of freedom (df).**

(a) Total df $= N - 1 = 26 - 1 = 25$

(b) Between-groups df $= k - 1 = 4 - 1 = 3$

(c) Within-groups df $= N - k = 26 - 4 = 22$

7. **Computation of mean squares (MS).**

(a) Total MS $= \dfrac{\text{Total SS}}{\text{Total df}} = \dfrac{168.15}{25} = 6.73$

(b) Between-groups MS $= \dfrac{\text{Between-groups SS}}{\text{Between-groups df}} = \dfrac{82.22}{3} = 27.41$

(c) Within-groups MS $= \dfrac{\text{Within-groups SS}}{\text{Within-groups df}} = \dfrac{85.93}{22} = 3.91$

8. **Computation of F-ratio**

$$F = \frac{\text{Between-groups MS}}{\text{Within-groups MS}} = \frac{27.41}{3.91} = 7.01$$

9. **Preparation of ANOVA summary table.** The results of analysis are summarised in Table 14.6 .

10. **Test of significance.** Consulting Table E in the appendix with df=3 associated with the numerator and df=22 with the denominator, we find that the value of F required for significance at the 0.05 level is 3.05, and at the 0.01 level is 4.82. Since the obtained F value

Table 14.6   Summary of one-way ANOVA

Source of Variation	SS	df	MS	F
Between-groups	82.22	3	27.41	7.01**
Within-groups (error)	85.93	22	3.91	
Total	168.15	25		

*Note:*** $p < 0.01$.

of 7.01 is greater than both the critical values, it is significant at 0.01 level of significance. Therefore, $p < 0.01$. This indicates that the four groups are significantly different in their mean performance. Hence, the H_0 is rejected and H_1 is accepted. The overall significance of F indicates that the means of the four groups do not fall on a straight line with zero slope. Hence, the null hypothesis that the four groups are random samples from a common normal population is rejected.

On the basis of the results of the analysis, we can conclude that the four methods of presentation produced significant differences in the four groups. In other words, the method of presentation has significantly affected the mean recall scores of four groups of subjects.

Example 14.3 A comparative psychologist conducts a research study to compare learning performance of two species, Vervet and Rhesus, monkeys. The following data show the number of trials taken by the animals to have a perfect learning. Test the significance of the difference between the sample means and prove that $F = t^2$.

$$\text{Vervet:} \quad 3, \quad 4, \quad 5, \quad 5, \quad 6, \quad 6, \quad 7, \quad 8$$
$$\text{Rhesus:} \quad 9, \quad 6, \quad 7, \quad 7, \quad 6, \quad 8, \quad 8, \quad 9$$

Solution

1. **The given data are presented in Table 14.7 along with its notations.**
2. **Computation of a variety of summary statistics for the given data in Table 14.7.** Specifically, $k=2$, $n=8$, $kn=N=16$; group totals $(\Sigma X): \Sigma X_1 = 44, \Sigma X_2 = 60$, $\bar{X}_1 = 5.5, \bar{X}_2 = 7.5$ and grand mean $(\bar{X}..) = 6.5$; sum of the squares of group scores $(\Sigma X^2): \Sigma X_1^2 = 260, \Sigma X_2^2 = 460$ and sum of the sums of squares of group scores $(\Sigma\Sigma X^2) = 720$.
3. **Statement of H_0 and H_1, as follows:**

$$H_0: \quad \mu_1 = \mu_2 \text{ (or } \bar{X}_1 = \bar{X}_2)$$
$$H_1: \quad \mu_1 \neq \mu_2 \text{ (or } \bar{X}_1 \neq \bar{X}_2)$$

4. **Calculation of the correction term (C).**

$$C = \frac{(\Sigma\Sigma X)^2}{N} = \frac{(G)^2}{N} = \frac{(104)^2}{16} = \frac{10816}{16} = 676.0$$

5. **Computation of the sum of squares (SS).**

   (a)   Totals $SS = \Sigma\Sigma X^2 - C = 720.0 - 676.0 = 44.0$

Table 14.7   Number of trials taken by two species of monkeys to have perfect learning

	Vervet	Rhesus	
	3	9	
	4	6	
	5	7	
	5	7	
	6	6	
	6	8	
	7	8	
	8	9	
n:	8	8	$N=16, n=8, k=2,$ $kn=2 \times 8=16$
ΣX:	44	60	$\Sigma \Sigma X = G = 104$
$\bar{X}$:	5.5	7.5	$\bar{X}.. = 6.5$
ΣX^2:	260	460	$\Sigma \Sigma X^2 = 720$

(b)   Between-groups SS $= \Sigma \dfrac{(\Sigma X)^2}{n} - C = \left[\dfrac{(\Sigma X_1)^2}{n_1} + \dfrac{(\Sigma X_2)^2}{n_2} \right] - C$

$$= \left[\frac{(44)^2}{8} + \frac{(60)^2}{8} \right] - 676.0 = \left[\frac{1936}{8} + \frac{3600}{8} \right] - 676.0$$

$$= \left[242.0 + 450.0 \right] - 676.0 = 692.0 - 676.0 = 16.0$$

(c)   Within-groups SS $= SS_t - SS_b = 44.0 - 16.0 = 28.0$

Alternative method for within-groups SS $= \Sigma \left[\Sigma X^2 - \dfrac{(\Sigma X)^2}{n} \right]$

$$= \left[\Sigma X_1^2 - \frac{(\Sigma X_1)^2}{n_1} \right] + \left[\Sigma X_2^2 - \frac{(\Sigma X_2)^2}{n_2} \right]$$

$$= \left[260 - \frac{(44)^2}{8} \right] + \left[460 - \frac{(60)^2}{8} \right]$$

$$= [260 - 242.0] + [460 - 450.0] = 18.0 + 10.0 = 28.0$$

6. **Determination of the degrees of freedom (df).**

(a)   Total df $= N-1 = 16-1 = 15$
or $kn-1 = 2 \times 8-1 = 16-1 = 15$

  (b) Between-groups df $= k-1 = 2-1 = 1$
  (c) Within-groups df $= N-k = 16-2 = 14$
       or $k(n-1) = 2(8-1) = 2 \times 7 = 14$

7. **Computation of mean squares (MS).**

  (a) Total MS $= \dfrac{\text{Total SS}}{\text{Total df}} = \dfrac{44}{15} = 2.93$

  (b) Between-groups MS $= \dfrac{\text{Between-groups SS}}{\text{Between-groups df}} = \dfrac{16}{1} = 16.0$

  (c) Within-groups MS $= \dfrac{\text{Within-groups SS}}{\text{Within-groups df}} = \dfrac{28}{14} = 2.0$

8. **Computation of F-ratio.**

$$F = \frac{\text{Between-groups MS}}{\text{Within-groups MS}} = \frac{16.0}{2.0} = 8.0$$

9. **Preparation of ANOVA summary table as given in Table 14.8.**

10. **Test of significance.** Consulting Table E in the appendix with df $=1/14$, the critical F value at 0.05 level is 4.60 and at 0.01 level is 8.86. Since the obtained value of $F = 8.0$ is greater than 4.60 but less than 8.86, it is significant at 0.05 level of significance but not at 0.01 level. Hence, we conclude that the mean difference is significant at 0.05 level. Therefore, $p < 0.05$. This indicates that the two group means are significantly different from each other in 95% of cases. So, the H_0 is rejected and H_1 is accepted.

The second part of the given Example 14.3 is to prove that $F = t^2$. In order to prove this, we have to compute t-ratio from the given data. We shall use the following formula for t, the formula for small samples:

$$t = \frac{\bar{X}_1 - \bar{X}_2}{\sqrt{\dfrac{\Sigma x_1^2 + \Sigma x_2^2}{(N_1 + N_2) - 2}\left(\dfrac{1}{N_1} + \dfrac{1}{N_2}\right)}}$$

First, we should find out Σx_1^2 and Σx_2^2 as follows:

$$\Sigma x_1^2 = \Sigma X_1^2 - \frac{(\Sigma X_1)^2}{n_1} = 260 - \frac{(44)^2}{8} = 260 - \frac{1936}{8}$$

$$= 260 - 242 = 18.0$$

Table 14.8　Summary of one-way ANOVA

Source of Variation	SS	df	MS	F
Between-groups	16.0	1	16.0	8.0*
Within-groups (Error)	28.0	14	2.0	
Total	44.0	15		

Note:* $p < 0.05$.

$$\Sigma x_2^2 = \Sigma X_2^2 - \frac{(\Sigma X_2)^2}{n_2} = 460 - \frac{(60)^2}{8} = 460 - \frac{3600}{8}$$

$$= 460 - 450 = 10.0$$

$$t = \frac{5.5 - 7.5}{\sqrt{\frac{18 + 10}{(8 + 8) - 2}\left(\frac{1}{8} + \frac{1}{8}\right)}}$$

$$= \frac{-2.0}{\sqrt{\frac{28}{14}\left(\frac{2}{8}\right)}} = \frac{-2.0}{\sqrt{2 \times \frac{1}{4}}} = \frac{-2.0}{\sqrt{\frac{1}{2}}} = \frac{-2.0}{\sqrt{.5}}$$

$$= -\frac{2.0}{0.707} = -2.829 = -2.83$$

$$\therefore t = -2.83; \quad t^2 = (-2.83)^2 = 8.0089 = 8.0$$

$$F = 8.00; \quad \sqrt{F} = \sqrt{8.0} = 2.828 = 2.83$$

Thus, $F = t^2$ or $\sqrt{F} = t$ (Proved)

The t-ratio may be positive or negative, but F-ratio is always positive.

With regard to the significance of the obtained t-ratio, we can say that since the obtained F-ratio is significant at 0.05 level, the corresponding t-ratio must be significant at 0.05 level of significance. To verify this, we may test the significance of the obtained t-ratio by taking the degrees of freedom and consulting the table containing the critical values of t.

df $= N_1 + N_2 - 2 = (8 + 8) - 2 = 16 - 2 = 14$. Consulting Table C in the appendix with df$=14$, the critical value of t at 0.05 level is 2.145, and at 0.01 level is 2.977. Since the obtained value of $t = 2.83$ is greater than 2.145 but less than 2.977, it is significant at 0.05 level of significance. Therefore, $p < 0.05$. Both techniques (F and t) lead to the same conclusion. It may be noted that when df for 'between groups'$=1$, $\sqrt{F} = t$ or, putting it the other way around, $t^2 = F$.

14.5.4 Strength of Association

The significant F-ratio indicates that the observed differences between the treatment means are not likely to arise by chance. However, it does not indicate anything about the strength of the treatment effect. The statistic called *Omega square* (ω^2) is a measure of the strength of treatment effect. It gives us the proportion of the total variability in a set of scores that can be accounted for by the treatments. That is, what portion of the variance in the scores can be accounted for by the differences in the treatment groups. The formula for the strength of association is:

$$\omega^2 = \frac{SS_b - (k-1)MS_w}{SS_t + MS_w}$$

where $\omega^2 =$ Omega square

$SS_b =$ Sum of squares between groups
$k =$ number of treatment groups
$MS_w =$ Mean squares within groups
$SS_t =$ Sum of squares total.

Let us now compute the strength of treatment effects in our illustrative Example 14.1. The values of SS_b, SS_t and MS_w have been obtained from Table 14.4. The steps in computing ω^2 are given below:

$$SS_b = 96.13; \quad SS_t = 141.73; \quad MS_w = 3.80; \quad k = 3$$

$$\therefore \quad \omega^2 = \frac{96.13 - (3-1)(3.80)}{141.73 + 3.80} = \frac{96.13 - 2 \times 3.80}{145.53}$$

$$= \frac{96.13 - 7.60}{145.53} = \frac{88.53}{145.53} = 0.608 = 0.61$$

Thus, approximately 61% of the variance in the dependent variable is accounted for by the difference in the method of instruction. In other words, there is fairly a strong relationship between methods of instruction (independent variable) and achievement scores (dependent variable) of the subjects.

There is an *alternative* formula to find out the strength of the relation between independent and dependent variables. This formula reads as:

$$\eta_{y.x}^2 = \frac{SS_b}{SS_t} \quad \text{or} \quad 1 - \frac{SS_w}{SS_t}$$

The symbol η is the Greek letter eta and SS denotes sum of squares. This statistic is known as the correlation ratio. It may be interpreted as a simple proportion in the same way that r^2 is interpreted as a proportion. It is a measure of the strength of association between the dependent and independent variables involved in the experiment.

By referring to Table 14.4, we found that $SS_b = 96.13$; $SS_w = 45.60$ and $SS_t = 141.73$. Let us now compute the strength of association or $\eta_{y.x}^2$ (eta square) as follows:

$$\eta_{y.x}^2 = \frac{SS_b}{SS_t} = \frac{96.13}{141.73} = 0.678 = 0.68$$

$$\text{or} \quad \eta_{y.x}^2 = 1 - \frac{SS_w}{SS_t} = 1 - \frac{45.60}{141.73} = 1 - 0.32 = 0.68$$

The obtained correlation ratio or $\eta_{y.x}^2$ is 0.68. Thus, 68% of the variation in the data can be attributed to the independent variable. If we compare omega square (ω^2) and eta square (η^2), the eta square is little higher than omega square.

To test whether a correlation ratio is significantly different from 0, we may use the F-ratio, the formula reads as:

$$F = \frac{\eta_{y.x}^2 / (k-1)}{(1 - \eta_{y.x}^2) / (N-k)}$$

where

$\eta_{y.x}^2$ = the obtained correlation ratio
k = Number of treatment groups
N = Total number of observations.

Referring to Table 14.4, $k = 3$ and $N = 15$.

$$\text{Thus,} \quad F = \frac{0.68 / (3-1)}{(1-.68) / (15-3)} = \frac{0.68 / 2}{0.32 / 12} = \frac{0.34}{0.027} = 12.59$$

So, the F-ratio used in testing the significance of this correlation ratio is 12.59. This is the same F-ratio, within the rounding of decimals, as that previously obtained in Table 14.4. The analysis of variance and the correlation-ratio approach are equivalent procedures and lead to the same result.

14.6 Two-way Analysis of Variance

Two-way analysis of variance is otherwise known as a two-way classification or two-factor analysis of variance. When a research study involves more than one factor, it is called a factorial design. The simplest version of a factorial design is the two-factor ANOVA. In this section, specifically we will examine analysis of variance as it applies to research studies with exactly two factors. In addition, we will limit our discussion to studies that use a separate sample for each treatment condition, that is, independent-measures design. Finally, we will consider research designs only where the sample size (n) is the same for all treatment conditions. In the terminology of ANOVA, this section will examine *two-factor, independent measures, equal n design*. In other words, those experiments which investigate simultaneously the effects of two independent variables (or factors), each having two or more levels to which separate groups of subjects are randomly assigned, on the dependent variable are called the two-factor experiments. The technique used to analyse the data of such experiments are called two-way or two-factor ANOVA.

The two-way ANOVA permits the simultaneous study of two independent variables or factors, whereas the one-way ANOVA permits the study of only one independent variable or factor. Moreover, the two-way ANOVA permits the evaluation of interaction between two factors or independent variables, whereas the one-way ANOVA does not permit such evaluation. Thus, study of interaction effect is an advantage of two-way ANOVA compared to one-way ANOVA.

To illustrate two-way ANOVA, assume that an investigator wishes to study the effect of two levels of intelligence (i.e., superior intelligence and inferior intelligence) and three methods of instruction (i.e., lecture, seminar and discussion) on the achievement scores of the subjects. Traditionally, the two independent variables in a two-factor experiment are identified as factor A and factor B. In this experiment, let intelligence be factor A, having two levels, that is, superior intelligence and inferior intelligence, represented by a_1, and a_2, respectively. Similarly, the second independent variable, method of instruction is factor B having three levels, that is, lecture, seminar, and discussion methods, represented by b_1, b_2 and b_3, respectively, The total number of treatment conditions or cells in this experiment will be $A \times B = 2 \times 3 = 6$. Thus, the experiment would require 6 separate samples of same size (n), say, 5 observations and the total number of subjects will be $2 \times 3 \times 5 = 30$. The data may be arranged in a table containing two rows and three columns. The rows correspond to intelligence (factor A), and the columns to methods (factor B).

Table 14.9 shows the arrangement of data of a 2×3 factorial experiment as given in the above example.

There are six cells in Table 14.9, and each cell is a joint or combined function of both the factors A and B.

The two-factor ANOVA will test for mean differences in the experiments or research studies that are structured like the intelligence and method of instruction example in Table 14.9. For this example, the two-factor ANOVA tests for

1. Mean difference between the two intelligence levels (or between two rows)
2. Mean differences between the three method levels (or between three columns)

Table 14.9 The six treatment conditions in a two-way analysis of variance

		Method (Factor B)			Total
		b_1 (Lecture)	b_2 (Seminar)	b_3 (Discussion)	
Intelligence (Factor A)	a_1 (Superior Intelligence)	$a_1 b_1$	$a_1 b_2$	$a_1 b_3$	Σa_1
	a_2 (Inferior Intelligence)	$a_2 b_1$	$a_2 b_2$	$a_2 b_3$	Σa_2
Total		Σb_1	Σb_2	Σb_3	Grand Total

3. Any other mean differences that may result from unique combinations of a specific intelligence and a specific method level (For example, superior intelligence may be especially facilitative when the method of instruction is seminar).

Thus, the two-factor ANOVA combines three separate hypothesis tests in one analysis. Each of these three hypothesis tests will be based on its own F-ratio computed from the data. The three F-ratios will all have the same basic structure:

$$F = \frac{\text{Variance (differences) between sample means}}{\text{Variance (differences) expected by chance}}$$

As always in ANOVA, a large value for the F-ratio indicates that the sample mean differences are greater than chance. To determine whether the obtained F-ratios are significantly greater than chance, we will need to compare each F-ratio with the critical values of F given in Table E in the appendix.

14.6.1 Main Effects and Interaction Effect

The goal of a two-factorial experiment is to evaluate the main effects of each of the two factors as well as their interaction effect. Thus, as noted earlier, a two-factor or two-way ANOVA actually involves three distinct hypothesis tests. Here, we will examine these three tests in more detail.

14.6.1.1 Main Effects

The mean differences among the levels of one factor are referred to as the *main effect* of that factor. When the design of an experiment is represented in a tabular form (or as a matrix) with one factor determining the rows and the second factor determining the columns, then the mean differences between (or among) the rows would describe the main effect of one factor and the mean differences among (or between) the columns would describe the main effect of the second factor.

In our example of intelligence and methods of instruction, one purpose of the experiment is to determine whether differences in intelligence (factor A) result in differences in achievement. To answer this question, we will compare the mean achievement score for all subjects tested with superior intelligence versus the mean achievement score for all subjects tested

Table 14.10   Hypothetical mean scores for six treatment conditions in a two-way analysis of variance

		Method (Factor *B*)			
		b_1 (Lecture)	b_2 (Seminar)	b_3 (Discussion)	
Intelligence (Factor *A*)	a_1 (Superior Intelligence)	$\bar{X}_{a_1 b_1} = 55$	$\bar{X}_{a_1 b_2} = 85$	$\bar{X}_{a_1 b_3} = 70$	$\bar{X}_{a_1} = 70$
	a_2 (Inferior Intelligence)	$\bar{X}_{a_2 b_1} = 35$	$\bar{X}_{a_2 b_2} = 65$	$\bar{X}_{a_2 b_3} = 50$	$\bar{X}_{a_2} = 50$
		$\bar{X}_{b_1} = 45$	$\bar{X}_{b_2} = 75$	$\bar{X}_{b_3} = 60$	$\bar{X}_{..} = 60$ (Grand mean)

with inferior intelligence, irrespective of the methods of instruction. Note that this process evaluates the mean differences between the rows in Table 14.9.

To make this process more concrete, let us take some hypothetical data, which are given in Table 14.10. This table shows the mean achievement score for each of the treatment conditions (or cells) as well as the mean for each row (i.e., each intelligence level) and for each column (i.e., each method).

These data presented in Table 14.10 indicate that subjects in the superior intelligence condition (the top row) obtained an average score of $\bar{X}_{a_1} = 70$. This overall mean was obtained by computing the average of the three means in the top row. In contrast, inferior intelligence resulted in a mean score of $\bar{X}_{a_2} = 50$ (the overall mean for the bottom row). The difference between these two means (i.e., $\bar{X}_{a_1}$ and $\bar{X}_{a_2}$) constitutes what is called the *main effect of intelligence or the main effect of factor A.*

Similarly, the main effect of factor B (methods) is defined by the mean differences among the columns of the table (or matrix). For the data in Table 14.10, the two groups of subjects instructed with lecture method obtained an overall mean score of $\bar{X}_{b_1} = 45$. Subjects instructed with the seminar method averaged $\bar{X}_{b_2} = 75$ and subjects instructed with the discussion method achieved a mean score of $\bar{X}_{b_3} = 60$. The differences among these three means constitute the *main effect of method or the main effect of factor B.*

In a two-factor experiment, any main effects that are observed in the data must be evaluated with a hypothesis test to determine whether or not they are statistically significant effects. Unless the hypothesis test demonstrates that the main effects are significant, we must conclude that the observed mean differences are simply the result of sampling error or chance factors. So, to evaluate main effects, we will state hypotheses concerning the main effect of factor A and the main effect of factor *B*, and then calculate two separate *F*-ratios to evaluate the hypotheses.

For the example we are considering, factor *A* involves the comparison of two different levels of intelligence. The null hypothesis (H_0) would state that there is no difference between the two levels, that is, intelligence has no effect on achievement. In symbols,

$$H_0: \quad \mu_{a_1} = \mu_{a_2}$$

The alternative hypothesis (H_1) is that the two different levels of intelligence do produce different scores. In symbols,

$$H_1: \quad \mu_{a_1} \neq \mu_{a_2}$$

To evaluate these hypotheses, we will compute an F-ratio that compares the actual mean differences between the two intelligence levels versus the amount of difference that would be expected by chance or sampling error. Thus,

$$F = \frac{\text{Variance (differences) between the means for factor } A}{\text{Variance (differences) expected by chance/error}}$$

or

$$F = \frac{\text{Variance (differences) between row means}}{\text{Variance (differences) expected by chance/error}}$$

Similarly, factor B involves the comparison of the three different methods of instruction. The null hypothesis (H_0) states that overall there are no differences in mean achievement scores among the three methods of instruction. In symbols,

$$H_0: \quad \mu_{b_1} = \mu_{b_2} = \mu_{b_3}$$

The alternative hypothesis (H_1) states that there are differences among the three means. In symbols,

$$H_1: \quad \mu_{b_1} \neq \mu_{b_2} \neq \mu_{b_3}$$

or

$$H_1: \quad \text{At least one mean is different from others}$$

The F-ratio will compare the obtained mean differences among the three methods of instruction versus the amount of difference that would be expected by chance or sampling error. Thus,

$$F = \frac{\text{Variance (differences) between the means for factor } B}{\text{Variance (differences) expected by chance/error}}$$

or

$$F = \frac{\text{Variance (differences) between column means}}{\text{Variance (differences) expected by chance/error}}$$

14.6.1.2 Interaction Effect

In addition to evaluating the main effect of each factor individually, the two-factor ANOVA allows us to evaluate other mean differences that may result from unique combination of the two factors. For example, specific combinations of intelligence and methods of instruction may have effects that are different from the overall effects of intelligence or methods of instruction acting alone. Any 'extra' mean differences that are not explained by the main effects are called an *interaction between factors*. The real advantage of combining two factors within the same study or experiment is the ability to examine the unique effects caused by an interaction. In other words, an interaction between two factors occurs whenever the mean differences between individual treatment conditions, or cells, are different from what would be predicted from the overall main effects of the factors.

Table 14.11 Hypothetical mean scores for six treatment conditions in a two-way analysis of variance

Intelligence (Factor A)		Method (Factor B)			
		b_1 (Lecture)	b_2 (Seminar)	b_3 (Discussion)	
	a_1 (Superior Intelligence)	$\bar{X}_{a_1 b_1} = 45$	$\bar{X}_{a_1 b_2} = 85$	$\bar{X}_{a_1 b_3} = 80$	$\bar{X}_{a_1} = 70$
	a_2 (Inferior Intelligence)	$\bar{X}_{a_2 b_1} = 45$	$\bar{X}_{a_2 b_2} = 65$	$\bar{X}_{a_2 b_3} = 40$	$\bar{X}_{a_2} = 50$
		$\bar{X}_{b_1} = 45$	$\bar{X}_{b_2} = 75$	$\bar{X}_{b_3} = 60$	$\bar{X}_{..} = 60$

To make the concept of an interaction more concrete, we will re-examine the data shown in Table 14.10. For these data, there is no interaction, that is, there are no extra mean differences that are not explained by the main effects. For example, within each method of instruction (each column of the table) the subjects scored 20 points higher in the superior intelligence condition than in the inferior intelligence condition. This 20-point mean difference is exactly what is predicted by the overall main effect of intelligence (factor A).

Let us now consider the hypothetical data shown in Table 14.11. These new data show exactly the same main effects that existed in Table 14.10 (the column means and the row means have not been changed). But now there is an interaction between the two factors.

For example, in discussion method (third column), there is a 40-point difference between the superior intelligence and the inferior intelligence conditions. This 40-point difference cannot be explained by the 20-point main effect of intelligence. Also, in the lecture method (first column), the data show no difference between the two intelligence conditions. Again, this zero difference is not what would be expected based on the 20-point main effect of intelligence. The extra, unexplained mean differences are an indication that there is an interaction between the two factors.

To evaluate the interaction, the two-factor ANOVA first identifies mean differences that cannot be explained by the main effects. After the extra mean differences are identified, they are evaluated by an F-ratio with the following structure:

$$F = \frac{\text{Variance (mean differences) not explained by main effects}}{\text{Variance (differences) expected by chance/error}}$$

The null hypothesis for this F-ratio simply states that there is no interaction:

H_0: There is no interaction between factors A and B. All the mean differences between treatment conditions or cells are explained by the main effects of the two factors.

The alternative hypothesis is that there is an interaction between the two factors:

H_1: There is an interaction between factors A and B. The mean differences between treatment conditions or cells are not what would be predicted from the overall main effects of the two factors.

Thus, we have introduced the concept of an interaction as the unique effect produced by two factors working together. Now, we want to say something more about interactions by presenting two alternative definitions of an interaction.

The first alternative definition of the concept of an interaction focuses on the notion of interdependency between the two factors. More specifically, if the two factors are interdependent, so that one factor does influence the effect of the other, then there will be an interaction. On the contrary, if the two factors are independent, so that the effect of either one is not influenced by the other, then there will be no interaction. In short, when the effect of one factor depends on the different levels of a second factor, then there is an *interaction between the factors*.

Referring to the data given in Table 14.10, we note that the size of the intelligence effect (top row versus bottom row) does not depend on the methods of instruction. For these data, the change in intelligence shows the same 20-point effect for all three levels of method. Thus, the intelligence effect does not depend on methods of instruction and there is no interaction. Let us now consider the data given in Table 14.11. Here the effect of changing intelligence depends on the methods of instruction, and there is an interaction. For example, at the lecture method, changing intelligence has no effect. However, there is a 20-point difference between superior and inferior intelligence at seminar method, and there is a 40-point difference at discussion method. Thus, the effect of intelligence depends on the methods of instruction, which means there is an interaction between the two factors.

The second alternative definition of an interaction is obtained when the results of a two-factor experiment/study are presented in a graph. In this case, the concept of an interaction can be defined in terms of the pattern displayed in the graph. Figure 14.4 shows the two sets of data we have been considering (i.e., data given in Tables 14.10 and 14.11). The original data from Table 14.10, where there is no interaction, are presented in Figure 14.4(a). To construct this figure, we selected one of the factors to be displayed on the horizontal axis (i.e., X-axis); in this case, different levels of method are displayed. The dependent variable, mean achievement scores, is shown on the vertical axis (i.e., Y-axis).

Note that the figure actually contains two separate graphs: the top line shows the relationship between method of instruction and mean performance when the intelligence is superior and the bottom line shows the relationship when the intelligence is inferior. In general, the picture in the graph matches the structure of the data matrix; the columns of the matrix appear as values along the X-axis and the rows of the matrix appear as separate lines in the graph.

For this particular set of data, Figure 14.4(a), note that the two lines are parallel, that is, the distance between lines is constant. In this case, the distance between lines reflects the 20-point difference in mean performance between superior and inferior intelligence, and this 20-point difference is the same for all three methods of instruction.

Now look at the Figure 14.4(b), which shows data from Table 14.11. Here, we note that the lines in the graph are not parallel. The distance between the lines changes as we scan from left to right. For these data, the distance between lines corresponds to the intelligence effect, that is, the mean difference in achievement for superior intelligence versus inferior intelligence. The fact that this difference depends on the methods of instruction indicates an interaction between factors. In short, when the results of a two-factor study are presented in a graph, the existence of nonparallel lines (lines that cross or converge) indicates an *interaction between the two factors*.

In sum, the concept of an interaction is easiest to understand using the perspective of interdependency, that is, an interaction exists when the effects of one variable (or factor) depend on another factor. However, the easiest way to identify an interaction within a set of data is to draw a graph showing the treatment means. The presence of nonparallel lines is an easy way to spot an interaction. The $A \times B$ interaction typically is called 'A by B interaction'. If there is an interaction of intelligence and method, it may be called the 'intelligence by method' interaction.

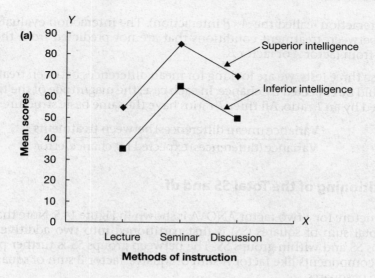

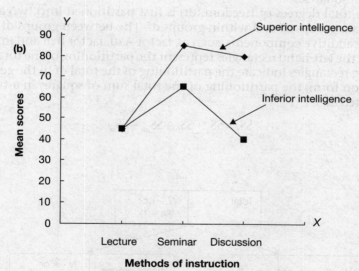

Figure 14.4   (a) Graph showing the data from Table 14.10, where there is no interaction, (b) Graph showing the data from Table 14.11, where there is an interaction.

14.6.2   Notation and Formulae

The two-way or two-factor ANOVA is composed of three distinct hypothesis tests:

(i)   The main effect of factor A (often called the A effect). Assuming that factor A is used to define the rows of the matrix or table, the main effect of factor A evaluates the mean differences between rows.

(ii) The main effect of factor B (called the B effect). Assuming that factor B is used to define the columns of the matrix, the main effect of factor B evaluates the mean differences between columns.

(iii)   The interaction (called the $A \times B$ interaction). The interaction evaluates mean differences between treatment conditions that are not predicted from the overall main effects from factor A or factor B.

For each of these three tests, we are looking for mean differences between treatments that are larger than would be expected by chance. In each case, the magnitude of the treatment effect will be evaluated by an F-ratio. All three F-ratios have the same basic structure.

$$F = \frac{\text{Variance (mean differences) between treatments}}{\text{Variance (differences) expected by chance/error}}$$

14.6.3   Partitioning of the Total SS and df

The general structure for a two-factor ANOVA is shown in Figure 14.5. Note that in a two-way ANOVA, the total sum of squares (SS) is first partitioned into two additive components—between-groups SS and within-groups SS. The between-groups SS is further partitioned into three additive components like factor A sum of squares, factor B sum of squares and interaction ($A \times B$) sum of squares.

Similarly, the total degrees of freedom (df) is first partitioned into two additive components, like between-groups df and within-groups df. The between-groups df is further partitioned into three additive components, such as, factor A df, factor B df and interaction df.

In Figure 14.5, the left-hand rectangles represent the partitioning of the total sum of squares and the adjoining rectangles indicate the partitioning of the total df in the general form.

In the equation form, the partitioning of the total sum of squares in a two-way ANOVA may be represented as:

$$SS_t = SS_a + SS_b + SS_{ab} + SS_w$$

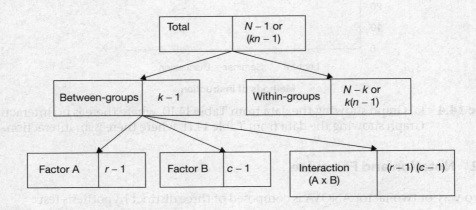

where
n=number of subjects or observations in each of the treatment conditions/groups (or cells)
k=number of treatment conditions or groups or cells
r=number of rows representing levels of factor A
c=number of columns representing levels of factor B

Figure 14.5   Schematic representation of a two-factor ANOVA

where

SS$_t$ = total sum of squares generated from the deviation of each score from the mean of the total scores.

SS$_a$ = sum of squares of factor A generated from the deviation of row means (i.e., the means of levels of factor $A-a_1, a_2$, etc.) from the mean of the total scores.

SS$_b$ = sum of squares of factor B generated from the deviation of column means (i.e., the means of levels of factor $B-b_1, b_2, b_3$, etc.) from the mean of the total scores.

SS$_{ab}$ = sum of squares for interaction ($A \times B$) generated from the deviation of each subgroup mean from the value predicted from that subgroup on the assumption of no interaction.

SS$_w$ = pooled sum of squares within groups generated from the deviation of the individual scores from the mean of the respective subgroups representing error.

The actual formulae for the two-way ANOVA are almost identical to the formulae for the one-way ANOVA (Section 14.5). We may find it useful to refer to this section for a more detailed explanation of the formulae. To help demonstrate the use of the formulae, we will use the data given in Table 14.12. In this example, we have taken two levels of intelligence (factor A), that is, superior intelligence (a_1) and inferior intelligence (a_2), and three methods of instruction (factor B), that is, lecture (b_1), seminar (b_2) and discussion (b_3) and $n=5$.

Table 14.12 indicates that there are two factors; factor A has two levels (a_1 and a_2) and factor B has three levels (b_1, b_2 and b_3). Thus, there are $A \times B = 2 \times 3 = 6$ treatment conditions or groups or cells. So $k=6$ and in each treatment group, there are five subjects ($n=5$). Therefore, the total number of observations is: $N = kn = 6 \times 5 = 30$. The levels of both the factors can be presented in an 'interaction table' as given below in the Table 14.13.

14.6.4 Computation

Several summary values have been computed for the given data and are given in Tables 14.12 and 14.13. For example, we have computed the size of the sample (n), the total of the raw scores (ΣX), the mean of the raw scores ($\bar{X}$) and the total of the squares of the raw scores (ΣX^2) for each sample (each treatment condition or each treatment group or each cell in the matrix). Also, the total is given for each row and for each column in the matrix. Finally, the values of $\Sigma\Sigma X^2$, N, the grand total ($\Sigma\Sigma X$ or G) and the grand mean ($\bar{X}..$) are computed for the entire set of scores. All of these summary values are necessary for the two-factor ANOVA.

Let us now analyse the given data stepwise.

Step 1. Correction term (C). The correction term (C) is found by squaring the grand total ($\Sigma\Sigma X$ or G) and then dividing it by the total number of observations ($N = kn = 6 \times 5 = 30$) in the study. Thus,

$$C = \frac{(\Sigma\Sigma X)^2}{N} = \frac{(G)^2}{N}. \text{ In the present example, from the data given in Table 14.12,}$$

$$C = \frac{(G)^2}{N} = \frac{(225)^2}{30} = \frac{50625}{30} = 1687.5$$

Step 2. Total sum of squares (SS$_t$). The total sum of squares is obtained by squaring each of the 30 scores or the entire set of observations (N) in the experiment, adding them up and then subtracting the correction term (C) from the sum. Thus, the formula for the total sum of squares (SS$_t$) reads

$$SS_t = \Sigma\Sigma X^2 - C$$

Table 14.12 Hypothetical achievement scores of superior and inferior intelligent subjects instructed by lecture, seminar and discussion methods

Levels of Intelligence(A)		Methods of Instruction (B)			Row Totals
		b_1	b_2	b_3	
a_1 (Superior intelligence)		5	10	7	
		7	8	10	
		9	6	6	
		6	11	5	
		3	15	12	
n:		5	5	5	$n_{a_1} = 15$
ΣX:		30	50	40	$\Sigma X_{a_1} = 120$
$\bar{X}$:		6	10	8	$\bar{X}_{a_1} = 8$
ΣX^2:		200	546	354	$\Sigma X^2_{a_1} = 1100$
a_2 (Inferior intelligence)		6	5	4	
		8	6	6	
		10	7	5	
		12	10	7	
		9	7	3	
n:		5	5	5	$n_{a_2} = 15$
ΣX:		45	35	25	$\Sigma X_{a_2} = 105$
$\bar{X}$:		9	7	5	$\bar{X}_{a_2} = 7$
ΣX^2:		425	259	135	$\Sigma X^2_{a_2} = 819$
Column totals	n:	$10(n_{b_1})$	$10(n_{b_2})$	$10(n_{b_3})$	$N = kn = 30; k = 6; n = 5$
	ΣX:	$75(\Sigma X_{b_1})$	$85(\Sigma X_{b_2})$	$65(\Sigma X_{b_3})$	$\Sigma\Sigma X = G = 225$
	$\bar{X}$:	$7.5(\bar{X}_{b_1})$	$8.5(\bar{X}_{b_2})$	$6.5(\bar{X}_{b_3})$	$\bar{X}.. = 7.5$
	ΣX^2:	$625(\Sigma X^2_{b_1})$	$805(\Sigma X^2_{b_2})$	$489(\Sigma X^2_{b_3})$	$\Sigma\Sigma X^2 = 1919$

Applying this above formula to the set of data in Table 14.12, we obtain

$$SS_t = \Sigma\Sigma X^2 - C = 1919 - 1687.5 = 231.5$$

Step 3. Between-groups sum of squares (SS$_{bet}$). The between-groups sum of squares (SS$_{bet}$) are obtained by the direct method. In this method, the sum of each of the six treatment groups (as in our example) is first squared and then divided by the number of observations in each group and summed $[\Sigma(\Sigma X)^2 / n]$. Finally,

Table 14.13 AB interaction table

	b_1	b_2	b_3	**Row Total**
a_1	30	50	40	$120(\Sigma a_1)$
a_2	45	35	25	$105(\Sigma a_2)$
Column Total	$75(\Sigma b_1)$	$85(\Sigma b_2)$	$65(\Sigma b_3)$	Grand 225 Total (G)

the correction term (C) is subtracted from the sum. Thus, the formula (direct method) to find out SS_b reads

$$SS_{bet} = \left[\Sigma \frac{(\Sigma X)^2}{n} \right] - C$$

$$= \left[\frac{(\Sigma X_1)^2}{n_1} + \frac{(\Sigma X_2)^2}{n_2} + \frac{(\Sigma X_3)^2}{n_3} + \frac{(\Sigma X_4)^2}{n_4} + \frac{(\Sigma X_5)^2}{n_5} + \frac{(\Sigma X_6)^2}{n_6} \right] - C$$

Applying this above formula to the set of data in Table 14.12 or in Table 14.13, we obtain

$$SS_{bet} = \left[\frac{(30)^2}{5} + \frac{(50)^2}{5} + \frac{(40)^2}{5} + \frac{(45)^2}{5} + \frac{(35)^2}{5} + \frac{(25)^2}{5} \right] - 1687.5$$

$$= \left[\frac{900}{5} + \frac{2500}{5} + \frac{1600}{5} + \frac{2025}{5} + \frac{1225}{5} + \frac{625}{5} \right] - 1687.5$$

$$= \left[180 + 500 + 320 + 405 + 245 + 125 \right] - 1687.5$$

$$= 1775 - 1687.5 = 87.5$$

Step 4. Within-groups sum of squares (SS_w). The within-groups sum of squares (SS_w) is found by the subtraction method. Referring to the schematic representation of a two-factor ANOVA in Figure 14.5, it is observed that the total sum of squares has been partitioned into two additive components—between-groups sum of squares and within-groups sum of squares. That is,

$$SS_t = SS_b + SS_w$$
$$\therefore \ SS_w = SS_t - SS_b$$

Substituting the values of total sum of squares and between-groups sum of squares, we get

$$SS_w = 231.5 - 87.5 = 144.0$$

However, the sum of squares within groups can also be found directly. Let us find the within groups sum of squares directly also.

We know that the within-groups sum of squares is the pooled sum of squares based on the variation of the individual observations about the mean of the respective group to which it belongs. Therefore, the formula to compute SS_w is

$$SS_w = \Sigma \left[\Sigma X^2 - \frac{(\Sigma X)^2}{n} \right]$$

This formula indicates that we can first find out the SS within each treatment group and then sum up them to get SS_w. Therefore,

$$\text{SS within } a_1 b_1 \text{ treatment group} = \Sigma X^2 - \frac{(\Sigma X)^2}{n} = 200 - \frac{(30)^2}{5} = 200 - 180 = 20$$

$$\text{SS within } a_1 b_2 \text{ treatment group} = \Sigma X^2 - \frac{(\Sigma X)^2}{n} = 546 - \frac{(50)^2}{5} = 546 - 500 = 46$$

$$\text{SS within } a_1 b_3 \text{ treatment group} = \Sigma X^2 - \frac{(\Sigma X)^2}{n} = 354 - \frac{(40)^2}{5} = 354 - 320 = 34$$

$$\text{SS within } a_2 b_1 \text{ treatment group} = \Sigma X^2 - \frac{(\Sigma X)^2}{n} = 425 - \frac{(45)^2}{5} = 425 - 405 = 20$$

$$\text{SS within } a_2 b_2 \text{ treatment group} = \Sigma X^2 - \frac{(\Sigma X)^2}{n} = 259 - \frac{(35)^2}{5} = 259 - 245 = 14$$

$$\text{SS within } a_2 b_3 \text{ treatment group} = \Sigma X^2 - \frac{(\Sigma X)^2}{n} = 135 - \frac{(25)^2}{5} = 135 - 125 = 10$$

$$\therefore \quad SS_w = 20 + 46 + 34 + 20 + 14 + 10 = 144$$

The outcome of both the methods is the same.

Step 5. 'A' sum of squares (SS_a). The 'A' sum of squares, also called the row effect in this experiment or main effect of factor A, is a component of between-groups sum of squares generated from the deviations of a_1 and a_2 means from the mean of the total scores. The A sum of squares is obtained by squaring the sum of $a_1 (\Sigma a_1)$ and $a_2 (\Sigma a_2)$ (see Table 14.13) and dividing each by 15 ($n=5+5+5$), the number of observations under each level of factor A, and then summing up and finally subtracting the correction term (C) from this sum. Therefore, the formula for 'A' sum of squares is

$$SS_a = \left[\frac{(\Sigma a_1)^2}{n_1} + \frac{(\Sigma a_2)^2}{n_2} \right] - C$$

Applying this formula to the set of data in Table 14.13, we obtain

$$SS_a = \left[\frac{(120)^2}{15} + \frac{(105)^2}{15} \right] - 1687.5 = \left[\frac{14400}{15} + \frac{11025}{15} \right] - 1687.5$$

$$= [960 + 735] - 1687.5 = 1695 - 1687.5 = 7.5$$

Step 6. 'B' sum of squares (SS_b). The 'B' sum of squares, also called the column effect in this experiment or main effect of factor B, is a component of between-groups sum of squares generated from the deviations of b_1, b_2 and b_3 means from the mean of the total scores. The 'B' sum of squares is obtained by squaring the sums of $b_1 (\Sigma b_1), b_2 (\Sigma b_2)$ and $b_3 (\Sigma b_3)$ (see Table 14.13), and dividing each by 10 ($n=5+5$), the number of observations under each level of factor B, then summing up and finally subtracting the correction term (C) from this sum. Thus, the formula for 'B' sum of squares is:

$$SS_b = \left[\frac{(\Sigma b_1)^2}{n_1} + \frac{(\Sigma b_2)^2}{n_2} + \frac{(\Sigma b_3)^2}{n_3} \right] - C$$

Applying this formula to the set of data in Table 14.13, we obtain

$$SS_b = \left[\frac{(75)^2}{10} + \frac{(85)^2}{10} + \frac{(65)^2}{10}\right] - 1687.5 = \left[\frac{5625}{10} + \frac{7225}{10} + \frac{4225}{10}\right] - 1687.5$$

$$= \left[562.5 + 722.5 + 422.5\right] - 1687.5 = 1707.5 - 1687.5 = 20.0$$

Step 7. *AB* interaction sum of squares (SS_{ab}). The *AB* interaction sum of squares (SS_{ab}) can be obtained by two different methods. First, the interaction sum of squares can be obtained by the *subtraction method*. Referring to Figure 14.5, we find that between-groups sum of squares is partitioned into three additive components—'A' sum of squares (SS_a), 'B' sum of squares (SS_b) and interaction sum of squares (SS_{ab}). Therefore,

$$SS_{between} = SS_a + SS_b + SS_{ab}$$
$$\therefore \quad SS_{ab} = SS_{between} - SS_a - SS_b$$

Thus, by subtracting the sum of squares of *A* and *B* from between-groups sum of squares, we obtain the interaction sum of squares.

Substituting the values of between-groups sum of squares (SS_{bet}), 'A' sum of squares (SS_a) and 'B' sum of squares (SS_b), we get

$$SS_{ab} = 87.5 - 7.5 - 20.0 = 87.5 - 27.5 = 60.0$$

To obtain *AB* interaction sum of squares *directly*, we first prepare interaction table or two-way table for *A* and *B* as shown in Table 14.13. (This table is also useful for computing the main effects of *A* and *B*. For example, the row totals give us the levels of factor *A* and the column totals give us the levels of factor *B*.)

In order to obtain *AB* interaction sum of squares, refer to Table 14.13. We first square the cell entries (sums) and divide each by 5, the number of observations contributing to the sums entered in the cells of this table. Then, take the sum and subtract the correction term (C) from this sum. Finally, the interaction sum of squares is obtained by subtracting the sum of squares for the main effects of *A* and *B* from the cell sum of squares. Thus, the formula for the interaction sum of squares (SS_{ab}) is

$$SS_{ab} = \left[\frac{(\Sigma Cell_1)^2}{n_1} + \frac{(\Sigma Cell_2)^2}{n_2} + \frac{(\Sigma Cell_3)^2}{n_3} + \frac{(\Sigma Cell_4)^2}{n_4} + \frac{(\Sigma Cell_5)^2}{n_5} + \frac{(\Sigma Cell_6)^2}{n_6}\right]$$
$$-C - SS_a - SS_b.$$

Applying this formula to the set of data in Table 14.13 and substituting the values of SS_a and SS_b, we obtain

$$SS_{ab} = \left[\frac{(30)^2}{5} + \frac{(50)^2}{5} + \frac{(40)^2}{5} + \frac{(45)^2}{5} + \frac{(35)^2}{5} + \frac{(25)^2}{5}\right] - 1687.5 - 7.5 - 20.0$$

$$= \left[\frac{900}{5} + \frac{2500}{5} + \frac{1600}{5} + \frac{2025}{5} + \frac{1225}{5} + \frac{625}{5}\right] - 1687.5 - 7.5 - 20.0$$

$$= \left[180 + 500 + 320 + 405 + 245 + 125\right] - 1715.0 = 1775.0 - 1715.0 = 60.0$$

The outcome of both the methods is the same.

Step 8. Degrees of freedom (df) for different SS. In our example, there are six treatment conditions and five observations in each condition. Thus, $k=6$; $n=5$;

$N = kn = 6 \times 5 = 30$. Factor A has two levels (which represent number of rows) and factor B has three levels (which represent number of columns). Therefore, $r = 2$ and $c = 3$ (see Table 14.13). Determination of df for different SS can be made as follows:

$$df \text{ for } SS_t = df_t = N - 1 = kn - 1 = 30 - 1 = 29$$
$$df \text{ for } SS_{bet.} = df_{bet.} = k - 1 = 6 - 1 = 5$$
$$df \text{ for } SS_w = df_w = N - k = 30 - 6 = 24$$
$$\text{or } k(n-1) = 6(5-1) = 6 \times 4 = 24$$

The df for SS_{bet} can be partitioned into three parts as follows:

$$df \text{ for } SS_a = df_a = r - 1 = 2 - 1 = 1$$
$$df \text{ for } SS_b = df_b = c - 1 = 3 - 1 = 2$$
$$df \text{ for } SS_{ab} = df_{ab} = (r-1)(c-1) = (2-1)(3-1) = 1 \times 2 = 2$$

Step 9. Mean Squares (MS) or Variance Estimates (VE). The goal of a two-way or two-factor ANOVA is to compute the variance values needed for the three F-ratios. We will need three between-treatment (or between-groups) variances (one for factor A, one for factor B and one for the interaction) and we will also need a within-treatments (or within-groups) variance (error variance). Each of these variance estimates (or mean squares) will be determined by a sum of squares value (SS) and a degrees of freedom (df) value as follows:

$$\text{Mean squares} = MS = \frac{SS}{df}$$

Let us now compute the MS for factor A, factor B, interaction ($A \times B$) and within-groups as noted below:

Mean squares for factor A $(MS_a) = \dfrac{SS_a}{df_a} = \dfrac{7.5}{1} = 7.5$

Mean squares for factor B $(MS_b) = \dfrac{SS_b}{df_b} = \dfrac{20.0}{2} = 10.0$

Mean squares for AB interaction $(MS_{ab}) = \dfrac{SS_{ab}}{df_{ab}} = \dfrac{60.0}{2} = 30.0$

Mean squares for within groups $(MS_w) = \dfrac{SS_w}{df_w} = \dfrac{144}{24} = 6.0$

Step 10. Computation of F-ratios. The three F-ratios are determined by their respective MS value divided by the within-group MS value, which is common for all three F-ratios, as follows:

$$F_a = \frac{MS_a}{MS_w} = \frac{7.5}{6.0} = 1.25$$

$$F_b = \frac{MS_b}{MS_w} = \frac{10.0}{6.0} = 1.67$$

$$F_{ab} = \frac{MS_{ab}}{MS_w} = \frac{30.0}{6.0} = 5.0$$

Step 11. Summary of analysis of variance. The summary of the analysis of data in a two-way ANOVA is given in Table 14.14.

Step 12. Test of significance. The obtained values of F in Table 14.14 are to be evaluated. The F-ratio in respect of factor A has been found to be 1.25. Consulting Table E in the Appendix with df=1/24, the critical F value at 0.05 level is 4.26 and at 0.01 level is 7.82. Since the obtained value of $F=1.25$ is smaller than both the table values of F, it is not significant. Therefore, we accept the null hypothesis (H_0) that the two groups selected on the basis of intelligence are random samples from the same normally distributed population.

Further, we observe that the F-ratio in respect of factor B is 1.67. Consulting the critical values of F table (Table E in the Appendix) with df=2/24, we find that the critical value of F at 0.05 level is 3.40 and at 0.01 level is 5.61. Since the obtained value of $F=1.67$ is smaller than both the table values of F, it is not significant. Therefore, we accept the null hypothesis (H_0) that three methods of instruction have not differentially affected the achievement scores of the subjects; the three groups of subjects are the random samples from the same population.

Moreover, the obtained F-ratio in respect of $A \times B$ interaction is 5.0. The critical value of F with df=2/24 (see Table E in Appendix) is 3.40 at 0.05 level and 5.61 at 0.01 level of significance. The obtained value of 5.0 exceeds the critical value at $\alpha=.05$ and is less than the critical value at $\alpha=0.01$. Thus, the obtained value of $F=5.0$ is significant at 0.05 level. Therefore, $p<0.05$. It indicates that the effectiveness of a particular method of instruction depends upon the level of intelligence in 95% of cases.

Since the $A \times B$ interaction effect is significant, it needs graphical presentation of data in order to get more information regarding the interdependence of both the factors.

Graphical Presentation of Interaction

The graphical presentation is useful in examining the nature of interaction and is also helpful in interpreting the results. First, we work out the means from the totals given in the cells of Table 14.13. Each cell total is based on five observations ($n=5$), thus, dividing it by 5, we obtain the means presented in Table 14.15 or we can find out the cell means already calculated in Table 14.12 and arrange it in Table 14.15.

As an aid in the interpretation of interaction, the profiles corresponding to the means are better than the totals. The given data are presented in Figure 14.6.

Table 14.14   Summary of two-way analysis of variance

Source of Variation	SS	df	MS	F
Between groups	87.5	5		
A (Intelligence)	7.5	1	7.5	1.25
B (Method)	20.0	2	10.0	1.67
AB (Interaction)	60.0	2	30.0	5.00*
Within groups (error)	144.0	24	6.0	
Total	231.5	29		

Note:* $p<0.05$.

Table 14.15   Two-way table of means

	b_1	b_2	b_3
a_1	6.0	10.0	8.0
a_2	9.0	7.0	5.0

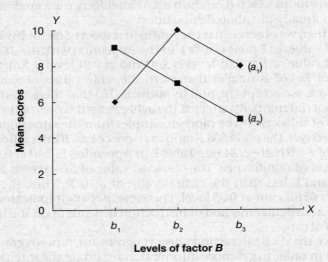

Figure 14.6 $A \times B$ interaction profiles

We take the levels of one factor on X-axis. Let us take levels of factor B on X-axis. It is purely for convenience that we have taken factor B on X-axis, otherwise it is alright to take any factor on X-axis. The mean achievement scores are presented on the Y-axis. Now, plot the means for each level of factor A. That is, first plot all the means in row a_1 (i.e., a_1b_1=6.0, a_1b_2=10 and a_1b_3=8.0) corresponding to the levels of factor B, join the points and label the resulting curve a_1. It represents achievement scores of subjects of superior intelligence. Similarly, plot all the means in row a_2 (i.e., a_2b_1=9.0, a_2b_2=7.0 and a_2b_3=5.0), join the points and label the resulting curve a_2. It represents achievement scores of subjects of inferior intelligence.

In Figure 14.6, it is observed that the curves marked a_1 and a_2 are not parallel, therefore, the AB interaction is significant. It is observed from Table 14.14 that the AB interaction is significant. It is obvious from the graph also. It indicates that the effectiveness of a particular method of instruction depends upon the level of intelligence. While the subjects of superior intelligence do better in seminar method of instruction, the subjects of inferior intelligence gain more from lecture method of instruction. It should be noted that the interaction is non-significant, when the curves are parallel to each other.

14.6.5   Illustrative Examples: Two-way ANOVA

We have already discussed about various notations and formulae used in the computation of two-way ANOVA through an example taking hypothetical data. Now, we will demonstrate the complete computational procedures (stepwise) of two-factor ANOVA through some of the following illustrative examples.

Example 14.4 One questionnaire was given to a group of high anxious and a group of low anxious persons, each under two levels of involvement, that is, ego-involvement (EI) and task-involvement (TI). The following are the scores. Test whether the mean differences among the groups are significant.

High Anxious		Low Anxious	
EI	**TI**	**EI**	**TI**
5	5	4	8
8	5	5	10
9	4	7	8
7	3	6	8
6	3	3	6

Solution

There are two factors in the given example and each factor is having two levels.
Let factor A=Anxiety, which has two levels.

a_1=high anxiety (HA)
a_2=low anxiety (LA)

Let factor B=Involvement, which has also two levels.

b_1=ego-involvement (EI)
b_2=task-involvement (TI)

For the solution of the problem, the following steps should be followed:

Step 1. The given data are entered in Table 14.16 having all its notations and general computations or summary statistics.

Step 2. Statement of the hypotheses. For factor A, the null hypothesis (H_0) states that there is no difference between the mean achievement scores of high anxious and low anxious persons. However, the alternative hypothesis (H_1) states that both the high anxious and low anxious subjects differ in their mean scores. In symbols,

$$H_0: \ \mu_{a_1} = \mu_{a_2}$$
$$H_1: \ \mu_{a_1} \neq \mu_{a_2}$$

For factor B, the H_0 states that the mean achievement scores of subjects under ego-involvement and task-involvement conditions will be the same. On the contrary, the H_1 states that the mean achievement scores of subjects under EI and TI conditions will be different. In symbols,

$$H_0: \ \mu_{b_1} = \mu_{b_2}$$
$$H_1: \ \mu_{b_1} \neq \mu_{b_2}$$

For the $A \times B$ interaction, the H_0 can be stated in two different ways. First, the difference in the mean achievement scores between the ego-involvement and task-involvement conditions will be the same for high anxious and low anxious

Table 14.16 Achievement scores of high anxious and low anxious persons under EI and TI conditions

	High Anxious (a_1)		Low Anxious (a_2)		
	EI(b_1)	TI(b_2)	EI(b_1)	TI(b_2)	
	5	5	4	8	
	8	5	5	10	
	9	4	7	8	
	7	3	6	8	
	6	3	3	6	
n:	5	5	5	5	$N=20; k=4; n=5$
ΣX:	35	20	25	40	$\Sigma\Sigma X = G = 120$
$\bar{X}$:	7.0	4.0	5.0	8.0	$\bar{X}.. = 6.0$
ΣX^2:	255	84	135	328	$\Sigma\Sigma X^2 = 802$

subjects. Second, the difference in the mean achievement scores between the high anxious and low anxious subjects will be the same for the ego-involvement and task-involvement conditions. In more general terms,

H_0 = The effect of factor A does not depend on the levels of factor B (and B does not depend on A).

H_1 = The effect of one factor does depend on the levels of the other factor.

Step 3. Computation of the correction term (C).

$$C = \frac{(\Sigma\Sigma X)^2}{kn} = \frac{(G)^2}{N} = \frac{(120)^2}{20} = \frac{14400}{20} = 720.0$$

Step 4. Computation of different sum of squares (SS):

(a) *Total Sum of Squares (SS_t)* $= \Sigma\Sigma X^2 - C$
$$= 802.0 - 720.0 = 82.0$$

(b) *Between-groups sum of squares (SS_{bet})*

$$SS_{bet} = \left[\Sigma \frac{(\Sigma X)^2}{n}\right] - C$$

$$= \left[\frac{(\Sigma X_1)^2}{n_1} + \frac{(\Sigma X_2)^2}{n_2} + \frac{(\Sigma X_3)^2}{n_3} + \frac{(\Sigma X_4)^2}{n_4}\right] - C$$

$$= \left[\frac{(35)^2}{5} + \frac{(20)^2}{5} + \frac{(25)^2}{5} + \frac{(40)^2}{5}\right] - 720.0$$

$$= \left[\frac{1225}{5} + \frac{400}{5} + \frac{625}{5} + \frac{1600}{5}\right] - 720.0$$

$$= [245.0 + 80.0 + 125.0 + 320.0] - 720.0$$

$$= 770.0 - 720.0 = 50.0$$

(c)   *Within-groups sum of squares* (SS_w):

$$SS_w = SS_t - SS_{bet.} = 82.0 - 50.0 = 32.0$$

Alternatively, the SS_w can be computed by the following formula:

$$SS_w = \Sigma \left[\Sigma X^2 - \frac{(\Sigma X)^2}{n} \right]$$

$$= \left[\Sigma X_1^2 - \frac{(\Sigma X_1)^2}{n_1} \right] + \left[\Sigma X_2^2 - \frac{(\Sigma X_2)^2}{n_2} \right]$$

$$+ \left[\Sigma X_3^2 - \frac{(\Sigma X_3)^2}{n_3} \right] + \left[\Sigma X_4^2 - \frac{(\Sigma X_4)^2}{n_4} \right]$$

$$= \left[255 - \frac{(35)^2}{5} \right] + \left[84 - \frac{(20)^2}{5} \right] + \left[135 - \frac{(25)^2}{5} \right] + \left[328 - \frac{(40)^2}{5} \right]$$

$$= \left[255 - \frac{1225}{5} \right] + \left[84 - \frac{400}{5} \right] + \left[135 - \frac{625}{5} \right] + \left[328 - \frac{1600}{5} \right]$$

$$= \left[255 - 245 \right] + \left[84 - 80 \right] + \left[135 - 125 \right] + \left[328 - 320 \right]$$

$$= 10.0 + 4.0 + 10.0 + 8.0 = 32.0$$

Note that the obtained SS_w by both the methods is the same, that is, $SS_w = 32.0$.

(d)   *The 'A' sum of squares* (SS_a)

The sum for a_1 (high anxiety) $= 35 + 20 = 55(\Sigma a_1)$
The number of observations for $a_1 = 5 + 5 = 10(n_1)$
The sum for a_2 (low anxiety) $= 25 + 40 + 65(\Sigma a_2)$
The number of observations for $a_2 = 5 + 5 = 10(n_2)$

Therefore,

$$SS_a = \left[\frac{(\Sigma a_1)^2}{n_1} + \frac{(\Sigma a_2)^2}{n_2} \right] - C$$

$$= \left[\frac{(55)^2}{10} + \frac{(65)^2}{10} \right] - 720.0 = \left[\frac{3025}{10} + \frac{4225}{10} \right] - 720.0$$

$$= \left[302.5 + 422.5 \right] - 720.0 = 725.0 - 720.0 = 5.0$$

(e)   *The 'B' sum of squares* (SS_b)

The sum for b_1 (EI) $= 35 + 25 = 60(\Sigma b_1)$
The number of observations for $b_1 = 5 + 5 = 10(n_1)$
The sum for b_2 (TI) $= 20 + 40 = 60(\Sigma b_2)$
The number of observations for $b_2 = 5 + 5 = 10(n_2)$

Therefore,

$$SS_b = \left[\frac{(\Sigma b_1)^2}{n_1} + \frac{(\Sigma b_2)^2}{n_2} \right] - C$$

$$= \left[\frac{(60)^2}{10} + \frac{(60)^2}{10} \right] - 720.0 = \left[\frac{3600}{10} + \frac{3600}{10} \right] - 720.0$$

$$= \left[360.0 + 360.0 \right] - 720.0 = 720.0 - 720.0 = 0.0$$

(f) *A × B interaction sum of squares (SS$_{ab}$):*

$$SS_{ab} = SS_{bet.} - SS_a - SS_b$$
$$= 50.0 - 5.0 - 0.0 = 50.0 - 5.0 = 45.0$$

Alternatively, the SS$_{ab}$ can be computed directly from Table 14.16 as follows:

$$SS_{ab} = \left[\frac{(\Sigma a_1 b_1)^2}{n_1} + \frac{(\Sigma a_1 b_2)^2}{n_2} + \frac{(\Sigma a_2 b_1)^2}{n_3} + \frac{(\Sigma a_2 b_2)^2}{n_4} \right] - C - SS_a - SS_b$$

$$= \left[\frac{(35)^2}{5} + \frac{(20)^2}{5} + \frac{(25)^2}{5} + \frac{(40)^2}{5} \right] - 720.0 - 5.0 - 0.0$$

$$= \left[\frac{1225}{5} + \frac{400}{5} + \frac{625}{5} + \frac{1600}{5} \right] - 720.0 - 5.0 - 0.0$$

$$= \left[245.0 + 80.0 + 125.0 + 320.0 \right] - 725.0$$

$$= 770.0 - 725.0 = 45.0$$

Note that the obtained SS$_{ab}$ by both the methods is the same, that is, SS$_{ab}$=45.0.

Step 5. Computation of df for different SS.

(a) *df for total SS (df$_t$):*

$$df_t = N - 1 = 20 - 1 = 19 \quad or \quad kn - 1 = 4 \times 5 - 1 = 19$$

(b) *df for between-groups SS (df$_{bet.}$):*

$$df_{bet.} = k - 1 = 4 - 1 = 3$$

(c) *df for within-groups SS (df$_w$):*

$$df_w = N - k = 20 - 4 = 16$$
$$or \quad k(n-1) = 4(5-1) = 4 \times 4 = 16$$

(d) *df for 'A' SS (df$_a$):*

$$df_a = r - 1 = 2 - 1 = 1$$
$$or \quad (number\ of\ levels\ of\ A) - 1 = 2 - 1 = 1$$

(e) *df for 'B' SS (df$_b$):*

$$df_b = c - 1 = 2 - 1 = 1$$
$$or \quad (number\ of\ levels\ of\ B) - 1 = 2 - 1 = 1$$

(f) *A × B interaction SS (df$_{ab}$):*

$$df_{ab} = (r - 1)(c - 1) = (2 - 1)(2 - 1) = 1 \times 1 = 1$$
$$or \quad df_a \times df_b = 1 \times 1 = 1$$
$$or \quad df_{bet.} - df_a - df_b = 3 - 1 - 1 = 3 - 2 = 1$$

Step 6. Computation of different MS.

(a) *MS for A_{SS} (MS_a):*

$$MS_a = \frac{SS_a}{df_a} = \frac{5.0}{1} = 5.0$$

(b) *MS for B_{SS} (MS_b):*

$$MS_b = \frac{SS_b}{df_b} = \frac{0.0}{1} = 0.0$$

(c) *MS for $A \times B$ interaction SS (MS_{ab}):*

$$MS_{ab} = \frac{SS_{ab}}{df_{ab}} = \frac{45.0}{1} = 45.0$$

(d) *MS for within-groups SS (MS_w):*

$$MS_w = \frac{SS_w}{df_w} = \frac{32.0}{16} = 2.0$$

Step 7. Computation of *F*-ratios.

The three *F*-ratios are determined by their respective MS values divided by the MS_w as follows:

$$F_a = \frac{MS_a}{MS_w} = \frac{5.0}{2.0} = 2.5$$

$$F_b = \frac{MS_b}{MS_w} = \frac{0.0}{2.0} = 0.0$$

$$F_{ab} = \frac{MS_{ab}}{MS_w} = \frac{45.0}{2.0} = 22.5$$

Step 8. Summary of analysis of variance.

The summary of the analysis of data in a two-way ANOVA is given in Table 14.17.

Table 14.17 Summary of two-way analysis of variance

Source of Variation	SS	df	MS	F
Between groups	50.0	3		
A (Anxiety)	5.0	1	5.0	2.5
B (Involvement)	0.0	1	0.0	0.0
A × B (Interaction)	45.0	1	45.0	22.5**
Within groups (error)	32.0	16	2.0	
Total	82.0	19		

Note: ** $p < 0.01$.

Step 9. Test of significance. The obtained F-ratios in Table 14.17 are to be evaluated. The F-ratio in respect of factor A has been found to be 2.5. Consulting Table E in the Appendix with df = 1/16, the critical value of F at 0.05 level is 4.49 and at 0.01 level is 8.53. Since the obtained value of $F = 2.5$, is smaller than both the table values of F, it is not significant. Therefore, we accept H_0 and reject H_1, and conclude that the two groups selected on the basis of anxiety are random samples from the same normally distributed population, and different levels of anxiety have no differential effects on the performance of the subjects.

Similarly, the F-ratio in respect of factor B is 0.0 (zero), which is also not significant. So, we accept H_0 and reject H_1, and conclude that the two groups selected on the basis of involvement are random samples from the same normally distributed population, and different levels of involvement have no differential effects, rather have exactly similar effects, on the performance of the subjects.

Furthermore, the obtained F-ratio in respect of $A \times B$ interaction is 22.5. This obtained value of $F = 22.5$ exceeds both the critical values of F for 0.05 and 0.01 levels. Therefore, the obtained $F = 22.5$ is significant at 0.01 level. Therefore, $p < 0.01$. It indicates that the effectiveness of a particular level of involvement depends upon the level of anxiety in 99% of cases.

Since the $A \times B$ interaction is significant, it needs graphical presentation of data in order to get more information regarding the interdependence of both the factors.

Graphical Presentation of Interaction

The treatment condition means or cell means already computed in Table 14.16 are arranged in Table 14.18.

The data given in Table 14.18 are presented in Figure 14.7.

In Figure 14.7, it is observed that the curves marked a_1 and a_2 are not parallel, rather they crossed each other. This shows that the $A \times B$ interaction is significant, as also observed from Table 14.17. It indicates that the effectiveness of a particular level of involvement depends upon the level of anxiety. From Figure 14.7, it is quite evident that while the high anxious persons performed better in ego-involvement condition, the low anxious persons performed better in task-involvement condition.

Example 14.5 Data obtained from an experiment examining the eating behaviour of normal and obese individuals who have either a full or empty stomach are presented in Table 14.19. Analyse the data by the help of a two-factor ANOVA and interpret the results.

Solution

There are two factors in the given example.
Factor A stands for type of individuals:

a_1 = Normal individual
a_2 = Obese individual

Table 14.18 Two-way table of means

	b_1	b_2
a_1	7.0	4.0
a_2	5.0	8.0

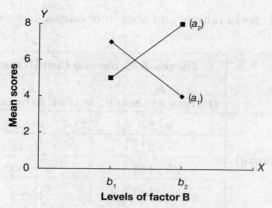

Figure 14.7 $A \times B$ interaction profile

Factor B stands for stomach condition:

b_1 = Empty stomach
b_2 = Full stomach

The solution of the problem leads to the following steps:

Step 1. Statement of the hypotheses. For factor A, the null hypothesis (H_0) states that there is no difference in the amount eaten by the normal versus obese subjects. The alternative hypothesis (H_1), on the contrary, states that there is a difference between the normal and obese subjects in the amount eaten by them. In symbols,

$$H_0: \quad \mu_{a_1} = \mu_{a_2}$$
$$H_1: \quad \mu_{a_1} \neq \mu_{a_2}$$

For factor B, the H_0 states that the amount eaten will be the same for full-stomach and empty-stomach subjects; the H_1, on the contrary, states that the amount eaten will not be the same for full-stomach and empty-stomach individuals. In symbols,

$$H_0: \quad \mu_{b_1} = \mu_{b_2}$$
$$H_1: \quad \mu_{b_1} \neq \mu_{b_2}$$

For the $A \times B$ interaction, the H_0 and H_1 are stated as:

H_0: The effect of factor A does not depend on the levels of factor B (and B does not depend on A)

H_1: The effect of one factor does depend on the levels of the other factor.

Step 2. Computation of the correction term (C).

$$C = \frac{(\Sigma\Sigma X)^2}{N} = \frac{(G)^2}{N} = \frac{(1440)^2}{80} = \frac{2073600}{80} = 25920.0$$

Table 14.19 Eating scores of normal and obese individuals under empty stomach and full stomach

		Factor B (Stomach Condition)		Total
		b_1 (Empty Stomach)	b_2 (Full Stomach)	
Factor A (Type of Individuals)	a_1 (Normal)	$n=20$	$n=20$	$n_{a_1}=40$
		$\bar{X}=22$	$\bar{X}=15$	
		$\Sigma X=440$	$\Sigma X=300$	$\Sigma X_{a_1}=740$
		SS=1540	SS=1270	
	a_2 (Obese)	$n=20$	$n=20$	$n_{a_2}=40$
		$\bar{X}=17$	$\bar{X}=18$	
		$\Sigma X=340$	$\Sigma X=360$	$\Sigma X_{a_2}=700$
		SS=1320	SS=1266	
Total		$n_{b_1}=40$	$n_{b_2}=40$	$\Sigma\Sigma X=G=1440$ $N=80$
		$\Sigma X_{b_1}=780$	$\Sigma X_{b_2}=660$	$\Sigma\Sigma X^2=31836$

Step 3. Computation of different sum of squares (SS):

(a) $SS_t = \Sigma\Sigma X^2 - C = 31836.0 - 25920.0 = 5916.0$

(b) $SS_{bet.} = \left[\Sigma\dfrac{(\Sigma X)^2}{n}\right] - C$

$$= \left[\dfrac{(440)^2}{20} + \dfrac{(300)^2}{20} + \dfrac{(340)^2}{20} + \dfrac{(360)^2}{20}\right] - 25920.0$$

$$= \left[\dfrac{193600}{20} + \dfrac{90000}{20} + \dfrac{115600}{20} + \dfrac{129600}{20}\right] - 25920.0$$

$$= \left[9680 + 4500 + 5780 + 6480\right] - 25920.0$$

$$= 26440.0 - 25920.0 = 520.0$$

(c) $SS_w = \Sigma SS_{inside\ each\ cell} = 1540 + 1270 + 1320 + 1266 = 5396.0$

(d) $SS_a = \left[\dfrac{(\Sigma X a_1)^2}{n_{a_1}} + \dfrac{(\Sigma X a_2)^2}{n_{a_2}}\right] - C$

$$= \left[\dfrac{(740)^2}{40} + \dfrac{(700)^2}{40}\right] - 25920.0 = \left[\dfrac{547600}{40} + \dfrac{490000}{40}\right] - 25920.0$$

$$= \left[13690 + 12250\right] - 25920.0 = 25940.0 - 25920.0 = 20.0$$

(e) $SS_b = \left[\dfrac{(\Sigma X_{b_1})^2}{n_{b_1}} + \dfrac{(\Sigma X_{b_2})^2}{n_{b_2}} \right] - C$

$= \left[\dfrac{(780)^2}{40} + \dfrac{(660)^2}{40} \right] - 25920.0 = \left[\dfrac{608400}{40} + \dfrac{435600}{40} \right] - 25920.0$

$= \left[15210.0 + 10890.0 \right] - 25920.0 = 26100.0 - 25920.0 = 180.0$

(f) $SS_{ab} = SS_{bet.} - SS_a - SS_b$
$= 520.0 - 20.0 - 180.0 = 520.0 - 200.0 = 320.0$

Step 4. Computation of df for different SS

(a) $df_t = N - 1 = 80 - 1 = 79$
or $kn - 1 = 4 \times 20 - 1 = 80 - 1 = 79$

(b) $df_{bet.} = k - 1 = 4 - 1 = 3$

(c) $df_w = N - k = 80 - 4 = 76$
or $k(n-1) = 4(20-1) = 4 \times 19 = 76$

(d) $df_a = r - 1 = 2 - 1 = 1$
or (Number of levels of A) $- 1 = 2 - 1 = 1$

(e) $df_b = c - 1 = 2 - 1 = 1$
or (Number of levels of B) $- 1 = 2 - 1 = 1$

(f) $df_{ab} = (r-1)(c-1) = (2-1)(2-1) = 1 \times 1 = 1$
or $df_a \times df_b = 1 \times 1 = 1$
or $df_{bet.} - df_a - df_b = 3 - 1 - 1 = 3 - 2 = 1$

Step 5. Computation of different MS.

$$MS_a = \frac{SS_a}{df_a} = \frac{20.0}{1} = 20.0$$

$$MS_b = \frac{SS_b}{df_b} = \frac{180.0}{1} = 180.0$$

$$MS_{ab} = \frac{SS_{ab}}{df_{ab}} = \frac{320.0}{1} = 320.0$$

$$MS_w = \frac{SS_w}{df_w} = \frac{5396.0}{76} = 71.0$$

Step 6. Computation of F-ratios

$$F_a = \frac{MS_a}{MS_w} = \frac{20.0}{71.0} = 0.28$$

$$F_b = \frac{MS_b}{MS_w} = \frac{180.0}{71.0} = 2.54$$

$$F_{ab} = \frac{MS_{ab}}{MS_w} = \frac{320.0}{71.0} = 4.51$$

Step 7. Summary of analysis of variance. The summary of the analysis of data in a two-way ANOVA is presented in Table 14.20.

Table 14.20   Summary of two-way analysis of variance

Source of Variation	SS	df	MS	F
Between groups	520.0	3		
A (Type of individuals)	20.0	1	20.0	0.28
B (Stomach condition)	180.0	1	180.0	2.54
A × B (Interaction)	320.0	1	320.0	4.51*
Within groups (error)	5396.0	76	71.0	
Total	5916.0	79		

Note: $p < 0.05$.

Table 14.21   Two-way table of means

	b_1	b_2
a_1	22	15
a_2	17	18

Step 8. Test of significance. The F-ratio in respect of Factor A is found to be 0.28, which is less than 1. There is no need to consult the table for the critical values of F, since the obtained $F<1$. We simply conclude that factor A (type of individual) has no significant effect. Statistically, there is no difference in the amount eaten by normal versus obese subjects. The H_0 is accepted and H_1 is rejected.

The F-ratio in respect of factor B is found to be 2.54. Consulting Table E in the appendix with df=1/76, the critical value of F at 0.05 level is 3.968 (or 3.97) and at 0.01 level is 6.98. Since the obtained value of $F=2.54$ is smaller than both the table values of F, it is not significant. In other words, factor B has no significant effect. Statistically, there is no difference in the amount eaten by the empty-stomach versus full-stomach subjects. Therefore, we accept H_0 and reject H_1, and conclude that the two groups selected on the basis of hunger needs are random samples from the same normally distributed population.

The F-ratio in respect of $A \times B$ interaction is found to be 4.51. This obtained value of $F=4.51$ exceeds the critical value of F only for the 0.05 level. Therefore, the obtained $F=4.51$ is significant at 0.05 level. Therefore, $p<0.05$. This means that the effect of stomach condition does depend on the type of individuals in 95% of cases.

Since the $A \times B$ interaction effect is significant, it needs graphical presentation of data in order to get more information regarding the interdependence of both the factors.

Graphical Presentation of Interaction

The cell means already computed in Table 14.19 are arranged in Table 14.21.

The data given in Table 14.21 are presented in Figure 14.8.

In Figure 14.8, it is observed that the curves marked a_1 and a_2 are not parallel, rather they crossed each other. This shows that the $A \times B$ interaction effect is significant, as also observed from Table 14.20. It indicates that the effectiveness of a particularly level of stomach condition

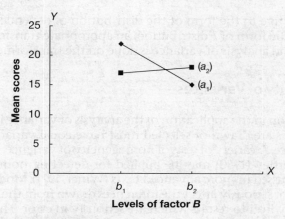

Figure 14.8 $A \times B$ interaction profile

depends upon the level of individuals. From the Figure 14.8, it is quite evident that the degree of fullness (i.e., full stomach) did adversely affect the normal subjects, but it had no such effect on the obese subjects.

14.7   Assumptions Underlying the Analysis of Variance

In the mathematical development of the analysis of variance, a number of assumptions are made. The validity of the analysis of variance presented in this chapter depends on these assumptions. The ratio of between-groups (treatments) to within-groups (error) mean squares is distributed as F if the assumptions underlying the analysis of variance are satisfied. If the assumptions are violated, the sampling distribution of mean square ratios may differ from the F distribution. If the assumptions are not sufficiently approximated, the conclusions or inferences based on the F-test may not be valid. These assumptions are: (i) Normality of F distribution of the dependent variable (or criterion measures); (ii) homogeneity of variances; (iii) additivity of the effects of various factors on the total variation and (iv) independence of the observation. These assumptions are discussed below in more detail.

14.7.1   Normality of F Distribution of the Dependent Variable

The assumption of normality states that the distribution of the dependent variable in the population from which the samples are drawn is normal. This assumption is satisfied when the scores within treatment groups are from normally distributed population. For large samples, the normality of the distribution may be tested using a test of goodness of fit, although in practice, this is rarely done. When the samples are fairly small, it is usually not possible to rigorously demonstrate lack of normality in the data. Unless there is reason to suspect a fairly extreme departure from normality, it is probable that the conclusions drawn from the data using an F-test will not be seriously affected. The effect of a departure from normality is to make the results appear somewhat more significant than they are. Consequently, where a fairly gross departure from normality occurs, a somewhat more rigorous level of confidence than usual may be employed.

In an empirical study, Norton (1952) found that F distribution is practically unaffected by lack of symmetry in the distribution of dependent variable; however, it is slightly affected if the distribution of the dependent measure is either leptokurtic or platykurtic. Symmetric non-normal distributions cause slight inflation of the Type I error probability. In general, the

F distribution is insensitive to the form of the distribution of dependent variable. In case of extreme departures in the form of F distribution, an appropriate transformation of the scores should be carried out and analysis of variance is done on the transformed scores.

14.7.2   Homogeneity of Variances

Another basic assumption in the application of the analysis of variance is that the populations from which the samples are drawn or selected must have equal variances. This is known as homogeneity of variance. A variety of tests of homogeneity of variance, such as, Bartlett (1937), Cochran (1947) and Hartley (1950) may be applied for detecting homogeneity of variance. These methods are discussed in more advanced texts (Winer, 1971). Moderate departures from homogeneity should not seriously affect the inferences drawn from the data. Gross departures from homogeneity may lead to results which are seriously in error. Therefore, under certain circumstances, a transformation of the variable, which leads to greater uniformity of variance, may be used. Under other circumstances, it may be possible to use a non-parametric procedure.

The experimental evidence, however, indicates that moderate departures, even two or three times as great as another group, from homogeneity of variance do not seriously affect the appropriateness of analysis of variance. Mathematical derivations by Box (1954) indicate that alpha (α) level is inflated by heterogeneity of variance. However, if all treatment populations are approximately normally distributed and all groups have equal ns, the inflation is slight. F-test is considered robust with respect to departures from homogeneity of variance.

14.7.3   Additivity of the Effects of Various Factors

A further assumption is that the effects of various factors on the total variation are additive, as distinct from, say, multiplicative. The basic model underlying the analysis of variance is that a given observation may be partitioned into independent and additive bits, each bit resulting from an identifiable source. In most situations, there are no grounds to suspect the validity of this model.

By 'additive' we mean that if X_1 is a score of a given observation under control condition, then under the experimental condition, the score would be $X_2 = X_1 + a_1$, where a_1 is a constant treatment effect due to experimental treatment. If the effect of the treatment is additive, then $s_1^2 = s_2^2$ (as variances of the two conditions should be equal), because addition or subtraction of a constant does not affect the variance, it affects only the mean. In other words, the experimental treatment should not affect the within-groups variation, it should change only the mean which ultimately will affect the between-groups variation.

If the treatment, instead of acting in an additive manner, acts in a multiplicative manner, then $X_2 = X_1 a_1$ and consequently $s_2^2 = s_1^2 a_1^2$, because multiplying each value of a variable by a constant results in multiplying the original variance by the square of the constant. Thus, if the treatment effect is multiplicative, then the variance of the treatment group may differ significantly from the variance of control group, thus, resulting in heterogeneity of variance. Further, if one treatment effect is additive and the other is multiplicative, this condition can also result in generating differences in the variance of the treatment groups.

14.7.4   Independence of the Observation

Another assumption underlying analysis of variance is independence of the observation. The observation within each sample must be independent. The critical concern is that each observation or measurement is not influenced by any other observation or measurement. The assumption of independence states that the score for any particular subject is independent of the scores of all other subjects. This assumption is essential. If we take only one observation or measurement from each subject and subjects are assigned at random to the different treatment conditions, the assumption of independence of scores, will, generally, be met.

In most research situations, the requirement for independent observations is typically satisfied by using a random sample of separate, unrelated individuals. Thus, the measurement obtained for each individual is not influenced by other subjects in the sample.

In the case of repeated-measures design or within-subjects design, where each subject is tested on different treatment conditions, we can expect that the scores will be correlated. However, this assumption of independence of observation in such design, generally, is not valid. Moreover, Cochran (1947) and Scheffé (1959) have reported that positive correlations among scores can result in inflating the Type I error rate and negative correlations in its deflation. Therefore, the appropriate procedure would be to obtain one single score for each subject.

With most sets of real data, the assumptions underlying the analysis of variance are, at best, only roughly satisfied. The raw data of experiments frequently do not exhibit the characteristics which the mathematical models require. One advantage of the analysis of variance is that reasonable departures from the assumptions of normality and homogeneity may occur without seriously affecting the validity of the inferences drawn from the data.

It has been observed in the foregoing discussion that even extreme non-normality does not affect Type I or Type II error rate much. Also, moderate departures from the assumption of homogeneity of variance do not seriously affect the appropriateness of the F-test. However, problems arise when heterogeneous variances are accompanied by unequal ns. Unequal ns should be avoided whenever possible. If we have equal number of subjects in each treatment group, the homogeneity of variance assumption can be violated without appreciably affecting the F-test. However, the assumption of independence of observation or measurement is essential. Randomisation is necessary to ensure validity of independence assumption. It is necessary to assign the subjects at random to the treatment conditions, as each subject has his/her own unique effect which will interact with the treatment condition. If the subjects are randomly distributed over the treatment conditions, these unique effects will be distributed evenly among the different treatment conditions.

14.8 Transformation of Data

As indicated in Section 14.7, the appropriate use of the analysis of variance involves assumptions of normality, homogeneity of variance, additivity and independence of observation. With some data, one or more of these assumptions are obviously not satisfied. One way to deal with such situations is to use some suitable non-parametric test. Another way is to change the scale of measurement by suitable transformation. Transformation is, thus, a change in the scale of measurement. Sometimes, it is possible to use a simple transformation, resulting in a set of transformed values which conform more closely to one or more of assumptions, which the appropriate use of the analysis of variance (or F-test) requires. Most transformations are intended to bring the variances closer to equality. In many cases, the transformed values will approximate the normal form more closely than do the original observations.

There are different reasons for making transformations in the scale of measurement. Ordinarily, the three assumptions, that is, additivity, normality and homogeneity, are violated together (Snedecor, 1956). Ideally, the transformation should be able to remedy all the problems, but in practice, it is not often possible. Additivity is the most essential requirement and next is the homogeneity of variance.

Commonly used transformations are the (i) square root transformation ($\sqrt{X}$), (ii) logarithmic transformation ($\log X$), (iii) reciprocal transformation ($1/X$), (iv) arc sine transformation (arc sine $\sqrt{X}$) and (v) linear transformation. A decision regarding which transformation is appropriate is made by exploring the relation between the variance and the treatment means. The nature of this relation determines which transformation to use.

Let us consider some transformations that are appropriate for different conditions. These are called *monotonic transformations*, as the transformations leave the ordinal relationships (i.e., greater than, equal to or less than relationship) unchanged.

14.8.1   Square Root Transformation

The square root transformation replaces each of the original observation by its square root. This transformation is appropriate when the variances are proportional to the means, that is, when $s_1^2 / \bar{X}_1 = C$, where C is a constant. Of course, with real data, this relation will be only roughly approximated. When data contain small numbers, and with Os, it is advisable to add 0.5 to each value before taking the square root. The transformation becomes $\sqrt{X+0.5}$ instead of $\sqrt{X}$.

Bartlett (1936) suggests a square root transformation for Poisson distribution, where the mean is equal to the variance. That is, $\mu = \sigma^2$. In Poisson distribution, we should transform each value of X to $\sqrt{X+0.5}$. Freeman and Tukey (1950) suggest that transformations are improved by taking $\sqrt{X} + \sqrt{X+1}$ for each value of X. Mosteller and Bush (1954) have provided a table of values of $\sqrt{X} + \sqrt{X+1}$.

14.8.2   Logarithmic Transformation

When the variances are proportional not to the means, but to the square of the means, a logarithmic transformation (log X) is appropriate. Here again, of course, with real data, relation $s_1^2 / \bar{X}_1 = C$ may be only roughly satisfied. If some of the observations are 0 (zero) and small numbers, the suggestion is that the transformation log (X+1) be used. Put it into other words, in logarithmic transformation, we transform each value of X to log X. For X equal to zero, the transformation may take the form log (1+X).

14.8.3   Reciprocal Transformation

When the standard deviations, and not the variances, are proportional to the square of the treatment means, that is, when $s_1 / \bar{X}_1^2 = C$, a reciprocal transformation (1/X) may prove useful. In other words, reciprocal transformation refers to the transformation of each value of X into 1/X. This transformation is useful in experiments where time is the dependent variable. For example, the transformation may be useful in reaction time (RT) experiments and where time taken to solve the problem is the dependent variable. By this transformation, the variances get stabilised.

14.8.4   Arcsine Transformation

In some experiments, the observations obtained are proportions or percentages, such as the proportion of successful responses in a given number of trials, or the percentage of correct answers in performing a series of tasks. When the data are proportions, a relation between means and variances roughly of the kind $s_1^2 = \bar{X}_1 (1 - \bar{X}_1)$ may be observed. Under this circumstance, an arcsine transformation (arcsin $\sqrt{X}$) may be used. Each of the original observations is replaced by an angle whose sine is the square root of the original observation.

Table 14.22 The original and transformed observations

Subject	X	X^2	$X'(X-200)$	X'^2
1	201	40401	1	1
2	203	41209	3	9
3	205	42025	5	25
4	208	43264	8	64
5	210	44100	10	100
$n=5$	$\Sigma X = 1027$	$\Sigma X^2 = 210999$	$\Sigma X' = 27$	$\Sigma X'^2 = 199$
	$\bar{X} = \dfrac{\Sigma X}{n} = \dfrac{1027}{5} = 205.4$		$\bar{X}' = \dfrac{\Sigma X'}{n} = \dfrac{27}{5} = 5.4$	
	$\begin{aligned} SS &= \Sigma X^2 - \dfrac{(\Sigma X)^2}{n} = 210999 - \dfrac{(1027)^2}{5} \\ &= 210999 - 210945.8 \\ &= 53.2 \end{aligned}$		$\begin{aligned} SS &= \Sigma X'^2 - \dfrac{(\Sigma X')^2}{n} = 199 - \dfrac{(27)^2}{5} \\ &= 199 - 145.8 = 53.2 \end{aligned}$	

In other words, when the observations have a binomial distribution, that is, when the observations are proportions or percentages, the transformation is done to the angle whose sine is the square root of the proportion or percentage. That is, $\sin^{-1}\sqrt{p}$ (read sin inverse) or arcsin $\sqrt{p}$, where p is the percentage or proportion of correct responses in a fixed number of trials. Values of the transformation have been tabulated by Bliss (1937). These tables have been reproduced by Snedecor (1956) and Guilford (1954). This transformation stabilises the variance. The table weighs more heavily the small percentages or proportions which have small variance. The arcsin transformation table is given in Table H in the Appendix.

14.8.5 Linear Transformation

Sometimes we obtain data that can be handled better by computing mean or variance from arbitrary values or observations, derived by subtracting a convenient number (i.e., a constant) from each original value, that is, by shifting the origin. As an example, consider the RT of five subjects: 201, 203, 205, 208 and 210 msec. It would be easier to handle the data if we subtract 200 msec from each original score before computing the mean and the variance. Let the original and transformed observations be labelled as X and X', respectively, and be presented in Table 14.22.

In Table 14.22, the X observations and the squares of X observations (X^2) have been presented. Then, the X' ($X-200$) observations have been presented. It can be observed that a constant number (i.e., 200) has been subtracted from each of the 5 observations, and then X' observations have been squared as noted in Table 14.22. We note in the example that the mean of the original scores ($\bar{X}$) is equal to 205.4 and that of the transformed scores ($\bar{X}'$) is equal to 5.4. Thus, if we add the subtracted number (constant) to the mean of transformed observations, the sum becomes equal to the mean of original observation, that is, $\bar{X} = \bar{X}' + 200 = 5.4 + 200 = 205.4$. However, the sum of squares and consequently the variance is not affected by the shifting of the origin. This shows that subtraction of a constant from the observations reduces the mean by the same value but does not affect the standard deviation or the variance. Evidently, subtraction of a constant results in moving down the scale of measurement with no change in the sample standard deviation or variance. It merely shifts the origin of measurement without changing the unit of measurement. The procedure makes the computation work much easy and the chances of committing error are minimised. Note that the subtraction or addition of a constant affects the mean by the same amount but leaves the standard deviation or variance unaltered. Subtraction of a constant results in the reduction and addition in the increase in the mean value by the same constant.

On the contrary, multiplication or division of the observed value by a constant will affect the mean as well as the standard deviation or variance. Multiplying a set of values by a constant greater than 1 will increase the standard deviation or variance and the mean in the same ratio. Similarly, dividing a set of values by a constant greater than 1will decrease the standard deviation or variance and the mean in the same ratio. For example, halving a set of values will reduce their standard deviation and mean to one-half, whereas the variance will be reduced to one-fourth, as $V(\text{variance}) = (\text{SD})^2$.

We have briefly discussed some of the transformations that can be applied to data to rectify situations in which the assumptions underlying the analysis of variance get violated. Transformations help in changing the scale of measurements and are monotonic in nature. However, the major problem is the choice of the transformation. The chosen transformation should be appropriate for a specific distribution.

The transformations commonly used are summarised below.

(i)   When the variance is proportional to the mean, take the square root of the observations.

(ii) When the variance is proportional to the square of the mean, (i.e., when the standard deviation is proportional to the mean), take the logarithms of the observations.

(iii) When the standard deviation is proportional to the square of the mean, take the reciprocal of the observations.

(iv) When the observations have a binomial distribution, the transformation is done to the angle whose sine is the square root of the proportion or percentage.

Thus, if we have the data that needs transformation, first we take a decision regarding the nature of transformation that will be appropriate for the data. The analysis of variance is carried out on the transformed data. After the analysis, the outcome is transformed for interpretation.

14.9   Models of Analysis of Variance

The general statistical model underlying the two-way ANOVA is referred to as the finite model. There are three cases of the finite model, which are identified as *random, fixed*, and *mixed* models. The models appropriate for different experiments differ. Investigators must decide which model best represents that experiment. The choice of the model determines the procedure for testing row, column, and interaction effects. The choice of model depends on the nature of the variables used as the basis of classification in the experimental design.

14.9.1   Random Model

Let us consider an experiment involving R levels of one factor/variable and C levels of another, these being regarded as random samples of levels from populations comprising R_p and C_p members. We may consider a case where R_p and C_p are very large, so that $R_p \gg R$ and $C_p \gg C$, where $\gg$ denotes much greater than. Under these circumstances, such terms as $(R_p - R)/R_p$ and $(C_p - C)/C_p$ approach unit. In other words, $(R_p - R)/R_p = 1$ and $(C_p - C)/C_p = 1$. When this is so, we have what is referred to as a *random model* situation.

In behavioural science research, experiments where the random model is appropriate are not numerous. Satisfactory examples are not readily found. One example is an experiment where each member of a sample of R job applicants is assigned a rating by each member of a sample of C interviewers. Here, both job applicants and interviewers may be viewed as samples drawn at random from populations such that $R_p \gg R$ and $C_p \gg C$. Similarly, ages, races, different breeds, genotypes, phenotypes, socioeconomic status and the like are examples of random variables.

14.9.2   Fixed Model

In many experiments, the R levels of one variable and the C levels of the other are not conceptualised as random samples. In agricultural experiments where R varieties of wheat and C variety of fertiliser are used, the investigator is usually concerned with the yield of a particular wheat varieties and with the effect of particular fertiliser on yield. He is not concerned with drawing inferences about hypothetical populations of wheat and fertiliser varieties. Both variables or factors are *fixed*. Any factor is fixed if the investigator on repeating the experiment would use the same levels of it. Under the fixed model, $R = R_p$ and $C = C_p$. In other words, $(R_p - R)/R_p = 0$ and $(C_p - C)/C_p = 0$. When this is so, we have what is referred to as a *fixed-model* situation.

In behavioural or psychological experiments, different methods of learning, environmental conditions, methods of inducing stress, effects of practice, levels of illumination, time intervals, size of the brain lesion, degrees of temperature, dosage of a drug and the like are examples of fixed factors or variables.

14.9.3   Mixed Model

In many experiments, one basis of classification is a random factor or variable and the other is fixed. Measurements may be obtained for a sample of R individuals for each of C treatments or experimental conditions. Here, one basis of classification is random and the other is fixed. This is a *mixed model*. In the mixed-model situation, either $R_p = R$ and $C_p \gg C$ or $R_p \gg R$ and $C_p = C$. In other words, $(R_p - R)/R_p = 1$ and $(C_p - C)/C_p = 0$ or vice versa. When this is so, we have what is referred to as a mixed model.

In brief, when the levels of the factors or variables are randomly selected from larger populations, it is called random-effect model. When the levels of each factor are not randomly selected from some larger populations, it is called fixed-effect model. If the levels of some factors are randomly selected from some larger populations and those of others are not selected, the analysis of variance model is referred to as a mixed-effect model.

Summary

In this chapter, we have discussed the topic of ANOVA (independent measures). ANOVA is a statistical technique that is used to test for mean differences among two or more treatment conditions or populations. The null hypothesis for this test states that there are no differences among the population means. The alternative hypothesis states that at least one mean is different from the others. Although ANOVA can be used with either an independent- or a repeated-measures design, this chapter examined only independent-measures designs in one-way and two-way ANOVA.

In the one-way ANOVA, the total variability of the data (SS_t) is partitioned into two parts: the variability that exists within each group, called the within-groups sum of squares (SS_w), and the variability that exists between the groups, called the between-groups sum of squares (SS_b). Each sum of squares is used to form an independent estimate of the variance of the null hypothesis populations. Finally, an F-ratio is calculated where the between-groups variance estimate (s^2_b) is in the numerator and the within-groups variance estimate (s^2_w) is in the denominator. Since the between-groups variance estimate increases with the effect of the independent variable, and the within-groups variance estimate remains constant, the larger the F-ratio, the more unreasonable the null hypothesis becomes. Since the obtained F (F_{obt}) is a ratio, there are two values for degrees of freedom (df), one for the numerator and one for the denominator. These df values are used to find the critical value for the F-ratio (F_{crit}) in the F distribution table. We evaluate F_{obt} by comparing it with F_{crit}. If $F_{obt} \geq F_{crit}$, we reject the null hypothesis and conclude that at least one of the conditions differs significantly from at least one of the other conditions.

Next, we discussed the two-way ANOVA, independent group design. The two-way ANOVA is very similar to the one-way ANOVA. However, in the two-way ANOVA, the total sum of squares (SS_t) is partitioned into four components: the within-cells sum of squares (SS_w), the row sum of squares (SS_r), the column sum of squares (SS_c) and the row $\times$ column sum of squares (SS_{rc}). When these sum of squares are divided by the appropriate degrees of freedom, they form four mean squares or variance estimates: the within-cells variance estimate (s^2_w), the row variance estimate (s^2_r), the column variance estimate (s^2_c) and the row $\times$ column variance estimate (s^2_{rc}).

The within-cells variance estimate (s^2_w) is the yardstick or standard against which the other variance estimates are compared. Since all the subjects within each cell receive the same level of variables/factors A and B, the within-cells variability cannot be due to treatment difference. Rather, it is a measure of the inherent variability of the scores and, hence, gives us an estimate of the null hypothesis population variance (σ^2). The row variance estimate (s^2_r) is based on the differences among the row means. It is an estimate of σ^2 + the effect of factor A. It is used to evaluate the main effect of variable A. The column variance estimate (s^2_c) is based on the differences among the column means. It is an estimate of σ^2 + the effect of factor B and is used to evaluate the main effect of variable B. The row $\times$ column variance estimate (s^2_{rc}) is based on the differences among the cell means beyond that which is predicted by the individual effects of the two variables. It is an estimate of σ^2 + the interaction of A and B. As such it is used to evaluate the interaction effect of variables A and B. Thus, the effect of either independent variable (averaged over the levels of the other variable) is called a main effect. An interaction occurs when the effect of one of the variables is not the same at each level of the other variable.

We have pointed out that s^2_w is not affected by the treatments, whereas the other three variance estimates—s^2_r, s^2_c and s^2_{rc}—are sensitive to the effects of the two independent variables and their interaction. If there are no main effects and no interaction, then each variance is an independent estimate of σ^2. To test whether there are any main effects, $F_r = s^2_r / s^2_w$ and $F_c = s^2_c / s^2_w$ are computed. To test if there is an interaction effect, $F_{rc} = s^2_{rc} / s^2_w$ is determined. These obtained F-ratios (i.e., F_r, F_c and F_{rc}) are then compared with their respective critical values of F (i.e., F_{crit}) found from the F distribution table (see Table E in the Appendix) according to their df. If the obtained F_r is equal to or greater than its critical value of F (i.e., $F_r \geq F_{crit}$), H_0 is rejected and we conclude that factor A (which stands for rows) has a significant effect. Similarly, if $F_c \geq F_{crit}$, we reject H_0 and conclude that factor B (which stands for columns) has a significant effect. If $F_{rc} \geq F_{crit}$, we conclude that there is a significant interaction effect between factors A and B.

We have also pointed out that when both t-test and F-test are applied to test the significance of the difference between two independent group means, the relationship between them is $F = t^2$ or $\sqrt{F} = t$.

Finally, we discussed the assumptions underlying the ANOVA, transformation of data and models of ANOVA. With regard to the assumptions, there are four assumptions: (i) normality of the distribution of the dependent variable or criterion measures; (ii) homogeneity of variances; (iii) additivity of the effects of various factors on the total variation and (iv) independence of the observation. The F-test is robust with regard to violations of normality and homogeneity of variances. Commonly used transformations are: (i) square root transformation; (ii) logarithmic transformation; (iii) reciprocal transformation; (iv) arc sine transformation and (v) linear transformation. With regard to the models of ANOVA, the general statistical model underlying the two-way ANOVA is referred to as the finite model. There are three cases of the finite model, which are identified as *random, fixed* and *mixed* models. The models appropriate for different experiments differ. Investigators must decide which model best represents that experiment. The choice of the model determines the procedure for testing row, column and interaction effects. The choice of model depends on the nature of the variables used as the basis of classification in the experimental design.

Key Terms

- Additivity of the effects
- Analysis of variance (ANOVA)
- ANOVA summary table
- Arc sine transformation
- Between-columns sum of squares (SS_c)
- Between-columns variance estimate (s^2_c)
- Between-groups degrees of freedom (df_b)
- Between-groups sum of squares (SS_b)
- Between-groups variance estimate (s^2_b)
- Between-rows sum of squares (SS_r)
- Between-rows variance estimate (s^2_r)
- Between-treatment variance
- Classification variable
- Correction term
- Degrees of freedom (df)
- Direct method
- Experimental error
- F-ratio (s^2_b / s^2_w)
- F-test
- Finite model
- Fixed model
- Grand mean
- Homogeneity of variances
- Independent-groups design
- Independent variable

- Interaction
- Interaction degrees of freedom (df_{rc})
- Interaction effect
- Interaction sum of squares (SS_{rc})
- Interaction variance estimate (s^2_{rc})
- Linear transformation
- Logarithmic transformation
- Logic of ANOVA
- Main effect
- Mean squares (MS)
- Mixed model
- Monotonic transformation
- Normality of F distribution
- Omega square (ω^2)
- One-way ANOVA
- Quasi-independent variable
- Random model
- Randomised group design
- Reciprocal transformation
- Single-factor ANOVA
- Square root transformation
- Strength of association
- Sum of squares
- t-test
- Total degrees of freedom (df_t)

- Total sum of squares (SS_t)
- Transformation of data
- Treatment effect
- Treatment variable
- Two-factor ANOVA
- Two-way ANOVA
- Variance estimate

- Within-cells sum of squares (SS_w)
- Within-cells variance estimate (s^2_w)
- Within-group variance estimate (s^2_w)
- Within-groups degrees of freedom (df_w)
- Within-groups sum of squares (SS_w)
- Within-treatment variance

Questions and Problems

1. What do you mean by 'analysis of variance'?
   Discuss its nature and purpose.
2. Show the relationship and difference between F-test and t-test.
3. With the help of some hypothetical data, elucidate the logic of analysis of variance.
4. Write notes on the following:

   (a) Assumptions of ANOVA
   (b) Models of ANOVA
   (c) Transformation of data
   (d) Difference between one-way and two-way ANOVA.
   (e) Strength of association

5. The following are measurements obtained from five equal groups of subjects.

Group	Measurements				
I	4	7	9	9	14
II	5	6	12	12	7
III	15	18	21	26	20
IV	35	27	29	30	25
V	17	26	17	20	12

Apply the analysis of variance to test the null hypothesis.

6. In a research study, a Marital Adjustment Inventory was administered on the four random samples of individuals. The data collected are given below. Test the hypothesis that they are from the same population.

Sample I	Sample II	Sample III	Sample IV
16	24	16	25
7	6	15	19
19	15	18	16
24	25	19	17
31	32	6	42
	24	13	45
	29	18	

7. The following are two sets of scores representing the responses of two independent groups.

Group	Scores									
I	22	18	24	22	16	18	13	18	19	22
II	12	16	10	10	4	6	17	14	14	10

Calculate F-ratio and t-ratio; test the null hypothesis H_0: $\mu_1 = \mu_2$ and prove that $\sqrt{F} = t$.

8. Apply the analysis of variance to test the significances among the treatment means for the following data.

Treatments	I	II	III
N	10	10	10
$\bar{X}$	7.40	8.30	10.50
ΣX^2	649	755	1263

9. The following are experimental data for three independent groups

Group	Data					$\bar{X}$
I	4	16	49	64	81	42.80
II	49	121	144	169	196	135.80
II	16	36	81	100	121	70.80

What would be an appropriate transformation on these data? Transform the data and apply an analysis of variance to the transformed values, and interpret the result.

10. Different combinations of three levels of a fixed treatment variable A and two levels of another treatment variable B were administered to the groups of a sample of 30 individuals, 5 in each treatment combinations, to study their effects on a particular

dependent variable. The scores of the dependent variable, measured after such treatments, are arranged in a two-way classification tabular form as given below. Find the significance of the effects of the treatments and also their interaction effects.

Variable B	Variable A		
	a_1	a_2	a_3
b_1	7	10	14
	9	11	17
	8	12	18
	6	9	12
	10	13	19
b_2	9	18	26
	12	17	25
	10	21	32
	8	16	26
	11	18	26

11. The following are data for a double-classification experiment involving two fixed variables.

	C_1		C_2		C_3	
R_1	29	31	23	62	17	32
	26	50	31	60	18	49
	42	25	18	20	50	58
R_2	17	62	35	83	17	28
	27	62	50	42	14	58
	50	29	62	19	49	62

Apply the analysis of variance to test the significance of row, column and interaction effects.

12. In an experiment involving double-classification within 10 observations in each cell, the following cell and marginal means were obtained.

	C_1	C_2	C_3	
R_1	8.3	3.2	17.4	9.6
R_2	12.5	4.6	12.6	9.9
	10.4	3.9	15.0	9.8

Compute (a) the cell means expected under zero interaction and (b) the interaction sum of squares.

13.   Six groups of students, five in each, have been selected randomly for six treatment conditions, one group for each condition. Study the main as well as the interaction effects of two factors, namely, factor A—socioeconomic status (SES) and factor B—method of instruction (MI) for the data given below.

Levels of SES (A)	Methods of Instruction (B)		
	b_1	b_2	b_3
a_1 (High SES)	5	10	7
	7	8	10
	9	6	6
	6	11	5
	3	15	12
a_2 (Low SES)	4	6	5
	6	8	6
	5	10	7
	7	12	10
	3	9	7

14.   We have two factors A and B, each at two levels. For each treatment combination, we have eight subjects assigned at random. The data are as follows:

A_1		A_2	
B_1	B_2	B_1	B_2
8	5	10	5
6	8	9	7
9	10	4	3
9	7	8	5
8	10	8	3
7	7	4	5
6	8	3	5
3	5	6	8

Compute F-ratios for main as well as the interaction effects of the factors and interpret the results.

15. Twenty rats were randomly divided into four independent groups, five rats per group. Each group was randomly assigned to one of the four treatment conditions as shown below. After the treatment, each rat of each treatment group was given a learning test and their error scores are given below. Test the significance of main effects and interaction effects.

	Enriched Environment	Impoverished Environment
Rich diet	2	4
	2	4
	3	5
	3	5
	2	4
Poor diet	3	5
	3	5
	4	6
	4	6
	3	5

16. The following data are from a study examining the extent to which different personality types are affected by distractions. Individuals were selected to represent two different personality types: introverts and extroverts. Half the individuals in each group were tested on a monotonous task in a relatively quiet, calm room. The individuals in the other half of each group were tested in a noisy room filled with distractions. The dependent variable was the number of errors committed by each individual. The results of this study are as follows:

		Factor B (Personality)	
		Introvert	Extrovert
Factor A (Distraction)	Quiet	$n=5$	$n=5$
		$T=\Sigma X=10$	$T=\Sigma X=10$
		SS$=15$	SS$=25$
	Noisy	$n=5$	$n=5$
		$T=\Sigma X=20$	$T=\Sigma X=40$
		SS$=10$	SS$=30$
		$\Sigma\Sigma X^2=520$	

Use a two-factor ANOVA and evaluate the main as well as the interaction effects with $\alpha=0.05$.

17. A psychologist conducts a two-factor study comparing the effectiveness of two different therapy techniques (factor A) for treating mild and severe phobias (factor B). The dependent variable is a measure of fear for each subject. If the study uses $n=10$ subjects in each of the four conditions, then identify the df values for each of the three F-ratios.

    (a) What are the df values for the F-ratio for factor A?
    (b) What are the df values for the F-ratio for factor B?
    (c) What are the df values for the F-ratio for the $A \times B$ interaction?

18. The following table represents the summary of two-factor ANOVA with two levels of factor A, two levels of factor B and $n=5$ subjects in each treatment condition. Some values in the table are missing. Find out these missing values and place them in the appropriate places marked by?

Summary of two-factor ANOVA

Sources of Variation	SS	df	MS	F
Between-treatments	855	3		
A (Lecture room)	5	?	5	0.55
B (Testing room)	?	1	5	?
A×B interaction	845	1	?	92.60
Within-treatment	146	?	9.125	
Total	?	19		

19. The following data are from a study examining the influence of a specific hormone on eating behaviour. Three different drug doses were used, including a control condition (no drug), and the study measured eating behaviour for males and females. The dependent variable was the amount of food consumed over a 48-h period.

	No Drug	Small Dose	Large Dose
	1	7	3
	6	7	1
Males	1	11	1
	1	4	6
	1	6	4
	0	0	0
	3	0	2
Females	7	0	0
	5	5	0
	5	0	3

Use an ANOVA to evaluate these data, and describe the results (i.e., the drug effect, the sex difference and the interaction). Test the main effects and interaction effect at the .05 level of significance. In this study, gender is factor A and drug dosage is factor B.

20.   The following data are from a two-factor independent-measures experiment:

Factor A		Factor B	
		b_1	b_2
	a_1	7	1
		12	0
		10	4
		9	3
		12	2
	a_2	1	8
		4	11
		2	11
		3	9
		5	16

(a)   For these data, compute the cell means and place them in an $A \times B$ matrix.

(b)   Looking at the cell means, row means and column means, describe whether or not there might be an interaction, a main effect for factor A and a main effect for factor B.

(c)   Perform a two-factor analysis of variance with $\alpha = 0.01$.

(d)   Describe the results of the analysis.

21.   Fill in the blanks:

(i)   Analysis of variance was developed by _____ in the year _____.

(ii)   The name F-test was given to ANOVA by _____ in Fisher's honour.

(iii)   The analysis of variance deals with _____ rather than with standard deviation or standard error.

(iv)   The ANOVA technique is useful in testing the significance of differences between _____ or _____ treatment means.

(v)   For two groups, F is equal to _____ and t is equal to _____.

(vi)   The total variance has _____ basic components.

(vii)   In one-way ANOVA, there is only _____ independent variable.

(viii) The goal of ANOVA is to find out whether or not a _____ effect exists.

(ix)   When the between-groups MS and within-groups MS are equal, the F-ratio becomes _____.

(x)   ANOVA table standards for _____.

22. Write whether the following statements are True or False.

    (i)   The denominator of the F-ratio is called the error term.

    (ii)   Two-way analysis of variance is otherwise known as a two-factor analysis of variance.

    (iii) In a two-way ANOVA, an interaction $A \times B \times C$ effect may occur.

    (iv)   In a one-way ANOVA, the between-groups df is equal to $N - k$.

    (v)   The analysis of variance helps us to test the equality of two or more sample variances.

    (vi)   One of the assumptions of ANOVA is that the dependent variable is normally distributed in the population from which the samples are drawn.

    (vii) For using ANOVA, it is assumed that the populations from which the samples are selected must have homogeneity of variances.

    (viii) The square root transformation is appropriate when the variances are disproportional to the means.

    (ix)   By reciprocal transformation, the variances get stabilised.

    (x)   Under the fixed model of ANOVA, $R = R_p$ and $C = C_p$.

23. Find out the correct answer from among the four alternatives

    (i)   Analysis of variance technique was developed by

(a)	R.A. Fisher	(b)	Karl Pearson
(c)	W.S. Gossett	(d)	None of the above

    (ii)   When the observations are proportions or percentage, which one of the following transformations is appropriate?

(a)	Logarithmic transformation	(b)	Arcsine transformation
(c)	Linear transformation	(d)	None of the above

    (iii) The general statistical model underlying the two-way ANOVA is referred to as the

(a)	Infinite model	(b)	Finite model
(c)	Either finite or infinite model	(d)	None of the above

    (iv)   For applying ANOVA, it is assumed that the observations within each sample must be

(a)	Dependent	(b)	Correlated
(c)	Independent	(d)	None of the above

    (v)   One assumption underlying the analysis of variance is that the effects of various factors on the total variation are:

(a)	Multiplicative	(b)	Dividend
(c)	Additive	(d)	None of the above

    (vi)   In a two-way ANOVA, the joint effect of factor A and factor B is known as their

(a)	Main effect	(b)	Interaction effect
(c)	Simple effect	(d)	None of the above

(vii) In a given data of one-way ANOVA, between-groups MS=22.5 and within-groups MS=4.5. The value of F would be :

   (a) 5.0   (b) 0.2
   (c) 2.5   (d) None of the above

(viii) If in a one-way ANOVA, $k=5$, $n=10$, then the total df would be

   (a) 49   (b) 45
   (c) 40   (d) None of the above

(ix) Mean square between groups (MS_b) is equal to :

   (a) $SS_b/(n-1)$ (b) $SS_b/(k-1)$
   (c) $SS_b/k(n-1)$ (d) None of the above

(x) Mean square for error (MS_w) equals

   (a) $SS_w/(k-1)$ (b) $SS_w/(kn-1)$
   (c) $SS_w/N-k$ (d) None of the above

Analysis of Variance (Repeated Measures)

After completing this chapter you will be able to:

- Compare analysis of variance (ANOVA) designs with and without repeated measures.
- Identify the limitations of the repeated-measures design.
- Understand the general layouts of single-factor repeated-measures design, and two-factor ANOVA with repeated measures either on one factor or on both the factors.
- Understand the steps involved in computation and interpretation of the obtained F-ratio/s in one-way and two-way ANOVA with repeated measures.

15.1   Introduction

In Chapter 14, we introduced the general logic underlying ANOVA and presented the equations used for analysing the data from a single-factor (one-way ANOVA) and two-factor (two-way ANOVA) independent-measures research study. We should recall that the term *single factor* indicates that the study involves only one independent variable (or quasi-independent variable). Similarly, the term two-factor indicates that the study involves two independent variables. Also, the term *independent-measures* indicate that the research study uses a separate sample of n size for each of the treatment conditions being compared. In this chapter, we will extend the analysis of the variance procedure to research studies using *repeated-measures* designs. A repeated-measures study uses a single sample of n size, with the same set of individuals measured in all of the different treatment conditions.

In a single-factor (one-way ANOVA) or two-factor (two-way ANOVA) experimental design without repeated measures (also called between-subject design), discussed in Chapter 14, the within-group variability (error) is made up of an experimental error as well as an error due to individual differences on the dependent measure. One way to achieve the objective has been considered in Chapter 20 (available on the companion website), that is, by forming blocks on the basis of the concomitant variable correlated with the dependent variable (randomised block design). However, error variance contributed by the individual differences can be separated more effectively by using repeated-measures design (also called within-subject design). If the variability due to individual differences is not controlled, it forms part of the uncontrolled sources of variability, resulting in an increase in the experimental error.

In this chapter, we shall consider one-way (single-factor) and two-way (two-factor) ANOVA with repeated-measures designs, separately as follows.

15.2   One-way (Single-factor) ANOVA with Repeated-measures Design

One-way repeated ANOVA is the simplest case of repeated-measures design in which k treatments are classified along a single dimension and each experimental unit or subject undergoes all the treatments. It is obvious that the primary objective of experiments in which each subject is observed under all the treatments is to provide a control on individual differences. The unique characteristics of the subject remain constant over the treatments, that is, each subject serves his/her own control.

15.2.1   Comparison of Designs With and Without Repeated Measures

In the repeated-measures design, each subject in the experiment is successively observed under all the k treatments, and, thus, the variation due to individual differences is eliminated from the estimate of the experimental error. On the other hand, in the one-way ANOVA designs (or in the single-factor experimental designs) without repeated measures, a subject is observed in one and only one of the k treatments and the variation due to individual differences forms the part of experimental error.

Repeated-measures design increases the precision of the experiment by eliminating the inter-subject differences as a source of error. This design is called repeated-measures design because repeated measures are obtained from the same subject, or in other words, the same subject is repeatedly measured on the same dependent variable under all the k treatment conditions. It follows then that the set of observations in an experiment will be dependent rather than independent, and the statistical tests take this correlation into account.

Let us consider an example to bring out the differences in the two designs. Suppose an experimenter is interested in studying the effect of five drugs on the reaction time (RT) of the subjects. For this purpose, a sample of size 5 is selected randomly from the population of interest. Each of the subjects is observed under all the five drugs, and, thus, five observations are taken for each drug. The order of presentation of the drugs is randomised independently for each subject, and the condition of drug administration is kept constant for all subjects. This design is called a single-factor (or one-way ANOVA) experimental design with repeated measures (within-subject design). If the experimenter had randomly assigned the subjects to each of the five drugs and used a separate sample of size n (say, $n=5$) for each drug, then it would have been a case of single-factor (or one-way ANOVA) experimental design without repeated measures (between-subjects design).

15.2.2   Limitations of the Repeated-measures Design

The repeated-measures design has certain advantages and disadvantages (or limitations). On the bright side, a repeated-measures study may be desirable if the supply of subjects is limited. Second, a repeated-measures study is economical (both in time and money) as the experimenter can get it done by using fewer subjects. Third, a repeated-measures design eliminates the role of variability due to individual differences. In other words, a repeated-measures design indirectly reduces the error variance (i.e., within-group variability) by directly controlling the individual differences on the dependent measure. However, the disadvantages of the repeated-measures design may be very great. These take the form of carry-over effects or progressive error, such as fatigue, that can make the interpretation of the data very difficult. These disadvantages or limitations of the repeated-measures design are discussed in detail below.

It may be noted that the repeated-measures design is not suitable in certain experimental situations. In this design, a number of levels of the factor are administered in succession to the same subject; the response of the subject to one treatment is conditioned by the fact that other treatments have previously been administered. Thus, this design should only be employed if the treatment effects are temporary. If the treatments are likely to have prolonged effect on the organism, then this design will not be suitable. Furthermore, when there is the possibility of *practice* or 'carry-over effect' of one treatment being carried to the subsequent treatments, this design should be avoided. For example, repeated-measures design is not recommended in learning experiments, unless the interest of the experimenter is to study the cumulative effects or to study the trend of responses over treatments rather than comparisons among the treatment means.

Moreover, if the number of treatments is large, the subjects may get fatigued over treatments, or if the treatments are spread over a period of time, it will be difficult to hold the conditions constant. Therefore, this design is a natural choice when the number of subjects is small and they are available for extended periods of experimentation.

15.2.3 General Layout of the Single-factor (or One-way ANOVA) Repeated-measures Design

The general layout of the single-factor experiment with repeated measures having k treatments and n subjects is presented in Table 15.1.

In Table 15.1, the layout of the design with k treatments (T) and n subjects has been presented. The rows represent the subjects and the columns the treatments. In the table, the

Table 15.1 General layout for a single-factor experiment with repeated measures

Subjects (n)	Treatments (k)				
	T_1	T_2	T_3	$T_4, \ldots, T_k$	
1	X_{11}	X_{12}	X_{13}	X_{14}	X_{1k}
2	X_{21}	X_{22}	X_{23}	X_{24}	X_{2k}
3	X_{31}	X_{32}	X_{33}	X_{34}	X_{3k}
4	X_{41}	X_{42}	X_{43}	X_{44}	X_{4k}
.	.	.	.	.	.
.	.	.	.	.	.
.	.	.	.	.	.
N	X_{n1}	X_{n2}	X_{n3}	X_{n4}	X_{nk}

observation or the subject's score is indicted by X which can be identified by its two subscripts. The first subscript refers to the subject number $(1, 2, 3, 4, \ldots, n)$ and the second to the treatment $(1, 2, 3, 4, \ldots, k)$. Thus, X_{11} refers to an observation of subject number 1 who has been administered treatment 1, and X_{24} refers to subject number 2 who has been administered treatment 4. Similarly, X_{nk} refers to an observation of subject n who has been administered treatment k.

The single-factor repeated-measures design entails the observation of each subject under each of the k treatments. It is very important to note that the order of presentation of the k treatments is randomised independently for each subject. The design could be treated as a two-factor design in which subjects constitute the second factor. Here, the subjects could be treated like any main effect in a two-factor design, and the variability associated with it can be isolated.

15.2.4   Partitioning of the Total Sum of Squares and df in a Single-factor Repeated-measures Design

In the single-factor experimental design (or one-way ANOVA design) with repeated measures, the total sum of squares is first partitioned into two component parts, such as the between-subjects sum of squares and the within-subjects sum of squares. The between-subjects sum of squares is based on the variation of the individual subject's mean about the overall mean. This represents the variation due to individual differences. The within-subjects sum of squares is further partitioned into two component parts: the between-treatment sum of squares and the subjects × treatment sum of squares or residual sum of squares. The between-treatment sum of squares is based on the variation of the treatment means about the overall mean. The subjects × treatment sum of squares is the residual effect, which reflects the residual variation after the between subjects and treatment effects have been separated. The residual variation serves as the error variance in a one-way repeated ANOVA model.

Similarly, the total df (i.e., $kn - 1$) is partitioned first into two components: $(n-1)$ df attributable to the variation between subjects and $[n(k-1)]$ df attributable to the within-subjects variation. The df associated with within-subjects variation is further partitioned into two components: $(k-1)$ df attributable to the variation between treatments and $[(n-1)(k-1)]$ df attributable to the subjects × treatment variation or residual.

Figure 15.1 represents the partitioning of the total sum of squares and df in a single-factor experimental design (or in a one-way ANOVA model) with repeated measures.

In the equation form, the partitioning of the total sum of squares may be expressed as

$$SS_{total} = SS_{between\ Ss} + SS_{within\ Ss}$$
$$= SS_{between\ Ss} + SS_{treatments} + SS_{residual}$$

where

SS_{total} = total sum of squares

$SS_{between\ Ss}$ = sum of squares between subjects

$SS_{within\ Ss}$ = sum of squares within subjects

$SS_{treatment}$ = sum of squares between treatments

$SS_{residual}$ = residual sum of squares.

Similarly, in the equation form, the partitioning of the total df may be expressed as

$$df_{total} = df_{between\ Ss} + df_{within\ Ss}$$
$$= df_{between\ Ss} + df_{treatment} + df_{residual}$$

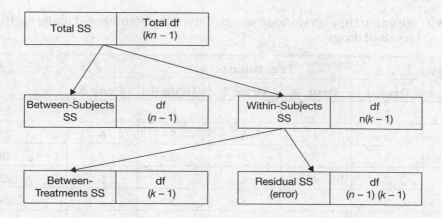

where

    k = number of treatments

    n = total number of subjects

    $kn = N$ = total number of observations.

Figure 15.1   Schematic representation of the analysis of the single-factor experimental design with repeated measures

or

$$(kn-1)=(n-1)+n(k-1)$$
$$=(n-1)+(k-1)+(n-1)(k-1)$$

where

    df_{total} = total df associated with the total sum of squares

    $df_{between\ Ss}$ = df associated with the between-subjects sum of squares

    $df_{within\ Ss}$ = df associated with the within-subjects sum of squares.

    $df_{treatment}$ = df associated with the between-treatments sum of squares

    $df_{residual}$ = df associated with the residual sum of squares.

15.2.5   Steps Involved in Computation of One-way ANOVA with Repeated Measures

Let us discuss the steps involved in analysing data in the case of one-way ANOVA with repeated measures. The data is from a hypothetical experiment in which the investigator is interested in studying the effect of drugs on the reaction time (RT) of the subjects. A sample of five subjects was selected randomly from the population of interest, and each subject was observed under all the five levels of drugs (treatments). In this experiment, the independent variable of interest was the drug, and the dependent variable was the reaction time in seconds. From each of the five subjects, observations were obtained for each of the five levels of drugs. The order of presentation of treatments was independently randomised for each subject. The RT scores of the subjects are given in Table 15.2.

To test the significance of the difference between k treatment means using one-way ANOVA with repeated-measures design, the following steps are to be followed for its computation:

Table 15.2   Reaction time (in seconds) scores of five subjects observed under each of the five levels of drugs

Subjects (n)	Treatments (k)					ΣS
	Drug 1	**Drug 2**	**Drug 3**	**Drug 4**	**Drug 5**	
1	2	3	5	6	7	23
2	3	4	5	5	6	23
3	1	2	3	5	7	18
4	2	4	4	6	6	22
5	3	4	5	5	7	24
n:	5	5	5	5	5	$kn = N = 25$; $k = 5$; $n = 5$
ΣX_k:	11	17	22	27	33	$\Sigma\Sigma X_k = 110 (G)$
$\bar{X}_k$:	2.2	3.4	4.4	5.4	6.6	$\bar{X}_{k..} = 4.4$
ΣX_k^2:	27	61	100	147	219	$\Sigma\Sigma X_k^2 = 554$

Step 1. The presentation of the given data in a table having all its notations, such as k, n, $kn = N$ and so on, as shown in Table 15.2.

Step 2. The computation of a variety of summary statistics, such as treatment totals (ΣX_k), subject totals (ΣS), grand total (G or $\Sigma\Sigma X_k$), sum of the squares of the treatment scores (ΣX_k^2), sum of the sums of squares ($\Sigma\Sigma X_k^2$), treatment means ($\bar{X}_k$), grand mean $\bar{X}_{k.}$ and so on, as shown in Table 15.2.

Step 3. The statement of the null hypothesis (H_0) and alternative hypothesis (H_1), and the selection of an alpha level. In the given example, the null hypothesis states that there are no differences among the five drugs. In symbols,

$$H_0: \quad \mu_1 = \mu_2 = \mu_3 = \mu_4 = \mu_5 \text{ (or } \bar{X}_1 = \bar{X}_2 = \bar{X}_3 = \bar{X}_4 = \bar{X}_5).$$

The general form of alternative hypothesis (H_1) states that there are differences among the drugs. In symbols,

$$H_1: \quad \mu_1 \neq \mu_2 \neq \mu_3 \neq \mu_4 \neq \mu_5 \text{ (or } \bar{X}_1 \neq \bar{X}_2 \neq \bar{X}_3 \neq \bar{X}_4 \neq \bar{X}_5).$$

or H_1: At least one of the treatment means is different.
We will set alpha at $\alpha = 0.05$.

Step 4. Computation of the correction term (C). The correction term is obtained by squaring the grand total (G) and then dividing it by the total number of observations ($kn = N$) in the experiment.

In the given example (see Table 15.2), $G = 110$ and $N = kn = 5 \times 5 = 25$. Therefore, the correction term (C) is

$$C = \frac{(G)^2}{N} = \frac{(110)^2}{25} = \frac{12100}{25} = 484.0.$$

Step 5. Computation of the sum of squares (SS). In the one-way ANOVA with repeated measures, the total sum of squares (SS_{total}) has two additive and independent parts-between-subjects sum of squares ($SS_{between\ Ss}$)and within-subjects sum of squares ($SS_{within\ Ss}$), which has again two additive parts: between-treatments sum of squares ($SS_{treatment}$) and residual (error) sum of squares ($SS_{residual}$). These are computed below one by one.

(a) **Total sum of squares (SS_{total}).** The total sum of squares is obtained by combining the scores of all the k treatments and treating them as a single set of scores. Each of the scores has been squared, then the squares have been summed up, and finally the correction term (C) has been subtracted from the sum. Thus, the computational formula for SS_{total} reads

$$SS_{total} = \Sigma\Sigma X_k^2 - C$$

Applying the above formula to the set of data given in Table 15.2, the total sum of squares, thus, obtained is equal to

$$SS_{total} = 554.0 - 484.0 = 70.0$$

(b) **Between-subjects sum of squares ($SS_{between\ Ss}$).** In one-way repeated ANOVA each subject undergoes all the treatments in the experiment. The sum of the rows given in the last column of the data table represents the variation due to individual differences. The between-subjects variation is a function of the squared deviation of the means of the individual subjects about the grand mean. The sum of the scores of each subject over all treatments given in the last column has been squared; then each squared value divided by the number of treatments (k), summed up and finally the correction term (C) has been subtracted from the sum. The computational formula for the between-subjects sum of squares ($SS_{between\ Ss}$) is as follows:

$$SS_{between\ Ss} = \left[\Sigma\frac{(\Sigma S)^2}{k}\right] - C$$

$$= \left[\frac{(\Sigma S_1)^2}{k} + \frac{(\Sigma S_2)^2}{k} + \frac{(\Sigma S_3)^2}{k} + \cdots + \frac{(\Sigma S_n)^2}{k}\right] - C$$

Applying the above formula to the set of data in Table 15.2, we obtain

$$SS_{between\ Ss} = \left[\frac{(23)^2}{5} + \frac{(23)^2}{5} + \frac{(18)^2}{5} + \frac{(22)^2}{5} + \frac{(24)^2}{5}\right] - 484.0$$

$$= \left[\frac{529}{5} + \frac{529}{5} + \frac{324}{5} + \frac{484}{5} + \frac{576}{5}\right] - 484.00$$

$$= [105.8 + 105.8 + 64.8 + 96.8 + 115.2] - 484.0$$

$$= 488.4 - 484.0 = 4.4$$

It represents the variability due to individual differences and is subtracted from the total sum of squares to reduce the experimental error.

(c) **Within-subjects sum of squares ($SS_{within\ Ss}$).** The difference between the observations of the same subject under all the k treatment conditions is in part due to the differences in the treatment effects and in part due to uncontrolled or residual sources of variation. Therefore, the pooled within-subjects varia-tion may be divided into two parts: one that is due to the differences between the treatment means and the other consisting of residual variation.

The within-subjects sum of squares has been calculated by the *subtraction method*. Referring to Figure 15.1, it can be observed that the total sum of squares is first partitioned into two components: variation between subjects and varia-tion within subjects. Thus, if we subtract between-subjects sum of squares from the total sum of squares, we can obtain the within-subjects sum of squares. In the given example (see Table 15.2), the within-subjects sum of squares that has been obtained is equal to

$$SS_{within\ Ss} = SS_{total} - SS_{between\ Ss}$$
$$= 70.0 - 4.4 = 65.6$$

We can also compute the within-subjects sum of squares directly. The within-subjects sum of squares is the pooled sum of squares based on the vari-ation within the observations of each subject about the mean of the particu-lar subject. Note that within-subjects sum of squares is not the error term in this design. However, the error variance is a component of the within-subjects variation. Let us now find out the within-subjects sum of squares by the *direct method*, referring to data given in Table 15.2:

SS within the observations of $S_1 = (2^2 + 3^2 + 5^2 + 6^2 + 7^2) - \dfrac{(23)^2}{5}$

$$= 123.0 - 105.8 = 17.2$$

SS within the observations of $S_2 = (3^2 + 4^2 + 5^2 + 5^2 + 6^2) - \dfrac{(23)^2}{5}$

$$= 111.0 - 105.8 = 5.2$$

SS within the observations of $S_3 = (1^2 + 2^2 + 3^2 + 5^2 + 7^2) - \dfrac{(18)^2}{5}$

$$= 88.0 - 64.8 = 23.2$$

SS within the observations of $S_4 = (2^2 + 4^2 + 4^2 + 6^2 + 6^2) - \dfrac{(22)^2}{5}$

$$= 108.0 - 96.8 = 11.2$$

SS within the observations of $S_5 = (3^2 + 4^2 + 5^2 + 5^2 + 7^2) - \dfrac{(24)^2}{5}$
$$= 124.0 - 115.2 = 8.8$$

$\therefore$ SS within subjects $= 17.2 + 5.2 + 23.2 + 11.2 + 8.8 = 65.6$

The outcome by the *direct method* is exactly the same as obtained through the *subtraction method*. It may be noted that it is easier to obtain within-subjects sum of squares through subtraction than by the direct method.

(d) **Between-treatment sum of squares (SS_treatment).** The sum of the col-umns of Table 15.2 represents the treatment effect. The sum of each of the *k* treatments has been squared, then divided by the number of observations or subjects in each treatment, summed up, and finally the correction term has been subtracted from the sum. The treatment sum of squares can be computed by the following formula:

$$SS_{treatment} = \left[\Sigma \frac{(\Sigma X_k)^2}{n} \right] - C$$

$$= \left[\frac{(\Sigma X_{k_1})^2}{n} + \frac{(\Sigma X_{k_2})^2}{n} + \cdots + \frac{(\Sigma X_{k_k})^2}{n} \right] - C$$

Apply this above formula to the set of data in Table 15.2, the between-treatments sum of squares, thus, obtained is equal to:

$$SS_{treatment} = \left[\frac{11^2}{5} + \frac{(17)^2}{5} + \frac{(22)^2}{5} + \frac{(27)^2}{5} + \frac{(33)^2}{5} \right] - 484.0$$

$$= \left[\frac{121}{5} + \frac{289}{5} + \frac{484}{5} + \frac{729}{5} + \frac{1089}{5} \right] - 484.0$$

$$= [24.2 + 57.8 + 96.8 + 145.8 + 217.8] - 484.0$$

$$= 542.4 - 484.0 = 58.4$$

(e) **Residual sum of squares ($SS_{residual}$).** Referring to Figure 15.1, it can be observed that the within-subjects sum of squares is partitioned into two parts: the treatment sum of squares and the residual sum of squares. In this design, the residual or error sum of squares is the subject × treatment interaction. Thus, the residual sum of squares has been obtained through subtraction as follows:

$$SS_{residual} = SS_{within\ Ss} - SS_{between\ treatment}$$

On substituting the values with reference to the given example,

$$SS_{residual} = 65.6 - 58.4 = 7.2$$

The residual sum of squares can also be obtained directly. We know that the residual sum of squares is the subject × treatment interaction sum of squares. Table 15.2 is itself the subject × treatment interaction table. In a single-factor experiment or one-way ANOVA with repeated measures, the data itself represent the subject × treatment interaction table. Thus,

Subject × treatment SS = Total SS − Treatment SS − Between Ss SS

On substituting the values in accordance with the given example,

Subject × Treatment SS = 70.0 − 58.4 − 4.4 = 70.0 − 62.8 = 7.2.

Thus, the residual sum of squares by the direct method is exactly the same as obtained through the subtraction method.

Step 6. Computation of degrees of freedom (df). The analysis of df follows the same pattern as the analysis of SS. Each type of SS has its associated df. Thus, the total df (df_{total}) is partitioned into two additive and independent parts: between-subjects df ($df_{between\ Ss}$) and within-subjects df ($df_{within\ Ss}$), which is again partitioned into two additive parts: between-treatment df ($df_{between\ treatment}$) and residual df ($df_{residual}$), as shown in Figure 15.1. In the given example (see Table 15.2),

k (treatments)$=5$ and n (subjects)$=5$. So, $N = kn = 5 \times 5 = 25$. Different types of df are computed as follows:

(a) Total df $(df_{total}) = N - 1$ or $kn - 1 = 25 - 1 = 24$.
(b) Between-subjects df $(df_{between\ Ss}) = n - 1 = 5 - 1 = 4$
(c) Within-subjects df $(df_{within\ Ss}) = n(k - 1) = 5(5 - 1) = 5 \times 4 = 20$
(d) Between-treatments df $(df_{between\ treatment}) = k - 1 = 5 - 1 = 4$
(e) Residual df $(df_{residual}) = (n - 1)(k - 1) = (5 - 1)(5 - 1) = 4 \times 4 = 16$

Step 7. Computation of mean squares (MS). The mean squares (MS) are otherwise known as variance estimates. The MS is obtained by dividing the SS by its associated df. Thus, MS=SS/df. In one-way ANOVA with repeated measures, we are mainly interested in the treatment effect. Therefore, we need to calculate the treatment MS and residual (error) MS, as follows:

$$\text{Treatment MS} = \frac{SS_{treatment}}{df_{treatment}} = \frac{58.4}{4} = 14.60$$

$$\text{Residual (Error) MS} = \frac{SS_{residual}}{df_{residual}} = \frac{7.2}{16} = 0.45$$

Step 8. Computation of F-ratio. For the given set of data, the F-ratio for the treatment effect is obtained by dividing the MS treatment by the MS residual (error), as follows:

$$F = \frac{14.60}{0.45} = 32.44$$

Step 9. Summary of ANOVA. The results of the computation, done in accordance with the single-factor (or one-way ANOVA) experimental design with repeated measures, have been summarised in Table 15.3.

Step 10. Test of Significance. To evaluate the obtained F-ratio for the treatment effect, we refer to the critical values of F given in Table E in the appendix for 4 and 16 df. We observe that the critical value of F for 4 and 16 df, for $\alpha = 0.05$ is 3.01 and for $\alpha = 0.01$ is 4.77. Our obtained value 32.44 far exceeds the critical value of F. Thus, the obtained value of $F = 32.44$ is significant at the 0.01 level of significance. Therefore, $p < 0.01$. So, we reject the null hypothesis (H_0), accept the alternate hypothesis (H_1) and conclude that the treatment means differ significantly in 99% of cases.

Table 15.3 Summary of one-way ANOVA with repeated measures

Source of Variation	SS	df	MS	F
Between subjects	4.4	4		
Within subjects	65.6	20		
Treatments	58.4	4	14.60	32.44**
Residual (Error)	7.2	16	0.45	
Total	70.0	24		

Note: ** $p < 0.01$.

In order to evaluate the differences among the various treatment means, additional post-hoc tests may be made in accordance with the procedures discussed in Chapter 19. For this design the residual MS is the error MS for these multiple comparison tests.

15.2.6 Illustrative Example: One-way Repeated-measures ANOVA

Example 15.1 The following data were obtained from a research study examining the effect of sleep deprivation on motor-skills performance. A sample of five subjects was tested on a motor-skills task after 24 hours of sleep deprivation, tested again after 36 hours and tested once more after 48 hours. The dependent variable is the number of errors made on the motor-skills task.

Subjects	24 hours	36 hours	48 hours
A	0	0	6
B	1	3	5
C	0	1	5
D	4	5	9
E	0	1	5

Do the data indicate that the number of hours of sleep deprivation has a significant effect on motor-skills performance?

Solution

For the solution of the above problem the following steps are to be followed:

1. The given data are entered in Table 15.4 having all its notations.

Table 15.4 Error scores of five subjects tested under each of the three levels of sleep deprivation

Subjects	24 hours	36 hours	48 hours	ΣS
A	0	0	6	6
B	1	3	5	9
C	0	1	5	6
D	4	5	9	18
E	0	1	5	6
n:	5	5	5	$kn=N=3\times5=15$
ΣX_k:	5	10	30	$\Sigma\Sigma X_k=45(G)$
$\bar{X}_k$:	1.0	2.0	6.0	$\bar{X}_{k..}=3.0$
ΣX_k^2:	17	36	192	$\Sigma\Sigma X_k^2=245$

2. Computation of a variety of summary statistics as shown in Table 15.4. In the given example, $k=3$, $n=5$, $N=kn=3\times5=15$, and $G=45$.

3. Statement of hypotheses and alpha level:

$$H_0:\ \mu_1 = \mu_2 = \mu_3\ \ (\text{or } \bar{X}_{K_1} = \bar{X}_{K_2} = \bar{X}_{K_3})$$
$$H_1:\ \mu_1 \neq \mu_2 \neq \mu_3\ \ (\text{or } \bar{X}_{K_1} \neq \bar{X}_{K_2} \neq \bar{X}_{K_3})$$

or H_1: At least one of the treatment means is different.
We will set alpha at $\alpha=0.05$.

4. Computation of the correction term (C)

$$C = \frac{(G)^2}{N} = \frac{(45)^2}{15} = \frac{2025}{15} = 135.0$$

5. Computation of sum of squares (SS):

   (a) Total SS $= \Sigma\Sigma X_k^2 - C = 245.0 - 135.0 = 110.0$

   (b) Between-subjects SS $= \left[\Sigma \dfrac{(\Sigma S)^2}{k}\right] - C$

   $$= \left[\frac{(\Sigma S_1)^2}{k} + \frac{(\Sigma S_2)^2}{k} + \frac{(\Sigma S_3)^2}{k} + \frac{(\Sigma S_4)^2}{k} + \frac{(\Sigma S_5)^2}{k}\right] - C$$

   $$= \left[\frac{(6)^2}{3} + \frac{(9)^2}{3} + \frac{(6)^2}{3} + \frac{(18)^2}{3} + \frac{(6)^2}{3}\right] - 135.0$$

   $$= \left[\frac{36}{3} + \frac{81}{3} + \frac{36}{3} + \frac{324}{3} + \frac{36}{3}\right] - 135.0$$

   $$= [12 + 27 + 12 + 108 + 12] - 135.0$$

   $$= 171.0 - 135.0 = 36.0$$

   (c) Within-subjects SS $=$ Total SS $-$ Between-subject SS
   $$= 110.0 - 36.0 = 74.0$$

   (d) Between-treatments SS $= \left[\Sigma \dfrac{(\Sigma X_K)^2}{n}\right] - C$

   $$= \left[\frac{(\Sigma X_{k_1})^2}{n} + \frac{(\Sigma X_{k_2})^2}{n} + \frac{(\Sigma X_{k_3})^2}{n}\right] - C$$

   $$= \left[\frac{(5)^2}{5} + \frac{(10)^2}{5} + \frac{(30)^2}{5}\right] - 135.0$$

   $$= \left[\frac{25}{5} + \frac{100}{5} + \frac{900}{5}\right] - 135.0$$

   $$= [5.0 + 20.0 + 180.0] - 135.0$$

   $$= 205.0 - 135.0 = 70.0$$

   (e) Residual (error) SS $=$ Within-subjects SS $-$ Between-treatment SS $= 74.0 - 70.0 = 4.0$

6. Computation of df values:

   (a) Total df $= N-1$ or $kn-1 = 3\times5-1 = 15-1 = 14$
   (b) Between-subjects df $= n-1 = 5-1 = 4$

Table 15.5   Summary of one-way ANOVA with repeated measures

Source of Variation	SS	df	MS	F
Between subjects	36.0	4		
Within subjects	74.0	10		
Treatments	70.0	2	35.0	70.0**
Residual (Error)	4.0	8	0.5	
Total	110.0	14		

Note: **$p < 0.01$.

    (c) Within-subjects df $= n(k-1) = 5(3-1) = 5 \times 2 = 10$
    (d) Between-treatments df $= k - 1 = 3 - 1 = 2$
    (e) Residual (error) df $= (n-1)(k-1) = (5-1)(3-1) = 4 \times 2 = 8$

7. Computation of mean squares (MS):
    (a) Treatment MS $= \dfrac{\text{Treatment SS}}{\text{Treatment df}} = \dfrac{70.0}{2} = 35.0$

    (b) Residual (error) MS $= \dfrac{\text{Residual SS}}{\text{Residual df}} = \dfrac{4.0}{8} = 0.5$

8. Computation of F-ratio:

$$F \text{ for treatment} = \frac{\text{Treatment MS}}{\text{Residual MS}} = \frac{35.0}{0.5} = 70.0$$

9. Summary of ANOVA:
    The results of analysis have been summarised in Table 15.5.

10. Test of Significance:
    Referring to Table E in the appendix, we find that the critical value of F for 2 and 8 df, for $\alpha = 0.05$ is 4.46 and for $\alpha = 0.01$ is 8.65. Our obtained value of $F = 70.0$ far exceeds the critical value of F. Thus, the obtained value of F for treatments is significant at the 0.01 level of significance. Therefore, $p < 0.01$. So, we reject the null hypothesis (H_0), accept the alternate hypothesis (H_1) and conclude that the number of hours of sleep deprivation has a significant effect on the number of errors committed by the subjects on the motor-skill performance in 99% of cases.

15.3   Two-way (Two-factor) ANOVA with Repeated Measures on One Factor

The simplest case of repeated-measures design has already been discussed in the previous section (see Section 15.2), in which the k treatments are classified along a single dimension and each experimental unit or subject undergoes all the treatments. This type of experiment has been designated as single-factor experiment (or one-way ANOVA) with repeated measures. In this section, we shall first consider an experimental design with repeated measures on one of the two factors (or two-way ANOVA with repeated measures on one of the two factors) and later in Section 15.4 we shall consider a design (two-way ANOVA) with repeated measures on both the factors. Experiments in which repeated measures are obtained on all the factors are called within-subjects designs. Those experiments in which repeated measures are obtained on levels of some factor/s and only under one of the levels of other factor/s are called mixed designs. These are experiments in which some factors are within subjects and some between subjects. Both types of designs will be considered in this chapter (Sections 15.3 and 15.4). First, we shall take up two-factor experiments ($p \times q$) with repeated measures on one factor (mixed design) followed by one with repeated measures on both the factors (within-subjects design).

15.3.1 General Layout of Two-factor Experiment (or Two-way ANOVA) with Repeated Measures on One Factor

The general layout of the two-factor experiment ($p \times q$) with repeated measures on the second factor (i.e., on factor B), factor A having p levels ($a_1, a_2, a_3, \ldots, a_p$) and factor B having q levels ($b_1, b_2, b_3, \ldots, b_q$), with n subjects in each p level, has been presented in Table 15.6. Factor A (between subjects) has been arranged on the vertical axis and factor B (within subjects) on the horizontal axis. Since factor A has p levels and factor B q levels, there are pq treatment combinations in the experiment. Each of the n subjects under level a_1 is observed under all the q levels of factor B. Similarly, each of the n subjects under level a_2 is observed under all the q levels of factor B and so on till level a_p. Thus, each of the np subjects is observed under all the q levels of factor B. Factors A and B are fixed, and the order in which subjects are observed under the levels of factor B is randomised independently.

The observation or the subject's score is indicated by letter X in the Table 15.6 which can be identified by three subscripts, the first refers to the subject number (1, 2, 3, ..., n) under each level of factor A, the second to the levels of factor A (1, 2, 3, ..., p) and the third to the levels of factor B (1, 2, 3, ..., q). For example, X_{111} refers to an observation of subject 1 under treatment combinations in which level 1 of factor A and level 1 of factor B have been administered. Similarly, X_{npq} refers to an observation of subject n in which level p of factor A and level q of factor B have been administered.

15.3.2 Partitioning of the Total Sum of Squares and df in a Two-factor Experiment (or Two-way ANOVA) with Repeated Measures on One Factor

In a two-factor (A $\times$ B) experiment (or two-way ANOVA) with repeated measures on the second factor (i.e., factor B) and n subjects in each of the p levels of factor A, the total sum of squares is first partitioned into two additive component parts—the between-subjects sum of squares ($SS_{bet.Ss}$) and within-subjects sum of squares ($SS_{w.Ss}$). The between-subjects sum of squares is based on the variation of the individual subject's mean about the overall mean. This represents the variation due to individual differences. The within-subjects sum of squares represents the pooled variation of the individual subject's observations about the respective mean.

The between subjects sum of squares is further partitioned into two component parts—A sum of squares (SS_A) and subjects within-groups sum of squares ($SS_{Ss\,w.grps}$). The 'A sum of squares' is based on the variation of the p levels of factor A, averaged over levels of factor B, about the overall mean. The subjects within-groups sum of squares is the pooled variation due to subjects within groups 1, 2, 3, ..., p.

Table 15.6 General layout of a two-factor experiment ($p \times q$) with repeated measures on the second factor

Factor A Levels	Subjects	Factor B Levels				ΣS
		b_1	b_2	$b_3 \dots b_q$		
	1	X_{111}	X_{112}	X_{113}	X_{11q}	
	2	X_{211}	X_{212}	X_{213}	X_{21q}	
a_1	3	X_{311}	X_{312}	X_{313}	X_{31q}	
	$\vdots$	$\vdots$	$\vdots$	$\vdots$	$\vdots$	
	n	X_{n11}	X_{n12}	X_{n13}	X_{n1q}	
Σ						
	1	X_{121}	X_{122}	X_{123}	X_{12q}	
	2	X_{221}	X_{222}	X_{223}	X_{22q}	
a_2	3	X_{321}	X_{322}	X_{323}	X_{32q}	
	$\vdots$	$\vdots$	$\vdots$	$\vdots$	$\vdots$	
	n	X_{n21}	X_{n22}	X_{n23}	X_{n2q}	
Σ						
	1	X_{131}	X_{132}	X_{133}	X_{13q}	
	2	X_{231}	X_{232}	X_{233}	X_{23q}	
a_3	3	X_{331}	X_{332}	X_{333}	X_{33q}	
	$\vdots$	$\vdots$	$\vdots$	$\vdots$	$\vdots$	
	n	X_{n31}	X_{n32}	X_{n33}	X_{n3q}	
Σ						
	$\vdots$	$\vdots$	$\vdots$	$\vdots$	$\vdots$	
	1	X_{1p1}	X_{1p2}	X_{1p3}	X_{1pq}	
	2	X_{2p1}	X_{2p2}	X_{2p3}	X_{2pq}	
a_p	3	X_{3p1}	X_{3p2}	X_{3p3}	X_{3pq}	
	$\vdots$	$\vdots$	$\vdots$	$\vdots$	$\vdots$	
	n	X_{np1}	X_{np2}	X_{np3}	X_{npq}	
Σ						
Σ						

Similarly, the within-subjects sum of squares is partitioned into three component parts—B sum of squares (SS_B), AB sum of squares (SS_{AB}) and B×subjects within groups sum of squares ($SS_B \times SS_{S.w.grps.}$). The B sum of squares is based on the variation of the q levels of factor B, averaged over levels of factor A, about the overall mean. The AB sum of squares is the variation due to the joint effect of two factors/variables acting together. The B×subjects within groups sum of squares is the pooled variation due to the interaction of B and subjects within groups.

It is important to note that factor A is the part of between-subjects variation, and B and AB that of the within-subjects variation. The appropriate denominator (error) to test the main effect of A is the subjects within groups variation (error between) and to test the main effect of B and AB interaction is the B×subjects within groups variation (error within).

In a similar vein, the total df ($npq-1$) is first partitioned into two parts—($np-1$) df attributable to the between-subjects sum of squares and [$np (q-1)$] df attributable to the within subjects sum of squares. Further, ($np-1$) df associated with the between-subjects sum of squares is partitioned into two components—($p-1$) df attributable to the A sum of squares and [$p (n-1)$] df attributable to the subjects within groups sum of squares. Similarly, [$np (q-1)$] df associated with the within-subjects sum of squares is partitioned into three components—($q-1$) df attributable to the B sum of squares, [$(p-1) (q-1)$] df attributable to the AB sum of squares and [$p(n-1)(q-1)$] df attributable to the B×subjects within groups sum of squares.

Figure 15.2 represents the partitioning of the total sum of squares and df in a two-factor experiment (or two-way ANOVA) with repeated measures on the second factor. The levels of factor A and factor B are considered fixed.

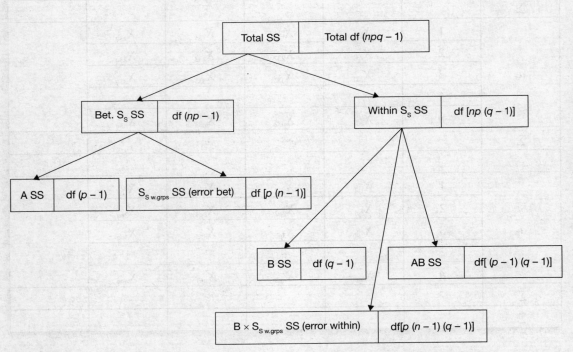

Figure 15.2 Schematic representation of the analysis of two-factor experiment with repeated measures on second factor

Note: n is the number of subjects in each of the p levels of factor A, p is the number of levels of factor A, q is the number of levels of factor B, npq is the total number of observations in the experiment.

In the equation form the partitioning of the total sum of squares may be expressed as:

$$SS_{total} = SS_{bet.Ss} + SS_{w.Ss}$$
$$= SS_A + SS_{Ss.w.grps} + SS_B + SS_{AB} + SS_{BxSs\ w.grps}$$

where

SS_{total} = total sum of squares

$SS_{bet.Ss}$ = between-subjects sum of squares

$SS_{w.Ss}$ = within-subjects sum of squares

SS_A = A sum of squares (or sum of squares between the p levels of factor A)

$SS_{Ss\ w.grps}$ = pooled sum of squares between subjects within groups (error between)

SS_B = B sum of squares (or sum of squares between the q levels of factor B)

SS_{AB} = AB sum of squares (or sum of squares due to the interaction of factors A and B)

$SS_{B \times Ssw.grps}$ = pooled sum of squares between B × subjects within groups (error within).

Similarly, in the equation form the partitioning of the total degrees of freedom may be expressed as:

$$df_{total} = df_{bet.\ ss} + df_{w.Ss}$$
$$= df_A + df_{Ss\ w.grps} + df_B + df_{AB} + df_{B \times Ss\ w.grps}$$
$$\text{or}\quad (npq-1) = (np-1) + np(q-1)$$
$$= (p-1) + p(n-1) + (q-1) + (p-1)(q-1) + p(n-1)(q-1)$$

where

df_{total} = total degrees of freedom associated with the total sum of squares $(npq-1)$

$df_{bet.Ss}$ = degrees of freedom associated with the sum of squares between subjects $(np-1)$

$df_{w.Ss}$ = degrees of freedom associated with the sum of squares within subjects $[np(q-1)]$

df_A = degrees of freedom associated with the sum of squares between the p levels of factor A $(p-1)$

$df_{Ss\ w.grps}$ = degrees of freedom associated with the sum of squares due to subjects within groups $[p(n-1)]$

df_B = degrees of freedom associated with the sum of squares between the q levels of factor B $(q-1)$

df_{AB} = degrees of freedom associated with the sum of squares due to the interaction of factors A and B $[(p-1)(q-1)]$

$df_{B \times Ss\ w.grps}$ = degrees of freedom associated with the sum of squares due to the interaction of B × Ss within groups $[p(n-1)(q-1)]$

15.3.3   Steps Involved in Computation of Two-way ANOVA with Repeated Measures on One Factor

Let us discuss the steps involved in analysing data for a two-factor experiment $(p \times q)$ or a two-way ANOVA with repeated measures on the second factor. The data are from a hypothetical experiment in which the researcher is interested in studying the effects of rearing environments and days on the exploratory behaviour of rats. Two groups of rats, three in each, reared either in an impoverished or in an enriched environment were tested for their exploratory behaviour for four days. The dependent measure is the number of cells explored in the exploratory box within a particular time interval. Thus, it is a 2 × 4 factorial experiment with repeated measures on the second factor. The first variable or factor A (i.e., rearing environment) has two

Table 15.7   Exploration scores of the subjects in a 2×4 factorial experiment with repeated measures on the second factor

Levels of Factor A	Subjects	Levels of Factor B				ΣX_s	$\bar{X}_s$
		b_1	b_2	b_3	b_4		
a_1	1	5	3	0	0	8	2.0
	2	5	4	3	1	13	3.25
	3	6	2	4	3	15	3.75
	ΣX_{a_1b}:	16	9	7	4	$\Sigma\Sigma X_{a_1b} = 36$	
	$\bar{X}_{a_1b}$:	5.33	3.0	2.33	1.33	$\bar{X}_{a_1b\cdot\cdot} = 3.0$	
	$\Sigma X_{a_1b}^2$:	86	29	25	10	$\Sigma\Sigma X_{a_1b}^2 = 150$	
a_2	1	7	8	4	2	21	5.25
	2	6	6	5	4	21	5.25
	3	8	9	7	5	29	7.25
	ΣX_{a_2b}:	21	23	16	11	$\Sigma\Sigma X_{a_2b} = 71$	
	$\bar{X}_{a_2b}$:	7.0	7.67	5.33	3.67	$\bar{X}_{a_2b\cdot\cdot} = 5.92$	
	$\Sigma X_{a_2b}^2$:	149	181	90	45	$\Sigma\Sigma X_{a_2b}^2 = 465$	
	ΣX_{ab}:	37	32	23	15	$\Sigma\Sigma X_{ab} = 107(G)$	
	$\bar{X}_{ab}$:	6.17	5.33	3.83	2.5	$\bar{X}_{ab\cdot\cdot} = 4.46$	
	ΣX_{ab}^2:	235	210	115	55	$\Sigma\Sigma X_{ab}^2 = 615$	

Note: For this table, $n=3$, $p=2$, $q=4$, $npq = N = 3 \times 2 \times 4 = 24$.

levels—impoverished environment (a_1) and enriched environment (a_2). The second variable or factor B (i.e., days) has four levels—Day 1 (b_1), Day 2 (b_2), Day 3 (b_3) and Day 4 (b_4). A total of six subjects were taken, three impoverished and three enriched. Each of the six subjects was observed under each of the four levels of factor B. The outcome of the hypothetical experiment is given in Table 15.7.

The AB summary table has been prepared from Table 15.7 in order to obtain the totals of treatments a_1b_1, a_1b_2, a_1b_3, a_1b_4, a_2b_1, a_2b_2, a_2b_3, a_2b_4, a_1, a_2, b_1, b_2, b_3 and b_4 which have been entered in the appropriate cells of the AB summary table. The levels of factor A, as in Table 15.7, have been presented on the vertical axis and that of factor B on the horizontal axis.

AB Summary Table

	b_1	b_2	b_3	b_4	Sum
a_1	16	9	7	4	36
a_2	21	23	16	11	71
Sum	37	32	23	15	107

For this AB summary table, $p=2$, $q=4$ and $n=3$. So, $N=npq=3 \times 2 \times 4=24$. The means are computed as:

$$\bar{X}_{a_1} = \frac{36}{nq} = \frac{36}{12} = 3.0 \qquad \bar{X}_{b_3} = \frac{23}{np} = \frac{23}{6} = 3.83$$

$$\bar{X}_{a_2} = \frac{71}{nq} = \frac{71}{12} = 5.92 \qquad \bar{X}_{b_4} = \frac{15}{np} = \frac{15}{6} = 2.50$$

$$\bar{X}_{a_1 b_1} = \frac{16}{n} = \frac{16}{3} = 5.33 \qquad \bar{X}_{a_2 b_1} = \frac{21}{n} = \frac{21}{3} = 7.00$$

$$\bar{X}_{a_1 b_2} = \frac{9}{n} = \frac{9}{3} = 3.0 \qquad \bar{X}_{a_2 b_2} = \frac{23}{n} = \frac{23}{3} = 7.67$$

$$\bar{X}_{a_1 b_3} = \frac{7}{n} = \frac{7}{3} = 2.33 \qquad \bar{X}_{a_2 b_3} = \frac{16}{n} = \frac{16}{3} = 5.33$$

$$\bar{X}_{a_1 b_4} = \frac{4}{n} = \frac{4}{3} = 1.33 \qquad \bar{X}_{a_2 b_4} = \frac{11}{n} = \frac{11}{3} = 3.67$$

$$\bar{X}_{b_1} = \frac{37}{np} = \frac{37}{6} = 6.17$$

$$\bar{X}_{b_2} = \frac{32}{np} = \frac{32}{6} = 5.33$$

Grand mean (overall mean) $= \frac{\Sigma\Sigma X_{ab}}{N} = \frac{107}{24} = 4.46$

To test the significance of the effects of factors A, B and AB interaction using two-way ANOVA with repeated measures on the second factor, the following steps are to be followed:

Step 1. Presentation of the given data in a table having all its notations, like p (a_1 and a_2)=2, q (b_1, b_2, b_3 and b_4)=4, $n=3$, $N=npq=3 \times 2 \times 4=24$, etc., as shown in Table 15.7.

Step 2. Computation of a variety of summary statistics, preparation of AB summary table and computation of various means as shown earlier in the text and also in Table 15.7.

Step 3. Statement of null hypothesis (H_0) and alternative hypothesis (H_1), and selection of an alpha level.

For factor A, the H_0 states that there is no difference between the mean exploratory behaviour of impoverished and enriched rats. However, the H_1 states that both impoverished and enriched rats differ in their mean scores. In symbols,

$$H_0: \quad \mu_{a_1} = \mu_{a_2} \quad (\text{or } \bar{X}_{a_1} = \bar{X}_{a_2})$$
$$H_1: \quad \mu_{a_1} \neq \mu_{a_2} \quad (\text{or } \bar{X}_{a_1} \neq \bar{X}_{a_2})$$

For factor B, the H_0 states that the mean exploration scores of rats over four days are same. On the contrary, the H_1 states that the mean exploration scores of rats over four days are not same. In symbols,

$$H_0: \quad \mu_{b_1} = \mu_{b_2} = \mu_{b_3} = \mu_{b_4} \quad (\text{or } \bar{X}_{b_1} = \bar{X}_{b_2} = \bar{X}_{b_3} = \bar{X}_{b_4})$$
$$H_1: \quad \mu_{b_1} \neq \mu_{b_2} \neq \mu_{b_3} \neq \mu_{b_4} \quad (\text{or } \bar{X}_{b_1} \neq \bar{X}_{b_2} \neq \bar{X}_{b_3} \neq \bar{X}_{b_4})$$

For the A×B interaction, the H_0 can be stated in two different ways. First, the difference in the mean exploration scores between impoverished and enriched subjects will be the same for four consecutive testing days (i.e., for Day 1, Day 2, Day 3 and

Day 4). Second, the difference in the mean exploration scores among four consecutive testing days will be the same for both impoverished and enriched rats. In more general terms,

H_0: The effect of factor A does not depend on the levels of factor B
   (and B does not depend on A)
H_1: The effect of one factor does depend on the levels of the other factor

We will set alpha at $\alpha = 0.05$

Step 4. Computation of the correction term (C). C is computed by squaring the grand total ($\Sigma\Sigma X_{ab}$ or G) and then dividing it by the total number of observations ($N = npq$) in the study.

In the given example (see Table 15.7), $G = 107$, $n = 3$, $p = 2$, $q = 4$ and $N = npq = 3 \times 2 \times 4 = 24$. Therefore, the correction term (C) is,

$$C = \frac{(G)^2}{N} = \frac{(107)^2}{24} = \frac{11449}{24} = 477.04$$

Step 5. Computation of the sum of squares (SS). In a two-factor experimental design (or two-way ANOVA) with repeated measures on the second factor, the total sum of squares is first partitioned into 'between-subjects sum of squares' ($SS_{bet.Ss}$) and 'within-subjects sum of squares' ($SS_{w.Ss}$). The between-subjects sum of squares is further partitioned into two parts—A sum of squares (SS_A) and subjects within groups sum of squares ($SS_{Ss\,w.grps}$). Similarly, the within-subjects sum of squares is further partitioned into three parts—B sum of squares (SS_B), AB interaction sum of squares (SS_{AB}) and B×subjects within groups sum of squares ($SS_{B \times Ss.w.grps}$). These sums of squares are computed below one after another.

(a) **Total sum of squares (SS_{total}).** The total sum of squares is obtained by squaring each of the scores in the entire set of observations irrespective of the p and q levels of both the factors in the experiment, adding them up and then subtracting the correction term (C) from the sum. Thus, the formula for the total sum of squares (SS_{total}) reads:

$$SS_{total} = \Sigma\Sigma X_{ab}^2 - C$$

Applying this above formula to the set of data in Table 15.7, we obtain

$$SS_{total} = \Sigma\Sigma X_{ab}^2 - C = 615 - 477.04 = 137.96$$

(b) **Between-subjects sum of squares ($SS_{bet.Ss}$).** As each subject in the experiment undergoes all the levels of factor B, the sum of the rows (i.e., the sum of the scores of each subject) given in the last but one column of Table 15.7, represents the variation due to individual differences or between-subjects variation. The between-subjects variation is a function of the squared deviations of the means of the individual subjects about the grand mean.

In the given example (see Table 15.7), the sum of each of the four observations of each of the ($np = 3 \times 2 = 6$) six subjects, given in the last but one column of Table 15.7, has been squared, divided by 4 (the number of observations making up the total) summed up and finally the correction term has been subtracted from the sum. The computational formula for $SS_{bet.Ss}$ reads:

$$SS_{\text{bet. Ss}} = \left[\Sigma \frac{(\Sigma S_{np})^2}{q} \right] - C$$

$$= \left[\frac{(\Sigma S_1)^2}{4} + \frac{(\Sigma S_2)^2}{4} + \frac{(\Sigma S_3)^2}{4} + \cdots + \frac{(\Sigma S_{np})^2}{4} \right] - C$$

Applying this above formula to the set of data given in Table 15.7, we obtain:

$$SS_{\text{bet .Ss}} = \left[\frac{(8)^2}{4} + \frac{(13)^2}{4} + \frac{(15)^2}{4} + \frac{(21)^2}{4} + \frac{(21)^2}{4} + \frac{(29)^2}{4} \right] - 477.04$$

$$= \left[\frac{64}{4} + \frac{169}{4} + \frac{225}{4} + \frac{441}{4} + \frac{441}{4} + \frac{841}{4} \right] - 477.04$$

$$= [16.0 + 42.25 + 56.25 + 110.25 + 110.25 + 210.25] - 477.04$$

$$= 545.25 - 477.04 = 68.21$$

(c) **Within-subjects sum of squares ($Ss_{\text{w.Ss}}$).** In this case, the within-subjects sum of squares has been obtained by subtraction. From Figure 15.2, it can be observed that the total sum of squares is bifurcated into 'between-subjects sum of squares' and 'within-subjects sum of squares'. Therefore, in order to get within-subjects sum of squares, we can subtract the between-subjects sum of squares from the total sum of squares. Thus, the within-subjects sum of squares obtained is,

$$SS_{\text{w.Ss}} = SS_{\text{total}} - SS_{\text{bet. Ss}}$$
$$= 137.96 - 68.21 = 69.75$$

We can also find out the within-subjects sum of squares by the *direct method*. We know that within-subjects sum of squares is the pooled variation of individual subject's observations about the respective means. Therefore,

$$SS_{\text{w.}}S_1 = (5)^2 + (3)^2 + (0)^2 + (0)^2 - \frac{(8)^2}{4} = 25 + 9 + 0 + 0 - \frac{64}{4} = 34 - 16 = 18.0$$

$$SS_{\text{w.}}S_2 = (5)^2 + (4)^2 + (3)^2 + (1)^2 - \frac{(13)^2}{4} = 25 + 16 + 9 + 1 - \frac{169}{4} = 51 - 42.25 = 8.75$$

$$SS_{\text{w.}}S_3 = (6)^2 + (2)^2 + (4)^2 + (3)^2 - \frac{(15)^2}{4} = 36 + 4 + 16 + 9 - \frac{225}{4} = 65 - 56.25 = 8.75$$

$$SS_{\text{w.}}S_4 = (7)^2 + (8)^2 + (4)^2 + (2)^2 - \frac{(21)^2}{4} = 49 + 64 + 16 + 4 - \frac{441}{4} = 133 - 110.25 = 22.75$$

$$SS_{\text{w.}}S_5 = (6)^2 + (6)^2 + (5)^2 + (4)^2 - \frac{(21)^2}{4} = 36 + 36 + 25 + 16 - \frac{441}{4} = 113 - 110.25 = 2.75$$

$$SS_{\text{w.}}S_6 = (8)^2 + (9)^2 + (7)^2 + (5)^2 - \frac{(29)^2}{4} = 64 + 81 + 49 + 25 - \frac{841}{4} = 219 - 210.25 = 8.75$$

$$\therefore SS_{\text{w.Ss}} = 18.0 + 8.75 + 8.75 + 22.75 + 2.75 + 8.75 = 69.75$$

It can be observed that the outcome by the *direct method* is exactly the same as obtained by the *subtraction method*.

(d) **A sum of squares (SS$_A$).** The main effect of factor A has been computed from the row totals of the AB summary table, presented after Table 15.7. The row totals corresponding to levels a_1 (or p_1) and a_2 (or p_2) are 36 and 71, respectively. These totals are squared, each divided by 12 ($nq = 3 \times 4 = 12$), summed up and finally the correction term is subtracted from the sum. The A sum of squares is found to be:

$$SS_A = \left[\frac{(\Sigma a_1)^2}{n_1 q} + \frac{(\Sigma a_2)^2}{n_2 q} \right] - C \quad \text{or} \quad \left[\frac{(\Sigma p_1)^2}{n_1 q} + \frac{(\Sigma p_2)^2}{n_2 q} \right] - C$$

$$= \left[\frac{(36)^2}{12} + \frac{(71)^2}{12} \right] - 477.04 = \left[\frac{1296}{12} + \frac{5041}{12} \right] - 477.04$$

$$= [108.0 + 420.08] - 477.04 = 528.08 - 477.04 = 51.04$$

(e) **Subjects within-groups sum of squares (SS$_{Ss.w.grps}$).** In this case, the subjects within groups sum of squares has been obtained by subtraction. From Figure 15.2, it can be observed that the between subjects sum of squares has been bifurcated into A sum of squares and subjects within groups sum of squares. Thus, the subjects within groups sum of squares can be obtained by subtracting A sum of squares from the between subjects sum of squares, as follows:

$$SS_{Ss\,w.grps} = SS_{bet.Ss} - SS_A$$
$$= 68.21 - 51.04 = 17.17$$

We can also find out the subjects within groups sum of squares by the *direct method*. We know that the subjects within groups sum of squares is the pooled variation between the subjects within each of the two groups a_1 (impoverished environment) and a_2 (enriched environment).

$$SS_{Ss.w.group\,a_1} = \left[\frac{(\Sigma S_1)^2}{q} + \frac{(\Sigma S_2)^2}{q} + \frac{(\Sigma S_3)^2}{q} \right] - \frac{(\Sigma S_{n_1 q})^2}{n_1 q}$$

$$= \left[\frac{(8)^2}{4} + \frac{(13)^2}{4} + \frac{(15)^2}{4} \right] - \frac{(36)^2}{12} = \left[\frac{64}{4} + \frac{169}{4} + \frac{225}{4} \right] - \frac{1296}{12}$$

$$= [16.0 + 42.25 + 56.25] - 108.0 = 114.5 - 108.0 = 6.5$$

$$SS_{Ss.w.group\,a_2} = \left[\frac{(\Sigma S_1)^2}{q} + \frac{(\Sigma S_2)^2}{q} + \frac{(\Sigma S_3)^2}{q} \right] - \frac{(\Sigma S_{n_2 q})^2}{n_2 q}$$

$$= \left[\frac{(21)^2}{4} + \frac{(21)^2}{4} + \frac{(29)^2}{4} \right] - \frac{(71)^2}{12} = \left[\frac{441}{4} + \frac{441}{4} + \frac{841}{4} \right] - \frac{5041}{12}$$

$$= [110.25 + 110.25 + 210.25] - 420.08 = 430.75 - 420.08 = 10.67$$

$$\therefore SS_{Ss.w.groups} = 6.5 + 10.67 = 17.17.$$

Thus, we observe that the outcome by the *direct method* is exactly the same as obtained by the *subtraction method*.

The subjects within groups sum of squares is the appropriate denominator (error between) to test the main effect of A. It is obtained by adding the separate variations between the subjects within groups a_1 and a_2. The sum of the observations of each subject in each of the two groups is squared and each divided by 4 ($q=4$, the number of observations making up the total), added up and finally the correction term (separate for each group) is subtracted from the total. The two variations or sum of squares, thus, obtained are then pooled to obtain the subjects within groups variation.

(f)   **B sum of squares (SS$_B$).** The main effect of B has been obtained from the column totals of the AB summary table. The column totals corresponding to levels b_1 (or q_1), b_2 (or q_2), b_3 (or q_3) and b_4 (or q_4) are 37, 32, 23 and 15, respectively. Each of these totals is squared, each divided by 6 ($np=3 \times 2=6$), summed up and finally the correction term is subtracted from the sum. The B sum of squares is found to be equal to:

$$SS_B = \left[\frac{(\Sigma b_1)^2}{np} + \frac{(\Sigma b_2)^2}{np} + \frac{(\Sigma b_3)^2}{np} + \frac{(\Sigma b_4)^2}{np} \right] - C$$

$$= \left[\frac{(37)^2}{6} + \frac{(32)^2}{6} + \frac{(23)^2}{6} + \frac{(15)^2}{6} \right] - 477.04$$

$$= \left[\frac{1369}{6} + \frac{1024}{6} + \frac{529}{6} + \frac{225}{6} \right] - 477.04$$

$$= [228.17 + 170.67 + 88.17 + 37.50] - 477.04 = 524.51 - 477.04 = 47.47$$

(g)   **AB sum of squares (SS$_{AB}$).** The AB interaction sum of squares has been obtained from the AB summary table. The AB sum of squares is found by subtracting the A sum of squares and B sum of squares from the cell sum of squares. The totals entered in the cells of the AB summary table are: 16, 9, 7, 4, 21, 23, 16 and 11. Each of these cells values (or totals) is based on three observations ($n=3$). The cell values (or totals) are first squared, each divided by 3 (the number of observations making up each of the totals), summed up and finally the correction term is subtracted from the sum. Thus, we obtain the cell sum of squares. To obtain the AB interaction sum of squares, we subtract A sum of squares and B sum of squares from the cell sum of squares. The obtained cell sum of squares is,

$$SS_{cell} = \left[\frac{(16)^2}{3} + \frac{(9)^2}{3} + \frac{(7)^2}{3} + \frac{(4)^2}{3} + \frac{(21)^2}{3} + \frac{(23)^2}{3} + \frac{(16)^2}{3} + \frac{(11)^2}{3} \right] - C$$

$$= \left[\frac{256}{3} + \frac{81}{3} + \frac{49}{3} + \frac{16}{3} + \frac{441}{3} + \frac{529}{3} + \frac{256}{3} + \frac{121}{3} \right] - 477.04$$

$$= [85.33 + 27.00 + 16.33 + 5.33 + 147.00 + 176.33 + 85.33 + 40.33] - 477.04$$

$$= 582.98 - 477.04 = 105.94$$

$$SS_{AB} = SS_{Cell} - SS_A - SS_B$$
$$= 105.94 - 51.04 - 47.47$$
$$= 105.94 - 98.51 = 7.43$$

Thus, the obtained AB sum of squares is found to be equal to 7.43.

(h)   **B × subjects within groups sum of squares (SS$_{B \times Ss.w.grps}$).** The B × subjects within groups sum of squares has been obtained by subtraction. Referring to Figure 15.2, it is observed that the within-subjects sum of squares has been partitioned into three components, such as B sum of squares, AB sum of squares and B × subjects within groups sum of squares. Thus, we can obtain the B × subjects within groups sum of squares by subtracting the B sum of squares and AB sum of squares from the within-subjects sum of squares. The obtained $B \times$ subjects within groups sum of square is equal to:

$$\begin{aligned} SS_{B \times Ss.w.grps} &= SS_{w.Ss} - SS_B - SS_{AB} \\ &= 69.75 - 47.47 - 7.43 \\ &= 69.75 - 54.90 = 14.85 \end{aligned}$$

We can also find out the $B \times$ subjects within groups sum of squares by the direct method. We know that the $B \times$ subjects within groups sum of squares is the pooled variation of $B \times$ subjects within-group a_1 and $B \times$ subjects within-group a_2. Let us first prepare the $B \times$ subjects within-groups interaction tables from Table 15.7.

$B \times$ Subjects Within Group a_1

Ss	b_1	b_2	b_3	b_4	Total
1	5	3	0	0	8
2	5	4	3	1	13
3	6	2	4	3	15
Total	16	9	7	4	36

$B \times$ Subjects within Group a_2

Ss	b_1	b_2	b_3	b_4	Total
1	7	8	4	2	21
2	6	6	5	4	21
3	8	9	7	5	29
Total	21	23	16	11	71

$$SS_{B \times Ss\,w.grp.}a_1 = \left[(5)^2 + (5)^2 + (6)^2 + \cdots + (3)^2 - \frac{(36)^2}{12} \right]$$

$$- \left[\frac{(8)^2}{4} + \frac{(13)^2}{4} + \frac{(15)^2}{4} - \frac{(36)^2}{12} \right] - \left[\frac{(16)^2}{3} + \frac{(9)^2}{3} + \frac{(7)^2}{3} + \frac{(4)^2}{3} - \frac{(36)^2}{12} \right]$$

$$= \left[150 - 108.0 \right] - \left[114.5 - 108.0 \right] - \left[133.99 - 108.0 \right]$$

$$= 42.0 - 6.5 - 25.99 = 42.0 - 32.49 = 9.51$$

$$SS_{B \times Ss\,w.grp.}a_2 = \left[(7)^2 + (6)^2 + (8)^2 + \cdots + (5)^2 - \frac{(71)^2}{12} \right]$$

$$- \left[\frac{(21)^2}{4} + \frac{(21)^2}{4} + \frac{(29)^2}{4} - \frac{(71)^2}{12} \right] - \left[\frac{(21)^2}{3} + \frac{(23)^2}{3} + \frac{(16)^2}{3} + \frac{(11)^2}{3} - \frac{(71)^2}{12} \right]$$

$$= \left[465 - 420.08 \right] - \left[430.75 - 420.08 \right] - \left[448.99 - 420.08 \right]$$

$$= 44.92 - 10.67 - 28.91 = 44.92 - 39.58 = 5.34$$

$$\therefore SS_B \times_{Ss.w.groups} = 9.51 + 5.34 = 14.85$$

It can be observed that the outcome by the *direct method* is exactly the same as that obtained by the *subtraction method*.

Step 6. Computation of degrees of freedom (df). The analysis of df follows the same pattern as the analysis of SS. Each type of SS has its associated df. In the given numerical example, p (levels of factor A) = 2, q (levels of factor B) = 4 and n = 3. Factor B is a repeated measure. Thus, the total number of observations $(N) = npq = 3 \times 2 \times 4 = 24$.
Determination of df for different SS can be made as follows:

Total df $(df_{total}) = npq - 1 = 3 \times 2 \times 4 - 1 = 24 - 1 = 23$ or $N - 1 = 24 - 1 = 23$
$df_{bet.Ss} = np - 1 = 3 \times 2 - 1 = 6 - 1 = 5$
$df_{w.Ss} = np(q - 1) = 3 \times 2(4 - 1) = 3 \times 2 \times 3 = 18$
$df_A = p - 1 = 2 - 1 = 1$
$df_{Ss\,w.grps} = p(n - 1) = 2(3 - 1) = 2 \times 2 = 4$
$df_B = q - 1 = 4 - 1 = 3$
$df_{AB} = (p - 1)(q - 1) = (2 - 1)(4 - 1) = 1 \times 3 = 3$
$df_{B \times Ss\,w.grps} = p(n - 1)(q - 1) = 2(3 - 1)(4 - 1) = 2 \times 2 \times 3 = 12$

Step 7. Computation of mean squares (MS). The mean squares (MS) are also called as variance estimates. The MS is obtained by dividing the SS by its associated df. Thus, $MS = \dfrac{SS}{df}$. We will compute the mean squares for factor A, factor B, AB interaction, Ss.w.groups (error between) and $B \times$ Ss.w.groups (error within), as follows:

$$\text{Mean squares for factor A } (MS_A) = \frac{SS_A}{df_A} = \frac{51.04}{1} = 51.04$$

$$\text{Mean squares for subjects within groups } (MS_{ss\,w.grps}) = \frac{SS_{Ss\,w.grps}}{df_{Ss\,w.grps}} = \frac{17.17}{4} = 4.29$$

$$\text{Mean squares for factor B } (MS_B) = \frac{SS_B}{df_B} = \frac{47.47}{3} = 15.82$$

$$\text{Mean squares for } AB \text{ interaction } (MS_{AB}) = \frac{SS_{AB}}{df_{AB}} = \frac{7.43}{3} = 2.48$$

$$\text{Mean square for } B \times Ss \text{ w.group } (MS_{B\,\times\,Ss\,w.grps}) = \frac{SS_{BSs\,w.grps}}{df_{BSs\,w.grps}} = \frac{14.85}{12} = 1.24$$

It is important to note that the $MS_{Ss\,w.groups}$ is the error between variance and $MS_{B \times Ss\,w.groups}$ is the error within variance.

Step 8. Computation of F-ratios. The F-ratios for factor A, factor B and AB interaction are determined by their respective MS values divided by their corresponding MS error values, as follows:

$$F \text{ for A } (F_A) = \frac{MS_A}{MS_{Ss\,w.grps.}} = \frac{51.04}{4.29} = 11.90$$

$$F \text{ for B } (F_B) = \frac{MS_B}{MS_{BSs\,w.grps.}} = \frac{15.82}{1.24} = 12.76$$

$$F \text{ for AB } (F_{AB}) = \frac{MS_{AB}}{MS_{BSs\,w.grps.}} = \frac{2.48}{1.24} = 2.0$$

Table 15.8 Summary of two-way ANOVA (2×4 factorial experiment) with repeated measures on the second factor

Source of Variation	SS	df	MS	F
Between subjects	68.21	5		
A (Rearing Environment)	51.04	1	51.04	11.90*
Subject within groups (Error between)	17.17	4	4.29	
Within subjects	69.75	18		
B (Days)	47.47	3	15.82	12.76**
A×B	7.43	3	2.48	2.00
B×Ss w.groups (Error within)	14.85	12	1.24	

Note:$p<0.05$; ** $p<0.01$.

Step 9. Summary of analysis of variance. The outcome of the ANOVA, in accordance with the 2×4 factor experiment, with repeated measures on the second factor, has been summarised in Table 15.8.

Step 10. Test of significance. The obtained values of F in Table 15.8 are to be evaluated. The F-ratio in respect of factor A has been found to be 11.90. Consulting Table E in the appendix with df=1/4, the critical F value at $\alpha=0.05$ is 7.71 and at $\alpha=0.01$ is 21.20. Since the obtained value of $F=11.90$ is greater than 7.71 but less than 21.20, the obtained F-ratio of 11.90 is significant at the 0.05 level of significance. So we reject the H_0 and accept the H_1. In other words, rearing environment has differentially affected the exploratory behaviour of rats in favour of enriched environment.

Further, the F value in respect of factor B is 12.76. The critical value of F with df=3/12 at $\alpha=0.05$ is 3.49 and at $\alpha=0.01$ is 5.95. Since the obtained value of $F=12.76$ exceeds both the critical values of F, it is significant at the 0.01 level of significance. So we reject the H_0 and accept the H_1. In other words, testing days had differential effects on the exploratory behaviour of rats.

The F value in respect of A×B interaction is 2.0, which falls short of the critical value of 3.49 at $\alpha=0.05$, and thus, it is non-significant. So, the H_0 is retained and H_1 is rejected. Thus, it was found that the main effects of both the factors A and B are significant. Therefore, we may conclude that enriched rearing environment facilitates the exploratory behaviour of rats and that the exploratory behaviour of rats shows intersession declines over days. In other words, the exploratory behaviour of rats decreases over days of testing. In sum, the effects of environmental conditions and days on exploratory behaviour of rats are statistically significant.

15.3.4   Illustrative Example: Two-way ANOVA with Repeated Measures on One Factor

Example 15.2 Table 15.9 shows illustrative data for a two-factor experiment with repeated measurements on one factor. Two groups of four subjects each were used. Each subject was measured under five experimental conditions. The totals required for computational purposes are also shown in this table. Apply ANOVA to test the significance of row effects, column effects and row by column interaction effects.

Solutions

1. In the given example (see Table 15.9), $R=2$, $C=5$, $n=4$ and $N=nRC=4\times2\times5=40$. It is a two-factorial (2×5 factorial) ANOVA design with repeated measures on the last factor.
2. Statement of H_0 and H_1:

    For factor R (rows):

    $$H_0:\ \mu_{r_1}=\mu_{r_2}\ (\text{or}\ \bar{X}_{r_1}=\bar{X}_{r_2})$$
    $$H_1:\ \mu_{r_1}\neq\mu_{r_2}\ (\text{or}\ \bar{X}_{r_1}\neq\bar{X}_{r_2})$$

Table 15.9   Illustrative data for a two-factor experiment with repeated measurements on one factor

	Subjects	Experimental Conditions					T_{rs}
		C_1	C_2	C_3	C_4	C_5	
Group 1 (R_1)	1	2	7	6	7	9	31
	2	4	3	7	12	14	40
	3	7	6	4	12	10	39
	4	1	3	3	6	6	19
	T_{r_1c}	14	19	20	37	39	$T_{r_1}=129$
Group 2 (R_2)	1	4	4	7	9	1	25
	2	10	12	12	12	16	62
	3	8	7	8	12	10	45
	4	5	7	6	7	8	33
	T_{r_2c}	27	30	33	40	35	$T_{r_2}=165$
	T_c	41	49	53	77	74	$T=294$

For factor C (columns):

$$H_0: \quad \mu_{C_1} = \mu_{C_2} = \mu_{C_3} = \mu_{C_4} = \mu_{C_5}$$
$$(\text{or} \quad \bar{X}_{C_1} = \bar{X}_{C_2} = \bar{X}_{C_3} = \bar{X}_{C_4} = \bar{X}_{C_5})$$
$$H_1: \quad \mu_{C_1} \neq \mu_{C_2} \neq \mu_{C_3} \neq \mu_{C_4} \neq \mu_{C_5}$$
$$(\text{or} \quad \bar{X}_{C_1} \neq \bar{X}_{C_2} \neq \bar{X}_{C_3} \neq \bar{X}_{C_4} \neq \bar{X}_{C_5})$$

For RC interaction:

H_0: The effect of factor R does not depend on the levels of factor C
    (C does not depend on R)
H_1: The effect of one factor does depend on the levels of the other factor.

3. Correction term $(C) = \dfrac{(294)^2}{40} = \dfrac{86436}{40} = 2160.90$

4. Computation of the sum of squares (SS):

  (a) Total SS $=[(2)^2+(4)^2+(7)^2+\ldots+(8)^2]-C$
             $=2664-2160.90=503.10$

  (b) Between Ss SS $=\left[\dfrac{(31)^2}{5}+\dfrac{(40)^2}{5}+\dfrac{(39)^2}{5}+\cdots+\dfrac{(33)^2}{5}\right]-C$
             $=2405.20-2160.90=244.30$

  (c) Within Ss SS $=$ Total SS $-$ Between Ss SS
             $=503.10-244.30=258.80$

  (d) R SS $=\left[\dfrac{(129)^2}{20}+\dfrac{(165)^2}{20}\right]-C$
             $=2193.30-2160.90=32.40$

  (e) Ss within groups SS $=$ Between Ss SS $- R$ SS
             $=244.30-32.40=211.90$

  (f) C SS $=\left[\dfrac{(41)^2}{8}+\dfrac{(49)^2}{8}+\dfrac{(53)^2}{8}+\dfrac{(77)^2}{8}+\dfrac{(74)^2}{8}\right]-C$
             $=2287.0-2160.90=126.10$

  (g) $R \times C$ SS $=\left[\dfrac{(14)^2}{4}+\dfrac{(19)^2}{4}+\cdots+\dfrac{(27)^2}{4}+\cdots+\dfrac{(35)^2}{4}-C\right]-R$ SS $-C$ SS
           $=[2347.50-2160.90]-32.40-126.10=186.60-158.50=28.10$

  (h) $C \times$ Ss within groups SS $=$ Within Ss SS $-C$ SS $-R \times C$ SS
             $=258.80-126.10-28.10$
             $=258.80-154.20=104.60$

5. Computation of the df:

  (a) Total df $=nRC-1$ or $N-1=40-1=39$

  (b) Between Ss df $=nR-1=4\times2-1=7$

  (c) Within Ss df $=nR\,(C-1)=4\times2\,(5-1)=8\times4=32$

  (d) R df $=R-1=2-1=1$

  (e) Ss within groups df $=R\,(n-1)=2(4-1)=2\times3=6$

  (f) C df $=(C-1)=5-1=4$

  (g) $R \times C$ df $=(R-1)\,(C-1)=(2-1)\,(5-1)=1\times4=4$

  (h) $C \times$ Ss within groups df $=R\,(n-1)\,(C-1)=2(4-1)\,(5-1)=2\times3\times4=24$

6. Computation of the MS:

   (a) $MS_R = \dfrac{SS_R}{df_R} = \dfrac{32.40}{1} = 32.40$

   (b) $MS_{Ss\,w.grps} = \dfrac{SS_{Ss\,w.grps}}{df_{Ss\,w.grps}} = \dfrac{211.90}{6} = 35.32$

   (c) $MS_C = \dfrac{SS_C}{df_C} = \dfrac{126.10}{4} = 31.53$

   (d) $MS_{R\times C} = \dfrac{SS_{R\times C}}{df_{R\times C}} = \dfrac{28.10}{4} = 7.03$

   (e) $MS_{C\times Ss\,w.groups} = \dfrac{SS_{C\times Ss\,w.grps}}{df_{C\times Ss\,w.grps}} = \dfrac{104.60}{24} = 4.36$

7. Computation of the F-ratios:

   (a) $F_R = \dfrac{MS_R}{MS_{Ss\,w.grps}} = \dfrac{32.40}{35.32} = 0.92 \;\; or \;\; <1$

   (b) $F_C = \dfrac{MS_C}{MS_{C\times Ss\,w.grps}} = \dfrac{31.53}{4.36} = 7.23$

   (c) $F_{R\times C} = \dfrac{MS_{R\times C}}{MS_{C\times Ss\,w.grps}} = \dfrac{7.03}{4.36} = 1.61$

8. Summary of ANOVA: The outcome of the ANOVA in accordance with the 2×5 factorial experiments with repeated measures on the second factor has been summarised in Table 15.10.

9. Test of Significance: The obtained values of F in Table 15.10 are to be evaluated. The F-ratio in respect of factor R has been found to be 0.92, which is less than 1, is not significant. Thus, we accept H_0 and reject H_1. In other words, the row effects are not significant.

   The F-ratio in respect of factor C has been found to be 7.23. Consulting Table E in the appendix with df=4/24, the critical F value at $\alpha=0.05$ is 2.78 and at $\alpha=0.01$ is 4.22. Since the obtained F value of 7.23 is greater than 4.22, it is significant at $\alpha=0.01$. Therefore

Table 15.10   Summary of two-way ANOVA (2×5 factorial experiment) with repeated measures on the second factor

Source of Variation	SS	df	MS	F
Between subjects	244.30	7		
R (rows)	32.40	1	32.40	<1
Subject within groups (Error between)	211.90	6	35.32	
Within subjects	258.80	32		
C (columns)	126.10	4	31.53	7.23**
R × C	28.10	4	7.03	1.61
C× Ss w.groups (Error within)	104.60	24	4.36	
Total	503.10	39		

Note: ** $p<0.01$.

$p < 0.01$. So we reject H_0 and accept H_1. In other words, the column effects are significant at better than the 0.01 level.

Further, the F value in respect of $R \times C$ interaction has been found to be 1.61, which falls short of the critical value of 2.78 at $\alpha = 0.05$, and thus, it is not significant. So we retain H_0 and reject H_1. Therefore, we may conclude that only the main effect of column is significant. In other words, different experimental conditions, irrespective of groups or rows, have differential effects on the performance of the subjects.

15.4 Two-way (Two-factor) ANOVA with Repeated Measures on Both the Factors

In the preceding section (Section 15.3), we have considered a two-way ANOVA or a two-factor experiment ($p \times q$) with repeated measures on one factor (i.e., on the second factor). In this section, we shall consider a two-factor experimental design or two-way ANOVA design in which repeated measures are obtained on both the factors, that is, each of the n subjects will be observed under all the pq treatment combinations. The analysis of this design will differ somewhat from the one with repeated measures on one factor. The general layout of the two-factor experiment or two-way ANOVA with repeated measures on both the factors is presented in Table 15.11.

15.4.1 General Layout of a Two-factor Experiment (or Two-way ANOVA) with Repeated Measures on Both the Factors

The general layout of a two-factor experiment, factor A having p levels and factor B having q levels, with repeated measures on both the factors has been presented in Table 15.11. It may be noted here that both the factors A and B have been arranged in the horizontal axis. Factors A and B are fixed, factor A having p levels and factor B, q levels. Thus, there are pq treatment combinations in the experiment and each of the n subjects in the experiment has been observed under all the pq treatment combinations.

The subject's score or observation is indicated by letter X in the table (see Table 15.11) that can be identified with three subscripts, the first refers to the subject number $(1, 2, 3, \ldots, n)$ under each of the pq treatment combinations, the second refers to the levels of factor A $(1, 2, 3, \ldots, p)$ and the third to the levels of factor B $(1, 2, 3, \ldots, q)$. Thus, X_{111} refers to an observation or

Table 15.11 General layout of a two-factor experiment ($p \times q$) with repeated measures on both the factors

Subjects	a_1			a_2			a_p			Σ
	b_1	$b_2 \cdots\cdots b_q$		b_1	$b_2 \cdots\cdots b_q$		b_1	$b_2 \cdots\cdots b_q$		
1	X_{111}	$X_{112}\cdots$	$\cdots X_{11q}$	X_{121}	$X_{122}\cdots$	$\cdots X_{12q}$	X_{1P1}	$X_{1P2}\cdots$	$\cdots X_{1pq}$	
2	X_{211}	$X_{212}\cdots$	$\cdots X_{21q}$	X_{221}	$X_{222}\cdots$	$\cdots X_{22q}$	X_{2P1}	$X_{2P2}\cdots$	$\cdots X_{2pq}$	
3	X_{311}	$X_{312}\cdots$	$\cdots X_{31q}$	X_{321}	$X_{322}\cdots$	$\cdots X_{32q}$	X_{3P1}	$X_{3P2}\cdots$	$\cdots X_{3pq}$	
$\vdots$	$\vdots$	$\vdots$	$\vdots$	$\vdots$	$\vdots$	$\vdots$	$\vdots$	$\vdots$	$\vdots$	
n	X_{n11}	$X_{n12}\cdots$	$\cdots X_{n1q}$	X_{n21}	$X_{n22}\cdots$	$\cdots X_{n2q}$	X_{nP1}	$X_{nP2}\cdots$	$\cdots X_{npq}$	
Σ										

score of subject 1 under treatment combination in which level 1 of factor A (i.e., a_1) and level 1 of factor B (i.e., b_1) has been administered. Similarly, X_{1pq} refers to an observation of subject 1 under treatment combination in which level p of factor A (i.e., a_p) and level q of factor B (i.e., b_q) has been administered. Moreover, X_{npq} refers to an observation of subject n under treatment combination in which level p of factor A and level q of factor B has been administered. The additional subject subscript has been included in the layout of this design to indicate that repeated measures are obtained from each of the n subjects.

15.4.2   Partitioning of the Total Sum of Squares and df in a Two-factor Experiment (or Two-way ANOVA) with Repeated Measures on Both the Factors

In a two-factor (A×B) experiment (or two-way ANOVA) with repeated measures on both the factors, each of the n subjects is observed under all the pq treatment combinations. The total sum of squares is first partitioned into two component parts—the between subjects sum of squares and the within-subjects sum of squares. In this experimental design or ANOVA design the between subjects sum of squares is separated from the total variation to eliminate the variation due to individual differences, thus, reducing the amount of experimental error. The between subjects sum of squares is not partitioned further.

The within-subjects sum of squares is further partitioned into six component parts—A sum of squares, A×Ss sum of squares, B sum of squares, B×Ss sum of squares, AB sum of squares and A×B×Ss sum of squares. Thus, A, B and AB components are the parts of within-subjects variation. The A sum of squares is based on the variation of the p levels of factor A, averaged over levels of factor B, about the overall mean. The A×Ss sum of squares is the variation due to the joint effect of factor A and subjects within the group; it is an appropriate denominator (error) to test the F-ratio of A. The B sum of squares is based on the variation of the q levels of factor B, averaged over levels of factor A, about the overall mean. The B×Ss sum of squares is the variation due to the joint effect of factor B and subjects within the group; it is an appropriate denominator (error) to test the F-ratio of B. The AB sum of squares is the variation due to the joint effect of A and B. The A×B×Ss sum of squares is the variation due to the joint effect of A, B and subjects within groups; it is an appropriate denominator (error) to test the F-ratio of AB interaction.

Similarly, the total df (i.e., $N-1$ or $npq-1$) is first partitioned into two parts—$(n-1)$ df attributable to the between subjects sum of squares and $[n(pq-1)]$ df attributable to the within-subjects sum of squares. Further, $[n(pq-1)]$ df associated with the variation within subjects is partitioned into six parts—$(p-1)$ df attributable to the A sum of squares, $[(p-1)(n-1)]$ df attributable to the A×Ss sum of squares, $(q-1)$ df attributable to the B sum of squares, $[(q-1)(n-1)]$ df attributable to the B×Ss sum of squares, $[(p-1)(q-1)]$ df attributable to the AB sum of squares and $[(p-1)(q-1)(n-1)]$ df attributable to the A×B×Ss sum of squares.

Figure 15.3 represents the partitioning of the total sum of squares and df in a two-factor experimental design or two-way ANOVA design with repeated measures on both the factors.

In the equation form the partitioning of the total sum of squares may be expressed as:

$$SS_{total} = SS_{bet.Ss} + SS_{w.Ss}$$
$$= SS_{bet.Ss} + SS_A + SS_{A \times Ss} + SS_B + SS_{B \times Ss} + SS_{AB} + SS_{A \times B \times Ss}$$

where

SS_{total} = total sum of squares

$SS_{bet.Ss}$ = between-subjects sum of squares

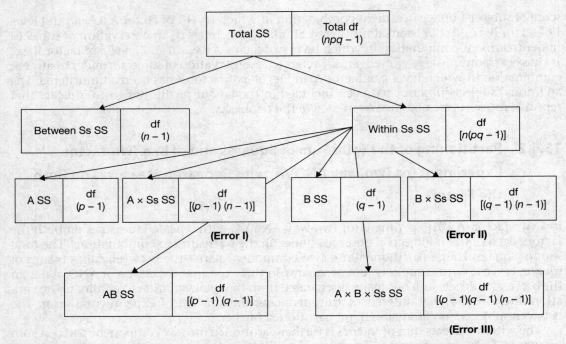

Figure 15.3 Schematic representation of the analysis of two-factor experiment with repeated measures on both the factors

Note: n is the total number of subjects (Ss) in the experiment, p is the number of levels of factor A, q is the number of levels of factor B and $npq = N =$ total number of observations in the experiment.

$SS_{w.Ss}$ = within-subjects sum of squares

SS_A = A sum of squares (or sum of squares between the p levels of factor A)

$SS_{A \times Ss}$ = A × Ss sum of squares (Error I)

SS_B = B sum of squares (or sum of squares between the q levels of factor B)

$SS_{B \times Ss}$ = B × Ss sum of squares (Error II)

SS_{AB} = AB interaction sum of squares

$SS_{A \times B \times Ss}$ = A × B × Ss sum of squares (Error III)

Similarly, in the equation form the total degrees of freedom (df) may be expressed as,

$$df_{total} = df_{bet.Ss} + df_{w.Ss}$$
$$= df_{bet.Ss} + df_A + df_{A \times Ss} + df_B + df_{B \times Ss} + df_{AB} + df_{A \times B \times Ss}$$

or

$$(npq-1) = (n-1) + [n(pq-1)]$$
$$= (n-1) + (p-1) + [(p-1)(n-1)] + (q-1) + [(q-1)(n-1)] + [(p-1)(q-1)] + [(p-1)(q-1)(n-1)]$$

where

df_{total} = df associated with the total sum of squares $(npq-1)$

$df_{bet.Ss}$ = df associated with the between-subjects sum of squares $(n-1)$

df_{wSs} = df associated with the within-subjects sum of squares [$n(pq-1)$]
df_A = df associated with the A sum of squares ($p-1$)
$df_{A \times Ss}$ = df associated with A×Ss sum of squares [$(p-1)(n-1)$]
df_B = df associated with the B sum of squares ($q-1$)
$df_{B \times Ss}$ = df associated with the B×Ss sum of squares [$(q-1)(n-1)$]
df_{AB} = df associated with AB interaction sum of squares [$(p-1)(q-1)$]
$df_{A \times B \times Ss}$ = df associated with A×B×Ss sum of squares [$(p-1)(q-1)(n-1)$]

15.4.3 Steps Involved in Computation of Two-way ANOVA with Repeated Measures on Both the Factors

Let us discuss the steps involved in analysing data for a two-factor experiment ($p \times q$) or a two-way ANOVA with repeated measures on both the factors. The data are from a hypothetical experiment in which the investigator is interested in studying the effects of days (intersession decline) and time interval in each day (intrasession decline) on the locomotor exploratory behaviour of rats. In this experiment, six rats were tested for two days, each day under three time intervals for their locomotor exploratory behaviour. The first independent variable or factor A is day, which has two levels—a_1 (Day 1) and a_2 (Day 2). The second factor (i.e., factor B) is time interval, which has three levels—b_1 (time interval 1), b_2 (time interval 2) and b_3 (time interval 3). Factors A and B are fixed. Thus, it is a 2×3 factorial experiment with repeated measures on both the factors. The dependent variable is the locomotor exploratory behaviour of rats. A total of six subjects were taken. Each of the six subjects was observed under each of the six treatment combinations (i.e., $p \times q = 2 \times 3 = 6$). The outcome of the hypothetical experiment is given in Table 15.12.

The *AB* summary table, the *A*×Ss summary table and the *B*×Ss summary table are prepared from Table 15.12 and are presented as follows:

(a) ***AB summary table.*** The AB summary table has been prepared from Table 15.12. The totals of treatment combinations a_1b_1, a_1b_2, a_1b_3, a_2b_1, a_2b_2 and a_2b_3 have been

Table 15.12 Locomotor exploration scores of the subjects in a 2×3 factorial experiment with repeated measures on both the factors

Subjects	a_1			a_2			Total	
	b_1	b_2	b_3	b_1	b_2	b_3		
1	4	5	7	1	4	2	23	
2	6	8	10	3	6	6	39	
3	1	6	5	3	5	4	24	
4	2	10	12	1	4	7	36	
5	5	10	10	5	6	5	41	
6	1	7	8	2	8	7	33	
Total	19	46	52	15	33	31	196	G

entered into the appropriate cells of the AB summary table. The levels of factor A have been arranged in the vertical axis and that of factor B in the horizontal axis.

AB Summary Table

	b_1	b_2	b_3	Total
a_1	19	46	52	117
a_2	15	33	31	79
Total	34	79	83	196 (G)

(b) **$A \times Ss$ summary table.** The $A \times Ss$ summary table represents the A and subjects (Ss) interaction. This table has been derived from Table 15.12. The a_1 and a_2 values for each of the six subjects have been derived by combining the values of the levels of factor B. That is, adding all the values of b_1, b_2 and b_3 under a_1 and a_2 gives the cell values in the table.

$A \times Ss$ Summary Table

Ss	a_1	a_2	Total
1	16	7	23
2	24	15	39
3	12	12	24
4	24	12	36
5	25	16	41
6	16	17	33
Total	117	79	196 (G)

(c) **$B \times Ss$ summary table.** The $B \times Ss$ summary table represents the B and subjects (Ss) interaction. This table has been derived from Table 15.12. The two values of a_1 and a_2 for each of the three levels of factor B have been combined to derive the values under b_1, b_2 and b_3 for each of the six subjects.

$B \times Ss$ Summary Table

Ss	b_1	b_2	b_3	Total
1	5	9	9	23
2	9	14	16	39
3	4	11	9	24
4	3	14	19	36
5	10	16	15	41
6	3	15	15	33
Total	34	79	83	196 (G)

To test the significance of the effects of factors A, B and AB interaction using two-way ANOVA with repeated measures on both the factors, the following steps are to be followed:

Step 1. Presentation of the given data in a table having all its notations, such as p (a_1 and a_2), q (b_1, b_2 and b_3), $n=6$, $N=npq=6\times2\times3=36$, etc., as shown in Table 15.12.

Step 2. Computation of a variety of statistics such as totals as shown in Table 15.12. Preparation of AB summary table, A×Ss summary table and B×Ss summary table as shown earlier in the text.

Step 3. Statement of null hypothesis (H_0) and alternative hypothesis (H_1) and selection of an alpha level.

For factor A, the H_0 states that there is no difference between the means of Day 1 and Day 2 locomotor exploratory behaviour of rats. However, the H_1 states that the rats differ in their Day 1 and Day 2 mean scores. In symbols,

$$H_0: \ \mu_{a_1} = \mu_{a_2} \quad (\text{or } \bar{X}_{a_1} = \bar{X}_{a_2})$$
$$H_1: \ \mu_{a_1} \neq \mu_{a_2} \quad (\text{or } \bar{X}_{a_1} \neq \bar{X}_{a_2})$$

For factor B, the H_0 states that the mean locomotor exploration scores of rats over three time intervals are same. The H_1, on the contrary, states that the mean locomotor exploration scores of rats over three time intervals are not same. In symbols,

$$H_0: \ \mu_{b_1} = \mu_{b_2} = \mu_{b_3} \quad (\text{or } \bar{X}_{b_1} = \bar{X}_{b_2} = \bar{X}_{b_3})$$
$$H_1: \ \mu_{b_1} \neq \mu_{b_2} \neq \mu_{b_3} \quad (\text{or } \bar{X}_{b_1} \neq \bar{X}_{b_2} \neq \bar{X}_{b_3})$$

For the A×B interaction, the H_0 and H_1 can be stated as follows:

H_0: The effect of factor A does not depend on the levels of factor B
(or B does not depend on A)
H_1: The effect of one factor does depend on the levels of the other factor.

We will set alpha at $\alpha=0.05$.

Step 4. Computation of the correction term (C). The correction term is computed by squaring the grand total (G) and then dividing by the total number of observations ($N=npq$) in the study.

In the given example (see Table 15.12), $G=196$, $n=6$, $p=2$ and $q=3$.

Thus, $N=npq=6\times2\times3=36$. Thus, the correction term (C) is:

$$C = \frac{(G)^2}{N} = \frac{(196)^2}{36} = \frac{38416}{36} = 1067.11$$

Step 5. Computation of the sum of squares (SS). In a two-factor experimental design or a two-way ANOVA design with repeated measures on both the factors, the total sum of squares (SS_{total}) is first partitioned into between subjects sum of squares ($SS_{bet.Ss}$) and within-subjects sum of squares ($SS_{w.Ss}$). Only the within-subjects sum of squares is further partitioned into six component parts—SS_A, $SS_{A\times Ss}$(error), SS_B, $SS_{B\times Ss}$(error), SS_{AB} and $SS_{A\times B\times Ss}$(error). These sum of squares are computed below one after another.

(a) *Total sum of squares (SS_{total}).* The total sum of squares is obtained by squaring each of the scores in the entire set of observations in the experiment irrespective of the p and q levels of both the factors, then summed up and finally the correction term (C) is subtracted from the sum. Thus, the formula for the total sum of squares reads:

$$SS_{total} = \Sigma\Sigma X_{pq}^2 - C$$

Applying this above formula to the set of data given in Table 15.12, we obtain:

$$SS_{total} = [4^2 + 6^2 + 1^2 + 2^2 + \cdots + 5^2 + 7^2] - 1067.11$$
$$= 1360.00 - 1067.11 = 292.89$$

(b) *Between-subjects sum of squares ($SS_{bet.Ss}$).* Each of the six subjects in the given experiment undergoes all the six treatment combinations. The sum of the rows, given in the last column of Table 15.12, represents the variation due to individual differences. The between-subjects variation is a function of the squared deviations of the means of the individual subjects about the grand mean.

The sum of the six treatment combinations of each of the six subjects, given in the last column of Table 15.12, has been squared, divided by 6 (the number of observations making up the total), summed up and finally the correction term is subtracted from the sum. The computational formula for $SS_{bet.Ss}$ reads:

$$SS_{bet.Ss} = \left[\Sigma \frac{(\Sigma S_n)^2}{pq} \right] - C$$

$$= \left[\frac{(\Sigma S_1)^2}{pq} + \frac{(\Sigma S_2)^2}{pq} + \cdots + \frac{(\Sigma S_n)^2}{pq} \right] - C$$

Applying this above formula to the set of data given in Table 15.12, we obtain:

$$SS_{bet.Ss} = \left[\frac{(23)^2}{6} + \frac{(39)^2}{6} + \frac{(24)^2}{6} + \frac{(36)^2}{6} + \frac{(41)^2}{6} + \frac{(33)^2}{6} \right] - 1067.11$$

$$= \left[\frac{529}{6} + \frac{1521}{6} + \frac{576}{6} + \frac{1296}{6} + \frac{1681}{6} + \frac{1089}{6} \right] - 1067.11$$

$$= [88.17 + 253.5 + 96.0 + 216.0 + 280.17 + 181.5] - 1067.11$$

$$= 1115.34 - 1067.11 = 48.23$$

(c) *Within-subjects sum of squares ($SS_{w.Ss}$).* In this case, the within-subjects sum of squares has been obtained by subtraction. From Figure 15.3, it can be observed that the total sum of squares is bifurcated into 'between-subjects sum of squares' and 'within-subjects sum of squares'. Therefore, the within-subjects sum of squares can be obtained by subtracting the between-subjects sum of squares from the total sum of squares. Thus, the within-subjects sum of squares obtained is:

$$SS_{w.Ss} = SS_{total} - SS_{bet.Ss}$$
$$= 292.89 - 48.23 = 244.66$$

The within-subjects sum of squares can also be obtained directly. We know that within-subjects sum of squares is the pooled variation of individual subject's observations about the respective mean. Therefore, we can calculate the within-subjects sum of squares as follows:

$$SS_{w}S_1=[4^2+5^2+7^2+1^2+4^2+2^2]-\frac{(23)^2}{6}=111.0-88.17=22.83$$

$$SS_{w}S_2=[6^2+8^2+10^2+3^2+6^2+6^2]-\frac{(39)^2}{6}=281.0-253.5=27.5$$

$$SS_{w}S_3=[1^2+6^2+5^2+3^2+5^2+4^2]-\frac{(24)^2}{6}=112.0-96.0=16.0$$

$$SS_{w}S_4=[2^2+10^2+12^2+1^2+4^2+7^2]-\frac{(36)^2}{6}=314.0-216.0=98.0$$

$$SS_{w}S_5=[5^2+10^2+10^2+5^2+6^2+5^2]-\frac{(41)^2}{6}=311.0-280.17=30.83$$

$$SS_{w}S_6=[1^2+7^2+8^2+2^2+8^2+7^2]-\frac{(33)^2}{6}=231.0-181.5=49.5$$

$$\therefore SS_{w.Ss}=22.83+27.5+16.0+98.0+30.83+49.5=244.66$$

It can be observed that the outcome by the *direct method* is exactly the same as obtained by the *subtraction method*.

(d) *A sum of squares (SS_A).* The main effect of factor A has been obtained from the AB summary table. The row totals corresponding to levels a_1 and a_2 are 117 and 79, respectively. Each of these totals is squared, divided by 18 (number of observations making up the total, that is, $nq=6\times3=18$), summed up and finally the correction term is subtracted from the sum. The A sum of squares is computed as follows:

$$SS_A = \left[\frac{(\Sigma a_1)^2}{nq}+\frac{(\Sigma a_2)^2}{nq}\right]-C$$

$$=\left[\frac{(117)^2}{18}+\frac{(79)^2}{18}\right]-1067.11=\left[\frac{13689}{18}+\frac{6241}{18}\right]-1067.11$$

$$=[760.5+346.72]-1067.11=1107.22-1067.11=40.11$$

(e) *A×subjects sum of squares ($SS_{A\times Ss}$).* The A×subjects sum of squares has been obtained from A×Ss summary table. The A×Ss sum of squares is the variation due to the joint effect of factor A and subjects within the group and is the appropriate denominator (error) to test the main effect of factor A.

The A×Ss sum of squares has been obtained by applying the usual first-order (two-factor) interaction formula. The values entered in the cells of A×Ss summary table are squared, each divided by 3 (the number of observations making up each of the cell values or the number of q levels of factor B), summed up and finally the correction term is subtracted from the sum. Thus, we obtain the cell sum of squares. In order to obtain the A×Ss sum of squares, we subtract between-subjects sum of squares and A sum of squares from the cell sum of squares. The $A \times Ss$ sum of squares is computed as follows:

$$SS_{A \times Ss} = \left[\left(\frac{16^2}{3} + \frac{24^2}{3} + \cdots + \frac{17^2}{3} - C \right) - SS_{bet.Ss} - SS_A \right]$$

$$= [(1180.0 - 1067.11) - 48.23 - 40.11] = 112.89 - 88.34 = 24.55$$

(f) *B sum of squares (SS_B).* The B sum of squares has been obtained from the AB summary table. The column totals corresponding to levels b_1, b_2 and b_3 are 34, 79 and 83, respectively. Each of these totals is squared, divided by 12 (the number of np, 6×2, observations making up the total), summed up and finally the correction term is subtracted from the sum. The B sum of squares is computed as follows:

$$SS_B = \left[\frac{(\Sigma b_1)^2}{np} + \frac{(\Sigma b_2)^2}{np} + \frac{(\Sigma b_3)^2}{np} \right] - C$$

$$= \left[\frac{(34)^2}{12} + \frac{(79)^2}{12} + \frac{(83)^2}{12} \right] - 1067.11 = \left[\frac{1156}{12} + \frac{6241}{12} + \frac{6889}{12} \right] - 1067.11$$

$$= [96.33 + 520.08 + 574.08] - 1067.11 = 1190.49 - 1067.11 = 123.38$$

(g) *$B \times Ss$ sum of squares ($SS_{B \times Ss}$).* The $B \times Ss$ sum of squares has been obtained from the $B \times Ss$ summary table. The $B \times Ss$ sum of squares is the variation due to the joint effect of factor B and subjects within the group. The $B \times Ss$ sum of squares is the appropriate denominator (error) to test the main effect of factor B.

The $B \times Ss$ sum of squares has been obtained by squaring each of the cell values of $B \times Ss$ summary table, dividing each by 2 (the number of observations making up the totals of each cell or the number of p levels of factor A), summing up and finally subtracting the correction term from the sum. Thus, we obtain the cell sum of squares. In order to obtain the $B \times Ss$ sum of squares, we subtract between subjects sum of squares and B sum of squares from the cell sum of squares. The $B \times Ss$ sum of squares is computed as follows:

$$SS_{B \times Ss} = \left[\left(\frac{5^2}{2} + \frac{9^2}{2} + \cdots + \frac{15^2}{2} + \frac{15^2}{2} - C \right) - SS_{bet.Ss} - SS_B \right]$$

$$= [(1272.0 - 1067.11) - 48.23 - 123.38] = 204.89 - 48.23 - 123.38 = 33.28$$

(h) *AB sum of squares (SS_{AB}).* The AB interaction sum of squares has been obtained from the *AB* summary table. The AB sum of squares is the variation due to the joint effect of factors A and B.

The AB sum of squares is found by subtracting both the A sum of squares and B sum of squares from the cell sum of squares. The cell sum of squares is obtained by squaring each of the cell values of the AB summary table, dividing each by 6 (the number of n subjects or the number of observations making up the cell totals), summing up and finally subtracting the correction term from the sum. Then, the A sum of squares and the B sum of squares are subtracted from the cell sum of squares to obtain the AB sum of squares. The AB sum of squares is computed as follows:

$$SS_{AB} = \left[\left(\frac{(\Sigma a_1 b_1)^2}{n} + \frac{(\Sigma a_1 b_2)^2}{n} + \cdots + \frac{(\Sigma a_2 b_3)^2}{n} - C \right) - SS_A - SS_B \right]$$

$$= \left[\left(\frac{19^2}{6} + \frac{46^2}{6} + \cdots + \frac{31^2}{6} - 1067.11 \right) - 40.11 - 123.38 \right]$$

$$= [(1242.67 - 1067.11) - 40.11 - 123.38] = 175.56 - 40.11 - 123.38 = 12.07$$

(i) $A \times B \times Ss$ *sum of squares* $(SS_{A \times B \times Ss})$. The $A \times B \times Ss$ sum of squares has been obtained by subtraction. Referring to Figure 15.3, it can be observed that the within-Subjects sum of squares is partitioned into six components—A SS, A × Ss SS, B SS, B × Ss SS, AB SS and A × B × Ss SS. Thus, if we subtract the sum of squares of first five components from the within-subjects sum of squares, we can get the A × B × Ss sum of squares. The A × B × Ss sum of squares is obtained as follows:

$$SS_{A \times B \times Ss} = SS_{w.Ss} - SS_A - SS_{A \times Ss} - SS_B - SS_{B \times Ss} - SS_{AB}$$
$$= 244.66 - 40.11 - 24.55 - 123.38 - 33.28 - 12.07$$
$$= 244.66 - 233.39 = 11.27$$

The $A \times B \times Ss$ sum of squares can be computed directly. The $A \times B \times Ss$ sum of squares is a second-order interaction or three-factor interaction. Let us present the $A \times B \times Ss$ interaction table. There will be two tables—B × Ss for a_1 and B × Ss for a_2.

$B \times Ss$ for a_1

Subjects (Ss)	b_1	b_2	b_3	Total(Σ)
1	4	5	7	16
2	6	8	10	24
3	1	6	5	12
4	2	10	12	24
5	5	10	10	25
6	1	7	8	16
Total(Σ)	19	46	52	117

The $B \times Ss$ for a_1 sum of squares is computed using the usual formula for two-factor interaction as explained earlier. Thus, the $B \times Ss$ for a_1 SS is computed as follows:

$$B \times Ss \text{ for } a_1 \text{ SS} = \left[4^2 + 6^2 + \cdots + 10^2 + 8^2 - \frac{(117)^2}{18} \right]$$

$$- \left[\frac{16^2}{3} + \frac{24^2}{3} + \cdots + \frac{16^2}{3} - \frac{(117)^2}{18} \right]$$

$$- \left[\frac{19^2}{6} + \frac{46^2}{6} + \frac{52^2}{6} - \frac{(117)^2}{18} \right]$$

$$= [939.0 - 760.5] - [811.0 - 760.5] - [863.5 - 760.5]$$
$$= 178.5 - 50.5 - 103.0 = 25.0$$

B×Ss for a_2

Subjects (Ss)	b_1	b_2	b_3	Total (Σ)
1	1	4	2	7
2	3	6	6	15
3	3	5	4	12
4	1	4	7	12
5	5	6	5	16
6	2	8	7	17
Total (Σ)	15	33	31	79

The $B\times$Ss for a_2 SS is computed as follows:

$$B\times Ss \text{ for } a_2 \text{ SS} = \left[1^2 + 3^2 + \cdots + 5^2 + 7^2 - \frac{(79)^2}{18}\right]$$
$$-\left[\frac{7^2}{3} + \frac{15^2}{3} + \cdots + \frac{17^2}{3} - \frac{(79)^2}{18}\right]$$
$$-\left[\frac{15^2}{6} + \frac{33^2}{6} + \frac{31^2}{6} - \frac{(79)^2}{18}\right]$$
$$=[421.0 - 346.72] - [369.0 - 346.72] - [379.17 - 346.72]$$
$$= 74.28 - 22.28 - 32.45 = 19.55$$

The $A\times B\times$Ss sum of squares is the interaction of three factors, that is, factor A, factor B and the subjects in the group that is considered the third factor. The formula for the third-factor interaction is presented, that is, from the sum of $B\times$Ss for a_1 and $B\times$Ss for a_2 sum of squares, the $B\times$Ss sum of squares obtained in step (g), is subtracted. Thus, the $A\times B\times$Ss sum of squares is found to be equal to:

$$A\times B\times Ss \text{ SS} = B\times Ss \text{ for } a_1 \text{ SS} + B\times Ss \text{ for } a_2 \text{ SS} - B\times Ss \text{ SS}$$
$$= 25.0 + 19.55 - 33.28 = 11.27$$

It is observed that the outcome of $A\times B\times$Ss SS by the direct method is the same as obtained by the subtraction method.

Step 6. Computation of degrees of freedom (df). The analysis of df follows the same pattern as the analysis of sum of squares (SS). Each type of SS has its associated df. In the given numerical example, p (levels of factor A)=2, q (levels of factor B)=3 and n=6. Both factors A and B are repeated measures. Thus, the total number of observations $(N)= npq=6\times 2\times 3=36$.

Determination of df for different SS can be made as follows:

$$df_{total} = npq-1=6\times 2\times 3-1=36-1=35 \text{ or } N-1=36-1=35$$
$$df_{bet.Ss} = n-1=6-1=5$$
$$df_{w.Ss} = n(pq-1)=6(2\times 3-1)=6\times 5=30$$

$$df_A = p - 1 = 2 - 1 = 1$$
$$df_{A \times Ss} = (p-1)(n-1) = (2-1)(6-1) = 1 \times 5 = 5$$
$$df_B = q - 1 = 3 - 1 = 2$$
$$df_{B \times Ss} = (q-1)(n-1) = (3-1)(6-1) = 2 \times 5 = 10$$
$$df_{AB} = (p-1)(q-1) = (2-1)(3-1) = 1 \times 2 = 2$$
$$df_{A \times B \times Ss} = (p-1)(q-1)(n-1) = (2-1)(3-1)(6-1) = 1 \times 2 \times 5 = 10$$

Step 7. Computation of mean squares (MS). The mean square (MS), which is called the variance estimate, is obtained by dividing the SS by its associated df. Thus, $MS = \dfrac{SS}{df}$. We will compute the mean squares for the A SS, A × Ss SS (Error I), B SS, B × Ss SS (Error II), AB SS and A × B × Ss SS (Error III), as follows:

$$\text{Mean squares for A SS } (MS_A) = \frac{SS_A}{df_A} = \frac{40.11}{1} = 40.11$$

$$\text{Mean squares for A} \times \text{Ss SS } (MS_{A \times Ss}) = \frac{SS_{A \times Ss}}{df_{A \times Ss}} = \frac{24.55}{5} = 4.91$$

$$\text{Mean squares for B SS } (MS_B) = \frac{SS_B}{df_B} = \frac{123.38}{2} = 61.69$$

$$\text{Mean squares for B} \times \text{Ss SS } (MS_{B \times Ss}) = \frac{SS_{B \times Ss}}{df_{B \times Ss}} = \frac{33.28}{10} = 3.33$$

$$\text{Mean squares for AB SS } (MS_{AB}) = \frac{SS_{AB}}{df_{AB}} = \frac{12.07}{2} = 6.04$$

$$\text{Mean squares for A} \times \text{B} \times \text{Ss SS } (MS_{A \times B \times Ss}) = \frac{SS_{A \times B \times Ss}}{df_{A \times B \times Ss}} = \frac{11.27}{10} = 1.13$$

It is important to note that the $MS_{A \times Ss}$ is the error for the main effect of factor A, the $MS_{B \times Ss}$ is the error for the main effect of factor B and the $MS_{A \times B \times Ss}$ is the error for the AB interaction effect.

Step 8. Computation of *F*-ratios. The *F*-ratio for factor A, factor B and AB interaction are determined by their respective MS values divided by their corresponding MS error values, as follows:

$$F \text{ for factor A } (F_A) = \frac{MS_A}{MS_{A \times Ss}} = \frac{40.11}{4.91} = 8.17$$

$$F \text{ for factor B } (F_B) = \frac{MS_B}{MS_{B \times Ss}} = \frac{61.69}{3.33} = 18.53$$

$$F \text{ for AB interaction } (F_{AB}) = \frac{MS_{AB}}{MS_{A \times B \times Ss}} = \frac{6.04}{1.13} = 5.35$$

Step 9. Summary of analysis of variance. The outcome of the ANOVA, in accordance with the 2 × 3 factor experiment, with repeated measures on both the factors, has been summarised in Table 15.13.

Step 10. Test of significance. The obtained values of F in Table 15.13 are to be evaluated. The F-ratio in respect of factor A has been found to be 8.17. Consulting Table E in

Table 15.13 Summary of two-way ANOVA (2×3 factorial experiment) with repeated measures on both the factors

Source of Variation	SS	df	MS	F
Between subjects	48.23	5		
Within subjects	244.66	30		
A (Days)	40.11	1	40.11	8.17*
$A \times Ss$ (Error I)	24.55	5	4.91	
B (Time Interval)	123.38	2	61.69	18.53**
$B \times Ss$ (Error II)	33.28	10	3.33	
AB Interaction	12.07	2	6.04	5.35*
$A \times B \times Ss$ (Error III)	11.27	10	1.13	
Total	292.89	35		

Notes: *$p < 0.05$; ** $p < 0.01$.

the appendix with df=1/5, the critical F value at $\alpha = 0.05$ is 6.61, and at $\alpha = 0.01$ is 16.26. Since the obtained value of $F = 8.17$ is greater than 6.61 but less than 16.26, the obtained F-ratio of 8.17 is significant at the 0.05 level of significance. Therefore, $p < 0.05$. Thus, the main effect of A is significant. So, we reject the H_0 and accept the H_1. In other words, days of testing have differentially affected the locomotor exploratory behaviour of rats, in favour of Day 1. The mean of locomotor exploration scores of rats on Day 1 is 6.50 (i.e., $117 \div 18 = 6.50$) and on Day 2 is 4.39 (i.e., $79 \div 18 = 4.39$). Thus, we may conclude that the locomotor exploratory behaviour of animals showed intersession decline or decreases over days of testing.

The F-ratio in respect of factor B has been found to be 18.53. The critical value of F with df = 2/10 at $\alpha = 0.05$ is 4.10 and at $\alpha = 0.01$ is 7.56. Since the obtained value of $F = 18.53$ exceeds both the critical values of F, it is significant at the 0.01 level of significance. Therefore, $p < 0.01$. Thus, the main effect of B is also highly significant. So, we reject H_0 and accept H_1. In other words, different time intervals have differential effects on the locomotor exploratory behaviour of rats, in favour of the third interval. The means of locomotor exploration scores of rats for the 1st, 2nd and 3rd time intervals are 2.83 ($34 \div 12 = 2.83$), 6.58 ($79 \div 12 = 6.58$) and 6.92 ($83 \div 12 = 6.92$), respectively. Thus, we may conclude that the locomotor exploration scores of the subjects did not show intrasession decline, rather showed intrasession facilitation over time intervals.

Further, the F-ratio in respect of AB interaction has been found to be 5.35. The critical value of F with df = 2/10 at $\alpha = 0.05$ is 4.10 and at $\alpha = 0.01$ is 7.56 (referring to Table E in the appendix). Since the obtained value of $F = 5.35$ is greater than 4.10 but less than 7.56, the obtained F-ratio of 5.35 is significant at the 0.05 level of significance. Therefore, $p < 0.05$. Thus, AB interaction is also significant. So, the H_0 is rejected and the H_1 is accepted. Therefore, we may conclude that the effects of factor B on both the levels of factor A (i.e., on a_1 and a_2) are different. The means of locomotor exploration scores of b_1, b_2 and b_3 on a_1 are 3.17 ($19 \div 6 = 3.17$), 7.67 ($46 \div 6 = 7.67$) and 8.67 ($52 \div 6 = 8.67$), respectively. On the other hand, the means of locomotor exploration scores of b_1, b_2 and b_3 on a_2 are 2.5 ($15 \div 6 = 2.5$), 5.5 ($33 \div 6 = 5.5$) and 5.17 ($31 \div 6 = 5.17$), respectively (referring to AB summary table cell values).

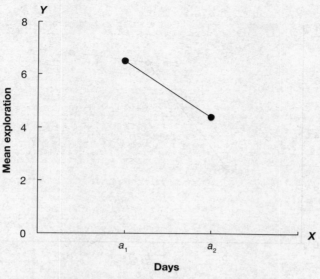

Figure 15.4   The main effect of factor a ($SS_a \neq 0$)

In addition to the above interpretation of the obtained outcomes of the ANOVA (see Table 15.13), the researcher may, if he/she desires proceed for further interpretation of the outcomes on the following points.

a.   Geometric Representation of Main Effects.
From the outcome of the experiment (see Table 15.13), it is observed that factor A is significant. This indicates that the two levels of factor A, that is, Day 1 (a_1) and Day 2 (a_2) differ significantly. In a_1 the mean exploration score is 6.50 as compared to 4.39 in a_2. The significant main effect indicates that the slope of the line joining a_1 and a_2 is not zero ($SS_a \neq 0$). In other words, the curve representing the main effect of A is not parallel to the baseline or X-axis (see Figure 15.4).

It is observed from Table 15.13 that the main effect of B is also highly significant. This shows that the mean exploration scores in respect of three time intervals (i.e., b_1, b_2 and b_3) differ significantly. The mean exploration scores for b_1, b_2 and b_3 are 2.83, 6.58 and 6.92, respectively. In order to evaluate the differences among these three means, Newman–Keuls test for multiple comparisons of means may be followed. However, Figure 15.5 shows the trend of the main effect of factor B.

b.   Simple Effects.
It can be observed from Table 15.13 that the AB interaction is significant. When AB interaction is significant, tests on simple effects are called for. The main effects, in such cases, are to be interpreted with caution. It can be observed from the AB interaction profile (see Figure 15.6) that the profile of B for a_1 is different from B for a_2. The means of locomotor exploration scores of b_1, b_2 and b_3 on a_1 are 3.17, 7.67 and 8.67, respectively. Similarly, the means of exploration scores of b_1, b_2 and b_3 on a_2 are 2.5, 5.5 and 5.17, respectively. These means are represented in Figure 15.6.

It can be observed from Figure 15.6 that the slope in respect of curve representing B for a_1 is different from the slope of the curve B for a_2. Observation of both curve a_1 and curve a_2 indicates that each one has a significant slope; however, curve a_1 has a highly significant slope compared to that of curve a_2.

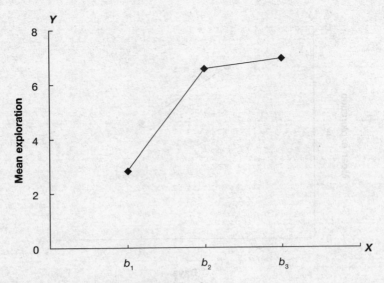

Figure 15.5   The main effect of factor B ($SS_b \neq 0$)

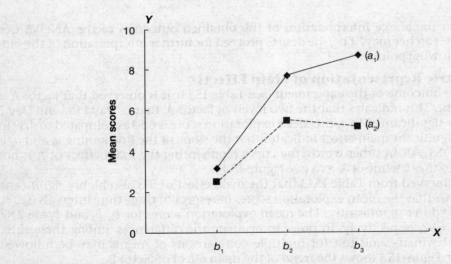

Figure 15.6   AB interaction profile (it also represents the simple effects of factor B)

Table 15.14   Summary of ANOVA for the simple effects of factor B

Source of Variation	SS	df	MS	F
B for a_1	103.00	2	51.50	15.47**
B for a_2	32.45	2	16.23	4.87*
$B \times$ Ss (Error)	33.28	10	3.33	

Notes: *$p < 0.05$; **$p < 0.01$.

The significance of the individual curves can be tested by studying the simple effects. Test on simple effects is the test on differences between means within the same profile. The simple effects can be worked out from the AB summary table resulting from Table 15.12.

$$\text{SS}_\text{B} \text{ for } a_1 = \left[\frac{(19)^2}{6} + \frac{(46)^2}{6} + \frac{(52)^2}{6} - \frac{(117)^2}{18}\right] = 863.5 - 760.5 = 103.0$$

$$\text{SS}_\text{B} \text{ for } a_2 = \left[\frac{(15)^2}{6} + \frac{(33)^2}{6} + \frac{(31)^2}{6} - \frac{(79)^2}{18}\right] = 379.17 - 346.72 = 32.45$$

Referring to Table E in the appendix with df$=2/10$, the critical value of F at $\alpha=0.05$ is 4.10 and at $\alpha=0.01$ is 7.56. Thus, the two simple effects of B for levels a_1 and a_2 show significant slopes; however, the simple effect of B for the level a_1 is highly significant compared to that of B for the level a_2 (Table 15.14). This shows that as the time interval increases, the mean exploration score increases linearly on Day 1. On the other hand, the mean exploration score increases from the first interval to the second interval and then decreases to the third interval on Day 2 (see Figure 15.6).

In sum, in this section (Section 15.4) we have discussed two-factor experimental design $(p \times q)$ with repeated measures on both the factors. It can be observed that the ANOVA in designs with repeated measures on one factor (discussed in Section 15.2) and with repeated measures on both the factors differ. In this design the main effects of factors A and B, and AB interaction are components of within-subjects variation, and in each case the denominator for F-ratio is the corresponding interaction with the subject factor. The variation due to subjects between groups is eliminated from the total variation, thus, reducing the experimental error. As the variation due to individual differences is taken out from the total variation, the sensitivity of the design increases.

15.4.4 Illustrative Example: Two-way ANOVA with Repeated Measures on Both the Factors

Example 15.3 The following are data for a 2×2 factorial experiment with repeated measurements on six subjects. Apply an ANOVA to these data.

Solutions

1. In the given example (see Table 15.15), $R=2$, $C=2$ and $n=6$. So, $N = nRC = 6 \times 2 \times 2 = 24$. It is a two-factorial (2×2 factorial) ANOVA design with repeated measures on both the factors.
2. Preparation of RC, R$\times$Ss and C$\times$Ss summary tables from Table 15.15 is made as follows:

RC Summary Table

	C_1	C_2	Total
R_1	18	35	53
R_2	23	36	59
Total	41	71	112

Table 15.15 Illustrative data for a two-factor experiment with repeated measures on both the factors

Subjects	R_1		R_2		Total [Σ]
	C_1	C_2	C_1	C_2	
1	1	6	5	3	15
2	2	7	4	5	18
3	5	9	8	3	25
4	2	1	3	7	13
5	4	4	2	8	18
6	4	8	1	10	23
Total [Σ]	18	35	23	36	112(G)

R × Ss Summary Table

Ss	R_1	R_2	Total
1	7	8	15
2	9	9	18
3	14	11	25
4	3	10	13
5	8	10	18
6	12	11	23
Total	53	59	112

C × Ss Summary Table

Ss	C_1	C_2	Total
1	6	9	15
2	6	12	18
3	13	12	25
4	5	8	13
5	6	12	18
6	5	18	23
Total	41	71	112

3. Statement of H_0 and H_1:

    For factor R (rows)

    $$H_0: \quad \mu_{r_1} = \mu_{r_2} \quad (\text{or } \bar{X}_{r_1} = \bar{X}_{r_2})$$
    $$H_1: \quad \mu_{r_1} \neq \mu_{r_2} \quad (\text{or } \bar{X}_{r_1} \neq \bar{X}_{r_2})$$

    For factor C (columns)

    $$H_0: \quad \mu_{C_1} = \mu_{C_2} \quad (\text{or } \bar{X}_{C_1} = \bar{X}_{C_2})$$
    $$H_1: \quad \mu_{C_1} \neq \mu_{C_2} \quad (\text{or } \bar{X}_{C_1} \neq \bar{X}_{C_2})$$

    For RC interaction

    H_0: The effect of factor R does not depend on the levels of factor C
    (and C does not depend on R)
    H_1: The effect of one factor does depend on the levels of the other factor

4. Correction term $(C) = \dfrac{(G)^2}{N} = \dfrac{(112)^2}{24} = 522.67$

5. Computation of sum of squares (SS):

    (a) Total SS $= (1^2 + 2^2 + \cdots + 10^2) - C = 688.0 - 522.67 = 165.33$

    (b) Between Ss SS $= \left[\dfrac{(15)^2}{4} + \dfrac{(18)^2}{4} + \dfrac{(25)^2}{4} + \dfrac{(13)^2}{4} + \dfrac{(18)^2}{4} + \dfrac{(23)^2}{4} \right] - C$

    $$= 549.0 - 522.67 = 26.33$$

    (c) Within Ss SS $=$ Total SS $-$ Bet.Ss SS $= 165.33 - 26.33 = 139.00$

    (d) R SS $= \left[\dfrac{(53)^2}{12} + \dfrac{(59)^2}{12} \right] - C = 524.17 - 522.67 = 1.50$

    (e) $(R \times Ss)$ SS $= \left[\left(\dfrac{7^2}{2} + \dfrac{9^2}{2} + \cdots + \dfrac{11^2}{2} - C \right) - \text{Bet.Ss SS} - \text{R SS} \right]$

    $$= [(565.00 - 522.67) - 26.33 - 1.50] = 42.33 - 27.83 = 14.50$$

    (f) C SS $= \left[\dfrac{(41)^2}{12} + \dfrac{(71)^2}{12} \right] - C = 560.17 - 522.67 = 37.50$

    (g) $(C \times Ss)$ SS $= \left[\left(\dfrac{6^2}{2} + \dfrac{6^2}{2} + \cdots + \dfrac{18^2}{2} - C \right) - \text{Bet.Ss SS} - \text{C SS} \right]$

    $$= [(614.00 - 522.67) - 26.33 - 37.50] = 91.33 - 63.83 = 27.50$$

    (h) RC SS $= \left[\left(\dfrac{18^2}{6} + \dfrac{35^2}{6} + \dfrac{23^2}{6} + \dfrac{36^2}{6} - C \right) - \text{R SS} - \text{C SS} \right]$

    $$= [(562.33 - 522.67) - 1.50 - 37.50] = 39.66 - 39.0 = 0.66$$

    (i) $(R \times C \times Ss)$ SS

    $= $ Within Ss SS $- (R \text{ SS} + R \times Ss \text{ SS} + C \text{ SS} + C \times Ss \text{ SS} + RC \text{ SS})$
    $= 139.00 - (1.50 + 14.50 + 37.50 + 27.50 + 0.66)$
    $= 139.00 - 81.66 = 57.34$

6. Computation of df:

$$df_{total} = npq - 1 = 6 \times 2 \times 2 - 1 = 23$$
$$\text{or} \quad N - 1 = 24 - 1 = 23$$
$$df_{bet.Ss} = n - 1 = 6 - 1 = 5$$
$$df_{w.Ss} = n(pq - 1) = 6(2 \times 2 - 1) = 6 \times 3 = 18$$
$$df_R = p - 1 = 2 - 1 = 1$$
$$df_{R \times Ss} = (p-1)(n-1) = (2-1)(6-1) = 1 \times 5 = 5$$
$$df_C = (q-1) = 2 - 1 = 1$$
$$df_{C \times Ss} = (q-1)(n-1) = (2-1)(6-1) = 1 \times 5 = 5$$
$$df_{RC} = (p-1)(q-1) = (2-1)(2-1) = 1 \times 1 = 1$$
$$df_{R \times C \times Ss} = (p-1)(q-1)(n-1) = (2-1)(2-1)(6-1) = 1 \times 1 \times 5 = 5$$

7. Computation of mean squares (MS)

$$MS_R = \frac{R\ SS}{df_R} = \frac{1.50}{1} = 1.50$$

$$MS_{R \times Ss} = \frac{R \times Ss\ SS}{df_{R \times Ss}} = \frac{14.50}{5} = 2.90$$

$$MS_C = \frac{C\ SS}{df_C} = \frac{37.50}{1} = 37.50$$

$$MS_{C \times Ss} = \frac{C \times Ss\ SS}{df_{C \times Ss}} = \frac{27.50}{5} = 5.50$$

$$MS_{RC} = \frac{RC\ SS}{df_{RC}} = \frac{0.66}{1} = 0.66$$

$$MS_{R \times C \times Ss} = \frac{R \times C \times Ss\ SS}{df_{R \times C \times Ss}} = \frac{57.34}{5} = 11.47$$

8. Computation of F-ratios

$$F_R = \frac{MS_R}{MS_{R \times Ss}} = \frac{1.50}{2.90} = 0.52 \quad \text{or} \quad <1$$

$$F_C = \frac{MS_C}{MS_{C \times Ss}} = \frac{37.50}{5.50} = 6.82$$

$$F_{RC} = \frac{MS_{RC}}{MS_{R \times C \times Ss}} = \frac{0.66}{11.47} = 0.06 \quad \text{or} \quad <1$$

9. Summary of ANOVA (see Table 15.16)

10. Test of significance:

The obtained values of F in Table 15.16 are to be evaluated. The F-ratios in respect of factor R and RC interaction are less than 1, so they need not be tested for significance. The F-ratio in respect of factor C is 6.82. Consulting Table E in the appendix with df = 1/5, the critical F value at $\alpha = 0.05$ is 6.61 and at $\alpha = 0.01$ is 16.26. Since the obtained value of $F = 6.82$ is greater than 6.61 but less than 16.26, it is significant at the 0.05 level of significance. Therefore, $p < 0.05$. Thus, the main effect of factor C (column) is significant. So, the H_0 is rejected and H_1 is accepted in 95% of cases. The subjects performed better in C_2 $\left(\text{mean} = \frac{71}{12} = 5.92 \right)$ than in C_1 $\left(\text{mean} = \frac{41}{12} = 3.42 \right)$. Therefore, we may conclude that the main effect of factor R and the RC interaction effect are not significant whereas the main

Table 15.16   Summary of ANOVA for a 2×2 factorial experiment with repeated measures on both the factors

Source of Variation	SS	df	MS	F
Between subjects	26.33	5		
Within subjects	139.00	18		
R (Rows)	1.50	1	1.50	0.52 (<1)
$R \times Ss$ (Error I)	14.50	5	2.90	
C (Columns)	37.50	1	37.50	6.82*
$C \times Ss$ (Error II)	27.50	5	5.50	
RC interaction	0.66	1	0.66	0.06 (<1)
$R \times C \times Ss$ (Error III)	57.34	5	11.47	
Total	165.33	23		

Note: *$p < 0.05$.

effect of factor C is significant. Thus, the H_0 is accepted in case of factor R and RC interaction effects whereas it is rejected in case of factor C effects.

Summary

In this chapter, we have discussed the topic of ANOVA (repeated measures). A repeated-measures study uses a single sample of n size measured in all of the different treatment conditions. Thus, the repeated-measures design is called within-subject design. The main difference between experimental designs with and without repeated measures is that: In the repeated-measures design, each subject in the experiment is successively observed under all the k treatments, and thus, the variation due to individual differences is eliminated from the estimate of experimental error, whereas in experiments without repeated measures, a subject is observed in one and only one of the k treatments and the variation due to individual differences forms the part of experimental error. Thus, repeated-measures design increases the precision of the experiment by eliminating the inter-subject differences as a source of error. However, the repeated-measures design is not suitable in certain experimental situations, particularly, when there is possibility of practise or 'carry-over effect' of one treatment being carried to the subsequent treatments.

In this chapter, we have presented three types of ANOVA designs with repeated measures: (a) one-factor ANOVA with repeated measures, (b) two-factor ANOVA with repeated measures on one factor and (c) two-factor ANOVA with repeated measures on both the factors. In the first case (i.e., one-factor ANOVA with repeated-measures design), the total sum of squares is first partitioned into two additive component parts: between-subjects sum of squares and within-subjects sum of squares. The between-subjects sum of squares represents the variation due to individual difference. The within-subjects sum of squares is further partitioned into two components parts: the between-treatment sum of squares and the residual sum of squares. The between-treatment sum of squares represents the variation of the treatment means about the overall mean. The residual sum of squares reflects the residual variation that serves as the error variance in one-way repeated ANOVA model. Thus, F-ratio for the treatment effect is obtained by dividing the MS treatment by the MS residual (error). When the obtained F-ratio is significant (that is, H_0 is rejected), it indicates that a significant difference lies between at least two of the treatment conditions. To determine exactly where the difference lies, post hoc comparisons may be made.

A repeated-measures ANOVA eliminates the influence of individual differences from the analysis because the same individuals are used in all treatments. If individual differences are extremely large, a treatment effect might be masked in an independent-measures experiment. In this case, a repeated-measures design might be a more sensitive test for a treatment effect.

In the second case (i.e., two-factor ANOVA with repeated measures on one factor, say Factor B), the total sum of squares is first partitioned into two additive component parts: between subjects sum of squares and within-subjects sum of squares. The between-subjects sum of squares is based on the variation of the individual subject's mean about the overall mean. It represents the variation due to individual differences. The within-subjects sum of squares represents the pooled variation of the individual subject's observations about the respective mean. The between subjects sum of squares is further partitioned into two component parts: A sum of squares and subjects within groups sum of squares. Similarly, the within-subjects sum of squares is partitioned into three component parts: B sum of squares, AB sum of squares and B × subjects within groups sum of squares. It is important to note that factor A is the part of between subjects variation whereas factor B and AB that of the within-subjects variation. The appropriate denominator to test the main effect of A is the subjects within groups variation (error between), and to test the main effect of B and AB interaction is the B × subjects within groups variation (error within).

In the third case (i.e., two-factor ANOVA with repeated measures on both the factors), the total sum of squares is first partitioned into two additive component parts: the between subjects sum of squares and the within-subjects sum of squares. In this ANOVA design, the between subjects sum of squares is separated from the total variation to eliminate the variation due to individual differences, thus, reducing the amount of experimental error. The between subjects sum of squares is not partitioned further. However, the within-subjects sum of squares is further partitioned into six component parts: A sum of squares, A × Ss sum of squares, B sum of squares, B × Ss sum of squares, AB sum of squares and AB × Ss sum of squares. To determine the F-ratio of A effects, A × Ss sum of squares is the appropriate denominator (error). Similarly, the B × Ss sum of squares and AB × Ss sum of squares are the appropriate denominators (errors) for the determination of F-ratios of B effects and AB interaction effects, respectively.

Finally, we have presented the computational formulae, and also explained the various processes of calculations of sum of squares, degrees of freedom, mean squares and F-ratios, and that of testing the significance of the obtained F-ratios through illustrative examples relating to all the above three types of ANOVA designs with repeated measures. We have also pointed out the limitations of the repeated-measures design.

Key Terms

- Between-subject design
- Direct method
- F-ratio
- Individual difference
- One-way ANOVA with repeated measures
- Repeated-measures design
- Single-factor repeated-measures design
- Subtraction method
- Two-factor ANOVA with repeated measures on both the factors
- Two-factor ANOVA with repeated measures on one factor
- Two-way ANOVA with repeated measures on both the factors
- Two-way ANOVA with repeated measures on one factor
- Within-subject design

Questions and Problems

1. What do you mean by a repeated-measures design? Make a comparison of designs with and without repeated measures.

2. What is the difference between a single-factor and a two-factor repeated-measures design? Discuss about the limitations of the repeated-measures design.

3. A researcher conducts a repeated-measures ANOVA for a study comparing four treatment conditions using a sample of $n=10$ subjects. What are the df values for the F-ratio?

4. A researcher reports an F-ratio with df$=2.40$ for a repeated-measures ANOVA.

   (a) How many treatment conditions were evaluated in this experiment?
   (b) How many subjects participated in this experiment?

5. The following data were obtained from a repeated-measures study comparing three treatment conditions.

Subjects (n)	Treatments (k)		
	I	**II**	**III**
A	6	8	10
B	5	5	5
C	1	2	3
D	0	1	2

   Use a repeated-measures ANOVA with $\alpha=0.05$ to determine whether these data are sufficient to demonstrate significant differences between the treatments.

6. It has been demonstrated that when subjects must memorise a list of words serially (in the order of presentation), words at the beginning and end of the list are remembered better than words in the middle. This observation has been called the *serial position effect*. The following data represent the number of errors made while recalling the first eight, second eight and last eight words in the list.

Persons	Serial Position		
	First	**Middle**	**Last**
A	1	5	0
B	3	7	2
C	5	6	1
D	3	2	1

   (a) Compute the mean number of errors for each position and draw a graph of the data.
   (b) Is there evidence for a significant effect of serial position? Test at the 0.05 level of significance. Based on the ANOVA, explain the results of the study.

7. An animal psychologist studies the effect of practice on maze learning for rats. Rats are tested in the maze in one daily session for four days. The psychologist records the number of errors made in each daily session. The data are as follows:

Rats	Sessions			
	1	2	3	4
1	3	1	0	0
2	3	2	2	1
3	6	3	1	2

Is there evidence for a practice effect? Use the 0.05 level of significance.

8. A teacher studies the effectiveness of a reading skills course on comprehension. A sample of $n=15$ students is studied. The instructor assesses their comprehension with a standardised reading test. The test is administered at the beginning of the course, at mid-term and at the end of the course. The instructor uses ANOVA to determine whether or not a significant change has occurred in the students' reading performance. The following summary table presents a portion of the ANOVA results. Provide the missing values in the table. (Start with df values.)

Source of Variation	SS	df	MS	F
Between subjects	36	–	–	–
Within subjects	–	–	–	–
Between treatments	–	–	24	8
Residual (Error)	–	–	–	–
Total	–	–	–	–

9. The following data are from a repeated-measures study.

Subjects	Treatments		Difference
	1	2	
A	2	4	+2
B	1	3	+2
C	0	10	+10
D	1	3	+2

(a) Use a repeated-measures t statistic with $\alpha=0.05$ to determine whether or not the data provide evidence of a significant difference between the two treatments.

(b) Use a repeated-measures ANOVA with $\alpha = 0.05$ to evaluate the data. Verify that $F = t^2$. (*Caution:* ANOVA calculations are done with the X values but for t you use the difference scores.)

10. Six different animals were given four different dosage levels of a particular drug. The order of administration of the dosage levels was randomised for each animal. The response measure was the number of discrimination problems solved within a time limit. The data are given below. Analyse the results of the experiment.

Subjects	Dosage Levels			
	a_1	a_2	a_3	a_4
1	3	7	8	5
2	2	7	7	6
3	2	6	7	4
4	3	3	8	7
5	4	7	7	6
6	2	6	7	7

11. The following are measurements made on a sample of 12 subjects under three experimental conditions. Apply repeated-measures ANOVA and interpret the results.

Subjects	Experimental Conditions		
	I	II	III
1	8	7	15
2	19	14	20
3	7	9	6
4	23	20	18
5	14	26	12
6	6	14	15
7	5	9	20
8	22	25	20
9	11	15	16
10	4	12	8
11	13	18	20
12	8	6	28

12. In an experiment, the investigator studied the effect of exposure duration on the judgement of size. Five exposure durations, that is, 60, 90, 120, 150 and 180 ms, were selected.

The stimuli for size judgement task consisted of six unfilled circles of different sizes varying from 1.5 to 9.0 cm. Each of the six sizes was presented with each of the five exposure durations. Though six sizes were taken, the independent variable of interest was the exposure duration. The dependent measure constituted the per cent error in judging the average size. A total of five subjects were randomly selected from the population of interest and each subject was observed under all the five treatment conditions. From each of the five subjects observations were obtained for each of the five exposure durations. The order of the presentation of treatments was independently randomised for each subject. Sufficient time was allowed to elapse between any two trials. For each combination of size and exposure duration five observations were taken from each subject and the criterion measure was the mean of these five observations. The outcome of the experiment in terms of per cent error in judging the size has been summarised below:

Subjects	Exposure Durations in msecs				
	T_1 (60)	T_2 (90)	T_3 (120)	T_4 (150)	T_5 (180)
1	22	19	16	10	7
2	18	13	13	13	9
3	18	13	13	11	7
4	14	11	8	9	3
5	15	12	11	10	7

Analyse the data using repeated-measures ANOVA.

13. The following are data for a two-factor experiment with repeated measurements on one factor. Three groups of two subjects are tested under four conditions.

Levels of Rows (R)	Subjects	Levels of Columns (C)				T_{rs}
		C_1	C_2	C_3	C_4	
R_1	1	4	1	3	2	10
	2	7	6	1	3	17
	T_{r_1c}	11	7	4	5	$T_1=27$
R_2	3	5	5	2	4	16
	4	9	5	1	2	17
	T_{r_2c}	14	10	3	6	$T_2=33$
R_3	5	7	8	1	4	20
	6	9	1	4	3	17
	T_{r_3c}	16	9	5	7	$T_3=37$
	T_c	41	26	12	18	$T=97$

Apply an ANOVA to these data and test the significance of row, column and interaction effects.

14. The following are data for a two-factor experiment with repeated measurements on one factor.

Levels of Rows (R)	Subjects	Levels of Columns (C)				Total
		C_1	C_2	C_3	C_4	
R_1	1	12	10	9	4	35
	2	10	5	8	2	25
		22	15	17	6	60
R_2	3	16	14	10	1	41
	4	27	23	14	8	72
		43	37	24	9	113
R_3	5	14	12	9	6	41
	6	23	14	10	9	56
		37	26	19	15	97
Total		102	78	60	30	270

Complete the ANOVA.

15. The following are data for a two-factor experiment with repeated measurements on both factors in which four experimental subjects are tested under four treatment combinations.

Subjects	R_1		R_2		Total
	C_1	C_2	C_1	C_2	
1	5	10	17	19	51
2	9	19	20	22	70
3	8	22	23	28	81
4	20	35	19	21	95
Total	42	86	79	90	297(G)

Apply an ANOVA to these data and test the significance of row and column effects.

16. The following are data for a 2×2 factorial experiment with repeated measurements on both the factors, in which six subjects were tested under four treatment combinations.

Subjects	R_1		R_2		Total
	C_1	C_2	C_1	C_2	
1	1	6	5	3	15
2	2	7	4	5	18
3	5	9	8	3	25
4	2	1	3	7	13
5	4	4	2	8	18
6	4	8	1	10	23
Total	18	35	23	36	112 (G)

Apply an ANOVA to these data.

17. Fill in the blanks:

   (i) The term single-factor indicates that the study involves only one _____ variable.

   (ii) The term independent measures indicates that the research study uses a _____ sample of n size for each of the treatment conditions being compared.

   (iii) In a repeated-measures study a _____ sample of n size is measured in all of the different _____ conditions.

   (iv) A single-factor or two-factor experimental design without repeated measures is also called _____.

   (v) The one-way or two-way ANOVA design with repeated measures is called as _____.

   (vi) A design is called repeated-measures design because _____ measures are obtained from the same subject.

   (vii) Repeated-measures design increases the precision of the experiment by eliminating the _____ differences as a source of error.

   (viii) A single-factor experimental design in which a subject is observed in one and only one of the k treatments, is called a _____ measures design.

   (ix) A single-factor experimental design in which each subject is successively observed under all the k treatments, is called a _____ measures design.

   (x) A repeated-measures design eliminates the role of _____ due to individual differences.

18. Write whether the following statements are True or False.

   (i) An independent variable is known as a factor.

   (ii) A repeated-measures design eliminates the role of variability due to individual differences.

(iii)   The amount of error variance of a non-repeated-measures design is less than that of a repeated-measures design.

(iv)   In one-way repeated-measures design, between-treatment sum of squares is a component of the between subjects sum of squares.

(v)   In a single-factor repeated-measures design, residual sum of squares is a component of the within-subjects sum of squares.

(vi)   Residual sum of squares is taken as the error variance in a single-factor repeated-measures design.

(vii)   In a two-factor, $A \times B$, design with repeated measures on factor B, factor A is a part of between subjects variation.

(viii)   There is only one error term in the analysis of two-factor experiment with repeated measures on the second factor.

(ix)   There are three error terms in the analysis of a two-factor experiment with repeated measures on both the factors.

(x)   In a two-factor design with repeated measures on both the factors, Total SS = Between Subj. SS + Within Subj. SS

19.   Find out the correct answer from among the four alternatives.

(i)   In one-way ANOVA design, the number of factors is:

(a)   One   (b)   Two

(c)   More than two   (d)   None of the above

(ii)   ANOVA with a repeated-measures design is also called as:

(a)   Between subjects design   (b)   Within-subjects design

(c)   Randomised block design   (d)   None of the above

(iii)   Inter-subject differences as a source of error is eliminated in the:

(a)   Randomised group design   (b)   Non-repeated-measures design

(c)   Repeated-measures design   (d)   None of the above

(iv)   A factor refers to:

(a)   A dependent variable   (b)   An independent variable

(c)   An effect   (d)   None of the above

(v)   A single-factor ANOVA design in which a group of subjects is tested under all the k treatment conditions is known as:

(a)   Repeated-measures design   (b)   Between subject design

(c)   Non-repeated-measures design   (d)   None of the above

(vi)   One of the disadvantages of the repeated-measures design is the:

(a)   Non-practice effects   (b)   Carry-over effects

(c)   Age effects   (d)   None of the above

(vii)   A repeated-measures design eliminates the role of variability due to:

    (a)   Individual differences   (b)   Sample size differences

    (c)   Population size differences   (d)   None of the above

(viii)   In a single-factor repeated-measures design, the residual sum of squares is called the:

    (a)   True variance   (b)   Between-subjects variance

    (c)   Error variance   (d)   None of the above

(ix)   In one-way ANOVA with repeated measures, the df associated with the within-subjects sum of squares is calculated as:

    (a) $df = n-1$ (b) $df = n(k-1)$

    (c) $df = k-1$ (d)   None of the above

(x)   In a two-factor, $A \times B$, design with repeated measures on factor B, the A sum of squares is a component of:

    (a)   Between-subjects sum of squares

    (b)   Within-subjects sum of squares

    (c)   Either between- or within-subjects sum of squares

    (d)   None of the above

Non-parametric Statistics

After completing this chapter you will be able to:

- Understand the concept of parametric and non-parametric tests.
- Differentiate between parametric and non-parametric statistical tests.
- Identify the advantages and disadvantages of non-parametric tests.
- Introduce the chi-square and use it in statistical inferences.
- Describe the Spearman rank-order correlation coefficient and use it in statistical inferences.
- Understand concepts like Phi coefficient, contingency coefficient, Kendall's rank correlation coefficient and coefficient of concordance, and use them in statistical inferences.
- Use and interpret each of six standard non-parametric hypothesis tests.
- Identify which distribution-free (non-parametric) tests are appropriate for different situations.
- Test hypotheses when no assumption can be made about the distribution which is sampled.

16.1   Introduction

Statistical inference tests are often classified as to whether they are parametric or non-parametric. We will recall from our earlier discussion (see Chapter 1) that a parameter is a characteristic or measurement of a population. Hence, a parametric inference test is one that depends considerably on population characteristics or parameters for its use. All the statistical tests we have examined thus far, for instance, z-test, t-test and F-test are the examples of parametric test because they are designed to test hypotheses about specific population parameters. Because these tests all concern parameters and require assumptions about parameters, they are called *parametric tests*.

Another general characteristic of parametric tests is that they require a numerical score for each individual in the sample. The scores then are added, squared, averaged and otherwise manipulated using basic arithmetic. In terms of measurement scales, parametric tests require data from an interval or a ratio scale (see Chapter 1).

Often researchers are confronted with experimental situations that do not conform to the requirements of parametric tests. In these situations, it may not be appropriate to use a parametric test, because we know that when the assumptions of a test are violated, the test may lead to an erroneous interpretation of the data. Fortunately, there are several hypothesis-testing techniques that provide alternatives to parametric tests. These alternatives are called non-parametric tests. Although all inference tests depend on population characteristics to some extent, the requirements for non-parametric tests are minimal. For non-parametric tests, the shape of population distribution is unimportant, and also it is not necessary that the samples be random samples from normally distributed populations as with the t- and F-tests. In this chapter, we introduce some commonly used non-parametric tests. You should note that these non-parametric tests usually do not state hypotheses in terms of specific parameters and they make few (if any) assumptions about the population distribution. For the latter reason, non-parametric tests are called *distribution-free tests.*

Another important characteristic of non-parametric tests is that the data are simply frequencies or ranks. In terms of measurement scales, non-parametric tests require data from a nominal or an ordinal scale (see Chapter 1). Most of the non-parametric tests, except chi-square (χ^2), are called ranking tests, because the data are in terms of ranks or the given scores are converted to ranks to apply a specific non-parametric test.

Since non-parametric inference tests have fewer requirements or assumptions about population characteristics, the question arises as to why not use them all the time and forget about parametric tests. The answer to this question is twofold. First, many of the parametric inference tests are robust with regard to violations of underlying assumptions. We will recall that a test is robust if violations in the assumptions do not greatly disturb the sampling distribution of its statistic. Thus, the t-test is robust regarding the violation of normality in the population. Even though, theoretically, normality in the population is required with small samples, it turns out empirically that unless the departures from normality are substantial, the sampling distribution of t remains essentially the same. Thus, the t-test can be used with data, even though the data violate the assumptions of normality.

The main reasons for preferring parametric to non-parametric tests are that, in general, they (i.e., parametric tests) are more sensitive, more powerful and more versatile than non-parametric tests. Therefore, whenever the experimental data give the researcher a choice between a parametric and a non-parametric test, the researcher always should choose the parametric alternative. As a general rule, the investigator will use parametric tests whenever possible. However, when there is an extreme violation of an assumption of the parametric test or if the investigator believes the scaling of the data makes the parametric test inappropriate, a non-parametric inference test will be employed.

The definitions, assumptions, advantages and disadvantages of parametric and non-parametric inference tests, a comparison between these two types of statistical tests and the precautions in using non-parametric statistical tests are discussed in detail in the next section.

16.2   Parametric and Non-parametric Statistical Tests

Statistical inference tests or simply the statistical tests are broadly divided into two types, such as, parametric and non-parametric statistical tests, which are discussed below in detail.

16.2.1   Parametric Statistical Tests (PST)

You will recall from our discussion in Chapter 1 that a parameter is a characteristic or a measure of a population. A parametric inference test is one that depends considerably on population characteristics, or parameters for its use. Thus, a parametric statistical test is defined as, 'A parametric statistical test is a test whose model specifies certain conditions about the parameters of the population from which the research sample was drawn.' Since these conditions are not ordinarily tested, they are assumed to hold. The meaningfulness of the results of a parametric test depends on the validity of these assumptions. The following are some of the assumptions of the parametric tests.

16.2.1.1   *Assumptions of Parametric Statistical Tests*

The assumptions of the parametric statistical tests are:

(i)   The observations must be independent. That is, the selection of any one case from the population for inclusion in the sample must not bias the chances of any other case for inclusion, and the score which is assigned to any case must not bias the score which is assigned to any other case. In brief, independence of observation implies two things, that is, selection of samples from the population must be random, and assignment of scores to the observation must be unbiased.

(ii)   The observations must be drawn from normally distributed populations. In other words, the trait or the dependent variable that the researcher is going to measure must be normally distributed in the population from which the research samples are drawn.

(iii) These populations from which the research samples are drawn must have the homogeneity of variances or same variance (or in special cases, they must have a known ratio of variances).

(iv)   The variables involved must have been measured in an interval or ratio scales of measurement, so that it is possible to use the operations of arithmetic (adding, dividing, finding means, etc.) on the scores.

(v)   The populations from which the research samples are drawn must have homoscedasticity of variances, which means the equality of variances between columns and rows. The means of these normal and homoscedastic populations must be linear combinations of effects due to columns and/or rows. That is, the effects must be additive.

All the above conditions [except Assumption (iv), which states the measurement requirement] are elements of the parametric statistical model. Assumption (v) regarding the homoscedastic population is found only in case of the analysis of variance model (the F-test). With the possible exception of the assumption of homoscedasticity (equal variances) these conditions are ordinarily not tested in the course of the performance of a statistical analysis. Rather, they are presumptions which are accepted, and their truth or falsity determines the meaningfulness of the probability statement arrived at by the parametric test.

When we have reason to believe that these conditions are met in the data under analysis, then we should certainly choose a parametric statistical test, such as 't' or F, for analysing those data. Such a choice is optimum because the parametric test will be most powerful for rejecting H_0 when it should be rejected.

But when the assumptions constituting the statistical model for a test are in fact not met, or when the measurement is not of the required strength, then it is difficult if not impossible to say what is really the power of the test. It is even difficult to estimate the extent to which a probability statement about the hypothesis in question is meaningful when that probability statement results from the unacceptable application of a test. Although some empirical evidence has been gathered to show that slight deviations in meeting the assumptions underlying parametric tests may not have radical effects on the obtained probability figure, there is as yet no general agreement as to what constitutes a 'slight' deviation.

16.2.2   Non-parametric Statistical Tests (NPSTs)

A non-parametric statistical test, on the contrary, is a test whose model does not specify conditions about the parameters of the population from which the research samples are drawn. For non-parametric statistical tests, the shape of the population is unimportant. For example, it is not necessary that the samples be random samples from normally distributed populations as with the parametric statistical tests. For non-parametric statistical tests all that is necessary is that the sample scores be random samples from population having the same distributions. For this reason, non-parametric inference tests are sometimes referred to as *distribution-free tests*.

16.2.2.1   *Assumptions of Non-parametric Statistical Tests*

The following are certain assumptions which are associated with most non-parametric tests.

(i)   The observations are independent. The independence of observation implies two things—one, the selection of samples from the population must be random and, second, assignment of scores to the observation must be unbiased.

(ii)   The trait or the dependent variable under study has underlying continuity. This means that the variable under study must be present in any amount in each and every element of the population from which the research samples are drawn; nowhere in the population, it is absent.

(iii)   The variables involved must have been measured in an ordinal scale or in a nominal scale. In other words, the given data should be in terms of ranks or in categories. Non-parametric tests do not require measurement so strong as that required for the parametric tests; most non-parametric tests apply to data in an ordinal scale and some apply also to data in a nominal scale.

16.2.2.2   *Advantages of Non-parametric Statistical Tests*

The following are some of the advantages of the non-parametric statistical tests.

(i)   Probability statements obtained from most non-parametric statistical tests are *exact* probabilities (except in the case of large samples, where excellent approximations are available), regardless of the shape of the population distribution from which the random sample was drawn. The accuracy of the probability statement does not depend on the shape of the population, although some non-parametric tests may assume identity of shape of two or more population distributions and some others assume symmetrical population distributions. In certain cases, the non-parametric tests do assume that the underlying distribution is continuous, an assumption which they share with parametric tests. In brief, exact probabilities can be determined by the help of non-parametric statistical tests.

(ii) If the sample size is small, as small as $n=6$ are used, there is no alternative to using a non-parametric statistical test unless the nature of the population distribution is *known exactly*.

(iii) There are suitable non-parametric statistical tests for treating samples made up of observations from several different populations. None of the parametric statistical tests can handle such data without requiring us to make seemingly unrealistic assumptions.

(iv) Non-parametric statistical tests are available to treat the data which are inherently in ranks as well as data whose seemingly numerical scores have the strength of ranks. That is, the researcher may only be able to say of his/her subjects that one has more or less of the characteristic than another, without being able to say how much more or less. For example, in studying such a variable as anxiety, we may be able to state that subject A is more anxious than subject B without knowing at all exactly how much more anxious A is. If data are inherently in ranks, or even if they can only be categorised as plus or minus (more or less, better or worse), they can be treated by non-parametric methods, whereas they cannot be treated by parametric methods unless precarious and perhaps unrealistic assumptions are made about the underlying distributions.

(v) Non-parametric statistical tests are available to treat data which are simply classificatory or categorical, that is, are measured in a nominal scale. No parametric statistical technique applies to such data.

(vi) Non-parametric statistical tests are typically much easier to learn and to apply than are parametric statistical tests.

16.2.2.3 *Disadvantages of Non-parametric Statistical Tests*

In spite of the so many advantages as cited above, the non-parametric statistical tests have the following disadvantages:

(i) If all the assumptions of the parametric statistical model are in fact met in the data, and if the measurement is of the required strength, then non-parametric statistical tests are wasteful of data, because the primary objectives of research are: (a) prediction about future outcomes and (b) drawing inference about population distribution. These two objectives are not met with non-parametric statistical tests.

(ii) The degree of wastefulness is expressed by the power efficiency of the non-parametric test. It will be remembered that if a non-parametric statistical test has power efficiency of, say, 90%, this means that where all the conditions of the parametric statistical test are satisfied the appropriate parametric test would be just as effective with a sample which is 10% smaller than that used in the non-parametric analysis.

(iii) Interaction effects among variables or factors cannot be measured by the help of non-parametric statistical tests. In other words, there are as yet no non-parametric methods for testing interactions in the analysis of variance model, unless special assumptions are made about additivity.

(iv) Another objection that has been raised against non-parametric methods is that the tests and their accompanying tables of significant values have been widely scattered in various publications and appear in different formats; many are highly specialised and they have, therefore, been comparatively inaccessible to the behavioural scientists.

16.2.3 Difference between Parametric and Non-parametric Statistical Tests

The following are some of the important points of difference between parametric and non-parametric statistical tests or simply statistical inference tests.

(i) A parametric statistical test depends considerably on population characteristics or parameters, for its use, whereas a non-parametric statistical test does not depend so much on the population characteristics or parameters for its use.

(ii) The model of the parametric statistical tests specifies certain conditions about the parameters of the population from which the research samples are drawn. However, the model of the non-parametric statistical tests does not specify conditions about the parameters of the population from which the samples are drawn.

(iii) For parametric statistical tests, the shape of the population is important but for non-parametric tests, the shape of population is unimportant.

(iv) Parametric statistical test can be applied to the data which are in terms of either interval or ratio scales of measurement, but when measurements are in terms of nominal or ordinal scales, the use of non-parametric tests will be more appropriate.

(v) Non-parametric statistical tests have fewer requirements or assumptions about population characteristics compared to the parametric statistical tests.

(vi) Many of the parametric statistical tests are robust with regard to violation of underlying assumptions. A test is said to be robust if violations in the assumptions do not greatly disturb the sampling distribution of its statistic. Thus, the 't'-test is robust regarding the violation of normality in the population. Even though, theoretically, normality in the population is required with small samples, it turns out empirically that unless the departures from normality are substantial, the sampling distribution of t remains essentially the same. Thus, the t-test can be used with data even though the data violate the assumptions of normality. This is one of the reasons of preferring parametric tests to non-parametric tests.

(vii) The main reasons for preferring parametric to non-parametric tests are that, in general, they are more powerful and versatile than non-parametric tests. We can see an example of the higher power of parametric tests when we will compare the t-test with the sign test for correlated groups (see Chapter 17). The factorial design discussed in Chapters 13–15 provides a good example of the versatility of parametric tests. With this design, we can test two, three, four or more variables and their interactions. No comparable statistical technique exists with non-parametric statistics.

(viii) As a general rule, investigators will use parametric statistical tests whenever possible. However, when there is an extreme violation of an assumption of the parametric test or if the investigator believes the scaling of the data makes the parametric test inappropriate, a non-parametric statistical test will be employed.

(ix) Prediction about future outcomes and drawing inferences about population distributions, which are the two basic objectives of research, are met with parametric statistical tests but not with non-parametric statistical tests.

(x) Non-parametric statistical tests are typically much easier to learn and to apply than are parametric statistical tests.

16.2.4 Precautions in Using Non-parametric Statistical Tests

The following precautions should be kept in mind while using non-parametric statistical tests:

(i) In situations where the assumptions underlying a parametric test are satisfied and both parametric and non-parametric tests can be applied, the preference should be for the parametric test because most parametric tests have greater power in such situations.

(ii) When measurements are in terms of interval or ratio scales, the transformation of the measurements on nominal or ordinal scales will lead to the loss of much information. Hence, as far as possible, parametric tests should be applied in such situations; no non-parametric test should be used here, unless it is asked for.

(iii) The non-parametric tests, no doubt, provide a means for avoiding the assumption of *normality* of distribution. But these tests do nothing to avoid the assumptions of independence of observation or homoscedasticity wherever applicable.

(iv) The *F*-test and *t*-test are generally considered to be robust test because the violation of the underlying assumptions does not invalidate the inferences about the population parameters. It is customary to justify the use of a normal theory test in a situation where normality cannot be guaranteed, by arguing that it is robust under non-normality.

(v) Behavioural scientists should specify the null hypothesis, alternative hypothesis, statistical test, sampling distribution and level of significance in advance of the collection of data. Hunting around for a statistical test after the data have been collected tends to maximise the effects of any chance differences which favour one test over another. As a result, the possibility of rejecting the null hypothesis (H_0) when it is true (Type I error) is greatly increased. However, this caution is equally applicable to both parametric and non-parametric statistical tests.

In the following sections of this chapter, we shall present some important and commonly used non-parametric statistical tests. Let us begin with chi-square (χ^2) test.

16.3 Chi-square (χ^2) Test

We have previously discussed about the binomial, Poisson, normal, t and F distributions. Another distribution of considerable theoretical and practical importance is the distribution of chi-square or χ^2. The name of the test comes from the Greek letter χ (Chi, pronounced 'Kye'), which is used to identify the test statistic. The distribution of χ^2, just as the binomial, Poisson, normal, t and F distributions, is a theoretical model.

The χ^2 test is used in the analysis of frequencies which are in terms of nominal data. We will recall that with this type of data, observations are grouped into several discrete, mutually exclusive categories, and one counts the frequency of occurrence in each category. The inference test most often used with nominal data is a non-parametric test called chi-square (χ^2).

In many experimental situations, we wish to compare a set of observed frequencies with a set of theoretical frequencies. The theoretical frequencies are usually called the expected frequencies, which the investigator would expect to get if the particular theory in question was true. The observed frequencies are those obtained empirically by direct observation or experiment. The theoretical or expected frequencies are those generated on the basis of some hypothesis or line of theoretical speculation which is independent of the data at hand. Now, the question arises as to whether the differences between the observed and expected frequencies are significant.

In this context, the null hypothesis (H_0) is that no difference exists between the observed and expected frequencies. The alternative hypothesis (H_1) is that a difference exists between the observed and expected frequencies. If the observed frequencies depart significantly from the theoretical or expected frequencies, this constitutes evidence for the rejection of the null hypothesis or theory that gave rise to the theoretical frequencies.

To illustrate, let us consider a coin. The hypothesis may be formulated that the coin is unbiased. Let us now toss the coin 100 times with the following results:

	Head	Tail	Total
f_o	60	40	100
f_e	50	50	100

The observed frequencies, denoted by the symbol f_o, are 60 heads and 40 tails. The expected frequencies, identified by the symbol f_e, are those the investigator would expect to get if the coins were unbiased and are 50 heads and 50 tails (i.e., total outcomes divided by the total number of categories; in this example, the total outcomes is 100 and there are two categories of outcomes—heads and tails, thus f_e is 100/2 = 50 each). Here, two important questions arise. One, how may these two sets of frequencies be compared? Second, what constitutes evidence for the rejection of the null hypothesis that the coin is unbiased? The statistic χ^2 is used to answer these questions.

16.3.1   Definition of Chi-square (χ^2)

Chi-square (χ^2) is a descriptive measure of the magnitude of the discrepancies between the observed and expected frequencies. χ^2 may be defined as the sum of ratios of squared deviations of observed frequencies (f_o) from the corresponding expected frequencies (f_e), and the respective f_e values. Thus, the formula for the chi-square statistic (χ^2) is

$$\chi^2 = \sum \frac{(f_o - f_e)^2}{f_e}$$

where

f_o = observed frequencies of a category
f_e = expected frequencies of the corresponding category
Σ = directs one to sum over all the categories

As the above formula indicates, the value of χ^2 is computed by the following steps:

(i)   Find the difference between f_o and f_e of each category.
(ii) Square the difference ($f_o - f_e$). This ensures that all values are positive.
(iii) Divide the squared difference of a particular category by its respective f_e.
(iv) Finally, sum the values from all the categories.

An alternative formula for chi-square reads as:

$$\chi^2 = \sum \frac{(f_o)^2}{f_e} - N$$

16.3.2 Characteristics of Chi-square (χ^2)

Inspection of the above formula for χ^2 leads to the following characteristics of the chi-square statistic:

(a) Since χ^2 is a descriptive measure of the magnitude of the discrepancies between the observed and expected frequencies, the greater the discrepancy between the f_o and f_e, relative to f_e, the greater is the amount of χ^2. If no discrepancies exist and the observed and expected frequencies are the same, χ^2 will be 0.

(b) χ^2 is always positive, since the difference between f_o and f_e is squared. The reader should note also that χ^2 is always 0 or a positive number. Negative values cannot occur.

(c) The magnitude of χ^2 varies from series to series, owing to the variations in the observed frequencies, the expected frequencies being constant over the categories. For example, one investigator tossed a coin 100 times and got 60 heads and 40 tails. Another investigator tossed a coin 100 times and got 45 heads and 55 tails. In both the cases, the expected frequencies are 50 in each category of responses, but the amount of χ^2 will be different in both the series. It is because of the different observed frequencies in the two categories of both the series.

(d) Different categories of responses are not independent. If the frequency of one category is known, the frequency of other category is determined. For example, in the tossing of 100 coins two frequencies are obtained, one for heads and one for tails. These frequencies are not independent. The frequency of tails is $100-45=55$, if the frequency of heads is 45. If the frequency of heads is 60, the frequency of tails is $100-60=40$. Thus, it is quite clear that, given either frequency, the other is determined.

(e) The typical chi-square distribution is positively skewed, and it is a continuous probability distribution at its right tail. The shape and form of the distribution depend on the df of the chi-square.

16.3.3 Assumptions of Chi-square (χ^2)

Since χ^2 is a non-parametric statistical test, most of the assumptions of non-parametric tests are also the assumptions of χ^2. The following are some of the important assumptions of χ^2 test:

(a) Observations must be independent. It implies that the selection of the samples from the population and the assignment of scores to the observations must be unbiased or impartial.

(b) The variable under study must have underlying continuity—nowhere in the sample or population, the trait is absent.

(c) The measurements or data should be in terms of nominal (categorical) scale of measurement. For example, the subjects are required to give their responses in different categories, such as 'Yes, Neutral or No', 'Favourable, Neutral or Unfavourable', 'Positive, Neutral or Negative', etc.

(d) The data are in terms of frequencies, percentage or proportions.

(e) Number of samples should be less so that maximum df would be 30 [df $=c-1$ or df $=(r-1)(c-1)$].

16.3.4   Sampling Distribution of Chi-square (χ^2)

The sampling distribution of χ^2 may be illustrated with reference to the tossing of coins. Let us assume that in tossing 100 unbiased coins 45 heads and 55 tails result. The expected frequencies are 50 heads and 50 tails. A value of χ^2 may be calculated as follows:

	f_o	f_e	$f_o - f_e$	$(f_o - f_e)^2$	$\dfrac{(f_o - f_e)^2}{f_e}$
Head	45	50	–5	25	0.5
Tail	55	50	5	25	0.5
					$\chi^2 = 1.0$

In the tossing of 100 coins two frequencies are obtained, one for heads and one for tails. These frequencies are not independent. If the frequency of heads is 45, the frequency of tails is $100 - 45 = 55$. If the frequency of heads is 60, the frequency of tails is $100 - 60 = 40$. Quite clearly, given either frequency the other is determined. One frequency only is free to vary. In this situation, 1 df is associated with the value of χ^2.

Let us toss the 100 coins a second time, a third time, and so on, to obtain different values of χ^2. A large number of trials may be made and a large number of values of χ^2 obtained. The frequency distribution of these values is an experimental sampling distribution of χ^2 for 1 df. It describes the variation in χ^2 with repeated sampling. By inspecting this experimental sampling distribution, estimates may be made of the proportion of times, or the probability, that values of χ^2 equal to or greater than any given value will occur due to sampling fluctuation for 1 df. In the present illustration this assumes, of course, that the coins are unbiased.

Instead of tossing 100 coins, let us throw an unbiased die (having six values –1, 2, 3, 4, 5, 6) 100 times, obtain observed and expected frequencies, and calculate the value of χ^2. In this situation, if any five frequencies are known, the sixth is determined. Thus, in this case, five degrees of freedom are associated with the value of χ^2 obtained. The 100 dice may be tossed a great many times, a value of χ^2 calculated for each trial and a frequency distribution made. This frequency distribution is an experimental sampling distribution of χ^2 for 5 df.

The theoretical sampling distribution of χ^2 contains the number of degrees of freedom as a variable. This means that a different sampling distribution of χ^2 exists for each value of df. Figure 16.1 shows different chi-square distributions for different values of df. The χ^2 distributions vary with degrees of freedom. For the lower degrees of freedom, the curves are positively skewed. The value of χ^2 is always positive because it results from squaring the difference between the observed and expected frequencies. Values of χ^2 range from 0 to infinity. The right-hand tail of the curve is asymptotic to the abscissa. For 1 df, the curve is asymptotic to the ordinate as well as to the abscissa.

The chi-square (χ^2) distribution is used in tests of significance in much the same way that the normal, t or the F distributions are used. The null hypothesis (H_0) is assumed. This H_0 states that no actual differences exist between the observed and expected frequencies. A value of χ^2 is calculated. If this obtained χ^2 value is equal to or greater than the critical value of χ^2 required for significance at an accepted level of significance for the appropriate df, the H_0 is rejected. The decision rule states the following:

$$\text{If } \chi^2_{obt} \geq \chi^2_{crit}, \quad \text{reject } H_0$$

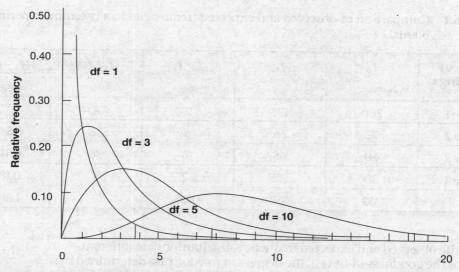

Figure 16.1   The shape of the chi-square distribution for different values of degrees of freedom

We may state that the differences between the observed and expected frequencies are significant and cannot reasonably be explained by sampling fluctuation. Table L in the appendix shows values of chi-square (χ^2) required for significance at various probability levels for different values of df. Since the direction of the difference between f_o and f_e is immaterial, the χ^2 test is a nondirectional test. Further, since each difference adds to the value of χ^2, the critical region for rejection always lies under the right-hand tail of the χ^2 distribution.

Table L of the appendix provides the 5% and 1% critical values for df=1 to df=30. This covers the great majority of situations ordinarily encountered in practice. Situations where a χ^2 is calculated based on a df > 30 are infrequent. Where df > 30, the expression $\sqrt{2\chi^2} - \sqrt{2df - 1}$ has a sampling distribution which is approximately normal. Values of this expression required for significance at the 5% and 1% levels are 1.64 and 2.33, respectively.

16.3.5   Applications of Chi-square (χ^2)

The chief situations for which it is permissible to use χ^2 may be classified into two types—test of goodness of fit and test of independence, which are discussed below.

16.3.5.1   *Test of Goodness of Fit*

Usually, in tests of goodness of fit, a set of observed frequencies on a single variable is compared with a corresponding set of expected or theoretical frequencies. This test is used to explore how far a distribution of the observed frequencies fits with a theoretical distribution such as the binomial distribution, Poisson distribution or normal distribution.

In this case, the null hypothesis (H_0) states that

H_0: There is no difference between the observed and expected frequency distributions.
The alternative hypothesis (H_1) states that:

Table 16.1 Comparison of observed and expected frequencies in a breeding experiment of plants

Type of Seedlings	f_0	f_e	$f_0 - f_e$	$(f_0 - f_e)^2$	$\dfrac{(f_0 - f_e)^2}{f_e}$
Type 1	200	198	2	4	0.0202
Type 2	72	66	6	36	0.5454
Type 3	60	66	-6	36	0.5454
Type 4	20	22	-2	4	0.1818
Total	352	352	0.00		1.2928

H_1: Tthe observed and expected frequency distributions are different.

For the goodness-of-fit test, the degrees of freedom are determined by:

$$df = c - 1$$

where c is the number of categories. To test the goodness of fit, first of all, the value of χ^2 will be calculated from the given data. If the calculated value of χ^2 is less than the critical value at a certain level of significance for an appropriate df, the fit is considered to be a good one which means that the divergence between the observed and expected frequencies is attributable to the sampling fluctuations. But if the calculated value of χ^2 is equal to or greater than the critical value (or table value), the fit is not considered to be a good one.

Numerous examples may be found to illustrate the goodness of fit of a theoretical to an observed frequency distribution. In a breeding experiment a cross between plants results in 352 seedlings. According to genetic theory, the seedlings should segregate into four types in the ratio of 9:3:3:1. The observed frequencies for the four types are 200, 72, 60 and 20, respectively. Is this outcome of the experiment in accord with theory? Or do the frequencies deviate significantly from those expected on the basis of theory? The data are shown in Table 16.1.

According to the theory, in the above experiment, the seedlings should segregate in the ratio of 9:3:3:1. This is the null hypothesis (H_0) we wish to test. If the theory is true, then $P_1 = 9/16$ should be the probability of Type 1; $P_2 = 3/16$ should be the probability of Type 2; $P_3 = 3/16$ should be the probability of Type 3 and $P_4 = 1/16$ should be the probability of Type 4.

We have $N = 352$ observations and the corresponding expected frequencies in Types 1 through 4 would be:

$$f_{e_1} = \frac{9}{16} \times 352 = 198; \qquad f_{e_2} = \frac{3}{16} \times 352 = 66;$$

$$f_{e_3} = \frac{3}{16} \times 352 = 66 \quad \text{and} \quad f_{e_4} = \frac{1}{16} \times 352 = 22$$

From Table 16.1, it is evident that the obtained χ^2 is 1.2928 (or 1.293). The $df = c - 1 = 4 - 1 = 3$. Referring to Table L of the appendix with $df = 3$, the critical value of χ^2 at $\alpha = 0.05$ is 7.82 and at $\alpha = 0.01$ is 11.34. Since the obtained value of $\chi^2 = 1.293$ is less than the table value of χ^2 at $\alpha = 0.05$, it is not significant. This shows that the outcome of the experiment is in accord with theory. The frequencies do not deviate significantly from those expected on the basis of the theory. In other words, the correspondence between the observed and expected frequencies is close. The value of $\chi^2 = 1.293$ and no grounds exist to reject the null hypothesis. Therefore, we may conclude that there is a goodness of fit between the theoretical and the observed frequency distributions.

16.3.5.2   Test of Independence

In tests of independence, two variables are involved. These are usually nominal variables. The question arises as to whether the two variables are independent of each other. The data are arranged in the form of a table called a *contingency table*. Contingency tables may be composed of any number of rows (R) and any number of columns (C). The rows correspond to the categories of one variable and the columns correspond to the categories of the second variable. For example, consider a contingency table of two rows and two columns. Such tables are known as 2×2 tables. Here is an illustrative example of such a table where the two variables are denoted by A and B, each having two categories or two levels.

	Observed Frequencies		
	B_1	B_2	Total
A_1	50	10	60
A_2	20	20	40
Total	70	30	100(N)

The frequencies shown are observed frequencies. The question is whether the variable A is independent of the variable B, or whether it may be argued that an association exists between A and B.

First of all, the expected frequencies must be obtained. What frequencies would we expect to find in the four cells of the table if A were independent of B? These expected frequencies are readily obtained using the multiplication theorem of probability. The argument runs as follows. The probability of any member chosen at random having the attribute of A_1 is $\frac{60}{100} = 0.60$. The probability of any member chosen at random having the attribute of B_1 is $\frac{70}{100} = 0.70$. Therefore, using the multiplication theorem of probability, if A is independent of B, the probability of any member chosen at random having the attributes of both A_1 and B_1 is the product of the separate probabilities or $0.60 \times 0.70 = 0.42$. Thus, if A is independent of B, the expected proportion in the top left-hand cell is 0.42, and the expected frequency is $0.42 \times 100 = 42$, there being 100 observations in all (N) in this example. Similarly, expected frequencies for the other three cells of the table may be obtained. The expected frequencies for the complete table are as follows:

	Expected Frequencies		
	B_1	B_2	Total
A_1	42	18	60
A_2	28	12	40
Total	70	30	100(N)

In practical work, the expected frequencies are usually not obtained by using the probabilistic argument described earlier. The expected frequency for the A_1B_1 cell is obtained directly by multiplying the A_1 row total by the B_1 column total and dividing by the total number of cases N. Thus, the expected frequency for the A_1B_1 cell is given simply by $\frac{60 \times 70}{100} = 42$. Similarly, the A_1B_2 cell expected frequency is $\frac{60 \times 30}{100} = 18$; the A_2B_1 cell expected frequency is $\frac{40 \times 70}{100} = 28$ and the A_2B_2 cell expected frequency is $\frac{40 \times 30}{100} = 12$. In general, for any contingency tables of R rows and C columns, the expected frequencies are obtained by multiplying the appropriate row and column marginal totals common to a cell, and dividing by the total number of observations N.

Given a set of observed and expected frequencies, χ^2 may be calculated in the usual way as follows:

f_o	f_e	$f_o - f_e$	$(f_o - f_e)^2$	$\dfrac{(f_o - f_e)^2}{f_e}$
50	42	8	64	1.52
10	18	-8	64	3.56
20	28	-8	64	2.29
20	12	8	64	5.33
100	100			$\chi^2 = 12.70$

Here the value of χ^2 is 12.70. How many degrees of freedom are associated with this value of χ^2? In any 2×2 table, given the restrictions of the marginal totals, only one cell frequency is free to vary. In the illustrative 2×2 table above, the observed cell frequency in the A_1B_1 cell is 50. If this frequency is known, and the marginal totals are fixed, all other frequencies are determined. The A_1B_2, A_2B_1, and A_2B_2 frequencies are obtained by simple subtraction. Thus, only one cell frequency is free to vary. For any 2×2 table, given the marginal totals, the number of degrees of freedom associated with the value of χ^2 is 1. In general, for any table of R rows and C columns, the number of degrees of freedom associated with the value of χ^2, given the marginal totals, is $(R-1)(C-1)$ or $(r-1)(c-1)$. Thus, for a 2×2 table, the number of degrees of freedom is $(2-1)(2-1) = 1 \times 1 = 1$; for a 3×2 table, the df is $(3-1)(2-1) = 2 \times 1 = 2$ and for a 4×3 table, the df is $(4-1)(3-1) = 3 \times 2 = 6$.

In the tests of independence, the null hypothesis (H_0) and the alternative hypothesis (H_1) are stated as follows:

H_0: The two variables are independent or are not associated.
H_1: The two variables are not independent or are associated.

To test the H_0, we have to test the significance of the obtained value of χ^2. If the obtained value of χ^2 is less than the critical (or table) value at a certain level of significance for a given degree of freedom, we conclude that the H_0 is true, which means that the two variables are independent or not associated. But if the obtained value of χ^2 is equal to or greater than its table value, our inference then would be that the H_0 is false, which means that the two variables are not independent or they are related, and this relationship or association between the two variables is not because of some chance factors or sampling fluctuations, but it exists in reality.

Referring to Table L in the appendix, the value of χ^2 required for significance at the 0.05 level for df = 1, is 3.84 and at the 0.01 level is 6.64. In our earlier illustrative example, the obtained value of $\chi^2 = 12.70$ exceeds the value required for significance at the 0.01 level. Clearly A is not independent of B. An association can be said to exist between variables A and B. Thus, the H_0 does not hold good. Thus, the H_0 is rejected and the H_1 is accepted. There is a real relationship between the two variables.

In addition to the above two major applications of χ^2, it has some *special applications* which are discussed below.

In this chapter (Section 16.5) we introduced the Phi coefficient (denoted by the symbol ϕ) as a correlational statistic for measuring the degree of association between two dichotomous variables. A dichotomous variable is one for which there are exactly two categories of measurement, for example, gender can be classified as males or females and people's opinions concerning a new law be classified as 'for' or 'against'. The phi coefficient allows you to compute a correlation measuring the degree of relationship between two such variables.

The same data that are used to compute the phi coefficient can be recognised into a matrix (or a contingency table) of frequencies that is suitable for the chi-square test for independence. The value for the phi coefficient (ϕ) may be computed directly from chi-square by the following formula:

$$\phi = \sqrt{\frac{\chi^2}{N}}$$

Thus, χ^2 is used for the computation of ϕ.

Another special application of χ^2 is in the contingency coefficient, denoted by the symbol C (for details, see Section 16.7 of this chapter). The correlation coefficient required to describe the degree of association in a contingency table is known as contingency coefficient. This contingency coefficient is defined by the following equation:

$$C = \sqrt{\frac{\chi^2}{N + \chi^2}}$$

Thus, χ^2 is used for the computation of C.

Besides the above applications of χ^2, it is also used in testing the significance of the difference between both independent (uncorrelated) and correlated proportions (which is discussed in detail later in this section).

16.3.6 Relation of χ^2 to both t and z

When there is 1 degree of freedom in a contingency table (i.e., in a 2×2 contingency table), chi-square is equal to t^2 or t is equal to chi, the square root of chi-square. A t-test and a chi-square test of the same statistics will, therefore, lead to the same inferences when there is 1 df.

Similarly, for 1 degree of freedom, it may be shown that χ^2 is equal to the normal deviate square. Thus, $\chi^2 = (x/s)^2 = z^2$ or $\sqrt{\chi^2} = z$. Therefore, when there is 1 df, $\chi^2 = t^2 = z^2$.

16.3.7   Calculation of Chi-Square (χ^2)

16.3.7.1   *One Sample with c Classes*

Frequently research is undertaken in which the researcher is interested in the number of subjects, objects or responses that fall in various categories. For example, people may be categorised according to whether they are 'in favour of', 'indifferent to' or 'opposed to' some statement of opinion to enable the researcher to test the hypothesis that these responses will differ in frequency. Children may be categorised according to their most frequent modes of play to test the hypothesis that these modes will differ in frequency. Throwing of coins may be categorised as 'heads' or 'tails' to test the hypothesis that these two categories will differ in frequency. Similarly, throwing of die may be categorised into 6 categories—1, 2, 3 4, 5 and 6 to test the hypothesis that these categories will differ in frequency.

The χ^2 test is suitable for analysing data like these. The number of categories may be two or more. The technique is of the goodness of fit type in that it may be used to test whether a significant difference exists between an observed number of objects or responses falling in each category and an expected number based on the null hypothesis.

The computation of χ^2 from one sample with c classes will be more clear from the following examples.

Example 16.1 In tossing a coin 200 times, the following results are obtained. Can it be argued that the coin is biased?

Heads	Tails	Total
90	110	200

Solution

Step 1. The hypothesis must be stated and a level of significance selected. The hypothesis may be stated as follows:

H$_0$: There is no difference between the observed and expected frequencies of heads and tails.

H$_1$: There is a significant difference between the observed and expected frequencies of heads and tails.

The level of significance is set at a standard value, $\alpha = 0.05$.

Step 2. The value of degrees of freedom is determined and then the critical value of χ^2 is determined. For this example, the value of degrees of freedom is df $= c-1 = 2-1 = 1$, where c stands for the number of categories; and in the present example, there are two categories of frequencies—heads and tails.

For df $=1$ and $\alpha = 0.05$, the critical value of χ^2 is 3.84 (see Table L in the appendix).

Step 3. The calculation of chi-square is actually a two-stage process. First, we must compute the expected frequencies from H$_0$ and then calculate the value of the chi-square statistic. For the given example, the null hypothesis (H$_0$) specifies a proportion of $p = \frac{1}{2} = 0.5$ for each of the two categories and the sample size is $N = 200$. Thus, the expected frequency for each category is

$$f_e = pN = \frac{1}{2} \times 200 = 100$$

Alternatively, the expected frequency for each category in one-sample experiments will be determined by dividing the total N(sample size) by the total number of categories (c), as follows: $f_e = \dfrac{N}{c}$. In this example, $N=200$ and $c=2$. Thus, $f_e = \dfrac{200}{2} = 100$. The total of the expected frequencies and the observed frequencies should be the same, N.

The observed frequencies (f_o) and the expected frequencies (f_e) are presented below, and using these values, the chi-square statistic may now be calculated:

	Head	Tail	Total
f_o	90	110	200
f_e	100	100	200
$f_o - f_e$	-10	10	
$(f_o - f_e)^2$	100	100	
$\dfrac{(f_o - f_e)^2}{f_e}$	1.00	1.00	

$$\therefore \chi^2 = \sum \frac{(f_o - f_e)^2}{f_e} = 1.00 + 1.00 = 2.00$$

$$\text{Alternatinely, } \chi^2 = \sum \frac{(f_o)^2}{f_e} - N = \left[\frac{(90)^2}{100} + \frac{(110)^2}{100} \right] - 200$$

$$= [81.00 + 121.00] - 200 = 202.00 - 200 = 2.00$$

Thus, the value of χ^2 in both the cases is same, that is, $\chi^2 = 2.00$

Step 4. The obtained value of χ^2 should be tested for its significance. Referring to Table L of the appendix the critical value of χ^2 with df=1 at $\alpha=0.05$ is 3.84, and at $\alpha=0.01$ is 6.64. Since the obtained $\chi^2=2.00$ is smaller than the critical value of $\chi^2=3.84$, it is not significant. Therefore, the H_0 is not rejected. So, we may argue that the coin is not biased; it is unbiased. Hence, the H_0 is accepted and H_1 is rejected.

Example 16.2 In a study of preference, 120 subjects are presented with vanilla, strawberry, and chocolate ice cream. Each subject was asked to indicate the ice cream he/she prefers. The following are the results. Can these frequencies deviate significantly from a uniform chance distribution?

Type of Ice cream	Vanilla	Strawberry	Chocolate
Number preferred	60	35	25

Solution

Step 1. Statement of the H_0 and H_1, and selection of the level of significance as follows:

H_0: The population of subjects shows no preference in choosing any one of the three types of ice cream over the others. Thus, the three types of ice cream are equally chosen.

H_1: The population of subjects shows preference in choosing any one of the three types of ice cream over the others. Thus, the three types of ice cream are not equally chosen.

The level of significance is set at a standard value, $\alpha = 0.05$.

Step 2. Determination of df and the critical value of χ^2 as follows:

$$df = c - 1 = 3 - 1 = 2$$

c refers to the number of categories, and in this example there are three categories—vanilla, strawberry and chocolate ice cream.

For df = 2 and $\alpha = 0.05$, the critical value of χ^2 is 5.99 (see Table L in the appendix).

Step 3. The calculation of χ^2 is done as follows:

Total subjects = $N = 120$

Total number of categories = $c = 3$

Expected frequency for each category is $f_e = \dfrac{N}{c} = \dfrac{120}{3} = 40$

The observed frequencies (f_o) and the expected frequencies (f_e) are presented below, and using these values, the χ^2 is computed.

	Vanilla	Strawberry	Chocolate	Total
f_o	60	35	25	120
f_e	40	40	40	120
$f_o - f_e$	20	−5	−15	
$(f_o - f_e)^2$	400	25	225	
$\dfrac{(f_o - f_e)^2}{f_e}$	10.00	0.625	5.625	

$$\therefore \chi^2 = \sum \frac{(f_o - f_e)^2}{f_e} = 10.00 + 0.625 + 5.625 = 16.25$$

Step 4. Test of significance of the obtained $\chi^2 = 16.25$. Referring to Table L of the appendix, the critical value of χ^2 with df = 2 at $\alpha = 0.05$ is 5.99 and at $\alpha = 0.01$ is 9.21. Since the obtained value of $\chi^2 = 16.25$ is larger than the table value of $\chi^2 = 9.21$, it is significant at 0.01 level of significance, therefore, $p < 0.01$. Therefore, H_0 is rejected and H_1 is accepted in 99% of cases. We may conclude that the three types of ice-cream are not equally chosen by the subjects. Instead, there are significant differences among the three types of ice cream, with some chosen more often and other less often than would be expected by chance. Thus, the observed frequencies deviate significantly from a uniform chance distribution in 99% of cases.

Example 16.3 A die was thrown for 300 times. The following are the results. Compute χ^2 and test its significance.

Value of Die	1	2	3	4	5	6
Observed frequency	43	55	39	56	63	44

Solution

Step 1. Statement of H_0 and H_1 and selection of α (alpha) levels as follows:

H_0: There is no difference between the observed and expected frequencies of six values of a die.

H_1: There is a significant difference between the observed and expected frequencies of six values of a die.

The level of significance is set at $\alpha=0.05$

Step 2. The value of df and the critical value of χ^2 are determined as follows:

$$df=c-1=6-1=5$$

In the given example, a die has six values, so there are six categories ($c=6$).
For df$=5$, and $\alpha=0.05$, the critical value of χ^2 is 11.07 (see Table L in the appendix).

Step 3. The calculation of χ^2 is done as follows:
Total number of throws of a die$=N=300$
Total number of categories$=c=6$

Expected frequency for each category is $f_e = \dfrac{N}{c} = \dfrac{300}{6} = 50$

The observed frequencies (f_o) and the expected frequencies (f_e) are presented below, and using these frequencies, the χ^2 is computed as follows.

Value of the Die	f_o	f_e	(f_o-f_e)	$(f_o-f_e)^2$	$\dfrac{(f_o-f_e)^2}{f_e}$
1	43	50	-7	49	0.98
2	55	50	5	25	0.50
3	39	50	-11	121	2.42
4	56	50	6	36	0.72
5	63	50	13	169	3.38
6	44	50	-6	36	0.72
Total	300	300	0.00		$\chi^2=8.72$

$$\therefore \chi^2 = \sum \frac{(f_o - f_e)^2}{f_e} = 8.72$$

Step 4. Test of significance of the obtained $\chi^2 = 8.72$. Referring to Table L of the appendix, the critical value of χ^2 with df=5 at $\alpha = 0.05$ is 11.07 and at $\alpha = 0.01$ is 15.09. Since the obtained value of $\chi^2 = 8.72$ is less than the table value of $\chi^2 = 11.07$, it is not significant. Therefore, the H_0 is not rejected. So, we may conclude that the die is not biased; it is unbiased. The differences between the observed frequencies and the expected frequencies of six values of a die are attributed to the chance factors or sampling fluctuations. Hence, the H_0 is accepted and the H_1 is rejected.

16.3.7.2   *Two or More Samples with c Classes*

When the data of research consists of frequencies in discrete categories, the χ^2 test may be used to determine the significance of differences between two independent groups or two independent samples. The measurement involved may be as weak as nominal scaling. Two or more samples with 'c' classes refer to a contingency table have R rows and C columns. The rows represent the samples or groups and the columns represent the categories. Thus, the number of rows may be two or more than two and also the number of columns may be two or more than two.

The hypothesis under test is usually that the two groups (or two samples) or more than two groups differ with respect to some characteristics and therefore with respect to the relative frequency with which group members fall in several categories. To test this hypothesis, we count the number of cases from each group which fall in the various categories and compare the proportion of cases from one group in the various categories with the proportion of cases from the other group or groups. For example, we might test whether two political groups differ in their agreement or disagreement with some opinion or we might test whether the sexes (i.e., males and females) differ in the frequency with which they choose certain leisure time activities, etc.

The χ^2 test for k independent samples (i.e., more than two independent samples) is a straightforward extension of the χ^2 test for two independent samples. In general, the χ^2 test is the same for both two and k (more than two) independent samples.

The same usual formula of χ^2 is used in this case, which reads as

$$\chi^2 = \sum \frac{(f_o - f_e)^2}{f_e}$$

where $\sum$ directs one to sum over all (r) rows and all (c) columns, that is, to sum over all cells in the contingency table.

In this case (two or more samples with 'c' classes), we can determine the value of the degrees of freedom as follows:

$$df = (r-1)(c-1)$$

where r=the number of rows and c=the number of columns in the contingency table.

The procedure for finding out the expected frequency for a cell in the contingency table (i.e., in case of 'two or more samples with c classes') is different from that used in the case of 'one sample with c classes'. To find the expected frequency for each cell, multiply the two marginal totals common to a particular cell and then divide this product by the total number of cases N.

$$f_e = \frac{\text{product of two marginal totals common to a cell}}{\text{total number of cases } (N)}$$

Table 16.2   A frequency distribution showing the level of self-esteem according to the level of academic performance

<table>
<tr><th colspan="2"></th><th colspan="4">Level of Self-esteem</th></tr>
<tr><th colspan="2"></th><th>High</th><th>Medium</th><th>Low</th><th>Total (Row Marginal)</th></tr>
<tr><td rowspan="2">Academic Performance</td><td>High</td><td>17</td><td>32</td><td>11</td><td>60</td></tr>
<tr><td>Low</td><td>13</td><td>43</td><td>34</td><td>90</td></tr>
<tr><td colspan="2">Total(Column Marginal)</td><td>30</td><td>75</td><td>45</td><td>$N=150$</td></tr>
</table>

The computational procedures of χ^2 from two or more samples with c classes will become more clear from the following illustrative examples.

Example 16.4 A researcher was investigating the relationship between academic performance and self-esteem. A sample of $N=150$ 10-year-old children was obtained and each child was classified by level of academic performance and level of self-esteem. The frequency distribution for this sample, the set of observed frequencies, is shown in Table 16.2. Find out χ^2 and interpret it.

Solution

Step 1. Statement of the H_0 and H_1, and selection of level of significance. According to the null hypothesis, the two variables are independent. This general hypothesis can be stated in two different ways as shown below.

H_0: In the general population, there is no relationship between academic performance and self-esteem.

or

H_0: In the general population, the distribution of self-esteem is the same for high and low academic performers.

H_1: There is a consistent, predictable relationship between academic performance and self-esteem.

or

H_1: The distribution of self-esteem for high academic performers is different from the distribution for low academic performers.

(Note: The first version of H_0 emphasises the similarity between the chi-square test and a correlation. The second version of H_0 emphasises the similarity between the chi-square test and the independent measures t-test. However, the two versions for the hypothesis are equivalent. The choice between them is largely determined by how the researcher wants to describe the outcome. For example, a researcher may want to emphasise the relationship between variables or may want to emphasise the difference between groups).

For this test, we will use $\alpha=0.05$.

Step 2. Determination of the df and the critical value of χ^2. For the χ^2 test for independence

$$df=(R-1)(C-1) \text{ or } (r-1)(c-1)$$

Table 16.3 Self-esteem and academic performance: Observed and expected frequencies

		Level of Self-esteem			
		High	Medium	Low	Total (Row Marginal)
Academic performance	High	17	32	11	60
	Low	13	43	34	90
Total (column marginal)		30	75	45	N=150

where

R=the number of rows
C=the number of columns

Therefore, for this example having two rows and three columns, df is

$$df=(R-1)(C-1)=(2-1)(3-1)=1\times2=2$$

With df=2 and α=0.05, the critical value of χ^2 is 5.99. (See Table L in the appendix.)

Step 3. Determination of the expected frequencies and computation of χ^2. For convenience, the 2×3 contingency Table 16.2 has been redrawn in Table 16.3 and the f_e values are entered within parentheses in the appropriate cells.

Table 16.3 consists of 2 rows and 3 columns, and thus it has $2\times3=6$ cells. The first row (high academic performance) has 3 cells, denoted by 1, 2 and 3. The second row (low academic performance) has 3 cells, denoted by 4, 5 and 6, respectively.

Let us find out the values of expected frequencies for each cell of Table 16.3. The f_e values of a particular cell can be found out directly by multiplying two marginal totals (i.e., row total and column total) common to a particular cell and then dividing this product by N. For example, the two marginal totals common to cell 1 are 60 (row total) and 30 (column total). Let us use this method to find the values of f_e for each of the six cells of Table 16.3.

$$f_e(\text{Cell 1})=\frac{60\times30}{150}=12; \quad f_e(\text{Cell 2})=\frac{60\times75}{150}=30; \quad f_e(\text{Cell 3})=\frac{60\times45}{150}=18$$

$$f_e(\text{Cell 4})=\frac{90\times30}{150}=18; \quad f_e(\text{Cell 5})=\frac{90\times75}{150}=45; \quad f_e(\text{Cell 6})=\frac{90\times45}{150}=27$$

These above calculated expected frequencies (f_e) are shown within parentheses in the appropriate cells in Table 16.3 which also shows the various original observed frequencies (f_o). We should note that a good check to make sure our calculations of f_e are correct is to see if the row and column totals of f_e equal the row and column marginal totals of f_o.

Once the f_e for each cell has been determined, the next step is to calculate χ^2. As before, this is done by summing $\frac{(f_o-f_e)^2}{f_e}$ for each cell. Thus, for the present example the χ^2 value will be

$$\chi^2 = \sum \frac{(f_o - f_e)^2}{f_e} = \frac{(17-12)^2}{12} + \frac{(32-30)^2}{30} + \frac{(11-18)^2}{18} + \frac{(13-18)^2}{18}$$

$$+ \frac{(43-45)^2}{45} + \frac{(34-27)^2}{27}$$

$$= 2.08 + 0.13 + 2.72 + 1.39 + 0.09 + 1.81 = 8.22$$

Thus, the obtained value of $\chi^2 = 8.22$.

Step 4. Test of significance of the obtained $\chi^2 = 8.22$. Referring to Table L of the appendix, the critical value of χ^2 with df=2 at $\alpha = 0.05$ is 5.99 and at $\alpha = 0.01$ is 9.21. Since the obtained value of $\chi^2 = 8.22$ exceeds the critical value of $\chi^2 = 5.99$, it is significant at $\alpha = 0.05$. Therefore, $p < 0.05$. Therefore, the H_0 is rejected and H_1 is accepted. The rejection of H_0 leads us to decide that there is a significant relationship between academic performance and self-esteem, and that there is a significant difference between the distribution of self-esteem for high academic performers versus low academic performers. To describe the details of the significant results, we must compare the original observed frequencies with the expected frequencies from the null hypothesis. Looking at the two types of frequencies, it should be clear that the high performers had higher self-esteem than would be expected if the two variables were independent and the low performers had lower self-esteem than would be expected.

Table 16.4   Eyedness and handedness

	Left-eyed	**Ambiocular**	**Right-eyed**	**Total**
Left-handed	34	62	28	124
Ambidextrous	27	28	20	75
Right-handed	57	105	52	214
Total	118	195	100	$N = 413$

Example 16.5 An investigator collected data on the relationship between eyedness and handedness in a sample of 413 subjects. Subjects were tested for eyedness and handedness and grouped in one of three categories on both variables. The data are presented in Table 16.4. Compute χ^2 and interpret it.

Solution

Step 1. Statement of the H_0 and H_1, and selection of the level of significance.

H_0: Eyedness is independent of handedness.
H_1: Eyedness is not independent of handedness.

The level of significance is set at $\alpha = 0.05$

Step 2. Determination of df and the critical value of χ^2. In the given example (see Table 16.4), there are three rows and three columns. Thus, df is

$$df = (R-1)(C-1) = (3-1)(3-1) = 2 \times 2 = 4$$

Table 16.5 Eyedness and handedness: Observed and expected frequencies

	Left-eyed	**Ambiocular**	**Right-eyed**	**Total**
Left-handed	34	62	28	124
	(35.4)	(58.5)	(30.0)	
Ambidextrous	27	28	20	75
	(21.4)	(35.4)	(18.2)	
Right-handed	57	105	52	214
	(61.1)	(101.0)	(51.8)	
Total	118	195	100	$N = 413$

With df=4 and $\alpha=0.05$, the critical value of χ^2 is 9.49 (see Table L in the appendix).

Step 3. The determination of the expected frequencies and computation of χ^2. For convenience the 3×3 contingency Table 16.4 has been redrawn in Table 16.5, and the values of expected frequencies (f_e) are entered within parentheses in the appropriate cells.

Table 16.5 consists of 3 rows and 3 columns, and thus it has $3\times3=9$ cells. The first row (left-handed) has 3 cells, denoted by Cells 1, 2 and 3; the second row (Ambidextrous) has 3 cells denoted by Cells 4, 5 and 6 and the third row (right-handed) has also 3 cells denoted by Cells 7, 8 and 9, respectively.

Let us determine the values of expected frequencies for each cell of Table 16.5 by the usual formula for the contingency tables as used in Example 16.4. The values of the expected frequencies (f_e) for each of the 9 cells (Cells 1 through 9) of Table 16.5 are, respectively,

$$f_e \text{ for Cell 1} = \frac{124\times118}{413} = 35.4; \quad f_e \text{ for Cell 2} = \frac{124\times195}{413} = 58.5$$

$$f_e \text{ for Cell 3} = \frac{124\times100}{413} = 30.0; \quad f_e \text{ for Cell 4} = \frac{75\times118}{413} = 21.4$$

$$f_e \text{ for Cell 5} = \frac{75\times195}{413} = 35.4; \quad f_e \text{ for Cell 6} = \frac{75\times00}{413} = 18.2$$

$$f_e \text{ for Cell 7} = \frac{214\times118}{413} = 61.1; \quad f_e \text{ for Cell 8} = \frac{214\times195}{413} = 101.0$$

$$f_e \text{ for Cell 9} = \frac{214\times100}{413} = 51.8$$

These above calculated values of f_e are shown within parentheses in the appropriate cells in Table 16.5, which also shows the various original observed frequencies (f_o). The reader may note that some of the row and column totals (see Table 16.5) of the expected frequencies are not exactly equal to those of the observed frequencies due to the decimal points as we have allowed one decimal point while determining the f_e. The computation of χ^2 for the data in Table 16.5 is straightforward:

$$\chi^2 = \sum \frac{(f_o - f_e)^2}{f_e} = \frac{(34-35.4)^2}{35.4} + \frac{(62-58.5)^2}{58.5} + \frac{(28-30.0)^2}{30.0} + \frac{(27-21.4)^2}{21.4} + \frac{(28-35.4)^2}{35.4}$$

$$+ \frac{(20-18.2)^2}{18.2} + \frac{(57-61.1)^2}{61.1} + \frac{(105-101.0)^2}{101.0} + \frac{(52-51.8)^2}{51.8}$$

$$= \frac{(-1.4)^2}{35.4} + \frac{(3.5)^2}{58.5} + \frac{(-2.0)^2}{30.0} + \frac{(5.6)^2}{21.4} + \frac{(-7.4)^2}{35.4} + \frac{(1.8)^2}{18.2} + \frac{(-4.1)^2}{61.1} + \frac{(4.0)^2}{101.0} + \frac{(0.2)^2}{51.8}$$

$$= \frac{1.96}{35.4} + \frac{12.25}{58.5} + \frac{4.0}{30.0} + \frac{31.36}{21.4} + \frac{54.76}{35.4} + \frac{3.24}{18.2} + \frac{16.81}{61.1} + \frac{16.0}{101.0} + \frac{0.04}{51.8}$$

$$= 0.055 + 0.209 + 0.133 + 1.465 + 1.547 + 0.178 + 0.275 + 0.158 + 0.001 = 4.021$$

Thus, the obtained $\chi^2 = 4.021$.

Step 4. The test of significance of the obtained $\chi^2 = 4.021$. Referring to Table L of the appendix, the critical value of χ^2 with df = 4 at $\alpha = 0.05$ is 9.49 and at $\alpha = 0.01$ is 13.28. Since the obtained value of $\chi^2 = 4.021$ is smaller than the critical value of $\chi^2 = 9.49$, it is not significant. Therefore, the H_0 is not rejected, it is accepted, whereas the H_1 is rejected. Thus, we may conclude that eyedness is independent of handedness. Apparently, there is no relationship between the two variables. The independence of eye and hand laterality indicates that the 124 observed frequencies in the first row of Table 16.5 are distributed in the three cells in that row in a manner proportional to the column sums. The expected values of 35.4, 58.5 and 30.0 are proportional to the column sums 118, 195 and 100. Likewise, the 118 cases of the observed frequencies in the first column are distributed in the three cells in that column in a manner proportional to the row sums 124, 75 and 214. A similar proportionality exists throughout the table. Thus, the expected cell frequencies in the rows and columns of any contingency table are proportional to the marginal totals of rows and columns.

16.3.7.3 More Samples with c = 2 Classes

Now, we will discuss about the computational procedures of χ^2 for the data involving more samples (or rows), and each sample or row having only two categories or columns. It will become clear through the following example.

Example 16.6 Table 16.6 shows the frequencies with which 43 short people and 52 tall people are categorised as 'leaders', 'followers' and as 'unclassifiable'. Test the H_0 that height is independent of leader–follower position.

Solution

Step 1. Statement of the H_0 and H_1 and selection of the α level.

H_0: Height is independent of leader–follower position, that is, that the proportion of tall people who are leaders is the same as the proportion of short people who are leaders, that the proportion of tall people who are followers is the same as the proportion of short people who are followers, etc.

H_1: Height is not independent of leader–follower position.

The level of significance is set at $\alpha = 0.05$.

Table 16.6 Height and leadership

	Short	Tall	Row Marginal Totals
Leader	12	32	44
Follower	22	14	36
Unclassifiable	9	6	15
Column marginal totals	43	52	$N=95$

Table 16.7 Height and leadership: Observed and expected frequencies

	Short	Tall	Row Marginal Totals
Leader	12 (19.9)	32 (24.1)	44
Follower	22 (16.3)	14 (19.7)	36
Unclassifiable	9 (6.8)	6 (8.2)	15
Column marginal totals	43	52	$N=95$

Step 2. Determination of df and the critical value of χ^2. In the given example, there are three rows and two columns. Thus, df is

$$df=(R-1)(C-1)=(3-1)(2-1)=2\times1=2$$

With df=2 and $\alpha=0.05$, the critical value of χ^2 is 5.99 (see Table L in the appendix).

Step 3. Determination of the expected frequencies and computation of χ^2. For convenience, the 3×2 contingency Table 16.6 has been redrawn in Table 16.7, and the values of expected frequencies (f_e) are entered within parentheses in the appropriate cells.

Table 16.7 consists of 3 rows and 2 columns, and thus it has 3×2=6 cells. The first row (leader) has 2 cells, denoted by cells 1 and 2; the second row (follower) has 2 cells which are denoted by cells 3 and 4 and the third row (unclassifiable) has 2 cells that are denoted by cells 5 and 6, respectively.

Let us determine the values of expected frequencies for each cell of Table 16.7, by the usual formula for contingency tables as used in Example 16.4. The values of the expected frequencies (f_e) for each of the six cells (Cells 1 through 6) of Table 16.7 are, respectively,

$$f_e \text{ for Cell } 1 = \frac{44 \times 43}{95} = 19.9; \quad f_e \text{ for Cell } 2 = \frac{44 \times 52}{95} = 24.1$$

$$f_e \text{ for Cell } 3 = \frac{36 \times 43}{95} = 16.3; \quad f_e \text{ for Cell } 4 = \frac{36 \times 52}{95} = 19.7$$

$$f_e \text{ for Cell } 5 = \frac{15 \times 43}{95} = 6.8; \quad f_e \text{ for Cell } 6 = \frac{15 \times 52}{95} = 8.2$$

These above calculated values of f_e are shown within parentheses in the appropriate cells in Table 16.7 which also shows the various original observed frequencies (f_o). The computation of χ^2 for the data in Table 16.7 is straightforward:

$$\chi^2 = \sum \frac{(f_o - f_e)^2}{f_e} = \frac{(12 - 19.9)^2}{19.9} + \frac{(32 - 24.1)^2}{24.1} + \frac{(22 - 16.3)^2}{16.3}$$

$$+ \frac{(14 - 19.7)^2}{19.7} + \frac{(9 - 6.8)^2}{6.8} + \frac{(6 - 8.2)^2}{8.2}$$

$$= \frac{(-7.9)^2}{19.9} + \frac{(7.9)^2}{24.1} + \frac{(5.7)^2}{16.3} + \frac{(-5.7)^2}{19.7} + \frac{(2.2)^2}{6.8} + \frac{(-2.2)^2}{8.2}$$

$$= 3.14 + 2.59 + 1.99 + 1.65 + 0.71 + 0.59 = 10.67$$

Thus, the obtained $\chi^2 = 10.67$

Step 4. The test of significance of the obtained $\chi^2 = 10.67$. Referring to Table L of the appendix, the critical value of χ^2 with df=2 at $\alpha = 0.05$ is 5.99 and at $\alpha = 0.01$ is 9.21. Since the obtained value of $\chi^2 = 10.67$ exceeds the critical value of $\chi^2 = 9.21$, it is significant beyond the 0.01 level. Therefore, we could reject the null hypothesis of no differences at $\alpha = 0.01$. Therefore, $p < 0.01$. The H_1 is accepted. Thus, we may conclude that height is not independent of leader-follower position, that is, that the proportion of tall people who are leaders is not the same as the proportion of short people who are leaders, that the proportion of tall people who are followers is not the same as the proportion of short people who are followers, etc.

Example 16.7 Number of nonreactors and reactors to a drug in monthly samples at a Mental Hospital is presented in Table 16.8. Compute χ^2 and test its significance.

Solution

When we have R samples (i.e., more samples) and only $c = 2$ classes, there is a simplified method for calculating χ^2. We take the column of frequencies with smaller total. The following is the formula for computing χ^2 for the data in Table 16.8:

$$\chi^2 = \frac{(n)^2}{\Sigma f_1 \Sigma f_2} \left[\sum \frac{f_1^2}{n_i} - \frac{(\Sigma f_1)^2}{n} \right]$$

where

n = the total number of samples over all the months ($\Sigma n_i = n$)

n_i = the number of monthly samples ($f_1 + f_2 = n_i$).

Table 16.8   Number of nonreactors and reactors to a drug in monthly samples at a mental hospital

Months	Nonreactors	Reactors
January	18	32
February	20	25
March	22	20
April	19	19
May	14	22
June	21	19
July	22	21
August	16	20
September	10	20

Σf_1 = the sum of frequencies of that column having smaller total.

Σf_2 = the sum of frequencies of that column having larger total.

f_1 and f_2 = the number of nonreactors and reactors in monthly samples, respectively.

Step 1. Statement of H_0 and H_1, and selection of the level of significance.

H_0: Monthly sample is independent of nonreactor–reactor position to a drug.

H_1: Monthly sample is not independent of nonreactor–reactor position to a drug.

The level of significance is set at $\alpha = 0.05$

Step 2. Determination of df and the critical value of χ^2. In the present example (Table 16.8), there are nine rows and two columns. Thus, df is

$$df = (R-1)(C-1) = (9-1)(2-1) = 8 \times 1 = 8$$

With df = 8 and $\alpha = 0.05$, the critical value of χ^2 is 15.51 (see Table L in the appendix).

Step 3. Computation of χ^2. For convenience, the 9×2 contingency Table 16.8 has been redrawn in Table 16.9 with all its notings like $f_1, f_2, \Sigma f_1, \Sigma f_2, n_i, n, f_1^2, \frac{f_1^2}{n_i}, \Sigma \frac{f_1^2}{n_i}$, etc. The computation of χ^2 for the data in Table 16.9 is as follows:

$$\chi^2 = \frac{(n)^2}{\Sigma f_1 \Sigma f_2} \left[\Sigma \frac{f_1^2}{n_i} - \frac{(\Sigma f_1)^2}{n} \right]$$

$$= \frac{(360)^2}{162 \times 198} \left[74.562 - \frac{(162)^2}{360} \right] = 4.04 \times 1.662 = 6.714$$

Thus, the obtained $\chi^2 = 6.714$.

Step 4. The test of significance of the obtained $\chi^2 = 6.714$. Referring to Table L of the appendix the critical value of χ^2 with df = 8 at $\alpha = 0.05$ is 15.51 and at $\alpha = 0.01$ is 20.09. Since the obtained value of $\chi^2 = 6.714$ is smaller than the critical value of $\chi^2 = 15.51$, it is not significant. Therefore, the H_0 is accepted and H_1 is rejected. So we may conclude that

Table 16.9 Number of nonreactors and reactors to a drug in monthly samples at a mental hospital

Months	Nonreactors (f_1)	Reactors (f_2)	n_i	f_1^2	$\dfrac{f_1^2}{n_i}$
January	18	32	50	324	6.480
February	20	25	45	400	8.889
March	22	20	42	484	11.524
April	19	19	38	361	9.500
May	14	22	36	196	5.444
June	21	19	40	441	11.025
July	22	21	43	484	11.256
August	16	20	36	256	7.111
September	10	20	30	100	3.333
Total	162 (Σf_1)	198 (Σf_2)	360 (n)		74.562 $\left(\Sigma \dfrac{f_1^2}{n_i}\right)$

monthly sample is independent of nonreactor-reactor position to a drug at a mental hospital. That means, in each month, the proportion of samples who are nonreactors to a drug is the same as the proportion of samples who are reactors to a drug.

16.3.7.4   Two Samples with c = 2 Classes

A frequently occurring type of contingency table is the 2×2 or fourfold contingency table. A χ^2 test for independence can be readily obtained for such a contingency table without calculating the expected frequencies. Let us represent the cell and marginal frequencies by the following notation:

a	b	a+b
c	d	c+d
a+c	b+d	N

or

A	B	A+B
C	D	C+D
A+C	B+D	N

Chi-square may then be calculated by the following formula that reads

$$\chi^2 = \frac{n(ad-bc)^2}{(a+b)(c+d)(a+c)(b+d)}$$

or

$$\chi^2 = \frac{N(AD-BC)^2}{(A+B)(C+D)(A+C)(B+D)}$$

Table 16.10   Number of individuals successful or unsuccessful on a job and pass or fail on an ability test item

	Test Item		Total
	Fail	**Pass**	
Successful	20	40	60
Unsuccessful	25	15	40
Total	45	55	100(N)

Note that the term in the numerator, $ad - bc$ (or $AD - BC$), is simply the difference between the two cross products and the term in the denominator is the product of the four marginal totals.

But there is one problem with regard to the *small expected frequencies* of any cell. Where the expected frequencies are small, the actual sampling distribution of χ^2 may exhibit marked discontinuity. Because we expect that the distribution of χ^2 used in determining critical significance values is a continuous theoretical frequency curve. When there is discontinuity, this continuous curve may provide a poor fit to the data and appreciable error may occur in the estimation of probabilities.

Therefore, some correction should be applied to the data. A correction, commonly recommended for use with 2×2 tables, is known as *Yates' correction for continuity*. To apply this correction, we reduce by 0.5 the obtained frequencies that are greater than expectation and increase by 0.5 the obtained frequencies that are less than expectation. This brings the observed and expected frequencies closer together and decreases the value of χ^2. Many texts recommend that this correction should be used when any of the expected frequencies is less than 5, and some writers suggest 10. Instead, it may be argued that the correction should always be used with 2×2 tables. For larger expected frequencies, the correction will be negligible.

The formula used in computing χ^2 from a 2×2 or fourfold contingency table may be written to incorporate *Yates' correction for continuity* as follows:

$$\chi^2 = \frac{n(|ad - bc| - n/2)^2}{(a+b)(c+d)(a+c)(b+d)}$$

or

$$\chi^2 = \frac{N(|AD - BC| - N/2)^2}{(A+B)(C+D)(A+C)(B+D)}$$

The term $|ad - bc|$ or $|AD - BC|$ is the absolute difference, that is, the difference taken regardless of sign. The correction amounts to subtracting $n/2$ (or $N/2$) from this absolute difference. The computational procedure will become clear through the following example.

Example 16.8 Table 16.10 shows the relationship between ratings of successful or unsuccessful on a job and pass or fail on an ability test. Find χ^2 without and with Yates' correction for continuity and comment on the results. Is there an association between performance on the job and performance on the test item? Does the item differentiates significantly between the successful and unsuccessful individuals?

Table 16.11   Number of individuals successful or unsuccessful on a job and pass or fail on an ability test item

	Test Item		Total
	Fail	**Pass**	
Successful	20 a	40 b	60 ($a+b$)
Unsuccessful	25 c	15 d	40 (c+d)
Total	45 ($a+c$)	55 ($b+d$)	100 ($a+b+c+d$)= N (or n)

Solution

The following steps are to be followed for computing χ^2 from a 2×2 contingency table:

Step 1. Statement of the H_0 and H_1, and selection of the level of significance.

H_0: There is no relationship between ratings of successful or unsuccessful on a job and pass or fail on an ability test item.

H_1: There is a relationship between ratings of successful or unsuccessful on a job and pass or fail on an ability test item.

The level of significance is set at $\alpha=0.05$

Step 2. Determination of df and the critical value of χ^2. In the present example (Table 16.10), there are two rows and also two columns. Thus, df is

$$df=(r-1)(c-1)=(2-1)(2-1)=1\times1=1$$

With df=1 and $\alpha=0.05$, the critical value of χ^2 is 3.84 (see Table L in the appendix).

Step 3. Computation of χ^2. For convenience, the 2×2 contingency Table 16.10 has been redrawn in Table 16.11 with all its notings like a, b, c, d, $a+b$, $c+d$, $a+c$, $b+d$ and n, etc.

The computation of χ^2 for the data in Table 16.11 is as follows:

χ^2 (without Yates' correction for continuity):

$$\chi^2=\frac{n(ad-bc)^2}{(a+b)(c+d)(a+c)(b+d)}=\frac{100(20\times15-40\times25)^2}{60\times40\times45\times55}$$

$$=\frac{100(300-1000)^2}{60\times40\times45\times55}=\frac{100(-700)^2}{60\times40\times45\times55}=\frac{4900}{594}=8.25$$

χ^2 (with Yates' correction for continuity):

$$\chi^2=\frac{n(|ad-bc|-n/2)^2}{(a+b)(c+d)(a+c)(b+d)}=\frac{100(|20\times15-40\times25|-100/2)^2}{60\times40\times45\times55}$$

$$=\frac{100(|300-1000|-50)^2}{60\times40\times45\times55}=\frac{100(700-50)^2}{60\times40\times45\times55}$$

$$=\frac{100(650)^2}{60\times40\times45\times55}=\frac{4225}{594}=7.11$$

STATISTICS FOR BEHAVIOURAL AND SOCIAL SCIENCES

Thus, the obtained χ^2 is 8.25 (without Yates' correction for continuity) and is 7.11 (with Yates' correction for continuity). However, we should take the χ^2 value of 7.11 for the test of significance.

Step 4. The test of significance of the obtained $\chi^2=7.11$. First of all, we should comment on both the values of χ^2 obtained without and with Yates' correction for continuity. The χ^2 value obtained with Yates' correction for continuity (i.e., $\chi^2=7.11$) is smaller than that of the χ^2 value obtained without Yates' correction for continuity (i.e., $\chi^2=8.25$). This shows that Yates' correction for continuity decreases the magnitude of χ^2.

Referring to Table L of the appendix, the critical value of χ^2 with df=1 at $\alpha=0.05$ is 3.84 and at $\alpha=0.01$ is 6.64. Since the obtained value of $\chi^2=7.11$ is larger than both the critical values of χ^2, it is significant at 0.01 level of significance. Therefore, the H_0 is rejected and H_1 is accepted. Thus, we may conclude that there is an association between performance on the job and performance on the test item. Moreover, the data provide fairly conclusive evidence that the test item differentiates significantly between the successful and unsuccessful individuals. In other words, the test item differentiates between individuals on the basis of their job performance. Thus, the obtained result shows that the performance on the job and performance on the test item are not independent of each other.

16.3.8 Application of χ^2 for Testing Goodness of Fit

One of the uses of χ^2 is testing a set of data to see if the data are normally distributed, that is, if they fit the normal distribution. In Chapter 7, we learned how to normalise a set of data. The reader who wishes to review at this point is referred to Table 7.1 and the discussion associated with it. In Table 7.1, we set up the expected frequencies for the distribution in the table. Both the observed and expected frequencies from Table 7.1 are reproduced in the first two columns of Table 16.12. It should be apparent by now that any time that we have a set of observed and a set of expected frequencies, we can apply the χ^2 test.

In columns 1 and 2 of Table 16.12, we have the observed and expected frequencies. In columns 3 and 4 are the same frequencies, in the extreme class intervals combined, so that none of the expected frequencies is less than 5. In column 5 are shown the differences between each f_o and f_e, in column 6 the square of these differences, and in column 7 the square of the differences divided by the expected frequencies. These are then summed, and a chi-square of 23.582 results.

The null hypothesis (H_0) which we have here is that the distribution of observed scores is a chance variation from a normal population. Basically, the number of degrees of freedom for this situation is the number of class intervals minus three (i.e., df=$c-3$). We place three restrictions upon our data when we normalised them. We noted that the best-fitting normal curve for a set of data has the same mean, standard deviation and number of cases as the original data. One degree of freedom was lost for each of these restrictions. In our given problem (see Table 16.12), we reduced the number of class intervals to 9, when we combined those in the tails having small frequencies. For these data, it follows that df=6, that is, 9 categories minus 3 (i.e., df=$c-3=9-3=6$). In the chi-square table (see Table L in the appendix), we find that the critical value of χ^2 for df=6, at 0.05 level is 12.59 and at 0.01 level is 16.81. Since our obtained χ^2 value of 23.582 is larger than both the critical values of χ^2, it is significant at 0.01 level of significance. So, we reject the H_0 at the 1% level. Therefore, we may conclude that the population from which this sample was drawn is not normal and there is no goodness of fit between the theoretical and observed frequencies.

Table 16.12   Testing goodness of fit

Class Intervals	(1) f_o	(2) f_e	(3) f_o	(4) f_e	(5) $f_o - f_e$	(6) $(f_o - f_e)^2$	(7) $(f_o - f_e)^2 / f_e$
90–94	1	1.7					
85–89	3	4.1					
80–84	8	8.2	12	14.0	−2.0	4.00	0.286
75–79	12	13.8	12	13.8	−1.8	3.24	0.235
70–74	28	19.7	28	19.7	8.3	68.89	3.497
65–69	36	23.8	36	23.8	12.2	148.84	6.254
60–64	12	24.2	12	24.2	−12.2	148.84	6.150
55–59	18	20.8	18	20.8	−2.8	7.84	0.377
50–54	10	15.3	10	15.3	−5.3	28.09	1.836
45–49	8	9.5	8	9.5	−1.5	2.25	0.237
40–44	8	4.9	14	7.9	6.1	37.21	4.710
35–39	5	2.2					
30–34	1	0.8					
$\Sigma f_o = n = 150$		$\Sigma f_e = 149.0$					$\chi^2 = 23.582$

16.3.9   Application of χ^2 for Testing the Significance of the Difference between Proportions

In Chapter 12, procedures were described for testing the significance of the difference between both *independent* and *correlated* proportions. These procedures involved dividing the difference between two proportions by the standard error of the difference to obtain a normal deviate (or z) which could be referred to a table of areas under the normal curve. Because of a simple relationship for 1 df between χ^2 and the normal deviate (i.e., z), χ^2 provides an alternative but equivalent procedure for testing the significance of the difference between proportions. For 1 df, it may be shown that χ^2 is equal to the normal deviate squared.

$$\text{Thus, } \chi^2 = (x/s)^2 = z^2 \text{ or } \sqrt{\chi^2} = z.$$

We shall now consider the use of χ^2 in testing the significance of the difference between proportions. Proportions are of two types—*independent* or *uncorrelated* proportions and *correlated* proportions. Proportions are called independent or uncorrelated when *independent* samples are used in the study, for example, males and females, boys and girls, etc. Proportions, on the contrary, are known as correlated only when the same group of subjects is taken and tested in two situations or two items or when the data are obtained in paired observations. For example, a group of men is taken and tested on two attitude items regarding their agreement or disagreement with the attitude statements.

First of all, we shall now begin with the use of χ^2 in testing the significance of the difference between proportions for *independent* samples.

16.3.9.1   *Uncorrelated or Independent Proportions*

Let the following be data obtained in response to an attitude-test statement for a group of males and females. Is there a significant difference in the attitude of males and females?

Frequency

	Agree	Disagree	Total
Males	70 a	70 b	140 $(a+b)$
Females	20 c	40 d	60 $(c+d)$
Total	90 $(a+c)$	110 $(b+d)$	200 (N) $(a+b+c+d)$

Proportion

	Agree	Disagree	Total
Males	0.500 p_1	0.500 q_1	1.00
Females	0.333 p_2	0.667 q_2	1.00
Total	0.450 (p)	0.550 (q)	1.00

In the above data:

$$\text{Number of males} = N_1 = 140$$
$$\text{Number of females} = N_2 = 60$$

Proportion of males indicating agreement to the attitude statement

$$= p_1 = \frac{70}{140} = 0.500$$

Proportion of females indicating agreement to the attitude statement

$$= p_2 = \frac{20}{60} = 0.333$$

In order to know the proportion (p) of the total samples indicating agreement to the attitude statement, we should calculate a proportion (p) based on a combination of data for the two samples. With the above data:

$$p = \frac{70+20}{140+60} = \frac{90}{200} = 0.450$$
$$q = 1 - p = 1 - 0.450 = 0.550$$

The standard error of difference between two independent proportions:

$$S_{p_1 \sim p_2} = \sqrt{pq(\frac{1}{N_1}+\frac{1}{N_2})} = \sqrt{(0.450)(0.550)\left(\frac{1}{140}+\frac{1}{60}\right)}$$
$$= \sqrt{(0.450)(0.550)(0.007+0.017)} = \sqrt{0.450 \times 0.550 \times 0.024} = \sqrt{0.0059400} = 0.077$$

The required normal deviate (z) is then:

$$z = \frac{p_1 - p_2}{S_{p_1 \sim p_2}} = \frac{0.500 - 0.333}{0.077} = \frac{0.167}{0.077} = 2.17$$

Let us now apply the formula for calculating χ^2 for a 2×2 contingency table to the same data without Yates' correction for continuity

$$\chi^2 = \frac{n(ad-bc)^2}{(a+b)(c+d)(a+c)(b+d)} = \frac{200(70 \times 40 - 70 \times 20)^2}{140 \times 60 \times 90 \times 110}$$
$$= \frac{200(2800-1400)^2}{140 \times 60 \times 90 \times 110} = \frac{200(1400)^2}{140 \times 60 \times 90 \times 110} = \frac{200 \times 1400 \times 1400}{140 \times 60 \times 90 \times 110} = 4.71$$

Our given problem is a 2×2 contingency table, for which df$=1$. So, we have to prove that $z^2 = \chi^2$. $z^2 = (2.17)^2 = 4.71$. Thus, $\chi^2 = z^2$.

Therefore, only when proportions are given, we must calculate z and then take the square of z which will be the value of χ^2 and test its significance by taking df$=(r-1)(c-1)$. For our given data, the df$=1$. Referring to Table L of the appendix, the critical values of χ^2, with df$=1$, at 0.05 is 3.84 and at 0.01 is 6.64. Since the obtained value of $\chi^2 = 4.71$ exceeds the critical value of $\chi^2 = 3.84$, it is significant at 0.05 level of significance. Thus, we may conclude that the difference between two independent proportions is significant at about the 5% level. Considerations pertaining to small frequencies apply also to the application of χ^2 in testing the significance of the difference between proportions.

16.3.9.2   Correlated Proportions

Let the following be data composed of paired observations. Test the significance of the difference between proportions of agreements to an attitude question for the same individuals tested on two occasions.

Frequency Item 2

		Disagree	Agree	Total
Item 1	Agree	10 _a_	50 _b_	60 _(a+b)_
	Disagree	110 _c_	30 _d_	140 _(c+d)_
	Total	120 _(a+c)_	80 _(b+d)_	200 _(a+b+c+d)=N_

Proportion Item 2

		Disagree	Agree	Total
Item 1	Agree	0.05 _a_	0.25 _b_	0.30(p_1) _(a+b)_
	Disagree	0.55 _c_	0.15 _d_	0.70(q_1) _(c+d)_
	Total	0.60 (q_2) _(a+c)_	0.40 (p_2) _(b+d)_	1.00 _(a+b+c+d)=N_

Proportions of samples agree to item $1 = p_1 = \dfrac{60}{200} = 0.30$

Proportions of samples agree to item $2 = p_2 = \dfrac{80}{200} = 0.40$

Number of samples $= N = 200$

We can calculate z for the difference between two correlated proportions by the following formula:

$$z = \frac{p_1 \sim p_2}{s_{p_1 \sim p_2}} \text{ where the } s_{p_1 \sim p_2} \text{ is determined as follows:}$$

$$s_{p_1 \sim p_2} = \sqrt{\frac{a+d}{N}} = \sqrt{\frac{0.05+0.15}{200}} = \sqrt{\frac{0.20}{200}} = \sqrt{0.001} = 0.0316$$

$$z = \frac{p_1 \sim p_2}{s_{p_1 \sim p_2}} = \frac{0.30 \sim 0.40}{0.0316} = \frac{0.10}{0.0316} = 3.16$$

$$\therefore \chi^2 = z^2 = (3.16)^2 = 9.986$$

Alternatively, we can calculate z directly from the above frequency table (if the data are composed of paired observations or data are correlated) as follows:

$$z = \frac{d-a}{\sqrt{a+d}} = \frac{30-10}{\sqrt{10+30}} = \frac{20}{\sqrt{40}} = \frac{20}{6.32} = 3.16$$

$$\therefore \chi^2 = z^2 = (3.16)^2 = 9.986$$

In both the situations, either we take proportions or frequencies to compute z, the value of z is same, that is, 3.16 and hence $\chi^2 = 9.986$.

Moreover, from the above frequency table, we can calculate χ^2 by the following formula:

$$\chi^2 = \frac{(d-a)^2}{a+d} = \frac{(30-10)^2}{10+30} = \frac{(20)^2}{40} = \frac{400}{40} = 10.0$$

$$z = \sqrt{\chi^2} = \sqrt{10.0} = 3.16$$

We note that there is a slight difference between the two values of χ^2, that is 9.986 and 10.0, which is negligible and might be caused by the rounding of the decimal points. So, we take the χ^2 value of 9.986 for the test of significance of the difference between two correlated proportions.

In our given problem, $df = (r-1)(c-1) = 1$, since it is a 2×2 contingency table. Referring to Table L of the appendix, the critical value of χ^2, with $df = 1$, at 0.05 is 3.84 and at 0.01 is 6.64. Since the obtained value of $\chi^2 = 9.986$ exceeds both the critical values of χ^2, it is significant at 0.01 level of significance. Therefore, it is reasonable to conclude that the difference between proportions of agreement to an attitude question for the same individuals tested on two occasions is significant at better than the 1% level.

16.4   Spearman Rank-order Correlation Coefficient (rho = ρ)

Of all the statistics based on ranks, the Spearman rank correlation coefficient was the earliest to be developed and is perhaps the best known today. This statistic is generally called as rho (ρ). It is a measure of association which requires that both variables be measured in at least an ordinal scale so that the objects or individuals under study may be ranked in two ordered series.

Spearman's rank-difference correlation coefficient (rho or ρ) is a measure of the magnitude and direction of the linear relationship between two variables in a sample when their values are expressed in ranks in order of magnitude or merit. It is a *non-parametric* counterpart of Pearson's r (or product-moment correlation coefficient) for *simple linear correlation*. Like Pearson's r, the value of Spearman's ρ ranges from –1.00 to +1.00; the absence of correlation is indicated by 0.00 (or zero).

In contrast to r, ρ is computed more quickly and easily, gives a lower value, and is applicable to smaller samples (i.e., number of cases is 25–30 or less), ranked data, and both normal and non-normal distributions. This is the most widely used of the rank correlational methods.

16.4.1   Assumptions of rho (ρ)

Being a non-parametric statistic, ρ requires very few assumptions to be fulfilled. The following are some of the important assumptions of rho:

(a)   The observations must be independent. This means that the selection of samples from the population should be random, and the assignment of scores to the performance of the samples should be unbiased or impartial.

(b)   There is a *linear relationship* between the variables to be correlated.

(c)   The measurements should be in terms of ordinal scale of measurement. In other words, the magnitude of each of the variables can be expressed in ranks, either in ascending or descending order; ρ is applicable to ordinal variables and also to such ratio and interval variables whose scores have been converted to ranks but not to nominal variables.

(d)   The paired scores (or ranks) of the variables for each individual occur at random and independent of all other paired scores (or ranks) in the sample.

16.4.2 Application of Rho (ρ)

The following are some of the general situations where the Spearman correlation (rho) is used.

(a) Spearman's ρ is used when the original data are ordinal, that is, when the X and Y values are ranks.

(b) Spearman correlation is particularly well-suited to situations where the number of cases in the sample is 25–30 or less. Usually, Spearman's ρ gives a lower value compared to Pearson's r, but when the sample is small, the values of ρ and r are equal. In other words, when N is small, the Spearman's rank-difference method will give as adequate a result as that obtained by finding Pearson's r.

(c) Differences among individuals in many traits can often be expressed by ranking the subjects in the order of merit when such differences cannot be measured directly. For example, persons may be ranked in order of merit for honesty, athletic ability, salesmanship, leadership ability or social adjustment when it is impossible to measure these complex behaviours. In like manner, various products or specimens, such as advertisements, colour combinations, compositions and jokes and pictures, which are admittedly hard to evaluate numerically may be put in order of merit for aesthetic quality, beauty, humour or some other characteristics. In all these cases, the Spearman method can be used to compute the correlation between two sets of ranks.

(d) Spearman rank-order correlation coefficient is used when a researcher wants to measure the consistency of a relationship between variables X and Y, independent of the specific form of the relationship. In this case, the original scores are first converted to ranks, then the Spearman correlation is used to measure the relationship for the ranks. Incidentally, when there is a consistently one-directional relationship between two variables, the relationship is said to be monotonic. Thus, the Spearman correlation can be used to measure the degree of monotonic relationship between two variables.

16.4.3 Computational Formula for ρ

There are various formulae for the computation of Spearman's ρ. However, a simplified and a widely used formula for computing rho when there are no ties or just a few ties relative to the number of paired scores is as follows:

$$\rho = 1 - \frac{6\sum D^2}{N(N^2 - 1)}$$

Where

ρ = rho, Spearman's rank-order correlation coefficient
D = difference between paired ranks (in each case)
N = number of pairs of ranks.

16.4.4 Characteristics of ρ

The following are some of the important properties or characteristics of Spearman's ρ:

(a) In Spearman's rank-order correlation coefficient, the observations or measurements of the bivariate variable are based on the ordinal scale in the form of ranks.

(b) The size of the correlation coefficient is directly affected by the size of the rank differences. For instance, if the paired ranks are same for both variables, each rank difference (i.e., D) will be zero, and ultimately each D^2 and, thus, ΣD^2 will be zero. This means that the correlation is perfect and positive, that is, +1.00. If the rank differences are, on the contrary, very large, and the fraction is greater than 1, then the correlation will be negative.

(c) The Spearman's ρ may be positive or negative and its value varies from –1.00 to +1.00, through 0.00. In short, when the paired ranks are in the same order, the ρ is perfect positive (ρ=+1.00), and when the paired ranks are in an inverse order, the ρ is perfect negative (ρ=–1.00).

16.4.5 Differences between Pearson's r and Spearman's ρ

Some of the important differences between Pearson's product-moment correlation coefficient (r) and Spearman's rank correlation coefficient (ρ) are discussed below:

(a) Pearson's r is a parametric statistic, whereas Spearman's ρ is a non-parametric statistic.

(b) Pearson's r assumes that the parent population from which the samples are drawn is normally distributed. But such a strict assumption is not made about the form of the population from which samples are selected in case of Spearman's ρ; the samples are drawn either from normal or non-normal populations.

(c) Pearson's r assumes that the variables under study are continuous measurement variables, whereas Spearman's ρ assumes that both variables should be ordinal variables.

(d) Basing on the sample findings, inferences about the parameters of the populations from which the samples are drawn are made in Pearson's r. However, no such inferences are made in case of Spearman's ρ.

(e) Pearson's r assumes that the measurements or the data should be in terms of either interval or ratio scales of measurements. On the contrary, Spearman's ρ assumes that the measurements or the data should be in terms of ordinal scale of measurement.

(f) Spearman's formula is easy to understand and apply as compared with Pearson's formula. The ρ is computed more rapidly than the r. The values obtained by the two formulae, namely, Pearson's r and spearman's ρ, are generally different. The difference arises due to the fact that when ranking is used instead of full set of observations, there is always some loss of information. Unless many ties exist, the coefficient of rank correlation should be only slightly lower than the product-moment correlation coefficient. However, in small sample cases having no ties, the value of ρ will be equal to that of r.

(g) Spearman's formula is the only formula to be used for finding correlation coefficient if we are dealing with qualitative characteristics which cannot be measured quantitatively, but can be arranged serially. It can also be used where actual data are given. In case of extreme observations, Spearman's formula is preferred to Pearson's formula.

(h) Spearman's formula has its limitations also. It is not practicable in the case of bivariate frequency distribution. In other words, correlation from the scatter diagram between two variables cannot be found out by rank-order method; for this we need the product-moment method.

(i) Rank-order method can be readily applied to small samples ($n<30$). For large samples ($n>30$), Spearman's formula should not be used unless the ranks are given, since in the contrary case the calculations are quite time consuming. However, Pearson's product-moment method can be applied even to the large samples having $n>30$.

16.4.6 Advantages of Spearman's ρ

As a non-parametric statistic, Spearman's ρ has the following advantages.

(a) The computation of Spearman's ρ is quicker and easier than that of Pearson's r.

(b) When data are available only in ordinal form or the number of paired scores is more than 5 but not greater than 30, with minimum or a few number of tied ranks, Spearman's rank method is the only acceptable method to find out the correlation coefficient between the two variables.

(c) Spearman's ρ is quite easy to interpret.

16.4.7 Limitations of Spearman's ρ

Spearman's ρ has the following limitations:

(a) Spearman's rank-order correlation method cannot be applied to the bivariate frequency distribution to find out the correlation from the scatter diagram between two variables.

(b) When the interval data are converted into ordinal data the information about the size of the score difference is lost.

(c) If the number of cases is more, assigning ranks to them becomes a tedious job and more time consuming.

16.4.8 Testing the Significance of Spearman's ρ

Testing a hypothesis for Spearman's ρ is similar to the procedure used for Pearson's r. The basic question is whether or not a correlation exists in the population. The sample correlation could be due to chance or perhaps it reflects an actual relationship between the variables in the population. The null hypothesis states that there is no correlation (no monotonic relationship) between the variables for the population or in symbols.

$H_0 : \rho = 0$ (population correlation is zero)

The alternative hypothesis predicts that a non-zero correlation exists in the population, which can be stated in symbols as

$H_1 : \rho \neq 0$ (there is a real correlation)

To determine if Spearman's ρ is statistically significant (i.e., H_0 should be rejected), there are two methods. One method of testing the significance of ρ is against the null hypothesis by referring to the table of critical values of Spearman correlation. Table M of the appendix shows critical values of ρ for different values of N required for significance at various levels. Observe that for a small N, values of ρ of very substantial size must be obtained before we have adequate grounds for rejecting the null hypothesis that no association exists between the rankings. For $N=10$ we require a ρ equal to or greater than 0.564 before we can argue that a significant association exists in a positive direction at the 5% level (i.e., 0.05 level of significance).

For N from 4 to 30, the Table M gives the value of ρ which has an associated probability under H_0 of $p=0.05$ and the value of ρ which has an associated probability under H_0 of $p=0.01$.

This is one-tailed table, that is, the stated probabilities apply when the observed value of ρ is in the predicted direction, either positive or negative. If an obtained value of ρ equals or exceeds the value tabled, that obtained value is significant (for a one-tailed test) at the level indicated.

The second method of testing the significance of ρ is in terms of t-test. This method is applied when $N=10$ or greater. In this case, we may test the significance of ρ by using a t given by:

$$t = \rho\sqrt{\frac{N-2}{1-\rho^2}}; \quad df = N-2$$

This quantity has a t distribution with $N-2$ degrees of freedom. For example, where $N=10$ and $\rho=0.564$, $t=1.93$. For 8 df, the table value of t (see Table C of the appendix) at 0.05 level is 2.306 (for a two-tailed test) and is 1.860 (for a one-tailed test). For a two-tailed test, we have insufficient grounds for arguing that the obtained ρ of 0.564 is significantly different from 0. For a one-tailed test, the obtained ρ of 0.564 is significant at about 5% level (i.e., 0.05 level of significance).

Therefore, when we test the significance of an observed ρ in terms of t, we should compare the obtained t value with the table value of t for one-tailed test with $N-2$ degrees of freedom, because ρ is always one-tailed, either positive or negative.

Suppose, $\rho=0.62$ and $N=12$. Let us test the significance of the obtained ρ of 0.62. Since N is larger than 10, we may use the t-test for testing the significance of ρ.

$$t = \rho\sqrt{\frac{N-2}{1-\rho^2}} = 0.62\sqrt{\frac{12-2}{1-(0.62)^2}} = 0.62\sqrt{\frac{10}{1-0.3844}} = 0.62\sqrt{\frac{10}{0.6156}}$$

$$= 0.62\sqrt{16.24} = 0.62 \times 4.03 = 2.4986 = 2.50$$

Table C of the appendix shows that for $df=N-2=12-2=10$, the table value of t at 0.025 level is 2.228 and at 0.01 level is 2.764 (for a one-tailed test). Thus, the obtained value of t of 2.50 is significant at 0.025 level for a one-tailed test. We could reject H_0 at $\alpha=0.05$, concluding that the two variables or two sets of rankings are associated in the population of which the 12 subjects were a sample.

16.4.9   Computational Procedures for Spearman's ρ

The calculation of the Spearman correlation is remarkably simple, provided we know how to compute it. However, the computational procedures of Spearman's ρ vary depending upon the nature of data given, whether the given data are in terms of original scores, or in ranks, and whether there are tied ranks or not. These procedures are discussed separately as given below.

16.4.9.1   *Calculation of ρ from Test Scores*

To illustrate the calculation of Spearman's rank-order correlation coefficient (ρ), we must go through the following steps:

(a)   The names of the subjects or their serial numbers are listed in column 1 (see Table 16.13).

(b)   The scores of each subject in Mathematics (variable X) and Statistics (variable Y) will be written in column 2 and column 3, respectively (see Table 16.13).

(c)   Ranks will be assigned to the scores of each variable separately, either in an ascending or descending order for both the variables. That is, the order of assignment of ranks to the scores must be the same for both the variables. In the present example (see Table 16.13), a rank of 1 is assigned to the highest score in the series, a rank of 2 is assigned to the next highest score and so on till the lowest score in the series gets a rank equal to

Table 16.13   Calculation of Spearman's rank-order correlation coefficient from test scores

(1) Students	(2) X	(3) Y	(4) R_1	(5) R_2	(6) D (R_1-R_2)	(7) D^2
1	20	12	1	6	−5	25
2	18	16	2	3	−1	1
3	17	10	3	7	−4	16
4	15	17	4	2	2	4
5	13	18	5	1	4	16
6	12	8	6	8	−2	4
7	10	15	7	4	3	9
8	9	6	8	9	−1	1
9	8	13	9	5	4	16
10	5	3	10	10	0	0
$N=10$					$\Sigma D=0$	$\Sigma D^2=92$

   N. Accordingly, the scores entered in column 2 and column 3 are separately ranked in a descending order, denoted by R_1 and R_2, and are entered in column 4 and column 5, respectively (see Table 16.13).

(d) The difference (D) between the ranks of the paired scores of two variables (i.e., R_1-R_2) is worked out for each subject and is entered in column 6. The sum of Ds is zero (i.e., $\Sigma D=0$). This calculation is of no value *per se*, but is a check on the computation of this point.

(e) Each difference between paired ranks (D) entered in column 6 is now squared, and each squared difference is entered in column 7 and this column is summed to give ΣD^2.

(f) Spearman's rank-order correlation coefficient (ρ) is calculated by the use of the following equation:

$$\rho = 1 - \frac{6\Sigma D^2}{N(N^2-1)}$$

(g) The obtained ρ will be evaluated for accepting or rejecting the H_0 at a particular α level for a one-tailed test. When N is small, special tables are available for testing the significance of rho (Table M of the appendix). If the size of the sample is 10 or greater, the *t*-test can be made using the formula mentioned earlier under the heading 'testing the significance of Spearman's ρ'.

Example 16.9 The following scores are obtained from 10 students in mathematics and statistics. Compute the Spearman's rank-order correlation coefficient and interpret it.

Mathematics	20	18	17	15	13	12	10	9	8	5
Statistics	12	16	10	17	18	8	15	6	13	3

Solution

Let the Mathematics be denoted by X and Statistics by Y. The data are entered in Table 16.13.

$$\rho = 1 - \frac{6\Sigma D^2}{N(N^2 - 1)} = 1 - \frac{6 \times 92}{10(10^2 - 1)} = 1 - \frac{552}{10 \times 99} = 1 - \frac{552}{990} = 1 - 0.558 = 0.442$$

Test of significance:

$$N = 10; \text{ Obtained } \rho = 0.442$$

Referring to Table M (given in the appendix) with $N = 10$, the critical value of ρ at 0.05 level is 0.564. Since the observed ρ of 0.442 is smaller than the critical value of ρ of 0.564, it is not significant. So, the null hypothesis (H_0: $\rho = 0$) is accepted, and we conclude that the mathematics and statistics scores are not associated in the population of which the 10 students were a sample.

16.4.9.2   *Calculation of ρ from Ranked Data*

To illustrate the calculation of Spearman's ρ from the ranked data, we must follow the same steps described under the calculation of ρ from test scores, except that the ranks are given instead of original scores. That means, the subjects of the sample have already been ranked with respect to each of the two variables and these ranks can be used directly for computing ρ.

Example 16.10 A sample of 10 pupils has been ranked in order of merit for their honesty by Judges X and Y. The judgements were in ranks which are given below. Determine the extent to which their judgements were in agreement.

Pupils	1	2	3	4	5	6	7	8	9	10
Judge X	1	3	4	7	6	9	8	10	2	5
Judge Y	1	2	5	9	6	8	10	7	4	3

Solution

The data are entered in Table 16.14.

$$\rho = 1 - \frac{6\Sigma D^2}{N(N^2 - 1)} = 1 - \frac{6 \times 28}{10(10^2 - 1)} = 1 - \frac{6 \times 28}{10 \times 99} = 1 - \frac{168}{990} = 1 - 0.17 = 0.83$$

Test of significance:

$$N = 10; \text{ obtained } \rho = 0.83$$

Referring to Table M (given in the appendix) with $N = 10$, the critical value of ρ at $\alpha = 0.05$ is 0.564 and at $\alpha = 0.01$ is 0.746. Since the obtained ρ of 0.83 is greater than both the critical values of ρ, it is significant at 0.01 level of significance. So, the H_0 is rejected, and we conclude that the judgements of both the judges, X and Y, significantly agree in 99% of cases. Thus, $p < 0.01$.

16.4.9.3   *Calculation of ρ from Tied Observations*

Occasionally, two or more subjects will receive the same scores on the same variable. These identical scores are known as tied scores. When tied scores occur, each of them is assigned the average of the ranks which would have been assigned had no ties occurred, our usual

Table 16.14 Calculation of ρ from ranked data

Pupil	Judge X Ranks	Judge Y Ranks	D $(X-Y)$	D^2
1	1	1	0	0
2	3	2	1	1
3	4	5	−1	1
4	7	9	−2	4
5	6	6	0	0
6	9	8	1	1
7	8	10	−2	4
8	10	7	3	9
9	2	4	−2	4
10	5	3	2	4
$N=10$			$\Sigma D=0$	$\Sigma D^2=28$

procedure for assigning ranks to tied observations. For example, if we want to replace 12, 15, 15, 15, 20, 22, 22 and 25 by ranks, we observe immediately that 15 occurs thrice and 22 occurs twice. Under these circumstances, we assign to each member the average rank which the tied observations occupy. Thus, 25 is ranked 1, the two 22s are ranked 2.5 and 2.5 (i.e., the average of ranks 2 and 3: $\frac{2+3}{2}=2.5$), the 20 is ranked 4, the three 15s are ranked 6, 6 and 6 (i.e., the average of ranks 5, 6 and 7: $\frac{5+6+7}{3}=6$) and 12 is ranked 8. Having replaced the tied scores by their average ranks, we proceed as before in the calculation of ρ.

When there are no ties either in X or Y variables and the ranks are treated as scores, in that situation, the r will be equal to ρ (i.e., $r=\rho$).

If the proportion of ties is not large, their effect on ρ is negligible, and the same usual formula $\left(\rho=1-\dfrac{6\Sigma D^2}{N(N^2-1)}\right)$ may still be used for computation. However, if the proportion of ties is large, then a *correction factor* must be incorporated in the computation of ρ, because it may inflate the value of ρ.

The effect of tied ranks in the X variable is to reduce the sum of squares, Σx^2, below the value of $\dfrac{N^3-N}{12}$, that is, $\Sigma x^2 < \dfrac{N^3-N}{12}$ when there are tied ranks in the X variable. Therefore, it is necessary to correct the sum of squares, taking ties into account. The correction factor is T, which reads as follows:

$$T=\frac{t^3-t}{12}$$

where

t = the number of observations tied at a given rank. When the sum of squares is corrected for ties, it becomes

$$\Sigma x^2 = \frac{N^3 - N}{12} - \Sigma T$$

where ΣT indicates that we sum the various values of T for all the various groups of tied observations.

When a considerable number of ties are present, we will use the following formula in computing ρ:

$$\rho = \frac{\Sigma x^2 + \Sigma y^2 - \Sigma d^2}{2\sqrt{\Sigma x^2 \Sigma y^2}}$$

where

$$\Sigma x^2 = \frac{N^3 - N}{12} - \Sigma T_x$$
$$\Sigma y^2 = \frac{N^3 - N}{12} - \Sigma T_y$$

To illustrate the calculation of Spearman's ρ from tied observations, the data may be given either in terms of tied scores or in tied ranks and we must follow the same steps described under the computation of ρ from test scores or from ranks, respectively, except that each tied score is assigned the average of the ranks which would have been assigned had no ties occurred, and incorporation of the correction factor for ties while computing ρ. The entire computational procedures of ρ from tied scores/tied ranks will become clear through the following example.

Example 16.11 The following scores are obtained by 10 subjects in variables X and Y. Compute Spearman's ρ and interpret it.

Subjects	A	B	C	D	E	F	G	H	I	J
X	10	15	11	14	16	20	10	8	7	9
Y	16	16	24	18	22	24	14	10	12	14

Solution

The data are entered in Table 16.15.

The value of ρ without correction for ties is

$$\rho = 1 - \frac{6\Sigma d^2}{N(N^2 - 1)} = 1 - \frac{6 \times 24}{10(10^2 - 1)} = 1 - \frac{144}{990} = 1 - 0.145 = 0.855$$

Correction for ties:

Correction factor = T

$$T = \frac{t^3 - t}{12} \quad \text{or} \quad \Sigma T = \Sigma \frac{t^3 - t}{12}$$

Table 16.15 Calculation of ρ from tied scores/tied ranks

(1) Subjects	(2) X	(3) Y	(4) R_1	(5) R_2	(6) d (R_1-R_2)	(7) d^2
A	10	16	6.5	5.5	1.0	1.00
B	15	16	3.0	5.5	−2.5	6.25
C	11	24	5.0	1.5	3.5	12.25
D	14	18	4.0	4.0	0.0	0.00
E	16	22	2.0	3.0	−1.0	1.00
F	20	24	1.0	1.5	−0.5	0.25
G	10	14	6.5	7.5	−1.0	1.00
H	8	10	9.0	10.0	−1.0	1.00
I	7	12	10.0	9.0	1.0	1.00
J	9	14	8.0	7.5	0.5	0.25
N=10					$\Sigma d=0.0$	$\Sigma d^2=24.00$

where

t=number of observations (or scores) tied with a particular rank
N=number of subjects or sample size

In X series or variable:
2 scores are tied with rank 6.5

$$\therefore \Sigma T_x = \Sigma \frac{t^3-t}{12} = \frac{2^3-2}{12} = \frac{8-2}{12} = \frac{6}{12} = 0.5$$

$$\text{Therefore, } \Sigma x^2 = \frac{N^3-N}{12} - \Sigma T_x = \frac{10^3-10}{12} - 0.5 = \frac{990}{12} - 0.5 = 82.5 - 0.5 = 82.0$$

In Y series or variable:

2 scores are tied with rank 1.5
2 scores are tied with rank 5.5
2 scores are tied with rank 7.5

$$\therefore \Sigma T_y = \Sigma \frac{t^3-t}{12} = \left(\frac{2^3-2}{12} + \frac{2^3-2}{12} + \frac{2^3-2}{12}\right)$$

$$= \left(\frac{8-2}{12} + \frac{8-2}{12} + \frac{8-2}{12}\right) = \left(\frac{6}{12} + \frac{6}{12} + \frac{6}{12}\right) = 1.5$$

$$\text{Therefore, } \Sigma Y^2 = \frac{N^3-N}{12} - \Sigma T_y = \frac{10^3-10}{12} - 1.5 = \frac{990}{12} - 1.5 = 82.5 - 1.5 = 81.0$$

Thus, corrected for ties, $\Sigma x^2=82.0$ and $\Sigma y^2=81.0$.

The following formula is applied to find out ρ after correction for ties.

$$\rho = \frac{\Sigma x^2 + \Sigma y^2 - \Sigma d^2}{2\sqrt{\Sigma x^2 \Sigma y^2}} = \frac{82.0 + 81.0 - 24.0}{2\sqrt{82.0 \times 81.0}} = \frac{163.0 - 24.0}{2\sqrt{6642.00}}$$

$$= \frac{139.0}{2 \times 81.498} = \frac{139.0}{162.996} = 0.853$$

Without correction for ties, the obtained $\rho = 0.855$

With correction for ties, the obtained $\rho = 0.853$

This illustrates the relatively insignificant or negligible effect of ties upon the value of the Spearman rank correlation. Note, however, that the effect of ties is to inflate or increase the value of ρ. For this reason, the correction should be used where there is a large proportion of ties in either or both the X and Y variables.

Test of significance:

$$N = 10; \text{ Obtained } \rho \text{ with correction for ties} = 0.853$$

Referring to Table M (given in the appendix) with $N = 10$, the critical value of ρ at $\alpha = 0.05$ is 0.564 and at $\alpha = 0.01$ is 0.746. Since the obtained ρ of 0.853 is greater than both the critical values of ρ, it is significant at 0.01 level of significance. Therefore, $p < 0.01$. So, the H_0 is rejected and we conclude that the subjects' scores in both the variables are significantly associated or correlated in 99% of cases.

16.4.10   Summary of Procedures

The following are the steps in the use of the Spearman rank correlation coefficient:

1. Rank the observations on the X variable from 1 to N. Similarly, rank the observations on the Y variable from 1 to N.
2. List the N subjects. Give each subject's rank on the X variable and his/her rank on the Y variable next to his entry.
3. Determine the value of d for each subject by subtracting his Y rank from his X rank. Square this value to determine each subject's d^2. Sum the d^2 for the N cases to determine Σd^2.
4. If the proportion of ties in either the X or the Y observations is large, use formula $\rho = \frac{\Sigma x^2 + \Sigma y^2 - \Sigma d^2}{2\sqrt{\Sigma x^2 \Sigma y^2}}$ to compute ρ. In other cases, use formula $\rho = 1 - \frac{6\Sigma d^2}{N(N^2 - 1)}$.
5. If the subjects constitute a random sample from some population, one may test whether the observed value of ρ indicates an association between the X and Y variables in the population. The method for doing so depends on the size of N.

   (a) For N from 4 to 30, critical values of ρ for the 0.05 and 0.01 levels of significance (one-tailed test) are shown in Table M (see the appendix).
   (b) For $N \geq 10$, the significance of a value as large as the observed value of ρ may be determined by computing the t associated with that value using formula $t = \rho\sqrt{\frac{N-2}{1-\rho^2}}$, and then determine the significance of that value of t by referring to Table C in the appendix with df $= N - 2$.

16.4.11 Power Efficiency

The efficiency of the Spearman rank correlation when compared with the most powerful parametric correlation, Pearson's *r*, is about 91% (Hotelling & Pabst, 1936). That is, when ρ is used with a sample to test for the existence of an association in the population, and when the assumptions and requirements underlying the proper use of Pearson's *r* are met, that is, when the population has a bivariate normal distribution and measurement is in the sense of at least an interval scale, then ρ is 91% as efficient as *r* in rejecting H_0. If a correlation between *X* and *Y* exists in that population, with 100 cases ρ will reveal that correlation at the same level of significance which *r* attains with 91 cases. Thus, the power efficiency of ρ is 91% compared to *r*.

16.5 The Phi Coefficient (ϕ)

The *phi coefficient* is also known as the Yule ϕ. It is a non-parametric *statistic* and is applicable to 2×2 tables only. It is a close relative of chi-square, which is applicable to a wide variety of situations. Yule's phi coefficient is a statistic of correlation between two genuinely dichotomous nominal variables, each having only two classes located at two distinct points on its scale with a real gap between them, for example, male–female, living–dead, pass–fail, successful–unsuccessful, normal–abnormal, colour blind–normal, right–wrong, pregnant–nonpregnant and the like.

Although ϕ may be used to describe the relation between any two dichotomous variables, its most common application is in describing the relation between two dichotomously scored test items. It is used in psychology mainly for *item-to-item correlation*; the items are dichotomously scored as yes/no, 1/0, or right/wrong, etc. ϕ is also used to find out the *item–criterion correlation* between a dichotomously scored test item and a genuinely dichotomous external criterion representing the attribute under investigation.

16.5.1 Assumptions of ϕ

Being a non-parametric statistic ϕ requires very few assumptions to be fulfilled for its application. The following are some of the important assumptions of ϕ.

(a) The two variables must be nominal variables.
(b) Both the variables are genuinely dichotomous with no reasonable expectation to yield any continuous series of data on more extensive exploration.
(c) Each of the variables has a bimodal distribution on the population with a real gap between its two classes.
(d) There is an association between the variables.
(e) The data are in terms of frequencies or proportions.

16.5.2 The Relation of Phi to Chi Square

Phi is related to chi square computed from a 2×2 table by the very simple equation. Phi is derived from chi square (i.e., phi as a function of chi square) by the equation

$$\phi = \sqrt{\frac{\chi^2}{N}}$$

Similarly, chi square as a function of phi is expressed by the equation

$$\chi^2 = N\phi^2$$

Since phi can be derived from chi square, when the latter is applied to a 2×2 table, any of the formulae for chi square given in Section 16.3 of this chapter will apply to its computation.

16.5.3 Computation of Phi Coefficient (ϕ)

The phi coefficient can be computed in various ways as mentioned below:

First, since phi is related to chi square calculated from a 2×2 table, first of all, we may compute χ^2 from the given 2×2 frequency or proportion tables and then derive ϕ directly from the obtained χ^2 value by the equation that reads

$$\phi = \sqrt{\frac{\chi^2}{N}} \quad \text{(phi as a function of chi square)}$$

Second, we can compute ϕ directly from the 2×2 frequency table by the formula that reads

$$\phi = \frac{ad - bc}{\sqrt{(a+b)(c+d)(a+c)(b+d)}}$$

where a, b, c and d are the four cell frequencies. The term in the denominator of the above expression is the square root of the product of the four marginal totals.

Table 16.16 shows a 2×2 table illustrating the responses of 200 students to an opinion item (Item 1) and an information item (Item 2). In other words, this table illustrates the relationship between two test items as follows:

Applied directly to the computing of phi from the 2×2 frequency table (see Table 16.16), it becomes

$$\phi = \frac{ad - bc}{\sqrt{(a+b)(c+d)(a+c)(b+d)}} = \frac{90 \times 70 - 30 \times 10}{\sqrt{120 \times 80 \times 100 \times 100}}$$

$$= \frac{6300 - 300}{\sqrt{96000000}} = \frac{6000}{9797.96} = 0.61$$

Third, the phi coefficient can be computed directly from the 2×2 proportion table (see Table 16.16). Let us represent the proportion of agree to item 1 by p_1 and those disagree by q_1,

Table 16.16 Responses of two hundred students to two test items

		Frequency Item 2				Proportion Item 2		
		Right	Wrong	Total		Right	Wrong	Total
Item 1	Agree	90 (a)	30 (b)	120 (a+b)	Agree	0.45 (a)(p_{12})	0.15 (b)	0.60 (p_1)
	Disagree	10 (c)	70 (d)	80 (c+d)	Disagree	0.05 (c)	0.35 (d)	0.40 (q_1)
	Total	100 (a+c)	100 (b+d)	200 (a+b+c+d=N)	Total	0.50 (p_2)	0.50 (q_2)	1.00

where $p_1=1-q_1$. Similarly, the proportion of rightly answered item 2 is p_2 and the proportion wrongly answered q_2. The proportion agree and rightly answered both items 1 and 2 is represented by p_{12}.

The formula for the phi coefficient is

$$\phi = \frac{ad-bc}{\sqrt{p_1 q_1 p_2 q_2}}$$

Substituting the values of 2×2 proportion table of Table 16.16, ϕ becomes

$$\phi = \frac{ad-bc}{\sqrt{p_1 q_1 p_2 q_2}} = \frac{0.45 \times 0.35 - 0.15 \times 0.05}{\sqrt{0.60 \times .040 \times .050 \times 0.50}} = \frac{0.1575 - 0.0075}{\sqrt{0.06}}$$

$$= \frac{0.15}{0.245} = 0.61$$

which checks with the result previously obtained from the frequency data.

Alternative formula for computing ϕ from the proportion data may be stated as follows:

$$\phi = \frac{p_{12} - p_1 p_2}{\sqrt{p_1 q_1 p_2 q_2}}$$

Substituting the proportion values of Table 16.16, φ becomes

$$\phi = \frac{p_{12} - p_1 p_2}{\sqrt{p_1 q_1 p_2 q_2}} = \frac{0.45 - 0.60 \times 0.50}{\sqrt{0.60 \times 0.40 \times 0.50 \times 0.50}} = \frac{0.45 - 0.30}{\sqrt{0.06}}$$

$$= \frac{0.15}{0.245} = 0.61$$

Thus, the obtained value of ϕ by both the formulae, based on the proportion data, is the same.

16.5.4 Special Case of Phi when One or Both Variables are Evenly Divided

When one of the variables, let us say the one for which we use p_1 and q_1 as total proportions, is evenly divided, so that $p_1=q_1=0.50$, the formula for ϕ is considerably simplified. The formula reads

$$\phi = \frac{2p_{12} - p_2}{\sqrt{p_2 q_2}}$$

Similarly, when the other variable, for which we use p_2 and q_2 as total proportions, is evenly divided, so that $p_2=q_2=0.50$, the formula for ϕ simplifies to

$$\phi = \frac{2p_{12} - p_1}{\sqrt{p_1 q_1}}$$

When both the variables are evenly divided, so that $p_1=q_1=p_2=q_2=0.50$, the formula becomes

$$\phi = 4p_{12} - 1$$

To illustrate the above three formulae regarding the special case of phi when one or both of the variables are evenly divided, we will refer to the data in proportions given in three 2×2 tables (A, B and C) of Table 16.17.

Table 16.17   Frequencies and proportions of pass and fail on two test items in three conditions

Condition A								
Frequency Item 2					**Proportion Item 2**			
		Pass	Fail	Total			Pass	Fail	Total
Item 1	Pass	20 (a)	5 (b)	25 (a+b)	Item 1	Pass	0.40 (p₁₂)	0.10	0.50 (p₁)
	Fail	15 (c)	10 (d)	25 (c+d)		Fail	0.30	0.20	0.50 (q₁)
	Total	35 (a+c)	15 (b+d)	50 (N)		Total	0.70 (p₂)	0.30 (q₂)	1.00

Condition B								
Frequency Item 2					**Proportion Item 2**			
		Pass	Fail	Total			Pass	Fail	Total
Item 1	Pass	40 (a)	30 (b)	70 (a+b)	Item 1	Pass	0.40 (p₁₂)	0.30	0.70 (p₁)
	Fail	10 (c)	20 (d)	30 (c+d)		Fail	0.10	0.20	0.30 (q₁)
	Total	50 (a+c)	50 (b+d)	100 (N)		Total	0.50 (p₂)	0.50 (q₂)	1.00

Condition C								
Frequency Item 2					**Proportion Item 2**			
		Pass	Fail	Total			Pass	Fail	Total
Item 1	Pass	70 (a)	30 (b)	100 (a+b)	Item 1	Pass	0.35 (p₁₂)	0.15	0.50 (p₁)
	Fail	30 (c)	70 (d)	100 (c+d)		Fail	0.15	0.35	0.50 (q₁)
	Total	100 (a+c)	100 (b+d)	200 (N)		Total	0.50 (p₂)	0.50 (q₂)	1.00

In condition A of Table 16.17, the 2×2 proportion table indicates that the first variable is evenly divided so that $p_1 = q_1 = 0.50$, $p_2 = 0.70$, $q_2 = 0.30$ and $p_{12} = 0.40$. So, the phi coefficient is

$$\phi = \frac{2p_{12} - p_2}{\sqrt{p_2 q_2}} = \frac{2 \times 0.40 - 0.70}{\sqrt{0.70 \times 0.30}} = \frac{0.80 - 0.70}{\sqrt{0.21}} = \frac{0.10}{0.458} = 0.218$$

If we apply the general formula, the phi coefficient is

$$\phi = \frac{p_{12} - p_1 p_2}{\sqrt{p_1 q_1 p_2 q_2}} = \frac{0.40 - 0.50 \times 0.70}{\sqrt{0.50 \times 0.50 \times 0.70 \times 0.30}} = \frac{0.40 - .035}{\sqrt{0.0525}} = \frac{0.05}{0.229} = 0.218$$

Thus, the value of ϕ is the same in both the above formulae.

In condition B of Table 16.17, the 2×2 proportion table shows that the second variable is evenly divided so that $p_2 = q_2 = 0.50$, $p_1 = 0.70$, $q_1 = 0.30$ and $p_{12} = 0.40$. So, the phi coefficient is

$$\phi = \frac{2p_{12} - p_1}{\sqrt{p_1 q_1}} = \frac{2 \times 0.40 - 0.70}{\sqrt{0.70 \times 0.30}} = \frac{0.80 - 0.70}{\sqrt{0.21}} = \frac{0.10}{0.458} = 0.218$$

The value of ϕ by the general formula is

$$\phi = \frac{p_{12} - p_1 p_2}{\sqrt{p_1 q_1 p_2 q_2}} = \frac{0.40 - 0.70 \times 0.50}{\sqrt{0.70 \times 0.30 \times 0.50 \times 0.50}} = \frac{0.40 - 0.35}{\sqrt{0.0525}} = \frac{0.05}{0.229} = 0.218$$

In this condition also, the value of ϕ remains same in both the above formulae.

In condition C of Table 16.17, the 2×2 proportion table shows that both variables are evenly divided so that $p_1 = q_1 = p_2 = q_2 = 0.50$ and $p_{12} = 0.35$. So, the phi coefficient is

$$\phi = 4p_{12} - 1 = 4 \times 0.35 - 1 = 1.40 - 1 = 0.40$$

The value of ϕ by the general formula is

$$\phi = \frac{p_{12} - p_1 p_2}{\sqrt{p_1 q_1 p_2 q_2}} = \frac{0.35 - 0.50 \times 0.50}{\sqrt{0.50 \times 0.50 \times 0.50 \times 0.50}} = \frac{0.35 - 0.25}{\sqrt{0.0625}} = \frac{0.10}{0.25} = 0.40$$

Thus, the obtained value of φ is the same in both the above formulae.

16.5.5   An Evaluation of the Phi Coefficient

Phi coefficient is actually a product-moment coefficient of correlation. Its formula is a variation of Pearson's fundamental equation, $r = \Sigma xy / N\sigma_x \sigma_y$. The similarity may be seen to some degree, at least, if we break the denominator of the formula, $ad - bc / \sqrt{p_1 q_1 p_2 q_2}$ or $p_{12} - p_1 p_2 / \sqrt{p_1 q_1 p_2 q_2}$ into two components, $\sqrt{p_1 q_1}$ and $\sqrt{p_2 q_2}$. These are the standard deviations of the two point distributions in Y and X variables. If we assign integers or numerical values of 1 and 0 to the two categories in X and in Y variables and calculate the product-moment correlation coefficient in the usual way, the result will be identical with the phi coefficient.

The value of phi coefficient varies from -1.0 to $+1.0$, but seldom reaches the extremes of this range. These limits, however, can be attained only when the two variables are evenly divided, that is, $p_1 = q_1 = p_2 = q_2 = 0.50$. When the variables are the same shape, $p_1 = p_2$ and $q_1 = q_2$, but are asymmetrical, $p_1 \neq q_1$ and $p_2 \neq q_2$, one or the other of the limits, -1.0 or $+1.0$, may be attained but not both. The maximum and minimum values of phi coefficient are clearly influenced by the particular combinations of marginal totals. Let us consider the above 2×2 tables pictured in Table 16.18.

In Tables 1 and 2, both variables are evenly divided and phi coefficients of $+1.0$ and -1.0 are possible, respectively. Table 3 represents the maximum positive association possible, given the restriction of the marginal totals. The phi coefficient is 0.612. Table 4 shows the most extreme negative association possible with the same marginal totals. The phi coefficient is -0.408. For this particular set of marginal totals, phi coefficient can extend from a minimum of -0.408 to a maximum of $+0.612$. The phi coefficient, although affected by the marginal totals, is a measure of the efficacy of prediction.

Table 16.18 Some fourfold table illustrating the dependence of the value of a phi coefficient upon the combination of marginal totals

<table>
<tr><td colspan="4" style="text-align:center">(1)
X</td><td></td><td colspan="4" style="text-align:center">(2)
X</td></tr>
<tr><td></td><td>+</td><td>−</td><td>Total</td><td></td><td></td><td>+</td><td>−</td><td>Total</td></tr>
<tr><td rowspan="3">Y</td><td>+</td><td>50</td><td>0</td><td>50</td><td rowspan="3">Y</td><td>+</td><td>0</td><td>50</td><td>50</td></tr>
<tr><td>−</td><td>0</td><td>50</td><td>50</td><td>−</td><td>50</td><td>0</td><td>50</td></tr>
<tr><td>Total</td><td>50</td><td>50</td><td>100(N)</td><td>Total</td><td>50</td><td>50</td><td>100(N)</td></tr>
<tr><td colspan="4" style="text-align:center">(3)
X</td><td></td><td colspan="4" style="text-align:center">(4)
X</td></tr>
<tr><td></td><td>+</td><td>−</td><td>Total</td><td></td><td></td><td>+</td><td>−</td><td>Total</td></tr>
<tr><td rowspan="3">Y</td><td>+</td><td>60</td><td>20</td><td>80</td><td rowspan="3">Y</td><td>+</td><td>40</td><td>40</td><td>80</td></tr>
<tr><td>−</td><td>0</td><td>20</td><td>20</td><td>−</td><td>20</td><td>0</td><td>20</td></tr>
<tr><td>Total</td><td>60</td><td>40</td><td>100(N)</td><td>Total</td><td>60</td><td>40</td><td>100(N)</td></tr>
</table>

16.5.6 Test of Significance of Phi Coefficient

A test of the null hypothesis (H_0) proposing no correlation between the variables can be made through phi's relationship to chi square. In other words, the obtained value of ϕ can be tested for its significance in terms of χ^2. If χ^2 is significant in a fourfold table, the corresponding ϕ is significant. The procedure, then, is to derive the corresponding χ^2 from the obtained ϕ by means of formula $\chi^2 = N\phi^2$ and then examine the chi square table (see Table L of the appendix) to find whether for 1 degree of freedom the required standard of significance is met.

Let us take an example. The computed ϕ for the problem given in Table 16.16 regarding the responses of 200 students to two test items is 0.61, and $N = 200$. Therefore, the corresponding χ^2 is

$$\chi^2 = N\phi^2 = 200 \times (0.61)^2 = 200 \times 0.3721 = 74.42$$
$$\mathrm{df} = (r-1)(c-1) = 1$$

Referring to Table L of the appendix, we find that a χ^2 of 74.42 is significant beyond the 0.01 level, therefore the obtained ϕ of 0.61 is likewise significant.

In sampling from a population where no association exists (when $\phi = 0$), the distribution of ϕ should be approximately normal with a standard error of $1/\sqrt{N}$. Of course, all considerations pertaining to small frequencies apply here. Clearly, N should not be too small.

The stepwise computational procedures of ϕ will become more clear to the reader through the following examples.

Example 16.12 Out of 40 pregnant and 60 nonpregnant women, respectively, 12 and 24 were found HIV-positive. Is there a significant correlation between pregnancy and HIV-positive test?

Solution
The following steps are to be followed for the solution of the above example.

(a) The HIV-positive–negative variable and the pregnant–non-pregnant variable are presented respectively along columns and rows of a 2×2-fold contingency table

Table 16.19   Fourfold contingency table for correlating HIV test results with pregnancy

	HIV-positive	**HIV-negative**	**Total**
Pregnant	12 (a)	28 (b)	40 (a+b)
Non-pregnant	24 (c)	36 (d)	60 (c+d)
Total	36 (a+c)	64 (b+d)	100 (N)

(see Table 16.19). The HIV-positive class and the pregnant class are considered the positive classes of the respective variables and presented along the left column and the top row, respectively. The frequencies of cases are then entered in the cells according to the classes of the two variables to which each case belongs. The marginal totals are computed for the rows and columns, respectively. Note that the cells are lettered and the marginal totals are, accordingly, marked as the combination of letters.

(b) As both the variables are genuinely dichotomous, the phi coefficient of correlation is computed between them.

   The phi coefficient (ϕ) is computed directly from the above table using the cell frequencies and the marginal totals. The formula reads

$$\phi = \frac{ad-bc}{\sqrt{(a+b)(c+d)(a+c)(b+d)}} = \frac{12\times36-28\times24}{\sqrt{40\times60\times36\times64}}$$

$$= \frac{432-672}{\sqrt{5529600}} = \frac{-240}{2351.51} = -0.10$$

(c) The computed ϕ is converted to χ^2 for interpretation. The formula reads

$$\chi^2 = N\phi^2 = 100(-0.10)^2 = 100\times0.01 = 1.0$$
$$df = (r-1)(c-1) = (2-1)(2-1) = 1$$

(d) The derived χ^2 value of 1.0 is being tested for significance. Referring to Table L of the appendix, the critical value of χ^2, with df=1, at 0.05 level is 3.84 and at 0.01 level is 6.64. Since the obtained χ^2 of 1.0 is smaller than both the critical values of χ^2, it is not significant. So, the computed φ of −0.10 is also not significant. Therefore, it is reasonable to conclude that there is no significant correlation between pregnancy and HIV-positive test.

Example 16.13 Fifty students were tested with two test items. The proportions of students passed and failed on both the items are given below. Test whether there is an item-to-item correlation between the two test items.

Proportion				
		Item 2		
		Pass	**Fail**	**Total**
Item 1	Pass	0.38	0.22	0.60
	Fail	0.10	0.30	0.40
	Total	0.48	0.52	1.00

Table 16.20 Proportion of students passed and failed in two test items

		Proportion		
		Item 2		
		Pass	Fail	Total
Item 1	Pass	0.38 (a) (p_{12})	0.22 (b)	0.60 (p_1)
	Fail	0.10 (c)	0.30(d)	0.40(q_1)
	Total	0.48(p_2)	0.52(q_2)	1.00

Solution

(a)   The data are entered in Table 16.20. The cells and marginal totals are lettered.

(b)   The phi coefficient of correlation is computed directly using the cell proportions and marginal totals. The formula reads

$$\phi = \frac{ad-bc}{\sqrt{p_1 q_1 p_2 q_2}} = \frac{0.38 \times 0.30 - 0.22 \times 0.10}{\sqrt{0.60 \times 0.40 \times 0.48 \times 0.52}} = \frac{0.114 - 0.022}{\sqrt{0.059904}} = \frac{0.092}{0.245} = 0.376$$

Alternative formula for computing ϕ from the proportion data may be stated as follows:

$$\phi = \frac{p_{12} - p_1 p_2}{\sqrt{p_1 q_1 p_2 q_2}}$$

For the example of Table 16.20, $p_{12} = 0.38$ (proportion of students passing both items 1 and 2) and the phi coefficient is

$$\phi = \frac{0.38 - 0.60 \times 0.48}{\sqrt{0.60 \times 0.40 \times 0.48 \times 0.52}} = \frac{0.38 - 0.288}{\sqrt{0.059904}} = \frac{0.092}{0.245} = 0.376$$

Thus, the obtained value of ϕ in both the cases is the same, $\phi = 0.376$

(c)   The computed ϕ is converted to χ^2 for the test of significance. The formula reads

$$\chi^2 = N\phi^2$$

In the given example, $N = 50$. So, χ^2 is

$$\chi^2 = N\phi^2 = 50 \times (0.376)^2 = 50 \times 0.141376 = 7.069$$
$$df = (r-1)(c-1) = (2-1)(2-1) = 1 \times 1 = 1$$

(d)   The derived value of $\chi^2 = 7.069$ is being tested for significance. Referring to Table L of the appendix, the critical value of χ^2, with df = 1, at 0.05 level is 3.84 and at 0.01 level is 6.64. Since the obtained $\chi^2 = 7.069$ exceeds both the critical values, it is significant beyond 0.01 level. So, the computed $\phi = 0.376$ is also significant beyond 0.01 level. Therefore, $P < 0.01$. Thus, there is a significant correlation between the two test items.

16.6   The Contingency Coefficient (C)

The contingency coefficient is designated by the letter C. It is a non-parametric statistical test. The contingency coefficient is a measure of the extent of association or relation between two variables or two sets of attributes, either or both of which are divided into two or more than two classes with intervening gaps. It is uniquely useful when we have only categorical (nominal scale) information about one or both sets of these attributes. That is, it may be used when the information about the attributes consists of an unordered series of frequencies.

Like Pearson's r, Spearman's ρ and other coefficients of correlation, the contingency coefficient (C) does not have limits of ±1.0. The value of C ranges between 0 and ±1.0 but does not reach the upper limit (i.e., ±1.0) because its upper limit is dependent upon the number of categories of both the variables. For a contingency table made up of an equal number of columns (k) and rows (r), that is, when $k=r$, the upper limit of C is given by the formula $\sqrt{\dfrac{k-1}{k}}$. Thus, the upper limit of C for a 2×2 table is $\sqrt{\dfrac{1}{2}}=0.707$; for a 3×3 table is $\sqrt{\dfrac{2}{3}}=0.816$; for a 4×4 table is $\sqrt{\dfrac{3}{4}}=0.866$; and for a 5×5 table is $\sqrt{\dfrac{4}{5}}=0.894$ and so on. However, when the number of columns and rows differ in a table, like 2×3, or 3×4, etc., to calculate the upper limit of C, the smaller number of categories, either columns or rows, is taken as k.

Another important characteristic of the contingency coefficient is that, like χ^2, C does not have negative values. That means, the value of C is always positive, that is, it is either 0 or something positive other than 0 up to a maximum value of +1.0.

16.6.1 Assumptions of C

To use the contingency coefficient, it is not necessary that we be able to assume underlying continuity for the various categories used to measure either or both sets of attributes or variables. In fact, we do not even need to be able to order the categories in any particular way. The contingency coefficient, as computed from a contingency table, will have the same value regardless of how the categories are arranged in the rows and columns.

Similarly, no assumption is needed for the genuineness of the discrete or discontinuous nature of distributions of the variables. It is applicable both to variables with genuine gaps between their classes and to those which either may be resolved into continuous data on further exploration or have been dichotomised on the basis of their continuous distributions. Moreover, no assumption is needed for normality or near-normality of distributions of the variables.

However, the computation of C needs the following few assumptions.

(a) Both the variables should be divided into two or more than two categories. In other words, it needs categorical (nominal scale) information.

(b) The data are in terms of frequencies.

(c) There is a linear relationship between the variables.

16.6.2 The Relation of C to χ^2

The contingency coefficient (C) is related to chi-square (χ^2) computed from contingency tables by the very simple equation. The C is derived from χ^2 (i.e., C as a function of chi-square) by the equation

$$C=\sqrt{\frac{\chi^2}{N+\chi^2}}$$

Similarly, chi-square as a function of contingency coefficient is expressed by the equation

$$\chi^2 = \frac{NC^2}{1-C^2}$$

Since contingency coefficient can be derived from chi-square, when the latter is applied to a contingency table, any of the formulae for χ^2 given in Section 16.3 will apply to its computation.

16.6.3 Computation of Contingency Coefficient (C)

The contingency coefficient (C) can be computed in two different ways as mentioned below.

First, the degree of association between two sets of attributes or variables, whether orderable or not, and irrespective of the nature of the variables (it may be either continuous or discrete) or of the underlying distribution of the attribute (the population distribution may be normal or any other shape), may be found from a contingency table of the frequencies by

$$C = \sqrt{\frac{\chi^2}{N+\chi^2}}$$

where χ^2 is computed by the method presented earlier (Section 16.3). In other words, in order to compute C, we first compute the value of χ^2 from the contingency table by the formula $\chi^2 = \sum \frac{(f_o - f_e)^2}{f_e}$ and then insert that value of χ^2 into the above noted formula to get C. The determination of the expected frequencies for each cell is done by the usual formula for the contingency tables discussed in Section 16.3 while computing χ^2 from the contingency tables. That is, the f_e values of a particular cell can be found out by multiplying two marginal totals (i.e., row total and column total) common to that cell and then dividing this product by the N.

Second, we can compute C directly from the contingency table by the following formula:

$$C = \sqrt{1 - \frac{N}{S}}$$

where $S = \sum \frac{f_o^2}{f_e}$

In other words, in order to compute C (without the help of χ^2), we first compute the *sum of quotient* (S) by the immediate above formula and then insert that value of S into the above noted formula to get C.

Table 16.21 shows a 3×3 table illustrating the responses of 150 students belonging to three religious groups to a particular question related to their attitude by providing three alternative responses—yes, no and undecided. In other words, this table illustrates the relationship between religious group membership and attitude as follows:

In Table 16.21, there are, 3 (rows)×3 (columns)=9 cells. First of all, we have to find out the expected frequencies (f_e) of each of the 9 cells, respectively, cells 1 through 9, by the usual formula for the contingency tables. The values of the expected frequencies (f_e) for each of the 9 cells (cells 1 through 9, row-wise) of Table 16.21 are, respectively,

Table 16.21 Contingency table for computing C between religious group membership and attitudes

		Responses (Attitudes)			Total
		Yes	No	Undecided	
Religious groups	Hindu	10 (20)	25 (20)	15 (10)	50
	Muslim	20 (18)	20 (18)	5 (9)	45
	Christian	30 (22)	15 (22)	10 (11)	55
	Total	60	60	30	150(N)

$$f_e \text{ for cell } 1 = \frac{50 \times 60}{150} = 20; \quad f_e \text{ for cell } 2 = \frac{50 \times 60}{150} = 20$$

$$f_e \text{ for cell } 3 = \frac{50 \times 30}{150} = 10; \quad f_e \text{ for cell } 4 = \frac{45 \times 60}{150} = 18$$

$$f_e \text{ for cell } 5 = \frac{45 \times 60}{150} = 18; \quad f_e \text{ for cell } 6 = \frac{45 \times 30}{150} = 9$$

$$f_e \text{ for cell } 7 = \frac{55 \times 60}{150} = 22; \quad f_e \text{ for cell } 8 = \frac{55 \times 60}{150} = 22$$

$$f_e \text{ for cell } 9 = \frac{55 \times 30}{150} = 11$$

These above calculated values of f_e are shown within parentheses in the appropriate cells in Table 16.21, which also shows the original observed frequencies (f_o). The readers may note that the marginal row and column totals of the expected frequencies are exactly equal to those of the observed frequencies.

The computation of χ^2 for the data in Table 16.21 is straightforward:

$$\chi^2 = \Sigma \frac{(f_o - f_e)^2}{f_e} = \frac{(10-20)^2}{20} + \frac{(25-20)^2}{20} + \frac{(15-10)^2}{10} + \frac{(20-18)^2}{18} + \frac{(20-18)^2}{18}$$

$$+ \frac{(5-9)^2}{9} + \frac{(30-22)^2}{22} + \frac{(15-22)^2}{22} + \frac{(10-11)^2}{11}$$

$$= 5.00 + 1.25 + 2.50 + 0.22 + 0.22 + 1.78 + 2.91 + 2.23 + 0.09 = 16.20$$

Thus, the computed value of $\chi^2 = 16.20$ and in the given data $N = 150$. Then the value of C is computed using formula

$$C = \sqrt{\frac{\chi^2}{N + \chi^2}} = \sqrt{\frac{16.20}{150 + 16.20}} = \sqrt{\frac{16.20}{166.20}} = 0.312$$

Alternatively, we may compute C in terms of the *sum of quotient* (S). The S is computed using the f_o and f_e values of each cell as follows:

$$S = \Sigma \frac{(f_o)^2}{f_e} = \frac{(10)^2}{20} + \frac{(25)^2}{20} + \frac{(15)^2}{10} + \frac{(20)^2}{18} + \frac{(20)^2}{18} + \frac{(5)^2}{9} + \frac{(30)^2}{22} + \frac{(15)^2}{22} + \frac{(10)^2}{11}$$

$$= 5.00 + 31.25 + 22.50 + 22.22 + 22.22 + 2.78 + 40.91 + 10.23 + 9.09 = 166.20$$

Thus, the computed value of $S=166.20$ and in the given data $N=150$. Then the value of C is computed using formula

$$C = \sqrt{1 - \frac{N}{S}} = \sqrt{1 - \frac{150}{166.20}} = \sqrt{1 - 0.9025} = \sqrt{0.0975} = 0.312$$

Thus, the value of C computed by both the above formulae is the same, that is, $C=0.312$.

16.6.4   Test of Significance of C

A test of the null hypothesis (H_0) proposing no correlation between the variables can be made through C's relationship to χ^2. In other words, the obtained value of C can be tested for its significance in terms of χ^2. If χ^2 is significant in a contingency table, the corresponding C is significant. The procedure, then, is to derive the corresponding χ^2 from the obtained C by means of formula

$$\chi^2 = \frac{NC^2}{1 - C^2}; \quad df = (r-1)(c-1)$$

Then, the computed χ^2 is compared with the critical values of χ^2 for 0.05 and 0.01 levels of significance (see Table L of the appendix). The computed χ^2 and the C may be considered significant at or below that level whose critical χ^2 value equals or falls below the computed value of $\chi^2 (p < \alpha)$.

Let us take an example. The computed C for the problem given in Table 16.21 is 0.312 and $N=150$. Now, we have to test whether this C value of 0.312 is significant. For this purpose, the computed value of C is converted to χ^2 as follows:

$$\chi^2 = \frac{NC^2}{1 - C^2} = \frac{150 \times (0.312)^2}{1 - (0.312)^2} = \frac{14.6016}{0.9027} = 16.18$$

At this point, the reader may note that the derived value of χ^2 is 16.18, whereas the χ^2 value directly computed from the data given in Table 16.21 is 16.20. This difference of 0.02 is very negligible and it is due to the rounding up the decimal points. Therefore, the derived value of χ^2 will be taken for testing its significance

$$\chi^2 = 16.18; \quad df = (r-)(c-1) = (3-1)(3-1) = 4$$

Referring to Table L in the appendix, the critical value of χ^2, with df=4, at 0.05 level is 9.49 and at 0.01 level is 13.28. Since the obtained value of $\chi^2 = 16.18$ exceeds both the critical values, it is significant beyond 0.01 level of significance, and accordingly the obtained C of 0.312 is also significant beyond 0.01 level. Therefore, we may conclude that there is a significant relationship between religious group membership and attitudes.

16.6.5   Summary of Procedures

The following are the steps in the use of the contingency coefficient:

(i)   Arrange the observed frequencies in a $r \times c$ contingency table like Table 16.21, where r=the number of categories on which one variable is scored row-wise and c=the number of categories on which the other variable is scored column-wise.

(ii)   Determine the expected frequencies under H_0 for each cell by multiplying the two marginal totals common to that cell and then dividing this product by N, the total number of cases.

(iii)   Using the appropriate formula, compute the value of χ^2 for the data.

(iv)   With this value of χ^2, compute the value of C using the conversion formula discussed earlier in this section or compute the value of C directly from the value of S as noted earlier.

(v)   To test whether the obtained value of C indicates that there is an association between the two variables in the population sampled, determine the associated probability under H_0 of a value as large as the obtained χ^2 with df$=(r-1)(c-1)$ by referring to Table L in the appendix. If that probability is equal to or less than α, reject H_0 in favour of H_1.

16.6.6   Limitations of the Contingency Coefficient

The wide applicability and relatively easy computation of C may seem to make it an ideal all-round measure of association. This is not the case because of several limitations or deficiencies of this statistic. The following are some of the major limitations of the contingency coefficient:

(i)   The value of C is always positive and it ranges between 0 and +1.0, but it cannot attain the upper limit or unity. The upper limit for the contingency coefficient is a function of the number of categories. When $k=r$, the upper limit for C, that is, the C which would occur for two perfectly correlated variables, is $\sqrt{\dfrac{k-1}{k}}$. This is the first limitation of C. k stands for columns.

(ii)   The fact that the upper limit of C depends on the sizes of k and r creates the second limitation of C. For instance, the upper limit of C for a 2×2 table is $\sqrt{\dfrac{1}{2}}=0.707$; for a 3×3 table is $\sqrt{\dfrac{2}{3}}=0.816$ and so on. Two contingency coefficients are not comparable unless they are yielded by contingency tables of the same size.

(iii)   A third limitation of C is that the data must be amenable to the computation of χ^2 before C may appropriately be used. The reader will remember that the χ^2 test can properly be used only if fewer than 20% of the cells have an expected frequency of less than 5, and no cell has an expected frequency of less than 1.

(iv)   A fourth limitation of C is that it is not directly comparable to any other measure of correlation, for example, Pearson's r, Spearman's ρ or the Kendall's τ.

In spite of the above limitations, the contingency coefficient is an extremely useful measure of association between two variables because of its wide applicability. The contingency coefficient makes no assumptions about the shape of the population of scores, it does not require underlying continuity in the variables under analysis, and it requires only nominal measurement of the variables. Because of this freedom from assumptions and requirements, C may often be used to indicate the degree of relation between two sets of scores to which none of the other measures of association which we have presented is applicable.

16.6.7   Power of Contingency Coefficient

Because of its nature and its limitations, we should not expect the contingency coefficient to be very powerful in detecting a relation in the population. However, its ease of computation and its complete freedom from restrictive assumptions recommend its use where other measures of correlation may be inapplicable. Because C is a function of χ^2, its limiting power distribution, like that of χ^2, tends to 1 as N becomes large (Cochran, 1952).

The stepwise computational procedures of C will become more clear to the reader through the following example.

Example 16.14 Below are given the responses of three groups on an interest inventory. Compute the contingency coefficient and test whether there is a significant relationship between marital status and interest held.

	Yes	?	No	Total
Single	20	10	10	40
Married	60	10	30	100
Divorced	10	20	30	60
Total	90	40	70	200 (N)

Solution

The following steps are to be followed for the solution of the above problem:

(a) The data are arranged in a 3×3-fold contingency table as shown in Table 16.22.

(b) After the data are entered in a contingency table, the expected frequencies of different cells (cells 1 through 9, row-wise) of Table 16.22 are computed as follows by the usual formula for the contingency tables:

$$f_e \text{ for Cell 1} = \frac{40 \times 90}{200} = 18; \quad f_e \text{ for Cell 2} = \frac{40 \times 40}{200} = 8$$

$$f_e \text{ for Cell 3} = \frac{40 \times 70}{200} = 14; \quad f_e \text{ for Cell 4} = \frac{100 \times 90}{200} = 45$$

$$f_e \text{ for Cell 5} = \frac{100 \times 40}{200} = 20; \quad f_e \text{ for Cell 6} = \frac{100 \times 70}{200} = 35$$

$$f_e \text{ for Cell 7} = \frac{60 \times 90}{200} = 27; \quad f_e \text{ for Cell 8} = \frac{60 \times 40}{200} = 12$$

$$f_e \text{ for Cell 9} = \frac{60 \times 70}{200} = 21$$

Table 16.22 Table for computing contingency coefficient between marital status and interest held

	Yes	?	No	Total
Single	20 (18)	10 (8)	10 (14)	40
Married	60 (45)	10 (20)	30 (35)	100
Divorced	10 (27)	20 (12)	30 (21)	60
Total	90	40	70	200 (N)

(c) The computed value of f_e are entered within parentheses in the appropriate cells of Table 16.22. Then the χ^2 is computed by the formula

$$\chi^2 = \sum \frac{(f_o - f_e)^2}{f_e} = \frac{(20-18)^2}{18} + \frac{(10-8)^2}{8} + \frac{(10-14)^2}{14} + \frac{(60-45)^2}{45}$$

$$+ \frac{(10-20)^2}{20} + \frac{(30-35)^2}{35} + \frac{(10-27)^2}{27} + \frac{(20-12)^2}{12} + \frac{(30-21)^2}{21}$$

$$= 0.22 + 0.50 + 1.14 + 5.00 + 5.00 + 0.71 + 10.70 + 5.33 + 3.86 = 32.46$$

Alternatively, the sum of the quotients (S) is computed by the formula

$$S = \sum \frac{(f_o)^2}{f_e} = \frac{(20)^2}{18} + \frac{(10)^2}{8} + \frac{(10)^2}{14} + \frac{(60)^2}{45} + \frac{(10)^2}{20} + \frac{(30)^2}{35} + \frac{(10)^2}{27} + \frac{(20)^2}{12} + \frac{(30)^2}{21}$$

$$= 22.22 + 12.50 + 7.14 + 80.00 + 5.00 + 25.71 + 3.70 + 33.33 + 42.86 = 232.46$$

(d) The statistic C is then computed using either the computed values of χ^2 or S as follows. In the given example N is 200.

Computation of C using χ^2 values and N:

$$C = \sqrt{\frac{\chi^2}{N + \chi^2}} = \sqrt{\frac{32.46}{200 + 32.46}} = \sqrt{\frac{32.46}{232.46}} = 0.374$$

Alternatively, computation of C using values of S and N:

$$C = \sqrt{1 - \frac{N}{S}} = \sqrt{1 - \frac{200}{232.46}} = \sqrt{1 - 0.86} = 0.374$$

Thus, the computed value of C is the same in both the formulae.

(e) C is converted to χ^2 for testing its significance. The formula reads

$$\chi^2 = \frac{NC^2}{1 - C^2} = \frac{200(0.374)^2}{1 - (0.374)^2} = \frac{27.9752}{0.860124} = 32.48$$

The reader may note it here that there is a difference of 0.02 between the computed values and converted values of χ^2, which may be due to the rounding up decimal points. However, this difference is very negligible and we take the converted value of $\chi^2 = 32.48$ for testing its significance

$$df = (r-1)(c-1) = (3-1)(3-1) = 4$$

Referring to Table L in the appendix, the critical value of χ^2, with df=4, at 0.05 level is 9.49 and at 0.01 level is 13.28. Since the obtained value of $\chi^2 = 32.48$ exceeds both the critical values, it is significant beyond 0.01 level of significance, and accordingly the obtained C of 0.374 is also significant beyond 0.01 level of significance ($p < 0.01$). The significance of C indicates that there is a significant relationship between marital status and interest held.

16.7 Kendall's Rank Correlation Coefficient (τ)

Kendall's rank correlation coefficient, τ (*tau*), is a non-parametric *statistical test*. It is the counterpart of Pearson's r for *linear correlation* between two variables. τ (*tau*) is computed more rapidly and is applicable to smaller samples, both normal and non-normal distributions, and ordinal (ranked) variables as well as such interval and ratio variables whose scores have been converted into ranks. In other words, Kendall's *tau* is suitable as a measure of correlation with the same sort of data for which Spearman's *rho* is useful. That is, if at least ordinal measurement of both the X and Y variables has been achieved so that every subject can be assigned a rank on both X and Y, then τ will give a measure of the degree of association or correlation between the two sets of ranks.

The value of τ (*tau*) ranges from –1.00 to +1.00, through 0.00, a value of 0.00 indicating the absence of correlation. For large samples, *tau* has a symmetric and near-normal sampling distribution. The sampling distribution of τ (*tau*) under the null hypothesis (H_0) is known, and therefore, τ, like ρ (rho), is subject to tests of significance.

16.7.1   Assumptions of tau (τ)

Being a non-parametric statistic, *tau* (τ) requires a few number of assumptions to be fulfilled for its use. The following are some of the important assumptions of τ:

(a) The observations must be independent. It implies two things—that the selection of samples from the population should be random, and that the assignment of scores to the performances of the samples should be unbiased and impartial.

(b) There is a linear correlation between the variables to be correlated.

(c) The data should be in terms of ordinal scale of measurement. In other words, the magnitude of scores of each variable should be expressed in ranks, either in ascending or descending order.

(d) The paired scores or ranks for each individual occur at random and independent of all other paired scores or ranks in the sample.

16.7.2   Computational Procedures for Kendall's Tau (τ)

The computation of Kendall's *tau* is very simple and rapid. However, the computational procedures of *tau* vary depending upon the nature of data given, whether the given data are in terms of original scores or in ranks and whether there are tied scores, and hence, tied ranks or not. These procedures are discussed separately in the following sections.

16.7.2.1   *Computation of Tau (τ) from Test Scores or from Ranks*

If the scores of the individuals of the sample have already been ranked with respect to each of the variables, those ranks are directly used in computing τ. Otherwise, ranks are first assigned in an ascending or descending order of magnitude to the scores of each variable separately from 1 to N. However, the order of assignment of ranks to the scores of both the variables should be the same.

After getting the paired ranks, R_1 and R_2, on both the variables, X and Y, for each of the individuals of the sample, the ranks (R_1) of the individuals on the first variable are serially arranged in an ascending order along a column or along a row. In other words, we arrange the order of individuals in such a way so that R_1 ranks appear in natural order (i.e., 1, 2, . . . , N). Then each such R_1 rank is paired in the adjoining column or row with the rank (R_2) of the other variable in the same individual.

Starting from the top of the column or extreme left of the row of the paired R_2 ranks, each R_2 rank is, in turn, taken as the pivotal rank and compared with all subsequent R_2 ranks in that column or row, as the case may be. Each pair comparison is assigned either a score of +1, 0 or –1 according as the pivotal rank is lower than, equal to or higher than the particular subsequent rank. In other words, when a pair comparison is in its natural order (e.g., 2 and 3, 2 and 4, 3 and 4, etc), it is assigned a score of +1; when it is in an inverse order (e.g., 2 and 1, 3 and 2, 4 and 3, etc.), it is assigned a score of –1 and when the paired ranks are equal or tied, it is assigned a score of 0. The algebraic sum of the +1 and –1 scores of all pairs is denoted as S (a measure of disarray).

Kendall's coefficient of rank correlation, τ, is defined as the obtained value of S divided by its maximum possible value, that is,

$$\tau = \frac{\text{Obtained value of } S}{\text{Maximum possible value of } S} = \frac{\text{Actual total of } S}{\text{Maximum possible total of } S}$$

The maximum possible value of S would occur in the case of perfect agreement between R_1 ranks and R_2 ranks, or between the ranks of variable X and the ranks of variable Y. In other words, maximum value of S would have been yielded only when the ranks of variable X (i.e., R_1 ranks) were arranged in their natural order, every pair of Y ranks (i.e., R_2 ranks) would also be in the correct order and thus every pair would receive a score of +1.

In general, the maximum possible value of S would be N things taken two at a time or $\binom{N}{2}$,

which can be expressed as $\frac{1}{2}N(N-1)$. Thus, this expression may be the denominator of the formula for τ. For the numerator, let us denote the observed sum of the +1 and –1 scores for all pairs as S. Then the formula for τ becomes

$$\tau = \frac{S}{\frac{1}{2}N(N-1)} = \frac{2S}{N(N-1)}$$

where N = the number of objects or individuals ranked on both X and Y variables. Thus, τ is a sort of coefficient of disarray.

Suppose we ask two judges—judge X and judge Y—to rank five paintings for their beauty. We represent the five paintings as a, b, c, d and e. The obtained rankings are these

Paintings	a	b	c	d	e
Judge X	4	5	2	3	1
Judge Y	3	5	1	4	2

If we arrange the order of the paintings so that Judge X's ranks appear in natural order (i.e., 1, 2, ..., N), we get

Paintings	e	c	d	a	b
Judge X	1	2	3	4	5
Judge Y	2	1	4	3	5

We are now in a position to determine the degree of correspondence between the judgements of X and Y. Judge X's rankings being in their natural order, we proceed to determine how many pairs of ranks in judge Y's set are in their natural order with respect to each other.

Let us first start with the judge Y's rank 2, which is the extreme left of the row, as the pivotal rank that is compared with four subsequent Y's ranks (i.e., 1, 4, 3 and 5) one after the other.

The first pair, 2 and 1, is not in 'natural' order: 2 precedes 1. Therefore, we assign this pair a score of –1. The second pair, 2 and 4, has the correct order: 2 precedes 4. Since this order is natural, we assign a score of +1 to this pair. Ranks 2 and 3 constitute the third pair. This pair is also in the correct order, so it also earns a score of +1. Now, the fourth pair consists of ranks 2 and 5. These ranks are in natural order: 2 precedes 5. Therefore, we assign a score of +1 to this pair. For all pairs which include the rank 2 as the pivotal rank, we total the scores:

$$(-1)+(+1)+(+1)+(+1)=+2$$

Likewise, each rank of judge Y's set is taken as the pivotal rank and compared with all subsequent Y's ranks in that row. Now, we consider all possible pairs of ranks which include rank 1 as the pivotal rank (which is the rank second from the left in judge Y's set) and one succeeding rank. There are three such pairs which include ranks 1 and 4, 1 and 3 and 1 and 5. All these three pairs are in natural order: 1 precedes 4, 3 and 5 in the respective pairs. Therefore, we assign a score of +1 to each of the three pairs. The total of these scores is

$$(+1)+(+1)+(+1)=+3$$

Now, we consider all possible pairs of ranks that include rank 4 (which is the rank third from the left in judge Y's set) as the pivotal rank and one succeeding rank. One such pair is 4 and 3; the two ranks of the pair are not in the natural order, so the score for this pair is –1. Another pair is 4 and 5; the two ranks of the pair are in the natural order: 4 precedes 5, so a score of +1 is assigned to this pair. The total of these scores is

$$(-1)+(+1)=0$$

At last we consider rank 3 (which is the rank fourth from the left in judge Y's set) as the pivotal rank and succeeding rank. There is only one pair that consists ranks 3 and 5. The two ranks of this pair are in the correct order or natural order: 3 precedes 5; therefore, this pair receives a score of +1.

The total of all the scores we have assigned to all the paired comparisons is

$$(+2)+(+3)+(0)+(+1)=+6$$

Thus, the obtained value of S is 6; S=6.

In the given example N=5. So, the maximum possible value of S will be

$$\binom{N}{2}=\tfrac{1}{2}N(N-1)=\tfrac{1}{2}\times 5\,(5-1)=10$$

For the given example, Kendall's *tau* (τ) is

$$\tau=\frac{S}{\tfrac{1}{2}\,N(N-1)}=\frac{6}{\tfrac{1}{2}\times 5(5-1)}=\frac{6}{10}=0.60$$

However, the calculation of S may be shortened considerably from the method shown above in the discussion of the logic of the measure.

In our given example, when the ranks of judge X were in the natural order, the corresponding ranks of judge Y were in this order.

Judge Y	2	1	4	3	5

We can determine the value of S by starting with the first number on the left and counting the number of ranks to its right which are larger. We then subtract from this the number of ranks to its right which are smaller. If we do this for all ranks and then sum the results, we obtain S.

Thus, for the above set of Y ranks, to the right of rank 2 are the ranks 4, 3 and 5 which are larger and rank 1 which is smaller. Rank 2 thus contributes $(+3-1)=+2$ to S. For rank 1, 3 ranks (e.g., 4, 3 and 5) to its right which are larger and no rank which is smaller. Rank 1 thus contributes $(+3-0)=+3$ to S. For rank 4, one rank to its right is smaller and one rank is larger, so rank 4 contributes $(-1+1)=0$ to S. For rank 3, one rank to its right is larger and no rank is smaller, so rank 3 contributes $(+1-0)=+1$ to S. These contributions total

$$(+2)+(+3)+(0)+(+1)=+6=S.$$

Knowing S, we may use the above formula to compute the value of τ between the ranks assigned by the two judges

$$\tau = \frac{S}{\frac{1}{2}N(N-1)} = \frac{6}{\frac{1}{2} \times 5(5-1)} = \frac{+6}{10} = +0.60$$

16.7.2.2 Computation of Tau (τ) from Tied Observations

When two or more observations on either the X or the Y variables are tied, we turn to our usual procedure in ranking tied scores: The tied observations are given the average of the ranks they would have received if there were no ties.

The effect of ties is to change the denominator of our formula for τ. In case of ties, the formula for τ becomes

$$\tau = \frac{S}{\sqrt{\frac{1}{2}N(N-1)-T_x}\sqrt{\frac{1}{2}N(N-1)-T_y}}$$

where

$T_x=\frac{1}{2}\sum t(t-1)$, t being the number of tied observations in each group of ties on the X variable.

$T_y=\frac{1}{2}\sum t(t-1)$, t being the number of tied observations in each group of ties on the Y variable.

In the above formula, the terms T_x and T_y are the correction terms for ties. If there are no ties among the scores of either X or Y variables, then $T_x=0$ or $T_y=0$.

The reader should keep it in mind that in the tied ranks either in X or Y variables or in both the computation of S value is done in the usual way with the following restrictions.

A comparison of two tied ranks on Y variable receives a score of 0. If ties occur on the X variable, a comparison of the corresponding paired Y values will also receive a score of 0, regardless of whether the paired Y ranks are tied. Let us consider the following example with no ties on X variable and one tied pair on Y variable.

X	1	2	3	4	5	6
Y	2	3	4.5	4.5	1	6

On comparing each rank on Y with every other rank and assigning a $+1$ for a pair in their natural order, a -1 for a pair in an inverse order, and a 0 for a tie, we obtain:

$$+1, +1, +1, -1, +1, +1, +1, -1, +1, 0, -1, +1, -1, +1, +1 \text{ and } S=6$$

Consider another example with tied ranks on both X and Y variables

X	1.5	1.5	3	5	5	5
Y	2	3	4.5	4.5	1	6

In this above example, the comparison on Y of 2 with 3 receives a score of 0, because the order of the first two paired ranks on X is arbitrary. Similarly, comparisons on Y involving the last three ranks will receive scores of 0, because of the triplet of ties on X. Thus, in the above example, the scores are, 0, +1, +1, −1, +1, +1, +1, −1, +1, 0, −1, +1, 0, 0, 0 and $S=4$. To calculate *tau* with tied ranks, S is calculated in the manner described above, and the formula incorporating the correction terms mentioned earlier is applied.

To illustrate, consider the example immediately above with ties on both X and Y variables. Here, $T_x = \frac{1}{2}[2(2-1)+3(3-1)] = 4$; also $T_y = \frac{1}{2}[2(2-1)] = 1$. In this example $N=6$, $S=4$ and *tau* is as follows:

$$\tau = \frac{S}{\sqrt{\frac{1}{2}N(N-1)-T_x}\sqrt{\frac{1}{2}N(N-1)-T_y}} = \frac{S}{\sqrt{\frac{1}{2}\times 6(6-1)-4}\sqrt{\frac{1}{2}\times 6(6-1)-1}}$$

$$= \frac{4}{\sqrt{11\times 14}} = \frac{4}{12.41} = 0.32$$

16.7.3   Testing the Significance of Kendall's tau (τ)

If a random sample is drawn from some population in which X and Y variables are unrelated, and the members of the sample are ranked on X and Y, then for any given order of the X ranks, any one possible order of the Y ranks is just as likely to occur as any other possible order of the Y ranks. Suppose we order the X ranks in natural order, that is, 1, 2, 3, …, N. For this order of the X ranks, all the N factorial (i.e., $N!$) possible orders of the Y ranks are equally probable under H_0. Therefore, any particular order of the Y ranks has probability of occurrence under H_0 of $1/N!$. For each of the $N!$ possible rankings of Y variable, there will be associated a value of τ. These possible values of τ will range from −1.0 to +1.0, and they can be cast in a frequency distribution. For instance, for $N=4$, there are $4!=(4\times 3\times 2\times 1)=24$ possible arrangements of the Y ranks and each has an associated value of τ.

The sampling distributions of τ and S are identical in a probability sense. Inasmuch as τ is a function of S, either might be tabled. It is more convenient to tabulate S. Like τ, the sampling distribution of S is obtained by considering the N factorial arrangements of Y in relation to X. A value of S may be determined for each of the $N!$ arrangements. The distribution of these N factorial values is the sampling distribution of S. This distribution is symmetrical. Frequencies taper off systematically from the maximum value towards the tails. The distribution of S rapidly approaches the normal form. For $N \geq 10$, the normal approximation to the exact distribution is very close. The exact sampling distribution of S for $N=4-10$ are given by Kendall (1970).

In testing the significance of the association between paired ranks, it is more convenient to apply a test directly to S rather than to τ. For small samples ($N \leq 10$), the significance of an observed relation between two samples of ranks may be determined by simply finding the value of S and then referring to Table O (see in the appendix) to determine the probability (one-tailed) associated with that value of S. If the $p \leq \alpha$, H_0 may be rejected. For example, suppose $N=8$ and $S=16$. Table O shows that an $S \geq 16$ for $N=8$ has probability of occurrence under H_0 of $p=0.031$. Thus, the H_0 is rejected at $\alpha=0.05$ level of significance ($p<0.05$). This shows that there is significant correlation between the ranking of two variables, X and Y.

When N is larger than 10 ($N>10$), τ may be considered to be normally distributed with

$$\text{Mean} = \mu_\tau = 0$$

$$\text{and Standard deviation} = \sigma_\tau = \sqrt{\frac{2(2N+5)}{9N(N-1)}}$$

That is, $z = \dfrac{\tau - \mu_\tau}{\sigma_\tau} = \dfrac{\tau}{\sigma_\tau}$ is approximately normally distributed with zero mean and unit variance. Thus, the probability associated with the occurrence under H_0 of any value as extreme
as an observed τ may be determined by computing the value of z as defined by the immediate
above formula and then determining the significance of that z by reference to Table A of the
appendix. As usual, the z values of 1.96 and 2.58 are required for significance at the 0.05 and 0.01
level, respectively, for a nondirectional test.

Suppose, we have already determined that among 12 students the correlation between
mechanical knowledge and arithmetic reasoning is $\tau=0.67$. If we assume these 12 students to
be a random sample from some population, we may test whether these two variables are associated in that population by using the formula that reads

$$z = \frac{\tau}{\sigma_\tau} ; \quad \sigma_\tau = \sqrt{\frac{2(2N+5)}{9N(N-1)}}$$

In the given example, $N=12$ and $\tau=0.67$. Substituting the values, σ_τ becomes

$$\sigma_\tau = \sqrt{\frac{2(2 \times 12+5)}{9 \times 12(12-1)}} = \sqrt{\frac{58}{1188}} = 0.221$$

$$z = \frac{\tau}{\sigma_\tau} = \frac{0.67}{0.221} = 3.03$$

Since the obtained value of $z=3.03$ is greater than both the critical values of $z_{0.05}=1.96$ and
$z_{0.01}=2.58$, it is significant beyond 0.01 level of significance ($p<0.01$).

Alternatively, by referring to Table A of the appendix, we see hat $z \geq 3.03$ has probability of
occurrence under H_0 of $p=0.0012$. Since this associated probability is less than $\alpha=0.01$, it is significant. Thus, we could reject H_0 beyond 0.01 level of significance and conclude that the two
variables are significantly associated or correlated in the population from which this sample
was drawn.

16.7.4   Comparison of ρ (rho) and τ (tau)

The coefficients ρ and τ, although used for the same purpose, are having different underlying
scales and numerically they are not directly comparable to each other. If ρ and τ are calculated
on the same data, the absolute value of ρ will usually be larger than the corresponding value
of τ. Values of ρ and τ are highly correlated in samples from a bivariate normal population. For
practical purposes, the correlation between the two statistics, that is, ρ and τ, can be regarded
as close to 1.0.

On considering the N factorial (i.e., $N!$) arrangements of one set of ranks in relation to
another, the distribution of both ρ and τ is symmetrical and tends to be in normal form for
large N. The distribution of τ tends to approach the normal form more rapidly than that of ρ.
The exact distributions are known for higher values of τ than of ρ. In general, τ as a statistic is
more amenable to mathematical manipulation than ρ. Problems resulting from tied scores are

more rapidly solved. Also, the measure of disarray S, used in the definition of τ, seems to have a degree of generality about it that does not characterise Σd^2. Thus, S has a number of applications apart from its use in correlation.

Both coefficients, ρ and τ, utilise the same amount of information in the data, and thus both have the same power to detect the existence of association in the population. That is, the sampling distributions of ρ and τ are such that with a given set of data, both will reject the null hypothesis (H_0: that the variables are unrelated in the population) at the same level of significance. In other words, even though ρ and τ are numerically different for the same set of data, their sampling distributions are such that with the same data, H_0 would be rejected at the same level of significance by the significance tests associated with both measures.

One advantage of τ over ρ is that τ can be generalised to a partial correlation coefficient.

16.7.5   Power Efficiency

Spearman's ρ and Kendall's τ are equally powerful in rejecting H_0 inasmuch as they make equivalent use of the information in the data.

When used on data to which Pearson's r is properly applicable, both τ and ρ have efficiency of 91%. That is, τ is approximately as sensitive a test of the existence of association between two variables in a bivariate normal population with a sample of 100 cases as is the Pearson's r with 91 cases (Moran, 1951).

16.7.6   Summary of Procedures

The following are the steps in the use of the Kendall rank correlation coefficient (τ).

1. Rank the observations on the X variable from 1 to N. Rank the observations on the Y variable from 1 to N, separately. The order of assigning ranks to the scores in both the variables should be the same, that is, either in ascending order or in descending order.

2. Arrange the list of N subjects so that the X ranks of the subjects are in their natural order, that is, $1, 2, 3, \ldots, N$.

3. Observe the Y ranks in the order in which they occur when the X ranks are in natural order. Determine the value of S for this order of the Y ranks.

4. If there are no ties among either the X or the Y observations, use formula: $\tau = \dfrac{S}{\frac{1}{2}N(N-1)} = \dfrac{2S}{N(N-1)}$ in computing the value of τ. If there are ties, use the following formula for computing the value of τ:

$$\tau = \frac{S}{\sqrt{\frac{1}{2}N(N-1) - T_x}\sqrt{\frac{1}{2}N(N-1) - T_y}}$$

5. Testing the significance of the obtained τ depends on the size of the sample (N). For $N \leq 10$, Table O in the appendix shows the associated probability (one-tailed) of a value as large as an observed S. If this probability (p) yielded by the appropriate method is equal to or less than α, then H_0 may be rejected in favour of H_1, indicating that there is a significant correlation between the two variables.

For $N > 10$, we may compute the value of z associated with τ by using the formula $z = \dfrac{\tau}{\sigma_\tau}$, where σ_τ is computed by the formula, $\sigma_\tau = \sqrt{\dfrac{2(2N+5)}{9N(N-1)}}$. The obtained value of z may be directly

Table 16.23 Assigning ranks to respiratory and pulse rates

Individual's Number	Respiratory Rate		Pulse Rate	
	Score (X)	Rank (R_1)	Score (Y)	Rank (R_2)
1	15	5	72	4
2	16	6	71	3
3	12	2	70	2
4	21	10	82	10
5	17	7	75	6
6	13	3	68	1
7	18	8	77	7
8	11	1	79	8
9	14	4	74	5
10	20	9	80	9

tested for significance or we may refer it to Table A of the appendix. If the obtained value of z is at least 1.96 or 2.58, then it is significant at 0.05 or 0.01 levels of significance, respectively or we may refer to Table A of the appendix for testing the significance of the obtained z. Table A shows the associated probability of a value as large as an observed z. If the probability (p) yielded by the appropriate method is equal to or less than α, H_0 may be rejected in favour of H_1, which indicates the existence of a significant correlation between two sets of ranks.

The stepwise computational procedures of τ will become more clear to the readers through the following examples.

Example 16.15 Compute *tau* between the pulse rate and the respiratory rate per minute of 10 subjects. Test whether there is a significant correlation between the two variables.

Individuals	1	2	3	4	5	6	7	8	9	10
Respiratory rate	15	16	12	21	17	13	18	11	14	20
Pulse rate	72	71	70	82	75	68	77	79	74	80

Solution

The following steps are to be followed for the solution of the above problem.

(a) Ranks are assigned separately in ascending order (i.e., lowest score in the series was assigned rank 1) to the scores of the two variables (see Table 16.23). Let us designate the respiratory rate as variable X and its ranks are denoted by R_1, similarly, the pulse rate as Y variable and its ranks by R_2.

(b) There are no tied scores in both the variables. The R_1 ranks (i.e., X ranks) are serially arranged in their natural order (or ascending order), e.g., 1, 2, 3, ..., N, in column 2 of Table 16.24, and then pairing each R_1 with the rank R_2 (i.e., Y ranks) of the same individual.

Table 16.24   Count of ranks for *S* between respiratory and pulse rates

Individual's Number	R_1	R_2	Count of Subsequent Ranks (*S*)
8	1	8	$(-1)+(-1)+(-1)+(-1)+(-1)+(-1)+(-1)+(+1)+(+1)=-5$
3	2	2	$(-1)+(+1)+(+1)+(+1)+(+1)+(+1)+(+1)+(+1)=+6$
6	3	1	$(+1)+(+1)+(+1)+(+1)+(+1)+(+1)+(+1)=+7$
9	4	5	$(-1)+(-1)+(+1)+(+1)+(+1)+(+1)=+2$
1	5	4	$(-1)+(+1)+(+1)+(+1)+(+1)=+3$
2	6	3	$(+1)+(+1)+(+1)+(+1)=+4$
5	7	6	$(+1)+(+1)+(+1)=+3$
7	8	7	$(+1)+(+1)=+2$
10	9	9	$+1=+1$
4	10	10	
Total: *N*=10			*S*=23

(c)   Starting from the top of the column of paired ranks (R_2), each of the latter is taken in turn as the pivotal rank and compared with all subsequent R_2 ranks of that column. Each subsequent R_2 rank is counted or scored as +1, 0 or –1 according to whether it is higher than, equal to (tied with) or lower than the pivotal rank under consideration. The scores of all the subsequent ranks for each pivotal R_2 rank are entered against it as noted in Table 16.24, and the sum of the +1 and –1 scores is treated as the contribution to *S* by that particular pivotal rank. Thus, for the first pivotal R_2 rank 8, the subsequent lower ranks 2, 1, 5, 4, 3, 6 and 7 are counted or scored as –1 each, and each of the subsequent higher ranks 9 and 10 is scored as +1; so, the sum of the +1 and –1 scores for the first pivotal R_2 rank 8 is –5, which is its contribution to S. This procedure is repeated for each R_2 rank in turn as the pivotal rank and comparing it with all the R_2 ranks following it but not with those preceding it in that column. The contributions of all pivotal R_2 ranks are then totalled to get S, which is 23 in the present example.

(d)   In the given example, *N*=10 and the obtained *S*=23. The τ is computed as follows:

$$\tau = \frac{S}{\tfrac{1}{2}N(N-1)} = \frac{23}{\tfrac{1}{2}\times 10(10-1)} = \frac{23}{45} = 0.51$$

(e)   Since *N*=10, we test the significance of the obtained *S*, and accordingly of τ, by referring to Table O in the appendix. This table shows that an $S \geq 23$ for *N*=10 has probability of occurrence under H_0 of *p*=0.023. Since this p is smaller than the α=0.05, it is significant at 0.05 level ($p<0.05$), which indicates a significant correlation between respiratory rate and pulse rate. Thus, the H_0 is rejected in favour of H_1.

Example 16.16 Test whether there is a significant correlation between the following test scores of mechanical knowledge and arithmetic reasoning computing Kendall's *tau*.

Students	1	2	3	4	5	6	7	8	9	10	11	12
Mechanical knowledge	18	38	21	26	30	27	25	19	20	35	14	8
Arithmetic reasoning	5	23	9	12	19	12	9	12	17	13	11	10

Solution

For the solution of the above problem the steps to be followed are given below:

(a) Ranks are assigned in ascending order and separately to the scores of the two variables, giving an average rank to each score of a tied set (see Table 16.25). Let the mechanical knowledge be designated as X variable and its ranks as R_1. Similarly, the arithmetic reasoning is designated as variable Y and its ranks as R_2.

(b) The R_1 ranks (i.e., X ranks) are arranged serially in their natural order (e.g., 1, 2, 3, ..., N) in column 2 of Table 16.26, and then pairing each R_1 rank with the rank R_2 of arithmetic reasoning scores of the same subject.

(c) Starting from the top of the column of paired ranks (R_2), each of the latter is taken in turn as the pivotal rank and compared with all subsequent ranks following it in that column, but not with those preceding it. Each subsequent R_2 rank is scored as +1, 0 or −1 according to whether it is higher than, equal to (tied with) or lower than the pivotal rank under consideration. The algebraic sum of these scores for each pivotal rank gives its contribution to S.

   For example, for the first pivotal R_2 of 4, there are eight subsequent ranks in that column which are greater than this pivotal rank and each is scored as +1, and also there

Table 16.25   Assigning ranks to mechanical knowledge scores and arithmetic reasoning scores

Students' Number	Mechanical Knowledge		Arithmetic Reasoning	
	Scores (X)	Ranks (R_1)	Scores (Y)	Ranks (R_2)
1	18	3	5	1
2	38	12	23	12
3	21	6	9	2.5
4	26	8	12	7
5	30	10	19	11
6	27	9	12	7
7	25	7	9	2.5
8	19	4	12	7
9	20	5	17	10
10	35	11	13	9
11	14	2	11	5
12	8	1	10	4

Table 16.26   Scoring of ranks for S between mechanical knowledge and arithmetic reasoning

Students' Numbers	R_1	R_2	Scoring of Subsequent Ranks (S)
12	1	4	$(+8)+(-3)=5$
11	2	5	$(+7)+(-3)=4$
1	3	1	$(+9)=9$
8	4	7	$(+4)+(-2)+(0)+(0)=2$
9	5	10	$(-5)+(+2)=-3$
3	6	2.5	$(0)+(+5)=5$
7	7	2.5	$(+5)=5$
4	8	7	$(0)+(+3)=3$
6	9	7	$(+3)=3$
5	10	11	$(-1)+(+1)=0$
10	11	9	$(+1)=1$
2	12	12	
Total: $N=12$			$S=34$

are three subsequent ranks which are smaller than the pivotal rank and each is scored as –1. Thus, a score of 5 (i.e., 8–3=5) is contributed by the pivotal R_2 rank of 4 to the S (see Table 16.26). The contributions of all pivotal R_2 ranks are added to give the S value.

(d)   Since there are no tied ranks in the set of R_1 ranks, $\sum T_1 = \sum[t_1(t_1-1)] = 0$. But the set of R_2 ranks show two tied sets, namely, two ranks of 2.5 and three ranks of 7. Thus, $\sum T_2 = \sum[t_2(t_2-1)] = 2(2-1)+3(3-1) = 2+6 = 8$.

(e) τ (*tau*) is then computed as follows:

$$\tau = \frac{S}{\sqrt{\frac{1}{2}N(N-1)-\sum T_1}\sqrt{\frac{1}{2}N(N-1)-\sum T_2}}$$

$$= \frac{34}{\sqrt{\frac{1}{2}\times 12(12-1)-0}\sqrt{\frac{1}{2}\times 12(12-1)-8}} = \frac{34}{\sqrt{66}\sqrt{58}}$$

$$= \frac{34}{8.12\times 7.62} = \frac{34}{61.87} = 0.55$$

(f)   Because $N>10$, z may be computed from τ to test the H_0 proposing no significant correlation between the two variables. In order to compute z, we must first of all, compute the standard error of τ (σ_τ or s_τ). The formula for s_τ reads

$$s_\tau = \sqrt{\frac{2(2N+5)}{9N(N-1)}} = \sqrt{\frac{2(2\times 12+5)}{9\times 12(12-1)}} = \sqrt{\frac{58}{1188}} = 0.22$$

$$\therefore z = \frac{\tau}{s_\tau} = \frac{0.55}{0.22} = 2.50$$

Since the obtained z of 2.50 is greater than 1.96 (z value for 0.05 level of significance), it is significant at 0.05 level of significance ($p < 0.05$).

Alternatively, we may refer to Table A in the appendix to find out the probability (p) associated with the obtained $z = 2.50$. The fractional area of the unit normal curve from μ to the z score of 2.50 amounts to 0.4938 (Table A of the appendix). So the probability (p) of the H_0 being correct works out to be very low:

$$p = 2\,[0.50 - (\text{area from }\mu\text{ to }z)] = 2\,(0.50 - 0.4938) = 0.0124.$$

Since this probability is less than the $\alpha = 0.05$, it is significant at 0.05 level ($p < 0.05$). This shows that there is a significant correlation between the two variables.

16.8 Kendall's Coefficient of Concordance (W)

In the previous sections of this chapter, we have been concerned with measures of the correlation between two sets of rankings of N objects or individuals. Now, we shall consider a measure of the correlation among several sets of rankings of N objects or individuals.

When we have m sets of rankings, where $m > 2$, we may determine the association among them by using Kendall's coefficient of concordance (W). In other words, for data comprising m sets of ranks, where $m > 2$, a descriptive measure of the agreement or concordance among the m sets is provided by Kendall's coefficient of concordance (W). As we have already discussed, Spearman's ρ and Kendall's τ express the degree of association between two variables measured in or transformed to ranks, whereas Kendall's W expresses the degree of association among m such variables. Kendall's W as a measure of correlation may be particularly useful in studies of interjudge or intertest reliability and also has applications in studies of clusters of variables.

The value of W ranges from 0 to 1. When perfect agreement exists among m sets of ranks, $W = 1$, and when maximum disagreement exists, $W = 0$. That is, W does not take negative values. With more than two sets of ranks complete disagreement cannot occur. For example, if X and Y are in complete disagreement and X and Z are also in complete disagreement, then Y and Z must be in complete agreement.

The degree of association or concordance among m sets of ranks may be described by calculating Spearman rank-order correlation coefficient between all $\binom{m}{2}$ possible pairs of ranks and finding the average value, denoted by $\bar{\rho}$. This average is related to W. This relation is expressed by the formula

$$\bar{\rho} = \frac{mW - 1}{m - 1}$$

For the particular case where $m = 2$, the relation is $\rho = 2\,W - 1$. For $W = 0$, $\rho = -1$, for $W = 0.5$, $\rho = 0$ and for $W = 1$, $\rho = 1$.

16.8.1 Assumptions of W

Kendall's coefficient of concordance (W) is a non-parametric statistical test. It has the following few number of assumptions:

(a) The observations must be independent, which means that the selection of samples from the population should be random and the assignment of scores to the performance of the samples should be unbiased and impartial.

(b) W bears a linear relationship to the average ρ (i.e., $\bar{\rho}$) taken for all groups.

(c) The data should be in terms of ordinal scale of measurement. In other words, the m variables should be measured in, or transformed to ranks.

(d) The m sets of scores or ranks for each individual occur at random and independent of all other m sets of scores or ranks in the sample.

16.8.2 Computational Procedures for Kendall's *W*

The computation of Kendall's W is much simpler. However, the computational procedures of W vary with the nature of the data given, whether the given data are in terms of original scores or in ranks and whether there are tied scores, and hence, tied ranks or not. These procedures are discussed separately, as follows.

16.8.2.1 *Computation of W from Test Scores or from Ranks*

If the scores of the individuals of the sample have already been ranked with respect to each of the m variables, those m sets of ranks are directly used in computing W. Otherwise, ranks are first assigned in an ascending or descending order of magnitude to the scores of each variable separately from 1 to N. However, the assignment of ranks to the scores of m variables should be the same. After getting the m sets of ranks, the computation of W starts.

Suppose four company executives are asked to interview six job applicants and to rank them separately in their order of suitability for a job. The four independent sets of ranks given by four company executives A, B, C and D to six job applicants 'a' through 'f' might be those shown in Table 16.27.

The bottom row of Table 16.27, labelled R_j, gives the sums of the ranks assigned to each applicant by the four executives.

If the four executives or judges had been in perfect agreement about the job applicants, that is, if they had each ranked the six applicants in the same order, then one applicant would have received four ranks of 1 and, thus, his/her sum of ranks, R_j would be $1+1+1+1=4=m$. Another applicant would be assigned a rank of 2 by all four executives and thus the sum of his or her ranks would be $R_j=2+2+2+2=8=2m$.

The least promising applicant would have

$$R_j=6+6+6+6=24=Nm$$

In fact, with perfect agreement among the four executives, the sums of ranks (R_j) for the six applicants would be 4, 8, 12, 16, 20 and 24, though not necessarily in that order. In general,

Table 16.27 Ranks assigned to six job applicants by four company executives

Executives	Job Applicants					
	a	**b**	**c**	**d**	**e**	**f**
A	6	4	1	2	3	5
B	5	3	1	2	4	6
C	6	4	2	1	3	5
D	3	1	4	5	2	6
R_j	20	12	8	10	12	22

when perfect agreement exists among m sets of ranks assigned by m judges, to N individuals, the rank sums (R_j) are: $m, 2m, 3m, 4m, \ldots, Nm$. The total sum of N ranks for m judges is $mN(N+1)/2$, and the mean rank sum is $m(N+1)/2$.

The degree of agreement among judges reflects itself in the variation in the rank sums. When all judges agree, this variation is a maximum. Disagreement among judges reflects itself in a reduction in the variation of rank sums. For maximum disagreement, the rank sums will tend to be more or less equal. This circumstance provides the basis for the definition of a coefficient of concordance.

Let R_j represent the rank sum of the jth individual. The sum of squares of deviations of rank sums from the mean of R_j for N individuals is

$$s = \sum \left(R_j - \frac{\Sigma R_j}{N} \right)^2$$

The maximum value of this sum of squares occurs when perfect agreement exists among judges and is equal to $m^2 (N^3 - N)/12$. The coefficient of concordance W is defined as the ratio of s to the maximum possible value of s and is expressed as

$$W = \frac{s}{1/12 m^2 (N^3 - N)} = \frac{12s}{m^2 (N^3 - N)}$$

where

s = sum of squares of the observed deviations from the mean of R_j

m = number of sets of rankings, for example, the number of judges

N = number of entities (objects or individuals) ranked.

$1/12 m^2 (N^3 - N)$ = maximum possible sum of the squared deviations, that is, the sum s which would occur with perfect agreement among m sets of ranks.

Thus, to compute W, we first find the sum of ranks, R_j, in each column of a $m \times N$ table. Then, we sum the R_j and divide that sum by N to obtain the mean value of R_j. Each of the R_j may then be expressed as a deviation from the mean value. Finally, s, the sum of squares of these deviations, is found. Knowing these s values, we may compute the value of W by the immediate above formula.

In the example of Table 16.27, the rank totals (R_j) are 20, 12, 8, 10, 12 and 22. The sum of rank totals (ΣR_j) is 84. The mean rank total, the rank sum expected in the case of independence, is $\frac{\Sigma R_j}{N} = \frac{84}{6} = 14$. To obtain s, we square the deviation of each rank total (R_j) from that mean $\left(\frac{\Sigma R_j}{N} \right)$ value, and then sum those squares. In other words, the sum of squares of deviations about this mean is

$$s = \sum \left(R_j - \frac{\Sigma R_j}{N} \right)^2 = (20-14)^2 + (12-14)^2 + (8-14)^2 + (10-14)^2 + (12-14)^2 + (22-14)^2$$

$$= 36 + 4 + 36 + 16 + 4 + 64 = 160$$

In our given example, $m=4$ and $N=6$, and the coefficient of concordance is

$$W = \frac{12s}{m^2 (N^3 - N)} = \frac{12 \times 160}{4^2 (6^3 - 6)} = \frac{1920}{3360} = 0.571$$

Thus, the obtained $W = 0.571$ expresses the degree of agreement among the four company executives in ranking the six job applicants.

With the help of the obtained value of W, we can determine the average value of Spearman's ρ as follows:

$$\bar{\rho} = \frac{mW-1}{m-1} = \frac{4 \times 0.571 - 1}{4-1} = \frac{1.284}{3} = 0.428$$

As is shown above, this value of $\bar{\rho}$ bears a linear relation to the value of W.

One difference between the W and $\bar{\rho}$ (average rho) methods of expressing agreement among m sets of ranks is that $\bar{\rho}$ may take values between –1 and +1, whereas W may take values only between 0 and +1. The reason that W cannot be negative is that when more than two sets of ranks are involved, the rankings cannot all disagree completely. For example, if judge A and judge B are in disagreement, and judge A is also in disagreement with judge C, then judges B and C must agree. That is, when more than two judges are involved, agreement and disagreement are not symmetrical opposites. The m judges may all agree but they cannot all disagree completely. Therefore, W must be zero or positive.

The readers should note that W bears a linear relation to the average ρ (rho) taken over all groups but seems to bear no orderly relation to τ (tau). This reveals one of the advantages which ρ has over τ.

16.8.2.2   Computation of W from Tied Observations

When tied observations occur, the observations are each assigned the average of the ranks they would have been assigned had no ties occurred, our usual procedure in ranking tied scores.

The effect of tied ranks is to depress the value of W as found by the above noted formula. If the proportion of ties is small or the ties are not numerous, that effect is negligible, and we may compute W directly from the data without further adjustment. If the proportion of ties is large or the ties are numerous, a correction may be introduced which will increase slightly the value of W over what it would have been if uncorrected. The correction is calculated for each set of ranks. This correction factor is the same one used with Spearman's ρ:

$$T = \frac{\Sigma(t^3 - t)}{12}$$

where

t = number of observations in a set or group tied with a given rank

Σ = directs one to sum over all groups of ties within any one of the m sets of ranks.

For example, if the ranks on X are 1, 2.5, 2.5, 4, 5, 6, 8, 8, 8, 10, we have two groups of ties, one of two ranks (i.e., 2.5 and 2.5), and the other of three ranks (i.e., 8, 8 and 8). The correction factor for this set of X ranks is

$$T_x = \frac{\Sigma(t^3 - t)}{12} = \frac{(2^3 - 2) + (3^3 - 3)}{12} = \frac{6 + 24}{12} = \frac{30}{12} = 2.5$$

A correction factor (T) is calculated for each of the m sets of ranks and these are added together over the m sets to obtain ΣT. We then apply a formula for W in which this correction factor is incorporated. This formula reads

$$W = \frac{s}{1/12m^2(N^3 - N) - m\Sigma T}$$

The application of this correction tends to increase the value of W. The correction has a small effect unless ties are quite numerous.

16.8.3   Testing the Significance of Kendall's *W*

The test of significance of the obtained value of *W* depends upon the size of the samples—whether it is a small sample case or a large sample case. When *N* is 7 or less ($N \leq 7$), it is called a small sample case and when *N* is larger than 7 ($N > 7$), it is a large sample case.

In small sample case, we can test the significance of the obtained value of *W* by referring to Table P of the appendix. This table gives values of *s* for *W*'s significant at the 0.05 and 0.01 levels. This table is applicable for *m* (or *k*) from 3 to 20, and for *N* from 3 to 7. If an observed *s* is equal to or greater than that value shown in Table P for a particular level of significance, then H_0 (i.e., the *m* or *k* sets of ranks are independent) may be rejected at that level of significance.

For example, we saw that when *m*=4 company executives ranked *N*=6 job applicants (see Table 16.27), their agreement was *W*=0.571, and the *s* associated with that value of *W* is 160 (*s*=160). Referring to Table P of the appendix with *m*=4 and *N*=6, the critical value of *s* at 0.05 is 143.3 and at 0.01 is 176.2. Since our obtained value of *s*=160 exceeds the critical value of *s*=143.3, it is significant at 0.05 level of significance ($p < 0.05$). The H_0 is rejected in favour of H_1. That means there is a significant agreement or association among the four company executives in ranking six job applicants in the order of their suitability for a job.

Alternatively, in small sample case, we can test the significance of the obtained value of *W* directly by referring to Table Q of the appendix. This table gives the critical values of *W* significant at the 20, 10, 5 and 1% levels. This table is applicable for *m* from 3 to 30 and for *N* from 3 to 10. If the obtained value of *W* is equal to or greater than that of the critical value shown in Table Q for a particular level of significance, then H_0 may be rejected at that level of significance. In our above example, the obtained value of *W*=0.571. Referring to Table Q of the appendix, with *m*=4 and *N*=6, the critical value of *W* at 0.05 is 0.51 and at 0.01 is 0.62. Since the obtained value of *W*=0.571 exceeds the critical value of *W*=0.51, it is significant at 0.05 level of significance. So, the H_0 is rejected in favour of H_1 ($p < 0.05$). Therefore, we may conclude that there is a significant agreement or association among the four executives in ranking six job applicants regarding their suitability for a job.

It may be noted here that the researchers may refer either to Table P or Table Q of the appendix for testing the significance of the obtained *W* when it is a small sample case.

In a large sample case (i.e., *N*>7), we test the significance of an obtained *W* in terms of chi-square (χ^2) with df = *N*–1, because in large samples, *W* is approximately distributed as chi-square with df = *N*–1

$$\chi^2 = \frac{s}{1/12 mN(N+1)} = m(N-1)W$$

Thus, the right-hand expression of the above formula is computationally simpler than the left-hand expression to compute χ^2, meaning, first we have to find out *W* and then convert this *W* to χ^2 which will be taken for testing the significance. If χ^2 is significant, then the obtained *W* is significant.

If the converted value of χ^2 equals or exceeds that critical value shown in Table L of the appendix for a particular level of significance and a particular value of df = *N*-1, then the null hypothesis (H_0) that the *m* sets of ranks are unrelated may be rejected at that level of significance.

For example, in a study, *m*=13, *N*=20, and we found that *W*=0.577. We may determine the significance of this relation by applying a χ^2 test as follows:

$$\chi^2 = m\,(N-1)\;W = 13\,(20-1) \times 0.577 = 142.52$$
$$df = N-1 = 20-1 = 19$$

Referring to Table L of the appendix, the critical value of χ^2, with df=19, at 0.05 level is 30.14, and at 0.01 level is 36.19. Since the obtained χ^2=142.52 exceeds the critical value of χ^2=36.19, it is significant beyond 0.01 level of significance. Thus, the obtained value of *W*=0.577 is also significant beyond 0.01 level of significance. So, the H_0 (which states that the judges' ratings are unrelated to each other) is rejected in favour of H_1 ($p<0.01$). Therefore, we may conclude that there is a significant agreement among the 13 judges in rating 20 subjects.

16.8.4   Summary of Procedures

The following are the steps in the use of Kendall's coefficient of concordance (W):

1. Let N=the number of entities (objects or individuals) to be ranked and let m=the number of sets of ranks or the number of judges assigning ranks. Cast the observed ranks in a $m \times N$ table.
2. For each entity, determine the R_j, the sum of the ranks assigned to that entity by the m judges.
3. Determine the mean of the R_j. Express each R_j as a deviation from that mean. Square these deviations, and sum the squares to obtain s.
4. If the proportion of ties in the m sets of ranks is large, use the appropriate formula incorporating the correction factor for ties in computing the value of W. Otherwise, use the formula meant for no ties, as discussed earlier in this section.
5. The method for determining whether the observed value of W is significantly different from zero depends on the size of N.

If N is 7 or smaller, either Table P or Table Q of the appendix may be referred. Table P gives critical values of s associated with W's significant at 0.05 and 0.01 levels. Table Q gives the critical values of W to be significant at 20, 10, 5 and 1% levels.

If N is larger than 7, a χ^2 test may be applied. The obtained value of W is converted to the χ^2 value by the help of the appropriate formula discussed earlier in this section. Then, the significance of the computed value of χ^2, for df = $N-1$, may be tested by reference to Table L of the appendix.

The stepwise computational procedures of W will become more clear to the readers through the following examples.

Example 16.17 Four judges A, B, C and D rank six convicts, a, b, c, d, e and f on 'parole readiness'. By using the coefficient of concordance, indicate the degree of consistency of the judges. Is the relationship statistically significant at the 1% level?

Judges	Convicts					
	a	b	c	d	e	f
A	1	2	3	4	5	6
B	1	4	3	2	6	5
C	1	3	2	4	5	6
D	1	2	4	3	5	6

Solution

The following steps are to be followed for the solution of the above problem:

(a) The given data are in terms of ranks and there are no tied ranks in the data. Let us denote the number of judges as m, which are four in number, that is, $m=4$. Similarly, the number of convicts is denoted as N, which are six in number, that is, $N=6$. The given data are arranged in a $m \times N$ table, as shown in Table 16.28.

(b) For each convict, the ranks assigned to that convict by the four judges are summed up and entered in the bottom row of Table 16.28 as R_j. Thus, the R_js for six convicts, a through f, are 4, 11, 12, 13, 21 and 23, respectively.

(c) The total of R_js and its mean are determined as follows:

$$\Sigma R_j = 4+11+12+13+21+23 = 84$$

$$\text{Mean of } R_j = \frac{\Sigma R_j}{N} = \frac{84}{6} = 14$$

(d) The s is determined as follows:

$$s = \Sigma\left(R_j - \frac{\Sigma R_j}{N}\right)^2 = (4-14)^2 + (11-14)^2 + (12-14)^2 + (13-14)^2 + (21-14)^2 + (23-14)^2$$

$$= 100+9+4+1+49+81 = 244$$

(e) The value of W is computed by the formula as follows:

$$W = \frac{12s}{m^2(N^3-N)} = \frac{12 \times 244}{4^2(6^3-6)} = \frac{2928}{3360} = 0.871$$

(f) Since it is a small sample case, for testing the significance of the obtained value of $W=0.871$, we may refer to Table Q of the appendix because this table gives the critical values of W required for significance at 0.05 or 0.01 levels with a particular m and N. In the given problem, $m=4$ and $N=6$. For $m=4$ and $N=6$, the critical value of W at 0.05 level is 0.51 and at 0.01 is 0.62. Since our obtained value of $W=0.871$ is larger than 0.62, it is significant beyond 0.01 level of significance. Thus, the H_0 (i.e., the judges' rankings are unrelated to each other) is rejected in favour of H_1 ($P<0.01$). Therefore, we may conclude that the degree of consistency of the judges is $W=0.871$, and this relationship is statistically significant at 1% level.

Table 16.28   Ranks assigned to six convicts by four judges

Judges (m)	Convicts (N)					
	a	**b**	**c**	**d**	**e**	**f**
A	1	2	3	4	5	6
B	1	4	3	2	6	5
C	1	3	2	4	5	6
D	1	2	4	3	5	6
R_j	4	11	12	13	21	23

Example 16.18 In a study, 10 objects are each ranked on three different variables: X, Y and Z. The ranks are given below. Compute W and interpret it.

Variables	Objects									
	a	**b**	**c**	**d**	**e**	**f**	**g**	**h**	**i**	**j**
X	1	4.5	2	4.5	3	7.5	6	9	7.5	10
Y	2.5	1	2.5	4.5	4.5	8	9	6.5	10	6.5
Z	2	1	4.5	4.5	4.5	4.5	8	8	8	10

Solution

The following steps are to be followed for the solution of the above problem.

(a)   The given data are in terms of ranks and there are numerous tied ranks in each set of ranks. Let us denote the number of variables as m, which are three in number, that is, $m = 3$. Similarly, the number of objects is denoted as N, which is 10 in number, that is, $N = 10$. The given data are arranged in a $m \times N$ table, as shown in Table 16.29, below.

(b)   Since each object was ranked on three different variables, the ranks assigned to each object was summed up and entered in the bottom row of Table 16.29 as R_j. Thus, the R_js for 10 objects, a through j, are 5.5, 6.5, 9.0, 13.5, 12.0, 20.0, 23.0, 23.5, 25.5 and 26.5, respectively.

(c)   The total of R_js and its mean are determined as follows:

$$\Sigma R_j = 5.5 + 6.5 + 9.0 + 13.5 + 12.0 + 20.0 + 23.0 + 23.5 + 25.5 + 26.5 = 165$$

$$\text{Mean of } R_j = \frac{\Sigma R_j}{N} = \frac{165}{10} = 16.5$$

(d)   To obtain s, we sum the squared deviations of each R_j from its mean as follows:

$$\begin{aligned} s = &(5.5 - 16.5)^2 + (6.5 - 16.5)^2 + (9.0 - 16.5)^2 + (13.5 - 16.5)^2 \\ &+ (12.0 - 16.5)^2 + (20.0 - 16.5)^2 + (23.0 - 16.5)^2 + (23.5 - 16.5)^2 \\ &+ (25.5 - 16.5)^2 + (26.5 - 16.5)^2 \\ = &121 + 100 + 56.25 + 9 + 20.25 + 12.25 + 42.25 + 49 + 81 + 100 = 591 \end{aligned}$$

Table 16.29   Ranks received by ten objects on three variables

Variables (*m*)	Objects (*N*)									
	a	**b**	**c**	**d**	**e**	**f**	**g**	**h**	**i**	**j**
X	1	4.5	2	4.5	3	7.5	6	9	7.5	10
Y	2.5	1	2.5	4.5	4.5	8.0	9	6.5	10	6.5
Z	2	1	4.5	4.5	4.5	4.5	8	8	8	10
R_j	5.5	6.5	9.0	13.5	12.0	20.0	23.0	23.5	25.5	26.5

(e) Since the proportion of ties in the ranks is large, we should correct for ties in computing the value of W.

In the set of X ranks, there are two sets of ties: 2 objects are tied at 4.5 and 2 are tied at 7.5. For both groups, t=the number of observations tied for a given rank=2. Thus,

$$T_x = \frac{\Sigma(t^3-t))}{12} = \frac{(2^3-2)+(2^3-2)}{12} = \frac{12}{12} = 1$$

In the set of Y ranks, there are three sets of ties, and each set contains two observations. That is, 2 objects are tied at 2.5; 2 are tied at 4.5 and 2 are tied at 6.5. Here, t=2 in each case. Thus,

$$T_y = \frac{\Sigma(t^3-t)}{12} = \frac{(2^3-2)+(2^3-2)+(2^3-2)}{12} = \frac{18}{12} = 1.5$$

In the set of Z ranks, there are two sets of ties. One set, tied at 4.5, consists of 4 observations; here t=4. The other set, tied at rank 8, consists of 3 observations; here t=3. Thus,

$$T_z = \frac{\Sigma(t^3-t)}{12} = \frac{(4^3-4)+(3^3-3)}{12} = \frac{84}{12} = 7$$

Knowing the values of T for the X, Y and Z rankings, we may find their sum:

$$\Sigma T = 1+1.5+7 = 9.5$$

With the above information, we may compute W by the formula incorporating the correction for ties as follows

$$W = \frac{s}{1/12 m^2(N^3-N)-m\Sigma T} = \frac{591}{1/12 \times 3^2(10^3-10)-3\times 9.5}$$

$$= \frac{591}{1/12 \times 9 \times 990 - 28.5} = \frac{591}{714} = 0.828$$

If we had disregarded the ties, then the computed value of W would be

$$W = \frac{12s}{m^2(N^3-N)} = \frac{12 \times 591}{3^2(10^3-10)} = \frac{7092}{8910} = 0.796$$

Thus, we would have found W=0.796 rather than 0.828. This difference illustrates the slightly depressing effect which ties, when uncorrected, exert on the value of W.

(f) Since N=10 which is greater than 7, it is a large sample case. In order to test the significance of the obtained value of W, a χ^2 test may be applied. So, first of all, the obtained value of W is converted to χ^2 value by the following formula:

$$\chi^2 = m(N-1) W = 3(10-1)(0.828) = 22.36$$
$$df = N-1 = 10-1 = 9$$

Referring to Table L of the Appendix, the critical value of χ^2, with df=9, at 0.05 level is 16.92 and at 0.01 level is 21.67. Since the obtained value of χ^2=22.36 is greater than both the critical values of χ^2, it is significant beyond 0.01 level of significance. Thus, the obtained value of W is also significant. So, the H_0, which states that the three sets of ranks are unrelated to each other, is rejected in favour of H_1 ($P<0.01$). This indicates that there is a significant agreement among the three sets of ranks assigned to 10 objects on three variables, X, Y and Z.

A high or significant value of W may be interpreted as meaning that the observers or judges are applying essentially the same standard in ranking the N objects under study.

Summary

In this chapter, we have discussed non-parametric statistics. Non-parametric inference tests depend considerably less on population characteristics than do parametric tests. The z-, t- and F-tests, and Pearson correlation coefficient (r) are examples of parametric statistics; the chi-square test, Spearman rank-order correlation coefficient, Phi coefficient, contingency coefficient, Kendall's both rank correlation coefficient and coefficient of concordance are examples of non-parametric statistics. Parametric statistical tests are used whenever possible because they are more powerful and versatile. However, when the assumptions of the parametric tests are violated, non-parametric tests, known as distribution-free tests, are frequently employed.

One of the most frequently used inference tests for analysing nominal data is the non-parametric tests called chi-square (χ^2). It is appropriate for analysing frequency data dealing with one or two variables. Chi-square essentially measures the discrepancy between the observed frequency (f_o) and the expected frequency (f_e) for each of the cells in one-way or two-way table. In equation form, $\chi^2_{obt} = \Sigma (f_o - f_e)^2 / f_e$, where the summation is over all the cells. In single-variable situations, the data are presented in a one-way table, and the various expected frequency values are determined on an *a priori* basis. In one-variable case, χ^2 is applied to test the goodness of fit. In the goodness-of-fit test the null hypothesis (H_0) states that there is no difference between the observed and expected frequency distributions. The alternative hypothesis (H_1) states that the observed and expected frequency distributions are different. To test the goodness of fit, first of all, the value of χ^2 will be calculated from the given data. If the obtained value of χ^2 is less than its critical value at a certain level of significance for an appropriate df, the H_0 is accepted. The acceptance of H_0 ensures that there is a goodness-of-fit between f_o and f_e distributions.

In two-variable situations, χ^2 is applied to test the independence of variables. In this case, the frequency data are presented in a contingency table and we are interested in determining if there is a relationship between the two variables. The test for independence is used to assess the relationship between two variables. The null hypothesis (H_0) states that there is no relationship that the two variables under study are independent of each other. The alternative hypothesis (H_1) states that the two variables are related. For the test of independence, the expected frequencies for H_0 can be directly calculated from the marginal frequency totals common to a cell in a contingency table as $f_e = f_c f_r / n$, where f_c is the total column frequency and f_r is the total row frequency for the cell in question and n is the total number of cases.

The obtained value of χ^2 is evaluated by comparing it with its critical value. If $X^2_{obt} \geq X^2_{crit}$, we reject the null hypothesis. The critical value of χ^2 is determined from the table given in the appendix (see Table L) with the help of degrees of freedom (df). In the one-variable experiment, $df = k - 1$ or $c - 1$ (where k or c is the number of categories in the variable). In the two-variable situation, $df = (r-1)(c-1)$, where r is the number of row categories and c is the number of column categories. Chi-square is not only applied to frequency data, but also the nominal data which are in terms of percentages or proportions either correlated or uncorrelated.

Spearman correlation is used for linear relationship when both variables are measured on ordinal scales. The computational equation for rho was presented and several practice problems worked out.

The phi-coefficient ($\emptyset$) is used when both variables are dichotomous. The $\emptyset$ is a statistic of correlation between two genuinely dichotomous nominal variables, each having only two classes located at two distinct points on its scale with a real gap between them, for example, male–female, living–dead, normal–abnormal, etc. Chi-square (computed from a 2×2 table) as a function of phi is expressed by the equation, $\chi^2 = N\emptyset$. The computational equation for $\emptyset$ was presented and several practice problems worked out.

Contingency coefficient (C) is used for a linear relationship when both variables are measured on nominal scale. The C as a function of χ^2 is expressed by the equation, $C = \sqrt{\dfrac{\chi^2}{N + \chi^2}}$. The computational equation for C was presented and several practice problems worked out.

Kendall's rank correlation coefficient ($tau = \tau$) is the counterpart of Pearson's r for linear correlation between two variables. Like Spearman's *rho*, Kendall's *tau* is used for linear relationship when both variables under study are measured on ordinal scales. The computational procedures, formulae and equations for τ (*tau*) were presented and several practice problems worked out.

Finally, we introduced Kendall's coefficient of concordance (W), which is used for linear relationship when m variables, where $m > 2$, are measured on ordinal scales. The computational procedures, equations and formulae for W were presented and several practice problems worked out.

Key Terms

- Chi-square (χ^2)
- Contingency coefficient
- Contingency table
- Distribution-free tests
- Expected frequency
- Kendall's coefficient of concordance
- Kendall's rank correlation coefficient
- Measure of disarray
- Non-parametric tests
- Observed frequency
- Parametric tests

- Phi coefficient
- Rank sums
- Sampling distribution of χ^2
- Spearman's rank-order correlation
- Sum of quotient
- Test of goodness of fit
- Test of independence
- Theoretical frequency
- Tied ranks
- Yates' correction for continuity

Questions and Problems

1. What is a non-parametric statistical test? Discuss the assumptions, advantages and disadvantages of non-parametric statistical tests.
2. What do you mean by a parametric statistical test? Discuss the assumptions of parametric statistical tests.
3. Define parametric and non-parametric statistical tests. Show the difference between parametric and non-parametric statistical tests.
4. What do you mean by distribution-free tests? Analyse the precautions one should keep in mind while using non-parametric statistical tests.
5. Define chi-square. Discuss its characteristics and assumptions.
6. With the help of suitable examples, discuss the various applications of chi-square.

7. Write notes on:

   (a) Sampling distribution of chi-square.

   (b) Relation of χ^2 to both t and z.

8. Define Spearman's rank-order correlation coefficient. How it is different from Pearson's product–moment correlation coefficient?

9. Write notes on:

   (a) Assumptions of Spearman's ρ (rho).

   (b) Applications of Spearman's rank-order correlation.

   (c) Characteristics of ρ (rho).

   (d) Advantages and limitations of Spearman's ρ (rho).

10. With the help of a suitable example, discuss the procedure for testing the significance of the obtained Spearman's ρ. What is its power efficiency?

11. What do you mean by Phi coefficient? Discuss its assumptions. How it is related to chi-square?

12. Write notes on:

    (a) An evaluation of Phi coefficient.

    (b) Test of significance of Phi coefficient.

13. Define the tetrachoric correlation and discuss its assumptions.

14. Write notes on:

    (a) An evaluation of the Tetrachoric coefficient.

    (b) Test of significance of Tetrachoric coefficient.

15. What is contingency coefficient? Discuss its assumptions. What are its limitations?

16. Writes notes on:

    (a) Relation of C to χ^2.

    (b) Test of significance of C.

    (c) Power efficiency of C.

17. Define Kendall's rank correlation coefficient. What are its assumptions? How it is tested for its significance?

18. Make a comparison between ρ (rho) and τ (tau). What is the power efficiency of Kendall's τ?

19. What do you mean by Kendall's coefficient of concordance? Discuss its assumptions.

20. With the help of suitable examples, discuss the procedures for testing the significance of Kendall's W.

21. A researcher obtained a random sample of $N=60$ students to determine whether there were any significant preferences among three leading brands of colas. Each student tested all three brands and then selected his/her favourite brand. The resulting frequency distribution is as follows:

Brand A	Brand B	Brand C
28	14	18

Are these data sufficient to indicate any preferences among the three brands? Test with $\alpha=0.05$.

22. A student responds to a 70-item true-false test by guessing the responses to every item. He obtains a score of 45. Does this differ significantly from what would be expected by chance?

23. A horse race was made taking eight horses in eight post positions. Total race was 144. Wins accrued on a circular track by horses from eight post positions are given below.

Post Positions	1	2	3	4	5	6	7	8
Number of Wins	29	19	18	25	17	10	15	11

Is there any significant difference in the expected number of winners starting from each of the post positions?

24. Genetic theory states that children having one parent of blood type A and the other of blood type B will always be of one of three types A, AB, B and that the proportion of three types will, on an average, be as 1: 2: 1. A report states that out of 300 children having one A parent and B parent, 30% were found to be type A. 45% type AB and remainder type B. Test the hypothesis by χ^2 test.

25. The theory predicts the proportion of beans in the four groups A, B, C and D should be 9: 3: 3: 1. In an experiment among 1600 beans, the numbers in the four groups were 882, 313, 287 and 118. Does the experimental result support the theory? Apply χ^2 test.

26. In 180 throws of a die the observed frequencies of the values from 1 to 6 are 34, 27, 41, 25, 18 and 35. Test the hypothesis that the die is unbiased.

27. Six coins are tossed 64 times and the number of heads counted. The following results were obtained.

Number of Heads	Frequency
0	1
1	9
2	16
3	18
4	16
5	3
6	1
Total	64

Do these frequencies differ significantly from those obtained from the binomial $(\frac{1}{2}+\frac{1}{2})^6$?

28. The following contingency table describes the relation between pass and fail on an examination and ratings of job performance for 100 employees.

	Ratings			Total
	Below Average	Average	Above Average	
Pass	11	25	35	71
Fail	15	7	7	29
Total	26	32	42	100

Test the hypothesis that job performance is independent of examination results.

29. Students belonging to three religious groups were asked to respond to a particular question related to their attitude by providing the three alternatives—Yes, No and Undecided. The data collected are given below.

Religious Groups	Responses			Total
	Yes	No	Undecided	
Hindu	10	25	15	50
Muslim	20	20	5	45
Christian	30	15	10	55
Total	60	60	30	150(N)

Compute χ^2 to test if there is a relationship between religious group membership and attitude.

30. Due to rampant inflation, the government is considering imposing wage and price controls. A government economist, interested in determining whether there is a relationship between occupation and attitude towards wage and price controls, collects the following data. The data show for each occupation the number of individuals in the sample which were for or against the controls.

Occupation	Attitude Towards Wage and Price Controls		Total
	For	Against	
Labour	90	60	150
Business	100	150	250
Professions	110	90	200
Total	300	300	600(N)

Do these occupations differ regarding attitudes towards wage and price controls?

31. The following data relate to patients in a mental hospital:

Method of Therapy	Rating		Total
	Improvement	**No Improvement**	
Therapy A	16	28	44
Therapy B	9	37	46
Total	25	65	90(N)

Test the hypothesis that method of therapy is independent of rating assigned.

32. Two lots of 14 rats each were subjects in an experiment related to the effectiveness of a drug. All rats were inoculated with the causative organism, but only one lot was previously given preventive serum. The results follow:

	Serum	**No Serum**
Recovered	12	6
Died	2	8

Can anything be said of the effectiveness of the serum?

33. The responses of 100 individuals to 2 items on a personality scale are given below:

		Item 1	
		Disagree	Agree
Item 2	Agree	40	20
	Disagree	25	15

Apply χ^2 test and interpret the results.

34. The authoritarianism and the social status striving scores of 12 students are given below. Calculate Spearman's rank correlation coefficient and interpret the results.

Students	A	B	C	D	E	F	G	H	I	J	K	L
Authoritarianism	82	98	87	40	116	113	111	83	85	126	106	117
Social Status Striving	42	46	39	37	65	88	86	56	62	92	54	81

35. Twelve individuals are independently ranked by two psychiatrists A and B, according to their degree of depression. Calculate Spearman's rank correlation coefficient and interpret it.

Individuals	1	2	3	4	5	6	7	8	9	10	11	12
Psychiatrist A	12	11	4	7	10	8	3	1	9	2	6	5
Psychiatrist B	9	12	5	8	11	7	4	1	6	2	10	3

36. Calculate Spearman's rank correlation coefficient for the following paired scores of 10 subjects. Does the coefficient obtained differ significantly from 0?

X	4	4	7	7	7	9	16	17	21	25
Y	8	16	8	8	16	20	12	15	25	20

37. Responses of 200 students to an opinion item and an information item have been recorded as shown below. Compute the phi coefficient for this data and interpret the results.

	Right	Wrong	Total
Agree	70	30	100
Disagree	30	70	100
Total	100	100	200(N)

38. Compute the phi coefficient for the following data. Is this a significant phi at the 5% level?

	Right	Wrong
Upper	65	35
Lower	25	75

39. The responses of 100 individuals to a test item were recorded as shown below. Our papers were divided into the top 50 and the bottom 50, and then the right and wrong answers for each group were counted. Compute the tetrachoric r for the following data and interpret the results.

	Right	Wrong	Total
Upper 50	20	30	50
Lower 50	10	40	50
Total	30	70	100

40. Compute the tetrachoric *r* for the data in Problem 38 above. Is the relationship significant at 5% level?

41. In a survey to determine the preference of the employees of an establishment for a particular type of soft drink, and the results were recorded as below.

	Sprite	Coca-Cola	Limca
Officers	25	30	52
Non-officers	46	22	28

Compute contingency coefficient to find out if there is a significant relationship between the preference for a particular type of soft drink and the class or status of the employee.

42. Seven instructors are rated by freshmen and sophomore students on 'clarity of presentation'. The results are tabulated in this manner.

Instructor	1	2	3	4	5	6	7
Freshmen	44	39	36	35	33	29	22
Sophomore	58	42	18	22	31	38	38

Compute Kendall's tau for these data and interpret the results.

43. Compute Kendall's tau for the following paired ranks. Is it significant at 5% level?

X	1	2	3	4	5	6
Y	6	3.5	1.5	1.5	3.5	5

44. Three judges rank-ordered a group of seven students on an examination as follows:

Judges	Students						
	a	b	c	d	e	f	g
A	1	2	3	4	5	6	7
B	2	3	4	5	1	7	6
C	5	4	1	2	3	6	7

Compute the coefficient of concordance and test its significance.

45. Four judges (parole board members) rank eight convicts on 'parole readiness'.

Convicts	Judges			
	(1)	(2)	(3)	(4)
1	1	1	1	1
2	2	4	3	2
3	3	3	2	4
4	4	2	4	3
5	5	6	5	5
6	6	5	6	7
7	7	7	8	6
8	8	8	7	8

   (a) By using the coefficient of concordance, indicate the degree of consistency of the judges.

   (b) Is the relationship statistically significant at the 1% level?

46. Fill in the blanks:

    (i) Non-parametric statistical tests are sometimes referred to as _____ tests.

   (ii) Parametric statistical tests are _____ to the non-parametric statistical tests.

  (iii) The equality of variances between columns and rows is known as _____ of variances.

  (iv) To apply parametric tests, the given data should be in _____ or _____ scales of measurement.

   (v) In non-parametric tests the data should be given in terms of _____ or _____ scales of measurement.

  (vi) The χ^2 test is one of the most simplest and most widely used _____ tests.

 (vii) The greater the discrepancy between the observed and expected frequencies _____ the value of χ^2.

(viii) The distribution of χ^2 depends on the _____.

  (ix) In computing χ^2 from a fourfold contingency table, a correction, commonly recommended for use, is known as _____.

   (x) Spearman's ρ is a _____ counterpart of Pearson's r.

47. Write whether the following statements are True or False.

    (i) The model of a parametric statistical test specifies certain conditions about the parameter of the population from which the research sample was drawn.

   (ii) Student's t-test is a non-parametric test.

(iii) In general, parametric statistical tests are more sensitive, more powerful and more versatile than non-parametric tests.

(iv) In non-parametric tests, it is assumed that the dependent variable is normally distributed in the population from which the samples were drawn.

(v) The χ^2 test is a parametric statistical test.

(vi) The value of χ^2 can be positive as well as negative.

(vii) In χ^2, the data are in terms of frequencies, percentage or proportions.

(viii) Spearman correlation is used when original data are ranks.

(ix) Chi-square as a function of phi coefficient is expressed by the equation: $\chi^2 = N\phi^2$.

(x) The contingency coefficient is a parametric statistical test.

48. Find out the correct answer from among the four alternatives.

(i) The distribution-free tests are otherwise known as:

(a) Parametric tests   (b) Non-parametric tests
(c) F-tests   (d) None of the above

(ii) In non-parametric statistical tests, it is assumed that the dependent variable under study has:

(a) Underlying continuity   (b) Normal distribution
(c) Mesokurtic distribution   (d) None of the above

(iii) When f_o and f_e completely coincide, the value of χ^2 will be:

(a) +1.0   (b) −1.0
(c) Zero   (d) None of the above

(iv) The calculated value of χ^2 is:

(a) Always positive   (b) Always negative
(c) Either positive or negative   (d) None of the above

(v) χ^2 test is defined as:

(a) $\chi^2 = \sum \dfrac{(f_o - f_e)^2}{f_e}$ (b) $\chi^2 = \sum \dfrac{(f_o - f_e)}{f_e}$

(c) $\chi^2 = \sum \dfrac{(f_o + f_e)^2}{f_e}$ (d) None of the above

(vi) Contingency coefficient is defined as:

(a) $C = \sqrt{\dfrac{\chi^2}{N + \chi^2}}$ (b) $C = \dfrac{\chi^2}{\sqrt{N + \chi^2}}$

(c) $C = \dfrac{\chi^2}{\sqrt{N - \chi^2}}$ (d) None of the above

(vii)   When the paired ranks are in the same order, Spearman's ρ is:

(a)   Perfect negative   (b)   Perfect positive
(c)   Zero   (d)   None of the above

(viii) In phi coefficient, it is assumed that the two variables must be:

(a)   Interval variables   (b)   Ordinal variables
(c)   Nominal variables   (d)   None of the above

(ix)   For the computation of Kendall's *tau*, the data should be in terms of

(a)   Ordinal scale   (b)   Nominal scale
(c)   Interval scale   (d)   None of the above

(x)   Kendall's *W* expresses the degree of association among *m* sets of variables, where:

(a) $m > 2$ (b) $m < 2$
(c) $m = 2$ (d)   None of the above

Some Other Non-parametric Statistical Tests

Completion of the chapter would enable the readers to:

- Test hypotheses when we cannot make any assumptions about the populations from which the samples are drawn.
- Identify which non-parametric tests are appropriate for different situations.
- Introduce sign test, Wilcoxon T-test, Wilcoxon rank sum test, Mann–Whitney U-test, Median test, Kruskal–Wallis H-test, and Friedman χ_r^2 test, and learn how to use them in statistical inferences.
- Use and interpret each of seven standard non-parametric hypothesis tests.

17.1 Introduction

Chi-square, Spearman's ρ (rho), Phi coefficient, contingency coefficient, Kendall's rank correlation coefficient and Kendall's coefficient of concordance discussed in the previous chapter (see Chapter 16) are non-parametric statistics. In this chapter, many other useful non-parametric statistical tests will be described. Let us first begin with the sign test.

17.2 The Sign Test

One of the simplest tests of significance in the non-parametric category is the sign test. This test gets its name from the fact that it uses the plus (+) and minus (–) signs rather than quantitative measures as its data. This test compares two correlated samples and is applicable to data composed of N paired observations.

The sign test is a simple non-parametric alternative of Student's t-test for finding the *significance of difference between paired observations* of single group and matched-pair experiments. It can be applied to both continuous and discrete variables, irrespective of the normality or non-normality of their distribution in the population, and even to very small samples.

The sign test is far less powerful than the *t*-test. Its major deficiency lies in the use of only the algebraic sign, and not the magnitude, of the difference between the scores of each pair.

The null hypothesis (H₀) contends that there is no significant difference between the scores of each pair and that any observed difference results from mere chances of random sampling. That means that the random samples have come from the same population. If this hypothesis is true, half of the paired differences should be positive and half should be negative. Another way to stating the null hypothesis is that the *median difference* between the pairs is zero. The alternative hypothesis (H₁), on the other hand, states that the samples are not the random samples from the same population; and the median difference between the pairs is not zero. Thus, the positive signs may be greater than the negative signs or vice versa.

17.2.1   Assumptions of the Sign Test

To apply the sign test, it should be justifiable to assume that:

  (i)   Each pair of scores is independent of all other pairs.
 (ii)   The variable under consideration has a continuous distribution.
(iii)   The test does not make any assumption about the form of the distribution of differences, nor does it assume that all subjects are drawn from the same population. The different pairs may be from different populations with respect to age, sex, intelligence, etc., the only requirement is that within each pair the experimenter has achieved matching with respect to the relevant extraneous variables. As was noted before, one way of accomplishing this is to use each subject as his/her own control.

17.2.2   Computation of the Sign Test

Only the algebraic sign of the difference between the scores of each pair (i.e., $X - Y$) is noted, ignoring the magnitude of the difference and also any zero difference (e.g., in case of tied scores).

For example, the following are paired observations, X and Y, for a sample of 10 individuals together with the sign of the difference between X and Y.

X	15	19	31	36	10	11	19	15	10	16
Y	19	30	26	8	10	6	17	13	22	8
Sign of $X - Y$	−	−	+	+	0	+	+	+	−	+

In the above example $N=10$; out of 10, we have six plus signs, three minus signs and one zero difference. The zero difference is discarded from the consideration as it does not carry any sign; accordingly, the N is reduced to 9, instead of 10. Thus, out of 9, we have six plus signs (+) and three minus signs (−). Now, we have to test the significance of these obtained results.

17.2.3   Testing the Significance of the Obtained Results of the Sign Test

Testing the significance of the results obtained by the sign test depends on the size of the sample whether it is a small sample case or a large sample case. If N is equal to or less than 25 ($N \leq 25$), it is known as a small sample case, and N greater than 25 ($N>25$) is a large sample case.

Moreover, the sign test may be either one tailed or two tailed. In a one-tailed test, the advance prediction (H₁) states which sign, + or −, will occur more frequently. In a two-tailed test, the prediction (H$_1$) is simply that the frequency with which the two signs occur will be significantly different.

In small sample cases, the significance of the obtained result can be tested by determining the probability associated with the occurrence of a particular number of + or – signs by reference to the binomial distribution with $p=q=\frac{1}{2}$, where N=the number of pairs. Table R of the appendix gives the probabilities associated with the occurrence under H$_0$ of values as small as x for $N\leq25$. To use this table, let x=the number of fewer signs. Table R gives the one-tailed probability associated with the occurrence under H$_0$ of values as small as an observed x. If a two-tailed test is required, the probability (p) yielded by Table R should be doubled. The probability associated with an observed value as found from Table R is then compared with the α (alpha) levels of 0.05 and 0.01. If the associated probability is equal to or less than 0.05 or 0.01 levels of significance, then the obtained value is statistically significant.

For the data given in the above example, x=the number of fewer signs=3, and N=the number of matched pairs which showed differences=9. Table R shows that for $N=9$, $x\leq3$ has a one-tailed probability of occurrence under H$_0$ of $p=0.254$. For a two-tailed test, the probability is $p=0.508$. Since this p, either 0.254 or 0.508, is greater than $\alpha=0.05$, the obtained value of $x=3$ is not significant. The H$_0$ is accepted. That means that there is not a significant difference between the frequencies of + and – signs; the subjects are the random samples from the same population; and the median difference between the pairs is zero.

In large sample cases, the normal approximation to the binomial (i.e., the z) or χ^2 may be used, preferably with *Yates' correction for continuity*, for the test of significance of the obtained results. In this case, the expected values are $N/2$. For example, suppose 30 pairs are observed. Out of these, 24 show differences in one direction (+) and the other six show differences in the other (–).

Let us first apply χ^2 to test the significance of the above results which is obtained from a large sample. In this case the observed frequencies (f_o) are 24 (+ signs) and 6 (– signs), and the expected frequencies (f_e) are 15 and 15, respectively. If we apply a correction for continuity, the corrected observed frequencies are 23.5 (i.e., 24–0.5=23.5) and 6.5 (i.e., 6+0.5=6.5). That means that the observed frequencies (f_o) of plus signs (or minus signs) which is greater than the expected frequencies (f_e) is reduced by 0.5, and which is smaller than f_e is increased by 0.5.

Put into other words, the correction is effected by reducing the absolute difference between the observed frequencies of pluses (or minuses) and the expected frequencies by 0.5. Thus, the χ^2 formula reads,

$$\chi^2 = \sum \frac{(|f_o-f_e|-0.5)^2}{f_e} = \frac{(|24-15|-0.5)^2}{15} + \frac{(|6-15|-0.5)^2}{15}$$

$$= \frac{(8.5)^2}{15} + \frac{(8.5)^2}{15} = 4.82 + 4.82 = 9.64$$

$$\text{df} = c-1 = 2-1 = 1$$

Referring to Table L of the appendix, the critical value of χ^2, with df=1, at 0.05 level is 3.84 and at 0.01 level is 6.64. Since the obtained value of χ^2=9.64 exceeds the critical value of 6.64, it is significant. So the H$_0$ (which states that the median difference between the pairs is zero) is rejected in favour of H$_1$ ($p<0.01$).

Alternatively, we can test the significance of the obtained result of the above example by the help of z-test. The computational procedure of z is much simpler than the χ^2 procedure described above. To apply the z-test, we must obtain the difference between the number of + and – signs, and denote this difference by D. The formula for z reads,

$$z = \frac{|D|-1}{\sqrt{N}}$$

where

    D = the difference between the number of + and – signs

    | | = directs one to take the absolute difference value without algebraic sign

    N = the number of matched pairs which showed differences

It may be shown that $z = \dfrac{|D|-1}{\sqrt{N}}$ approaches the normal form as N increases in size. This formula incorporates a continuity correction. Values of 1.96 and 2.58 are required for significance at the 0.05 and 0.01 level of significance, respectively, for a non-directional (or two-tailed) test.

In the above example, we have 24 plus signs, six minus signs and N = 30. The difference between these two signs is

$$D = 24 - 6 = 18$$

The computed z value is

$$z = \frac{|D|-1}{\sqrt{N}} = \frac{18-1}{\sqrt{30}} = \frac{17}{5.48} = 3.10$$

Since the obtained z = 3.10 is greater than 2.58, it is significant beyond 0.01 level of significance. The H_0 is rejected in favour of H_1 ($p < 0.01$). Thus, both χ^2 test and z-test have yielded similar results, rejecting the H_0 beyond 0.01 level of significance.

The reader should recall that for df = 1 the quantity $z^2 = \chi^2$. In the above example $z^2 = (3.10)^2 = 9.61$ and $\chi^2 = 9.64$. The difference between these two values is very negligible, which is due to the rounding up of the decimal points, otherwise both quantities are the same (i.e., $z^2 = \chi^2$).

17.2.4   Summary of Procedures

The following are the steps in the use of the sign test

   (i)   Determine the sign of difference between the two members of each pair.

  (ii)   By counting, determine the value of N = the number of pairs whose differences show a sign. The pairs having zero differences are discarded from the analysis.

 (iii)   Determine the observed number of + and – signs.

 (iv)   The testing of the significance of the obtained results under the H_0 depends on the size of N.

     (a)   If N is 25 or smaller, Table R of the appendix may be referred to. This table shows the one-tailed probabilities (p) associated with a value as small as the observed value of x = the number of fewer signs. For a two-tailed test, double the value of p shown in Table R.

     (b)   If N is greater than 25, compute the value of χ^2 or z. In the case of χ^2, Table L of the appendix may be referred to. This table gives the critical values of χ^2 at various levels of significance for a particular number of df. In the case of z, Table A of the appendix may be consulted. This table gives one-tailed p associated with values as extreme as various values of z. For a two-tailed test, double the value of p shown in Table A. Both χ^2 and z tests take into consideration the *Yates' correction for continuity* while computing the respective values.

If the computed value of χ^2 is equal to or greater than the critical value of χ^2 at a chosen level of significance for a particular df, then the observed differences between the paired scores are considered to be significant ($p \leq \alpha$). If the computed χ^2 is lower than the critical χ^2, the observed differences are not significant ($p > \alpha$). If, on the other hand, the computed value of z is 1.96 or 2.58, then it is significant at 0.05 level or 0.01 level of significance, respectively. If the computed z is less than 1.96, then it is not significant. Alternatively when we refer to Table A of the appendix), if the p yielded by the z-test is equal to or less than α, then H_0 is rejected in favour of H_1.

17.2.5   Power-efficiency

The power-efficiency of the sign test is about 95% for $N=6$, but it declines as the size of the sample increases to an eventual (asymptotic) efficiency of 63%.

The step-wise computational procedures of the sign test will become more clear to the researchers through the following examples.

Example 17.1 The following are the scores of individuals who are matched and assigned to one of the two groups at random. Apply a sign test and test the null hypothesis that the two samples come from population with the same median.

X	16	12	22	16	14	10	20	18	10	22
Y	4	18	10	14	12	14	10	12	4	12

Solution
The following steps are to be followed for the solution of the above problem.

(a)   The given paired data are entered in Table 17.1

(b)   Statement of the null hypothesis (H_0) and alternative hypothesis (H_1).

H_0: The median difference between the pairs is zero.
H_1: The median difference between the pairs is not zero.

It is a two-tailed test because no direction of the difference is predicted. Let $\alpha=0.05$.

(c)   The algebraic sign of the difference between the score of each pair ($X- Y$) is recorded in the bottom row of Table 17.1. The number of plus and minus signs are counted out and noted.

Number of + signs=8; Number of - signs=2
$N=$ The number of matched pair which showed difference$=8+2=10$
$x=$the number of fewer signs$=2$

Table 17.1   Sign test for the paired scores

X	16	12	22	16	14	10	20	18	10	22
Y	4	18	10	14	12	14	10	12	4	12
Sign of X– Y	+	−	+	+	+	−	+	+	+	+

(d) Test of significance of the obtained result. Since in the given example $N=10$, it is a small sample case. We can test the H_0 with reference to Table R of the appendix. This table shows that for $N=10$, $x \leq 2$ has one-tailed probability of occurrence under H_0 of $p=0.055$. For a two-tailed test, the probability is 0.11. Since this p, either 0.055 or 0.11, is greater than $\alpha=0.05$, the obtained value of $x=2$ is not significant. The H_0 is accepted. That means the median difference between the pairs is zero. Therefore, we may conclude that the two samples come from populations with the same median.

Example 17.2 The following data are obtained from a matched-group paired observation. Test the hypothesis of no difference by using a sign test.

$$\text{Number of + signs} = 30; \quad \text{Number of − signs} = 10; \quad N=40$$

Solution

(a) Statement of the H_0 and H_1, and α level:

H_0: There is no difference between + and − signs.
H_1: There is a difference between + and − signs.

Let $\alpha=0.05$; since no direction of the difference is predicted, it is a two-tailed test.

(b) Since in the given data $N=40$, it is a large sample case. We can test the H_0 with the help of either χ^2 test or z test.

(c) Let us first apply χ^2 test. The observed frequencies (f_o) of + signs is 30 and − signs is 10. According to the H_0 the expected frequencies (f_e) of each type of sign is $N/2=20$. The formula for computing χ^2 incorporating *Yates' correction for continuity* reads,

$$\chi^2 = \sum \frac{(|f_o - f_e| - 0.5)^2}{f_e} = \frac{(|30-20|-0.5)^2}{20} + \frac{(|10-20|-0.5)^2}{20}$$

$$= \frac{(9.5)^2}{20} + \frac{(9.5)^2}{20} = 4.5125 + 4.5125 = 9.025$$

$$df = c - 1 = 2 - 1 = 1$$

Referring to Table L of the appendix, the critical value of χ^2, with df=1 at 0.05 level is 3.84, and at 0.01 level is 6.64. Since the obtained $\chi^2=9.025$ exceeds the critical value of 6.64, it is significant beyond 0.01 level of significance. So, the H_0 is rejected in favour of H_1 ($p<0.01$). Therefore, it is reasonable to conclude that there is a significant difference between the number of plus and minus signs and thus, the median difference between the matched pairs is not zero; the two samples have come from populations with different medians.

Alternatively, we may apply z-test for testing the H_0. In the given data, the number of + signs is 30 and − signs is 10, and $N=40$. The difference between + and − signs is

$$D = 30 - 10 = 20.$$

The formula for the computation of z incorporating the correction for continuity reads

$$z = \frac{|D|-1}{\sqrt{N}} = \frac{20-1}{\sqrt{40}} = \frac{19}{6.325} = 3.004$$

Since the obtained value of $z=3.004$ is greater than the critical value of z of 2.58, it is significant beyond 0.01 level of significance. The reader may notice that both χ^2 test and z-test rejected the H_0 at the same level of significance. So, similar conclusions are drawn, as it is drawn in the case of χ^2 test noted above, and with df=1, $\chi^2=z^2$.

17.3   The Wilcoxon Matched-pairs Signed-ranks Test

The Wilcoxon matched-pairs signed-ranks test is a powerful non-parametric alternative to student's *t*-test for finding the *significance of difference between paired observations* of single group and matched-pair experiment. It can be applied to both continuous and discrete variables irrespective of the normality or non-normality of their distributions in the population, and even to small samples.

It is a more powerful test than the sign test though both are applied to two *correlated samples* or matched, paired observations, because it takes into account more information than the sign test. The sign test that we have just discussed utilises information simply about the *direction* of the differences within pairs (i.e., either + or – signs), whereas the Wilcoxon matched-pairs signed-ranks test utilises information about the relative *magnitude* as well as the *direction* of the differences within pairs. The Wilcoxon matched-pairs signed-ranks test gives more weight to a pair which shows a large difference between the two conditions than to a pair which shows a small difference. It is less powerful than the *t*-test.

The null hypothesis (H_0) contends that there is no significant difference between the scores of each pair of observations, and that any observed difference results from mere chances of random sampling. To be more simple, the H_0 states that the sum of the positive ranks = the sum of the negative ranks. On the contrary, the H_1 states that the sum of the positive ranks $\neq$ the sum of the negative ranks.

17.3.1   Assumptions of the Wilcoxon Matched-pairs Signed-ranks Test

To apply the Wilcoxon signed-ranks test, it should be justifiable to assume that

  (i)   Each pair of scores or observations occurs at random in the sample, independent of all other pairs.
 (ii)   The variable under study has a continuous distribution.
(iii)   The test does not make any assumption about the form of the distribution of differences. It only requires that within each pair the experimenter has achieved matching with respect to the relevant extraneous variable.

17.3.2   Computation of the Wilcoxon Matched-pairs Signed-ranks Test

To illustrate this test of significance we use the data presented in Table 17.2.

The following steps are to be followed for the computation of Wilcoxon matched-pairs signed-ranks test:

  (a)   The difference between each pair of scores is obtained. Let us denote this difference as *d*. Each pair has one *d* (see Table 17.2). While obtaining *d*'s, we might get two equal scores of any pair, so that *d*=0 (this happens in case of tied scores). Such pairs are dropped from the analysis. This is the same practice that we follow with the sign test. *N*=the number of matched pairs minus the number of pairs whose *d*=0.

  (b)   All the non-zero *d*'s are then assigned ranks in an ascending order according to their absolute magnitudes or values, 'absolute' meaning to disregard or ignore algebraic signs. To be more simple, rank of 1 is assigned to the smallest *d* in the series, the rank of 2 to the next smallest and so on. When we rank the *d*'s without respect to signs, a *d* of –1 or 1 is given a lower rank than a *d* of –2 or 2. If two or more *d*'s have the same absolute value, irrespective of their algebraic signs, each is assigned a rank which is the

Table 17.2   Wilcoxon matched-pairs signed-ranks test for paired scores

Pairs	X	Y	Difference (d) (X– Y)	Ranks of d	R(+)	R(–)
a	16	4	12	9.5	9.5	
b	12	18	–6	–5		5
c	22	10	12	9.5	9.5	
d	16	14	2	1.5	1.5	
e	14	12	2	1.5	1.5	
f	10	14	–4	–3		3
g	20	10	10	7.5	7.5	
h	18	12	6	5	5	
i	10	4	6	5	5	
j	22	12	10	7.5	7.5	
N=10					47.0 $\Sigma R(+)$	8 $\Sigma R(-)$

average of the ranks that would have been assigned if the d's had differed slightly. Such a case happens in case of tied differences (d's).

(c) Then to each rank affix the sign of the difference. That is, indicate which ranks arose from negative d's and which ranks arose from positive d's. In short, the original algebraic signs of the differences are then assigned to their respective ranks.

(d) The ranks with identical algebraic signs are then added together. This process gives two types of *sums of ranks*, one for *plus signed-ranks*, and the other for *minus signed-ranks*. The smaller of these rank sums, in absolute value irrespective of signs, is taken as the statistic T. Put it into other words, let T= the smaller sum of like-signed ranks. That is, T is either the sum of the positive ranks or the sum of the negative ranks, whichever sum is smaller. Thus, in the given illustration (see Table 17.2) the computed or obtained T=8.

(e) Then the significance of the obtained value of T is tested in the following alternative ways depending upon the sample size—whether it is a small sample case or a large sample case, which are discussed in detail under the heading 'Testing the Significance of the Obtained T'.

17.3.3   Testing the Significance of the Obtained *T*

The test of the significance of the computed T or the test of the correctness of the H_0 (i.e., the sum of the positive ranks=the sum of the negative ranks) depends upon the size of the sample—whether it is a small sample case or a large sample case. If N (number of non-zero d's) is equal to or less than 25 ($N \le 25$), it is known as a small sample case, and N greater than 25 ($N>25$) is a large sample case.

Moreover, the Wilcoxon matched-pairs signed-ranks test may be either one tailed or two tailed. In a one-tailed test the advance prediction (H_1) states that the sum of the negative ranks would be the smaller sum. In a two-tailed test, the advance prediction (H_1) states that the two sums of ranks (i.e., sum of plus ranks and sum of minus ranks) would differ.

In small sample cases, the significance of the obtained T can be tested with reference to Table S of the appendix. This table gives various critical values of T and their associated levels of significance. That is, if an observed T is equal to or less than the critical value of T given in Table S under a particular significance level for the observed value of N, the H_0 may then be rejected at that level of significance. If the obtained T exceeds the critical T, then it is not significant, and hence, the H_0 is accepted. Table S of the appendix is adapted for use with both one-tailed and two-tailed tests. The significance level for a two-tailed test is double that for a one-tailed test.

In the illustrative example (see Table 17.2), $T=8$ and $N=10$. It is a small sample case, and we test the significance of the computed T with reference to Table S. Let us assume it a two-tailed test with our alpha $=0.05$. Referring to Table S of the appendix, for $N=10$, the critical value of T at 0.05 level is 8 and at 0.01 level is 3. Since the obtained $T=8$ is equal to the critical value of T for 0.05 level for a two-tailed test, it is significant; hence we reject the H_0 at the 5% level ($p<0.05$).

In a large sample case (when $N>25$), Table S of the appendix cannot be used. However, it can be shown that in such cases the sum of the ranks, T, is practically normally distributed with

$$\text{Mean of } T = \mu_T = \bar{T} = \frac{N(N+1)}{4}$$

$$\text{and Standard deviation} = \sigma_T = \sqrt{\frac{(2N+1)\bar{T}}{6}} = \sqrt{\frac{N(N+1)(2N+1)}{24}}$$

$$\text{Therefore, } z = \frac{T-\bar{T}}{\sigma_T}$$

is approximately normally distributed with zero mean and unit variance. If the obtained value of z is 1.96 or 2.58, then it is significant at 0.05 or 0.01 levels, respectively, in a two-tailed test. Therefore, we may directly test the significance of the obtained z or we may refer to Table A of the appendix which gives the probabilities associated with the occurrence under H_0 of various values as extreme as an observed z computed from the above noted formula.

For example, suppose 30 pairs were observed and none of them showed a d of 0. The smaller of the sums of the like-signed ranks is 90. That means, in this example, $N=30$ and $T=90$. So, it is a large sample case, and hence we apply z-test for testing the significance of the obtained T as follows:

$$\bar{T} = \frac{N(N+1)}{4} = \frac{30(30+1)}{4} = 232.5$$

$$\sigma_T = \sqrt{\frac{N(N+1)(2N+1)}{24}} = \sqrt{\frac{30(30+1)(2\times30+1)}{24}} = \sqrt{\frac{30\times31\times61}{24}} = 48.62$$

$$z = \frac{T-\bar{T}}{\sigma_T} = \frac{90-232.5}{48.62} = -2.93$$

Since the computed z value (absolute value) of 2.93 is greater than 2.58, it is significant beyond 0.01 level of significance (for a two-tailed test). *Alternatively*, we may refer to Table A of the appendix. This table shows that z as extreme as -2.93 has a one-tailed probability associated with its occurrence under H_0 of $p=0.0017$. For a two-tailed test the p is 0.0034 (i.e., $0.0017 \times 2 = 0.0034$). This p is less than $\alpha=0.01$ and thus the value of z is in the region of rejection; our decision is to reject H_0 in favour of H_1. We conclude that the sum of the $+$ signed ranks and the sum of the $-$ signed ranks are not equal.

17.3.4   Summary of Procedures

The following are the steps to be followed in the use of the Wilcoxon matched-pairs signed-ranks test:

(i)   For each matched pair, determine the signed difference (d) between the two scores.

(ii) Drop those 0 value ds from the analysis. Rank those non-zero ds without respect to algebraic sign. With tied ds, assign the average of the tied ranks.

(iii) Affix to each rank the sign (+ or –) of the d which it represents.

(iv) Determine T=the smaller of the sums of the like-signed ranks.

(v)   By counting, determine N=the total number of ds having a sign.

(vi) The procedure for determining the significance of the observed value of T depends on the size of N.

    (a)   If N is 25 or less, Table S of the appendix is referred to. This table gives the critical values of T for various sizes of N. If the obtained value of T is equal to or less than that given in the table for a particular significance level and a particular N, H_0 may be rejected at that level of significance.

    (b)   If N is larger than 25, compute the value of z as defined by the formula discussed earlier for the said purpose. Directly test its significance taking the computed value of z. That means, z values of 1.96 and 2.58 are required for its significance at 0.05 or 0.01 levels, respectively. Alternatively, determine its associated probability under H_0 by referring to Table A of the appendix. For a two-tailed test, double the p shown in that table. If the p thus obtained is equal to or less than α, reject H_0.

17.3.5   Power-efficiency

When the assumptions of the parametric t-test are in fact met, the asymptotic efficiency near H_0 of the Wilcoxon matched-pairs signed-ranks test compared with the t-test is $3/\pi = 95.5\%$. This means that $3/\pi$ is the limiting ratio of sample sizes necessary for the Wilcoxon test and the t-test to attain the same power. For small samples, the efficiency is near 95%.

The step-wise computational procedures of the Wilcoxon matched-pairs signed-ranks test will become more clear to the readers through the following examples.

Example 17.3 In a fictitious study, the social perceptiveness scores of 'nursery school' and 'home' children are given below. These children are twins. Test whether nursery school experience does affect the social perceptiveness of children.

Pairs	a	b	c	d	e	f	g	h
Nursery School	82	69	73	43	58	56	76	85
Home	63	42	74	37	51	43	80	82

Solution

The following steps are to be followed for the solution of the above problem.

(a)   The given paired data are entered in Table 17.3.

(b)   Statement of the H_0 and H_1, and α level.

    H_0: Nursery School experience does not affect the social perceptiveness of children.
    H_1: Nursery School experience does affect the social perceptiveness of children.

Table 17.3 Social perceptiveness scores of nursery school and home twin children

Pairs	Nursery School	Home	d	Ranks of d	R(+)	R(−)
a	82	63	19	7	7	
b	69	42	27	8	8	
c	73	74	−1	−1		1
d	43	37	6	4	4	
e	58	51	7	5	5	
f	56	43	13	6	6	
g	76	80	−4	−3		3
h	85	82	3	2	2	
N=8					32 $\Sigma R(+)$	4 $\Sigma R(-)$

It is a two-tailed test. Let $\alpha=0.05$.

(c) The difference (d) between each pair of scores is recorded in Table 17.3, and all ds are non-zero, and there is no tied ds. So, N=8.

(d) All the non-zero ds are assigned ranks in an ascending order, according to their absolute values disregarding the algebraic signs.

(e) Then the original algebraic signs of the ds are assigned to their respective ranks.

(f) The like-signed ranks are summed up. It was found that the sum of the + signed ranks is 32 and the sum of the − signed ranks is 4, which are recorded in Table 17.3. Thus, T is 4.

(g) Since N=8, it is a small sample case and we test the significance of the obtained T with reference to Table S of the appendix. Referring to Table S, the critical value of T, for N=8, at 0.05 level is 4 and at 0.01 level is 0. Since the obtained T=4 is equal to the critical value of T at 0.05 level, it is significant at $\alpha=0.05$ for a two-tailed test. Therefore, we reject H$_0$ in favour of H$_1$ (p<0.05) in this fictitious study, concluding that nursery school experience does affect the social perceptiveness of children.

Example 17.4 In a study on 30 matched pairs of prisoners, their latency of times of incorrectly predicted and correctly predicted decisions were recorded. Four pairs showed differences of zero. The obtained value of T=53. Test the significance of the computed T.

Solution

(a) Statement of the H$_0$ and H$_1$, and α level.

H$_0$: There is no difference between the latency times of incorrectly predicted and correctly predicted decisions.

H$_1$: The latency times of incorrectly predicted decisions are longer than the latency times of correctly predicted decisions.

Let $\alpha=0.01$.

Since the direction of the difference is predicted, the region of rejection is one-tailed. Thus, it is a one-tailed test.

(b) In the above example, 30 matched pairs of prisoners served as the subjects. Four pairs of subjects showed differences of zero. Thus,

N = the number of matched pairs minus the number of pairs whose $d=0=30-4=26$.

The obtained $T=53$.

(c) Since the given data is a larger sample case, we should apply z-test for testing the correctness of H_0. So, we should compute the statistics like $\bar{T}$, σ_T, and z basing on the given data, as follows:

$$\bar{T} = \frac{N(N+1)}{4} = \frac{26(26+1)}{4} = \frac{26 \times 27}{4} = 175.5$$

$$\sigma_T = \sqrt{\frac{N(N+1)(2N+1)}{24}} = \sqrt{\frac{26 \times 27 \times 53}{24}} = 39.37$$

$$z = \frac{T-\bar{T}}{\sigma_T} = \frac{53-175.5}{39.37} = -3.11$$

(d) In order to test the correctness of H_0, we can test the obtained z directly or we may refer to Table A of the appendix. As we know that z values of 1.65 and 2.33 are required in order to be significant at 0.05 and at 0.01 levels in a one-tailed test, respectively, the obtained z value of –3.11 (or absolute z value = 3.11) is significant beyond 0.01 level of significance.

Alternatively, referring to Table A shows that z as extreme as –3.11 has a one-tailed probability associated with its occurrence under H_0 of $p = 0.0009$. Inasmuch as this p is less than $\alpha = 0.01$ and thus the value of z is in the region of rejection, our decision is to reject H_0 in favour of H_1. We conclude that the prisoners' latency times for incorrectly predicted decisions were significantly longer than their latency times for correctly predicted decisions.

17.4   The Wilcoxon Composite Rank Test or Rank Sum Test

The sign test and the Wilcoxon matched-pairs signed-ranks test, which we have already discussed in this chapter under sections 17.2 and 17.3, respectively, are the non-parametric alternatives to Student's t-test for two correlated samples. That means, these two tests are used for comparing two correlated samples or matched-pair observations.

The most commonly used rank test for comparing two independent samples is the Wilcoxon rank sum test which is also known as Wilcoxon composite rank test. It is a good non-parametric alternative to Student's t-test for finding the significance of difference between unpaired observations of two independent samples. It can be applied to both continuous and discrete variables, irrespective of the normal or non-normal nature of their distribution in the population, and even to small samples.

The null hypothesis (H_0) proposes that there is no significant difference between the scores of two independent samples, and that any observed difference has resulted from mere chances of random sampling. In short, the H_0 states that the two samples come from populations with the same distribution.

17.4.1   Assumptions of the Wilcoxon Rank Sum Test

To apply the Wilcoxon rank sum test or composite rank test, it should be justifiable to assume that:

(i)   Each score of a sample occurs at random and independent of all other scores.
(ii)   The variable under study has a continuous distribution.
(iii)   The data should be in terms of ranks. If scores are given, then those should be converted into ranks.

17.4.2 Computation of the Wilcoxon Rank Sum Test

To illustrate this test of significance, we use the data given in Table 17.4.

The following steps are to be followed for the computation of Wilcoxon rank sum test or composite rank test:

(a)   All the observations or scores of both the samples are combined together or are taken as a composite group, and then these are ranked in order of their increasing sizes. For example, rank 1 is assigned to the smallest score, rank 2 to the next smallest in the series and so on.

(b)   When tied scores occur in the series, we give each of the tied scores the average of the ranks they would have had if no ties had occurred. The score next higher than those of a tied set of scores is assigned the same rank as it would have got if the tied scores had separate consecutive ranks instead of an average rank. For example, suppose there are two scores of 3, which are the smallest scores in the series. Then each score of 3 is assigned a rank of 1.5 (the average of ranks 1 and 2; i.e., $\frac{1+2}{2} = 1.5$). Suppose the next higher score in the series is 5, then this is assigned a rank of 3.

Table 17.4 Wilcoxon composite rank test or rank sum test for scores of two independent samples

Scores		Ranks	
Sample I	**Sample II**	**Sample I**	**Sample II**
27	6	5	1
33	9	7	2
37	14	8	3
52	16	13	4
53	29	14	6
57	43	16	9
69	45	18	10
70	47	19	11
71	50	20	12
77	55	22	15
	63		17
	72		21
Total N_1=10	N_2=12	142 (R_1)	111

(c) The sum of ranks, R_1, is obtained for the smaller of the two samples, if the samples are unequal in size. If the samples are equal in size, either rank sum may be used. In the illustrative example, both samples are unequal in size. So, R_1 is 142 (the sum of ranks of the smaller sample). The sum of ranks, R_1, is then evaluated in relation to its distribution, which is discussed below. The total of rank sums of both samples should be N $(N+1)/2$, where $N = N_1 + N_2$.

(d) The evaluation or the test of significance of the obtained R_1 depends upon the size of the samples—whether it is a small samples case or large samples case. If neither N_1 nor N_2 is greater than 25 (i.e., both N_1 and $N_2 \le 25$), it is a small samples case. If either N_1 or N_2 or both, are greater than 25 (i.e., N_1 or $N_2 > 25$), it is a large samples case.

In small samples case, we refer to Table T of the appendix for testing the significance of the obtained R_1. Table T shows the exact lower-tail critical values of R_1 for N_1 and N_2 up to 25 at probability levels equal to or less than 0.10, 0.05, 0.025, 0.01, 0.005 and 0.001. These probabilities given in Table T are for a directional (or one-tailed) test. For a non-directional (or two-tailed) test the probabilities in the table are doubled. To enter Table T of the appendix, we need to calculate the mean of R_1, which is denoted by $\bar{R}_1$.

$$\bar{R}_1 = \frac{N_1(N_1 + N_2 + 1)}{2}$$

For example, Table T shows a $p = 0.05$ for $R_1 = 19$ where $N_1 = 5$ and $N_2 = 5$. This means that the probability of obtaining a value equal to or less than R_1 in samples of this size is equal to or less than 0.05. This is a directional or one-tailed test which uses the lower tail of the distribution. Since the distribution is symmetrical, the corresponding upper-tail values are given by noting that a lower-tail value R_1 is $\bar{R}_1 - R_1$ points below the mean. The corresponding value above the mean is $\bar{R}_1 + (\bar{R}_1 - R_1) = 2\bar{R}_1 - R_1$. If R_1 is an upper-tail value, that is, if it is above the mean, Table T is entered with $2\bar{R}_1 - R_1$. The null hypothesis (H$_0$) is rejected if it is smaller than the critical value. To assist calculation, Table T shows values of $2\bar{R}_1$. In the above illustrative example (Table 17.4) R_1 is 142 for $N_1 = 10$ and $N_2 = 12$. The mean value is 115 (i.e., $2\bar{R} = 230$; $\bar{R} = 115$, see Table T of the appendix) for $N_1 = 10$ and $N_2 = 12$. The R_1 of 142, which is greater than $\bar{R}_1$ of 115, is the upper-tail value. So the lower-tail value corresponding to this R_1 value is $2\bar{R}_1 - R_1 = 230 - 142 = 88$. Entering Table T, we note that p is slightly less than 0.05. Thus, R_1 is significant at 0.05 level for a directional or one-tailed test. For a non-directional or two-tailed test, either R_1 or $2\bar{R}_1 - R_1$, whichever is appropriate, is referred to Table T and the probabilities in the table are doubled. The appropriate choice between R_1 and $2\bar{R}_1 - R_1$ is, of course, always the smaller one.

The above discussion sounds rather complex. In practice the procedure is simple. *First*, calculate R_1, and then calculate $\bar{R}_1$ by the formula noted earlier. *Second*, if R_1 is less than $\bar{R}_1$, refer R_1 to Table T to obtain the required probability. *Third*, if R_1 is greater than $\bar{R}_1$, calculate $2\bar{R}_1 - R_1$ and refer this quantity to Table T to obtain the required probability.

In a large sample case (when either N_1 or N_2 is greater than 25), the distribution approaches the normal form. In this case, a large-sample procedure using the normal approximation and a continuity correction is applied to determine the required probabilities. The normal deviate z with a continuity correction is given by

$$z = \frac{|R_1 - \bar{R}_1| - \frac{1}{2}}{\sigma_{R_1}}$$

where the $\bar{R}_1$ and standard deviation of R_1 (σ_{R_1}) are calculated as follows:

$$\bar{R}_1 = \frac{N_1(N_1 + N_2 + 1)}{2}$$

$$\sigma_{R_1} = \sqrt{\frac{N_1 N_2 (N_1 + N_2 + 1)}{12}}$$

If the obtained z value is equal to or greater than 1.96 or 2.58, we reject the H_0 for a two-tailed test at the 0.05 or 0.01 level and accept the H_1 that the samples are from different populations. For a one-tailed test, the z values required for significance at 0.05 and 0.01 levels are 1.65 and 2.33, respectively.

Suppose, in an experiment two independent groups of 30 subjects each are studied. R_1 is 810 and $\bar{R} = 915$. It is a large sample case, $N_1 = 30$ and $N_2 = 30$.

$$\sigma_{R_1} = \sqrt{\frac{N_1 N_2 (N_1 + N_2 + 1)}{12}} = \sqrt{\frac{30 \times 30 \times 61}{12}} = 67.64$$

$$z = \frac{|R_1 - \bar{R}_1| - \frac{1}{2}}{\sigma_{R_1}} = \frac{|810 - 915| - 0.5}{67.64} = 1.54$$

Since the obtained z value is 1.54, it is not significant. Thus, H_0 is accepted and we conclude that the two samples are from the same population.

When ties occur, the tied observations may be assigned the average of the ranks they would occupy if no ties had occurred. If ties are fairly numerous, a correction may be applied to the standard deviation of R_1 in the denominator of the z ratio. Corrected for ties, the σ_{R_1} becomes

$$\sigma_{R_1} = \sqrt{\frac{N_1 N_2}{N(N-1)}\left(\frac{N^3 - N}{12} - \sum T\right)}$$

where
$N = N_1 + N_2$ and $T = \frac{t^2 - t}{12}$, where t = number of scores tied at a particular rank. The summation of $T(\sum T)$ extends over all groups of ties.

17.4.3   Summary of Procedures

The following are the steps to be followed in the use of the Wilcoxon rank sum test or composite rank test.

(i)   All the scores of both the samples are combined together as a series and then these are ranked in a single ascending order of their values.

(ii)   Rank 1 is assigned to the lowest score in the series, rank 2 to the next lowest score and so on. Tied scores are assigned the average of the ranks they would have had if no ties had occurred.

(iii)   The sum of ranks, R_1, is obtained for the smaller sample if $N_1 \neq N_2$. If $N_1 = N_2$, either rank sum may be used.

(iv)   The mean of R_1 ($\bar{R}_1$) is computed by using the formula discussed earlier in this chapter. If R_1 is less than $\bar{R}_1$, then R_1 should be taken for the test of significance. If R_1 is greater than $\bar{R}_1$, then $2\bar{R}_1 - R_1$ is calculated and this value will be taken for the test of significance. The appropriate choice between R_1 and $2\bar{R}_1 - R_1$ is, of course, always the smaller one.

(v)   The procedure for determining the significance of the obtained R_1 depends on the size of the samples.

   (a)   In small samples case (i.e., $N_1 \leq 25$ and $N_2 \leq 25$) Table T of the appendix is referred to. This table gives the critical values of R_1 for various sizes of N_1 and N_2 at different levels of significance. If the obtained value of R_1 is equal to or less than that given in the table for a particular significance level and for particular sizes of N_1 and N_2, H_0 may be rejected at that level or less than that level of significance.

   (b)   In large samples case (i.e., either N_1 or N_2 is greater than 25), z value is computed by the formula noted above for the said purpose. Then the computed value of z is taken directly for the test of its significance. z values of 1.96 and 2.58 are required to be significant at 0.05 and 0.01 levels, respectively, in a two-tailed test, and in a one-tailed test these values are 1.65 and 2.33, respectively.

17.4.4   Power-efficiency

The Wilcoxon rank sum test has an asymptotic relative efficiency when compared with the t-test for independent samples of $3/\pi=0.955\%$ or 95.5%. This comparison assumes that the distributions are normal. If the distributions are rectangular, the asymptotic relative efficiency is 1.00% or 100%. For certain other types of distributions the asymptotic relative efficiency is greater than 1.00. All the available evidence indicates that the Wilcoxon rank sum test is an excellent alternative to the t-test.

The step-wise computational procedures of the Wilcoxon rank sum test will become more clear to the readers through the following examples.

Example 17.5 The following are data for two independent groups of experimental children. Apply the Wilcoxon rank sum test and interpret the results:

Control	14	13	10	12	15	9	9
Experimental	5	7	6	5	11	8	10

Solution

The following steps are followed for the solution of the above problem:

(a)   The given data are entered in Table 17.5.

(b)   Statement of H_0 and H_1, and α level:

   H_0: The two samples have come from populations with the same distribution.
   H_1: The two sample have come from populations with different distributions.

   It is a two-tailed test, and let $\alpha = 0.05$.

(c)   All the scores of both the samples are combined and taken as a series. Thus, there are 14 scores in toto. These scores are ranked in a single ascending order of their values. We assign the lowest rank to the lowest score in the series. The tied scores are assigned the average of the ranks they would have had if no ties had occurred. In the given data there are two lowest scores of 5, each of which receives a rank of 1.5. The next lowest score of 6 then receives a rank of 3, and so on, until the highest score of 15 receives a rank of 14, which equals N (i.e., $N = N_1 + N_2$) unless there are ties for top place.

(d)   The ranks of each sample are then totalled separately. This gives two sums of ranks, R_c (rank sum for the control group) and R_e (rank sum for the experimental group), which

Table 17.5   Wilcoxon rank sum test for scores of two independent samples

Scores		Ranks	
Control	**Experimental**	**Control**	**Experimental**
14	5	13	1.5
13	7	12	4
10	6	8.5	3
12	5	11	1.5
15	11	14	10
9	8	6.5	5
9	10	6.5	8.5
Total $N_1=7$	$N_2=7$	71.5(R_c)	33.5(R_e)

are 71.5 and 33.5, respectively. Since both samples are of equal size ($N_1=N_2=7$), either rank sum may be used. But we select the smaller of the two sums, which happens to be R_e in this problem, as our sampling statistic R_1.

(e)   The mean of R_1, that is, $\bar{R}_1$ is calculated as follows:

$$\bar{R}_1 = \frac{N_1(N_1+N_2+1)}{2} = \frac{7(7+7+1)}{2} = \frac{7 \times 15}{2} = 52.5$$

(f)   Since R_1 is less than $\bar{R}_1$, and it is a small samples case, we refer R_1 to Table T of the appendix to obtain the required probability. This table shows that the lower-tail critical values of R_1 at 0.05 and 0.01 levels for $N_1=7$ and $N_2=7$ are 39 and 34, respectively. Since the obtained value of $R_1=33.5$ is smaller than both the critical values, it is significant at 0.01 level of significance. So the H_0 is rejected at 0.01 level in a one-tailed test and at 0.02 level in a two-tailed test. Thus, we conclude that the two samples have come from populations with different distributions. The rank sums of two samples are not evenly distributed.

Example 17.6 The following data are obtained from an experiment of two groups of experimental animals. Apply the Wilcoxon rank sum test and interpret the results:

Control Group	$N_1=25$	$R_c=530$
Experimental Group	$N_2=30$	$R_e=1010$

Solution

(a)   Statement of H_0 and H_1, and α level.

H_0: the two samples come from the same population.
H_1: the two samples come from different populations.

It is a two-tailed test. Let $\alpha=0.05$.

(b) Since in the given example, the samples are unequal in size, the sum of the ranks of the smaller sample (i.e., the control group, $N_1 = 25$) is taken as the sampling statistic, R_1, which is equal to 530.

(c) The mean of R_1 (that is $\bar{R}_1$) is computed as follows:

$$\bar{R}_1 = \frac{N_1(N_1 + N_2 + 1)}{2} = \frac{25(25 + 30 + 1)}{2} = 700$$

(d) Since the given example is a large sample case, a large-sample procedure using the normal approximation and a continuity correction should be applied for testing the significance of R_1. The normal deviate z with a continuity correction is given by

$$z = \frac{|R_1 - \bar{R}_1| - \frac{1}{2}}{\sigma_{R_1}} = \frac{|R - \bar{R}_2| - \frac{1}{2}}{\sqrt{\dfrac{N_1 N_2 (N_1 + N_2 + 1)}{12}}} = \frac{|530 - 700| - 0.5}{\sqrt{\dfrac{25 \times 30(25 + 30 + 1)}{12}}} = \frac{169.5}{59.16} = 2.86$$

Since the obtained z value is 2.86, which is greater than 2.58, we reject the H_0 for a two-tailed test at 0.01 level and accept the H_1, which states that the samples are from different populations.

17.5   The Mann–Whitney U-test

The Mann–Whitney U-test is sometimes referred to as the rank test or sum-of-ranks test; and if the two groups are equal, it is the same as the Wilcoxon T-test. This is one of the most powerful of the non-parametric tests, and it is a most powerful and an efficient non-parametric alternative to the parametric t-test with two independent groups. The U-test can be applied to both continuous and discrete measurement variables, irrespective of normality or non-normality of their distributions in the population, and also to very small samples. It is particularly used to test the significance of difference between the unpaired observations of two independent samples (or groups) either of equal or unequal sizes.

The Mann–Whitney U-test is applicable when we have scores for two separate, independent or uncorrelated groups. It is also applicable when the researcher wishes to avoid the t-test's assumptions or when the measurement in the research is weaker than interval scaling.

The power of the U-test is slightly lower than that of the t-test, but higher than those of the Wilcoxon rank sum test (composite rank test) and the median test (see Section 17.6).

The null hypothesis (H_0) and the alternative hypothesis (H_1) are stated in terms of consistent, systematic differences between the two independent samples. The resulting hypotheses are as follows:

H_0: There is no tendency for the ranks in one sample to be systematically higher or lower than the ranks in the other sample. There is no difference between the two samples. The two independent samples have been drawn from the same population.

H_1: The ranks in one sample are systematically higher (or lower) than the ranks in the other sample. There is a difference between the two samples. The two independent samples have not been drawn from the same population.

17.5.1   Assumptions of U-test

Since the Mann–Whitney U-test is a non-parametric statistical test, most of the assumptions of the non-parametric tests are the assumptions of the U-test. These assumptions are discussed below:

(a) The observations must be independent. This implies two things—one, the selection of samples from the population should be random and independent, and second, the assignment of scores to the performance of the subjects should be unbiased and impartial. In other words, each score occurs in the sample at random and independent of all other scores.

(b) The trait or the dependent variable that the researcher is going to measure must have underlying continuity. This implies that the trait must be present in each and every element of the population irrespective of its magnitude; nowhere in the element of the population from which the samples are drawn the trait is absent. It must be present in any amount—whether large or small.

(c) The measurements should be in terms of the ordinal scale of measurement. If data are given in interval scale, then it must be converted into ordinal scale before the value of U is computed. In other words, when at least ordinal measurement has been achieved, the Mann-Whitney U-test may be used to test whether two independent groups have been drawn from the same population.

(d) The two groups of samples must be independent or uncorrelated for the U-test to be applied.

17.5.2   Computation of U Values

In Mann-Whitney U-test, we have always only two independent groups (or samples), and therefore, two ns. Let n_1=the number of cases in the smaller of two independent groups, and n_2=the number of cases in the larger one. If both the samples are equal in size, either n may be used as n_1 or n_2. To apply the U-test, we first combine the observations or scores from both groups, and rank these in the order of increasing size. Rank 1 is assigned to the smallest value in the series, rank 2 to the next smallest and so on. In this ranking, algebraic size is considered, that is, the lowest ranks are assigned to the largest negative numbers, if any. When tied scores occur, we give each of the tied observations the average of the ranks they would have had if no ties had occurred.

We can divide the computational procedures of U into two classes (i) U for small samples, and (ii) U for large samples. These are discussed in detail below:

17.5.2.1   *Computation of U for Small Samples*

The computation of U for small samples can be divided into two categories, such as, (a) very small samples (neither n_1 nor n_2 is larger than 8), and (b) relatively small samples (n_2 is between 9 and 20). The computation of U for these two types of small samples is discussed below one after another.

Very Small Samples (neither n_1 nor n_2 is larger than 8)

In very small samples (when $n_1 \leq 8$ and $n_2 \leq 8$), the U can be calculated in two ways: one, by the *counting method*, and second, by the *ranking method using equations*. Whichever method is used, there are always two values (or numbers) that result. The smaller of the two numbers is arbitrarily called U (the statistic used in this test) and the larger U'. Note that U and U' indicate the same degree of separation between the two independent samples. Let us first see how to calculate U and U' by the *counting method* and then by the *ranking method using the equations*.

We will begin with the following illustrative example.

Example for very small samples. Two independent groups of rats, one experimental group (E) having five rats, and one control group (C) having four rats were taken. The following are their learning scores. Test whether the previous training facilitated the performance:

E Scores	68	54	65	35	72
C Scores	80	60	43	41	

In the above illustrative example, $n_1 = 4$ (number of C scores) and $n_2 = 5$ (number of E scores). The value of U is given by the number of times that a score in the group with n_2 cases precedes a score in the group with n_1 cases in the ascending order of the combined scores of both samples.

There are two steps involved in calculating U and U' by the *counting method.*

First, we combine the scores from both groups and arrange these scores in the order of increasing size (i.e., from lowest to highest scores), retaining the identity of each score as follows:

35	41	43	54	60	65	68	72	80
E	C	C	E	C	E	E	E	C

Second, count the number of E scores that precede (or lower than) C scores, or the number of C scores that precede (or lower than) E scores.

To count the total number of E scores that are lower than C scores, count the number of E scores that are lower than each C score and sum these values. Now consider the control group, and count the number of E scores that precede (or lower than) each C score. For the C score of 41, one E score precedes. This is also true for the C score of 43. For the next C score of 60, two E scores precede. And for the final C score of 80, five E scores precede. Thus, their sum equals to 9 (1+1+2+5=9). This means that there are 9 E scores that precede or lower than C scores. The same procedure is followed in counting the number of C scores that are lower than E scores. Now consider the experimental group and count the number of C scores that precede each E score, and sum these values. For the E score of 35, no C score precedes. For the next E score of 54, two C scores precede. For each of the E scores of 65, 68 and 72, three C scores precede. Their sum equals to 11 (0+2+3+3+3=11). Thus, there are 11 C scores that precede (or lower than) E scores. Since U is always the lowest of these two totals and U' the largest,

$$U = 9; \quad U' = 11$$

The sum of U and U' must equal to $n_1 n_2$. Thus,

$$U + U' = n_1 n_2$$

In the above illustrative example,

$$9 + 11 = 4 \times 5$$
$$20 = 20$$

Therefore, we can transform any U' to U by

$$U = n_1 n_2 - U'$$

In our illustrative example, by this transformation, $U = (4)(5) - 11 = 9$. Of course this is the U we found directly when we counted the number of E scores preceding each C score.

The *counting method* cannot be used when there are tied scores between samples. After all, which score would be put first when doing the rank ordering (or arranging the scores of both samples together in a single ascending order from lower to higher), the tied E score or the tied C score? Moreover, for fairly large values of n_1 and n_2, the counting method of determining the value of U may be rather tedious. An alternative method, which gives identical results, is the *equation method* or *equation solution*. Since the equation solution is more general, it can be used under all circumstances.

Next, let us illustrate how to calculate U and U' from equations. The equations are as follows:

$$U = n_1 n_2 + \frac{n_1(n_1+1)}{2} - R_1 \quad \text{or equivalently,} \quad U = n_1 n_2 + \frac{n_2(n_2+1)}{2} - R_2$$

where

n_1 = number of scores in the smaller group or sample
n_2 = number of scores in the larger group or sample
R_1 = sum of the ranks assigned to group whose sample size is n_1
R_2 = sum of the ranks assigned to group whose sample size is n_2

The above two equations will yield two different values of U. In an actual analysis, the equation that yields the lower value is the U equation; and the one that yields the higher value is the U' equation.

Let us try this method on the data given in the previous example. The E and C scores for that example are given again in Table 17.6 with their ranks.

The equation method of calculating U and U' involves the following three steps:

First, combine the scores of both the groups and assign the rank of 1 to the lowest score in the combined $(n_1 + n_2)$ group of scores, assign rank 2 to the next lowest score and so on.

Second, sum the ranks for each group; that is, determine R_1 and R_2. To find R_1, we add the ranks for group n_1, and to find R_2, we add the ranks for group n_2, as shown in Table 17.6.

Third, solve the equation for U and U'. For the given data, $R_1 = 19$ and $R_2 = 26$; $n_1 = 4$ and $n_2 = 5$.

$$U = n_1 n_2 + \frac{n_1(n_1+1)}{2} - R_1$$
$$= (4)(5) + \frac{4(4+1)}{2} - 19 = 20 + 10 - 19 = 11$$

Table 17.6   Learning scores of E and C rats

E Scores	Ranks	C Scores	Ranks
68	7	80	9
54	4	60	5
65	6	43	3
35	1	41	2
72	8		
$n_2 = 5$	$R_2 = 26$	$n_1 = 4$	$R_1 = 19$

or equivalently

$$U = n_1 n_2 + \frac{n_2(n_2+1)}{2} - R_2$$

$$= (4)(5) + \frac{5(5+1)}{2} - 26 = 20 + 15 - 26 = 9$$

Thus, $U=9$; $U'=11$

$U=9$ is of course exactly the value we found earlier by the counting method. The above two equations or formulae yield different U's. It is the smaller of these that we want (U), and the larger is U'. The investigator should check whether he has found U' rather than U by applying the following transformation formula,

$$U = n_1 n_2 - U'$$

Although the value of U can be found by computing both above formulae and choosing the smaller of the two results, a simple method is to use only one of those formulae and then find the other value of U by the transformation formula noted just immediately above.

Finally, we move for testing the significance of the obtained value of U. When neither n_1 nor n_2 is larger than 8, Table U of the appendix may be used to determine the exact probability associated with the occurrence under H_0 of any U as extreme as an observed value of U. The reader will observe that Table U is made up of six separate subtables, one for each value of n_2, from $n_2=3$ to $n_2=8$. To determine the probability under H_0 associated with his/her data, the researcher needs know only n_1 (the size of the smaller group), n_2 (the size of the larger group) and U. With this information he/she may read the value of probability (p) from the subtable appropriate to his/her value of n_2. The probabilities given in Table U are one-tailed. For a two-tailed test, the value of p given in the table should be doubled.

In our example, $n_1=4$, $n_2=5$ and $U=9$. The subtable for $n_2=5$ in Table U shows that $U \le 9$, when $n_1=4$, has a probability of occurrence under H_0 of $p=0.452$. Since this $p=0.452$ is greater than $\alpha=0.05$, it is not significant, because in order to be significant the probability associated with the obtained U value should be either equal to or less than the α levels. Therefore, H_0 is accepted. Basing on our analysis of data, it is reasonable to conclude that previous training does not facilitate the performance of the rats.

Relatively Small Samples (n_2 between 9 and 20)

The equations or formulae for computing the values of U are the same as used in case of a very small sample (where neither n_1 nor n_2 is larger than 8). However, testing the significance of the obtained U is different under both conditions that we will discuss later.

Let us begin with the following illustrative example. Table 17.7 shows the scores of two groups of subjects. We have to test whether the two independent groups differ significantly in their performance.

The following steps are to be followed for solving the above example through the equation method.

First, in the given illustrative example, the sizes of both the groups are same. So the size of either group may be denoted as n_1 and the other as n_2. Let us denote Group 1 as n_1 and Group 2 as n_2, and accordingly the rank sums are R_1 and R_2, respectively.

Second, we combine the scores of both the groups, and assign each of them the appropriate ranks using rank 1 for the lowest score in the combined series. Each of the tied scores will be assigned the average of the ranks they would have had if no ties had occurred. These assigned ranks are noted in Table 17.7 against each score.

Table 17.7   Performance scores of two independent groups of subjects

Group 1 Scores	Ranks	Group 2 Scores	Ranks
104	6	62	1
109	9	82	2
127	11	89	3
143	12	90	4
186	13	101	5
204	14	106	7
209	16	109	9
266	17	109	9
277	18	205	15
$n_1=9$	$R_1=116$	$n_2=9$	$R_2=55$

Third, we sum the ranks for each group separately and determine R_1 and R_2. Thus, Table 17.7 shows that $n_1=9$, $n_2=9$, $R_1=116$ and $R_2=55$.

Fourth, we find out the values of U and U' by using the following equations:

$$U = n_1 n_2 + \frac{n_1(n_1+1)}{2} - R_1$$

$$= 9 \times 9 + \frac{9(9+1)}{2} - 116 = 81 + 45 - 116 = 10$$

or equivalently,

$$U = n_1 n_2 + \frac{n_2(n_2+1)}{2} - R_2$$

$$= 9 \times 9 + \frac{9(9+1)}{2} - 55 = 81 + 45 - 55 = 71$$

Thus, $U=10$; $U'=71$

As a computation check, the obtained U can be verified using the transformation method, as follows:

$$U = n_1 n_2 - U'   = 9 \times 9 - 71 = 10$$

Finally, we test the significance of the obtained $U=10$, with $n_1=n_2=9$.

If n_2 (the size of the larger of two independent samples) is larger than 8, and it is in between 9 and 20, the significance of the obtained U can be tested by using Table V of the appendix. This table gives critical values of U for significance levels 0.001, 0.01, 0.025 and 0.05 for a one-tailed test, and significance levels 0.002, 0.02, 0.05 and 0.10 for a two-tailed test. Thus, Table V has four subtables (as V_1, V_2, V_3 and V_4), each one for one level of significance either for one-tailed or two-tailed test.

Notice that this set of tables gives critical values of U and does not give exact probabilities (as does Table U). That is, if an observed or obtained U for a particular $n_1 \leq 20$ and n_2 between 9 and 20 is equal to or less than that value given in the table, H_0 may be rejected at the level of significance indicated at the head of that table.

In our illustrative example, $n_1=9$, $n_2=9$ and $U=10$. With $n_1=9$ and $n_2=9$, the critical value of U (from Table V of the appendix) is 21 at 0.05 and 14 at 0.01 levels of significance for a one-tailed test. Since the obtained $U=10$ is less than both the critical table values, it is significant at 0.01 level. Thus, the H_0 is rejected at $\alpha=0.01$ for a one-tailed test and at $\alpha=0.02$ for a two-tailed test ($p<0.01$ or $p<0.02$ in one-tailed or two-tailed tests, respectively). Therefore, we may conclude that these two independent groups differ significantly in their performance and, thus, they have drawn from different populations.

17.5.2.2   Computation of U for Large Samples ($n_2 > 20$)

When the size of n_2 is greater than 20, then the sample is said to be large. Neither Table U nor Table V of the appendix is usable when $n_2 > 20$. However, it has been shown (Mann and Whitney, 1947) that as n_1, n_2 increase in size, the sampling distribution of U rapidly approaches the normal distribution with

$$\text{Mean} = \mu_u = \frac{n_1 n_2}{2}$$

$$\text{and Standard deviation} = \sigma_u = \sqrt{\frac{n_1 n_2 (n_1 + n_2 + 1)}{12}}$$

That is, when $n_2 > 20$ we may determine the significance of an observed value of U by

$$z = \frac{U - \mu_u}{\sigma_u} = \frac{U - \dfrac{n_1 n_2}{2}}{\sqrt{\dfrac{n_1 n_2 (n_1 + n_2 + 1)}{12}}}$$

which is practically normally distributed with zero mean and unit variance. That is, the probability associated with the occurrence under H_0 of values as extreme as an observed z may be determined by reference to Table A of the appendix.

When the normal approximation to the sampling distribution of U is used in a test of H_0, it does not matter whether the first equation (or formula) or the second equation (or formula) cited earlier in this section under U for small samples is used in the computation of U, for the absolute value of z yielded in the immediate above formula will be the same if either is used. The sign of the z depends on whether U or U' was used, but the value does not.

With this much of introductory information, let us illustrate the computation of U and U' for large samples ($n_2 > 20$) using equations/formulae. Table 17.8 represents the scores of two independent groups of subjects. We have to test whether there is a significant difference between these two groups.

We have to follow the steps noted below for the solution of the example given in Table 17.8.

First, in the given illustrative example, the sizes of both groups are unequal. So, group 1 scores are denoted by $n_1=10$ and group 2 scores by $n_2=21$. It is a large samples case. The sum of ranks, R_1 and R_2, are denoted in accordance with n_1 and n_2, respectively.

Second, we combine the scores of both the groups and assign each of them the appropriate ranks, starting from rank 1 for the lowest score in the combined series ($n_1 + n_2$). In the given example (see Table 17.8) there are 31 scores ($n_1 + n_2 = 10 + 21 = 31$) in total, and there are no tied scores in the series. Therefore, the maximum rank will be 31, which is equal to N (i.e., $N = n_1 + n_2$). These assigned ranks are noted in Table 17.8 against each score.

Third, we sum the ranks for each group separately, and determine R_1 and R_2. Thus, Table 17.8 shows that $R_1 = 90$ and $R_2 = 406$; $n_1 = 10$ and $n_2 = 21$.

Fourth, we determine the values of U and U' by the following equations:

$$U = n_1 n_2 + \frac{n_1(n_1 + 1)}{2} - R_1$$

$$= 10 \times 21 + \frac{10(10 + 1)}{2} - 90 = 210 + 55 - 90 = 175$$

Table 17.8   Scores of two independent groups of subjects

Group 1 Scores	Ranks	Group 2 Scores	Ranks
13	9	17	13
22	18	16	12
11	7	18	14
9	5	20	16
7	3	19	15
8	4	10	6
6	2	12	8
5	1	21	17
24	20	23	19
25	21	14	10
		28	24
		26	22
		27	23
		15	11
		29	25
		30	26
		32	28
		31	27
		34	30
		33	29
		35	31
$n_1 = 10$	$R_1 = 90$	$n_2 = 21$	$R_2 = 406$

or equivalently,

$$U = n_1 n_2 + \frac{n_2(n_2+1)}{2} - R_2$$

$$= 10 \times 21 + \frac{21(21+1)}{2} - 406 = 210 + 231 - 406 = 35$$

Thus,

$$U = 35; \quad U' = 175$$

As a computation check, the obtained U can be verified using the transformation method, as follows:

$$U = n_1 n_2 - U'$$
$$= 10 \times 21 - 175 = 210 - 175 = 35$$

Fifth, in order to test the significance of the obtained U (when $n_2 > 20$), we should compute the z, as follows:

$$z = \frac{U - \mu_u}{\sigma_u}$$

where

$$\text{Mean} = \mu_u = \frac{n_1 n_2}{2} = \frac{10 \times 21}{2} = 105$$

$$\text{Standard deviation} = \sigma_u = \sqrt{\frac{n_1 n_2 (n_1 + n_2 + 1)}{12}} = \sqrt{\frac{10 \times 21(10 + 21 + 1)}{12}}$$

$$= \sqrt{\frac{10 \times 21 \times 32}{12}} = \sqrt{560} = 23.66$$

Thus,

$$z = \frac{U - \mu_u}{\sigma_u} = \frac{35 - 105}{23.66} = -\frac{70}{23.66} = -2.96$$

or

$$z = \frac{U' - \mu_u}{\sigma_u} = \frac{175 - 105}{23.66} = \frac{70}{23.66} = 2.96$$

In the above computation of z by taking U (smaller value) or U' (larger value), the absolute value of z remains same in both the cases, but only its sign changes. It becomes negative when U is used, and it becomes positive when U' is used.

Finally, we test the significance of the observed z. The obtained value of z can be directly tested for its significance. The z values of 1.96 and 2.58 are required to be significant at 0.05 and 0.01 levels, respectively, in a two-tailed test. Since the obtained z value is 2.96, which is greater than 2.58, it is significant at 0.01 level in a two-tailed test, and at 0.005 level in a one-tailed test.

Alternatively, we may refer to Table A of the appendix for the significance of the obtained z. This table reveals that $z \geq 2.96$ has a one-tailed probability under H_0 of $p = 0.0015$ (or $p = 0.0030$ in a two-tailed test). Since this p is smaller than $\alpha = 0.01$ (either in a one-tailed test or a two-tailed test), it is significant. So our decision is to reject H_0 in favour of H_1. We conclude that Group 2 subjects performed better than Group 1 subjects (one-tailed test), or there is a significant difference between these two groups of subjects (two-tailed test).

17.5.3 Correction for Ties

The Mann–Whitney U-test assumes that the scores represent a distribution which has underlying continuity. With very precise measurement of a variable which had underlying continuity, the probability of a tie is zero. But in behavioural scientific research, since we are using relatively crude measures, ties may well occur.

When tied scores occur, we give each of the tied observations the average of the ranks they would have had if no ties had occurred.

If the ties occur between two or more observations in the same group, the value of U is not affected. But if ties occur between two or more observations involving both groups, the value of U is affected. Although the effect is usually negligible, a *correction for ties* is available for use with the normal curve approximation, which we employ for large samples only.

The effect of tied ranks is to change the variability of the set of ranks. Thus, the correction for ties must be applied to the standard deviation of the sampling distribution of U. Corrected for ties, the standard deviation becomes,

$$\sigma_u = \sqrt{\left(\frac{n_1 n_2}{N(N-1)}\right)\left(\frac{N^3 - N}{12} - \Sigma T\right)}$$

where

$N = n_1 + n_2$

$T = \dfrac{t^3 - t}{12}$ (where t is the number of observations tied for a given rank)

ΣT is found by summing the Ts over all groups of tied observations.

With the correction for ties, we find z by

$$z = \frac{U - \mu_u}{\sigma_u} = \frac{U - \dfrac{n_1 n_2}{2}}{\sqrt{\left(\dfrac{n_1 n_2}{N(N-1)}\right)\left(\dfrac{N^3 - N}{12} - \Sigma T\right)}}$$

Let us illustrate the computation of U and U' for large samples ($n_2 > 20$) having tied scores. Table 17.9 represents the scores of two independent samples. We have to test whether sample 2 performed better than sample 1.

The following steps are to be followed for the solution of the illustrative example given in Table 17.9.

First, in the given example, the sizes of both groups are unequal. So, the sample 1 scores are denoted by $n_1 = 16$, and sample 2 scores by $n_2 = 23$. It is a large samples case. The sum of ranks, R_1 and R_2 are denoted in accordance with n_1 and n_2, respectively.

Second, we combine the scores of both the groups and assign each of them the appropriate ranks, beginning from rank 1 for the lowest score in the combined ($n_1 + n_2$) series. In the given example, there are 39 ($n_1 + n_2 = 16 + 23 = 39$) scores in total, and also a large number of tied scores. Each of the tied scores is assigned the average of the ranks they would have had if no ties had occurred. For instance, Table 17.9 shows that 6 is the lowest score in the combined series and there are two scores of 6. So, each score of 6 is assigned a rank of 1.5, the average of ranks 1 and 2 (i.e., $\dfrac{1+2}{2} = \dfrac{3}{2} = 1.5$). The assigned ranks are noted in Table 17.9 against each score.

Third, we sum the ranks for each sample separately and determine R_1 and R_2. Thus, Table 17.9 shows that $R_1 = 200$ and $R_2 = 580$; $n_1 = 16$ and $n_2 = 23$; $N = n_1 + n_2 = 16 + 23 = 39$.

Table 17.9   Scores of two independent samples

Group 1 Scores	Ranks	Group 2 Scores	Ranks
13	29.5	17	39.0
12	24.5	16	38.0
12	24.5	15	36.0
10	16.0	15	36.0
10	16.0	15	36.0
10	16.0	14	33.0
10	16.0	14	33.0
9	12.0	14	33.0
8	9.5	13	29.5
8	9.5	13	29.5
7	5.0	13	29.5
7	5.0	12	24.5
7	5.0	12	24.5
7	5.0	12	24.5
7	5.0	12	24.5
6	1.5	11	20.5
		11	20.5
		10	16.0
		10	16.0
		10	16.0
		8	9.5
		8	9.5
		6	1.5
$n_1 = 16$	$R_1 = 200.0$	$n_2 = 23$	$R_2 = 580.0$

Fourth, we determine the values of U and U' by the following equations:

$$U = n_1 n_2 + \frac{n_1(n_1 + 1)}{2} - R_1$$

$$= 16 \times 23 + \frac{16(16 + 1)}{2} - 200 = 368 + 136 - 200 = 304$$

or equivalently,

$$U = n_1 n_2 + \frac{n_2(n_2 + 1)}{2} - R_2$$

$$= 16 \times 23 + \frac{23(23 + 1)}{2} - 580 = 368 + 276 - 580 = 64$$

Thus,

$U = 64; \ U' = 304$

As a computation check, the obtained U can be verified using the transformation method, as follows,

$$U = n_1 n_2 - U' = 16 \times 23 - 304 = 368 - 304 = 64$$

Fifth, now we will find out the $\sum T = \sum \dfrac{t^3 - t}{12}$. We observe these tied groups.

2 scores of 6

5 scores of 7

4 scores of 8

7 scores of 10

2 Scores of 11

6 scores of 12

4 scores of 13

3 scores of 14

3 scores of 15

Thus, we have ts of 2, 5, 4, 7, 2, 6, 4, 3 and 3. To find $\sum T$, we sum the values of $\dfrac{t^3 - t}{12}$ for each of these tied groups:

$$\sum T = \sum \frac{t^3 - t}{12} = \frac{2^3 - 2}{12} + \frac{5^3 - 5}{12} + \frac{4^3 - 4}{12} + \frac{7^3 - 7}{12} + \frac{2^3 - 2}{12} + \frac{6^3 - 6}{12} + \frac{4^3 - 4}{12} + \frac{3^3 - 3}{12} + \frac{3^3 - 3}{12}$$

$$= 0.5 + 10.0 + 5.0 + 28.0 + 0.5 + 17.5 + 5.0 + 2.0 + 2.0 = 70.5$$

Thus, $\sum T = 70.5$

Sixth, we will determine the mean (μ_u), and the standard deviation (σ_u) of U without and with correction for ties, as follows:

$$\text{Mean} = \mu_u = \frac{n_1 n_2}{2} = \frac{16 \times 23}{2} = 184$$

$$\text{Standard deviation} = \sigma_u = \sqrt{\frac{n_1 n_2 (n_1 + n_2 + 1)}{12}} \ (\text{without correction for ties})$$

$$= \sqrt{\frac{16 \times 23(16 + 23 + 1)}{12}} = \sqrt{\frac{16 \times 23 \times 40}{12}} = \sqrt{1226.67} = 35.02$$

$$\sigma_u = \sqrt{\left(\frac{n_1 n_2}{N(N-1)}\right)\left(\frac{N^3 - N}{12} - \sum T\right)} \ (\text{with correction for ties})$$

$$= \sqrt{\left(\frac{16 \times 23}{39(39-1)}\right)\left(\frac{39^3 - 39}{12} - 70.5\right)} = \sqrt{0.248 \times 4869.5} = \sqrt{1207.636} = 34.75$$

Seventh, the z values (without correction for ties and with correction for ties) are computed as follows:

$$z = \frac{U - \mu_u}{\sigma_u} \quad \text{(without correction for ties)}$$

$$= \frac{64 - 184}{35.02} = \frac{-120}{35.02} = -3.43$$

$$z = \frac{U - \mu_u}{\sigma_u} \quad \text{(with correction for ties)}$$

$$= \frac{64 - 184}{34.75} = \frac{-120}{34.75} = -3.45$$

Alternatively, we can also compute z values by taking U' rather than U in the numerator, as follows:

$$z = \frac{U' - \mu_u}{\sigma_u} \quad \text{(without correction for ties)}$$

$$= \frac{304 - 184}{35.02} = \frac{120}{35.02} = 3.43$$

$$z = \frac{U' - \mu_u}{\sigma_u} \quad \text{(with correction for ties)}$$

$$= \frac{304 - 184}{34.75} = \frac{120}{34.75} = 3.45$$

We can notice that the absolute value of z remains same whether we use either U or U' in the numerator of the z ratio.

Eighth, let us now make a comparison between z values obtained without correction for ties and with correction for ties. We can notice one thing that the value of z when corrected for ties ($z = 3.45$) is a little larger than that found without correction for ties ($z = 3.43$). As this example demonstrates, ties have only a slight effect. Even when a large proportion of the scores are tied (this example had over 90% of its observations involved in ties) the effect is practically negligible. However, the magnitude of the correction factor, ΣT, depends importantly on the *length* of the various ties, that is, on the size of the various ts. Thus, a tie of length 2 contributes only 0.5 to ΣT in this example, whereas a tie of length 4 contributes 5.0; and a tie of length 6 contributes 17.5, whereas a tie of length 7 contributes 28.0 to ΣT.

Ties reduce the amount of z. When the correction is employed, it tends to increase the value of z slightly, making it more significant. Therefore, when we do not correct for ties our test is 'conservative' in that the value of p (probability) will be slightly inflated. That is, the value of the probability associated with the observed data under the null hypothesis (H_0) will be slightly larger than that which would be found were the correction employed. Therefore, our recommendation is that one should correct for ties only if the proportion of ties is quite large, if some of the ts are large, or if the p which, obtained without the correction, is very close to one's previously set value of α (alpha).

Finally, we test the significance of the obtained value of z. Usually one should test the significance of the z value that is obtained with correction for ties. However, in this example, the difference between $z \geq 3.43$ (without correction for ties) and $z \geq 3.45$ (with correction for ties) is negligible so far as the probability given in Table A of the appendix is concerned. Both zs are read as having an associated probability of $p < 0.0003$ (one-tailed test). Since this p is less than $\alpha = 0.01$, it is significant at 0.01 level of significance.

Alternatively, we may directly test the significance of the obtained value of z with correction for ties. As we know that z values of 2.33 and 2.58 are required to be significant at 0.01 level of significance in a one-tailed test and a two-tailed test, respectively. Since the value of $z=3.45$, obtained with correction for ties, is greater than both the critical values of z for one-tailed and two-tailed tests, it is significant at 0.01 level of significance. Thus, H_0 is rejected in favour of H_1. We may conclude that sample 2 performed better than sample 1 (one-tailed test) or there is a significant difference between the performances of two independent samples (two-tailed test).

17.5.4   Summary of Procedures

The following steps are to be followed in the use of the Mann–Whitney U-test:

(i)   Determine the values of n_1 and n_2. n_1=the number of cases in the smaller group/ sample; n_2=the number of cases in the larger group/sample. If the two samples are of equal size, then designate any one of the samples as n_1 and the other as n_2.

(ii)   Combine the scores of both the groups/samples, and assign the rank of 1 to the lowest score in the combined (n_1+n_2) series of scores, assign rank 2 to the next lowest score and so on. Ranks range from 1 to $N=n_1+n_2$.

(iii)   When tied scores occur, assign each of the tied observations the average of the ranks they would have had if no ties had occurred.

(iv)   Sum the ranks for each group/sample separately and denote them by R_1 and R_2 in accordance with n_1 and n_2, respectively.

(v)   Determine the values of U and U' either by the counting method or by the equation method. However, the equation method is preferred, as the counting method cannot be applied to data having ties scores.

(vi)   After the values of U and U' are determined, make a computation check and verify the obtained value of U by the transformation method.

(vii)   Test the significance of the obtained U. The method for determining the significance of the observed value of U depends on the size of n_2.

(a)   If n_2 is 8 or less, the exact probability associated with a value as small as the observed value of U is shown in Table U of the appendix. The probabilities shown in Table U are for one-tailed tests; for a two-tailed test, double the value of p shown in that table. If the associated p is equal to, or less than, the $\alpha=0.05$ or 0.01, then it is significant.

(b)   If n_2 is between 9 and 20, the significance of any observed value of U may be determined by reference to Table V of the appendix. This table gives the critical values of U for different combinations of n_1 and n_2 (i.e., $n_1 \leq 20$; n_2 from 9 to 20) for 0.001, 0.01, 0.025 and 0.05 levels of significance for a one-tailed test. For a two-tailed test, double the value of p shown in that table. If the observed value of U is equal to, or less than, the critical value as shown in that table, then it is significant.

(c)   If n_2 is larger than 20, the probability associated with a value as extreme as the observed value of U may be determined by computing the value of z by the formula not incorporating the correction for ties, and testing this value of z by referring to Table A of the appendix. For a two-tailed test, double the p shown in that table. If the proportion of ties is very large or if the obtained p is very close to α, apply the correction for ties, and the value of z may be computed by the formula incorporating the correction for ties, as discussed earlier in this section.

If the observed value of U has an associated probability equal to or less than α, reject H_0 in favour of H_1.

17.5.5   Power Efficiency

If the Mann–Whitney U-test is applied to the data which might properly be analysed by the most powerful parametric test, that is, the t-test, its power-efficiency approaches $3/\pi = 95.5\%$ as N increases (Mood, 1954), and is close to 95% even for moderate-sized samples. It is, therefore, an excellent alternative to the t-test, and of course it does not have the restrictive assumptions and requirements associated with the t-test.

Whitney (1948) gives examples of distribution for which the U-test is superior to its parametric alternative, that is, for which U-test has greater power to reject H_0.

The step-wise computational procedures of the Mann–Whitney U-test will become more clear to the readers through the following examples.

Example 17.7 An independent-groups experiment is conducted to see if treatment A differs from treatment B. Eight subjects are randomly assigned to treatment A and seven to treatment B. The following data are collected.

Treatment A	30	35	34	40	19	32	21	23
Treatment B	14	8	25	16	26	28	9	

Solution
The following steps are followed for the solution of the above problem:

(a)   The given data are entered in Table 17.10. In this example, treatment A is having eight subjects and treatment B, seven subjects. So, treatment B is denoted by n_1 and treatment A by n_2. Thus, $n_1 = 7$ and $n_2 = 8$. Therefore, it is a very small samples case, that is, neither n_1 nor n_2 is greater than 8.

(b)   Statement of H_0 and H_1, and α level.

H_0: Treatment A does not differ from treatment B
H_1: Treatment A differs significantly from treatment B.

It is a two-tailed test. Let $\alpha = 0.05$.

Table 17.10   Scores of two independent groups of subjects under treatment A and treatment B

Treatment A Scores	Ranks	Treatment B Scores	Ranks
30	11	14	3
35	14	8	1
34	13	25	8
40	15	16	4
19	5	26	9
32	12	28	10
21	6	9	2
23	7		
$n_2 = 8$	$R_2 = 83$	$n_1 = 7$	$R_1 = 37$

(c) The scores of both the treatments are combined and taken as a series. Thus, there are 15 ($n_1 + n_2$) scores in total. These scores are assigned ranks in a single ascending order of their values. We assign rank 1 to the lowest score, rank 2 to the next lowest score and so on. The highest score receives a rank equal to $N(n_1 + n_2)$.

(d) The ranks of each treatment are totalled separately. Thus, we have two sums of ranks, which are denoted by R_1 and R_2 in accordance with n_1 and n_2, respectively (see Table 17.10). $R_1 = 37$ and $R_2 = 83$; $n_1 = 7$ and $n_2 = 8$.

(e) Now, we will find out the values of U and U' through the following equations:

$$U = n_1 n_2 + \frac{n_1(n_1 + 1)}{2} - R_1$$
$$= 7 \times 8 + \frac{7(7+1)}{2} - 37 = 56 + 28 - 37 = 47$$

or equivalently,

$$U = n_1 n_2 + \frac{n_2(n_2 + 1)}{2} - R_2$$
$$= 7 \times 8 + \frac{8(8+1)}{2} - 83 = 56 + 36 - 83 = 9$$

Thus,

$$U = 9; \; U' = 47$$

Verification of the value of U by the transformation method, as follows:

$$U = n_1 n_2 - U' = 7 \times 8 - 47 = 56 - 47 = 9$$

(f) Next, we have to test the significance of the obtained value of U. Since it is a case of very small samples, Table U of the appendix may be used. The subtable $n_2 = 8$ in Table U shows that $U \leq 9$, when $n_1 = 7$, has a probability of occurrence under H_0 of $p = 0.014$. Since this $p = 0.014$ is less than $\alpha = 0.05$, it is significant. Hence, H_0 is rejected in favour of H_1. Therefore, we may conclude that treatment A differs significantly from treatment B in its effects on the dependent variable.

Example 17.8 A psychologist is interested in determining whether left-handed and right-handed people differ in spatial ability. He randomly selects six left-handers and 10 right-handers from the students enrolled in the University where he works and administers a test that measures spatial ability. The following are the scores (a higher score indicates better spatial ability):

Left-handers	50	55	45	37	40	35				
Right-handers	60	65	70	75	85	80	95	90	96	98

Solution

We have to follow the following steps for the solution of the above problem:

(a) The given data are entered in Table 17.11. In this example, the number of left-handers is 6 and right-handers is 10. So the number of left-handers is denoted by n_1 and right-handers by n_2. Thus, $n_1=6$ and $n_2=10$. Therefore, it is a relatively small samples case, that is, $n_1 \leq 20$ and $n_2=9$ to 20.

(b) Statement of H_0 and H_1, and α level

H_0: Left-handed and right-handed people do not differ in spatial ability.
H_1: Left-handed and right-handed people differ significantly in spatial ability.

It is a two-tailed test. Let $\alpha=0.05$.

(c) The scores of both the groups are combined and taken as a series. Thus, there are 16 (n_1+n_2) scores in toto. These scores are assigned ranks in a single ascending order of their values. We assign rank 1 to the lowest score, rank 2 to the next lowest score and so on till the highest score receives a rank equal to $N(n_1+n_2)$.

(d) Then, the ranks of each group are totalled separately. Thus, there are two sums of ranks which are designated as R_1 and R_2 in accordance with n_1 and n_2, respectively (see Table 17.11). So, we have $R_1=21$ and $R_2=115$; $n_1=6$ and $n_2=10$.

(e) Next, we have to compute the values of U and U' by using the following equations:

$$U = n_1 n_2 + \frac{n_1(n_1+1)}{2} - R_1$$

$$= 6 \times 10 + \frac{6(6+1)}{2} - 21 = 60 + 21 - 21 = 60$$

or equivalently,

$$U = n_1 n_2 + \frac{n_2(n_2+1)}{2} - R_2$$

$$= 6 \times 10 + \frac{10(10+1)}{2} - 115 = 60 + 55 - 115 = 0$$

Table 17.11 Spatial ability scores of left-handers and right-handers

Left-handers Scores	Ranks	Right-handers Scores	Ranks
50	5	60	7
55	6	65	8
45	4	70	9
37	2	75	10
40	3	85	12
35	1	80	11
		95	14
		90	13
		96	15
		98	16
$n_1=6$	$R_1=21$	$n_2=10$	$R_2=115$

Thus,

$$U=0; \quad U'=60$$

The obtained value of U can be verified by the following transformation formula,

$$U = n_1 n_2 - U' = 6 \times 10 - 60 = 0$$

(f) Finally, we test the significance of the obtained U. Since it is a small samples case of second type where $n_2 = 9$ to 20, Table V of the appendix may be used. With $n_1 = 6$ and $n_2 = 10$, the critical value of U is 11 at 0.05 and 8 at 0.02 levels of significance for a two-tailed test (see Table V—subtables V_2 and V_3—of the appendix). Since the obtained $U = 0$ is less than both the critical values, it is significant at 0.02 level. Thus, the H_0 is rejected at $\alpha = 0.02$ for a two-tailed test ($p < 0.02$). Therefore, we may conclude that left-handed and right-handed people significantly differ in spatial ability.

Example 17.9 An experiment using 10 control rats and 25 experimental rats was conducted to find out the effect of stimulus complexity on the exploratory behaviour of rats. The subjects were tested in an open field box and their exploration scores were recorded. The scores of both the groups were combined and ranked in a single ascending order of their values. The sum of the ranks of the control group is 200 and that of the experimental group is 430. Determine the values of U and U'. Test whether stimulus complexity has facilitated the exploratory behaviour of rats.

Solution
The following steps are to be followed for the solution of the above problem:

(a) In the given example, the control group consists of 10 rats and the experimental group consists of 25 rats. So the number of control rats is denoted by n_1 and the experimental rats by n_2. Thus, we have (as given), $n_1 = 10$, $R_1 = 200$, $n_2 = 25$ and $R_2 = 430$.

(b) Statement of H_0, H_1 and α level, as follows:

H_0: Stimulus complexity does not facilitate the exploratory behaviour of rats.
H_1: Stimulus complexity facilitates the exploratory behaviour of rats.

It is a one-tailed test. Let $\alpha = 0.05$.

(c) Now we compute the values of U and U' by the following equations:

$$U = n_1 n_2 + \frac{n_1(n_1 + 1)}{2} - R_1$$

$$= 10 \times 25 + \frac{10(10 + 1)}{2} - 200 = 250 + 55 - 200 = 105$$

or equivalently,

$$U = n_1 n_2 + \frac{n_2(n_2 + 1)}{2} - R_2$$

$$= 10 \times 25 + \frac{25(25 + 1)}{2} - 430 = 250 + 325 - 430 = 145$$

Thus,

$$U = 105; \quad U' = 145$$

The obtained value of U may be checked by the following transformation formula:

$$U = n_1 n_2 - U' = 10 \times 25 - 145 = 105$$

(d) Next, we compute the value of z as follows:

$$z = \frac{U - \mu_u}{\sigma_u} \text{ (without correction of ties)}$$

where

$$\mu_u = \frac{n_1 n_2}{2} = \frac{10 \times 25}{2} = 125$$

$$\sigma_u = \sqrt{\frac{n_1 n_2 (n_1 + n_2 + 1)}{12}} = \sqrt{\frac{10 \times 25 (10 + 25 + 1)}{12}}$$

$$= \sqrt{\frac{10 \times 25 \times 36}{12}} = \sqrt{750} = 27.386$$

Thus,

$$z = \frac{105 - 125}{27.386} = \frac{-20}{27.386} = -0.73$$

or equivalently,

$$z = \frac{U' - \mu_u}{\sigma_u} = \frac{145 - 125}{27.386} = \frac{20}{27.386} = 0.73$$

Whether we use the values of U or U', the absolute value of z remains the same, only the algebraic sign changes.

(e) Now, we proceed to test the significance of the obtained value of z. Since the given example is a large sample case, Table A of the appendix may be used for this purpose. This table shows that $z \geq 0.73$ has a one-tailed probability under H_0 of $p = 0.2327$. Since this p is greater than $\alpha = 0.05$, it is not significant. So, our decision is to retain or accept H_0. Therefore, we may conclude that the stimulus complexity has no facilitatory effects on the exploratory behaviour of rats.

17.6 The Median Test

The median test is a non-parametric test, and it is an alternative to the parametric t-test. The median test is applied for testing whether two or more independent samples of equal or unequal sizes differ in median. In other words, it compares the medians of two or more independent samples of either equal or unequal sizes. It can be applied to both continuous and discontinuous measurement variables, irrespective of the normality or non-normality of their population distributions, and also to small samples.

The median test is less powerful than the t-test and the Mann–Whitney U-test.

The null hypothesis (H_0) is that the two or more independent samples/groups are from populations with the same median. The H_0 proposes in effect that there are equal number of scores in each sample above and below the common (or joint) median, and any observed deviation from this distribution being due to mere chances of random sampling. The alternative hypothesis (H_1) may be that the median of one population is *different* from that of the other (two-tailed test) or that the median of one population is *higher or lower* than that of the other (one-tailed test).

17.6.1   Assumptions of the Median Test

To apply the median test, it should be reasonable to assume that:

(a)   Each score occurs in the sample at random and independent of all other scores.

(b)   The scores for the two or more samples are in at least an ordinal scale.

(c)   The two or more samples must be independent or uncorrelated.

The median test can be applied to two or more than two (k) independent samples. Let us begin with two independent samples.

17.6.2   Median Test with Two Independent Samples

The median test is based on the idea that in two samples drawn from the same population the expectation is that as many observations (or scores) in each sample will fall above as below the common (or joint) median. The data consist of two independent samples of n_1 and n_2 observations. To perform (or apply) the median test, the following steps are followed:

(a)   A common median (or a joint median) is first computed for the combined ($n_1 + n_2$) scores of both the samples, by following the procedures described in Chapter 3 for the ungrouped data.

(b)   In each sample or group, positive (+) signs are assigned to the scores higher than the common median while negative (–) signs are assigned to those equal to or less than the median. Then for each sample, the frequencies of scores with positive and negative signs are counted separately and entered as the respective f_o (observed frequencies) values in a contingency table. A (2×2)-fold contingency table results in case of two samples only. A (2×2)-fold contingency table is framed with two columns representing the positive and negative deviations of scores from the common median, and the rows representing number of samples or groups.

(c)   A chi-square (χ^2) test of independence is then performed. The χ^2 value is computed from a four-fold contingency table by the following formula incorporating *Yates' correction for continuity* (as described in Chapter 16, Section 16.3, under the heading 'Two Samples with $c = 2$ Classes'). The formula reads,

$$\chi^2 = \frac{n(|ad - bc| - n/2)^2}{(a+b)(c+d)(a+c)(b+d)}; \quad df = (r-1)(c-1)$$

(d)   The computed χ^2 value is compared with the critical χ^2 values for different significance levels for a particular df (for a 2×2 contingency table, df is always 1). The computed χ^2 is considered significant only if it exceeds or equals the critical χ^2 value for a chosen α. Table L of the appendix may be referred for this purpose. If the obtained χ^2 is not significant, the H_0 is accepted, and we will conclude that the samples have come from populations with the same median. If the obtained χ^2 is, on the other hand, significant, then the H_0 is rejected in favour of H_1, and our conclusion will be that the samples have come from populations with different medians. It may be a one-tailed test or a two-tailed test depending upon the nature of the H_1, and accordingly, the α levels are chosen.

The computational procedure will become more clear to the reader through the following example.

Example 17.10 The following scores are obtained from two independent samples of students on an arithmetic addition test. Use the median test to find out whether the test scores differ significantly in the two samples.

Sample I	12	16	18	7	6	4	11	12	8	20	18	16	10	
Sample II	7	12	14	18	5	16	9	10	14	3	18	9	7	4

Solution

The following steps are needed for the solution of the above problem:

(a)   The H_0, H_1 and α level are stated as follows:

H_0: The test scores of the two samples are not different from the common median
H_1: The test scores of the two samples are significantly different from the common median

It is a two-tailed median test. Let $\alpha = 0.05$.

(b)   A common median is computed for the scores of both samples combined.

$$n = n_1 + n_2 = 13 + 14 = 27$$

$$\text{Median } (M_{dn}) = \frac{n+1}{2}\text{th score} = \frac{27+1}{2} = \text{14th score}$$

In order to find out the 14th score in an ascending order, we should arrange all the scores of both the samples taken together in an increasing order of their magnitude. Thus, the ascending order of 27 scores is,

3, 4, 4, 5, 6, 7, 7, 7, 8, 9, 9, 10, 10, 11, 12, 12, 12, 14, 14, 16, 16, 16, 18, 18, 18, 18, 20.

The 14th score in the above series is 11. Thus, the common median of the two sets of scores is 11.

(c)   The scores of each group are assigned positive (+) and negative (−) signs according to whether they are respectively higher than and lower than (or equal to) the common median (M_{dn}), as follows:

Sample I	+	+	+	−	−	−	−	+	−	+	+	+	−	
Sample II	−	+	+	+	−	+	−	−	+	−	+	−	−	−

(d)   A (2×2)-fold contingency table is framed for computing χ^2, and the number of + and − signs in the two samples are entered as f_o values in its respective cells (see Table 17.12).

Table 17.12   The (2×2)-fold contingency table for median test

Samples	Positive Signs	Negative Signs	Totals
Sample I	7 (a)	6 (b)	13 (a + b)
Sample II	6 (c)	8 (d)	14 (c + d)
Totals	13 (a + c)	14 (b + d)	27 = n

The marginal totals of cell frequencies of each row and each column are computed in the table.

The cell frequencies (f_o) are designated by the letters a, b, c and d, and accordingly the columns and rows marginal totals, as indicated in Table 17.12.

The χ^2 is computed by the following formula:

$$\chi^2 = \frac{n(|ad - bc| - n/2)^2}{(a+b)(c+d)(a+c)(b+d)} = \frac{27(|7 \times 8 - 6 \times 6| - 27/2)^2}{13 \times 14 \times 13 \times 14}$$

$$= \frac{27(|56 - 36| - 13.5)^2}{13 \times 14 \times 13 \times 14} = \frac{27(6.5)^2}{33124} = \frac{1140.75}{33124} = 0.034$$

(e) Now, we will test the significance of the obtained $\chi^2 = 0.034$. df $= (r-1)(c-1) = (2-1)(2-1) = 1$. Referring to Table L of the appendix, the critical value of χ^2, with df $= 1$, at 0.05 level is 3.84 and at 0.01 level is 6.64. Because the computed χ^2 is less than the critical χ^2 for even the 0.05 level, it is not significant. Thus, the H_0 is accepted. So, the test scores of the two samples do not differ significantly. Our conclusion is that both samples have come from the populations with the same median. This is a two-tailed test.

17.6.3   Median Test with More Than Two Independent Samples

This is an obvious extension of the median test for two independent samples. The data comprise k samples of $n_1, n_2, \ldots, n_k$ observations. As before, the null hypothesis (H_0) is that no difference exists in the medians of the populations from which the samples are drawn. To apply the median test for k independent samples, the following steps are followed.

(a) A common median is computed for the combined $n_1 + n_2 + \cdots + n_k$ observations of k independent samples, by following the same procedures described earlier, that is, by arranging all the scores of k independent samples combined together in a single ascending order and then by taking the $\frac{n+1}{2}$th score as the median.

(b) For each sample scores above the common median are assigned a + sign and those either at or below the common median, a − sign. Then for each sample, the frequencies of scores with + and − signs are counted separately and entered as the respective f_o values in a $2 \times k$ contingency table, which is framed with two columns representing the + and − signs of the scores from the common median and as many rows as the number of independent samples or groups.

(c) A chi-square (χ^2) test of independence is then performed, computing the expected frequencies (f_e) for each cell of the contingency table, which can be obtained by multiplying the two marginal totals common to a particular cell and then dividing this product by the total number of cases (n), as described in Chapter 16, section 16.3, under the heading 'Two or More Samples with c Classes'. The same usual formula of χ^2 used in this case reads,

$$\chi^2 = \sum \frac{(f_o - f_e)^2}{f_e}; \quad df = (r-1)(c-1)$$

(d) Then, the computed χ^2 is tested for significance as usual referring to Table L of the appendix.

The entire computational procedure will become more clear to the researcher through the following example.

Example 17.11 The following are the test scores of four independent samples. Apply a median test and interpret you results.

Sample I	3	6	11	14	17	18	21	33
Sample II	3	3	4	5	5	8	9	14
Sample III	18	18	25	26	29	31		
Sample IV	14	18	20	22	22	25	27	35

Solution

The steps to be followed for the solution of the above problem are as follows:

(a) The H_0, H_1 and α level are stated below:

H_0: The test scores of four independent samples are not different from the common median.

H_1: The test scores of four independent samples are significantly different from the common median.

It is a two-tailed test. Let $\alpha=0.05$.

(b) A common median is computed for the scores of four independent samples combined.

$$n=n_1+n_2+n_3+n_4=8+8+6+8=30$$

$$M_{dn}=\frac{n+1}{2}\text{th score}=\frac{30+1}{2}=15.5\text{th score}$$

The 15.5th score indicates that the average of the 15th and 16th scores in a single ascending order of all the scores combined together will be taken as the common median. In the given example there are 30 scores or observations in total, which are arranged in an increasing order of their magnitude, as follows:

3, 3, 3, 4, 5, 5, 6, 8, 9, 11, 14, 14, 14, 17, 18, 18, 18, 18, 20, 21, 22, 22, 25, 25, 26, 27, 29, 31, 33, 35.

In the above order, the 15th score is 18 and the 16th score is also 18; and thus, their average is 18, which is the common median of four sets of scores combined together.

(c) The scores of each samples are assigned + and – signs according to whether they are respectively above the median and at or below the common median, as follows:

Sample I	–	–	–	–	–	–	+	+
Sample II	–	–	–	–	–	–	–	–
Sample III	–	–	+	+	+	+		
Sample IV	–	–	+	+	+	+	+	+

(d) The number of + and – signs in the four independent samples are counted and are entered as f_o values in its respective cells. These data may be arranged in a 2×4 contingency table having two columns and four rows. The columns represent the + and

Table 17.13   The 2×4 contingency table for median test

Samples	+ Sign	– Sign	Total
Sample I	2 (3.2)	6 (4.8)	8
Sample II	0 (3.2)	8 (4.8)	8
Sample III	4 (2.4)	2 (3.6)	6
Sample IV	6 (3.2)	2 (4.8)	8
Totals	12	18	30 (n)

– signs whereas the rows represent the samples. The marginal totals of cell frequencies of each column and each row are computed in Table 17.13, as follows.

Table 17.13 has eight cells. Now, we will compute the expected frequencies (f_e) of each cell, as follows:

$$f_e \text{ for Cell } 1 = \frac{8 \times 12}{30} = 3.2; \quad f_e \text{ for Cell } 2 = \frac{8 \times 18}{30} = 4.8;$$

$$f_e \text{ for Cell } 3 = \frac{8 \times 12}{30} = 3.2; \quad f_e \text{ for Cell } 4 = \frac{8 \times 18}{30} = 4.8$$

$$f_e \text{ for Cell } 5 = \frac{6 \times 12}{30} = 2.4; \quad f_e \text{ for Cell } 6 = \frac{6 \times 18}{30} = 3.6$$

$$f_e \text{ for Cell } 7 = \frac{8 \times 12}{30} = 3.2; \quad f_e \text{ for Cell } 8 = \frac{8 \times 18}{30} = 4.8$$

The above computed expected frequencies (f_e) are entered in the appropriate cells of Table 17.13 within parentheses.

The χ^2 is computed by the following formula:

$$\chi^2 = \Sigma \frac{(f_o - f_e)^2}{f_e}$$

$$= \frac{(2-3.2)^2}{3.2} + \frac{(6-4.8)^2}{4.8} + \frac{(0-3.2)^2}{3.2} + \frac{(8-4.8)^2}{4.8}$$

$$+ \frac{(4-2.4)^2}{2.4} + \frac{(2-3.6)^2}{3.6} + \frac{(6-3.2)^2}{3.2} + \frac{(2-4.8)^2}{4.8}$$

$$= 0.45 + 0.30 + 3.20 + 2.13 + 1.07 + 0.71 + 2.45 + 1.63 = 11.94$$

(e) The obtained value of $\chi^2 = 11.94$ may be tested for significance. The df $=(r-1)$ $(c-1) = (4-1)(2-1) = 3$. Referring to Table L of the appendix, the critical value of χ^2, with df $= 3$, at 0.05 level is 7.82 and at 0.01 level is 11.34. Because the obtained $\chi^2 = 11.94$ is greater than both the critical values of χ^2, it is significant at 0.01 level of significance. So, the H_0 is rejected in favour of H_1 ($p < 0.01$). Hence, the test scores of four independent samples are significantly different from the common median. Therefore, we may conclude that there exists a significant difference in the medians of the populations from which the samples are drawn. This is a two-tailed median test.

17.6.4   Summary of Procedures

The following are the steps in the use of the median test:

(i)   Determine the common median of the combined scores of all the samples or groups.

(ii)   Assign a positive (+) sign and a negative (–) sign to the sores which are, respectively, higher than, and equal to or lower than the common median in each sample.

(iii)   Determine the number of + and – signs in each sample and enter them as f_o values of the cells in a contingency table. A 2×2 contingency table results in case of two independent samples only, and a $2 \times k$ contingency table results in case of more than two independent samples.

(iv)   Compute the value of χ^2 by applying the appropriate formula. In case of more than two samples only, determine the f_e of each cell before computing χ^2.

(v)   Test the significance of the obtained χ^2 by finding the number of df and referring to Table L of the appendix. If the computed χ^2 exceeds or equals the critical value of χ^2 for the chosen a with a particular df, then it is significant, and reject H_0 in favour of H_1.

17.6.5   Power-efficiency

Mood (1954) has shown that when the median test is applied to data measured in at least an interval scale from normal distributions with common variance (i.e., data that might properly be analysed by the parametric t-test), it has the same power-efficiency as the sign test. That is, its power-efficiency is about 95% for $n_1 + n_2$ as low as 6. This power-efficiency decreases as the sample sizes increase, reaching an eventual asymptotic efficiency of $2/\pi = 63\%$.

17.7   The Kruskal–Wallis One-way Analysis of Variance by Ranks

A rank test for k independent samples is the Kruskal–Wallis one-way analysis of variance (ANOVA) by ranks. It is a non-parametric *statistical test* which is rank-dependent. The Kruskal–Wallis test is designated as a statistic H, and it is simply known as the Kruskal–Wallis H-test. The Kruskal–Wallis one-way ANOVA is an extremely useful test for deciding whether k independent samples are from different populations. This test may be applied to continuous, discrete or ordinal variables, normal or non-normal distributions, and to small samples.

The null hypothesis (H_0) is that the k independent samples come from the same population or from identical populations with respect to averages.

17.7.1   Assumptions of Kruskal–Wallis H-test

For computing the Kruskal-Wallis statistic H, it should be justifiable to assume that:

(a)   The observations may be independent. This means that the selection of samples from the population must be random and independent, and the assignment of scores to the performances of the members of the samples must be unbiased and impartial. In other words, each score of the dependent variable occurs in the sample at random and independent of all other scores.

(b)   The variable under study must have an underlying continuous distribution. This means that the dependent variable under study must be present in each and every element of the population from which the samples are drawn, and nowhere in the element of the population it is absent.

(c)   It requires at least ordinal measurement of that dependent variable. In other words, the data should be in terms of ranks. If scores are given, then these scores are converted into ranks.

(d)   The samples must be independent or uncorrelated.

17.7.2   Computation of H Values

The computation of the Kruskal-Wallis statistic H can be made for small samples as well as for large samples. When the number of samples or groups is 3 (i.e., $k=3$) and the number of cases in each of the three samples is 5 or less (i.e., $n_j \leq 5$), it is a small sample case. Any deviation to this is a large sample case. For example, $k>3$ and $n_j \leq 5$, or $k=3$ and $n_j>5$, are the instances of large sample cases.

Whether it is a small samples case or large samples case, there is no difference in the computational procedures of H values. However, these two cases differ from each other with regard to the test of significance of the computed H values. We will discuss about this in detail later on, under the heading 'Test of Significance of H'. Now let us discuss about the computation of H values. The following are the steps to be followed for computing the Kruskal-Wallis statistic H:

(a)   In the computation of the Kruskal-Wallis H test, each of the N observations are replaced by ranks. That is, all of the scores from all of the k independent samples are combined, and then are ranked in a single series. The lowest score in the series is assigned a rank of 1, the next lowest rank 2 and so on till the highest score is assigned a rank of N. N = the total number of independent observations in the k samples.

(b)   After the scores are converted into ranks, the ranks of the scores of each sample/group are added separately to give the rank sums (R_j) of the respective groups.

(c)   The H may be computed directly from the *rank sums* (R_j) of the groups by the following formula:

$$H = \frac{12}{N(N+1)} \sum_{j=1}^{k} \left(\frac{R_j^2}{n_j} \right) - 3(N+1)$$

where

k = number of independent samples or groups
n_j = number of cases in the j-th sample
R_j = sum of ranks in j-th sample (column)
$N = \Sigma n_j$ = the number of cases in all samples combined.
$\displaystyle\sum_{j=1}^{k}$ directs one to sum over the k samples (columns)
df = $k-1$.

17.7.3   Correction for Ties

When ties occur between two or more scores, the usual convention is adopted of assigning to each of the tied scores the average of the ranks they would have had if no ties had occurred.

Since the value of H is somewhat influenced by ties, one may wish to correct for ties in computing H. To correct for the effect of ties, H is computed by the formula noted above, and then divided by

$$1 - \frac{\sum T}{N^3 - N}$$

where

$T = t^3 - t$ (where t is the number of observations tied for a given rank)

$N = \sum n_j =$ number of observations in all k samples together

$\sum T$ directs one to sum over all groups of ties

Thus, a general expression for the quantity H corrected for ties is

$$H = \frac{H}{1 - \dfrac{\sum T}{N^3 - N}} = \frac{\dfrac{12}{N(N+1)} \sum_{j=1}^{k} \left(\dfrac{R_j^2}{n_j} \right) - 3(N+1)}{1 - \dfrac{\sum T}{N^3 - N}}$$

The effect of correcting for ties is to increase the value of H, and thus to make the result more significant than it would have been if uncorrected. Therefore, if one is able to reject H_0 without making the correction for ties, he/she will be able to reject H_0 at an even more stringent level of significance if the correction is used.

In most cases, the effect of the correction is negligible. According to Kruskal–Wallis (1952), if no more than 25% of the observations are involved in ties, the probability associated with an H computed without the correction for ties is rarely changed by more than 10% when the correction for ties is made.

17.7.4   Test of Significance of H

The null hypothesis (H_0) states that the k samples are from the same population or from identical populations. If the H_0 is true, then the Kruskal–Wallis statistic H is distributed as chi-square (χ^2) with df $= k-1$, provided that the sizes of the various k samples are not too small. That means, in large sample cases, the computed value of H is compared with the critical value of χ^2 for a particular chosen α for testing its significance. Therefore, when there are more than five cases in the various groups, that is $n_j > 5$, the probability associated with the occurrence under H_0 of values as large as an observed H may be determined by reference to Table L of the appendix. If the computed value of H is equal to or larger than the value of χ^2 given in Table L for the previously set level of significance and for df $= k-1$, then H_0 may be rejected at that level of significance.

In small sample cases, that is, when $k=3$ and the number of cases in each of the three samples is 5 or less, the chi-square approximation to the sampling distribution of H is not sufficiently close. For such cases, exact probabilities are presented in Table W of the appendix. The first column in that table gives the number of cases in the three samples, that is, gives various possible values of n_1, n_2 and n_3. The second column gives various values of H as computed by the appropriate formula discussed earlier. The third column gives the probability associated with the occurrence under H_0 of values as large as an observed H. Therefore, in small sample cases, the computed H is tested for its significance with reference to Table W of the appendix. If the probability associated with the obtained H value is equal to or less than the previously chosen α level, then it is significant, and hence the H_0 is rejected in favour of H_1.

17.7.5   Summary of Procedures

The following are the steps in the use of the Kruskal–Wallis one-way analysis of variance by ranks:

(i)   Rank all of the observations for the k samples in a single series, assigning ranks in an ascending order from 1 to N.

(ii)   Determine the value of R (the sum of the ranks) for each of the k groups of ranks. Determine $N = n_1 + n_2 + \cdots + n_k$.

(iii)   If tied scores occur, compute the correction factor, $\sum T$, where $T = t^3 - t$ in each case.

(iv)   If there are tied observations, compute the value of H by the formula incorporating the correction factor as mentioned earlier. Otherwise use the formula without incorporating the correction factor, as noted previously.

(v)   The testing of the significance of the obtained value of H depends on the number of k and on the size of the samples:

(a)   If $k = 3$ and if $n_1, n_2, n_3 \leq 5$, Table W of the appendix may be used to determine the associated probability under H_0 of an H as large as that observed. If the probability associated with the observed value of H is equal to or less than the previously set level of significance (α), reject H_0 in favour of H_1.

(b)   In other cases (i.e., in large sample cases), the significance of a value as large as the observed value of H may be tested by reference to Table L (critical values of χ^2) of the appendix with df $= k - 1$. If the computed value of H is equal to or larger than the critical value of χ^2 for the previously set level of significance and for the observed value of df $= k - 1$, then H_0 may be rejected at that level of significance in favour of H_1.

17.7.6   Power-efficiency

Compared with the most powerful parametric test, the F-test, under conditions where the assumptions associated with the statistical model of the F-test are met, the Kruskal–Wallis test has asymptotic efficiency of $3/\pi = 95.5\%$ (Andrews, 1954).

The Kruskal–Wallis H-test is more efficient than the extension of the median test because it utilises more of the information in the observations, converting the scores into ranks rather than simply dichotomising them as above and below the median, or exceeding and not exceeding the median. For $k = 2$, this test is equivalent to the Wilcoxon rank sum test.

The step-wise computational procedures of the Kruskal–Wallis H-test will become more clear to the reader through the following examples.

Example 17.12 The following are the authoritarianism scores of three groups of educators—teaching-oriented teachers (TOT), administration-oriented teachers (AOT) and administrators (A).

TOT	86	118	73	51	91
AOT	72	114	122	125	99
A	105	139	156	137	

Apply Kruskal–Wallis H-test to find whether these three groups differ with respect to averages on the authoritarianism.

Table 17.14 Authoritarianism scores of three groups of educators

TOT	AOT	A
86	72	105
118	114	139
73	122	156
51	125	137
91	99	

Table 17.15 Authoritarianism ranks of three groups of educators

TOT	AOT	A
4	2	7
9	8	13
3	10	14
1	11	12
5	6	
$R_1 = 22$	$R_2 = 37$	$R_3 = 46$

Solution

The following are the steps leading to the solution of the above problem.

(a) The given data are entered in Table 17.14.

  In this example, the number of TOT $= n_1 = 5$; the number of AOT $= n_2 = 5$; and the number of A $= n_3 = 4$. It is a small sample case, because $k = 3$ and $n_j \leq 5$. $N = n_1 + n_2 + n_3 = 5 + 5 + 4 = 14$.

(b) The H_0, H_1 and α level are stated as follows:

  H_0: Three groups do not differ with respect to averages on the authoritarianism.
  H_1: Three groups differ significantly with respect to averages on the authoritarianism.

  It is a two-tailed test. Let $\alpha = 0.05$.

(c) The scores of all the three groups are combined and taken as a series. Thus, there are 14 scores in total. These scores are assigned ranks in a single ascending order of their magnitudes. Rank 1 is assigned to the lowest score in the series, rank 2 to the next lowest score and so on. The highest score receives a rank equal to $N(n_1 + n_2 + n_3)$. These ranks are represented in Table 17.15.

(d) The ranks assigned to the scores of each group are added separately to give the rank sums (R_j) of the respective groups. Thus, we get $R_1 = 22$, $R_2 = 37$ and $R_3 = 46$ for groups 1 through 3 (see Table 17.15).

(e) Since there are no tied scores, the value of H may be computed directly from the rank sums (R_j) of the groups by the following formula:

$$H = \frac{12}{N(N+1)}\sum_{j=1}^{k}\left(\frac{R_j^2}{n_j}\right) - 3(N+1)$$

$$= \frac{12}{14(14+1)}\left[\frac{(22)^2}{5} + \frac{(37)^2}{5} + \frac{(46)^2}{4}\right] - 3(14+1) = \frac{2}{35}\times 899.6 - 45 = 51.4 - 45 = 6.4$$

Now, we test the significance of the obtained value of H. Since it is a case of very small samples, Table W of the appendix may be used. Reference to Table W discloses that when the n_js are 5, 5 and 4, $H \geq 6.4$ has probability of occurrence under the H_0 of $p < 0.049$. Since this probability is smaller than $\alpha = 0.05$, our decision is to reject H_0 in favour of H_1. We conclude that the specified three groups of educators differ in the degree of authoritarianism.

Example 17.13 The following data are for four groups of experimental animals:

Group 1	5	7	16	14	19
Group 2	8	15	18	20	24
Group 3	17	21	22	25	29
Group 4	23	27	28	31	32

Apply a Kruskal–Wallis one-way analysis of variance by ranks to the data, and interpret the results.

Solution

The following steps are to be followed for the solution of the above problem:

(a) The given data are entered in Table 17.16.

In this example, $n_1 = 5$, $n_2 = 5$, $n_3 = 5$ and $n_4 = 5$. $N = n_1 + n_2 + n_3 + n_4 = 5+5+5+5 = 20$, and $k = 4$. It is a large sample case.

(b) The H_0, H_1 and α level are stated as follows:

H_0: Four groups of experimental animals do not differ with respect to the averages of performance.

H_1: Four groups of experimental animals differ significantly with respect to the averages of performance.

It is a two-tailed test. Let $\alpha = 0.05$.

Table 17.16   Scores of four groups of experimental animals

Group 1	Group 2	Group 3	Group 4
5	8	17	23
7	15	21	27
16	18	22	28
14	20	25	31
19	24	29	32

Table 17.17   Ranks of four groups of experimental animals

Group 1	Group 2	Group 3	Group 4
1	3	7	13
2	5	11	16
6	8	12	17
4	10	15	19
9	14	18	20
$R_1 = 22$	$R_2 = 40$	$R_3 = 63$	$R_4 = 85$

(c)   The scores of all four groups of experimental animals are combined and taken as a series. Thus, there are 20 scores in total. These scores are ranked in a single ascending order of their magnitudes. We assign rank 1 to the lowest score in the series, rank 2 to the next lowest score and so on. The highest score in the series is assigned a rank equal to N. These assigned ranks are represented in Table 17.17.

(d)   The ranks assigned to the scores of each group are totalled separately to give the rank sums (R_j) of the respective groups. Thus, we get $R_1 = 22$, $R_2 = 40$, $R_3 = 63$ and $R_4 = 85$ (see Table 17.17).

(e)   Since there are no tied scores, the value of H may be computed directly from the rank sums (R_j) of the groups by the following formula:

$$H = \frac{12}{N(N+1)} \sum_{j=1}^{k} \left(\frac{R_j^2}{n_j} \right) - 3(N+1)$$

$$= \frac{12}{20(20+1)} \left[\frac{(22)^2}{5} + \frac{(40)^2}{5} + \frac{(63)^2}{5} + \frac{(85)^2}{5} \right] - 3(20+1)$$

$$= \frac{1}{35} \times 2655.6 - 63 = 75.87 - 63 = 12.87$$

$$df = k - 1 = 4 - 1 = 3.$$

(f)   Because it is a large samples case, the significance of the obtained value of H is tested in terms of the critical values of χ^2 given in Table L of the appendix. Reference to Table L indicates that the critical value of χ^2, with df=3, at 0.05 level is 7.82 and at 0.01 level is 11.34. Since the obtained value of $H = 12.87$ is greater than both the table values of χ^2, it is significant at 0.01 level of significance ($p < 0.01$). This indicates that our decision is to reject H_0 and accept H_1. Therefore, we conclude that the four groups of experimental animals significantly differ with respect to the averages of performance.

Example 17.14 The following are data for three samples:

Sample I	3	7	11	16	22	29	31	36	
Sample II	3	4	7	18	19	32			
Sample III	22	38	46	47	47	50	53	54	56

Table 17.18   Scores of three samples

Sample I	Sample II	Sample III
3	3	22
7	4	38
11	7	46
16	18	47
22	19	47
29	32	50
31		53
36		54
		56

Apply Kruskal–Wallis one-way ANOVA by ranks to the data and interpret the obtained results.

Solution

The following are the steps leading to the solution of the given problem:

(a)   The given data are entered in Table 17.18.
In this example, $n_1=8$, $n_2=6$ and $n_3=9$
$N=n_1+n_2+n_3=8+6+9=23$, and $k=3$. It is a large sample case.

(b)   The H_0, H_1 and α level are stated below:

     H_0: Three samples do not differ with respect to the averages of performance.
     H_1: Three samples differ significantly with respect to the averages of performance.

     It is a two-tailed test. Let $\alpha=0.05$.

(c)   The scores of all three samples are combined and taken together as a series. Thus, there are 23 scores in toto. These scores are ranked in a single ascending order of their values. The rank 1 is assigned o the lowest score in the series, rank 2 to the next lowest score and so on. The highest rank would be equal to N. In the given data, there are some tied scores. Each of these tied scores is assigned the average of the ranks they would have had if no ties had occurred. The ranks assigned to the scores of all the three samples are presented in Table 17.19.

(d)   The sums of ranks (R_j) are calculated for each sample separately. These are $R_1=69.5$, $R_2=40$ and $R_3=166.5$ (see Table 17.19).

(e)   Since there are some tied scores, we should apply the correction for ties. We note that in the given data we have four sets of ties of two observations each. These are given below:

2 scores of 3

2 scores of 7

2 scores of 22

2 scores of 47

Table 17.19   Ranks of three samples

Sample I	Sample II	Sample III
1.5	1.5	10.5
4.5	3	16
6	4.5	17
7	8	18.5
10.5	9	18.5
12	14	20
13		21
15		22
		23
$R_1 = 69.5$	$R_2 = 40$	$R_3 = 166.5$

Thus, we have ts of 2 for each of the four sets. To find $\sum T$, we sum the values of $t^3 - t$ for each of these tied sets.

$$\sum T = \sum t^3 - t = 2^3 - 2 + 2^3 - 2 + 2^3 - 2 + 2^3 - 2$$
$$= 6 + 6 + 6 + 6 = 24$$

(f)   The value of H is computed by the following formula incorporating the correction for ties:

$$H = \frac{\frac{12}{N(N+1)} \sum_{j=1}^{k} \left(\frac{R_j^2}{n_j} \right) - 3(N+1)}{1 - \frac{\sum T}{N^3 - N}}$$

$$= \frac{\frac{12}{23(23+1)} \left[\frac{(69.5)^2}{8} + \frac{(40)^2}{6} + \frac{(166.5)^2}{9} \right] - 3(23+1)}{1 - \frac{24}{23^3 - 23}}$$

$$= \frac{\frac{1}{46} [603.78 + 266.67 + 3080.25] - 72}{1 - 0.002} = \frac{85.88 - 72}{0.998} = \frac{13.88}{0.998} = 13.91$$

Thus, the value of H, without correction for ties, is 13.88 and with correction it becomes 13.91. In this example, the effect of the correction for ties is only 0.03 (i.e., $13.91 - 13.88 = 0.03$), which is negligible.

$$df = k - 1 = 3 - 1 = 2.$$

(g)   Since the given example is a large samples case, we can test the significance of the obtained value of H referring to the table of χ^2 with df = 2. Consulting Table L of the appendix we find that the critical value of χ^2, with df = 2, at 0.05 level is 5.99 and at 0.01 level is 9.21. Since the computed $H = 13.91$ is larger than both the table values of χ^2, it is significant at better than the 1% level ($p < 0.01$). Thus, the H_0 is rejected in favour of H_1. We may conclude that the three samples differ significantly with respect to the averages of performance; these three samples are from different populations.

17.8   The Friedman Two-way Analysis of Variance by Ranks

A rank test for k correlated or matched samples is the Friedman two-way analysis of variance by ranks (1937). It is a non-parametric *statistical test*; it is a rank-dependent statistic. The Friedman test is designated as a statistic χ_r^2 and it is simply known as the Friedman χ_r^2 test. The corresponding parametric test is an analysis of variance for two-way classification where observations are made on each of a group of individuals under more than two conditions (i.e., F-test for repeated measures). If there is reason to believe that the assumptions underlying the analysis of variance are not satisfied by the data, the Friedman rank method may be appropriate. The data are a set of k observations for a sample of N individuals. Such data arise in many experiments where subjects are tested under a number of different experimental conditions.

The Friedman χ_r^2 test is useful when the measurement of the dependent variable is in at least an ordinal scale. It tests whether the k related samples could probably have come from the same population with respect to mean ranks. That is, it is an overall test of whether the size of the scores depends on the conditions under which they were yielded. In other words, when the data from k matched samples are in at least on ordinal scale, the Friedman two-way ANOVA by ranks is useful for testing the null hypothesis that the k samples have drawn from the same population.

Since the k samples are matched, the number of cases is the same in each of the samples or groups. The matching may be achieved by studying the same group of subjects under each of the k conditions. Or the researcher may obtain several sets, each consisting of k matched subjects, and then randomly assign one subject in each set to the first condition, one subject in each set to the second condition and so on. For example, if one wished to study the differences in learning achieved under four teaching methods—A, B, C, and D, one might obtain N sets of $k = 4$ children, each set consisting of children who are matched on the relevant variables (e.g., age, previous learning, intelligence, socioeconomic status, motivation, etc.), and then at random assign one child from each of the N sets to teaching method A, another from each set to B, another from each set to C and the fourth to D.

For the Friedman χ_r^2 test, the data are cast in a two-way table containing N rows and k columns. The rows represent the various subjects or matched set of subjects (or groups) and the columns represent various conditions. If the scores of subjects serving under all conditions are under study, then each row gives the scores of one subject under the k conditions.

The data of the Friedman test are ranks. The scores in each row (or group) are ranked separately. That is, with k conditions being studied, the ranks in any row range from 1 to k. The Friedman test determines whether it is likely that the different columns or ranks (samples) came from the same population.

The null hypothesis (H_0) is that the k correlated samples have been drawn from the same population with respect to the column rank sums. In other words, if the H_0 is true, the rank totals of the various columns would be about equal, and if the H_0 is false, then the rank totals would vary from one column to another.

17.8.1   Assumptions of Friedman χ_r^2 Test

Being a non-parametric *statistical test*, the following are some of the assumptions of the Friedman two-way analysis of variance (χ_r^2) by ranks:

(a) The observations must be independent. This implies that the selection of samples from the population should be random and the assignment of scores to the performance of the subjects should be unbiased and impartial.

(b) The trait or the dependent variable that the researcher is going to measure must have underlying continuity. This means that the trait must be present in each and every element of the population from which the samples are drawn; nowhere in the population it is absent.

(c) The measurements or data should be in terms of ordinal scale of measurement. That is, the data of the test are ranks.

(d) The k samples are correlated or matched.

17.8.2   Computation of χ_r^2 Values

We can divide the computation of the Friedman two-way analysis of variance (χ_r^2) by ranks into two categories: (i) when N and k are small, and (ii) when N and k are large. N represents the number of rows and k represents the number of columns. When $k=3$, $N=2$ to 9, and when $k=4$, $N=2$ to 4, it is a small sample case. Any deviation to the above either in k or N or in both is a case of large sample.

So far as the computational formula is concerned, it is the same for both the categories—small and large samples. But these two categories differ from each other so far as the testing of the significance of the observed χ_r^2 value is concerned. We will discuss it in detail later on under the heading 'Test of Significance of χ_r^2 Values'. Now, we discuss about the computation of χ_r^2 values. For computing the χ_r^2 values, the steps to be followed are as follows:

(a) To perform the Friedman test, we first rank the scores row-wise. We may give the lowest score in each row the rank of 1, the next lowest score in each row the rank of 2, etc. The ranks in each row of the table range from 1 to k. The tied scores are dealt with as usual; each score is given the average of the tied ranks.

(b) After the scores have been assigned ranks row-wise, these ranks are added column-wise, and these rank sums are denoted by R_j.

(c) The χ_r^2 may be computed directly from the rank sums (R_j) of the columns (samples) by the following formula:

$$\chi_r^2 = \frac{12}{Nk(k+1)} \sum_{j=1}^{k}(R_j)^2 - 3N(k+1)$$

where

N = number of rows

k = number of columns

R_j = sum of ranks in j-th column

$\sum_{j=1}^{k}$ directs one to sum the squares of the sums of ranks over all k conditions

df = $k-1$

17.8.3   Test of Significance of χ_r^2

The null hypothesis (H_0) states that the k correlated samples have been drawn from the same population with respect to the column rank sums. If the H_0 is true, then the Friedman statistic χ_r^2 is distributed as chi-square (χ^2) with df = $k-1$ only when the number of rows (N) and/or columns (k) is not too small. That means, in large sample cases, the computed value of χ_r^2 is compared with the critical value of χ^2 for a previously selected level of significance and for a computed value of df $= k-1$, for testing its significance. The probability associated with occurrence under H_0 of values as large as an observed χ_r^2 is shown in Table L of the appendix. If the computed value of χ_r^2 is equal to or larger than that given in Table L for a particular level of significance and for a particular value of df $= k-1$, then it is significant; the implication is that the sums of ranks (or, equivalently, the mean ranks, R_j/N) for the various columns differ significantly (which is to say that the size of the scores depends on the conditions under which the scores were obtained) and, thus, H_0 may be rejected at that level of significance.

In small sample cases (when $k=3$, $N=2$ to 9; and when $k=4$, $N=2$ to 4), exact probability tables are available, and these should be used rather than Table L of the appendix. Table X of the appendix gives exact probabilities associated with values as large as an observed χ_r^2 for $k=3$, $N=2$ to 9, and for $k=4$, $N=2$ to 4. When N and k are larger than the values included in Table X, χ_r^2 may be considered to be distributed as χ^2, and thus Table L may be used for testing H_0. Therefore, in small sample cases (when N and k are small), the obtained or computed χ_r^2 is tested for its significance with reference to Table X of the appendix. If the probability associated with the computed χ_r^2 value is equal to or less than the previously chosen α level, then it is significant, and hence the H_0 is rejected in favour of H_1.

Friedman (1937) states that the substitution of the average rank for tied values does not affect the validity of the χ_r^2 test. So, there is no need for correction for ties. We should take the computed value of χ_r^2 as such for testing its significance, even if there are some tied scores in the given data.

17.8.4   Summary of Procedures

The following are the steps in the use of Friedman two-way ANOVA by ranks (χ_r^2):

(i)   Cast the scores in a two-way contingency table having k columns (samples or conditions) and N rows (subjects or groups)

(ii)   Rank the scores in each row from 1 to k.

(iii)   Determine the sum of the ranks in each column (R_j).

(iv)   Compute the value of χ_r^2 using the formula noted earlier.

(v)   The testing of the significance of the obtained value of χ_r^2 depends on the size of N and k:

(a)   If $k=3$, $N=2$ to 9, and if $k=4$, $N=2$ to 4, Table X of the appendix may be used to determine the associated probability under H_0 of χ_r^2 as large as that observed. If the probability associated with the observed value of χ_r^2 is equal to or less than the previously set α level, reject H_0 in favour of H_1.

(b)   For N and/or k larger than those shown in Table X of the appendix, the associated probability may be determined by reference to the chi-square (χ^2) distribution (given in Table L of the appendix) with df $= k-1$. If the computed value of χ_r^2 is equal to or larger than the critical value of χ^2 for the previously set level of significance and for the observed value of df $= k-1$, then H_0 may be rejected at that level of significance and the H_1 is accepted.

17.8.5   Power-efficiency

The asymptotic relative efficiency of the Friedman test relative to the parametric F-test resulting from a two-way analysis of variance with one observation per cell is

$$\left(\frac{3}{\pi}\right)\left(\frac{k}{k+1}\right)$$

The efficiency of the test increases as k increases, and extends from 0.637 for $k=2$ to a maximum of 0.955 for $k=\infty$. For $k=2$, this test is the same as the sign test for correlated samples.

The step-wise computational procedures of the Friedman χ_r^2 test for N and k small and for N and k large will become more clear to the reader through the following examples.

Example 17.15 The following are the scores of three groups under four conditions. Each group contains four matched subjects, one being assigned to each of the four conditions. Apply Friedman χ_r^2 test and interpret the results.

Scores of Three Matched Groups under Four Conditions

Groups	Conditions			
	I	**II**	**III**	**IV**
A	9	4	1	7
B	6	5	2	8
C	9	1	2	6

Solution
The following steps are followed for the solution of the above problem:

(a) The given data are entered in Table 17.20.
In this example, N (number of rows)=3, and k (number of columns/conditions)=4. It is a small sample case, because $k=4$ and $N=3$.

(b) The H_0, H_1 and α level are stated below:

H_0: The $k=4$ correlated samples are from the same population with respect to the column sums of ranks.
H_1: The $k=4$ samples are not from the same population with respect to the column sums of ranks.

It is a two-tailed test. Let $\alpha=0.05$.

(c) We rank the scores row-wise. In each row, the lowest score is assigned a rank of 1, the next lowest score a rank of 2 and so on. The ranks in each row of the table range from 1 to $k=4$. These assigned ranks are presented in Table 17.21.

Table 17.20 Scores of three matched groups under four conditions

Groups	Conditions			
	I	**II**	**III**	**IV**
A	9	4	1	7
B	6	5	2	8
C	9	1	2	6

Table 17.21   Ranks of three matched groups under four conditions

Groups	Conditions			
	I	**II**	**III**	**IV**
A	4	2	1	3
B	3	2	1	4
C	4	1	2	3
R_j	11	5	4	10

(d)   The ranks assigned to the scores of each row are added separately column-wise to give the rank sums of the respective conditions (columns or samples). Thus, we get $R_1 = 11$, $R_2 = 5$, $R_3 = 4$ and $R_4 = 10$ for conditions/columns I through IV (see Table 17.21)

(e)   The Friedman statistic χ_r^2 is computed by the formula that reads

$$\chi_r^2 = \frac{12}{Nk(k+1)} \sum_{j=1}^{k} \left(R_j\right)^2 - 3N(k+1)$$

$$= \frac{12}{3 \times 4(4+1)} \left[(11)^2 + (5)^2 + (4)^2 + (10)^2\right] - 3 \times 3(4+1)$$

$$= \frac{1}{5} \times 262 - 45 = 52.4 - 45 = 7.4$$

(f)   Now, we test the significance of the computed value of χ_r^2. Since it is a small samples case, Table X of the appendix may be used. Reference to Table X (subtable X_{11}, $k=4$) reveals that when $k=4$ and $N=3$, $\chi_r^2 \geq 7.4$ has the probability of occurrence under H_0 of $p=0.033$. Since this probability is less than $\alpha=0.05$, the obtained χ_r^2 is significant. With these data, therefore, we could reject the H_0, which states that the four samples were drawn from the same population with respect to location (mean ranks), and accept the H_1 which states that the four samples are not from the same population with respect to the column rank sums.

Example 17.16 Apply a Friedman two-way analysis of variance by ranks to the following data and interpret the results:

Subjects	Treatments			
	I	**II**	**III**	**IV**
1	5	9	4	1
2	6	8	7	3
3	9	10	8	7
4	5	10	4	2
5	8	6	4	1
6	10	8	7	5
7	14	12	13	10

Table 17.22   Scores of subjects under four treatments

Subjects	Treatments			
	I	**II**	**III**	**IV**
1	5	9	4	1
2	6	8	7	3
3	9	10	8	7
4	5	10	4	2
5	8	6	4	1
6	10	8	7	5
7	14	12	13	10

Solution

For the solution of the above problem the steps to be followed are as follows:

(a)   The given data are entered in Table 17.22.
In this example, N (number of rows)$=7$, and k (number of columns/treatments)$=4$. It is a large sample case, because $k=4$ and $N=7$.

(b)   The H_0, H_1 and α level are stated below.

H_0: The $k=4$ related samples are from the same population with respect to column sums of ranks.
H_1: The $k=4$ related samples are not from the same population with respect to column sums of ranks.

It is a two-tailed test. Let $\alpha=0.05$.

(c)   The scores are ranked row-wise. The lowest score in each row is ranked as 1, next lowest score as 2 and so on. The ranks in each row of the table range from 1 to $k=4$. These ranks are presented in Table 17.23.

(d)   The ranks assigned to the scores of each row are added separately column-wise to give the rank sums of the respective treatments (columns or samples). Thus, we get $R_1=23$, $R_2=24$, $R_3=16$ and $R_4=7$ for treatments or columns I through IV (see Table 17.23).

(e)   The Friedman statistic χ_r^2 is computed by the following formula:

$$\chi_r^2 = \frac{12}{Nk(k+1)}\sum_{j=1}^{k}(R_j)^2 - 3N(k+1)$$

$$= \frac{12}{7\times 4(4+1)}\left[(23)^2 + (24)^2 + (16)^2 + (7)^2\right] - 3\times 7(4+1)$$

$$= \frac{12}{7\times 4\times 5}\left[529 + 576 + 256 + 49\right] - 3\times 7\times 5$$

$$= \frac{3}{35}\times 1410 - 105 = 120.86 - 105 = 15.86$$

$$\therefore \chi_r^2 = 15.86. \quad \mathrm{df} = k-1 = 4-1 = 3$$

Table 17.23   Ranks of subjects under four treatments

Subjects	Treatments			
	I	**II**	**III**	**IV**
1	3	4	2	1
2	2	4	3	1
3	3	4	2	1
4	3	4	2	1
5	4	3	2	1
6	4	3	2	1
7	4	2	3	1
R_j	23	24	16	7

(f) Next is the test of significance of the computed value of χ_r^2. Since it is a large samples case, the significance of the obtained value of χ_r^2 is tested in terms of the critical values of χ^2 given in Table L of the appendix. Reference to Table L indicates that the critical value of χ^2, with df $= k-1=4-1=3$, at 0.05 level is 7.82 and at 0.01 level is 11.34. Since the obtained value of $\chi_r^2 = 15.86$ is larger than both the table values of χ^2, it is significant at 0.01 level of significance (therefore, $p < 0.01$). This indicates that our decision is to reject the H_0 and accept the H_1. The conclusion is that the four samples significantly differ with respect to the column sums of ranks.

Summary

In this chapter, we have discussed some other non-parametric statistical tests which were not presented in Chapter 16. These non-parametric statistical tests include: the sign test, Wilcoxon matched-pairs signed ranks test, Wilcoxon composite rank test or rank sum test, Mann–Whitney U-test, median test, Kruskal–Wallis one-way analysis of variance by ranks and Friedman two-way analysis of variance by ranks.

The sign test is a simple non-parametric alternative to student's correlated t-test. In analysing the data of an experiment with the sign test, we ignore the magnitude of difference scores and just consider their direction. There are only two possible scores for each subject, a plus or a minus. We sum the pluses and minuses for all subjects, and the obtained result is the total number of pluses and minuses. To test the null hypothesis, we calculate the probability of getting the total number of pluses or minuses, whichever is less in number. The computational procedures for the sign test were presented and several illustrative and practice problems worked out. The sign test is far less powerful than the t-test. Its major deficiency lies in the use of only the algebraic sign, and not the magnitude, of the difference between the scores of each pair.

The Wilcoxon matched-pairs signed ranks test is a non-parametric test that is used with a correlated-groups design. The statistic calculated is T_{obt}. Determination of T_{obt} involves four steps: (i) finding the difference between each pairs of scores, (ii) ranking the absolute values of the difference scores, (iii) assigning the appropriate sign to the ranks and (iv) separately summing the positive and negative ranks. T_{obt} is evaluated by comparison with T_{crit}. If $T_{obt} \leq T_{crit}$, we reject H_0. The Wilcoxon signed ranks test requires that: (a) the within-pair scores are at least of ordinal scaling and (b) the difference scores are also at least of ordinal scaling. This test serves as an alternate to the t-test for correlated groups when the assumptions of the t-test have not been met. It is more powerful than the sign test, but not as powerful as the t-test. The step-wise computational procedures for the Wilcoxon matched-pairs signed ranks test were presented, and several illustrative as well as practice problems worked out.

The Wilcoxon composite rank test or rank sum test is a non-parametric test that is used with an uncorrelated (or independent) groups design. The statistic calculated is R_{1obt}. Determination of R_{1obt} involves four steps: (i) all the scores of both the samples are taken as a composite group and then they are ranked in an ascending order, (ii) separately summing the ranks sample-wise, (iii) R_1 obtained is the sum of ranks of the smaller sample and (iv) computation of R_1. The obtained R_1 is evaluated by comparison with its critical value (see Table T of the appendix). If $R_{1obt} \leq R_{1crit}$, we reject H_0. The Wilcoxon rank sum test requires that: (a) both the samples are independent/uncorrelated and (b) the data are of ordinal scaling. This test serves as an excellent alternative to the t-test for independent samples when the assumptions of the t-test have been violated. The step-wise computational procedures for the Wilcoxon rank sum test were presented, and several illustrative and practice problems worked out.

The Mann–Whitney U-test is a non-parametric test that is used with an independent-groups design. This test analyses the degree of separation or difference between the samples. The less the separation, the more reasonable chance is as the underlying explanation. For any analysis, there are two values indicating the degree of separation. They both indicate the same degree of separation. The lower value is arbitrarily called U_{obt} and the higher value is called U'_{obt}. The lower the U_{obt} value, the greater the separation. The higher the U'_{obt} value, the greater the separation. With the Mann–Whitney U-test, we calculate the U_{obt} and U'_{obt} value of the data. Since they both indicate the same degree of separation, we just used the U_{obt} value. The obtained U value is evaluated by comparison with its critical value (see Table V of the appendix). If $U_{obt} \leq U_{crit}$, we reject H_0. If not, we retain H_0. The Mann–Whitney U-test is appropriate for an independent group design where the data are at least ordinal in scaling. It is a powerful test, often used in place of student's t-test when the data do not meet the assumptions of the t-test. The power of the U-test is slightly lower than that of the t-test, but higher than those of the Wilcoxon rank sum test and the median test. The step-wise computational procedures, formulae and equations for the Mann–Whitney U-test calculated from both small and large samples were presented, and several illustrative and practice problems worked out.

The median test is a non-parametric test that is used with independent groups design where the data are at least in an ordinal scale. The median test can be applied to two or more than two independent samples. The statistic calculated is the χ^2_{obt}. The obtained value of χ^2 is evaluated by comparing it with its critical value. If $\chi^2_{obt} \geq \chi^2_{crit}$, we reject H_0. The critical value of χ^2 is determined from Table L given in the appendix with the help of the appropriate df. The rejection of H_0 leads to the conclusion that the samples have come from populations with different medians. The step-wise computational procedures for the median test were presented, and several illustrative and practice problems worked out.

The Kruskal–Wallis test used as a substitute for one-way parametric ANOVA. It uses the independent-group design with k samples (where $k \geq 3$). The null hypothesis (H_0) asserts that the k samples are random samples from the same or identical population distributions. No attempt is made to specifically test for population mean differences, as is the case with parametric ANOVA. The statistic computed is H_{obt}. If the number of scores in each sample is 5 or more, the sampling distribution of H_{obt} is close enough to that of chi-square to use the latter in determining H_{crit}. If $H_{obt} \geq H_{crit}$, H_0 is rejected. In computing H_{obt}, the scores of the K samples are combined and rank ordered, assigning 1 to the lowest score. The ranks are then summed for each sample. Kruskal–Wallis tests whether it is reasonable to consider the summed ranks for each sample to be due to random sampling from a single population set of scores. The greater the differences between the sum of ranks for each sample the less tenable is the null hypothesis. This test assumes that the dependent variable is measured on a scale that is of at least ordinal scaling. There must also be five or more scores in each sample to validly use the chi-square sampling distribution. The step-wise computational procedures, formulae and equations for the Kruskal–Wallis H test calculated from both small and large samples were presented, and several illustrative and practice problems worked out.

Friedman test is used as a substitute for two-way parametric ANOVA. It uses the repeated measures design with k correlated or matched samples. The null hypothesis (H_0) asserts that the k correlated samples have been drawn from the same population with respect to the column rank sums. The statistic computed is χ_r^2. If the number of scores in each of the three samples ($k=3$) is 10 or more ($N \geq 10$) and if the number of scores in each of the four samples ($k=4$) is 5 or more ($N \geq 5$), the sampling distribution of $\chi_{r\,obt}$ is close enough to that of chi-square to use the latter in determining $\chi_{r\,crit}^2$. If $\chi_{r\,obt}^2 \geq \chi_{crit}^2$, H_0 is rejected. In computing $\chi_{r\,obt}^2$, the scores are ranked row-wise, assigning rank 1 to the lowest score. The ranks are then summed for each column and designated as R_r. Friedman χ_r^2 tests whether it is reasonable to consider the summed ranks for each column (sample) to be due to random sampling from the same population of scores. The greater the differences between the rank sums of columns the less tenable is the null hypothesis. Friedman χ_r^2 test assumes that the k samples are correlated or matched, and the dependent variable is measured on an ordinal scale. The step-wise computational procedures, formulae and equations for the Friedman χ_r^2 test from both small and large samples were presented, and several illustrative and practice problems worked out.

Key Terms

- Correction for ties
- Counting method
- Equation method
- Friedman two-way analysis of variance by ranks
- Kruskal–Wallis one-way analysis of variance by ranks
- Mann–Whitney U-test
- Median test
- Paired observations
- Power-efficiency
- Sign test
- Wilcoxon composite rank test
- Wilcoxon matched-pairs signed rank test
- Wilcoxon rank sum test

Questions and Problems

1. What do you mean by sign test? What are its assumptions?
2. With the help of an example, illustrate the computation and test of significance of the sign test.
3. What is Wilcoxon matched-pairs signed-ranks test? Discuss its assumptions.
4. By citing some examples, illustrate the computational procedures of Wilcoxon matched-pairs signed-ranks test. How the result of this test is tested for significance?

5. What is Wilcoxon rank sum test? What are its assumptions?

6. Discuss about the computation and testing of significance procedures of Wilcoxon rank sum test through an example.

7. What do you mean by Mann–Whitney U-test? What are its assumptions?

8. With the help of examples, illustrate the computation and test of significance of the U-test.

9. What is the median test? Discuss its assumptions.

10. With the help of suitable examples, illustrate the computational procedures of the median test for two and more than two independent samples. How the obtained results of the median test are tested for their significance?

11. What is meant by Kruskal–Wallis one-way analysis of variance by ranks? Discuss its assumptions.

12. By the help of hypothetical data, illustrate the computational procedures of Kruskal–Wallis H-test for both small and large samples. How the obtained value of H is tested for its significance?

13. What do you mean by Friedman two-way analysis of variance by ranks? What are its assumptions?

14. Taking hypothetical data, illustrate the computational procedures of the Friedman two-way analysis of variance by ranks for both small and large samples. How the obtained value of χ_r^2 is tested for its significance?

15. Write notes on the followings:

   (a) Power of the sign test.
   (b) Power of the Wilcoxon matched-pairs signed-ranks test.
   (c) Power of the Wilcoxon rank sum test.
   (d) Power of the Mann–Whitney U-test.
   (e) Power of the median test.
   (f) Power of the Kruskal–Wallis H-test.
   (g) Power of the Friedman χ_r^2 test.

16. The scores under two conditions obtained by a sample of seven respondents are given below. Apply sign test and comment on your findings.

| X: | 12 | 16 | 18 | 8 | 6 | 4 | 11 |
| Y: | 7 | 12 | 14 | 17 | 5 | 12 | 8 |

17. The following are data for a sample of nine animals tested under control and experimental conditions:

Control	21	24	26	32	55	82	46	55	88
Experimental	18	9	23	26	82	199	42	30	62

Test the significance of the difference between the two medians using a sign test.

18. In the data below, column X represents 12 scores of members of a control group in an experiment. Column Y represents the scores of 12 matched individuals who were

given the same test after a period of stress. Use the sign test to test the hypothesis of no difference.

X:	46	68	60	58	42	43	40	56	38	58	42	48
Y:	36	50	58	40	44	43	29	36	46	48	38	42

19. The following data are obtained from a matched-group paired observations. Test the hypothesis of no difference by using a sign test.

$$\text{Number of + signs} = 40, \text{Number of } - \text{signs} = 10, N = 50$$

20. Apply the Wilcoxon matched-pairs signed-ranks test to the data of (a) Problem 16 and (b) Problem 17 above.

21. With the data in Problem 18 above, test the hypothesis of no difference using Wilcoxon matched-pairs signed-ranks test.

22. n a study on 40 matched pairs of MBA students, their latency of times of incorrectly predicted and correctly predicted decisions were recorded. Five pairs showed differences of zero. The obtained value of $T = 170$. Test the significance of the obtained T.

23. The following are data for two groups of experimental animals:

Group I	104	109	127	143	187	204	209	266	277
Group II	62	82	89	90	101	106	109	109	205

Apply the Wilcoxon rank sum test and interpret the results.

24. Below are the scores of a group of normals and a group of psychotics on the Picture Completion Scale of the Wechsler-Bellevue. Test the hypothesis of no difference using the Wilcoxon rank sum test.

Normal	6	6	14	13	15	6	8	7	10	14	10	14
Psychotics	7	2	12	13	8	6	4	2	2	12		

25. The following data are obtained from an experiment on the control and experimental groups of rats. Apply the Wilcoxon rank sum test and interpret the results.

Control Group	$N_1 = 30; R_c = 635$
Experimental Group	$N_2 = 40; R_e = 1,850$

26. Two independent groups of rats, one experimental group (E) having five rats, and one control group (C) having four rats were taken. The following are the scores. Test whether the previous training facilitated the performance.

E rats	78	64	75	45	82
C rats	90	70	53	51	

27. Apply the Mann-Whitney U-test to the data in Problem 24 above.

28. The scores of two independent groups of subjects are given below. Apply Mann-Whitney U-test and test whether there is a significant difference between these two groups.

Group 1	Group 2	
12	16	25
21	15	26
10	17	14
8	19	28
6	18	29
7	9	31
5	11	30
4	20	33
23	22	32
24	13	34
	27	

29. Two independent groups of children made the following scores on the vocabulary test of the Stanford-Binet. By using the Mann-Whitney U-test, test for differences in the two groups.

Group 1	Group 2	
10	33	14
18	36	18
36	26	22
22	24	16
28	31	38
29	13	26
32	19	28
15	23	12
18	25	11
36	27	19
21	32	16
27		

30. Apply the median test to the data of Problem 23, above, (a) with a continuity correction and (b) without a continuity correction.

31. Apply the median test to the data of Problem 24, above, with a correction for continuity.

32. The following are the arithmetic achievement scores of three independent samples. Apply the median test and interpret the results.

Sample A	Sample B	Sample C
8	2	12
7	4	3
14	6	10
10	14	4
8	10	14
6	8	11
	6	10
	2	8

33. The following scores are for four independent groups of experimental animals. Apply a median test to test the hypothesis that the four samples come from populations with the same median.

Group 1	5	7	16	14	19
Group 2	8	15	18	20	24
Group 3	17	21	22	25	29
Group 4	23	27	28	31	32

34. Paintings of children of three different schools, five from each school, were evaluated and the scores are given below. Apply Kruskal–Wallis one-way analysis of variance to find out the significance of difference among schools.

Stewart School	Convent School	Tribal School
80	75	78
75	70	77
79	71	72
74	69	68
73	76	67

35. Apply Kruskal–Wallis one-way ANOVA to the following data and interpret your results.

Treatment Conditions		
A	**B**	**C**
2	7	10
4	14	18
3	9	12
1	28	20
6	22	15
8	27	23
11	24	21
13	25	16

36. Analyse the following data using Kruskal–Wallis one-way ANOVA and interpret the results.

Group 1	4	6	15	13	18
Group 2	7	14	17	19	23
Group 3	16	20	21	24	28
Group 4	22	26	27	30	31

37. The following data show the changed response scores of three independent groups of subjects on the Edwards Personal Preference Schedule. Test the significance of the differences among these three groups using Kruskal–Wallis H-test.

Control Group	Social Desirability Group	Personal Desirability Group
45	74	85
36	74	74
32	73	50
30	71	49
30	60	48
28	45	40
		36

38. We studied the scores of four groups under four treatment conditions. Each group contains four matched subjects, one being assigned to each of the four treatment conditions. The following are the scores of four matched groups under four treatment conditions. Analyse the data using Friedman two-way analysis of variance by ranks and interpret your results.

Groups	Treatment Conditions			
	I	II	III	IV
A	11	6	3	9
B	8	7	4	10
C	11	3	4	8
D	9	4	1	7

39. Apply Friedman χ_r^2 test to the following data and interpret the results.

Subjects	Treatments		
	I	II	III
1	6	10	5
2	7	9	8
3	10	11	9
4	6	11	5
5	9	7	5

40. In a study of the effect of three different patterns of reinforcement upon extent of discrimination learning in rats, three matched samples of 10 groups of rats were trained under three patterns of reinforcement such as 100% reinforcement (RR), partial reinforcement where each sequence of trials ended with an unreinforced trial (RU) and partial reinforcement where each sequence of trials ended with reinforced trial (UR). The following are the scores of 10 groups of rats under three conditions of reinforcement. Analyse the data using Friedman two-way ANOVA by ranks and interpret the results.

Groups	Types of Reinforcement		
	RR	RU	UR
1	12	16	14
2	10	12	8
3	11	13	12
4	9	10	11
5	14	10	12
6	12	13	11
7	15	14	11
8	9	15	12
9	14	7	10
10	13	10	12

41. Fill in the blanks:
    (i)   The sign test compares two _____ samples.
    (ii) The sign test is a simple _____ alternative to correlated t-test.
    (iii) The Wilcoxon matched-pairs signed ranks test is a powerful _____ alternative to student's correlated t-test.
    (iv) The Wilcoxon matched-pairs signed ranks test is _____ powerful than the sign test.
    (v)   The Wilcoxon composite rank test is a good non-parametric alternative to student's t-test for two _____ samples.
    (vi) The Wilcoxon composite rank test is otherwise known as _____ test.
    (vii) The power of the Mann-Whitney U-test is slightly _____ than the t-test for two independent samples.
    (viii) The U-test assumes that the data should be in terms of _____ scale of measurement.
    (ix) The median test assumes that the two or more samples must be _____.
    (x)   The Kruskal-Wallis test is designated as a statistic _____.

42. Write whether the following statements are True or False.
    (i)   Friedman test is designated as a statistic χ_r^2.
    (ii) Friedman test is a rank-dependent statistic.
    (iii) Kruskal-Wallis H-test is applicable to k correlated samples.
    (iv) The median test is applicable to two or more independent samples of equal sizes only.
    (v)   In the median test, the H_0 states that the two or more independent samples are from populations with the same median.

(vi) In the Mann–Whitney U-test, we have always only two independent samples/groups.

(vii) In Wilcoxon rank sum test, the scores of both the samples are separately ranked.

(viii) In Wilcoxon matched-pair signed ranks test, any pair of observations having a difference of zero is dropped from the analysis.

(ix) Sign test utilises information simply about the direction of the differences within pairs (i.e., either + or – signs).

(x) In the sign test, any pair of scores having zero difference is discarded from the analysis.

43. Find out the correct answer from among the four alternatives.

(i) The test of significance of the results of the sign test is done by

   (a) Chi-square test   (b) Student's t-test
   (c) Median test   (d) None of the above

(ii) In sign test the H_0 states that the median difference between the pairs is

   (a) +1.0   (b) Zero
   (c) –1.0   (d) None of the above

(iii) The Wilcoxon matched-pairs signed ranks test is applicable to two:

   (a) Uncorrelated samples   (b) Independent samples
   (c) Correlated samples   (d) None of the above

(iv) The Wilcoxon rank sum test is used for comparing two:

   (a) Independent samples   (b) Correlated samples
   (c) Matched samples   (d) None of the above

(v) The Wilcoxon composite rank test is a good non-parametric alternative to:

   (a) Uncorrelated t-test   (b) Correlated t-test
   (c) F-test   (d) None of the above

(vi) The Mann–Whitney U-test is applicable when we have scores for two:

   (a) Correlated groups   (b) Uncorrelated groups
   (c) Matched groups   (d) None of the above

(vii) For the use of U-test, it is assumed that the measurements should be in terms of:

   (a) Interval scale   (b) Nominal scale
   (c) Ordinal scale   (d) None of the above

(viii) The median test compares the medians of two or more:

   (a) Independent groups   (b) Dependent groups
   (c) Correlated groups   (d) None of the above

(ix) The Kruskal–Wallis *H*-test is a:

    (a) Score-dependent statistic   (b) Rank-dependent statistic

    (c) Rank-independent statistic   (d) None of the above

(x) To apply Friedman χ_r^2 test, it is assumed that the *k* samples are:

    (a) Correlated   (b) Uncorrelated

    (c) Independent   (d) None of the above

CHAPTER 18

Psychological Test Construction

After completing this chapter you will be able to:

- Understand the important principles of test construction.
- Differentiate between the power and speed test.
- Make final selection of test items through item analysis.
- Estimate the reliability of a test and which method is preferred.
- Understand the factors that influence the test reliability.
- Estimate the validity of a test.
- Explain the factors that affect test validity.
- Describe the relationship between test reliability and validity.
- Understand the basic concepts in factor analysis, its purpose and methods.
- Explain the meaning of standardisation and norms.
- Identify the characteristics of standardised tests and establish norms.

18.1 Introduction

Psychological tests are undertaken mainly to study individual differences in abilities, aptitudes, personality, attitudes, achievements, memory, interests, intelligence, creative thinking, reasoning and psychomotor abilities.

Many behavioural variables are abstract in nature and cannot be measured with precision. While some variables such as intelligence, job performance and memory span can be measured on quantitative scales, others such as job satisfaction, personality and emotionality are assessed only qualitatively. The scale of quantitative measurement is frequently an interval scale with an arbitrary zero point instead of a true zero point. However, some psychological variables such as the ratios between stimuli in psychophysics and the calorie expenditures in various job activities in organisational behaviour are measured in ratio scales with true zero points.

Psychological measurements are expressed in various ways such as the number of trials required to achieve a particular level of performance, the number of correct responses, the speed of action and the average number of items remembered after brief exposures. The units at equal distances on a psychological scale are assumed to represent equal differences in the psychological variable.

In the words of Anastasi (1976), a psychological test is essentially an objective and standardised measure of a sample of behaviour. Munn (1966) says that such a test is an examination to reveal the relative standing of an individual in the group with respect to intelligence, personality, aptitude or achievement. Cronbach (1970) defines, 'A test is a systematic procedure for comparing the behaviour of two or more persons.'

18.2   Principles of Test Construction

This chapter mainly deals with the tests of abilities. The important principles of or essentials for the test construction may be summarised as follows:

(a) **Area to be assessed.** The specific area of ability which will be assessed by the test should first be identified or decided.

(b) **Selection of test items.** Each test generally comprises a number of test items. These items should be chosen or selected in such a way that they would explore the particular area of ability properly and efficiently. A dichotomously scored test item is usually scored as 1 or 0 according to right or wrong answers, respectively, and the total of item scores gives the test score.

(c) **Item analysis.** Methods of item analysis should be used to determine the difficulty level (or value) and the discriminatory power of each test item. The test items are selected depending on these two important properties.

(d) **Arrangement of test items.** The test items selected by item analysis should be serially arranged in a suitable order according to the type of test—whether it is a power test or a speed test. However, the test items are generally arranged in a progressive difficulty level. That is, the difficulty level of the test items gradually increases as the number of items increases; the first item is the easiest and the last one is the most difficult; the first item elicits 100% correct responses from the respondents whereas the last item elicits 0% correct response.

(e) **Estimation of reliability.** Reliability of a test refers to the consistency of its results obtained on its repeated application on the same sample under the same or identical conditions. Before the test is put to actual use, its reliability should be estimated by applying it on a properly drawn representative sample.

(f) **Estimation of validity.** Validity of a test refers to the extent to which it measures, what it purports or intends to measure. The validity of a test concerns what the test measures and how well it does so. In short, validity is the capacity of the test to measure a specific variable in exclusion of others. The validity of a test should be estimated from the scores of the test administered on a representative sample.

(g) **Standardisation.** Methods of administration and scoring of the test should be precisely laid down and standardised.

(h) **Establishment of norms.** The test scores should be statistically treated to establish the norms.

18.3 Power and Speed Tests

The psychological tests belong to two types—power tests and speed tests, according to whether they differentiate between individuals in terms of difficulty levels of items and the speed of performance, respectively.

In *power tests*, the test items are usually grouped according to the types of contents and are arranged serially in an increasing order of difficulty. Enough time is given to enable at least 75% of the subjects being tested to attempt all the items. Still, some may fail to answer all the test items because of the difficulty level. Achievement tests are pure power tests.

In *speed tests*, all the test items are of uniform difficulty level, and the subject being tested has to answer the test items within a stipulated time which is so short that none can answer all the items in time. The level of ability of the subject is determined by his/her speed of performance.

In most tests, however, both speed and power are mixed in varying degrees. So, there is no rigid line of demarcation. Estimation of reliability depends on the proportions of power and speed in the test. In actual practice, the distinction between speed and power tests is one of degree, most tests depending on both power and speed in varying proportions. But we can find a distinction between speed and power tests with regard to the proper procedure for evaluating its reliability.

Single-trial reliability coefficients, such as those found by split-half or Kuder–Richardson techniques, are inappropriate to speeded tests, because the extent of individual differences in test scores depends on the speed of performance, and thus reliability coefficients found by these methods will be spuriously high. Therefore, it is necessary to use a test–retest or parallel-forms techniques to find out the reliability coefficients of highly speeded tests.

It might be noted that even with such a procedure, speeded tests will generally be found to have higher reliability than power tests. This is not a mathematical artefact, however, but seems to reflect the fact that in actual behaviour a greater consistency exists in the rate of work than it does in the quality of performance. Thus, in actual practice, parallel test or retest procedures are used whenever, looking at the test content and time limits, the researcher feels the test is speeded.

18.4 Item Analysis

Most tests are composed of test items. A test should be neither too easy nor too difficult. The final selection of test items should be done through *item analysis* which is the procedure used to judge the quality of an item. Thus, *item analysis* can be defined as a process or technique for analysing the items included in a test with regard to the indexes of *item characteristics*. The four basic *item characteristics* needed to predict the major characteristics of a test are:

(i) **Item difficulty:** The proportion of persons answering each item correctly.

(ii) **Item discrimination:** The degree to which an item differentiates correctly among test takers in the behaviour that the test is designed to measure (i.e., the difference between the highest group scores and the lowest group scores and the difference between the number of persons/subjects who answered correctly each item in the highest group and in the lowest group).

(iii) **Item reliability:** Taken as the point-biserial correlation between an item and the total test scores, multiplied by the item standard deviation.

(iv)   **Item validity:** Taken as the point-biserial correlation between an item and a criterion score, multiplied by the item standard deviation.

With regard to the *usefulness* of item analysis, it can be said that item analysis can help test users in their evaluation of published tests. In addition, item analysis is particularly relevant to the construction of informal, local tests such as the quizzes and examinations prepared by teachers for classroom use. Some of the general guidelines for effective item writing, as well as the simpler statistical techniques of item analysis, can materially improve classroom tests and are worth using even with small groups.

The test items can be analysed qualitatively in terms of their content and form, and quantitatively in terms of their statistical properties. Qualitative analysis includes the consideration of content validity as well as the evaluation of items in terms of effective item-writing procedures. Quantitative analysis includes principally the measurement of item difficulty and item discrimination. Both the validity and reliability of any test depend ultimately on the characteristics of its items. High reliability and validity can be built into a test in advance through item analysis. Tests can be improved through the selection, substitution or revision of items.

Item analysis makes it possible to shorten a test and at the same time to increase its validity and reliability. Other things being equal, a longer test is more valid and reliable than a shorter one. The estimation of the effect of lengthening or shortening a test on the reliability coefficient can be determined by Spearman–Brown prophecy formula (discussed later in this chapter under split-half reliability). These estimated changes in reliability occur when the discarded items are equivalent to those that remain or when equivalent new items are added to the test. Similar changes in validity will result from the deletion or addition of items of equivalent validity. All such estimates of change in reliability or validity refer to the lengthening or shortening of tests through a random selection of items, without item analysis. When a test is shortened by eliminating the least satisfactory items, however, the short test may be more valid and reliable than the original longer instrument.

The following facts are taken care of prior to the application of item analysis for the selection of test items:

(a)   The psychological processes, involved in the attribute under study, are first analysed.

(b)   A list of items is next prepared with more items than what is required for the given test.

(c)   These items are then administered to a representative sample on a trial basis.

Item analysis is then done for the final selection of test items. The selection of test items is finally done quantitatively by determining for each item: (a) the *difficulty value* given by the percentage or proportion of individuals answering a test item correctly and (b) the *discriminatory power* which is the power of a test item to discriminate between individuals with respect to the given variable. These two important properties of the test items are discussed further one after the other.

18.4.1   Item Difficulty

For most testing purposes, the difficulty level of an item is defined in terms of the percentage passing, that is, the percentage (or proportions) of persons who answer it correctly. The easier the item, the larger this percentage will be. A word that is correctly defined by 70% of the standardised sample ($p=0.70$) is regarded as easier than one that is correctly defined by only 15% ($p=0.15$). It is customary to arrange items in order of difficulty level, so that test takers begin with relatively easy items and proceed to an item of increasing difficulty level. This arrangement gives the test takers confidence in approaching the test and also reduces the likelihood of their wasting much time on items beyond their ability to the neglect of easier items they can correctly complete.

In the process of test construction, a major reason for measuring item difficulty is to choose items of a suitable difficulty level. Most standardised ability tests are designed to assess as accurately as possible each individual's level of attainment in the particular ability. For this purpose, if no one passes an item, it is excess baggage in the test. The same is true of items that everyone passes. Neither of these types of items provides any information about individual differences. Since such items do not affect the variability of test scores, they contribute nothing to the reliability or validity of the test. The closer the difficulty of an item approaches 1.00 or 0, the less differential information about test takers it contributes. Conversely, the closer the difficulty level approaches 0.50, the more differentiations the item can make. Suppose out of 100 persons, 50 pass an item and 50 fail it ($p=0.50$). This item enables us to differentiate between each of those who passed it and each of those who failed it. We, thus, have 50×50 or 2,500 paired comparisons or bits of differential information. An item passed by 70% of the persons or test takers provides 70×30 or 2,100 bits of information, one passed by 90% provides 90×10 or 900 bits of information and one passed by 100% provides 100×0 or 0 bits of information. The same relationships would hold good for harder items, passed by fewer than 50%.

For maximum differentiation, then, it would seem that one should choose all items at the 0.50 test difficulty level. The decision is complicated, however, by the fact that items within a test tend to be intercorrelated. The more homogeneous the test, the higher these intercorrelations will be. In an extreme case, if all items were perfectly intercorrelated and all were of 0.50 difficulty level, the same 50 persons out of 100 would pass each item. Consequently, half of the test takers would obtain perfect scores and the other half, zero scores. Because of item intercorrelations, it is best to select items with a moderate spread of difficulty level, but whose average difficulty is 0.50. Moreover, the higher the item intercorrelations (or the correlations of items with total score), the wider should be the spread of item difficulty.

Another consideration in the choice of appropriate item difficulty pertains to the probability of guessing in multiple-choice items. To allow for the fact that a certain proportion of test takers will select the correct option by guessing, the desired proportion of correct responses is set higher than would be the case for a free response item. For a five-option, multiple-choice item, for example, the average proportion correct should be approximately 0.69, and it should be set at about 0.67 for a four-option alternative item.

18.4.2 Item Discrimination

Item discrimination refers to the degree to which an item differentiates correctly among test takers in the behaviour that the test is designed to measure. When the test as a whole is to be evaluated by means of criterion-related validation, the items may themselves be evaluated and selected on the basis of their relationship to the same external criterion. The discriminatory value of a test item may be estimated by (a) the item validity measured by item-criterion correlation, (b) the item-total correlation between the scores in that item and total scores of the test and (c) the index of discrimination, according to the purpose of the test. These estimators of the discriminatory power of an item are discussed further:

18.4.2.1 *Item Validity or Item-criterion Correlation*

This is determined by correlating the scores of a given test item with a criterion. A high correlation with the criterion indicates a high discriminatory value of that item. The criterion to be chosen depends on the type of validity envisaged for the test—content, construct or predictive validity. When emphasis is laid on construct validity, the criterion used is the total score of the same test or of any other equivalent test. Measures of job performance, teacher's ratings or grade points may be used as the criterion for content validity. For tests of interest and personality, validation is done by correlating the items with any suitable external criterion revealing the given attribute. For achievement tests, the criterion used may consist of grade points (or grade performances) or teacher's ratings. Academic achievement is often used as the criterion for intelligence test. When emphasis is laid on predictive validity, an external criterion that consists of the measures of everyday success in the variable under investigation may be used.

18.4.2.2   *Item-total Correlation or Internal Consistency*

The test items may sometimes be correlated with the total scores of that test for internal consistency (item-total correlation). The homogeneity of a test depends upon the highest average item-total correlation.

According to the type of validity required and the nature of variable, point-biserial r, biserial r, tetrachoric r or phi coefficient may be computed to correlate the scores in the item with either the total test scores or the criterion revealing the desired attribute.

(a) **Point-biserial r (or r_{pbi})** is used in correlating the scores of a continuous variable such as the total test scores with a genuinely dichotomous variable such as the right/wrong, yes/no and 1/0 answers to a test item (see Chapter 9; Section 9.5). Thus, it may be used for *item-total correlation* for item analysis. The r_{pbi} is also preferred for correlating a dichotomously answered test item with an external criterion revealing the attribute under investigation (*item-criterion correlation*), if the predictive power of the item for the given attribute is to be explored.

(b) **Biserial r (or r_b)** is used in correlating the scores of a continuous variable such as the total test score with the answers to an *apparently dichotomous* test item. In such cases, r_b is applied for item-total correlation (see Chapter 9, Section 9.4). Such *item-total correlation* measured by r_b is independent of the difficulty value of the test item. The r_b is also computed between a dichotomised test item and the continuous scores of an external criterion in order to assess whether the item measures the same attribute as represented by the criterion (*item-criterion correlation*).

(c) **Phi coefficient (ϕ)** is used for *item-to-item correlation* between two dichotomous test items, each scored as yes/no, right/wrong or 1/0 (see Chapter 16, Section 16.5). It is also used in correlating a dichotomously scored test item and a genuinely dichotomous external criterion such as success/failure in a public examination (*item-criterion correlation*), so as to explore the power of the test item to predict one of the two categories of the dichotomous attribute represented by the criterion.

Phi coefficients may be computed directly from the observed frequencies (f_o) of classes of two dichotomous variables (either two dichotomous items or an item and a dichotomous criterion), arranging these classes along the rows and columns of a 2×2-fold contingency table. However, it is often computed also from the proportions of cases in different combinations of the classes of two dichotomous variables being correlated—for example, the proportions of cases passing or failing in one or both test items being correlated. In the latter case, where a, b, c and d are the proportions of cases in the four cells of the 2×2-fold contingency table, p_1 and p_2 are the proportions of passes or right answers in items 1 and 2, respectively, and q_1 and q_2 are, respectively, the proportions of failure or wrong answers in those items (see Tables 16.16 and 16.17).

However, when an item-criterion correlation is worked out with a criterion dichotomised at its median into upper and lower groups, each with a proportion of

0.50 of the sample size ($p=q=0.50$), and p_u and p_l are the proportions of pass in the respective groups, then ϕ is computed as,

$$\phi = \frac{p_u - p_l}{2\sqrt{pq}}$$

(d) **Tetrachoric r (or r_t)** is computed for *item-criterion correlation* to measure the extent to which a dichotomised test item and a dichotomised criterion estimate the same attribute, when the test item and/or the attribute may be considered artificially dichotomised (see Chapter 9; Section 9.6). It is also used in correlating the items of two questionnaires scored on scales other than dichotomous responses. It may also be applied to personality tests with dichotomised test items. However, because of its higher standard error (SE) and lower reliability than product-moment r, and a complex procedure for its significance test, the r_t is seldom used in item analysis.

18.4.2.3 *Index of Discrimination (D)*

If the number of persons passing each item in the upper (U) and lower (L) criterion groups are expressed as percentages, the difference between these two percentages provides an index of item discrimination that can be interpreted independently of the size of the particular sample in which it was obtained. The computation of the index of discrimination (D) can be illustrated by reference to the data reported in Table 18.1.

First, the number of persons passing each item in the U and L groups are changed to percentages. The difference between the two percentages is the index of discrimination of an item as shown in Table 18.1. This index can have any value between +100 and –100. If all members of the U group and none of the L group pass an item, D equals 100. Conversely, if all members of the L group and none of the U group pass it, D equals –100. If the percentages of both groups passing an item are equal, D will be zero.

The values of D are not independent of item difficulty but are biased in favour of intermediate difficulty levels. Table 18.2 shows the maximum possible value of D for items with different percentages of correct responses. If either 100% or 0% of the total sample pass an item,

Table 18.1 Computation of index of discrimination

Items	Percentage Passing		Index of Discrimination (D)
	Upper Group ($n=50$)	**Lower Group ($n=50$)**	
1	75	35	40
2	100	80	20
3	95	45	50
4	50	80	–30
5	55	55	0
6	80	45	35
7	25	0	25

Table 18.2   Relation of maximum value of *D* to item difficulty

Percentage Passing Item	Maximum Value of *D*
100	0
90	20
70	60
50	100
30	60
10	20
0	0

then there can be no difference in percentage passing in U and L groups; hence, *D* is zero. At the other extreme, if 50% pass an item, it would be possible for all the U cases and none of the L cases to pass it, thus, yielding a *D* of 100 (100−0=100). If 70% pass, the maximum value that *D* could take can be illustrated as follows: (U) 50/50=100%; (L) 20/50=40%; *D*=100−40=60. It will be recalled that, for most testing purposes, items closer to the 50% difficulty level are preferable. Hence, item discrimination indices that favour this difficulty level are often appropriate for item selection. Relation of the maximum value of *D* to item difficulty is given in Table 18.2.

During test construction, some psychologists prefer *factor analysis* for assessing the construct validity in order to estimate the discriminatory value.

18.5   Reliability of a Test

18.5.1   Meaning of Reliability

A standardised psychological test has four basic characteristics—reliability, validity, objectivity and efficiency. The dictionary meaning of *reliability* is consistency, dependence or trust. A test is considered to be reliable if it yields consistent results in its successive administration. So by *reliability* of a test we mean how dependable, faithful or trustworthy the test is. Therefore, the *reliability* of a test refers to the consistency of scores obtained by the same persons when they are re-examined with the same test on different occasions, with different sets of equivalent items or under variable examining conditions (Anastasi, 1976). In short, the reliability of a test gives information about the consistency of an individual's scores on a series of measurements. This concept of reliability underlies the computation of the *error of measurement* of a single score, whereby we can predict the range of fluctuation likely to occur in a single individual's score as a result of irrelevant or unknown chance factors. The test reliability, in its broadest sense, indicates the extent to which individual differences in test scores are attributable to '*true*' differences in the characteristics under consideration and the extent to which they are attributable to chance errors. To put it in more technical terms, measures of test reliability make it possible to estimate what proportion of the *total variance* of test scores is *error variance*.

Any obtained score or measure of an individual at a particular moment is determined in part by the true value and in part by the error value. In terms of an equation:

$$X_t = X_\infty + X_e$$

where

X_t = total obtained score or measure

X_∞ = true score or measure

X_e = error score or measure.

Variations in the scores of an individual, on repetition of the same test, may result from either genuine changes in his/her ability or random errors of measurement. The *true score* (X_∞) is the expected average of the scores of an individual in an infinitely large number of repetitions of the test under identical conditions and is assumed to remain unchanged because it is supposed to be free from any *random error*. The *error score* (X_e) is one which is due to the random errors of measurement. The *obtained score* (X_t) is one that we get by administering the test on an individual. The *obtained score* (X_t) of an individual differs at random from X_∞ due to X_e; for reliability, X_t should correspond closely to X_∞. Thus, the *total score* (X_t) can be said to be the sum total of *true score* (X_∞) and *error score* (X_e), as follows:

$$X_t = X_\infty + X_e, \quad X_\infty = X_t - X_e \quad \text{or} \quad X_e = X_t - X_\infty$$

Similarly, the *total variance* (σ_t^2) is the sum total of *true variance* (σ_∞^2) and *error variance* (σ_e^2). In terms of equation:

$$\sigma_t^2 = \sigma_\infty^2 + \sigma_e^2$$

The test reliability is statistically defined as the proportion of *true variance* (σ_∞^2) to *total variance* (σ_t^2). To find out the proportion of true variance to total variance, let us divide both sides of the equation just discussed by σ_t^2. So, the equation now becomes

$$\frac{\sigma_t^2}{\sigma_t^2} = \frac{\sigma_\infty^2 + \sigma_e^2}{\sigma_t^2} \quad \text{or} \quad 1 = \frac{\sigma_\infty^2}{\sigma_t^2} + \frac{\sigma_e^2}{\sigma_t^2}$$

$$\text{or} \quad \frac{\sigma_\infty^2}{\sigma_t^2} + \frac{\sigma_e^2}{\sigma_t^2} = 1 \quad \text{or} \quad \frac{\sigma_\infty^2}{\sigma_t^2} = 1 - \frac{\sigma_e^2}{\sigma_t^2}$$

$$\text{or} \quad r_{tt} = 1 - \frac{\sigma_e^2}{\sigma_t^2}$$

where

r_{tt} = reliability coefficient

$\dfrac{\sigma_e^2}{\sigma_t^2}$ = ratio of error variance to total variance.

So, test reliability is the proportion of true variance to total variance $\left(r_{tt} = \dfrac{\sigma_\infty^2}{\sigma_t^2} \right)$ or $1 - \dfrac{\sigma_e^2}{\sigma_t^2}$ (i.e., one minus the ratio of error variance to total variance).

The *true variance* (σ_∞^2) is the variance contributed by the test itself. But *error variance* (σ_e^2) is obtained due to the operation of factors that are irrelevant to the purpose of the test. Factors that might be considered as error variance for one purpose would be classified under true variance for another. For example, if we are interested in measuring fluctuations of mood, then the day-by-day changes in scores on a test of cheerfulness-depression would be relevant to the purpose of the test and would, hence, be a part of the true variance of the scores. If, on the other hand, the test is designed to measure more permanent personality characteristics, they fall under the heading of error variance.

The *total variance* (σ_t^2) of scores of a test estimates the deviations of individual scores (X_t) from their mean ($\bar{X}_t$). It is the mean squared deviation of X_t scores from $\bar{X}_t$, as shown in the following equation.

$$\sigma_t^2 = \frac{\Sigma(X_t - \bar{X}_t)^2}{df}$$

A part of σ_t^2 is due to true variance (σ_∞^2) while its other part comes from the error variance (σ_e^2). The error variance may arise from errors of measurement and is not the same as sampling errors.

Reliability coefficient (r_{tt}) is a measure of correlation between σ_∞^2 and σ_t^2 of the test scores. In absence of any correlation between σ_∞^2 and σ_e^2,

$$\frac{\sigma_\infty^2}{\sigma_t^2} + \frac{\sigma_e^2}{\sigma_t^2} = 1.00$$

The lower is the proportion of σ_e^2 to σ_t^2, the closer is the true variance (σ_∞^2) to the total variance (σ_t^2) and, consequently, the closer are X_∞ and X_t, and the higher the reliability of that test. Indeed, r_{tt} is the proportion of σ_∞^2 to σ_t^2 and can be considered as a self-correlation of a test.

$$r_{tt} = \frac{\sigma_\infty^2}{\sigma_t^2} = 1 - \frac{\sigma_e^2}{\sigma_t^2} \quad \text{or} \quad \sigma_e^2 = \sigma_t^2(1 - r_{tt})$$

Reliability depends on the close agreement between the obtained score (X_t) and the true score (X_∞). The *standard error of measurement* (SEM; σ_e) is the square root of the error variance (σ_e^2) and is, thus, another measure of random errors.

$$\sigma_e^2 = \sigma_t^2(1 - r_{tt}); \quad \sigma_e = \sqrt{\sigma_t^2(1 - r_{tt})}$$

When σ_e is zero or negligible, the test is perfectly reliable ($r_{tt}=1$) and X_t coincides with X_∞; differences between X_t scores are then solely due to genuine differences between X_∞ scores. But when σ_e equals the square root (σ_t) of the total variance, the test has no reliability ($r_{tt}=0$).

We know that r_{tt} is a measure of *self-correlation* of a test with itself, whereas the *index of reliability* ($r_{t\infty}$) is a measure of correlation between the whole obtained score X_t and its part which is the true score X_∞. Thus, $r_{t\infty}$ is a *part-whole correlation*, $r_{t\infty} = \sqrt{r_{tt}}$ and the r_{tt} is a better measure for comparing the reliabilities of different test scores.

The following example will clarify some of the computations relating to reliability.

Example 18.1 For a psychological test, r_{tt} and σ_t were found to be 0.75 and 10, respectively. Compute σ_∞^2 and σ_e^2, their proportional contribution to σ_t^2 and the SEM of the test.

Solution

$$r_{tt} = 0.75; \quad \sigma_t = 10; \quad \therefore \sigma_t^2 = (10)^2 = 100$$
$$\sigma_e^2 = \sigma_t^2(1 - r_{tt}) = 100(1 - 0.75) = 100 \times 0.25 = 25$$
$$\therefore \text{SEM} = \sigma_e = \sqrt{\sigma_e^2} = \sqrt{25} = 5$$
$$\sigma_\infty^2 = r_{tt}\,\sigma_t^2 = 0.75 \times 100 = 75$$
$$\frac{\sigma_e^2}{\sigma_t^2} = \frac{25}{100} = 0.25; \quad \frac{\sigma_\infty^2}{\sigma_t^2} = \frac{75}{100} = 0.75$$

18.5.2 Characteristics of Reliability

The test reliability has the following characteristics:

(a) Although correlation coefficient (product-moment correlation) is the reliability coefficient, unlike correlation, reliability is always positive, whereas correlation may be positive or negative.

(b) Reliability of a test ranges from 0 to +1.00, whereas correlation varies from –1.00 to +1.00 through zero. Reliability is zero when the measurement involves nothing but error, and it is +1.00 when there is no variable error at all in the measurement.

(c) Reliability is the coefficient of internal consistency.

(d) The test reliability is a measure of variable error or chance error or the errors of measurement. It suffers from errors of measurement.

(e) The test reliability is a matter of degree. It does not exist in all or none basis.

(f) Reliability does not ensure the validity, truthfulness or purposiveness of a test.

(g) Reliability is a necessary but not a sufficient condition for validity. Low reliability can restrict the degree of validity that is obtained, but high reliability provides no assurance for a satisfactory degree of validity.

(h) The reliability coefficient (r_{tt}) is a measure of *self-correlation* of a test with itself, but the index of reliability ($r_{t\infty}$) is a *part-whole correlation*. The r_{tt} is a better measure for comparing the reliabilities of different test scores. Reliability indicates the stability of scores which tend to be unstable because of the errors of measurement.

18.5.3 Errors of Measurement

Errors of measurement may be either random or systematic, which are discussed further:

18.5.3.1 Random Errors

Reliability is affected mostly by random errors. These errors result from uncontrolled and uncorrelated factors such as errors of scoring and interpretation, fluctuating mood, motivation, attention or interest of the subjects, noise and other distractions. Sampling of test items may be a major source of random errors. It may cause item-to-item variations within a test. The time gap between administration and re-administration of the same test, between administration of alternate forms of a test as well as differences in their contents and scoring may result in random errors. In multiple-choice tests, guessing definitely serves as a source of random errors due to variations in item-to-item performance. These random errors lower the reliability of a test.

Random errors of measurement should be minimised by proper item sampling, larger sample size, clear instructions for proper test administration, and objective scoring and interpretation.

18.5.3.2 Systematic Errors

Systematic or constant errors affect mainly the validity of a test, but not its reliability. These errors result from defects in test construction, limited time allotment to an ability test, some personal modes of responses and environmental variations. Systematic errors act unidirectionally, causing either overestimation or underestimation of the scores in all cases systematically.

18.5.4 Standard Error of Measurement

The reliability of a test may be expressed in terms of the SEM, also called the standard error of a score. This measure is particularly well suited to the interpretation of individual scores. For many testing purposes, it is, therefore, more useful than the reliability coefficient. The SEM can be easily computed from the reliability coefficient of the test by the following formula:

$$SEM = SD_t \sqrt{1 - r_{tt}}$$

where

SEM = standard error of measurement
SD_t = standard deviation of the test scores
r_{tt} = reliability coefficient.

For example, if the intelligence test scores have SD = 15 and a reliability coefficient (r_{tt}) = 0.89, then the SEM = 15 $\sqrt{1 - 0.89}$ = 15$\sqrt{0.11}$ = 15 × 0.33 = 4.95 = 5.0.

SEM can be used for interpretation of individual scores and for interpretation of score differences.

To understand what the SEM tells us about a score, let us suppose that we had a set of 100 IQ scores obtained by a single subject in the above noted test. Because of the types of chance errors, these scores vary, falling into a normal distribution around the subject's *true score*. The mean of this distribution of 100 scores can be taken as the *true score* for a specified test used, and the standard deviation of the distribution can be taken as the SEM. Like any standard deviation, this standard error can be interpreted in terms of the normal curve frequency.

We know that between the mean ±1.96σ there are 95% of cases in the normal curve. Thus, we can conclude that the chances are 95:5 or 19:1 that the subject's IQ score on this test will fluctuate between ±1.96SEM (1.96 × 5 = 9.80) or 10 points on either side of this true IQ score. If the true IQ score is 110, we would expect that his/her score would vary between 100 and 120 in 95% of cases. Similarly, a distance of 2.58σ on either side of the mean includes exactly 99% of the cases. Hence, the chances are 99:1 that the subject's IQ score will fall within 2.58σ or 2.58SEM (2.58 × 5 = 12.90) or 13 points on either side of his/her true IQ score. Thus, his/her score will vary between 97 and 123 (i.e., 110 − 13 and 110 + 13) in 99% of cases. In other words, if the subject will be given 100 equivalent tests, then his/her IQ score would lie outside the band of values 100–120 and 97–123, five times or only once, respectively.

The SEM and the reliability coefficient are obviously alternative ways of expressing test reliability. Hence, if we want to compare the reliability of different tests, the reliability coefficient is the better measure. To interpret individual scores, the SEM is more appropriate. Neither reliability coefficients nor errors of measurement, however, can be assumed to remain constant when the ability level varies widely.

SEMs can also be used when we want to compare the differences between two scores.

It is good to bear in mind that the standard error of the difference between two scores is larger than the error of measurement of either of the two scores. This follows from the fact that this difference is affected by the chance errors present in both the scores. The standard error of the difference between two scores can be found from the SEMs of the two scores by the following formula:

$$SE_{diff.} = \sqrt{(SEM_1)^2 + (SEM_2)^2}$$

where

$SE_{diff.}$ = standard error of difference between two scores
SEM_1 = standard error of measurement of the first score
SEM_2 = standard error of measurement of the second score.

By substituting SD $\sqrt{1-r_{11}}$ for SEM_1 and SD $\sqrt{1-r_{22}}$ for SEM_2, we may rewrite the formula just discussed, directly in terms of reliability coefficients, as follows:

$$SE_{diff.} = \sqrt{(SD\sqrt{1-r_{11}})^2 + (SD\sqrt{1-r_{22}})^2}$$
$$= \sqrt{SD^2(1-r_{11}) + SD^2(1-r_{22})}$$
$$= \sqrt{SD^2(1-r_{11} + 1 - r_{22})}$$
$$= SD\sqrt{2-r_{11}-r_{22}}$$

In this substitution, the same SD was used for tests 1 and 2, since their scores would have to be expressed in terms of the same scale before they could be compared.

We may illustrate the above procedure with the verbal and performance IQs on the Wechsler Adult Intelligence Scale-Revised (WAIS-R). The split-half reliabilities of these scores are 0.97 and 0.93, respectively. WAIS-R deviation IQs are expressed on a scale with a mean of 100 and SD of 15. Hence, the standard error of difference between these two scores can be found as follows:

$$SE_{diff.} = SD\sqrt{2-r_{11}-r_{22}} = 15\sqrt{2-0.97-0.93} = 15\sqrt{2-1.90} = 15\sqrt{0.10} = 15 \times 0.316 = 4.74$$

To determine how large a score difference could be obtained by chance at the 0.05 level, we multiply the standard error of difference (4.74) by 1.96. The result is 9.29 (4.74 × 1.96) or approximately 10 points. Thus, the difference between an individual's WAIS-R verbal and performance IQs should be at least 10 points to be significant at the 0.05 level. Similarly, this difference should be at least (4.74 × 2.58) 12.23 or approximately 13 points, to be significant, at the 0.01 level.

18.5.5 Methods of Estimating Reliability

At the present time, there are four classical ways of estimating or determining reliability. Each of these procedures is basically different in that it defines what is meant by error in a slightly different way. These four methods for determining test reliability are: (a) test-retest method, (b) parallel-forms or alternate-forms method, (c) split-half method and (d) Kuder-Richardson method. These types of reliability methods are discussed further in the text.

18.5.5.1 Test–Retest Method

The most obvious method for finding out the reliability of test scores is by repeating the same test on a second occasion. In this method, a group of subjects is tested on one situation and after some time interval the same subjects are retested with the same test, and then the scores on test and retest conditions are correlated and, thus, the correlation (r) between these two sets of scores is found out. The *reliability coefficient* (r_{tt}) in this case is simply the *correlation* between the scores obtained by the same persons on the two administrations of the same test.

The error variance (σ_e^2) corresponds to the random fluctuations of performance from one test session to the other. These variations may result in part from uncontrolled testing conditions such as extreme changes in weather, poor visibility or audibility, sudden noises and other distractions. To some extent, however, they arise from changes in the condition of the test takers or subjects themselves, as illustrated by illness, fatigue, lack of motivation, emotional strain, boredom, worry, anxiety, recent experiences of a pleasant or unpleasant nature and the like. Maturity factors during the time interval between test and retest conditions may also contribute to error variance.

The test-retest reliability assesses only the effects of time variation or temporal variability. Therefore, the reliability coefficient found by test-retest technique is known as the *coefficient of stability*. The coefficient of stability determines the dependability of the measurement over a time interval. Closeness of the two sets of scores indicates a low σ_e^2 and a high stability coefficient (r_{tt}). Retest reliability shows the extent to which scores on a test can be generalised over different occasions; the higher the reliability, the less susceptible the scores are to the random daily changes in the condition of the subjects or of the testing environment.

In this method, an optimum time interval should be chosen for retesting. A short interval may apparently increase true variance (σ_∞^2) to enhance r_{tt} owing to the memory effect. On the contrary, if the interval is too long, different rates of physical and emotional changes of the testee may affect the scores, raising σ_e^2 and lowering r_{tt}. The time interval should not exceed six months.

When retest reliability is reported in a test manual, the time interval over which it was measured should always be specified. Since retest correlations decrease progressively as this interval lengthens, there is not one but an infinite number of retest reliability coefficients for any test. It is also desirable to give some indication of the relevant intervening experiences of the person whose reliability was measured, such as educational or job experiences, counselling, psychotherapy and so forth.

Advantages of Test–Retest Reliability

The following are some of the important advantages or merits of the test-retest method for estimating the reliability coefficient of a test.

(i)   The test-retest method for estimating or determining the *coefficient of retest reliability* is apparently simple and straightforward and is worthy to use in different situations conveniently.

(ii)   The test-retest method can be used for tests of psychomotor abilities, sensory discriminations and cognitive skills that are less affected by practice and memory effects.

(iii) This method is suitable for speed tests. It can also be applied to heterogeneous tests where items measure different abilities and have high correlations with a criterion, but a low correlation with other items of the test, making the reliability of internal consistency insignificant.

(iv)   Various types of reliabilities of ratings such as performance evaluation and personal assessment ratings can be estimated with the help of the coefficient of stability. This can be done by working out (a) *inter-rater reliability*, that is, the consistency of the results when the same individual is rated by two or more raters and (b) *rate-rerate reliability*, that is, the consistency of the results when the same individual is rated repeatedly by the same rater over a time gap.

Disadvantages of Test–Retest Reliability

The following are some of the important disadvantages, demerits or limitations of the test-retest method. Although simple and straightforward, the test-retest technique presents difficulties when applied to most psychological tests. Thus, it is open to several serious objections, which are discussed further.

(i) If the time interval between test and retest is fairly short and the retesting is administered immediately or after only a short period, then the subjects may recall many of their former responses and tend to answer the questions in the same way. In other words, the same pattern of right and wrong responses is likely to recur through sheer memory. Thus, the scores on the two administrations of the test are not independently obtained and the correlation between them will be spuriously high. As a result of this the estimated reliability will increase. In other words, *memory effects* may unnecessarily facilitate the reliability coefficient if the time interval is very short; there may be a *carry-over effect* on the reliability coefficient.

(ii) In some cases the traits assessed by a test will change very rapidly over time. In these cases the estimated error variance will be unnecessarily high, thereby decreasing the reliability coefficient. For example, many traits of personality, interest, intelligence and attitude are conceived of as not being static but continually in a state of flux. Even with measures of achievement, ability and aptitude, there are problems. If in these cases the time interval between the test and retest is very wide, then the estimated reliability coefficient will be adversely affected by the *growth changes* of the subjects and also by changes of the test itself. Thus, in testing young children, the period should be even shorter than for older persons, since at early ages progressive developmental changes are discernible over a period of a month or even less. For any type of persons, the interval between test and retest should rarely exceed six months.

(iii) Besides immediate memory effects and effects of growth changes, practise as well as transfer effect will probably produce varying amounts of improvement in the retest scores of different individuals. Thus, the test–retest procedure may either overestimate or underestimate the true reliability of the test and in many instances it is difficult to determine which has occurred.

(iv) Moreover, the nature of the test itself may also change with repetition. This is especially true of problems involving reasoning or ingenuity. Once the subject has grasped the principle involved in the problem or has worked out a solution, he/she can reproduce the correct response in the future without going through the intervening steps. Therefore, only tests that are not appreciably affected by repetition lend themselves to the test–retest technique. A number of sensory discrimination and memory tests would fall into this category. For the large majority of psychological tests, however, the retest technique is inappropriate.

(v) The *coefficient of stability* gives no indication about the internal consistency of the test. The test–retest method is considered unsuitable for many psychological tests such as personality, interest, intelligence and attitudes tests. This method is used in such cases mainly in the absence of an alternate form of the test.

18.5.5.2 *Alternate-forms or Parallel-forms Method*

Parallel-forms reliability is otherwise known as alternate-forms reliability, equivalent-forms reliability, comparable-forms reliability or two-forms reliability.

One way of avoiding the difficulties encountered in test–retest reliability is through the use of alternate forms of the test. In this method, the same group of individuals can be tested with one form of a test on the first occasion and another parallel or equivalent form of that test on the second. The correlation between the scores obtained on the two forms represents the reliability coefficient of the test. Equivalent or parallel forms of a test should possess an identical *true variance* (σ_∞^2), similar item difficulties, similar item-total correlations and *independent error variance* (σ_e^2) with no overlap.

Strictly speaking, two sets of a test are parallel, if and only if, they sample the same content universe in the same way and result in scores (when both are administered to the same group of subjects) such that the means, variances and inter-item covariances are equal. Fundamentally, parallel forms of a test should be independently structured tests designated to meet the same specifications. Both forms of the test should contain the same number of items, and the items should be expressed in the same form and should cover the same type of content. The range and level of difficulty of the items should also be equal. Instructions, time limit for the completion of items, illustrative examples, format, behavioural domain of sampling, item-total correlations and all other aspects of the test must likewise be checked for comparability.

The reliability coefficient obtained by using alternate forms or parallel forms of a test is known as the *coefficient of equivalence*, because it measures the extent to which the two forms of a test are equivalent. Since it is impossible to administer two forms of the test to the same individuals simultaneously, all the time-to-time fluctuations of the test–retest procedure are called errors. Moreover, different scores on the two forms of the test might also be obtained because the test forms were not exactly equivalent. For example, since different items are used, one form may be slightly more difficult for one person and at the same time slightly easier for a second, or the items may not get at precisely the same trait. Thus, both time-to-time and form-to-form fluctuations in performance are called errors. For this reason, the alternate-forms procedure of reliability coefficient is a measure of both *temporal stability* and *equivalence* (i.e., consistency of responses to different item samples or test forms). In other words, the alternate-forms reliability coefficient combines two types of reliability. Since both types are important for most testing purposes, however, alternate-forms reliability provides a useful measure for evaluating many tests. If the two forms are administered in immediate succession, the resulting correlation shows reliability across forms only, not across occasions. The error variance (σ_e^2) in this case represents fluctuations in performance from one set of items to another, but not fluctuations over time.

Thus, the alternate-forms, parallel-forms or equivalent-forms reliability may be expressed in two ways, as follows:

(a) **Coefficient of stability and equivalence:** It is the correlation coefficient between two sets of scores obtained by administering two equivalent or parallel forms of a test to the same group of individuals on two different occasions separated by a time interval. It measures both *equivalence of contents* of the two forms of a test and *temporal stability* (i.e., the dependability of measurements over a time interval). The error variance (σ_e^2) results here from both temporal variations of performance and variations of scores due to different sets of items in the two forms of a test—the latter may be termed *item specificity*.

(b) **Coefficient of equivalence:** It is the correlation coefficient between the scores of two equivalent forms of a test administered in immediate succession to the same group of subjects. It measures only the *equivalence* of the two forms and not the temporal stability. Here the error variance (σ_e^2) results from the variations of performance in different sets of items or item specificity alone in the two forms of a test.

The difference between a test–retest procedure and alternate-forms method is that: (a) the second administration of the alternate-forms test is not the retest of the first one, (b) the test–retest reliability measures the temporal stability whereas alternate-forms reliability not only measures the temporal stability but also the equivalence of responses to different item samples in both forms of a test and (c) by using the parallel-forms method we can overcome the problem of recalling specific items encountered in a test–retest procedure.

Let us now discuss the advantages and disadvantages (or limitations) of the alternate-forms or parallel-forms method.

Advantages of Alternate-forms Reliability

The following are some of the advantages or merits of the alternate-forms or parallel-forms reliability.

(a) The alternate or parallel-forms method is highly suitable for speed tests. For well-made standard tests the parallel forms method is usually the most satisfactory way of determining reliability. Moreover, alternate-forms are useful in follow-up studies or in investigations of the effects of some intervening experimental factors on test performance.

(b) The use of several alternate forms also provides means of reducing the possibility of coaching or cheating. Parallel forms are usually available for standard psychological and educational achievement tests.

(c) In parallel or alternate-forms method the second administration of the test is not the retest or repetition of the first one. So, the memory effect, practice effect, carry-over effect and recall factors are minimised in this method.

(d) The alternate-forms or parallel-forms reliability coefficient combines both temporal stability and equivalence (i.e., consistency of responses to different item samples or test forms). Since both types are important for most testing purposes, however, alternate-forms reliability provides a useful measure for evaluating many tests.

(e) Unlike the test–retest method, the item contents are not identical, only similar, on the two occasions of administration of the parallel tests. This decreases the memory effect and the practice effect resulting from prior use. So, the alternate-forms method is frequently preferred to the test–retest method and used in a larger number of cases than the latter.

Although much more widely applicable than test–retest method, alternate-forms method has certain limitations which are discussed further in the text.

Disadvantages of Alternate-forms Reliability

The following are some of the disadvantages, demerits or limitations of the parallel-forms or alternate-forms reliability.

(a) It is a laborious process and also very tedious one. There is every possibility that the two forms may not be parallel to each other. In practise, it is difficult to get precisely equivalent forms fulfilling all the criteria of parallelism. Therefore, in the development of parallel forms or alternate forms, care must be exercised to match test materials for content, difficulty and form; precautions must be taken not to have the items in the two forms too similar. When alternate forms are virtually identical reliability is too high; whereas when parallel forms are not sufficiently alike, reliability will be too low.

(b) It is difficult to have two parallel forms of a test. In certain situations (i.e., in Rorschach test) it is almost impossible. Moreover, alternate-forms method cannot serve for heterogeneous tests unless item-intercorrelations have been taken care of while developing the parallel forms.

(c) The parallel-forms reliability may be affected by any deviation from precise equivalence such as an overlap of error variances (σ_e^2), inequality of either σ_e^2 or true variances (σ_∞^2), variations of σ_e^2 owing to change in content of the alternate forms, rise of σ_e^2 because of different item difficulties of the parallel forms of the test or fluctuations in testing environments. The time interval between the administrations of the two forms of a test, individual changes in motivation, practice effects resulting from the use of similar item contents in the parallel forms, distractions, fatigue, and boredom influence the error variance (σ_e^2) to affect the equivalent-forms reliability just like the test–retest reliability.

(d) The testing conditions while administering the second form (i.e., Form B) of the test may not be the same as the first form (i.e., Form A). Besides, the testees may not be in a similar physical, mental or emotional state at both the times of administration.

(e) Practice effects and carryover effects cannot be completely eliminated. In some cases the responses of the subjects are largely affected by practice. In such cases the alternate forms of the test will lead to better responses on the second testing session. Therefore, if the behaviour functions under consideration are subject to a large practice effect, the use of alternate forms will reduce but not eliminate such an effect. To be sure, if all subjects were to show the same improvement with repetition, the correlation between their scores would remain unaffected, since adding a constant amount to each score does not alter the correlation coefficient. But it is much more likely, however, that individuals will differ in amount of improvement, owing to the extent of previous practice with similar materials, motivation in taking the test, and other factors. Under these conditions, the practice effect represents another source of variance that will tend to reduce the correlation between the two test forms. But if the practice effect is small, reduction will be negligible.

(f) The development of parallel forms of a test is almost impossible for problems involving certain behavioural area and ingenuity, because the nature of the test will change to a great extent by changing the items only. They may also change with mere repetition. In certain types of ingenuity problems, for example, any item involving the same principle can be readily solved by most subjects once they have worked out the solution to the first. In such a case, changing the specific content of the items in the second form would not suffice to eliminate this carry-over effect from the first form.

(g) Finally, it should be added that alternate forms are unavailable for many tests, because of the practical difficulties of constructing comparable forms. For all these reasons, other techniques for estimating test reliability are often required.

18.5.5.3   *Split-half Method*

Although parallel-forms/alternate-forms reliability eliminates the effects of remembering responses from one test form to another, it does not overcome the difficulty of calling real fluctuation in the trait under consideration error. To do this, it would be necessary to administer both test forms to the same group of persons simultaneously. For this reason, split-half method is very important.

In this method the subjects are not tested twice but only once. We first administer a test to the subjects for only once and then, after the answers have been obtained, we divide the items into two equivalent parts, each part scored separately. In such a way, two scores are obtained for each subject by dividing the test into two comparable halves. Then the correlation between the scores on one part of the test and those obtained on the other part may be computed. This correlation may represent a measure of form-to-form fluctuations only. The correlation coefficient obtained by split-half method is known as coefficient of equivalence, because of the fact that in this case the method finds out to what extent the two halves of the test are equivalent to each other.

It is apparent that split-half reliability provides a measure of consistency with regard to content sampling. Temporal stability of the scores does not enter into such reliability, because only one test session is involved. This type of reliability coefficient is sometimes called as *coefficient of internal consistency*, since only a single administration of a single form is required.

To find out split-half reliability, as was true with parallel-form reliability, the first problem is how to split the test in order to obtain approximately two equal halves. Any test can be divided in many different ways. But in most tests, the first half and second half would not be comparable owing to differences in nature of difficulty level of items as well as to the cumulative effects of warming up, practise, fatigue, boredom and any other factors varying progressively from the beginning to the end of the test.

One could, of course, be very rigorous. It is possible to perform an item analysis on the results, pair items according to difficulty, content, discrimination and so forth, and to assign one item from each pair to each half.

However, a much less laborious way that is most adequate for most purposes and one which in practice seems to work out very well is to divide the test into two equivalent halves according to the odd–even principle—that is to simply place all the odd numbered items in one half and all the even numbered items in the other, because of the fact that the difficulty level of all odd numbered items is equal to all even numbered items of the test. If the items are originally arranged in an approximate order of difficulty, such a division yields very nearly equivalent half-scores.

One precaution to be observed in making such an odd–even split pertains to groups of items dealing with a single problem, such as, questions referring to a particular mechanical diagram or to a given passage in a reading test. In this case, a whole group of items should be assigned intact to one or the other half. Were the items in such a group to be placed in different halves of the test, the similarity of the half-scores would be spuriously inflated, since any single error in understanding of the problem might affect items in both halves. Therefore, unlike test–retest method or like the parallel-forms method, the split-half method assesses another error variance, that is, the equivalence of two halves of the test.

The obtained correlation between the two half-scores actually gives the reliability of only a half-test. For example, if the entire test consists of 100 items, the correlation is computed between two sets of scores each of which is based on only 50 items. In both test–retest and alternate-forms reliability, on the other hand, each score is based on the full number of items in the test.

By using split-half reliability, we face another problem which does not occur with other procedures like test–retest and parallel-forms. It so happens that test reliability is a function of the test length as measured by the number of items that comprise a test. In other words, other things being equal, the longer a test, the more reliable it will be. It is reasonable to expect that with a large sample of behaviour, we can arrive at a more adequate and consistent measure. So the lengthening or shortening a test will have its effect on its reliability. Lengthening a test, however, will increase only its consistency in terms of content sampling, but not its stability over time.

The reliability coefficient obtained by split-half method is only for half-length of the items of the test. But we are interested to know the reliability coefficient for the full-length of the items of the test. For this purpose we can apply the *Spearman–Brown Prophecy Formula*, because this formula is applied for estimating the r_{tt} for the full-length of the items of the test. In completely general terms, it is expressed as :

$$r_{tt} = \frac{n r'_{tt}}{1 + (n-1) r'_{tt}}$$

where

r_{tt} = coefficient of reliability for the full-length of the items of the test

r'_{tt} = coefficient of reliability obtained for the present length of the test

n = number of times the test is lengthened or shortened.

Thus, if the number of items of the test is increased from 25 to 100, n is 4, and if it is decreased from 60 to 30, n is ½.

The *Spearman–Brown Prophecy formula* is widely used in determining reliability by the split-half method. When applied to split-half reliability, the formula always involves doubling the length of the test. Under these conditions, $n=2$, since the whole test is twice as long as the half-test on which the original reliability was computed. Thus, when used to correct the correlation found between scores on two halves of a test in determining split-half reliability, the *Spearman–Brown prophecy formula* becomes

$$r_{tt} = \frac{2r'_{tt}}{1+r'_{tt}}.$$

The *Spearman–Brown prophecy formula* assumes that: (a) the items added to make the test longer measure the same trait and (b) the variances of the two half-scores are equal, that is, for example, $\sigma^2_{odd} = \sigma^2_{even}$. If the division of the items into two halves is done carefully, both assumptions can readily be met. But in some cases this does not hold good. For example, on occasion where the odd–even approach is used, the variances may not turn out to be equal.

In order to eliminate this pitfall, drawback or lacuna of the Spearman–Brown formula, a second formula has been developed by Guttman (1945), which reads as:

$$r_{tt} = 2\left(1 - \frac{\sigma^2_{xa} + \sigma^2_{xb}}{\sigma^2_x}\right)$$

where

r_{tt} = coefficient of reliability for the full-length of the test items
σ^2_{xa} = variance of the scores obtained on half 'a' of the test
σ^2_{xb} = variance of the scores obtained on half 'b' of the test
σ^2_x = variance of the scores obtained on the entire test.

Similarly, a short-cut method for finding out split-half reliability was developed by Rulon (1939). It requires only the variance of the differences between each person's scores on the two half-tests (σ^2_d), and the variance of the total scores (σ^2_x). These two values are substituted in the following formula :

$$r_{tt} = 1 - \frac{\sigma^2_d}{\sigma^2_x}$$

where

r_{tt} = coefficient of reliability for the full-length of the test items
σ^2_d = variance of the differences between each person's scores on the two half-tests
σ^2_x = variance of the total scores obtained on the entire test.

It is interesting to note the relationship of this formula to the definition of error variance. Any difference between a person's scores on the two half-tests represents chance error. The variance of these differences divided by the variance of the total scores, gives the proportion of error variance in the scores. When this error variance is subtracted from 1.0, it gives the *true* variance, which is equal to the reliability coefficient.

The following example will clarify the computational procedure of split-half reliability for the full-length of the test.

Example 18.2 A test contains 100 items arranged in order of difficulty. The test was administered to the subjects and their responses were scored. The items were divided into two equal halves basing on the principle of odd–even items. The coefficient of correlation between two half-tests is 0.80. What is the split-half reliability for the full-length of the test?

Solution

Let the obtained split-half reliability $= r'_{tt} = 0.80$. The Spearman–Brown prophecy formula to find out the split-half reliability for the full-length of the test reads as:

$$r_{tt} = \frac{2r'_{tt}}{1 + r'_{tt}} = \frac{2 \times 0.80}{1 + 0.80} = \frac{1.60}{1.80} = 0.89$$

Let us now discuss the advantages and disadvantages (or limitations) of the split-half reliability.

Advantages of Split-half Reliability

The following are some of the advantages, merits or applicability of the split-half reliability:

(a) The split-half method is employed or applied where construction of parallel-forms test is not feasible or practicable, such will be the cases of tests of performance, questionnaires, attitudes, interests, and other personality tests, as for example, the Rorschach test.

(b) This split-half method is mostly used in cases where the repetition of the test is not advisable. For example, the performance tests such as picture completion, puzzle solving and form boards cannot readily be given in alternate-forms, nor repeated, owing to changes in the subject's attitudes upon taking the test for the second time.

(c) The most important advantage of the split-half method is that all data for computing reliability are obtained upon one occasion, so that variations brought about by differences between the two testing situations are eliminated.

(d) In split-half method the entire test is administered to the subjects only for once; there is no repetition of the same test or alternate form of the test. Therefore, the memory effects, practice effects, and carry-over effects found in case of test–retest and parallel-forms methods are eliminated by the split-half method.

Disadvantages of Split-half Reliability

Although split-half method is regarded by many as the best of the methods for measuring test reliability, yet it has certain lacunas or limitations, which are discussed further:

(a) A marked disadvantage of the split-half technique lies in the fact that chance error may affect the scores on the two halves in the same way, thus, tending to make the reliability coefficient too high. This follows because the test is administered only once.

(b) Objection has been raised to the split-half method on the grounds that a test can be divided into two equal halves in a number of ways and the coefficient of correlation in each case may be different, so that the reliability coefficient is not a unique value. This criticism is true only when items are all of equal difficulty; or when as in personality inventories, items may take any order. It is also true in speed tests. But in most standard

tests items are arranged in order of difficulty so that the split into odds and evens provides a unique determination of the reliability coefficient.

(c)   The split-half method cannot be used for estimating the coefficient of reliability of
the speed tests and heterogeneous tests, because all the testees cannot attempt all
items of the speed tests, and the items of the heterogeneous tests cannot be grouped
into two equivalent halves.

In spite of all these limitation or drawbacks of the split-half method, it is considered as the best
of all the methods of measuring test reliability, as the data for determining reliability coefficient are obtained upon one occasion and thus reduces the time, labour, and difficulties
and problems involved in case of second or repeated administration.

18.5.5.4   *Kuder–Richardson Method*

A fourth classical method for estimating test reliability is Kuder–Richardson method. This
method is also known as *rational equivalence method or inter-item consistency method*. The
Kuder–Richardson's method, like split-half method, also utilises a single administration of a
single form, and is based on the consistency of subject's responses to all items of the test. In
other words, in the rational equivalence method, the entire test is administered at a time to a
group of individuals. The reliability coefficient computed by this method is also a *coefficient
of internal consistency or inter-item consistency*, and measures both homogeneity of test item
and equivalence of contents. As splitting of the test is avoided, no bias is introduced in the
computed r_{tt} owing to arbitrary grouping of items in separate halves.

Assumptions of this method include similar item difficulties, dichotomy (e.g., yes/no, 1/0)
of test items, uniform and high item-total correlations of scores, homogeneity of test items,
and the dependence of total variance (σ_t^2) on item variances and covariances. Such assumptions prevent the application of this method to heterogeneous and speed tests.

The inter-item consistency is influenced by two sources of error variance, such as, *content sampling* (as in alternate-forms and split-half reliability), and *heterogeneity of behaviour
domain sampled*. The more homogeneous the domain, the higher the inter-item consistency.
For example, if one test includes only multiplication items, while another comprises addition,
multiplication, subtraction, and division items, the former test will probably show more inter-
item consistency than the latter. Because in the latter, more heterogeneous test, one subject
may perform better in subtraction than in any of the other arithmetic operations; another
subject may score relatively well on the division items, but more poorly in addition, subtraction, and multiplication; and so on. Similarly, if a test measures both quickness in arithmetical
computation and vocabulary, an individual may miss some easy arithmetic items and get
more difficult vocabulary items correct or vice-versa, not because of happenstance, but
because he has achieved more in one area than another.

Because of this characteristic, the Kuder–Richardson reliability has sometimes been referred
to as a measure of an entirely different characteristic of a test—that is, *homogeneity*. In other
words, Kuder–Richardson reliability measures to what extent the test items are homogeneous
or to what extent the test is internally consistent.

We think of variable error in terms of inconsistency of performance on the items within the
test. Kuder–Richardson's method is perfectly acceptable where the test is obviously *unifactor*.
In other words, this method is applied to those tests where the test items are homogeneous or
where it is desirable to measure a unique trait only. Certainly, if a test is a complex one, that
is, if it measures more than one trait, it is difficult to say to what extent the *inconsistencies* in

performance result from error and to what extent they reflect intra-individual differences in the traits involved. In such cases, Kuder-Richardson reliability should not be used.

The most common procedure for finding inter-item consistency or test reliability is that developed by Kuder and Richardson (1937). As in the split-half method, inter-item consistency is found from a single administration of a single test. Rather than requiring two half-scores, however, such a technique is based on an examination of performance on each item.

The most popular, widely applicable, and commonly known as *Kuder-Richardson Formula-20 (K-R 20)* reads as:

$$r_{tt} = \left(\frac{n}{n-1}\right)\left(\frac{\sigma_t^2 - \Sigma pq}{\sigma_t^2}\right) = \left(\frac{n}{n-1}\right)\left(1 - \frac{\Sigma pq}{\sigma_t^2}\right)$$

where

r_{tt} =reliability coefficient of the whole test

n =number of items in the test

σ_t^2 =the total variance of the observed test scores

P=proportion of persons being successful on each item

q =proportion of persons being unsuccessful on each item (q=1– p)

Σpq =the sum of item variances given by the product of p and q for each item.

The term $\frac{n}{n-1}$ is the common correction for bias when an estimate of the variance of a set of values is obtained by taking the square of the standard deviation in small samples.

The only thing in the formula which may be unfamiliar is the item analysis, *pq*. The product of *p* and *q* is computed for each item, and these products are then added for all items to give Σpq. The *pq* is the expression of the variance of scores on a single item where a score of 1 is assigned to a person who gets the item correct and a score of zero is given to a person who gets it wrong. Suppose, for example, 10 persons took a test composed of just one item. Suppose six persons out of 10 became successful and rest four became unsuccessful in that particular item. Therefore, *p*=6/10=0.6, and *q*=1–0.6=0.4. So, *pq*=0.6×0.4=0.24. Thus, 0.24 is the item variance of scores of a particular item of the test.

Thus, it is apparent that error variance, for Kuder-Richardson reliability, is measured by the sum of the item variances over all items of the test.

According to Cronbach (1951), it can be shown mathematically that the Kuder–Richardson reliability coefficient is actually the mean or average of all split-half reliability coefficients resulting from different splittings of a test. The ordinary split-half coefficient, on the other hand, is based on a planned split designed to yield equivalent sets of items. Hence, unless the test items are highly homogeneous, the Kuder–Richardson coefficient will be lower than the split-half reliability. An extreme example will serve to highlight the difference. Suppose we construct a 50-item test out of 25 different kinds of items such that items 1 and 2 are vocabulary items, items 3 and 4 arithmetic reasoning, items 5 and 6 spatial orientation, and so on. The odd and even scores on this test could theoretically agree quite closely, thus, yielding a high split-half reliability coefficient. The homogeneity of this test, however, would be very low, since there would be little consistency of performance among the entire set of 50 items. In this example, we would expect the Kuder-Richardson reliability to be much lower than the split-half reliability. It can be seen that difference between Kuder-Richardson and split-half reliability coefficients may serve as a rough index of the heterogeneity of a test.

The rational equivalence method has the following advantages and disadvantages.

Advantages of Kuder–Richardson Reliability

The following are some of the advantages of Kuder-Richardson reliability or rational equivalence method.

(a) Kuder-Richardson reliability coefficient measures both equivalence and homogeneity of test items whereas split-half reliability coefficient simply measures the equivalence of content sampling.

(b) Kuder-Richardson reliability measures the inter-item consistency which is based on the consistency of subject's responses to all items in the test administered only for once. This method neither requires administration of two alternate forms of a test like parallel-forms method nor it requires to split the test into two equivalent halves like split-half method.

(c) The difference between Kuder-Richardson and split-half reliability coefficients may serve as a rough index of the heterogeneity of a test.

(d) It is a measure of the average item intercorrelation of the test and an estimate of the average of split-half correlations obtained from all possible splittings of the test.

(e) The computation of Kuder-Richardson reliability coefficient takes into account the sum of item variances given by the product of p and q for each test item. So this type of reliability is better than the split-half reliability.

Disadvantages of Kuder–Richardson Reliability

The following are some of the limitations or disadvantages of Kuder-Richardson reliability.

(a) Kuder-Richardson method cannot be applied to heterogeneous and speed tests.

(b) If the items of the test are not highly homogeneous, this method will yield low reliability coefficient.

(c) The reliability coefficient obtained by this method is generally somewhat lower than the coefficients obtained by other methods.

Besides the above four basic methods of determining test reliability, there are another two methods for finding the reliability of a test. These two methods are Hoyt reliability and Scorer reliability, which are discussed further.

18.5.5.5 *Hoyt Reliability*

Hoyt (1941) has presented a procedure for estimating reliability which defines a variable error in a slightly different way from other approaches presented so far. As it turns out, however, the results are identical with Kuder-Richardson reliability. Nonetheless, it is instructive in terms of understanding the concept of reliability to examine this conceptual approach.

The final basic way of defining what is meant by variable error involves a slightly different breakdown of observed score variance from what has been previously presented.

According to Kuder-Richardson reliability, the variance in the performance of an individual from item to item is considered as error variance. But according to Hoyt's formulation, the variation in the performance of an individual from item to item is not considered to be error at all. Rather, it is a real (non-error) difference, an intra-individual difference, and one which should not be involved in the estimation of reliability. Therefore, according to Hoyt, total variance observed is conceived to be made up of three components rather than two.

These three components of total variance are: (a) true inter-individual differences, (b) intra-individual differences (measured by item variances) and (c) error inter-individual differences. This concept can be expressed as:

$$\sigma_x^2 = \sigma_t^2 + \sigma_i^2 + \sigma_e^2$$

where

σ_x^2 = total variance of the test scores
σ_t^2 = true variance
σ_i^2 = item variance
σ_e^2 = error variance.

Transposing the intra-individual difference term or item variance, we get

$$\sigma_x^2 - \sigma_i^2 = \sigma_t^2 + \sigma_e^2$$

as the appropriate observed variance to be used. Then according to Hoyt, a better definition of reliability is :

$$r_{tt} = \frac{\sigma_t^2}{\sigma_x^2 - \sigma_i^2} = \frac{(\sigma_x^2 - \sigma_i^2) - \sigma_e^2}{\sigma_x^2 - \sigma_i^2}$$

Using an analysis of variance procedure, then this reliability can be tested by :

$$r_{tt} = \frac{MS_{individuals} - MS_{residuals}}{MS_{individuals}}$$

where

$MS_{individuals}$ = mean squares of deviations from the individual's means
$MS_{residuals}$ = mean squares of deviations left over after individual and item variations have been removed.

18.5.5.6   Scorer Reliability

One source of error variance that can be checked quite simply is scorer variance. Certain types of tests—notably tests of creativity and projective tests of personality—leave a good deal to the judgement of the scorer. With such tests, there is as much need for a measure of scorer reliability as there is for more usual reliability coefficients. Scorer reliability can be found by having a sample of test papers independently scored by two examiners. These two scores thus obtained by each subject are then correlated in the usual way, and the resulting correlation coefficient is a measure of scorer reliability. This type of reliability is commonly computed when subjectively scored instruments are employed in research.

Thus, this type of reliability measures the error variances which are in scores or with the scorer, and with the experimental conditions known as irrelevant factors that can be experimentally controlled.

From the above discussion we may conclude that there is no one best way of estimating reliability coefficient. The type preferred will depend upon one's purposes, the meaning and use one wishes to attach to r_{tt}. The previous procedures differ most in the kinds of things that are allowed to be considered as true variance and as error variance. What may be regarded as true variance in computing one kind of r_{tt}, may be regarded as error variance in computing one of the others.

18.5.5.7 *Which Method of Reliability Is Preferred?*

The answer to this question depends upon the problem at hand.

Psychologists and educators want to know: (a) the internal consistency of a test and (b) the predictive value of a test.

When we want to determine the internal consistency, it is preferable to use the split-half and Kuder–Richardson method—the tests being given at one setting.

To estimate the predictive value of a test, the test–retest method, and the parallel-forms method are preferable—the test being given within a week or two (using the same form or alternate forms).

18.5.6 Factors Influencing the Reliability

The factors influencing or affecting the test reliability are broadly categorised into two groups, such as (a) intrinsic factors and (b) extrinsic factors that affect the reliability of the tests.

18.5.6.1 *Intrinsic Factors*

The intrinsic factors refer to those factors that lie within the test itself. The principal intrinsic factors that affect the test reliability are as follows:

(i) **Length of the test.** The test reliability has a definite relation with the length of the test. The more the number of items the test contains, the greater will be its reliability and vice-versa. Logically, the more sample of items we take of a given area of knowledge, skill and the like, the more reliable the test will be. However, it is difficult to ensure the maximum length of the test to ensure an appropriate value of reliability. The length of the tests in such cases should not give rise to fatigue effects in the testees, etc. Thus, it is advisable to use longer tests rather than shorter tests, because shorter tests are less reliable.

 The number of times a test should be lengthened to get a desired amount of reliability is given by the following formula that reads.

$$n = \frac{r_{tt}(1 - r'_{tt})}{r'_{tt}(1 - r_{tt})}$$

where

n = the number of times the test is to be lengthened
r_{tt} = the desired reliability
r'_{tt} = the obtained reliability

Example 18.3 The reliability of a test containing 100 items is 0.80. How many times the number of the items of the test should be lengthened so that the desired reliability of the test will be 0.95?

Solution

(i) In the above example, the data given are:

$$r'_{tt} = 0.80; \quad r_{tt} = 0.95$$

Thus,

$$n = \frac{r_{tt}(1 - r'_{tt})}{r'_{tt}(1 - r_{tt})} = \frac{0.95(1 - 0.80)}{0.80(1 - 0.95)} = \frac{0.95 \times 0.20}{0.80 \times 0.05} = \frac{0.19}{0.04} = 4.75$$

Hence the test is to be lengthened 4.75 times in order to get the reliability of 0.95. That means, the number of items in the test should be $100 \times 4.75 = 475$. However, while lengthening the test one should see that the items added to increase the length of the test must satisfy the conditions, such as, equal range of difficulty, desired discrimination power, and comparability with other test items already included in the test.

(ii) **Homogeneity of items.** *Homogeneity* of test items has two aspects—item reliability and the homogeneity of traits measured from one item to another. If the items measure different functions and the intercorrelations of items are 'zero' or near to it, then the reliability is 'zero' or very low and vice-versa.

(iii) **Difficulty level of items.** The difficulty level and the clarity of expression of a test item also affect the reliability of test scores. If the test items are either too easy or too difficult for the test takers it will tend to produce scores of low reliability, because in both the cases the tests have a restricted spread of scores.

(iv) **Discrimination value of items.** Test items having high discriminatory value can well discriminate between superior and inferior or between upper and lower test takers; the item-total correlation is high, and thus the reliability of the test is likely to be high, and vice-versa.

(v) **Test instructions.** Clear and concise instructions increase reliability of the test. Complicated and ambiguous directions give rise to difficulties in understanding the questions and the nature of the responses expected from the testees ultimately will lead to low reliability of the test.

(vi) **Range of scores.** Restricted range of scores of the subjects being tested has low coefficient of reliability. Wide range of scores means high reliability coefficient.

(vii) **Consistency of scores.** Lack of agreement among scores adversely affects the reliability of the test. If the test scores have consistency among themselves, then the reliability coefficient will be high and vice-versa.

(viii) **Item selection.** If there are too many interdependent items in a test, then its reliability coefficient will be low. Therefore, proper precautions should be taken while selecting the items to be included in the test.

(ix) **Reliability of the scorer.** The reliability of the scorer also influences the reliability of the test. If the scorer is moody, fluctuating type, then the test scores will vary from one situation to another. Errors in him/her will give rise to errors in the scores. The scorer variance is a source of error variance, and thus will lead to low reliability of the test. Therefore, the scorers must be reliable persons in order to have the appropriate reliability coefficient of the test.

18.5.6.2 *Extrinsic Factors*

The extrinsic factors refer to those factors which remain outside the test itself. The important extrinsic factors that influence the test reliability are as follows:

(i) **Range of age.** If the group of subjects taking the test has wider range of age, and thus has greater variations of the trait or ability being measured, the reliability coefficient will be high. That means homogeneity in chronological age has lowered reliability coefficient.

(ii) **Time interval between testing.** In case of test–retest method, and parallel-forms method, the wide time interval between two testing sessions results in low reliability coefficients whereas low time interval results in high reliability coefficients. Therefore, the time interval between two testing sessions should not be too short or too long, it should be optimal, that is, it should be within six months.

(iii) **Effects of memory and practice.** If the same test is repeated (as in test–retest method) or the alternate form of a test is administered (as in parallel-forms method) immediately or after a short time gap, there may be the possibility of carry-over effect, transfer effect, memory effect or practice effect, that might affect most of the educational achievement tests, so that the reliability coefficient will be spuriously high.

(iv) **Group variability.** When the group of pupils being tested is homogeneous in ability, the reliability of the test scores is likely to be lowered and vice-versa.

(v) **Guessing and chance errors.** Guessing in test gives rise to increased error variance and as such reduces test reliability. For example, in two-alternative response options there is a 50% chance of answering the items correctly in terms of guessing.

(vi) **Environmental conditions.** As far as practicable, testing environment should be uniform. Arrangements of light, sound, and other comforts should be equal for all testees, otherwise it will adversely affect the reliability coefficient of the test scores. Similarly, if the physical, mental, and emotional states of the test takers are not similar at both the times of administration (as it is in case of test–retest method and parallel-forms method) then the reliability of the test scores will be low.

(vii) **Momentary fluctuations.** Momentary fluctuations may enhance or reduce the amount of reliability coefficient of the test scores. For example, extreme changes in weather, sudden noises and other momentary distractions, emotional strain, a broken pencil point, etc., are the factors which may adversely affect the reliability of test scores.

The solutions of the following examples will definitely help the reader to have clear-cut ideas regarding the computational procedures of split-half and Kuder–Richardson reliabilities.

Example 18.4 The reliability coefficient for a test of 20 items was found to be 0.48. What will be the reliability coefficient if the test is lengthened by 10 more items?

Solution
In the above example the given data are:

The obtained reliability coefficient $= r_{tt}' = 0.48$
The initial test length $= 20$
The final test length $= 20 + 10 = 30$

The number of times test is lengthened $= \dfrac{\text{final test length}}{\text{initial test length}} = \dfrac{30}{20} = 1.5$

$\therefore n = 1.5$

Reliability coefficient of the final test (r_{tt}) is:

$$r_{tt} = \frac{n r_{tt}'}{1 + (n-1) r_{tt}'}$$

where

r_{tt}=reliability coefficient of the final test length
r'_{tt} =reliability coefficient obtained for the initial test length
n=number of times the test is lengthened.

Thus,

$$r_{tt} = \frac{1.5 \times 0.48}{1+(1.5-1)(0.48)} = \frac{1.5 \times 0.48}{1+0.5 \times 0.48} = \frac{0.72}{1+0.24} = \frac{0.72}{1.24} = 0.58$$

$$\therefore r_{tt} = 0.58$$

Example 18.5 Find the coefficient of internal consistency for a whole test whose split-half tests are correlated by 0.52.

Solution

The obtained split-half reliability $= r'_{tt} = 0.52$. The reliability for the full-length of the test (r_{tt}) is:

$$r_{tt} = \frac{2r'_{tt}}{1+r'_{tt}} = \frac{2 \times 0.52}{1+0.52} = \frac{1.04}{1.52} = 0.68$$

$$\therefore r_{tt} = 0.68$$

Example 18.6 If a test consisting of 20 items has a reliability coefficient of 0.45, how long it should be made to have a reliability coefficient of 0.80?

Solution

Given data:

Obtained reliability (r'_{tt})=0.45
Desired reliability (r_{tt})=0.80
Initial test length=20 item

Number of times the test is lengthened=n

$$n = \frac{r_{tt}(1-r'_{tt})}{r'_{tt}(1-r_{tt})} = \frac{0.80(1-0.45)}{0.45(1-0.80)} = \frac{0.80 \times 0.55}{0.45 \times 0.20} = \frac{0.44}{0.09} = 4.9$$

So the test should be made 4.9 times longer. Thus, the lengthened test should have the following number of items:

$$\text{Number of items} = 20 \times 4.9 = 98 \text{ items.}$$

Example 18.7 In a test consisting of 20 items, the sum of the item variance (Σpq) and the SD of all the test scores are 8.3725 and 6.5, respectively. Calculate the coefficient of internal consistency of the test by Kuder–Richardson formula 20.

Solution

The given data are: SD$= \sigma_t = 6.5$; $\Sigma pq = 8.3725$;

Number of items=n=20; $\sigma_t^2 = (6.5)^2 = 42.25$

Therefore, coefficient of internal consistency (r_{tt}) is:

$$r_{tt} = \left(\frac{n}{n-1}\right)\left(1 - \frac{\Sigma pq}{\sigma_t^2}\right) = \left(\frac{20}{20-1}\right)\left(1 - \frac{8.3725}{42.25}\right) = 1.053 \times 0.802 = 0.844$$

$$\therefore r_{tt} = 0.844$$

18.6   Validity of a Test

18.6.1   Meaning of Validity

The dictionary meaning of validity is 'well based', 'efficacious' or 'sound'. It refers to 'truthfulness'. Thus, any test which is truthful, well-based, and serves the right purpose is valid. Every test has certain objectives of its own. It is constructed for some specific purposes and it is valid for that purpose. If a test measures what it intends to measure, then it is said to be valid. An index of validity of a test refers to the extent to which it measures what it purports to measure. The validity of a test concerns what the test measures and how well it does so.

The validity of a test cannot be reported in general terms. No test can be said to have high or low validity in the abstract. Its validity must be determined with reference to the particular use for which the test is being considered. Various authors have defined validity of a test in their own words. For example, Anastasi (1976) writes, 'The validity of a test concerns what the test measures and how well it does so.' According to Freeman (1962), 'An index of validity shows the degree to which a test measures what it purports to measure when compared with accepted criterion.' In the opinion of Cronbach (1970), 'Validity is the extent to which a test measures what it purports to measure.'

From the foregoing discussion it is well evident that validity refers to the 'very purpose of the test', and if the purpose is fulfilled, the test should be considered to be valid.

18.6.2   Characteristics of Validity

The test validity has the following characteristics:

(i) The validity provides a direct check on how well a test fulfils its *purposes or functions*. Validity is the first requisite of a test becoming universal. Reliability may be necessary but not a sufficient condition of validity. A test cannot be valid unless it is reliable. It may be reliable but cannot be said as valid. Validity of a test ensures its reliability. If a test is valid, it must be reliable.

(ii) Validity of a test is affected by *systematic errors of measurement*. In other words, validity is a measure of *constant error*, while reliability is a measure of *variable error*.

(iii) Validity is the capacity of a test to measure and predict the specific variable under investigation, in exclusion of other variables. It indicates (a) the *relevance* of the test to the variable or trait to be investigated (b) the *discriminatory power* of the test to exclude the measurement of other variables and (c) the *predictive value* of the test for only the specific trait. For example, a test for clerical aptitude is valid if it can predict success in clerical jobs but gives no measure of any other variable such as the aptitude for salesmanship.

(iv) Validity should not be generalised beyond the specific purpose of a test. It needs empirical investigation. So, for constructing a valid test, (a) the attribute to be investigated should be precisely fixed, (b) the test items should be carefully chosen to reveal and measure that attribute in exclusion of others and finally (c) the validity should be determined by correlating the test scores with some *external criterion*. The latter may be either an objective measure of the same attribute or any other variable representing the latter. External criteria differ according to the purpose of the test, because different tests require different types of validity. External criteria for intelligence tests include school marks, teacher's ratings, grades in public examinations, achievement test scores, and similar but more elaborate tests of established validity such as the Binet-Simon and Wechsler scales. Achievement tests are validated against the criteria of actual courses of study, analysed and chosen by experts. The criteria for personality tests are the actual forms of behaviour, case histories, clinician's reports, and comparison of test scores before and after therapy.

(v) Validity is a measure of accuracy with which the test scores predict the variable to be explored by the test. It is ordinarily taken to be directly proportional to the magnitude of the *validity coefficient* (r_{xy} or r_{yx}) which is the correlation coefficient between the scores (X) of the given test and those (Y) of an external criterion.

(vi) Validity varies with the nature of the group tested; a group with a wider ability range yields a higher validity coefficient (r_{xy}) than a small selected group.

(vii) Sometimes different meanings of validity are expressed by terms such as intrinsic and relevant validities. (a) *Intrinsic validity* indicates the capacity of test scores (X_t) to denote true scores (X_∞). It is given by the intrinsic validity coefficient ($r_{t\infty}$) which is the square root of the reliability coefficient (r_{tt}): $r_{t\infty} = \sqrt{r_{tt}}$. (b) *Relevant validity* shows the extent to which a test measures the factors common with another test. The coefficient of relevant validity is the correlation coefficient of test scores with other measures, considering the common factors and eliminating the specific variance of the test scores. It is given by the square root of common factor variance in the scores.

(viii) Validity of a homogeneous test may be enhanced by increasing the test length without disturbing the homogeneity, because such an elongation either increases the proportion of the true variance (σ_∞^2) or adds new factors to increase the common factor loading of the test The validity coefficient [$r_{y(nx)}$] of the elongated test depends upon the reliability coefficient (r_{tt}) of the test of unit length, the validity coefficient (r_{yx} or r_{xy}) of the same and the number (n) of times the test has been elongated.

$$r_{y(nx)} = \frac{r_{yx}}{\sqrt{\dfrac{1-r_{tt}}{n}+r_{tt}}}; \quad n = \frac{1-r_{tt}}{\dfrac{r_{yx}^2}{r_{y(nx)}^2}-r_{tt}}$$

But unlike reliability, validity increases at a lower rate and never attains the perfect stage with the increase in the test length. The *SE of estimate* (σ_e) for validity coefficient (r_{yx}) measures the average random error in predicting individual criterion score from test scores, owing to an imperfect validity of the test. $\sigma_e = \sigma_y \sqrt{1-r_{yx}^2}$.

Example 18.8 An achievement test has validity coefficient of 0.64 between the test scores and the grade performance, and a reliability coefficient of 0.55. What will be the expected validity if the test is lengthened twice of its original length? How many times it should be lengthened to get a validity of 0.80?

Solution
The given data are:

Validity coefficient, $r_{yx} = 0.64$
Reliability coefficient, $r_{tt} = 0.55$

(a) When the test is elongated twice of its original length: $n = 2$

$$r_{y(nx)} = \frac{r_{yx}}{\sqrt{\dfrac{1-r_{tt}}{n}+r_{tt}}} = \frac{0.64}{\sqrt{\dfrac{1-0.55}{2}+0.55}}$$

$$= \frac{0.64}{\sqrt{0.775}} = \frac{0.64}{0.88} = 0.73$$

(b)   To get a validity coefficient ($r_{y(nx)}$) of 0.80

$$n = \frac{1-r_{tt}}{\dfrac{r_{yx}^2}{r_{y(nx)}^2} - r_{tt}} = \frac{1-0.55}{\dfrac{(0.64)^2}{(0.80)^2} - 0.55} = \frac{0.45}{0.64-0.55} = \frac{0.45}{0.09} = 5$$

So, the test should be lengthened 5 times of its original length for getting a validity of 0.80.

18.6.3   Types of Validity

There are three basic types of validity, such as, content validity, criterion-related validity (or empirical validity) and construct validity. These are discussed further.

18.6.3.1   Content Validity

Nature

Content validity procedures involve essentially the systematic examination of the test content to determine whether it covers a representative sample of the behaviour domain to be measured. Such a validation procedure is commonly used in tests designed to measure how well the individual has mastered a specific skill or course of study. It might seem that mere inspection of the content of the test should suffice to establish its validity for such a purpose. A test of multiplication or spelling would seem to be valid by definition if it consists of multiplication or spelling items, respectively.

However, the solution is not so simple as it appears to be. One difficulty is that of adequate sampling the item universe. The behaviour domain to be tested must be systematically analysed to make certain that all major aspects are covered by the test items, and in the correct proportions. A well-constructed educational test, for example, should cover the objectives of instruction, not just its subject matter. Content must, therefore, be broadly defined to include major objectives such as the application of principles and the interpretation of data, as well as factual knowledge. Moreover, validity depends on the relevance of the individual's test responses to the behaviour area under consideration, rather than on the apparent relevance of item content. Mere inspection of the test may fail to reveal the processes actually used by examinees in taking the test.

It is also important to guard against any tendency to over-generalise regarding the domain sampled by the test. For instance, a multiple-choice spelling test may ensure the ability to recognise correctly and incorrectly spelled words. But it cannot be assumed that such a test also measures ability to spell correctly from dictation, frequency of misspelling in written compositions, and other aspects of spelling ability. Still another difficulty arises from the possible inclusion of irrelevant factors in the test scores. For example, a test designed to measure proficiency in mathematics or mechanics may be unduly influenced by the ability to understand verbal directions or by speed of performing simple, routine tasks.

In sum, content validity is based on the logical analysis and proper sampling of the contents of the test. It is estimated to ensure the relevance of both the individual test items and the total test contents to the behavioural domain under consideration. It also investigates whether different aspects of the relevant behaviour are assessed in correct proportions by the test items, and how far those items and the cognitive processes involved form a representative sample of the variable to be measured. Content validity thus assesses the suitability of a test in evaluating the existing status of an individual in a specific area of behaviour. It is normally used for educational achievement tests by computing the correlation coefficient between the test scores (predictor) and some independent criterion for the pertinent variable. But content validity does not serve for personality tests.

Specific Procedures

Content validity is built into a test from the outset through the choice of appropriate items. For educational tests, the preparation of items is preceded by a thorough and systematic examination of relevant course syllabi and textbooks, as well as by consultation with subject-matter experts. On the basis of the information thus gathered, test specifications are drawn up for the item writers. These specifications should show the content area or topic to be covered, the instructional objectives or processes to be tested, and the relative importance of individual topics and processes. The final specifications should indicate the number of items of each kind to be prepared for each topic. For example, assessment of reading ability may include understanding vocabulary in context, literal comprehension of content, and drawing correct inferences from the given information. It may also sample material from different sources, such as, essays, poems, newspaper articles or instructions for operating equipments. A mathematics test may cover computation skills, the solution of verbally presented problems, and the application of learned processes to new and unfamiliar contexts.

Content validity is worked out in the following ways:

(i) When both the test scores (X) and the criterion scores (Y) constitute continuous variables, content validity coefficient is given by the product-moment correlation (r_{xy}) between the two.

(ii) When correlating continuous test scores with a dichotomised criterion, either biserial r_b or point biserial r_{pbi} is computed according to the genuine or arbitrary nature of the dichotomy of the criterion (see Chapter 9; Sections 9.4 and 9.5, respectively).

(iii) When both the criterion and the test scores are dichotomised, either phi coefficient or tetrachoric r is computed between them according to the genuine or arbitrary nature of the dichotomy (see Chapter 9; Section 9.6 for details of tetrachoric r, and Chapter 16; Section 16.5 for phi coefficient).

(iv) In case of more than one test as the predictors, validity is given by the *multiple correlation coefficient* ($R_{1.23...m}$) between the combined test scores and the criterion (see Chapter 9; Section 9.9).

Application

Content validity provides an adequate technique for evaluating achievement tests. For aptitude and personality tests, content validity is inappropriate and may be misleading. It permits us to answer two questions that are basic to the validity of an achievement test (educational and occupational achievement tests): (a) Does the test cover a representative sample of the specified skills and knowledge or of the curricular content? (b) Is test performance reasonably free from the influence of irrelevant variables?

Unlike achievement tests, aptitude and personality tests are not based on a specified course of instruction or uniform set of prior experiences from which test content can be drawn. Hence, in the latter tests, individuals are likely to vary more in the work methods or psychological processes employed in responding to the same test items.

Advantages

Some general points of ensuring content validity are given as follows:

(a)   The test should serve the required level of subjects, neither above nor below their standard.

(b)   The language of the test should be up to the level of the subjects.

(c)   The test items should not include anything which is not in the curriculum.

(d)   Each part of the curriculum should be given necessary weightage. More items should be selected from more important parts of the curriculum.

Limitations

The content validity has the following limitations:

(a)   The weightage to be given to different parts of content is subjective.

(b)   It is difficult to construct the perfect objective tests.

(c)   Content validity is not adequate for tests of intelligence, achievement, attitude, and personality.

(d)   Weightage given on different behaviour change is not objective.

Kinds of Content Validity

There are mainly three kinds of content validity, such as: (a) face validity, (b) logical or sampling validity and (c) factorial validity, which are briefly discussed as follows:

(i)   **Face validity.** Face validity refers not to what a test actually measures, but to what it appears superficially, on the basis of subjective evaluation, to measure. In other words, face validity refers *to the extent the test appears to measure what is to be measured.*

   Of all the concepts of validity, face validity is the least justifiable. It pertains to whether the test looks valid to the subjects. Face validity is never to be regarded as a substitute for more objective kinds of evidence. In spite of this, it has a place in testing.

   Face validity is important because of two reasons. First, in the original writing of items, face validity is about all upon which to rely. If by reading over the items of a test to see if the items look satisfactory and if the content appears to be appropriate, then face validity is important. But, once items have been written, face validity in test construction is not at all important. Face validity can often be improved by merely reformulating test items in terms that appear relevant and plausible.

   Second, face validity has some importance in gaining rapport and maintaining public relations particularly when tests are used in industry, in military situations or in civil service examinations, it is of some importance that the items and the test as a whole appear to be plausible and relevant to the stated purpose.

   It is almost always possible to develop tests which combine face validity with other types of validity. Face validity is a desirable feature of tests.

(ii)   **Logical or sampling validity.** The second variety of content validity has been variously termed as logical validity, validity by definition, content validity proper, and sampling validity. Actually, it is the last term which comes closest to describing what is meant. Here the primary concern is whether a specifically defined universe of behaviour is adequately sampled by the test in question.

Although logical/sampling validity, like face validity, depends upon the judgement of an expert in the field, it involves far more than merely looking at the items to see if they appear adequate to do the job.

First, it requires a careful definition in behavioural terms of the trait or content area to be measured. Second, it involves a breakdown of the total area defined into categories which represent all major aspects of the area. Finally, it involves a judgement as to whether there is a sufficient number of items in each of the categories which do, in fact, discriminate between those persons who have the particular characteristics or possess the knowledge and those who do not.

Logical validity is of greatest use in measures of achievement tests; for aptitude and personality tests, it is inappropriate.

(iii) **Factorial validity.** The third variety of content validity is the factorial validity, which makes use of the technique called factor analysis to determine to what extent a given test measures various content areas. Because a factor analysis involves gathering empirical data on test performance for a variety of measures, some writers classify factorial validity as a kind of empirical validity. Since most such studies include only test behaviours and their primary purpose is to analyse test content it logically fits into content validity.

To understand fully the meaning of factorial validity, it is necessary to know some of the basic tenets of factor analysis.

Any linear combination of the variables in a data matrix is said to be a factor of that matrix.

Factor analysis is a device which shows up the variables that can be grouped together because they behave in the same way. It is a technique to find out these new, independent, underlying factors which may be responsible for the grouping of variables. It analyses out the distinct factors at work among the variables; it also groups the variables together in ways which permit one to synthesise new entities.

There are three types of factors, such as, general factor (g), group factor (c) and individual factor (s). A general factor is that factor which is common in all variables in a particular study. A group factor refers to that factor which is common in some variables only but not in all variables, for example, only 5 out of 20 variables have substantial loadings on a particular factor. An individual factor is that factor which is specific in one variable.

According to Eysenck (1970), factorial validity has three purposes, such as, it describes a new field, suggestion of hypotheses, and testing of hypotheses.

Theories of Factor Analysis

The theories of factor analysis are otherwise known as theories of mental organisation or trait organisation. The following are four theories of factor analysis.

(a) Two-factor theory

This theory was developed by Spearman (1927). According to him 'g' factor is a function of heredity whereas 's' factors represent the acquisition of specific learnings and experiences.

Spearman says that all mental activity is made up of one common element or trait called mental energy or general factor plus a large number of independent, specific elements. Thus, any activity involves two components—the general factor and a factor unique to the particular activity in question.

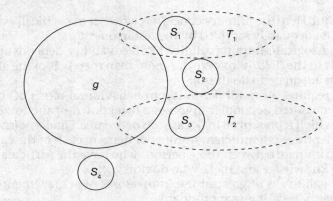

where

g = general factor

S_i = any specific factor

T_i = any test activity

Figure 18.1   Graphical representation of Spearman's theory

Spearman's theory can be represented graphically as shown in Figure 18.1.

Spearman felt that each test contained some 'g' and the 's' unique to the activity of answering the particular item in the test. Thus, the observed correlation between any two tests resulted because they both, to a certain extent, were measures of 'g'.

$$g_i^2 + s_i^2 = 1.0$$

where

g_i^2 = loadings on the general factor

s_i^2 = loadings on the specific factor.

The implication of Spearman's theory for testing is quite clear. Since the specific traits are too numerous to be of practical value, test construction should concentrate on the development of tests highly saturated with 'g'. Although the exact nature of 'g' was never precisely stated, tests dealing with abstract relationships (e.g., verbal, numerical or graphic analogies) seem to come closest to representing what was meant.

Spearman's major contribution in the field of factor analysis is the *criterion of proportionality*. Any test which satisfies the *criterion of proportionality* can be said to contain two factors. For example:

$$G : S = \frac{r_{3,1}}{r_{3,2}} = \frac{r_{4,1}}{r_{4,2}} \quad \text{or} \quad r_{3,1}r_{4,2} = r_{3,2}r_{4,1}$$

(b) Bi-factor theory

This theory was developed by Holzinger (1937). These two factors are: general factor (g) and group factor (c).

As more and more data were gathered, it became apparent that some modification of Spearman's theory was necessary. In many instances, tests involving quite similar activities showed correlation greater than would be anticipated on the basis of overlap with 'g' alone.

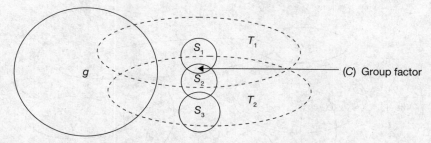

Figure 18.2 Graphical representation of Holzinger's theory

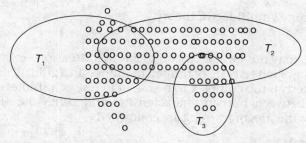

Figure 18.3 Graphical representation of Thompson's sampling theory

Thus, a new intermediate class of factors—group factors—was postulated. These group factors can be shown diagrammatically by permitting the specific factors to overlap slightly (see Figure 18.2). Thus,

$$g_i^2 + s_i^2 - c_i^2 = 1.00$$

where

c_i^2 = loadings on the group factor.

Such group factors (c), however, have remained in a relatively unimportant position in Spearman's theory.

(c) Sampling theory

Another theory of trait organisation is known as sampling theory. This theory was formulated by Thompson (1951). According to this theory, mental makeup consists of a vast number of relatively minute ability elements which have been variously identified with genes, neural elements, stimulus-response bonds, specific experiences and so forth. The behaviour of any person in a given activity such as taking a test is a reflection of the particular sample or pool of such elements called forth. Correlation among various measures results from an overlapping of the different elements. Diagrammatically, this can be represented as shown in Figure 18.3.

The major implication of this sampling theory for testing is quite different from Spearman's theory. Rather than developing pure measures of a single trait which is important in all activities, a specific test needs to be developed for each different activity and ideally should duplicate as closely as possible the situation which it is designed to predict. Thus, in business and industry, many work sample tests are used. Such tailor-made tests produce the highest predictive correlation for a specific situation. However, a test of this sort which is useful for one job

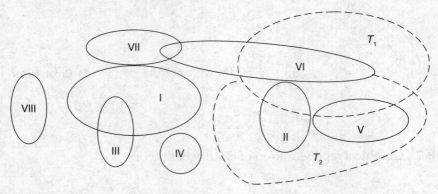

Figure 18.4   Thurstone's multi-factor theory

in a particular factory, may not be at all useful in another situation—even one which appears to be quite similar. Thus, such tests are of limited usefulness in a guidance situation. Again, the composition of such tests is too complex to be useful in research studies designed to discover lawful relationships between human characteristics and behaviour. This theory is most important so far as the theories of learning are concerned.

(d) Multi-factor theory
The last major theory of trait organisation is multi-factor theory developed by Thurstone (1931).

This theory proposes a relatively small number of broad group-factors, each of which enters with different weights into performance of specific tasks. Schematically, the mental organisation suggested by the group-factor theory is shown (see Figure 18.4).

In this connection, the intercorrelation of tests results from an overlap of these common factors. Ideally, then each test should be a pure measure of one of the group factors. Once all of the group factors have been identified and tests developed which accurately measure each one independently of other traits, it should be possible to predict any given criterion. This would be done by administering all of the group factor tests and assigning weights appropriate to the particular situation at hand. Tests developed following this theory are not as useful in employee selection as they are in guidance situations where a considerable gain in generalizability of the results often offsets a relatively small loss in accuracy of prediction. Thurstone, following group factor theory, felt that the number of traits ultimately needed for complete prediction in all tasks would be relatively small.

In sum, factorial validity refers to the extent of correlation of the different factors with the whole test. Factorial validity is determined by a statistical technique known as factor analysis. It uses methods of intercorrelation and other statistical methods to estimate factorial validity. The correlation of the test with each factor is calculated to determine the weight contributed by each such factor to the total performance of the test. This tells us about the factor loadings. This relationship of the different factors with the whole test is called the factorial validity.

18.6.3.2   *Criterion-related Validity*

The criterion-related validity is otherwise known as empirical validity. This type of validity provides the evidence that a test score can be interpreted in a particular way by showing that a relationship exists between the test performance on the one hand, and on the other, behaviour in some second (criterion) activity. In other words, when a test measures what it is designed to measure might be entirely restricted to relationship between the test behaviour and the criterion behaviour—this is known as empirical validity or criterion-related validity. This relationship between test and criterion performance can be expressed in several ways, as given as follows:

(a) Because it represents a measure of association between two continuous variables, the Pearson product-moment correlation coefficient is the most common index of empirical validity. Thus, a measure of scholastic ability is validated by correlating test scores with subsequent grade-point average; a test of mechanical ability is assessed for validity by means of the correlation between scores on the measure and rating of performance on the job. If either the criterion or the test or both variables are not measurable on a ratio scale, then some other form of correlation such as rank order, biserial, tetrachoric or the correlation ratio may be used.

(b) Sometimes direct measurement of the criterion behaviour is expensive, unreliable or nearly impossible to obtain. Under these circumstances other ways of describing the relationship between the two behaviours must be found. One possibility is that of noting the mean difference in performance among readily recognised groups. Thus, for example, evidence of the empirical validity of a measure of art aptitude might be expressed in terms of the differences in mean scores obtained by people in general, by art students, and by professional artists. If the test is empirically valid, scores should increase considerably or significantly from the first group to the last. Similarly, a test of scholastic ability might be empirically validated by showing that the average of the scores obtained on the test increases as it is administered to persons at successively higher levels of education.

(c) Another somewhat different approach is to express the relationship between test and criterion performance in terms of the percentage of individuals who would be correctly classified by the test according to their known group membership. Thus, an interest measure which was designed as an aid in occupational guidance might be empirically validated by showing that a high proportion of persons presently on the job could be correctly classified according to their occupation from the test scores alone.

Kinds of Criterion-related Validity

There are three kinds of criterion-related validity (or empirical validity), such as, (a) predictive validity, (b) concurrent validity and (c) cross validation. These are discussed as follows.

(i) **Predictive Validity:** The predictive validity has been defined by Cureton (1965) as an estimate of the correlation coefficient between the test scores and the true criterion. It refers to the extent to which the test predicts the future performance of the subjects.

Predictive validity is concerned with the predictive capacity of a test. It indicates the effectiveness of a test in predicting an individual's behaviour in specified situation. For this purpose, the performance on the test is checked against a criterion, that is, a direct and independent measure of that which the test is designed to predict. The test scores can be used to predict future behaviour or performance of the individuals and hence called as predictive validity. For predictive validity, the scores of the test (predictor) are usually correlated with scores of an independent criterion by computing either Spearman's rho or Pearson's product-moment r.

The accuracy of prediction is indicated by the *coefficient of predictive validity* which is the correlation coefficient between the test scores and the criterion scores. It is generally true that the higher the validity coefficient, the more useful the test for predicting an individual criterion score or for screening purposes.

The procedure for predictive validity is that the test data was gathered first and then at some later time, by means of a follow-up study, the criterion data was gathered. This approach to gathering empirical validity results in information often referred to as predictive validity. An example can clarify the concept better.

For example, medical entrance test is constructed and administered to select candidates for admission into MBBS courses. Basing on the scores made by the candidates on this test we admit the candidates. After completion of the course they appear at the final MBBS examination. The scores of the final MBBS examination is the criterion. The scores of the entrance test (predictor) and the final examination (criterion) are correlated. High correlation implies high predictive validity.

Similar examples like other recruitment tests or entrance tests in agriculture, engineering, banking, railway, etc. may be cited here which must have high predictive validity. That is, tests used for recruitment, classification and entrance examination must have high predictive validity. This type of validity is sometimes referred to as 'empirical validity' or 'statistical validity' as our evaluation is primarily empirical and statistical.

This predictive validity is appropriate for aptitude and personality tests. However, it has certain *limitations*. If we get a suitable criterion measure with which our test results are to be correlated, we can determine the predictive validity of a test. But it is very difficult to get a good criterion. Moreover, we may not get criterion measures for all types of psychological tests.

(ii) **Concurrent Validity.** Sometimes it is expensive, inconvenient, ethically undesirable or otherwise nearly impossible, from a practical point of view, to obtain data as it is gathered in predictive validity procedure. Rather it is necessary to obtain criterion data at the same time (or concurrently) or even prior to securing the test information. For example, it may not be possible to administer a test to hundreds of children and then to wait five or ten years to follow them up to see how many have become successful mechanics. It is obviously much less costly and less time consuming to simply search out mechanics who are presently on the job and administer to them the test at the same time ratings or other criterion information are gathered from their employers. In contrast to the predictive validity described earlier, empirical validity data gathered in this latter way would provide information referred to as concurrent validity. The concurrent validity refers to the extent to which the test scores correlate with already established or available criterion scores.

The dictionary meaning of the term 'concurrent' is 'existing' or 'done at the same time'. Thus, the term 'concurrent validity' is used to indicate the process of validating a new test by correlating its scores with some existing or available criterion scores which might have been obtained shortly before or shortly after the new test scores are obtained. For example, the scores of any intelligence test can be validated against the scores already obtained in the Stanford-Binet Scale. Similarly, the concurrent validity of an arithmetic test is given by the correlation coefficient between the test scores and the already achieved class grades of the testees.

The usual procedure in obtaining the concurrent validity is to administer a battery of tests to a group of employees already on the job or to students while they are in the school. At the same time, supervisory ratings, productive indices, grade–point averages or other criterion data are gathered. Then the correlation between the test results and the criterion scores is computed and reported as the validity evidence.

When both the predictor (test scores) and the criterion (criterion scores) are perfectly reliable, criterion-related validities tend to reach maximum magnitudes, approaching but rarely attaining the square root of the reliability coefficient of the test. Concurrent validity is appropriate for psychiatric diagnosis tests.

So far the difference between concurrent validity and predictive validity is concerned we can say that concurrent validity is relevant to tests employed for diagnosis of existing status rather than the prediction of future outcomes. In other words, concurrent validity shows the validity of the test as a measure of the *present status* of an individual while predictive validity assesses the test as a measure of his/her *future status*. For example, Is Rama neurotic? (concurrent validity). Is Rama likely become neurotic? (predictive validity).

This type of validity is also known as 'external validity' or 'functional validity'. Concurrent validity is relevant to tests employed for diagnosis, not for prediction of future success.

(iii) **Cross Validation.** Failure to consider the effects of the restriction in range when it is necessary to gather empirical data by the process of concurrent validation results in underestimating the usefulness of a test. On the other hand, neglecting to gather new information as to the effectiveness of the test after the prediction or selection system has been worked out, that is, failure to cross validation, can lead to exaggerated claims as to the effectiveness of the prediction or selection.

Whenever a test is used either to predict a specific criterion score or for necessary screening purposes, the resulting prediction equation or cutting score is determined in such a way that error is minimised for the specific data at hand. In doing this many of the chance fluctuations occurring in the particular observations obtained are used to advantage. This tends to spuriously increase the estimated accuracy of prediction over that which can actually be accomplished when the findings are applied to new observations. Therefore, to properly evaluate the usefulness of a test, the prediction equation or cutting score must be derived from one sample of information and validated on a second sample of subjects from the same universe. If this has been done, the test is said to be *cross-validated* for that universe.

A person who attempts to apply the test, even to a second sample of the same universe, without cross-validation should anticipate a reduction in the test–criterion correlation found in practice as compared with that calculated in the original analysis. In general, when a single test is used, the smaller the size of the original sample, the greater the shrinkage of the validity coefficient in cross-validation. If more than one measure is used in the prediction or selection system, the amount of shrinkage will also be a function of the number of variables tried out: the larger the number of original predictors used and the smaller the proportion of variables retained, the greater the reduction in actual validity from that found with the original sample.

In many instances, a potential user of a test examines validity coefficients reported in the literature in the hope of determining whether the tests would be useful in his/her own situation. Judgements of this sort require inferences beyond the original universe and, thus, the actual validity in the new situation can be expected to be smaller than the reported coefficients, even if the latter was cross-validated on a second sample in the original situation.

To accurately assess the usefulness of the test in a new situation, it is necessary to carry out other forms of cross-validation studies. If the additional information is obtained by checking the effectiveness of the test on a differently defined population, but using the same criterion as in the original study, the process is called *validity generalisation*. If the test validity is checked against a new criterion as well as with a different population, *validity extension* has been carried out. Other designs for cross-validation studies which may be useful in special circumstances have also been worked out and described by Mosier (1951).

Cross-validation is especially important in the selection of items for a test and in discovering so-called psychometric signs (score characteristics, empirically derived, which distinguish between two or more groups).

In summary, then, cross-validation serves to provide more accurate information about the usefulness of a test in a particular situation than can be obtained from the validity coefficient calculated on the original group of subjects used to develop the prediction or screening system. Cross-validation is accomplished by trying out a previously developed and refined test (or series of psychometric signs) on a completely new group as close as possible to that for which the test will ultimately be used.

To the extent that the original sample used for the test development was small (or different) to the extent that a large number of predictors was tried and only a small proportion ultimately retained, there is likely to be considerable shrinkage in the cross-validation validity coefficient from that obtained with the original analysis group.

18.6.3.3   *Construct Validity*

Construct validity is the most recent addition to the conceptual ideas concerning kinds of evidences which are required before a test user can feel justified in interpreting test scores in certain ways. More recently Cronbach and Meehl (1955) has elaborated and clarified the concept.

The construct validity of a test is the extent to which the test may be said to measure a theoretical construct or trait. In other words, it aims to establish a given hypothetical construct that a test aims to measure or assess really exists in a population. Or when the evidence gathered implies or depends upon the existence of some mental trait or hypothetical construct—it is referred to as *construct validity*, which is also known as *psychological validity or trait validity*, because a hypothetical construct refers to a mental trait or to a psychological attribute of abstract quality. Examples of such hypothetical constructs are intelligence, mechanical comprehension, mechanical ability, musical talent, emotional stability, clerical aptitude, verbal fluency, speed of walking, neuroticism, anxiety, and in fact, all mental (including attitudes, interests and personality) traits which one might attempt to measure with tests, scales and inventories are hypothetical constructs, each carrying with it a number of associated meanings relating how a person who possessed the specified trait would behave in certain situations. Thus, the process of establishing the construct validity of a test is no simple one. Every validation study becomes an evaluation not just of the test alone, but also of theory and concept of the trait as well.

As Cronbach and Meehl (1955) describe it; the logical process of construct validation requires: First, setting forth the proposition that this test measures trait A; second, inserting this proposition into present theory about trait A; third, working through the theory to predict behaviour characteristics which should be related to test scores and those which should show no relation to test scores if the test truly measures trait A as presently conceived; and finally, securing data which will empirically or experimentally confirm or reject the hypothesis.

They also have been pointed out that if the predictions (positive or negative) do not hold up, there are three possibilities as given as follows:

(i)   The test does not measure the construct variable.

(ii)   The theoretical network which generated the hypothesis is incorrect.

(iii) The experimental design failed to test the hypothesis properly.

Thus, a decision must be made as to which of these three conditions has occurred. As can be imagined, a great many of the claims and counter claims about tests and their interpretation stem from disagreement as to which of the three possibilities is the culprit.

Features

Sometimes it is relatively easy to tell what has happened. A well-trained researcher with adequate knowledge of the subject matter involved, through an examination of the procedure followed, would be able to determine whether the design of the study itself was adequate.

Perhaps the best way to clarify the nature of construct validity is to point of various features of the process which need special emphasis.

First, it should be noted that a specific criterion used in the early stages of the development of a test may be later rejected as less valid than the test itself.

Second, a consumer of tests needs to know not only the test itself, but also the theory behind the test and the evidence which supports the theory. That is, it is absolutely essential that a test user should know what interpretations of a test are theoretically possible, and which of these have been empirically verified. As Cronbach and Meehl (1955) have pointed out, 'Unless essentially the same theory is accepted by all test users, no general scientific validation is possible.'

Third, scientists can properly evaluate a claim supporting the usefulness of a test and the associated theory of the trait it measures only if the evidence is made public.

Fourth, it should be perfectly clear that each positive study results in greater and greater confidence that a test is a valid measure of a certain construct. On the other hand, in spite of hundreds of prior successes, one well-established negative finding can completely destroy any belief in the absolute reality of the trait as measured. Such a pronouncement may seem harsh and actually contrary to what happens in practise—for, very few workers would, as a result of one contrary finding, stop using the test in those situations where positive results had been repeatedly obtained. This apparent conflict can readily be solved by conceiving of any mental trait not as representing or failing to represent underlying truth but as being a relatively useful or useless conception in certain practical and/or theoretical situations. While one solid, negative finding does destroy the logical necessity of the trait as representing the truth—it only sets a boundary on the usefulness of the construct and its measure.

Finally, it should be apparent that it is quite naïve to ask whether a test is valid. As Cronbach and Meehl (1955) pointed out, a test is never really validated at all. Rather, a principle for making certain kinds of inferences about persons who obtain given test scores is verified or refuted. Thus, if a test yields many types of inferences, some may be valid and others not. The question should not be, 'Is the test valid?', but 'Is the test valid for such and such?'

Techniques

Focusing on a broader, more enduring and more abstract kind of behavioural description than the previously discussed types of validity, construct validation requires the gradual accumulation of information from a variety of sources. Any data throwing light on the nature of the trait under consideration and the conditions affecting its development and manifestations are grist for this validity mill. Illustrations of specific techniques suitable for construct validation will be considered as follows.

(i) **Age differentiation.** A major criterion employed in the validation of a number of intelligence tests is age. Such a test as the Stanford–Binet and most preschool tests are checked against chronological age to determine whether the scores show a progressive increase with advancing age. Since abilities are expected to increase with age during childhood, it is argued that the test scores should likewise show such an increase, if the test is valid. The very concept of an age scale of intelligence, as initiated by Binet, is based on the assumption that intelligence increases with age, at least, until maturity.

The criterion of age differentiation, of course, is inapplicable to any functions that do not inhibit clear-cut and consistent age changes. In the area of personality, for example, it has found limited use. Moreover, it should be noted that age differentiation is essentially a negative rather than a positive criterion. Thus, if the test scores fail to improve with age, such a finding probably indicates that the test is not a valid measure of the abilities it was designed to sample. On the other hand, to prove that a test measures something that increases with age does not define the area covered by the test very precisely. A measure of height or weight would also show regular age increments, although it would obviously not be designated as an intelligence test.

A final point should be emphasised regarding the interpretation of the age criterion. A psychological test validated against such a criterion measures behaviour characteristics that increase with age under the conditions existing in the type of environment in which the test was standardised. Because different cultures may stimulate and foster the development of dissimilar behaviour characteristics, it cannot be assumed that the criterion of age differentiation is a universal one. Like all other criterion, it is circumscribed by the particular cultural setting in which it is derived.

(ii) **Correlation with other tests**. Correlation between a new test and similar earlier tests are sometimes cited as evidence that the new test measures approximately the same general area of behaviour as other tests designated by the same name, such as, 'intelligence tests' or 'mechanical aptitude tests'. Unlike the correlations found in criterion—related validity these correlations should be moderately high but not too high. If the new test correlates too highly with an already available test, without such added advantages as brevity or ease of administration, then the new test represents needless duplication.

Correlations with other tests are employed in still another way to demonstrate that the new test is relatively free from the influence of certain irrelevant factors. For example, a special aptitude test or a personality test should have a negligible correlation with tests of general intelligence or scholastic aptitude. Similarly, reading comprehension should not appreciably affect performance on such tests. Thus, correlations with tests of general intelligence, reading or verbal comprehension are sometimes reported as indirect or negative evidence of validity. In these cases, high correlations would make the test suspect. Low correlations, however, would not in themselves insure validity. It will be noted that this use of correlations with other tests is similar to one of the supplementary techniques described under content validity.

(iii) **Factorial analysis**. Of particular relevance to construct validity is factor analysis, a statistical procedure for the identification of psychological traits. Essentially, factor analysis is a refined technique for analysing the intercorrelations of behaviour data. For example, if 20 tests have been given to 300 persons, the first step is to compute the correlations of each test with every other. An inspection of the resulting table of 190 correlations may itself reveal certain clusters among the tests, suggesting the location of common traits. Thus, if such tests as vocabulary analogies, opposites and sentence comprehension have high correlations with each other and low correlations with all other tests, we could tentatively infer the presence of a verbal comprehension factor, because such an inspectional analysis of correlation table is difficult and uncertain; however, more precise statistical techniques have been developed to locate the common factors required to account for the obtained correlations.

In the process of factor analysis, the number of variables or categories in terms of which each individual's performance can be described is reduced from the number of original tests to a relatively small number of factors or common traits. In the example cited above, five or six factors might suffice to account for the intercorrelations among the 20 tests. Each individual might, thus, be described in terms of his/her scores in the five or six factors rather than in terms of the original 20 scores. A major purpose of factor analysis is to simplify the description of behaviour by reducing the number of categories from an initial multiplicity of test variables to a few common factors or traits.

After the factors have been identified they can be utilised in describing the factorial composition of a test. Each test can thus be characterised in terms of the major factors determining its scores, together with the weight or loadings of each factor. Such factor loadings also represent the correlations of the test with each factor, a correlation known as the factorial validity of the test. Thus, if the verbal comprehension factor has a weight of 0.66 in a vocabulary test, the factorial validity of this vocabulary test as a measure of the trait of verbal comprehension is 0.66. It should be noted that factorial validity is essentially the correlation of the test with whatever is common to a group or other indices of behaviour. The set of variables analysed can, of course, include both test and non-test data. Ratings and other criterion measures can thus be utilised along with other tests, to explore the factorial validity of a particular test and to define the common traits it measures.

(iv) **Internal consistency**. Certain tests, especially in the area of personality, have been validated by the method of internal consistency. The essential characteristic of this method is that the criterion is nothing but the total score on the test itself. Sometimes the contrasted group method is used. Extreme groups are selected on the basis of the total test scores. The performance of the upper criterion group on each test item is then compared with that of the lower criterion group. Items that fail to show a significantly greater proportion of 'passes' in the upper than in the lower criterion group are considered invalid and are either eliminated or revised. Correlational procedures may also be employed for this purpose. For example, the biserial correlation between pass and fail on each item and total test score can be computed. Only those items yielding significant item-test correlations would be retained. A test whose items were selected by this method can be said to show internal consistency since each item differentiates in the same direction as the entire test.

Another application of the criterion of internal consistency involves the correlation of subtest scores with total score. Many intelligence tests, for instance, consist of separately administered subtests (such as, vocabulary, arithmetic and picture completion) whose scores are combined in finding the total test score. In the construction of such tests, the scores on each subtest are often correlated with total score and any subtest whose correlation with total score is too low is eliminated. The correlations of the remaining subtests with total score are then reported as evidence of the internal consistency of the entire instrument.

It is apparent that internal consistency correlations, whether based on items or subtests, essentially, measure of homogeneity. Because it helps to characterise the behaviour domain or trait sampled by the test, the degree of homogeneity of a test has some relevance to its construct validity.

(v) **Effects of experimental variables on test scores**. A further source of data for construct validation is provided by experiments on the effect of selected variables on test scores. Whether pitch discrimination as measured by a particular test is or is not susceptible to practice, for instance, can be checked by administering the test to the same subjects before and after a period of intensive practice. A test designed to measure anxiety-proneness can be administered to subjects who are subsequently put through a situation designed to arouse anxiety, such as taking an examination under distracting and stressful conditions. The initial anxiety test scores can then be correlated with physiological and other indices of anxiety expression during and after the examination. A different hypothesis regarding an anxiety test could be evaluated by administering the test before and after an anxiety-arousing experience and seeing whether test scores arise significantly on the retest. Positive findings from such an experiment would indicate that the test scores reflect current anxiety level. In a similar way, experiments can be designed to test any other hypothesis regarding the trait measured by a given test.

(vi) **Convergent and discriminant validation**. In a thoughtful analysis of construct validation, Campbell (1960) points out that in order to demonstrate construct validity we must show not only that a test correlates highly with other variables with which it should theoretically correlate, but also it does not correlate significantly with variables from which it should differ. In an earlier article, Campbell and Fiske (1959) described the former process as *convergent validation* and the latter as *discriminant validation*. In other words, if the scores in the given test have a significant moderately high positive correlation with the scores in other tests known to measure the same trait satisfactorily, it is called as *convergent validity*. On the other hand, if the scores in the given test have a negligible or negative correlation with the scores in tests for dissimilar traits, it is known as *discriminant validity*. Correlation of a mechanical aptitude test with subsequent grades in a shop course would be an example of convergent validation. For the same test, discriminant validity would be illustrated by a low and insignificant correlation with scores on a reading comprehension test, since the latter would be an irrelevant variable in a test designed to measure mechanical aptitude. Discriminant validation is especially relevant to the validation of personality tests, in which irrelevant variables may affect scores in a variety of ways.

Campbell and Fiske (1959) proposed systematic experimental design for the dual approach of convergent and discriminant validation which they called the *multitrait-multimethod matrix*. Essentially this procedure requires the assessment of two or more traits by two or more methods. A hypothetical example provided by Campbell and Fiske will serve to illustrate the procedure. They found out the all possible correlations among the scores obtained when three traits are each measured by three methods. The three traits could represent three personality characteristics such as: (A) dominance, (B) sociability and (C) achievement motivation. The three methods could be: (1) a self-report inventory, (2) a projective technique and (3) associates' ratings. Thus, A_1 would indicate dominance scores on the self-report inventory, A_2 dominance scores on the projective test and C_3 associates' ratings on achievement motivation and so forth. The scores obtained for the same trait by different methods are correlated which is the construct validity. They also found out the correlations between different traits measured by the same method and correlations between different traits measured by different methods. For satisfactory construct validity, the validity coefficients should obviously be higher than the correlations between different traits measured by different methods; they should also be higher than the correlations between different traits measured by the same method. For example, the correlation between dominance scores from a self-report inventory and dominance scores from a projective test should be higher than the correlation between dominance scores and sociability scores from a self-report inventory. If the latter correlation, representing common method variance, were higher, then it might indicate, for example, that a person's scores on this inventory are unduly affected by some irrelevant common factor such as ability to understand the questions or desire to make oneself appear in a favourable light on all traits.

It might be noted that within the framework of the *multitrait-multimethod matrix* reliability represents agreement between two measures of the same trait obtained through maximally similar methods, such as parallel forms of the same test; validity represents agreement between two measures of the same trait obtained by maximally different methods, such as, test scores and supervisor's ratings. Since similarity and difference of methods are matters of degree, theoretically reliability and validity can be regarded as falling along a single continuum.

It must be noted that construct validity is inferential. It is used primarily when other types of validity are insufficient to indicate the validity of the test. Construct validity is usually involved in such as those study habits, appreciation, honesty, sincerity, intelligence, emotional stability, sympathy, attitudes, mathematical aptitude, critical thinking, study skills, anxiety, logical reasoning and reading comprehension.

18.6.4 Methods of Estimating Validity of a Test

The following are some of the methods of estimating or determining the validity of a test.

(i) **Correlation coefficient method.** In this method the scores of a newly constructed test are correlated with that of criterion scores. The coefficient of correlation gives the extent of validity index of the test. For this purpose Pearson's method of correlation is most widely and popularly used. The technique of correlation depends on the nature of data obtained on the test as well as on the criterion.

(ii) **Cross-validation method.** Cross-validation would be a trial of the selected items on new groups. In order to evaluate the usefulness of a test, the prediction equation or cut-off score must be derived from one sample of information and validated on a second sample of subjects from the same universe or population. Cross-validation is accomplished by trying out previously developed and refined test on a completely new group.

(iii) **Expectancy table method.** In this method the scores of newly constructed test are evaluated or correlated with the rating of the supervisors. It provides empirical probabilities of the validity index.

(iv) **Item analysis method.** The items of a valid test should have proper difficulty value and discriminating power. Difficulty value and discriminating power of test items can be calculated through item analysis. Item analysis is a process by which the difficulty value and discriminating power of the individual items of a test are calculated.

(v) **Method of intercorrelation of items and factor analysis.** The factor analysis is done by highly statistical methods. Methods of intercorrelation and other statistical methods are used to estimate factorial validity.

18.6.5 Factors Affecting Test Validity

A large number of factors influence the validity of a test. Gronlund (1981) has suggested the following factors.

(i) Factors in the test itself
(ii) Functioning content and teaching procedure
(iii) Factors in the administration and scoring
(iv) Factors in pupils' responses
(v) Nature of the group and the criterion

These above factors are discussed as follows:

(i) **Factors in the test itself.** Each test contains items and a close scrutiny of test items will indicate whether the test appears to measure the subject matter content and the mental functions that the teacher wishes to test. The following factors in the test itself can prevent the test items from functioning as desired and thereby lower the validity.

(a) **Length of the test.** A test usually represents a sample of many questions called items. If the test is too short to become a representative one, then validity will be affected accordingly. Homogeneous lengthening of a test increases both reliability and validity. The formula which determines the length to which the test may be increased is:

$$n = \frac{1 - r_t}{\dfrac{r_{tc}^2}{r_{tx}^2} - r_t}$$

where

n=number of times a test is to be increased

r_t=reliability of the test

r_{tc}=correlation of the test with the criterion

r_{tx}=validity of the test.

For example, the reliability coefficient of a test is 0.57 and it correlates 0.65 with the teacher's rating. How many times the test must be lengthened if a validity coefficient of 0.80 is sought?

In the given example

$$r_t = 0.57; \quad r_{tc} = 0.65; \quad r_{tx} = 0.80$$

Hence,

$$n = \frac{1 - r_t}{\dfrac{r_{tc}^2}{r_{tx}^2} - r_t}$$

$$= \frac{1 - 0.57}{\dfrac{(0.65)^2}{(0.80)^2} - 0.57} = \frac{0.43}{0.66 - 0.57} = \frac{0.43}{0.09} = 4.78$$

(b) **Unclear direction**. If direction regarding how to respond to the items, whether it is permissible to guess and how to record the responses/answers, are not clear to the subjects, then the validity will tend to reduce.

(c) **Reading vocabulary and sentence structures which are too difficult**. The complicated vocabulary and sentence structures meant for the subjects taking the test may fail in measuring the aspects of subject performance; thus, lowering the validity.

(d) **Inappropriate level of difficulty of the test items**. When the test items have an inappropriate level of difficulty, it will affect the validity of the test. For example, in criterion-referenced tests, failure to match the difficulty level specified by the learning outcome will lower the validity.

(e) **Poorly constructed test items**. The test items which are poorly constructed will lower the validity of the test. For example, the test items which provide unintentional clues to the answer will tend to measure the pupils' alertness in detecting clues as well as the aspects of pupils' performance which ultimately affect the validity.

(f) **Ambiguity**. Ambiguity in statements in the test items leads to misinterpretation, different interpretations and confusions. Sometimes it may confuse the better students more than poor ones resulting in the discrimination of items in the negative direction. As a consequence, the validity of the test is lowered.

(g) **Inappropriate test items.** The test items which are inappropriate for the outcomes being measured will affect the results and lead to the distortion of the validity.

(h) **Improper arrangement of items.** Items in the test are generally arranged in order of difficulty level with the easiest items at the top of the test. If the difficult items are placed at the beginning of the test, it may make the students too much of their time on these items and fail to reach other items which they could answer easily. Also, such an improper arrangement of items may adversely affect the validity of the test by having a negative effect on the students' motivation.

(i) **Guessing.** When the subjects identify the systematic pattern of correct responses, they can cleverly guess the answers, and this guessing will affect the validity of the test.

(ii) **Functioning Content and Teaching Procedure.** In achievement testing, the functioning content of test items cannot be determined only by examining the form and content of the test. The teacher has to teach fully how to solve a particular problem before including it in the test as an item. Test of complex learning outcomes seem to be valid if the test items function as intended. If the students have previous experience of the solution of the problem included in the test, then such tests are no more a valid instrument for measuring the more complex mental processes and they, thus, affect the validity.

(iii) **Factors in Test Administration and Scoring.** Erroneous factors in the test administration and scoring procedures may also affect the interpretation of the results, and thus the validity of the test. For instance, in teacher-made tests factors like insufficient time to complete the test, unfair help to individual students, cheating during the examination and the unreliable scoring of essay-type answers might lead to lower the validity of the test. Similarly, in standardised tests, the lack of standard directions and time limits, unauthorised help to students and errors in scoring would tend to lower the validity of the test. Whether it is a teacher-made test or a standard-ised test, adverse physical and psychological conditions during testing time may affect the validity of the test.

(iv) **Factors in Pupils' Responses.** There are certain personal factors which may affect the pupils' responses to the test items. For example, the emotional disturbances, lack of motivation, afraid of test situation, etc. are some of the personal factors that might adversely affect the normal responses of the students, which ultimately affect the validity of the test.

(v) **Nature of the Group and the Criterion.** Validity is always specific to a particular group. For example, an arithmetic test based on story problems may help us in meas-uring reasoning ability in a slow group, and a combination of recall of information and computation skills in a more advanced group. There are certain factors such as age, sex, ability level, educational background and cultural background which influ-ence the test measures. Therefore, the nature of the validation group should find a mention in the test manuals.

The nature of criterion used is another important consideration while evaluating validity coefficient. For example, scores on a scientific aptitude test are likely to provide a more accu-rate prediction of achievement in an environmental study course. Other things being equal, the greater the similarity between the performance measured by the test and the performance represented in the criterion, the larger the validity coefficient.

18.6.6　Relation between Reliability and Validity

There is a close relationship between reliability and validity of the tests. These are the two dimensions of the same thing, that is, test efficiency. The following are some of the relationships between reliability and validity.

First, reliability refers to the dependability, consistency or stability of the test scores whereas validity refers to the extent to which the test truthfully measures what it purports to measure.

Second, a test is far from valid if it cannot measure a trait reliably. A reliable test should also be theoretically valid because proper item selection and elongation of tests lead to increased proportions of true variances and, hence, to enhanced common factor loadings. However, reliability does not always ensure validity in practice.

Third, reliability depends on the proportion of true variance in a test while validity depends basically on the common factor variances which, however, form a component of the true variance.

Fourth, reliability is concerned with the stability of the test scores, and thus, it is a measure of self-correlation of a test. Validity, on the other hand, is the correlation of the test with some external criteria.

Fifth, every reliable test is not necessarily a valid test. Because a test having high correlation with itself may not have equally high correlation with a criterion. On the other hand, a test to be valid has to be reliable. A test which possesses poor reliability is not expected to yield high validity. In other words, reliability is a prerequisite of validity; to be valid a test must be reliable. Thus, reliability controls validity.

Sixth, reliability depends on the test items having identical or equal difficulty levels, high internal consistency or high intercorrelations among themselves. But validity depends on test items differing in difficulty levels and low intercorrelations among test items. So, both reliability and validity may not be uniformly high for a test.

Seventh, lengthening a test increases the proportion of common factor variances and hence, the proportion of true variances also. Rise in the number of common factors, shared by the test and the criterion, increases the validity while the rise in the proportion of true variance enhances reliability. But unlike reliability, validity cannot be raised to the maximum level by the increase in test length alone.

Eighth, reliability may be low in a heterogeneous test with its items measuring different factors, but a high validity may still result from the common factors shared by the test items and the criterion. Reliability may be high in a homogeneous test with high internal consistency, but validity may often still be low due to the dearth of common factors for the test items and the criterion. In short, maximum reliability is found in case of homogeneous test items. If the test items are heterogeneous in nature, then the test has low reliability but high validity.

Ninth, validity coefficient does not exceed the square root of reliability coefficient. In other words, the validity of a test may not be higher than the reliability index.

Tenth, we cannot claim that a reliable test is also a valid one. This claim may or may not be true. A test measures consistently, but it may not measure what it intends to measure. For example, a wall-clock consistently measures time 10 minutes faster than the actual time; this clock may be reliable but not valid. Similarly, when a man wrongly reports his date of birth consistently, it may be reliable but not valid. On the other hand, a valid test is always reliable. If a test truthfully measures what it purports to measure is both valid and reliable. For example, if the wall-clock correctly measures time consistently, it is both reliable and valid. Similarly, when a man truly reports his date of birth consistently, it is both valid and reliable. Thus, a valid test always ensures the reliability, but not the vice-versa.

Tests should possess sufficient validities along with reasonable degrees of reliability. A test serves no purpose if it gives consistent results on repetition, but fails to measure the desired trait. Both reliability and validity may be reasonably ensured by placing a single test with a test battery of heterogeneous type, but consisting of individual tests of homogeneous nature.

18.7 Factor Analysis

Factor analysis is by far the most often used multivariate technique of research studies, specially pertaining to social and behavioural sciences. It is a technique applicable when there is a systematic interdependence among a set of observed or manifest variables and the researcher is interested in finding out something more fundamental or latent which creates this commonality. For instance, we might have data, say, about an individual's income, education, occupation and dwelling area, and want to infer from these some factor (such as, social class) which summarises the commonality of all the said four variables. The technique used for such purposes is generally described as factor analysis. Factor analysis, thus, seeks to resolve a large set of measured variables in terms of relatively few categories, known as factors.

Factor analysis is the right statistical procedure for construct validity of tests. If scores of a test correlate highly with scores of another similar and already validated test or criterion measuring the same attribute, the two tests may have common factors shared by their scores (convergent validity). The poor correlation between the scores of two tests, measuring dissimilar attributes, may result from their poor loading with common factors (discriminant validity). Thus, factor analysis can explain the intercorrelations between tests by analysing the common factors.

Factor analysis identifies the factors or psychological components in a test, assesses their relative independence, correlates them individually to a criterion for determining their individual contributions to the total test scores and analyses the weights of factors responsible for the common variance of scores in two tests. It, thus, searches for common factors, shared by two tests and is responsible for their correlation. Common factors can explain the intercorrelations between a group of tests. For example, tests for arithmetic problems, number completion, addition and multiplication may show high positive correlation with each other due to a common 'numerical factor' in all of them; but these tests show low and insignificant correlations with vocabulary and sentence completion tests, loaded with a 'verbal factor' instead of the 'numerical' one. *Factor validity* is given by the loading of a test with factors and its correlation with each factor. So, factor analysis validates a test in the form of factor loading or intercorrelation between each test and the factor. It is usually applied to the data of interdependent variables, not differentiated into dependent and independent ones. It identifies the most specific ability required for a particular task and reduces the number of original test items to a smaller number of common factors sufficient to explain the correlation between the tests.

A good criterion can be ensured by its factor analysis. This intercorrelates criterion measures among themselves as also correlates them with validated tests of anticipated common factors. Investigations of factor loadings of the criterion help to choose the most relevant and representative criterion, to include the most predictive tests in a test battery, to give weights to criteria for combinations and to detect the insufficiency of a proposed test battery in predicting any factor of the criterion.

18.7.1   Theorems of Factor Theory

Of the numerous theorems of factor theory, theorems I and II suffice to explain validity.

1. **Theorem I of factor theory**. True variance (S_∞^2) of a test score is the sum of (a) *common factor variances* ($s_a^2, s_b^2, \ldots, s_k^2$) for the common factors ($a, b, \ldots, k$) shared by many tests and (b) a *specific factor variance* (s_s^2) of the given test, which is shared only by its parallel and equivalent forms.

$$s_\infty^2 = (s_a^2 + s_b^2 + \cdots + s_k^2) + s_s^2$$

   The total variance (s_t^2) equals the sum of s_∞^2 and the error variance (s_e^2). Where a_x^2, b_x^2, etc. are the proportions of s_t^2 due to the common factors; s_x^2 or specificity is the proportion of s_s^2 in s_t^2; and e_x^2 is the proportion of s_e^2 in s_t^2. Thus,

$$s_t^2 = s_\infty^2 + s_e^2$$
$$= (s_a^2 + s_b^2 + \cdots + s_k^2 + s_s^2) + s_e^2$$
$$\text{or} \quad \frac{s_t^2}{s_t^2} = \left(\frac{s_a^2}{s_t^2} + \frac{s_b^2}{s_t^2} + \cdots + \frac{s_k^2}{s_t^2} + \frac{s_s^2}{s_t^2} \right) + \frac{s_e^2}{s_t^2}$$
$$\text{or} \quad 1.00 = (a_x^2 + b_x^2 + \cdots + k_x^2 + s_x^2) + e_x^2$$
$$\text{or} \quad 1.00 - e_x^2 = (a_x^2 + b_x^2 + \cdots + k_x^2) + s_x^2$$
$$\text{or} \quad \frac{s_\infty^2}{s_t^2} = (a_x^2 + b_x^2 + \cdots + k_x^2) + s_x^2$$

   Where h_x^2 or *communality* is the sum of proportions of common factor variances in the test scores, and u_x^2 or *uniqueness* is the sum of proportions of specific and error variances in the test scores,

$$r_{tt} = \frac{s_\infty^2}{s_t^2} = a_x^2 + b_x^2 + \cdots + k_x^2 + s_x^2$$
$$\text{or} \quad r_{tt} - s_x^2 = h_x^2 = a_x^2 + b_x^2 + \cdots + k_x^2$$
$$\therefore h_x^2 = \frac{s_\infty^2}{s_t^2} - s_x^2 = \frac{s_\infty^2}{s_t^2} - \frac{s_s^2}{s_t^2} \quad \text{and}$$
$$u_x^2 = 1 - h_x^2 = s_x^2 + e_x^2$$

   Factor loadings are the square roots of the proportions of common factor variances; each factor loading, viz., a_x, b_x, etc., is the correlation coefficient between the relevant common factor and the total test score. This correlation coefficient, called the *factor validity*, is an estimate of the capacity of the test to measure the trait underlying the given factor.

2. **Theorem II of factor theory**. *Validity coefficient* is the correlation coefficient (r_{xy} or r_{yx}) between the test (X) and either an external criterion or another validated test (Y). It equals the sum of cross products of common factor loadings of X and Y, because r_{xy} results from common factors shared by them and amounts to 0 in absence of such common factors. Construct validity coefficient can thus be computed from factorial validities or common factor loadings. Thus,

$$r_{xy} \text{ or } r_{yx} = a_x a_y + b_x b_y + \cdots + k_x k_y$$

18.7.2 Basic Concepts in Factor Analysis

Before going to the factor analysis in detail, one should properly understand the following basic terms relating to factor analysis.

(i) **Factor.** A factor is an underlying dimension that account for several observed variables. There can be one or more factors, depending upon the nature of the study and the number of variables involved in it.

(ii) **Factor-loadings.** Factor-loadings are those values which explain how closely the variables are related to each one of the factors discovered. They are also known as factor-variable correlations. In fact, factor loadings work as key to understanding what the factors mean. It is the absolute size (rather than the signs, plus or minus) of the loadings that is important in the interpretation of a factor.

(iii) **Communality (h^2).** Communality, symbolised as h^2, shows how much of each variable is counted for by the underlying factor(s) taken together. A high value of communality means that not much of the variable is left over after whatever the factors represent is taken into consideration. It is worked out in respect of each variable as under :

h^2 of the ith variable = (ith factor loading of factor A)^2 + (ith factor loading of factor B)^2 + $\cdots$

(iv) **Eigen value.** When we take the sum of squared values of factor loadings relating to a factor, then such sum is referred to as Eigen value or latent root. Eigen value indicates the relative importance of each factor in accounting for the particular set of variables being analysed.

(v) **Total sum of squares.** When eigen values of all factors are totalled, the resulting value is termed as the total sum of squares. This value, when divided by the number of variables (involved in the study) results in an index that shows how the particular solution accounts for what all the variables taken together represent. If the variables are all very different from each other, this index will be low. If they fall into one or more highly redundant groups, and if the extracted factors account for all the groups, the index will then approach unity.

(vi) **Rotation.** Different rotations reveal different structures in the data. If the factors are independent, orthogonal rotation is done, and if the factors are correlated, an oblique rotation is made. Communality for each variable will remain undisturbed regardless of rotation but the eigen values will change as a result of rotation.

(vii) **Factor scores.** Factor score represents the degree to which each respondent gets high scores on the group of items that load high on each factor. Factor scores can help explain what the factors mean.

18.7.3 Purpose of Factor Analysis

The following are some of the important purposes of factor analysis.

(i) The purpose of factor analysis is the orderly simplification of a number of interrelated measures. As a statistical technique it reduces a large number of variables called factors. A factor is a hypothetical construct underlying performance on a cluster of tests. The input measure for factor analysis is an intercorrelation matrix.

(ii)   The purpose of rotation is to achieve simple structure, that is, the cluster of tests loading on different factors appear to be clearer as a result of which the factor naming process becomes easier.

(iii) The purpose of factor analysis may be exploratory (creating hypotheses) or confirmatory (testing hypotheses).

(iv)   Factor analysis has been mainly used in developing psychological tests (such as, IQ tests, personality tests and the like) in the realm of psychology. In marketing, this technique has been used to look at media readership profiles of people.

18.7.4   Merits and Limitations of Factor Analysis

As a multivariate technique, factor analysis has the following advantages and disadvantages.

18.7.4.1   *Merits*

The main merits of factor analysis can be stated thus:

(i)   The technique of factor analysis is quite useful when we want to condense and simplify the multivariate data.

(ii)   The technique is helpful in pointing out important and interesting relationships among observed data that were there all the time, but not easy to see from the data alone.

(iii) The technique can reveal the latent factors (i.e., underlying factors not directly observed) that determine relationships among several variables concerning a research study. For example, if people are asked to rate different cold drinks (say, Limca, Nova-Cola, Gold Spot and so on) according to preference, a factor analysis may reveal some salient characteristics of cold drinks that underlie relative preferences.

(iv)   The technique may be used in the context of empirical clustering of products, media or people, that is, for providing a classification scheme when data scored on various rating scales have to be grouped together.

18.7.4.2   *Limitations*

One should also be aware of several limitations of factor analysis. Important ones are as follows:

(i)   Factor analysis, like all multivariate techniques, involves laborious computations involving heavy cost burden. In spite of the computer facilities now-a-days, large factor analyses are still found to be quite expensive both in terms of time and money.

(ii)   The results of a single-factor analysis are considered generally less reliable and dependable for very often a factor analysis starts with a set of imperfect data. 'The factors are nothing but blurred averages, difficult to be identified.' To overcome these difficulties, it has been realised that analysis should at least be done twice. If we get more or less similar results from all rounds of analyses, our confidence concerning such results increases.

(iii) Factor analysis is a complicated decision tool that can be used only when one has thorough knowledge and enough experience of handling this tool. Even then, at times it may not work well and may even disappoint the user.

To conclude, we can state that in spite of all the said limitations, when it works well, factor analysis helps the investigator make sense of large bodies of intertwined data. When it works unusually well, it also points out some interesting relationships that might not have been obvious from examination of the input data alone.

18.7.5   Important Methods of Factor Analysis

The important methods of factor analysis are: (a) the centroid method, (b) the principal components (P.C.) method and (c) the maximum likelihood (ML) method, which are discussed further.

(i) **The centroid method.** This method of factor analysis was developed by L.L. Thurstone (1948). This method tends to maximise the sum of loadings, disregarding signs; it is the method which extracts the largest sum of absolute loadings for each factor in turn. It is defined by the linear combinations in which all weights are either +1.0 or –1.0. The main merit of this method is that it is relatively simple, can be easily understood, and involves simpler computations.

This method starts with the computation of a matrix of correlation, R, wherein unities are placed in the diagonal spaces. The product-moment formula is used for working out the correlation coefficients. If the correlation matrix so obtained happens to be positive manifold, the centroid method requires that the weights for all variables be +1.0. In other words, the variables are not weighted; they are simply summed. But in case the correlation matrix is not a positive manifold, then reflections must be made before the first centroid factor is obtained.

(ii) **The principal component method.** The P.C. method of factor analysis was developed by H. Hotelling (1933). This method seeks to maximise the sum of squared loadings of each factor extracted in turn. Accordingly, P.C. factor explains more variance than would the loadings obtained from any other method of factoring.

The aim of the P.C. method is the construction out of a given set of variables X_j's $(j=1, 2, \ldots, k)$ of new variables (p_i) called P.C. which are linear combinations of the X_i. For example, $p_i = a_{11}X_1 + a_{12}X_2 + \cdots + a_{1k}X_k$. The a_{ij} are called loadings and are worked out in such a way that the extracted P.C. satisfy two conditions: (a) P.C. are uncorrelated (orthogonal) and (b) the first P.C. (p_1) has the maximum variance, the second P.C. (p_2) has the next maximum variance and so on.

(iii) **Maximum likelihood method.** The ML method consists in obtaining sets of factor loadings successively in such a way that each, in turn, explains as much as possible of the population correlation matrix as estimated from the sample correlation matrix. If Rs stands for the correlation matrix actually obtained from the data in a sample, Rp stands for the correlation matrix that would be obtained if the entire population were tested, then the ML method seeks to extrapolate what is known from Rs in the best possible way to estimate Rp. Thus, the ML method is a statistical approach in which one maximises some relationship between the sample data and population from which the sample was drawn.

18.8   Standardisation and Norms

The final stage in test construction consists of the standardisation of the test. A test has been standardised if (a) its items have been properly analysed and chosen, (b) procedures of administration and scoring have been made uniform, (c) instructions for its application and also the scoring keys have been provided and (d) norms have been established and tabulated for interpreting the test scores. Thus, a standardised test is one that has been carefully constructed by experts in the light of acceptable objectives or purposes; procedure for administering, scoring and interpreting scores are specified in detail so that no matter who gives the test or where it may be given, the results should be comparable; and norms or average for different age or grade levels have been pre-determined.

18.8.1   Characteristics of Standardised Tests

The following are some of the important characteristics of standardised tests.

(i)   These tests consist of items of high quality. The items are pre-tested and selected on the basis of difficulty value, discrimination power and relationship to clearly defined objectives in behavioural terms.

(ii)   The directions for administering, exact time limit and scoring are precisely stated so that any person can administer and score the test.

(iii) Norms based on representative groups of individuals are provided as an aid for interpreting the test scores. These norms are frequently based on age, grade, sex, etc.

(iv)   Information needed for judging the value of the test is provided. Before the test becomes available, the reliability and validity are established.

(v)   A manual of the test is supplied that explains the purposes and uses of the test, describes briefly how it was constructed, provides specific directions for administering, scoring and interpreting results, specifies time limits, contains tables of norms and summarises available research data on the test.

18.8.2   Norm

A raw score can be made meaningful and significant by comparing it with a standard. For example, numerical scores of 125, 134 and 142 in the US Army Alpha Group Intelligence Test indicate only the relative position of the tested individuals and acquire real significance only when judged against the score distribution of a representative sample. To achieve this, the establishment of a *norm* is essential for each sample.

Scores on psychological tests are most commonly interpreted by reference to norms that represent the test performance of the standardisation sample. Norm is nothing but an uniform frame of reference. Norms are thus empirically established by determining what persons in a representative group actually do on the test. Any individual's raw score is then referred to the distribution of scores obtained by the standardisation sample, to discover where he/she falls in that distribution.

Thus, a *norm* is the average score of a representative group in terms of a convenient scale of converted or transformed scores. In order to ascertain more precisely the individual's exact position with reference to the standardisation sample, the raw score is converted into some relative measure. These derived scores are designed to serve a dual function or purpose. First, they indicate the individual's relative standing in the normative sample and, thus, permit an evaluation of his/her performance in reference to other persons. Second, they provide comparable measures that permit a direct comparison of the individual's performance on different tests. Derived scores can be expressed in the same units and referred to the same or to closely similar normative samples for different tests. The individual's relative performance in many different functions can, thus, be compared.

The essential criterion for establishing norms is the representative nature of the sample rather than its size. Norms are limited to the particular group or population from which the representative sample was drawn when establishing the norm. Local norms, group norms, regional norms or national norms are established separately according to the nature of the sample. Even the established norms may get outdated and need updating.

Summary

In this chapter, we have discussed the topic of psychological test construction. Under this topic we have presented the subtopics that include: principles of test construction, power and speed tests, item analysis, reliability of a test, validity of a test, factor analysis, standardisation and norms.

The important principles of test construction may be summarised as: area to be assessed, selection of test items, item analysis, arrangement of test items, estimation of reliability, estimation of validity, standardisation and establishment of norms.

Psychological tests belong to two types—power tests and speed tests. In power tests, the test items are usually grouped according to the types of contents and are arranged serially in an increasing order of difficulty. Enough time is given to enable at least 75% of the subjects being tested to attempt all the items. In speed tests, all the test items are of uniform difficulty level, and the subjects being tested have to answer the test items within a stipulated time which is so short that none can answer all the items in time.

The final selection of test items should be done through item analysis. It is defined as a technique for analysing items included in a test with regard to the indexes of *item characteristics*. The four basic item characteristics needed to predict the major characteristics of a test are: item difficulty, item discrimination, item reliability and item validity.

Reliability is one of the four basic characteristics of a standardised psychological test, and other characteristics are validity, objectivity and efficiency. By reliability of a test we mean how dependable, faithful or trustworthy the test is. A test is considered to be reliable if it yields consistent results in its successive administrations. The four methods of estimating the reliability of a test are: test–retest method, parallel-forms/alternate-forms method, split-half method and Kuder–Richardson method. If we want to determine the internal consistency of a test, then it is preferable to use the split-half method and Kuder–Richardson method. To estimate the predictive value of a test, the test–retest method and parallel-forms method are preferable. The factors influencing the test reliability are broadly categorised into two groups, such as, intrinsic factors and extrinsic factors. The intrinsic factors include the length of the test, homogeneity of items, difficulty level of items, discrimination value of items, test instructions, range of scores, consistency of scores, item selection and reliability of the score. The extrinsic factors, on the other hand, include range of age, time interval between testing, effects of memory and practice, group variability, guessing and chance errors, environmental conditions and momentary fluctuations. The characteristics of reliability, errors of measurement and SEM have also been discussed.

Validity refers to truthfulness. Any test which is truthful, well based and serves the right purpose is valid. An index of validity of a test refers to the extent to which it measures what it purports to measure. The three basic types of validity are: content validity, criterion-related validity/empirical validity and construct validity. Content validity includes face validity, logical/sampling validity and factorial validity. Similarly, the criterion-related validity or empirical validity includes predictive validity, concurrent validity and cross-validation. The five methods of estimating the validity of a test are: correlation coefficient method, cross-validation method, expectancy table method, item analysis method and method of intercorrelation of items and factor analysis. A large number of factors affecting the validity of a test are grouped under five broad categories that include: factors in the test itself, functioning content and teaching procedure, factors in the administration and scoring, factors in pupils' responses and nature of the group and the criterion. There is a close relationship between reliability and validity of the tests. These are the two dimensions of the same thing, that is, test efficiency. We have also discussed in detail the characteristics of test validity.

Factor analysis is by far the most often used multivariate technique of research studies, especially pertaining to social and behavioural sciences. The basic concepts in factor analysis are: factor, factor-loadings, communality, eigen value, total sum of squares, rotation and factor scores. The important purposes of factor analysis are: (a) the orderly simplification of a number of interrelated measures, (b) the purpose of rotation is to achieve simple structure, (c) purpose may be exploratory (creating hypotheses) or confirmatory (testing hypotheses) and (d) factor analysis has been used in developing psychological tests (e.g., IQ tests, personality tests and aptitude tests) in the realm of psychology. The important methods of factor analysis are: (a) the centroid method, (b) the P.C. method and (c) the ML method. We have also discussed the merits and limitations of factor analysis.

The final stage in test construction consists of the standardisation of test and the establishment of norms. A test has been standardised if: (a) its items have been properly analysed and chosen, (b) procedures of administration and scoring have been made uniform, (c) instructions for its application and also scoring keys have been provided and (d) norms have been established and tabulated for interpreting the test scores. Thus, a standardised test is one that has been carefully constructed by experts in the light of acceptable objectives or purposes, whose procedures for administering, scoring and interpreting scores are specified in detail so that no matter who gives the test or where it may be given, the results should be comparable; and whose norms or average-for different age or grade levels have been pre-determined.

Scores on psychological tests are most commonly interpreted by reference to norms that represent the test performance of the standardised sample. Norm is nothing but a uniform frame of reference. Norms are, thus, empirically established by determining what persons in a representative group actually do on the test. Any individual's raw score is then referred to the distribution of scores obtained by the standardisation sample, to discover where he/she falls in that distribution. Thus, a *norm* is the average score of a representative group in terms of a convenient scale of converted or transformed scores. The essential criterion for establishing norms is the representative nature of the sample rather than its size. Norms are limited to the particular group or population from which a representative sample is drawn when establishing the norm. Local norms, group norms, regional norms or national norms are established separately according to the nature of the sample. Even the established norms may get outdated and need updating.

Key Terms

- Alternate-forms method
- Bi-factor theory
- Centroid method
- Coefficient of equivalence
- Coefficient of internal consistency
- Coefficient of stability
- Concurrent validity

- Content validity
- Construct validity
- Convergent validation
- Criterion-related validity
- Cross validation
- Discriminant validation
- Errors of measurement

- Estimation of reliability
- Estimation of validity
- Extrinsic factors
- Face validity
- Factor analysis
- Factorial validity
- Heterogeneity of behaviour domain
- Hoyt reliability
- Index of discrimination
- Intrinsic factors
- Item analysis
- Item-criterion correlation
- Item difficulty
- Item discrimination
- Item reliability
- Item validity
- Interitem consistency
- Kudder–Richardson method
- Kudder–Richardson formula 20
- Logical/sampling validity
- ML method
- Multi-factor theory

- Multitrait-multimethod matrix
- Norms
- Parallel-forms method
- Power tests
- Predictive validity
- P.C. method
- Random errors
- Rational equivalence method
- Reliability coefficient
- Reliability of a test
- Sampling theory
- Scorer reliability
- Spearman–Brown prophecy formula
- Speed tests
- Split-half method
- standardisation
- Standard errors of measurement
- Systematic errors
- Test-retest method
- Two-factor theory
- Validity of a test

Questions and Problems

1. What do you mean by a test? Discuss the principles of test construction.
2. Differentiate between power and speed tests.
3. What is item analysis? Discuss the basic item characteristics. What facts should be taken care of prior to the application of item analysis?
4. Write notes on:
   (a) Need for item analysis
   (b) Item difficulty
5. What is item discrimination? Discuss about the estimators of the discriminatory power of the test items.
6. What is index of discrimination? How can it be determined? Explain with examples.
7. Discuss the steps involved in the construction of a test.
8. Explain the meaning of the reliability of a test. Discuss the characteristics of test reliability.

9. What is test reliability? Explain the errors of measurement, and also the SEM.
10. Explain the various methods of estimating test reliability.
11. What do you mean by test reliability? How is it determined?
12. Differentiate between the test–retest method and split-half method of determining test reliability.
13. Explain the factors affecting the reliability of a test.
14. Explain the meaning of validity of a test. Discuss the characteristics of test validity.
15. Briefly discuss the various types of validity.
16. What is content validity? Briefly discuss its nature, specific procedures, application, advantages and limitations.
17. What are the kinds of content validity? Explain each of them.
18. What do you mean by the criterion-related validity? How can the relationship between test and criterion performance be expressed?
19. Analyse the various kinds of empirical validity.
20. What is construct validity? Analyse its features and techniques.
21. What is test validity? Discuss the methods of estimating the validity of a test.
22. Define test validity. Explain the factors that affect the validity of a test.
23. Define reliability and validity of a test. How is validity related to reliability?
24. Explain the relationships between reliability and validity.
25. What is factor analysis? Explain theorems I and II of factor theory.
26. What is the purpose of factor analysis? Analyse the basic concepts in factor analysis.
27. Define factor analysis. Discuss its merits and limitations.
28. Examine some of the important methods of factoring with reference to their relative merits.
29. Write notes on the following:
    (a) Characteristics of standardised tests
    (b) Norm
30. The following data indicate the number of persons passed the items in both upper group and lower group out of 50 persons in each group. Find out the index of discrimination (D) for each item.

Item	Upper Group	Lower Group
1	50	30
2	45	25
3	30	35
4	25	25
5	10	0

31. For a test r_{tt} and σ_t were found to be 0.80 and 10, respectively. Find out the values of σ_∞^2 and σ_e^2, their proportional contribution to σ_t^2 and the SEM of the test.

32. (a) The achievement test scores have a SD=12 and r_{tt}=0.85. Find the SEM.

   (b) The split-half reliability of the verbal and nonverbal IQ test scores are 0.95 and 0.92, respectively. The IQ scores are expressed on a scale with a mean of 100 and SD of 10. Find out the SE_D.

33. (a) The split-half reliability for a 50-item test is 0.90. What is the reliability for the full-length of the test?

   (b) A certain 25-item test has a reliability coefficient of 0.72. To this are added 75 similar and well-made items. What is the reliability of the new test?

34. (a) Suppose that a test is made of 150 items. The author of the test decides to shorten it to 50 items. The reliability of the original test is 0.93. What would be the reliability for the shortened test?

   (b) A certain test has a reliability coefficient of 0.60. This test is made up of 20 items. How many well-made and similar items will have to be added to increase the reliability to 0.90?

35. (a) If a test consisting of 30 items has a reliability coefficient of 0.50, how long it should be made to have a reliability coefficient of 0.80?

   (b) In a test consisting of 25 items, the sum of the item variance (Σpq) and the SD of all the test scores are 10.58 and 7.5, respectively. Calculate the coefficient of internal consistency of the test by Kuder–Richardson formula 20.

36. An achievement test has validity coefficient of 0.60 between the test scores and the grade performance, and a reliability coefficient of 0.50.

   (a) What will be the validity of the test if it is lengthened thrice of its original length?

   (b) How many times it should be lengthened to get a validity of 0.80?

37. (a) A certain test has a reliability coefficient of 0.92 and a validity coefficient of 0.48 with criterion Y. The standard deviation of this criterion is 10.2 and that of the test is 9.6. Calculate the standard error of estimate when predicting Y from X.

   (b) Calculate the index of forecasting the efficiency for this validity coefficient. What does it mean?

38. Fill in the blanks:

   (i) An interval scale of measurement has an _____ zero point instead of a true zero point.

   (ii) A ratio scale of measurement has a _____ zero point.

   (iii) Anastasi says that a psychological test is essentially an _____ and _____ measure of a sample of behaviour.

   (iv) In the opinion of Cronbach, a test is a _____ procedure for comparing the behaviour of two or more persons.

   (v) Test items are selected by _____.

   (vi) Item analysis is used to determine the _____ and _____ of each test item.

    (vii) The test items are generally arranged in a _____ difficulty level.

   (viii) Reliability of a test refers to the _____ of its results obtained on its repeated application on the same sample under the same or identical conditions.

    (ix) Validity of a test refers to the extent to which it measures what it _____ to measure.

     (x) The test scores should be statistically treated to establish the _____.

39. Write whether the following statements are True or False.

     (i) In power tests, the test items are arranged serially in an increasing order of difficulty.

    (ii) In speed tests, all the test items are of uniform difficulty level.

   (iii) In power tests, there is a short time limit and the subject has to answer the test items within that stipulated time.

   (iv) In speed tests enough time is given to enable at least 75% of the subjects being tested to answer all the items.

    (v) Item difficulty is one of the four basic item characteristics.

   (vi) Item reliability refers to the proportion of persons answering each item correctly.

   (vii) The reliability coefficient obtained by split-half method is only for half-length of the items of the test.

  (viii) The reliability coefficient obtained by using the test–retest method is known as the coefficient of equivalence.

   (ix) Validity of a test is a measure of constant error.

    (x) Face validity is a kind of content validity.

40. Find out the correct answer from among the four alternatives.

     (i) Coefficient of internal consistency of test items can be measured by:

       (a) Test-retest method   (b) Parallel-forms method

       (c) Split-half method   (d) None of the above

    (ii) Spearman–Brown prophecy formula determines the reliability coefficient for the:

       (a) Half-length of the items of the test

       (b) Full-length of the items of the test

       (c) Quarter-length of the items of the test

       (d) None of the above

   (iii) Validity is a measure of:

       (a) Constant error   (b) Variable error

       (c) Sampling error   (d) None of the above

   (iv) A factor which is specific in one variable is called:

       (a) A general factor   (b) A group factor

       (c) An individual factor   (d) None of the above

(v) The two-factor theory of factor analysis was developed by:

   (a) Thurstone   (b) Spearman
   (c) Holzinger   (d) None of the above

(vi) Predictive validity is a kind of:

   (a) Content validity   (b) Criterion-related validity
   (c) Construct validity   (d) None of the above

(vii) Reliability and validity are the two dimensions of the:

   (a) Test efficiency   (b) Test inefficiency
   (c) Test sufficiency   (d) None of the above

(viii) Heterogeneous test items lead to:

   (a) Low reliability but high validity
   (b) Low reliability but low validity
   (c) High reliability but low validity
   (d) None of the above

(ix) Factor analysis is the right statistical procedure for:

   (a) Content validity of tests   (b) Empirical validity of tests
   (c) Construct validity of tests (d) None of the above

(x) The sum of squared values of factor loadings relating to a factor is referred to as:

   (a) Eigen value   (b) Communality
   (c) Factor score   (d) None of the above

Answers to Exercises

Chapter 1

10. (a), (b), (c), (d), (e) and (k)—Continuous variables;
    (f), (g), (h), (i), (j) and (l)—discrete variables

11. (a), (i) and (j)—interval scale
    (b), (e), (f) and (g)—ratio scale
    (c), (d), (k) and (l)—nominal scale
    (h)—ordinal scale

12. (i) Data, inferences
    (iii) Measure
    (v) Representative
    (vii) Decreases
    (ix) Ordinal

    (ii) Infinite, finite (or finite, infinite)
    (iv) Infinite
    (vi) Probability
    (viii) Non-probability (or non-random)
    (x) Abstract

13. (i) T
    (iii) F
    (v) F
    (vii) F
    (ix) T

    (ii) T
    (iv) T
    (vi) T
    (viii) T
    (x) T

14. (i) a
    (iii) b
    (v) c
    (vii) c
    (ix) b

    (ii) c
    (iv) b
    (vi) a
    (viii) a
    (x) a

Chapter 2

16.

Class Interval	Frequency	Cumulative Frequency
95–99	2	40
90–94	2	38
85–89	4	36
80–84	6	32
75–79	5	26
70–74	4	21
65–69	5	17
60–64	2	12
55–59	2	10
50–54	4	8
45–49	1	4
40–44	2	3
35–39	1	1
Total	40	

17.

Class Interval	Exact Limits	Midpoints
95–99	94.5–99.5	97
90–94	89.5–94.5	92
85–89	84.5–89.5	87
80–84	79.5–84.5	82
75–79	74.5–79.5	77
70–74	69.5–74.5	72
65–69	64.5–69.5	67
60–64	59.5–64.5	62
55–59	54.5–59.5	57
50–54	49.5–54.5	52
45–49	44.5–49.5	47
40–44	39.5–44.5	42
35–39	34.5–39.5	37

18.

Class Interval	Frequency	Cumulative Frequency	Cumulative Percentage Frequency
17–18	3	50	100
15–16	7	47	94
13–14	1	40	80
11–12	5	39	78
9–10	6	34	68
7–8	6	28	56
5–6	8	22	44
3–4	8	14	28
1–2	6	6	12
	$N=50$		

26.

Class Interval	Frequency	Cumulative Frequency	Cumulative Percentage Frequency
85–89	2	40	100
80–84	2	38	95
75–79	4	36	90
70–74	6	32	80
65–69	5	26	65
60–64	4	21	52.5
55–59	5	17	42.5
50–54	2	12	30
45–49	2	10	25
40–44	4	8	20
35–39	1	4	10
30–34	2	3	7.5
25–29	1	1	2.5
	$N=40$		

27.

Score	f	Score	f	Score	f	Score	f
90	3	80	0	70	4	60	1
89	0	79	0	69	0		
88	3	78	2	68	3		
87	0	77	0	67	0		
86	0	76	1	66	0		
85	2	75	3	65	2		
84	0	74	0	64	1		
83	0	73	0	63	2		
82	0	72	2	62	0		
81	0	71	0	61	1		

31.
   (i) Data
   (ii) Numerical
   (iii) Continuous scores, discrete scores (or discrete scores, continuous scores)
   (iv) Inclusive, exclusive (or exclusive, inclusive)
   (v) Qualitative (or descriptive)
   (vi) Quantitative
   (vii) Discrete (or discontinuous), continuous
   (viii) Coordinate
   (ix) Abscissa
   (x) Midpoints

32.
   (i) T   (ii) T
   (iii) F   (iv) F
   (v) T   (vi) T
   (vii) T   (viii) T
   (ix) F   (x) T

33.
   (i) b   (ii) a
   (iii) c   (iv) b
   (v) a   (vi) b
   (vii) c   (viii) a
   (ix) c   (x) b

Chapter 3

11. (a) Mean   (b) Mode
     (c) Median
12. (a) $\bar{X} + a$ (b) $\bar{X} - a$
     (c) $\bar{X}a$ (d) $\bar{X}/a$

13.   (a) Positively skewed   (b) Negatively skewed
     (c) Symmetrical
14.   (a) $\bar{X} = 2.54$ hours per day   (b) Median = 2.7 hours per day
     (c) Mode = 0 hours per day
15.   (a) The mean, because there are no extreme scores.
     (b) The mean, because there are no extreme scores.
     (c) The median, because the distribution contains an extreme score (i.e., 25).
16.   (a) $\bar{X} = 3.56$, Median = 3, Mode = 2
     (b) $\bar{X} = 22.75$, Median = 24.5, Mode = 30
     (c) $\bar{X} = 3.03$, Median = 2.70, No Mode
17. Mean = 2.69, Median = 2.5, Mode = 2
18.   (a) 96   (b) 100
     (c) 9   (d) 11.11
19. For the original sample, $\Sigma X = \bar{X} n = 23 \times 10 = 230$
    After the score is removed $\Sigma X = \bar{X} n = 25 \times 9 = 225$
    The score that was removed is $X = 5$.
20.   (a) $\bar{X} = 120$ (the old mean is multiplied by 6)
     (b) $\bar{X} = 25$ (the old mean is increased by 5)
21.   (a) $\bar{X} = 19.88$, Median = 20.5, Mode = Nil (no mode)
     (b) $\bar{X} = 15.63$, Median = 14, Mode = 14
     (c) $\bar{X} = 20.38$, Median = 21, Mode = Nil (no mode)
     (d) $\bar{X} = 10.78$, Median = 10, Mode = 10
22. $\bar{X} = 66.58$, Median = 67.36, Mode = 68.92
23. $\bar{X} = 42.80$, Median = 42.85, Mode = 42.95
24.   (a) $\bar{X} = 106.00$, Median = 105.83, Mode = 105.49
     (b) $\bar{X} = 55.43$, Median = 55.17, Mode = 54.65
25.   (i)   Location   (ii)   Middle (or mid)
    (iii) Average   (iv)   10
     (v)   7.5   (vi)   22
   (vii) Gravity   (viii) Positional
    (ix) Frequencies (or concentration)   (x)   Coincide (or fall)
26.   (i)   T   (ii)   F
    (iii) T   (iv)   T
     (v) F   (vi)   T
   (vii) F   (viii) F
    (ix) T   (x)   T
27.   (i)   a   (ii)   b
    (iii) c   (iv)   a
     (v) b   (vi)   c
   (vii) b   (viii) c
    (ix) c   (x)   a

Chapter 4

11. (a) Quartile deviation   (b) Quartile deviation
     (c) Standard deviation   (d) Range
     (e) Average deviation

12. (a) s remains the same   (b) s remains the same
     (c) s is multiplied by 'a'   (d) s is divided by 'a'

13. (a) Range=6, s=2.04, s^2=4.16   (b) Range=24, s=10.76, s^2=115.78
     (c) Range=9.1, s=3.64, s^2=13.25

14. (a) s=1.86
     (b) s=11.96. Because the standard deviation is sensitive to extreme scores and 35 is an extreme score.

15. (a) Distribution b is most variable, followed by distribution a and then distribution c.
     (b) For distribution b, s=11.37; for distribution a, s=3.16; and for distribution c, s=0.

16. (a) 17   (b) 4.67
     (c) 6.26   (d) 39.19

17. 1485

18. 12.50

19. (a) 500   (b) 0.80

20. m_2=20.80, m_3=0, m_4=620.80, g_1=0, g_2=–1.57

21. AD=3.9, SD=4.68

22. AD=2.04

23. (a) SD=5.02, Q=3.10   (b) SD=13.55, Q=9.79
     (c) SD=11.84, Q=7.92

24. Group I=0.95; Group II=0.00

25. Mean=68.10, Median=68.75, Mode=70.05, Q=9.01, SD=12.50

26. (i) Dispersion (or variation)   (ii) Variability
     (iii) 40   (iv) Range
     (v) Inter-quartile range   (vi) Median
     (vii) Standard deviation   (viii) 5.65
     (ix) 8   (x) 60

27. (i) T   (ii) F
     (iii) T   (iv) F
     (v) T   (vi) F
     (vii) T   (viii) T
     (ix) T   (x) T

28. (i) a   (ii) b
     (iii) c   (iv) a
     (v) b   (vi) c
     (vii) a   (viii) b
     (ix) a   (x) a

Chapter 5

5.

	(a)	(b)
Q_1	20.3	90.40
Q_3	29.3	108.14
D_1	15.8	82.29
P_{90}	33.6	115.75

6.

		I	II
(a)	P_{30}	24.13	11.53
	P_{70}	30.50	18.37
	P_{90}	34.40	24.80
(b)	PR of 14	3	45
	PR of 20	17	79
	PR of 26	40	97

7.

Students	A	B	C	D	E
Scores	42	60	31	50	71
PR	30	70	10	50	90

8. PRs are 1st=97.5; 5th=77.5; 10th=52.5; 15th=27.5; 20th=2.5

9. (a) Sonali's PR in mathematics is 81.67 or 82. Her PR in English is 89.
   (b) Sonali's rank must be 4, approximately.
   (c) A PR of 65 means that 65% made scores below him.

10. (b)

	Group A		Group B	
	Graphical Values	Calculated Values	Graphical Values	Calculated Values
P_{30}	46.0	45.81	48.50	48.69
P_{60}	56.0	55.77	59.75	59.85
P_{90}	74.0	73.64	75.50	74.81

(c)   In Group A, PR = 58; in Group B, PR = 47.

(d)   A PR of 70 in Group A corresponds to a PR of 62 in Group B.

11.   (i)   Positional   (ii)   4
      (iii)   10   (iv)   100, centile
      (v) Q_2, D_5, P_{50} (vi) P_{25}, P_{75}
      (vii) P_{100}, D_{10} (viii) P_{10}
      (ix)   Position   (x)   Position, 100

12.   (i)   T   (ii)   F
      (iii)   F   (iv)   T
      (v)   F   (vi)   T
      (vii)   T   (viii)   T
      (ix)   F   (x)   T

13.   (i)   a   (ii)   b
      (iii)   a   (iv)   c
      (v)   a   (vi)   b
      (vii)   c   (viii)   c
      (ix)   a   (x)   a

Chapter 6

7.   (a), (c), (e)

8.   (a), (c), (d), (e)

9.   (a), (c)

10.   (a)   0.0192   (b)   0.0769
      (c)   0.3077   (d)   0.5385

11.   (a)   0.0278   (b)   0.0556
      (c)   0.1111   (d)   0.1667

12.   (a)   0.4000   (b)   0.0640
      (c)   0.0350   (d)   0.2818

13.   (a)   0.4000   (b)   0.0491
      (c)   0.0409   (d)   0.2702

14.   0.0001

15.   0.0238

16.   (a)   0.0687   (b)   0.5581
      (c)   0.2005

17.   0.1479

18.   (a)   0.1429   (b)   0.1648
      (c)   0.0116

19.   1/3 = 0.3333

20.   2/9 = 0.2222

21.   31/36 = 0.8611

22.   5/18 = 0.2778

23.   1/6 = 0.1667

24. $\dfrac{4}{52} \times \dfrac{3}{51} \times \dfrac{2}{50} \times \dfrac{1}{49} = \dfrac{24}{6497400} = 0.000004$

25. $\dfrac{4}{7} \times \dfrac{3}{6} \times \dfrac{3}{5} \times \dfrac{2}{4} \times \dfrac{2}{3} \times \dfrac{1}{2} \times \dfrac{1}{1} = \dfrac{144}{5040} = 0.0286$

26. $\frac{1}{2} = 0.5000$

27. $6/100 = 0.0600$

28. $36/1024 = 0.0352$

29. (a) $45/60 = 0.75$ (b) $25/60 = 0.4167$
    (c) $5/60 = 0.0833$ (d) $20/60 = 0.3333$
    (e) $15/60 = 0.25$

30. (a) $20/30 = 0.6667$ (b) $10/28 = 0.3571$

31. $3/4 = 0.75$

32. $3/8 = 0.375$

33. $10/32 = 0.3125$

34. (a) $1/2 = 0.50$ (b) $2/3 = 0.6667$
    (c) $1/3 = 0.3333$

35. $4/5 = 0.80$

36. $1/6 = 0.1667$

37. (a) $1/1024 = 0.0010$ (b) $1/252 = 0.0040$

38. $32/243 = 0.1317$

39. $n! = 8! = 8 \times 7 \times 6 \times 5 \times 4 \times 3 \times 2 \times 1 = 40320$

40. $P_r^n = \dfrac{n!}{(n-r)!} = \dfrac{4!}{(4-2)!} = \dfrac{4!}{2!} = \dfrac{4 \times 3 \times 2 \times 1}{2 \times 1} = 12$

41. 20

42. $C_r^n = \dfrac{n!}{r!(n-r)!} = \dfrac{5!}{3!(5-3)!} = \dfrac{5!}{3!2!} = \dfrac{5 \times 4 \times 3 \times 2 \times 1}{3 \times 2 \times 1 \times 2 \times 1} = 10$

43. The expected distribution of heads in tossing 6 coins 64 times is:

H:	0	1	2	3	4	5	6
f:	1	6	15	20	15	6	1

44. The expected distribution of 6s in rolling 6 dice 64 times is:

6s	f
0	$15{,}625/46{,}656 \times 64$
1	$18{,}750/46{,}656 \times 64$
2	$9{,}375/46{,}656 \times 64$
3	$2{,}500/46{,}656 \times 64$
4	$375/46{,}656 \times 64$
5	$30/46{,}656 \times 64$
6	$1/46{,}656 \times 64$

45. $598/4096 = 0.1460$

46. $7/64 \times 31/46,656 = 0.1094 \times 0.0007 = 0.00008$

47. (a) $210/1024 = 0.2051$, (b) $848/1024 = 0.8281$, (c) $176/1024 = 0.1719$

48. $\dfrac{n!}{r!(n-r)!} p^r q^{n-r} = \dfrac{15!}{2!13!}\left(\dfrac{1}{7}\right)^2\left(\dfrac{6}{7}\right)^{13} = \dfrac{105 \times 6^{13}}{7^{15}} = 0.29$

49. $\dfrac{n!}{r!(n-r)!} p^r q^{n-r} = \dfrac{3!}{2!1!}(0.5)^2(0.5)^1 = 3(0.25)(0.5) = 0.375$

50. $\dfrac{n!}{r!(n-r)!} p^r q^{n-r} = \dfrac{6!}{3!3!}(0.8)^3(0.2)^3 = 20(0.512)(0.008) = 0.08192$

51.

	N	P	$\mu = np$	$\sigma = \sqrt{npq}$
(a)	16	0.40	6.4	1.960
(b)	10	0.75	7.5	1.369
(c)	22	0.15	3.3	1.675
(d)	350	0.90	315.0	5.612
(e)	78	0.05	3.9	1.925

52. (a) $p(r = 4) = \left(\dfrac{10!}{4!6!}\right)(0.30)^4(0.70)^6 = 0.2001$

 (b) $p(r = 0) = \left(\dfrac{10!}{0!10!}\right)(0.55)^0(0.45)^{10} = 0.0003$

 (c) $p(r = 2) = \left(\dfrac{10!}{2!8!}\right)(0.15)^2(0.85)^8 = 0.2759$

 (d) $p(r \geq 8) = p(r = 8) + p(r = 9) + p(r = 10)$

$= \left(\dfrac{10!}{8!2!}\right)(0.30)^8(0.70)^2 + \left(\dfrac{10!}{9!1!}\right)(0.30)^9(0.70)^1 + \left(\dfrac{10!}{10!0!}\right)(0.30)^{10}(0.70)^0$

$= 0.00145 + 0.00014 + 0.00001 = 0.0016$

53. (a) 0.0043   (b) 0.1480
     (c) 1.0   (d) 0.0333

54.

	N	P	$\mu = np$	$\sigma = \sqrt{np}$
(a)	15	0.20	3.00	1.732
(b)	8	0.42	3.36	1.833
(c)	72	0.06	4.32	2.078
(d)	29	0.49	14.21	3.770
(e)	642	0.21	134.82	11.611

55. (a) $p(X = 0) = \dfrac{\mu^X}{X!e^\mu} = \dfrac{(5)^0}{0!(2.71828)^5} = \dfrac{1}{148.41266} = 0.00674$

(b) $p(X = 1) = \dfrac{\mu^X}{X!e^\mu} = \dfrac{(5)^1}{1!(2.71828)^5} = \dfrac{5}{148.41266} = 0.03369$

(c) $p(X = 2) = \dfrac{\mu^X}{X!e^\mu} = \dfrac{(5)^2}{2!(2.71828)^5} = \dfrac{25}{2 \times 1 \times 148.41266} = 0.08423$

(d) $p(X = 3) = \dfrac{\mu^X}{X!e^\mu} = \dfrac{(5)^3}{3!(2.71828)^5} = \dfrac{125}{3 \times 2 \times 1 \times 148.41266} = 0.14037$

(e) $p(X = 4) = \dfrac{\mu^X}{X!e^\mu} = \dfrac{(5)^4}{4!(2.71828)^5} = \dfrac{625}{4 \times 3 \times 2 \times 1 \times 148.41266} = 0.17547$

(f) $p(X \leq 3) = p(X = 0) + p(X = 1) + p(X = 2) + p(X = 3)$
$= 0.00674 + 0.03369 + 0.08423 + 0.14037 = 0.26503$

(g) $p(X = 0 \text{ or } 1 \text{ or } 2) = p(X = 0) + p(X = 1) + p(X = 2)$
$= 0.00674 + 0.03369 + 0.08423 = 0.12466$

56. (i) Ratio   (ii) Chance of occurrence
(iii) 1/2   (iv) 1/6
(v) Four   (vi) Eight
(vii) Zero (0)   (viii) 4/52 or 1/13
(ix) One   (x) Dichotomised

57. (i) T   (ii) T
(iii) F   (iv) T
(v) T   (vi) T
(vii) F   (viii) F
(ix) F   (x) T

58. (i) c   (ii) a
(iii) a   (iv) b
(v) b   (vi) a
(vii) c   (viii) a
(ix) b   (x) a

Chapter 7

11.

X	z	X	z
58	+1.00	46	−0.50
34	−2.00	62	+1.50
70	+2.50	44	−0.75

12.

z	X	z	X
2.50	130	0.25	85
−0.50	70	−0.75	65
−1.50	50	1.00	100

13. (a) $z=2.00$ (b) $z=-1.00$
    (c) $z=1.50$ (d) $z=-3.00$

14. $\sigma=6$

15. $\mu=45$

16. 0.0395, 0.1238, 0.3980, 0.2444, 0.0088

17. 3.50, 25.90, 79.40, 62.46, 34.28

18. (a) 0.4319   (b) 0.3962
    (c) 0.4013   (d) 0.9332
    (e) 0.1038   (f) 0.8289
    (g) 0.3830   (h) 0.7066
    (i) 0.1337

19. (a) 0.675   (b) 1.281
    (c) 1.281   (d) ±1.281

20. (a) 0.0099   (b) 0.0918
    (c) 0.2514   (d) 0.9050

21. $\mu=54$ and $\sigma=8$

22. Your psychology score corresponds to $z=0.5$ and English score corresponds to $z=2.00$. So, you receive a better grade in English examination.

23. (a) With $\sigma=2$, the score $X=86$ corresponds to $z=3.00$, which is an extremely high score.

    (b) With $\sigma=12$, the score $X=86$ corresponds to $z=0.50$, which is a central score.

24. $\sigma=8$ gives $z=-1.00$
    $\sigma=16$ gives $z=-0.50$ (better score). So, you prefer $\sigma=16$.

25. (a) $\mu=5$ and $\sigma=2$.

(b)

X	z
8	1.50
6	0.50
2	−1.50
4	−0.50
5	0.00

(c)

Original X	New X
8	130
6	110
2	70
4	90
5	100

26.

Original Score	Standardised Score
84	125
78	110
80	115
66	80
62	70
72	95

27. (a) $-0.61\sigma, -0.10\sigma, 0.10\sigma, 0.88\sigma$ (b) 11, 31, 80
28. 71.6, 80.0, 88.4, 100.5
29. (a) 95.99%   (b) 99.45%
    (c) 15.87%   (d) 4.36%
    (e) 50.00%
30. (a) 16.85%   (b) 0.99%
    (c) 59.87%   (d) 97.50%
    (e) 50.00%
31. (a) 51.57%   (b) 34.71%
    (c) 23.28%
32. 68

33.

Grades	Score Interval
A	62.8-
B	55.2–62.8
C	44.8–55.2
D	37.2–44.8
E	-37.2

34. Difference between A and B is 0.25σ; between C and D is 0.32σ.

35.

Grades	A+	A	A-	B+	B	B-	C+	C	C-	D
Students Receiving	3	14	40	80	113	113	80	40	14	3

36. (a) 79   (b) 201
37. $S_k = 0.261$ (positively skewed set of numbers)
38. $K_u = -1.03$ (platykurtic set of numbers)
39. (a) 48.21%, 21.90%, 46.41%
    (b) 43.53% (57 cases); 12.13% (16 cases); 3.58% (5 cases)
    (c) 25; 22
41. (i) z   (ii) 0, 1
    (iii) Coincide   (iv) Minus, plus
    (v) 1, 1   (vi) 0.3989
    (vii) 0.9973 or 99.73%   (viii) 0, 0.263
    (ix) Greater   (x) Zero
42. (i) F   (ii) F
    (iii) T   (iv) T
    (v) T   (vi) T
    (vii) T   (viii) F
    (ix) T   (x) T
43. (i) a   (ii) b
    (iii) c   (iv) b
    (v) a   (vi) a
    (vii) c   (viii) a
    (ix) b   (x) c

Chapter 8

11. (a) $\bar{X} - \mu$ measures the difference between the sample mean and the hypothesised population mean.
    (b) A sample mean is not expected to be identical to the population mean. The standard error indicates how much difference between $\bar{X}$ and μ is expected by chance.
12. (a) A research can reduce the risk of a Type I error by lowering the alpha level of the hypothesis test.
    (b) A research can reduce the standard error by increasing the sample size (taking a large sample or increasing n).
13. With inferential reasoning, you use limited information from a sample to test a general hypothesis about a population. In this situation, it is impossible to prove that your general hypothesis is absolutely correct. However, you may get enough information to show that the hypothesis is wrong. Thus, we focus on the null

hypothesis and hope that the sample data will demonstrate that it is wrong. If we can show that H_0 is wrong, then we have established a treatment effect. (Remember, H_0 says that there is no effect).

14. (a) H_0: $\mu=100$; the standard error is $\sigma_{\bar{x}}=2.0$; $z_{obt}=3.0$; it is a two-tailed test; the critical value of z at $0.05_{2tail} \pm 1.96$. Reject H_0.

   (b) $\sigma_{\bar{x}}=5$; $z_{obt}=1.20$. Fail to reject H_0.

   (c) A larger standard deviation produces a larger standard error and reduces the chances of rejecting the null hypothesis.

15. (a) H_0: $\mu=50$; the standard error is $\sigma_{\bar{x}}=3.0$; $z_{obt}=-2.33$; it is a two-tailed test; the critical value of z at $0.05_{2tail}=\pm1.96$. Reject H_0.

   (b) With $\alpha=0.01$, the critical value of $z=\pm2.58$. The $z_{obt}=-2.33$ is not in the critical region. Fail to reject H_0.

   (c) As the alpha level decreases, the critical values are moved further out and it becomes more difficult to reject H_0.

16. $\sigma_{\bar{x}}=1.28$; $z_{obt}=-2.34$. The critical value of z at 0.01 for a one-tailed test is ±2.33. Reject H_0.

17. (a) H_1: New teaching method increases the amount learned.

   (b) H_0: Two methods are equal in the amount of materials learned.

   (c) Since the two groups of subjects are matched pairs, a correlated t-test was applied to analyse the given data. $\bar{X}_1=81.75$; $\bar{X}_2=78.75$; $n=20$; the mean difference $(M_D)=3.0$; the standard deviation of the difference (SD$_D$ or σ_D)=7.61; the standard error of the mean difference (SE$_{MD}$ or $\sigma_{\bar{x}_1-\bar{x}_2}$)=1.70; $t_{obt}=1.76$. $df=19$. With $df=19$, the critical value of t at 0.05 for one-tailed test is 1.73. Reject H_0. Our conclusion is that the new method is better than the old method.

   (d) We may be making a Type I error, rejecting H_0 when it is true.

   (e) Our conclusion applies to the VIII grade students in the school district at the time of the experiment.

18. (a) H_1: Four brands of scotch whiskey are not equal in preference among the scotch whiskey drinkers in the New York city.

   (b) H_0: Four brands of scotch whiskey are equal in preference among the scotch whiskey drinkers in the New York city.

   (c) χ^2-test is applied to analyse the given data. $\chi^2_{obt}=2.72$. $df=c-1=3$. The critical value of χ^2 at 0.05 for a two-tailed test with $df=3$ is $(\chi^2_{crit})=7.82$. Since the $\chi^2_{obt} < \chi^2_{crit}$, retain H_0. We can conclude that the scotch whiskey drinkers in the New York city do not differ in their preference for the four brands of scotch whiskey.

19. (a) H_1: ACTH affects avoidance learning, $\mu_1 \neq \mu_2$.

   (b) H_0: ACTH has no effect on avoidance learning, $\mu_1=\mu_2$.

   (c) An uncorrelated t-test is applied to analyse the given data. $t_{obt}=-3.24$; $df=18$; $t_{crit}=2.878$. Since $t_{obt} > t_{crit}$, reject H_0, and conclude that ACTH has a significant effect on avoidance learning; it appears to facilitate avoidance learning.

   (d) You may be making a Type I error, rejecting H_0 when it is true.

   (e) These results apply to the 100-day-old male rats living in the University vivarium at the time when the sample was selected.

20. (a) H_0: There is no relationship between the sexual gender and time-of-day preference for having intercourse.

    (b) The χ^2-test is applied to analyse the given data. $\chi^2_{obt} = 2.14$; df=1; $\chi^2_{crit} = 3.84$. Since $\chi^2_{obt} < \chi^2_{crit}$, retain H_0. You can conclude that there is no relationship between the sexual gender and time-of-day preference for having intercourse.

21. (a) H_0: Food deprivation (hunger) has no effect on the number of food-related objects reported. Therefore, $\mu_1 = \mu_2 = \mu_3$.

    (b) One-way analysis of variance (F-test) test was applied to analyse the given data. $F_{obt} = 11.85$; $F_{crit}(2/21) = 3.47$. Since $F_{obt} > F_{crit}$, reject H_0, and conclude that food deprivation has a significant effect on the number of food-related objects reported.

    (c) Reject H_0 for all conditions. All three conditions differ significantly from each other. Increasing the number of hours from eating results in an increase in the number of food-related objects reported.

22. An uncorrelated t-test was applied to analyse the given data. $\sigma_{\bar{x}} = 17.35$; $t_{obt} = 10.78$; df=23. The critical value of t, with df=23, at 0.01 for the one-tiled test is 2.50. Since $t_{obt} > t_{crit}$, reject H_0. Yes, the engineer is correct in her claim. The new process results in significantly longer life for TV picture tubes.

    (Alternatively, the z-test may be applied to analyse the given data. $\sigma_{\bar{x}} = 17.35$; $z_{obt} = 10.78$. The critical value of z at the 0.01 level for a one-tailed test is ±2.33. Since $z_{obt} > z_{crit}$, reject H_0).

23. (a) H_1: Alcohol has an effect on aggressiveness, $\mu_1 \neq \mu_2$.

    (b) H_0: Alcohol has no effect on aggressiveness, $\mu_1 = \mu_2$.

    (c) An uncorrelated t-test was applied to analyse the given data. $t_{obt} = -3.93$; df=15. The critical value of t, with df=15, at 0.05 for a two-tailed test is 2.231. Since the $t_{obt} > t_{crit}$, reject H_0 and conclude that alcohol has a significant effect on aggressiveness. It appears to decrease aggressiveness.

24. (a) $r_{obt} = 0.70$.

    (b) df=13. The critical value of r, with df=13, at the 0.05 level for a two-tailed test is 0.514. Since $r_{obt} > r_{crit}$, reject H_0. The correlation is significant.

    (c) $r^2 = 0.49$ is accounted for.

    (d) Yes, although it is clear that there is still a lot of variability unaccounted for.

25. (a) H_1: Smoking affects the heart rate, $\mu_D \neq 0$.

    (b) H_0: Smoking has no effect, $\mu_D = 0$.

    (c) A correlated t-test was applied to analyse the given data. $t_{obt} = -3.40$. df=9. The critical value of t, with df=9, at the 0.05 level for a two-tailed test is 2.262. Since $t_{obt} > t_{crit}$, reject H_0, and conclude that smoking affects the heart rate. It appears to increase the heart rate.

26. (a) H_0: Men and women do not differ in logical reasoning ability.

    (b) The Mann–Whitney U-test was applied to analyse the given data, because it is a most non-parametric powerful alternative to the parametric t-test for independent samples. $U_{obt} = 25.5$; $U' = 37.5$; $n_1 = 7$, $n_2 = 9$. The critical value of U at 0.05 for a two-tailed test is 12. Since $U_{obt} > U_{crit}$, retain H_0. You can conclude that men and women do not differ in logical reasoning ability.

27. The given data were analysed by the Kruskal–Wallis one-way analysis of variance by ranks (H-test), because it is a non-parametric powerful alternative to the parametric F-test. $H_{obt}=1.46$; df$=2$. The critical value of H, with df$=2$, at the 0.05 level is 5.99. Since $H_{obt}<H_{crit}$, retain H_0. We can conclude that physical science professors are not more authoritarian than social science professors.

28. A two-way analysis of variance test (F-test) is applied to analyse the given data. The obtained F values for row (activity), columns (time) and interaction (rows × columns) are 11.76, 9.60 and 0.09, respectively. The df for rows is (1, 24), for columns is (2, 24) and for interaction is (2, 24). The critical values of F for rows, columns and interaction are 4.26, 3.40 and 3.40, respectively. Since $F_{obt}>F_{crit}$ for the rows and column effects, we reject H_0, for the main effects. We must retain H_0 for the interaction effect because $F_{obt}<F_{crit}$. So, we may conclude that performance is affected differently by at least one of the activity conditions and by the time of day when it is conducted. It appears that napping in afternoon produce superior performance.

29. (a) The power of a hypothesis test is defined as the probability that the test will correctly reject the null hypothesis. Power is defined as

    Power$=1-\beta$, where β is the probability of Type II error.

    (b) Power is influenced by several factors that can be controlled by the experimenter:

        (i) *Size of the treatment effect:* As the size of the treatment effect increases, statistical power increases.

        (ii) *Alpha level:* Increasing the alpha level will increase power.

        (iii) *Directional and non-directional tests:* A one-tailed test will have greater power than a two-tailed test.

        (iv) *Sample size:* A large sample will result in more power than a small sample.

    (c) Power increases.

30. (a) As the size of the treatment effect gets smaller, the treatment distribution moves closer to the null distribution and power decreases. When the difference between the two distributions is extremely small, the size of the critical region (alpha) corresponds almost exactly with the portion of the treatment distribution that is located in the critical region (power). Thus, the smallest possible power is equal to alpha.

    (b) Change in the alpha level from 0.01 to 0.05 will increase the amount of power, because increasing the alpha level will increase power. It increases the risk of making a Type I error from 1% to 5%. However, researchers generally agree to the convention that $\alpha=0.05$ is the greatest risk one should take in making a Type I error. Thus, the 0.05 level of significance is frequently used and has become the 'standard' alpha level.

    (c) Use a small alpha level, but increase the sample size. Because increasing the sample size will increase the power of the test, and at the same time, using a small alpha level will lead to less risk of making Type I error.

31.   (i) Independent, dependent   (ii) Descriptive, inferential
    (iii) Hypothesis testing, parameter estimation
    (iv) Parameters   (v) No

(vi)   Opposite   (vii)   True
(viii) False (or not true)   (ix)   One
(x)   Standard error   (xi)   Sampling distribution
(xii) Population mean (or μ)

32. (i)   T   (ii)   T
     (iii) T   (iv)   F
     (v)   T   (vi)   F
     (vii) F   (viii) T
     (ix)   T   (x)   T

33. (i)   a   (ii)   b
     (iii) c   (iv)   a
     (v)   a   (vi)   b
     (vii) c   (viii) a
     (ix)   b   (x)   a

Chapter 9

20. (a)   Fairly high positive   (b)   +1 and –1
     (c)   When the two variables are uncorrelated
     (d)   No   (e) $\dfrac{\Sigma Z_x Z_y}{N}$

21. (i)   b   (ii)   a
     (iii) c   (iv)   a
     (v)   b   (vi)   a
     (vii) b   (viii) c
     (ix)   b   (x)   a

22. (a) Correlation   (b) Karl Pearson
     (c) Spearman   (d) 0.09
     (e) Regression coefficients   (f) Multiple
     (g) Linear   (h) Cause, effect
     (i) +1.0   (j) Same

23. (a) F   (b) F
     (c) T   (d) T
     (e) T   (f) F
     (g) F   (h) T
     (i) T   (j) T

24. (a) $r=1.00$; df$=3$; $p<0.01$ (significant)
     (b) $r=1.00$; value has not changed; it is the same value as in (a)

25. $r=0.603$; df$=6$; $p>0.05$ (not significant)

26. (a) $r=-0.748$; df$=8$; $p<0.05$ (significant in 95% of cases)
     (b) $r=-0.981$; df$=8$; $p<0.01$ (significant in 99% of cases)

27. (a) $r=0.896$; df$=5$; $p<0.01$ (significant in 99% of cases)
     (b) $r=0.567$; df$=6$; $p>0.05$ (not significant)

28. (a) $r=0.805$; df$=11$; $p<0.01$ (significant in 99% of cases)
    (b) $r=0.891$; df$=13$; $p<0.01$ (significant in 99% of cases)
    (c) $r=0.775$; df$=10$; $p<0.01$ (significant in 99% of cases)
29. $r=0.524$; df$=62$; $p<0.01$ (significant in 99% of cases)
30. (a) $r_b=0.34$; SE$_{r_b}=0.07$ (b) $r_b=0.41$; SE$_{r_b}=0.11$
    (c) $r_b=0.47$; 0.99 confidence interval of true $r_b=0.29-0.65$
31. (a) $r_{pbi}=0.54$; $s_{r_{pbi}}=0.2334$; df$=13$; $t=2.314$; $p<0.05$ (significant in 95% of cases)
    (b) $r_{pbi}=0.56$; $s_{r_{pbi}}=0.0944$; df$=77$; $t=5.932$; $p<0.01$ (significant in 99% of cases)
32. (a) $r_t=-0.09$ (b) $r_t=0.34$
33. (a) Partial $r=r_{12.3}=0.67$. The original correlation has been reduced from 0.80 to 0.67 after partialling out the age effect.
    (b) (i) $r_{12.3}=-0.18$; $s_{r_{12.3}}=0.10$; $t=-1.8$; df$=97$; $p>0.05$ (not significant)
        (ii) $r_{13.2}=0.70$; $s_{r_{13.2}}=0.07$; $t=10.0$; df$=97$; $p<0.01$ (significant in 99% of cases)
34. $R_{1.23}=0.94$; $s_{R_{1.23}}=0.71$; $t=1.33$; df$=2$; $p>0.05$ (not significant)
35. (a) $R_{1.23}=0.725$ (b) $R_{3.12}=0.757$
    (c) $R_{2.13}=0.681$
36. (a) Multiple determination   (b) 0 and 1
    (c) X_1 (d) First-order coefficients
    (e) First order
37. (a) F   (b) T
    (c) T   (d) F
    (e) F   (f) T
    (g) T

Chapter 10

13. (i) (b)   (ii) (a)
    (iii) (b)   (iv) (c)
    (v) (a)   (vi) (a)
    (vii) (b)
14. (a) $r=0.809$ (b) $b_{yx}=0.545$
    (c) $a_{yx}=0.82$ (d) $Y'=0.545X+0.82$
    (e) $b_{xy}=1.2$ (f) $a_{xy}=0.4$
    (g) $X'=1.2Y+0.4$

(h)

X	Y'
1	1.365
5	3.545
6	4.090
6	4.090
2	1.910

(i) $s_{y.x}^2 = 0.864$

(j)

Y	X'
2	2.8
4	5.2
5	6.4
3	4.0
1	1.6

(k) $s_{x.y}^2 = 1.9$ (l) $b_{yx} = 0.545$

(m) $a_{yx} = 0$ (n) $y' = 0.545x$

(o) $b_{xy} = 1.2$ (p) $a_{xy} = 0$

(q) $x' = 1.2y$

15. (a) (i) The regression equation of Y on X: $2.6 + (-0.2)X$; Y' when $X_{10} = 0.6$

         (ii) The regression equation of X on Y: $3.34 + (-0.17)Y$; X' when $Y_{25} = 2.92$

         (iii) $r_{xy} = r_{yx} = -0.18$

     (b) Regression equation of Y on X: $4.0 + 0.2X$

         Regression equation of X on Y: $7.3 + 0.45Y$

     (c) Regression equation of X on Y: $9.0 + 0.44Y$; X' when $Y_{30} = 22.2$

16. (a) Let advertising expenditure be X and sales be Y.

         (i) Regression line of Y on X: $Y' = (3.2)X - 23$

             Regression line of X on Y: $X' = 8.2 + (0.2)Y$

         (ii) Y' when X is ₹15 lakh $= 25$ lakh

         (iii) X' when Y is ₹ 120 lakh $= 32.2$ lakh

     (b) (i) Regression equation of Y on X: $Y' = (1.42)X - 0.52$

             Regression equation of X on Y: $X' = 4.4 + (0.2)Y$

         (ii) Y' when $X_{100} = 141.48$

     (c) Regression line of Y on X: $Y' = 1.78 + (1.6)X$

         Regression line of X on Y: $X' = 2.6 + (0.4)Y$

         Y' when $X_8 = 14.58$ ounces

     (d) Let price in Kolkata be X and that in Cuttack be Y. Likely price in Cuttack (Y') corresponding to price ₹ 75 at Kolkata (X) is: $Y' = ₹78.9$

17. (a) $\bar{X} = 4$, $\bar{Y} = 7$, $r = -0.5$, $s_y = 15$

     (b) (i) $\bar{X} = 5$, $\bar{Y} = 1/3$ (ii) $r = -0.289$

         (iii) $s_y^2 / s_x^2 = 3/4$

     (c) $R = -0.866$, $s_y^2 = 4$ (d) $\bar{X} = 0$, $\bar{Y} = 2$, $s_y = 2.74$

     (e) $\bar{X} = 1$, $\bar{Y} = 2$

18. (a) $r = 0.87$, $\sigma_y = 6.14$

     (b) Regression coefficient of Y on X: $b_{yx} = 1.25$

         Regression coefficient of X on Y: $b_{xy} = 0.556$

(c)   (i)   Regression line of Y on X: $Y' = 12 + 0.8X$

(ii)   Regression line of X on Y: $X' = 1 + 0.45Y$

19.   (a)   Let sales be denoted by Y and advertisement expenditure by X.

(i)   The likely sales for the advertisement expenditure of ₹100 lakh: $Y' = 41.65$ crores

(ii)   The likely advertisement expenditure for obtaining the sales target of ₹47 crores: $X' = 102.325$ lakh

(b)   Let the age of a car be denoted by X and maintenance cost by Y. The likely maintenance cost for a car of a particular age will be: $Y' = 5.0 + 3.25X$ (in hundreds of rupees)

20.   (a)   (i)   Multiple regression of Y on X_1 and X_2 : $Y' = 0.47X_1 + 1.26X_2 - 4.51$

(ii)   Predicted Y value for $X_1 = 36$ and $X_2 = 16$: $Y' = 32.57$

(b)   Multiple linear regression equation of X_1 on X_2 and X_3 :

$$X_1' = 16.63 + 0.30X_2 - 0.59X_3$$

Also, the predicted value of X_1 when $X_2 = 10$ and $X_3 = 12$: $X_1' = 12.55$

(c)   (i)   Regression equation of x_1 on x_2 and x_3: $x_1' = 0.84x_2 + 0.54x_3$

(ii)   Regression equation of x_2 on x_1 and x_3: $x_2' = 0.62x_1 + 0.05x_3$

(d)   Multiple linear regression of X_1 on X_2 and X_3 :

$$X_1' = 2.95 + 0.14X_2 + 0.07X_3$$

21.   (a)   Regression   (b)   Negative

(c)   Exceed   (d)   Dependent

(e)   Independent   (f)   Nature

(g)   Unknown, known, regression

(h) b_{yx} (i)   Two

(j) X on Y (k) b_{yx}

(l) b_{xy}

22.   (a)   (i)   (b)   (i)

(c)   (ii)   (d)   (i)

(e)   (ii)   (f)   (ii)

(g)   (iii)   (h)   (i)

(i)   (i)   (j)   (i)

(k)   (i)   (l)   (ii)

23.   (a)   T   (b)   T

(c)   T   (d)   F

(e)   F   (f)   T

(g)   T   (h)   T

(i)   T   (j)   F

(k)   T   (l)   T

Chapter 11

11. $s_{\bar{X}} = 0.4$; the 95% confidence interval $= 41.22 - 42.78$;
     The 99% confidence interval $= 40.97 - 43.03$.

12. $s_{\bar{X}} = 0.46$
     - (a) 95% confidence interval $= 49.10 - 50.90$
     - (b) The 99% confidence interval $= 48.81 - 51.19$
     - (c) Sampling error $=$ critical value $\times s_{\bar{X}}$
            Acceptable sampling error at the 0.05 level of significance $= 1.96 s_{\bar{X}} = 0.90$
            Allowable sampling error at the 0.01 level of significance $= 2.58 s_{\bar{X}} = 1.19$

13. $s_{\bar{X}} = 1.12$.
     - (a) The 0.99 confidence interval $= 92.11 - 97.89$
     - (b) Our sample mean of 95.00 will not miss the true mean (population mean by more than 2.89 (i.e., 2.58×1.12), that is, the true mean is not larger than 97.89.

14. Sample A: $s_{\bar{X}} = 0.36$; the 0.05 confidence interval $= 39.29 - 40.71$.
     The 0.01 confidence interval $= 39.07 - 40.93$.
     Sample B: $s_{\bar{X}} = 0.3$; 0.05 confidence interval $= 44.41 - 45.59$;
     The 0.01 confidence interval $= 44.23 - 45.77$
     Sample C: $s_{\bar{X}} = 0.27$; 0.05 confidence interval $= 49.47 - 50.53$
     The 0.01 confidence interval $= 49.30 - 50.70$.
     Sample D: $s_{\bar{X}} = 0.48$; the 0.05 confidence interval $= 79.06 - 80.94$
     The 0.01 confidence interval $= 78.76 - 81.24$.

15. $s_{\bar{X}} = 1.0$; df $= N - 1 = 4$; the critical value of t with df $= 4$, at the 95% confidence level (i.e., 0.05 level of significance) is 2.78.
     The 95% confidence interval $= \bar{X} \pm 2.78 s_{\bar{X}} = 12 \pm 2.78 \times 1.0 = 9.22 - 14.78$.

16. $s_{\bar{X}} = 6.0$; df $= 15$; with df $= 15$, $t_{0.05} = 2.13$ and $t_{0.01} = 2.95$
     - (a) 0.05 fiduciary limit $= \bar{X} \pm 2.13 s_{\bar{X}} = 87.22 - 112.78$.
     - (b) True mean is at least as large as 82.3 (the lower limit of the 0.99 confidence interval which ranges from 82.3 to 117.7).

17. $\bar{X} = 5.4$; $s = 1.14$; $s_{\bar{X}} = 0.51$; df $= 4$; with df $= 4$, $t_{0.01} = 4.60$.
     The 0.99 confidence interval $= \bar{X} \pm 4.60 s_{\bar{X}} = 3.05 - 7.75$.

18. (a) 100   (b) 202

19. $s_{mdn} = \dfrac{1.858 Q}{\sqrt{N}} = \dfrac{1.858 \times 4.90}{\sqrt{801}} = 0.32$. Since N is large, the sampling distribution may be taken to be normal.

     The 0.99 confidence interval

$$= M_{dn} \pm 2.58 s_{mdn} = 21.40 \pm 2.58 \times 0.32 = 21.40 \pm 0.83 = 20.57 - 22.23.$$

     We may be confident that the median of the population is neither less than 20.57 nor more than 22.23. This narrow range shows a high degree of trustworthiness in the sample median to represent the population median.

20. $s_{mdn} = \dfrac{1.253s}{\sqrt{N}} = \dfrac{1.253 \times 2.4}{\sqrt{36}} = 0.50$. Since N is large, the sampling distribution may be taken to be normal.

    The 0.95 confidence interval
    $= M_{dn} \pm 1.96\ s_{mdn} = 30.4 \pm 1.96 \times 0.50 = 30.4 \pm 0.98 = 29.42 - 31.38$
    The 0.99 confidence interval
    $= M_{dn} \pm 2.58\ s_{mdn} = 30.4 \pm 2.58 \times 0.50 = 30.4 \pm 1.29 = 29.11\text{-}31.69$.
    The narrow ranges in both the confidence intervals show a high degree of trustworthiness in the sample median to represent the population median.

21. $s_s = \dfrac{s}{\sqrt{2N}} = \dfrac{5.20}{\sqrt{2 \times 100}} = \dfrac{5.20}{14.14} = 0.37$

    The 0.95 confidence interval for true $\sigma = \sigma \pm 1.96\ s_s = 5.20 \pm 1.96 \times 0.37 = 5.20 \pm 0.725 = 4.475\text{-}5.925$.
    Hence, population σ is neither less than 4.475 nor larger than 5.925.

22. $s_s = \dfrac{0.71\sigma}{\sqrt{N}} = \dfrac{0.71 \times 6}{\sqrt{400}} = \dfrac{4.26}{20} = 0.21$

    Since N is large, the 0.99 confidence interval for the population SD can safely be taken at limits $\sigma \pm 2.58\ s_s = 6 \pm 2.58 \times 0.21 = 6 \pm 0.54 = 5.46\text{-}6.54$.
    If we assume that the population SD lies between the limits 5.46 and 6.54, we should be right 99% of the time and wrong 1%.

23. $s_Q = \dfrac{1.17Q}{\sqrt{N}} = \dfrac{1.17 \times 4.90}{\sqrt{801}} = 0.203$

    The 0.99 confidence interval for $Q_{pop} = Q \pm 2.58 s_Q = 4.90 \pm 2.58 \times 0.203 = 4.90 \pm 0.52 = 4.38\text{-}5.42$. This range shows that the sample Q is a highly dependable statistic for population Q.

24. $s_Q = \dfrac{0.786s}{\sqrt{N}} = \dfrac{0.786 \times 6.68}{\sqrt{200}} = 0.37$

    The 0.99 confidence interval for the $Q_{pop} = Q \pm 2.58_{s_Q} = 4.49 \pm 2.58 \times 0.37 = 4.49 \pm 0.95 = 3.54 - 5.44$. This range shows that the sample Q is a highly dependable statistic for the Q of the population from which the sample was drawn.

25. $\text{SE}_\% \ \text{ or }\ s_\% = \sqrt{\dfrac{PQ}{N}} = \sqrt{\dfrac{25\% \times 75\%}{400}} = 2.17\%$

    The 99% confidence interval for population percentage ranges from:
    $25\% \pm 2.58 s_\% = 25\% \pm 2.58 \times 2.17\% = 25\% \pm 5.60\% = 19.40\%$ to 30.60%. This range shows that the sample percentage is a dependable statistic for the population percentage. We may conclude with 99% confidence that elementary school children from homes of high socio-economic status would cheat with at least 19.40% and it will not be larger than 30.60%.

26. SE$_r$ or $s_r = \dfrac{1-r^2}{\sqrt{N}} = \dfrac{1-(0.48)^2}{\sqrt{52}} = 0.107$

The 0.05 confidence interval $= r \pm 1.96\ s_r = 0.48 \pm 1.96 \times 0.107 = 0.48 \pm 0.21 = 0.27 - 0.69$.
The 0.01 confidence interval $= r \pm 2.58\ s_r = 0.48 \pm 2.58 \times 0.107 = 0.48 \pm 0.28 = 0.20 - 0.76$

27. SE$_r$ or $s_r = \dfrac{1-r^2}{\sqrt{N}} = \dfrac{1-(0.52)^2}{\sqrt{173}} = 0.055$

The 0.99 confidence interval $= r \pm 2.58\ s_r = 0.52 \pm 2.58 \times 0.055 = 0.52 \pm .142 = 0.378 - 0.662$.
Hence, we may conclude that the population r is at least as large as 0.378 and no larger than 0.662. The sample r is, thus, a dependable statistic for the population r.

28. (i)   Statistics   (ii)   Parameters
     (iii) Index   (iv) $\sigma/\sqrt{N}$
     (v)   Fudiciary limit   (vi)   Continuous
     (vii) Leptokurtic   (viii) Mesokurtic
     (ix) 0.064   (x)   W. S. Gossett

29. (i)   T   (ii)   T
     (iii) F   (iv)   F
     (v)   T   (vi)   T
     (vii) F   (viii) T
     (ix) T   (x)   T

30. (i)   a   (ii)   b
     (iii) c   (iv)   a
     (v)   a   (vi)   a
     (vii) b   (viii) c
     (ix) a   (x)   b

Chapter 12

4. $z = -4.12$; it is a two-tailed test; significant at the 0.01 level ($p < 0.01$)
5. $z = 4.42$; it is a one-tailed test; significant at the 0.01 level ($p < 0.01$)
6. $z = -1.91$; it is a two-tailed test; not significant at the 0.05 level ($p > 0.05$)
    The null hypothesis (H$_0$) is accepted; we have insufficient evidence of any sex difference in the attitudes as assessed by the given attitude scale.
7. (a) $z = 1.50$; it is a two-tailed test; it is not significant at the 0.05 level ($p > 0.05$)
    (b) The difference between two means should be at least 7.22 for being significant at the 0.01 level of significance.
8. $t = 1.74$; it is a two-tailed test; it is not significant ($p > 0.05$)
9. $t = 1.62$; it is a one-tailed test; it is not significant ($p > 0.05$)
10. $t = 2.81$; it is a one-tailed test; it is significant at the 0.01 level ($p < 0.01$)
11. $t = 3.66$; it is a two-tailed test; it is significant at the 0.01 level ($p < 0.01$)
12. $t = 2.51$; it is a two-tailed test; it is significant at the 0.05 level ($p < 0.05$)

13. $t=4.63$; it is a one-tailed test; it is significant at the 0.01 level $(p<0.01)$
14. $t=2.81$; it is a two-tailed test; it is significant at the 0.05 level $(p<0.05)$
15. $t=2.96$; it is a two-tailed test; it is significant at the 0.01 level $(p<0.01)$
16. $t=5.26$; it is a one-tailed test; it is significant at the 0.01 level $(p<0.01)$
17. $t=-0.202$; it is a two-tailed test; it is not significant at the 0.05 level $(p>0.05)$
18. $t=-3.08$; it is a two-tailed test; it is significant at the 0.01 level $(p<0.01)$
19. $t=-0.89$; it is a two-tailed test; it is not significant at the 0.05 level $(p>0.05)$
20. $t=3.61$; it is a two-tailed test; it is significant at the 0.01 level $(p<0.01)$
21. $F=1.79$; it is not significant at the 0.05 level $(p>0.05)$
22. $t=1.52$; it is a two-tailed test; it is not significant at the 0.05 level $(p>0.05)$
23. $t=-1.35$; it is a two-tailed test; it is not significant at the 0.05 level $(p>0.05)$
24. $z=-2.065$; it is significant at the 0.05 level $(p<0.05)$
25. $z=0.83$; it is not significant at the 0.05 level $(p>0.05)$
26. $z=3.086$; it is significant at the 0.01 level $(p<0.01)$
27. $z=-1.764$; it is not significant at the 0.05 level $(p>0.05)$
28. $t=1.19$; it is a two-tailed test; it is not significant at the 0.05 level $(p>0.05)$
29. $z=1.414$; it is not significant at the 0.05 level $(p>0.05)$
30. $z=3.629$; it is significant at the 0.01 level $(p<0.01)$
31. $t=0.98$; it is a one-tailed test; it is not significant at the 0.05 level $(p>0.05)$
32. (i) Standard error of difference (ii) Sum
    (iii) z, t (iv) z
    (v) Rejection (vi) Continuous
    (vii) Random, independent (viii) Equal
    (ix) Parametric (x) Independent
33. (i) T (ii) T
    (iii) F (iv) F
    (v) T (vi) T
    (vii) T (viii) F
    (ix) F (x) T
34. (i) a (ii) b
    (iii) a (iv) c
    (v) a (vi) b
    (vii) a (viii) c
    (ix) a (x) b

Chapter 13

13. (i) Architect (ii) Structure
    (iii) Relations (iv) Independent,dependent
    (v) Independent (vi) Dependent
    (vii) Classification (viii) Factor
    (ix) Level (x) Slope

14.   (i) T   (ii) T
        (iii) T   (iv) F
        (v) F   (vi) F
        (vii) T   (viii) F
        (ix) T   (x) T

15.   (i) a   (ii) b
        (iii) c   (iv) b
        (v) a   (vi) c
        (vii) b   (viii) a
        (ix) c   (x) a

Chapter 14

5. $F=23.31$, $df_b=4$, $df_w=20$, significant at the 0.01 level ($p<0.01$).

6. $F=2.06$, $df_b=3$, $df_w=21$, not significant at the 0.05 level ($p>0.05$).

7. $F=21.96$, $df_b=1$, $df_w=18$, significant at the 0.01 level ($p<0.01$); H_0 is rejected; $t=4.69$; $\sqrt{F}=t$ (proved).

8. $F=2.27$, $df_b=2$, $df_w=27$, not significant at the 0.05 level ($p>0.05$).

9. $s^2/\bar{X}$ is roughly 2.5 for the three groups, and a square root transformation is appropriate. $F=4.60$, $df_b=2$, $df_w=12$, significant at the 0.05 level ($p<0.05$).

10. $F_a=85.699$, $df=2/24$, significant at the 0.01 level ($p<0.01$).
    $F_b=72.635$, $df=1/24$, significant at the 0.01 level ($p<0.01$);
    $F_{ab}=11.172$; $df=2/24$, significant at the 0.01 level ($p<0.01$).

11. $F_r=1.23$, $df=1/30$, not significant at the 0.05 level ($p>0.05$);
    $F_c=0.23$, $df=2/30$, not significant at the 0.05 level ($p>0.05$);
    $F_{rc}=0.31$, $df=2/30$, not significant at the 0.05 level ($p>0.05$).

12. (a)

	C_1	C_2	C_3	
R_1	10.2	3.8	14.7	9.6
R_2	10.5	3.9	15.2	9.9
	10.4	3.9	15.0	9.8

    (b) Interaction sum of square $=212.13$.

13. $F_a=1.25$, $df=1/24$, not significant at the 0.05 level ($p>0.05$);
    $F_b=6.67$, $df=2/24$, significant at the 0.01 level ($p<0.01$);
    $F_{ab}=0.00$, $df=2/24$, not significant at the 0.05 level ($p>0.05$).

14. $F_a=3.77$, $df=1/28$, not significant at the 0.05 level ($p>0.05$);
    $F_b=0.35$, $df=1/28$, not significant at the 0.05 level ($p>0.05$);
    $F_{ab}=1.60$, $df=1/28$, not significant at the 0.05 level ($p>0.05$).

15. $F_a=66.67$, $df=1/16$, significant at 0.01 level ($p<0.01$);
    $F_b=16.67$, $df=1/16$, significant at 0.01 level ($p<0.01$);
    $F_{ab}=0.00$, $df=1/16$, not significant at 0.05 level ($p>0.05$).

16.

Sources of Variation	SS	df	MS	F
Between treatments	120	3		
A (distraction)	80	1	80	16
B (personality)	20	1	20	4
A×B	20	1	20	4
Within treatments	80	16	5	
Total	200	19		

Factor A (distraction) has a significant effect on performance ($p<0.05$). Factor B (personality) has no significant effect on performance ($p>0.05$). Similarly, the A×B interaction effect on performance was not found to be significant ($p>0.05$).

17.   (a)   df=1/36;   (b) df=1/36;   (c) df=1/36.

18.   Summary of Two-factor ANOVA

Sources of Variation	SS	df	MS	F
Between treatments	855	3		
A (lecture room)	5	1	5	0.55
B (testing room)	5	1	5	0.55
A×B interaction	845	1	845	92.60
Within treatment	146	16	9.125	
Total	1001	19		

19. $F_a=6.0$, df=1/24, significant at the 0.05 level ($p<0.05$);
$F_b=2.0$, df=2/24, not significant at the 0.05 level ($p>0.05$);
$F_{ab}=8.0$, df=2/24, significant at the 0.05 level ($p<0.05$).

20.   (a)   The cell means are as follows:

	b_1	b_2
a_1	10	2
a_2	3	11

(b)   There appears to be no main effect for factor A (the means are nearly equal) and no effect for factor B (the means are equal). There does appear to be an interaction effect because the means decrease across levels of B for a_1, but they increase across B for a_2.

(c) The null hypotheses state that factor A has no effect (H_0: $\mu_{a_1} = \mu_{a_2}$), factor B has no effect (H_0: $\mu_{b_1} = \mu_{b_2}$) and that there is no interaction (A×B) effect. For df=1/16 and $\alpha = 0.01$, the critical value is $F = 8.53$.

Summary of Two-factor ANOVA

Sources of Variation	SS	df	MS	F
Between treatments	325	3		
A	5	1	5	1.05
B	0	1	0	0.00
A×B	320	1	320	67.37
Within treatment	76	16	4.75	
Total	401	19		

(d) The A and B main effects are not significant, but there is a significant interaction (A×B) effect ($p < 0.01$).

21.   (i)   R.A. Fisher, 1923   (ii)   Snedecor
     (iii) Variances   (iv)   Two, more
      (v) $t^2, \sqrt{F}$ (vi)   Two
    (vii) One   (viii) Treatment
     (ix) One   (x)   Analysis of variance table
22.   (i)   T   (ii)   T
     (iii) F   (iv)   F
      (v)   F   (vi)   T
    (vii) T   (viii) F
     (ix) T   (x)   T
23.   (i)   a   (ii)   b
     (iii) b   (iv)   c
      (v)   c   (vi)   b
    (vii) a   (viii) a
     (ix) b   (x)   c

Chapter 15

3.   df=3,27
4.   (a) $K = 3$ treatment conditions
     (b) $n = 21$ subjects
5. $F = 5.97$; df=2,6; it is significant at the 0.05 level ($p < 0.05$)

6. (a) First $\bar{X} = 3.0$, second $\bar{X} = 5.0$ and third $\bar{X} = 1.0$
   (b) $F = 8.0$, df = 2,6, it is significant at the 0.05 level ($p < 0.05$). The H_0 ($\mu_1 = \mu_2 = \mu_3$) is rejected and we conclude that the number of errors differs significantly with the position in the list. Most errors are made in the middle of the list, with fewer errors at the beginning and fewest errors on the last items in the list.

7. $F = 8.96$; df = 3,6; it is significant at the 0.05 level ($p < 0.05$)

8.

Source of Variation	SS	df	MS	F
Between subjects	36	14		
Within subjects	132	30		
Between treatments	48	2	24	8
Residual (Error)	84	28	3	
Total	168	44		

9. (a) $T = 2.00$; df = 3; it is not significant at the 0.05 level ($p > 0.05$)
   (b) $F = 4.00$; df = 1,3; it is not significant at the 0.05 level ($p > 0.05$)
   The value of $t^2 = (2.0)^2 = 4.00$. Thus, $F = t^2$ (proved)

10. $F = 17.79$; df = 3,15; it is significant at the 0.01 level ($p < 0.01$)

11. $F = 2.61$; df = 2,22; it is not significant at the 0.05 level ($p > 0.05$)

12. $F = 28.16$; df = 4,16; it is significant at the 0.01 level ($p < 0.01$)

13.

Source of Variation	SS	df	MS	F
Between subjects	13.71	5		
Rows	6.34	2	3.17	1.29
Subject within rows (Error between)	7.37	3	2.46	
Within subjects	137.25	18		
Columns	78.79	3	26.26	4.37*
R × C	4.33	6	0.72	0.12
C × subject within rows (Error within)	54.13	9	6.01	
Total	150.96	23		

Note: *$p < 0.05$.

14.

Source of Variation	SS	df	MS	F
Between subjects	345.50	5		
Rows	184.75	2	92.38	1.72
Subject within rows (Error between)	160.75	3	53.58	
Within subjects	585.00	18		
Columns	460.50	3	153.50	37.08**
R×C	87.25	6	14.54	3.51*
C×subject within rows (Error within)	37.25	9	4.14	
Total	**930.50**	**23**		

Notes: *p<0.05; **p<0.01.

15.

Source of Variation	SS	df	MS	F
Between subjects	258.69	3		
Within subjects	617.25	12		
R (rows)	105.06	1	105.06	1.43
R×SS (Error-I)	220.69	3	73.56	
C (columns)	189.06	1	189.06	26.15*
C×SS (Error-II)	21.69	3	7.23	
R×C (interaction)	68.06	1	68.06	16.09*
R×C×SS (Error-III)	12.69	3	4.23	
Total	**875.94**	**15**		

Note: *p<0.05 (significant at the 0.05 level).

16.

Source of variation	SS	df	MS	F
Between subjects	26.33	5		
Within subjects	139.00	18		
R (rows)	1.50	1	1.50	0.52
R×SS (Error-I)	14.50	5	2.90	
C (columns)	37.50	1	37.50	6.82*
C×SS (Error-II)	27.50	5	5.50	
R×C (interaction)	0.66	1	0.66	0.06
R×C×SS (Error-III)	57.34	5	11.47	
Total	165.33	23		

Note: * p<0.05 (significant at the 0.05 level).

17. (i)   Independent   (ii)   Separate
     (iii) Single, treatment   (iv)   Between subject design
     (v)   Within subject design   (vi)   Repeated
     (vii) Inter-subject   (viii) Without repeated
     (ix)   Repeated   (x)   Variability
18. (i)   T   (ii)   T
     (iii) F   (iv)   F
     (v)   T   (vi)   T
     (vii) T   (viii) F
     (ix)   T   (x)   T
19. (i)   a   (ii)   b
     (iii) c   (iv)   b
     (v)   a   (vi)   b
     (vii) a   (viii) c
     (ix)   b   (x)   a

Chapter 16

21. $\chi^2 = 5.2$, df $= 2$; $p > 0.05$
22. $\chi^2 = 5.71$, df $= 1$; $p < 0.05$
23. $\chi^2 = 16.33$, df $= 7$; $p < 0.05$
24. $\chi^2 = 4.5$, df $= 2$; $p > 0.05$
25. $\chi^2 = 4.72$, df $= 3$; $p > 0.05$
26. $\chi^2 = 11.33$, df $= 5$; $p < 0.05$
27. $\chi^2 = 3.334$, df $= 6$; $p > 0.05$
28. $\chi^2 = 14.466$, df $= 2$; $p < 0.001$
29. $\chi^2 = 16.20$, df $= 4$; $p < 0.01$
30. $\chi^2 = 18.00$, df $= 2$; $p < 0.01$
31. $\chi^2 = 3.163$, df $= 1$; $p > 0.05$
32. $\chi^2 = 3.889$, df $= 1$; $p < 0.05$
33. $\chi^2 = 11.364$, df $= 1$; $p < 0.001$
34. $\rho = 0.82$, $p < 0.01$ for the one-tailed test
35. $\rho = 0.85$, $p < 0.01$ for the one-tailed test
36. $\rho = 0.59$, $p < 0.05$ for the one-tailed test
37. $\phi = 0.40$, $\chi^2 = 32.0$, df $= 1$, $p < 0.001$
38. $\phi = 0.40$, $\chi^2 = 32.0$, df $= 1$, $p < 0.05$
39. $r_t = 0.37$, $t = 2.241$, df $= 98$, $p < 0.05$
40. $r_t = 0.59$, $t = 5.291$, df $= 198(\infty)$, $p < 0.05$
41. $C = 0.254$, $\chi^2 = 14.03$, df $= 2$, $p < 0.001$
42. $\tau = 0.10$, $s = +2$, $N = 7$, $p > 0.05$
43. $\tau = 0.07$, $s = -1$, $N = 6$, $p > 0.05$

44. $W=0.651$, $m=3$, $N=7$, $p<0.05$
45. (a) $W=0.923$
    (b) $\chi^2=25.844$, df$=7$, $p<0.01$ (or $m=4$, $N=8$, $p<0.01$)
46. (i)   Distribution-free   (ii)   Preferred
    (iii) Homoscedasticity   (iv) Interval, ratio
    (v)   Ordinal, nominal   (vi) Non-parametric
    (vii) Greater   (viii) df (degrees of freedom)
    (ix) Yates' correction for continuity   (x)   Non-parametric
47. (i)   T   (ii)   F
    (iii) T   (iv) F
    (v)   F   (vi) F
    (vii) T   (viii) T
    (ix) T   (x)   F
48. (i)   b   (ii)   a
    (iii) c   (iv) a
    (v)   a   (vi) a
    (vii) b   (viii) c
    (ix) a   (x)   a

Chapter 17

16 $x=2$, $N=7$, $p=0.454$ (two-tailed), $p>0.05$
17. $x=2$, $N=9$, $p=0.18$ (two-tailed), $p>0.05$
18. $x=2$, $N=11$, $p=0.066$ (two-tailed), $p>0.05$
19. $\chi^2=16.82$ (or $z=4.10$), df$=1$, $p<0.01$
20. (a) $N=7$, $T=13$, $p>0.05$
     (b) $N=9$, $T=17$, $p>0.05$
21. $N=11$, $T=6.5$, $p<0.01$ (one-tailed test)
22. $N=35$, $z=-2.375$, $p<0.01$ (one-tailed test)
23. $N_1=9$, $N_2=9$, $R_1=116$, $\bar{R}_1=85.5$, $p<0.005$ (one-tailed test)
24. $N_1=10$, $N_2=12$, $R_1=86$, $\bar{R}_1=115$, $p<0.05$ (one-tailed test)
25. $z=5.10$, $p<0.01$ (two-tailed test)
26. $n_1=4$, $n_2=5$, $U=9$, $p=0.452$ ($p>0.05$)
27. $n_1=10$, $n_2=12$, $U=31$, $p<0.05$ (one-tailed test)
28. $U=35$, $\mu_u=105$, $\sigma_u=23.66$, $z=-2.96$, $p<0.01$ (two-tailed test)
29. $U=76$, $\mu_u=126.5$, $\sigma_u=27.13$, $z=-1.86$, $p>0.05$ (two-tailed test)
30. (a) $\chi^2=5.625$, df$=1$, $p<0.05$ (two-tailed test)
     (b) $\chi^2=8.10$, df$=1$, $p<0.01$ (two-tailed test)
31. $\chi^2=0.81$, df$=1$, $p>0.05$ (two-tailed test)
32. $\chi^2=2.54$, df$=2$, $p>0.05$ (two-tailed test)
33. $\chi^2=13.36$, df$=3$, $p<0.01$ (two-tailed test)
34. $H=2.75$, $n_1=5$, $n_2=5$, $n_3=5$, $p>0.102$ ($p>0.05$)
35. $H=12.08$, df$=2$, $p<0.01$ (two-tailed test)

36. $H=12.87$, df$=3$, $p<0.01$ (two-tailed test)
37. $H=10.64$, df$=2$, $p<0.01$ (two-tailed test)
38. $\chi_r^2 =10.2$, $N=4$, $k=4$, $p=0.0027$ ($p<0.01$) (two-tailed test)
39. $\chi_r^2 =6.4$, $N=5$, $k=3$, $p=0.0496$ ($p<0.05$) (two-tailed test)
40. $\chi_r^2 =0.8$, $N=10$, $k=3$, df$=2$, $p>0.05$ (two-tailed test)
41. (i) Correlated   (ii) Non-parametric
    (iii) Non-parametric   (iv) More
      (v) Independent   (vi) Rank sum
    (vii) Lower   (viii) Ordinal
      (ix) Independent (or uncorrelated) (x) H
42. (i) T   (ii) T
    (iii) F   (iv) F
      (v) T   (vi) T
    (vii) F   (viii) T
      (ix) T   (x) T
43. (i) a   (ii) b
    (iii) c   (iv) a
      (v) a   (vi) b
    (vii) c   (viii) a
      (ix) b   (x) a

Chapter 18

30. 1. $D=40$, 2. $D=40$, 3. $D=-10$, 4. $D=0$, 5. $D=20$
31. $\sigma_t^2 =100$, $\sigma_e^2 =20$, $\sigma_\infty^2 =80$, $\sigma_e^2 / \sigma_t^2 = 0.20$, $\sigma_\infty^2 / \sigma_t^2 = 0.80$, SE $= 4.472$
32. (a) SEM$=4.648$,   (b) $SE_D=3.605$
33. (a) $r_{tt} =0.95$,   (b) $r_{tt} =0.91$
34. (a) $r_{tt} =0.82$,   (b) 100 items to be added.
35. (a) 4 times (or 120 items),   (b) $r_{tt} =0.846$
36. (a) Validity$=0.73$,   (b) 8.33 times
37. (a) 9.0,
    (b) 12.3% (the size of the error of prediction has decreased by 12.3%)
38. (i) Arbitrary   (ii) True
    (iii) Objective, standardised   (iv) Systematic
      (v) Item analysis
      (vi) Difficulty level, discriminatory power
    (vii) Progressive   (viii) Consistency
      (ix) Purports (or intends or aims) (x) Norms
39. (i) T   (ii) T
    (iii) F   (iv) F
      (v) T   (vi) F
    (vii) T   (viii) F
      (ix) T   (x) T

40. (i) c   (ii) b
     (iii) a   (iv) c
     (v) b   (vi) b
     (vii) a   (viii) a
     (ix) c   (x) a

Appendix

List of Tables

(contd.)

(contd.)

Table A.   Ordinates and areas of the unit normal curve, and the probabilities associated with the z values in the normal distribution

Table A(I).   Ordinates at specific χ/σ or z scores and areas from the mean to the z scores of the unit normal curve

$\frac{\chi}{\sigma}$	Area	Ordinate	$\frac{\chi}{\sigma}$	Area	Ordinate	$\frac{\chi}{\sigma}$	Area	Ordinate	$\frac{\chi}{\sigma}$	Area	Ordinate
.00	.0000	.3989	.40	.1554	.3683	.80	.2881	.2897	1.20	.3849	.1942
.01	.0040	.3989	.41	.1591	.3668	.81	.2910	.2874	1.21	.3869	.1919
.02	.0080	.3989	.42	.1628	.3653	.82	.2939	.2850	1.22	.3888	.1895
.03	.0120	.3988	.43	.1664	.3637	.83	.2967	.2827	1.23	.3907	.1872
.04	.0160	.3986	.44	.1700	.3621	.84	.2995	.2803	1.24	.3925	.1849
.05	.0199	.3984	.45	.1736	.3605	.85	.3023	.2780	1.25	.3944	.1826
.06	.0239	.3982	.46	.1772	.3589	.86	.3051	.2756	1.26	.3962	.1804
.07	.0279	.3980	.47	.1808	.3572	.87	.3078	.2732	1.27	.3980	.1781
.08	.0319	.3977	.48	.1844	.3555	.88	.3106	.2709	1.28	.3997	.1758
.09	.0359	.3973	.49	.1879	.3538	.89	.3133	.2685	1.29	.4015	.1736
.10	.0398	.3970	.50	.1915	.3521	.90	.3159	.2661	1.30	.4032.	.1714
.11	.0438	.3965	.51	.1950	.3503	.91	.3186	.2637	1.31	.4049	.1691
.12	.0478	.3961	.52	.1985	.3485	.92	.3212	.2613	1.32	.4066	.1669
.13	.0517	.3956	.53	.2019	.3467	.93	.3238	.2589	1.33	.4082	.1647
.14	.0557	.3951	.54	.2054	.3448	.94	.3264	.2565	1.34	.4099	.1626
.15	.0596	.3945	.55	.2088	.3429	.95	.3289	.2541	1.35	.4115	.1604
.16	.0636	.3939	.56	.2173	.3410	.96	.3315	.2516	1.36	.4131	.1582
.17	.0675	.3932	.57	.2157	.3391	.97	.3340	.2492	1.37	.4147	.1561
.18	.0714	.3925	.58	.2190	.3372	.98	.3365	.2468	1.38	.4162	.1539
.19	.0753	.3918	.59	.2224	.3352	.99	.3389	.2444	1.39	.4177	.1518
.20	.0793	.3910	.60	.2257	.3332	1.00	.3413	.2420	1.40	.4192	.1497
.21	.0832	.3902	.61	.2291	.3312	1.01	.3438	.2396	1.41	.4207	.1476
.22	.0871	.3894	.62	.2324	.3292	1.02	.3461	.2371	1.42	.4222	.1456
.23	.0910	.3885	.63	.2357	.3271	1.03	.3485	.2347	1.43	.4236	.1435
.24	.0948	.3876	.64	.2389	.3251	1.04	.3508	.2323	1.44	.4251	.1415
.25	.0987	.3867	.65	.2422	.3230	1.05	.3531	.2299	1.45	.4265	.1394
.26	.1026	.3857	.66	.2454	.3209	1.06	.3554	.2275	1.46	.4279	.1374
.27	.1064	.3847	.67	.2486	.3187	1.07	.3577	.2251	1.47	.4292	.1354
.28	.1103	.3836	.68	.2517	.3166	1.08	.3599	.2227	1.48	.4306	.1334
.29	.1141	.3825	.69	.2549	.3144	1.09	.3621	.2203	1.49	.4319	.1315
.30	.1179	.3814	.70	.2580	.3123	1.10	.3643	.2179	1.50	.4332	.1295
.31	.1217	.3802	.71	.2611	.3101	1.11	.3665	.2155	1.51	.4345	.1276
.32	.1255	.3790	.72	.2642	.3070	1.12	.3686	.2131	1.52	.4357	.1257
.33	.1293	.3778	.73	.2673	.3056	1.13	.3708	.2107	1.53	.4370	.1238
.34	.1331	.3765	.74	.2703	.3034	1.14	.3729	.2083	1.54	.4382	.1219
.35	.1368	.3752	.75	.2734	.3011	1.15	.3749	.2059	1.55	.4394	.1200
.36	.1406	.3739	.76	.2764	.2989	1.16	.3770	.2036	1.56	.4406	.1182
.37	.1443	.3725	.77	.2794	.2966	1.17	.3790	.2012	1.57	.4418	.1163
.38	.1480	.3712	.78	.2823	.2943	1.18	.3810	.1989	1.58	.4429	.1145
.39	.1517	.3697	.79	.2852	.2920	1.19	.3830	.1965	1.59	.4441	.1127

(Table A(I) contd.)

(Table A(I) contd.)

$\frac{\chi}{\sigma}$	Area	Ordinate	$\frac{\chi}{\sigma}$	Area	Ordinate	$\frac{\chi}{\sigma}$	Area	Ordinate	$\frac{\chi}{\sigma}$	Area	Ordinate
1.60	.4452	.1109	2.05	.4798	.0488	2.50	.4938	.0175	2.95	.4984	.0051
1.61	.4463	.1092	2.06	.4803	.0478	2.51	.4940	.0171	2.96	.4985	.0050
1.62	.4474	.1074	2.07	.4808	.0468	2.52	.4941	.0167	2.97	.4985	.0048
1.63	.4484	.1057	2.08	.4812	.0459	2.53	.4943	.0163	2.98	.4986	.0047
1.64	.4495	.1040	2.09	.4817	.0449	2.54	.4945	.0158	2.99	.4986	.0046
1.65	.4505	.1023	2.10	.4821	.0440	2.55	.4946	.0154	3.00	.4987	.0044
1.66	.4515	.1006	2.11	.4826	.0431	2.56	.4948	.0151	3.01	.4987	.0043
1.67	.4525	.0989	2.12	.4830	.0422	2.57	.4949	.0147	3.02	.4987	.0042
1.68	.4535	.0973	2.13	.4834	.0413	2.58	.4951	.0143	3.03	.4988	.0040
1.69	.4545	.0957	2.14	.4838	.0404	2.59	.4952	.0139	3.04	.4988	.0039
1.70	.4554	.0940	2.15	.4842	.0395	2.60	.4953	.0136	3.05	.4989	.0038
1.71	.4564	.0925	2.16	.4846	.0387	2.61	.4955	.0132	3.06	.4989	.0037
1.72	.4573	.0909	2.17	.4850	.0379	2.62	.4956	.0129	3.07	.4989	.0036
1.73	.4582	.0893	2.18	.4854	.0371	2.63	.4957	.0126	3.08	.4990	.0035
1.74	.4591	.0878	2.19	.4857	.0363	2.64	.4959	.0122	3.09	.4990	.0034
1.75	.4599	.0863	2.20	.4861	.0355	2.65	.4960	.0119	3.10	.4990	.0033
1.76	.4608	.0848	2.21	.4864	.0347	2.66	.4961	.0116	3.11	.4991	.0032
1.77	.4616	.0833	2.22	.4868	.0339	2.67	.4962	.0113	3.12	.4991	.0031
1.78	.4625	.0818	2.23	.4871	.0332	2.68	.4963	.0110	3.13	.4991	.0030
1.79	.4633	.0804	2.24	.4875	.0325	2.69	.4964	.0107	3.14	.4992	.0029
1.80	.4641	.0790	2.25	.4878	.0317	2.70	.4965	.0104	3.15	.4992	.0028
1.81	.4649	.0775	2.26	.4881	.0310	2.71	.4966	.0101	3.16	.4992	.0027
1.82	.4656	.0761	2.27	.4884	.0303	2.72	.4967	.0099	3.17	.4992	.0026
1.83	.4664	.0748	2.28	.4887	.0297	2.73	.4968	.0096	3.18	.4993	.0025
1.84	.4671	.0734	2.29	.4890	.0290	2.74	.4969	.0093	3.19	.4993	.0025
1.85	.4678	.0721	2.30	.4893	.0283	2.75	.4970	.0091	3.20	.4993	.0024
1.86	.4686	.0707	2.31	.4896	.0277	2.76	.4971	.0088	3.21	.4993	.0023
1.87	.4693	.0694	2.32	.4898	.0270	2.77	.4972	.0086	3.22	.4994	.0022
1.88	.4699	.0681	2.33	.4901	.0264	2.78	.4973	.0084	3.23	.4994	.0022
1.89	.4706	.0669	2.34	.4904	.0258	2.79	.4974	.00 81	3.24	.4994	.0021
1.90	.4713	.0656	2.35	.4906	.0252	2.80	.4974	.0079	3.25	.4994	.0020
1.91	.4719	.0644	2.36	.4909	.0246	2.81	.4975	.0077	3.26	.4994	.0020
1.92	.4726	.0632	2.37	.4911	.0241	2.82	.4976	.0075	3.27	.4995	.0019
1.93	.4732	.0620	2.38	.4913	.0235	2.83	.4977	.0073	3.28	.4995	.0018
1.94	.4738	.0608	2.39	.4916	.0229	2.84	.4977	.0071	3.29	.4995	.0018
1.95	.4744	.0596	2.40	.4918	.0224	2.85	.4978	.0069	3.30	.4995	.0017
1.96	.4750	.0584	2.41	.4920	.0219	2.86	.4979	.0067	3.40	.4997	.0012
1.97	.4756	.0573	2.42	.4922	.0213	2.87	.4979	.0065	3.50	.4998	.0009
1.98	.4761	.0562	2.43	.4925	.0208	2.88	.4980	.0063	3.60	.4998	.0006
1.99	.4767	.0551	2.44	.4927	.0203	2.89	.4981	.0061	3.70	.4999	.0004
2.00	.4772	.0540	2.45	.4929	.0198	2.90	.4981	.0060	3.80	.49993	.0003
2.01	.4778	.0529	2.46	.4931	.0194	2.91	.4982	.0058	3.90	.49995	.0002
2.02	.4783	.0519	2.47	.4932	.0189	2.92	.4982	.0056	4.00	.49997	.0001
2.03	.4788	.0508	2.48	.4934	.0184	2.93	.4983	.0055			
2.04	.4793	.0498	2.49	.4936	.0180	2.94	.4984	.0053			

Table A(II). Probabilities associated with values as extreme as observed values of z in the normal distribution

The body of the table gives one-tailed probabilities under H_0 of z. The left-hand marginal column gives various values of z to one decimal place. The top row gives various values to the second decimal place. Thus, for example, the one-tailed p of $z \geq 0.11$ or $z \leq -0.11$ is $p = 0.4562$

z	.00	.01	.02	.03	.04	.05	.06	.07	.08	.09
.0	.5000	.4960	.4920	.4880	.4840	.4801	.4761	.4721	.4681	.4641
.1	.4602	.4562	.4522	.4483	.4443	.4404	.4364	.4325	.4286	.4247
.2	.4207	.4168	.4129	.4090	.4052	.4013	.3974	.3936	.3897	.3859
.3	.3821	.3783	.3745	.3707	.3669	.3632	.3594	.3557	.3520	.3483
.4.	.3446	.3409	.3372	.3336	.3300	.3264	.3228	.3192	.3156	.3121
.5	.3085	.3050	.3015	.2981	.2946	.2912	.2877	.2843	.2810	.2776
.6	.2743	.2709	.2676	.2643	.2611	.2578	.2546	.2514	.2483	.2451
.7	.2420	.2389	.2358	.2327	.2296	.2266	.2236	.2206	.2177	.2148
.8	.2119	.2090	.2061	.2033	.2005	.1977	.1949	.1922	.1894	.1867
.9	.1841	.1814	.1788	.1762	.1736	.1711	.1685	.1660	.1635	.1611
1.0	.1587	.1562	.1539	.1515	.1492	.1469	.1446	.1423	.1401	.1379
1.1	.1357	.1335	.1314	.1292	.1271	.1251	.1230	.1210	.1190	.1170
1.2	.1151	.1131	.1112	.1093	.1075	.1056	.1038	.1020	.1003	.0985
1.3	.0968	.0951	.0934	.0918	.0901	.0885	.0869	.0853	.0838	.0823
1.4	.0808	.0793	.0778	.0764	.0749	.0735	.0721	.0708	.0694	.0681
1.5	.0668	.0655	.0643	.0630	.0618	.0606	.0594	.0582	.0571	.0559
1.6	.0548	.0537	.0526	.0516	.0505	.0495	.0485	.0475	.0465	.0455
1.7	.0446	.0436	.0427	.0418	.0409	.0401	.0392	.0384	.0375	.0367
1.8	.0359	.0351	.0344	.0336	.0329	.0322	.0314	.0307	.0301	.0294
1.9	.0287	.0281	.0274	.0268	.0262	.0256	.0256	.0244	.0239	.0233
2.0	.0228	.0222	.0217	.0212	.0207	.0202	.0197	.0192	.0188	.0183
2.1	.0179	.0174	.0170	.0166	.0162	.0158	.0154	.0150	.0146	.0143
2.2	.0139	.0136	.0132	.0129	.0125	.0122	.0119	.0116	.0113	.0110
2.3	.0107	.0104	.0102	.0099	.0096	.0094	.0091	.0089	.0087	.0084
2.4	.0082	.0080	.0078	.0075	.0073	.0071	.0069	.0068	.0066	.0064
2.5	.0062	.0060	.0059	.0057	.0055	.0054	.0052	.0051	.0049	.0048
2.6	.0047	.0045	.0044	.0043	.0041	.0040	.0039	.0038	.0037	.0036
2.7	.0035	.0034	.0033	.0032	.0031	.0030	.0029	.0028	.0027	.0026
2.8	.0026	.0025	.0024	.0023	.0023	.0022	.0021	.0021	.0020	.0019
2.9	.0019	.0018	.0018	.0017	.0016	.0016	.0015	.0015	.0014	.0014
3.0	.0013	.0013	.0013	.0012	.0012	.0011	.0011	.0011	.0010	.0010
3.1	.0010	.0009	.0009	.0009	.0008	.0008	.0008	.0008	.0007	.0007
3.2	.0007									
3.3	.0005									
3.4	.0003									
3.5	.00023									
3.6	.00016									
3.7	.00011									
3.8	.00007									
3.9	.00005									
4.0	.00003									

Table B. Critical values of the correlation coefficient (*r*)

	Level of Significance for One-tailed Test			
	.05	.025	.01	.005
	Level of Significance for Two-tailed Test			
df	**.10**	**.05**	**.02**	**.01**
1	.988	.997	.9995	.9999
2	.900	.950	.980	.990
3	.805	.878	.934	.959
4	.729	.811	.882	.917
5	.669	.754	.833	.874
6	.622	.707	.789	.834
7	.582	.666	.750	.798
8	.549	.632	.716	.765
9	.521	.602	.685	.735
10	.497	.576	.658	.708
11	.476	.553	.634	.684
12	.458	.532	.612	.661
13	.441	.514	.592	.641
14	.426	.497	.574	.623
15	.412	.482	.558	.606
16	.400	.468	.542	.590
17	.389	.456	.528	.575
18	.378	.444	.516	.561
19	.369	.433	.503	.549
20	.360	.423	.492	.537
21	.352	.413	.482	.526
22	.344	.404	.472	.515
23	.337	.396	.462	.505
24	.330	.388	.453	.496
25	.323	.381	.445	.487
26	.317	.374	.437	.479
27	.311	.367	.430	.471
28	.306	.361	.423	.463
29	.301	.355	.416	.456
30	.296	.349	.409	.449
35	.275	.325	.381	.418
40	.257	.304	.358	.393
45	.243	.288	.338	.372
50	.231	.273	.322	.354
60	.211	.250	.295	.325
70	.195	.232	.274	.303
80	.183	.217	.256	.283
90	.173	.205	.242	.267
100	.164	.195	.230	.254
125	.147	.174	.206	.228
150	.134	.159	.189	.208
200	.116	.138	.164	.181
300	.095	.113	.134	.148
400	.082	.098	.116	.128
500	.073	.088	.104	.115
1000	.052	.062	.073	.081

Table C.   Critical values of t

	Level of Significance for One-tailed Test					
	.10	.05	.025	.01	.005	.0005
	Level of Significance for Two-tailed Test					
df	.20	.10	.05	.02	.01	.001
1	3.078	6.314	12.706	31.821	63.657	636.619
2	1.886	2.920	4.303	6.965	9.925	31.598
3	1.638	2.353	3.182	4.541	5.841	12.941
4	1.533	2.132	2.776	3.747	4.604	8.610
5	1.476	2.015	2.571	3.365	4.032	6.859
6	1.440	1.943	2.447	3.143	3.707	5.959
7	1.415	1.895	2.365	2.998	3.449	5.405
8	1.397	1.860	2.306	2.896	3.355	5.041
9	1.383	1.833	2.262	2.821	3.250	4.781
10	1.372	1.812	2.228	2.764	3.169	4.587
11	1.363	1.796	2.201	2.718	3.106	4.437
12	1.356	1.782	2.179	2.681	3.055	4.318
13	1.350	1.771	2.160	2.650	3.012	4.221
14	1.345	1.761	2.145	2.624	2.977	4.140
15	1.341	1.753	2.131	2.602	2.947	4.073
16	1.337	1.746	2.120	2.583	2.921	4.015
17	1.333	1.740	2.110	2.567	2.898	3.965
18	1.330	1.734	2.101	2.552	2.878	3.922
19	1.328	1.729	2.093	2.539	2.861	3.883
20	1.325	1.725	2.086	2.528	2.845	3.850
21	1.323	1.721	2.080	2.518	2.831	3.819
22	1.321	1.717	2.074	2.508	2.819	3.792
23	1.319	1.714	2.069	2.500	2.807	3.767
24	1.318	1.711	2.064	2.492	2.797	3.745
25	1.316	1.708	2.060	2.485	2.787	3.725
26	1.315	1.706	2.056	2.479	2.779	3.707
27	1.314	1.703	2.052	2.473	2.771	3.690
28	1.313	1.701	2.048	2.467	2.763	3.674
29	1.311	1.699	2.045	2.462	2.756	3.659
30	1.310	1.697	2.042	2.457	2.750	3.646
40	1.303	1.684	2.021	2.423	2.704	3.551
60	1.296	1.671	2.000	2.390	2.660	3.460
120	1.289	1.658	1.980	2.358	2.617	3.373
∞	1.282	1.645	1.960	2.326	2.576	3.291

Table D.   Transformation of r to z_r

r	z_r	r	z_r	r	z_r	r	z_r	r	z_r
.000	.000	.200	.203	.400	.424	.600	.693	.800	1.099
.005	.005	.205	.208	.405	.430	.605	.701	.805	1.113
.010	.010	.210	.213	.410	.436	.610	.709	.810	1.127
.015	.015	.215	.218	.415	.442	.615	.717	.815	1.142
.020	.020	.220	.224	.420	.448	.620	.725	.820	1.157
.025	.025	.225	.229	.425	.454	.625	.733	.825	1.172
.030	.030	.230	.234	.430	.460	.630	.741	.830	.1188
.035	.035	.235	.239	.435	.466	.635	.750	.835	1.204
.040	.040	.240	.245	.440	.472	.640	.758	.840	1.221
.045	.045	.245	.250	.445	.478	.645	.767	.845	1.238
.050	.050	.250	.255	.450	.485	.650	.775	.850	1.256
.055	.055	.255	.261	.455	.491	.655	.784	.855	1.274
.060	.060	.260	.266	.460	.497	.660	.793	.860	1.293
.065	.065	.265	.271	.465	.504	.665	.802	.865	1.313
.070	.070	.270	.277	.470	.510	.670	.811	.870	1.333
.075	.075	.275	.282	.475	.517	.675	.820	.875	1.354
.080	.080	.280	.288	.480	.523	.680	.829	.880	1.376
.085	.085	.285	.293	.485	.530	.685	.838	.885	1.398
.090	.090	.290	.299	.490	.536	.690	.848	.890	1.422
.095	.095	.295	.304	.495	.543	.695	.858	.895	1.447
.100	.100	.300	.310	.500	.549	.700	.867	.900	1.472
.105	.105	.305	.315	.505	.556	.705	.877	.905	1.499
.110	.110	.310	.321	.510	.563	.710	.887	.910	1.528
.115	.116	.315	.326	.515	.570	.715	.897	.915	1.557
.120	.121	.320	.332	.520	.576	.720	.908	.920	1.589
.125	.126	.325	.337	.525	.583	.725	.918	.925	1.623
.130	.131	.330	.343	.530	.590	.730	.929	.930	1.658
.135	.136	.335	.348	.535	.597	.735	.940	.935	1.697
.140	.141	.340	.354	.540	.604	.740	.950	.940	1.738
.145	.146	.345	.360	.545	.611	.745	.962	.945	1.783
.150	.151	.350	.365	.550	.618	.750	.973	.950	1.832
.155	.156	.355	.371	.555	.626	.755	.984	.955	1.886
.160	.161	.360	.377	.560	.633	.760	.996	.960	1.946
.165	.167	.365	.383	.565	.640	.765	1.008	.965	2.014
.170	.172	.370	.388	.570	.648	.770	1.020	.970	2.092
.175	.177	.375	.394	.575	.655	.775	1.033	.975	2.185
.180	.182	.380	.400	.580	.662	.780	1.045	.980	2.298
.185	.187	.385	.406	.585	.670	.785	1.058	.985	2.443
.190	.192	.390	.412	.590	.678	.790	1.071	.990	2.647
.195	.198	.395	.418	.595	.685	.795	1.085	.995	2.994

Table E. Critical values of F (light face type $\alpha=0.05$, bold face $\alpha=0.01$)

n_2	\multicolumn{24}{c}{n_1 Degrees of Freedom (for Numerator Mean Square)}
	1	2	3	4	5	6	7	8	9	10	11	12	14	16	20	24	30	40	50	75	100	200	500	∞
1	161 **4,052**	200 **4,999**	216 **5,403**	225 **5,625**	230 **5,764**	234 **5,859**	237 **5,928**	239 **5,981**	241 **6,022**	242 **6,056**	243 **6,082**	244 **6,106**	245 **6,142**	246 **6,169**	248 **6,208**	249 **6,234**	250 **6,258**	251 **6,286**	252 **6,302**	253 **6,323**	253 **6,334**	254 **6,352**	254 **6,361**	254 **6,366**
2	18.51 **98.49**	19.00 **99.00**	19.16 **99.17**	19.25 **99.25**	19.30 **99.30**	19.33 **99.33**	19.36 **99.34**	19.37 **99.36**	19.38 **99.38**	19.39 **99.40**	19.40 **99.41**	19.41 **99.42**	19.42 **99.43**	19.43 **99.44**	19.44 **99.45**	19.45 **99.46**	19.46 **99.47**	19.47 **99.48**	19.47 **99.48**	19.48 **99.49**	19.49 **99.49**	19.49 **99.49**	19.50 **99.50**	19.50 **99.50**
3	10.13 **34.12**	9.55 **30.82**	9.28 **29.46**	9.12 **28.71**	9.01 **28.24**	8.94 **27.91**	8.88 **27.67**	8.84 **27.49**	8.81 **27.34**	8.78 **27.23**	8.76 **27.13**	8.74 **27.05**	8.71 **26.92**	8.69 **26.83**	8.66 **26.69**	8.64 **26.60**	8.62 **26.50**	8.60 **26.41**	8.58 **26.35**	8.57 **26.27**	8.56 **26.23**	8.54 **26.18**	8.54 **26.14**	8.53 **26.12**
4	7.71 **21.20**	6.94 **18.00**	6.59 **16.69**	6.39 **15.98**	6.26 **15.52**	6.16 **15.21**	6.09 **14.98**	6.04 **14.80**	6.00 **14.66**	5.96 **14.54**	5.93 **14.45**	5.91 **14.37**	5.87 **14.24**	5.84 **14.15**	5.80 **14.02**	5.77 **13.93**	5.74 **13.83**	5.71 **13.74**	5.70 **13.69**	5.68 **13.61**	5.66 **13.57**	5.65 **13.52**	5.64 **13.48**	5.63 **13.46**
5	6.61 **16.26**	5.79 **13.27**	5.41 **12.06**	5.19 **11.39**	5.05 **10.97**	4.95 **10.67**	4.88 **10.45**	4.82 **10.27**	4.78 **10.15**	4.74 **10.05**	4.70 **9.96**	4.68 **9.89**	4.64 **9.77**	4.60 **9.68**	4.56 **9.55**	4.53 **9.47**	4.50 **9.38**	4.46 **9.29**	4.44 **9.24**	4.42 **9.17**	4.40 **9.13**	4.38 **9.07**	4.37 **9.04**	4.36 **9.02**
6	5.99 **13.74**	5.14 **10.92**	4.76 **9.78**	4.53 **9.15**	4.39 **8.75**	4.28 **8.47**	4.21 **8.26**	4.15 **8.10**	4.10 **7.98**	4.06 **7.87**	4.03 **7.79**	4.00 **7.72**	3.96 **7.60**	3.92 **7.52**	3.87 **7.39**	3.84 **7.31**	3.81 **7.23**	3.77 **7.14**	3.75 **7.09**	3.72 **7.02**	3.71 **6.99**	3.69 **6.94**	3.68 **6.90**	3.67 **6.88**
7	5.59 **12.25**	4.74 **9.55**	4.35 **8.45**	4.12 **7.85**	3.97 **7.46**	3.87 **7.19**	3.79 **7.00**	3.73 **6.84**	3.68 **6.71**	3.63 **6.62**	3.60 **6.54**	3.57 **6.47**	3.52 **6.35**	3.49 **6.27**	3.44 **6.15**	3.41 **6.07**	3.38 **5.98**	3.34 **5.90**	3.32 **5.85**	3.29 **5.78**	3.28 **5.75**	3.25 **5.70**	3.24 **5.67**	3.23 **5.65**
8	5.32 **11.26**	4.46 **8.65**	4.07 **7.59**	3.84 **7.01**	3.69 **6.63**	3.58 **6.37**	3.50 **6.19**	3.44 **6.03**	3.39 **5.91**	3.34 **5.82**	3.31 **5.74**	3.28 **5.67**	3.23 **5.56**	3.20 **5.48**	3.15 **5.36**	3.12 **5.28**	3.08 **5.20**	3.05 **5.11**	3.03 **5.06**	3.00 **5.00**	2.98 **4.96**	2.96 **4.91**	2.94 **4.88**	2.93 **4.86**
9	5.12 **10.56**	4.26 **8.02**	3.86 **6.99**	3.63 **6.42**	3.48 **6.06**	3.37 **5.80**	3.29 **5.62**	3.23 **5.47**	3.18 **5.35**	3.13 **5.26**	3.10 **5.18**	3.07 **5.11**	3.02 **5.00**	2.98 **4.92**	2.93 **4.80**	2.90 **4.73**	2.86 **4.64**	2.82 **4.56**	2.80 **4.51**	2.77 **4.45**	2.76 **4.41**	2.73 **4.36**	2.72 **4.33**	2.71 **4.31**
10	4.96 **10.04**	4.10 **7.56**	3.71 **6.55**	3.48 **5.99**	3.33 **5.64**	3.22 **5.39**	3.14 **5.21**	3.07 **5.06**	3.02 **4.95**	2.97 **4.85**	2.94 **4.78**	2.91 **4.71**	2.86 **4.60**	2.82 **4.52**	2.77 **4.41**	2.74 **4.33**	2.70 **4.25**	2.67 **4.17**	2.64 **4.12**	2.61 **4.05**	2.59 **4.01**	2.56 **3.96**	2.55 **3.93**	2.54 **3.91**
11	4.84 **9.65**	3.98 **7.20**	3.59 **6.22**	3.36 **5.67**	3.20 **5.32**	3.09 **5.07**	3.01 **4.88**	2.95 **4.74**	2.90 **4.63**	2.86 **4.54**	2.82 **4.46**	2.79 **4.40**	2.74 **4.29**	2.70 **4.21**	2.65 **4.10**	2.61 **4.02**	2.57 **3.94**	2.53 **3.86**	2.50 **3.80**	2.47 **3.74**	2.45 **3.70**	2.42 **3.66**	2.41 **3.62**	2.40 **3.60**
12	4.75 **9.33**	3.88 **6.93**	3.49 **5.95**	3.26 **5.41**	3.11 **5.06**	3.00 **4.82**	2.92 **4.65**	2.85 **4.50**	2.80 **4.39**	2.76 **4.30**	2.72 **4.22**	2.69 **4.16**	2.64 **4.05**	2.60 **3.98**	2.54 **3.86**	2.50 **3.78**	2.46 **3.70**	2.42 **3.61**	2.40 **3.56**	2.36 **3.49**	2.35 **3.46**	2.32 **3.41**	2.31 **3.38**	2.30 **3.36**
13	4.67 **9.07**	3.80 **6.70**	3.41 **5.74**	3.18 **5.20**	3.02 **4.86**	2.92 **4.62**	2.84 **4.44**	2.77 **4.30**	2.72 **4.19**	2.67 **4.10**	2.63 **4.02**	2.60 **3.96**	2.55 **3.85**	2.51 **3.78**	2.46 **3.67**	2.42 **3.59**	2.38 **3.51**	2.34 **3.42**	2.32 **3.37**	2.28 **3.30**	2.26 **3.27**	2.24 **3.21**	2.22 **3.18**	2.21 **3.16**
14	4.60 **8.86**	3.74 **6.51**	3.34 **5.56**	3.11 **5.03**	2.96 **4.69**	2.85 **4.46**	2.77 **4.28**	2.70 **4.14**	2.65 **4.03**	2.60 **3.94**	2.56 **3.86**	2.53 **3.80**	2.48 **3.70**	2.44 **3.62**	2.39 **3.51**	2.35 **3.43**	2.31 **3.34**	2.27 **3.26**	2.24 **3.21**	2.21 **3.14**	2.19 **3.11**	2.16 **3.06**	2.14 **3.02**	2.13 **3.00**
15	4.54 **8.68**	3.68 **6.36**	3.29 **5.42**	3.06 **4.89**	2.90 **4.56**	2.79 **4.32**	2.70 **4.14**	2.64 **4.00**	2.59 **3.89**	2.55 **3.80**	2.51 **3.73**	2.48 **3.67**	2.43 **3.56**	2.39 **3.48**	2.33 **3.36**	2.29 **3.29**	2.25 **3.20**	2.21 **3.12**	2.18 **3.07**	2.15 **3.00**	2.12 **2.97**	2.10 **2.92**	2.08 **2.89**	2.07 **2.87**
16	4.49 **8.53**	3.63 **6.23**	3.24 **5.29**	3.01 **4.77**	2.85 **4.44**	2.74 **4.20**	2.66 **4.03**	2.59 **3.89**	2.54 **3.78**	2.49 **3.69**	2.45 **3.61**	2.42 **3.55**	2.37 **3.45**	2.33 **3.37**	2.28 **3.25**	2.24 **3.18**	2.20 **3.10**	2.16 **3.01**	2.13 **2.96**	2.09 **2.89**	2.07 **2.86**	2.04 **2.80**	2.02 **2.77**	2.01 **2.75**
17	4.45 **8.40**	3.59 **6.11**	3.20 **5.18**	2.96 **4.67**	2.81 **4.34**	2.70 **4.10**	2.62 **3.93**	2.55 **3.79**	2.50 **3.68**	2.45 **3.59**	2.41 **3.52**	2.38 **3.45**	2.33 **3.35**	2.29 **3.27**	2.23 **3.16**	2.19 **3.08**	2.15 **3.00**	2.11 **2.92**	2.08 **2.86**	2.04 **2.79**	2.02 **2.76**	1.99 **2.70**	1.97 **2.67**	1.96 **2.65**
18	4.41 **8.28**	3.55 **6.01**	3.16 **5.09**	2.93 **4.58**	2.77 **4.25**	2.66 **4.01**	2.58 **3.85**	2.51 **3.71**	2.46 **3.60**	2.41 **3.51**	2.37 **3.44**	2.34 **3.37**	2.29 **3.27**	2.25 **3.19**	2.19 **3.07**	2.15 **3.00**	2.11 **2.91**	2.07 **2.83**	2.04 **2.78**	2.00 **2.71**	1.98 **2.68**	1.95 **2.62**	1.93 **2.59**	1.92 **2.57**

(Table E contd.)

(Table E contd.)

n₁, Degrees of Freedom (for Numerator Mean Square)

n_2	1	2	3	4	5	6	7	8	9	10	11	12	14	16	20	24	30	40	50	75	100	200	500	∞
19	4.38 **8.18**	3.52 **5.93**	3.13 **5.01**	2.90 **4.50**	2.74 **4.17**	2.63 **3.94**	2.55 **3.77**	2.48 **3.63**	2.43 **3.52**	2.38 **3.43**	2.34 **3.36**	2.31 **3.30**	2.26 **3.19**	2.21 **3.12**	2.15 **3.00**	2.11 **2.92**	2.07 **2.84**	2.02 **2.76**	2.00 **2.70**	1.96 **2.63**	1.94 **2.60**	1.91 **2.54**	1.90 **2.51**	1.88 **2.49**
20	4.35 **8.10**	3.49 **5.85**	3.10 **4.94**	2.87 **4.43**	2.71 **4.10**	2.60 **3.87**	2.52 **3.71**	2.45 **3.56**	2.40 **3.45**	2.35 **3.37**	2.31 **3.30**	2.28 **3.23**	2.23 **3.13**	2.18 **3.05**	2.12 **2.94**	2.08 **2.86**	2.04 **2.77**	1.99 **2.69**	1.96 **2.63**	1.92 **2.56**	1.90 **2.53**	1.87 **2.47**	1.85 **2.44**	1.84 **2.42**
21	4.32 **8.02**	3.47 **5.78**	3.07 **4.87**	2.84 **4.37**	2.68 **4.04**	2.57 **3.81**	2.49 **3.65**	2.42 **3.51**	2.37 **3.40**	2.32 **3.31**	2.28 **3.24**	2.25 **3.17**	2.20 **3.07**	2.15 **2.99**	2.09 **2.88**	2.05 **2.80**	2.00 **2.72**	1.96 **2.63**	1.93 **2.58**	1.89 **2.51**	1.87 **2.47**	1.84 **2.42**	1.82 **2.38**	1.81 **2.36**
22	4.30 **7.94**	3.44 **5.72**	3.05 **4.82**	2.82 **4.31**	2.66 **3.99**	2.55 **3.76**	2.47 **3.59**	2.40 **3.45**	2.35 **3.35**	2.30 **3.26**	2.26 **3.18**	2.23 **3.12**	2.18 **3.02**	2.13 **2.94**	2.07 **2.83**	2.03 **2.75**	1.98 **2.67**	1.93 **2.58**	1.91 **2.53**	1.87 **2.46**	1.84 **2.42**	1.81 **2.37**	1.80 **2.33**	1.78 **2.31**
23	4.28 **7.88**	3.42 **5.66**	3.03 **4.76**	2.80 **4.26**	2.64 **3.94**	2.53 **3.71**	2.45 **3.54**	2.38 **3.41**	2.32 **3.30**	2.28 **3.21**	2.24 **3.14**	2.20 **3.07**	2.14 **2.97**	2.10 **2.89**	2.04 **2.78**	2.00 **2.70**	1.96 **2.62**	1.91 **2.53**	1.88 **2.48**	1.84 **2.41**	1.82 **2.37**	1.79 **2.32**	1.77 **2.28**	1.76 **2.26**
24	4.26 **7.82**	3.40 **5.61**	3.01 **4.72**	2.78 **4.22**	2.62 **3.90**	2.51 **3.67**	2.43 **3.50**	2.36 **3.36**	2.30 **3.25**	2.26 **3.17**	2.22 **3.09**	2.18 **3.03**	2.13 **2.93**	2.09 **2.85**	2.02 **2.74**	1.98 **2.66**	1.94 **2.58**	1.89 **2.49**	1.86 **2.44**	1.82 **2.36**	1.80 **2.33**	1.76 **2.27**	1.74 **2.23**	1.73 **2.21**
25	4.24 **7.77**	3.38 **5.57**	2.99 **4.68**	2.76 **4.18**	2.60 **3.86**	2.49 **3.63**	2.41 **3.46**	2.34 **3.32**	2.28 **3.21**	2.24 **3.13**	2.20 **3.05**	2.16 **2.99**	2.11 **2.89**	2.06 **2.81**	2.00 **2.70**	1.96 **2.62**	1.92 **2.54**	1.87 **2.45**	1.84 **2.40**	1.80 **2.32**	1.77 **2.29**	1.74 **2.23**	1.72 **2.19**	1.71 **2.17**
26	4.22 **7.72**	3.37 **5.53**	2.98 **4.64**	2.74 **4.14**	2.59 **3.82**	2.47 **3.59**	2.39 **3.42**	2.32 **3.29**	2.27 **3.17**	2.22 **3.09**	2.18 **3.02**	2.15 **2.96**	2.10 **2.86**	2.05 **2.77**	1.99 **2.66**	1.95 **2.58**	1.90 **2.50**	1.85 **2.41**	1.82 **2.36**	1.78 **2.28**	1.76 **2.25**	1.72 **2.19**	1.70 **2.15**	1.69 **2.13**
27	4.21 **7.68**	3.35 **5.49**	2.96 **4.60**	2.73 **4.11**	2.57 **3.79**	2.46 **3.56**	2.37 **3.39**	2.30 **3.26**	2.25 **3.14**	2.20 **3.06**	2.16 **2.98**	2.13 **2.93**	2.08 **2.83**	2.03 **2.74**	1.97 **2.63**	1.93 **2.55**	1.88 **2.47**	1.84 **2.38**	1.80 **2.33**	1.76 **2.25**	1.74 **2.21**	1.71 **2.16**	1.68 **2.12**	1.67 **2.10**
28	4.20 **7.64**	3.34 **5.45**	2.95 **4.57**	2.71 **4.07**	2.56 **3.76**	2.44 **3.53**	2.36 **3.36**	2.29 **3.23**	2.24 **3.11**	2.19 **3.03**	2.15 **2.95**	2.12 **2.90**	2.06 **2.80**	2.02 **2.71**	1.96 **2.60**	1.91 **2.52**	1.87 **2.44**	1.81 **2.35**	1.78 **2.30**	1.75 **2.22**	1.72 **2.18**	1.69 **2.13**	1.67 **2.09**	1.65 **2.06**
29	4.18 **7.60**	3.33 **5.42**	2.93 **4.54**	2.70 **4.04**	2.54 **3.73**	2.43 **3.50**	2.35 **3.33**	2.28 **3.20**	2.22 **3.08**	2.18 **3.00**	2.14 **2.92**	2.10 **2.87**	2.05 **2.77**	2.00 **2.68**	1.94 **2.57**	1.90 **2.49**	1.85 **2.41**	1.80 **2.32**	1.77 **2.27**	1.73 **2.19**	1.71 **2.15**	1.68 **2.10**	1.65 **2.06**	1.64 **2.03**
30	4.17 **7.56**	3.32 **5.39**	2.92 **4.51**	2.69 **4.02**	2.53 **3.70**	2.42 **3.47**	2.34 **3.30**	2.27 **3.17**	2.21 **3.06**	2.16 **2.98**	2.12 **2.90**	2.09 **2.84**	2.04 **2.74**	1.99 **2.66**	1.93 **2.55**	1.89 **2.47**	1.84 **2.38**	1.79 **2.29**	1.76 **2.24**	1.72 **2.16**	1.69 **2.13**	1.66 **2.07**	1.64 **2.03**	1.62 **2.01**
32	4.15 **7.50**	3.30 **5.34**	2.90 **4.46**	2.67 **3.97**	2.51 **3.66**	2.40 **3.42**	2.32 **3.25**	2.25 **3.12**	2.19 **3.01**	2.14 **2.94**	2.10 **2.86**	2.07 **2.80**	2.02 **2.70**	1.97 **2.62**	1.91 **2.51**	1.86 **2.42**	1.82 **2.34**	1.76 **2.25**	1.74 **2.20**	1.69 **2.12**	1.67 **2.08**	1.64 **2.02**	1.61 **1.98**	1.59 **1.96**
34	4.13 **7.44**	3.28 **5.29**	2.88 **4.42**	2.65 **3.93**	2.49 **3.61**	2.38 **3.38**	2.30 **3.21**	2.23 **3.08**	2.17 **2.97**	2.12 **2.89**	2.08 **2.82**	2.05 **2.76**	2.00 **2.66**	1.95 **2.58**	1.89 **2.47**	1.84 **2.38**	1.80 **2.30**	1.74 **2.21**	1.71 **2.15**	1.67 **2.08**	1.64 **2.04**	1.61 **1.98**	1.59 **1.94**	1.57 **1.91**
36	4.11 **7.39**	3.26 **5.25**	2.86 **4.38**	2.63 **3.89**	2.48 **3.58**	2.36 **3.35**	2.28 **3.18**	2.21 **3.04**	2.15 **2.94**	2.10 **2.86**	2.06 **2.78**	2.03 **2.72**	1.98 **2.62**	1.93 **2.54**	1.87 **2.43**	1.82 **2.35**	1.78 **2.26**	1.72 **2.17**	1.69 **2.12**	1.65 **2.04**	1.62 **2.00**	1.59 **1.94**	1.56 **1.90**	1.55 **1.87**
38	4.10 **7.35**	3.25 **5.21**	2.85 **4.34**	2.62 **3.86**	2.46 **3.54**	2.35 **3.32**	2.26 **3.15**	2.19 **3.02**	2.14 **2.91**	2.09 **2.82**	2.05 **2.75**	2.02 **2.69**	1.96 **2.59**	1.92 **2.51**	1.85 **2.40**	1.80 **2.32**	1.76 **2.22**	1.71 **2.14**	1.67 **2.08**	1.63 **2.00**	1.60 **1.97**	1.57 **1.90**	1.54 **1.86**	1.53 **1.84**
40	4.08 **7.31**	3.23 **5.18**	2.84 **4.31**	2.61 **3.83**	2.45 **3.51**	2.34 **3.29**	2.25 **3.12**	2.18 **2.99**	2.12 **2.88**	2.07 **2.80**	2.04 **2.73**	2.00 **2.66**	1.95 **2.56**	1.90 **2.49**	1.84 **2.37**	1.79 **2.29**	1.74 **2.20**	1.69 **2.11**	1.66 **2.05**	1.61 **1.97**	1.59 **1.94**	1.55 **1.88**	1.53 **1.84**	1.51 **1.81**
42	4.07 **7.27**	3.22 **5.15**	2.83 **4.29**	2.59 **3.80**	2.44 **3.49**	2.32 **3.26**	2.24 **3.10**	2.17 **2.96**	2.11 **2.86**	2.06 **2.77**	2.02 **2.70**	1.99 **2.64**	1.94 **2.54**	1.89 **2.46**	1.82 **2.35**	1.78 **2.26**	1.73 **2.17**	1.68 **2.08**	1.64 **2.02**	1.60 **1.94**	1.57 **1.91**	1.54 **1.85**	1.51 **1.80**	1.49 **1.78**
44	4.06 **7.24**	3.21 **5.12**	2.82 **4.26**	2.58 **3.78**	2.43 **3.46**	2.31 **3.24**	2.23 **3.07**	2.16 **2.94**	2.10 **2.84**	2.05 **2.75**	2.01 **2.68**	1.98 **2.62**	1.92 **2.52**	1.88 **2.44**	1.81 **2.32**	1.76 **2.24**	1.72 **2.15**	1.66 **2.06**	1.63 **2.00**	1.58 **1.92**	1.56 **1.88**	1.52 **1.82**	1.50 **1.78**	1.48 **1.75**
46	4.05 **7.21**	3.20 **5.10**	2.80 **4.24**	2.57 **3.76**	2.42 **3.44**	2.30 **3.22**	2.22 **3.05**	2.14 **2.92**	2.09 **2.82**	2.04 **2.73**	2.00 **2.66**	1.97 **2.60**	1.91 **2.50**	1.87 **2.42**	1.80 **2.30**	1.75 **2.22**	1.71 **2.13**	1.65 **2.04**	1.62 **1.98**	1.57 **1.90**	1.54 **1.86**	1.51 **1.80**	1.48 **1.76**	1.46 **1.72**

n₁ Degrees of Freedom (for Numerator Mean Square)

n_2	1	2	3	4	5	6	7	8	9	10	11	12	14	16	20	24	30	40	50	75	100	200	500	∞
48	4.04 **7.19**	3.19 **5.08**	2.80 **4.22**	2.56 **3.74**	2.41 **3.42**	2.30 **3.20**	2.21 **3.04**	2.14 **2.90**	2.08 **2.80**	2.03 **2.71**	1.99 **2.64**	1.96 **2.58**	1.90 **2.48**	1.86 **2.40**	1.79 **2.28**	1.74 **2.20**	1.70 **2.11**	1.64 **2.02**	1.61 **1.96**	1.56 **1.88**	1.53 **1.84**	1.50 **1.78**	1.47 **1.73**	1.45 **1.70**
50	4.03 **7.17**	3.18 **5.06**	2.79 **4.20**	2.56 **3.72**	2.40 **3.41**	2.29 **3.18**	2.20 **3.02**	2.13 **2.88**	2.07 **2.78**	2.02 **2.70**	1.98 **2.62**	1.95 **2.56**	1.90 **2.46**	1.85 **2.39**	1.78 **2.26**	1.74 **2.18**	1.69 **2.10**	1.63 **2.00**	1.60 **1.94**	1.55 **1.86**	1.52 **1.82**	1.48 **1.76**	1.46 **1.71**	1.44 **1.68**
55	4.02 **7.12**	3.17 **5.01**	2.78 **4.16**	2.54 **3.68**	2.38 **3.37**	2.27 **3.15**	2.18 **2.98**	2.11 **2.85**	2.05 **2.75**	2.00 **2.66**	1.97 **2.59**	1.93 **2.53**	1.88 **2.43**	1.83 **2.35**	1.76 **2.23**	1.72 **2.15**	1.67 **2.06**	1.61 **1.96**	1.58 **1.90**	1.52 **1.82**	1.50 **1.78**	1.46 **1.71**	1.43 **1.66**	1.41 **1.64**
60	4.00 **7.08**	3.15 **4.98**	2.76 **4.13**	2.52 **3.65**	2.37 **3.34**	2.25 **3.12**	2.17 **2.95**	2.10 **2.82**	2.04 **2.72**	1.99 **2.63**	1.95 **2.56**	1.92 **2.50**	1.86 **2.40**	1.81 **2.32**	1.75 **2.20**	1.70 **2.12**	1.65 **2.03**	1.59 **1.93**	1.56 **1.87**	1.50 **1.79**	1.48 **1.74**	1.44 **1.68**	1.41 **1.63**	1.39 **1.60**
65	3.99 **7.04**	3.14 **4.95**	2.75 **4.10**	2.51 **3.62**	2.36 **3.31**	2.24 **3.09**	2.15 **2.93**	2.08 **2.79**	2.02 **2.70**	1.98 **2.61**	1.94 **2.54**	1.90 **2.47**	1.85 **2.37**	1.80 **2.30**	1.73 **2.18**	1.68 **2.09**	1.63 **2.00**	1.57 **1.90**	1.54 **1.84**	1.49 **1.76**	1.46 **1.71**	1.42 **1.64**	1.39 **1.60**	1.37 **1.56**
70	3.98 **7.01**	3.13 **4.92**	2.74 **4.08**	2.50 **3.60**	2.35 **3.29**	2.23 **3.07**	2.14 **2.91**	2.07 **2.77**	2.01 **2.67**	1.97 **2.59**	1.93 **2.51**	1.89 **2.45**	1.84 **2.35**	1.79 **2.28**	1.72 **2.15**	1.67 **2.07**	1.62 **1.98**	1.56 **1.88**	1.53 **1.82**	1.47 **1.74**	1.45 **1.69**	1.40 **1.62**	1.37 **1.56**	1.35 **1.53**
80	3.96 **6.96**	3.11 **4.88**	2.72 **4.04**	2.48 **3.56**	2.33 **3.25**	2.21 **3.04**	2.12 **2.87**	2.05 **2.74**	1.99 **2.64**	1.95 **2.55**	1.91 **2.48**	1.88 **2.41**	1.82 **2.32**	1.77 **2.24**	1.70 **2.11**	1.65 **2.03**	1.60 **1.94**	1.54 **1.84**	1.51 **1.78**	1.45 **1.70**	1.42 **1.65**	1.38 **1.57**	1.35 **1.52**	1.32 **1.49**
100	3.94 **6.90**	3.09 **4.82**	2.70 **3.98**	2.46 **3.51**	2.30 **3.20**	2.19 **2.99**	2.10 **2.82**	2.03 **2.69**	1.97 **2.59**	1.92 **2.51**	1.88 **2.43**	1.85 **2.36**	1.79 **2.26**	1.75 **2.19**	1.68 **2.06**	1.63 **1.98**	1.57 **1.89**	1.51 **1.79**	1.48 **1.73**	1.42 **1.64**	1.39 **1.59**	1.34 **1.51**	1.30 **1.46**	1.28 **1.43**
125	3.92 **6.84**	3.07 **4.78**	2.68 **3.94**	2.44 **3.47**	2.29 **3.17**	2.17 **2.95**	2.08 **2.79**	2.01 **2.65**	1.95 **2.56**	1.90 **2.47**	1.86 **2.40**	1.83 **2.33**	1.77 **2.23**	1.72 **2.15**	1.65 **2.03**	1.60 **1.94**	1.55 **1.85**	1.49 **1.75**	1.45 **1.68**	1.39 **1.59**	1.36 **1.54**	1.31 **1.46**	1.27 **1.40**	1.25 **1.37**
150	3.91 **6.81**	3.06 **4.75**	2.67 **3.91**	2.43 **3.44**	2.27 **3.14**	2.16 **2.92**	2.07 **2.76**	2.00 **2.62**	1.94 **2.53**	1.89 **2.44**	1.85 **2.37**	1.82 **2.30**	1.76 **2.20**	1.71 **2.12**	1.64 **2.00**	1.59 **1.91**	1.54 **1.83**	1.47 **1.72**	1.44 **1.66**	1.37 **1.56**	1.34 **1.51**	1.29 **1.43**	1.25 **1.37**	1.22 **1.33**
200	3.89 **6.76**	3.04 **4.71**	2.65 **3.88**	2.41 **3.41**	2.26 **3.11**	2.14 **2.90**	2.05 **2.73**	1.98 **2.60**	1.92 **2.50**	1.87 **2.41**	1.83 **2.34**	1.80 **2.28**	1.74 **2.17**	1.69 **2.09**	1.62 **1.97**	1.57 **1.88**	1.52 **1.79**	1.45 **1.69**	1.42 **1.62**	1.35 **1.53**	1.32 **1.48**	1.26 **1.39**	1.22 **1.33**	1.19 **1.28**
400	3.86 **6.70**	3.02 **4.66**	2.62 **3.83**	2.39 **3.36**	2.23 **3.06**	2.12 **2.85**	2.03 **2.69**	1.96 **2.55**	1.90 **2.46**	1.85 **2.37**	1.81 **2.29**	1.78 **2.23**	1.72 **2.12**	1.67 **2.04**	1.60 **1.92**	1.54 **1.84**	1.49 **1.74**	1.42 **1.64**	1.38 **1.57**	1.32 **1.47**	1.28 **1.42**	1.22 **1.32**	1.16 **1.24**	1.13 **1.19**
1000	3.85 **6.66**	3.00 **4.62**	2.61 **3.80**	2.38 **3.34**	2.22 **3.04**	2.10 **2.82**	2.02 **2.66**	1.95 **2.53**	1.89 **2.43**	1.84 **2.34**	1.80 **2.26**	1.76 **2.20**	1.70 **2.09**	1.65 **2.01**	1.58 **1.89**	1.53 **1.81**	1.47 **1.71**	1.41 **1.61**	1.36 **1.54**	1.30 **1.44**	1.26 **1.38**	1.19 **1.28**	1.13 **1.19**	1.08 **1.11**
∞	3.84 **6.64**	2.99 **4.60**	2.60 **3.78**	2.37 **3.32**	2.21 **3.02**	2.09 **2.80**	2.01 **2.64**	1.94 **2.51**	1.88 **2.41**	1.83 **2.32**	1.79 **2.24**	1.75 **2.18**	1.69 **2.07**	1.64 **1.99**	1.57 **1.87**	1.52 **1.79**	1.46 **1.69**	1.40 **1.59**	1.35 **1.52**	1.28 **1.41**	1.24 **1.36**	1.17 **1.25**	1.11 **1.15**	1.00 **1.00**

Table F.   Trigonometric functions

Angle	Sin	Cos	Tan	Angle	Sin	Cos	Tan
0°	.000	1.000	.000	45°	.707	.707	1.000
1°	.018	.999	.018	46°	.719	.695	1.036
2°	.035	.999	.035	47°	.731	.682	1.072
3°	.052	.998	.052	48°	.743	.669	1.111
4°	.070	.997	.070	49°	.755	.656	1.150
5°	.087	.996	.087	50°	.766	.643	1.192
6°	.105	.994	.105	51°	.777	.629	1.235
7°	.122	.992	.123	52°	.788	.616	1.280
8°	.139	.990	.141	53°	.799	.602	1.327
9°	.156	.988	.158	54°	.809	.588	1.376
10°	.174	.985	.176	55°	.819	.574	1.428
11°	.191	.982	.194	56°	.829	.559	1.483
12°	.208	.978	.213	57°	.839	.545	1.540
13°	.225	.974	.231	58°	.848	.530	1.600
14°	.242	.970	.249	59°	.857	.515	1.662
15°	.259	.966	.268	60°	.866	.500	1.732
16°	.276	.961	.287	61°	.875	.485	1.804
17°	.292	.956	.306	62°	.883	.469	1.881
18°	.309	.951	.325	63°	.891	.454	1.963
19°	.326	.946	.344	64°	.899	.438	2.050
20°	.342	.940	.364	65°	.906	.423	2.144
21°	.358	.934	.384	66°	.914	.407	2.246
22°	.375	.927	.404	67°	.921	.391	2.356
23°	.391	.921	.424	68°	.927	.375	2.475
24°	.407	.914	.445	69°	.934	.358	2.605
25°	.423	.906	.466	70°	.940	.342	2.747
26°	.438	.899	.488	71°	.946	.326	2.904
27°	.454	.891	.510	72°	.951	.309	3.078
28°	.469	.883	.532	73°	.956	.292	3.271
29°	.485	.875	.554	74°	.961	.276	3.487
30°	.500	.866	.577	75°	.966	.259	3.732
31°	.515	.857	.601	76°	.970	.242	4.011
32°	.530	.848	.625	77°	.974	.225	4.331
33°	.545	.839	.649	78°	.978	.208	4.705
34°	.559	.829	.675	79°	.982	.191	5.145
35°	.574	.819	.700	80°	.985	.174	5.671
36°	.588	.809	.727	81°	.988	.156	6.314
37°	.602	.799	.754	82°	.990	.139	7.115
38°	.616	.788	.781	83°	.992	.122	8.144
39°	.629	.777	.810	84°	.994	.105	9.514
40°	.643	.766	.839	85°	.996	.087	11.430
41°	.656	.755	.869	86°	.997	.070	14.300
42°	.669	.743	.900	87°	.998	.052	19.081
43°	.682	.731	.933	88°	.999	.035	28.636
44°	.695	.719	.966	89°	.999	.018	57.290

Table G. Values to facilitate the estimation of the Cosine-pi coefficient of correlation, with two-place accuracy

$\frac{ad}{bc}$	$r_{\text{cos-pi}}$	$\frac{ad}{bc}$	$r_{\text{cos-pi}}$	$\frac{ad}{bc}$	$r_{\text{cos-pi}}$	$\frac{ad}{bc}$	$r_{\text{cos-pi}}$
1.013	.005	1.940	.255	4.067	.505	11.512	.755
1.039	.015	1.993	.265	4.205	.515	12.177	.765
1.066	.025	2.048	.275	4.351	.525	12.906	.775
1.093	.035	2.105	.285	4.503	.535	13.702	.785
1.122	.045	2.164	.295	4.662	.545	14.592	.795
1.150	.055	2.225	.305	4.830	.555	15.573	.805
1.180	.065	2.288	.315	5.007	.565	16.670	.815
1.211	.075	2.353	.325	5.192	.575	17.900	.825
1.242	.085	2.421	.335	5.388	.585	19.288	.835
1.275	.095	2.490	.345	5.595	.595	20.866	.845
1.308	.105	2.563	.355	5.813	.605	22.675	.855
1.342	.115	2.638	.365	6.043	.615	24.768	.865
1.377	.125	2.716	.375	6.288	.625	27.212	.875
1.413	.135	2.797	.385	6.547	.635	30.106	.885
1.450	.145	2.881	.395	6.822	.645	33.578	.895
1.488	.155	2.957	.405	7.115	.655	37.818	.905
1.528	.165	3.095	.415	7.428	.665	43.100	.915
1.568	.175	3.153	.425	7.761	.675	49.851	.925
1.610	.185	3.251	.435	8.117	.685	58.765	.935
1.653	.195	3.353	.445	8.499	.695	71.046	.945
1.697	.205	3.460	.455	8.910	.705	88.984	.955
1.743	.215	3.571	.465	9.351	.715	117.52	.965
1.790	.225	3.690	.475	9.828	.725	169.60	.975
1.838	.235	3.808	.485	10.344	.735	293.28	.985
1.888	.245	3.935	.495	10.903	.745	934.06	.995

Example, if an obtained ratio *ad/bc* equals 3.472, we find that this value lies between tabled values of 3.460 and 3.571. The cosine-pi coefficient is therefore between 0.455 and 0.465; that is say, it is 0.46. If *bc* is greater than *ad*, find the ratio *bc/ad* and attach a negative sign to $r_{\text{cos-pi}}$.

Table H. Arcsin transformation, angle = Arcsin $\sqrt{\text{Percentage}}$

%	0	1	2	3	4	5	6	7	8	9
0.0	0	0.57	0.81	0.99	1.15	1.28	1.40	1.52	1.62	1.72
0.1	1.81	1.90	1.99	2.07	2.14	2.22	2.29	2.36	2.43	2.50
0.2	2.56	2.63	2.69	2.75	2.81	2.87	2.92	2.98	3.03	3.09
0.3	3.14	3.19	3.24	3.29	3.34	3.39	3.44	3.49	3.53	3.58
0.4	3.63	3.67	3.72	3.76	3.80	3.85	3.89	3.93	3.97	4.01
0.5	4.05	4.09	4.13	4.17	4.21	4.25	4.29	4.33	4.37	4.40
0.6	4.44	4.48	4.52	4.55	4.59	4.62	4.66	4.69	4.73	4.76
0.7	4.80	4.83	4.87	4.90	4.93	4.97	5.00	5.03	5.07	5.10
0.8	5.13	5.16	5.20	5.23	5.26	5.29	5.32	5.35	5.38	5.41
0.9	5.44	5.47	5.50	5.53	5.56	5.59	5.62	5.65	5.68	5.71
1	5.74	6.02	6.29	6.55	6.80	7.04	7.27	7.49	7.71	7.92
2	8.13	8.33	8.53	8.72	8.91	9.10	9.28	9.46	9.63	9.81
3	9.98	10.14	10.31	10.47	10.63	10.78	10.94	11.09	11.24	11.39
4	11.54	11.68	11.83	11.97	12.11	12.25	12.39	12.52	12.66	12.79
5	12.92	13.05	13.18	13.31	13.44	13.56	13.69	13.81	13.94	14.06
6	14.18	14.30	14.42	14.54	14.65	14.77	14.89	15.00	15.12	15.23
7	15.34	15.45	15.56	15.68	15.79	15.89	16.00	16.11	16.22	16.32
8	16.43	16.54	16.64	16.74	16.85	16.95	17.05	17.16	17.26	17.36
9	17.46	17.56	17.66	17.76	17.85	17.95	18.05	18.15	18.24	18.34
10	18.44	18.53	18.63	18.72	18.81	18.91	19.00	19.09	19.19	19.28
11	19.37	19.46	19.55	19.64	19.73	19.82	19.91	20.00	20.09	20.18
12	20.27	20.36	20.44	20.53	20.62	20.70	20.79	20.88	20.96	21.05
13	21.13	21.22	21.30	21.39	21.47	21.56	21.64	21.72	21.81	21.89
14	21.97	22.06	22.14	22.22	22.30	22.38	22.46	22.55	22.63	22.71
15	22.79	22.87	22.95	23.03	23.11	23.19	23.26	23.34	23.42	23.50
16	23.58	23.66	23.73	23.81	23.89	23.97	24.04	24.12	24.20	24.27
17	24.35	24.43	24.50	24.58	24.65	24.73	24.80	24.88	24.95	25.03
18	25.10	25.18	25.25	25.33	25.40	25.48	25.55	25.62	25.70	25.77
19	25.84	25.92	25.99	26.06	26.13	26.21	26.28	26.35	26.42	26.49
20	26.56	26.64	26.71	26.78	26.85	26.92	26.99	27.06	27.13	27.20
21	27.28	27.35	27.42	27.49	27.56	27.63	27.69	27.76	27.83	27.90
22	27.97	28.04	28.11	28.18	28.25	28.32	28.38	28.45	28.52	28.59
23	28.66	28.73	28.79	28.86	28.93	29.00	29.06	29.13	29.20	29.27
24	29.33	29.40	29.47	29.53	29.60	29.67	29.73	29.80	29.87	29.93
25	30.00	30.07	30.13	30.20	30.26	30.33	30.40	30.46	30.53	30.59
26	30.66	30.72	30.79	30.85	30.92	30.98	31.05	31.11	31.18	31.24
27	31.31	31.37	31.44	31.50	31.56	31.63	31.69	31.76	31.82	31.88
28	31.95	32.01	32.08	32.14	32.20	32.27	32.33	32.39	32.46	32.52
29	32.58	32.65	32.71	32.77	32.83	32.90	32.96	33.02	33.09	33.15
30	33.21	33.27	33.34	33.40	33.46	33.52	33.58	33.65	33.71	33.77
31	33.83	33.89	33.96	34.02	34.08	34.14	34.20	34.27	34.33	34.39
32	34.45	34.51	34.57	34.63	34.70	34.76	34.82	34.88	34.94	35.00
33	35.06	35.12	35.18	35.24	35.30	35.37	35.43	35.49	35.55	35.61
34	35.67	35.73	35.79	35.85	35.91	35.97	36.03	36.09	36.15	36.21
35	36.27	36.33	36.39	36.45	36.51	36.57	36.63	36.69	36.75	36.81
36	36.87	36.93	36.99	37.05	37.11	37.17	37.23	37.29	37.35	37.41
37	37.47	37.52	37.58	37.64	37.70	37.76	37.82	37.88	37.94	38.00
38	38.06	38.12	38.17	38.23	38.29	38.35	38.41	38.47	38.53	38.59
39	38.65	38.70	38.76	38.82	38.88	38.94	39.00	39.06	39.11	39.17
40	39.23	39.29	39.35	39.41	39.47	39.52	39.58	39.64	39.70	39.76
41	39.82	39.87	39.93	39.99	40.05	40.11	40.16	40.22	40.28	40.34
42	40.40	40.46	40.51	40.57	40.63	40.69	40.74	40.80	40.86	40.92
43	40.98	41.03	41.09	41.15	41.21	41.27	41.32	41.38	41.44	41.50
44	41.55	41.61	41.67	41.73	41.78	41.84	41.90	41.96	42.02	42.07
45	42.13	42.19	42.25	42.30	42.36	42.42	42.48	42.53	42.59	42.65
46	42.71	42.76	42.82	42.88	42.94	42.99	43.05	43.11	43.17	43.22
47	43.28	43.34	43.39	43.45	43.51	43.57	43.62	43.68	43.74	43.80
48	43.85	43.91	43.97	44.03	44.08	44.14	44.20	44.25	44.31	44.37
49	44.43	44.48	44.54	44.60	44.66	44.71	44.77	44.83	44.89	44.94
50	45.00	45.06	45.11	45.17	45.23	45.29	45.34	45.40	45.46	45.52

%	0	1	2	3	4	5	6	7	8	9
51	45.57	45.63	45.69	45.75	45.80	45.86	45.92	45.97	46.03	46.09
52	46.15	46.20	46.26	46.32	46.38	46.43	46.49	46.55	46.61	46.66
53	46.72	46.78	46.83	46.89	46.95	47.01	47.06	47.12	47.18	47.24
54	47.29	47.35	47.41	47.47	47.52	47.58	47.64	47.70	47.75	47.81
55	47.87	47.93	47.98	48.04	48.10	48.16	48.22	48.27	48.33	48.39
56	48.45	48.50	48.56	48.62	48.68	48.73	48.79	48.85	48.91	48.97
57	49.02	49.08	49.14	49.20	49.26	49.31	49.37	49.43	49.49	49.54
58	49.60	49.66	49.72	49.78	49.84	49.89	49.95	50.01	50.07	50.13
59	50.18	50.24	50.30	50.36	50.42	50.48	50.53	50.59	50.65	50.71
60	50.77	50.83	50.89	50.94	51.00	51.06	51.12	51.18	51.24	51.30
61	51.35	51.41	51.47	51.53	51.59	51.65	51.71	51.77	51.83	51.88
62	51.94	52.00	52.06	52.12	52.18	52.24	52.30	52.36	52.42	52.48
63	52.53	52.59	52.65	52.71	52.77	52.83	52.89	52.95	53.01	53.07
64	53.13	53.19	53.25	53.31	53.37	53.43	53.49	53.55	53.61	53.67
65	53.73	53.79	53.85	53.91	53.97	54.03	54.09	54.15	54.21	54.27
66	54.33	54.39	54.45	54.51	54.57	54.63	54.70	54.76	54.82	54.88
67	54.94	55.00	55.06	55.12	55.18	55.24	55.30	55.37	55.43	55.49
68	55.55	55.61	55.67	55.73	55.80	55.86	55.92	55.98	56.04	56.11
69	56.17	56.23	56.29	56.35	56.42	56.48	56.54	56.60	56.66	56.73
70	56.79	56.85	56.91	56.98	57.04	57.10	57.17	57.23	57.29	57.35
71	57.42	57.48	57.54	57.61	57.67	57.73	57.80	57.86	57.92	57.99
72	58.05	58.12	58.18	58.24	58.31	58.37	58.44	58.50	58.56	58.63
73	58.69	58.76	58.82	58.89	58.95	59.02	59.08	59.15	59.21	59.28
74	59.34	59.41	59.47	59.54	59.60	59.67	59.74	59.80	59.87	59.93
75	60.00	60.07	60.13	60.20	60.27	60.33	60.40	60.47	60.53	60.60
76	60.67	60.73	60.80	60.87	60.94	61.00	61.07	61.14	61.21	61.27
77	61.34	61.41	61.48	61.55	61.62	61.68	61.75	61.82	61.89	61.96
78	62.03	62.10	62.17	62.24	62.31	62.37	62.44	62.51	62.58	62.65
79	62.72	62.80	62.87	62.94	63.01	63.08	63.15	63.22	63.29	63.36
80	63.44	63.51	63.58	63.65	63.72	63.79	63.87	63.94	64.01	64.08
81	64.16	64.23	64.30	64.38	64.45	64.52	64.60	64.67	64.75	64.82
82	64.90	64.97	65.05	65.12	65.20	65.27	65.35	65.42	65.50	65.57
83	65.65	65.73	65.80	65.88	65.96	66.03	66.11	66.19	66.27	66.34
84	66.42	66.50	66.58	66.66	66.74	66.81	66.89	66.97	67.05	67.13
85	67.21	67.29	67.37	67.45	67.54	67.62	67.70	67.78	67.86	67.94
86	68.03	68.11	68.19	68.28	68.36	68.44	68.53	68.61	68.70	68.78
87	68.87	68.95	69.04	69.12	69.21	69.30	69.38	69.47	69.56	69.64
88	69.73	69.82	69.91	70.00	70.09	70.18	70.27	70.36	70.45	70.54
89	70.63	70.72	70.81	70.91	71.00	71.09	71.19	71.28	71.37	71.47
90	71.56	71.66	71.76	71.85	71.95	72.05	72.15	72.24	72.34	72.44
91	72.54	72.64	72.74	72.84	72.95	73.05	73.15	73.26	73.36	73.46
92	73.57	73.68	73.78	73.89	74.00	74.11	74.21	74.32	74.44	74.55
93	74.66	74.77	74.88	75.00	75.11	75.23	75.35	75.46	75.58	75.70
94	75.82	75.94	76.06	76.19	76.31	76.44	76.56	76.69	76.82	76.95
95	77.08	77.21	77.34	77.48	77.61	77.75	77.89	78.03	78.17	78.32
96	78.46	78.61	78.76	78.91	79.06	79.22	79.37	79.53	79.69	79.86
97	80.02	80.19	80.37	80.54	80.72	80.90	81.09	81.28	81.47	81.67
98	81.87	82.08	82.29	82.51	82.73	82.96	83.20	83.45	83.71	83.98
99.0	84.26	84.29	84.32	84.35	84.38	84.41	84.44	84.47	84.50	84.53
99.1	84.56	84.59	84.62	84.65	84.68	84.71	84.74	84.77	84.80	84.84
99.2	84.87	84.90	84.93	84.97	85.00	85.03	85.07	85.10	85.13	85.17
99.3	85.20	85.24	85.27	85.31	85.34	85.38	85.41	85.45	85.48	85.52
99.4	85.56	85.60	85.63	85.67	85.71	85.75	85.79	85.83	85.87	85.91
99.5	85.95	85.99	86.03	86.07	86.11	86.15	86.20	86.24	86.28	86.33
99.6	86.37	86.42	86.47	86.51	86.56	86.61	86.66	86.71	86.76	86.81
99.7	86.86	86.91	86.97	87.02	87.08	87.13	87.19	87.25	87.31	87.37
99.8	87.44	87.50	87.57	87.64	87.71	87.78	87.86	87.93	88.01	88.10
99.9	88.19	88.28	88.38	88.48	88.60	88.72	88.85	89.01	89.19	89.43
100.0	90.00	–	–	–	–	–	–	–	–	–

Table I.   Distribution of the studentised range statistics

df for s_x	$1-\alpha$	2	3	4	5	6	7	8	9	10	11	12	13	14	15
		\multicolumn{14}{c}{r = Number of Steps between Ordered Means}												
1	.95	18.0	27.0	32.8	37.1	40.4	43.1	45.4	47.4	49.1	50.6	52.0	53.2	54.3	55.4
	.99	90.0	135	164	186	202	216	227	237	246	253	260	266	272	277
2	.95	6.09	8.3	9.8	10.9	11.7	12.4	13.0	13.5	14.0	14.4	14.7	15.1	15.4	15.7
	.99	14.0	19.0	22.3	24.7	26.6	28.2	29.5	30.7	31.7	32.6	33.4	34.1	34.8	35.4
3	.95	4.50	5.91	6.82	7.50	8.04	8.48	8.85	9.18	9.46	9.72	9.95	10.2	10.4	10.5
	.99	8.26	10.6	12.2	13.3	14.2	15.0	15.6	16.2	16.7	17.1	17.5	17.9	18.2	18.5
4	.95	3.93	5.04	5.76	6.29	6.71	7.05	7.35	7.60	7.83	8.03	8.21	8.37	8.52	8.66
	.99	6.51	8.12	9.17	9.96	10.6	11.1	11.5	11.9	12.3	12.6	12.8	13.1	13.3	13.5
5	.95	3.64	4.60	5.22	5.67	6.03	6.33	6.58	6.80	6.99	7.17	7.32	7.47	7.60	7.72
	.99	5.70	6.97	7.80	8.42	8.91	9.32	9.67	9.97	10.2	10.5	10.7	10.9	11.1	11.2
6	.95	3.46	4.34	4.90	5.31	5.63	5.89	6.12	6.32	6.49	6.65	6.79	6.92	7.03	7.14
	.99	5.24	6.33	7.03	7.56	7.97	8.32	8.61	8.87	9.10	9.30	9.49	9.65	9.81	9.95
7	.95	3.34	4.16	4.69	5.06	5.36	5.61	5.82	6.00	6.16	6.30	6.43	6.55	6.66	6.76
	.99	4.95	5.92	6.54	7.01	7.37	7.68	7.94	8.17	8.37	8.55	8.71	8.86	9.00	9.12
8	.95	3.26	4.04	4.53	4.89	5.17	5.40	5.60	5.77	5.92	6.05	6.18	6.29	6.39	6.48
	.99	4.74	5.63	6.20	6.63	6.96	7.24	7.47	7.68	7.87	8.03	8.18	8.31	8.44	8.55
9	.95	3.20	3.95	4.42	4.76	5.02	5.24	5.43	5.60	5.74	5.87	5.98	6.09	6.19	6.28
	.99	4.60	5.43	5.96	6.35	6.66	6.91	7.13	7.32	7.49	7.65	7.78	7.91	8.03	8.13
10	.95	3.15	3.88	4.33	4.65	4.91	5.12	5.30	5.46	5.60	5.72	5.83	5.93	6.03	6.11
	.99	4.48	5.27	5.77	6.14	6.43	6.67	6.87	7.05	7.21	7.36	7.48	7.60	7.71	7.81
11	.95	3.11	3.82	4.26	4.57	4.82	5.03	5.20	5.35	5.49	5.61	5.71	5.81	5.90	5.99
	.99	4.39	5.14	5.62	5.97	6.25	6.48	6.67	6.84	6.99	7.13	7.26	7.36	7.46	7.56
12	.95	3.08	3.77	4.20	4.51	4.75	4.95	5.12	5.27	5.40	5.51	5.62	5.71	5.80	5.88
	.99	4.32	5.04	5.50	5.84	6.10	6.32	6.51	6.67	6.81	6.94	7.06	7.17	7.26	7.36
13	.95	3.06	3.73	4.15	4.45	4.69	4.88	5.05	5.19	5.32	5.43	5.53	5.63	5.71	5.79
	.99	4.26	4.96	5.40	5.73	5.98	6.19	6.37	6.53	6.67	6.79	6.90	7.01	7.10	7.19
14	.95	3.03	3.70	4.11	4.41	4.64	4.83	4.99	5.13	5.25	5.36	5.46	5.55	6.64	5.72
	.99	4.21	4.89	5.32	5.63	5.88	6.08	6.26	6.41	6.54	6.66	6.77	6.87	6.96	7.05
16	.95	3.00	3.65	4.05	4.33	4.56	4.74	4.90	5.03	5.15	5.26	5.35	5.44	5.52	5.59
	.99	4.13	4.78	5.19	5.49	5.72	5.92	6.08	6.22	6.35	6.46	6.56	6.66	6.74	6.82
18	.95	2.97	3.61	4.00	4.28	4.49	4.67	4.82	4.96	5.07	5.17	5.27	5.35	5.43	5.50
	.99	4.07	4.70	5.09	5.38	5.60	5.79	5.94	6.08	6.20	6.31	6.41	6.50	6.58	6.65
20	.95	2.95	3.58	3.96	4.23	4.45	4.62	4.77	4.90	5.01	5.11	5.20	5.28	5.36	5.43
	.99	4.02	4.64	5.02	5.29	5.51	5.69	5.84	5.97	6.09	6.19	6.29	6.37	6.45	6.52
24	.95	2.92	3.53	3.90	4.17	4.37	4.54	4.68	4.81	4.92	5.01	5.10	5.18	5.25	5.32
	.99	3.96	4.54	4.91	5.17	5.37	5.54	5.69	5.81	5.92	6.02	6.11	6.19	6.26	6.33
30	.95	2.89	3.49	3.84	4.10	4.30	4.46	4.60	4.72	4.83	4.92	5.00	5.08	5.15	5.21
	.99	3.89	4.45	4.80	5.05	5.24	5.40	5.54	5.56	5.76	5.85	5.93	6.01	6.08	6.14
40	.95	2.86	3.44	3.79	4.04	4.23	4.39	4.52	4.63	4.74	4.82	4.91	4.98	5.05	5.11
	.99	3.82	4.37	4.70	4.93	5.11	5.27	5.39	5.50	5.60	5.69	5.77	5.84	5.90	5.96
60	.95	2.83	3.40	3.74	3.98	4.16	4.31	4.44	4.55	4.65	4.73	4.81	4.88	4.94	5.00
	.99	3.76	4.28	4.60	4.82	4.99	5.13	5.25	5.36	5.45	5.53	5.60	5.67	5.73	5.79
120	.95	2.80	3.36	3.69	3.92	4.10	4.24	4.36	4.48	4.56	4.64	4.72	4.78	4.84	4.90
	.99	3.70	4.20	4.50	4.71	4.87	5.01	5.12	5.21	5.30	5.38	5.44	5.51	5.56	5.61
∞	.95	2.77	3.31	3.63	3.86	4.03	4.17	4.29	4.39	4.47	4.55	4.62	4.68	4.74	4.80
	.99	3.64	4.12	4.40	4.60	4.76	4.88	4.99	5.08	5.16	5.23	5.29	5.35	5.40	5.45

Table J. Significant studentised ranges for Duncan's new multiple range test ($\alpha = 0.10$)

df \ k	2	3	4	5	6	7	8	9	10	11	12	13	14	15	16	17	18	19
2	4.130																	
3	3.328	3.330																
4	3.015	3.074	3.081															
5	2.850	2.934	2.964	2.970														
6	2.748	2.846	2.890	2.908	2.911													
7	2.680	2.785	2.838	2.864	2.876	2.878												
8	2.630	2.742	2.800	2.832	2.849	2.857	2.858											
9	2.592	2.708	2.771	2.808	2.829	2.840	2.845	2.847										
10	2.563	2.682	2.748	2.788	2.813	2.827	2.835	2.839	2.839									
11	2.540	2.660	2.730	2.772	2.799	2.817	2.827	2.833	2.835	2.835								
12	2.521	2.643	2.714	2.759	2.789	2.808	2.821	2.828	2.832	2.833	2.833							
13	2.505	2.628	2.701	2.748	2.779	2.800	2.815	2.824	2.829	2.832	2.832	2.832						
14	2.491	2.616	2.690	2.739	2.771	2.794	2.810	2.820	2.827	2.831	2.832	2.833	2.833					
15	2.479	2.605	2.681	2.731	2.765	2.789	2.805	2.817	2.825	2.830	2.832	2.834	2.834	2.834				
16	2.469	2.596	2.673	2.723	2.759	2.784	2.802	2.815	2.824	2.829	2.833	2.835	2.836	2.836	2.836			
17	2.460	2.588	2.665	2.717	2.753	2.780	2.798	2.812	2.822	2.829	2.834	2.836	2.838	2.838	2.838	2.838		
18	2.452	2.580	2.659	2.712	2.749	2.776	2.796	2.810	2.821	2.828	2.834	2.838	2.840	2.840	2.840	2.840	2.840	
19	2.445	2.574	2.653	2.707	2.745	2.773	2.793	2.808	2.820	2.828	2.834	2.839	2.841	2.842	2.843	2.843	2.843	2.843
20	2.439	2.568	2.648	2.702	2.741	2.770	2.791	2.807	2.819	2.828	2.834	2.839	2.843	2.845	2.845	2.845	2.845	2.845
24	2.420	2.550	2.632	2.688	2.729	2.760	2.783	2.801	2.816	2.827	2.835	2.842	2.848	2.851	2.854	2.856	2.857	2.857
30	2.400	2.532	2.615	2.674	2.717	2.750	2.776	2.796	2.813	2.826	2.837	2.846	2.853	2.859	2.863	2.867	2.869	2.871
40	2.381	2.514	2.600	2.660	2.705	2.741	2.769	2.791	2.810	22.825	2.838	2.849	2.858	2.866	2.873	2.878	2.883	2.887
60	2.363	2.497	2.584	2.646	2.694	2.731	2.761	2.786	2.807	2.825	2.839	2.853	2.864	2.874	2.883	2.890	2.897	2.903
120	2.344	2.479	2.568	2.632	2.682	2.722	2.754	2.781	2.804	2.824	2.842	2.857	2.871	2.883	2.893	2.903	2.912	2.920
∞	2.326	2.462	2.552	2.619	2.670	2.712	2.746	2.776	2.801	2.824	2.844	2.861	2.877	2.892	2.905	2.918	2.929	2.939

Table J. Significant studentised ranges for Duncan's new multiple range test ($\alpha = 0.05$) (continued)

df \ k	2	3	4	5	6	7	8	9	10	11	12	13	14	15	16	17	18	19
2	6.085																	
3	4.501	4.516																
4	3.927	4.013	4.033															
5	3.635	3.749	3.797	3.814														
6	3.461	3.587	3.649	3.680	3.694													
7	3.344	3.477	3.548	3.588	3.611	3.622												
8	3.261	3.399	3.475	3.521	3.549	3.566	3.575											
9	3.199	3.339	3.420	3.470	3.502	3.523	3.536	3.544										
10	3.151	3.293	3.376	3.430	3.465	3.489	3.505	3.516	3.522									
11	3.113	3.256	3.342	3.397	3.435	3.462	3.480	3.493	3.501	3.506								
12	3.082	3.225	3.313	3.370	3.410	3.439	3.459	3.474	3.484	3.491	3.496							
13	3.055	3.200	3.289	3.348	3.389	3.419	3.442	3.458	3.470	3.478	3.484	3.488						
14	3.033	3.178	3.268	3.329	3.372	3.403	3.426	3.444	3.457	3.467	3.474	3.479	3.482					
15	3.014	3.160	3.250	3.312	3.356	3.389	3.413	3.432	3.446	3.457	3.465	3.471	3.476	3.478				
16	2.998	3.144	3.235	3.298	3.343	3.376	3.402	3.422	3.437	3.449	3.458	3.465	3.470	3.473	3.477			
17	2.984	3.130	3.222	3.285	3.331	3.366	3.392	3.412	3.429	3.441	3.451	3.459	3.465	3.469	3.473	3.475		
18	2.971	3.118	3.210	3.274	3.321	3.356	3.383	3.405	3.421	3.435	3.445	3.454	3.460	3.465	3.470	3.472	3.474	
19	2.960	3.107	3.199	3.264	3.311	3.347	3.375	3.397	3.415	3.429	3.440	3.449	3.456	3.462	3.467	3.470	3.472	3.473
20	2.950	3.097	3.190	3.255	3.303	3.339	3.368	3.391	3.409	3.424	3.436	3.445	3.453	3.459	3.464	3.467	3.470	3.472
24	2.919	3.066	3.160	3.226	3.276	3.315	3.345	3.370	3.390	3.406	3.420	3.432	3.441	3.449	3.456	3.461	3.465	3.469
30	2.888	3.035	3.131	3.199	3.250	3.290	3.322	3.349	3.371	3.389	3.405	3.418	3.430	3.439	3.447	3.454	3.460	3.466
40	2.858	3.006	3.102	3.171	3.224	3.266	3.300	3.328	3.352	3.373	3.390	3.405	3.418	3.429	3.439	3.448	3.456	3.463
60	2.829	2.976	3.073	3.143	3.198	3.241	3.277	3.307	3.333	3.355	3.374	3.391	3.406	3.419	3.431	3.442	3.451	3.460
120	2.800	2.947	3.045	3.116	3.172	3.217	3.254	3.287	3.314	3.337	3.359	3.377	3.394	3.409	3.423	3.435	3.446	3.457
∞	2.772	2.918	3.017	3.089	3.146	3.193	3.232	3.265	3.294	3.320	3.343	3.363	3.382	3.399	3.414	3.428	3.442	3.454

Table J. Significant studentised ranges for Duncan's new multiple range test ($\alpha = 0.01$) (continued)

k / df	2	3	4	5	6	7	8	9	10	11	12	13	14	15	16	17	18	19
2	14.04																	
3	8.261	8.321																
4	6.512	6.677	6.740															
5	5.702	5.893	5.989	6.040														
6	5.243	5.439	5.549	5.614	5.655													
7	4.949	5.145	5.260	5.334	5.383	5.416												
8	4.746	4.939	5.057	5.135	5.180	5.227	5.256											
9	4.596	4.787	4.906	4.986	5.043	5.086	5.118	5.142										
10	4.482	4.671	4.790	4.871	4.931	4.975	5.010	5.037	5.058									
11	4.392	4.579	4.697	4.780	4.841	4.887	4.924	4.952	4.975	4.994								
12	4.320	4.504	4.622	4.706	4.767	4.815	4.852	4.883	4.907	4.927	4.944							
13	4.260	4.442	4.560	4.644	4.706	4.755	4.793	4.824	4.850	4.872	4.889	4.904						
14	4.210	4.391	4.508	4.591	4.654	4.704	4.743	4.775	4.802	4.824	4.843	4.859	4.872					
15	4.168	4.347	4.463	4.547	4.610	4.660	4.700	4.733	4.760	4.783	4.803	4.820	4.834	4.846				
16	4.131	4.309	4.425	4.509	4.572	4.622	4.663	4.696	4.724	4.748	4.768	4.786	4.800	4.813	4.825			
17	4.099	4.275	4.391	4.475	4.539	4.589	4.630	4.664	4.693	4.717	4.738	4.756	4.771	4.785	4.797	4.807		
18	4.071	4.246	4.362	4.445	4.509	4.560	4.601	4.635	4.664	4.689	4.711	4.729	4.745	4.759	4.772	4.783	4.792	
19	4.046	4.220	4.335	4.419	4.483	4.534	4.575	4.610	4.639	4.665	4.686	4.705	4.722	4.736	4.749	4.761	4.771	4.780
20	4.024	4.197	4.312	4.395	4.459	4.510	4.552	4.587	4.617	4.642	4.664	4.684	4.701	4.716	4.729	4.741	4.751	4.761
24	3.956	4.126	4.239	4.322	4.386	4.437	4.480	4.516	4.546	4.573	4.596	4.616	4.634	4.651	4.665	4.678	4.690	4.700
30	3.889	4.056	4.168	4.250	4.314	4.366	4.409	4.445	4.477	4.504	4.528	4.550	4.569	4.586	4.601	4.615	4.628	4.640
40	3.825	3.988	4.098	4.180	4.244	4.296	4.339	4.376	4.408	4.436	4.461	4.483	4.503	4.521	4.537	4.553	4.566	4.579
60	3.762	3.922	4.031	4.111	4.174	4.226	4.270	4.307	4.340	4.368	4.394	4.417	4.438	4.456	4.474	4.490	4.504	4.518
120	3.702	3.858	3.965	4.044	4.107	4.158	4.202	4.239	4.272	4.301	4.327	4.351	4.372	4.392	4.410	4.426	4.442	4.456
∞	3.643	3.796	3.900	3.978	4.040	4.091	4.135	4.172	4.205	4.235	4.261	4.285	4.307	4.327	4.345	4.363	4.379	4.394

Table J. Significant studentised ranges for Duncan's new multiple range test ($\alpha=0.005$) (*continued*)

k\df	2	3	4	5	6	7	8	9	10	11	12	13	14	15	16	17	18	19
2	19.93																	
3	10.55	10.63																
4	7.916	8.126	8.210															
5	6.751	6.980	7.100	7.167														
6	6.105	6.334	6.466	6.547	6.600													
7	5.699	5.922	6.057	6.145	6.207	6.250												
8	5.420	5.638	5.773	5.864	5.930	5.978	6.014											
9	5.218	5.430	5.565	5.657	5.725	5.776	5.815	5.846										
10	5.065	5.273	5.405	5.498	5.567	5.620	5.662	5.695	5.722									
11	4.945	5.149	5.280	5.372	5.442	5.496	5.539	5.574	5.603	5.626								
12	4.849	5.048	5.178	5.270	5.341	5.396	5.439	5.475	5.505	5.531	5.552							
13	4.770	4.966	5.094	5.186	5.256	5.312	5.356	5.393	5.424	5.450	5.472	5.492						
14	4.704	4.897	5.023	5.116	5.185	5.241	5.286	5.324	5.355	5.382	5.405	5.425	5.442					
15	4.647	4.838	4.964	5.055	5.125	5.181	5.226	5.264	5.297	5.324	5.348	5.368	5.386	5.402				
16	4.599	4.787	4.912	5.003	5.073	5.129	5.175	5.213	5.245	5.273	5.298	5.319	5.338	5.354	5.368			
17	4.557	4.744	4.867	4.958	5.027	5.084	5.130	5.168	5.201	5.229	5.254	5.275	5.295	5.311	5.327	5.340		
18	4.521	4.705	4.828	4.918	4.987	5.043	5.090	5.129	5.162	5.190	5.215	5.237	5.256	5.274	5.289	5.303	5.316	
19	4.488	4.671	4.793	4.883	4.952	5.008	5.054	5.093	5.127	5.156	5.181	5.203	5.222	5.240	5.256	5.270	5.283	5.295
20	4.460	4.641	4.762	4.851	4.920	4.976	5.022	5.061	5.095	5.124	5.150	5.172	5.193	5.210	5.226	5.241	5.254	5.266
24	4.371	4.547	4.666	4.753	4.822	4.877	4.924	4.963	4.997	5.027	5.053	5.076	5.097	5.116	5.133	5.148	5.162	5.175
30	4.285	4.456	4.572	4.658	4.726	4.781	4.827	4.867	4.901	4.931	4.958	4.981	5.003	5.022	5.040	5.056	5.071	5.085
40	4.202	4.369	4.482	4.566	4.632	4.687	4.733	4.772	4.806	4.837	4.864	4.888	4.910	4.930	4.948	4.965	4.980	4.995
60	4.122	4.284	4.394	4.476	4.541	4.595	4.640	4.679	4.713	4.744	4.771	4.796	4.818	4.838	4.857	4.874	4.890	4.905
120	4.045	4.201	4.308	4.388	4.452	4.505	4.550	4.588	4.622	4.652	4.679	4.704	4.726	4.747	4.766	4.784	4.800	4.815
∞	3.970	4.121	4.225	4.303	4.365	4.417	4.461	4.499	4.532	4.562	4.589	4.614	4.636	4.657	4.676	4.694	4.710	4.726

Table J. Significant studentised ranges for Duncan's new multiple range test ($\alpha = 0.001$) (*continued*)

k \ df	2	3	4	5	6	7	8	9	10	11	12	13	14	15	16	17	18	19
2	44.69																	
3	18.28	18.48																
4	12.18	12.52	12.67															
5	9.714	10.05	10.24	10.35														
6	8.427	8.743	8.932	9.055	9.139													
7	7.648	7.943	8.127	8.252	8.342	8.409												
8	7.130	7.407	7.584	7.708	7.799	7.869	7.924											
9	6.762	7.024	7.195	7.316	7.407	7.478	7.535	7.582										
10	6.487	6.738	6.902	7.021	7.111	7.182	7.240	7.287	7.327									
11	6.275	6.516	6.676	6.791	6.880	6.950	7.008	7.056	7.097	7.132								
12	6.106	6.340	6.494	6.607	6.695	6.765	6.822	6.870	6.911	6.947	6.978							
13	5.970	6.195	6.346	6.457	6.543	6.612	6.670	6.718	6.750	6.795	6.826	6.854						
14	5.856	6.075	6.223	6.332	6.416	6.485	6.542	6.590	6.631	6.667	6.699	6.727	6.752					
15	5.760	5.974	6.119	6.225	6.309	6.377	6.433	6.481	6.522	6.558	6.590	6.619	6.644	6.666				
16	5.678	5.888	6.030	6.135	6.217	6.284	6.340	6.388	6.429	6.465	6.497	6.525	6.551	6.574	6.595			
17	5.608	5.813	5.953	6.056	6.138	6.204	6.260	6.307	6.348	6.384	6.416	6.444	6.470	6.493	6.514	6.533		
18	5.546	5.748	5.886	5.988	6.068	6.134	6.189	6.236	6.277	6.313	6.345	6.373	6.399	6.422	6.443	6.462	6.480	
19	5.492	5.691	5.826	5.927	6.007	6.072	6.127	6.174	6.214	6.250	6.281	6.310	6.336	6.359	6.380	6.400	6.418	6.434
20	5.444	5.640	5.774	5.873	5.952	6.017	6.071	6.117	6.158	6.193	6.225	6.254	6.279	6.303	6.324	6.344	6.362	6.379
24	5.297	5.484	5.612	5.708	5.784	5.846	5.899	5.945	5.984	6.020	6.051	6.079	6.105	6.129	6.150	6.170	6.188	6.205
30	5.156	5.335	5.457	5.549	5.622	5.682	5.734	5.778	5.817	5.851	5.882	5.910	5.935	5.958	5.980	6.000	6.018	6.036
40	5.022	5.191	5.308	5.396	5.466	5.524	5.574	5.617	5.654	5.688	5.718	5.745	5.770	5.793	5.814	5.834	5.852	5.869
60	4.894	5.055	5.166	5.249	5.317	5.372	5.420	5.461	5.498	5.530	5.559	5.586	5.610	5.632	5.653	5.672	5.690	5.707
120	4.771	4.924	5.029	5.109	5.173	5.226	5.271	5.311	5.346	5.377	5.405	5.431	5.454	5.476	5.496	5.515	5.532	5.549
∞	4.654	4.798	4.898	4.974	5.034	5.085	5.128	5.166	5.199	5.229	5.256	5.280	5.303	5.324	5.343	5.361	5.378	5.394

Table K.   Distribution of t statistic in comparing treatment means with a control
Table K(I).   Distribution of t statistic for one-sided comparisons between k treatment means and a control ($\alpha = 0.05$)

	k, Number of Treatment Means (Excluding the Control)								
df	**1**	**2**	**3**	**4**	**5**	**6**	**7**	**8**	**9**
5	2.02	2.44	2.68	2.85	2.98	3.08	3.16	3.24	3.30
6	1.94	2.34	2.56	2.71	2.83	2.92	3.00	3.07	3.12
7	1.89	2.27	2.48	2.62	2.73	2.82	2.89	2.95	3.01
8	1.86	2.22	2.42	2.55	2.66	2.74	2.81	2.87	2.92
9	1.83	2.18	2.37	2.50	2.60	2.68	2.75	2.81	2.86
10	1.81	2.15	2.34	2.47	2.56	2.64	2.70	2.76	2.81
11	1.80	2.13	2.31	2.44	2.53	2.60	2.67	2.72	2.77
12	1.78	2.11	2.29	2.41	2.50	2.58	2.64	2.69	2.74
13	1.77	2.09	2.27	2.39	2.48	2.55	2.61	2.66	2.71
14	1.76	2.08	2.25	2.37	2.46	2.53	2.59	2.64	2.69
15	1.75	2.07	2.24	2.36	2.44	2.51	2.57	2.62	2.67
16	1.75	2.06	2.23	2.34	2.43	2.50	2.56	2.61	2.65
17	1.74	2.05	2.22	2.33	2.42	2.49	2.54	2.59	2.64
18	1.73	2.04	2.21	2.32	2.41	2.48	2.53	2.58	2.62
19	1.73	2.03	2.20	2.31	2.40	2.47	2.52	2.57	2.61
20	1.72	2.03	2.19	2.30	2.39	2.46	2.51	2.56	2.60
24	1.71	2.01	2.17	2.28	2.36	2.43	2.48	2.53	2.57
30	1.70	1.99	2.15	2.25	2.33	2.40	2.45	2.50	2.54
40	1.68	1.97	2.13	2.23	2.31	2.37	2.42	2.47	2.51
60	1.67	1.95	2.10	2.21	2.28	2.35	2.39	2.44	2.48
120	1.66	1.93	2.08	2.18	2.26	2.32	2.37	2.41	2.45
∞	1.64	1.92	2.06	2.16	2.23	2.29	2.34	2.38	2.42

Table K(II). Distribution of t statistic for one-sided comparisons between k treatment means and a control ($\alpha=0.01$)

df	\multicolumn{9}{c}{k, Number of Treatment Means (Excluding the Control)}
	1	2	3	4	5	6	7	8	9
5	3.37	3.90	4.21	4.43	4.60	4.73	4.85	4.94	5.03
6	3.14	3.61	3.88	4.07	4.21	4.33	4.43	4.51	4.59
7	3.00	3.42	3.66	3.83	3.96	4.07	4.15	4.23	4.30
8	2.90	3.29	3.51	3.67	3.79	3.88	3.96	4.03	4.09
9	2.82	3.19	3.40	3.55	3.66	3.75	3.82	3.89	3.94
10	2.76	3.11	3.31	3.45	3.56	3.64	3.71	3.78	3.83
11	2.72	3.06	3.25	3.38	3.48	3.56	3.63	3.69	3.74
12	2.68	3.01	3.19	3.32	3.42	3.50	3.56	3.62	3.67
13	2.65	2.97	3.15	3.27	3.37	3.44	3.51	3.56	3.61
14	2.62	2.94	3.11	3.23	3.32	3.40	3.46	3.51	3.56
15	2.60	2.91	3.08	3.20	3.29	3.36	3.42	3.47	3.52
16	2.58	2.88	3.05	3.17	3.26	3.33	3.39	3.44	3.48
17	2.57	2.86	3.03	3.14	3.23	3.30	3.36	3.41	3.45
18	2.55	2.84	3.01	3.12	3.21	3.27	3.33	3.38	3.42
19	2.54	2.83	2.99	3.10	3.18	3.25	3.31	3.36	3.40
20	2.53	2.81	2.97	3.08	3.17	3.23	3.29	3.34	3.38
24	2.49	2.77	2.92	3.03	3.11	3.17	3.22	3.27	3.31
30	2.46	2.72	2.87	2.97	3.05	3.11	3.16	3.21	3.24
40	2.42	2.68	2.82	2.92	2.99	3.05	3.10	3.14	3.18
60	2.39	2.64	2.78	2.87	2.94	3.00	3.04	3.08	3.12
120	2.36	2.60	2.73	2.82	2.89	2.94	2.99	3.03	3.05
∞	2.33	2.56	2.68	2.77	2.84	2.89	2.93	2.97	3.00

Table K(III).   Distribution of t statistic for two-sided comparisons between k treatment means and a control ($\alpha = 0.05$)

df	\multicolumn{9}{c}{k, Number of Treatment Means (Excluding the Control)}								
	1	**2**	**3**	**4**	**5**	**6**	**7**	**8**	**9**
5	2.57	3.03	3.39	3.66	3.88	4.06	4.22	4.36	4.49
6	2.45	2.88	3.18	3.41	3.60	3.75	3.88	4.00	4.11
7	2.36	2.75	3.04	3.24	3.41	3.54	3.66	3.76	3.86
8	2.31	2.67	2.94	3.13	3.28	3.40	3.51	3.60	3.68
9	2.26	2.61	2.86	3.04	3.18	3.29	3.39	3.48	3.55
10	2.23	2.57	2.81	2.97	3.11	3.21	3.31	3.39	3.46
11	2.20	2.53	2.76	2.92	3.05	3.15	3.24	3.31	3.38
12	2.18	2.50	2.72	2.88	3.00	3.10	3.18	3.25	3.32
13	2.16	2.48	2.69	2.84	2.96	3.06	3.14	3.21	3.27
14	2.14	2.46	2.67	2.81	2.93	3.02	3.10	3.17	3.23
15	2.13	2.44	2.64	2.79	2.90	2.99	3.07	3.13	3.19
16	2.12	2.42	2.63	2.77	2.88	2.96	3.04	3.10	3.16
17	2.11	2.41	2.61	2.75	2.85	2.94	3.01	3.08	3.13
18	2.10	2.40	2.59	2.73	2.84	2.92	2.99	3.05	3.11
19	2.09	2.39	2.58	2.72	2.82	2.90	2.97	3.04	3.09
20	2.09	2.38	2.57	2.70	2.81	2.89	2.96	3.02	3.07
24	2.06	2.35	2.53	2.66	2.76	2.84	2.91	2.96	3.01
30	2.04	2.32	2.50	2.62	2.72	2.79	2.86	2.91	2.96
40	2.02	2.29	2.47	2.58	2.67	2.75	2.81	2.86	2.90
60	2.00	2.27	2.43	2.55	2.63	2.70	2.76	2.81	2.85
120	1.98	2.24	2.40	2.51	2.59	2.66	2.71	2.76	2.80
∞	1.96	2.21	2.37	2.47	2.55	2.62	2.67	2.71	2.75

Table K(IV). Distribution of t statistic for two-sided comparisons between k treatment means and a control ($\alpha = 0.01$)

df	\multicolumn{9}{c}{k, Number of Treatment Means (Excluding the Control)}
	1	2	3	4	5	6	7	8	9
5	4.03	4.63	5.09	5.44	5.73	5.97	6.18	6.36	6.53
6	3.71	4.22	4.60	4.88	5.11	5.30	5.47	5.61	5.74
7	3.50	3.95	4.28	4.52	4.71	4.87	5.01	5.13	5.24
8	3.36	3.77	4.06	4.27	4.44	4.58	4.70	4.81	4.90
9	3.25	3.63	3.90	4.09	4.24	4.37	4.48	4.57	4.65
10	3.17	3.53	3.78	3.95	4.10	4.21	4.31	4.40	4.47
11	3.11	3.45	3.68	3.85	3.98	4.09	4.18	4.26	4.33
12	3.05	3.39	3.61	3.76	3.89	3.99	4.08	4.15	4.22
13	3.01	3.33	3.54	3.69	3.81	3.91	3.99	4.06	4.13
14	2.98	3.29	3.49	3.64	3.75	3.84	3.92	3.99	4.05
15	2.95	3.25	3.45	3.59	3.70	3.79	3.86	3.93	3.99
16	2.92	3.22	3.41	3.55	3.65	3.74	3.82	3.88	3.93
17	2.90	3.19	3.38	3.51	3.62	3.70	3.77	3.83	3.89
18	2.88	3.17	3.35	3.48	3.58	3.67	3.74	3.80	3.85
19	2.86	3.15	3.33	3.46	3.55	3.64	3.70	3.76	3.81
20	2.85	3.13	3.31	3.43	3.53	3.61	3.67	3.73	3.78
24	2.80	3.07	3.24	3.36	3.45	3.52	3.58	3.64	3.69
30	2.75	3.01	3.17	3.28	3.37	3.44	3.50	3.55	3.59
40	2.70	2.95	3.10	3.21	3.29	3.36	3.41	3.46	3.50
60	2.66	2.90	3.04	3.14	3.22	3.28	3.33	3.38	3.42
120	2.62	2.84	2.98	3.08	3.15	3.21	3.25	3.30	3.33
∞	2.58	2.79	2.92	3.01	3.08	3.14	3.18	3.22	3.25

Table L.   Critical values of chi-square (χ^2)

df*	Level of Significance					
	.20	.10	.05	.02	.01	.001
1	1.64	2.71	3.84	5.41	6.64	10.83
2	3.22	4.61	5.99	7.82	9.21	13.82
3	4.64	6.25	7.82	9.84	11.34	16.27
4	5.99	7.78	9.49	11.67	13.28	18.46
5	7.29	9.24	11.07	13.39	15.09	20.52
6	8.56	10.64	12.59	15.03	16.81	22.46
7	9.80	12.02	14.07	16.62	18.48	24.32
8	11.03	13.36	15.51	18.17	20.09	26.12
9	12.24	14.68	16.92	19.68	21.67	27.88
10	13.44	15.99	18.31	21.16	23.21	29.59
11	14.63	17.28	19.68	22.62	24.72	31.26
12	15.81	18.55	21.03	24.05	26.22	32.91
13	16.98	19.81	22.36	25.47	27.69	34.53
14	18.15	21.06	23.68	26.87	29.14	36.12
15	19.31	22.31	25.00	28.26	30.58	37.70
16	20.46	23.54	26.30	29.63	32.00	39.25
17	21.62	24.77	27.59	31.00	33.41	40.79
18	22.76	25.99	28.87	32.35	34.81	42.31
19	23.90	27.20	30.14	33.69	36.19	43.82
20	25.04	28.41	31.41	35.02	37.57	45.32
21	26.17	29.62	32.67	36.34	38.93	46.80
22	27.30	30.81	33.92	37.66	40.29	48.27
23	28.43	32.01	35.17	38.97	41.64	49.73
24	29.55	33.20	36.42	40.27	42.98	51.18
25	30.68	34.38	37.65	41.57	44.31	52.62
26	31.80	35.56	38.89	42.86	45.64	54.05
27	32.91	36.74	40.11	44.14	46.96	55.48
28	34.03	37.92	41.34	45.42	48.28	56.89
29	35.14	39.09	42.56	46.69	49.59	58.30
30	36.25	40.26	43.77	47.96	50.89	59.70

* For *df* greater than 30, the value obtained from the expression $\sqrt{2\chi^2} - \sqrt{2df - 1}$ may be used as a *t* ratio.

Table M.   Critical values of ρ (rho), the Spearman rank correlation coefficient

N	Significance Level (One-tailed Test)	
	.05	.01
4	1.000	
5	.900	1.000
6	.829	.943
7	.714	.893
8	.643	.833
9	.600	.783
10	.564	.746
12	.506	.712
14	.456	.645
16	.425	.601
18	.399	.564
20	.377	.534
22	.359	.508
24	.343	.485
26	.329	.465
28	.317	.448
30	.306	.432

Table N.   Estimates of r_{tet} for various values of ad/bc

r_{tet}	ad / bc	r_{tet}	ad / bc	r_{tet}	ad / bc
.00	0–1.00	.35	2.49–2.55	.70	8.50–8.90
.01	1.01–1.03	.36	2.56–2.63	.71	8.91–9.35
.02	1.04–1.06	.37	2.64–2.71	.72	9.36–9.82
.03	1.07–1.08	.38	2.72–2.79	.73	9.83–-10.33
.04	1.09–1.11	.39	2.80–2.87	.74	10.34–-10.90
.05	1.12–1.14	.40	2.88–2.96	.75	10.91–11.51
.06	1.15–1.17	.41	2.97–3.05	.76	11.52–12.16
.07	1.18–1.20	.42	3.06–3.14	.77	12.17–12.89
.08	1.21–1.23	.43	3.15–3.24	.78	12.90–13.70
.09	1.24–1.27	.44	3.25–3.34	.79	13.71–14.58
.10	1.28–1.30	.45	3.35–3.45	.80	14.59–15.57
.11	1.31–1.33	.46	3.46–3.56	.81	15.58–16.65
.12	1.34–1.37	.47	3.57–3.68	.82	16.66–17.88
.13	1.38–1.40	.48	3.69–3.80	.83	17.89–19.28
.14	1.41–1.44	.49	3.81–3.92	.84	19.29–20.85
.15	1.45–1.48	.50	3.93–4.06	.85	20.86–22.68
.16	1.49–1.52	.51	4.07–4.20	.86	22.69–24.76
.17	1.53–1.56	.52	4.21–4.34	.87	24.77–27.22
.18	1.57–1.60	.53	4.35–4.49	.88	27.23–30.09
.19	1.61–1.64	.54	4.50–4.66	.89	30.10–33.60
.20	1.65–1.69	.55	4.67–4.82	.90	33.61–37.79
.21	1.70–1.73	.56	4.83–4.99	.91	37.80–43.06
.22	1.74–1.78	.57	5.00–5.18	.92	43.07–49.83
.23	1.79–1.83	.58	5.19–5.38	.93	49.84–58.79
.24	1.84–1.88	.59	5.39–5.59	.94	58.80–70.95
.25	1.89–1.93	.60	5.60–5.80	.95	70.96–89.01
.26	1.94–1.98	.61	5.81–6.03	.96	89.02–117.54
.27	1.99–2.04	.62	6.04–6.28	.97	117.55–169.67
.28	2.05–2.10	.63	6.29–6.54	.98	169.68–293.12
.29	2.11–2.15	.64	6.55–6.81	.99	293.13–923.97
.30	2.16–2.22	.65	6.82–7.10	1.00	923.98 –
.31	2.23–2.28	.66	7.11–7.42		
.32	2.29–2.34	.67	7.43–7.75		
.33	2.35–2.41	.68	7.76–8.11		
.34	2.42–2.48	.69	8.12–8.49		

Table O. Probabilities associated with values as large as observed values of *s* in the Kendall rank correlation coefficient

S	Values of N				S	Values of N		
	4	5	8	9		6	7	10
0	.625	.592	.548	.540	1	.500	.500	.500
2	.375	.408	.452	.460	3	.360	.386	.431
4	.167	.242	.360	.381	5	.235	.281	.364
6	.042	.117	.274	.306	7	.136	.191	.300
8		.042	.199	.238	9	.068	.119	.242
10		.0083	.138	.179	11	.028	.068	.190
12			.089	.130	13	.0083	.035	.146
14			.054	.090	15	.0014	.015	.108
16			.031	.060	17		.0054	.078
18			.016	.038	19		.0014	.054
20			.0071	.022	21		.00020	.036
22			.0028	.012	23			.023
24			.00087	.0063	25			.014
26			.00019	.0029	27			.0083
28			.000025	.0012	29			.0046
30				.00043	31			.0023
32				.00012	33			.0011
34				.000025	35			.00047
36				.0000028	37			.00018
					39			.000058
					41			.000015
					43			.0000028
					45			.00000028

Table P.   Critical values of s in the Kendall coefficient of concordance

k	N					Additional Values for N=3	
	3†	4	5	6	7	k	s
Values at the .05 Level of Significance							
3			64.4	103.9	157.3	9	54.0
4		49.5	88.4	143.3	217.0	12	71.9
5		62.6	112.3	182.4	276.2	14	83.8
6		75.7	136.1	221.4	335.2	16	95.8
8	48.1	101.7	183.7	299.0	453.1	18	107.7
10	60.0	127.8	231.2	376.7	571.0		
15	89.8	192.9	349.8	570.5	864.9		
20	119.7	258.0	468.5	764.4	1,158.7		
Values at the .01 Level of Significance							
3			75.6	122.8	185.6	9	75.9
4		61.4	109.3	176.2	265.0	12	103.5
5		80.5	142.8	229.4	343.8	14	121.9
6		99.5	176.1	282.4	422.6	16	140.2
8	66.8	137.4	242.7	388.3	579.9	18	158.6
10	85.1	175.3	309.1	494.0	737.0		
15	131.0	269.8	475.2	758.2	1,129.5		
20	177.0	364.2	641.2	1,022.2	1,521.9		

† Notice that additional critical values of s for $N=3$ are given in the right-hand column of this table.

Table Q. Values of the coefficient of concordance W significant at the 20, 10, 5, and 1% levels

m	α	n							
		3	4	5	6	7	8	9	10
3.	.20	.78	.60	.53	.49	.47	.46	.45	.44
	.10		.73	.62	.58	.55	.53	.52	.51
	.05	1.00	.82	.71	.65	.62	.60	.58	.56
	.01		.96	.84	.77	.73	.70	.67	.65
4	.20	.56	.40	.38	.37	.36	.35	.34	.33
	.10	.75	.52	.47	.44	.42	.41	.40	.39
	.05	.81	.65	.54	.51	.48	.46	.45	.44
	.01	1.00	.80	.67	.62	.59	.56	.54	.52
5	.20	.36	.34	.30	.29	.28	.28	.27	.27
	.10	.52	.42	.38	.36	.34	.33	.32	.31
	.05	.64	.52	.44	.41	.39	.38	.36	.35
	.01	.84	.66	.56	.52	.49	.46	.44	.43
6	.20	.33	.27	.25	.24	.24	.23	.23	.23
	.10	.44	.36	.32	.30	.29	.28	.27	.26
	.05	.58	.42	.37	.35	.33	.32	.31	.30
	.01	.75	.56	.49	.45	.42	.40	.38	.37
7	.20	.27	.23	.22	.21	.20	.20	.20	.19
	.10	.39	.30	.27	.26	.25	.24	.23	.23
	.05	.51	.36	.32	.30	.29	.27	.26	.26
	.01	.63	.48	.43	.39	.36	.34	.33	.32
8	.20	.25	.20	.19	.18	.18	.17	.17	.17
	.10	.33	.26	.24	.23	.22	.21	.20	.20
	.05	.39	.32	.29	.27	.25	.24	.23	.23
	.01	.56	.43	.38	.35	.32	.31	.29	.28
9	.20	.20	.18	.17	.16	.16	.16	.15	.15
	.10	.31	.23	.21	.20	.19	.19	.18	.18
	.05	.35	.28	.26	.24	.23	.22	.21	.20
	.01	.48	.38	.34	.31	.29	.27	.26	.25
10	.20	.19	.16	.15	.15	.14	.14	.14	.13
	.10	.25	.21	.19	.18	.17	.17	.16	.16
	.05	.31	.25	.23	.21	.20	.20	.19	.18
	.01	.48	.35	.31	.28	.26	.25	.24	.23
12	.20	.14	.13	.13	.12	.12	.12	.11	.11
	.10	.19	.17	.16	.15	.15	.14	.14	.13
	.05	.25	.21	.19	.18	.17	.16	.16	.15
	.01	.36	.30	.26	.24	.22	.21	.20	.19

(Table Q contd.)

(Table Q contd.)

m	α	n							
		3	**4**	**5**	**6**	**7**	**8**	**9**	**10**
14	.20	.12	.11	.11	.10	.10	.10	.10	.10
	.10	.17	.15	.14	.13	.13	.12	.12	.12
	.05	.21	.18	.17	.16	.15	.14	.14	.13
	.01	.31	.26	.23	.21	.19	.18	.17	.17
16	.20	.10	.10	.09	.09	.09	.09	.09	.08
	.10	.15	.13	.12	.12	.11	.11	.10	.10
	.05	.19	.16	.15	.14	.13	.12	.12	.12
	.01	.28	.23	.20	.18	.17	.16	.15	.15
18	.20	.09	.09	.08	.08	.08	.08	.08	.07
	.10	.13	.12	.11	.10	.10	.09	.09	.09
	.05	.17	.14	.13	.12	.11	.11	.11	.10
	.01	.25	.20	.18	.16	.15	.14	.14	.13
20	.20	.08	.08	.07	.07	.07	.07	.07	.07
	.10	.11	.10	.10	.09	.09	.08	.08	.08
	.05	.15	.13	.12	.11	.10	.10	.10	.09
	.01	.22	.18	.16	.15	.14	.13	.12	.11
25	.20	.07	.06	.06	.06	.06	.06	.05	.05
	.10	.09	.08	.08	.07	.07	.07	.07	.06
	.05	.12	.10	.09	.09	.08	.08	.08	.07
	.01	.18	.15	.13	.12	.11	.10	.10	.09
30	.20	.05	.05	.05	.05	.05	.05	.05	.04
	.10	.08	.07	.06	.06	.06	.06	.06	.05
	.05	.10	.09	.08	.07	.07	.07	.07	.06
	.01	.15	.12	.11	.10	.09	.09	.08	.08

Table R. Probabilities associated with values as small as observed values of x in the binomial test

Given in the body of this table are one-tailed probabilities under H_0 for the binomial test when $P = Q = \frac{1}{2}$.

N\x	0	1	2	3	4	5	6	7	8	9	10	11	12	13	14	15
5	.031	.188	.500	.812	.969	†										
6	.016	.109	.344	.656	.891	.984	†									
7	.008	.062	.227	.500	.773	.938	.992	†								
8	.004	.035	.145	.363	.637	.855	.965	.996	†							
9	.002	.020	.090	.254	.500	.746	.910	.980	.998	†						
10	.001	.011	.055	.172	.377	.623	.828	.945	.989	.999	†					
11		.006	.033	.113	.274	.500	.726	.887	.967	.994	†	†				
12		.003	.019	.073	.194	.387	.613	.806	.927	.981	.997	†	†			
13		.002	.011	.046	.133	.291	.500	.709	.867	.954	.989	.998	†	†		
14		.001	.006	.029	.090	.212	.395	.605	.788	.910	.971	.994	.999	†	†	
15			.004	.018	.059	.151	.304	.500	.696	.849	.941	.982	.996	†	†	†
16			.002	.011	.038	.105	.227	.402	.598	.773	.895	.962	.989	.998	†	†
17			.001	.006	.025	.072	.166	.315	.500	.685	.834	.928	.975	.994	.999	†
18			.001	.004	.015	.048	.119	.240	.407	.593	.760	.881	.952	.985	.996	.999
19				.002	.010	.032	.084	.180	.324	.500	.676	.820	.916	.968	.990	.998
20				.001	.006	.021	.058	.132	.252	.412	.588	.748	.868	.942	.979	.994
21				.001	.004	.013	.039	.095	.192	.332	.500	.668	.808	.905	.961	.987
22					.002	.008	.026	.067	.143	.262	.416	.584	.738	.857	.933	.974
23					.001	.005	.017	.047	.105	.202	.339	.500	.661	.798	.895	.953
24					.001	.003	.011	.032	.076	.154	.271	.419	.581	.729	.846	.924
25						.002	.007	.022	.054	.115	.212	.345	.500	.655	.788	.885

† 1.0 or approximately 1.0.

Table S. Critical values of T in the Wilcoxon matched-pairs signed-ranks test

N	Level of Significance for One-tailed Test		
	.025	.01	.005
	Level of Significance for Two-tailed Test		
	.05	.02	.01
6	0	–	–
7	2	0	–
8	4	2	0
9	6	3	2
10	8	5	3
11	11	7	5
12	14	10	7
13	17	13	10
14	21	16	13
15	25	20	16
16	30	24	20
17	35	28	23
18	40	33	28
19	46	38	32
20	52	43	38
21	59	49	43
22	66	56	49
23	73	62	55
24	81	69	61
25	89	77	68

Table T. Critical lower-tail values of R_1 for rank test for two independent samples ($N_1 < N_2$)

| | $N_1=1$ | | | | | | | $N_1=2$ | | | | | | | |
N_2	0.001	0.005	0.010	0.025	0.05	0.10	$2\bar{R}_1$	0.001	0.005	0.010	0.025	0.05	0.10	$2\bar{R}_1$	N_2
2							4						-	10	2
3							5						3	12	3
4							6					-	3	14	4
5							7					3	4	16	5
6							8					3	4	18	6
7							9				-	3	4	20	7
8						-	10				3	4	5	22	8
9						1	11				3	4	5	24	9
10						1	12				3	4	6	26	10
11						1	13				3	4	6	28	11
12						1	14			-	4	5	7	30	12
13						1	15			3	4	5	7	32	13
14						1	16			3	4	6	8	34	14
15						1	17			3	4	6	8	36	15
16						1	18			3	4	6	8	38	16
17						1	19			3	5	6	9	40	17
18					-	1	20		-	3	5	7	9	42	18
19					1	2	21		3	4	5	7	10	44	19
20					1	2	22		3	4	5	7	10	46	20
21					1	2	23		3	4	6	8	11	48	21
22					1	2	24		3	4	6	8	11	50	22
23					1	2	25		3	4	6	8	12	52	23
24					1	2	26		3	4	6	9	12	54	24
25	-	-	-	-	1	2	27	-	3	4	6	9	12	56	25

| | $N_1=3$ | | | | | | | $N_1=4$ | | | | | | | |
N_2	0.001	0.005	0.010	0.025	0.05	0.10	$2\bar{R}_1$	0.001	0.005	0.010	0.025	0.05	0.10	$2\bar{R}_1$	N_2
3					6	7	21								
4				-	6	7	24			-	10	11	13	36	4
5				6	7	8	27		-	10	11	12	14	40	5
6			-	7	8	9	30		10	11	12	13	15	44	6
7			6	7	8	10	33		10	11	13	14	16	48	7
8		-	6	8	9	11	36		11	12	14	15	17	52	8
9		6	7	8	10	11	39	-	11	13	14	16	19	56	9
10		6	7	9	10	12	42	10	12	13	15	17	20	60	10
11		6	7	9	11	13	45	10	12	14	16	18	21	64	11
12		7	8	10	11	14	48	10	13	15	17	19	22	68	12
13		7	8	10	12	15	51	11	13	15	18	20	23	72	13
14		7	8	11	13	16	54	11	14	16	19	21	25	76	14
15		8	9	11	13	16	57	11	15	17	20	22	26	80	15
16	-	8	9	12	14	17	60	12	15	17	21	24	27	84	16
17	6	8	10	12	15	18	63	12	16	18	21	25	28	88	17
18	6	8	10	13	15	19	66	13	16	19	22	26	30	92	18
19	6	9	10	13	16	20	69	13	17	19	23	27	31	96	19
20	6	9	11	14	17	21	72	13	18	20	24	28	32	100	20
21	7	9	11	14	17	21	75	14	18	21	25	29	33	104	21
22	7	10	12	15	18	22	78	14	19	21	26	30	35	108	22
23	7	10	12	15	19	23	81	14	19	22	27	31	36	112	23
24	7	10	12	16	19	24	84	15	20	23	27	32	38	116	24
25	7	11	13	16	20	25	87	15	20	23	28	33	38	120	25

(Table T contd.)

(Table T contd.)

	$N_1=5$							$N_1=6$							
N_2	0.001	0.005	0.010	0.025	0.05	0.10	$2\bar{R}_1$	0.001	0.005	0.010	0.025	0.05	0.10	$2\bar{R}_1$	N_2
5		15	16	17	19	20	55								
6		16	17	18	20	22	60	–	23	24	26	28	30	78	6
7	–	16	18	20	21	23	65	21	24	25	27	29	32	84	7
8	15	17	19	21	23	25	70	22	25	27	29	31	34	90	8
9	16	18	20	22	24	27	75	23	26	28	31	33	36	96	9
10	16	19	21	23	26	28	80	24	27	29	32	35	38	102	10
11	17	20	22	24	27	30	85	25	28	30	34	37	40	108	11
12	17	21	23	26	28	32	90	25	30	32	35	38	42	114	12
13	18	22	24	27	30	33	95	26	31	33	37	40	44	120	13
14	18	22	25	28	31	35	100	27	32	34	38	42	46	126	14
15	19	23	26	29	33	37	105	28	33	36	40	44	48	132	15
16	20	24	27	30	34	38	110	29	34	37	42	46	50	138	16
17	20	25	28	32	35	40	115	30	36	39	43	47	52	144	17
18	21	26	29	33	37	42	120	31	37	40	45	49	55	150	18
19	22	27	30	34	38	43	125	32	38	41	46	51	57	156	19
20	22	28	31	35	40	45	130	33	39	43	48	53	59	162	20
21	23	29	32	37	41	47	135	33	40	44	50	55	61	168	21
22	23	29	33	38	43	48	140	34	42	45	51	57	63	174	22
23	24	30	34	39	44	50	145	35	43	47	53	58	65	180	23
24	25	31	35	40	45	51	150	36	44	48	54	60	67	186	24
25	25	32	36	42	47	53	155	37	45	50	56	62	69	192	25

	$N_1=7$							$N_1=8$							
N_2	0.001	0.005	0.010	0.025	0.05	0.10	$2\bar{R}_1$	0.001	0.005	0.010	0.025	0.05	0.10	$2\bar{R}_1$	N_2
7	29	32	34	36	39	41	105								
8	30	34	35	38	41	44	112	40	43	45	49	51	55	136	8
9	31	35	37	40	43	46	119	41	45	47	51	54	58	144	9
10	33	37	39	42	45	49	126	42	47	49	53	56	60	152	10
11	34	38	40	44	47	51	133	44	49	51	55	59	63	160	11
12	35	40	42	46	49	54	140	45	51	53	58	62	66	168	12
13	36	41	44	48	52	56	147	47	53	56	60	64	69	176	13
14	37	43	45	50	54	59	154	48	54	58	62	67	72	184	14
15	38	44	47	52	56	61	161	50	56	60	65	69	75	192	15
16	39	46	49	54	58	64	168	51	58	62	67	72	78	200	16
17	41	47	51	56	61	66	175	53	60	64	70	75	81	208	17
18	42	49	52	58	63	69	182	54	62	66	72	77	84	216	18
19	43	50	54	60	65	71	189	56	64	68	74	80	87	224	19
20	44	52	56	62	67	74	196	57	66	70	77	83	90	232	20
21	46	53	58	64	69	76	203	59	68	72	79	85	92	240	21
22	47	55	59	66	72	79	210	60	70	74	81	88	95	248	22
23	48	57	61	68	74	81	217	62	71	76	84	90	98	256	23
24	49	58	63	70	76	84	224	64	73	78	86	93	101	264	24
25	50	60	64	72	78	86	231	65	75	81	89	96	104	272	25

	$N_1=9$							$N_1=10$							
N_2	0.001	0.005	0.010	0.025	0.05	0.10	$2\bar{R}_1$	0.001	0.005	0.010	0.025	0.05	0.10	$2\bar{R}_1$	N_2
9	52	56	59	62	66	70	171								
10	53	58	61	65	69	73	180	65	71	74	78	82	87	210	10
11	55	61	63	68	72	76	189	67	73	77	81	86	91	220	11
12	57	63	66	71	75	80	198	69	76	79	84	89	94	230	12
13	59	65	68	73	78	83	207	72	79	82	88	92	98	240	13
14	60	67	71	76	81	86	216	74	81	85	91	96	102	250	14
15	62	69	73	79	84	90	225	76	84	88	94	99	106	260	15
16	64	72	76	82	87	93	234	78	86	91	97	103	109	270	16
17	66	74	78	84	90	97	243	80	89	93	100	103	113	280	17
18	68	76	81	87	93	100	252	82	92	96	103	110	117	290	18
19	70	78	83	90	96	103	261	84	94	99	107	113	121	300	19
20	71	81	85	93	99	107	270	87	97	102	110	117	125	310	20
21	73	83	88	95	102	110	279	89	99	105	113	120	128	320	21
22	75	85	90	98	105	113	288	91	102	108	116	123	132	330	22
23	77	88	93	101	108	117	297	93	105	110	119	127	136	340	23
24	79	90	95	104	111	120	306	95	107	113	122	130	140	350	24
25	81	92	98	107	114	123	315	98	110	116	126	134	144	360	25

| | $N_1=11$ | | | | | | | | $N_1=12$ | | | | | | |
N_2	0.001	0.005	0.010	0.025	0.05	0.10	$2\bar{R}_1$	0.001	0.005	0.010	0.025	0.05	0.10	$2\bar{R}_1$	N_2
11	81	87	91	96	100	106	253								
12	83	90	94	99	104	110	264	98	105	109	115	120	127	300	12
13	86	93	97	103	108	114	275	101	109	113	119	125	131	312	13
14	88	96	100	106	112	118	286	103	112	116	123	129	136	324	14
15	90	99	103	110	116	123	297	106	115	120	127	133	141	336	15
16	93	102	107	113	120	127	308	109	119	124	131	138	145	348	16
17	95	105	110	117	123	131	319	112	122	127	135	142	150	360	17
18	98	108	113	121	127	135	330	115	125	131	139	146	155	372	18
19	100	111	116	124	131	139	341	118	129	134	143	150	159	384	19
20	103	114	119	128	135	144	352	120	132	138	147	155	164	396	20
21	106	117	123	131	139	148	363	123	136	142	151	159	169	408	21
22	108	120	126	135	143	152	374	126	139	145	155	163	173	420	22
23	111	123	129	139	147	156	385	129	142	149	159	168	178	432	23
24	113	126	132	142	151	161	396	132	146	153	163	172	183	444	24
25	116	129	136	146	155	165	407	135	149	156	167	176	187	456	25

| | $N_1=13$ | | | | | | | | $N_1=14$ | | | | | | |
N_2	0.001	0.005	0.010	0.025	0.05	0.10	$2\bar{R}_1$	0.001	0.005	0.010	0.025	0.05	0.10	$2\bar{R}_1$	N_2
13	117	125	130	136	142	149	351								
14	120	129	134	141	147	154	364	137	147	152	160	166	174	406	14
15	123	133	138	145	152	159	377	141	151	156	164	171	179	420	15
16	126	136	142	150	156	165	390	144	155	161	169	176	185	434	16
17	129	140	146	154	161	170	403	148	159	165	174	182	190	448	17
18	133	144	150	158	166	175	416	151	163	170	179	187	196	462	18
19	136	148	154	163	171	180	429	155	168	174	183	192	202	476	19
20	139	151	158	167	175	185	442	159	172	178	188	197	207	490	20
21	142	155	162	171	180	190	455	162	176	183	193	202	213	504	21
22	145	159	166	176	185	195	468	166	180	187	198	207	218	518	22
23	149	163	170	180	189	200	481	169	184	192	203	212	224	532	23
24	152	166	174	185	194	205	494	173	188	196	207	218	229	546	24
25	155	170	178	189	199	211	507	177	192	200	212	223	235	560	25

| | $N_1=15$ | | | | | | | | $N_1=16$ | | | | | | |
N_2	0.001	0.005	0.010	0.025	0.05	0.10	$2\bar{R}_1$	0.001	0.005	0.010	0.025	0.05	0.10	$2\bar{R}_1$	N_2
15	160	171	176	184	192	200	465								
16	163	175	181	190	197	206	480	184	196	202	211	219	229	528	16
17	167	180	186	195	203	212	495	188	201	207	217	225	235	544	17
18	171	184	190	200	208	218	510	192	206	212	222	231	242	560	18
19	175	189	195	205	214	224	525	196	210	218	228	237	248	576	19
20	179	193	200	210	220	230	540	201	215	223	234	243	255	592	20
21	183	198	205	216	225	236	555	205	220	228	239	249	261	608	21
22	187	202	210	221	231	242	570	209	225	233	245	255	267	624	22
23	191	207	214	226	236	248	585	214	230	238	251	261	274	640	23
24	195	211	219	231	242	254	600	218	235	244	256	267	280	656	24
25	199	216	224	237	248	260	615	222	240	249	262	273	287	672	25

(Table T contd.)

(Table T contd.)

	$N_1=17$							$N_1=18$							
N_2	0.001	0.005	0.010	0.025	0.05	0.10	$2\bar{R}_1$	0.001	0.005	0.010	0.025	0.05	0.10	$2\bar{R}_1$	N_2
17	210	223	230	240	249	259	595								
18	214	228	235	246	255	266	612	237	252	259	270	280	291	666	18
19	219	234	241	252	262	273	629	242	258	265	277	287	299	684	19
20	223	239	246	258	268	280	646	247	263	271	283	294	306	702	20
21	228	244	252	264	274	287	663	252	269	277	290	301	313	720	21
22	233	249	258	270	281	294	680	257	275	283	296	307	321	738	22
23	238	255	263	276	287	300	697	262	280	289	303	314	328	756	23
24	242	260	269	282	294	307	714	267	286	295	309	321	335	774	24
25	247	265	275	288	300	314	731	273	292	301	316	328	343	792	25

	$N_1=19$							$N_1=20$							
N_2	0.001	0.005	0.010	0.025	0.05	0.10	$2\bar{R}_1$	0.001	0.005	0.010	0.025	0.05	0.10	$2\bar{R}_1$	N_2
19	267	283	291	303	313	325	741								
20	272	289	297	309	320	333	760	298	315	324	337	348	361	820	20
21	277	295	303	316	328	341	779	304	322	331	344	356	370	840	21
22	283	301	310	323	335	349	798	309	328	337	351	364	378	860	22
23	288	307	316	330	342	357	817	315	335	344	359	371	386	880	23
24	294	313	323	337	350	364	836	321	341	351	366	379	394	900	24
25	299	319	329	344	357	372	855	327	348	358	373	387	403	920	25

	$N_1=21$							$N_1=22$							
N_2	0.001	0.005	0.010	0.025	0.05	0.10	$2\bar{R}_1$	0.001	0.005	0.010	0.025	0.05	0.10	$2\bar{R}_1$	N_2
21	331	349	359	373	385	399	903								
22	337	356	366	381	393	408	924	365	386	396	411	424	439	990	22
23	343	363	373	388	401	417	945	372	393	403	419	432	448	1012	23
24	349	370	381	396	410	425	966	379	400	411	427	441	457	1034	24
25	356	377	388	404	418	434	987	385	408	419	435	450	467	1056	25

	$N_1=23$							$N_1=24$							
N_2	0.001	0.005	0.010	0.025	0.05	0.10	$2\bar{R}_1$	0.001	0.005	0.010	0.025	0.05	0.10	$2\bar{R}_1$	N_2
23	402	424	434	451	465	481	1081								
24	409	431	443	459	474	491	1104	440	464	475	492	507	525	1176	24
25	416	439	451	468	483	500	1127	448	472	484	501	517	535	1200	25

	$N_1=25$						
N_2	0.001	0.005	0.010	0.025	0.05	0.10	$2\bar{R}_1$
25	480	505	517	536	552	570	1275

The table shows (i) values, R_1, which are just significant at the probability level quoted at the head of column, (ii) twice the mean $2\bar{R}_1$. A blank space indicates that no value is significant at that level. The upper critical value is $2\bar{R}_1 - R_1$.

Table U. Probabilities associated with values as small as observed values of U in the Mann-Whitney test

$n_2=3$			
n_1 / U	1	2	3
0	.250	.100	.050
1	.500	.200	.100
2	.750	.400	.200
3		.600	.350
4			.500
5			.650

$n_2=4$				
n_1 / U	1	2	3	4
0	.200	.067	.028	.014
1	.400	.133	.057	.029
2	.600	.267	.114	.057
3		.400	.200	.100
4		.600	.314	.171
5			.429	.243
6			.571	.343
7				.443
8				.557

$n_2=5$					
n_1 / U	1	2	3	4	5
0	.167	.047	.018	.008	.004
1	.333	.095	.036	.016	.008
2	.500	.190	.071	.032	.016
3	.667	.286	.125	.056	.028
4		.429	.196	.095	.048
5		.571	.286	.143	.075
6			.393	.206	.111
7			.500	.278	.155
8			.607	.365	.210
9				.452	.274
10				.548	.345
11					.421
12					.500
13					.579

(Table U contd.)

(Table U contd.)

$n_2 = 6$						
U \ n_1	1	2	3	4	5	6
0	.143	.036	.012	.005	.002	.001
1	.286	.071	.024	.010	.004	.002
2	.428	.143	.048	.019	.009	.004
3	.571	.214	.083	.033	.015	.008
4		.321	.131	.057	.026	.013
5		.429	.190	.086	.041	.021
6		.571	.274	.129	.063	.032
7			.357	.176	.089	.047
8			.452	.238	.123	.066
9			.548	.305	.165	.090
10				.381	.214	.120
11				.457	.268	.155
12				.545	.331	.197
13					.396	.242
14					.465	.294
15					.535	.350
16						.409
17						.469
18						.531

$n_2 = 7$							
U \ n_1	1	2	3	4	5	6	7
0	.125	.028	.008	.003	.001	.001	.000
1	.250	.056	.017	.006	.003	.001	.001
2	.375	.111	.033	.012	.005	.002	.001
3	.500	.167	.058	.021	.009	.004	.002
4	.625	.250	.092	.036	.015	.007	.003
5		.333	.133	.055	.024	.011	.006
6		.444	.192	.082	.037	.017	.009
7		.556	.258	.115	.053	.026	.013
8			.333	.158	.074	.037	.019
9			.417	.206	.101	.051	.027
10			.500	.264	.134	.069	.036
11			.583	.324	.172	.090	.049
12				.394	.216	.117	.064
13				.464	.265	.147	.082
14				.538	.319	.183	.104
15					.378	.223	.130
16					.438	.267	.159
17					.500	.314	.191
18					.562	.365	.228
19						.418	.267
20						.473	.310
21						.527	.355
22							.402
23							.451
24							.500
25							.549

n_1 \ U	1	2	3	4	5	6	7	8	t	Normal
					$n_2=8$					
0	.111	.022	.006	.002	.001	.000	.000	.000	3.308	.001
1	.222	.044	.012	.004	.002	.001	.000	.000	3.203	.001
2	.333	.089	.024	.008	.003	.001	.001	.000	3.098	.001
3	.444	.133	.042	.014	.005	.002	.001	.001	2.993	.001
4	.556	.200	.067	.024	.009	.004	.002	.001	2.888	.002
5		.267	.097	.036	.015	.006	.003	.001	2.783	.003
6		.356	.139	.055	.023	.010	.005	.002	2.678	.004
7		.444	.188	.077	.033	.015	.007	.003	2.573	.005
8		.556	.248	.107	.047	.021	.010	.005	2.468	.007
9			.315	.141	.064	.030	.014	.007	2.363	.009
10			.387	.184	.085	.041	.020	.010	2.258	.012
11			.461	.230	.111	.054	.027	.014	2.153	.016
12			.539	.285	.142	.071	.036	.019	2.048	.020
13				.341	.177	.091	.047	.025	1.943	.026
14				.404	.217	.114	.060	.032	1.838	.033
15				.467	.262	.141	.076	.041	1.733	.041
16				.533	.311	.172	.095	.052	1.628	.052
17					.362	.207	.116	.065	1.523	.064
18					.416	.245	.140	.080	1.418	.078
19					.472	.286	.168	.097	1.313	.094
20					.528	.331	.198	.117	1.208	.113
21						.377	.232	.139	1.102	.135
22						.426	.268	.164	.998	.159
23						.475	.306	.191	.893	.185
24						.525	.347	.221	.788	.215
25							.389	.253	.683	.247
26							.433	.287	.578	.282
27							.478	.323	.473	.318
28							.522	.360	.368	.356
29								.399	.263	.396
30								.439	.158	.437
31								.480	.052	.481
32								.520		

Table V.   Table of critical values of U in the Mann–Whitney test

Table V(I).   Critical values of U for a one-tailed test at $\alpha=0.001$ or for a two-tailed test at $\alpha=0.002$

n_1 \ n_2	9	10	11	12	13	14	15	16	17	18	19	20
1												
2												
3									0	0	0	0
4		0	0	0	1	1	1	2	2	3	3	3
5	1	1	2	2	3	3	4	5	5	6	7	7
6	2	3	4	4	5	6	7	8	9	10	11	12
7	3	5	6	7	8	9	10	11	13	14	15	16
8	5	6	8	9	11	12	14	15	17	18	20	21
9	7	8	10	12	14	15	17	19	21	23	25	26
10	8	10	12	14	17	19	21	23	25	27	29	32
11	10	12	15	17	20	22	24	27	29	32	34	37
12	12	14	17	20	23	25	28	31	34	37	40	42
13	14	17	20	23	26	29	32	35	38	42	45	48
14	15	19	22	25	29	32	36	39	43	46	50	54
15	17	21	24	28	32	36	40	43	47	51	55	59
16	19	23	27	31	35	39	43	48	52	56	60	65
17	21	25	29	34	38	43	47	52	57	61	66	70
18	23	27	32	37	42	46	51	56	61	66	71	76
19	25	29	34	40	45	50	55	60	66	71	77	82
20	26	32	37	42	48	54	59	65	70	76	82	88

Table V(II).   Critical values of U for a one-tailed test at $\alpha=0.01$ or for a two-tailed test at $\alpha=0.02$

n_1 \ n_2	9	10	11	12	13	14	15	16	17	18	19	20
1												
2					0	0	0	0	0	0	1	1
3	1	1	1	2	2	2	3	3	4	4	4	5
4	3	3	4	5	5	6	7	7	8	9	9	10
5	5	6	7	8	9	10	11	12	13	14	15	16
6	7	8	9	11	12	13	15	16	18	19	20	22
7	9	11	12	14	16	17	19	21	23	24	26	28
8	11	13	15	17	20	22	24	26	28	30	32	34
9	14	16	18	21	23	26	28	31	33	36	38	40
10	16	19	22	24	27	30	33	36	38	41	44	47
11	18	22	25	28	31	34	37	41	44	47	50	53
12	21	24	28	31	35	38	42	46	49	53	56	60
13	23	27	31	35	39	43	47	51	55	59	63	67
14	26	30	34	38	43	47	51	56	60	65	69	73
15	28	33	37	42	47	51	56	61	66	70	75	80
16	31	36	41	46	51	56	61	66	71	76	82	87
17	33	38	44	49	55	60	66	71	77	82	88	93
18	36	41	47	53	59	65	70	76	82	88	94	100
19	38	44	50	56	63	69	75	82	88	94	101	107
20	40	47	53	60	67	73	80	87	93	100	107	114

Table V(III). Critical values of U for a one-tailed test at $\alpha=0.025$ or for a two-tailed test at $\alpha=0.05$

n_1 \ n_2	9	10	11	12	13	14	15	16	17	18	19	20
1												
2	0	0	0	1	1	1	1	1	2	2	2	2
3	2	3	3	4	4	5	5	6	6	7	7	8
4	4	5	6	7	8	9	10	11	11	12	13	13
5	7	8	9	11	12	13	14	15	17	18	19	20
6	10	11	13	14	16	17	19	21	22	24	25	27
7	12	14	16	18	20	22	24	26	28	30	32	34
8	15	17	19	22	24	26	29	31	34	36	38	41
9	17	20	23	26	28	31	34	37	39	42	45	48
10	20	23	26	29	33	36	39	42	45	48	52	55
11	23	26	30	33	37	40	44	47	51	55	58	62
12	26	29	33	37	41	45	49	53	57	61	65	69
13	28	33	37	41	45	50	54	59	63	67	72	76
14	31	36	40	45	50	55	59	64	67	74	78	83
15	34	39	44	49	54	59	64	70	75	80	85	90
16	37	42	47	53	59	64	70	75	81	86	92	98
17	39	45	51	57	63	67	75	81	87	93	99	105
18	42	48	55	61	67	74	80	86	93	99	106	112
19	45	52	58	65	72	78	85	92	99	106	113	119
20	48	55	62	69	76	83	90	98	105	112	119	127

Table V(IV). Critical values of U for a one-tailed test at $\alpha=0.05$ or for a two-tailed test at $\alpha=0.10$

n_1 \ n_2	9	10	11	12	13	14	15	16	17	18	19	20
1											0	0
2	1	1	1	2	2	2	3	3	3	4	4	4
3	3	4	5	5	6	7	7	8	9	9	10	11
4	6	7	8	9	10	11	12	14	15	16	17	18
5	9	11	12	13	15	16	18	19	20	22	23	25
6	12	14	16	17	19	21	23	25	26	28	30	32
7	15	17	19	21	24	26	28	30	33	35	37	39
8	18	20	23	26	28	31	33	36	39	41	44	47
9	21	24	27	30	33	36	39	42	45	48	51	54
10	24	27	31	34	37	41	44	48	51	55	58	62
11	27	31	34	38	42	46	50	54	57	61	65	69
12	30	34	38	42	47	51	55	60	64	68	72	77
13	33	37	42	47	51	56	61	65	70	75	80	84
14	36	41	46	51	56	61	66	71	77	82	87	92
15	39	44	50	55	61	66	72	77	83	88	94	100
16	42	48	54	60	65	71	77	83	89	95	101	107
17	45	51	57	64	70	77	83	89	96	102	109	115
18	48	55	61	68	75	82	88	95	102	109	116	123
19	51	58	65	72	80	87	94	101	109	116	123	130
20	54	62	69	77	84	92	100	107	115	123	130	138

Table W. Probabilities associated with values as large as observed values of H in the Kruskal-Wallis one-way analysis of variance by ranks

n_1	n_2	n_3	H	p	n_1	n_2	n_3	H	p
2	1	1	2.7000	.500	4	2	1	4.8214	.057
								4.5000	.076
								4.0179	.114
2	2	1	3.6000	.200	4	2	2	6.0000	.014
								5.3333	.033
								5.1250	.052
								4.4583	.100
								4.1667	.105
2	2	2	4.5714	.067	4	3	1	5.8333	.021
			3.7143	.200				5.2083	.050
								5.0000	.057
								4.0556	.093
								3.8889	.129
3	1	1	3.2000	.300	4	3	2	6.4444	.008
								6.3000	.011
								5.4444	.046
								5.4000	.051
								4.5111	.098
								4.4444	.102
3	2	1	4.2857	.100	4	3	3	6.7455	.010
			3.8571	.133				6.7091	.013
								5.7909	.046
								5.7273	.050
								4.7091	.092
								4.7000	.101
3	2	2	5.3572	.029	4	4	1	6.6667	.010
			4.7143	.048				6.1667	.022
			4.5000	.067				4.9667	.048
			4.4643	.105				4.8667	.054
								4.1667	.082
								4.0667	.102
3	3	1	5.1429	.043	4	4	2	7.0364	.006
			4.5714	.100				6.8727	.011
			4.0000	.129				5.4545	.046
								5.2364	.052
								4.5545	.098
								4.4455	.103
3	3	2	6.2500	.011	4	4	3	7.1439	.010
			5.3611	.032				7.1364	.011
			5.1389	.061				5.5985	.049
			4.5556	.100				5.5758	.051
			4.2500	.121				4.5455	.099
								4.4773	.102
3	3	3	7.2000	.004	4	4	4	7.6538	.008
			6.4889	.011				7.5385	.011
			5.6889	.029				5.6923	.049
			5.6000	.050				5.6538	.054
			5.0667	.086				4.6539	.097
			4.6222	.100				4.5001	.104
4	1	1	3.5714	.200					

Sample Sizes			H	p	Sample Sizes			H	p
n_1	n_2	n_3			n_1	n_2	n_3		
5	1	1	3.8571	.143	5	4	3	7.4449	.010
								7.3949	.011
								5.6564	.049
								5.6308	.050
								4.5487	.099
								4.5231	.103
5	2	1	5.2500	.036	5	4	4	7.7604	.009
			5.0000	.048				7.7440	.011
			4.4500	.071				5.6571	.049
			4.2000	.095				5.6176	.050
			4.0500	.119				4.6187	.100
								4.5527	.102
5	2	2	6.5333	.008	5	5	1	7.3091	.009
			6.1333	.013				6.8364	.011
			5.1600	.034				5.1273	.046
			5.0400	.056				4.9091	.053
			4.3733	.090				4.1091	.086
			4.2933	.122				4.0364	.105
5	3	1	6.4000	.012	5	5	2	7.3385	.010
			4.9600	.048				7.2692	.010
			4.8711	.052				5.3385	.047
			4.0178	.095				5.2462	.051
			3.8400	.123				4.6231	.097
								4.5077	.100
5	3	2	6.9091	.009	5	5	3	7.5780	.010
			6.8218	.010				7.5429	.010
			5.2509	.049				5.7055	.046
			5.1055	.052				5.6264	.051
			4.6509	.091				4.5451	.100
			4.4945	.101				4.5363	.102
5	3	3	7.0788	.009	5	5	4	7.8229	.010
			6.9818	.011				7.7914	.010
			5.6485	.049				5.6657	.049
			5.5152	.051				5.6429	.050
			4.5333	.097				4.5229	.099
			4.4121	.109				4.5200	.101
5	4	1	6.9545	.008	5	5	5	8.0000	.009
			6.8400	.011				7.9800	.010
			4.9855	.044				5.7800	.049
			4.8600	.056				5.6600	.051
			3.9873	.098				4.5600	.100
			3.9600	.102				4.5000	.102
5	4	2	7.2045	.009					
			7.1182	.010					
			5.2727	.049					
			5.2682	.050					
			4.5409	.098					
			4.5182	.101					

Table X.   Probabilities associated with values as large as observed values of χ_r^2 in the Friedman two-way analysis of variance by ranks

Table X(I). $k=3$

N=2		N=3		N=4		N=5	
χ_r^2	p	χ_r^2	p	χ_r^2	p	χ_r^2	p
0	1.000	.000	1.000	.0	1.000	.0	1.000
1	.833	.667	.944	.5	.931	.4	.954
3	.500	2.000	.528	1.5	.653	1.2	.691
4	.167	2.667	.361	2.0	.431	1.6	.522
		4.667	.194	3.5	.273	2.8	.367
		6.000	.028	4.5	.125	3.6	.182
				6.0	.069	4.8	.124
				6.5	.042	5.2	.093
				8.0	.0046	6.4	.039
						7.6	.024
						8.4	.0085
						10.0	.00077

N=6		N=7		N=8		N=9	
χ_r^2	p	χ_r^2	p	χ_r^2	p	χ_r^2	p
.00	1.000	.000	1.000	.00	1.000	.000	1.000
.33	.956	.286	.964	.25	.967	.222	.971
1.00	.740	.857	.768	.75	.794	.667	.814
1.33	.570	1.143	.620	1.00	.654	.889	.865
2.33	.430	2.000	.486	1.75	.531	1.556	.569
3.00	.252	2.571	.305	2.25	.355	2.000	.398
4.00	.184	3.429	.237	3.00	.285	2.667	.328
4.33	.142	3.714	.192	3.25	.236	2.889	.278
5.33	.072	4.571	.112	4.00	.149	3.556	.187
6.33	.052	5.429	.085	4.75	.120	4.222	.154
7.00	.029	6.000	.052	5.25	.079	4.667	.107
8.33	.012	7.143	.027	6.25	.047	5.556	.069
9.00	.0081	7.714	.021	6.75	.038	6.000	.057
9.33	.0055	8.000	.016	7.00	.030	6.222	.048
10.33	.0017	8.857	.0084	7.75	.018	6.889	.031
12.00	.00013	10.286	.0036	9.00	.0099	8.000	.019
		10.571	.0027	9.25	.0080	8.222	.016
		11.143	.0012	9.75	.0048	8.667	.010
		12.286	.00032	10.75	.0024	9.556	.0060
		14.000	.000021	12.00	.0011	10.667	.0035
				12.25	.00086	10.889	.0029
				13.00	.00026	11.556	.0013
				14.25	.000061	12.667	.00066
				16.00	.0000036	13.556	.00035
						14.000	.00020
						14.222	.000097
						14.889	.000054
						16.222	.000011
						18.000	.0000006

Table X(II). $k = 4$

χ_r^2	p	χ_r^2	p	χ_r^2	p	χ_r^2	p
N=2		**N=3**		**N=4**			
.0	1.000	.2	1.000	.0	1.000	5.7	.141
.6	.958	.6	.958	.3	.992	6.0	.105
1.2	.834	1.0	.910	.6	.928	6.3	.094
1.8	.792	1.8	.727	.9	.900	6.6	.077
2.4	.625	2.2	.608	1.2	.800	6.9	.068
3.0	.542	2.6	.524	1.5	.754	7.2	.054
3.6	.458	3.4	.446	1.8	.677	7.5	.052
4.2	.375	3.8	.342	2.1	.649	7.8	.036
4.8	.208	4.2	.300	2.4	.524	8.1	.033
5.4	.167	5.0	.207	2.7	.508	8.4	.019
6.0	.042	5.4	.175	3.0	.432	.8.7	.014
		5.8	.148	3.3	.389	9.3	.012
		6.6	.075	3.6	.355	9.6	.0069
		7.0	.054	3.9	.324	9.9	.0062
		7.4	.033	4.5	.242	10.2	.0027
		8.2	.017	4.8	.200	10.8	.0016
		9.0	.0017	5.1	.190	11.1	.00094
				5.4	.158	12.0	.000072

Bibliography

Anastasi, A. (1976). *Psychological testing* (4th Ed.). New York: MacMillan Publishing Co. Inc.

——. (1988). *Psychological testing* (6th Ed.). New York: MacMillan Publishing Co. Inc.

Andrews, F.C. (1954). Asymptotic behaviour of some rank tests for analysis of variance. *Annals of Mathematical Statistics, 25,* 724-736.

Baron, R.A. (2002). *Psychology* (3rd Ed.). New Delhi: Prentice-Hall of India Private Limited.

Bartlett, M.S. (1936). Squareroot transformation in analysis of variance. *Journal of the Royal Statistical Society Supplement, 3,* 68-78.

——. (1937). Some examples of statistical methods of research in agriculture and applied biology. *Journal of Royal Statistical Society Supplement, 4,* 137-183.

——. (1947). The use of transformation. *Biometrics, 3,* 39-52.

Bliss, C.I. (1937). The analysis of field experimental data expressed in percentages. *Plant Protection* (Leningrad), *12,* 67-77.

Box, G.E.P. (1954). Some theorems on quadratic forms applied in the study of analysis of variance problems. *The Analysis of Mathematical Statistics, 25,* 290-302.

Broota, K.D. (1989). *Experimental design in behavioural research.* New Delhi: Wiley Eastern Limited.

Campbell, D.T. (1960). Recommendations for APA test standards regarding construct, trait, and discriminant validity. *American Psychologist, 15,* 546-553.

Campbell, D.T., & Fiske, D.W. (1959). Convergent and discriminant validation by the multitrait-multimethod matrix. *Psychological Bulletin, 56,* 81-105.

Campbell, D.T., & Stanley, J.C. (1966). *Experimental and quasi-experimental designs for research.* Chicago: Rand McNally & Co.

Carmer, S.G., & Swanson, M.R. (1973). An evaluation of ten multiple comparison procedures by Monte Carlo Method. *Journal of the American Statistical Association, 68,* 66-74.

Cochran, W.G. (1947). Some consequences when assumptions for the analysis of variance are not satisfied. *Biometrics, 3,* 22-38.

——. (1952). The χ^2 test of goodness of fit. *Annals of Mathematical Statistics, 23,* 315-345.

Cochran, W.G., & Cox, G.M. (1957). *Experimental designs.* New Delhi: Asia Publishing House.

Cook, T.D., & Campbell, D.T. (1979). *The design and analysis of quasi-experiments for field settings.* Chicago: Rand McNally & Co.

Cronbach, L.J. (1951). Coefficient alpha and the internal structure of tests. *Psychometrika, 16,* 297-334.

——. (1970). *Essentials of psychological testing* (3rd Ed.). New York: Harper & Row.

Cronbach, L.J., & Meehl, P.E. (1955). Construct validity in psychological tests. *Psychological Bulletin, 52,* 281-302.

Cureton, E.E. (1965). Reliability and validity: Basic assumptions and experimental designs. *Educational and Psychological Measurement, 25,* 327-346.

Das, D., & Das, A. (1998). *Statistics in biology and psychology* (3rd Ed.). Calcutta: Academic Publishers.

Davidoff, M.D., & Goheen, H.W. (1953). A table for the rapid determination of the tetrachoric correlation coefficient. *Psychometrika, 18,* 115–121.

Downie, N.M., & Heath, R.W. (1965). *Basic statistical methods* (2nd Ed.). New York: Harper & Row.

Duncan, D.B. (1955). Multiple and multiple F tests. *Biometrica, 11,* 1–42.

Dunnett, C.W. (1955). A multiple comparison procedure for comparing several treatments with a control. *Journal of the American Statistical Association, 50,* 1026–1121.

Edwards, A.L. (1968). *Experimental design in psychological research* (3rd Ed.). New York: Holt, Rinehart and Winston, Inc.

——. (1973). *Statistical methods* (3rd Ed.). New York: Holt, Rinehart and Winston, Inc.

——. (1979). *Multiple regression and the analysis of variance and covariance.* San Frasisco, CA: Freeman.

Eysenck, H.J. (1970). *The structure of human personality.* London: Methuen.

Federer, W.T. (1955). *Experimental design.* New York: Macmillan.

Ferguson, G.A. (1981). *Statistical analysis in psychology and education* (5th Ed.). Tokyo: McGraw-Hill.

Fisher, R.A. (1935). *The design of experiments.* Edinburgh: Oliver & Boyd.

——. (1949). *The design of experiments.* London: Oliver & Boyd.

Fisher, R.A., & Yates, F. (1953). *Statistical tables for biological, agricultural, and medical research* (4th Ed.). Edinburgh: Oliver & Boyd.

Freeman, F.S. (1965). *The theory and practice of psychological testing.* Calcutta: Oxford-IBH.

Freeman, M.F., & Tukey, J.W. (1950). Transformations related to the angular and the square-root. *Annals of Mathematical Statistics, 21,* 607–711.

Friedman, M. (1937). The use of ranks to avoid the assumptions of normality implicit in the analysis of variance. *Journal of the American Statistical Association, 32,* 675–701.

Garrett, H.E. (1966). *Statistics in psychology and education.* New York: David McKay Company, Inc.

Gravetter, F.J., & Wallnau, L.B. (2000). *Statistics for the behavioral sciences* (5th Ed.). Belmont, CA: Wadsworth/Thomson Learning.

Gronlund, N.E. (1981). *Measurement and evaluation in teaching* (4th Ed.). New York: MacMillan Publishing Co., Inc.

Guilford, J.P. (1954). *Psychometric methods.* New York: McGraw-Hill.

Guilford, J.P., & Fruchter, B. (1978). *Fundamental statistics in psychology and education* (6th Ed.). New York: McGraw-Hill.

Gupta, S.C. (1996). *Fundamentals of statistics* (7th Ed.). New Delhi: Himalaya Publishing House.

Gupta, S.P. (2005). *Statistical methods* (34th Ed.). New Delhi: Sultan Chand & Sons.

Guttman, L. (1954). Some necessary conditions for common factor analysis. *Psychometrika, 19,* 149–161.

Hartley, H.O. (1950). The use of range in analysis of variance. *Biometrika, 37,* 271–280.

Hersen, M., & Barlow, D.H. (1976). *Single-case experimental design: Strategies for studying behavioural change.* New York: Pergamon Press.

Holzinger, K.J. & Frances, S. (1937). The bi-factor method. *Psychometrika, 2,* 41–54.

Hotelling, H. (1933). Analysis of a complex of statistical variables into principal components. *Journal of Educational Psychology, 24,* 417–441, 498–528.

Hotelling, H., & Pabst, M.R. (1936). Rank Correlation and tests of significance involving no assumption of normality. *Annals of Mathematical Statistics, 7,* 29–46.

Hoyt, C.J. (1941). Note on a simplified method of computing test reliability. *Educational and Psychological Measurement, 1,* 93–95.

Kendall, M.G. (1970). *Rank correlation methods* (4th Ed.). London: Charles Griffin & Company, Ltd.

Kruskal, W.H., & Wallis, W.A. (1952). Use of ranks in one-criterion variance analysis. *Journal of American Statistical Association, 47,* 583–621.

Kuder, G.F., & Richardson, M.W. (1937). The theory of estimation of test reliability. *Psychometrika, 2,* 151–160.

Levin, R.I., & Rubin, D.S. (1997). *Statistics for management* (7th Ed.). Upper Saddle River, NJ: Prentice-Hall, Inc.

Lindquist, E.F. (1956). *Design and analysis of experiments in psychology and education.* Boston: Houghton Mifflin Co.

Mann, H.B., & Whitney, D.R. (1947). On a test of whether one of two random variables is stochastically larger than the other. *Annals of Mathematical Statistics, 18,* 50–60.

McCall, W.A. (1923). *How to experiment in education.* New York: MacMillan.

McNemar, Q. (1962). *Psychological statistics* (3rd Ed.). New York: Wiley.

——. (1969). *Psychological statistics* (4th Ed.). New York: Wiley.

Mood, A.M. (1954). On the asymptotic efficiency of certain nonparametric two-sample tests. *Annals of Mathematical Statistics, 25,* 514–522.

Moran, P.A.P. (1951). Partial and multiple rank correlation. *Biometrika, 38,* 26–32.

Mosier, C.I. (1937). A factor analysis of certain neurotic tendencies. *Psychometrika, 2,* 263–286.

——. (1943). On the reliability of a weighted composite. *Psychometrika, 8,* 161–168.

Mosteller, F., & Brush, R.R. (1954). Selected quantitative techniques. In G. Lindezey (Ed.), *Handbook of social psychology.* Cambridge: Addison-Wesley.

Munn, N.L. (1966). *Psychology: The fundamentals of human adjustment* (5th Ed.). Boston: Houghton Mifflin.

Myers, A. (1980). *Experimental psychology.* New York: D.Van Nostrand Co.

Newman, D. (1939). The distribution of range in samples from a normal population expressed in terms of an independent estimate of standard deviation. *Biometric, 31,* 20.

Norton, D.W. (1952). *An empirical investigation of some effects of non-normality and heterogeneity on the F-distribution* (Unpublished PhD thesis). State University of Lowa.

Pagano, R.R. (1994). *Understanding statistics in the behavioral sciences* (4th Ed.). New York: West Publishing Company.

Rulon, P.J. (1939). A simplified procedure for determining the reliability of a test of split-halves. *Harvard Educational Review, 9,* 99–103.

Scheffé, H.A. (1959). *The analysis of variance.* New York: Wiley.

Siegel, S. (1956). *Nonparametric statistics for the behavioral sciences.* New York: McGraw-Hill Book Company, Inc.

Snedecor, G.W. (1956). *Statistical methods.* Ames: Lowa State College Press.

Spearman, C. (1927). *The abilities of man.* Boston: Houghton.

Tate, M.W. (1948). *Statistics in education.* New York: McGraw-Hill.

Thompson, G.H. (1951). *The factor analysis of human ability* (5th Ed.). London: University of London Press Ltd.

Thurstone, L.L. (1931). Multiple factor analysis. *Psychological Review, 38,* 406–427.

——. (1948). Psychological implications of factor analysis. *American Psychologist, 3,* 402–408.

Tukey, J.W. (1953). *The problem of multiple comparison.* Mimeographed for Limited Circulation (Reference from Snedeco, G.W. *Satistical Methods,* Lowa State College Press, Ames, 1956).

Whitney, D.R. (1948). *A comparison of the power of non-parametric tests and tests based on the normal distribution under non-normal alternatives* (Unpublished doctoral dissertation). Ohio State University, Columbus, Ohio.

Winer, B.J. (1971). *Statistical principles in experimental design* (2nd Ed.). New York: McGraw-Hill.

Index